THE NAZI ERA
1919–1945

THE NAZI ERA
1919–1945

A SELECT BIBLIOGRAPHY
OF PUBLISHED WORKS
FROM THE EARLY ROOTS TO 1980

Compiled by
Helen Kehr and Janet Langmaid

Mansell Publishing Limited

ISBN 0 7201 1618 X

Mansell Publishing Limited, 35–37 William Road, London NW1 3ER

First published 1982

Distributed in the United States and Canada by The H. W. Wilson Company, 950 University Avenue, Bronx, New York 10452.

British Library Cataloguing in Publication Data

Kehr, Helen
  The Nazi era, 1919–1945.
   1. National socialism—Bibliography
   2. Germany—Politics and government—1918–1933
  —Bibliography   3. Germany—Politics and
  government—1933–1945—Bibliography
  I. Title II. Langmaid, Janet
  016.3356'0943   Z224.N27

  ISBN 0–7201–1618–X

Typeset by Computacomp (UK) Ltd, Fort William, Scotland

CONTENTS

Introduction   xv

I. Reference books

A.   General—Biographical works; Statistics; Third Reich lexicons and
      handbooks   1

B.   Histories and documents—History of Germany; Documentations;
      Captured documents   4

C.   Aids to research—Bibliographies; Periodical indexes   7

II. Nationalsozialistische Deutsche Arbeiterpartei

A.   General—Party and state; Party rallies; Sociological studies of the party
      and its members; Occultism   11

B.   Roots   16

      1. General   16
      2. Political and nationalist   17
      3. Racist—Eugenics; Aryans, Nordics, etc.   19
      4. Anti-Semitism—Political; Racial; Anti-Judaism; Social, economic and
         cultural Anti-Semitism; 'Jewish world conspiracy'   20
      5. Social and economic   25
      6. Cultural and religious—Occult roots   26
      7. External—'Protocols of Zion'   27

C.   Nazi ideology and programme   30

      1. General   30
      2. Nationalism and militarism—Lebensraum; Geopolitics   32
      3. Racism—Master race; Eugenics and population policy; Euthanasia   34
         a. Anti-Semitism—Racial; Social, economic and cultural; Moral and
            religious;'Jewish world conspiracy'   38
         b. Other races—Gypsies; Coloured races   43
      4. Freemasonry and secret societies   44
      5. Führerprinzip   45
      6. Economic theories—Finance; Workers; Peasantry and agriculture;
         Analysis of Marxism   46
      7. Legal theories   48
      8. Cultural theories—Literature; Music; Visual arts; Drama   50
      9. Ethical attitudes   51

D. Leaders 52

    1. General 52

    2. Adolf Hitler—Before 1933; After 1933 and general biographies; Medical history; Psychological studies; As military leader; Religious beliefs; Last days; 'Mein Kampf'; Other writings; Speeches and conversations; Table talk 53

    3. Ministers 63

    4. Other leaders 68

III. From struggle to consolidation of power

A. Weimar: the political background 73

B. Before 1933: the time of struggle (Kampfzeit)—Nazi songbooks; Rise of the party: Regional and local accounts; 1923: the Munich Putsch; Hitler's trial; Party finances; Nazis in the legislature; Workers and trade unions; Opposition to National Socialism 74

C. The fall of the Weimar Republic 85

D. Consolidation of power—Hindenburg; Reichstag fire; Reichstag fire trial; Potsdam ceremonies; 30 June 1934 (Night of the Long Knives); Crushing of the opposition and rivals (Gleichschaltung) 88

IV. The Third Reich

A. General accounts—Local and regional 94

B. The land and the people 98

C. Personal experiences and accounts—By Germans; Contemporary foreign accounts 99

D. Administration 104

    1. General—Awards, flags and orders 104

    2. The bureaucracy—The law relating to civil servants (Beamtenrecht) 107

    3. Law—Constitution; Racial and citizenship law; Nuremberg Laws; Criminal law 109

    4. Courts of law—Judges and advocates; Military courts; People's Court (Volksgericht); Reichsgericht; Sondergericht; Perversion of justice 114

E. The new social system 117

    1. Welfare and health—Medical care; Social welfare; Winterhilfswerk; Animal welfare 117

    2. Population policy and eugenics—Marriage; Sterilization and castration 120

F. The economy 123

    1. General 123

    2. Finance—Currency control; Taxation 126

    3. Industry and commerce—Autarky and Four-Year-Plan 128

    4. Foreign trade—Economic relations with other countries 133

	5. Agriculture and food production—Peasantry	136
	6. Workers—Deutsche Arbeitsfront; Strength through Joy (Kraft durch Freude); Craftsmen	138
	7. Economic preparations for war—Autobahnen	143
G.	Religion	144
	1. The Churches in the Kampfzeit	144
	2. Religion in the Third Reich	
	a. General	146
	b. Christians and Jews	147
	c. Kirchenkampf: Oppression, persecution, opposition and resistance—The Churches and Alfred Rosenberg's 'Der Mythus des 20. Jahrhunderts'	148
	d. The Protestant Churches—Bekennende Kirche; German Christians; The struggle within the Protestant Church; Opposition, resistance and persecution	151
	e. The Roman Catholic Church—The Vatican and the Third Reich; Nazi anti-Catholicism; Opposition, persecution and resistance	159
	f. Heresies, anti-Christianity, neo-paganism—Deutsche Glaubensbewegung; Germanic festivals	167
H.	Women—War service	170
J.	Youth and education	173
	1. General	173
	2. Education and indoctrination—Children's books	174
	3. Nazi youth organizations—Hitler Youth; Bund Deutscher Mädel	176
	4. Schools and teachers—Educational establishments; Handbooks for teachers; School subjects	179
	5. Arbeitsdienst—Arbeitsmaiden	188
	6. Vocational training—Reichsberufswettkampf; Berufsschulen (training schools)	190
	7. Adult education and indoctrination	191
	8. Universities and learned institutes—Professors, scientists, scholars and researchers; Students	192
	9. Oppression and resistance—Catholic youth; Protestant youth; Workers' movement; Resistance at universities; Weisse Rose	197
K.	Culture	199
	1. General—Linguistics; Folklore	199
	2. Literature—Writers; Poetry; Innere Emigration; Books and publishing; Banned and burned books	202
	3. The arts	
	a. General	209
	b. Music	210
	c. Architecture and town planning	211

	d. Painting and sculpture	213
	e. Stage and screen	215
	4. Science, technology and scholarship—Economics; History; Philosophy; Physics; Psychology; Technology	218
	5. Press—Religious press; Individual journals	220
	6. Radio	227
	7. Sport and athletics—Gymnastics; Olympic Games	228
	8. Humour and satire—Anti-Nazi humour	231
L.	Propaganda	233
	1. General	233
	2. Art and the media	235
	3. Nazi propaganda writings—Themes of propaganda; Defensive propaganda; Illustration as propaganda	236
	4. Propaganda in World War II	
	a. General	240
	b. The radio war	240
	c. Countercharges and quotations	241
	d. Allied propaganda (general)	243
	e. German propaganda (general)	243
	f. Hostile Nazi propaganda	245
	g. Favourable Nazi propaganda	250
V.	**The criminal state**	
A.	Instruments of repression	252
	1. SA (Sturmabteilung)	252
	2. SS (Schutzstaffel)	254
	a. General	254
	b. SS leaders	256
	c. Nationalsozialistisches Kraftfahr Korps (NSKK)	257
	3. Police	258
	a. Sicherheitsdienst	258
	b. Gestapo (Geheime Staatspolizei)	258
	c. Other police	259
	4. Prisons	260
B.	Persecution and resistance	261
	1. General	261
	2. Local and regional	263
	3. Individual accounts—Kreisauer Kreis	267
	4. Political	269
	a. General	269
	b. Left-wing—Rote Kapelle	271
	c. Pacifists	275

	d.	Freemasonry	275
	e.	Right-wing, monarchists and military	275
	f.	Conspiracies against Hitler—20 July 1944	276
5.		The Jews	281
	a.	General	281
	b.	Emigration	282
	c.	Extermination	283
	d.	Local and regional persecution	283
	e.	Individual accounts and cases	287
	f.	Underground survival	289
	g.	Economic persecution—'Aryanization'	290
	h.	Cultural and professional persecution—Jurists; Scientists and scholars; Writers, artists, etc.	291
	j.	November 1938 Pogrom	292
	k.	Attempts at adaptation and resistance—Cultural life; Education	293
	l.	'Non-Aryan' Christians	295
	m.	'Mischlinge' and mixed marriages	296
6.		Exiles	297
	a.	General	297
	b.	Political—Nationalkomitee Freies Deutschland; Journalists and periodicals; Illegal pamphlets and periodicals	297
	c.	Cultural—Literature (secondary works); Theatre; Artists; Musicians; Science and Scholarship	302
	d.	Exile literature, (primary)—Poetry; Fiction; Drama; Letters, political and autobiographical writings	305

VI. The road to war

A.	Military policy	308
	1. Armed forces in politics	308
	2. Militarism and preparation for war—Military indoctrination	309
B.	Foreign relations	311
	1. Reference works	311
	2. General	313
	3. Expansionism	316
	a. First steps—Repudiation of the Versailles peace treaty; Germany and the League of Nations; Failure of disarmament; German demand for equal rights (Gleichberechtigung)	316
	b. Rearmament—Conscription; Westwall (Siegfried Line)	319
	c. Methods of expansionism—Subversion, infiltration, espionage and propaganda; Encouragement of foreign nationalist movements; German minorities abroad (Volksdeutsche); Lebensraum; Geopolitics; Colonies	320
	d. First successes—Return of the Saar; March into the Rhineland	325

C.   Relations with Axis states   326

    1. Italy—The early phase; South Tyrol; Italian Empire   326
    2. Axis pacts   328
    3. Japan   328

D.   Relations with European states   329

    1. Grossdeutschland (Greater Germany)   329
    2. Austria—Up to 1938; The Churches and National Socialism; Nazi subversion in Austria; The Anschluss   330
    3. Balkan and Danubian States   332
    4. Baltic states   335
    5. Czechoslovakia—Up to 1938; Annexation   336
    6. Eire (including Northern Ireland)   338
    7. France—Alsace-Lorraine; French Empire   338
    8. Great Britain—Secret contacts; British Empire and Commonwealth   340
    9. Low Countries   344
    10. Memel (Lithuania)   345
    11. Poland—German minority; Danzig and the Polish Corridor; Upper Silesia   345
    12. Portugal   348
    13. Scandinavia   348
    14. Spain—Spanish Civil War   349
    15. Soviet Union—The Nazi–Soviet Pact; German minority; Ukraine   351
    16. Switzerland—Nazi subversion and propaganda   354

E.   Origins of World War II   355

    1. Contemporary view   355
    2. Postwar views and controversies   356
    3. The Munich Pact   358
    4. The last year of peace   359
    5. The Polish crisis: September 1939   360

F.   Relations with the western hemisphere   361
    1. General   361
    2. United States of America—German-Americans, and Nazi subversion and propaganda   361
    3. Latin America   363

G.   Middle East   365

H.   Far East   367

VII.   **World War II**

A.   Reference books   369
B.   General histories   369
C.   Germany in World War II   371

1. General 371

2. The home front—Young people 372

3. War economy—Weapons and matériel (including prewar period) 374

D. German Armed forces, including prewar period 375

1. General 375

2. Handbooks and instructions for personnel 377

3. Strategy 378

4. Military leaders 379

 a. General 379

 b. Individuals 381

5. Army 383

 a. General—Paratroops; Pioneers; Tanks 383

 b. Waffen-SS 386

 c. Foreign contingents 386

6. Luftwaffe and Air War 388

 a. Early years (including civil air force) 388

 b. War years 389

 c. Battle of Britain 390

 d. Air attacks against Germany 391

7. Navy 393

 a. Prewar years 393

 b. War at sea—U-boats 393

E. Campaigns of World War II 396

1. Poland 396

2. The Phony War 397

3. Scandinavia 397

4. The Western Front, 1940 398

 a. Attack on the Low Countries 398

 b. The Six Weeks' War 399

5. Seelöwe (Operation Sea-Lion) 400

6. North Africa 401

7. Balkans 401

8. Soviet Union 402

 a. Up to the Battle of Stalingrad—Leningrad; Moscow 402

 b. Stalingrad 403

 c. General 404

9. Italy 405

10. Defeat in the East and South — Austria 405

11. Defeat in the West 406

12. Defeat in Germany—Berlin; Other towns and regions; German prisoners of war 407

F. Espionage and Sabotage 409

G.   German war aims: Europe and beyond   411

H.   Occupation, persecution and resistance   412

   1. The New Order in Europe   412
      a. General   412
      b. Looting of art treasures   414
      c. Population movements   414
   2. Persecution and resistance   416
      a. General   416
      b. SS and police as occupying forces   417
   3. Individual countries   418
      a. Austria   418
      b. Balkan and Danubian states—Albania, Bulgaria, Greece, Hungary, Romania, Yugoslavia   420
      c. Channel Islands   423
      d. Czechoslovakia—Czechoslovak exiles; Slovakia   423
      e. Eastern Europe—Baltic states; Danzig   427
      f. Poland—Occupation and German administration; Cultural persecution, and resistance; Catholic Church; Warsaw Uprising, 1944   429
      g. Soviet Union   433
      h. France—Alsace-Lorraine; Vichy France   434
      j. Italy   439
      k. Low Countries—Belgium; Holland; Luxemburg   439
      l. Scandinavia—Denmark; Norway   444

VIII.   **War crimes**

A.   General   447

B.   War crimes trials   448

   1. General   448
   2. Nuremberg Trials—The accused   449

C.   The Holocaust   451

   1. Histories, documentations, bibliographies   451
   2. General studies covering 1933–1945   452
   3. Europe, 1939–1945   454
      a. General—Nazi vocabulary of extermination   454
      b. Adolf Eichmann—Eichmann trial   457
      c. Individual accounts   458
      d. Individual countries   460
      e. Ghettoes   473
      f. Warsaw Ghetto—Uprising   478

D.   Concentration camps   481

E.   Medical crimes   499

	1. General	499
	2. Euthanasia	499
	3. Medical experiments—individual camps	500
F.	Forced labour	501
G.	Children	503
H.	Gypsies	504
J.	Hostages	505
K.	Prisoners of war	505
L.	Responses to persecution	506
	1. External protests and reactions	506
	2. Attempts at relief and rescue	508
	3. Individual countries	510

IX. After the fall of the Third Reich

A.	Wartime planning	516
B.	Escaped war criminals	516
C.	Expulsion of Germans	517
D.	The survivors of persecution	518
	1. Victims' organizations	518
	2. Displaced persons	518
	3. The Jews	518
	4. Children	520
	5. Lasting effects of persecution	520
E.	Reparations and restitution	521
F.	Occupation and rehabilitation of Germany	522
G.	German views of the Third Reich	523
	1. General	523
	2. Apologists	524
H.	After the Holocaust	525
	1. Postwar Germany	525
	2. Denial	525
	3. Religious aftermath	526

Index | | 529 |

INTRODUCTION

This bibliography is intended to help both the serious student and the interested layman to a better understanding of National Socialism and the Third Reich.

Before dealing with the development of the movement itself, we have attempted to trace its complex historical roots, some of which go back to the sixteenth century and beyond. The National Socialist era itself began, in our view, with the inception of the Party in 1919, for the menacing figure of Hitler overshadowed the whole tragic story of the Weimar Republic. The Party's way of thought did not materially change after the seizure of power and the section on 'Ideology and Programme' illuminates many of the subsequent policies and actions of the Third Reich.

In dealing with the history of a major European power over twelve traumatic years, selection from an enormous quantity of available material has necessarily been difficult and, in the last resort, arbitrary. There exists a very large number of books dealing with certain aspects of the period under review, such as the National Socialist educational system, the Holocaust, and European resistance, yet in other fields only a limited amount of material can be found: for example, there is comparatively little on social welfare, sport, economics and internal administration, all subjects of vital importance for an understanding of the Third Reich.

Particularly in regard to World War II, we have made no attempt to cover the whole of the vast literature on the subject. Our aim has primarily been to represent the German outlook of the time, while including a number of bibliographies and basic works which can point the way for further research.

In our selection we have tried to maintain a due proportion in the length of sections, even though this has regrettably entailed the omission of titles which might well be considered indispensable. Limitations on size have also meant that, with few exceptions, periodicals and articles from journals have not been included.

For the sake of balance, we have tried to give a representative sample of works published throughout the period from 1919 to the present day, with particular emphasis on those issued in the Third Reich. In order to round out the picture of life in National Socialist Germany, a fair amount of lighter reading matter such as novels and memoirs has been included.

Some twenty languages are represented among the *circa* 6500 works chosen, but the majority of these are in English or in German. A much larger selection could have been made from other European languages and from Hebrew and Yiddish: but in deference to Western readers, we have tended to choose books which are accessible through translations and summaries.

Problems have arisen in defining headings for various sections and in the index. For example, given the tight hold of the totalitarian state at every level, virtually all publications in the Third Reich had to mirror the aims and attitudes of National Socialism and each could therefore be classed as propaganda. Similarly, so many books contain passages of antisemitism that they cannot be specially noted or indexed under that heading. On the other hand, what might be regarded by an outsider as a mere timid whisper of opposition can legitimately be included under the general term of resistance.

The National Socialist era ended in 1945, but its aftermath is still with us. A glimpse of the immediate results for Germany itself and some of the victims is given in the short final section.

Both of us were for many years on the staff of the Institute of Contemporary History and Wiener Library. Close acquaintance with that great collection, begun in 1933 by the late Dr. Alfred Wiener and now extending over the whole field of modern European history, has inevitably influenced the set-up of this bibliography. By far the majority of the books quoted have passed through our hands and many have been used to assist students and scholars in their researches.

We take this opportunity of expressing our gratitude to the Institute of Contemporary History and Wiener Library and to our former colleagues there for their unfailing help and consideration. Our thanks are also due to the Libraries of the German Historical Institute and the Goethe Institute in London, as well as to the London School of Economics and the Imperial War Museum.

I. REFERENCE BOOKS

A. GENERAL

1 SNYDER, LOUIS L.: *Encyclopedia of the Third Reich.* New York: McGraw-Hill, 1976. 410 pp., illus., facsims., tabs., bibl.

2 WALKER, MALVIN: *Chronological encyclopedia of Adolf Hitler and the Third Reich.* New York: Carlton Press, 1978. 191 pp., bibl.

Biographical works

3 ARNIM, MAX and others, eds.: *Internationale Personalbibliographie.* Stuttgart: Hiersemann, 1952/63. 3 vols.
 Bde. 1, 2: Max Arnim, ed.: *1800–1943.* 2. verb. und stark verm. Aufl. Publ. 1952. 706 + 834 pp.
 Bd. 3: Max Arnim, Gerhard Bock, Franz Hodes, eds.: *1944–1959 und Nachtrage* ... Publ. 1963. 639 pp.
 [Supplements (ed.: Franz Hodes) are currently being published.]

4 *Biographisches Wörterbuch zur deutschen Geschichte.* Begr.: Hellmuth Rössler, Günther Franz. 2. völlig neubearb. und stark erw. Aufl. Bearb.: Karl Bosl, Günther Franz, Hanns Hubert Hoffmann. München: Francke, 1973/75. 3330 cols. + [137 pp.] in 3 vols.

 Das Deutsche Führerlexikon 1934/1935. See 607.

5 *Der grossdeutsche Reichstag.* IV. Wahlperiode: Beginn am 10. April 1938, verlängert bis zum 30. Januar 1947. Neuhrsg. des Handbuchs von E. Kienast. Berlin: Schenck, 1943. 575 pp., ports., tabs.
 [Contains much biographical material on members of the Reichstag.]

6 *The International Who's Who.* London: Europa Publications.
 1937. 1166 pp.
 1942. 1012 pp.

7 *Kürschners deutscher Gelehrten-Kalender.* Berlin: de Gruyter, 1927–continuing. (Hrsg.: Gerhard Lüdtke).
 3. 1928/29
 4. 1931
 5. 1935
 6. 1940/41 [2 vols.]
 7. 1950 [Contains a necrology from 1935 onward.]

1

8 *Kürschners deutscher Literatur-Kalender.* Berlin: de Gruyter, 1929–continuing.
   1930
   1934
   1937/38
   1943
   1949
   [1934 volume contains 'Nekrolog 1901–1935', which is updated in subsequent issues.]

9 *Neue deutsche Biographie.* Hrsg. von der Historischen Kommission bei der Bayerischen Akademie der Wissenschaften. Berlin: Duncker & Humblot, 1953– continuing. 11 vols. (to 'Kleinfercher') so far published.

10 SCHWARZ, MAX: *MdR. Biographisches Handbuch der Reichstage.* Hannover: Verlag für Literatur und Zeitgeschehen, 1965. 832 pp., illus., plans, bibl.

11 STOCKHORST, ERICH: *Fünftausend Köpfe. Wer war was im Dritten Reich.* Velbert: Blick und Bild Verlag, 1967. 461 pp., diagrs.

12 *Wer ist's?* Begr. und Hrsg.: Herbert A. L. Degener. Berlin: Degener.
   IX. [Subtitled] *Unsere Zeitgenossen.* Publ. 1928. xlix + 1789 pp.
   X. [Entitled] *Degeners Wer ist's?* Publ. 1935. lxxv + 1833 pp.
   [Each volume contains lists of several thousand pseudonyms and a necrology.]

Statistics

13 *Statistisches Handbuch von Deutschland 1928–1944.* Hrsg.: Länderrat des Amerikanischen Besatzungsgebiets. München: Ehrenwirth, 1949. 640 pp.

14 *Statistisches Jahrbuch für das Deutsche Reich.* 50.–59. Jhrg. Hrsg.: Statistisches Reichsamt. Berlin: 1931–1942. 10 vols., tabs., graphs.
   [1931–34 publ. by Hobbing; 1935–38 Verlag für Sozialpolitik, Wirtschaft und Statistik (Paul Schmidt); no imprint in remaining vols.]

15 STATISTISCHES REICHSAMT: [Series of publications based on census of June 1933 (publ. 1936–37) and that of May 1939 (publ. 1941–44.)] Berlin: Verlag für Sozialpolitik, Wirtschaft und Statistik (Schmidt). [Titles include: (from 1933 census) *Die Bevölkerung des Deutschen Reichs nach der Religionszugehörigkeit, Die Ausländer im Deutschen Reich, Die Bevölkerung einiger Gebiete des Deutschen Reichs nach der Muttersprache, Die Glaubensjuden im Deutschen Reich*; (from 1939 census) *Die Juden und jüdische Mischlinge im Deutschen Reich.*]

Third Reich lexicons and handbooks

16 *Das Archiv. Nachschlagewerk für Politik, Wirtschaft, Kultur.* Berlin: Stollberg, 1934–1944.
   Bde. 1–19: [April 1934–October 1935]. Bearb.: Kurt Jahncke
   Bde. 20–65: [November 1935–August 1939]. Bearb.: Alfred-Ingemar Berndt
   Bde. 66–126: [September 1939–September 1944. From October 1939 subtitled *Deutschland im Kampf*]. Bearb.: Alfred-Ingemar Berndt & Oberst-Lt. von Wedel

2

Nachtragsbde. I–III: *Januar 1933–März 1934.* Hrsg.: Alfred-Ingemar Berndt. Bearb.: Fritz Reipert (II), Max Junge (III). Publ. 1939–40. 1412 pp. (in 3 vols.)

[*Deutschland im Kampf* also issued separately in 116 numbers.]

17 BAUER, WILHELM & DEHEN, PETER, eds.: *Tatsachen und Zahlen über Deutschland.* 2. Aufl. [Berlin: no imprint], 1941. 135 pp., tabs.

18 [BROCKHAUS] *Der grosse Brockhaus. Handbuch des Wissens in 20 Bänden.* 15. völlig neubearb. Aufl. Leipzig: Brockhaus, 1928–1937. 22 vols. incl. *Ergänzungsband & Der Brockhaus-Atlas* [Also *Der neue Brockhaus* (2. verb. Aufl. Publ. 1941–42. 5 vols.) & *Der Volks-Brockhaus* (6. verb. Aufl. Publ. 1938. One vol.)]

19 EICHLER, MAX: *Du bist sofort im Bilde. Lebendig-anschauliches Reichsbürger-Handbuch.* Zeichnungen: Alfred Grobe. Erfurt: Cramer, 1940. 204 pp., illus. (50.–80. Taus.)

20 GALÉRA, K[ARL] S[IEGMAR] Baron von: *Deutschlands Schicksalsweg 1919–1939. Nachschlagewerk zur deutschen Geschichte.* Berlin: Hochmuth, 1940. 352 pp.

21 [HERDER] *Der grosse Herder. Nachschlagewerk für Wissen und Leben.* 4. völlig neubearb. Aufl. von Herders Konversationslexikon. Freiburg i.Br.: Herder, 1931–1935. 12 vols.

22 *Hitler spricht. Ein Lexikon des Nationalsozialismus.* Leipzig: Kittler, 1934. 172 pp.

23 JAMROWSKI, OTTO, ed.: *Tagebuch aus Politik, Kultur und Wirtschaft.* Berlin: Deutscher Verlag für Politik und Wirtschaft, 1937–1942. Jhrg. 1–6, illus., maps, tabs., bibls.

24 LEISTRITZ, HANS KARL: *Staatshandbuch des Volksgenossen.* 11. Aufl. des *Deutschen Staatsbürger-Taschenbuches* hrsg. von Dr. Model. Berlin: Sudau, 1936. 975 pp.

25 *Meyers Lexikon.* 8. Aufl. Leipzig: Bibliographisches Institut, 1936–1942. Bde. 1–9 + Bd. 12 (*Atlasband*), illus. [No further volumes of this edition published.]

26 *Nationalsozialistisches Handbuch.* Hrsg. unter Mitw. der Hauptparteileitung der N.S.D.A.P. München: Eher, 1927–1944. [1934–1938 ed. by Philipp Bouhler; 1939–1944 by Robert Ley.]

27 PARTEI-KANZLEI: *Verfügungen, Anordnungen, Bekanntgaben.* [1942–1944?]. 6 vols.

28 PREUSSISCHES STAATSMINISTERIUM: *Handbuch über den Preussischen Staat.* Jhrg. 138–141. Berlin: Schenck, 1934–1941. 4 vols., illus.

29 *Reichsband. Adressenwerk der Dienststellen der NSDAP mit den angeschlossenen Verbänden des Staates der Reichsregierung und Behörden und der Organisation: Kultur, Reichsnährstand, gewerblichen Wirtschaft.*

Hrsg. unter Aufsicht der Reichsleitung der NSDAP Hauptorganisations-amt... Berlin: 'Die Deutsche Tat', [1938?]. [858 pp.], illus., maps, tabs.

30 REICHS- UND PREUSSISCHES-MINISTERIUM DES INNERN: *Handbuch für das Deutsche Reich 1936.* Berlin: Heymann, 1936. 467 pp.

31 *Schlag nach! Wissenswerte Tatsachen aus allen Gebieten. Ein umfassendes Nachschlagewerk* ... 3. Aufl. Leipzig: Bibliographisches Institut, 1941. 704 pp., maps, diagrs., tabs. [Also issued in parts, each dealing with one country or region: such parts were also put out by the Oberkommando der Wehrmacht for military information.]

B. HISTORIES AND DOCUMENTS

History of Germany

32 CRAIG, GORDON A.: *Germany 1866–1945.* Oxford: Clarendon Press, 1978. xv + 825 pp.

32a DIWALD, HELLMUT: *Geschichte der Deutschen.* Frankfurt a.M.: Propyläen, 1978. 767 pp., illus. [Also 4th ed. 1979. Incl. controversial statements on the persecution of the Jews.]

33 FRIEDRICH-SCHILLER-UNIVERSITÄT JENA, Historisches Institut: *Die bürgerlichen Parteien in Deutschland. Handbuch der Geschichte der bürgerlichen Parteien und anderer bürgerlicher Interessenorganisationen vom Vormärz bis zum Jahre 1945.* Berlin [East]: Das Europäische Buch, 1968/70. 806 + 974 pp., tabs., bibls. [In 2 vols.]

34 *Handbuch der deutschen Geschichte.* Begr. von Otto Brandt, fortgef. von Arnold Oskar Meyer. Neu hrsg. von Leo Just. Konstanz: Athenaion Verlag, 1965–
Bd. 4: *Deutsche Geschichte der neuesten Zeit* ...
Teil 1: Werner Frauendienst, Wolfgang [Justin] Mommsen: *Von 1890 bis 1933.* Publ. 1973. [Incl.: Abschn. III: 'Die Weimarer Republik' by Albert Schwarz. 232 pp.]
Teil 2: Walther Hofer, Herbert Michaelis: *Von 1933 bis 1945.* Publ. 1965. 393 + xvi pp.
Bd. 5: *Athenaion Bilderatlas zur deutschen Geschichte.* Hrsg.: Herbert Jankuhn, Hartmut Boockmann, Wilhelm Treue. Publ. 1968. viii + 807 pp., illus., maps.

35 *Handbuch der deutschen Geschichte.* Begr.: [Bruno] Gebhardt. Hrsg.: Herbert Grundmann. 9., neu bearb. Aufl. Stuttgart: 1973/76.
Bd. 4: *Die Zeit der Weltkriege.* Bearb.: Karl Dietrich Erdmann. xii + x + 906 pp.
Teil 1: *Der erste Weltkrieg: Die Weimarer Republik.* Union Verlag, 1973.
Teil 2: *Deutschland unter der Herrschaft des Nationalsozialismus 1933–1939.* Klett, 1976.

35a Institut für Deutsche Geschichte: *Jahrbuch, I–IX.* Hrsg.: Walter Grab. Tel Aviv: University of Tel Aviv, 1972/80 continuing.

36 Institut für Zeitgeschichte: *Deutsche Geschichte seit dem Ersten Weltkrieg.* Stuttgart: Deutsche Verlags-Anstalt, 1971/73.
Bd. I: Publ. 1971. 844 pp. [Comprising: Helmut Heiber: 'Die Republik von Weimar'; Hermann Graml: 'Europa zwischen den Kriegen'; Martin Broszat: 'Der Staat Hitlers'.]
Bd. II: Publ. 1973. 784 pp., tabs. [Comprising: Lothar Gruchmann: 'Der Zweite Weltkrieg'; Thilo Vogelsang: 'Das geteilte Deutschland'; Dietmar Petzina: 'Grundriss der deutschen Wirtschaftsgeschichte 1918–1945'.]
Bd. III: Publ. 1973. 366 pp., bibl. (pp. 151–316). [Comprising: Wolfgang Benz: 'Quellen zur Zeitgeschichte'.]

37 *Lexikon der deutschen Geschichte. Personen, Ereignisse, Institutionen. Von der Zeitwende bis zum Ausgang des Zweiten Weltkrieges.* Hrsg.: Gerhard Taddey. Stuttgart: Kröner, 1977. x + 1352 pp.

38 Mann, Golo: *Deutsche Geschichte 1919–1945.* Frankfurt a.M.: Fischer, 1976. 249 pp. (183.–187. Taus.)

39 Meyer, Henry Cord, ed.: *The long generation. Germany from Empire to ruin, 1913–1945.* New York: Harper & Row, 1973. 359 pp.

40 Ryder, A. J.: *Twentieth-century Germany. From Bismarck to Brandt.* London: Macmillan, 1973. 656 pp., illus., maps

41 Usadel, Georg: *Zeitgeschichte in Wort und Bild. Vom Alten zum Neuen Reich.* Oldenburg i.O.: Kultur und Aufbau Verlag, 1937–1939. In 4 vols. (272 pp. each), ports., illus., facsims., bibls.

41a Valentin, Veit: *Geschichte der Deutschen.* Mit einem ergänzenden Abriss zur deutschen Geschichte von 1945 bis zur Gegenwart von Erhard Klöss. Köln: Kiepenheuer & Witsch, 1979. 772 pp., illus. [First publ.: New York: Knopf, 1946.]

42 Vogel, Bernhard and others: *Wahlen in Deutschland. Theorie—Geschichte—Dokumente. 1848–1970.* [By] Bernhard Vogel, Dieter Nohlen, Rainer-Olaf Schultze. Berlin: de Gruyter, 1971. xiii + 465 pp., graphs, tabs., bibl.

Documentations

43 Anger, Walter: *Das Dritte Reich in Dokumente.* Frankfurt a.M.: Europäische Verlagsanstalt, 1957. 216 pp.

44 *Dokumente der deutschen Politik.* Hrsg.: Paul Meier-Benneckenstein [from Bd. 6, Teil 2 onwards: Franz Alfred Six]. Bearb.: Axel Friedrichs [from Bd. 5 onwards: Hans Volz]. Berlin: Junker & Dünnhaupt, 1935–1944. Illus., maps, tabs. (Hrsg.: Deutsche Hochschule für Politik [from Bd. 7 onwards: Deutsches Auslandswissenschaftliches Institut]).
Bd. 1: *Die nationalsozialistische Revolution 1933.* Publ. 1935. 355 pp., bibl.
Bd. 2: *Der Aufbau des deutschen Führer-Staates: Das Jahr 1934.* Publ. 1936. 340 pp.

Bd. 3: *Deutschlands Weg zur Freiheit 1935*. Publ. 1937. 338 pp.
Bd. 4: *Deutschlands Aufstieg zur Grossmacht 1936*. Publ. 1937. 378 pp.
Bd. 5: *Von der Grossmacht zur Weltmacht 1937*. Publ. 1938. 468 pp.
Bd. 6: *Grossdeutschland 1938, Teile 1, 2*. Publ. 1939. 755 pp.
Bd. 7: *Das Werden des Reichs 1939, Teile 1, 2*. Publ. 1940. 914 pp. [From this volume onward subtitled *Das Reich Adolf Hitlers*.]
Bd. 8: *Der Kampf gegen den Westen 1940, Teile 1, 2*. Publ. 1940. 904 pp.
Bd. 9: *Der Kampf gegen den Osten 1941, Teile 1, 2*. Publ. 1944. 1050 pp.
[In supplementary series subtitled *Die Zeit des Weltkrieges und der Weimarer Republik 1914–1933*]:
Bd. 3 (1, 2): *Novemberumsturz und Versailles*. Publ. 1942. xix + 856 pp. [No others of this series appeared.]

45 *Dokumente der deutschen Politik und Geschichte bis zur Gegenwart. Ein Quellenwerk für die politische Bildung und Staatsbürgerliche Erziehung*. Hrsg.: Johann Hohlfeld. Berlin: Dokumenten-Verlag (Wendler), 1951–
Bd. 3: *Die Weimarer Republik 1918–1933*. Publ. 1951. xii + 476 pp.
Bde. 4, 5: *Die Zeit der nationalsozialistischen Diktatur 1933–1945*. Publ. 1953.
1. *Aufbau und Entwicklung 1933–1938*. xviii + 508 pp.
2. *Deutschland im Zweiten Weltkrieg 1939–1945*. xx + 565 pp.
Kommentar, Erläuterung und Erklärungen zu Bde. 1–6. Bearb.: Herbert Michaelis. Publ. 1956. 506 pp.

46 DRESLER, ADOLF, ed.: *Dokumente des Dritten Reiches*. Verfasst von Fritz Maier-Hartmann. München: Eher, 1939. 575 pp., ports., illus., maps, facsims.

47 KÜHNL, REINHARD: *Der deutsche Faschismus in Quellen und Dokumenten*. 2. erw. Aufl. Köln: Pahl-Rugenstein, 1977. 530 pp., illus., facsims., tabs., bibl.

48 NOAKES, JEREMY & PRIDHAM, GEOFFREY, eds.: *Documents on Nazism, 1919–1945*. London: Cape, 1974. 704 pp.

49 *Ursachen und Folgen. Vom deutschen Zusammenbruch 1918 und 1945 bis zur staatlichen Neuordnung Deutschlands in der Gegenwart. Eine Urkunden- und Dokumentensammlung zur Zeitgeschichte*. Hrsg.: Herbert Michaelis, Ernst Schraepler. Mitw.: Günter Scheel. Berlin: Wendler, 1958–
Bde. 1–3: [Covers period up to 1919].
Bde. 4–8: *Die Weimarer Republik*.
Bde. 9–23: *Das Dritte Reich*.
[Indexes]:
Die Weimarer Republik. Namen- und Personenregister zu Bde. 4–8. [Publ. 1977?] 141 pp.
Biographisches Register. Publ. 1979. 818 pp. (in 2 vols.)

Captured documents

50 *Guides to German records microfilmed at Alexandria, Va.* Washington, D.C.: The National Archives [and others], 1958– continuing. Nos. 1–76 continuing, mimeog. (Prepared under direction of Committee for the Study of War Documents, American Historical Association). [Includes particulars of documentary records of the NSDAP, various ministries and agencies, military and police, etc.]

51 HEINZ, GRETE & PETERSON, AGNES F., comps.: *NSDAP Hauptarchiv. Guide to the Hoover Institution microfilm collection.* Stanford, Calif.: Hoover Institution on War, Revolution, and Peace, 1964. 175 pp., tabs.

52 THE NATIONAL ARCHIVES OF THE UNITED STATES: *Captured German sound recordings.* Washington, D.C.: [197–?]. 22 pp.

53 *Nazi conspiracy and aggression.* Ed.: Office of United States Chief of Counsel for Prosecution of Axis Criminality. Washington, D.C.: Government Printing Office, 1946–1948. 9 vols. + Supplements A & B [A collection of documentary evidence and guide materials prepared by the American and British prosecution staffs for presentation before the International Military Tribunal at Nuernberg.]

54 NISHIKAWA, MASAO: 'Survey of source materials on modern German history: the so-called captured German documents and other sources'. [Reprint from] *Shigaku-Zasshi (Historical Journal of Japan)*, Vol. 72, Nos. 4 & 6. Pp. 45–91.

Trial of the major war criminals before the International Military Tribunal Nuremberg. See 5630.

Trials of War Criminals before the Nuernberg Military Tribunals. See 5636.

55 WEINBERG, GERHARD L. and others, comps.: *Guide to captured German documents.* Prepared by Gerhard L. Weinberg and the War Documentation Projects Staff under direction of Fritz T. Epstein. Maxwell Air Force Base, Ala.: Air University, Human Resources Research Institute, 1952. 90 pp.
[And] *Supplement.* [Issued by] American Historical Association, Committee for the Study of War Documents. Washington, D.C.: National Archives, 1959. 69 pp.

56 WOLFE, ROBERT, ed.: *Captured German and related records. A National Archives conference.* Athens, Ohio: Ohio University Press, 1974. 279 pp., illus., facsims.

C. AIDS TO RESEARCH

57 BAUMGART, WINFRIED: *Bücherverzeichnis zur deutschen Geschichte. Hilfsmittel, Handbücher, Quellen.* Frankfurt a.M.: Ullstein, 1971. 195 pp.

58 DEUTSCHE BIBLIOTHEK: *Bibliography of German publications in English translation 1972–1976.* Frankfurt a.M.: Buchhändler-Vereinigung, 1978. 220 pp.

59 GERMANIA JUDAICA: *Arbeitsinformationen über Studienprojekte auf dem Gebiet des deutschen Judentums und des Antisemitismus.* Köln: 1963– continuing. Ausg. 1–10, mimeog.

60 HAASE, CARL: *The records of German history in German and certain other record offices with short notes on libraries and other collections.* Boppard a.Rh.: Boldt, 1975. 194 pp. [Text in German and English.]

61 LENZ, WILHELM, comp.: *Archivalische Quellen zur deutschen Geschichte seit 1500 in Grossbritannien.* Boppard a.Rh.: Boldt, 1975. xxviii + 372 pp. (Veröffentlichungen des Deutschen Historischen Instituts in London). [Text in German and English.]

62 MÖNNING, RICHARD, ed.: *Translations from the German. A series of bibliographies. English 1948–1964.* 2nd rev. ed. Göttingen: Vandenhoeck & Ruprecht, 1968. 509 pp.

62a TRUMPP, THOMAS & KÖHNE, RENATE, comps.: *Archivbestände zur Wirtschafts- und Sozialgeschichte der Weimarer Republik. Übersicht über Quellen in Archiven der Bundesrepublik Deutschland.* Mit Beiträgen von Jens Flemming [and others]. Boppard a.Rh.: Boldt, 1979. 380 pp. (Schriften des Bundesarchivs.)

Bibliographies

BENZ, WOLFGANG: *Quellen zur Zeitgeschichte. See* 36.

63 *Bibliographie zur Zeitgeschichte. Beilage der Vierteljahrshefte für Zeitgeschichte. Jhrg. 1–22.* Zusammengest.: Thilo Vogelsang. Stuttgart: Deutsche Verlags-Anstalt, 1953–1972.

64 *Bibliothek des Instituts für Zeitgeschichte München—Library of the Institute for Contemporary History, Munich.* Boston, Mass.: Hall, 1967–1973.
Alphabetischer Katalog. Publ. 1967. 5 vols. [And] *Nachtragsband I.* Publ. 1973.
Sachkatalog. Publ. 1967. 6 vols. [And] *Nachtragsbände.* Publ. 1973. 2 vols.
Länderkatalog. Publ. 1967. 2 vols.
Biographischer Katalog. Publ. 1967. 1 vol. [And] *Nachtragsband.* Publ. 1973.

65 BIBLIOTHEK FÜR ZEITGESCHICHTE—WELTKRIEGSBÜCHEREI STUTTGART: *Systematischer Katalog.* Boston, Mass.: Hall, 1968. In 20 vols.

66 BIBLIOTHEK FÜR ZEITGESCHICHTE—WELTKRIEGSBÜCHEREI STUTTGART: *Bücherschau der Weltkriegsbücherei.* Stuttgart: 1953–1959. 7 vols.
[And] *Neue Folge der Bücherschau der Weltkriegsbücherei.* Frankfurt a.M.: Bernard & Graefe, 1960– continuing. Nos. 35–50.
[Extensive bibliographies on many aspects of contemporary history are included.]

67 *Deutsches Bücherverzeichnis. Eine Zusammenstellung der im deutschen Buchhandel erschienenen Bücher, Zeitschriften und Landkarten. Mit einem Stich- und Schlagwortregister.*
1915–1935. New York: Johnson Reprint Corp., 1960–62. In 16 vols.
1936–1940. Leipzig: Verlag des Börsenvereins der deutschen Buchhändler, 1942. In 3 vols.
1941–1950. Leipzig: Verlag für Buch- und Bibliothekswesen, 1953–57. In 6 vols.
[Further volumes have appeared and continue to appear.]

68 *Gesamtverzeichnis des deutschsprachigen Schrifttums 1911–1965.* Hrsg.: Reinhard Oberschelp. Bearb. unter der Leitung von Willi Gorzny. Geleitw.:

Wilhelm Totok. München: Verlag Dokumentation, 1976– continuing. 104 vols. (to Rat). [Approx. 500 pp. per volume.]

69 KRAUS PERIODICALS: *National Socialism*. Nendeln, Liechtenstein: [1973?] 167 pp. (Catalogue 48 [of reprint publishers]).

70 LEA VALLEY BOOKS, ed.: *Hitler's Germany*. Hastings, Sx.: 1976–1977. 94 pp. [In 11 parts.]

71 *Nationalsozialistische Bibliographie. Monatshefte der parteiamtlichen Prüfungskommission zum Schutze des NS.-Schrifttums.* Hrsg.: Philipp Bouhler. Berlin: Eher, 1936–1944. 1.–8. Jhrg.

72 NEUBURGER, OTTO: *Official publications of present-day Germany. Government, corporate organizations and National Socialist Party. With an outline of the governmental structure of Germany.* Washington, D.C.: Government Printing Office, 1944. 130 pp.

73 REICHSMINISTERIUM FÜR VOLKSAUFKLÄRUNG UND PROPAGANDA, Abt. Schrifttum: *Das Buch ein Schwert des Geistes. Grundliste für das deutsche Leih- und Werkbüchereiwesen.* 3. Folge. Leipzig: Börsenverein der Deutschen Buchhändler, 1943. 189 pp.

74 REICHSMINISTERIUM FÜR VOLKSAUFKLÄRUNG UND PROPAGANDA: *Soldatisches Volk. Politische Buch- und Dokumentenschau.* Berlin: Limpert, 1941. 248 pp., illus., facsims.

75 SAGITZ, WALTER: *Bibliographie des Nationalsozialismus.* Cottbus: Heine, 1933. 168 pp.

76 *Schrifttum über Deutschland 1918–1963. Ausgewählte Bibliographie deutscher Publikationen.* Bearb.: Inter Nationes Bonn... Wiesbaden: Steiner, 1964. 292 pp.

STACHURA, PETER D.: *The Weimar era and Hitler* ... See 930.

77 ULLMANN, HANS PETER: *Bibliographie zur Geschichte der deutschen Parteien und Interessenverbände.* Göttingen: Vandenhoeck & Ruprecht, 1978. 263 pp.

78 THE WIENER LIBRARY: *Catalogue series*
No. 2: *From Weimar to Hitler—Germany, 1918–1933.* 2nd rev. and enl. ed. London: Vallentine, Mitchell, 1964. x + 268 pp. (Ed.: Ilse R. Wolff)
No. 4: *After Hitler—Germany, 1945–1963.* London: Vallentine, Mitchell, 1963. x + 261 pp. (Ed.: Ilse R. Wolff; Comp.: Helen Kehr) [Incl.: 'Wartime plans for Germany', pp. 12–26; 'The Third Reich in retrospect', pp. 72–88.]
No. 5: *Prejudice—Racist, religious, nationalist.* London: Vallentine, Mitchell, 1971. viii + 385 pp. (Comp. and ed.: Helen Kehr)
No. 7: *Persecution and resistance under the Nazis. Part I: Reprint of Catalogue 1 (2nd ed.); Part II: New material and amendments.* London: Institute of Contemporary History, 1978. 500 pp. (Ed.: Ilse R. Wolff (Part I), Helen Kehr (Part II)).

Periodical indexes

79 *Monatsschrift für Geschichte und Wissenschaft des Judentums. Gesamtregister 1851–1939.* Tübingen: Mohr, 1966. 250 pp. (Veröffentlichungen des Leo Baeck Instituts).

80 *Neue Politische Literatur. Register der Jahrgänge xi (1966)–xx (1975).* Bearb.: Michael Mattig, Ingrid Schmidt. Wiesbaden: Steiner, 1978. 250 pp.

81 *Revue d'Histoire de la Deuxième Guerre Mondiale: Table systématique des numéros 1 à 100.* Paris: Presses Universitaires de France, 1977. 114 pp.

82 *[Survey of international affairs]* Dɪᴛᴍᴀs, E. M. R., comp.: *Consolidated index to the Survey of International Affairs 1920–1938 and Documents on International Affairs 1928–1938.* London: Oxford University Press (under the auspices of the Royal Institute of International Affairs), 1967. 271 pp.

83 *Vierteljahrshefte für Zeitgeschichte: Inhaltsverzeichnis der Jhrg. 1 (1953)–22 (1974).* Zusammengest.: Ruth Körner. Stuttgart: Deutsche Verlags-Anstalt, 1975. 68 pp.

84 *The Wiener Library Bulletin Index 1946/47–1968. (Old Series: Vols. I–XIX (No. 3) and New Series Nos. 1–13).* Comp.: Helen Kehr. Nendeln/Liechtenstein: Kraus Reprint, 1979. 201 pp.

II. NATIONALSOZIALISTISCHE DEUTSCHE ARBEITERPARTEI

A. GENERAL

85 Cěsar, Jaroslav and Černý, Bohumil: *Nacismus a Třeti Riše* [Nazism and the Third Reich]. Praha: Orbis, 1963. 269 pp., illus., tab., bibl.

86 Drexler, Anton: *Mein politisches Erwachen. Aus dem Tagebuch eines deutschen sozialistischen Arbeiters*. 4. Aufl. München: Deutscher Volksverlag, 1923. 70 pp. [1884–1942. In 1919, Drexler, a locksmith, and Karl Harrer founded the Deutsche Arbeiterpartei which became (March 1920) the NSDAP. From 1920 to 1921 he was the party's chairman. After the NSDAP's reorganization in 1925, Drexler, an opponent of Hitler, took no further part in the movement, despite a reconciliation in 1930.]

87 Galkin, A. A.: *Germaniskii fashizm* [German fascism]. Moskva: Izd. 'Nauka', 1967. 398 pp., tabs.

88 *Gau- und Kreisverzeichnis der NSDAP*. München: Hrsg. der Reichs-organisationsleiter der NSDAP, 1938. 164 pp.

89 Glum, Friedrich: *Der Nationalsozialismus. Werden und Vergehen*. München: Beck, 1962. 474 pp., illus., bibl.

90 Grebing, Helga: *Der Nationalsozialismus. Ursprung und Wesen*. 16. durchges. Aufl. München: Olzog, 1965. 160 pp., bibl.

91 Grosser, Alfred, ed.: *Wie war es möglich? Die Wirklichkeit des Nationalsozialismus. 9 Studien von Henri Burgelin* [and others]. Frankfurt a.M.: Fischer, 1980. 204 pp. [Transl. from the French: *Dix leçons sur le nazisme*. Paris: Fayard, 1976.]

92 Heiden, Konrad: *Geschichte des Nationalsozialismus. Die Karriere einer Idee*. Berlin: Rowohlt, 1932, 296 pp., bibl.

93 Koch, Erich: *Die NSDAP. Idee, Führer und Partei*. Berlin: Kittler, 1934. 96 pp., illus.

94 Lindenberg, Christoph: *Die Technik des Bösen. Zur Vorgeschichte und Geschichte des Nationalsozialismus*. 2. Aufl. Stuttgart: Verlag Freies Geistesleben, 1978. 110 pp.

95 Lingg, Anton: *Die Verwaltung der Nationalsozialistischen Deutschen Arbeiterpartei*. München: Eher, 1939. 327 pp., tabs., bibl.

96 McKale, Donald M.: *The Nazi Party courts. Hitler's management of conflict in*

his movement, 1921–1945. Lawrence, Kans.: University Press of Kansas, 1974. 252 pp., bibl.

97   McRANDLE, JAMES H.: *The track of the wolf. Essays on National Socialism and its leader Adolf Hitler.* Evanston, Ill.: Northwestern University Press, 1965. 261 pp., bibl.

98   MAZOR, MICHEL: *Le phénomène nazi. Documents nazis commentés.* Paris: Eds. du Centre, 1957. 273 pp.

99   NEUMANN, FRANZ: *Behemoth. The structure and practice of National Socialism, 1933–1944.* London: Cass, 1967. 649 pp., tabs. [Reprint of 2nd ed., first publ. 1944; first ed. 1942. German version: *Behemot.* Hrsg. und mit einem Nachwort 'Franz Neumanns Behemoth und die heutige Faschismusdiskussion' von Gert Schäfer. Köln: Europäische Verlags-Anstalt, 1977.]

100   NEY, E. L.: *Die braune Armee. Vom Hakenkreuz zum Krieg.* Thann [Alsace]: Journal de Thann, 1933. 94 pp. [Shows connection between Free Corps, Stahlhelm, SA, Reichswehr.]

101   NOLTE, ERNST: *Der Nationalsozialismus.* Frankfurt a.M.: Ullstein, 1970. 250 pp.

102   NYOMARKAY, JOSEPH: *Charisma and factionalism in the Nazi Party.* Minneapolis, Minn.: University of Minnesota Press, 1967. 161 pp., tabs., bibl.

103   ORLOW, DIETRICH: *The History of the Nazi Party.*
[I]: *1919–1933.* Pittsburgh, Pa.: University of Pittsburgh Press, 1969. 338 pp., tabs., bibl.
II: *1933–1945.* Newton Abbot: David & Charles, 1973. xiv + 538 pp., tabs., bibl.

104   REICHSORGANISATIONSLEITER DER NSDAP: *Organisationsbuch der NSDAP.* 7. Aufl. 1943. 596 pp., illus.

105   REICHSORGANISATIONSLEITER DER NSDAP: *Parteistatistik. Stand 1. Januar 1935 (ohne Saargebiet).* In 3 vols.

105a   RHODES, JAMES M.: *The Hitler movement: a modern millenarian revolution.* Stanford, Cal.: Hoover Institution Press, 1980. 253 pp., bibl.

106   ROSTEN, CURT: *Das ABC des Nationalsozialismus.* 3. Aufl. Berlin: Schmidt, 1933. 252 pp., illus., diagrs.

107   SCHÄFER, WOLFGANG: *NSDAP. Entwicklung und Struktur der Staatspartei des Dritten Reiches.* Hannover: Norddeutsche Verlagsanstalt, 1956. 100 pp., tabs. (Schriften des Instituts für Wissenschaftliche Politik in Marburg/Lahn).

108   THORNTON, M. J.: *Nazism 1918–1945.* Oxford: Pergamon Press, 1966. 181 pp., illus.

109 UNGER, ARYEH: *The totalitarian party. Party and people in Nazi Germany and Soviet Russia.* London: Cambridge University Press, 1974. 286 pp., bibl.

110 UNRUH, FRIEDRICH FRANZ von: *Nationalsozialismus.* Frankfurt a.M.: Societäts-Verlag, 1931. 64 pp.

111 VOLZ, HANS: *Daten der Geschichte der NSDAP.* 11. Aufl. Berlin: Ploetz, 1943. 156 pp., diagrs., tabs.

Party and state

112 DIEHL-THIELE, PETER: *Partei und Staat im Dritten Reich. Untersuchungen zum Verhältnis von NSDAP und allgemeiner innerer Staatsverwaltung 1933–1945.* München: Beck, 1969. 269 pp., bibl.

113 GAHLMANN, FRANZ: *Probleme der rechtlichen Stellung der Organe der Nationalsozialistischen Deutschen Arbeiterpartei in strafrechtlicher und strafprozessualer Hinsicht.* Inaugural-Dissertation [pres. to] Universität Köln. Emsdetten: Lechte, 1940. 71 pp., bibl.

114 *Gesetz über die Vernehmung von Angehörigen der Nationalsozialistischen Deutschen Arbeiterpartei und ihrer Gliederungen vom 1. Dezember 1936 mit Ausführungsbestimmungen.* Berlin: Decker, 1937, 26 pp.

115 HAIDN, E. & FISCHER, L., eds.: *Das Recht der NSDAP. Vorschriften-Sammlung mit Anmerkungen, Verweisungen und Sachregister.* Vorwort: Dr. Frank. München: Eher, 1936. 782 pp.

116 JOHANNY, CARL: *Partei und Staat.* Inaugural-Dissertation [pres. to] Bayerische Julius-Maximilians-Universität Würzburg. Königsberg (Pr.): Gräfe & Unger, 1936. 100 pp., bibl.

117 KLENNER, JOCHEN: *Verhältnis von Partei und Staat 1933–1945. Dargestellt am Beispiel Bayerns.* München: Wölfle, 1974. xiii + 364 pp., tab., bibl.

118 NEESZE, GOTTFRIED: *Die Nationalsozialistische Deutsche Arbeiterpartei. Versuch einer Rechtsdeutung.* Stuttgart: Kohlhammer, 1935. 208 pp.

119 REULING, ROBERT: *Die öffentlich-rechtliche Gestaltung der NSDAP.* Dissertation [pres. to] Ludwigs-Universität zu Giessen. Düsseldorf: Nolte, 1936. 86 pp., bibl.

Party rallies

120 BURDEN, HAMILTON T.: *The Nuremberg party rallies 1923–1939.* Foreword: Adolf A. Berle. London: Pall Mall Press, 1967. 206 pp., illus., maps, bibl.

121 HOFFMANN, HEINRICH, ed.: *Parteitag der Freiheit. 80 Bilddokumente vom Reichsparteitag zu Nürnberg 1935.* Geleitwort und Unterschriften: Alfred Ingemar Berndt. Berlin: 'Zeitgeschichte' Verlag, [1935]. [66 pp.], illus.

122 *Nürnberg 1933. Der erste Reichstag der geeinten deutschen Nation.* Berlin: Hobbing, 1933. 111 pp., illus., tab.

123 [REICHSPARTEITAGE] *Offizieller Bericht über den Verlauf des Reichsparteitages mit sämtlichen Reden.* München: Eher, 1934–1938. Ports., illus.

1934: *Der Kongress zu Nürnberg vom 5. bis 10. Oktober 1934.* 215 pp.
1935: *Der Parteitag der Freiheit vom 10.–16. September 1935.* 2. Aufl. 290 pp.
1936: *Der Parteitag der Ehre vom 8. bis 14. September 1936.* 309 pp.
1937: *Der Parteitag der Arbeit vom 6. bis 13. September 1937.* Publ. 1938.
386 pp.
1938: *Der Parteitag Grossdeutschland vom 5. bis 12. September 1938.* 347 pp.

124 ROSENBERG, ALFRED, ed.: *Führer zum Reichsparteitag der Nationalsozialistischen Deutschen Arbeiterpartei zu Nürnberg.* München: Eher,
1927–1929. Illus.
3. *1927.* 47 pp.
4. *1929.* 55 pp.

'TRIUMPH DES WILLENS' (film)
125 BARSAM, RICHARD MERAN: *Filmguide to Triumph of the Will.* Bloomington,
Ind.: Indiana University Press, 1975. x + 82 pp., list of films, bibl.

126 RIEFENSTAHL, LENI: *Hinter den Kulissen des Reichsparteitag-Films. Der Film
'Triumph des Willens' wurde im Auftrag des Führers geschaffen.* München:
Eher, 1935. 105 pp., illus.

---

127 WHITE, JOHN BAKER: *Dover–Nürnberg return.* London: Burrup, Mathieson,
1937. 108 pp., illus.

128 WYKES, ALAN: *The Nuremberg rallies.* London: Macdonald, 1970. 160 pp.,
illus., facsims., map, bibl. (Purnell's History of the Second World War,
Campaign Book 8). [Chiefly on pre-1933 rallies.]

Sociological studies of the party and its members

129 ABEL, THEODORE: *Why Hitler came into power. An answer based on the original
life stories of six hundred of his followers.* New York: Prentice-Hall, 1938.
322 pp.

130 BANASZKIEWICZ, JAKUB: *Powstanie partii hitlerowskiej. Studium socjologiczne
genezy faszyzmu niemieckiego 1919–1923* [The formation of the Nazi party.
A sociological study of the genesis of German fascism in the years
1919–1923]. Poznań: Instytut Zachodni, 1968. 525 pp., bibl., summary in
English.

131 BROSZAT, MARTIN and others, eds.: *Bayern in der NS-Zeit. Soziale Lage und
politisches Verhalten der Bevölkerung im Spiegel vertraulicher Berichte.*
Hrsg.: Martin Broszat, Elke Fröhlich, Falk Wiesemann. München:
Oldenbourg, 1977. 712 pp., maps, tabs.

132 FISCHER, CONAN J.: 'The occupational background of the SA's rank and file
membership during the depression years, 1929 to mid-1934'. [In] Stachura,
Peter D., ed.: *The shaping of the Nazi state*, pp. 131–159. See 1157.

133 FROMM, ERICH: *The anatomy of human destructiveness.* New York: Holt,
Rinehart & Winston, 1973. xvi + 521 pp., bibl.

134 HEBERLE, RUDOLF: *Landbevölkerung und Nationalsozialismus. Eine soziologische Untersuchung der politischen Willensbildung in Schleswig-Holstein 1918 bis 1932.* Stuttgart: Deutsche Verlagsanstalt, 1963. 171 pp., map, tabs. (Schriftenreihe der Vierteljahrshefte für Zeitgeschichte).

135 [HEBERLE, RUDOLF] SAHNER, HEINZ: *Politische Tradition, Sozialstruktur und Parteiensystem in Schleswig-Holstein. Ein Beitrag zur Replikation von Rudolf Heberles: Landbevölkerung und Nationalsozialismus.* Meisenheim a.Gl.: Hain, 1972. 144 pp., maps, tabs., bibl.

136 HENNIG, EIKE: *Bürgerliche Gesellschaft und Faschismus in Deutschland. Ein Forschungsbericht.* Frankfurt a.M.: Suhrkamp, 1977. 423 pp., tabs., bibl.

137 MERKL, PETER H.: *Political violence under the swastika. 581 early Nazis.* Princeton, N.J.: Princeton University Press, 1975. xiv + 735 pp., tabs., bibl. [Based on Theodore Abel collection.]

REICH, WILHELM: *Massenpsychologie des Faschismus. See 258.*

138 SCHIEDER, WOLFGANG, ed.: *Faschismus als soziale Bewegung. Deutschland und Italien im Vergleich.* Hamburg: Hoffmann & Campe, 1976. 211 pp., summary in English.

139 SCHUON-WIEHL, ANNALIESE K.: *Faschismus und Gesellschaftsstruktur. Am Beispiel des Aufstiegs des Nationalsozialismus.* Einl.: Karl Theodor Schuon. Frankfurt a.M: Europäische Verlagsanstalt, 1970. 101 pp., tabs., bibl.

140 WEBER, ALEXANDER: *Soziale Merkmale der NSDAP-Wähler. Eine Zusammenfassung bisheriger impirischer Untersuchungen und eine Analyse in den Gemeinden der Länder Baden und Hessen.* Inaugural-Dissertation [pres. to] Albert-Ludwigs-Universität zu Freiburg i.Br. 1969. 281 pp., tabs., bibl.

See also 252–261.

Occultism

141 BRENNAN, J. H.: *Occult Reich.* [London?]: Futura Books, 1974. 188 pp., bibl.

142 GERSON, WERNER: *Le nazisme, société secrète.* Paris: Productions de Paris, 1969. [50] + 365 pp., illus., bibl.

HANUSSEN, ERIK JAN
143 BOROVIČKA, V. P.: *Vražda jasnovidce Hanussena* [Murder of the clairvoyant Hanussen]. Praha: Svoboda, 1968. 283 pp., bibl.

144 FREI, BRUNO: *Hanussen. Ein Bericht.* Vorwort: Egon Erwin Kisch. Strasbourg: Brant, 1934. 209 pp.

_____

145 HOWE, ELLIC: *Uraniä's children. The strange world of the astrologers.* London: Kimber, 1967. 259 pp., illus., facsims., diagrs.

146 RAVENSCROFT, TREVOR: *The spear of destiny. The occult power behind the spear which pierced the side of Christ.* London: Neville Spearman, 1972.

xxii + 362 pp., illus., diagr., facsims., bibl. [Occultist view of Hitler and the NSDAP.]

147 REHWALDT, HERMANN: *Die 'kommende Religion'. Okkultwahn als Nachfolger des Christentums.* München: Ludendorff, 1936. 48 pp., illus.

148 SEBOTTENDORFF, RUDOLF VON: *Bevor Hitler kam. Urkundliches aus der Frühzeit der nationalsozialistischen Bewegung.* München: Deukula, 1933. 267 pp., illus., facsims. [Founder of 'Thule Gesellschaft, Orden für Deutsche Art'.]

148a TAUTZ, JOHANNES: *Der Eingriff des Widersachers. Fragen zum Okkultenaspekt des Nationalsozialismus.* Freiburg i.Br.: Verlag Die Kommenden, 1980. 76 pp.

VONDUNG, KLAUS: *Magie und Manipulation.* See 2070.

149 WULFF, WILHELM Th. H.: *Tierkreis und Hakenkreuz. Als Astrologe an Himmlers Hof.* Gütersloh: Bertelsmann, 1968. 248 pp., illus., facsim.

See also 279–282.

B. ROOTS

1. GENERAL

150 ARENDT, HANNAH: *The burden of our time.* London: Secker & Warburg, 1951. 477 pp., bibl. [Part I: 'Antisemitism' (includes racism). German version: *Elemente und Ursprünge totaler Herrschaft.* Frankfurt a.M.: Europäische Verlagsanstalt, 1955.]

151 BRONDER, DIETRICH: *Bevor Hitler kam. Eine historische Studie.* Hannover: Pfeiffer, 1964. 446 pp., bibl. [Incl.: 'Christlich-europäischer Anti-semitismus'; 'Deutscher Antisemitismus bis 1900'; 'Deutscher Antisemitis-mus ab 1900'.]

152 BUTLER, ROHAN D'O.: *The roots of National-Socialism, 1783–1933.* London: Faber & Faber, 1941. 310 pp., bibl.

153 LEERS, JOHANN VON: *Die geschichtlichen Grundlagen des Nationalsozialismus.* Berlin: Deutscher Rechtsverlag, 1938. 116 pp.

154 LUKÁCS, GEORG: *Von Nietzsche bis Hitler, oder Der Irrationalismus in der deutschen Politik. Auszüge aus: 'Zerstörung der Vernunft'.* Frankfurt a.M.: Fischer, 1966. 268 pp.

155 McGOVERN, WILLIAM MONTGOMERY: *From Luther to Hitler. The history of Fascist-Nazi political philosophy.* London: Harrap, 1946. 683 pp., bibl.

156 NEUROHR, JEAN F.: *Der Mythos vom Dritten Reich. Zur Geistesgeschichte des Nationalsozialismus.* Stuttgart: Cotta, 1957. 286 pp., bibl.

157 RADEL, J.-LUCIEN: *Roots of totalitarianism. The ideological sources of Fascism, National Socialism and Communism.* New York: Crane, Russak, 1975. ix + 218 pp., diagrs., bibl.

158 THIER, ERICH, ed.: *Wegbereiter des deutschen Sozialismus. Eine Auswahl aus ihren Schriften.* Stuttgart: Kröner, 1940. xxxv + 301 pp.

159 WEBER, EUGEN: *Varieties of Fascism. Doctrines of revolution in the twentieth century.* Princeton, N.J.: Nostrand, 1964. 191 pp., bibl. [Incl.: Part I/5: 'A red herring: racialism'; I/7: 'Hitler and the Nazis. ...'; II/2: 'Racialist National Socialism'.]

2. POLITICAL AND NATIONALIST

160 [ALLDEUTSCHER VERBAND] KRUCK, ALFRED: *Geschichte des Alldeutschen Verbandes 1890–1939.* Wiesbaden: Steiner, 1954. 258 pp., bibl.

161 CLASS, HEINRICH (under pseud. EINHART): *Deutsche Geschichte.* 5. vollkommen neu bearb. und erweit. Aufl. Leipzig: Dieterich (Weicher), 1914. xxii + 511 pp., illus., map. [First ed. 1909.]

FICHTE, JOHANN GOTTLIEB
162 *Fichtes Reden an die deutsche Nation.* Eingeleitet: Rudolf Eucken. Leipzig: Insel-Verlag, 1922. 269 + xvi pp.

163 BERGMANN, ERNST: *Fichte und der Nationalsozialismus.* Breslau: Hirt, 1933. 48 pp., port.

164 EDMONDSON, NELSON: 'The Fichte Society. A chapter in Germany's conservative revolution'. [In] *The Journal of Modern History*, Vol. 38, No. 2, June 1966. Chicago, Ill.: University of Chicago Press. Pp. 161–180.

165 FOERSTER, FRIEDRICH WILHELM: *Mein Kampf gegen das militaristische und nationalistische Deutschland. Gesichtspunkte zur deutschen Selbsterkenntnis und zum Aufbau eines neuen Deutschland.* Stuttgart: Verlag 'Friede durch Recht', 1920. 262 pp.

FREIKORPS
166 SALOMON, ERNST von, ed.: *Das Buch vom deutschen Freikorpskämpfer.* Hrsg. im Auftr. der Freikorpszeitschrift 'Der Reiter gen Osten'. Berlin: Limpert, 1938. 496 pp., illus., maps, facsim.

167 WAITE, ROBERT G. L.: *Vanguard of Nazism. The Free Corps movement in postwar Germany 1918–1923.* Cambridge, Mass.: Harvard University Press, 1952. xii + 344 pp.

168 FRYMANN, DANIEL: *Wenn ich der Kaiser wär! Politische Wahrheiten und Notwendigkeiten.* 4. Aufl. Leipzig: Dieterich, 1913. 235 pp.

169 GEYER, CURT: *Macht und Masse. Von Bismarck zu Hitler.* Hannover: Verlag 'Das Andere Deutschland', 1948. 282 pp. ['... the influence of nationalistic thought on all classes and parties of the German people.']

170 GÖHRING, MARTIN: *Bismarcks Erben 1890–1945. Deutschlands Weg von Wilhelm II bis Adolf Hitler.* Wiesbaden: Steiner, 1958. viii + 386 pp., illus.

171 [JAHN, FRIEDRICH LUDWIG] BAUER, FRANZ: *Friedrich Ludwig Jahn, das Leben eines Nationalsozialisten aus früher Zeit.* Leipzig: Schneider, 1934. 79 pp., illus.

172 JUNG, RUDOLF: *Der nationale Sozialismus. Seine Grundlagen, sein Werdegang und seine Ziele.* 3. vollst. umgearb. Aufl. München: Deutscher Volksverlag, 1922. 160 pp., bibl.

173 KLEMPERER, KLEMENS von: *Germany's new conservatism. Its history and dilemma in the twentieth century.* Foreword: Sigmund Neumann. Princeton, N.J.: Princeton University Press, 1957. 250 pp., bibl. [Incl. Moeller van den Bruck, Oswald Spengler, Ernst Jünger, Schwarze Front, etc. etc. German version: *Konservative Bewegungen. Zwischen Kaiserreich und Nationalsozialismus.* München: Oldenbourg, 1962(?)]

LAGARDE, PAUL DE
174 LAGARDE, PAUL de: *Deutscher Glaube, Deutsches Vaterland, Deutsche Bildung.* Das Wesentliche aus seinen Schriften ausgew. und eingel. von Friedrich Daab. Jena: Diederichs, 1914. 224 pp., ports.

175 BREITLING, RICHARD: *Paul de Lagarde und der grossdeutsche Gedanke.* Geleitwort: K. A. von Müller. Wien: Braumüller, 1927. vii + 116 pp.

176 LOUGEE, ROBERT W.: *Paul de Lagarde, 1827–1891. A study of radical conservatism in Germany.* Cambridge, Mass.: Harvard University Press, 1962. 357 pp., bibl.

MOELLER VAN DEN BRUCK, ARTHUR
177 MOELLER van den BRUCK: *Das dritte Reich.* Hrsg.: Hans Schwarz. Hamburg: Hanseatische Verlagsanstalt, 1931. 249 pp. [The Bible of Nazi ideology. French version: *Le troisième Reich.* Paris: Librairie de la Revue Française, 1933. English condensed version: *Germany's Third Empire.* London: Allen & Unwin, 1934. The original publication was in 1923.]

178 MOELLER van den BRUCK, ARTHUR: *Das Recht der jungen Völker. Sammlung politischer Aufsätze.* Hrsg.: Hans Schwarz. Berlin: Verlag Der Nahe Osten, 1932. 218 pp. [First publ. 1919.]

179 SCHWIERSKOTT, HANS-JOACHIM: *Arthur Moeller van den Bruck und der revolutionäre Nationalismus in der Weimarer Republik.* Göttingen: Musterschmidt, 1962. 202 pp., bibl.

---

180 MOSSE, GEORGE L.: *The nationalization of the masses. Political symbolism and mass movements in Germany from the Napoleonic wars through the Third Reich.* New York: Fertig, 1975. xiv + 252 pp., illus. [German version: *Die Nationalisierung der Massen.* Berlin: Ullstein, 1976.]

181 [REVENTLOW, Graf ERNST zu] BOOG, HORST: *Graf Ernst zu Reventlow, 1869–1943. Eine Studie zur Krise der deutschen Geschichte seit dem Ende des 19. Jahrhunderts.* Inaugural-Dissertation [pres. to] Ruprecht-Karl-Universität Heidelberg. 1965. 326 pp., bibl.

182   RÖHL, J. C. G.: *From Bismarck to Hitler. The problem of continuity in German history.* London: Longmans, 1970. xiv + 191 pp. [Anthology of documents, speeches, etc. Part I: 'The roots of National Socialism'.]

183   SCHWEDHELM, KARL, ed.: *Propheten des Nationalismus.* München: List, 1969. 319 pp., ports., bibl. [Incl.: Eugen Dühring, Paul de Lagarde, Heinrich von Treitschke, Houston Stewart Chamberlain, Dietrich Eckart, Adolf Bartels, Erwin Guido Kolbenheyer.]

184   SNYDER, LOUIS L.: *Roots of German nationalism.* Bloomington, Ind.: Indiana University Press, 1978. 309 pp., illus., bibl.

STAPEL, WILHELM
185   STAPEL, WILHELM: *Volksbürgerliche Erziehung.* 2. durchges. und wesent. verm. Aufl. Hamburg: Verlag des Deutschen Volkstums, 1920. 144 pp. [First ed. 1917. This second edition does not include 'Von den Juden', which forms Part III of the fourth edition, publ. Hamburg: Hanseatische Verlagsanstalt, 1942, under title: *Volk. Untersuchungen über Volkheit und Volkstum.*]

186   KESSLER, HEINRICH: *Wilhelm Stapel als politischer Publizist. Ein Beitrag zur Geschichte des konservativen Nationalismus zwischen den beiden Weltkriegen.* Nürnberg: Spindler, 1967. 326 pp., port., bibl.

3.   RACIST

Eugenics

187   BINDING, KARL & HOCHE, ALFRED: *Die Freigabe der Vernichtung lebensunwerten Lebens. Ihr Mass und ihre Form.* Leipzig: Meiner, 1920. 62 pp.

188   DRIESMANS, HEINRICH: 'Die Aufartung der Völker germanischer Rasse unter Vormacht und Führung der Deutschen'. [In *Die Vernichtung der englischen Weltmacht und des Zarismus ...* by G. Kampffmeyer and others, ed. by Kurt L. Walter van der Bleek. Berlin: Borngräber, (1915). 235 pp.]

189   ELLERBEK, ELLEGAARD: *Sönne Sonnings Söhne auf Sonnen-See. Ein deutscher Roman mit drei Gesichtern, in einem Vorschau und sieben Büchern.* Mit vier Briefen von Guido von List. Berlin: Widar-Verlag, 1924. 840 pp. [In 2 vols.]

190   HAISER, FRANZ: *Das Gastmahl des Freiherrn von Artaria. Ein Kampf zwischen rassenaristokratischer und demokratischer Weltanschauung.* München: Lehmann, 1920. 172 pp.

191   HENTSCHEL, WILLIBALD: *Varuna. Das Gesetz des aufsteigenden und sinkenden Lebens in der Geschichte.* 2. Aufl. Leipzig: Fritsch, 1907. 626 pp.

192   SIEBERT, Fr.: *Der völkische Gehalt der Rassenhygiene.* München: Lehmann, 1917. 214 pp. (Bücherei deutscher Erneuerung).

Aryans, Nordics, etc.

193   KOCH, PAUL: *Die arischen Grundlagen der Bibel. Die Übereinstimmung der*

blischen Sagen mit der Mythologie der Indogermanen. Berlin: Johnke, 914. 189 pp.

194 POESCHE, THEODOR: *Die Arier. Ein Beitrag zur historischen Anthropologie.* Jena: Costenoble, 1878. 238 pp.

195 POLIAKOV, LEON: *The Aryan myth. A history of racist and nationalist ideas in Europe.* Transl.: Edmund Howard. New York: Basic Books (and London: Heinemann), 1974. 388 pp.

196 WILSER, LUDWIG: *Die Germanen. Beiträge zur Völkerkunde.* Neue, den Fortschritten der Wissenschaft angepasste und mehrfach erweit. Bearb. Leipzig: Dieterich, 1913/14. 2 vols., illus., tabs.

197 WILSER, LUDWIG: *Die Überlegenheit der germanischen Rasse. Zeitgemässe Betrachtungen.* Stuttgart: Strecker & Schröder, 1915. 46 pp.

198 WIRTH, HERMAN: *Der Aufgang der Menschheit. Untersuchungen zur Geschichte der Religion, Symbolik und Schrift der atlantisch-nordischen Rasse. Textband I: Die Grundzüge.* Jena: Diederichs, 1928. 632 pp., illus., diagrs., tabs. under separate cover.

199 ZSCHAETZSCH, KARL GEORG: *Die Herkunft und Geschichte des arischen Stammes.* Nikolssee b. Berlin: Arier-Verlag, 1920. 527 pp.

SWASTIKA

200 BERNHARDI, DIETRICH: *Das Hakenkreuz. Seine Geschichte, Verbreitung und Bedeutung.* 8. Aufl. der ehemaligen Schrift des 1923 verstorbenen Dr. Ludwig Wilser: 'Das Hakenkreuz nach Ursprung, Vorkommen und Bedeutung'. Leipzig: Fritsch, [after 1933]. 31 pp., illus., map, tab.

201 CLAASSEN, OSWALD: *Weltwissen im Hakenkreuz. Von Labyrinthen, Runen und Religionen.* Krefeld: Hohn, 1934. 239 pp., illus.

202 PAULSEN, PETER: *Axt und Kreuz bei den Nordgermanen.* Berlin: Ahnenerbe-Stiftung-Verlag, 1939. 267 pp., illus., maps, bibl.

4. ANTI-SEMITISM

203 ANDICS, HELLMUT: *Der ewige Jude. Ursachen und Geschichte des Antisemitismus.* Wien: Molden, 1965. 420 pp., maps, tabs.

BRONDER, DIETRICH: *Bevor Hitler kam. See 151.*

204 FELDEN, KLEMENS: *Die Übernahme des antisemitischen Stereotyps als soziale Norm durch die bürgerliche Gesellschaft Deutschlands (1875–1900).* Inaugural-Dissertation [pres. to] Ruprecht-Karl-Universität zu Heidelberg. 1963. 175 pp., diagr., tabs.

205 FUCHS, EDUARD: *Die Juden in der Karikatur. Ein Beitrag zur Kulturgeschichte.* München: Lange, 1921. 309 pp., illus.

206 KERNHOLT, OTTO: *Deutschlands Schuld und Sühne. Geschichtliche*

Betrachtungen zur Entstehung und Lösung der Judenfrage. Leipzig: Weicher, 1923. 301 pp.

207 PARKES, JAMES: *The emergence of the Jewish problem 1878–1939.* London: Oxford University Press, 1946. 259 pp. (Issued under auspices of the Royal Institute of International Affairs).

THE WIENER LIBRARY: *Catalogue Series: No. 5: Prejudice—Racist, religious, nationalist. See 78.*

Political

208 MASSING, PAUL W.: *Rehearsal for destruction. A study of political antisemitism in Imperial Germany.* New York: Harper, 1949. 341 pp. [German version: *Vorgeschichte des politischen Antisemitismus.* Frankfurt a.M.: Europäische Verlagsanstalt, 1959.]

209 NAUDH, H. [pseud. of H. Nordmann]: *Die Juden und der deutsche Staat.* 13. ergänz. Aufl. Leipzig: Hammer-Verlag, 1920. 98 pp., bibl.

210 PULZER, P[ETER] G. J.: *The rise of political antisemitism in Germany and Austria.* New York: Wiley, 1964. 364 pp., ports., facsims., tabs., bibl.

SCHÖNERER, GEORG (the father of political anti-Semitism)
211 PICHL, EDUARD, ed.: *Georg Schönerer.* Hrsg. mit Unterstützung des Reichsinstituts für Geschichte des neuen Deutschlands. Oldenburg i.O.: Stalling, 1938. 3 vols., illus.

212 SCHNEE, HEINRICH: *Georg Ritter von Schönerer. Ein Kämpfer für Alldeutschland. Mit ausgewählten Zeugnissen aus Schönerers Kampfzeit für deutsche Einheit und deutsche Reinheit.* 3. verb. und ergänz. Aufl. Reichenberg; Sudetendeutscher Verlag (Kraus), 1943. x + 275 pp., port., tabs., bibl.

---

213 STERLING, ELEONORE: *Judenhass. Die Anfänge des politischen Antisemitismus in Deutschland 1815–1850.* Frankfurt a.M.: Europäische Verlagsanstalt, 1969. 237 pp., bibl. [Rev. ed. of *Er ist wie Du. Aus der Frühgeschichte des Antisemitismus in Deutschland 1815–1850.* Publ. 1956.]

214 TREITSCHKE, HEINRICH von: 'Ein Wort über unser Judentum'. Separatabdr. aus dem 44. & 45. Bde. der *Preussischen Jahrbücher.* Berlin: Reimer, 1880. 27 pp.

Racial

215 BARTELS, ADOLF: *Rasse und Volkstum. Gesammelte Aufsätze zur nationalen Weltanschauung.* 2. verm. Aufl. Weimar: Duncker, 1920. 320 pp.

DEUTSCHVÖLKISCHER SCHUTZ- UND TRUTZ-BUND
216 LOHALM, UWE: *Völkischer Radikalismus. Die Geschichte des Deutschvölkischen Schutz- und Trutz-Bundes 1919–1923.* Hamburg: Leibniz, 1970. 492 pp., bibl. (notes and bibl. pp. 335–481).

217 MEISTER, WILHELM, pseud.: *Judas Schuldbuch. Eine deutsche Abrechnung.* 3. und 4. verb. und stark verm. Aufl. München: Deutscher Volksverlag, 1919. 180 pp. (Hrsg.: Deutscher Schutz- und Trutz-Bund 'Deutschland den Deutschen').

---

218 DINTER, ARTUR: *Die Sünden der Zeit.* In 3 vols.
I: *Die Sünde wider das Blut. Ein Zeitroman.* 3. umgearb. und verm. Aufl. Leipzig: Matthes, 1919.
II: *Die Sünde wider den Geist. Ein Zeitroman.* Leipzig: Beust, 1921.
III: *Die Sünde wider die Liebe. Ein Zeitroman.* Leipzig: Matthes & Thost, 1922.

219 DÜHRING, E[UGEN]: *Sache, Leben und Feinde. Als Hauptwerk und Schlüssel zu seinen sämmtlichen Schriften.* 2. ergänz. und verm. Aufl. Leipzig: Thomas, 1902. 539 pp., port.

220 GOLDSTEIN, JULIUS: *Rasse und Politik.* 2. verb. Aufl. Schlüchtern: Neuwerk-Verlag, 1921. 157 pp.

221 KAHN, SIEGBERT: *Antisemitismus und Rassenhetze. Eine Übersicht über ihre Entwicklung in Deutschland.* Berlin: Dietz, 1948. 94 pp., bibl.

222 MOSSE, GEORGE L.: *Toward the Final Solution. A history of European racism.* London: Dent, 1978. xvi + 277 pp., illus. [German version: *Rassismus. Ein Krankheitssymptom in der europäischen Geschichte des 19. und 20. Jahrhunderts.* Königstein/Ts.: Athenäum Verlag, 1978.]

223 MÜLLER, JOSEF: *Die Entwicklung des Rassenantisemitismus in den letzten Jahrzehnten des 19. Jahrhunderts. Dargestellt hauptsächlich auf Grundlage der 'Antisemitischen Korrespondenz'.* Berlin: Ebering, 1940. 95 pp., bibl.

224 SCHMAHL, EUGEN & SEIPEL, WILHELM: *Entwicklung der völkischen Bewegung.* Giessen: Roth, 1933. 167 pp., illus. [Comprising: Jakob Sprenger: 'Geleitwort'; Eugen Schmahl: 'Die antisemitische Bauernbewegung in Hessen von der Böckelzeit bis zum Nationalsozialismus'; Wilhelm Seipel: 'Entwicklung der nationalsozialistischen Bauernbewegung in Hessen'.]

Anti-Judaism
BRIMAN, ARON
225 JUSTUS, Dr. [pseud of Aron Briman]: *Judenspiegel oder 100 neuenthüllte, heutzutage noch geltende, den Verkehr der Juden mit den Christen betreffende Gesetze der Juden; mit einer die Bestehung und Weiterentwickelung der jüdischen Gesetze darstellenden, höchst interessanten Einleitung.* 2. Aufl. Paderborn: Bonifacius-Druckerei, 1883. 96 pp. [Briman also used the pseudonym 'Jakob Ecker'.]

226 LIPPE, K[ARPEL]: *Die Gesetzsammlung des Judenspiegels zusammengestellt und gefälscht von Aron Briman, pseudodoctor Justus. Beleuchtet und berichtigt.* Jassy: Goldner, 1885. 288 pp.

---

227 DECKERT, JOSEF: *Ein Ritualmord. Aktenmässig nachgewiesen.* Dresden: Glöss, 1893. 39 pp.

22

228 [EISENMENGER, JOHANN ANDREAS] SCHIEFERL, FRANZ XAVER, ed.: *Joh. Andr. Eisenmenger's Entdecktes Judentum. Das ist: wortgetreue Verdeutschung der wichtigsten Stellen des Talmuds und der sonstigen ... hebräisch-rabbinischen Litteratur, welche einen sicheren Einblick in die jüdische Religions- und Sittenlehre gewähren.* Zeitgemäss. überarb. und hrsg. Dresden: Brandner, 1893. 591 pp. [First publ. 1711.]

229 FREIMUT, BERNARDIN: *Altjüdische Religionsgeheimnisse und neujüdische Praktiken im Lichte christlicher Wahrheit. Eine Kritik des Talmud.* 2. verm. und verb. Aufl. von 'Jüdische Religionsgeheimnisse nach dem Talmud'. Münster i.W.: Russell, 1893. 142 pp.

230 HEER, FRIEDRICH: *Gottes erste Liebe. 2000 Jahre Judentum und Christentum. Genesis des österreichischen Katholiken Adolf Hitler.* München: Bechtle, 1967. 740 pp., bibl.

231 LANGEN, F. E. Frhr. von: *Das jüdische Geheimgesetz und die deutschen Landesvertretungen. Talmudische Täuschungen. Ein Handbüchlein für Politiker.* 5. Aufl. München: Deutsches Volksverlag, 1919. 80 pp.

232 [OBERAMMERGAU] *Das Passions-Spiel in Oberammergau. Ein geistliches Festspiel in 3 Abteilungen mit 24 lebenden Bildern. Mit Benützung der alten Texte verfasst von J. A. Daisenberger.* Offizieller Gesamt-Text für das Jahr 1922 überarb. und neu hrsg. von der Gemeinde Oberammergau. Diessen vor München: Huber, 1922. 149 pp., port., plan.

233 PARKES, JAMES: *The conflict of the Church and the Synagogue. A study in the origins of antisemitism.* London: Soncino Press, 1934. 430 pp.

234 PAWLIKOWSKI, KONSTANTIN Ritter de Cholewa: *Der Talmud in der Theorie und in der Praxis. Eine literar-historische Zusammenstellung.* 2. Ausg. Regensburg: Manz, 1881. 340 pp., bibl.

235 ROHLING, AUG[UST]: *Der Talmudjude. Zur Beherzigung für Juden und Christen aller Stände dargestellt.* 6. Aufl. Münster i.W.: Russell, 1877. 111 pp.

236 RUETHER, ROSEMARY RADFORD: *Faith and fratricide. The theological roots of anti-semitism.* New York: Seabury Press, 1974. 293 pp.

237 SCHROER, HERMANN, ed.: *Blut und Geld im Judentum.* Dargestellt am jüdischen Recht (Schulchan Aruch), übersetzt von Heinrich George F. Löwe sen., 1836, neu hrsg. und erläut. München: Hoheneichen-Verlag, 1936, 1937. Bibl.
1. Bd.: *Eherecht (Eben haäser) und Fremdenrecht.*
2. Bd.: *Zivil- und Strafrecht.*

Social, economic and cultural anti-Semitism

238 BAHRDT, HANS PAUL: 'Soziologische Reflexionen über die gesellschaftlichen Voraussetzungen des Antisemitismus in Deutschland'. Sonderdruck aus *Entscheidungsjahr 1932*, Hrsg. Werner E. Mosse. Tübingen: Mohr, 1965. Pp. 135–155.

FRITSCH, THEODOR

239 FRITSCH, THEODOR, ed.: *Handbuch der Judenfrage. Eine Zusammenstellung des wichtigsten Materials zur Beurteilung des jüdischen Volkes.* [49. Aufl.] Leipzig: Hammer-Verlag, 1944. 604 pp., port.

240 SALBURG, EDITH Gräfin: *Der Tag des Ariers. Ein Buch der Zeit.* Berlin: Schlieffen, 1935. 288 pp. [On Fritsch.]

241 L'HOUET, A.: *Psychologie des Bauerntums.* 3. neubearb. und ergänz. Aufl. Tübingen: Mohr (Siebeck), 1935. 368 pp. [First ed. 1905. Incl.: 'Jude, Talmud, Vergiftung'; 'Aufartung-Aufnordung'.]

242 REICHMANN, EVA G.: *Hostages of civilisation. The social sources of national socialist anti-semitism.* London: Gollancz, 1950. 281 pp., bibl. [German version: *Die Flucht in den Hass. Die Ursachen der deutschen Judenkatastrophe.* Frankfurt a.M.: Europäische Verlagsanstalt, 1956 (and) 5. Aufl., 1968.]

243 *Semigothaisches Genealogisches Taschenbuch ari(st)okratischjüdischer Heiraten mit Enkel-Listen (Deszendenz-Verfolgen). Aufsammlung aller adeligen Ehen mit vollblutjüdischen und gemischtblütigen Frauen—und 18 Ahnentafeln.* 3. Jhrg. München: Kyffhäuser-Verlag, 1914. 453 pp., port.

SEMI-KÜRSCHNER

244 STAUFF, PHILIPP, ed.: *Semi-Kürschner oder Literarisches Lexikon der Schriftsteller, Dichter, Bankiers, Geldleute, Ärzte, Schauspieler, Künstler, Musiker, Offiziere, Rechtsanwälte, Revolutionäre, Frauenrechtlerinnen, Sozialdemokraten usw., jüdischer Rasse und Versippung, die von 1813 bis 1913 in Deutschland tätig oder bekannt waren. Unter Mitwirkung von völkischen Verbänden, von Gelehrten, ... Industriellen, Kaufleuten, von Männern und Frauen des In- und Auslandes.* Berlin: Selbstverlag, 1913. xxvi + 308 pp.

245 *Sigilla Veri. (Ph. Stauff's Semi-Kürschner). Lexikon der Juden-Genossen und -Gegner aller Zeiten und Zonen, insbesondere Deutschlands, der Lehren, Gebräuche, Kunstgriffe und Statistiken der Juden sowie ihrer Gaunersprache, Trugnamen, Geheimbände, usw. Unter Mitwirkung gelehrter Männer und Frauen aller in Betracht kommenden Länder im Auftrage der 'Weltliga gegen die Lüge' in Verbindung mit der 'Alliance chrétienne arienne',* hrsg von E. Ekkehard. 2. Aufl. Erfurt: Bodung, 1929. 5 vols. (A–R).

WAGNER, RICHARD

246 WAGNER, RICHARD: *Das Judenthum in der Musik.* Leipzig: Weber, 1869. 57 pp. [And: Weimar: Deutschvölkischer Verlag, 1914. Hrsg.: Phil. Stauff.]

247 SCHÜLER, WINFRIED: *Der Bayreuther Kreis von seiner Entstehung bis zum Ausgang der Wilhelminischen Ära. Wagnerkult und Kulturreform im Geiste völkischer Weltanschauung.* Münster: Aschendorff, 1971. 293 pp., bibl. [III,

pp. 231–267: 'Völkisch-kultureller Nationalismus im Zeichen von Antisemitismus und Rassismus'.]

248 STEIN, LEON: *The racial thinking of Richard Wagner.* New York: Philosophical Library, 1950. xiv + 252 pp., illus., bibl.

249 WINTER, GEORG: *Der Antisemitismus in Deutschland vom kulturhistorischen und sozialpolitischen Standpunkte beleuchtet.* 2. Aufl. Magdeburg: Salinger, 1896. 125 pp.

'Jewish world conspiracy'

250 ELTZBACHER, PAUL: *Der Bolschewismus und die deutsche Zukunft.* Jena: Diederichs, 1919. 47 pp.

251 OSMAN-BEY, (Major): *Die Eroberung der Welt durch die Juden. Enthüllungen über die universelle israelitische Allianz.* 2. Neudruck nach der 11. im Jahre 1888 erschienenen Ausg. Lorch (Württ.): Rohm, 1922. 46 pp.

5 SOCIAL AND ECONOMIC ROOTS

252 BENNECKE, HEINRICH: *Wirtschaftliche Depression und politischer Radikalismus. Die Lehre von Weimar.* München: Olzog, 1968. 232 pp., tabs., bibl.

253 CALLEO, DAVID: *The German Problem reconsidered. Germany and the world order 1870 to the present.* Cambridge: Cambridge University Press, 1978. xi + 239 pp., bibl. [Incl.: Ch. 5: 'Hitler and the German Problem'; Ch. 6: 'The German Problem—social and cultural explanations'.]

254 CILLER, A.: *Vorläufer des Nationalsozialismus. Geschichte und Entwicklung der nationalen Arbeiterbewegung im deutschen Grenzland.* Wien: Ertl, 1932. 158 pp.

255 CLEMENZ, MANFRED: *Gesellschaftliche Ursprünge des Faschismus.* Frankfurt a.M.: Suhrkamp, 1972. 314 pp., tabs., bibl. [2nd ed. publ. 1976. Concentrates on fascism in Germany.]

256 LEBOVICS, HERMAN: *Social conservatism and the middle classes in Germany, 1914–1933.* Princeton, N.J.: Princeton University Press, 1969. 248 pp., bibl. [Chs. on Mittelstand, Werner Sombart, Edgar Salin, Othmar Spann, Ernst Niekisch, Otto Spengler, 'Die Tat'.]

257 MOHLER, ARMIN: *Die konservative Revolution in Deutschland 1918–1923. Ein Handbuch.* 2. völlig neu bearb. und erw. Fassung. Darmstadt: Wissenschaftliche Buchgesellschaft, 1972. 554 pp., bibl. (pp. 173–483).

258 REICH, WILHELM: *Massenpsychologie des Faschismus. Zur Sexualoekonomie der politischen Reaktion und zur proletarischen Sexualpolitik.* Zürich: Verlag für Sexualpolitik, 1933. 288 pp. [New ed.: *Die Massenpsychologie des Faschismus.* (With introd. by Mary Boyd Higgins and author's introd. to 3rd rev. enl. ed., 1942.) Köln: Kiepenheuer & Witsch, 1971. 384 pp. Latest

English version: *The mass psychology of Fascism*. New York: Farrar, Straus & Giroux, 1970. 400 pp.]

259 SPENGLER, OSWALD: *Der Untergang des Abendlandes. Umrisse einer Morphologie der Weltgeschichte*. 33.–47. völlig umgest. Aufl. München: Beck, 1923. 2 vols. [First published 1918. Praises the virtues of primitive man and foretells the doom of civilization.]

260 [STOECKER, ADOLF] FRANK, WALTER: *Hofprediger Stoecker und die christlich-soziale Bewegung*. 2. durchges. Aufl. Hamburg: Hanseatische Verlagsanstalt, 1935. 347 pp., port.

261 WISKEMANN, ERWIN & LÜTKE, HEINZ, eds.: *Der Weg der deutschen Volkswirtschaftslehre. Ihre Schöpfer und Gestalter im 19. Jahrhundert*. Berlin: Junker & Dünnhaupt, 1937. 193 pp.

6 CULTURAL AND RELIGIOUS ROOTS

262 ANDREWS, WAYNE: *Siegfried's curse. The German journey from Nietzsche to Hesse*. New York: Atheneum, 1972. x + 370 pp., illus., bibl.

263 DANKWORTH, HERBERT: *Das alte Grossdeutschtum. Versuch einer Bestimmung seiner kulturellen Grundlagen*. Frankfurt a.M.: Frankfurter Societäts-Druckerei, 1925. 129 pp.

264 DEWEY, JOHN: *German philosophy and politics*. New York: Putnam's, 1942. 149 pp.

265 FISCHLI, BRUNO: *Die Deutschen-Dämmerung. Zur Genealogie des völkisch-faschistischen Dramas und Theaters 1897–1933*. Bonn: Bouvier, 1976. 387 pp., illus., facsims., bibl.

266 GLASER, HERMANN: *The cultural roots of National Socialism*. Transl. with introd. and notes: Ernest [August] Menze. London: Croom Helm, 1978. 289 pp.

267 GLUM, FRIEDRICH: *Philosophen im Spiegel und Zerrspiegel. Deutschlands Weg in den Nationalismus und Nationalsozialismus*. München: Isar Verlag, 1954. 287 pp.

268 HAMILTON, ALASTAIR: *The appeal of fascism. A study of intellectuals and fascism, 1919–1945*. Foreword: Stephen Spender. London: Blond, 1971. xxiii + 312 pp., illus., bibl.

KÜNNETH, WALTER: *Der grosse Abfall. See* 2052.

269 [LEHMANN, J. F.] STARK, GARY D.: 'Der Verleger als Kulturunternehmer: Der J. F. Lehmanns Verlag und Rassenkunde in der Weimarer Republik'. Sonderdruck aus *Archiv für Geschichte des Buchwesens*, Bd. XVI, Lfrg. 2. Frankfurt a.M.: Buchhändler-Vereinigung, 1976. Pp. 291–318.

LUTHER, MARTIN
270 WIENER, PETER F.: *Martin Luther. Hitler's spiritual ancestor*. London: Hutchinson, [1945]. 84 pp., ports. (Win the Peace Pamphlet).

271 RUPP, GORDON: *Martin Luther. Hitler's cause—or cure. In reply to Peter F. Wiener.* London: Lutterworth Press, 1945. 94 pp.

---

272 MOSSE, GEORGE L.: *The crisis of German ideology. Intellectual origins of the Third Reich.* New York: Grosset & Dunlap, 1964. 373 pp.

273 [PLOETZ, ALFRED] DOELEKE, WERNER: *Alfred Ploetz, 1860–1940. Sozialdarwinist und Gesellschaftsbiologe.* Inaugural-Dissertation [pres. to] Goethe Universität Frankfurt a.M. 1975. 141 pp., illus., facsim., bibl.

274 SAALFELD, LERKE von: *Die ideologische Funktion des Nibelungenliedes in der preussisch-deutschen Geschichte von seiner Wiederentdeckung bis zum Nationalsozialismus.* Inaugural-Dissertation [pres. to] Freie Universität Berlin. Berlin: 1977. ix + 339 + 71 pp., bibl.

SOCIAL DARWINISM

275 GASMAN, DANIEL: *The scientific origins of National Socialism. Social Darwinism in Ernst Haeckel and the German Monist League.* London: Macdonald, 1971. 208 pp., illus., bibl.

276 MANN, GUNTER: 'Rassenhygiene–Sozialdarwinismus.' Sonderdruck aus *Biologismus im 19. Jahrhundert.* Stuttgart: Enke, 1973. Pp. 73–93, bibl.

---

277 VIERECK, PETER: *Metapolitics. From the Romantics to Hitler.* New York: Knopf, 1941. 335 + xxiv pp., bibl.

278 WOLZOGEN, HANS von: *Aus deutscher Welt. Gesammelte Aufsätze über deutsche Art und Kultur.* Berlin: Schwetschke, 1905. 212 pp.

Occult roots

279 ALLEAU, RENÉ: *Hitler et les sociétés secrètes. Enquête sur les sources occultes du nazisme.* Paris: Grasset, 1969. 318 + 45 pp., illus. [Incl.: 'La "Thule-Gesellschaft" ', pp. 245–268, with list of members.]

280 ANGEBERT, JEAN-MICHEL: *Hitler et la tradition cathare.* Préface: Serge Hutin. Paris: Laffont, 1976. 330 pp., illus., bibl.

281 ANTONIUS, PETER: *Gross-Deutschlands Macht und herrliche Zukunft im Lichte der Prophezeiungen. Deutschland unter dem kommenden Herrscher als Führer des neuen Völkerbundes. Ein tröstender Ausblick in die nächste Zukunft Deutschlands.* Dortmund: Lensing, 1920. 37 pp.

282 WEBB, JAMES: *The occult establishment.* La Salle, Ill.: Library Press (Open Court), 1976. 535 pp. [Incl. much material on occultism and its effects in pre-1933 Germany: secret societies, anti-Semitism, the theories of Alfred Rosenberg, etc.]

7 EXTERNAL ROOTS

283 BRAFMANN, JACOB: *Das Buch vom Kahal.* Auf Grund einer neuen

Verdeutschung des russischen Originals hrsg. vom Dr. Siegfried Passarge. Leipzig: Hammer-Verlag, 1928. In 2 vols.
I: *Materialien zur Erforschung der jüdischen Sitten.*
II: *Das Buch von der Verwaltung der jüdischen Gemeinde.*

284 [CARLYLE, THOMAS] SEILLIÈRE, ERNEST: *Un précurseur du national-socialisme. L'actualité de Carlyle.* Paris: Eds. de la Nouvelle Revue Critique, 1939. 252 pp., bibl.

CHAMBERLAIN, HOUSTON STEWART
285 CHAMBERLAIN, HOUSTON STEWART: *Die Grundlagen des neunzehnten Jahrhunderts. Volksausgabe.* VII. Aufl. München: Bruckmann, 1906. 2 vols. [First ed. 1899. A tenth ed. was publ. in 1912. English version: *Foundations of the nineteenth century.* London: Bodley Head, 1911. 2 vols.]

286 ROSENBERG, ALFRED: *Houston Stewart Chamberlain als Verkünder und Begründer einer deutschen Zukunft.* München: Bruckmann, 1927. 128 pp., illus.

---

287 DRUMONT, EDUARD: *Das verjudete Frankreich. Versuch einer Tagesgeschichte.* Autor. deutsche Ausgabe von A. Gardon. Berlin: Deubner.
I: xii + 460 pp. 1886.
II: 424 pp. 1887.
[Transl. of *La France juive.* Paris: Bleriot, 1883.]

GOBINEAU, COMTE JOSEPH-ARTHUR DE
288 GOBINEAU, Comte de: *Essai sur l'inégalité des races humaines.* Paris: Librairie de Paris, 1933. 2 vols. [First ed. 1855. German version: *Die Ungleichheit der Menschenrassen.* Berlin: Wolff, 1935.]

289 DESCHNER, GÜNTHER: *Gobineau und Deutschland. Der Einfluss von J. A. de Gobineaus 'Essai sur l'inégalité des races humaines' auf die deutsche Geistesgeschichte 1853–1917.* Inaugural-Dissertation [pres. to] Friedrich-Alexander-Universität Erlangen-Nürnberg. 1967. 194 + xix pp., bibl.

290 SCHEMANN, LUDWIG: *Gobineau und die deutsche Kultur.* Leipzig: Eckardt, 1910. 168 pp.

LANZ VON LIEBENFELS, GEORG (Jorg)
291 LANZ VON LIEBENFELS, GEORG: *Ostara. Briefbücherei der Blonden und Mannesrechtler.* [Priv. pr.:] 1905– Approx. 120 pamphlets.
1. Serie: Rodaun b. Wien: 1905–1918.
2. Serie: [One issue only]. 1922.
3. Serie: Wien: 1927–1930.

292 DAIM, WILFRIED: *Der Mann der Hitler die Ideen gab. Von den religiösen Verirrungen eines Sektierers zum Rassenwahn eines Diktators.* München: Isar Verlag, 1958. 286 pp., illus.

---

293 [LAWRENCE, DAVID HERBERT] SEILLIÈRE, ERNEST: *David-Herbert Lawrence et les récentes idéologies allemandes.* Paris: Boivin, 1936. xviii + 282 pp.

294 [LUEGER, KARL] SKALNIK, KURT: *Dr. Karl Lueger. Der Mann zwischen den Zeiten.* München: Herold, 1954. 182 pp., illus., bibl. [Lord Mayor of Vienna and leader of an anti-Semitic party.]

295 STODDARD, LOTHROP: *The revolt against civilisation. The menace of the underman.* London: Chapman & Hall, 1923. 255 pp. [German version: *Der Kulturumsturz. Die Drohung des Untermenschen.* München: Lehmann, 1925.]

296 TREBITSCH, ARTHUR: *Geist und Judentum. Eine grundlegende Untersuchung.* Wien: Sirache, 1919. 282 pp., diagrs.

'Protocols of Zion' ('Jewish world conspiracy')

297 BEEK, GOTTFRIED zur (pseud. of Ludwig Müller von Hausen), ed.: *Die Geheimnisse der Weisen von Zion.* Charlottenburg: Verlag 'Auf Vorposten', 1919. 252 pp. [23rd ed. publ. 1939.]

298 BERNSTEIN, HERMAN: *The truth about 'The Protocols of Zion'. A complete exposure.* New York: Covici, Friede, 1935. 397 pp., facsims.

299 COHN, NORMAN: *Warrant for genocide. The myth of the Jewish world-conspiracy and the Protocols of the Elders of Zion.* London: Eyre & Spottiswoode, 1967. 303 pp., illus., bibl.

300 [JOLY, MAURICE]: *Dialogue aux enfers entre Machiavel et Montesquieu ou La politique de Machiavel au XIXe siècle, par un contemporain.* Bruxelles: Mertens, 1864. 337 pp. [The work from which the Protocols were plagiarized.]

301 NILUS, SERGEJ A.: *Der jüdische Antichrist und die Protokolle der Weisen von Zion. Deutsche Ausgabe des russischen Buches 'Er ist nahe vor der Tür'.* Übersetzt von Sergej von Markow. Hrsg. und mit einer Einführung versehen von Hans Jonak von Freyenwald. Leipzig: Günther, 1938. 277 pp.

302 RETCLIFFE, Sir JOHN, pseud.: *Die Geheimnisse des Judenkirchhofes in Prag. Die Verschwörung der Weisen von Zion.* Volks- und Schulausg. mit dem Bild des Rabbi Löw. Hrsg.: M. Meiner. Grossdeuben (Leipzig): Gotland-Verlag, 1934. 42 pp. [Extract from 5-vol. novel entitled *Biarritz.* Berlin: Liebrecht, 1868/70. Another source of the Protocols.]

303 SEGEL, B[ENJAMIN]: *Die Protokolle der Weisen von Zion kritisch beleuchtet. Eine Erledigung.* Berlin: Philo Verlag, 1924. 233 pp., illus. [Authorised English version: *The Protocols of the Elders of Zion. The greatest lie in history. With ten letters of endorsement from eminent non-Jewish scholars.* New York: Bloch, 1934. 97 pp.]

304 *Die Zionistischen Protokolle. Das Programm der internationalen Geheim-Regierung. Aus dem Englischen übersetzt nach dem im Britischen Museum befindlichen Original.* Vor- und Nachwort: Theodor Fritsch. 4. Aufl. Leipzig: Hammer-Verlag, 1924. 79 pp., bibl.

305 FLEISCHHAUER, ULRICH: *Die echten Protokolle der Weisen von Zion. Sachverständigengutachtung erstattet im Auftrage des Richteramtes V in Bern.* Erfurt: Bodung, 1935. 416 pp. [Fleischhauer was the 'expert' called by the defendants in the 'Protocol' libel trial in 1935 in Berne.]

306 JONAK VON FREYENWALD, HANS, ed.: *Der Berner Prozess um die Protokolle der Weisen von Zion. Akten und Gutachten. I. Bd.: Anklage und Zeugenaussagen.* Erfurt: Bodung, 1939. 213 pp.

307 RAAS, EMIL & BRUNSCHVIG, GEORGES: *Vernichtung einer Fälschung. Der Prozess um die erfundenen 'Weisen von Zion'.* Zürich: Verlag 'Die Gestaltung', 1938. 74 pp.

C. NAZI IDEOLOGY AND PROGRAMME

1. GENERAL

308 *Anti-Europa.* Maggio-Giugno 1931/Anno III. Roma. Pp. 1887–2004. [Incl.: Georg Moenius: 'Faschismus und Nationalsozialismus'; Alfred Missong: 'Faschismus, Nationalsozialismus und Romanita'; Otto Steinbrick: 'Der Nationalsozialismus ist kirchlich und kulturell anti-römisch'; Prof. Schultz: 'Perchè il fascismo tedesco ha caratteri di movimento romanico'.]

309 BECK, FRIEDRICH ALFRED: *Deutsche Vollendung. Idee und Wirklichkeit des nationalsozialistischen Reiches.* 2. Aufl. Posen: Feldmüller, 1944. 851 pp.

310 BRADY, ROBERT A.: *The spirit and structure of German fascism.* With a foreword by Harold J. Laski. New York: Viking Press, 1937. 420 pp., tabs., diagrs. [Also: London: Gollancz, 1937.]

311 BROSZAT, MARTIN: *Der Nationalsozialismus. Weltanschauung, Programm und Wirklichkeit.* 2. Aufl. Stuttgart: Deutsche Verlagsanstalt, 1960. 84 pp., bibl. [English version: *German National Socialism 1919–1945.* Santa Barbara, Calif.: Clio Press, 1966.]

312 DAVID, F.: *Ist die NSDAP eine sozialistische Partei? Eine grundsätzliche Auseinandersetzung mit der NSDAP über Gewerkschaftsfragen, Sozialpolitik, Wirtschaft und Sozialismus.* Wien: Internationaler Arbeiter Verlag, 1933. 191 pp., bibl.

313 FEDER, GOTTFRIED: *Der deutsche Staat auf nationaler und sozialer Grundlage. Neue Wege in Staat, Finanz und Wirtschaft.* München: Deutschvölkische Verlagsbuchhandlung, 1923. 206 pp.

314 FEDER, GOTTFRIED: *Das Programm der NSDAP und seine weltanschaulichen Grundgedanken.* 179. Aufl. München: Eher, 1927. 60 pp. [English version: *The programme of the party of Hitler, the National Socialist German Workers' Party and its general conceptions.*]

315 FRANK, WALTER: *Geist und Macht. Historischpolitische Aufsätze.* Hamburg: Hanseatische Verlagsanstalt, 1938. 243 pp.

316 Franzel, Emil: *Das Reich der braunen Jakobiner. Der Nationalsozialismus als geschichtliche Erscheinung.* München: Pfeiffer, 1964. 230 pp., illus.

317 Hermant, Max: *Idoles allemandes.* Paris: Grasset, 1935. 358 pp.

318 Hudal, Alois: *Die Grundlagen des Nationalsozialismus. Eine ideengeschichtliche Untersuchung von katholischer Warte.* Leipzig: Günther, 1937. 294 pp., port., bibl.

319 Johst, Hanns: *Maske und Gesicht. Reise eines Nationalsozialisten von Deutschland nach Deutschland.* München: Langen & Müller, 1935. 207 pp.

320 Klagges, Dietrich: *Idee und System. Vorträge an der Deutschen Hochschule für Politik über Grundfragen nationalsozialistischer Weltanschauung.* Leipzig: Armanen-Verlag, 1934. 144 pp.

321 Kolbenheyer, E. G.: *Neuland. Zwei Abhandlungen.* München: Langen & Müller, 1934. 167 pp.

322 Lane, Barbara Miller & Rupp, Leila J., eds.: *Nazi ideology before 1933. A documentation.* Manchester: Manchester University Press, 1978. xxviii + 180 pp.

323 Mankiewicz, H.: *La Weltanschauung national-socialiste. Ses aspects généraux et sa critique du libéralisme.* Thèse [pres. to] Université de Lyon. Lyon: Bosc (Riou), 1937. 254 pp.

324 Mosse, George L.: *Nazism. A historical and comparative analysis of National Socialism. An interview with Michael A. Ledeen.* Oxford: Blackwell, 1978. 134 pp.

325 Nolte, Ernst: *Der Faschismus in seiner Epoche. Die Action française, der italienische Faschismus, der Nationalsozialismus.* 4. Aufl. München: Piper, 1971. 635 pp. [English version: *Three faces of Fascism.* New York: New American Library, 1965.]

326 Perroux, François: *Les mythes hitlériens.* Paris: Librairie Générale de Droit et de Jurisprudence, 1935. 156 pp.

327 Poliakov, Leon & Wulf, Josef: *Das Dritte Reich und seine Denker. Dokumente.* Berlin-Grunewald: Arani, 1959. 560 pp.

328 Rauschning, Hermann: *Die Revolution des Nihilismus.* Neu hrsg. von Golo Mann. Zürich: Europa Verlag, 1964. 359 pp. [First ed.: 1938. French version: *La révolution du nihilisme.* Paris: Gallimard, 1939. English version: *Germany's revolution of destruction.* London: Heinemann, 1939 (new ed.).]

329 Reventlow, Graf E[rnst]: *Deutscher Sozialismus. Civitas Dei Germanica.* Weimar: Duncker, 1930. 310 pp.

Rosenberg, Alfred
330 Rosenberg, Alfred: *Der Mythus des 20. Jahrhunderts. Eine Wertung der seelisch-geistigen Gestaltenkämpfe unserer Zeit.* 5. Aufl. München: Hoheneichen Verlag, 1942. 712 pp. [First ed. 1930.]

331 CECIL, ROBERT: *The myth of the master race: Alfred Rosenberg and Nazi ideology.* London: Batsford, 1972. x + 266 pp., ports., illus., bibl.

332 CHANDLER, ALBERT R.: *Rosenberg's Nazi myth.* New York: Greenwood Press, 1968. 146 pp., port. [Written 1945.]

333 GRIESSDORF, HARRY: *Unsere Weltanschauung. Gedanken über Alfred Rosenberg: Der Mythos des 20. Jahrhunderts.* Berlin: Nordland Verlag, 1941. 211 pp.

---

334 SCHEUNEMANN, WALTHER: *Der Nationalsozialismus. Quellenkritische Studie seiner Staats- und Wirtschaftsauffassung.* Berlin: Der Neue Geist Verlag, 1931. 143 pp.

335 SCHULZ, GERHARD: *Faschismus—Nationalsozialismus. Versionen und theoretische Kontroversen 1922–1972.* [Berlin]: Propyläen Verlag, 1974. 222 pp., bibl.

336 SCHWARZ, HERMANN: *Nationalsozialistische Weltanschauung. Freie Beiträge zur Philosophie des Nationalsozialismus aus den Jahren 1919–1933.* Berlin: Junker & Dünnhaupt, 1933. 111 pp.

337 TINGSTEN, HERBERT: *De nationale dictaturen. De gedachtenwereld van Nationaal-Socialisme en Fascisme.* Geautoriseerde vertaling uit het Zweedsch. Utrecht: Bijleveld, 1938. 243 pp., bibl.

338 VERMEIL, EDMOND: *Doctrinaires de la Révolution allemande (1918–1938). W. Rathenau, Keyserling, Th. Mann, O. Spengler, Moeller van den Bruck, le groupe de la 'Tat', Hitler, A. Rosenberg, Günther, Darré, G. Feder, R. Ley, Goebbels.* Nouvelle éd. Paris: Nouvelles Éditions latines, 1948. 335 pp., bibl.

339 VRIES DE HEEKELINGEN, H. de, comp. & ed.: *Die Nationalsozialistische Weltanschauung. Ein Wegweiser durch die nationalsozialistische Literatur. 500 markante Zitate.* Berlin-Charlottenburg: Pan-Verlagsgesellschaft, 1932. 186 pp.

2. NATIONALISM AND MILITARISM

340 BANSE, EWALD: *Raum und Volk im Weltkriege. Gedanken über eine nationale Wehrlehre.* Oldenburg i.O.: Stalling, 1932. 424 pp., maps. [English version: *Germany, prepare for war!* London: Lovat Dickson, 1934. American version: *Germany prepares for war. A Nazi theory of 'National Defense'.* New York: Harcourt Brace, 1934.]

341 DRYSSEN, CARL: *Die Botschaft des Ostens. Fascismus, Nationalsozialismus und Preussentum.* Breslau: Korn, 1933. 186 pp.

342 HEINZ, FRIEDRICH WILHELM: *Die Nation greift an. Geschichte und Kritik des soldatischen Nationalismus.* Berlin: Verlag Das Reich, 1933. 232 pp.

343 HIERL, CONSTANTIN: *Grundlagen einer deutschen Wehrpolitik.* 3. Aufl. München: Eher, 1931. 35 pp.

344 KAINDL, RAIMUND FRIEDRICH: *Oesterreich, Preussen, Deutschland. Deutsche Geschichte in grossdeutscher Beleuchtung.* Wien: Braumüller, 1926. xxvii + 321 pp.

345 KAUTTER, EBERHARD: *Wirtschaftsgeist, Sozialgeist, Wehrgeist.* Berlin: Hochmuth, 1935. 96 pp.

346 KUNTZE, PAUL H.: *Soldatische Geschichte der Deutschen.* 11.–15. Taus. der Gesamtaufl. Berlin: Eher, 1939. 347 pp.

347 MESSERSCHMIDT, HERMANN: *Das Reich im nationalsozialistischen Weltbild.* 5. vollkommen neu bearb. Aufl. Leipzig: Kohlhammer, 1940. 107 pp.

348 OERTZEN, K. L. von: *Grundzüge der Wehrpolitik.* Hamburg: Hanseatische Verlagsanstalt, 1933. 266 pp., tabs.

349 PRÜMM, KARL: *Die Literatur des soldatischen Nationalismus der 20er Jahre (1918–1933). Gruppenideologie und Epochenproblematik.* Kronberg, Taunus: Scriptor Verlag, 1974. vi + 445 + 132 pp., bibl. [Also appeared as dissertation under title: *Ernst Jünger und der soldatische Nationalismus der Weimarer Republik.* 1973. In 2 vols.]

350 STIRK, S. D.: *The Prussian spirit. A survey of German literature and politics, 1914–1940.* London: Faber & Faber, 1941. 235 pp.

351 UNGER, ERICH, comp.: *Das Schrifttum des Nationalismus von 1919 bis zum 1. Januar 1934.* Geleitwort: Arthur Görlitzer, Paul Meier-Benneckenstein. Berlin: Junker & Dünnhaupt, 1934. 187 pp. (Forschungsberichte zur Wissenschaft des Nationalsozialismus, Heft 1).

Lebensraum

352 GRIMM, HANS: *Volk ohne Raum.* München: Langen, 1926. 1299 pp.

353 LANGE, KARL: 'Der Terminus "Lebensraum" in Hitlers "Mein Kampf" '. [In] *Vierteljahrshefte für Zeitgeschichte,* 13. Jhrg., 1965. Stuttgart: Deutsche Verlags-Anstalt. Pp. 426–437.

354 MEYER, KONRAD, ed.: *Volk und Lebensraum. Forschungen im Dienste von Raumordnung und Landesplanung.* Heidelberg: Vowinckel, 1938. 588 pp., maps, tabs., bibls. [Incl.: II. Teil: 'Aufgaben und Arbeitsergebnisse der Raumforschung an deutschen Hochschulen'.]

Geopolitics

355 BAKKER, G.: *Duitse geopolitiek, 1919–1945. Een imperialistische ideologie.* Assen: van Gorcum, 1967. 207 pp., port., maps, bibl.

356 BANSE, EWALD: *Geographie und Wehrwille. Gesammelte Studien zu den Problemen Landschaft und Mensch, Raum und Volk, Krieg und Wehr.* Breslau: Korn, 1934. 287 pp., port.

357 BRAUN, FRANZ & ZIEGFELD, A. HILLEN, eds.: *Weltgeschichte im Aufriss auf geopolitischer Grundlage. Hierzu erschien: Geopolitischer Geschichtsatlas.* Dresden: Ehlermann, 1930. xv + 49 + 83 + 185 pp., bibl.

358 HAUSHOFER, KARL and others, eds.: *Die Grossmächte vor und nach dem Weltkriege.* 25. Aufl. der Grossmächte Rudolf Kjelléns. 4. Aufl. der Neubearb. In Verbindung mit Hugo Hassinger, Otto Maull, Erich Obst hrsg. Leipzig: Teubner, 1935. vii + 351 pp., port., maps, tabs., bibl. [Incl.: Staude, Heinrich: 'Die Grossmächte im Lichte der Statistik', 24 pp., diagrs., tabs.]

359 HAUSHOFER, KARL and others, eds.: *Jenseits der Grossmächte. Ergänzungsband zur Neubearbeitung der Grossmächte Rudolf Kjelléns.* Mitw.: W. Geisler [and others]. Leipzig: Teubner, 1932. 520 pp., maps, diagrs., tabs., bibl.

360 HAUSHOFER, KARL: *Grenzen—in ihrer geographischen und politischen Bedeutung.* Berlin-Grunewald: Vowinckel, 1927. xv + 350 pp., maps, diagrs., notes (pp. 274–326).

361 HENNIG, RICHARD: *Geopolitik. Die Lehre vom Staat als Lebewesen.* Leipzig: Teubner, 1928. 338 pp., maps, graphs, tabs.

3. RACISM

362 BARABBINO, CARLO: *Il 'popolo' nell'ideologia nazional-sozialista.* Milano: Giuffré, 1940. 188 pp., bibl.

363 BERENSMANN, WILHELM and others, eds.: *Deutsche Politik. Ein völkisches Handbuch.* Bearb. von Angehörigen des Kyffhäuser-Verbandes der Vereine Deutscher Studenten und hrsg. in seinem Auftrage [by] Wilhelm Berensmann, Wolfgang Stahlberg, Friedrich Koepp. Frankfurt a.M.: Englert & Schlosser, 1926. 552 pp.

364 BLAAS, SIEGFRIED: *Der Rassegedanke. Seine biologische und philosophische Grundlegung.* Berlin: Junker & Dünnhaupt, 1940. 338 pp.

365 BLUNCK, HANS FRIEDRICH, ed.: *Die nordische Welt. Geschichte, Wesen und Bedeutung der nordischen Völker.* Unter Mitwirkung von F. J. Domes. Berlin: Propyläen-Verlag, 1937. xviii + 651 pp., illus., maps, facsisms.

366 BREITLING, RUPERT: *Die nationalsozialistische Rassenlehre. Entstehung, Ausbreitung, Nutzen und Schaden einer politischen Ideologie.* Meisenheim a.Gl.: Hain, 1971. 76 pp.

367 BURGDÖRFER, FRIEDRICH: *Volks- und Wehrkraft, Krieg und Rasse.* Berlin: Metzner, 1936. 138 pp., diagrs., tabs.

368 CLAUSS, LUDWIG FERDINAND: *Die nordische Seele. Eine Einführung in die Rassenkunde.* 5. durchges. Aufl. München: Lehmann, 1936. 91 pp., illus.

369 CLAUSS, LUDWIG FERDINAND: *Rasse und Seele. Eine Einführung in den Sinn der leiblichen Gestalt.* 17. Aufl. München: Lehmann, 1941. 195 pp., illus.

370 DAHLBERG, GUNNAR: *Race, reason and rubbish. An examination of the biological credentials of the Nazi creed.* Transl. from the Swedish by Lancelot Hogben. London: Allen & Unwin, 1942. 240 pp., illus., diagrs.

371 EICKSTEDT, EGON Frhr. von: *Rassenkunde und Rassengeschichte der Menschheit.* Stuttgart: Enke, 1934. 908 pp., illus., maps, tabs., diagrs., bibl.

372 FAHRENKROG, ROLF L., ed.: *Europas Geschichte als Rassenschicksal. Vom Wesen und Wirken der Rassen im europäischen Schicksalsraum.* Leipzig: Hesse & Becker, [1935?]. 439 pp., illus., maps.

373 GERSTENHAUER, M. R.: *Der völkische Gedanke in Vergangenheit und Zukunft. Aus der Geschichte der völkischen Bewegung.* Leipzig: Armanen Verlag, 1933. 165 pp.

374 GRIESMAYR, GOTTFRIED: *Das völkische Ideal.* Berlin: NS.-Führungsstab der Wehrmacht, 1944. 160 pp.

375 GÜNTHER, ADOLF: *Der Rassegedanke in der weltanschaulichen Auseinandersetzung unserer Zeit.* Berlin: Junker & Dünnhaupt, 1940. 224 pp. (Forschungen des Deutschen Auslandswissenschaftlichen Instituts ...).

376 GÜNTHER, HANS F. K.: *Rassenkunde des deutschen Volkes.* München: Lehmann, 1922. 440 pp., illus., maps, bibliographical footnotes.

377 GÜNTHER, HANS F. K.: *Rassenkunde Europas. Mit besonderer Berücksichtigung der Rassengeschichte der Hauptvölker indogermanischer Sprache.* 3. wesent. verm. und verb. Aufl. München: Lehmann, 1929. 342 pp., illus., diagrs. [First ed. 1924. English version of 2nd ed.: *The racial elements of European history.* London: Methuen, 1927.]

378 HUXLEY, JULIAN & HADDON, A. C.: *We Europeans. A survey of 'racial' problems.* With a chapter 'Europe overseas', by A. M. Carr-Saunders. London: Jonathan Cape, 1935. 299 pp., illus., tabs., diagrs.

379 KEITER, FRIEDRICH: *Rasse und Kultur. Eine Kulturbilanz der Menschenrassen als Weg zur Rassenseelenkunde.* Illus., diagrs., maps, tabs., bibls.
I. Bd.: *Allgemeine Kulturbiologie.* Publ. 1938. xi + 298 pp.
II. Bd.: *Vorzeitrassen und Naturvölker.* Publ. 1938. ix + 334 pp.
III. Bd.: *Hochkultur und Rasse.* Publ. 1940. viii + 500 pp.

380 KÖHN-BEHRENS, CHARLOTTE: *Was ist Rasse? Gespräche mit den grössten deutschen Forschern der Gegenwart.* München: Eher, 1934. 126 pp., ports.

381 LUTZHÖFT, HANS-JÜRGEN: *Der nordische Gedanke in Deutschland, 1920–1940.* Stuttgart: Klett, 1971. 439 pp., bibl.

382 MÄRKER, FRIEDRICH: *Charakterbilder der Rassen. Rassenkunde auf physiognomischer und phrenologischer Grundlage.* Berlin: Frundsberg-Verlag, 1934. 131 pp., illus.

383 PETERSEN, CARL: *Deutscher und nordischer Geist. Ihre Wechselwirkungen bis zum Ende der Romantik.* 2. Aufl. Breslau: Hirt, 1937. 170 pp.

384 PUDOR, HEINRICH: *Nordland-Fahrten. Wie ein deutscher Forscher und Streiter für den germanischen Hochgedanken das Land seiner Sehnsucht ... aufsuchte ... Zum Miterleben ... allen germanischen Blutsverwandten ... erzählt ...* Hellerau b. Dresden: Hakenkreuz-Verlag, 1923. 215 pp.

385 RADIN, PAUL: *The racial myth.* New York: McGraw-Hill, 1934. 141 pp.

386 RODENWALDT, ERNST: 'Die nationalsozialistische Rassenerkenntnis als

Grundlage für die koloniale Betätigung des neuen Europa'. [In] *Das Deutsche Koloniale Jahrbuch* (1941), pp. 122–131. *See* 4031.

387 SCHEMANN, LUDWIG: *Die Rasse in den Geisteswissenschaften.* München: Lehmann, 1928–1931. In 3 vols.
Bd. I: *Studien zur Geschichte des Rassen-Gedankens.*
Bd. II: *Hauptepochen und Hauptvölker der Geschichte in ihrer Stellung zur Rasse.*
Bd. III: *Die Rassenfragen im Schrifttum der Neuzeit.*

388 SCHULTZE-NAUMBURG, PAUL: *Kunst und Rasse.* München: Eher, 1928. 144 pp., illus.

389 THOENE, ALBRECHT W.: *Das Licht der Arier. Licht-, Feuer- und Dunkelsymbolik des Nationalsozialismus.* München: Minerva Publ., 1979. 106 pp., illus.

390 TIRALA, LOTHAR GOTTLIEB: *Rasse, Geist und Seele.* München: Lehmann, 1935. 256 pp., illus., bibl. [English abridged version: *Race, mind and soul. An example of the new racial science of Germany.* Foreword: Sir Grafton Elliot Smith. London: Friends of Europe, 1936. 30 pp.]

391 ZIMMERMANN, KARL: *Deutsche Geschichte als Rassenschicksal.* 3. Aufl. Leipzig: Quelle & Meyer, 1933. 177 pp.

Master race

392 DARRÉ, R. WALTHER: *Neuadel aus Blut und Boden.* München: Lehmann, 1934. 231 pp. [French version: *La race. Nouvelle noblesse du sang et du sol.* Paris: Sorlot, 1939.]

393 DRASCHER, WAHRHOLD: *Die Vorherrschaft der Weissen Rasse. Die Ausbreitung des abendländischen Lebensbereiches auf die überseeischen Erdteile.* Stuttgart: Deutsche Verlags-Anstalt, 1936. 387 pp., bibl.

394 GÜNTHER, HANS F. K.: *Führeradel durch Sippenpflege. Vier Vorträge.* München: Lehmann, 1936. 124 pp.

395 HAISER, FRANZ: *Die Sklaverei—ihre biologische Begründung und sittliche Rechtfertigung.* München: Lehmann, 1923. 71 pp.

NIETZSCHE, FRIEDRICH
396 HÄRTLE, HEINRICH: *Nietzsche und der Nationalsozialismus.* München: Eher, 1937. 171 pp. [Incl. notions of 'Supermen' and 'Herrenvolk'.]

397 NICOLAS, M.-P.: *De Nietzsche à Hitler.* Paris: Charpentier, 1936. 190 pp. [Also appeared in English.]

398 ROSENTHAL, ALFRED: *Nietzsches 'Europäisches Rasse-Problem'. ('Der Kampf um die Erdherrschaft').* Leiden: Sijthoff, 1935. 197 pp.

399 SANDVOSS, E.: *Hitler und Nietzsche.* Göttingen: Musterschmidt-Verlag, 1969. 208 pp.

Eugenics and population policy

400 BAUR, ERWIN and others: *Menschliche Erblehre.* [By] Erwin Baur, Eugen Fischer, Fritz Lenz. 4. neubearb. Aufl. München: Lehmann, 1936. 795 pp., illus., tabs., diagrs., bibl.

401 BURGDÖRFER, FRIEDRICH: *Volk ohne Jugend. Geburtenschwund und Überalterung des deutschen Volkskörpers. Ein Problem der Volkswirtschaft—der Sozialpolitik—der nationalen Zukunft.* 3. verm. Aufl. Heidelberg: Vowinckel, 1937. 536 pp., tabs., diagrs., maps.

402 GRAF, JAKOB: *Vererbungslehre, Rassenkunde und Erbgesundheitspflege. Einführung nach methodischen Grundsätzen.* 5. verb. und verm. Aufl. München: Lehmann, 1938. 352 pp., illus., diagrs., tabs., maps, bibl. [First ed. 1930.]

403 HAUSER, OTTO: *Der blonde Mensch.* 2. Aufl. Danzig: Verlag Der Mensch, 1930. 148 pp.

404 HIPPIUS, RUDOLF and others: *Volkstum, Gesinnung und Charakter. Bericht über psychologische Untersuchungen an Posener deutsch-polnischen Mischlingen und Polen, Sommer 1942.* [By] Rudolf Hippius, I. G. Feldmann, K. Jellinek, K. Leider. Stuttgart: Kohlhammer, 1943. 416 pp., illus., diagrs., tabs. (Veröffentlichungen der Arbeitsgemeinschaft für Ostsiedlung).

405 JESS, F[RIEDRICH]: *Rassenkunde und Rassenpflege.* 2. verb. und verm. Aufl. Dortmund: Crüwell, 1935. 170 pp., illus.

406 LENZ, FRITZ: *Menschliche Auslese und Rassenhygiene (Eugenik).* 4. Aufl. München: Lehmann, 1932. 593 pp., tabs., diagrs., bibl. (Menschliche Erblichkeitslehre und Rassenhygiene, Bd. II).

407 MUCKERMANN, HERMANN: *Eugenik.* Berlin: Dümmler, 1934. 173 pp., illus., diagrs., bibl.

408 RITTERSHAUS, ERNST: *Konstitution oder Rasse?* München: Lehmann, 1936. 209 pp., illus., tabs.

409 SCHMEIL, OTTO; *Der Mensch. Menschenkunde—Gesundheitslehre— Vererbungslehre—Rassenhygiene—Familienkunde—Rassenkunde— Bevölkerungspolitik.* 87. Aufl. bearb. von Paul Eichler. Leipzig: Quelle & Meyer, 1936. 184 pp., illus., tabs., diagrs.

410 SCHNELL, FRITZ: *Volk und Gesellschaft. Eine lebensgesetzliche Gesellschaftsbetrachtung des deutschen Volkes.* Leipzig: Heling, 1942. 435 pp.

411 STROOTHENKE, WOLFGANG: *Erbpflege und Christentum. Fragen der Sterilisation, Aufnordung, Euthanasie, Ehe.* Inaugural-Dissertation [pres. to University of Berlin]. 1940. 153 pp., bibl.

412 VERSCHUER, OTMAR Frhr von: *Leitfaden der Rassenhygiene.* 2. verb. Aufl. Leipzig: Thieme, 1944. 278 pp., illus., diagrs.

413 WEINERT, HANS: *Biologische Grundlagen für Rassenkunde und Rassenhygiene.* 2. umgearb. Aufl. Stuttgart: Enke, 1943. viii + 174 pp., diagrs., bibl.

Euthanasia

414 BAEYER, WALTER VON: 'Die Bestätigung der N.S. Ideologie in der Medizin, unter besonderer Berücksichtigung der Euthanasie'. [In] *Nationalsozialismus und die deutsche Universität*, pp. 63–75. See 2414.

415 MEHRMANN, JOHANN: *Anstiftung zum Selbstmord und Vernichtung lebensunwerten Lebens.* Inaugural-Dissertation [pres. to] Ruprecht-Karls-Universität in Heidelberg. 1933. 146 pp., tabs., bibl.

a. Anti-Semitism

416 BREWITZ, WALTHER: *Viertausend Jahre jüdischer Geschichte.* Leipzig: Reclam, 1939. 234 pp.

417 DIEBOW, HANS, ed.: *Der ewige Jude. 265 Bilddokumente.* München: Eher, 1937. 128 pp., illus.

418 DOSE, F. M.: *Sind 500000 Juden ein deutsches Problem? Ist der Jude auch ein Mensch?* Köln-Kalk: Paling, 1935. 226 pp.

419 ESSER, HERMANN: *Die jüdische Weltpest. Judendämmerung auf dem Erdball.* München: Eher, 1939. 243 pp.

420 FEDER, GOTTFRIED and others: *Das neue Deutschland und die Judenfrage. Des Diskussionsbuches erster Teil.* Leipzig: Rüdiger-Verlag, 1933. 228 pp. [Other contributors: Ferdinand Werner, Graf E. zu Reventlow, Ernst Frhr. von Wolzogen, Hans Blüher, Artur Dinter, Alfred Roth, Major Buchrucker, Hans Hauptmann, Max Jungnickel, Wilhelm Stapel, Richard von Schaukal, S. Passarge, Ottokar Stauf von der March.]

421 FISCHER, EUGEN & KITTEL, GERHARD: *Das antike Weltjudentum. Tatsachen, Texte, Bilder.* Hamburg: Hanseatische Verlagsanstalt, 1943. 236 pp., illus., map. (Forschungen zur Judenfrage).

422 FRANK, WALTER: *'Höre Israel!' Studien zur modernen Judenfrage.* 2. erweit. Aufl. Hamburg: Hanseatische Verlagsanstalt, 1943. 327 pp.

423 FRIEDLÄNDER, SAUL: *L'antisémitisme nazi. Histoire d'une psychose collective.* Paris: Eds. du Seuil, 1971. 204 pp.

424 HAUSER, OTTO: *Geschichte des Judentums.* Neuausg. Weimar: Duncker, 1935. 320 pp.

425 INSTITUT ZUM STUDIUM DER JUDENFRAGE: *Die Juden in Deutschland.* 4. Aufl. München: Eher, 1936. 413 pp.

426 JONAK VON FREYENWALD, HANS: *Jüdische Bekenntnisse aus allen Zeiten und Ländern.* Nürnberg: Der Stürmer Buchverlag, 1941. 273 pp.

427 KARL, GEORG; *Satan über Deutschland. Das Schicksal Einzelner und Aller.* Berlin: Kulturpolitischer Verlag, 1934. 272 pp.

428 KÖNITZER, WILLI Fr. & TRURNIT, HANSGEORG, eds.: *Weltentscheidung in der Judenfrage. Der Endkampf nach 3000 Jahren Judengegnerschaft.* In Verbindung mit dem Institut zum Studium der Judenfrage hrsg. Dresden: Zwinger-Verlag (Glöss), 1940. 304 pp., illus.

429 LEERS, JOHANN VON: *Juden sehen Dich an.* Berlin-Schöneberg: NS.-Druck und Verlag, [1934?]. 95 pp., illus.

430 PAUMGARTEN, KARL: *Juda. Kritische Betrachtungen über das Wesen und Wirken des Judentums.* 4. Aufl. Leipzig: Socker, [1921]. 256 pp.

431 PÖTSCH, WALTER: *Die Grundlagen des jüdischen Volkes. Eine notwendige Abrechnung mit dem Judentum.* 2. Aufl. Breslau: Hans W. Pötsch, 1935. 188 pp., bibl.

432 REVENTLOW, Graf E[RNST] zu: *Judas Kampf und Niederlage in Deutschland. 150 Jahre Judenfrage.* Berlin: Verlag 'Zeitgeschichte', 1937. 398 pp., illus.

433 ROSENBERG, ALFRED: *Die Spur des Juden im Wandel der Zeiten.* München: Eher, 1937. 154 pp. [First publ. 1920.]

434 SEIFERT, HERMANN ERICH: *Der Jude zwischen den Fronten der Rassen, der Völker, der Kulturen.* Berlin: Eher, 1943. 183 pp.

435 SERAPHIM, PETER-HEINZ: *Das Judentum im osteuropäischen Raum.* Hrsg. unter Mitwirkung des Instituts für Osteuropäische Wirtschaft an der Universität Königsberg i.Pr. Essen: Essener Verlagsanstalt, 1938. 736 pp., illus., diagrs., map, tabs., bibl.

436 STOCK, RICHARD WILHELM: *Die Judenfrage durch fünf Jahrhunderte.* Nürnberg: Verlag Der Stürmer, 1939. 539 pp., illus.

437 WACHE, WALTER: *Judenfibel. Was Jeder vom Weltjudentum wissen muss!* Leipzig: Fritsch, 1936. 164 pp.

Racial

438 AMANN, BRUNO: *Das Weltbild des Judentums. Grundlagen des völkischen Antisemitismus.* Wien: Kühne, 1939. 363 pp.

439 GÜNTHER, HANS F. K.: *Rassenkunde des jüdischen Volkes.* 2. Aufl. München: Lehmann, 1930. 352 pp., maps.

440 HALBACH, FRITZ: *Esther die Herrin der Welt. Ein völkisches Testament.* Leipzig: Klein, 1934. 133 pp.

441 HARTNER, HERWIG: *Erotik und Rasse. Eine Untersuchung über gesellschaftliche, sittliche und geschlechtliche Fragen.* München: Deutscher Volksverlag, 1925. 252 pp., illus.

442 KURTH, PAUL: *Arier und Juden.* 3. Aufl. Berlin-Pankow: Aar-Verlag, 1925. 288 pp., bibl.

443 PASSARGE, SIEGFRIED: *Das Judentum als landschaftskundlich-ethnologisches Problem.* München: Lehmann, 1929. 460 pp., illus., maps.

444 PLISCHKE, KURT: *Der Jude als Rassenschänder. Eine Anklage gegen Juda und eine Mahnung an die deutschen Frauen und Mädchen.* Berlin-Schöneberg: NS.-Druck und Verlag [193-]. 109 pp.

445 SCHATTENFROH, FRANZ: *Wille und Rasse.* Berlin: Verlag für Wirtschaft und Kultur, 1939. 441 pp.

446 WINGHENE, EGON van: *Arische Rasse, christliche Kultur und das Judenproblem.* Mitarbeiter: A. Tjören. Aus dem Holländischen übersetzt. 4. Aufl. Erfurt: Bodung, 1934. 78 pp., tabs., map of Madagascar on cover. [First mention of Madagascar Plan—that all Jews should be obliged to settle there—in anti-Semitic literature.]

Social, economic and cultural

447 BARTELS, ADOLF: *Jüdische Herkunft und Literaturwissenschaft. Eine gründliche Erörterung.* Leipzig: Bartels-Bund, 1925. 231 pp.

448 BREWITZ, WALTHER: *Die Familie Rothschild.* Stuttgart: Kohlhammer, 1939. 193 pp., geneal. tabs., bibl.

449 DEEG, PETER: *Hofjuden.* Hrsg.: Julius Streicher. 4. und 5. Aufl. Nürnberg: Verlag Der Stürmer, 1939. 547 pp., illus., facsims., bibl.

450 *Das Judentum in der Rechtswissenschaft. Ansprache, Vorträge und Ergebnisse der Tagung der Reichsgruppe Hochschullehrer des NSRB am 3. und 4. Oktober 1936.* Berlin: Deutscher Rechts-Verlag. 8 vols. [Incl.: Vol. 1: *Die deutsche Rechtswissenschaft im Kampf gegen den jüdischen Geist.* 35 pp.; Vol. 3: *Judentum und Verbrechen.* 82 pp.; Vol. 5: *Der Einfluss des Judentums in Staatsrecht und Staatslehre.* 35 pp.]

451 KERNHOLT, OTTO: *Vom Ghetto zur Macht. Die Geschichte des Aufstiegs der Juden auf deutschem Boden.* 4.–6. Aufl. Leipzig: Weicher, 1923. 298 pp.

452 KYNASS, FRITZ: *Der Jude im deutschen Volkslied. Eine Teilstudie.* Inaugural-Dissertation [pres. to] Ernst-Moritz-Arndt Universität Greifswald. 1934. 155 pp., bibl.

453 LISKOWSKY, OSKAR: *Die Geissel der Welt. Juda auf verlorenem Posten.* Geleitwort: Hans Hinkel, M.d.R. Berlin: Deutscher Verlag für Politik und Wirtschaft, 1936. 237 pp., illus., diagrs., map. (2. Folge der Schrift *Deutschlands Kampf um die abendländische Kultur*).

454 MEISTER, ANTON: *Die Presse als Machtmittel Judas.* 2. erweit. Aufl. München: Eher, 1931. 108 pp.

455 PUDOR, HEINRICH: *Die internationalen verwandtschaftlichen Beziehungen der jüdischen Hochfinanz.* Leipzig: Selbstverlag, 1933/40. 62 pamphlets. [Incl.: 1. *Das Haus Rothschild*; 9/10. *Amsterdamer und Oppenheimer Juden, Berliner Juden*; 14. *Rumänische Finanzjuden...*; 17. *Polnische Finanzjuden*; 39/42. *Ungarische Finanzjuden*; etc.]

456 RODERICH-STOLTHEIM, E. (pseud. of Theodor Fritsch): *Das Rätsel des jüdischen Erfolges.* Leipzig: Hammer-Verlag, 1928. 275 pp. [English version: *The riddle of the Jew's success.* Leipzig: Hammer-Verlag, 1927.]

457 SCHICKEDANZ, ARNO: *Sozialparasitismus im Völkerleben.* Leipzig: Lotus-Verlag, 1927. 342 pp., illus.

458 STAPEL, WILHELM: *Die literarische Vorherrschaft der Juden in Deutschland 1918 bis 1933.* Hamburg: Hanseatische Verlagsanstalt, 1937. 43 pp.

Moral and religious

459 BLÜHER, HANS: *Die Erhebung Israels gegen die christlichen Güter.* Hamburg: Hanseatische Verlagsanstalt, [1931]. 202 pp., illus.

460 GROSS, W[ALTER]: *Der Weltenumbruch im jüdischen Mythos.* Düsseldorf: Verlag Deutsche Revolution, 1936. 164 pp., illus., bibl.

461 HILDEBRANDT, OTTO: *Jehova. Das Gesetz einer Nation.* Eisenach i.Th.: Drei Adler-Verlag, 1938. 160 pp., bibl.

462 KOCKSKEMPER, WILHELM: *Jehovah an der Westfront! Der Wirklichkeit nacherzählt.* Landsberg (Warthe): Pfeiffer, 1939. 126 pp.

MURAWSKI, FRIEDRICH: *Der Kaiser aus dem Jenseits. See* 2064.

463 POHL, J[OHANN]: *Talmudgeist.* Berlin: Nordland Verlag, 1941. 121 pp.

464 SCHULZ, ERNST: *Der Trug von Sinai.* München: Ludendorff, 1934. 109 pp.

'JEWISH CRIMINALITY'
465 KELLER, J. & ANDERSEN, HANNS: *Der Jude als Verbrecher.* Mit einem Geleitwort des Frankenführers Gauleiter Julius Streicher. Berlin: Nibelungen-Verlag, 1937. 212 pp., ports.

466 LEERS, JOHANN VON: *Die Verbrechernatur der Juden.* Berlin: Hochmuth, 1944. 171 pp., bibl.

PLISCHKE, KURT: *Der Jude als Rassenschänder. See* 444.

467 PÖTSCH, WALTER: *Die jüdische Rasse im Lichte der Straffälligkeit. Zuchtstätten der Minderrassigkeit.* 2. unveränd. Aufl. Ratibor: Pötsch, 1933. 78 pp., bibl.

'RITUAL MURDER'
468 SCHRAMM, HELMUT: *Der jüdische Ritualmord. Eine historische Untersuchung.* 4. Aufl. Berlin: Fritsch, 1944. 475 pp., illus., facsims., bibl.

469 STAUF VON DER MARCH, OTTOKAR: *Der Ritualmord. Beiträge zur Untersuchung der Frage.* Wien: Hammer-Verlag, 1933. 222 pp.

470 DER STÜRMER, Nr. 20, 17. Jhrg., Mai 1939. [Special issue]: *Ritualmord.* Nürnberg. [20] pp., illus.

471 UTIKAL, GERHARD: *Der jüdische Ritualmord. Eine nichtjüdische Klarstellung.* 16. Aufl. Berlin: Pötsch, 1941. 182 pp., illus., bibl.

'Jewish World Conspiracy'

472 ENGELHARDT, E. Frhr. von: *Jüdische Weltmachtpläne. Die Entstehung der sogenannten Zionistischen Protokolle. Neue Zusammenhänge zwischen Judentum und Freimaurerei.* Leipzig: Hammer-Verlag, 1936. 103 pp.

473 FERVERS, KURT: *Berliner Salons. Die Geschichte einer grossen Verschwörung.* München: Deutscher Volksverlag, 1940. 237 pp.

474 MEYER-CHRISTIAN, WOLF: *Die englisch-jüdische Allianz. Werden und Wirken der kapitalistischen Weltherrschaft.* 3. Aufl. Berlin: Nibelungen-Verlag, 1942. 218 pp., illus., maps.

475 RIECKE, HEINZ: *Der Zionismus. Lösung der Judenfrage—oder eine Weltgefahr?* Berlin: Fritsch, [1939]. 61 pp.

476 ROSE, FRANZ: *Wieder Weltkrieg um Juda?* Berlin: Schlieffen-Verlag, 1939. 220 pp.

477 RUDOLF, E. V. von: *Totengräber der Weltkultur. Der Weg des jüdischen Untermenschentums zur Weltherrschaft.* München: Eher, 1937. 148 pp., illus.

478 SCHULZ, F. O. H.: *Jude und Arbeiter. Ein Abschnitt aus der Tragödie des deutschen Volkes.* Hrsg.: Institut zum Studium der Judenfrage in Zusammenarb. mit der Antikomintern (Gesamtverband deutscher antikommunistischer Vereinigungen), Berlin. 2. durchges. Aufl. Berlin: Nibelungen-Verlag, 1942. 192 pp., ports., bibl.

479 SCHWARTZ-BOSTUNITSCH, GREGOR: *Jüdischer Imperialismus. 3000 Jahre hebräischer Schleichwege zur Erlangung der Weltherrschaft.* 5. aufs neue verm., verb., bis auf die jüngste Zeit ergänzte ... Aufl. Berlin: Fritsch, [1940?]. 687 pp., illus., facsims., bibl. [2. Aufl.: Landsberg a.Lech: Ebersberger, 1935. 300 pp.]

480 UNGER-WINKELRIED, EMIL: *Judas im Weltkriege. 15 Jahre Verrat.* Berlin-Schöneberg: Verlag Deutsche Kultur-Wacht, 1935. 79 pp.

BOLSHEVISM AND THE JEWS
481 BLEY, WULF, ed.: *Der Bolschewismus. Seine Entstehung und Auswirkung.* München: Moser, 1938. 404 pp., illus. [Incl.: 'Die Juden in der biblischen Frühzeit', by Erich Kochanowski; 'Das Mosaische Gesetz und der Talmud', by Wulf Bley; 'Die Revolution, der Stern Judas', by Karl Baumböck; 'Kulturjuden im Vormarsch', by Erich Kochanowski; 'Die Organisation der kommunistischen Weltverschwörung', by Paul Hoecke.]

482 BOCKHOFF, E. H.: *Völker-Recht gegen Bolschewismus.* Mit einem Geleitwort des ... Reichsminister Hans Frank. Berlin: Nibelungen-Verlag, 1937. 252 pp. [Incl.: 'Jüdische Diktatur über das Proletariat'; 'Judentum als "staatstragende" Schicht'; etc.]

483 ECKART, DIETRICH: *Der Bolschewismus von Moses bis Lenin. Zwiegespräch zwischen Adolf Hitler und mir.* München: Hoheneichen-Verlag, 1924. 57 pp.

484 FEHST, HERMAN: *Bolschewismus und Judentum. Das jüdische Element in der Führerschaft des Bolschewismus.* Hrsg. vom Institut zur Erforschung der Judenfrage in Zusammenarbeit mit dem Gesamtverband deutscher

antikommunistischer Vereinigungen Berlin. Berlin: Eckart-Kampf-Verlag, 1934. 167 pp., ports., tabs., diagrs., bibl.

HAUPTMANN, HANS: *Bolschewismus in der Bibel*. See 2049.

485 IWANOW-MOSKWIN, NIKOLAI: *Die Weltrevolution. Judas Kampf um die Weltmacht*. 2. Aufl. Berlin: Donar-Verlag, [1937?]. [30 pp.], illus.

486 KOMMOSS, RUDOLF: *Juden hinter Stalin. Die jüdische Vormachtstellung in der Sowjetunion, auf Grund amtlichen Sowjetquellen dargestellt. Lage und Aussichten*. Berlin: Nibelungen-Verlag, 1938. 229 pp., illus.

487 KUMMER, RUDOLF: *Rasputin, ein Werkzeug der Juden*. 10. Aufl. Nürnberg: Der Stürmer Buchverlag, 1942. 208 pp., bibl.

488 MÜLLER-KRONACH, PAUL: *Moskau vollstreckt Mardochais Testament. Der jüdische Bolschewismus bedroht die Welt*. Bayreuth: Gauverlag Bayerische Ostmark, 1938. 264 pp., tabs., bibl.

489 MÜNCHMEYER, LUDWIG: *Marxisten als Mörder am deutschen Volke im Solde des Feindes*. 5. Aufl. München: Eher, 1935. 196 pp., illus., facsims.

490 POEHL, G. V. & AGTHE, M.: *Das Judentum—das wahre Gesicht der Sowjets*. 2. erweit. Aufl. Berlin: Stollberg, [1941]. 172 pp., maps, diagrs., tabs., bibl. [Dutch version: *Het Jodendom der Sowjets zonder masker*. Amsterdam: Uitg. Westland, 1943.]

491 ROSENBERG, ALFRED: *Pest in Russland. Der Bolschewismus, seine Häupter, Handlanger und Opfer*. Gekürzt hrsg. von Georg Leibbrandt. 4. Aufl. München: Eher, [1937]. 48 pp. [Written 1922.]

b. Other races

Gypsies

492 BLOCK, MARTIN: *Zigeuner. Ihr Leben und ihre Seele dargestellt auf Grund eigener Reisen und Forschungen*. Leipzig: Bibliographisches Institut, 1936. 220 pp., illus.

Coloured races

493 BANG, PAUL: *Die farbige Gefahr*. Göttingen: Vandenhoeck & Ruprecht, 1938. 195 pp., illus.

494 BURGDÖRFER, FRIEDRICH: *Sterben die weissen Völker? die Zukunft der weissen und farbigen Völker im Lichte der biologischen Statistik*. München: Callwey, 1934. 88 pp., maps, tabs., diagr.

495 HEDRICH, KURT: *Der Rassegedanke im deutschen Kolonialrecht. Die rechtliche Regelung der ehelichen und ausserehelichen Beziehungen zwischen Weissen und Farbigen*. Inaugural-Dissertation [pres. to] Universität zu Tübingen. 1941. 113 pp., tabs., bibl.

496 KUCHER, WALTER: *Die Eingeborenenpolitik des Zweiten und Dritten Reiches*. Königsberg (Pr.): Gräfe & Unzer, 1941. 201 pp., tabs., bibl. (Veröffent-

lichungen des Geographischen Instituts der Albertus-Universität zu Königsberg).

497 SELL, MANFRED: *Die schwarze Völkerwanderung. Der Einbruch des Negers in die Kulturwelt.* Wien: Frick, 1940. 315 pp., illus., maps, bibl.

498 ZUMPT, F.: *Kolonialfrage und nationalsozialistischer Rassenstandpunkt.* Hamburg: Hartung, 1938. 32 pp., illus., map.

4. FREEMASONRY AND SECRET SOCIETIES

499 BARTELS, ADOLF: *Freimaurerei und deutsche Literatur. Feststellungen und Vermutungen.* München: Eher, 1929. 106 pp.

500 BLUME, HEINRICH: *Das politische Gesicht der Freimaurerei.* Braunschweig: Appelhans, 1936. 164 pp., bibl.

501 CUSTOS, (Dr.): *Die jüdische Weltherrschaft über die Trümmern der Völker.* Berlin: Hochmuth, [1933?]. 96 pp., tabs. [Jews and Freemasonry.]

502 EVERWIEN, MAX: *Die Unterirdischen. Geschichte der Geheimbünde neuerer Zeit.* Berlin: Claassen, 1939. 379 pp.

503 HASSELBACHER, FRIEDRICH: *Entlarvte Freimaurerei.* Berlin: Hochmuth, 1934/37. 3 vols.
Bd. I: *Das enthüllte Geheimnis der Freimaurerei in Deutschland.* 1934.
Bd. II: *Vom Freimaurer-Mord in Sarajewo—über den Freimaurer-Verrat im Weltkriege—zum Freimaurer-Frieden von Versailles.* 1936.
Bd. III: *Auf den Pfaden der internationalen Freimaurerei—das geschichtliche Wirken der überstaatlichen Mächte.* 1937.

504 HUBER, ENGELBERT: *Freimaurerei. Die Weltmacht hinter den Kulissen.* Stuttgart: Union Deutsche Verlagsgesellschaft, [1934]. 312 pp., illus., bibl.

505 LUDENDORFF, ERICH: *Vernichtung der Freimaurerei durch Enthüllung ihrer Geheimnisse.* München: Ludendorff, 1937. 116 pp., illus., bibl. [First ed. 1927.]

506 LÜTZELER, FELIX FRANZ EGON: *Hinter den Kulissen der Weltgeschichte. Biologische Beiträge zur Geschichte der Geheimbünde aller Zeiten und Völker.* Leipzig: Heling, [1937]. 2 vols., bibls.

507 ROSENBERG, ALFRED: *Das Verbrechen der Freimaurerei. Judentum— Jesuitismus—Deutsches Christentum.* München: Lehmann, 1922. 181 pp.

508 SCHICK, HANS: *Das ältere Rosenkreuzertum. Ein Beitrag zur Entstehungsgeschichte der Freimaurerei.* Berlin: Nordland Verlag, 1942. 338 pp., illus., facsim., bibl.

509 SCHNEIDER, ROBERT: *Die Freimaurerei vor Gericht. Neue Tatsachen über Weltfreimaurerei, deutsch-christliche Orden und geheime Hochgrade.* 3. ergänz. und neubearb. Aufl. München: Lehmann, 1936. 104 pp. [First publ. in Weimar Republic.]

510 SCHWARTZ-BOSTUNITSCH, GREGOR: *Die Freimaurerei. Ihr Ursprung, ihre Geheimnisse, ihr Wirken.* 3. Aufl. Weimar: Duncker, 1933. 307 pp., illus. [First German ed.]

511 SIEBERTZ, PAUL: *Freimaurer im Kampf um die Macht.* Hamburg: Hanseatische Verlagsanstalt, 1938. 488 pp., bibl.

512 WICHTL, FRIEDRICH: *Weltfreimaurerei—Weltrevolution—Weltrepublik. Eine Untersuchung über Ursprung, Verlauf und Fortsetzung des Weltkrieges und über das Wirken des Freimaurerbundes in der Gegenwart.* Neu hrsg. von Robert Schneider. 14. Aufl. München: Lehmann, 1943. 320 pp., illus.

5. FÜHRERPRINZIP

513 ANSBACHER, H. L.: *Attitudes of German prisoners of war: a study of the dynamics of national-socialistic followership.* Washington, D.C.: American Psychological Ass'n, 1948. 42 pp., tabs., bibl.

514 BRAUSSE, HANS BERNHARD: *Die Führungsordnung des deutschen Volkes. Grundlegung einer Führungslehre.* 2. Aufl. Hamburg: Hanseatische Verlagsanstalt, 1940/42. 199 pp.

515 BROSZAT, MARTIN: 'Soziale Motivation und Führer-Bindung des Nationalsozialismus'. [In] *Vierteljahrshefte für Zeitgeschichte*, 18. Jhrg., 4. Heft, Oktober 1970. Stuttgart: Deutsche Verlags-Anstalt. Pp. 392–409.

516 DIETRICH, OTTO: *Hitler, Caudillo. El proceso del partido Nacionalsocialista vivido y analizado por el jefe supremo de la prensa del Reich. Apendice: Plan cuetrienal por el presidente general Goering: Programa del partido Nacionalsocialista.* Granada: Marin, 1937. 222 pp.

517 FRANK, HANS: *Rechtsgrundlegung des nationalsozialistischen Führerstaates.* München: Eher, 1938. 56 pp.

518 HORN, WOLFGANG: *Führerideologie und Parteiorganisation in der NSDAP 1919–1933.* Düsseldorf: Droste, 1972. 451 pp., bibl.

519 KOTZ, ALFRED: *Führen und Folgen. Ein Katechismus für Hitlersoldaten.* 6. Aufl. Potsdam: Voggenreiter, 1934. 100 pp.

520 MEHRINGER, HELMUT: *Die NSDAP als politische Ausleseorganisation.* München: Deutscher Volksverlag, 1938. 122 pp.

521 NOVA, FRITZ: *The National Socialist Führerprinzip and its background in German thought. A dissertation.* Philadelphia, Pa.: University of Pennsylvania, 1943. 169 pp., bibl.

522 WÖRTZ, ULRICH: 'Die "Vorsehung" als Transcendenz des Führerprinzips'. [In] *Programmatik und Führerprinzip. See 865.*

523 ZEDDIES, ADOLF: *Der Weg zur Führerpersönlichkeit. Das Führertum in Wirtschaft und Beruf.* Bad Homburg: Siemens-Verlagsgesellschaft, [n.d.]. 338 pp.

6. ECONOMIC THEORIES

524 BANGERT, OTTO: *Gold oder Blut. Der Weg aus dem Chaos.* 4. neubearb. Aufl. München: Eher, 1927. 113 pp.

524a BARKAI, AVRAHAM: *Des Wirtschaftssystem des Nationalsozialismus. Der historische und ideologische Hintergrund 1933–1936.* Köln: 1977. 214 pp., tabs., bibl.

525 BUCHNER, HANS: *Grundriss einer nationalsozialistischen Volkswirtschaftstheorie.* 5. Aufl. München: Eher, 1933. 46 pp.

526 BUCHNER, HANS: *Warenhauspolitik und Nationalsozialismus.* München: Eher, 1929. 63 pp.

527 FASSBENDER, SIEGFRIED: *Nationalsozialistische Wirtschaft und völkische Freiheit.* Bad Oeynhausen: Lutzeyer, 1940. 197 pp., tabs.

528 GRÜNBERG, HANS BERNHARD von: *Wirtschaft und Kultur. Elemente einer rassen- und willensgebundener Wirtschaftslehre.* Berlin: Verlag für Sozialpolitik, Wirtschaft und Statistik, 1937. 157 pp. (Schriften des Instituts für Wirtschaftswissenschaft).

529 HEINDEL, RUDOLF and others: *Nationalsozialistisches Denken und Wirtschaft.* Von Rudolf Heindel, Wilhelm Link, Erich Schmiedel, Horst Ebel, Heinrich Link. Stuttgart: Kohlhammer, 1932. 163 pp., tabs.

530 KLAGGES, DIETRICH: *Reichtum und soziale Gerechtigkeit. Grundfragen einer nationalsozialistischen Volkswirtschaftslehre.* 2. Aufl. Leipzig: Armanen-Verlag, 1933. 179 pp. [First publ. 1927.]

531 MAURER, EMIL: *Grundlagen und Zukunft der deutschen Nationalwirtschaft. Eine nationalökonomische Studie.* Leipzig: Weicher, 1932. 113 pp.

532 MERKEL, HANS: *Nationalsozialistische Wirtschaftsgestaltung. Einführung in ihre wissenschaftliche Grundlagen.* Stuttgart: Kohlhammer, 1936. 104 pp.

533 [POPITZ, JOHANNES & SCHMITT, CARL] BENTIN, LUTZ-ARWED: *Johannes Popitz und Carl Schmitt. Zur wirtschaftlichen Theorie des totalen Staates in Deutschland.* München: Beck, 1972. ix + 186 pp., bibl.

534 ROBERTS, HELMUTH: *Untergang des Mittelstandes? Eine philosophische und wirtschaftliche Studie zur Frage der mittelständischen Wirtschaftsform.* Stuttgart: Selbstverlag, 1934. 62 pp.

535 SAAGE, RICHARD: *Faschismustheorien. Eine Einführung.* München: Beck, 1976. 184 pp., bibl. [Concentrates on German fascism and economic theories.]

536 WAGENER, OTTO: *Das Wirtschafts-Programm der N.S.D.A.P. Rednermaterial!* Als Manuskript gedruckt. Zusammengestellt nach 2 öffentlichen Versammlungsreden 1931/32. München: Eher, 1932. 104 pp.

Finance

537 DRÄGER, HEINRICH: *Arbeitsbeschaffung durch produktive Kreditschöpfung. Ein*

Beitrag zur Frage der Wirtschaftsbelebung durch das sogenannte Federgeld.
München: Eher, 1932. 82 pp., illus., bibl.

538 FEDER, GOTTFRIED: *Kampf gegen die Hochfinanz.* 2. Aufl. München: Eher, 1933. 382 pp. [5. Aufl. 1934.]

539 FEDER, GOTTFRIED: *Das Manifest zur Brechung der Zinsknechtschaft des Geldes.* 27.–31. Taus. München: Eher, 1932. 61 pp., diagr. [First publ. 1920.]

540 HOCHSTETTER, FRANZ: *Leihkapital und Goldwährung als Grundlagen der Geldversklavung in Deutschland.* München: Eher, 1931. 52 pp., tabs.

541 NICOLAI, HELMUT: *Die Wurzeln des modernen Bankwesens. Rasse und Bankwesen.* Berlin: Hobbing, 1934. 80 pp. [Written in 1925.]

542 REINHARDT, FRITZ: *Die Herrschaft der Börse.* 2. Aufl. München: Eher, 1929. 48 pp.

543 ROSENBERG, ALFRED: *Die internationale Hochfinanz als Herrin der Arbeiterbewegung in allen Ländern.* München: Deutscher Volksverlag (Boepple), [1924?]. 71 pp.

Workers

544 HARTZ, GUSTAV: *Die national-soziale Revolution. Die Lösung der Arbeiterfrage.* München: Lehmann, 1932. 207 pp.

545 LAWACZECK, FRANZ: *Technik und Wirtschaft im Dritten Reich. Ein Arbeitsbeschaffungsprogramm.* 2. Aufl. München: Eher, 1932. 93 pp., charts.

546 MUCHOW, REINHOLD: *Nationalsozialismus und 'freie' Gewerkschaften.* München: Eher, 1932. 115 pp., tabs.

Peasantry and agriculture

DARRÉ, RICHARD WALTHER
547 DARRÉ, R. WALTHER: *Aufbruch des Bauerntums. Reichsbauerntagsreden 1933 bis 1938.* Berlin: Reichsnährstand Verlagsgesellschaft, 1942. 130 pp. [Incl.: 'Wo der Jude herrscht, muss der Bauer sterben', 'Der jüdische Asphaltliterat und das Bauerntum', 'Die Verfälschung des Sozialismus durch den jüdischen Marxismus'.]

548 DARRÉ, R. WALTHER: *Das Bauerntum als Lebensquell der nordischen Rasse.* 6. Aufl. München: Lehmann, 1937. 493 pp. [Copyright 1929.]

549 GIES, HORST: *R. Walther Darré und die nationalsozialistische Bauernpolitik in den Jahren 1930 bis 1933.* Inaugural-Dissertation [pres. to] Johann-Wolfgang-Goethe Universität Frankfurt a.M. 1966. 177 pp., bibl.

---

550 GÜNTHER, HANS F. K.: *Das Bauerntum als Lebens- und Gemeinschaftsform.* Leipzig: Teubner, 1939. 673 pp.

551 GAUCH, HERMANN: *Die germanische Odal- oder Allodverfassung*. Berlin: Blut und Boden Verlag, 1934. 86 pp.

552 HILDEBRANDT, FRIEDRICH: *Nationalsozialismus und Landarbeiterschaft*. München: Eher, 1930. 45 pp.

553 JUST, OSKAR & WILLRICH, WOLFGANG, artists: *Nordisches Blutserbe im süddeutschen Bauerntum*. Geleitw.: R. Walther Darré. München: Bruckmann, 1938. 66 pp., illus.

KOLLER, HELLMUT: *Die nationalsozialistische Wirtschaftsidee im 'Völkischen Beobachter'*. See 2843.

554 LEERS, JOHANN VON: *Odal. Das Lebensgesetz eines ewigen Deutschland*. 2. Aufl. Goslar: Blut und Boden Verlag, 1936. 759 pp., illus., diagrs., facsims., bibl.

555 *National-Sozialismus und Landwirtschaft. Warum jeder deutsche Bauer Nationalsozialist werden muss. Eine Aufklärungsschrift über das National-Sozialistische Agrarprogramm, von einem schlesischen Landwirt*. Breslau: Jenke, [1930?]. 31 pp. [Incl.: 'Parteiamtliche Kundgebung über die Stellung der NSDAP zum Landvolk ...' over signature Adolf Hitler, dated 6 March 1930. Pp. 1–4.]

556 WILLIKINS, WERNER: *Nationalsozialistische Agrarpolitik*. Geleitwort: R. Walther Darré. München: Boepple, 1931. 64 pp., tabs.

Analysis of Marxism

557 BOCKELMANN, WILHELM: *Von Marx zu Hitler*. München: Eher, 1933. 128 pp. [NS analysis of Marxism addressed to workers, attacking social democracy, Jews, Freemasons, Jesuits.]

558 LORENZ, OTTOKAR: *Karl Marx und der Kapitalismus. Eine Untersuchung über die Grundbegriffe der marxistischen Klassenkampflehre*. Hamburg: Hanseatische Verlagsanstalt, 1937. 135 pp.

559 MEIER, PAUL, ed.: *Das kommunistische Manifest von Karl Marx und Friedrich Engels. Für den Nationalsozialisten hrsg*. Köthen-Anhalt: Verlag 'Die Lichtputze', 1931. 32 pp.

560 SCHMITT, WALTHER: *Die Klassenkampftheorie und ihre Widerlegung*. München: Eher, 1930. 134 pp., bibl.

561 STRASSER, OTTO & FREI, BRUNO: *Internationaler Marxismus oder Nationaler Sozialismus. Eine grundlegende Diskussion*. Berlin: 'Der Nationale Sozialist', 1930. 37 pp.

7. LEGAL THEORIES

562 ANDERBRÜGGE, KLAUS: *Völkisches Rechtsdenken. Zur Rechtslehre in der Zeit des Nationalsozialismus*. Berlin: Duncker & Humblot, 1978. 237 pp., bibl. [Orig. pres. as diss. to Münster University in 1976.]

563 BEYER, JUSTUS: *Die Ständeideologie der Systemzeit und ihre Überwindung.* Darmstadt: Wittich, 1941. 363 pp., bibl. (Forschungen zum Staats- und Verwaltungsrecht).

564 BRISTLER, EDUARD: *Die Völkerrechtslehre des Nationalsozialismus.* Vorwort: Georges Scelle. Zürich: Europa-Verlag, 1938. 230 pp., bibl. [Incl.: 'Völkerrecht auf der Grundlage von Rasse und Volkstum', pp. 108–167.]

565 FLESSNER, VOLLMAR: *Rasse und Politik im Staatsbürgerrecht. Rassisch-völkische und politische Voraussetzungen der Ausübung staatsbürgerlichen Rechte in Deutschland und im Auslande.* Berlin: Deutscher Rechtsverlag, 1939. 120 pp., bibl.

566 FRANK, HANS: *Heroisches und geordnetes Recht.* Rede ... anlässlich der Eröffnung der Ausstellung 'Buch und Recht' im Reichsgericht zu Leipzig. Nachwort: Wilhelm Heuber. Berlin: Deutscher Rechtsverlag, 1938. 31 pp.

567 JÄGER, AUGUST: *Kirche im Volk. Ein Beitrag zur Geschichte der national-sozialistischen Rechtsentwicklung.* Berlin: Deutscher Rechtsverlag, 1936. 119 pp.

568 JONES, WALTER J.: *The Nazi conception of law.* London: Oxford University Press, 1940. 32 pp. (Oxford Pamphlets on World Affairs).

569 KIRSCHENMANN, DIETRICH: *'Gesetz' im Staatsrecht und in der Staatsrechtlehre des NS.* Berlin: Duncker & Humblot, 1970. 143 pp., bibl.

570 LEERS, JOHANN VON: *Blut und Rasse in der Gesetzgebung. Ein Gang durch die Völkergeschichte.* München: Lehmann, 1936. 135 pp.

571 LEISTRITZ, HANS KARL: *Entrechtung der Jurisprudenz. Abwehr des juristischen Denksystems mit einer Einführung in die volksrechtliche Wirklichkeit und deren Denkweise.* Berlin-Südende: Sudau, 1936. 88 pp.

572 MEYER, HERBERT: *Rasse und Recht bei den Germanen und Indogermanen.* Weimar: Böhlaus, 1937. 136 pp.

573 RÜHLE, GERD, ed.: *Rasse und Sozialismus im Recht.* Berlin: Deutsche Rechts- und Wirtschaftswissenschaft Verlags-Gesellschaft, 1935. 142 pp., tabs. [Incl.: K. Ziegra: 'Hang zur Straffälligkeit? Die Straffälligkeit als rassische Lebenserscheinung der Juden', pp. 28–57, tabs.]

574 RUTTKE, FALK: *Rasse, Recht und Volk. Beiträge zur rassengesetzlichen Rechtslehre.* München: Lehmann, 1937. 212 pp., illus., diagrs., bibl.

575 SCHMELZEISEN, G. K.: *Das Recht im nationalsozialistischen Weltbild. Grundzüge des deutschen Rechts.* 3. umgearb. und verm. Aufl. Leipzig: Kohlhammer, 1936. 85 pp., bibl.

576 [SCHMITT, CARL] MAUS, INGEBORG: *Bürgerliche Rechtstheorie und Faschismus. Zur sozialen Funktion und aktuellen Wirkung der Theorie Carl Schmitts.* München: Fink, 1976. 195 pp.

8. CULTURAL THEORIES

577 BERGMANN, ERNST: *Deutschland das Bildungsland der neuen Menschheit. Eine nationalsozialistische Kulturphilosophie.* Breslau: Hirt, 1933. 153 pp.

578 DELIUS, RUDOLF VON: *Die Weltmächte des Geistes. Zum Endkampf der Kulturen.* Berlin: Hoffmann, 1934. 130 pp.

579 FOCHLER-HAUKE, GUSTAV, ed.: *Von deutscher Art.* München: Deutsche Akademie, [1939]. 129 pp., illus.

580 KRANNHALS, PAUL: *Das organische Weltbild. Grundlagen einer neuentstehenden deutschen Kultur.* Ungekürzte Volksausg. München: Bruckmann, 1936. 775 pp. [In 2 vols. First ed. 1928.]

581 LANGEWEYDE, WOLF SLUYTERMAN VON: *Kultur ist Dienst am Leben.* 2. Aufl. Berlin: Nordland-Verlag, 1937. 295 pp.

582 SCHULTZ, WOLFGANG: *Grundgedanken nationalsozialistischer Kulturpolitik.* München: Eher, 1939. 217 pp., bibl.

583 SCHWERBER, PETER: *Nationalsozialismus und Technik. Die Geistigkeit der nationalsozialistischen Bewegung.* München: Eher, 1930. 64 pp., bibl.

584 STEINBÖMER, GUSTAV: *Politische Kulturlehre.* Hamburg: Hanseatische Verlagsanstalt, 1933. 182 pp.

585 STONNER, ANTON: *Von germanischer Kultur und Geistesart. Deutsche Vergangenheit als Bildungsgut.* Regensburg: Pustet, 1934. 254 pp., bibl.

586 WILLRICH, WOLFGANG: *Säuberung des Kunsttempels. Eine kunstpolitische Kampfschrift zur Gesundung deutscher Kunst im Geiste nordischer Art.* München: Lehmann, 1937. 178 pp., front., bibl.

Literature

587 ATKINS, H. G.: *German literature through Nazi eyes.* London: Methuen, 1941. 136 pp.

588 GILMAN, SANDER L., ed.: *NS-Literaturtheorie. Eine Dokumentation.* Vorwort: Cornelius Schnauber. Frankfurt a.M.: Athenäum Verlag, 1971. xxii + 264 pp., bibl. [Incl.: IIA: 'Die völkische Literaturbetrachtung'; IIB: 'Die rassische Literaturbetrachtung'; IVB: 'Die jüdische Kritik als Dekadenzerscheinung', by Wilhelm Stapel.]

589 VONDUNG, KLAUS: *Völkisch-nationale und nationalsozialistische Literatur-theorie.* München: List, 1973. 247 pp., bibl.

Music

590 BLESSINGER, KARL: *Mendelssohn, Meyerbeer, Mahler. Drei Kapitel Judentum in der Musik als Schlüssel zur Musikgeschichte des 19. Jahrhunderts.* Berlin: Hahnefeld, 1939. 94 pp. [Enlarged and revised edition renamed: *Judentum und Musik. Ein Beitrag zur Kultur- und Rassenpolitik.* 1944. 156 pp.]

591 EICHENAUER, RICHARD: *Musik und Rasse*. 2. verb. und verm. Aufl. München: Lehmann, 1937. 323 pp., illus.

592 WALDMANN, GUIDO, ed.: *Rasse und Musik*. Mitarb.: Joachim Dukart, Richard Eichenauer, Gotthold Fritscher, Fritz Matzler, Joseph Müller-Blattau. Berlin: Vieweg, 1939. 112 pp., illus., mus. notations.

Visual arts

593 STANG, WALTER: *Weltanschauung und Kunst*. Berlin: Junker & Dünnhaupt, 1937. 55 pp.

594 TAYLOR, ROBERT R.: *The word in stone. The role of architecture in the National Socialist ideology*. Berkeley, Calif.: University of California Press, 1974. xv + 298 pp., illus., bibl.

Drama

595 KETELSEN, UWE-KARSTEN: *Heroisches Theater. Untersuchungen zur Dramentheorie des Dritten Reichs*. Bonn: Bouvier, 1968. xi + 230 pp., bibl.

9. ETHICAL ATTITUDES

596 BASSENGE, FRIEDRICH: *Ehre und Beleidigung*. Berlin: Junker & Dünnhaupt, 1937. 84 pp.

597 BLEUEL, HANS PETER: *Strength through joy. Sex and society in Nazi Germany*. London: Pan, 1970. 352 pp., illus., facsims. [Orig. German: *Das saubere Reich. Theorie und Praxis des sittlichen Lebens im Dritten Reich*. Bern: Scherz, 1972.]

598 EILEMANN, JOHANNES: *Weltanschauung, Erziehung und Dichtung. Einige Kapitel einer arteigenen Ethik*. Frankfurt a.M.: Diesterweg, 1935. 134 pp.

599 FRANK, HANS & GOLTZ, RÜDIGER Graf von der: *Nationalsozialistischer Ehrenschutz*. Wien: Deutscher Rechts-Verlag, 1938. 36 pp. (Schriften des NS.-Rechtswahrerbundes in Österreich.) [Title of von der Goltz's article: 'Ehre und Gemeinschaft'.]

600 HENNEMANN, GERHARD: *Grundzüge einer Deutschen Ethik*. Leipzig: Klein, 1938. 125 pp.

601 USADEL, GEORG: *Zucht und Ordnung. Grundlagen einer nationalsozialistischen Ethik*. Hamburg: Hanseatische Verlagsanstalt, 1935. 74 pp.

602 WIENEKE, FRIEDRICH: *Charaktererziehung im Nationalsozialismus*. Soldin: Madrasch, 1936. 195 pp.

603 WUNDT, MAX: *Die Ehre als Quelle des sittlichen Lebens in Volk und Staat*. Langensalza: Beyer, 1937. 52 pp. (Schriften zur Politischen Bildung ...).

604 *Zucht und Sitte. Schriften für die Neuordnung unserer Lebensgesetze*. *Erscheinungsjahr 1942*. Goslar: Verlag Zucht und Sitte. 115 pp., illus., diagrs., facsims. (2. Folge.)
Erscheinungsjahr 1943. Berlin: Engelhardt. 95 pp., illus., tabs. (3. Folge).

D. LEADERS

1. GENERAL

605 AMBROSI, DOMINIQUE: *Les chefs nazis*. Paris: Éds. Gaucher, 1949. 246 pp.

606 BAYLES, WILLIAM D.: *Caesars in goose-step*. New York: Harper, 1940. xi + 262 pp., ports.

607 *Das Deutsche Führerlexikon 1934/1935*. Berlin: Stollberg, 1934. 552 + 148 pp., ports.

608 DUTCH, OSWALD: *Hitler's twelve apostles*. London: Arnold, 1939. 271 pp., illus.

609 DWINGER, EDWIN ERICH: *Die 12 Gespräche 1933–1945*. Velbert: Blick + Bild Verlag, 1966. 246 pp., ports. facsims.

610 FEST, JOACHIM C.: *Das Gesicht des Dritten Reiches. Profile einer totalitären Herrschaft*. München: Piper, 1963. 513 pp., illus., bibl.

611 HÜTTENBERGER, PETER: *Die Gauleiter. Studie zum Wandel des Machtgefüges in der NSDAP*. Stuttgart: Deutsche Verlags-Anstalt, 1969. 239 pp. map, tab., bibl. (Schriftenreihe der Vierteljahrshefte für Zeitgeschichte).

612 *Ich kämpfe. Der Alten Garde des Führers zum 10. Jahrestag der Machtergreifung am 30. Januar 1943*. München: Eher, 1943. 98 pp., illus.

613 KORNEV, N.: *Tret'ia Imperiia v litsakh* [Personalities of the Third Reich]. Moskva: Gosyd. Izd. 'Khudozhestvennaia Literatura', 1937. 530 pp., ports., illus. (cartoons).

614 LAMPE, FRIEDRICH WILHELM: *Die Amtsträger der Partei*. 2. Aufl. Stuttgart: Kohlhammer, 1944. 172 pp., bibl.

615 *Männer im Dritten Reich*. Hrsg.: Orientalische Cigaretten-Compagnie 'Rosma', Bremen. Bremen: Rosma, 1934. 241 pp., illus.

616 MANTAU-SADILA, HANS HEINZ, ed.: *Deutsche Führer—Deutsches Schicksal. Das Buch der Künder und Führer des Dritten Reiches*. Berlin: Riegler, 1933. 399 pp., illus., facsim. [Illus. compiled by Arnold Schley.]

617 [MÜNZENBERG, WILLI]: *Naziführer sehen Dich an. 33 Biographien aus dem Dritten Reich*. Paris: Éds. du Carrefour, 1934. 226 pp., illus., facsims. [Criminal careers of leading Nazis.]

618 RICHTER, ALFRED: *Unsere Führer im Lichte der Rassenfrage und Charakterologie. Eine rassenmässige und charakterologische Beurteilung von Männern des Dritten Reiches. Mit polizeilicher und parteiamtlicher NSDAP-Genehmigung*. Leipzig: Lippold, 1933. 158 pp., diagr.

619 SCHIRACH, BALDUR von: *Die Pioniere des Dritten Reiches*. Essen: Zentralstelle für den deutschen Freiheitskampf, [1933?]. 247 pp., ports.

620 SCHMIDT-PAULI, EDGAR von: *Die Männer um Hitler*. Berlin: Verlag für Kulturpolitik, 1932. 189 pp.

2. ADOLF HITLER

Before 1933

621 *Adolf Hitler und seine Bewegung im Lichte neutraler Beobachter und objektiver Gegner.* 2. Aufl. München: Eher, 1928. 55 pp. (Anhang: 'Ziele und Wege der Nationalsozialistischen Deutschen Arbeiterpartei').

622 BEUCLER, ANDRÉ: *L'ascension d'Hitler. Du village autrichien au coup d'état de Munich.* Paris: Éds. nationales, 1937. 251 pp. (L'histoire inconnu).

623 BOUHLER, PHILIPP: *Adolf Hitler. Das Werden einer Volksbewegung.* 25. Aufl. Lübeck: Coleman, 1943. 95 pp., illus.

624 CALIC, ÉDOUARD: *Ohne Maske. Hitler-Breiting Geheimgespräche 1931.* Vorwort: Golo Mann. Frankfurt a.M.: Societäts-Verlag, 1968. 233 pp., bibl.

625 CZECH-JOCHBERG, ERICH: *Hitler. Reichskanzler.* Oldenburg: Stalling, 1930. 237 pp. [New enl. ed of *Hitler. Eine deutsche Bewegung.*]

626 DIEBOW, HANS & GOELTZER, KURT: *Hitler. Eine Biographie in 134 Bildern.* Berlin: Verlag Tradition, 1932. 160 pp., illus.

627 DIETRICH, OTTO: *Mit Hitler in die Macht. Persönliche Erlebnisse mit meinem Führer.* 20. Aufl. München: Eher, 1935. 209 pp. [English version: *With Hitler on the road to power.* London: 1934.]

628 GRIESWELLE, DETLEF: *Propaganda der Friedlosigkeit. Eine Studie zu Hitlers Rhetorik 1920–1933.* Stuttgart: Enke, 1972. 233 pp., bibl.

629 HANFSTAENGEL, ERNST: *Hitler: the missing years.* London: Eyre & Spottiswoode, 1957. 299 pp., port.

630 HANSER, RICHARD: *Prelude to terror. The rise of Hitler 1919–1923.* London: Hart-Davis, 1971. 409 pp., illus., facsim., bibl.

631 HARTINGER, J. F.: *Der deutsche Diktator. Ist Adolf Hitler jener von den Sehern aller Zeiten angekündigte grosse Volksherzog, der Deutschland zum mächtigsten christlichen Weltreich machen wird? Ein Trostbuch für das bedrückte deutsche Volk!* Traunstein: Miller, 1932. 40 pp., bibl. [A Catholic on Hitler as the saviour of the German people.]

632 HEUSS, THEODOR: *Hitlers Weg. Eine Schrift aus dem Jahre 1932.* Neu hrsg. ... Einleitung: Eberhard Jäckel. Tübingen: Wunderlich, 1968. 167 + 110 pp., bibl. [First ed. Stuttgart, 1932. Dutch version: *De rol van Adolf Hitler in het huidige Duitschland.* Amsterdam: Seyffardt, 1932.]

633 HIRTH, FRÉDÉRIC: *Hitler ou le guerrier déchaîné.* Paris: Éds. du Tambourin, 1930. 254 pp.

634 HOFFMANN, HEINRICH, ed.: *Hitler über Deutschland.* Text: Josef Berchtold. München: Eher, 1932. 88 pp., illus.

635 JENKS, WILLIAM A.: *Vienna and the young Hitler.* New York: Columbia University Press, 1960. 252 pp.

636 JETZINGER, FRANZ: *Hitlers Jugend. Phantasien, Lügen—und die Wahrheit.* Wien: Europa-Verlag, 1956. 308 pp., illus. [English version: *Hitler's youth.* London: Hutchinson, 1958.]

637 KALLENBACH, HANS & UWESON, ULF: *Mit Adolf Hitler auf Festung Landsberg.* Nach Aufzeichnungen des Mitgefangenen Hans Kallenbach, bearb. von Ulf Uweson. München: Parcus, 1933. 167 pp., illus., facsim.

638 KUBIZEK, AUGUST: *Adolf Hitler. Mein Jugendfreund.* Graz: Stock, 1953. 352 pp. [English version: *Young Hitler. The story of our friendship.* Introd.: H. R. Trevor-Roper. London: Wingate, 1954. 204 pp., illus.]

639 LEWIS, [PERCY] WYNDHAM: *Hitler.* London: Chatto & Windus, 1931. 202 pp., illus. [German version: *Hitler und sein Werk in englischer Beleuchtung.* Berlin: Hobbing, 1932.]

640 MEYER, ADOLF: *Mit Adolf Hitler im Bayerischen Reserve-Infantrie-Regiment 16 List.* Geleitw.: Julius Streicher. Neustadt-Aisch: Aupperle, 1934. 109 pp., illus.

641 MILTENBERG, WEIGAND VON: *Adolf Hitler—Wilhelm III.* Berlin: Rowohlt, 1931. 92 pp.

642 PFEIFER, EVA: *Das Hitlerbild im Spiegel einiger konservativer Zeitungen in den Jahren 1929–1933.* Inaugural-Dissertation [pres. to] Ruprecht-Karl Universität zu Heidelberg. München: 1966. 192 pp., bibl.

643 RABITSCH, HUGO: *Aus Adolf Hitlers Jugendzeit. Jugenderinnerungen eines zeitgenössischen Linzer Realschülers.* München: Deutscher Volksverlag, 1938. 152 pp.

644 SMITH, BRADLEY F.: *Adolf Hitler. His family, childhood and youth.* Stanford, Calif.: Hoover Institution on War, Revolution, and Peace, 1967. 180 pp., illus., family tree, bibl.

645 TOURLY, ROBERT & LVOVSKY, Z.: *Hitler.* Préface: Pierre MacOrlan. Paris: Éds. du Siècle, 1932. 220 pp.

646 TURNER, H. A., ed.: *Hitler aus nächster Nähe. Aufzeichnungen eines Vertrauten 1929–1932.* Frankfurt a.M.: Ullstein, 1978. xvii + 508 pp., illus., facsims. [Diary of Otto Wagener.]

647 TYRELL, ALBRECHT: *Vom 'Trommler' zum 'Führer'. Der Wandel von Hitlers Selbstverständnis zwischen 1919 und 1924 und die Entwicklung der NSDAP.* München: Fink, 1975. 296 pp., bibl.

After 1933 and general biographies

648 *Adolf Hitler. Bilder aus dem Leben des Führers.* Altona-Bahrenfeld: Cigaretten-Bilderdienst, 1936. 132 pp., illus. [English version: *Pictures from the life of the Führer 1931–1935.* Encomion: Hermann Göring; Foreword: Joseph Goebbels; Text: Joseph Goebbels (and others). Introd. and commentary: Julius Rosenthal. New York: Peebles Press, 1978. xiii + 145 pp.]

649 BETHGE, HERMANN: *Der Führer und sein Werk. Kernstoffe, Leitgedanken und Anregungen.* Osterwieck/Harz: Zickfeldt, 1938/39. 4 vols., tabs., family tree.

650 BILLINGER, KARL: *Hitler is no fool.* New York: Modern Age Books, 1939. x + 198 pp.

651 BOROWSKI, PETER: *Adolf Hitler.* Hamburg: Dressler, 1978. 204 pp., illus.

652 BULLOCK, ALAN: *Hitler. A study in tyranny.* London: Odhams, 1952. 776 pp., illus., maps, diagrs., bibl. [Completely rev. ed. 1964. German version: *Hitler. Eine Studie über Tyrannei.* 5. Aufl. Düsseldorf: Droste, 1957 (and) Frankfurt a.M.: Fischer, 1964.]

653 CARR, WILLIAM: *Hitler—a study in personality and politics.* London: Arnold, 1978. x + 200 pp.

654 DAVIDSON, EUGENE: *The making of Adolf Hitler.* London: Macdonald and Jane's, 1977. 408 pp., illus., bibl.

655 DEVI, SAVITRI: *The lightning and the sun.* Calcutta: [priv. pr.], 1958. 432 pp., illus.

656 DIETRICH, OTTO: *12 Jahre mit Hitler.* München: Isar Verlag, 1955. 285 pp.

657 CROSS, COLIN: *Adolf Hitler.* London: Hodder & Stoughton, 1973. 348 pp., illus., map, bibl.

658 FABRY, PHILIPP W.: *Mutmassungen über Hitler. Urteile von Zeitgenossen.* Düsseldorf: Droste, 1969. 265 pp., front., bibl. [Also: Königstein/Ts.: Athenäum Verlag, 1979.]

659 FEST, JOACHIM C.: *Hitler. Eine Biographie.* Frankfurt a.M.: Ullstein (Propyläen), 1973. 1190 pp., illus., bibl. [English version: *Hitler.* London: Weidenfeld & Nicolson, 1974.]

660 GERVASI, FRANK: *Adolf Hitler.* New York: Hawthorn Books, 1974. 279 pp., bibl.

661 GIESLER, HERMANN: *Ein anderer Hitler. Bericht seines Architekten. Erlebnisse, Gespräche, Reflexionen.* Leoni a. Starnberger See: Druffel, 1977. 527 pp., illus.

662 GISEVIUS, HANS-BERND: *Adolf Hitler. Versuch einer Deutung.* München: Rütten & Loening, 1963. 565 pp., illus.

663 GÖRLITZ, WALTER & QUINT, HERBERT A.: *Adolf Hitler. Eine Biographie.* Stuttgart: Steingrüben-Verlag, 1952. 656 pp., family tree, bibl.

664 GOSSET, PIERRE & RENÉE: *Adolf Hitler.* Paris: Julliard, 1961/65. Illus.
Tome 1: Publ. 1961. 347 pp.
Tome 2: *De la prise du pouvoir à Munich.* Publ. 1962. 337 pp.
Tome 3: *De l'apogée au Götterdämmerung.* Publ. 1965. 557 pp., bibl.

665 GREINER, JOSEF: *Das Ende des Hitler-Mythos.* Zürich: Amalthea-Verlag, 1947. 342 pp., illus.

666 GÜNTHER, HANS F. K.: *Mein Eindruck von Adolf Hitler*. Pähl: von Bebenburg, 1969. 158 pp., port.

667 HAFFNER, SEBASTIAN: *Anmerkungen zu Hitler*. München: Kindler, 1978. 203 pp. [English version: *The meaning of Hitler*. London: Weidenfeld & Nicolson, 1979.]

668 HAMMER, WOLFGANG: *Adolf Hitler ... Dialog mit dem 'Führer'*. München: Delp, 1970/74. Bibls.
   I: ... *ein deutscher Messias? Geschichtliche Aspekte*. Publ. 1970. 250 pp.
   II: ... *der Tyrann und die Völker. Politische Aspekte*. Publ. 1972. 291 pp.
   III: ... *ein Prophet unserer Zeit? Ideologische Aspekte*. Publ. 1974. 215 pp.

669 HAMŠÍK, DUŠAN: *Géniùs prùmĕrnosti. Nová fakta a pohledy na Hitlerùv konec* [Genius of mediocrity. New facts and opinions concerning Hitler's end]. Praha: Československý spisovatel, 1967. 161 pp., illus., bibl.

670 HEIBER, HELMUT: *Adolf Hitler. A short biography*. Transl. from the German. London: Wolff, 1972. 192 pp., illus., bibl. [German orig.: *Adolf Hitler. Eine Biographie*. Berlin: Colloquium, 1960.]

671 HEIDEN, KONRAD: *Adolf Hitler. Eine Biographie*. Zürich: Europa-Verlag, 1936/37. In 2 vols. [English version: *Hitler—a biography*. London: Constable, 1936; Vol. 2 only: *One man against Europe*. Harmondsworth, Middx.: Penguin Books, 1939. 279 pp. French version: *Adolf Hitler*. Paris: Grasset, 1936.]

672 HEINZ, HEINZ A.: *Germany's Hitler*. London: Hurst & Blackett, 1934. 288 pp., illus. ['The only authorised biography'.]

673 HÖRSTER-PHILIPPS, ULRIKE: *Wer war Hitler wirklich? Grosskapital und Faschismus 1918–1945. Dokumente*. Köln: Pahl-Rugenstein, 1978. 388 pp.

674 HOFFMANN, HEINRICH, ed.: *Hitler abseits vom Alltag*. 100 Bilddokumente aus der Umgebung des Führers. Geleitwort: Wilhelm Brückner. Berlin: Zeitgeschichte-Verlag, 1937. 94 pp., illus.

675 HOFFMANN, PETER: *Die Sicherheit des Diktators. Hitlers Leibwachen, Schutzmassnahmen, Residenzen, Hauptquartiere*. München: Piper, 1975. 328 pp., illus., maps, bibl. [English version: *Hitler's personal security*. London: Macmillan, 1979.]

676 KERN, ERICH: *Adolf Hitler ...* 1970/78. Illus., bibls.
   ... *und seine Bewegung. Der Parteiführer*. Göttingen: Schütz, 1970. 390 pp., facsims., diagrs., tabs., family tree.
   ... *und das Dritte Reich. Der Staatsmann*. Preussisch Oldendorf: Schütz, 1971. 466 pp.
   ... *und der Krieg. Der Feldherr*. Preussisch Oldendorf: Schütz, 1978. 462 pp.

676a KERSHAW, IAN: *Der Hitler-Mythos 1920–1945*. Stuttgart: Deutsche Verlagsanstalt, 1980. (Schriftenreihe der Vierteljahrshefte für Zeitgeschichte).

677 LE GRIX, FRANÇOIS: *Vingt jours chez Hitler. Tableaux d'une révolution.* Paris: Grasset, 1933. 253 pp.

678 LEWIS, DAVID: *The secret life of Adolf Hitler.* London: Hanau, 1977. 223 pp., illus.

679 MANVELL, ROGER & FRAENKEL, HEINRICH: *Adolf Hitler. The man and the myth.* London: Granada, 1978. 255 pp., illus., bibl. [First publ. under title *Inside Adolf Hitler,* 1973.]

680 MASER, WERNER: *Adolf Hitler. Legende, Mythos, Wirklichkeit.* München: Bechtle, 1971. 529 pp., facsims., family tree, map, bibl.

680a MASER, WERNER: *Adolf Hitler—Das Ende der Führerlegende.* Düsseldorf: Econ-Verlag, 1980. 400 pp.

681 OLDEN, RUDOLF: *Hitler the pawn.* London: Gollancz, 1936. 439 pp., illus. [German version: *Hitler.* Amsterdam: Querido, 1935.]

682 PAYNE, ROBERT: *The life and death of Adolf Hitler.* London: Cape, 1973. xiii + 623 pp., illus., facsims., maps, bibl.

683 PETITFRÈRE, RAY: *Pas à pas avec Hitler.* Paris: Presses de la Cité, 1973/74. Ports., illus., maps.
[Tome I]: *Autriche, Bavière, France, Belgique.* Publ. 1973. viii + 434 pp.
Tome II: *Brandebourg, Prusse, Rhénanie.* Publ. 1974. 478 pp.
Tome III: *Tchécoslovaquie, Allemagne, Finlande, Pologne, Russie, Italie.* Publ. 1974. 426 pp.

684 SCHOTT, GEORG: *Das Volksbuch von Hitler.* 7. Aufl. München: Eher, 1937. 307 pp. (Copyright 1924).

685 SCHUMAN, FREDERICK L.: *Hitler and the Nazi dictatorship. A study in social pathology and the politics of Fascism.* London: Hale, 1936. 516 pp.

686 SIEBARTH, WERNER: *Hitlers Wollen. Nach Kernsätzen aus seinen Schriften und Reden.* München: Eher, 1935. 266 pp. [Further issues: '3. ergänz. Aufl.', 1936, 319 pp.; '6. Aufl.', 1939.]

687 STELLRECHT, HELMUT: *Adolf Hitler: Heil und Unheil. Die verlorene Revolution.* Tübingen: Grabert, 1974. 333 pp., illus. [An apologist view.]

688 STERN, J. P.: *Hitler. The Fuehrer and the people.* Glasgow: Collins (Fontana), 1975. 254 pp. [Incl. J. G. Elser and the Munich bomb attempt.]

689 STIERLIN, HELM: *Adolf Hitler. Familienperspektiven.* Frankfurt a.M.: Suhrkamp, 1975. 186 pp., bibl.

690 STONE, NORMAN: *Hitler.* Introd.: J. H. Plumb. London: Hodder & Stoughton, 1980. xii + 195 pp., illus., bibl.

691 THIES, JOCHEN: *Architekt der Weltherrschaft. Die 'Endziele' Hitlers.* Düsseldorf: Droste, 1976. 221 pp., bibl.

692 TOLAND, JOHN: *Adolf Hitler.* New York: Doubleday, 1976. 1035 pp., illus., maps, facsims., bibl. [German version: Bergisch Gladbach: Lübbe, 1977.]

693 WAGNER, LUDWIG: *Hitler, man of strife. A biography.* New York: Norton, 1942. 331 pp., illus.

694 WALTHER, HERBERT, ed.: *Der Führer.* London: Bison Books, 1978. 256 pp., illus.

695 ZIEGLER, HANS SEVERUS, ed.: *Wer war Hitler? Beiträge zur Hitler-Forschung.* Tübingen: Verlag der deutschen Hochschullehrer-Zeitung (Grabert-Verlag), 1970. 375 pp., illus., bibl. [An apologist view.]

Medical history

696 HESTON, LEONARD L. & RENATE: *The medical casebook of Adolf Hitler.* London: Kimber, 1980. 184 pp., illus.

697 KRUEGER, KURT: *Inside Hitler.* From the German. Prelude for the second printing by Upton Sinclair. Introd.: Otto Strasser. Preface: K. Arvid Enlind. New York: Avalon Press, 1942. 445 pp., front. [Also publ. under title *I was Hitler's doctor.*]

698 RÖHRS, HANS-DIETRICH: *Hitler—die Zerstörung einer Persönlichkeit. Grundlegende Feststellungen zum Krankheitsbild.* Neckargemünd: Vowinckel, 1965. 151 pp., ports., bibl.

699 RÖHRS, HANS-DIETRICH: *Hitlers Krankheit. Tatsachen und Legenden. Medizinische und psychische Grundlagen seines Zusammenbruchs.* Neckargemünd: Vowinckel, 1966. 201 pp., ports.

Psychological studies

700 ACHILLES-DELMAS, F.: *Adolf Hitler. Essai de biographie psycho-pathologique.* Paris: Rivière, 1946. 256 pp.

701 BINION, RUDOLPH: *Hitler among the Germans.* New York: Elsevier, 1976. xiv + 207 pp., tabs., facsim., bibl.

702 BROSSE, JACQUES: *Hitler avant Hitler. Essai d'interprétation psychoanalytique.* Postface: Albert Speer. Paris: Fayard, 1972. 388 pp., bibl.

703 LANGER, WALTER C.: *The mind of Adolf Hitler. The secret wartime report.* Foreword: William L. Langer. Afterword: Robert G. L. Waite. New York: Basic Books, 1972. ix + 269 pp., bibl. [Written 1943. German version: *Adolf-Hitler Psychogramm. Eine Analyse seiner Person und seines Verhaltens, verfasst 1943 für die psychologische Kriegsführung der USA.* Vorw.: Friedrich Hacker. Wien: Molden, 1973.]

704 WAITE, ROBERT G. L.: *The psychopathic god—Adolf Hitler.* New York: Basic Books, 1977. xx + 482 pp., illus.

As military leader

705 BELOW, NICOLAUS von: *Als Hitlers Adjutant 1937–1945.* Mainz: von Hase & Koehler, 1980. 500 pp., illus., facsims.

706 BUCHHEIT, GERT: *Hitler der Feldherr. Die Zerstörung einer Legende.* Rastatt/Baden: Grote, 1958. 560 pp., maps, bibl.

707 CARTIER, RAYMOND: *Hitler et ses généraux. Les secrets de la guerre.* Ed. revue et complétée. Paris: Fayard, 1962. 265 pp.

708 GILBERT, FELIX, ed.: *Hitler directs his war. The secret record of his daily military conferences ... from the manuscript in the University of Pennsylvania Library.* New York: Oxford University Press, 1951. 187 pp.

709 HALDER, FRANZ: *Hitler als Feldherr.* München: Münchener Dom-Verlag, 1949. 63 pp. [English version: *Hitler as war lord.* London: 1950.]

710 HILLGRUBER, ANDREAS: *Hitlers Strategie, Politik und Kriegsführung 1940–1941.* Frankfurt a.M.: Bernard & Graefe, 1965. 715 pp., tabs., bibl.

711 HUBATSCH, WALTHER, ed.: *Hitlers Weisungen für Kriegsführung 1939–1945. Dokumente des Oberkommandos der Wehrmacht.* Frankfurt a.M.: Bernard & Graefe, 1962. 330 pp. [English version: *Hitler's war directives, 1939–1945.* Ed.: Hugh Trevor-Roper. London: Sidgwick & Jackson, 1964.]

712 KOTZE, HILDEGARD von, ed.: *Heeresadjutant bei Hitler, 1938–1943. Aufzeichnungen des Majors Engel.* Stuttgart: Deutsche Verlags-Anstalt, 1974. 157 pp., bibl. (Schriftenreihe der Vierteljahrshefte für Zeitgeschichte).

LAGEBESPRECHUNGEN

713 HEIBER, HELMUT, ed.: *Hitlers Lagebesprechungen.* Stuttgart: Deutsche Verlags-Anstalt, 1962. 970 pp.

714 DER SPIEGEL, 20 Jhrg., Nr. 3, 10. Januar 1966. [Special issue]: *Hitlers letzte Lagebesprechung.* Hamburg. 90 pp., illus.

———

715 SCHRAMM, PERCY ERNST: *Hitler als militärischer Führer. Erkenntnisse und Erfahrungen aus dem Kriegstagebuch des Oberkommandos der Wehrmacht.* Frankfurt a.M.: Athenäum Verlag, 1962. 207 pp. [English version: *Hitler. The man and the military leader.* Transl. & ed. by Donald S. Detwiler. London: Lane (Penguin Press), 1972. Comprises extracts from *Hitlers Tischgespräche im Führerhauptquartier 1941–1942* and *Kriegstagebuch des Oberkommandos der Wehrmacht (Wehrmachtführungsstab) 1940–1945* (*see* 756, 4760). Incl. 1946 memorandum by Alfred Jodl.]

716 SORB, (Commandant): *Hitler, l'auteur de l'écroulement de l'Allemagne. Caporal stratège.* Paris: Éds. de la nouvelle France, 1945. 257 pp.

717 STRAWSON, JOHN: *Hitler as military commander.* London: Batsford, 1971. 256 pp., illus., maps., bibl.

Religious beliefs

718 HEER, FRIEDRICH: *Der Glaube des Adolf Hitler. Anatomie einer politischen Religiosität.* München: Bechtle, 1968. 751 pp., bibl.

719 TROSSMAN, K.: *Hitler und Rom.* Nürnberg: Sebaldus Verlag, 1931. 208 pp., bibl.

720 VERMEIL, EDMOND: *Hitler et le Christianisme.* London: Penguin, 1944. 78 pp. [Reprint of French ed.: Paris: Gallimard, 1940.]

Last days

721 BESYMENSKI, LEW: *Der Tod des Adolf Hitler. Unbekannte Dokumente aus Moskauer Archiven.* Eingel.: Karl-Heinz Janssen. Hamburg: Wegner, 1968. 134 pp., illus., facsims., bibl. [Incl. Russian autopsy reports on Hitler, Eva Braun, Hans Krebs and Goebbels family. English version: BEZYMENSKI, LEV: *The death of Adolf Hitler.* London: Michael Joseph, 1968.]

722 BOLDT, GERHARD: *Die letzten Tage der Reichskanzlei.* Zürich: Europa Verlag, 1947. 91 pp., maps. [English version: *Hitler's last days. An eyewitness account.* London: Sphere Books, 1973. (Earlier title: *In the shelter with Hitler*).]

723 O'DONNELL, JAMES P. & BAHNSEN, UWE: *Die Katakombe. Das Ende in der Reichskanzlei.* Stuttgart: Deutsche Verlags-Anstalt, 1975. 436 pp. [English version: O'DONNELL, JAMES: *The Berlin Bunker.* London: Dent, 1979. 317 pp., illus., plans. Also publ. as *The history of the Reichs-Chancellery group.* Boston: Houghton Mifflin, 1979.]

724 RSHEWSKAJA, JELENA: *Hitlers Ende ohne Mythos.* Berlin [East]: Deutscher Militärverlag, 1960. 97 pp., illus [Transl. from the Russian.]

725 TREVOR-ROPER, H[UGH] R.: *The last days of Hitler.* New and rev. ed. London: Pan Books, 1968. 285 pp., map. [First ed.: London: Macmillan, 1947.]

'Mein Kampf'

726 HITLER, ADOLF: *Mein Kampf. Eine Abrechnung.* München: Eher, 1925, 1929.
1. Bd.: *Mein Kampf.*
2. Bd.: *Die nationalsozialistische Bewegung.*
[First ed., followed by numerous German editions and translations into at least ten languages.]

727 HITLER, ADOLF: *Mein Kampf* [in English]. Introd.: D. C. Watt. Transl.: Ralph Manheim. London: Hutchinson, 1973. xlviii + 629 pp., bibl. [First publ. as *My Struggle*, Hurst & Blackett, 1933. Transl.: E. S. Dugdale, expurgated by author; followed by *Mein Kampf, complete edition*, Hurst & Blackett, 1939. Transl.: James Murphy. This transl. introd. by D. C. Watt was first publ. in 1969.]

728 APPUHN, CHARLES: *Hitler par lui-même. D'après son Livre 'Mein Kampf'.* Nouvelle éd. corrigée. Paris: Haumont, 1933. 169 pp.

729 COMBES de PATRIS, B.: *Que veut Hitler? D'après la traduction de son oeuvre par le Colonel Chappat.* Paris: Éds. Babu, 1932. 150 pp.

730 HACKETT, FRANCIS: *What 'Mein Kampf' means to America.* New York: Reynal & Hitchcock, 1941. xx + 288 pp.

731 HUMBERT, MANUEL: *Hitlers 'Mein Kampf'. Dichtung und Wahrheit.* Vorwort: Heinrich Mann. Paris: Verlag 'Pariser Tageblatt', 1936. 391 pp.

732 JOHN, EVAN: *Answer to Hitler. Reflections on Hitler's 'Mein Kampf' and on some recent events upon the continent of Europe.* London: Nicholson & Watson, 1939. vi + 89 pp.

733 LANGE, KARL: *Hitlers unbeachtete Maximen. 'Mein Kampf' und die Öffentlichkeit*. Stuttgart: Kohlhammer, 1968. 211 pp.

734 MASER, WERNER: *Hitlers 'Mein Kampf'. Entstehung, Aufbau, Stil, Änderungen, Quellen, Quellenwert, kommentierte Auszüge*. München: Bechtle, 1966. 344 pp., illus., facsims., bibl.

735 MORVILLIERS, ROGER: *Face à Hitler et à Mein Kampf*. Sèvres: Morvilliers, 1939. 251 pp.

736 ZENTNER, CHRISTIAN, ed.: *Adolf Hitlers 'Mein Kampf'. Eine kommentierte Auswahl*. München: List, 1974. 255 pp. [Notes and index pp. 179–255.]

Other writings

737 *Hitlers zweites Buch. Ein Dokument aus dem Jahr 1928*. Hrsg.: Gerhard L. Weinberg. Geleitwort: Hans Rothfels. Stuttgart: Deutsche Verlags-Anstalt, 1961. 228 pp. (Quellen und Darstellungen zur Zeitgeschichte). [English version: *Hitler's secret book*. Introd.: Telford Taylor. New York: Grove Press, 1961.]

738 GENOUD, FRANÇOIS, ed.: *The testament of Adolf Hitler. The Hitler–Bormann documents, February–April 1945*. Transl. from the German. Introd.: H. R. Trevor-Roper. London: Cassell, 1961. 115 pp., port. [French version: *Le testament politique de Hitler. Notes recueillies par Martin Bormann*. Préface: H. R. Trevor-Roper. Commentaires: André François-Poncet. Paris: Fayard, 1959.]

738a JÄCKEL, EBERHARD & KUHN, AXEL, eds.: *Hitler. Sämtliche Aufzeichnungen 1905–1924*. Stuttgart: Deutsche Verlagsanstalt, 1980. 1300 pp.

739 MASER, WERNER: *Hitlers Briefe und Notizen. Sein Weltbild in handschriftlichen Dokumenten*. Düsseldorf: Econ Verlag, 1973. 399 pp., illus., facsims. [English version: *Hitler's letters and notes*. London: Heinemann, 1973.]

740 SUDHOLT, GERT, ed.: *Adolf Hitlers drei Testamente. Ein Zeitdokument*. Leoni am Starnberger See: Druffel, [1978]. 107 pp., facsims.

Speeches and conversations

741 BAYNES, NORMAN H., ed.: *The speeches of Adolf Hitler, April 1922–August 1939. An English translation of representative passages arranged under subjects*. London: Oxford University Press, under auspices of Royal Institute of International Affairs, 1942. In 2 vols.

742 BOEPPLE, ERNST, ed.: *Adolf Hitlers Reden*. München: Boepple, 1933. 127 pp.

743 DOMARUS, MAX: *Hitler. Reden und Proklamationen 1932–1945. Kommentiert von einem deutschen Zeitgenossen*. Würzburg: [priv. pr.], 1962/63. Illus.
Bd. I: *Triumph (1932–1938)*. Publ. 1962.
Bd. II: *Untergang (1939–1945)*. Publ. 1963.

744 *Führerworte. Uddrag af Rigskansler Adolf Hitler. Taler Opraab og Breve fra 1.9.1939 til 29.11.1943*. Fredericia: Forlaget Landsoldaten, 1944. 95 pp.

745 Der grossdeutsche Freiheitskampf. Reden Adolf Hitlers. München: Eher, 1943.
     In 2 vols.
     Bd. I und II in einem Band: Vom 1. September 1939–15. März 1941.
     Bd. III: Vom 16. März 1941–15. März 1942.

746 JOCHMANN, WERNER: Im Kampf um die Macht. Hitlers Rede vor dem Hamburger Nationalklub von 1919. Frankfurt a.M.: Europäische Verlagsanstalt, 1960. 120 pp.

747 KLÖSS, ERHARD, ed.: Reden des Führers. Politik und Propaganda Adolf Hitlers 1922–1945. München: Deutscher Taschenbuch Verlag, 1967. 334 pp., bibl.

748 KOTZE, HILDEGARD von and others, eds.: 'Es spricht der Führer'. 7 exemplarische Hitler-Reden. Hrsg. und erläut. von Hildegard von Kotze und Helmut Krausnick unter Mitwirkung von F. A. Krummacher. Gütersloh: Mohn, 1966. 379 pp., tabs.

749 PHELPS, REGINALD H.: 'Hitler's "grundlegende" Rede über den Antisemitismus'. [In] Vierteljahrshefte für Zeitgeschichte, 16. Jhrg., 4. Heft, Okt. 1968. Stuttgart: Deutsche Verlags-Anstalt. Pp. 590–420.

750 PRANGE, GORDON W., ed.: Hitler's words. Two decades of national socialism, 1923–1943. Introd.: Frederick Schuman. [Washington, D.C.]: American Council on Public Affairs, 1944. 400 pp., illus.

751 Die Reden des Führers nach der Machtübernahme. Eine Bibliographie. Berlin: Eher, 1939. 192 pp.

752 SCHNAUBER, CORNELIUS: Wie Hitler sprach und schrieb. Zur Psychologie und Prosodik der faschistischen Rhetorik. Frankfurt a.M.: Athenäum, 1972. x + 149 pp.

Table talk

753 Adolf Hitler: Monologe im Führerhauptquartier 1941–1944. Die Aufzeichnungen Heinrich Heims. Hrsg.: Werner Jochmann. Hamburg: Knaus, 1980. 491 pp., facsims.

754 Hitler's table talk, 1941–1944. With an introductory essay on 'The mind of Adolf Hitler' by H. R. Trevor-Roper. London: Weidenfeld & Nicolson, 1953. 746 pp., facsim. [Transl. from the German. US ed. entitled: Hitler's secret conversations.]

755 Libres propos sur la guerre et la paix, recueillis sur l'ordre de Martin Bormann. Préface: Robert d'Harcourt. Paris: Flammarion, 1952. 370 pp. [Hitler's table talk in French.]

756 PICKER, HENRY: Hitlers Tischgespräche im Führerhauptquartier. Vollst. überarb. und erweit. Neuausg. mit bisher unbekannten Selbstzeugnissen Adolf Hitlers, Abbildungen, Augenzeugenberichten und Erläuterungen des Autors: 'Hitler, wie er wirklich war'. Stuttgart: Seewald, 1976. 548 pp., illus., facsims. [First ed. 1951.]

3. MINISTERS

757 HINKEL, HANS & BLEY, WULF: *Kabinett Hitler!* Berlin-Schöneberg: Verlag Drei Kultur-Wacht, 1933. 62 pp., illus.

758 SADILA-MANTAU, HANS HEINZ, ed.: *Unsere Reichsregierung.* 2. Aufl. Berlin: Riegler, 1940. 367 pp., illus.

Darré, Richard Walther

759 DARRÉ, R. WALTHER: *Erkenntnisse und Werden. Aus der Zeit vor der Machtergreifung.* 2. Aufl. Hrsg.: Marie-Adelheid Prinzessin Reuss zur Lippe. Goslar: Verlag Blut und Boden, 1940. 236 pp.

760 DARRÉ, R. WALTHER: *Um Blut und Boden. Reden und Aufsätze.* 3. Aufl. München: Eher, 1941. 598 pp., port.

761 WENZEL, FRITZ: *R. Walther Darré und seine Mitkämpfer. Der Sieg von Blut und Boden.* Erweit. Ausg. ... Berlin: Verlag Volksbuch, 1934. 142 pp., illus.

Dönitz, Karl

762 DÖNITZ, KARL: *Mein wechselvolles Leben.* Göttingen: Musterschmidt, 1968. 227 pp., illus., facsims.

763 DÖNITZ, KARL: *Zehn Jahre und zwanzig Tage.* Bonn: Athenäum Verlag, 1958. 512 pp., illus., map. [English version: *Memoirs. Ten years and twenty days.* London: Weidenfeld & Nicolson, 1959.]

Frank, Hans

764 FRANK, HANS: *Die Technik des Staates.* Vorwort: Adolf Dresler. 2. unveränd. Aufl. Krakau: Burgverlag, 1942. 46 pp.

765 FRANK, HANS: *Im Angesicht des Galgens. Deutung Hitlers und seiner Zeit auf Grund eigener Erlebnisse und Erkenntnisse.* 2. Aufl. Neuhaus b. Schliersee: [publ. by author's widow], 1955. 445 pp.

766 PIETROWSKI, STANISLAW, ed.: *Dziennik Hansa Franka.* Vol. I. Warszawa: Wyd. Prawnicze, 1956. 551 pp. [Text in Polish and German.]

Frick, Wilhelm

767 FRICK, WILHELM: *Erziehung zum lebendigen Volke.* Berlin: Steegemann, 1933. 47 pp. [Incl.: 'Bevölkerungs- und Rassenpolitik', pp. 31–47.]

768 FRICK, [WILHELM]: *Wir bauen das Dritte Reich.* Oldenburg i.O.: Stalling, 1934. 112 pp.

769 PFUNDTNER, HANS, ed.: *Dr. Wilhelm Frick und sein Ministerium. Aus Anlass des 60. Geburtstages des Reichs- und Preussischen Ministers des Innern Dr. Wilhelm Frick am 12. März 1937.* München: Eher, 1937. 202 pp., illus.

Funk, Walther

770 FUNK, WALTHER: *Das wirtschaftliche Gesicht des neuen Europa.* Vortrag zur Eröffnung der Vortragsreihe 'Europäische Wirtschaftsgemeinschaft' am 15. Januar 1942. Berlin: Haude & Spener, 1942. 31 pp.

771 OESTREICH, PAUL: *Walther Funk. Ein Leben für die Wirtschaft.* München: Eher, 1941. 120 pp., port.

Goebbels, Joseph

SPEECHES

772 GOEBBELS, JOSEPH: *Signale der neuen Zeit. 25 ausgewählte Reden.* München: Eher, 1934. 362 pp. [Speeches of 1927–1933.]

773 GOEBBELS, JOSEPH: *Das eherne Herz. Reden und Aufsätze aus den Jahren 1941/42.* München: Eher, 1943. 472 pp. (Hrsg.: M.A. von Schirmeister).

774 HEIBER, HELMUT, ed.: *Goebbels-Reden.* Düsseldorf: Droste, 1971/72.
Bd. 1: 1932–1939. Publ. 1971. xxxiv + 337 pp.
Bd. 2: 1939–1945. Publ. 1972. xxvi + 466 pp.

DIARIES

775 *Das Tagebuch von Joseph Goebbels 1925/26.* Mit weiteren Dokumenten hrsg. von Helmut Heiber. Stuttgart: Deutsche Verlags-Anstalt, [1961]. 141 pp. (Schriftenreihe der Vierteljahrshefte für Zeitgeschichte.) [English version: *The early Goebbels diaries. The journal of Joseph Goebbels 1925–1926.* Preface: Alan Bullock. London: Weidenfeld & Nicolson, 1962.]

776 GOEBBELS, JOSEPH: *Vom Kaiserhof zur Reichskanzlei. Eine historische Darstellung in Tagebuchblättern. Vom 1. Januar 1932 bis zum 1. Mai 1933.* München: Eher, 1934. 312 pp. [English version: *My part in Germany's fight.* London: Hurst & Blackett, 1938.]

777 GOEBBELS, JOSEPH: *Tagebücher 1945. Die letzten Aufzeichnungen.* Einführung: Rolf Hochhuth. Hamburg: Hoffmann & Campe, 1977. 607 pp., illus., maps. [English version: *The Goebbels diaries. The last days.* Ed. Hugh Trevor-Roper. London: Secker & Warburg, 1978. xii + 368 pp., illus.]

OTHER WRITINGS

778 GOEBBELS, JOSEPH: *Aufsätze aus der Kampfzeit.* München: Eher, 1935, 1939.
[1. Bd.]: *Der Angriff.* Publ. 1935. 340 pp.
2. Bd.: *Wetterleuchten.* Hrsg.: Georg-Wilhelm Müller. Publ. 1939. 392 pp.

779 GOEBBELS, JOSEPH: *Michael. Ein deutsches Schicksal in Tagebuchblättern.* München: Eher, 1934. 158 pp. [Fiction.]

KESSEMEIER, CARIN: *Der Leitartikler Goebbels in den NS-Organen 'Der Angriff' und 'Das Reich'. See* 2813.

SECONDARY WORKS

780 BOELCKE, WILLI A., ed.: *'Wollt Ihr den totalen Krieg?'. Die Geheimen Goebbels-Konferenzen 1939–1943.* München: Deutscher Taschenbuch Verlag, 1969. 470 pp., bibl. [English version: *The secret conferences of Dr. Goebbels October 1939–March 1943.* London: Weidenfeld & Nicolson, 1967.]

781 BORRESHOLM, BORIS von, ed.: *Dr. Goebbels nach Aufzeichnungen aus seiner Umgebung.* Hrsg. unter Mitarb. von Karena Niehoff. [Berlin]: Verlag des 'Journal', 1949. 238 pp.

782 BRAMSTED, ERNEST: 'Goebbels and his newspaper Der Angriff'. [In] *On the track of tyranny*, ed. Max Beloff. London: Vallentine, Mitchell, for the Wiener Library, 1959. Pp. 45–65.

783 EBERMAYER, ERICH & MEISSNER, HANS-OTTO: *Evil genius. The story of Joseph Goebbels*. Transl. and freely adapted by Louis Hagen. London: Wingate, 1953. 245 pp., illus. [Original: *Gefährtin des Teufels*. Hamburg: Hoffmann & Campe, 1952.]

784 HEIBER, HELMUT: *Joseph Goebbels*. Berlin: Colloquium Verlag, 1962. 433 pp., illus., bibl. [English version: *Goebbels*. London: Hale, 1972.]

785 HOMBOURGER, RENÉ: *Goebbels, Chef de Publicité du IIIème Reich*. Paris: Sorlot, 1939. 316 pp.

786 MANVELL, ROGER & FRAENKEL, HEINRICH: *Doctor Goebbels. His life and death*. London: Heinemann, 1960. 329 pp., illus., facsims.

787 OVEN, WILFRED VON: *Mit Goebbels bis zum Ende*. Buenos Aires: Dürer-Verlag, 1949/50. 295 + 320 pp., in 2 vols.

788 REIMANN, VIKTOR: *Dr. Joseph Goebbels*. Wien: Molden, 1971. 383 pp., illus., bibl. [English version: *The man who created Hitler: Joseph Goebbels*. Transl.: Stephen Wendt. London: Kimber, 1977.]

789 SCHAUMBURG-LIPPE, FRIEDRICH CHRISTIAN Prinz zu: *Dr. G. Ein Porträt des Propagandaministers*. 2. Aufl. Wiesbaden: Limes Verlag, 1964. 288 pp.

790 SEMMLER, RUDOLF: *Goebbels—the man next to Hitler*. Introd.: D. McLachlan; Notes: G. S. Wagner. London: Westhouse, 1947. 234 pp., illus.

Goering, Hermann

791 GOERING, HERMANN: *Aufbau einer Nation*. 2. Aufl. Berlin: Mittler, 1934. 111 pp., port.

792 GOERING, HERMANN: *Germany reborn*. London: Elkin Mathews & Marrot, 1934. 160 pp., port. [French version: *Renaissance de l'Allemagne*. Paris: Sorlot, 1939.]

793 BLOOD-RYAN, H. W.: *Göring, the iron man of Germany*. London: Long, 1938. 292 pp., illus.

794 BUTLER, EWAN & YOUNG, GORDON: *Marshal without glory*. London: Hodder & Stoughton, 1951. 287 pp., illus.

795 EMESSEN, T. R., ed.: *Aus Goerings Schreibtisch. Ein Dokumentenfund*. Berlin: Allgemeiner Deutscher Verlag, 1947. 127 pp.

796 FRISCHAUER, WILLI: *Goering*. London: Odhams, 1950. 303 pp., illus., bibl.

797 GÖRING, EMMY: *An der Seite meines Mannes. Begebenheiten und Bekenntnisse*. Göttingen: Schütz, 1967. 337 pp., illus., diagr.

798 GRITZBACH, ERICH: *Hermann Göring. Werk und Mensch*. 2. Aufl. München:

Eher, 1938. 345 pp., illus. [Also in English and French; illus. in English version differ from those in German ed.]

799   LANGE, EITEL: *Der Reichsmarschall im Kriege. Ein Bericht in Wort und Bild.* Stuttgart: Schwab, 1950. 215 pp., illus.

800   MANVELL, ROGER & FRAENKEL, HEINRICH: *Hermann Goering.* London: Heinemann, 1962. 429 pp., illus., bibl.

801   MOSLEY, LEONARD: *The Reich Marshal. A biography of Hermann Goering.* New York: Doubleday, 1974. xi + 394 pp., illus.

802   WILAMOWITZ-MOELLENDORFF, FANNY Gräfin von: *Carin Göring.* Nachwort: Martin H. Sommerfeldt. Berlin: Warneck, 1934. 158 pp., illus. [Goering's first wife.]

Hess, Rudolf

803   HESS, RUDOLF: *Reden.* München: Eher, 1938. 269 pp.

804   *The case of Rudolf Hess. A problem in diagnosis and forensic psychiatry.* By the following physicians in the Services who have been concerned with him from 1941 to 1946: Henry V. Dicks, J. Gibson Graham, M. K. Johnston, D. Ellis Jones, Douglas McG. Kelley, N. R. Phillips, G. M. Gilbert. Ed.: J. R. Rees. London: Heinemann, 1947. 224 pp.

DOUGLAS-HAMILTON, JAMES: *Motive for a mission. See* 4282.

805   HUTTON, J. BERNARD: *Hess. The man and his mission.* Introd.: Airey Neave. London: Bruce & Watson, 1970. 262 pp., illus., facsim.

806   LEASOR, JAMES: *Rudolf Hess. The uninvited envoy.* London: Allen & Unwin, 1962. 239 pp., illus.

807   MANVELL, ROGER & FRAENKEL, HEINRICH: *Hess. A biography.* London: MacGibbon & Kee, 1971. 256 pp., illus., facsim., bibl.

Himmler, Heinrich. *See* Index.

Ley, Robert

808   LEY, ROBERT: *Durchbruch der sozialen Ehre. Reden und Gedanken für das schaffende Deutschland.* Hrsg.: Hans Bauer. Mitarb.: Walter Kiehl. Berlin: Mehden, 1935. x + 278 pp., port.

809   LEY, ROBERT: *Soldaten der Arbeit.* München: Eher, 1938. 229 pp., ports.

810   LEY, ROBERT: *Die grosse Stunde. Das deutsche Volk im totalen Kriegseinsatz. Reden und Aufsätze aus den Jahren 1941–1943.* München: Eher, 1943. 400 pp.

811   KIEHL, WALTER, ed.: *Mann an der Fahne. Kameraden erzählen von Dr. Ley.* München: Eher, 1938. 301 pp., illus., facsims.

Neurath, Constantin von

812   HEINEMANN, JOHN L.: *Hitler's first foreign minister. Constantin von Neurath,*

diplomat and statesman. Berkeley, Calif.: University of California Press, 1979. x + 359 pp., illus., bibl. (bibl. and notes pp. 247–347).

Rosenberg, Alfred

813 ROSENBERG, ALFRED: *Blut und Ehre. Ein Kampf für deutsche Wiedergeburt. Reden und Aufsätze von 1919–1933.* Hrsg.: Thilo von Trotha. 22. Aufl. München: Eher, 1939. 384 pp., port.

814 ROSENBERG, ALFRED: *Schriften und Reden.* Einleitung: Alfred Bäumler. München: Hoheneichen-Verlag, 1943. Illus.
Schriften aus den Jahren 1917–1921. cvii + 624 pp.
Schriften aus den Jahren 1921–1923. 746 pp.

815 LANG, SERGE & SCHENK, ERNST von: *Porträt eines Menschheitsverbrechers, nach den hinterlassenen Memoiren des ehemaligen Reichsministers Alfred Rosenberg.* St. Gallen: Zollikofer, 1947. 356 pp., illus. [French version: *Testament nazi. Mémoires d'Alfred Rosenberg.* Paris: Éds. des Trois Collines, 1948.]

Sauckel, Fritz

816 SAUCKEL, FRITZ: *Kampfreden. Dokumente aus der Zeit der Wende und des Aufbaus.* Weimar: Fink, 1934. 188 pp.

Schacht, Hjalmar Horace Greeley

817 SCHACHT, HJALMAR: *Abrechnung mit Hitler.* Berlin: Michaelis, 1949. 197 pp. [English version: *Account settled.* London: Weidenfeld & Nicolson, 1949.]

818 SCHACHT, HJALMAR: *Grundsätze deutscher Wirtschaftspolitik.* Oldenburg i. O.: Stalling, 1932. 75 pp.

819 MUHLEN, NORBERT: *Der Zauberer. Leben und Anleihen des Dr. Hjalmar H. G. Schacht.* Zürich: Europa Verlag, 1938. 221 pp.

820 SIMPSON, AMOS E.: *Hjalmar Schacht in perspective.* The Hague: Mouton, 1969. 202 pp., bibl.

Seyss-Inquart, Arthur

821 SEYSS-INQUART, [ARTHUR]: *Vier Jahre in den Niederlanden. Gesammelte Reden.* Amsterdam: Volk und Reich Verlag, 1944. 222 pp.

822 NEUMAN, H. J.: *Arthur Seyss-Inquart.* Graz: Styria Verlag, 1970. 396 pp., tabs.

Schirach, Baldur von

823 SCHIRACH, BALDUR von: *Ich glaubte an Hitler.* Hamburg: Mossik, 1967. 367 pp.

824 SCHIRACH, HENRIETTE von: *Der Preis der Herrlichkeit.* Wiesbaden: Limes Verlag, 1956. 266 pp. [English version: *The price of glory.* Transl. and adapted by Willi Frischauer. London: Muller, 1960.]

Schwerin von Krosigk, Lutz Graf

825   SCHWERIN VON KROSIGK, LUTZ Graf: *Memoiren.* Stuttgart: Seewald, 1977. 340 pp.

Speer, Albert

826   SPEER, ALBERT: *Erinnerungen.* Berlin: Propyläen Verlag, 1969. 610 pp., illus., facsims., plans, tabs. [English version: *Inside the Third Reich. Memoirs.* Introd.: Eugene Davidson. London: Weidenfeld & Nicolson, 1970.]

827   HAMSHER, WILLIAM: *Albert Speer—victim of Nuremberg?* London: Frewin, 1970. 286 pp., illus.

828   REIF, ADELBERT: *Albert Speer. Kontroversen um ein deutsches Phänomen.* München: Bernard & Graefe, 1978. 501 pp., bibl.

Todt, Friedrich Wilhelm

829   TODT, FRIEDRICH WILHELM: *Gemeinnutz oder Eigennutz im praktischen Wirtschaftsleben.* Hamburg: Hanseatische Verlagsanstalt, 1934. 59 pp., tabs.

830   MILWARD, HANS S.: 'Fritz Todt als Minister für Bewaffnung und Munition'. [In] *Vierteljahrshefte für Zeitgeschichte*, 14. Jhrg., 1966. Pp. 40–58.

831   SCHÖNLEBEN, EDUARD: *Fritz Todt: Der Mensch, der Ingenieur, der Nationalsozialist. Ein Bericht über Leben und Werk.* Oldenburg: Stalling, 1943. 116 pp., illus., facsims.

4.   OTHER LEADERS

Bormann, Martin

832   *The Bormann letters. The private correspondence between Martin Bormann and his wife from January 1943 to April 1945.* Ed. with an introd. and notes by H. R. Trevor-Roper. London: Weidenfeld & Nicolson, 1954. 500 pp., illus. [Transl. from the German.]

833   BESYMENSKI, LEW: *Die letzten Notizen von Martin Bormann. Ein Dokument und sein Verfasser.* Stuttgart: Deutsche Verlags-Anstalt, 1974. 345 pp., illus., facsims. [Transl. from the Russian.]

834   LANG, JOCHEN von: *Der Sekretär. Martin Bormann: Der Mann, der Hitler beherrschte.* Mitarb.: Claus Sibyll. Stuttgart: Deutsche Verlags-Anstalt, 1977. 511 pp., illus., facsims., bibl. [English version: *Bormann. The man who manipulated Hitler.* London: Weidenfeld & Nicolson, 1979.]

835   MCGOVERN, JAMES: *Martin Bormann.* London: Barker, 1968. 237 pp., illus., bibl.

836   WULF, JOSEPH: *Martin Bormann—Hitlers Schatten.* Gütersloh: Mohn, 1962. 254 pp., illus., facsims.

Epp, Franz Ritter von

837　FRANK, WALTER: *Franz Ritter von Epp. Der Weg eines deutschen Soldaten.* Hamburg: Hanseatische Verlagsanstalt, 1934. 165 pp., illus., facsims., diagr. [Contains illus. (p. 152/153) showing Hitler with Roehm: this was removed from later printings.]

Förster, Albert

838　FOERSTER, ALBERT: *Das nationalsozialistische Gewissen in Danzig. Aus sechs Jahren Kampf für Hitler.* Bearb. und hrsg.: Wilhelm Löbsack. Danzig: Kafemann, 1936. 278 pp., illus.

839　LÖBSACK, WILHELM: *Gauleiter Albert Förster. Der deutsche Angestelltenführer.* Hamburg: Hanseatische Verlagsanstalt, 1934. 140 pp., illus.

Gmelin, Hermann

840　GMELIN, HERMANN: *Briefe eines Kämpfers.* 2. Aufl. München: Heger, 1937. 101 pp., illus.

Grohé, Josef

841　SCHMIDT, PETER: *Zwanzig Jahre Soldat Adolf Hitlers: Zehn Jahre Gauletier. Ein Buch von Kampf und Treue.* Köln: Verlag 'Westdeutscher Beobachter', 1941. 285 pp., illus., facsims.

Heydrich, Reinhard. *See* Index.

Hierl, Konstantin

842　HIERL, KONSTANTIN: *Ausgewählte Schriften und Reden.* Hrsg.: Herbert Frhr. von Stetten-Erb. München: Eher, 1941. 302 + 438 pp.

843　ERD, HERBERT & GROTE, HANS HENNING Frhr: *Konstantin Hierl. Der Mann und sein Werk.* München: Eher, 1939. 181 pp., ports.

Hinkel, Hans

844　HINKEL, HANS: *Einer unter Hunderttausend.* München: Knorr & Hirth, 1938. 263 pp. ['My path to Adolf Hitler'.]

Jordan, Rudolf

845　JORDAN, RUDOLF: *Erlebt und erlitten. Weg eines Gauleiters von München bis Moskau.* Leoni am Starnberger See: Druffel, 1971. 368 pp., illus.

Killinger, Manfred von

846　KILLINGER, MANFRED von: *Ernstes und Heiteres aus dem Putschleben.* München: Eher, 1934. 127 pp., illus. [by A. Paul Weber]. [First ed. 1927.]

Klagges, Dietrich

847　BERG, RUDOLF, [pseud. of Dietrich Klagges]: *Angeklagter oder Ankläger? Das Schlusswort im Klagges-Prozess.* Göttingen: Göttinger Verlagsanstalt, 1954. 87 pp.

Koch, Erich

848   KOCH, ERICH: *Aufbau im Osten.* Breslau: Korn, 1934. 217 pp.

Kube, Wilhelm

849   KUBE, WILHELM: *Nach der Aufrichtung des Dritten Reiches. National-sozialistische Aufsätze und Reden.* 2. Teil. Ausgew.: Müller-Rüdersdorf. Eingel.: Gerd Rühle. Langensalza: Beltz, 1933. 61 pp. (Geschichte der deutschen Ostlande).

850   ALTENSTEIG, G.: *Wilhelm Kube.* Leipzig: Weicher, 1933. 80 pp., illus.

Lippert, Julius, National Socialist Mayor of Berlin

851   LIPPERT, JULIUS: *Im Strom der Zeit. Erlebnisse und Eindrücke.* Berlin: Reimer, 1942. 195 pp.

852   LIPPERT, JULIUS: *Lächle ... und verbirg die Tränen. Erlebnisse und Bemerkungen eines deutschen 'Kriegsverbrechers'.* Leoni am Starnberger See: Druffel, 1955. 222 pp., illus.

Loeper, (Hauptmann)

853   HENNINGSEN, HANS: *Unser Hauptmann Loeper. Leben und Sterben eines Kämpfers. Dokumente aus Deutschlands schwerer und grosser Zeit ...* Magdeburg: Trommler-Verlag, 1936. 169 pp., illus., facsims.

Oberländer, Theodor

854   AUSSCHUSS FÜR DEUTSCHE EINHEIT: *Der Oberländer Prozess. Gekürztes Protokoll der Verhandlung vor dem Obersten Gericht der Deutschen Demokratischen Republik vom 20., 27., und 29.4.1960.* Berlin: 1960. 240 pp. [Oberländer was tried in absentia in the German Democratic Republic for alleged war crimes in Russia.]

Oberlindober, Hanns

855   OBERLINDOBER, HANNS: *Ein Vaterland, das allen gehört! Brief an Zeitgenossen aus zwölf Kampfjahren.* München: Eher, 1939. 200 pp.

Papen, Franz von

856   BLOOD-RYAN, H. W.: *Franz von Papen. His life and times.* London: Rich & Cow, 1940. 320 pp., port.

857   DUTCH, OSWALD: *The errant diplomat. The life of Franz von Papen.* Introd.: Captain von Rintelen. London: Arnold, 1940. 291 pp., illus., facsims.

Röhm, Ernst. *See* Index

Schellenberg, Walter

858   SCHELLENBERG, WALTER: *Aufzeichnungen. Die Memoiren des letzten Geheimdienstchefs unter Hitler.* Hrsg.: Gita Petersen. Im Anhang unter Verw. bislang unveröffentlichten Dokumenten kommentiert von Gerald Fleming. Wiesbaden: Limes Verlag, 1979. 438 pp., illus.

Schemm, Hans

859 KAHL-FURTHMANN, G., ed.: *Hans Schemm spricht. Seine Reden und sein Werk.*
Hrsg.: Gauleitung ... des NS-Lehrerbundes. 11. Aufl. Bayreuth: Gauverlag
Bayerische Ostmark, 1935. 428 pp., illus.

Schwede-Coburg, Franz

860 *Ein Lebensbild des Gauleiters und Oberpräsidenten von Pommern.* Berlin:
Junker & Dünnhaupt, 1939. 44 pp.

Seldte, Franz

860a SELDTE, FRANZ: *Vor und hinter den Kulissen.* Leipzig: Koehler, 1931. 344 pp.
[3rd vol. of *Der Vater aller Dinge*, a novel about the Stahlhelm.]

Strasser, Gregor

861 STRASSER, GREGOR: *Kampf um Deutschland. Reden und Aufsätze eines
Nationalsozialisten.* München: Eher, 1932. 390 pp.

862 KISSENKOETTER, UDO: *Gregor Strasser und die NSDAP.* Stuttgart: Deutsche
Verlags-Anstalt, 1978. 219 pp., diagrs., bibl. (Schriftenreihe der
Vierteljahrshefte für Zeitgeschichte).

863 KÜHNL, REINHARD: *Die nationalsozialistische Linke 1925–1930.* Meisenheim
am Glan: Hain, 1966. 378 pp., facsims. (Marburger Abhandlungen zur
politischen Wissenschaft).

864 STACHURA, PETER D.: ' "Der Fall Strasser": Gregor Strasser, Hitler and
National Socialism 1930–1932'. [In] *The shaping of the Nazi state*, ed. Peter
D. Stachura, pp. 88–130. *See* 1157.

865 WÖRTZ, ULRICH: *Programmatik und Führerprinzip. Das Problem des
Strasserkreises in der NSDAP. Eine historisch-politische Studie zum
Verhältnis von sachlichem Programm und persönlicher Führung in einer
totalitären Bewegung.* Inaugural-Dissertation [pres. to] Friedrich-Alexander
Universität zu Erlangen-Nürnberg. [1966]. 249 + 124 pp., bibl. (Exkurse:
'Hitler als "Inkarnation des Nationalsozialismus" '; 'Die "Vorsehung" als
Transcendenz des Führerprinzips'; 'Die Vollendung der Strasserlegende';
'Zur Genesis des Hitlergrusses'.)

Strasser, Otto

866 STRASSER, OTTO: *Aufbau des deutschen Sozialismus.* 2. neubearb. und ergänz.
Aufl. Als Anlage das historische Gespräch Hitlers mit Dr. Strasser. Prag:
Grunov, 1936. 152 pp.

867 STRASSER, OTTO: *Hitler and I.* Boston: Houghton Mifflin, 1940. 248 pp. [Also in
German and French.]

868 STRASSER, OTTO: *Mein Kampf.* Vorwort: Gerhard Zwerens. Frankfurt a.M.:
Heinrich Heine Verlag, 1969. 234 pp., illus., facsims.

869 STRASSER, OTTO: *Ministersessel oder Revolution? Eine wahrheitsgemässe*

Darstellung meiner Trennung von der NSDAP. 3. Aufl. Berlin: Verlag 'Der National Sozialist', [1931?]. 47 pp.

870 REED, DOUGLAS: *The prisoner of Ottawa: Otto Strasser.* London: Cape, 1953. 272 pp.

Streicher, Julius

871 STREICHER, JULIUS: *Kampf dem Weltfeind. Reden aus der Kampfzeit.* Gesammelt und bearb. von Heinz Preiss. Nürnberg: Verlag 'Der Stürmer', 1938. 148 pp., port., facsims.

872 BONDY, LOUIS W.: *Racketeers of hatred. Julius Streicher and the Jew-baiters' International.* London: Newman Wolsey, 1946. 268 pp., illus., facsims.

873 BYTWERK, RANDALL LEE: *Julius Streicher: the rhetoric of an anti-semite.* A dissertation [pres. to] Northwestern University. Evanston, Ill.: 1975. iii + 216 pp., bibl.

Wagner, Gerhard

874 WAGNER, GERHARD: *Reden und Aufrufe. Gerhard Wagner, 1888–1939.* Hrsg.: L. Conti. Berlin: Reichsgesundheitsverlag, 1943. 300 pp. [Leader of the Nazi medical association.]

Wagner, Joseph

875 WAGNER, JOSEPH: *Nationalsozialistische deutsche Zeitenwende.* Leipzig: Armanen-Verlag, 1934. 87 pp., port.

Wahl, Karl

876 WAHL, KARL: *Patrioten oder Verbrecher. Aus fünfzigjähriger Praxis davon siebzehn als Gauleiter.* 3. Aufl. Heusenstamm: Orion-Heimreiter-Verlag, 1975. 243 pp.

III. FROM STRUGGLE TO CONSOLIDATION OF POWER*

A. WEIMAR: THE POLITICAL BACKGROUND

877 ARETIN, KARL OTMAR Frhr. von & FAUTH, GERHARD: *Die Machtergreifung. Entwicklung Deutschlands zur totalitären Diktatur 1918–1934.* München: Bayerische Landeszentrale für Heimatdienst, 1959. 127 pp., tabs.

878 CONZE, WERNER & RAUPACH, HANS, eds.: *Die Staats- und Wirtschaftskrise des Deutschen Reichs 1929–33.* 6 Beiträge von Hans Raupach [and others]. Stuttgart: Klett, 1967. 255 pp., tabs.

879 DELMER, SEFTON: *Weimar Germany. Democracy on trial.* London: Macdonald, 1972. 127 pp., illus. [The author was *Daily Express* correspondent in Berlin, 1928/33.]

880 DIEHL, JAMES M.: *Paramilitary politics in Weimar Germany.* Bloomington, Ind.: Indiana University Press, 1977. x + 406 pp., bibl.

881 EHRT, ADOLF: *Totale Krise—Totale Revolution?* Die 'Schwarze Front' des völkischen Nationalismus. Berlin-Steglitz: Eckart Verlag, 1933. 79 pp., diagr.

882 EYCK, ERICH: *Geschichte der Weimarer Republik.* Erlenbach-Zürich: Rentsch, 1956, 1962.
Bd. 1: *Vom Zusammenbruch des Kaisertums bis zur Wahl Hindenburgs.* 2. Aufl. Publ. 1957. 468 pp.
Bd. 2: *Von der Konferenz von Locarno bis zu Hitlers Machtübernahme.* 3. Aufl. Publ. 1962. 621 pp.
[English version: *A history of the Weimar Republic.* Cambridge, Mass.: Harvard University Press, 1962, 1964.]

883 HEBERLE, RUDOLF: *From democracy to Nazism. A regional case study on political parties in Germany.* New York: Fertig, 1970. 130 pp., map, diagrs., tabs., bibl. [First publ. 1945.]

884 HOEGNER, WILHELM: *Der politische Radikalismus in Deutschland 1919–1933.* München: Olzog, 1966. 256 pp., bibl. [Incl.: 'Feme'-murders, Hitler-Putsch, KPD.]

885 KNICKERBOCKER, H. R.: *Germany—Fascist or Soviet?* London: The Bodley Head, 1932. 272 pp., illus. [German version: *Deutschland so oder so?* Berlin: Rowohlt, 1932.]

* Works relating to specific aspects of this period, e.g. the churches, armed forces, foreign relations, press and propaganda, etc., will be found in the appropriate sections. (*See* Contents Table).

886 LUTHER, HANS: *Vor dem Abgrund 1930–1933. Reichsbankpräsident in Krisenzeiten.* Einführung: Edgar Salin. Berlin: Propyläen Verlag, 1964. 316 pp., illus.

887 PETZOLD, JOACHIM: *Wegbereiter des Faschismus. Die Jungkonservativen in der Weimarer Republik.* Köln: Pahl-Rugenstein, 1978. 410 pp. [Orig. publ. in East Berlin by Deutscher Verlag der Wissenschaften under title: *Konservative Theoretiker des deutschen Faschismus.*]

888 SCHEELE, GODFREY: *The Weimar Republic. Overture to the Third Reich.* London: Faber & Faber, 1975. 360 pp.

889 SCHÜDDEKOPF, OTTO ERNST: *Nationalbolschewismus in Deutschland 1918–1933.* 2. Aufl. [of *Links Leute von rechts*]. Frankfurt a.M.: Ullstein, 1973. 576 pp. [Incl.: 'Die Spaltung der NSDAP 1925–1926', pp. 174–184.]

890 SCHUMACHER, MARTIN: *Wahlen und Abstimmungen 1918–1933. Eine Bibliographie zur Statistik und Analyse der politischen Wahlen in der Weimarer Republik.* Hrsg.: Kommission für Geschichte des Parlamentarismus und der politischen Parteien. Düsseldorf: Droste, 1976. 155 pp.

891 SONTHEIMER, KURT: *Antidemokratisches Denken in der Weimarer Republik. Die politischen Ideen des deutschen Nationalismus zwischen 1918 und 1933.* München: Nymphenburger Verlagshandlung, 1962. 414 pp., bibl.

892 STERN, FRITZ: *The politics of cultural despair. A study in the rise of the Germanic ideology.* Berkeley, Calif.: University of California Press, 1961. 367 pp., bibl.

THE WIENER LIBRARY: *Catalogue Series: No. 2—From Weimar to Hitler. See* 78.

893 WINKLER, HEINRICH AUGUST: *Mittelstand, Demokratie und Nationalsozialismus. Die politische Entwicklung von Handwerk und Kleinhandel in der Weimarer Republik.* Köln: Kiepenheuer & Witsch, 1972. 307 pp.

B. BEFORE 1933: THE TIME OF STRUGGLE (KAMPFZEIT)

894 BADE, WILFRID: *Deutschland erwacht. Werden, Kampf und Sieg der NSDAP.* Auswahl und künstlerische Durcharbeitung der Lichtbilder: Heinrich Hoffmann. Altona-Bahrenfeld: Cigaretten-Bilderdienst, 1933. 150 pp., illus. [Album issued by cigarette company: space left for users to affix pictures.]

895 BUCHRUCKER, (Major): *Die neue Ordnung. Grundlegende Ausführungen über den Aufbau des Nationalen Sozialismus.* Berlin: Verlag 'Der Nationale Sozialist', [1931?]. 63 pp. [Author was member of 'Kampfgemeinschaft Revolutionärer Nationalsozialisten'.]

896 CARSTEN, F. L.: *The rise of fascism.* London: Batsford, 1967. 256 pp., bibl.

897 DEUERLEIN, ERNST, ed.: *Der Aufstieg der NSDAP in Augenzeugenberichten.* 2.

Aufl. Düsseldorf: Rauch, 1968. 462 pp., illus., facsim., tabs., bibl. [Also publ.: München: Deutscher Taschenbuch Verlag, 1976.]

898 DZELEPY, E.-N.: *Le vrai 'combat' d'Hitler. D'après les documents communiqués par le Baron von G ... S ... du Herrenklub.* Préface: Wladimir d'Ormesson. Paris: Vogel, 1936. 317 pp.

899 EISENHART ROTHE, JOHANN FRIEDRICH ERNST von, ed.: *Deutsche Gedenkhalle. Das neue Deutschland: Sturz und Erhebung. Bilder aus der vaterländischen Geschichte.* Berlin: Deutscher National-Verlag, [1933]. 378 pp., illus., maps.

900 ESPE, WALTER M.: *Das Buch der N.S.D.A.P. Werden, Kampf und Ziel der N.S.D.A.P.* Berlin: Schönfeld, 1934. 334 + 32 pp., illus.

901 FANDERL, WILHELM: *Von sieben Mann zum Volk. Illustrierte Geschichte der NSDAP und SA.* Oldenburg i.O.: Stalling, 1933. 112 pp., illus.

902 FRANZ-WILLING, GEORG: *Ursprung der Hitlerbewegung. 1919–1922.* Preussisch Oldendorf: Schütz, 1974. 391 pp., illus., facsims., bibl. [First ed. Hamburg, 1962.]

903 FRANZ-WILLING, GEORG: *Krisenjahr der Hitlerbewegung 1923.* Preussisch Oldendorf: Schütz, 1975. 408 pp., illus., bibl.

904 FRIEDRICH, H.: *Unter dem Hakenkreuz. Meine Erlebnisse als Agitator bei der Nationalsozialistischen Deutschen Arbeiterpartei.* Karlsruhe: Friedrich, 1929. 30 pp.

905 GOOTE, THOR: *Kam'raden, die Rotfront und Reaktion erschossen ... Ein Buch vom Opfertode unserer braunen Kameraden. Mit ... einer vollständigen Liste der ... gefallenen Nationalsozialisten.* Berlin: Mittler, 1934. 79 pp.

906 GROTE, HANS HENNING Frhr. von, ed.: *Deutschlands Erwachen. Das Buch vom Niedergang und Aufstieg des deutschen Volkes 1918–1933.* Zusammengest.: Arnold Schley. Essen: Deutsche Vertriebsstelle 'Rhein und Ruhr', 1934. 415 pp., illus.

907 GUILLEMINAULT, GILBERT, ed.: *De Charlot à Hitler.* Avec la collaboration de François Brigneau [and others]. Paris: Denoël, 1960. 314 pp., illus.

908 HAAKE, HEINZ, ed.: *Das Ehrenbuch des Führers: Der Weg zur Volksgemeinschaft.* Düsseldorf: Floeder, [1933]. 343 pp., illus., facsims. (2. von Rudolf Hilgers erw. Aufl.)

909 HALLGARTEN, GEORGE W. F.: *Hitler, Reichswehr und Industrie. Zur Geschichte der Jahre 1918–1933.* Frankfurt a.M.: Europäische Verlagsanstalt, 1955. 139 pp.

910 HANNOVER, HEINRICH & HANNOVER-DRÜCK, ELISABETH: *Politische Justiz 1918–1933.* Hamburg: Attica Verlag, 1977. 330 pp., illus. [Incl. material on Nazi crimes.]

911 HASSELBACH, ULRICH von: *Die Entstehung der Nationalsozialistischen Deutschen Arbeiterpartei, 1919–1923.* Inaugural-Dissertation [pres. to] Universität Leipzig. Leipzig: 1931. 70 pp., bibl.

912 HEIDEN, KONRAD: *Geburt des Dritten Reiches. Die Geschichte des Nationalsozialismus bis Herbst 1933.* 2. Aufl. Zürich: Europa-Verlag, 1934. 272 pp.

913 HEIDEN, KONRAD: *Der Führer. Hitler's rise to power.* Transl. from the German. London: Gollancz, 1944. 614 pp.

914 HOFFMANN, HEINRICH: *Deutschlands Erwachen in Bild und Wort.* Text: Marc Sesselmann. München: Hoffmann, [1924]. [32 pp.], ports., illus.

915 HOFFMANN, HEINRICH: *Der Triumph des Willens. Kampf und Aufstieg Adolf Hitlers und seiner Bewegung.* Berlin: Verlag 'Zeitgeschichte', [1933]. 8 + 56 pp., illus.

915a HORN, WOLFGANG: *Der Marsch zur Machtergreifung.* Königstein/Ts.: Athenäum/Droste, 1980. 452 pp.

916 KLUKE, PAUL: 'Der Fall Potempa'. [In] *Vierteljahrshefte für Zeitgeschichte,* Jhrg. 5, 1957. Pp. 279–300. [Murder by Nazis: the perpetrators were honoured by Hitler.]

917 KREBS, ALBERT: *Tendenzen und Gestalten der NSDAP. Erinnerungen an die Frühzeit der Partei.* Stuttgart: Deutsche Verlags-Anstalt, 1959. 246 pp. (Veröffentlichungen des Instituts für Zeitgeschichte). [English version: *The infancy of Nazism.* Ed.: William Sheridan Allen. New York: 1976. 328 pp., bibl.]

918 LEERS, JOHANN VON: *Entwicklung des Nationalsozialismus von seinem Anfang bis zur Gegenwart.* 2. Aufl. Bielefeld: Velhagen & Klasing, 1936. 127 pp. [First ed. 1935.]

919 LOEWENSTEIN, (Prince) HUBERTUS: *The tragedy of a nation. Germany 1918–1934.* Introd.: Wickham Steed. London: Faber, 1934. 373 pp. [German version: *Die Tragödie eines Volkes.* Amsterdam: Steenul, 1934.]

920 MALTITZ, HORST VON: *The evolution of Hitler's Germany. The ideology, the personality, the moment.* New York: McGraw-Hill, 1973. xiv + 479 pp., illus., bibl.

921 MASER, WERNER: *Der Sturm auf die Republik. Frühgeschichte der NSDAP.* Stuttgart: Deutsche Verlags-Anstalt, 1973. 524 pp., illus., facsims., family tree, bibl. [Rev. ed. of *Die Frühgeschichte der NSDAP: Hitlers Weg bis 1924.* Frankfurt a.M.: 1965.]

922 MAURER, ILSE & WENGST, UDO, eds.: *Staat und NSDAP 1930–1932. Quellen zur Ära Brüning.* Eingel.: Gerhard Schulz. Düsseldorf: Droste, 1977. lxxxix + 350 pp. (Quellen zur Geschichte des Parlamentarismus und der politischen Parteien).

923 MÜLLER, (Dr.): *Beamtentum und Nationalsozialismus.* München: Eher, 1931. 62 pp.

924 NICHOLLS, A. J.: *Weimar and the rise of Hitler.* London: Macmillan, 1968. xii + 203 pp., illus., maps, bibl. [Reprinted 1975.]

925 NICHOLLS, ANTHONY & MATTHIAS, ERICH, eds.: *German democracy and the triumph of Hitler. Essays in recent German history.* London: Allen & Unwin, 1971. 271 pp. (St. Antony's Papers).

926 [PAPEN, FRANZ von] DITTRICH, ZDENEK RADSLAV: *Hitlers weg naar de macht. De regering-von Papen.* [Thesis pres. to University of Utrecht.] Utrecht: Oosthoek, 1951. 229 pp., tabs., bibl., summary in French.

927 REICH, ALBERT & ACHENBACH, O. R.: *Vom 9. November 1918 zum 9. November 1923. Die Entstehung der deutschen Freiheitsbewegung.* München: Eher, 1933. 160 pp., illus., facsims.

928 SOLDAN, GEORG: *Zeitgeschichte in Wort und Bild.* München: 1931/34. Illus., maps, facsims., reprods. of political posters.
Bd. I: [Publ.: National-Archiv Berlin and Alleinige Vertriebsstelle München, 1931]. 512 pp.
Bd. II: [Same publs. 1932]. 518 pp.
Bd. III: [Publ.: Alleinige Vertriebsstelle München, 1934]. 599 pp.

929 SPERBER, MANÈS: *Die vergebliche Warnung ... All das Vergangene.* München: Deutscher Taschenbuch Verlag, 1979. 242 pp. [Second volume of autobiography.]

930 STACHURA, PETER D.: *The Weimar era and Hitler, 1918–1933. A critical bibliography.* Oxford: Clio Press, 1977. 275 pp.

931 TROTSKY, LEON: *The struggle against Fascism in Germany.* Introd.: Ernest Mandel. New York: Pathfinder Press, 1971. 479 pp., port. [Mainly written before 1933.]

932 TYRELL, ALBRECHT, ed.: *Führer befiehl ... Selbstzeugnisse aus der Kampfzeit der NSDAP. Dokumentation und Analyse.* Düsseldorf: Droste, 1969. 403 pp., illus., tabs., facsims., bibl.

933 *Der Weg in die Diktatur 1918 bis 1933.* Zehn Beiträge [by] Theodor Eschenburg, Ernst Fraenkel, Kurt Sontheimer, Erich Matthias, Rudolf Morsey, Ossip K. Flechtheim, Karl Dietrich Bracher, H. Krausnick, Hans Rothfels, Eugen Kogon. München: Piper, 1962. 244 pp. [From a Norddeutscher Rundfunk television series. English version: *The road to dictatorship.* London: Wolff, 1964.]

934 *Der Weg zum Nationalsozialismus.* Fürstenwalde: Militär-Verlag, 1934/35. Illus.
[I]: GERVINUS, FRITZ & WOLF, WERNER: *Von Weimar bis Potsdam. Deutsche Geschichte von 1918 bis zur Gegenwart.* 322 pp.
[III]: *Die Ruhmeshalle des SA., SS. und HJ., des früheren Stahlhelms und der für das Dritte Reich gefallenen Parteigenossen.* Hrsg. mit Unterstützung des Gaupresseamts Berlin [and others]. 331 pp.

935 ZÖBERLEIN, HANS: *Der Befehl des Gewissens. Ein Roman von den Wirren der Nachkriegszeit und der ersten Erhebung.* München: Eher, 1937. 990 pp., illus.

Nazi songbooks

936 ARENDT, PAUL, ed.: *Deutschland erwache! Das kleine Nazi-Liederbuch.*
Sulzbach-Oberpfalz: Arendt, [193–]. Illus.
Ausg. A: 63. Aufl. 32 pp.
Ausg. B: 54. Aufl. 32 pp.
[First ed. 1923. Contains examples of particularly repulsive anti-Semitism.]

937 HANFSTAENGL, ERNST, ed.: *Hitler Liederbuch 1924. 5 völkische Lieder. ...* Mit
dem Bilde Adolf Hitlers von Otto von Kursell. München: Hanfstaengl, 1924.
15 pp.

938 *Horst-Wessel-Marschalbum. Lieder der Nationalsozialistischen Deutschen
Arbeiterpartei. Vaterlands- und Soldatenlieder und Märsche aus alter und
neuer Zeit.* München: Eher, 1933/34. Mus. scores.
[Ausg. A]: Hrsg.: Hans Bajer. 12. Aufl. Publ. 1934. 86 pp.
Ausg. BB: Bearb.: Hans Buchner. 3. Aufl. Publ. 1933. 48 pp.

939 STURM 22/97: *Zehn S.A. Kampflieder.* Neuss: Meyerdruck, [193–?]. 8 pp.
[Contains song with words: 'Und wenn das Judenblut vom Messer spritzt,
dann geht's noch mal so gut'.]

Rise of the party: regional and local accounts

AIX-LA-CHAPELLE (AACHEN)
940 HERMANNS, WILL: *Stadt in Ketten. Geschichte der Besatzungs- und
Separatistenzeit 1918–1929 in und um Aachen.* Nachw.: 'Aachener
Nationalsozialisten im Kampf', [by] Quirin Jansen. Aachen: Mayer (Inh.:
Gölitzer & Eickmann), 1933. 357 pp., illus., facsims.

BADEN
941 REHBERGER, HORST: *Die Gleichschaltung des Landes Baden 1932/33.*
Heidelberg: Winter, 1966. 162 pp., bibl. (Heidelberger Rechtswissen-
schaftliche Abhandlungen).

BAVARIA
942 BUCHNER, FRANZ: *Kamerad! Halt aus! Aus der Geschichte des Kreises
Starnberg der NSDAP.* München: Eher, 1938. 428 pp., illus., map. [Covers
period 1925–1930.]

943 PRIDHAM, GEOFFREY: *Hitler's rise to power. The Nazi movement in Bavaria,
1923–1933.* London: Hart-Davis, MacGibbon, 1973. xvi + 380 pp., map,
tabs., bibl.

944 WIESEMANN, FALK: *Die Vorgeschichte der nationalsozialistischen Machtübernahme in Bayern 1932–1933.* Berlin: Duncker & Humblot, 1975.
328 pp., bibl.

See also 953, 954.

BERLIN
945 BERGER, ERICH: *Berlin wird deutsch!* Geleitw.: Dagobert Dürr. Berlin:
Heymann, 1934. 60 pp., ports., tabs.

946 GOEBBELS, JOSEPH: *Kampf um Berlin. Der Anfang.* 9. Aufl. München: Eher, 1936. 285 pp.

947 ROEGELS, FRITZ CARL: *Der Marsch auf Berlin.* Mitarb.: Hans Henning Frhr. von Grote, Curt Hotzel. Vorw.: Hans von Sodenstern. Berlin: Voegel, 1932. 192 pp., illus. (Ein Buch vom Wehrwillen deutscher Jugend).

BIELEFELD

948 HIEMISCH, MAX: *Der nationalsozialistische Kampf um Bielefeld. Die Geschichte der N.S.D.A.P. Bielefeld.* Bielefeld: Holtman, 1933. 77 pp.

BRUNSWICK

949 KAISER, KLAUS: *Braunschweiger Presse und Nationalsozialismus. Der Aufstieg der NSDAP im Lande Braunschweig im Spiegel der Braunschweiger Tageszeitungen 1930 bis 1933.* Inaugural-Dissertation [pres. to] Freie Universität Berlin. Braunschweig: 1970. 196 pp., tabs., bibl.

950 ROLOFF, ERNST-AUGUST: *Bürgertum und Nationalsozialismus 1930–1933. Braunschweigs Weg ins Dritte Reich.* Hannover: Verlag für Literatur und Zeitgeschehen, 1961. 174 pp., illus., facsims.

COBURG

951 SCHWEDE-COBURG, FRANZ: *Kampf um Coburg.* München: Eher, 1939. 256 pp., illus. [Coburg was the first town in which the Nazis gained a municipal election majority.]

DARMSTADT

952 PINGEL, HENNER: *Das Jahr 1933. NSDAP-Machtergreifung in Darmstadt und im Volksstaat Hessen. Mit zahlreichen Dokumenten und einer ausgewählten Gesetzsammlung.* Darmstadt: [priv. pr.], 1978. 245 pp., illus., facsims., tabs., bibl. [2nd rev. and amended ed. First publ. under title *Darmstadt 1933,* 1977.]

FRANCONIA

953 HAMBRECHT, RAINER: *Der Aufstieg der NSDAP in Mittel- und Oberfranken 1925–1933.* Nürnberg: Stadtarchiv, 1976. xi + 612 pp., map, tabs., bibl.

954 PREISS, HEINZ: *Die Anfänge der völkischen Bewegung in Franken.* Inaugural-Dissertation [pres. to] Friedrich Alexander-Universität Erlangen. 1937. 92 pp., tabs., bibl.

HAMBURG

955 JOCHMANN, WERNER: *Nationalsozialismus und Revolution. Ursprung und Geschichte der NSDAP in Hamburg 1922–1933. Dokumente.* Frankfurt a.M.: Europäische Verlagsanstalt, 1963. 444 pp., facsims., tabs. (Veröffentlichungen der Forschungsstelle für die Geschichte des Nationalsozialismus in Hamburg).

956 KRÜGER, ALF: *Der Weg, auf dem wir angetreten.* Berlin: Limpert, 1938. 341 pp., illus. [NSDAP among police in Hamburg.]

957 TIMPKE, HENNING, ed.: *Dokumente zur Gleichschaltung des Landes Hamburg 1933.* Frankfurt a.M.: Europäische Verlagsanstalt, 1964. 327 pp.

HESSEN

958 GIMBEL, A. & HEPP, KARL, eds.: *So kämpften wir! Schilderung aus der Kampfzeit der NSDAP im Gau Hessen-Nassau.* Frankfurt a.M.: NS-Verlagsgesellschaft, 1941. 190 pp., illus.

959 SCHÖN, EBERHART: *Die Entstehung des Nationalsozialismus in Hessen.* Meisenheim a.Gl.: Hain, 1972. xix + 227 pp., map, tabs., bibl.

SEIPEL, WILHELM: 'Entwicklung der nationalsozialistischen Bauernbewegung in Hessen'. *See 224.*

See also 952.

KURMARK

960 RUEHLE, GERD VON: *Kurmark. Die Geschichte eines Gaues.* Berlin: Lindemann, 1934. 140 pp., illus.

LIPPE

961 CIOLEK-KÜMPER, JUTTA: *Wahlkampf in Lippe. Die Wahlkampfpropaganda der NSDAP zur Landtagswahl am 15. Januar 1933.* München: Verlag Dokumentation, 1976. 406 pp., illus., map, diagrs., bibl.

962 SCHRÖDER, ARNO: *'Hitler geht auf die Dörfer ...'. Der Auftakt zur nationalen Revolution. Erlebnisse und Bilder von der entscheidenden Januarwahl in Lippe.* Detmold: Lippische Staatszeitung NS-Verlag, 1938. 212 pp., illus.

LOWER SAXONY

963 HENNINGSEN, HANS: *Niedersachsenland, Du wurdest unser! Zehn Jahre Nationalsozialismus im Gau Ost-Hannover. Streiflichter aus der Kampfzeit.* Nach Angaben, Aufzeichnungen und Zeitungsausschnitten verf. und zusammengest. im Auftr. des Gauleiters, Otto Telschow. Harburg-Wilhelmsburg: 'Niedersachsen-Stürmer' Verlag, 1935. 185 pp., illus.

964 NOAKES, JEREMY: *The NSDAP in Lower Saxony 1921–1933. A study of National Socialist organisation.* Thesis. Oxford: 1967. 352 pp.

MECKLENBURG

965 DITZ, BERTHOLD: *Werdegang der Ortsgruppe Bützow der NSDAP.* Bützow: Ratsbuchdruckerei, [1935?]. 118 pp., illus.

OBERHARZ

966 PLESSE, SIGURD: *Die nationalsozialistische Machtergreifung im Oberharz. Clausthal-Zellerfeld 1929–1933.* Clausthal-Zellerfeld: Pieper, 1970. 94 pp., tabs.

OSNABRÜCK

967 KÜHLING, KARL: *Osnabrück 1925–1933. Von der Republik bis zum Dritten Reich.* Osnabrück: Fromm, 1963. 164 pp., illus., facsims. [First publ. in 'Neue Tagespost'.]

RUHR

968 BÖHNKE, WILFRIED: *Die NSDAP im Ruhrgebiet 1920–1933.* Bonn-Bad Godesberg: Verlag Neue Gesellschaft, 1974. 239 pp., bibl. (Schriftenreihe des Forschunginstituts der Friedrich-Ebert-Stiftung).

SYLT

969 VOIGT, HARALD: *Der Sylter Weg ins Dritte Reich. Die Geschichte der Insel Sylt vom Ende des Ersten Weltkriegs bis zu den Anfängen der nationalsozialistischen Diktatur. Eine Fallstudie.* Münsterdorf: Hansen & Hansen, 1977. 158 pp., illus., facsims., tabs., bibl.

THURINGIA

970 ALBRECHT, KARL HEINZ: 'Zehn Jahre Kampf um Gera. Eine Geschichte der NSDAP im Thüringer Osten.' Sonderdruck aus *Geraer Zeitung*, Okt. 1933. 93 pp., illus.

971 SCHULZE, MARTIN: *Nationalsozialistische Regierungstätigkeit in Thüringen 1932–1935.* Weimar: Fink, 1935. 35 pp.

WESTPHALIA

972 BECK, FRIEDRICH ALFRED: *Kampf und Sieg. Geschichte der NSDAP im Gau Westfalen-Süd von den Anfängen bis zur Machtübernahme.* Im Aufrr. des Gauleiters Josef Wagner hrsg. Dortmund: Westfalen-Verlag, 1938. 612 pp., illus., facsims.

973 SCHRÖDER, ARNO, ed.: *Mit der Partei vorwärts! Zehn Jahre Gau Westfalen-Nord.* Detmold: Lippische Staatszeitung, 1940. 480 pp., illus., facsims., bibl,, chronology (pp. 301–479). [Incl. list of Hoheitsträger as at 30 January 1933.]

WETZLAR

974 MAYER, ULRICH: *Das Eindringen des Nationalsozialismus in die Stadt Wetzlar.* Wetzlar: Wetzlarischer Geschichtsverein, 1970. 124 pp., maps, diagrs., tabs.

WÜRTTEMBERG

975 BESSON, WALDEMAR: *Württemberg und die deutsche Staatskrise 1928–1933. Eine Studie zur Auflösung der Weimarer Republik.* Stuttgart: Deutsche Verlags-Anstalt, 1959. 429 pp., bibl.

1923: the Munich Putsch

976 BONNIN, GEORGES: *Le Putsch de Hitler à Munich en 1923.* Les Sables d'Olonne: Bonnin, 1966. 230 pp., illus., facsims., plan, bibl.

977 DEUERLEIN, ERNST, ed.: *Der Hitler-Putsch. Bayerische Dokumente zum 8./9. November 1923.* Stuttgart: Deutsche Verlags-Anstalt, 1962. 760 pp. (Quellen und Darstellungen zur Zeitgeschichte).

978 FRANZ-WILLING, GEORG: *Putsch und Verbotszeit der Hitlerbewegung, November 1923–Februar 1925.* Preussisch Oldendorf: Schütz, 1977. 464 pp., illus., bibl.

979 GORDON, HAROLD J., jr.: *Hitler and the Beer Hall Putsch.* Princeton, N.J.: Princeton University Press, 1972. xii + 666 pp., illus., bibl. [German version: *Hitlerputsch 1923.* Frankfurt a.M.: Bernard & Graefe, 1971.]

980 LUDENDORFF, [ERICH]: *Auf dem Wege zur Feldherrnhalle. Lebenserinnerungen an die Zeit des 9. November 1923, mit Dokumenten in 5 Anlagen.* München: Ludendorff, 1937. 156 pp.

981 SCHÖNER, HELLMUT, ed,: *Hitler-Putsch im Spiegel der Presse. Berichte bayerischer, norddeutscher und ausländischer Zeitungen über die Vorgänge im November 1923 in Originalreproduktionen.* München: Lipp, 1974. 184 pp., facsims.

Hitler's trial

982 *Der Hitler-Prozess. Auszüge aus den Verhandlungsberichten. Mit den Bildern der Angeklagten nach Zeichnungen von Otto von Kursell.* München: Deutscher Volksverlag, 1924. 272 pp., ports.

983 *Der Hitler-Prozess vor dem Volksgericht in München.* München: Knorr & Hirth, 1924. 293 + 121 pp. [Also: Unveränderter Neudruck. Glashütten i.Ts.: Auvermann, 1973.]

984 VOGGENREITER, LUDWIG, comp.: *Der Hitler-Prozess. Das Fanal zum Erwachen Deutschlands.* Nach dem Prozessbericht zusammengest. 2. Aufl. verm. um den Bericht vom 9. November 1933. Potsdam: Voggenreiter, 1934. 104 pp.

Party finances

985 CZICHON, EBERHARD: *Wer verhalf Hitler zur Macht? Zum Anteil der deutschen Industrie an der Zerstörung der Weimarer Republik.* 4. Aufl. Köln: Pahl-Rugenstein, 1976. 105 pp., tabs., bibl.

986 GOSSWEILER, KURT: 'Hitler und das Kapital 1925–1928'. [Reprint from] *Blätter für deutsche und internationale Politik.* Köln: Pahl-Rugenstein, Juli/Aug. 1978. Pp. 842–860, 993–1109.

987 POOL, JAMES & SUZANNE: *Who financed Hitler? The secret funding of Hitler's rise to power, 1919–1933.* London: Macdonald and Jane's, 1979. 535 pp., illus., bibl.

988 THYSSEN, FRITZ: *I paid Hitler.* London: Hodder & Stoughton, 1941. 319 pp., illus., facsims. [Disputed authenticity.]

989 TURNER, HENRY ASHBY, jr.: *Faschismus und Kapitalismus in Deutschland. Studien zum Verhältnis zwischen Nationalsozialismus und Wirtschaft.* Göttingen: Vandenhoeck & Ruprecht, 1972. 185 pp. [Transl. from articles written in English 1968–1972. Orig. titles incl.: 'Big business and the rise of Hitler'; 'Hitler's secret pamphlet for industrialists 1927'; 'Emil Kirdorf and the Nazi Party'; 'Fritz Thyssen und das Buch "I paid Hitler"'.]

990 WARBURG, SIDNEY: *De geldbronnen van het Nationaal-Socialisme. Drie gesprekken met Hitler.* Vertaald door J.G. Schoup. Amsterdam: Van Holkema & Warendorf, 1933. 99 pp. [Disputed authenticity.]

Nazis in the legislature

CIOLEK-KÜMPER, JUTTA: *Wahlkampf in Lippe. See* 961.

991 FIGGE, REINHARD: *Die Opposition der NSDAP im Reichstag.* Inaugural-

Dissertation [pres. to] Universität zu Köln. Essen: 1963. 199 + 20 pp., tabs., bibl.

992 FRICK, WILHELM; *Die Nationalsozialisten im Reichstag 1924–1931*. Neu hrsg. im Auftr. der nationalsozialistischen Reichstagsfraktion von Curt Fischer. München: Eher, 1932. 160 pp. (Nationalsozialistische Bibliothek, Heft 37.) [First ed. 1928. A further ed. appeared in 1939.]

993 HIMMLER, HEINRICH: *Der Reichstag*. München: Eher, 1931. 84 pp., tabs. [Author was a member of the Reichstag at that time.]

994 HINKLER, PAUL: *Nationalsozialistische Arbeit im Preussen-Parlament 1928–1932*. Itzehoe i.Holstein: Schleswig-Holsteinische Tageszeitung, [1932]. 40 pp.

995 *Adolf Hitler und seine Kämpfer. 288 Braunhemden im Reichstag. Die nationalsozialistische Reichstagsfraktion VIII. Wahlperiode 5. März 1933. Mit Abbildungen und Personalangaben der Mitglieder.* München: Eher, 1933. 240 pp., illus.

996 MERTES, ALOIS: *Abstimmungsverhalten der Fraktion der KPD bzw. der NSDAP im Deutschen Reichstag, im Sächsischen Landtag und im Preussischen Landtag in dem Zeitraum vom 1.1.1929 bis zum 30.1.1933. Zahl und Gegenstand der Oppositions- und Obstruktionsanträge.* Bearb.: Dr. Klatt. [Bonn]: Deutscher Bundestag, 1976. 35 pp., tabs., mimeog.

997 STACHURA, PETER D.: 'Der kritische Wendepunkt? Die NSDAP und die Reichstagswahlen von 20. Mai 1928'. [In] *Vierteljahrshefte für Zeitgeschichte*, 26. Jhrg., 1978. pp. 66–99, tabs.

998 TRUMPP, THOMAS: *Franz von Papen, der preussisch-deutsche Dualismus und die NSDAP in Preussen. Ein Beitrag zur Vorgeschichte des 20. Juli 1932.* Inaugural-Dissertation [pres. to] Eberhard-Karls-Universität Tübingen. Marburg: 1963. 235 pp., bibl.

999 *Verzeichnis der Mitglieder des Reichstags und der Reichsregierung sowie der Bevollmächtigten zum Reichsrat. Abgeschlossen am 12. Dez. 1933.* Berlin: Drucksachen des Reichstags, 1933. 95 pp. [Also a 1936 ed.]

1000 *Wider den Nationalsozialismus.* Berlin: Voco Verlag, [1932]. 150 pp., port. [Comprising: August Weber: 'Zwei mutige Reden'; Rudolf Breitscheid: 'Eine Reichstagsrede (24. Feb. 1932)'; Wilhelm Groener: 'Verteidigungsrede (24. Feb. 1932)' (on his decree admitting NSDAP members to the Reichswehr).]

Workers and trade unions

1001 DEUTSCHER METALLARBEITER-VERBAND: *Der Nationalsozialismus in Theorie und Praxis.* 7. Ausg. Berlin: Jan. 1933. 32 pp., looseleaf.

1002 GERHARD, H. W.: *Über Hildburghausen ins dritte Reich! Nationalsozialismus und Arbeiterklasse.* Berlin: Verlag 'Der Syndikalist', 1932. 30 pp.

1003 GIEN, R.: *Unser Kampf gegen die Gewerkschaftsbonzen.* Berlin: Selbstverlag, [1931?]. 30 pp.

1004 HAMEL, IRIS: *Völkischer Verband und nationale Gewerkschaft. Der Deutschnationale Handlungsgehilfen-Verband 1893–1933.* Frankfurt a.M.: Europäische Verlagsanstalt, 1967. 289 pp., bibl. (Veröffentlichungen der Forschungsstelle für die Geschichte des Nationalsozialismus in Hamburg).

1005 HEER, HANNES: *Burgfrieden oder Klassenkampf. Zur Politik der sozialdemokratischen Gewerkschaften 1930–1933.* Neuwied: Luchterhand, 1971. 239 pp., bibl.

1006 KELE, MAX H.: *Nazis and workers. National Socialist appeals to German labor, 1919–1933.* Chapel Hill, N.C.: University of North Carolina Press, 1972. 243 pp., bibl.

MUCHOW, REINHOLD: *Nationalsozialismus und 'freie' Gewerkschaften. See* 546.

1007 SCHILDT, GERHARD: *Die Arbeitsgemeinschaft Nord-West. Untersuchungen zur Geschichte der NSDAP 1925–26.* Inaugural-Dissertation [pres. to] Albert-Ludwigs-Universität zu Freiburg i.Br. [1964]. 194 + xlvi pp., bibl.

1008 UNGER-WINKELRIED, EMIL: *Von Bebel zu Hitler. Vom Zukunftsstaat zum Dritten Reich. Aus dem Leben eines sozialdemokratischen Arbeiters.* [Berlin-Schöneberg]: Verlag Deutsche Kultur-Wacht, 1934. 119 pp. [Convert to anti-Semitism.]

1009 WINNIG, AUGUST: *Der weite Weg.* 2. Aufl. Hamburg: Hanseatische Verlagsanstalt, 1932. 447 pp. [Autobiographical novel: a social democrat becomes a National Socialist.]

Opposition to National Socialism

1010 ALLGEMEINER DEUTSCHER BEAMTENBUND: *Der Nationalsozialismus—eine Gefahr für das Berufsbeamtentum.* Berlin: 1932. 88 pp.

1011 *Der Anti-Nazi.* Berlin: Deutscher Volksgemeinschaftsdienst, 1930/32. 1930: *Redner- und Pressematerial über die NSDAP.* 2. erw. Aufl. Looseleaf. 1932: *Handbuch im Kampf gegen die NSDAP.* 181 pp.

1012 BLOCH, ERNST: *Politische Messungen. Pestzeit, Vormärz.* Frankfurt a.M.: Suhrkamp, 1970. 490 pp. (Gesamtausgabe, Bd. 11).

1013 CALLMANN, RUDOLF: *Zur Boykottfrage. Ein Gutachten.* Berlin: Philo Verlag, 1932. 43 pp.

1014 CENTRALVEREIN DEUTSCHER STAATSBÜRGER JÜDISCHEN GLAUBENS: *Die Stellung der Nationalsozialistischen Deutschen Arbeiterpartei (NSDAP) zur Judenfrage. Eine Materialsammlung.* Berlin: [1932]. Looseleaf.

DAVID, F.: *Ist die NSDAP eine sozialistische Partei? See* 312.

1015 KEMPNER, ROBERT M. W.: [Photo-mechanical reprint of] *Justizdämmerung. Auftakt zum Dritten Reich*, von Eike von Repkow [pseud.]. Berlin: Volksfunk-Verlag, 1932. [Reissued with introd. by author: Landsdowne, Pa.: 1963. 120 pp.].

1016 LOEWENFELD, PHILIPP: *Das Strafrecht als politische Waffe*. Berlin: Dietz, 1933. 48 pp. (Schriftenreihe der Vereinigung Sozialdemokratischer Juristen).

1017 NIEKISCH, ERNST: *Hitler—ein deutsches Verhängnis*. Zeichnungen: A. Paul Weber. Berlin: Widerstands-Verlag, 1932. 36 pp., illus.

1018 OTTWALT, ERNST: *Deutschland erwache! Geschichte des Nationalsozialismus*. Wien: Hess, 1932. 391 pp., bibl.

1019 SOZIALDEMOKRATISCHE PARTEI DEUTSCHLANDS: *Zeugnisse über das persönliche Verhalten von Nationalsozialisten. Vorwiegend aus der Zeit ab Januar 1929*. Berlin: Werbeabt. der SPD, 1931. 91 pp., mimeog.

1020 STEINER, JOHANNES, comp.: *Prophetien wider das Dritte Reich. Aus den Schriften des Dr. Fritz Gerlich und des Paters Ingbert Naab* ... München: Schnell & Steiner, 1946. 585 pp., ports., facsims.

1021 TOLLER, ERNST & MÜHR, ALFRED: *Nationalsozialismus. Eine Diskussion über Kulturbankrott des Bürgertums zwischen Ernst Toller und Alfred Mühr*. Berlin: Kiepenheuer, 1930. 35 pp.

1022 *Wenn Judenblut vom Messer spritzt* ... Wien: Wiener Volksbuchhandlung, [193–]. 15 pp. (Verantwortl.: Hans Philipp).

1023 *Zwischenspiel Hitler. Ziele und Wirklichkeit des Nationalsozialismus*. 2. erw. Aufl. Wien: Reinhold, 1932. 397 pp., illus.

See also Zentrum (German Centre Party).

C. THE FALL OF THE WEIMAR REPUBLIC

1024 ALLEN, WILLIAM SHERIDAN: *The Nazi seizure of power. The experience of a single German town, 1930–1935*. Chicago, Ill.: Quadrangle Books, 1965. 345 pp., tabs., diagrs., map. [French version: *Une petite ville nazie*. Paris: Laffont, 1967.]

1025 BARRÈS, PHILIPPE: *Sous la vague Hitlérienne. Octobre 1932–Juin 1933*. Paris: Plon, 1933. 312 pp.

1026 BOJANO, FILIPPO: *Sulle rovine di Weimar*. Milano: Agnelli, 1933. 222 pp., illus.

1027 BRACHER, KARL DIETRICH: *Die Auflösung der Weimarer Republik. Eine Studie zum Problem des Machtverfalls in der Demokratie*. Einl.: Hans Herzfeld.

Stuttgart: Ring-Verlag, 1955. 745 pp. (Schriften des Instituts für politische Wissenschaft). [Fifth ed.: Villingen: Ring-Verlag, 1971.]

1028 BRAUN, OTTO: *Von Weimar zu Hitler*. 3. Aufl. Hildesheim: Gerstenberg, 1979. 458 pp.

1029 BRECHT, ARNOLD: *Prelude to silence. The end of the German Republic*. New York: Oxford University Press, 1944. 156 pp. [German version: *Vorspiel zum Schweigen*. Wien: Verlag für Geschichte und Politik, 1948.]

1030 BRÜNING, HEINRICH: *Reden und Aufsätze eines deutschen Staatsmanns*. Hrsg.: Wilhelm Vernekohl, Rudolf Morsey. Münster: Regensberg, 1968. 358 pp. [Incl. 'Wie Hitler die Macht eroberte. Ein Brief Brünings an Dr. Pechel. Hrsg. der Deutschen Rundschau 1947', pp. 223–269.]

1031 CARLEBACH, EMIL: *Hitler war kein Betriebsunfall. Hinter den Kulissen der Weimarer Republik. Die vorprogrammierte Diktatur*. Frankfurt a.M.: Röderberg, 1978. 131 pp., illus., bibl.

1032 CLARK, R. T.: *The fall of the German republic. A political study*. London: Allen & Unwin, 1935. 494 pp. [Reprinted: New York: Russell & Russell, 1964.]

1033 EGGERS, KURT: *Die Geburt des Jahrtausends*. Leipzig: Schwarzhäupter, 1941. 149 pp. [Seventh ed., first ed. 1936.]

1034 GESSNER, DIETER: *Das Ende der Weimarer Republik. Fragen, Methoden und Ergebnisse interdisziplinärer Forschung*. Darmstadt: Wissenschaftliche Buchgesellschaft, 1978. vii + 131 pp.

1035 HENTSCHEL, VOLKER: *Weimars letzte Monate. Hitler und der Untergang der Republik*. Düsseldorf: Droste, 1978. 180 pp.

1036 HILLGRUBER, ANDREAS: *Die Auflösung der Weimarer Republik*. 2. Aufl. Hannover: Verlag für Literatur und Zeitgeschehen, 1960. 72 pp., ports., tabs., diagrs., bibl. [Fifth ed. 1965.]

1037 HOEGNER, WILHELM: *Flucht vor Hitler. Erinnerungen an die Kapitulation der ersten deutschen Republik 1933*. Nachw.: Wolfgang Jean Stock. München: Nymphenburger Verlagshandlung, 1978. 295 pp., port. [2nd ed.]

1038 HOLBORN, HAJO, ed.: *Republic to Reich. The making of the Nazi revolution. Ten essays*. Transl. from the German: Ralph Manheim. New York: Random House, 1973. 491 pp. [Orig. publ. in the *Vierteljahreshefte für Zeitgeschichte* as separate articles.]

1039 JASPER, GOTTHARD, ed.: *Von Weimar zu Hitler 1930–1933*. Köln: Kiepenheuer & Witsch, 1968. 527 pp., tabs., bibl.

1040 KING, JOSEPH: *The German revolution. Its meaning and menace*. Preface: Viscount Snowden. London: Williams & Norgate, 1933. 152 pp.

1041 KUBE, WILHELM and others, eds.: *Almanach der nationalsozialistischen · Revolution*. Hrsg.: Wilhelm Kube. Mitarb.: Willi Bischoff, Heinz Weiss. Mit vergleichenden Bilddokumenten der Zeit. Berlin: Brunnen-Verlag, 1934. 227 pp., illus.

1042 KÜHNL, REINHARD & HARDACH, GERD, eds.: *Die Zerstörung der Weimarer Republik.* Köln: Pahl-Rugenstein, 1977. 290 pp.

LE GRIX, FRANÇOIS: *Vingt jours chez Hitler. Tableaux d'une révolution. See 686.*

1043 MEISSNER, HANS OTTO & WILDE, HARRY: *Die Machtergreifung. Ein Bericht über die Technik des nationalsozialistischen Staatsstreichs.* Stuttgart: Cotta, 1958. 364 pp., bibl.

1044 PAPEN, FRANZ VON: *Vom Scheitern einer Demokratie 1930–1933.* Mainz: von Hase & Koehler, 1968. 408 pp., port., bibl.

1045 PETROFF, PETER & IRMA: *The secret of Hitler's victory.* London: Hogarth Press, 1934. 128 pp.

1046 REVERMANN, KLAUS: *Die stufenweise Durchbrechung des Verfassungssystems der Weimarer Republik in den Jahren 1930 bis 1933. Eine staatsrechtliche und historisch-politische Analyse.* Münster/Westf.: Aschendorff, 1959. 175 pp., bibl.

1047 ROSTEN, CURT: *Vom Bonzentum zum Dritten Reich.* Berlin: Schmidt, 1933. 307 pp., illus.

1048 SCHACHT, HJALMAR: *1933. Wie eine Demokratie stirbt.* Düsseldorf: Econ-Verlag, 1968. 179 pp., tabs.

1049 SCHLEGEL, WERNER: *Sinn und Gestaltung der grossen deutschen Revolution.* 2. Aufl. Leipzig: Heling, 1934. 173 pp., tabs.

SCHLEICHER, KURT VON
1050 BERNDORFF, H. R.: *General zwischen Ost und West. Aus den Geheimnissen der Deutschen Republik.* Hamburg: Hoffmann & Campe, [1951?]. 320 pp.

1051 VOGELSANG, THILO: *Kurt von Schleicher. Ein General als Politiker.* Göttingen: Musterschmidt, 1965. 112 pp.

––––––––––

1052 TREVIRANUS, GOTTFRIED REINHOLD: *Das Ende von Weimar. Heinrich Brüning und seine Zeit.* Düsseldorf: Econ-Verlag, 1968. 431 pp., bibl.

1053 *Wir fliegen mit Hitler. Mit dem Führer kreuz und quer durch Deutschland.* Berlin-Schöneberg: Verlag Deutsche Kultur-Wacht, 1933. 184 pp., illus. [Election campaign tour.]

1054 WUCHER, ALBERT: *Die Fahne hoch. Das Ende der Republik und Hitlers Machtübernahme. Ein Dokumentarbericht.* München: Süddeutscher Verlag, 1963. 254 pp., illus., tab., facsims., bibl.

D. CONSOLIDATION OF POWER

ALLEN, WILLIAM SHERIDAN: *The Nazi seizure of power. See* 1024.

1055 BECK, R.: *The death of the Prussian republic. A study of Reich–Prussian relations, 1932–1934.* Tallahassee, Fla.: Florida State University, 1959. 283 pp., bibl.

1056 BRACHER, KARL DIETRICH and others: *Die nationalsozialistische Machtergreifung. Studien zur Errichtung des totalitären Herrschaftssystems in Deutschland 1933/34.* 2. durchges. Aufl. [By] Karl Dietrich Bracher, Wolfgang Sauer, Gerhard Schulz. Köln: Westdeutscher Verlag, 1962. xx + 1034 pp., tabs., bibl. (Schriften des Instituts für politische Wissenschaft.) [First ed. 1960. Also: Frankfurt a.M.: Ullstein, 1974, in 3 vols.—Bracher, K. D.: *Stufen der Machtergreifung*; Schulz, Gerhard: *Die Anfänge des totalitären Massnahmenstaates*; Sauer, Wolfgang: *Die Mobilmachung der Gewalt.*]

1057 BRÜDIGAM, HEINZ: *Das Jahr 1933. Terrorismus an der Macht. Eine Dokumentation über die Errichtung der faschistischen Diktatur.* Frankfurt a.M.: Röderberg, 1978. 136 pp., bibl.

1058 DOMMISCH, HANS & BLANKENBURG, PAUL: *Ein Jahr Nationalsozialismus in Regierung und Gesetzgebung.* Langensalza: Beltz, 1934. 108 pp., ports., diagrs.

1059 DOMRÖSE, ORTWIN: *Der NS-Staat in Bayern von der Machtergreifung bis zum Röhm-Putsch.* München: Wölfle, 1974. 398 pp. (Neue Schriftenreihe des Stadtarchivs München).

1060 FRICK, WILHELM: *Der Neuaufbau des Reichs.* Berlin: Steegemann, 1934. 64 pp. [Speeches by Frick, entitled: 'Der Neuaufbau des Reichs'; 'Die freie deutsche Wissenschaft'; 'Die Aufgabe der Studentenschaft'; 'Rassengesetzgebung des Dritten Reichs'.]

1061 GRUBER, WALTER: *Zwei Jahre Drittes Reich. Die Stufen zur Verwirklichung des Dritten Reiches.* Berlin: Hochmuth, 1935. 31 pp.

1062 HEUSS, THEODOR: *Die Machtergreifung und das Ermächtigungsgesetz. Zwei nachgelassene Kapitel der 'Erinnerungen 1905–1933'* hrsg. von Eberhard Pikart. Tübingen: Wunderlich, 1967. 55 pp.

1063 HOCHE, WERNER, ed.: *Verordnung zum Schutze des deutschen Volkes vom 4. Februar 1933 nebst den einschlägigen Bestimmungen.* Berlin: Vahlen, 1933. 79 pp.

1064 JÄRTE, OTTO: 'Nazism i närbild'. Uppsala: Almquist & Wiksells, [1961?]. Pp. 217–260, summary in English. [Offprint from *Festkrift till Georg Andren.* English title: 'Nazism at close quarters. Impressions from Berlin in the critical summer of 1934'.]

1065 KRÖGER, HANS: *Gestern und heute. Ein Jahr nationalsozialistischer Aufarbeit: Beseitigung des Klassenkampfes: Einigung des deutschen Volkes: Hemmungen, auf die wir achten müssen.* Leipzig: Schaufuss, 1934. 46 pp.

KUBE, WILHELM and others, eds.: *Almanach der nationalsozialistischen Revolution. See* 1041.

1066 MANVELL, ROGER & FRAENKEL, HEINRICH: *The hundred days to Hitler.* London: Dent, 1974. 235 pp., bibl. [Incl.: Pt. 3: 'The Night of the Long Knives'; Appendix II: 'Who fired the Reichstag?'.]

1067 MEINCK, JÜRGEN: *Weimarer Staatslehre und Nationalsozialismus. Eine Studie zum Problem der Kontinuität im staatsrechtlichen Denken in Deutschland. 1928 bis 1936.* Frankfurt a.M.: Campus Verlag, 1978. 367 pp. [Orig. a dissertation pres. to Marburg University 1976.]

1068 MORSEY, RUDOLF, ed.: *Das 'Ermächtigungsgesetz' vom 24. März 1933.* Göttingen: Vandenhoeck & Ruprecht, 1976. 84 pp. (Unveränd. Nachdruck).

PINGEL, HENNER: *Das Jahr 1933. See* 952.

1069 POETZSCH-HEFFTER, FRITZ, ed.: *Vom deutschen Staatsleben 30. Januar bis 31. Dezember 1933.* Tübingen: Mohr, 1935. 272 pp., tabs.

1070 REICHSMINISTERIUM DES INNERN: *Volksabstimmung vom 12. November 1933. Die geltenden Durchführungsbestimmungen.* Berlin: Reichs- und Staatsverlag, [1933]. 52 pp.

1071 REIMER, K. F. and others: 'Hitlers Aufruf an das deutsche Volk vom 10. Februar 1933'. [Special issue of] *Publikationen zu Wissenschaftlichen Filmen (Sektion Geschichte, Pädagogik, Publizistik),* Bd. II, Heft 2, Mai 1971. Göttingen: Institut für den wissenschaftlichen Film. 281 pp., illus., bibl.

1072 WENDT, HANS: *Die Märzrevolution von 1933.* Oldenburg: Stalling, 1933. 107 pp.

1073 WILLIGMANN, KARL: *Behörden im Dritten Reich. Praktischer Leitfaden für Studierende, Anwärter, Beamte, Privat- und Geschäftsleute durch des neuen Einheits-Staates Verwaltungs-Einrichtungen und N.S.D.A.P. Organisationen.* Berlin: Schultze, [1934]. 223 pp. (Belehre Dich selbst!).

1074 WHEATON, ELIOT BARCULE: *Prelude to calamity: the Nazi revolution 1933–35. With a background survey of the Weimar era.* Garden City, N.Y.: Doubleday, 1968. 523 pp., map, tab., bibl.

1075 ZINNER-BIBERACH, F. (M. Winter): *Führer, Volk und Tat. Geschichte und Gestalt der neuen Nation.* 2. verm. und verb. Aufl. München: Pechstein, 1934. 445 pp., illus., diagrs.

Hindenburg, Paul von Beneckendorff und von

1076 DORPALEN, ANDREAS: *Hindenburg and the Weimar Republic.* Princeton, N.J.: Princeton University Press, 1964. 506 pp., port., bibl. [German version: *Hindenburg in der Geschichte der Weimarer Republik.* Berlin: Leber, 1966.]

1077 HUBATSCH, WALTHER: *Hindenburg und der Staat. Aus den Papieren des Generalfeldmarschalls und Reichspräsidenten von 1878 bis 1934.* Göttingen: Musterschmidt, 1966. xiv + 397 pp.

1078 KIMENKOWSKI, EWALD, ed.: *Hindenburg im neuen Deutschland. Ein Denkmal des Dankes für den treuen Eckart des deutschen Volkes.* Berlin: Vaterländische Verlagsanstalt, 1934. 151 pp.

1079 LÜDERS, MARTIN: *Der Soldat und das Reich. Paul von Hindenburg, Generalfeldmarschall und Reichspräsident.* Leoni am Starnberger See: Druffel, 1961. 255 pp., illus., map, facsims.

1080 SCHULTZE-PFAELZER, GERHARD: *Hindenburg und Hitler zur Führung vereint.* Berlin: Stollberg, 1933. 96 pp., illus.

1081 WHEELER-BENNETT, JOHN W.: *Hindenburg: the wooden Titan.* London: Macmillan, 1936. 507 pp., illus., maps.

Reichstag fire

1082 *Braunbuch über Reichstagbrand und Hitler-Terror.* Vorw.: Lord Marley. 2. Aufl. Basel: Universum-Bücherei, 1933. 382 pp., illus. [English version: *Brown Book of the Hitler terror and the burning of the Reichstag.* Prepared by the World Committee for the Victims of German Fascism. London: Gollancz, 1933.]

1083 CALIC, EDUARD: *Le Reichstag brûle!* Paris: Stock, 1969. 301 pp., illus., plans, facsims., bibl.

1084 EHRT, ADOLF: *Bewaffneter Aufstand! Enthüllungen über den kommunistischen Umsturzversuch am Vorabend der nationalen Revolution.* Hrsg.: Gesamtverband deutscher Antikommunistischer Vereinigungen. 4. Aufl. Berlin: Eckart Verlag, 1933. 188 pp., illus.

1085 HOFER, WALTHER and others, eds.: *Der Reichstagsbrand. Eine wissenschaftliche Dokumentation.* Hrsg.: Walther Hofer, Eduard Calic, Karl Stephan, Friedrich Zipfel. Wissenschaftliche Mitarb.: Christoph Graf [and others].
Bd. I: Berlin: Arani-Verlag, 1972. 293 pp., illus., graphs.
Bd. II: München: Saur, 1978. 487 pp., bibl.

1086 MOMMSEN, HANS: 'Der Reichstagsbrand und seine politischen Folgen'. [In] *Vierteljahrshefte für Zeitgeschichte*, 12. Jhrg., 1964. Pp. 351–413.

1087 PRITCHARD, JOHN: *Reichstag fire—ashes of democracy.* New York: Ballantyne Books, 1972. 159 pp., illus., facsims., plan, bibl.

1088 REED, DOUGLAS: *The burning of the Reichstag.* London: Gollancz, 1934. 352 pp.

1089 TOBIAS, FRITZ: *Der Reichstagsbrand. Legende und Wirklichkeit.* Rastatt: Grote, 1962. 723 pp., illus., facsims. [English version: *The Reichstag fire.* London: Secker & Warburg, 1963.]

Reichstag fire trial

1090 *Braunbuch II. Dimitroff contra Goering. Enthüllungen über die wahren Brandstifter.* Paris: Éds. du Carrefour, 1934. 462 pp., illus. [2nd ed. Introd.: D. N. Pritt. English version: *Brown Book II. The Reichstag Fire Trial. The material collected by the World Committee for the Relief of the Victims of*

German Fascism. Introd. chapter: Georgi Dimitrov. Foreword: D. N. Pritt, K.C. Appendix: 'Murder in Hitler Germany', introd. by Lion Feuchtwanger. London: Lane, 1934. Reprint of German ed.: Köln: Pahl-Rugenstein, 1980.]

1091 DIMITROFF, G.: *Der Reichstagsbrandprozess. Dokumente, Briefe und Aufzeichnungen.* Moskau: Verlag für fremdsprachige Literatur, 1942. 199 pp., illus. [Also Berlin ed., 1946.]

1092 DIMITROFF, GEORGI: ... *Signed G. Dimitroff. Letters, documents and notes from prison and the Leipzig Supreme Court, with 8 unpublished facsimiles.* Comp.: Alfred Kurella. London: Lawrence, 1935. 156 pp., ports., facsims.

1093 JUSTINIAN, pseud.: *Reichstagsbrand: Wer ist verurteilt?* Karlsbad: Verlagsanstalt Graphia, 1934. 47 pp.

1094 KALBE, ERNSTGERT: *Freiheit für Dimitroff. Der internationale Kampf gegen die provokatorische Reichstagsbrandstiftung und den Leipziger Prozess.* Berlin [East]: Rütten & Loening, 1963. 359 pp., bibl.

1095 *Roodboek. Van der Lubbe en de Rijksdagbrand.* Publicatie van het Internationaal van der Lubbe-Comité. Amsterdam: Internationaal Uitg., [1934?]. 149 pp., illus.

1096 SACK, (Dr.): *Der Reichstagsbrandprozess.* Vorw.: Professor Grimm. Berlin: Ullstein, 1934. 346 pp., illus.

1097 STOJANOFF, PETR: *Reichstagsbrand. Die Prozesse in London und Leipzig.* Wien: Europa Verlag, 1966. 347 pp., port., bibl.

1098 TRACHTENBERG, JAKOW: *Gegen das Braunbuch (Rotbuch).* Berlin: Trachtenberg, 1934. 146 pp., ports., maps.

Potsdam ceremonies

1099 HUFFELD, HANS, ed.: *Reichstags-Eröffnungsfeier in Potsdam. Das Erlebnis des 21. März in Wort und Bild.* Potsdam: Hayn, 1933. 60 pp.

1100 *Die Nationalversammlung von Potsdam. Deutschlands grosse Tage 21. bis 23. März 1933.* Mit verbindendem Text von Hans Wendt. Berlin: Mittler, 1933, 48 pp., illus.

30 June 1934 (Night of the Long Knives)

1101 BENNECKE, HEINRICH: *Die Reichswehr und der 'Röhm-Putsch'.* München: Olzog, 1964. 93 pp., bibl. (Beiheft 2: *Politische Studien*).

1102 BLOCH, CHARLES & FAVEZ, JEAN-CLAUDE: *La nuit des longs couteaux.* Paris: Julliard, 1967. 255 pp., illus.

1103 BLOCH, CHARLES: *Die SA und die Krise des NS-Regimes 1934.* Frankfurt a.M.: Suhrkamp, 1970. 176 pp. [Incl. Reichstag fire.]

1104 BREDOW, KLAUS: *Hitler rast. Der 30. Juni. Ablauf, Vorgeschichte und Hintergründe.* Saarbrucken: 1934. 72 pp.

1105   *Der 30. Juni 1934. Hitlers Sieg über Rebellion und Reaktion.* Berlin: Schmidt, [1934?]. 16 pp.

1106   FRANÇOIS, JEAN: *L'affaire Roehm–Hitler.* Alger: Pfister, 1943. 226 pp. [First publ. by Éds. France, 1936.]

1107   GALLO, MAX: *La nuit des longs couteaux. 30 Juin 1934.* Paris: Laffont, 1970. 348 pp., illus., map, bibl. [English version: *The night of long knives.* London: Souvenir Press, 1973.]

1108   *Le Livre Blanc austro-allemand sur les assassinats des 30 Juin et 25 Juillet 1934 (Weissbuch über die Erschiessungen des 30. Juni 1934).* Préface: Georg Branting. Paris: Éds. de la Nouvelle Revue Critique, 1935. 254 pp., tabs., diagr. [German version: *Weissbuch über die Erschiessungen des 30. Juni.* Paris: Éds. du Carrefour, 1934.]

1109   LUDECKE, KURT G. W.: *I knew Hitler. The story of a Nazi who escaped the Blood Purge.* New York: Scribner, 1937. 814 pp., illus., facsims.

1110   STRASSER, OTTO: *Die deutsche Bartolomäusnacht.* Hrsg.: René Sonderegger. 6. Aufl. Zürich: Reso-Verlag, 1935. 241 pp., port. [Contains list of all those murdered.]

Crushing of the opposition and rivals (Gleichschaltung)

1111   KAISENBERG, GEORG: *Gleichschaltung der Länder mit dem Reich.* 7.–8. Taus. Berlin: Heymann, 1933. 20 pp.

1112   *Die neuen Männer. Verzeichnis der Dienststellenbesetzungen in Reichs- und Länderministerien.* Berlin: Junker & Dünnhaupt, 1933. 85 pp.

TIMPKE, HENNING, ed.: *Dokumente zur Gleichschaltung des Landes Hamburg. See* 957.

POLITICAL PARTIES

1113   BAHNE, SIEGFRIED: *Die KPD und das Ende von Weimar. Das Scheitern einer Politik 1932–1935.* Frankfurt a.M.: Campus Verlag, 1976. 184 pp., bibl.

1114   MATTHIAS, ERICH & MORSEY, RUDOLF, eds.: *Das Ende der Parteien 1933.* Düsseldorf: Droste, 1960. 816 pp., illus., tabs. (Veröffentlichungen der Kommission für Geschichte des Parlamentarismus und der politischen Parteien).

1115   MORSEY, RUDOLF: *Der Untergang des politischen Katholizismus. Die Zentrumspartei zwischen christlichem Selbstverständnis und 'Nationaler Erhebung' 1932/33.* Stuttgart: Belser, 1977. 279 pp.

1116   POTTHOFF, HEINRICH: *Die Sozialdemokratie von den Anfängen bis 1945.* 2. Aufl. Bonn: Verlag Neue Gesellschaft, 1978. 229 pp., graphs. [Incl.: viii: 'Die Zerstörung der Demokratie'; ix: 'Im Kampf für ein besseres Deutschland'. Pp. 109–145. Vol. I of *Kleine Geschichte der SPD.*]

1117   RUPPRECHT, ADOLF: *Wie die Nazis das Eigentum der SPD raubten und zerstörten. Aus die Aufzeichnungen eines ehemaligen leitenden sozialdemokratischen Funktionärs.* Berlin [East]: Dietz, 1960. 55 pp.

1118 BLACK, ROBERT: *Fascism in Germany. How Hitler destroyed the world's most powerful labour movement.* London: Steyne Publs., 1975. 1139 + [approx. 150] pp., bibl. In 2 vols.

1119 KRÜGER, OSKAR: *Die Befreiung des deutschen Arbeiters 2. Mai 1933.* München: Eher, 1934. 216 pp.

1120 NASSEN, PAUL: *Kapital und Arbeit im Dritten Reich. Hitlers Mai-Programm und seine Durchführung.* Berlin: Mittler, 1933. 100 pp.

1121 REINHARDT, FRITZ: *Die Arbeitsschlacht der Reichsregierung.* Berlin: Junker & Dünnhaupt, 1933. 87 pp.

1122 SCHUMANN, HANS-GERT: *Nationalsozialismus und Arbeiterbewegung. Die Vernichtung der deutschen Gewerkschaften und der Aufbau der 'Deutschen Arbeits-Front'.* Hannover: Goedel, 1958. 219 pp.

1123 WENDT, HANS: *Der Tag der Nationalen Arbeit. Die Feier des 1. Mai 1933.* Berlin: Mittler, 1933. 50 pp., illus.

STAHLHELM

1124 BERGHAHN, VOLKER R.: *Der Stahlhelm. Bund der Frontsoldaten 1918–1935.* Hrsg.: Kommission für Geschichte des Parlamentarismus und der politischen Parteien. Düsseldorf: Droste, 1966. 304 pp., tabs., diagrs., bibl. [Orig. a thesis pres. to University of London, 1964.]

1125 DUESTERBERG, THEODOR: *Der Stahlhelm und Hitler.* Geleitw.: Wolfgang Müller. Wolfenbüttel: Wolfenbütteler Verlags-Anstalt, 1949. 157 pp.

1126 NATIONALSOZIALISTISCHER DEUTSCHER FRONTSOLDATENBUND (Stahlhelm): *Der NSDFB (Stahlhelm): Geschichte, Wesen und Aufgabe des Frontsoldatenbundes.* Berlin: Freiheitsverlag, 1935. 128 pp., illus., facsim.

KYFFHÄUSER BUND (veterans of former armed services)

1127 *Nachschlagewerk des Deutschen Reichskriegerbundes (Kyffhäuserbund). Zum 150jährigen Bestehen.* Berlin: Deutsche Verlagsgesellschaft, 1936. 588 pp., illus., maps.

1128 REICHSKRIEGERBUND, Propagandaabteilung: *Reichskriegertag Kassel 1937.* Berlin: Kyffhäuser Verlag, 1937. 72 pp., illus.

IV. THE THIRD REICH

A. GENERAL ACCOUNTS

1129 ALEFF, EBERHARD, ed.: *Das Dritte Reich*. Mit Beiträgen von Walter Tormin, Eberhard Aleff, Friedrich Zipfel. 4. neu hrsg. und überarb. Aufl. Hannover: Verlag für Literatur und Zeitgeschehen, 1970. 301 pp., illus. [Orig. ed.: Blase, Alexander, ed. 1963.]

1130 BADE, WILFRID: *Geschichte des Dritten Reiches*. Lübeck: Coleman, 1933– Illus.
Bd. I: *1933—Das Jahr der Revolution*. 118 pp.
Bd. 2: [Hereafter called *Der Weg des Dritten Reiches*]. *1934—Der Aufbau beginnt*. Publ. 1935. 147 pp.
Bd. 3: *1935—Der Kampf um die Freiheit*. Publ. 1936. 165 pp.
Bd. 4: *1936—Das vierte Jahr*. Publ. 1938. 163 pp.

1131 BERNDT, ALFRED-INGEMAR: *1: Meilensteine des Dritten Reiches. Erlebnisschilderungen grosser Tage* [and] *2: Der Marsch ins Grossdeutsche Reich*. Geleitw.: Joachim von Ribbentrop. München: Eher, 1938/39. 238 + 504 pp. In 2 vols.

1132 BRACHER, KARL DIETRICH: *Die deutsche Diktatur. Entstehung, Struktur, Folgen des Nationalsozialismus*. 2. Aufl. Köln: Kiepenheuer & Witsch, 1969. 580 pp., bibl. [English version: *The German dictatorship*. London: Weidenfeld & Nicolson, 1970.]

1133 BREHM, BRUNO: *Das zwölfjährige Reich*. Graz: Verlag Styria, 1960/61.
I: *Der Trommler*. Publ. 1960. 362 pp.
II: *Der böhmische Gefreite*. Publ. 1960. 467 pp.
III: *Wehe den Besiegten allen*. Publ. 1961. 467 pp.

1134 COLLOTTI, ENZO: *La Germania nazista*. Torino: Einaudi, 1962. 395 pp., bibl.

1134a DOUCET, F. W.: *Im Banne des Mythos. Die Psychologie des Dritten Reiches*. Esslingen a.Neckar: Bechtle, 1979. 296 pp.

1135 FREUND, MICHAEL: *Deutschland unterm Hakenkreuz. Die Geschichte der Jahre 1933–1945*. Gütersloh: Bertelsmann, 1965. 479 pp., illus., bibl.

1136 GEHL, WALTHER, ed.: *Die Jahre I–IV des nationalsozialistischen Staates. Grundlagen und Gestaltung. Urkunden des Aufbaus. Reden und Vorträge*. Breslau: Hirt, [1937]. 152 + 228 + 236 + 220 pp., illus., maps. diagrs., tabs.

1137 GISEVIUS, HANS BERND: *Bis zum bittern Ende*. Zürich: Fretz & Wasmuth, 1946. In 2 vols.
I: *Vom Reichstagsbrand zur Fritsch-Krise*.

II: *Vom Münchner Abkommen zum 20. Juli 1944.*
[Also: *Bis zum bitteren Ende. Vom Reichstagsbrand bis zum 20. Juli 1944.*
Hamburg: Rütten & Loening, n.d. 568 pp. (Vom Verfasser auf den neuesten
Stand gebrachte Sonderausg.). And English version: *To the bitter end.*
Westport, Conn.: Greenwood Publ., 1975. 632 pp.]

1138 GÖHRING, MARTIN: *Alles oder Nichts. Zwölf Jahre totalitärer Herrschaft in
Deutschland.* Tübingen: Mohr, 1966–
Bd. 1: *1933–1939.* 354 pp., bibl.

1139 GOLDSTON, ROBERT: *The life and death of Nazi Germany.* Indianapolis, Ind.:
Bobbs-Merrill, 1967. 224 pp., illus., maps. bibl.

1140 HAGEN, LOUIS: *Follow my leader.* London: Wingate, 1951. 374 pp. [Also publ.
as *The mark of the swastika.* London: Corgi Books, 1965.]

1141 HENNIG, EIKE: *Thesen zur deutschen Sozial- und Wirtschaftsgeschichte, 1933
bis 1938.* Frankfurt a.M.: Suhrkamp, 1973. 263 pp., tabs., graphs., bibl.

1142 HEYDECKER, JOE J. & LEEB, J.: *Der Nürnberger Prozess. Bilanz der Tausend
Jahre.* Köln: Kiepenheuer & Witsch, 1958. 609 pp., illus. [A study of the
Third Reich, based on Nuremberg trial proceedings and documents, and
interviews with witnesses.]

1143 HILDEBRAND, KLAUS: *Das Dritte Reich.* München: Oldenburg, 1979. 244 pp.

1144 HUBER, HEINZ & MÜLLER, ARTUR, eds.: *Das Dritte Reich. Seine Geschichte in
Texten, Bildern und Dokumenten.* Mitwirkung: Waldemar Besson. Vorw.:
Hans Bausch. München: Desch, 1964. Illus.
1. Bd.: *Der Aufbau der Macht.* 400 pp.
2. Bd.: *Der Zusammenbruch der Macht.* 855 pp., bibl.

1145 KLEIST, PETER: *Auch Du warst dabei. Ein Beitrag zur Verarbeitung der
Vergangenheit.* Verb. Neuaufl. Göttingen: Schütz, 1959. 372 pp., illus., bibl.
[Reissued 1968 under title *Aufbruch und Sturz des 3. Reiches. Auch Du
warst dabei.* Neo-Nazi view.]

1146 LAMBERT, GABRIEL: *L'Allemagne d'aujourd'hui expliquée par l'Allemagne
d'avant-guerre.* Paris; Renard, 1942. 227 pp.

1147 MAU, HERMANN & KRAUSNICK, HELMUT: *Deutsche Geschichte der jüngsten
Vergangenheit 1933–1945.* Tübingen: Wunderlich, 1956. 207 pp. [English
version: *German history 1933–1945. An assessment by German historians.*
London: Wolff, 1959.]

1148 MERKER, PAUL: *Deutschland—Sein oder nicht sein?* Mexico: Ed. 'El Libro
Libre', 1944/45. Bibls.
1. Bd.: *Von Weimar zu Hitler.* Publ. 1944. 424 pp.
2. Bd.: *Das Dritte Reich und sein Ende.* Publ. 1945. 574 pp., tabs.

1149 NEUMANN, ROBERT: *Hitler. Aufstieg und Untergang des Dritten Reiches. Ein
Dokument in Bildern.* Mitarb.: Helga Koppel. München: Desch, 1961.
250 pp., illus. [Book of illustrations.]

1150 ORB, HEINRICH: *Nationalsozialismus: 13 Jahre Machtrausch.* Olten: Walter, 1945. 451 pp.

1151 PATERNA, ERICH and others: *Deutschland von 1933 bis 1939. Von der Machtübertragung an den Faschismus bis zur Entfesselung des Zweiten Weltkrieges.* [By] Erich Paterna, Werner Fischer, Kurt Gossweiler, Gertrud Markus, Kurt Pätzold. Berlin [East]: VEB Deutscher Verlag der Wissenschaften, 1969. 411 pp., tabs., bibl.

1152 PETWAIDIG, WALTER: *Die autoritäre Anarchie. Streiflichter des deutschen Zusammenbruchs.* Hamburg: Hoffmann & Campe, 1946. 148 pp.

1153 REVENTLOW, Graf E.: *Der deutsche Freiheitskampf. Das grosse Jahrfünft 1933–1938.* Berlin: Andermann, 1938. 476 pp., illus.

1154 RÜHLE, GERD: *Das Dritte Reich. Dokumentarische Darstellung des Aufbaus der Nation.* Mit Unterstützung des Deutschen Reichsarchivs. Berlin: Hummel, 1934/39. Illus.
Die Kampfjahre 1918–1933. Publ. 1936. 427 pp.
Das 1. Jahr—1933. Publ. 1934. 455 pp.
Das 2. Jahr—1934. Publ. 1935. 498 pp.
Das 3. Jahr—1935. Publ. 1937. 518 pp.
Das 4. Jahr—1936. Publ. 1937. 488 pp.
Das 5. Jahr—1937. Publ. 1938. 504 pp.
Das 6. Jahr—1938. Publ. 1939. 562 pp.
[Continued as *Das Grossdeutsche Reich.*]
Die österreichische Kampfjahre 1918–1938. Publ. 1941. 436 pp.

1155 SCHLANGE-SCHOENINGEN, HANS: *The morning after.* Transl.: Edward Fitzgerald. London: Gollancz, 1948. 235 pp. [German original: *Am Tage danach.* Hamburg: Hammerich & Lesser, 1946. An account, begun in 1939, of German history 1919–1945, particularly including life in the Third Reich.]

1156 SHIRER, WILLIAM L.: *The rise and fall of the Third Reich. A history of Nazi Germany.* London: Secker & Warburg, 1960. 1244 pp., bibl. [Also: London: Pan Books, 1964 (12th printing 1979). German version: *Aufstieg und Fall des Dritten Reiches.* Köln: Kiepenheuer & Witsch, 1961.]

1157 STACHURA, PETER D., ed.: *The shaping of the Nazi state.* London: Croom Helm, 1978. 304 pp. [Anthology of articles by Geoffrey Stoakes and others.]

1158 *The Third Reich. Studies by 27 leading historians of the origins and policies of National Socialism.* London: Weidenfeld & Nicolson, 1955. 910 pp.

1159 TURNER, HENRY A. jr., ed.: *Nazism and the Third Reich.* New York: Quadrangle Books, 1972. 262 pp., bibl. [Anthology of articles by Alan Bullock and others.]

1160 VOGELSANG, THILO: *Die nationalsozialistische Zeit. Deutschland 1933 bis 1939.* Frankfurt a.M.: Ullstein, 1967. 178 pp., bibl.

Local and regional

BERLIN

1161 EGGEBRECHT, AXEL: *Volk ans Gewehr. Chronik eines Berliner Hauses 1930–1934.* Frankfurt a.M.: Europäische Verlagsanstalt, 1959. 299 pp., illus. [Also: Berlin: Dietz, 1980. Descriptive novel.]

1162 ENGELBRECHTEN, J. K. von & VOLZ, HANS, eds.: *Wir wandern durch das nationalsozialistische Berlin. Ein Führer durch die Gedenkstätten des Kampfes um die Reichshauptstadt.* Im Auftr. der Obersten SA-Führung bearb. München: Eher, 1937. 275 pp., illus., maps, bibl.

DÜSSELDORF

1163 GÖRGEN, HANS-PETER: *Düsseldorf und der Nationalsozialismus. Studie zur Geschichte einer Grossstadt im 'Dritten Reich'.* Düsseldorf: Schwann, 1969. 254 + 28 pp., illus., facsims., tabs., map, bibl.

EAST PRUSSIA

1164 FRANZ, WALTHER & KRAUSE, ERICH: *Deutsches Grenzland Ostpreussen. Land und Volk in Wort und Bild.* 3. verb. Aufl. Pillkallen-Ostpr.: Boettcher, 1936. 270 pp., illus., maps.

HERNE

1165 MEYERHOFF, HERMANN, ed.: *Herne 1933–1945. Die Zeit des Nationalsozialismus. Ein kommunalhistorischer Rückblick.* Im Auftr. von Oberstadtdirektor Edwin Ostendorf bearb. Stadt Herne: 1963. 154 pp., illus., facsims., tabs., bibl.

MAINZ-KOBLENZ-TRIER

1166 HEYEN, FRANZ JOSEF: *Nationalsozialismus im Alltag. Quellen zur Geschichte des Nationalsozialismus vornehmlich im Raum Mainz-Koblenz-Trier.* Boppard a.Rh.: Boldt, 1967. 372 pp.

MANNHEIM

1167 WALTER, FRIEDRICH: *Schicksal einer deutschen Stadt. Geschichte Mannheims 1907–1945. Bd. II: 1925–1945.* Bearb. im Auftr. der Stadt Mannheim. Frankfurt a.M.: Knapp, 1950. 419 pp., illus., maps, facsims., tabs.

MUNICH

1168 BASIL, FRITZ and others: *Munich. The spirit of a German city.* München: Arbeitsgemeinschaft für Zeitgeschichte, [1939]. 133 pp., illus.

1168a PREIS, KURT: *München unterm Hakenkreuz. Die Hauptstadt der Bewegung— Zwischen Pracht und Trümmern.* München: Ehrenwirth, 1980. 280 pp., illus.

SAXONY

1169 GRUBER, KURT, ed.: *Der Gau Sachsen. Ein Buch der Grenzlandheimat.* Dresden: Kommunal Verlag, 1938. xxxii + 232 pp., illus., maps.

WÜRTTEMBERG

1170 SAUER, PAUL: *Württemberg in der Zeit des Nationalsozialismus.* Ulm: Süddeutsche Verlagsgesellschaft, 1975. 519 pp., illus., facsims., bibl.

B. THE LAND AND THE PEOPLE

1171 AUBIN, HERMANN & ZORN, WOLFGANG, eds.: *Handbuch der deutschen Wirtschafts- und Sozialgeschichte. Bd. II: Das 19. und 20. Jahrhundert.* Stuttgart: Klett, 1976. xiv + 998 pp.

1172 BLUNCK, HANS FRIEDRICH, ed.: *Das Deutschlandbuch.* Berlin: Franke, 1935. 307 pp., illus. [Later ed.: 101.–130. Taus. Mitw.: Hans Brandenburg (and others). 577 pp., illus.]

1173 BROSZAT, MARTIN and others, eds.: *Bayern in der NS-Zeit.* München: Oldenbourg, 1977– (... im Auftr. des Bayerischen Staatsministeriums für Unterricht und Kultus bearb. vom Institut für Zeitgeschichte ...)
Bd. I: *Soziale Lage und politisches Verhalten der Bevölkerung im Spiegel vertraulicher Berichte.* Hrsg.: Martin Broszat, Elke Fröhlich, Falk Wiesemann. Publ. 1977. 712 pp., maps, tabs. [Teil V: 'Judenverfolgung und nichtjüdische Bevölkerung'.]
Bd. 2: *Herrschaft und Gesellschaft im Konflikt. Teil A.* Hrsg.: Martin Broszat, Elke Fröhlich. Publ. 1979. xxv + 517 pp., illus. [Incl.: Ian Kershaw: 'Antisemitismus und Volksmeinung', pp. 281–348.]

1174 *Das Buch der deutschen Gaue.* Bayreuth: Gauverlag Bayerische Ostmark, 1938. 328 pp., illus.

1174a DAVIS, BRIAN LEIGH: *German uniforms of the Third Reich, 1933–1945.* Poole, Dorset: Blandford Press, 1980. 222 pp., illus., tabs.

1175 DONAY, EDUARD: *Die Beziehungen zwischen Herkunft und Beruf. Auf Grund einer statistischen Erhebung in der Dortmunder Bevölkerung.* Vorw.: Otto Graf. Essen: Bacmaister, 1941. 129 pp., diagrs., tabs., bibls.

1176 GAUSS, PAUL, ed.: *Das Buch vom deutschen Volktstum. Wesen—Lebensraum— Schicksal.* Mitarb.: Hektor Ammann-Aarau [and others]. Leipzig: Brockhaus, 1935. 425 pp., illus., maps, bibl.

1177 GRUNBERGER, RICHARD: *A social history of the Third Reich.* London: Weidenfeld & Nicolson, 1971. 535 pp., illus., bibl. [Also: Harmondsworth, Middx.: Penguin Books, 1974. German version: *Das zwölfjährige Reich. Der deutsche Alltag unter Hitler.* Wien: Molden, 1972.

1178 GRUNFELD, FREDERIC V.: *The Hitler file. A social history of Germany and the Nazis, 1918–1945.* Introd.: H. Trevor-Roper. London: Weidenfeld & Nicolson, 1974. 374 pp., illus., facsims.

1179 MOSSE, GEORGE L.: *Nazi culture. Intellectual, cultural and social life in the Third Reich.* Transl. by Salvator Attanasio and others. London: Allen, 1966. 386 pp., illus. [German version: *Der nationalsozialistische Alltag. So lebte man unter Hitler.* Königstein i. Ts.: Athenäum Verlag, 1976.]

1180 MÜLLER, JOSEF: *Ein deutsches Bauerndorf im Umbruch der Zeit: Sulzthal in Mainfranken. Eine Bevölkerungspolitische, soziologische und kulturelle Untersuchung.* Würzburg: Stürtz, 1939. 150 pp., illus., tabs., map.

1181 MUNK, FRANK: *The legacy of Nazism. The economic and social consequences of totalitarianism.* New York: Macmillan, 1943. 288 pp., tabs.

1182 PFLUG, HANS: *Deutschland. Landschaft, Volkstum, Kultur. Ein Handbuch.* Leipzig: Reclam, 1937. 645 pp., illus., maps., diagrs., tabs.

1183 ROSEN, J.: *Das Existenzminimum in Deutschland. Untersuchungen über die Untergrenze der Lebenshaltung.* Zürich: Oprecht, 1939. 90 pp., tabs.

1184 SCHOENBAUM, DAVID: *Hitler's social revolution. Class and status in Nazi Germany, 1933–1939.* London: Weidenfeld & Nicolson, 1967. 336 pp., tabs., bibl. [German version: *Die braune Revolution. Eine sozialgeschichte des Dritten Reiches.* Köln: Kiepenheuer & Witsch, 1980.]

1185 SOHN-RETHEL, ALFRED: *Ökonomie und Klassenstruktur des deutschen Faschismus. Aufzeichnungen und Analysen.* Hrsg.: Johannes Agnoli, Bernhard Blanke, Niels Kadritzke. Frankfurt a.M.: Suhrkamp, 1973. 209 pp. [Written 1937–1941. English version: *Economy and class structure of German fascism.* London: 1978.]

1186 WALTHER, KARL AUGUST: *Deutsches Volk in Arbeit und Wehr.* Berlin: Rödiger, 1937. 196 pp., illus.

1187 WIEBER, IDA: *Ernährung und Kleidung im Dritten Reich. Ein hauswirtschaftliches Fachbuch.* Breslau: Handel, 1938. 103 pp., illus.

C. PERSONAL EXPERIENCES AND ACCOUNTS
By Germans

1188 ABSHAGEN, KARL HEINZ: *Schuld und Verhängnis. Ein Vierteljahrhundert deutscher Geschichte in Augenzeugenberichten.* Stuttgart: Union Verlag, 1961. 300 pp., illus.

1189 BARTHEL, MAX: *Kein Bedarf an Weltgeschichte. Geschichte eines Lebens.* Wiesbaden: Limes Verlag, 1950. 311 pp.

1190 BRÄUTIGAM, OTTO: *So hat es sich zugetragen ... Ein Leben als Soldat und Diplomat.* Würzburg: Holzner, 1968. 723 pp.

1191 BRAUN, MAGNUS von: *Von Ostpreussen bis Texas.* Stollhamm: Rauschenbusch, 1955. 444 pp.

1192 BRENTANO, BERNARD: *Du Land der Liebe. Bericht von Abschied und Heimkehr eines Deutschen.* Tübingen: Wunderlich, 1952. 284 pp.

1193 DREWS, WOLFGANG: *Die klirrende Kette. Nachträgliches Tagebuch eines Journalisten, Dramaturgen und Soldaten, 1933–1945.* Baden-Baden: Keppler, 1947. 281 pp.

1194 EBERMAYER, ERICH: [Memoirs]. Bayreuth: Hestia Verlag, 1966.
Denn heute gehört uns Deutschland ... Persönliches und politisches Tagebuch. Von der Machtergreifung bis zum 31. Dezember 1935. 656 pp.
... und morgen die ganze Welt. Erinnerungen an Deutschlands dunkle Zeit. 442 pp.

1195 GRIMM, FRIEDRICH: *Mit offenem Visier. Aus den Lebenserinnerungen eines deutschen Rechtsanwalts.* Als Biographie bearb. von Hermann Schild. Leoni am Starnberger See: Druffel, 1961. 280 pp., illus.

1196 GRIMM, HANS: *Über mich selbst und über meine Arbeit.* Lippoldsberg: Klosterhaus Verlag, 1975. 179 pp.

1197 HANFSTAENGL, ERNST: *Zwischen Weissem und Braunem Haus. Memoiren eines politischen Aussenseiters.* München: Piper, 1970. 402 pp., illus., facsim. [English version: *Unheard witness.* Also 2nd German ed.: *15 Jahre mit Hitler.* 1980.]

1198 HIELSCHER, FRIEDRICH: *Fünfzig Jahre unter Deutschen.* Hamburg: Rowohlt, 1954. 484 pp. [Mainly Resistance. Description of Lodz Ghetto, pp. 349–368.]

1199 HIERL, KONSTANTIN: *Im Dienst für Deutschland 1918–1945.* Heidelberg: Vowinckel, 1954. 208 pp.

1200 HOEGNER, WILHELM: *Der schwierige Aussenseiter. Erinnerungen eines Abgeordneten, Emigranten und Ministerpräsidenten.* München: Isar Verlag, 1959. 344 pp.

1201 HUBMANN, HANS: *Augenzeuge 1933–1945.* München: Herbig, 1980. 216 pp., illus.

1202 JÜNGER, FRIEDRICH GEORG: *Spiegel der Jahre. Erinnerungen.* München: Hanser, 1958. 275 pp.

1203 KEHRL, HANS: *Krisenmanager im Dritten Reich. 6 Jahre Frieden—6 Jahre Krieg. Erinnerungen.* Mit kritischen Anmerkungen und einem Nachwort von Erwin Viefhaus. Düsseldorf: Droste, 1973. 552 pp.

1204 KROGMANN, CARL VINCENT: *Es ging um Deutschlands Zukunft 1932–1939. Erlebtes täglich diktiert von dem früheren Regierenden Bürgermeister von Hamburg.* Leoni am Starnberger See: Druffel, 1977. 372 pp., illus.

1204a KUHN, HEINZ: *Widerstand und Emigration. Die Jahre 1928–1945.* Hamburg: Hoffmann & Campe, 1980. 357 pp., port. [First vol. of the memoirs of a Social Democrat.]

1205 LANGGÄSSER, ELISABETH: *... soviel berauschende Vergänglichkeit. Briefe 1926–1950.* Hamburg: Claassen, 1954. 251 pp., port.

1206 LEMMER, ERNST: *Manches war doch anders. Erinnerungen eines deutschen Demokraten.* Frankfurt a.M.: Scheffler, 1968. 397 pp., illus., facsim.

1207 LÖWENSTEIN, HUBERTUS Prinz zu: *Botschafter ohne Auftrag. Lebensbericht.* Düsseldorf: Droste, 1972. 231 pp. [Nazi period, pp. 89–219.]

1208 MASCHMANN, MELITA: *Fazit. Kein Rechtfertigungsversuch.* Vorw.: Ida Friederike Görres. Stuttgart: Deutsche Verlags-Anstalt, 1963. 222 pp. [English version: *Account rendered. A dossier on my former self.* Foreword: Lord Russell of Liverpool. London: Abelard-Schumann, 1964.]

1209 MEINECKE, FRIEDRICH: *Die deutsche Katastrophe. Betrachtungen und Erinnerungen.* Wiesbaden: Brockhaus, 1946. 177 pp. [Also 5th ed. 1955. English version: *The German catastrophe.* Cambridge, Mass.: Harvard University Press, 1950.]

1210 MEISSNER, OTTO: *Staatssekretär unter Ebert—Hindenburg—Hitler. Der Schicksalsweg des deutschen Volkes von 1918–1945, wie ich ihn erlebte.* Hamburg: Hoffmann & Campe, 1950. 643 pp., port.

1211 NIEKISCH, ERNST: *Gewagtes Leben. Begegnungen und Begebnisse.* Köln: Kiepenheuer & Witsch, 1958. 390 pp. [Also: Köln: Verlag Wissenschaft und Politik, 1974 (ed. Berend von Nottbeck).]

1212 NIES, ERICH: *Politisches Tagebuch 1935–1945. Historisches Dokument eines deutschen Sozialisten.* Ulm-Donau: Ebner, 1947. 347 pp.

1213 OELFKEN, TAMI: *Das Logbuch.* Berlin: Verlag der Nation, 1955. 323 pp.

1214 PAPEN, FRANZ VON: *Memoirs.* London: André Deutsch, 1952. 630 pp., illus. [German orig.: *Der Wahrheit eine Gasse.* München: List, 1952.]

1215 PÜNDER, HERMANN: *Von Preussen nach Europa. Lebenserinnerungen.* Stuttgart: Deutsche Verlags-Anstalt, 1968. 571 pp., port., facsims.

1216 RUGE, LUDWIG: *Seinen Freunden aus dem Leben erzählt. 19. Januar 1879– 19. Januar 1959.* [Berlin]: Ullstein, 1959. 211 pp.

1217 SCHACHT, HJALMAR: *76 Jahre meines Lebens.* Bad Wörishofen: Kindler & Schiermeyer, 1953. 689 pp., illus. [English version: *My first seventy six years. An autobiography.* London: Wingate, 1955.]

1218 SCHAUMBURG-LIPPE, FRIEDRICH CHRISTIAN Prinz zu: *Als die goldne Abendsonne . . . Aus meinen Tagebüchern der Jahre 1933–1937.* Wiesbaden: Limes Verlag, 1971. 234 pp., illus.

1219 SCHOLTIS, AUGUST: *Ein Herr aus Bolatitz. Lebenserinnerungen.* München: List, 1959. 459 pp.

1220 THAPE, ERNST: *Von Rot zu Schwarz-Rot-Gold. Lebensweg eines Sozialdemokraten.* Hannover: Dietz, 1969. 364 pp., illus. [Incl. material on Buchenwald.]

1221 TSCHIRSCHKY, FRITZ GÜNTER VON: *Erinnerungen eines Hochverräters.* Stuttgart: Deutsche Verlags-Anstalt, 1972. 342 pp., port. [A friend and follower of Ernst Röhm.]

1222 VALTIN, JAN (pseud. of Richard Krebs): *Out of the night.* New York: Alliance Book Corp., 1941. 749 pp. [Autobiography. German version: *Tagebuch der Hölle.* Köln: Kiepenheuer & Witsch, 1957.]

1223 VETTER, LILLI, ed.: *Briefe aus jener Zeit (1933–1945).* Berlin: Arnold, 1948. 203 pp.

1224 WEIZSÄCKER, ERNST VON: *Erinnerungen.* München: List, 1950. 391 pp., port.

Contemporary foreign accounts

1225 BANNISTER, SYBIL: *I lived under Hitler. An Englishwoman's story.* London: Rockcliff, 1957. 264 pp.

1226 BARTLETT, VERNON: *Nazi Germany explained.* London: Gollancz, 1933. 288 pp.

1227 BISE, PIERRE: *Le cauchemar allemand. L'antagonisme des cultures; l'impossible résignation; la guerre!* Paris: Éds. Civis, 1934, 489 pp.

1228 BÖÖK, FREDRIK: *An eyewitness in Germany.* Transl. from the Swedish. London: Lovat Dickson, 1933. 249 pp. [Swedish orig.: *Hitlers Tyskland, Maj 1933.* Stockholm: Norstedt, 1933.]

1229 BOLITHO, GORDON: *The other Germany.* London: Lovat Dickson, 1934. 275 pp., illus.

1230 CERRUTI, ELISABETTA: *Ambassador's wife.* London: Allen & Unwin, 1952. 255 pp.

1231 CHATEAUBRIANT, A[LPHONSE] de: *La gerbe des forces (Nouvelle Allemagne).* Paris: Grasset, 1937. 356 pp.

1232 COLE, J. A.: *Just back from Germany.* London: Faber & Faber, 1938. 333 pp.

1233 COLLINS, SARAH MABEL: *The alien years, being the autobiography of an Englishwoman in Germany and Austria, 1938–1946.* London: Hodder & Stoughton, 1949. 222 pp., port.

1234 CUNNINGHAM, CHARLES: *Germany today and tomorrow.* New York: AMS Press, 1973. 336 pp. [Reprinted from edition of 1936.]

1235 DARCY, PAUL: *Qui gouverne l'Allemagne?* Paris: Baudinière, 1937. 375 pp.

1236 DELMER, SEFTON: [Autobiography]. London: Secker & Warburg, 1961/62.
Vol. I: *Trail sinister.* 423 pp.
Vol. II: *Black boomerang.* 320 pp.
[German version: *Die Deutschen und ich.* Hamburg: Nannen, 1961/62.]

1237 DODD, MARTHA: *Through embassy eyes.* New York: Harcourt, Brace, 1939. 382 pp. [Memoirs of life in Nazi Germany by the daughter of the US ambassador.]

1238 DODD, WILLIAM E. jr. & DODD, MARTHA, eds.: *Ambassador Dodd's diary, 1933–1938.* London: Gollancz, 1941. 452 pp.

1239 DOMVILLE-FIFE, CHARLES W.: *This is Germany. The country, the people and the Third Reich system of life and government, described from personal experience and with the assistance of many of the leaders of both thought and action in the New Germany.* London: Seeley Service, 1939. 288 pp., illus., map, tab. [Pro-Nazi.]

1240 EBENSTEIN, WILLIAM: *The Nazi state.* New York: Farrar & Rinehart, 1943. 355 pp.

1241 FARQUHARSON, ALEXANDER, ed.: *The German mind and outlook.* By G. P. Gooch [and others]. With a summary. London: Chapman & Hall, 1945. vii + 225 pp. [Lectures delivered 1942–1943.]

1242 GIBBS, PHILIP: *Across the frontiers.* London: Michael Joseph, 1938. 336 pp., port.

1243 HAFFNER, SEBASTIAN: *Germany: Jekyll and Hyde.* London: Secker & Warburg, 1940. 327 pp.

1244 HEDIN, SVEN: *Tyskland och världsfreden.* Stockholm: Medén, 1937. 368 pp., illus., maps, tabs., diagr., bibl. [German version: *Fünfzig Jahre Deutschland.* Leipzig: Brockhaus, 1938.]

1245 JONES, THOMAS: *A diary with letters, 1931–1950.* Oxford: Oxford University Press, 1954. 582 pp., illus.

1246 JUVET, RENÉ: *Ich war dabei ... 20 Jahre Nationalsozialismus 1923–1943. Ein Tatsachenbericht.* Zürich: Europa Verlag, 1944. 162 pp.

1247 KENT, MADELEINE: *I married a German.* London: Allen & Unwin, 1938. 349 pp.

1248 KLUIC, STEVO: *Putevi Nemackog preporoda* [German rebirth]. Berlin: Limpert, 1936. 227 pp. [German version: *Ein Reich? Ein Volk? Ein Führer? Gedanken über das neue Deutschland.* Berlin: Brunnen-Verlag, 1937.]

1249 LAURIE, A. P.: *The case for Germany. A study of modern Germany.* Preface: Barry Domvile. Berlin: Internationaler Verlag, 1939. 179 pp., graph.

1250 MOWRER, EDGAR ANSEL: *Germany puts the clock back.* Harmondsworth, Middx.: Penguin Books, 1933. 278 pp.

1251 MÜRER, NIELS J.: *Det nye Tyskland.* Oslo: Aschehoug (Nygaard), 1935. 188 pp., illus.

1252 PASCAL, ROY: *The Nazi dictatorship.* London: Routledge, 1934. viii + 278 pp.

1253 SANTORO, CESARE: *Vier Jahre Hitler-Deutschland von einem Ausländer gesehen.* 2. Aufl. Berlin: Internationaler Verlag, 1937. 336 + 76 pp., illus., diagr., maps. [English version: *Hitler Germany as seen by a foreigner. With ... a supplement 'The new Germany in pictures'.* 3rd Engl. ed. Berlin: 1939. Also publ. in French.]

1254 SHIRER, WILLIAM L.: *Berlin diary. The journal of a foreign correspondent, 1934–1941.* London: Hamish Hamilton, 1941. 491 pp.

1255 SIDGWICK, CHRISTOPHER: *German journey.* London: Hutchinson, 1936. 284 pp., illus. [Incl. visit to Dachau.]

1256 STEED, WICKHAM: *The meaning of Hitlerism.* London: Nisbet, 1934. 208 pp.

1257 STODDARD, LOTHROP: *Into the darkness. Nazi Germany today.* New York: Duell, Sloan & Pearce, 1940. 311 pp.

1258 TAVERNER, ERIC: *These Germans.* London: Seeley, Service, 1937. 242 pp., illus., maps.

1259 TESSAN, FRANÇOIS de: *Voici Adolf Hitler.* [Paris]: Flammarion, 1936. 284 pp. [Ch. VII: 'Les campagnes contre le judaïsme'; Ch. VIII: 'Le conflit avec les églises protestantes'; Ch. IX: 'La "mise au pas" des catholiques'.]

1260 VERMEIL, EDMOND: *L'Allemagne. Essai d'explication.* 10e éd. Paris: Gallimard, 1940. 334 pp. [English version: *Germany's three Reichs. Their history and culture.* London: Dakers, 1944. 420 pp.]

1261 WARD PRICE, G.: *I know these dictators.* London: Harrap, 1937. 256 pp., illus.

1262 WILSON, ARNOLD: *Walks and talks abroad. The diary of a Member of Parliament in 1934–6.* 3rd ed. London: Oxford University Press, 1939. xliii + 292 pp. [Pro-Nazi.]

D. ADMINISTRATION

1. GENERAL

1263 ARNIM, HERBERT VON: *Unser Staat in seinen Gesetzen und Verordnungen. Eine systematische Darstellung seines Wesens und seiner Aufgaben unter Anführung der gesetzlichen Bestimmungen.* Berlin: Kameradschaft Verlagsgesellschaft, 1936. 160 pp., illus.

1264 BAYERISCHER LANDESVERBAND FÜR WANDERDIENST & BAYERISCHES STAATSMINISTERIUM DES INNERN: *Der nichtsesshafte Mensch. Ein Beitrag zur Neugestaltung der Raum und Menschenordnung im Grossdeutschen Reich.* München: Beck, 1938. 466 + xxvi pp., illus., diagrs., tabs., bibl. [Incl. gypsies.]

1265 BOLLMUSS, REINHARD: *Das Amt Rosenberg und seine Gegner. Studien zum Machtkampf im nationalsozialistischen Herrschaftssystem.* Stuttgart: Deutsche Verlags-Anstalt, 1970. 359 pp., tabs., bibl. (notes & bibl. pp. 251–350).

COMMUNAL ADMINISTRATION (GEMEINDEPOLITIK)

1266 *Die deutsche Gemeindeordnung. Ein Leitfaden für nationalsozialistische Parteibeauftragte in der Gemeinde, für Gemeinderäte und Bürgermeister.* Vorw.: Adolf Wagner. München: Eher, 1935. 192 pp.

1267 FIEHLER, KARL (Oberbürgermeister): *Nationalsozialistische Gemeindepolitik.* 7. Aufl. München: Eher, 1933. 80 pp.

1268 FRICK, WILHELM: *Freiheit und Bindung der Selbstverwaltung.* München: Eher, 1937. 52 pp., (Schriften zur deutschen Gemeindepolitik.)

1269 KERRL, HANS & WEIDEMANN, [JOHANNES]: *Die deutsche Gemeindeordnung vom 30. Januar 1935. Kommentar.* Berlin: Verlag für Recht und Verwaltung, 1937. 1098 pp.

1270 MATZERATH, HORST: *Nationalsozialismus und kommunale Selbstverwaltung.* Stuttgart: Kohlhammer, 1970. 503 pp., tabs., bibl.

1271 WEIDEMANN, JOHANNES: *Die Aufsicht des Staates über die Gemeinden.* München: Eher, 1936. 91 pp.

1272 DUSSAUZE, VÉRONIQUE: *L'organisation professionelle en Allemagne.* Préface: René Arnaud. Paris: Presses Universitaires de France, 1943. 137 pp., tabs., diagrs.

1273 HEILIGENTHAL, R.: *Grundlagen der Regionalplanung, Raumplanung und Staatsplanung.* Heidelberg: Winter, 1940. 92 pp., illus., maps, diagrs.

1274 HIPPEL, FRITZ VON: *Die nationalsozialistische Herrschaftsordnung als Warnung und Lehre. Eine juristische Betrachtung.* Tübingen: Mohr, 1946. 55 pp. [Orig. lecture delivered at Marburg University, Feb. 1946.]

1275 KONRAD, FRANZ: *Die persönliche Freiheit im nationalsozialistischen Deutschen Reiche.* Inaugural-Dissertation [pres. to] Ludwig-Maximilians-Universität zu München. 1936. 83 pp., bibl.

1276 LALOIRE, MARCEL: *Nouvelle Allemagne. Réformes sociales et économiques.* Bruxelles: L'Édition universelle, 1935. 272 pp., port., bibl.

1277 LAMMERS, H.-H. & PFUNDTNER, HANS, eds.: *Grundlagen, Aufbau und Wirtschaftsordnung des nationalsozialistischen Staates.* Berlin: Spaeth & Linde, 1936. Maps, diagrs., tabs.
Bd. 1: *Die weltanschaulichen, politischen und staatsrechtlichen Grundlagen des nationalsozialistischen Staates.* [600 pp.]
Bd. 2: *Der Aufbau des nationalsozialistischen Staates.* [590 pp.]
Bd. 3: *Die Wirtschaftsordnung des nationalsozialistischen Staates.* [590 pp.]

1278 MARX, FRITZ MORSTEIN: *Government in the Third Reich.* Foreword: W. Y. Elliott. New York: McGraw-Hill, 1936. 158 pp.

1279 MEIER-BENNECKENSTEIN, PAUL, ed.: *Das Dritte Reich im Aufbau. Übersichten und Leistungsbericht.* Berlin: Junker & Dünnhaupt, 1939/42.
Bd. I: *Grundfragen der deutschen Politik.* 383 pp.
Bd. II: *Der organisatorische Aufbau. Teil I.* 439 pp., diagrs., map.
Bd. III: *Wehrhaftes Volk. Der organisatorische Aufbau. Teil II.* 420 pp., diagrs., tabs.

1280 MÜNZ, LUDWIG, ed.: *Führer durch die Behörden und Organisationen.* Berlin: Duncker & Humblot, 1939. 466 pp. [Previous ed. 1936.]

1281 *Nationalsozialismus in Staat, Gemeinde und Wirtschaft.* Essen: National-Zeitungs-Verlag, 1934. 279 + 174 pp., illus.

1282 [NUREMBERG] GRIESER, UTHO: *Himmlers Mann in Nürnberg: Der Fall Benno Martin. Eine Studie zur Struktur des Dritten Reiches in der 'Stadt der Reichsparteitage'.* Nürnberg: Stadtarchiv, 1974. xxviii + 329 pp., map, bibl.

1282a PETERSON, EDWARD, N.: *The limits of Hitler's power.* Princeton, N.J.: Princeton University Press, 1969. 472 pp., bibl.

1283 [PRUSSIA] RINGLEB, ARNULF: *Die Stellung Preussens im Dritten Reich.* Inaugural-

Dissertation [pres. to] Albertus-Universität zu Königsberg in Preussen. Zeulenroda: Sporn, 1937. 121 pp., bibl.

1284 [REICHSKANZLEI] HEGNER, H. S.: *Die Reichskanzlei 1933–1945. Anfang und Ende des Dritten Reiches*. 4. neubearb. Aufl. Frankfurt a.M.: Verlag Frankfurter Bücher, 1966. 448 pp., illus., tabs., bibl.

REICHSMELDEORDNUNG

1285 SCHLEMPP, HANS, ed.: *Die Reichsmeldeordnung vom 6. Januar 1938 mit der Kennkarten-VO und der Ausländerpolizei-VO sowie den einschlägigen gesetzlichen Bestimmungen und Erlassen.* Einl.: Ralf Zeitler. 6. erw. und ergänz. Aufl. Berlin: Deutscher Gemeindeverlag, 1939. 138 pp.

1286 SCHULZE, GEORGE, ed.: *Die Reichsmeldeordnung und die sonstigen Vorschriften über das Meldewesen und über die Volkspartei.* Für die Praxis bearb. 2. verm. Aufl. Dresden: Gruber, 1942. 247 pp.

REICHSMINISTERIUM DES INNERN

1287 MEDICUS, FRANZ ALBRECHT: *Das Reichsministerium des Innern. Geschichte und Aufbau.* Berlin: Junker & Dünnhaupt, 1940. 88 pp. (Neue Folge der Schriften der Hochschule für Politik).

PFUNDTNER, HANS, ed.: *Dr. Wilhelm Frick und sein Ministerium. See* 769.

REICHSPOST

1288 NAGEL, (Diplom-Ing.) & LAMPE, (Ministerialdirektor): *Die Personalpolitik der Deutschen Reichspost im Dritten Reich.* Berlin: Decker, 1937. 191 pp.

1289 OHNESORGE, W[ILHELM]: *Die Reichspost im Dritten Reich. Vier Aufsätze und Vorträge.* Berlin: Decker, 1937. 105 pp., front.

1290 *Die Reichspost im Staate Adolf Hitlers. Festausgabe der 'Deutschen Verkehrs-Zeitung'. Aus Anlass des 65. Geburtstages des Reichspostministers Dr.-Ing. e.h. Ohnesorge am 8. Juni 1937 hrsg. vom Staatssekretär ... Nagel.* Berlin: Koenig, 1937. 149 pp., illus., fascims., bibl.

1291 RYSZKA, FRANCISZEK: *Państwo stanu wyjatkowego. Rzecz o systemie państwa i prawa Trzeciej Rzeszy* [The martial law state. Comment on the state and legal system of the Third Reich]. Wrocław: Zakład Narodowy imienia Ossolińskich, Wyd. Polskiej Akademii Nauk, 1964. 504 pp., tabs., bibl. (Polski Instytut Spraw Międzynarodowych). [Summaries in Russian, English, German.]

1292 SCHMEER, KARLHEINZ: *Die Regie des öffentlichen Lebens im Dritten Reich.* München: Pohl, 1956. 164 pp.

1293 [THURINGIA] GERBETH, O. & LEONHARDT, WERNER: *Fünf Jahre national-sozialistische Regierung in Thüringen. Ein Rechenschaftsbericht. 1932–26. August 1937.* Frankfurt a.M.: Diesterweg, 1938. 94 pp., tabs.

1294 *Volksabstimmung und Wahl zum Grossdeutschen Reichstag am 10. April 1938.*

Zusammenstellung der gesamten geltenden Wahlberechtigten Bestimmungen mit gesonderter Darstellung des Abstimmungsverfahrens in Österreich. Berlin: Heymann, 1938. 89 pp.

1295 [WESTPHALIA] TEPPE, KARL: *Provinz, Partei, Staat. Zur provinziellen Selbstverwaltung im Dritten Reich untersucht am Beispiel Westfalens.* Münster i.W.: Aschendorff, 1977. x + 300 pp., bibl. (Veröffentlichungen der historischen Kommission für Westfalen).

Awards, flags and orders

1296 BENDER, ROGER JAMES: *For Führer and Fatherland. Political and civil awards of the Third Reich.* San José, Calif.: Bender, 1978. 367 pp., illus., facsims., bibl.

1297 BRINKMANN, JÜRGEN: *Orden und Ehrenzeichen des 'Dritten Reiches'.* Minden: [priv. pr.], 1976. 93 pp., illus.

1298 DOMBROWSKI, HANNS: 'Orden, Ehrenzeichen und Titel des national-sozialistischen Deutschlands. Zusammenstellung von Gesetzen, Verordnungen und Erlassen'. [From] *Sammlung des Wehrrechts,* von Dr. Walter Rehdans. Berlin: Vahlen, 1940. 191 pp.

1299 LITTLEJOHN, DAVID & DODKINS, C. M.: *Orders, decorations, medals and badges of the Third Reich.* Mountain View, Calif.: Bender, 1968/73. Illus., facsims. [Vol. 1]: *... including the Free City of Danzig.* Publ. 1968. 230 pp.
Vol. 2: *... including awards of German 'Volksgruppen' outside the Reich, the pro-Nazi parties of occupied Western Europe and also the puppet states of Croatia and Slovakia.* Assisted by Roger James Bender. Publ. 1973. 192 pp.

1300 WALKER, A. S. and others: *Flags and banners of the Third Reich.* London: Almark, 1973. 136 pp., illus.

2. THE BUREAUCRACY

1301 BORCH, HERBERT von: *Obrigkeit und Widerstand. Zur politischen Soziologie des Beamtentums.* Tübingen: Mohr, 1954. 243 pp.

1302 CAPLAN, JANE: 'Bureaucracy, politics and the National Socialist state'. [In] Stachura, Peter D., ed.: *The shaping of the Nazi state.* Pp. 234–256. *See* 1157.

1303 EBELING, CARL-OTTO: *Grundlagen und wesentliche Merkmale des Beamtenverhältnisses im nationalsozialistischen Staat.* Dissertation [pres. to] Hansische Universität Hamburg. 1936. 56 pp., bibl.

1304 HILBERATH, LEO, ed.: *Bibliographie des kommunalen Schrifttums von 1936 und 1937. Ausbildung der Kommunalbeamten in Deutschland und England.* Mit Beiträgen von Friedrich Schöne und L. Hill. Stuttgart: Kohlhammer, 1938. xi + 584 pp., tabs., bibl.

1305 *Kalender für Reichsjustizbeamte für das Jahr 1938.* Bearb. im Büro des Reichsjustizministeriums. Vorw.: Roland Freisler. 3. Jhrg., 1. Teil. Berlin: Schenck, [1937]. 456 pp., tabs.

1306 MOMMSEN, HANS: *Beamtentum im Dritten Reich. Mit ausgewählten Quellen zur nationalsozialistischen Beamtenpolitik.* Stuttgart: Deutsche Verlags-Anstalt, 1966. 246 pp. (Schriftenreihe der Vierteljahrshefte für Zeitgeschichte).

1307 NEEF, HERMANN: *Die politische Forderung an den Beamten in Recht und Gesetzgebung.* Berlin: Verlag Beamtenpresse, 1937. 23 pp.

1308 NISCHK, KURT: *Der Gemeindebeamte im Dritten Reich. Ein Handbuch und Nachschlagewerk für die Beamten der Gemeinden und Gemeindeverbände.* Leipzig: Rossberg, 1936. xx + 496 pp.

1309 *Personalverzeichnis des höheren Justizdienstes. Ein alphabetisches Verzeichnis der planmässigen Beamten des höheren Justizdienstes mit Angaben über ihre Dienstlaufbahn.* Bearb. im Büro des Reichsjustizministeriums. Berlin: Heymann, 1938. 296 pp.

1310 POLIAKOV, LEON & WULF, JOSEF: *Das Dritte Reich und seine Diener. Dokumente.* Berlin-Grunewald: Arani, 1956. 540 pp.

1311 REICHSBUND DER DEUTSCHEN BEAMTEN: *Almanach der deutschen Beamten.* Berlin: Verlag Beamtenpresse, [1934]. 204 pp., illus.

1312 [REICHSDIENSTSTRAFHOF] *Entscheidungen des Reichsdenststrafhofs.* Hrsg. von Mitgliedern des Gerichtshofs. Berlin: Heymann, 1939–
1. Bd.: Publ. 1939. xvi + 209 pp.
3. Bd.: Publ. 1941. x + 213 pp.

REICHSSTATTHALTER
1313 ARZT, HEINZ: *Der Reichsstatthalter im Gemeinschaftsstaat.* Inaugural-Dissertation [pres. to] Universität Leipzig. Dresden: Deckert, 1937. 88 pp., bibl.

1314 CHEN, YOAU-TING: *Die Stellung und Aufgabe des Reichsstatthalters.* Inaugural-Dissertation. Dresden: Dittert, 1940. 124 pp.

1315 SCHNEIDER, RICHARD and others: *Die Laufbahnen der deutschen Beamten. Ein Nachschlagewerk für Behörden, ein Ratgeber für Zivil- und Versorgungsanwärter.* Vorw.: Dr. Schütze. Berlin: Verlag Beamtenpresse, 1939. Tabs., diagrs.
Bd. 1: *Kommentar zur Verordnung über die Vorbildung und die Laufbahnen der deutschen Beamten. Vom 28. Februar 1939.* 345 pp.
Bd. II: *Justizverwaltung: Mittlerer Dienst (Justizassistent, Gerichtsvollzieher, Justizvollstreckungsassistent) erläutert …* 260 pp.

1316 *Verzeichnis der oberen Reichsbahnbeamten 1944. 39. Jhrg.* Leipzig: Verkehrswissenschaftliche Lehrmittelgesellschaft, 1943. 771 pp., port., tabs.

The law relating to civil servants (Beamtenrecht)

1317 *ABC des deutschen Beamtengesetzes. Alphabetischer Führer durch das DBG.* Hrsg.: Hauptamt für Beamte der Reichsleitung der NSDAP. 2. verm. und verb. Aufl. Berlin: Verlag Beamtenpresse, 1940. 127 pp.

1318 *Deutsches Beamtengesetz und Reichsdienststrafordnung vom 26. Januar 1937.* *Mit ausführlichem Sachregister.* Stuttgart: Kohlhammer, 1937. 236 pp.

1319 MÜLLER, HEINZ and others: *Neues Beamtenrecht für Grossdeutschland.* [By] Heinz Müller, Walther Eckhardt, Fritz Reuter. 7. ergänz. Aufl. Leipzig: Kohlhammer, 1944. 123 pp.

1320 RASCH, HAROLD: *Wiederherstellung des Berufsbeamtentums. Die Gesetze und Verordnungen des Reichs und die Ausführungsvorschriften Preussens in der am 15. Oktober 1933 gültigen Fassung.* Berlin: Heymann, 1934. 56 pp.

1321 SAUER, FRANZ, ed.: *Beamtenrecht des Reichs. Sammlung der für die Beamten geltenden reichsrechtlichen Bestimmungen (einschliesslich Notverordnungen). Mit zahlreichen Quellennachweisungen, Fundstellen, Behörden und Sachregister.* Berlin: Schwabacher, 1933. 295 pp.

1322 WITTLAND, HERMANN: *Beamtenkriegsrecht. Textausgabe der aus Anlass des Krieges auf dem Gebiete des Beamtenrechts erlassenen Vorschriften. Zusammengestellt nach dem Stande vom 1. Juli 1941.* Berlin: de Gruyter, 1941. 305 pp.

3. LAW

1323 BOCKHOFF, E. H.: *Völker-Recht gegen Bolschewismus.* Vorw.: Hans Frank. Berlin: Nibelungen Verlag, 1937. 251 pp.

1324 BRODERSEN, UWE, comp.: *Gesetze des NS-Staates.* Einl.: Ingo von Münch. Bad Homburg: Gehlen, 1968. 195 pp., bibl.

1325 DEHLINGER, A., ed.: *Systematische Übersicht über 77 Jahrgänge Reichsgesetzblatt (1867–1943), das geltende alte und neue Reichsrecht und das Recht der Reichsverteidigung. 21. Aufl. nach dem Stand vom 1. Januar 1944.* Stuttgart: Kohlhammer, 1944. 136 pp.

1326 ECHTERHÖLTER, RUDOLF: *Das öffentliche Recht im nationalsozialistischen Staat.* Stuttgart: Deutsche Verlags-Anstalt, 1970. 343 pp.

1327 FRANK, HANS: *Nationalsozialistisches Handbuch für Recht und Gesetzgebung.* München: Eher, 1935. 1604 pp., bibls. after each ch.

1328 FREITAG, HERMANN: *Staatsbegriff und Staatsperson im Dritten Reich.* Inaugural-Dissertation [pres. to] Johann Wolfgang Goethe-Universität zu Frankfurt a.M. Frankfurt a.M.: Kalbfleisch, 1937. 47 pp., bibl.

1329 FUHRMANN, E.: *Wirtschafts-Strafverordnungen.* Berlin: Schweitzer, 1943. 203 pp.

1330 *Handbuch der Justizverwaltung.* Bearb. im Büro des Reichsjustizministeriums. Berlin: Schenck, 1942. 427 pp.

1331 HOCHE, WERNER, ed.: *Gesetzgebung Adolf Hitlers für Reich, Preussen, Österreich und die Sudetendeutschen Gebiete.* Berlin: Vahlen, 1939. 331 pp.

1332 IPSEN, HANSPETER: *Politik und Justiz. Das Problem der justizlosen Hoheitsakte.* Hamburg: Hanseatische Verlagsanstalt, 1937. 335 pp., bibl.

1333 KÖLBLE, J.: *Behördenfeindliche Verwaltungsjustiz.* Berlin: Deutscher Rechtsverlag, 1937. 57 pp., bibl.

1334 MEYER, OTTO: *Geschäftsgang und Geschäftsleitung bei den Justizbehörden. Stand vom 1. Juli 1944.* 4. verb. Aufl. Berlin: Deutscher Verlag, 1944. 112 pp.

1335 [REICHSJUSTIZMINISTERIUM] SAUER, FRANZ: *Das Reichsjustizministerium.* Berlin: Junker & Dünnhaupt, 1939. 63 pp. (Schriften der Hochschule für Politik).

1336 SAUER, WILHELM: 'Recht und Volksmoral im Führerstaat. Zu den Grundfragen der deutschen Rechtserneuerung'. Sonderdruck aus dem *Archiv für Rechts- und Sozialphilosophie*, Bd. XXVIII, Heft 2. Berlin: Verlag für Staatswissenschaften und Geschichte, [1934?]. Pp. 230–274.

1337 RÜTHERS, BERND: *Die unbegrenzte Auslegung. Zum Wandel der Privatrechtordnung im Nationalsozialismus.* Tübingen: Mohr, 1968. xvii + 496 pp., bibl.

1338 SCHLEGELBERGER/HOCHE: *Das Recht der Neuzeit. Ein Führer durch das geltende Recht des Grossdeutschen Reichs und das preussische Landesrecht 1914–1943.* 18. Ausg. von Werner Hoche. Berlin: Vahlen, 1943. 594 pp.

1339 SCHORN, HUBERT: *Die Gesetzgebung des Nationalsozialismus als Mittel der Machtpolitik.* Frankfurt a.M.: Klostermann, 1963. 175 pp., bibl. [Incl.: ix: 'Gesetzgebung und Judentum'; x: 'Gesetzgebung und Kirchenpolitik'; xi: 'Die Gesetzgebung zur nationalsozialistischen Rassenlehre'.]

1340 STÖCKMANN, ALBERT: *Der Vollstreckungsrichter und seine Abteilung.* Berlin: Deutscher Rechtsverlag, 1936. 140 pp.

1341 STOLLEIS, MICHAEL: *Gemeinwohlformeln im nationalsozialistischen Recht.* Berlin: Schweitzer, 1974. xxv + 315 pp., bibl. (Münchener Universitätsschriften, Juristische Fakultät).

VERWALTUNGSRECHT (Administrative law)

1342 FRANK, HANS, ed.: *Deutsches Verwaltungsrecht.* Unter Mitwirkung von Werner Best, Wilhelm Coblitz (Schriftleitung) [and others]. München: Eher, 1937. xxiii + 516 pp.

1343 MEISSNER, OTTO & RAISENBERG, GEORG: *Staats- und Verwaltungsrecht im Dritten Reich.* Berlin: Verlag für Sozialpolitik, Wirtschaft und Statistik, 1935. xvi + 357 pp.

1344 WEINKAUFF, HERMANN & WAGNER, ALBRECHT: [Comprising] Hermann Weinkauff: *Die deutsche Justiz und der Nationalsozialismus. Ein Überblick.* 187 pp.; Albrecht Wagner: *Die Umgestaltung der Gerichtsverfassung und des Verfahrens- und Richterrechts im nationalsozialistischen Staat.* Pp. 191–382. Stuttgart: Deutsche Verlags-Anstalt, 1968.

Constitution

1345 BROSZAT, MARTIN: *Der Staat Hitlers: Grundlegung und Entwicklung seiner inneren Verfassung.* München: Deutscher Taschenbuch Verlag, 1969. 472 pp., tab., bibl.

1346 HUBER, ERNST: *Verfassung.* Hamburg: Hanseatische Verlagsanstalt, 1937. 238 pp. [Also: 2. stark erw. Aufl. *Verfassungsrecht des Grossdeutschen Reiches.* 1939. 527 pp.]

1347 SARTORIUS, CARL: *Verfassungs- und Verwaltungsrecht. Sammlung von Reichs-Gesetzen, -Verordnungen und -Erlassen. Textausgabe mit Anmerkungen und Sachverzeichnis. Ergänzt nach dem Stand vom März 1940.* München: Beck, 1940. [320 pp.]

1348 STUCKART, WILHELM & SCHIEDERMAIR, ROLF: *Neues Staatsrecht.* Leipzig: Kohlhammer, 1944.
I: *Der neue Reichsaufbau.* 19. ergänz. Aufl. 152 pp.
II: *Die Errichtung des Grossdeutschen Reiches.* 19. umgearb. und ergänz. Aufl. 134 pp.

Racial and citizenship law

1349 *Änderung von Familiennamen und Vornamen. Textausgabe des Gesetzes vom 3. Januar 1938 ...* München: König, 1938. 47 pp.

1350 BEHN, JOACHIM: *Auswirkungen der Rassegesetzgebung auf das zwischenstaatliche Recht.* Inaugural-Dissertation [pres. to] Universität zu Greifswald. 1936. 79 pp., bibl.

1351 BLAU, BRUNO, ed.: *Das Ausnahmerecht für die Juden in den europäischen Ländern 1933–1945. I. Teil: Deutschland.* 2. Aufl. Düsseldorf: Verlag Allgemeine Wochenzeitung der Juden in Deutschland, 1954. 125 pp., bibl. [First ed.: New York: priv. pr., 1952.]

1352 COHN, HEINZ & GOTTFELD, ERICH: *Auswanderungs-Vorschriften für Juden in Deutschland.* Berlin: Jastrow, 1938. 112 pp.

1353 DAWID, HEINZ: *Die Rechtsstellung der Juden und der jüdischen Mischlinge in Deutschland.* Berlin: Als Manuskript gedruckt, Juli 1936. 170 pp.

1354 DEEG, PETER, comp.: *Die Judengesetze Grossdeutschlands.* Hrsg.: Julius Streicher. Nürnberg: Verlag 'Der Stürmer', 1939. 243 pp.

1355 HOFFMANN, BRUNO: *Die Ausnahmegesetzgebung gegen die Juden von 1933–1945 unter besonderer Berücksichtigung der Synagogengemeinde Köln.* Inaugural-Dissertation [pres. to University of Cologne]. [1963?]. 121 pp., bibl.

1356 LISSNER, JACOB: *Jüdische Ausländer und Staatenlose in Deutschland. Ihre Rechte und Pflichten.* Berlin: Jüdischer Buchverlag, 1938. 48 pp.

1356a MAJER, DIEMUT: *'Fremdvölkische' im Dritten Reich. Ein Beitrag zur nationalsozialistischen Rechtssetzung und Rechtspraxis in Verwaltung und Justiz unter besonderer Berücksichtigung der eingegliederten Ostgebiete und*

111

des Generalgouvernements. Boppard a.Rh.: Boldt, 1981. 1034 pp.,map, bibl. (Schriften des Bundesarchivs).

1357 MISCH, CARL, ed.: *Gesamtverzeichnis der Ausbürgerungslisten 1933–1938. Nach dem amtlichen Abdruck des 'Reichsanzeigers' zusammengestellt ...* Paris: Verlag der 'Pariser Tageszeitung', 1939. [64 pp.]

NUREMBERG LAWS

1358 BECKER, HEINZ: *Die Rassenschande. (2. Teil des Gesetzes zum Schutze des deutschen Blutes und der deutschen Ehre).* Dissertation [pres. to] Universität Giessen. Düsseldorf: Nolte, 1937. 48 pp.

1359 DEISZ, ROBERT: *Das Recht der Rasse. Kommentar zur Rassengesetzgebung.* München: Eher, 1938. 324 pp.

1360 GÜTT, ARTHUR and others: *Blutschutz und Ehegesundheitsgesetz. Gesetz zum Schutze des deutschen Blutes und der deutschen Ehre und Gesetz zum Schutze der Erbgesundheit des deutschen Volkes nebst Durchführungsverordnungen sowie einschlägigen Bestimmungen. Dargestellt, medizinisch und juristisch erläutert.* Mitw.: Herbert Linden, Franz Massfeller. München: Lehmann, 1936. 354 pp.

1361 LÖSENER, .BERNHARD & KNOST, FRIEDRICH A.: *Die Nürnberger Gesetze mit den Durchführungsverordnungen und den sonstigen einschlägigen Vorschriften.* 5. Aufl. Berlin: Vahlen, 1942. 296 pp.

1362 MÜLLER, WILLI: *Das ius sanguinis der Nürnberger Gesetze in Bedeutung für das Völkerrecht.* Dissertation [pres. to] Universität Heidelberg. Ladenburg: Nerlinger, 1938. 71 + 3 pp., bibl.

1363 STUCKART, WILHELM & GLOBKE, HANS: *Kommentare zur deutschen Rassengesetzgebung. Reichsbürgergesetz, Blutschutzgesetz, Ehegesundheitsgesetz.* München: Beck, 1936. 287 pp.

1364 VERSPOHL, HERMANN: *Deutschblütige Angestellte im jüdischen Haushalt im Lichte des Strafrechts.* Dissertation [pres. to] Universität zu Göttingen. Bochum: Pöppinhaus, 1938. 85 + 4 pp., bibl.

1365 SCHMIDT-KLEVENOW, KURT: *Mischehen-Vorschriften. Eine Zusammenstellung sämtlicher Bestimmungen mit einer graphischen Darstellung.* Berlin: Deutscher Rechts-Verlag, 1938. 15 pp.

1366 SEEBACH, WERNER Frhr. von: *Änderungen des deutschen Staatsangehörigkeitsrechtes seit dem 30. Januar 1933.* Bleicherode a. Harz: Nieft, 1936. 65 pp.

1367 SIGG, MARIANNE: *Das Rassestrafrecht in Deutschland in den Jahren 1933–1945, unter besonderer Berücksichtigung des Blutschutzgesetzes.* Aarau: Sauerländer, 1951. 126 pp. (Zürcher Beiträge zur Rechtswissenschaft).

1368 WITTELSHÖFER, FRITZ: *Sozial- und Wirtschaftsrecht. Ausgew. und bearb. für die Bedürfnisse der Juden in Deutschland.* Mitw.: Kurt Friedländer, Georg Lubinski, Gerhard Wallbach. Berlin: Zentralwohlfahrtsstelle ... bei der Reichsvertretung der Juden in Deutschland, 1936. 113 pp. + 2 suppl.

1369 WITTKEN, JUNGNIK Frhr. von: *Die nationalsozialistischen Blutschutzgesetze im Spiegel des urarischen Strafrechts.* Berlin: Mittler, 1938. 214 pp., bibl.

Criminal law

1370 FRANK, HANS: *Nationalsozialistische Strafrechtspolitik.* München: Eher, 1938. 50 pp.

1371 FRANK, HANS, ed.: *Nationalsozialistische Leitsätze für ein neues deutsches Strafrecht.*
1. Teil: 2. Aufl. Berlin: Deutsche Rechts- und Wirtschaftswissenschaft, 1935. 43 pp.
Besonderer (2.) Teil: Berlin: Deutscher Rechts-Verlag, 1936. 147 pp.

1372 FREISLER, ROLAND and others: *Deutsches Strafrecht. Bd. 1: Erläuterungen zu den seit dem 1.9.1939 ergangenen strafrechtlichen und straf-verfahrensrechtlichen Vorschriften.* [By] Roland Freisler, Fritz Grau, Karl Krug, Otto Rietzsch. Berlin: Schenck, 1941. 747 pp.

1373 FREISLER, ROLAND and others: *Der Ehrenschutz im neuen deutschen Strafverfahren. Gemeinschafts-Arbeit.* Technische Gesamtleitung: Dr. Lehmann. Geleitw.: Franz Gürtner. Berlin: Schenck (Decker), 1937. 212 pp.

1374 GÜRTNER, FRANZ, ed.: *Bericht der amtlichen Strafprozesskommission.* Mitw.: [Roland] Freisler [and others]. Berlin: Schenck (Decker), 1938. 624 pp.

1375 GÜRTNER, FRANZ & FREISLER, ROLAND: *Das neue Strafrecht. Grundsätzliche Gedanken zum Geleit.* Einführende Worte: Rüdiger Graf von der Goltz. Berlin: Schenck (Decker), 1936. 216 pp., bibl.

1376 MENSCHELL, WOLFGANG: *Das gesamte deutsche Gnadenrecht nebst verwandten Gebieten. Texte mit Anmerkungen.* 5. neubearb. Aufl. Berlin: Deutscher Rechtsverlag, 1943. 544 pp.

1377 OLCZEWSKI, HELMUTH: *Strafverfahren, Strafvollstreckung und Gnadenrecht.* Berlin: Deutscher Rechtsverlag, 1940. 192 pp.

1378 PETERS, KARL: 'Die Umgestaltung des Strafgesetzes in den Jahren 1933–1945'. [In] Andreas Flitner, ed.: *Deutsches Geistesleben und Nationalsozialismus.* Pp. 160–177. *See 2480.*

1379 RÖSCHEL, ALFRED & BLAESE, ERNST: *Die Strafvollstreckung. Durchführung der Vollstreckung gerichtlicher Strafen mit Beispielen.* Berlin: de Gruyter, 1944. 280 pp.

1380 STATISTISCHES REICHSAMT: *Kriminalstatistik für das Jahr 1934. Mit Hauptergebnisse für das Jahr 1936.* Bearb. im Reichs-Justizministerium und im Statistischen Reichsamt. Berlin: Verlag für Sozialpolitik, Wirtschaft und Statistik, 1938. 285 pp., tab.

1381 *Strafgesetzbuch, Strafprozessordnung, Gerichtsverfassungsgesetz, nebst einigen ergänzenden Vorschriften in ihrer vom 1.1.1934 ab geltenden Fassung. Für den Dienstgebrauch zusammengestellt im Preussischen Justizministerium.* [Berlin: 1934]. 316 pp.

TREASON

1382 BRUNE, HORST: *Hochverrat und Landesverrat in rechtsvergleichender Darstellung auf Grund der neuesten strafrechtlichen Entwicklung.* Breslau-Neukirch: Kurtze, 1937. 157 pp.

1383 SCHULTZ, GERHARD: *Staatsauffassung und Staatsverbrechen insbesondere das Verbrechen des Hochverrats.* Inaugural-Dissertation [pres. to] Friedrich Wilhelm-Universität Berlin. Breslau-Neukirch: Kurtze, 1940. 180 pp.

4. COURTS OF LAW

Judges and advocates

DEUTSCHE RECHTSFRONT

1384 GAEB, WILHELM: *Die Deutsche Rechtsfront. Ziele, Leistungen und Organisation.* Berlin: Junker & Dünnhaupt, 1935. 31 pp., bibl. (Schriften der Deutschen Hochschule für Politik).

1385 KNÖPFEL, HANS ERWIN: *Drei Jahre Kampf für deutsches Recht. Ein Bericht über die rechtsschöpferische Arbeit in den Zeitschriften der Deutschen Rechtsfront.* Berlin: Deutscher Rechts-Verlag, 1936. 86 pp.

1386 EHRENGERICHTSHOF DER REICHS-RECHTSANWALTS-KAMMER: *Entscheidungen, Band XXXI (neue Folge Band IV), Jahr 1937 nebst Inhaltsverzeichnis.* Hrsg.: Präsidium der Reichs-Rechtsanwalts-Kammer. Berlin: 1938. 183 pp.

1387 GLÖCKLER, OTTO: *Die Zulassung zur Rechtsanwaltschaft insbesondere seit 1933.* Würzburg: Triltsch, 1937. v + 76 pp.

1388 HENKEL, HEINRICH: *Die Unabhängigkeit des Richters in ihrem neuen Sinngehalt.* Hamburg: Hanseatische Verlagsanstalt, 1934. 35 pp.

1389 *Justizausbildungsordnung vom 4. Januar 1939, mit dem gesamten sonstigen Prüfungs- und Ausbildungsrecht für Gerichts- und Regierungsreferendare und -assessoren im Altreich, Österreich, Sudetenland, die Bestimmungen über Unterhalt und Vergütung während der Vorbereitungszeit und vielen Vorschriften über die zugehörigen Berufslaufbahnen. Textausgabe mit Anmerkungen und Sachverzeichnis.* 2. Aufl. München: Beck, 1939. 104 pp.

1390 KÜHNE, LOTAR: *Der Verteidiger ohne fremdrechtliches Gewand.* Berlin-Südende: Sudau, 1937. 86 pp., bibl.

1391 NATIONALSOZIALISTISCHER RECHTSWAHRERBUND: *Der Deutsche Rechtsstand.* Berlin: Deutscher Rechtsverlag, 1939. 372 pp., illus.

1392 NEUBERT, REINHARD: *Anwalt in der Politik.* Berlin: Spaeth & Linde, 1939. 262 pp.

1393 *Reichs-Rechtsanwaltsordnung in der Fassung vom 21. Februar 1936, nebst der Allgemeinen Verfügung über die Zulassung als Rechtsanwalt ... sowie anderen einschlägigen Vorschriften.* München: Beck, 1936. 83 pp.

1394 RONGE, PAUL: *Im Namen der Gerechtigkeit. Erinnerungen eines Strafverteidigers.* München: Kindler, 1963. 442 pp., port.

1395 ROTHENBERGER, CURT: *Der deutsche Richter.* Geleitw.: Reichsjustizminister Dr. Thierack. Hamburg: Hanseatische Verlagsanstalt, 1943. 215 pp.

1396 SCHORN, HUBERT: *Der Richter im Dritten Reich. Geschichte und Dokumente.* Frankfurt a.M.: Klostermann, 1959. 742 pp., facsim., tab.

1397 SCHRAUT, RUDOLF, ed.: *Deutscher Juristentag 1933. 4. Reichstagung des Bundes Nationalsozialistischer Deutscher Juristen. Ansprachen und Fachvorträge.* Berlin: Deutsche Rechts- und Wirtschafts-Wissenschaft Verlag, 1933. 326 pp., illus.

1398 SEGELKEN, HANS: *Amor fati. Aufzeichnungen aus einer gescheiterten Juristengeneration.* Hamburg: Talkner, [1970]. 390 pp.

1399 SINGER, J., ed.: *Rechtspfleger Jahrbuch.* Berlin: Deutsche Rechts- und Wirtschafts-Wissenschaft Verlag, [1935]; Deutscher Rechtsverlag, 1936–1943. [Issued yearly.]

Military courts

1400 *Entscheidungen des Reichskriegsgerichts.* Hrsg. als Kameradschaftsarbeit von Angehörigen des Reichskriegsgericht. 2. Bd., 1. Heft. Berlin: Vahlen, 1940. 64 pp.

1401 FRASCHKA, GÜNTER: *Fertigmachen zum Erschiessen. Zwischen Willkür und Gewissen. Acht Kriegsgerichtsfälle.* 2. Aufl. Rastatt/Baden: Pabel, 1960. 248 pp.

1402 MÖRBITZ, H.: *'Hohes Kriegsgericht!' Ein Tatsachenbericht nach den Erlebnissen eines Kriegsgerichtsverteidigers.* Wien: CFH-Verlag, 1968. 340 pp.

1403 NÜSE, KARL-HEINZ: *Das Kriegsstrafrecht und Kriegsstrafverfahren mit Erläuterungen und Durchführungsbestimmungen.* Bad Oeynhausen: Lutzeyer, 1940. 128 pp.

People's Court (Volksgericht)

1404 BUCHHEIT, GERT: *Richter in roter Robe. Freisler, Präsident des Volksgerichtshofes.* München: List, 1968. 294 pp., illus., facsims., bibl.

1405 FREISLER, ROLAND and others: *Der Volksrichter in der neuen deutschen Strafrechtspflege. Gemeinschaftsarbeit.* Vorw.: Rüdiger Graf von der Goltz. Berlin: Schenck (Decker), [1936]. 212 pp., diagr., tabs.

1406 *'... Für immer ehrlos'. Aus der Praxis des Volksgerichtshofes.* Berlin: Landeszentrale für politische Bildungsarbeit, 1978. 46 pp., facsims. (Beiträge zum Thema Widerstand).

1406a HILLERMEIER, HEINZ, ed.: *'Im Namen des deutschen Volkes'. Todesurteile des Volksgerichtshofes*. Darmstadt: Luchterhand, 1980.

1407 SCHULTZE-PFAELZER, GERHARD: *Kampf um den Kopf. Meine Erlebnisse als Gefangener des Volksgerichtshofes 1943–1945*. Berlin: Weichert, 1948. 287 pp.

1408 WAGNER, WALTER: *Der Volksgerichtshof im nationalsozialistischen Staat*. Stuttgart: Deutsche Verlags-Anstalt, 1974. 991 pp., tabs. [Incl.: 'Die Kommunisten'; 'Die demokratische Linke'; 'Die "Nacht und Nebel" Verfahren'; '20. Juli 1944'; 'Die Ära Freisler'.]

Reichsgericht

1409 [BUMKE, ERWIN] KOLBE, DIETER: *Reichsgerichtspräsident Dr. Erwin Bumke. Studien zum Niedergang des Reichsgerichts und der deutschen Rechtspflege*. Karlsruhe: Müller, 1975. 431 pp., illus., bibl.

1410 KAUL, FRIEDRICH-KARL: *Geschichte des Reichsgerichts. Bd. IV: 1933–1945*. Mitarb.: Winfried Matthäus ... Berlin [East]: Akademie-Verlag, 1971. 356 pp., facsims., tabs., bibl. (Veröffentlichung ... der Humboldt-Universität zu Berlin). [Incl. lists of judges and lawyers.]

1411 SCHACK, HANS: *Vier Jahre Rechtsprechung des Reichsgerichts auf dem Gebiete des privaten Versicherungsrechts (1933–1936)*. Leipzig: Möser, 1937. 95 pp.

Sondergericht

1412 PAWLAS, KARL R., ed.: *Sondergerichte im 3. Reich*. Nürnberg: Publizistisches Archiv, [196–?]. [80 pp.], illus., facsims.

Perversion of justice

1413 BOBERACH, HEINZ, ed.: *Richterbriefe. Dokumente zur Beeinflussung der deutschen Rechtsprechung 1942–1944*. Mit Beiträgen von Robert M. H. Kempner, Theo Rasehorn. Boppard a.Rh.: Boldt, 1975. xxviii + 515 pp., bibl. (Schriften des Bundesarchivs).

HAMBURG

1414 JOHE, WERNER: *Die gleichgeschaltete Justiz. Organisation des Rechtswesens und Politisierung der Rechtsprechung 1933–1945 dargestellt am Beispiel des Oberlandesgerichtsbezirk Hamburg*. Frankfurt a.M.: Europäische Verlags-Anstalt, 1967. 258 pp., bibl.

1415 ROBINSON, HANS: *Justiz als politische Verfolgung. Die Rechtsprechung in 'Rassenschandefällen' beim Landgericht Hamburg 1936–1943*. Stuttgart: Deutsche Verlags-Anstalt, 1977. 167 pp., tabs., bibl. (Schriftenreihe der Vierteljahrshefte für Zeitgeschichte).

1416 HIPPEL, FRITZ VON: *Die Perversion von Rechtsordnungen*. Tübingen: Mohr, 1955. 213 pp.

1417 KLÜTZ, ALFRED: *Volksschädlinge am Pranger. Aufklärungsschrift im grossdeutschen Freiheitskampf.* Vorw.: Staatssekretär Dr. Freisler. Berlin: Hillger, 1940. 96 pp.

1418 PÜSCHEL, WILHELM: *Der Niedergang des Rechts im Dritten Reich.* Reutlingen: Verlag 'Die Zukunft', 1947. 124 pp.

1419 ROETTER, FRIEDRICH: *Might is right.* London: Quality Press, 1939. 417 pp.

1420 STAFF, ILSE, ed.: *Justiz im Dritten Reich. Eine Dokumentation.* 2. Aufl. Frankfurt a.M.: Fischer, 1978. 234 pp., facsims., bibl. [First ed. 1964.]

1421 TIMOROUMENOS, pseud.: *La robe brune. Trois années de justice nationale-socialiste, en matière civile et criminelle, d'après les jugements et arrêtes des tribunaux allemands.* Préface: Henry Torrès. Paris: Éds. Logos, 1936. 154 pp.

1422 *Der Unrechts-Staat. Recht und Justiz im Nationalsozialismus.* Mit Beiträgen von Bernhard Blanke [and others]. Red.: Kritische Justiz. Frankfurt a.M.: Europäische Verlagsanstalt, 1979. 211 pp.

E. THE NEW SOCIAL SYSTEM

1. WELFARE AND HEALTH

1423 GÜTT, ARTHUR: *Der Aufbau des Gesundheitswesens im Dritten Reich.* Berlin: Junker & Dünnhaupt, 1935. 64 pp., diagr.

1424 HILDEBRANDT, WILHELM: *Rassenmischung und Krankheit. Ein Versuch.* Bearb. des hinterlassenen Manuskripts H. Herling. Geleitw.: Kurt Klare. Stuttgart: Hippokrates-Verlag, 1935. 122 pp., illus., tab., diagrs.

1425 MANNEWITZ, RUDOLF: *Morbidität und Mortalität im Deutschen Reich, ihre zeitliche Entwicklung und ihre räumlichen Unterschiede.* Dresden: Dittert, 1941. 224 pp., tabs., bibl.

1426 SCHILLING, VICTOR: *Blut und Erbe. Über die Eigenschaften des Blutes, seine Aufgaben im menschlichen Körper und über seine Rolle als Vererbungsträger mit Einschluss der erblichen Blutkrankheiten.* Hamburg: Hanseatische Verlagsanstalt, 1936. 94 pp., illus., diagrs.

1427 SCHOTTKY, JOHANNES, ed.: *Rasse und Krankheit.* München: Lehmann, 1937. 468 pp., illus., tabs., diagrs., maps, bibls. after each of 16 contributions.

1428 SEIDLER, FRANZ: *Prostitution, Homosexualität, Selbstverstümmelung. Probleme der deutschen Sanitätsführung 1939–1945.* Neckargemünd: Vowinckel, 1977. 323 pp., illus., tabs., diagrs., bibl.

1429 *Umbruch des Gesundheitswesen im Geiste des Paracelsus.* Nürnberg: Verlag Deutsche Volksgesundheit, 1936. 147 pp.

Medical care

1430 BRUGSCH, THEODOR: *Arzt seit fünf Jahrzehnten.* Berlin: Rütten & Loening, 1957. 405 pp., illus.

117

1431 FROMMOLT, G.: *Rassefragen in der Geburtshilfe und Gynäkologie.* Leipzig: Barth, 1936. 96 pp., tabs., bibl.

1432 *Führer durch das medizinische Berlin.* Ausg. 1941. Hrsg.: Pütz, im Auftr. der Berliner Akademie für ärztliche Fortbildung. 138 pp.

1433 HOFFMANN, ERICH: *Ringen um Vollendung. Lebenserinnerungen aus einer Wendezeit der Heilkunde 1933–1946.* Hannover: Schmorl & von Seefeld, 1949. 311 pp. [2nd vol of memoirs.]

1434 KETTER, FRIEDRICH: *Kurzes Lehrbuch der Rassenbiologie und Rassenhygiene für Mediziner.* Geleitw.: L. Schmidt-Kehl. Stuttgart: Enke, 1941. 204 pp., illus., diagrs.

1434a LEIBFRIED, STEPHAN & TENNSTEDT, FLORIAN: *Berufsverbote und Sozialpolitik 1933. Die Auswirkungen der nationalsozialistischen Machtergreifung auf die Krankenkassenverwaltung und die Kassenärzte. Analyse: Materialien zu Angriff und Selbsthilfe: Erinnerungen.* Bremen: Universitätsdruckerei, 1979. xix + 325 pp., mimeog.

NATURE CURES

1435 KLARE, KURT, ed.: *Neue Wege der Heilkunde. Zeitstimmen.* Stuttgart: Hippokrates-Verlag, 1937. 50 pp.

1436 KÖTSCHAU, KARL: *Zum nationalsozialistischen Umbruch in der Medizin.* Stuttgart: Hippokrates-Verlag, 1936. 96 pp.

1437 PIETRUSKY, F.: *Gerichtliche Medizin.* [And] CRINIS, MAX de: *Gerichtliche Psychiatrie.* 2.–3. durchges. Aufl. Berlin: Heymann, 1943. 335 pp., illus., tabs., bibl.

1438 *Reichsärzteordnung mit allen Anordnungen, Durchführungs- und Ausführungsbestimmungen bis zum 1. April 1938 ...* Berlin: Verlag der Deutschen Ärzteschaft, [1938]. 101 pp.

1439 SCHOON, CARL H.: *Entschleierte Geheimnisse. Deutschland bannt den Tropentod.* Berlin: Limpert, 1942. 156 pp., illus., diagrs.

TERNON, YVES & HELMAN, SOCRATE: *Les médecins allemands et le nationalsocialisme. Les métamorphoses du darwinisme. See* 6217.

1440 VERSCHUER, OTMAR Frhr. von: *Erbpathologie. Ein Lehrbuch für Ärzte.* Dresden: Steinkopf, 1934. 213 pp., illus., tabs., diagrs., bibl.

Social welfare

1441 [BERLIN] ARCHIV FÜR WOHLFAHRTSPFLEGE: *Die Einrichtungen des Wohlfahrts- und Gesundheitswesens, sowie die sonstigen gemeinnützigen Einrichtungen in der Reichshauptstadt Berlin. Graubuch.* Berlin: 1941. 452 pp.

1442 BOBERSKI, GÜNTHER, ed.: *Die Versorgungsgesetze des Grossdeutschen Reichs. Sammlung der wichtigsten Versorgungsvorschriften einschliesslich des Familienunterhaltsrechts.* 6. Aufl. mit eingearb. 1. Nachtrag. Dresden: Müller, 1942. [Also *Nachträge, 1943–1944.]*

1443 BOTZ, GERHARD: *Wohnungspolitik und Judendeportation 1938–1945. Zur Funktion des Antisemitismus als Ersatz nationalsozialistischer Sozialpolitik.* Wien: Geyer, 1975. 200 pp. (Veröffentlichungen des Historischen Instituts der Universität Salzburg).

1444 BRÜCKMANN, WILHELM: *Die deutsche Sozialversicherung. Systematische Übersicht über die wichtigsten Bestimmungen mit kurzen Erläuterungen.* Berlin: Verlag für Sozialpolitik, Wirtschaft und Statistik, 1944. 128 pp.

1445 BÜHLER, THEODOR: *Deutsche Sozialwirtschaft. Ein Überblick über die sozialen Aufgaben der Volkswirtschaft.* 2. unveränd. Aufl. Stuttgart: Kohlhammer, 1943. 406 pp.

1446 DEUTSCHE ARBEITSFRONT: *Soziale Sicherung bei Dienstverpflichtung, Notdienst und Arbeitsplatzwechsel.* Berlin: 1940. 183 pp.

1447 [DÜSSELDORF] FRIEDRICH, ROBERT: *Zwei Jahre Tatsozialismus im Gau Düsseldorf.* Düsseldorf: Industrie Verlag und Druckerei Pressehaus, [1935]. 111 pp., illus.

1448 GERHARDT, JOHANNES: *Deutsche Arbeits- und Sozialpolitik.* Berlin: Duncker & Humblot, 1944. 286 pp.

1449 GUILLEBAUD, C. W.: *The social policy of Nazi Germany.* Cambridge: Cambridge University Press, 1941. 132 pp.

1450 HEINEMANN, W.: *Jahrbuch der deutschen Sozialversicherung, vormals Deutscher Krankenkassen-Kalender, für das Jahr 1939.* Mainz: Diemer, 1938. xv + 440 pp.

1451 KROHN, MARIE-ELISABETH: *Staat und Sozialversicherung in Grossbritannien und Deutschland.* Berlin: Deutscher Rechtsverlag, 1942. 160 pp., bibl.

1452 MAGNUS, G.: *Betriebliche Gefolgschaftssicherung, Gefolgschaftsfürsorge— Altersvorsorge.* Stuttgart: Kohlhammer, 1939. 164 pp.

1453 MENDE, FRANZ, ed.: *Wege zur neuen Sozialpolitik. Arbeitstagung des Sozialamtes der Deutschen Arbeitsfront vom 16. bis 21. Dezember 1935.* Stuttgart: Kohlhammer, 1936. 259 pp., diagrs.

NS-VOLKSWOHLFAHRT

1454 ALTGELT, INGEBORG: *Wegweiser durch die NS-Volkswohlfahrt.* Berlin: Weidmann, 1935. 75 pp., charts.

1455 MENNECKE, KURT: *Ein westdeutscher NSV-Kreis. Seine Entstehung und sein Menschengefüge vom 15. September 1933 bis zum 30. November 1934.* Inaugural-Dissertation [pres. to] Universität Köln. 1936. 95 pp., diagr., bibl.

1456 *Sozialisten der Tat. Das Buch der unbekannten Kämpfer der N.S.V.* Berlin: N.S.D.A.P. Amt für Volkswohlfahrt, Gau Gross-Berlin, [1934]. 157 pp., illus., diagrs., tabs.

1457 STÖRMER, HELLMUTH: *Das rechtliche Verhältnis der NS.-Volkswohlfahrt und des Winterhilfswerkes zu den Betreuten im Vergleiche zur öffentlichen Wohlfahrtspflege.* Berlin: Eher, 1940. 72 pp.

1458   PHISTER, BERNHARD: *Sozialpolitik als Krisenpolitik.* Stuttgart: Kohlhammer, 1936. 283 pp., tabs.

1459   RUPPERT, FRITZ: *Das Recht der öffentlichen Fürsorge. Sammlung der fürsorgerechtlichen Vorschriften der Altreichsgebiets und der seit 1938 in das Reich eingegliederten Gebiete, unter besondere Berücksichtigung der Fürsorge für Wehrdienst und Einsatzbeschädigte und ihre Hinterbliebenen. Textausgabe mit Anmerkungen und Sachverzeichnis.* Berlin: Heymann, 1943. 155 pp.

1460   SELDTE, FRANZ: *Sozialpolitik im Dritten Reich 1933–1938.* München: Beck, 1939. 274 pp.

1461   STATISTISCHES REICHSAMT: *Die Richtsätze der öffentlichen Fürsorge am 1. Januar 1941.* Berlin: Verlag für Sozialpolitik, Wirtschaft und Statistik, 1941. 110 pp., tabs. (Bd. 582).

Winterhilfswerk

1462   WINTERHILFSWERK: *Buchreihe Winterhilfe.* 1937–1941. [Miniature books issued each year. Also: Kriegswinterhilfswerk: *Alte deutsche Volksmärchen* (1941); *Das deutsche Lied* (1942); *Ritterkreuzträger* (1943).]

1463   *Ewiges Deutschland. Ein deutsches Hausbuch. 1.–5. Folge.* Hrsg.: Winterhilfswerk des deutschen Volkes. Braunschweig: Westermann, 1939–1945. In 5 vols.

1464   *Führer-Reden zum Winterhilfswerk 1933–1938.* München: Eher, 1937/39.

1465   REICHSPROPAGANDALEITUNG DER NSDAP: *Das deutsche Hausbuch.* Hrsg. in Verbindung mit dem Winterhilfswerk des deutschen Volkes vom Hauptkulturamt in der Reichspropagandaleitung der NSDAP. Berlin: Eher, 1943. 368 pp., illus., mus. scores.

1466   WULFF, ERNST: *Das Winterhilfswerk des deutschen Volkes.* Berlin: Eher, 1940. 111 pp., tabs., diagrs.

Animal welfare

1467   SCHOENICHEN, WALTHER: *Naturschutz im Dritten Reich. Einführung in Wesen und Grundlagen zeitgemässer Naturschutz-Arbeit.* Berlin: Bermühler, [1934]. 107 pp., illus.

1468   VETTER, HANS: *Hitlerjunge Horst schützt die Tiere. Dramatische Szene.* Warendorf: Genesiue-Verlag, [1933]. 16 pp.

2. POPULATION POLICY AND EUGENICS

1469   BURGDÖRFER, FRIEDRICH: *Geburtenschwund. Die Kulturkrankheit Europas und ihre Überwindung in Deutschland.* Heidelberg: Vowinckel, 1942. 215 pp., graphs, tabs., maps. (Beiheft zur *Zeitschrift für Geopolitik*).

1470   DUBITSCHER, F.: *Asoziale Sippen. Erb- und sozialbiologische Untersuchungen.* Leipzig: Thieme, 1942. 226 pp., diagrs., tabs., bibl.

1471 FINCKH, LUDWIG: *Das deutsche Ahnenbuch.* Görlitz: Verlag für Sippenforschung und Wappenkunde, 1934. 134 pp.

1472 GAIL, F. W., ed.: *Unser Dorf- und Hausbuch.* Frankfurt a.M.: Diesterweg, 1936. 147 pp., illus.

1473 KRONENBERG, KURT: *Kirchenbuch-Urkunden für Sippenforschung und deutschblütigen Abstammungsnachweis. Ein Wegweiser für Pfarrer und Kirchenbuchführer in die geltenden Bestimmungen, Erlasse und Gebührenordnungen.* Berlin-Steglitz: Evangelischer Pressverband für Deutschland, 1937. 67 pp.

1474 LEHMANN, WALTER: *Vererbung und Rasse.* Potsdam: Bonness & Hachfeld, [1939?]. 504 pp., illus., diagrs., tabs. [Part-work of 18 issues.]

1475 LINDEMANN, CHRISTA: *Die Feststellung der blutmässigen Abstammung bei ehelichen und unehelichen Kinder.* Inaugural-Dissertation [pres. to] Friedrich-Alexanders-Universität zu Erlangen. Düsseldorf: Nolte, 1937. 35 pp., bibl.

1476 MAHNKE, KARL GEORG: *Kulturaufwand und Kinderzahl. Eine statistische Analyse der kulturellen Lebenshaltung der deutschen Familie unter besonderer Berücksichtigung der Kinderzahl.* Inaugural-Dissertation [pres. to] Friedrich-Wilhelms-Universität zu Berlin. Würzburg-Aumühle: Triltsch, 1939. 56 pp., tabs., diagrs., bibl.

1477 PAUL, ALEXANDER: *Jüdisch-deutsche Blutmischung. Eine sozial-biologische Untersuchung.* Inaugural-Dissertation [pres. at] Berlin. Berlin: Schoetz, 1940. 160 pp., tabs., diagrs., bibl. (Sonderdruck aus den *Veröffentlichungen aus dem Gebiete des Volksgesundheitsdienstes,* Bd. LV).

1478 *Rasse- und Gesundheitspass für* ... Leipzig: Degener, 1934. 24 pp.

1479 SCHÜTT, Ed. & VIERNSTEIN, Th.: *Die Bekämpfung der Kriminalität vom bevölkerungspolitischen und erbbiologischen Standpunkt. Vorträge auf der wissenschaftlichen Sitzung ... 1933 ... des Preussischen Medizinalbeamtenvereins ...* Leipzig: Fischers Medizinische Buchhandlung, 1933. 42 pp.

1480 SCHULZE-MANITIUS, HANS: *Bevölkerungs-Statistik Deutschlands und des Auslandes im Bild.* Heidelberg: Vowinckel, [1943]. 373 pp., diagrs.

1481 SIEMENS, HERMANN WERNER: *Grundzüge der Vererbungslehre, Rassenhygiene und Bevölkerungspolitik.* 10. Aufl. München: Lehmann, 1941. 203 pp., illus., diagrs., bibl.

1482 *Über Personenstandswesen und Sippenkunde. Der Weg vom Standesamt zum Sippenamt. Vorträge geh. auf der Verwaltungswissenschaftlichen Woche für Standesbeamte vom 8. bis 13. Oktober 1934* ... Berlin: Verlag für Standesamtswesen, 1934. 97 pp., graphs, diagrs.

1483 ULMENSTEIN, Frhr. von: *Der Abstammungsnachweis.* Berlin: Verlag für Standesamtswesen, 1941. 243 pp. [3rd ed. 1937. 147 pp.]

1484 WEBER, ROBERT: *Die Blutgruppenbestimmung für die gerichtliche Praxis unter besonderer Berücksichtigung des Familienrechts.* Leipzig: Deichert, 1936. 64 pp., bibl.

1485 WOLF, HEINRICH: *Angewandte Geschichte. Band V: Angewandte Rassenkunde.* 2. erw. Aufl. Berlin: Weicher, 1938. 452 pp., illus.

Marriage

1486 GÜNTHER, HANS F. K.: *Gattenwahl zu ehelichem Glück und erblicher Ertüchtigung.* München: Lehmann, 1941. 171 pp., diagrs.

1487 KNOST, FRIEDRICH A. & WAGNER, JOHANNES, eds.: *Handbücherei des Standesbeamten.* Berlin: Verlag für Standesamtswesen, 1936/38. Facsims. of official forms.
  Bd. I: Johannes Wagner & Bernhard Offers: *Eheerfordernisse und Ehehindernisse. 1. Teil: Ehemündigkeit und Eheeinwilligungen.* Publ. 1936. 150 pp.
  Bd. II: Johannes Wagner & Bernhard Offers: *Eheerfordernisse und Ehehindernisse. 2. Teil: Ehehindernisse.* 2. völlig neubearb. Aufl. Publ. 1938. 173 pp., diagrs.
  Bd. III: Hans Bässler: *Worte an die Eheschliessenden. Vorschläge für Ansprachen bei der standesamtlichen Eheschliessung.* 4. Aufl. Publ. 1938. 72 pp.
  Bd. IV: Alexander Bergmann: *Standesamt und Auslandsrecht.* Publ. 1938. 137 pp.

1488 *Das neue Ehegesetz. Gesetz zur Vereinheitlichung des Rechts der Eheschliessung und der Ehescheidung im Lande Österreich und im übrigen Reichsgebiet vom 6. Juli 1938. Mit der amtlichen Begründung, den eherechtlichen Bestimmungen des Blutschutzgesetzes, des Ehegesundheitsgesetzes, des Personenstandsgesetzes und anderen einschlägigen Vorschriften. Textausgabe mit Anmerkungen und Sachverzeichnis.* München: Back, 1938. vii + 126 pp.

1489 RICHTER, BODO & VÖLKER, HANS: *Das deutsche Eherecht. Bürgerliches Gesetzbuch, Eheprozessrecht, Ehegesundheitsrecht, Erb- und Rassenpflege, Ehestandsdarlehen, Beihilfen an kinderreiche Familien, Steuerrechtliche Bestimmungen.* Geleitw.: Landgerichtsdirektor Jenne. Berlin: Heymann, [1936?]. 272 pp.

Sterilization and castration

1490 BEYER, RUDOLF, ed.: *Hitlergesetz V. Gesetz zur Verhütung erbkranken Nachwuchses mit der Durchführungsverordnung vom 5. Dezember 1933: Gesetze gegen Missbräuche bei der Eheschliessung und der Annahme an Kindes Statt: Tierschutzgesetz. Sämtliche Gesetze mit den amtlichen Begründungen. Textausgabe.* Leipzig: Reclam, 1934. 73 pp.

1491 GÜTT, ARTHUR and others, eds.: *Gesetz zur Verhütung erbkranken Nachwuchses vom 14. Juli 1933 nebst Ausführungsverordnungen.* Bearb. und erläutert von Arthur Gütt, Ernst Rüdin, Falk Ruttke. Mit Beiträgen:

Erich Lexer: 'Die Eingriffe zur Unfruchtbarmachung des Mannes und zur Entmannung'; Heinrich Eymer: 'Die Eingriffe zur Unfruchtbarmachung der Frau'. 2. neubearb. Aufl. München: Lehmann, 1936. 418 pp., illus., diagrs., tabs., bibl.

1492 REUTER, FRITZ: *Aufartung durch Ausmerzung. Sterilisation und Kastration im Kampf gegen Erbkrankheiten und Verbrechen.* Berlin: Hobbing, 1936. 112 pp., illus., diagrs.

1493 RISTOW, ERICH: *Erbgesundheitsrecht. Berechtigung, Bedeutung und Anwendung des Gesetzes zur Verhütung erbkranken Nachwuchses mit einem Anhang der Gesetze, Verordnungen und wichtigsten Runderlasse.* Stuttgart: Kohlhammer, 1935. 343 pp.

1494 ' "Von der Verhütung unwerten Lebens". Ein Zyklus von 5 Vorträgen. Anhang: Das Gesetz zur Verhütung erbkranken Nachwuchses vom 25. Juli 1933'. [Special number of] *Bremer Beiträge zur Naturwissenschaft.* Bremen: 1933. 119 pp.

F. THE ECONOMY
1. GENERAL

1495 BACKE, HERBERT: *Das Ende des Liberalismus in der Wirtschaft.* Berlin: Reichsnährstand Verlag, 1938. 160 pp.

1496 *The Banker*, Feb. 1937, Vol. XLI, No. 133 [Special issue on] 'Germany. The results of four years of National Socialism'. London: The Financial News. Pp. 100–204.

1497 BLAICH, FRITZ and others: *Probleme der nationalsozialistischen Wirtschaftspolitik.* [By] Fritz Blaich, Gustav Otruba, Dietmar Petzina, Harald Winkel. Hrsg.: Friedrich-Wilhelm Henning. Berlin: Duncker & Humblot, 1976. 174 pp., tabs., graphs.

1498 BLANKENBURG, PAUL & DREYER, MAX: *Nationalsozialistischer Wirtschaftsaufbau und seine Grundlagen. Ein bildstatistischer Tatsachenbericht.* Berlin: Zentralverlag, 1934. 248 pp., port., maps, diagrs.

1499 BRINKMANN, RUDOLF: *Wirtschaftspolitik aus nationalsozialistischem Kraftquell! Eine Sammlung ausgewählter Vorträge, Reden und Ansprachen.* Jena: Gustav Fischer, 1939. 224 pp.

1500 BUND NEUES DEUTSCHLAND: *Zur Kritik der deutschen Wirtschaft.* Paris: [1939?]. 64 pp., tabs.

1501 DAUPHIN-MEUNIER, A.: *L'économie allemande contemporaine.* Paris: Sorlot, 1942. 202 pp.

1502 DEPARTMENT OF OVERSEAS TRADE: *Economic conditions in Germany* ... London: HMSO, 1934, 1936. Diagrs., tabs.
... *to June 1934. A report.* By C. M. C. Thelwall, 228 pp.
... *to March 1936.* By E. C. Donaldson Rawlins. xii + 285 pp.

1503 DEUTSCHES INSTITUT FÜR BANKWISSENSCHAFT UND BANKWESEN: *Probleme des deutschen Wirtschaftslebens. Erstrebtes und Erreichtes. Eine Sammlung von Abhandlungen.* Berlin: de Gruyter, 1937 xiv + 860 pp., tabs.

1504 DUBAIL, RENÉ: *Une expérience d'économie dirigée: l'Allemagne nationale socialiste.* Paris: Dupont, 1962. 171 pp.

1505 EINZIG, PAUL: *The economics of Hitlerism.* London: Macmillan, 1934. 128 pp.

1506 ERBE, RENÉ: *Die nationalsozialistische Wirtschaftspolitik 1933–1939 im Lichte der modernen Theorie.* Zürich: Polygraphischer Verlag, 1958. 197 pp., tabs., bibl. (Hrsg.: Basle Centre Economic and Financial Research ...).

1507 ERMARTH, FRITZ: *The new Germany. National Socialist government in theory and practice.* Introd.: E. S. Griffith. Washington, D.C.: Digest Press, 1936. 203 pp., bibl. [Economic viewpoint.]

1508 GASSERT, G.: *Werden und Wesen der sozialistischen deutschen Wirtschaft.* Berlin: Verlag für Wirtschaft und Verwaltung, 1939. 306 pp.

1509 GERMANICUS [pseud. of W. G. F. Knop]: *Germany—the last four years. An independent examination of the results of National Socialism.* Introd.: Walter Layton. London: Eyre & Spottiswoode, 1937. 116 pp., tabs. [Emphasis on economics.]

1510 GUILLEBAUD, C. W.: *The economic recovery of Germany from 1933 to the incorporation of Austria in March 1938.* London: Macmillan, 1939. xiv + 303 pp., tabs.

1511 HEISS, FRIEDRICH: *Der grosse Auftrag. Jahre deutscher Werkarbeit 1933–1936.* Berlin: Verlag Volk und Reich, 1937. 91 pp., illus.

1512 HELZEL, ALFRED and others: *Beruf 'Wirtschaftsleiter'. Neues Betriebsführertum in der volksgebundenen Wirtschaft! Eine gesellschaftspolitische Untersuchung.* [By] Alfred Helzel, Richard Zellien, Hermann Schäfer. Berlin-Charlottenburg: Reichsverband der Wirtschaftsleiter, [193–]. 133 pp., diagr.

1513 HÖVEL, PAUL: *Grundfragen deutscher Wirtschaftspolitik.* Berlin: Springer, 1935. 192 pp., tabs., bibl.

1514 HUNKE, HEINRICH: *Grundzüge der deutschen Volks- und Wehrwirtschaft.* 7. unveränd. Aufl. Berlin: Haude & Spener, 1943. 101 pp.

1515 *Jahrbuch der deutschen Wirtschaft 1937.* Hrsg.: H. Rolf Fritzsche. Geleitw.: H. E. Posse. Leipzig: Breitkopf & Härtel, [1936]. 165 pp., illus., tab. [No others publ.]

1516 *Jahrbuch für nationalsozialistische Wirtschaft.* Hrsg.: Otto Mönckmeier. Diagrs., tabs.
1935: Stuttgart: Kohlhammer. vi + 324 pp.
1937: München: Eher. xi + 643 pp.
[No others publ.]

1517 KADRITZKE, NIELS: *Faschismus und Krise. Zum Verhältnis von Politik und*

Ökonomie im Nationalsozialismus. Frankfurt a.M.: Campus Verlag, 1976. 216 pp., bibl.

1518 KNAUERHASE, RAMON: *An introduction to National Socialism, 1920 to 1939.* Columbus, Ohio: Merrill, 1972. xii + 143 pp., tabs., maps. [Economic viewpoint.]

1519 KÖLBLE, JOSEF: *Grundzüge der neuen deutschen Wirtschaftsordnung.* Leipzig: Kohlhammer, 1941. 141 pp.

1520 *Konjunktur-Statistisches Handbuch.* Tabs.
1933: Hrsg.: Institut für Konjunkturforschung. Berlin: Hobbing. 384 pp.
1936: Hrsg.: Ernst Wagemann. Berlin: Hanseatische Verlagsanstalt, 1935. 349 pp.

1521 KRAUSE, A. B.: *Organisation von Arbeit und Wirtschaft.* Berlin: Elsner, 1935. 184 pp., diagrs., tabs.

1522 LIMBECK, H.: *Deutscher Aufbau in Zahlen. Schicksalskampf eines Volkes.* Karlsruhe: Braun, 1938. viii + 79 + 15 pp., illus., maps, graphs, tabs.

1523 NERESOFF, WLADISLAW: *Das wirtschaftliche Gesicht des neuen Deutschland. Das Urteil eines Ausländers.* Berlin: Verlag für Wirtschaftswissenschaft, 1939. 107 pp., illus.

1524 NONNENBRUCH, FRITZ: *Die dynamische Wirtschaft.* München: Eher, 1936. 295 pp.

1525 PAUL, OTTO ERNST & CLAUSSEN, WILHELM: *Grossdeutschland und die Welt. Ein Wirtschafts-ABC in Zahlen.* Berlin: Deutsche Verlagsgesellschaft, 1938. 480 pp., diagrs., tabs.

1526 PETZINA, DIETMAR: *Die deutsche Wirtschaft in der Zwischenkriegszeit.* Wiesbaden: Steiner, 1977. 205 pp.

1527 PRIESTER, HANS E.: *Das deutsche Wirtschaftswunder.* Amsterdam: Querido Verlag, 1936. 360 pp., tabs.

1528 REICHLE, HERMANN: *Der volkswirtschaftliche Ausgleich zwischen Stadt und Land.* München: Eher, 1942. 96 pp.

1529 REICHSFINANZMINISTERIUM: *Wirtschaftsbestimmungen für die Reichsbehörden (RWB).* Berlin: Heymann, 1941. 194 pp.

1530 REICHSWIRTSCHAFTSKAMMER: *Verzeichnis der Mitglieder der Reichswirtschaftskammer und deren Untergliederungen. Stand: Februar 1936.* Berlin: Heymann, 1936. 294 pp.

1531 *Schaffendes Volk. Reichsausstellung, Düsseldorf 1937. Ein Bericht.* Hrsg.: E. W. Maiwald. Zusammengest. und bearb. von Richard W. Geutebruck. 264 + 125 + [12] pp., illus., plan, tabs., diagrs. [In 2 vols.]

1532 THALHEIM, KARL C., ed.: *Das ABC der Volkswirtschaft. Ein Nachschlagewerk über das Wirtschafts- und Sozialleben der Gegenwart.* Leipzig: Seemann, 1934. 325 pp.

1532a VOLKMANN, HANS-ERICH: *Wirtschaft im Dritten Reich. Eine Bibliografie.* München: Bernard & Graefe, 1980. 139 pp. (Schriften der Bibliothek für Zeitgeschichte).

1533 WAGEMANN, ERNST: *Wirtschafts-politische Strategie. Von den obersten Grundsätzen wirtschaftlicher Staatskunst.* Hamburg: Hanseatische Verlagsanstalt, 1937. 368 pp., tabs., graphs.

1534 WAGEMANN, ERNST: *Zwischenbilanz der Krisenpolitik. Eine international vergleichende konjunkturpolitische Studie.* Berlin: Heymann, 1935. vii + 102 pp., diagrs., tabs.

1535 WAGENFÜHR, HORST: *Grossdeutschlands Wirtschaft.* Leipzig: Goldmann, 1939. 142 pp., maps, tabs., bibl.

1536 WEBER, ADOLF: *Kurzgefasste Volkswirtschaftspolitik in einem Bande.* München: Duncker & Humblot, 1935. 370 pp.

1537 WELS, H. PAUL: *Staat und Wirtschaft. Praktische Volkswirtschaft durch die neue Wirtschafts-Gesetzgebung.* Dresden: Ehlermann, 1935. 84 pp., diagrs.

1538 *Wer leitet? Die Männer der Wirtschaft und der einschlägigen Verwaltung 1940.* Berlin: Hoppenstedt, 1940. 1012 pp.

2. FINANCE

1539 *Allgemeiner deutscher Bankiertag 1938, am 10. und 11. Mai 1938 in der Kroll-Oper zu Berlin. Ansprachen, Vorträge und Teilnehmer.* Berlin: de Gruyter, 1938. 149 pp.

1540 BEYER, RUDOLF, ed.: *Hitlergesetze VII. Wechselgesetz vom 21. Juni 1933, nebst dem Scheckgesetz vom 14. August 1933, samt den Einführungsgesetzen, den wesentlichen Bestimmungen und Auszügen aus den Genfer Abkommen zur Vereinheitlichung des Wechsel- und des Scheckrechts und anderen Bestimmungen. Textausgabe mit kurzen Anmerkungen.* Leipzig: Reclam, 1934. 134 pp.

1541 BOESLER, FELIX, ed.: *Deutsche Finanzpolitik.* Berlin: Junker & Dünnhaupt, 1935. 141 pp.

Currency control

1542 BLEICHERT, GASTON ADOLF VON: *Die Massnahmen Deutschlands zum Ausgleich der Zahlungsbilanz unter besonderer Berücksichtigung des Neuen Plans.* Bern: Haupt, 1940. 134 pp.

1543 HARRIS, M. A.: *Germany's foreign indebtedness charts.* London: Oxford University Press, 1935. 124 pp. (With assistance of the Information Department, Royal Institute of International Affairs).

1544 *Kapitalflucht und Devisenanzeige nach dem Volksverratsgesetz (Gesetz gegen Verrat der deutschen Volkswirtschaft vom 12.6.1933). Erläutert für die Praxis auf Grund der Durchführungsverordnung vom 28. Juni 1933 und den einschlägigen Rechtsvorschriften.* Berlin: Berliner Börsen-Courier, 1933. 67 pp.

1545 KÜHNE, RUDOLF: *Grundriss des Devisenrechts. Ein Leitfaden durch die deutsche Devisengesetzgebung.* Berlin-Lichterfelde: Langewort, 1937. 124 pp.

1546 PIATIER, ANDRÉ: *Le contrôle des devises dans l'économie du IIIe Reich.* Paris: Centre d'Études de Politique étrangère, 1937. 185 pp., tabs., bibl.

1547 RASCH, HAROLD, ed.: *Die neue Devisengesetzgebung. Einschliesslich der grundlegenden Vorschriften über den Warenverkehr (Überwachungsstellen) und der Moratoriumsgesetze und unter Berücksichtigung der Rückgliederung des Saargebiets. Textausgabe mit ausführlichem Sachregister nach dem Stand vom 20. März 1935.* Einl.: Hans Hartenstein. Berlin: Heymann, 1935. viii + 300 pp., tabs.

1548 ERBE, HANS, ed.: *Entschädigungsgesetz. Gesetz über Gewährung von Entschädigungen bei der Einziehung oder dem Übergang von Vermögen vom 9. Dezember 1937 nebst den Durchführungsverordnungen vom 11. und 18. März 1938.* Berlin: Vahlen, 1938. 127 pp.

1549 GROTH, KARL: *Die Reichsfinanzverwaltung. BandI. 1.* Berlin: Spaeth & Linde, 1938. 118 pp.

1550 LURIE, SAMUEL: *Private investment in a controlled economy. Germany, 1933–1939.* New York: Columbia University Press, 1947. 243 pp.

1551 NORDEN, ALBERT: *Lehren deutscher Geschichte. Zur politischen Rolle des Finanzkapitals und der Junker.* 3. Aufl. Berlin: Dietz, 1947. 303 pp.

1552 OPITZ, REINHARD, ed.: *Europastrategien des deutschen Kapitals 1900–1945.* Köln: Pahl-Rugenstein, 1977. 1069 pp., bibl. [A documentation, with much material relating to World War II.]

1553 POOLE, KENYON E.: *German financial policies 1932–1939.* Cambridge, Mass.: Harvard University Press, 1939. 260 pp.

1554 PRION, W.: *Das deutsche Finanzwunder. Die Geldbeschaffung für den deutschen Wirtschaftsaufschwung.* 3. unveränd. Aufl. Berlin: Franke, 1938. 111 pp., tabs.

1555 *Die Reichsbank im grösseren Deutschland. Vorträge gehalten in der Zeit vom 20. bis 25. Juni 1938 in der Unterrichtswoche für Reichsbankbeamte sowie für Beamte der Staats- und Landesbanken.* Hrsg.: Reichssachbearbeiter beim Reichswalter des Reichsbundes der Deutschen Beamten. Berlin: Verlag Beamtenpresse, 1938. 210 pp.

1556 REINHARDT, FRITZ: *Was geschieht mit unserem Geld? Finanzen, Kaufkraft, Währung.* Nürnberg: Willmy-Verlag, [1942]. 72 pp.

1557 SCHACHT, HJALMAR: *Nationale Kreditwirtschaft.* Berlin: Steegeman, 1934. 51 pp.

1558 SCHWERIN VON KROSIGK, LUTZ Graf: *Staatsbankrott. Die Geschichte der Finanzpolitik des Deutschen Reiches von 1920 bis 1945, geschrieben vom letzten Reichsfinanzminister.* Göttingen: Musterschmidt, 1974. 371 pp., illus., facsims., bibl. [Third Reich, pp. 174–368.]

Taxation

1559 BARTH, KARL (Dr. rer. pol.): *Das Bevölkerungsproblem und seine Auswirkung in der neuen deutschen Steuerreform.* Leipzig: Buske, 1936. 158 pp., tabs., diagrs., bibl.

1560 BEYER, RUDOLF, ed.: *Erbschaftsteuergesetz. Textausgabe mit ausführlichem Sachregister. Gesetzgebung bis Ende November 1934.* 5. Aufl. Leipzig: Reclam, 1934. 46 pp.

1561 MENSENS, CHRISTOPH and others: *Handbuch des gemeindlichen Steuerrechts.* 3. verb. und erw. Aufl. [By] Christoph Mensens, Erich Bohley, Hermann Krutsch. München: Jehle, 1943. 1155 pp.

1562 REINHARDT, FRITZ: *Die neuen Steuergesetze. Einführung in die neuen Steuergesetze. Übersichten über die wesentlichen Änderungen gegenüber dem bisherigen Recht—Wortlaut der zehn neuen Gesetze.* Berlin: Spaeth & Linde, [1934/35]. 392 pp.

1563 WAGEMANN, ERNST: *'Wo kommt das viele Geld her?' Geldschöpfung und Finanzlenkung in Krieg und Frieden.* Düsseldorf: Völkischer Verlag, 1940. 160 pp., diagrs., tabs.

1564 WISSMANN, HELLMUTH: *Das Gold in Wirtschaft und Politik.* Leipzig: Goldmann, 1940. 156 pp., tabs.

1565 ZIMMERMANN, RICHARD: *Die deutschen Gemeindefinanzen nach der nationalsozialistischen Revolution. Eine finanzpolitische Untersuchung.* Köln: Schroeder, 1936. 204 pp., tabs., bibl.

3. INDUSTRY AND COMMERCE

1566 ABEL, HEINZ: *Die Industrie- und Handelskammern im nationalsozialistischen Staate.* Inaugural-Dissertation [pres. to] Universität zu Würzburg. 1940. 111 pp., bibl.

COOPERATIVES

1567 BLUDAU, KUNO: *Nationalsozialismus und Genossenschaften.* Hannover: Verlag für Literatur und Zeitgeschehen, 1968. 240 pp., facsims., bibl.

1568 LANG, JOHANN & WEIDMÜLLER, LUDWIG: *Das Reichsgesetz betreffend die Erwerbs- und Wirtschaftsgenossenschaften. Kleiner Kommentar.* 25. Aufl. Berlin: de Gruyter, 1943. 411 pp.

1569 DICHGANS, HANS: *Zur Geschichte des Reichskommissars für die Preisbildung.* Düsseldorf: 1937. 45 pp.

1570 ESENWEIN-ROTHE, INGEBORG: *Die Wirtschaftsverbände von 1933 bis 1945.* Berlin: Duncker & Humblot, 1965. 209 pp., tabs., charts, bibl.

1571 GROSCHUFF, HANS: *Reichsgesetz betreffend die Gesellschaften mit beschränkter Haftung in der am 1. November 1942 geltenden Fassung.* 2. durchgearb. und erw. Aufl. nebst einem Beitrag: Ernst Kaemmel: 'Die steuerrechtliche Behandlung der GmbH'. Berlin: de Gruyter, 1943. 348 pp.

1572 GURLAND, A. R. L. and others: *The fate of small business in Nazi Germany.* [By] A. R. L. Gurland, Otto Kirchheimer, Franz Neumann. Printed for the use of the Special Committee to study problems of American small business. Washington, DC.: US Gov't Ptg. Office, 1943. viii + 152 pp., tabs.

1573 HAMBURGER, L.: *How Nazi Germany has controlled business.* Washington, D.C.: The Brookings Institution, 1943. 101 pp.

1574 MÖNCKMEIER, OTTO, ed.: *Wirtschaftstreuhänder-Jahrbuch 1939.* Bearb.: Dr. Adler, Dr. Buchholz, Richard Karoli. Leipzig: Gloeckner, 1938. xvi + 596 pp., tabs.

1575 NS-HAGO: *Gewerbeordnung für das Deutsche Reich.* Berlin: Verlag Der Aufbau, [1934?]. 95 pp.

1576 SCHIER, WALDEMAR: *Der nationalsozialistische Unternehmertyp.* Emsdetten: Lechte, 1938. 114 pp.

1577 SCHWEITZER, ARTHUR: *Big business in the Third Reich.* London: Eyre & Spottiswoode, 1964. 739 pp., tabs., diagr., bibl.

1578 SWATEK, DIETER: *Unternehmenskonzentration als Ergebnis und Mittel nationalsozialistischer Wirtschaftspolitik.* Berlin: Duncker & Humblot, 1972, 172 pp., bibl.

1579 TESCHEMACHER, HERMANN, ed.: *Handbuch des Aufbaus der gewerblichen Wirtschaft. Bd. III: Reichswirtschaftskammern, Industrie- und Handelskammern, sowie Aussenhandelsstellen, deutsche Handelskammern und wirtschaftliche Vereinigungen im Ausland und deutsche Gruppe der Internationalen Handelskammer. Jhrg. 1937.* Bearb.: H. Franke. [Introds.]: Hjalmar Schacht, Albert Pietzsch. Leipzig: Lühe, 1937. 461 pp., ports., bibl.

1580 ZISCHKA, ANTON: *Wissenschaft bricht Monopole.* Leipzig: Goldmann, 1936. 287 pp., illus., bibl.

Autarky and Four-Year-Plan

1581 *Bayern im ersten Vierjahresplan. Denkschrift der Bayerischen Landesregierung zum 9. März 1937.* München: Eher, 1937. 575 pp., illus., maps, diagrs., graphs, tabs.

1582 BERNDT, ALFRED-INGEMAR: *Gebt mir vier Jahre Zeit! Dokumente zum ersten Vierjahresplan des Führers.* Geleitw.: Joseph Goebbels. München: Eher, 1937. 253 pp., tabs.

1583 DAITZ, WERNER: *Der Weg zur völkischen Wirtschaft. Ausgewählte Reden und Aufsätze. Teil I: Deutschlands Wirtschaftsordnung aus eigener Kraft und eigenem Raum. Teil II: Deutschland und die europäische Grossraumwirtschaft.* München: Verlag der Deutschen Technik, 1938. 262 + 179 pp., port.

1584 FRIEDRICHS, KARLERNST: *Der zweite Vierjahresplan, ein Weg zur Weltwirtschaft oder Autarkie? Idee und Verwirklichungsbedingungen.* Inaugural-Dissertation. Bottrop: Postberg, 1938. 75 pp., tabs., bibl.

1585 KREMMLER, H.: *Autarkie in der organischen Wirtschaft.* Dresden: Focken & Oltmann, 1940. 79 pp., bibl.

1586 OBWURZER, HERBERT von: *Selbstversorgung (Autarkie) im Dritten Reich.* Vorw.: Adr. v. Renteln. Berlin: Nationaler Freiheitsverlag, 1933. 90 pp.

1587 PETZINA, DIETMAR: *Autarkiepolitik im Dritten Reich. Der nationalsozialistische Vierjahresplan.* Stuttgart: Deutsche Verlags-Anstalt, 1968. 204 pp., tabs., bibl. (Schriftenreihe der Vierteljahrshefte für Zeitgeschichte ...).

1588 RHEINLÄNDER, PAUL: *Die deutsche Eisen- und Stahlwirtschaft im Vierjahresplan.* Berlin: Junker & Dünnhaupt, 1939. 40 pp.

1589 SCHMIDT, PAUL: *Das Wirtschaftsleben im neuen Deutschland unter Berücksichtigung des Vierjahresplanes.* 7. verb. Aufl. Breslau: Handel, 1939. 80 pp., tabs., diagrs.

Industry

1590 BEHREND, HANS: *The real rulers of Germany.* Transl. from the German. Preface: R. Page Arnot. London: Lawrence & Wishart, 1939, 230 pp.

1591 *Chemie in Deutschland. Werbemitteilungen.* Heft 1, Feb. 1940. Hrsg.: Wirtschaftsgruppe Chemische Industrie. Berlin. 96 pp., illus., tabs.

1592 COPPOCK, J. B. M.: *The pharmaceutical industry in Germany during the period 1939–1945.* London: HMSO, for the British Intelligence Objectives Sub-Committee, 1950. 120 pp., illus., diagrs., bibl. (BIOS Surveys, Report No. 24).

1593 *Deutsche Energiewirtschaft. Deutsche Berichte zur III. Weltkraftkonferenz Washington 1936.* Berlin: VDI-Verlag, 1936. vii + 325 pp., illus., graphs, tabs.

ERSATZ

1594 BIRKENFELD, WOLFGANG: *Der synthetische Treibstoff 1933–1945. Ein Beitrag zur nationalsozialistischen Wirtschafts- und Rüstungspolitik.* Göttingen: Musterschmidt, 1964. 279 pp., illus., tabs., bibl. (Studien und Dokumente zur Geschichte des Zweiten Weltkrieges).

1595 BRANDENBURGER, KURT: *Im Zeitalter der Kunststoffe. Allgemeinverständliche Schilderung der Entstehung und Verwendung der Kunststoffe in Wirtschaft, Industrie und im täglichen Leben.* 2. verb. und verm. Aufl. München: Lehmann, 1938. 109 pp., illus.

1596 DORN, KARL: *Werkstoffe. Miracles of German chemistry.* New York: German Library of Information, 1941. ix + 30 pp., illus.

1597 HILFRICH, CARL, ed.: *Handbuch der deutschen Zellwoll-Wirtschaft. Zellwolle-Spinnereien.* Berlin: Arends, 1941. 516 pp.

1598 *Gliederung der Reichsgruppe Industrie.* Hrsg. von der Geschäftsführung. Leipzig: Lühe, 1941. 263 pp., diagrs., tabs. [3rd ed. 1936 ed.: 95 pp.]

1599 HITLER, ADOLF: *Vortrag ... vor westdeutschen Wirtschaftlern im Industrie-Klub zu Düsseldorf am 27. Januar 1932.* München: Eher, 1932. 31 pp.

1600 *Industrielle Mobilmachung. Statistische Untersuchungen.* Bearb.: Institut für Konjunkturforschung, Berlin. Hamburg: Hanseatische Verlagsanstalt, 1936. 96 pp.

1601 *Jahrbuch des deutschen Fremdenverkehrs.* Hrsg.: Reichsfremdenverkehrsverband. Im Auftr. des Präsidenten des Reichsfremdenverkehrsverbandes bearb. von Bodo Ronnefeld. 2. Ausg. Berlin: Müller, 1939. 283 pp., port., tabs. [First issue 1938. No others appeared.]

RAW MATERIALS

1602 HESSENLAND, MAX: *Deutschlands Kampf um seine Rohstoffe.* 3. ergänz. und verb. Aufl. München: Lehmann, 1939. 198 pp., diagrs., tabs.

1603 JÄGER, JÖRG-JOHANNES: *Die wirtschaftliche Abhängigkeit des Dritten Reiches vom Ausland dargestellt am Beispiel der Stahlindustrie.* Berlin: Berlin Verlag, 1969. 336 pp., tabs., bibl.

1604 JÜNGER, WOLFGANG: *Kampf um Kautschuk.* Leipzig: Goldmann, 1940. 207 pp., illus., maps, diagrs., tabs., bibl. [First ed. 1937.]

1605 JUNGERMANN, WILHELM & KRAFFT, HERBERT: *Rohstoffreichtum aus deutscher Erde. Eine Darstellung unserer Rohstoffwirtschaft.* Berlin: Schmidt, 1939. 191 pp., illus., diagrs., tabs., bibl.

1606 LÜBKE, ANTON: *Das deutsche Rohstoffwunder. Wandlungen der deutschen Rohstoffwirtschaft.* Stuttgart: Forkel, 1939. 572 pp., illus., tabs., diagrs.

1607 MISSBACH, ARTUR: *Die deutschen Spinnstoffe (Wolle, Flachs, Hanf, Seide, Kunstseide und Zellwolle), ihre Gewinnung, ihre wirtschaftliche Bedeutung und ihre Bewirtschaftung.* Berlin: Schmidt, 1938. 188 pp., illus., diagrs., tabs.

1608 [PLEIGER, PAUL] RIEDEL, MATTHIAS: *Eisen und Kohle für das Dritte Reich. Paul Pleigers Stellung in der NS-Wirtschaft.* Göttingen: Musterschmidt, 1973. 375 pp., illus., facsim., bibl.

1609 SCHWARZ, WALTER: *Industriespionage. Geschichte, Rechtsnatur und Systematik des strafrechtlichen Schutzes der Geschäft- und Betriebsgeheimnisse.* Breslau-Neukirch: Kurtze, 1937. 189 pp.

1610 SÖRGEL, WERNER: *Metallindustrie und Nationalsozialismus. Eine Untersuchung über Struktur und Funktion industrieller Organisationen in Deutschland 1929 bis 1939.* Frankfurt a.M.: Europäische Verlagsanstalt, 1965. 96 pp., tabs.

VOLKSWAGEN

1611 HOPFINGER, K. B.: *Beyond expectation. The Volkswagen story.* 3rd ed. London: Foulis, 1956. 182 pp., illus. [Third Reich, pp. 68–145.]

1612 KLUKE, PAUL: 'Hitler und das Volkswagenprojekt'. [In] *Vierteljahrshefte für Zeitgeschichte*, Nr. 8, 1960. Pp. 341–383.

1613 NELSON, WALTER HENRY: *Small wonder. The amazing story of the Volkswagen.* Completely revised. Boston: Little, Brown, 1967. 288 pp., bibl. [German version: *Die Volkswagen-Story. Biographie eines Autos.* München: Piper, 1965.]

1614 WELTER, ERICH: *Der Weg der deutschen Industrie.* Frankfurt a.M.: Frankfurter Societäts-Verlag, 1943. 210 pp.

1615 WINSCHUH, JOSEF: *Industrievolk an der Ruhr. Aus der Werkstatt von Kohle und Eisen.* Oldenburg: Stalling, 1935. 128 pp., illus.

Commerce

1616 BISSINGER, EDGAR: *Der deutsche Handel. Aufgabe und Zukunft.* Stuttgart: Forkel, [1935?]. 497 pp., ports., maps, tabs.

1617 DEUTSCHER INDUSTRIE- UND HANDELSTAG: *Wirtschaft und Handelspolitik.* Berlin: Heymann, 1934. 95 pp., tabs.

1618 GREIFELT, KURT & SCHULZ-KRESS, H. von, eds.: *Wirtschaftliches Kriegsrecht. Unter besonderer Berücksichtigung des Rechts des deutschen Gross- und Aussenhandels.* Berlin: Elsner, 1941. 268 pp.

1619 GREIFF, WALTER: *Die neuen Methoden der Handelspolitik.* Berlin: Junker & Dünnhaupt, 1934. 60 pp., diagr., bibl.

1620 *Handelsgesetzbuch. Aktiengesetz, GmbH-Gesetz, Wechselgesetz, Scheckgesetz mit den wichtigsten Ergänzungsgesetzen und -verordnungen. Textausgabe mit Verweisungen und Sachverzeichnis.* 28. durchges. Aufl. München: Beck, 1940. 602 pp.

1621 LEHMANN, HEINRICH: *Handel und Gewerbe nebst dem Recht der Handelsgeschäfte.* 3. Aufl. Berlin: Vahlen, 1943. 270 pp.

1622 QUITMANN, WALTER, ed.: *Erster deutscher Werbekalender.* Hrsg.: Reichsfachschaft Deutscher Werbefachleute (NSRDW). Berlin: Weltkreisverlag, 1935. 276 pp., illus., tabs.

RETAIL TRADE

1623 KRAUS, J.: *Warenhaus und Einzelhandel unter besonderer Berücksichtigung nationalsozialistischer Wirtschaftsauffassung.* Inaugural-Dissertation [pres.

to] Julius-Maximilians-Universität zu Würzburg. Würzburg: Triltsch, 1937. 74 pp., tabs., bibl.

1624 STEFFENS, HEINZ, ed.: *Gesetz zum Schutze des Einzelhandels nebst allen Verordnungen ... und einer ausführlichen, systematischen Abhandlung.* Berlin: Heymann, 1935. 64 pp.

1625 *Taschenbuch für den Einzelhandelskaufmann.* 1. Jhrg. Hrsg.: Reichsbetriebsgemeinschaft Handel in der DAF. Berlin: Verlag der Deutschen Arbeitsfront, 1937. 288 pp., illus., tabs. [Issued annually, with slight variations (e.g. *Taschenjahrbuch ... 1940.* Hrsg.: Der deutsche Handel in der DAF).]

1626 UHLIG, HEINRICH: *Die Warenhäuser im Dritten Reich.* Köln: Westdeutscher Verlag, 1956. 230 pp.

4. FOREIGN TRADE

1627 BARTLING, K.: *Die deutsche Wirtschaft und ihre Verflechtung mit der Welt. Eine geographische Wirtschaftskunde für Handels- und Berufsschulen.* Leipzig: List & von Bressensdorf, 1939. 116 pp.

1628 DINKLAGE, LUDWIG: *Die deutsche Handelsflotte 1939–1945. Unter besonderer Berücksichtigung der Blockadebrecher.* Göttingen: Musterschmidt, 1971. 537 + 391 pp., bibl. [In 2 vols.]

1629 DOERING, DÖRTE: *Deutsche Aussenwirtschaftspolitik 1933–35. Die Gleichschaltung der Aussenwirtschaft in der Frühphase des nationalsozialistischen Regimes.* Inaugural-Dissertation [pres. to] Freie Universität Berlin. 1969. 377 pp., tabs., diagrs., bibl.

1630 EICKE, RUDOLF: *Warum Aussenhandel?* Geleitw.: Hjalmar Schacht. Berlin: Verlag für Sozialpolitik, Wirtschaft und Statistik, 1936. 79 pp., tabs., diagrs.

1631 FLESSNER, VOLLMAR: *Der Aussenhandel im neuen Deutschland. Ziele und Wege der nationalsozialistischen Aussenpolitik.* München: Eher, 1935. 103 pp., tabs.

1632 FORSTMANN, ALBRECHT: *Der Kampf um den internationalen Handel.* Berlin: Haude & Spener, 1935. xii + 415 pp., tabs., bibl.

1633 FRIED, FERDINAND: *Die Zukunft des Aussenhandels. Durch innere Marktordnung zur Aussenhandelsfreiheit.* Jena: Diederichs, 1934. 89 pp.

1634 *Geschichte und Gesellschaft,* 2. Jhrg., 1976, Heft 1. [Special issue entitled] 'Aussenwirtschaft und Aussenpolitik im "Dritten Reich"'. Göttingen: Vandenhoeck & Ruprecht. 142 pp. [Ed. of this issue: Wolfgang Schneider.]

1635 HAMBLOCH, ERNEST: *Germany rampant. A study in economic militarism.* London: Duckworth, 1939. 297 pp., map.

1636 LADOR-LEDERER, J. JOSEF: *Capitalismo mondiale e cartelli tedeschi tra le due guerre.* [Turin]: Einaudi, 1959. 411 pp., tabs., bibl.

1637 MARSCHNER, HEINZ, ed.: *Deutschland in der Wirtschaft der Welt*. Berlin: Deutscher Verlag für Politik und Wirtschaft, 1937. 135 pp., maps, tabs., diagrs., bibl.

1638 MARTIN, JAMES STEWART: *All honorable men*. Boston: Little, Brown, 1950. 326 pp.

1639 MICKWITZ, EUGEN VON, ed.: *Aussenhandel unter Zwang, unter besonderer Berücksichtigung des Vierjahresplans und des Anschlusses Österreichs an das Reich. Auf Grund von Material des Hamburgischen Welt-Wirtschafts-Archivs*. Hamburg: 'Aussenhandel unter Zwang', 1938. 84 pp., tabs., graphs.

1640 PASSARGE, KARL, ed.: *Messebuch der deutschen Wirtschaft*. Berlin: Wiking Verlag, 1938. 278 pp., illus., tabs.

1641 REICHSSTELLE FÜR DEN AUSSENHANDEL: *Aus- und Einfuhrverbote des Deutschen Reichs, nach dem Gesetz über Aus- und Einfuhrverbote vom 25. März 1939. Devisenpolitische Abfertigungsverbote—Liste und Zuständigkeit der Reichsstellen zur Überwachung und Regelung des Warenverkehrs*. Berlin: Eildienst für amtliche und private Handelsnachrichten, 1940.

1642 REIMANN, GUENTER: *The vampire economy. Doing business under Fascism*. New York: Vanguard Press, 1939. 345 pp.

1643 SCHREIBER, MANFRED: *Grundzüge einer nationalorganischen Aussen-handelspolitik*. Jena: Fischer, 1935. xi + 204 pp., tabs.

1644 WENDT, BERND-JÜRGEN: *Appeasement 1938. Wirtschaftliche Rezession und Mitteleuropa*. Frankfurt a.M.: Europäische Verlagsanstalt, 1966. 151 pp., bibl.

1645 ZEELAND, PAUL van: *Bericht über die Möglichkeit eines allgemeinen Abbaus der Handelshemmnisse vom 26. Januar 1938*. Berlin: Junker & Dünnhaupt, 1938. 47 pp. (Schriften des Deutschen Instituts für Aussenpolitische Forschung ...).

Economic relations with other countries

ARGENTINE
1646 COMISIÓN INVESTIGADORA DE ACTIVIDADES ANTI-ARGENTINAS: *Formas y medios de la penetración totalitaria—'Oficina de Información de los Ferrocarriles Alemanes', enero de 1943*. Buenos Aires: Camara de Diputados de la Nación, 1943. 134 pp., facsims., tabs.

1647 EBEL, ARNOLD: *Die diplomatischen Beziehungen des Dritten Reiches zu Argentinien unter besonderer Berücksichtigung der Handelspolitik, 1933–1939*. Thèse présentée à l'Université de Genève. 1970. xvi + 472 pp., bibl.

BALKANS AND DANUBIAN STATES
1648 BASCH, ANTONIN: *The Danube Basin and the German economic sphere*. New York: Columbia University Press, 1943. 275 pp.

1649 GROSS, HERMANN: *Die wirtschaftliche Bedeutung Südosteuropas für das deutsche Reich*. Stuttgart: Kohlhammer, 1938. 26 pp. (Schriften der Deutschen Wirtschaftswissenschaftlichen Gesellschaft).

1650 KRUGMANN, R. W.: *Südosteuropa und Grossdeutschland. Entwicklung und Zukunftsmöglichkeiten der Wirtschaftsbeziehungen*. Breslau: Breslauer Verlags- und Druckerei GmbH, 1939. 204 pp.

1651 TRANDAFILOVITCH, IVAN: *L'expansion économique allemande vers le Sud-Est européen*. Paris: Librairie sociale et économique, 1939. 168 pp., diagr., graphs, tabs., bibl.

1652 VASSILIER, STEFAN: *L'Allemagne et le commerce extérieur des états balkaniques*. Paris: Domat-Montchrestien, 1939. 114 pp., tabs., bibl.

FRANCE

1653 *La grande duperie des échanges franco-allemands. Français, votre or sert à forger les armes allemandes*. Paris: Sorlot, 1939. 32 pp., diagrs., tabs.

GREAT BRITAIN

1654 FUNK, WALTHER: *Grundsätze der deutschen Aussenhandelspolitik und das Problem der internationalen Verschuldung. Rede ... Anhang: 'Deutsch-englisches Transferabkommen und Abkommen zur Abänderung des deutsch-englischen Zahlungsabkommens vom 1. Juli 1938'*. Berlin: Junker & Dünnhaupt, 1938. 32 pp. (Schriften des Deutschen Instituts für Aussenpolitische Forschung).

1655 WENDT, BERNDT-JÜRGEN: *Economic appeasement. Handel und Finanz in der britischen Deutschland-Politik 1933–1939*. Düsseldorf: Bertelsmann, 1971. 695 pp., tabs., bibl.

SPAIN

1656 HARPER, GLENN T.: *German economic policy in Spain during the Spanish Civil War, 1936–1939*. The Hague: Mouton, 1967. 150 pp., bibl.

SWEDEN

1657 WITTMANN, KLAUS: *Schwedens Wirtschaftsbeziehungen zum 'Dritten Reich' 1933–1945*. München: Oldenbourg, 1978. 479 pp.

SWITZERLAND

1658 *Deutsche Handelskammer in der Schweiz. 25 Jahre deutsch-schweizerischer Handel*. [Berlin: 1937]. 199 pp.

UNITED STATES OF AMERICA

1659 LONG, OLIVIER: *Les États-Unis et la Grande-Bretagne devant le IIIe Reich, 1934–1939. Un aspect du conflit des politiques commerciales avant la guerre*. Préface: William E. Rappard. Genève: Librairie de l'Université, 1943. 302 pp.

1660 SCHRÖDER, HANS-JÜRGEN: *Deutschland und die Vereinigten Staaten 1933–1939. Wirtschaft und Politik in der Entwicklung des deutsch-amerikanischen Gegensatzes*. Wiesbaden: Steiner, 1970. 338 pp., bibl. (Veröffentlichungen des Instituts für europäische Geschichte Mainz ...).

1661 UNITED STATES TARIFF COMMISSION: *Compilation of data on United States trade with Germany. A detailed analysis of imports of individual commodities together with a brief summary of United States imports from and exports to Germany.* Washington, D.C.: 1939. [200 pp.]

URUGUAY

1662 COMISIÓN INVESTIGADORA DE ACTIVIDADES ANTINACIONALES: *Movimento de fondos del Nazismo en el Uruguay.* Montevideo: Lagomarsimo, 1942. 49 + 19 pp., facsims., diagrs., tabs.

5. AGRICULTURE AND FOOD PRODUCTION

1663 BACKE, HERBERT, ed.: *Gesetzgebung auf dem Gebiet der Ernährungswirtschaft. Kommentar zu den Gesetzen und Bestimmungen für die Ernährung und Landwirtschaft.* München: Beck, 1941. 2 vols.

1664 BRANDT, KARL: *The German fat plan and its economic setting.* Stanford, Calif.: Food Research Institute, 1938. xii + 344 pp., diagrs., plans, tabs., bibl.

1665 DARRÉ, R. WALTHER: *Der Schweine Mord.* München: Eher, 1937. 147 pp.

1666 DECKEN, S. EBERHARD von der: *Die Front gegen den Hunger. Ernährungskrieg 1939–43.* Geleitw.: Reichsbauernführer. Mitarb.: E. Fritz Baer [and others.] Berlin: Engelhard, 1944. 175 pp.

1667 DOMMASCHK, HEINZ: *Das Bezugscheinwesen der Ernährungswirtschaft.* 2. wesent. erw. Aufl. Berlin: Deutsche Verlagsgesellschaft, 1941. 606 pp., tabs.

1668 DRESCHER, LEO: *Entschuldung der ostdeutschen Landwirtschaft. Auf Grund einer Untersuchung von Osthilfe-Entschuldungsbetrieben.* Bearb. im Auftr. der Bank für Deutsche Industrie-Obligationen. Berlin: Als Manuskript gedruckt, 1938. 88 + 96 pp., charts, diagrs.

1669 FARQUHARSON, J. E.: *The plough and the swastika. The NSDAP and agriculture in Germany, 1928–1945.* London: Sage, 1976. viii + 312 pp., tabs., bibl.

1670 HASSELBACH, W. von: *Marktordnung oder Zwangswirtschaft? Grundlagen und Probleme der ernährungswirtschaftlichen Marktordnung.* Berlin: Haude & Spener, 1942. 144 pp.

1671 REICHARDT, FRITZ, ed.: *Wie schlägt man die Erzeugungsschlacht? Richtige Ratschläge in drastischen Bilderfolgen.* Essen: Bildgut-Verlag, 1935. 87 pp., illus., diagrs.

1672 *Reichsministerialblatt der landwirtschaftlichen Verwaltung.* Berlin: Reichsverlagsamt, 1936–1945. 9 vols.

REICHSNÄHRSTAND

1673 REICHSNÄHRSTAND: *Archiv des Reichsnährstandes.* Berlin: 1933–1938. [Issued annually.]

1674 REICHSNÄHRSTAND: *Die Landbauernschaften in Zahlen.* Berlin: 1937–1943. [Issued annually.]

1675 HANEFELD, KURT: *Geschichte des deutschen Nährstandes*. Leipzig: Franke, 1935. 514 pp., tabs., bibl.

1676 REICHLE, HERMANN & SAUER, WILHELM: *Der Reichsnährstand. Aufbau, Aufgaben und Bedeutung*. 2. Aufl. Berlin: Reichsnährstand Verlag, 1936. 373 pp., maps, diagrs., tabs.

1677 SCHÜRMANN, ARTUR: *Deutsche Agrarpolitik*. Neudamm: Neumann, 1941. 518 pp., tabs., bibl.

1678 TOPF, ERWIN: *Die Grüne Front. Der Kampf um den deutschen Acker*. Berlin: Rowohlt, 1933. 295 pp.

1679 TORNOW, WERNER, ed.: *Chronik der Agrarpolitik und Agrarwirtschaft des Deutschen Reiches von 1933–1945*. Hamburg: Parey, 1972. 193 pp., bibl.

1680 ZIEGELMAYER, WILHELM: *Rohstoff-Fragen der deutschen Volksernährung. Eine Darstellung der ernährungswirtschaftlichen und ernährungswissenschaftlichen Aufgaben unserer Zeit mit einem Ausblick auf die Grossraumwirtschaft*. Dresden: Steinkopff, 1941. xiii + 374 pp., maps, tabs.

1681 ZISCHKA, ANTON: *Brot für zwei Milliarden Menschen*. Leipzig: Goldmann, 1941. 346 pp., illus., tabs., bibl. [First ed. 1938.]

Peasantry

1682 BACH, HANS: *Bauer und Boden. Leitfaden zur nationalsozialistischen Landpolitik*. Leipzig: Quelle & Meyer, 1942. 170 pp., bibl.

1683 EICHENAUER, RICHARD & PALLMANN, GERHARD, eds.: *Unser das Land. Ein Liederbuch des deutschen Dorfes*. Wolfenbüttel: Hallmeyer, 1937. 201 pp., mus. scores.

ERBHOFRECHT

1684 BAUMECKER, OTTO: *Handbuch des Grossdeutschen Erbhofrechts (unter Berücksichtigung der österreichischen, memelländischen, sudeten-deutschen und Danziger Bestimmungen)*. Mitarb.: Wolf Domke. Köln: Otto Schmidt, 1940. 1055 pp.

1685 KLINGLER, GÜNTHER: *Die Versorgungsrechte nach dem Reichserbhofgesetz, insbesondere die Heimatzuflucht*. Inaugural-Dissertation [pres. to] Eberhard-Karls-Universität zu Tübingen. 1937. 89 pp., bibl.

1686 LÜTZELER, FRANZ-KARL: *Erb- und Erbverzichtsverträge im Erbhofrecht*. Abhandlung [pres. to] Albert-Ludwigs-Universität zu Freiburg i.Br. 1936. 83 pp., bibl.

1687 ROSTOSKY, FRIEDRICH: *Die Bauern-Fibel vom Erbhofrechte*. Berlin: 'Offene Worte', [1935]. 127 pp., illus.

1688 VOGELS, WERNER, ed.: *Reichserbhofgesetz vom 29. September 1933*. 4. Aufl. Berlin: Vahlen, 1937. 988 pp.

1689　*Gesetz zur Regelung der Landwirtschaftlichen Schuldverhältnisse vom 1. Juni 1933 nebst Vollzugsverordnungen und ausführlichem Sachverzeichnis.* [By] Otto Woerner. 2. durchges. und verm. Aufl. München: Beck, 1935. vii + 236 pp.

1690　HOERNLE, EDWIN: *La situation des paysans en Allemagne hitlérienne.* Paris: Bureau d'Éditions, 1939. 154 pp.

1691　MERKEL, H. & WÖHRMANN, O.: *Deutsches Bauernrecht.* 4. teilw. umgearb. Aufl. Leipzig: Kohlhammer, 1942. 136 pp., bibl.

1692　MIELKE, ROBERT: *Der deutsche Bauer und sein Dorf in Vergangenheit und Gegenwart.* 4. Aufl. Weimar: Duncker, 1942. 134 pp., illus., plans. [First ed. 1934.]

1693　MÜLLER-PARTENKIRCHEN, FRITZ: *Rund um den Bückeberg. Erlebnisse und Berichte vom Ersten Deutschen Erntedanktag am 1. Oktober 1933.* Hrsg.: Kreisausschuss des Kreises Hameln-Pyrmont. Möser (Bezirk Magdeburg): Drescher, 1934. 64 pp., illus., plan.

1694　OECHSNER, HANS, ed.: *Der Bauer im Staat. Nationalsozialistische Bauernstaatskunde.* 5. neubearb. Aufl. Hannover: Schaper, 1936. 79 pp., illus., diagrs., maps.

1695　RUNGE, FRIEDRICH WILHELM, ed.: *Das Buch des deutschen Bauern.* Berlin: Zentralverlag, 1935. 278 pp., illus., diagrs., tabs.

1696　TILTON, TIMOTHY ALAN: *Nazism, neo-Nazism, and the peasantry.* Bloomington, Ind.: Indiana University Press, 1975. 186 pp., map, tabs., bibl.

6.　WORKERS

1696a　ARETZ, JÜRGEN: *Katholische Arbeiterbewegung und Nationalsozialismus. Der Verband Katholischer Arbeiter und Knappenvereine Westdeutschlands 1923–1945.* Mainz: Matthias-Grünewald-Verlag, 1978. 252 pp., bibl. (Veröffentlichungen der Kommission für Zeitgeschichte ...).

1697　ARNHOLD, KARL: *Der deutsche Betrieb. Aufgaben und Ziele nationalsozialistischer Betriebsführung.* Leipzig: Bibliographisches Institut, 1939. 118 pp.

1698　BEUTH, W.: *Hitler-Sozialismus. Den schaffenden Ständen der Stirne und der Faust gewidmet.* Frankfurt a.M.: Nationaler Buchverlag, 1933. 136 pp., tabs.

1699　DENCKLER, WERNER: *Handbuch für den Vertrauensmann und Betriebsführer.* Berlin: Denckler, [193–]. 64 pp.

1700　EMMERICH, WOLFGANG, ed.: *Proletarische Lebensläufe. Autobiographische Dokumente zur Entstehung der Zweiten Kultur in Deutschland. Band 2: 1914 bis 1945.* Reinbek b. Hamburg: Rowohlt, 1975. 474 pp., bibl.

1701　HADAMOVSKY, EUGEN: *Hilfsarbeiter Nr. 50000.* München: Eher, 1938. 235 pp.

1702 HOLTZ, ACHIM: *Nationalsozialistische Arbeitspolitik. Notwendigkeit und Bedeutung der Arbeitspolitik für den Umbruch und die Lenkung der Volkswirtschaft und ihr praktischer Einsatz.* Würzburg: Triltsch, 1938. 118 pp.

1703 INSTITUT FÜR MARXISMUS-LENINISMUS BEIM ZENTRALKOMITEE DER SED: *Geschichte der deutschen Arbeiterbewegung.* Berlin [East]: Dietz, 1966. Illus., facsims., tabs.
Bd. 4: *Von 1924 bis Januar 1933.* 634 pp.
Bd. 5: *Von Januar 1933 bis Mai 1945.* 664 pp.

1704 IRWAHN, FRITZ: *Feste der Arbeit.* 2. Aufl. Hamburg: Hanseatische Verlagsanstalt, 1936. 71 pp., bibl.

1705 KLOTZBACH, KURT: *Bibliographie zur Geschichte der deutschen Arbeiterbewegung 1914–1945. Sozialdemokratie, Freie Gewerkschaften, Christlich-Soziale Bewegungen, Kommunistische Bewegung und linke Splittergruppen. Mit einer forschungsgeschichtlichen Einleitung.* Bonn-Bad Godesberg: Verlag Neue Gesellschaft, 1974. 278 pp.

1706 KUCZYNSKI, JÜRGEN: *Die Geschichte der Lage der Arbeiter in Deutschland von 1800 bis in die Gegenwart. Bd. II: 1933 bis 1946.* Berlin: 'Die Freie Gewerkschaft' Verlagsgesellschaft, 1947. 292 pp., tabs. [English version: *Germany under Fascism, 1933 to the present day.* London: Muller, 1944.]

LAW RELATING TO WORKERS (Arbeitsrecht)
1707 BEYER, RUDOLF, ed.: *Hitlergesetz I. Arbeitsbeschaffungsprogramm: Gesetz zur Verminderung der Arbeitslosigkeit vom 1. Juni 1933 samt den Durchführungsverordnungen (Arbeitspendengesetz—Ehestandsdarlehen): Schuldnerschutz: Verordnung über Massnahmen auf dem Gebiete der Zwangsvollstreckung vom 26 Mai 1933. Textausgabe mit kurzen Anmerkungen und einem Nachtrag: Gesetzgebung bis Mitte Dezember 1933.* Leipzig: Reclam, 1933. 125 pp.

1708 DIETZ, ROLF, ed.: *Gesetz zur Ordnung der nationalen Arbeit und Gesetz zur Ordnung der Arbeit in öffentlichen Verwaltungen und Betrieben mit ihren Durchführungsverordnungen, den Einführungsverordnungen für die neuen Reichsgebiete, der Lohngestaltungsverordnung und den einschlägigen kriegsrechtlichen Vorschriften. Textausgabe mit Einleitung, Erläuterungen und Sachverzeichnis.* 7. durchgearb. und verm. Aufl. München: Beck, 1942. 453 pp.

1709 RIEDLER, ANTON: *Politische Arbeitslehre. Einführung in die weltanschauliche Begründung des Arbeitsrechtes.* Berlin-Südende: Südau, 1937. 115 pp.

1710 LÜDDECKE, THEODOR: *Nationalsozialistische Menschenführung in den Betrieben. Die Werkzeitung als Mittel der Wirtschaftsführung.* Hamburg: Hanseatischer Verlag, 1934. 190 pp.

1711 MASON, TIMOTHY: *Arbeiterklasse und Volksgemeinschaft. Dokumente und Materialien zur deutschen Arbeiterpolitik 1936–1939.* Opladen:

Westdeutscher Verlag, 1975. lxiii + 1299 pp., tabs., bibl. (Schriften des Zentralinstituts für sozialwissenschaftliche Forschung der Freien Universität Berlin).

1712 MAUR, HELMUT V.: *Die Sondertreuhänder der Arbeit—ihre Rechtsstellung und Aufgaben*. Inaugural-Dissertation [pres. to] Eberhard-Karls-Universität zu Tübingen. Borna-Leipzig: Noske, 1939. 101 pp., tabs., bibl.

1713 MICHEL, ERNST: *Sozialgeschichte der modernen Arbeitswelt*. Limburg a.d. Lahn: Steffen, 1937. 125 pp., bibl.

1714 MÜLLER, KARL VALENTIN: *Der Aufstieg des Arbeiters durch Rasse und Meisterschaft*. München: Lehmann, 1935. 160 pp., tabs.

1715 OPPENHEIMER-BLUHM, HILDE: *The standard of living of German labor under Nazi rule*. New York: Graduate Faculty of Political and Social Science, New School for Social Research, 1943. 71 pp., tabs.

1716 REICHSARBEITS- UND REICHSWIRTSCHAFTSRAT: *Neue Formen der Gemeinschaftsarbeit*. Berlin: 1935. 33 + 28 + 28 pp. [Text in German, English, French.]

1717 SCHAUMBURG-LIPPE, FRIEDRICH CHRISTIAN Prinz zu, ed.: *Deutsche Sozialisten am Werk. Ein sozialistisches Bekenntnis deutscher Männer*. Berlin: Deutscher Verlag für Politik und Wirtschaft, 1936. 196 pp.

1718 TIMM, HERBERT: *Das Grundproblem der modernen Vollbeschäftigung*. Darmstadt: Buske, 1940. 148 pp.

WINNIG, AUGUST
1719 WINNIG, AUGUST: *Vom Proletariat zum Arbeitertum*. Hamburg: Hanseatische Verlagsanstalt, 1941. 227 pp.

1720 *Ein deutsches Gewissen. Dank an August Winnig*. Berlin-Steglitz: Eckart-Verlag, 1938. 83 pp., port.

1721 WOLFFSOHN, MICHAEL: *Industrie und Handwerk im Konflikt mit staatlicher Wirtschaftspolitik? Studien zur Politik der Arbeitsbeschaffung in Deutschland 1930–1934*. Berlin: Duncker & Humblot, 1977. 504 pp. [Orig. a dissertation, Freie Universität Berlin, 1975.]

Deutsche Arbeitsfront

1722 ARNHOLD, KARL: *Das Ringen um die Arbeitsidee. Gesammelte Aufsätze*. Berlin: Verlag der Deutschen Arbeitsfront, 1938. 173 pp. [Author was 'Leiter des Amtes für Berufserziehung und Betriebsführung in der Deutschen Arbeitsfront'.]

1723 BIALLAS, HANS & STARCKE, GERHARD, eds.: *Leipzig, das Nürnberg der Deutschen Arbeitsfront. Ein Bericht in Bildern und Reden über die Reichstagung der Deutschen Arbeitsfront in Leipzig vom 25. bis. 30. März 1935*. Vorw.: Claus Selzner. München: Eher, 1935. 192 pp., illus.

1724 DEUTSCHE ARBEITSFRONT: *Deutsche Sozialpolitik. Jahresbericht der Deutschen Arbeitsfront Zentralbüro, Sozialamt.* Berlin: Verlag der Deutschen Arbeitsfront, 1937. 252 pp., maps, tabs., diagrs.

1725 DEUTSCHE ARBEITSFRONT: *Kalender der deutschen Arbeit. 1939.* [Berlin: Verlag der Deutschen Arbeitsfront, 1939]. 175 pp. [Incl.: 'Grundsteinlegung der KdF-Wagen-Fabrik'.]

1726 JAGUSCH, HEINRICH: *Die Rechtsberatungsstellen der Deutschen Arbeitsfront, ihre Aufgaben, ihr Wesen und ihre Rechtsverhältnisse.* Berlin: Deutscher Rechtsverlag, 1940. 151 pp.

1727 JÖSTLEIN, HANS: *Die Deutsche Arbeitsfront. Werden, Wesen und Aufgaben.* Inaugural-Dissertation [pres. to] Bayerische Julius-Maximilians-Universität Würzburg. 1935. 84 pp., bibl.

1728 MARRENBACH, OTTO, ed.: *Fundamente des Sieges. Die Gesamtarbeit der Deutschen Arbeitsfront von 1933 bis 1940.* Unter Mitw. der Amtsleiter des Zentralbüros der DAF. 2. Aufl. Berlin: Verlag der Deutschen Arbeitsfront, 1941. 418 pp.

1729 MÜLLER, WILLY: *Das soziale Leben im neuen Deutschland, unter besonderer Berücksichtigung der Deutschen Arbeitsfront.* Berlin: Mittler, 1938. 198 pp.

1730 MÜNCHEBERG, FRIEDRICH: *Die Organisation der Arbeit durch die Deutsche Arbeitsfront.* Inaugural-Dissertation [pres. to] Friedrich Schiller-Universität Jena. 1935. 64 pp., diagr., tabs., bibl.

1731 *Organisation der Deutschen Arbeitsfront und der N.S. Gemeinschaft Kraft durch Freude.* Deutsche Arbeitsfront, 1934. 159 pp.

1732 PREIS, ERWIN, ed.: *Königswinter. Tage der Pflicht und Kameradschaft. Erlebnis und Erfolg der Lehrgänge 'Druck und Papier' der Deutschen Arbeitsfront für Betriebsführer, Betriebsobmänner und DAF.-Walter vom September 1936 bis Oktober 1938.* Hrsg.: Leiter des Fachamtes ... Fritz Ebenbock. Berlin: Zander, 1939. 119 pp., illus., facsims.

1733 STARCKE, GERHARD: *N.S.B.O. und Deutsche Arbeitsfront.* Berlin: Hobbing, 1934. 259 pp., illus., tab. [The NS-Betriebszellen-Organisation, the 'industrial shock troops' of the Kampfzeit, was later incorporated into the Deutsche Arbeitsfront.]

1734 STARCKE, GERHARD: *Die Presse der Deutschen Arbeitsfront. Ihre politische Bedeutung nach der Umgestaltung.* Leipzig: Noske, 1936. 31 pp.

Strength through Joy (Kraft durch Freude)

1735 AMELN, HEINZ, ed.: *Werkleute singen. Lieder der NS-Gemeinschaft 'Kraft durch Freude'.* Geleitw.: Robert Ley. Im Auftr. des Gaues Südhannover-Braunschweig ... Kassel: Bärenreiter-Verlag, 1936. 66 pp., mus. scores.

1736 BIALLAS, HANS: *Der Sonne entgegen! Deutsche Arbeiter fahren nach Madeira.* Berlin: Freiheitsverlag, 1936. 112 pp., illus., facsims.

1737 DEUTSCHE ARBEITSFRONT/NS.-GEMEINSCHAFT 'KRAFT DURCH FREUDE': *Ein*

Querschnitt durch den Arbeitsplan und die Arbeitswesen einer Volksbildungsstätte des Amtes Deutsches Volksbildungswerk. Berlin: Verlag der Deutschen Arbeitsfront, [1939?]. [48 pp.], illus.

1738 HÜBBENET, ANATOL VON: *Die N.S.-Gemeinschaft 'Kraft durch Freude'. Aufbau und Arbeit.* Berlin: Junker & Dünnhaupt, 1939. 62 pp.

1739 INTERNATIONAL CENTRAL BUREAU JOY AND WORK: *Joy and Work. Bibliographical materials. Compiled and published ... in Berlin on the Third World Congress 'Work and Joy' in Rome 1938/XVI.* Berlin: 1938. 396 pp.

1740 INTERNATIONAL CENTRAL BUREAU JOY AND WORK: *World Congress for Leisure Time and Recreation, Hamburg, July 23 to July 30, 1936. Report.* Hamburg: Hanseatische Verlagsanstalt, 1937. 732 pp.

1741 LEY, ROBERT: *Ein Volk erobert die Freude.* Berlin: Verlag der Deutschen Arbeitsfront, 1937. 33 pp.

1742 NS-GEMEINSCHAFT 'KRAFT DURCH FREUDE': *Fünf Jahre 'Kraft durch Freude'. Leistungsbericht zum 27. November 1938.* Berlin: Verlag der Deutschen Arbeitsfront, 1938. 51 pp.

1743 REICHSAMTSLEITUNG K.d.F.: *Unter dem Sonnenrad. Ein Buch von Kraft durch Freude.* Berlin: Verlag der Deutschen Arbeitsfront, 1938. 198 pp., illus.

1744 SCHAFFNER, JAKOB: *Volk zu Schiff! Zwei Seefahrten mit der 'KdF'-Hochseeflotte.* Hamburg: Hanseatische Verlagsanstalt, 1936. 168 pp., illus.

1745 WEIR, L. H.: *Europe at play. A study of recreation and leisure time activities.* New York: Barnes, 1937. 589 pp., tabs., illus., bibl.

Craftsmen

1746 BOLLER, HANS-HERMANN: *Pflege des Handwerks in Deutschland.* [Berlin: 1939?]. 87 pp., illus.

1747 CHESI, VALENTIN: *Struktur und Funktionen der Handwerksorganisation in Deutschland seit 1933. Ein Beitrag zur Verbandstheorie.* Berlin: Duncker & Humblot, 1966. 245 pp., tabs., diagrs., bibl. [Third Reich, pp. 17–131.]

1748 *Jahrbuch des Deutschen Handwerks 1935. 1. Juli 1934 bis 31. Dezember 1935.* Berlin: Haus des Deutschen Handwerks, 1936. 228 pp., diagrs., tabs.

1749 LEERS, JOHANN VON: *Das Lebensbild des deutschen Handwerks.* Hrsg.: Deutsches Handwerksinstitut im Reichsstand des deutschen Handwerks. München: Zeleny, 1938. xi + 644 pp., illus., tabs.

1750 MEUSCH, H.: *Deutsches Handwerksrecht. Textausgabe des Gesetzes ... vom 29. November 1933 und der bis zum 1. Oktober 1935 erlassenen Verordnungen ...* 3. wesent. erw. Aufl. Essen: Haarfeld, 1935. 280 pp.

1751 PURPUS, H.: *Was der Handwerker von den Gesetzen wissen muss.* In 44. Aufl. bearb. und hrsg. von C. Frettlöh. Augsburg: Rösler, 1938. xviii + 222 pp., diagrs., tabs.

1752 [REICHSHANDWERKERTAG] *Festbuch zum Reichshandwerkertag. 12. bis 23.*

Juni 1935 Frankfurt a.M. Hrsg.: Deutsche Arbeitsfront, Reichsbetriebsgemeinschaft Handwerk. [1935]. 119 pp., illus.

1753 SCHRAMM, FERDINAND: *Der Reichsstand des Deutschen Handwerks.* Berlin: Junker & Dünnhaupt, 1941. 60 pp.

1754 SCHRAUT, RUDOLF and others: *Das Handwerk in Staat und Wirtschaft.* Berlin: Verlag für Handwerk und Gewerbe, 1938. 461 pp., map, tabs., diagrs.

1755 SCHÜLER, FELIX: *Das deutsche Handwerk in der Kriegswirtschaft.* Mit einem Geleitw. des Reichshandwerksmeisters. Stuttgart: Kohlhammer, 1941. 59 pp., diagrs., tabs. (Deutsche Wirtschaftswissenschaftliche Gesellschaft ...).

1756 SPITZ, H.: *Die Organisation des Deutschen Handwerks. Stand: 1.6. 1936.* München: Zeleny, 1936. 953 pp., ports., diagrs.

1757 STADLINGER, FRIEDRICH & STOLLREITER, HEINRICH: *Lehrling, Geselle, Meister im Dritten Reich. Kurzgefasste Wiederholung zur Meisterprüfung. Ein Merkbuch für Berufs- und Fachschulen—Ein Nachschlagebuch für die Praxis.* Hannover: Meyer, 1938. 107 pp., tabs.

1758 STEUERNAGEL, FRIEDRICH: *Die Gestaltung des Lebensraumes des deutschen Handwerks seit 1933.* München: Zeleny, 1939. 182 pp., bibl.

1759 ZEE-HERÄUS, BERNH[ARD] & HOMANN, FRITZ: *Das Handwerk und seine Verfassung.* Hamburg: Hanseatische Verlagsanstalt, 1937. 109 pp.

7. ECONOMIC PREPARATIONS FOR WAR

AUTOBAHNEN

1760 *Deutschlands Autobahnen. Adolf Hitlers Strassen.* Hrsg. im Auftr. des Gen. Inspektors für das deutsche Strassenwesen. Bayreuth: Hausverlag Bayer. Ostmark, 1937. 278 pp., illus., maps.

1761 *Die Reichsautobahnen. Principles of design, construction and traffic control.* Ed.: Volk und Reich Verlag on behalf of the Inspector General of the German roads. Berlin: 1938. 45 pp., illus., maps, diagrs.

1762 SCHUDER, KURT: *Die Strassen Adolf Hitlers—ein Dombau unserer Zeit.* Braunschweig: Westermann, 1940. 169 pp.

1763 TODT, FRITZ: *Die Strassen Adolf Hitlers.* Zusammengest. und bearb. von Otto Reismann. Hrsg.: NS.-Kulturgemeinde. Berlin: Hillger, [193–]. 32 pp., map, illus.

1764 VOLLBEHR, ERNST: *Arbeitsschlacht. Fünf Jahre Malfahrten auf den Bauplätzen der 'Strassen Adolf Hitlers'.* Berlin: Andermann, 1938. 151 pp., illus.

1765 BAGEL-BOHLAN, ANJA E.: *Hitlers industrielle Kriegsvorbereitungen 1936–1939.* Koblenz: Wehr und Wissen, 1975. 143 pp., tabs., bibl.

1766 CARROLL, BERENICE A.: *Design for total war. Arms and economics in the Third Reich.* The Hague: Mouton, 1968. 311 pp., diagrs., tabs., bibl.

1767 EICHHOLTZ, DIETRICH & SCHUMANN, WOLFGANG, eds.: *Anatomie des Krieges. Neue Dokumente über die Rolle des deutschen Monopolkapitals bei der Vorbereitung und Durchführung des Zweiten Weltkrieges.* Berlin [East]: VEB Deutscher Verlag der Wissenschaften, 1969. 523 pp., illus.

1768 FORSTMEIER, FRIEDRICH & VOLKMANN, HANS ERICH, eds.: *Wirtschaft und Rüstung am Vorabend des Zweiten Weltkrieges.* Für das Militärgeschichtliche Forschungsamt hrsg. Düsseldorf: Droste, 1975. 415 pp., tabs.

1769 HESSE, KURT: *Der kriegswirtschaftliche Gedanke.* Hamburg: Hanseatische Verlagsanstalt, 1935. 52 pp., bibl.

1770 KLEIN, BURTON H.: *Germany's economic preparations for war.* Cambridge, Mass.: Harvard University Press, 1959. 272 pp., tabs., bibl.

1771 NATHAN, OTTO & FRIED, MILTON: *The Nazi economic system. Germany's mobilization for war.* Durham, N.C.: Duke University Press, 1944. ix + 378 pp., tabs.

1772 POSSONY, STEFAN Th.: *Die Wehrwirtschaft des totalen Krieges.* Wien: Gerold, 1938. 155 pp., tabs., diagrs.

1773 REICHSAMT FÜR WEHRWIRTSCHAFTLICHE PLANUNG: *Die deutsche Industrie. Gesamtergebnisse der amtlichen Produktionsstatistik.* Berlin: Schmidt, 1939. 159 pp., maps, diagrs., tabs.

1774 ROTHE, CARL: *Wirtschaftskrieg und Kriegswirtschaft. Die Rolle der Landesverteidigung in der Friedenswirtschaft.* Leipzig: Goldmann, 1936. 77 pp.

1775 THOMAS, GEORG: *Geschichte der deutschen Wehr- und Rüstungswirtschaft 1918–1943/45.* Hrsg.: Wolfgang Birkenfeld. Boppard a.Rh.: Boldt, 1966. 552 pp., illus., facsims., diagrs., tabs. (Schriften des Bundesarchivs . . .).

G. RELIGION

1. THE CHURCHES IN THE KAMPFZEIT

1776 ALBANI, JOHANNES: *Aus gärender Zeit. Zwischen Eisner und Hitler. Geistliche Gedanken aus deutschen Schicksalstagen.* Paderborn: Jungfermann, 1928. 124 pp.

1777 BREUNING, KLAUS: *Die Vision des Reichs. Deutscher Katholizismus zwischen Demokratie und Diktatur 1929–1934.* München: Hueber, 1969. 403 pp., facsims., bibl.

1778 ENGEL, WILHELM: *Christenkreuz, Hakenkreuz, Sowjetstern. Ein Appell an Eltern, Lehrer und Erzieher deutscher Jugend.* Werdau: Arbeitsgemeinschaft nationalsozialistischer Pfarrer, 1932. 23 pp.

1779 FISCHER, FRANZ: *Die Sendung der christlichen Kirche im deutschen Freiheitskampf.* Vorw.: Hans Koch. Wien: Evangelischer Presseverband für Österreich, 1933. 38 pp.

1780 KLOTZ, LEOPOLD, ed.: *Die Kirche und das Dritte Reich. Fragen und Forderungen deutscher Theologen.* Gotha: Klotz, 1932. In 2 vols. [Symposium by Protestant theologians on the National Socialist movement.]

1781 KOFLER, J. A.: *Katholische Kirche und Judentum.* 2. Aufl. München: Eher, 1931. 55 pp. [First ed. 1928.]

KÜPPERS, HEINRICH: *Der katholische Lehrerverband in der Übergangszeit von der Weimarer Republik zur Hitler-Diktatur. Zugleich ein Beitrag zur Geschichte des Volksschullehrerstandes. See* 2247.

1782 MEIER, KURT: 'Die Religionspolitik der NSDAP in der Zeit der Weimarer Republik'. [In] *Zur Geschichte des Kirchenkampfes II. See* 1956.

1783 NÖTGES, JAKOB: *Nationalsozialismus und Katholizismus.* Köln: Gilde-Verlag, 1931. 223 pp. [Against 'errors and exaggerations of National Socialism'.]

1784 SCHOLDER, KLAUS: *Die Kirchen und das Dritte Reich.* Frankfurt a.M.: Propyläen-Verlag, 1977–
Bd. I: *Vorgeschichte und Zeit der Illusionen 1918–1934.* ix + 897 pp., illus., maps, bibl.

1785 SCHREINER, HELMUTH: *Der Nationalsozialismus vor der Gottesfrage. Illusion oder Evangelium?* Berlin-Spandau: Wichern, 1932. 62 pp. [14.–15. Taus. Cover design by A. Paul Weber. Critical examination of National Socialist literature on religion.]

1786 SENN, WILHELM MARIA: *Katholizismus und Nationalsozialismus. Eine Rede an den deutschen Katholizismus.* Münster (Westf.): Abwehr-Verlag, 1931. 95 pp.
Halt! Meine zweite Rede an den deutschen Katholizismus und—nach Rom. München: Eher, [193–]. 96 pp.
[Anti-Catholic.]

1787 STEFFEN, FRANZ: *Antisemitische und deutsch-völkische Bewegung im Lichte des Katholizismus.* Berlin: Philo Verlag, 1925. 91 pp., illus., bibl.

ZENTRUM (German Centre Party)
1788 JORDAN, RUDOLF: *Das demaskierte Zentrum. Kampfschrift gegen den Verrat des Zentrums an Religion und Volk.* Dresden: Drei-Eichen Verlag, [1931?]. 32 pp., facsims. [Author became Gauleiter of Magdeburg.]

1789 JUNKER, DETLEF: *Die Deutsche Zentrumspartei und Hitler 1932/33. Ein Beitrag zur Problematik des politischen Katholizismus in Deutschland.* Stuttgart: Klett, 1969. 247 pp., bibl.

MORSEY, RUDOLF: *Der Untergang des politischen Katholizismus. See* 1115.

2. RELIGION IN THE THIRD REICH

a. General

1790 BAUER, GÜNTHER: *Kirchliche Rundfunkarbeit, 1924–1939.* Frankfurt a.M.: Knecht, 1966. 135 pp., bibl.

1791 BENDISCIOLI, MARIO: *La Germania religiosa nel IIIo Reich. Conflitti religiosi e culturali nella Germania nazista.* Brescia: Morcelliana, 1936. viii + 310 pp., tab.

1792 BUCHHEIM, HANS: *Glaubenskrise im Dritten Reich. Drei Kapitel national-sozialistischer Religionspolitik.* Stuttgart: Deutsche Verlags-Anstalt, 1953. 223 pp.

1793 GAZELLES, HENRI: *Église et état en Allemagne de Weimar et aux premières années du IIIe Reich.* Paris: Rousseau, 1936. 283 pp.

1794 GURIAN, WALDEMAR: *Hitler and the Christians.* Transl. from the German. London: Sheed & Ward, 1936. 175 pp. [German orig.: *Der Kampf um die Kirche im Dritten Reich.* 2. Aufl. Luzern: Vita Nova, 1936.]

1795 HALBAN, LEON: *Religja Trzeciej Rzeszy* [Religion in the Third Reich]. Łwów: Nakład Towarzystwa Naukowego, 1936. 402 pp., summary in French. [Archives of the Learned Society of Lwow.]

1796 HELMREICH, ERNST CHRISTIAN: *The German churches under Hitler. Background, struggle and epilogue.* Detroit, Mich.: Wayne State University Press, 1979. 616 pp., bibl.

1797 HERRMANN, GOTTHILF: *Der nationalsozialistische Staat und die religiösen Bekenntnisse. Anhang: Das Gesetz über die Feiertage—Die Verordnung über den Schutz der Sonn- und Feiertage.* 3. erw. Aufl. Zwickau (Sachsen): Herrmann, [1934]. 28 pp.

1798 HERRMANN, GOTTHILF, ed.: *Religionsfreiheit. Amtliche Dokumente—Worte führender Männer.* 5. erw. Aufl. Zwickau (Sachsen): Herrmann, 1936. 110 pp.

JEHOVAH'S WITNESSES
1799 JONAK VON FREYENWALD, HANS: *Die Zeugen Jehovas. Pioniere für ein jüdisches Weltreich. Die politischen Ziele der Internationalen Vereinigung Ernster Bibelforscher.* Berlin: Buchverlag Germania, 1936. 103 pp., bibl.

1800 KATER, MICHAEL H.: 'Die Ernsten Bibelforscher im Dritten Reich'. [In] *Vierteljahrshefte für Zeitgeschichte*, 17. Jhrg., 2. Heft, 1969. Pp. 181–218.

─────────────

1801 KRETSCHMAR, GEORG, ed.: *Dokumente zur Kirchenpolitik des Dritten Reiches.* Bearb.: Carsten Nicolaisen. München: Kaiser, 1971–
Bd. I: *Das Jahr 1933.* Publ. 1971. xxiv + 221 pp.
Bd. II: *1934/35. Vom Beginn des Jahres 1934 bis zur Errichtung des Reichsministeriums für die kirchlichen Angelegenheiten am 16. Juli 1935.* Publ. 1975. xxviii + 368 pp.

1802 KROSE, HERMANN: *Statistik der Religionsgemeinschaften im Deutschen Reich, in den Ländern und Verwaltungsbezirken.* Köln: Bachem, 1937. 103 pp.

1803 MACFARLAND, CHARLES S.: *The new Church and the new Germany. A study of Church and State.* New York: Macmillan, 1934. xii + 209 pp.

1804 MILES ECCLESIAE, pseud.: *Hitler gegen Christus. Eine katholische Klarstellung und Abwehr.* Paris: Société d'Éditions européennes, 1936. 191 pp., illus., facsims.

1805 *Der neue Glaube oder Die religiöse Weltanschauung der Gegenwart. Entstanden in einer Arbeitsgemeinschaft deutscher Theologen.* Leipzig: Heitz, 1935. 500 pp.

1806 SCHOTT, ERDMANN: *Die nationalsozialistische Revolution als theologisches Problem. 1933 im Lichte von 1866.* Tübingen: Mohr, 1933. 27 pp.

1807 SIEGELE-WENSCHKEWITZ, LEONORE: *Nationalsozialismus und Kirche. Religionspolitik von Partei und Staat bis 1935.* Düsseldorf: Droste, 1974. 235 pp., bibl. (Tübinger Schriften zur Sozial- und Zeitgeschichte).

1808 STAPEL, WILHELM: *Die Kirche Christi und der Staat Adolf Hitlers.* 4. Aufl. Hamburg: Hanseatische Verlagsanstalt, [1933]. 89 pp.

STATISTISCHES REICHSAMT: 'Die Bevölkerung des Deutschen Reiches nach der Religionszugehörigkeit' [1933]. *See* 15.

1809 TESCHITZ, KARL: *Religion, Kirche, Religionsstreit in Deutschland.* Kopenhagen: Sexpol-Verlag, 1935. 112 pp., bibl.

1810 [THEOSOPHY] RUDOLPH, HERMANN: *Nationalsozialismus und Theosophie. Ihr Wesen und ihre gegenseitigen Beziehungen.* Leipzig: Theosophischer Kultur-Verlag, 1934. 42 pp.

b. Christians and Jews

1811 BLÜHER, HANS: *Streit um Israel. Ein jüdisch-christliches Gespräch.* Hamburg: Hanseatische Verlagsanstalt, 1933. 120 pp.

1812 BUSCH, EBERHARD: *Juden und Christen im Schatten des Dritten Reiches. Ansätze zu einer Kritik des Antisemitismus in der Zeit der Bekennenden Kirche.* München: Kaiser, 1979. 76 pp.

1813 FAULHABER, [MICHAEL von]: *Judentum, Christentum, Germanentum. Adventspredigt ... München 1933.* München: Huber, [1933]. 124 pp., port.

1814 FAULHABER, [MICHAEL von]: *Juifs et Chrétiens devant le racisme.* Paris: Sorlot, 1934. 118 pp. [Transl. from the German.]

1815 GERLACH, WOLFGANG: *Zwischen Kreuz und Davidstern. Bekennende Kirche in ihrer Stellung zum Judentum im Dritten Reich.* Dissertation [pres. to] Universität Hamburg. 1972. 513 + 163 pp., bibl.

1816 GRUNDMANN, WALTER, ed.: *Christentum und Judentum* [Bd. I]: *Germanentum, Christentum und Judentum* [Bd. II & III]. *Studien zur Erforschung ihres*

gegenseitigen Verhältnisses. Sitzungsberichte der ... Arbeitstagung des Institutes zur Erforschung des jüdischen Einflusses auf das deutsche kirchliche Leben ... Leipzig: Wigand, 1940/43. 3 vols.
Bd. I: *... 1. Arbeitstagung ... vom 1. bis 3. März 1940 in Wittenberg.*
Bd. II: *... 2. Arbeitstagung ... vom 3. bis 5. März 1941 in Eisenach.*
Bd. III: *... 3. Arbeitstagung ... vom 9. bis 11. Juli 1942 in Nürnberg.*

1817 GUTTERIDGE, RICHARD: *Open thy mouth for the dumb! The German Evangelical Church and the Jews, 1879–1950.* Oxford: Blackwell, 1976. 374 pp., bibl. [Incl. anti-Semitism and the failure to speak out for the Jews during the Third Reich.]

1818 INSTITUT ZUR ERFORSCHUNG DES JÜDISCHEN EINFLUSSES AUF DAS DEUTSCHE KIRCHLICHE LEBEN: *Die Botschaft Gottes.* Leipzig: Wigand, 1940. 296 pp. [108 pp. version: Weimar: Verlag Deutsche Christen, 1940.]

1819 JONCA, KAROL: 'Kościoł Ewangelicki na Śląsku wobec polityki rasistowskiej NSDAP' [The attitude of the Evangelical Church in Silesia to the racist policies of the NSDAP]. [In] *Studia Śląskie,* seria nowa, tom. 35, 1979. Pp. 131–179, summaries in English and German.

KITTEL, GERHARD
1820 KITTEL, GERHARD: *Die Judenfrage.* Mit 2 Beilagen: 'Antwort an Martin Buber', 'Kirche und Judenchristen'. 3. Aufl. Stuttgart: Kohlhammer, 1934. 135 pp. [First & second eds. 1933.]

1821 SIEGELE-WENSCHKEWITZ, LEONORE: *Die Evangelisch-Theologische Fakultät Tübingen in den Anfangsjahren des Dritten Reichs. 2: Gerhard Kittel und die Judenfrage.* Tübingen: Mohr, 1978. 80 pp.

1822 LITTELL, FRANKLIN H. & LOCKE, HUBERT G.: *The German church struggle and the Holocaust.* Detroit, Mich.: Wayne State University Press, 1974. 327 pp., bibl.

1823 [LUTHER, MARTIN] LINDEN, WALTHER, ed.: *Luthers Kampfschriften gegen das Judentum.* Berlin: Klinkhardt & Biermann, 1936. 234 pp., illus.

1824 PETERS, BERNHARD: *Arier und Jude. Ein Beitrag zur Judenfrage und ihrer Lösung.* Worms a.Rh.: Verlag Missions-Buchhandlung, 1934. 96 pp.

1825 STROBL, GUSTAV: *Kann ein Christ Antisemit sein? Die Briefe des Erzbischofs Agobard in Lyon über die Juden.* Erfurt: Bodung, 1937. 120 pp., bibl. [Also publ. under title: *Das goldene Zeitalter der Juden.*]

c. **Kirchenkampf: oppression, persecution, opposition and resistance**

1826 BERGER, ALEXANDER: *Kreuz hinter Stacheldraht. Der Leidensweg deutscher Pfarrer.* Bayreuth: Hestia, 1963. 239 pp.

1827 BERNADAC, CHRISTIAN: *Les sorciers du ciel.* Paris: Éds. France-Empire, 1969. 398 pp. [Priests in concentration camps.]

1828 BOYENS, ARMIN: *Kirchenkampf und Ökumene 1933–1939. Darstellung und Dokumentation.* München: Kaiser, 1969. 486 pp., bibl.

1829 CONWAY, J. S.: *The Nazi persecution of the Churches, 1933–1945.* London: Weidenfeld & Nicolson, 1968. 474 pp., illus., facsims., bibl.

1830 DIEHN, OTTO: *Bibliographie zur Geschichte des Kirchenkampfes 1933–1945.* Göttingen: Vandenhoeck und Ruprecht, 1958. 249 pp.

1831 DROBISCH, KLAUS, ed.: *Christen im Nationalkomitee 'Freies Deutschland'. Eine Dokumentation.* Berlin [East]: Union Verlag, 1973. 310 pp., illus., facsims.

1832 DUNCAN-JONES, A. S.: *The struggle for religious freedom in Germany.* London: Gollancz, 1938. 319 pp.

1833 EHRLE, GERTRUD, ed.: *Licht über dem Abgrund. Aufzeichnungen und Erlebnisse christlicher Frauen 1933–1945.* Freiburg: Herder, 1951. 236 pp. [Incl. Father Delp and Count von Moltke.]

1834 GEIS, ROBERT RAPHAEL and others: *Männer des Glaubens im deutschen Widerstand.* München: Ner-Tamid-Verlag, 1959. 71 pp. [Comprising: R. R. Geis: 'Leo Baeck'; Oskar Hammelbeck: 'Dietrich Bonhoeffer'; Oskar Simmel: 'Alfred Delp'.]

1835 KAMPMANN, THEODERICH: *Gelebter Glaube. Zwölf Porträts.* Warendorf, Westf.: Schnell, 1957. 169 pp. [Incl.: Theodor Haecker, Karl Muth, Romano Guardini, Paul Simon, Hans Ehrenberg.]

1836 KIRCHLICHE HOCHSCHULE BERLIN: *Repertorium des Archivs für die Geschichte des Kirchenkampfes. Stand: Februar 1972.* xv + 246 pp., mimeog.

1837 LAATSMAN, W.: *De Duitsche kerkstrijd: Waarheid of leugen?* Zwolle: La Rivière & Voorhoeve, 1937. 207 pp., illus. [Pro-Nazi.]

1838 MASON, JOHN BROWN: *Hitler's first foes. A study in religion and politics.* Minneapolis, Minn.: Burgess, 1936. 118 pp.

1839 PEETERS, Fl. J. P.: *Het bruine Bolsjewisme. Over de Christenverfolging in het Derde Rijk.* Antwerp: 'Geloofsverdediging', 1937. viii + 169 pp., illus.

1840 PELKE, ELSE: *Der Lübecker Christenprozess 1943.* Nachw.: Stephanus Pfürtner. Mainz: Matthias-Grünewald-Verlag, 1961. 275 pp., ports. [Trial and execution of three Catholic priests and a Protestant pastor.]

1841 SCHJELDERUP, KRISTIAN: *På vei mot hedenskapet. Trekk av den tyske religionskamp.* Oslo: Nygaard, 1935. 142 pp., bibl.

1842 SHUSTER, GEORGE N.: *Like a mighty army. Hitler versus established religion.* New York: Appleton-Century, 1935. 286 pp. [Incl.: 'The war on the Jews', pp. 53–93.]

1843 *Sous le joug hitlérien. La révolte des consciences.* Paris: Maison de la Bonne Presse, 1937. 127 pp.

1844 STEWARD, JOHN S.: *Sieg des Glaubens. Authentische Gestapoberichte über den kirchlichen Widerstand in Deutschland.* Zürich: Thomas, 1946. 119 pp.

[Mainly about Catholic resistance in Southern Germany, but includes reports on the Evangelical Church.]

1845 VESTERS, J. A.: *Hakenkruis tegen Kruis. Zes jaar Hitler-regiem.* Utrecht: Vobie, 1939. 151 pp.

1846 ZIPFEL, FRIEDRICH: *Kirchenkampf in Deutschland 1933–1945. Religionsverfolgung und Selbstbehauptung der Kirchen in der nationalsozialistischen Zeit.* Einl.: Hans Herzfeld. Berlin: de Gruyter, 1965. xiv + 571 pp., tabs., diagrs., bibl. (Veröffentlichungen der Historischen Kommission zu Berlin beim Friedrich-Meinecke-Institut der Freien Universität Berlin ...).

See also Concentration camps, particularly Dachau.

The Churches and Alfred Rosenberg's 'Der Mythus des 20. Jahrhunderts'

1847 BAUMGÄRTNER, RAIMUND: *Weltanschauungskampf im Dritten Reich. Die Auseinandersetzung der Kirchen mit Alfred Rosenberg.* Mainz: Matthias-Grünewald-Verlag, 1977. xxxii + 275 pp., bibl. (Veröffentlichungen der Kommission für Zeitgeschichte ...).

1848 GRUNDMANN, WALTER: *Gott und Nation. Ein evangelisches Wort zum Wollen des Nationalsozialismus und zu Rosenbergs Sinndeutung.* 2. erw. Aufl. Berlin: Furche-Verlag, 1933. 123 pp. (Stimmen aus der deutschen christlichen Studentenbewegung).

1849 HOMANN, RUDOLF: *Der Mythus und das Evangelium. Die evangelische Kirche in Abwehr und Angriff gegenüber dem 'Mythus des 20. Jahrhunderts' von Alfred Rosenberg. Unter Berücksichtigung der soeben erschienenen neuesten Schrift 'An die Dunkelmänner unserer Zeit'.* 3. Aufl. Witten: Westdeutscher Lutherverlag, 1935. xvi + 200 pp.

1850 *Kirchlicher Anzeiger—Amtliche Beilage: Studien zum Mythus des XX. Jahrhunderts.* Köln: Erzbischöfliches Generalvikariat, 1934–
[Nov. 1934]: 'Studien zum Mythus ... Grundfragen der Lebensauffassung und Lebensgestaltung—5. Teil der "Studien ..." '. 56 pp.
Dez. 1934: 'Nachtrag zu den Studien ...: "Der Apostel Paulus und das Urchristentum" '. 30 pp.
5. Neudruck 1935: 'Kirchengeschichtlicher und biblischer Teil mit Epilogen (zugleich Stellungnahme zu Rosenbergs Broschüre "An die Dunkelmänner unserer Zeit")'. 217 pp.
[Also issued by other dioceses.]

KÜNNETH, WALTER
1851 KÜNNETH, WALTER: *Die Entscheidung zwischen dem nordischen Mythus und dem biblischen Christus.* Berlin: Wichern Verlag, 1935. xv + 215 pp., bibl.

1852 MARKGRAF, BRUNO: *Rosenberg und Künneth. Nationalkirche und Lutherkirche.* Leipzig: Grethlein, 1936. 160 pp.

———

1853 ROSENBERG, ALFRED: *An die Dunkelmänner unserer Zeit. Eine Antwort auf die*

Angriffe gegen den 'Mythus des 20. Jahrhunderts'. München: Hoheneichen Verlag, 1935. 112 pp. (31. Aufl.).

ROSENBERG, ALFRED: *Der Mythus des 20. Jahrhunderts. See* 330.

1854 ROSENBERG, ALFRED: *Protestantische Rompilger. Der Verrat an Luther und der 'Mythus des 20. Jahrhunderts'.* 6. Aufl. München: Hoheneichen Verlag, 1937. 86 pp.

d. The Protestant Churches

1855 [BAPTISTS] FLÜGGE, C. A.: *Die Botschaft der Baptisten im Echo der Presse. Erklärungen führender Männer über religiöse Duldsamkeit im Neuen Deutschland.* 51.–70. Taus. Kassel: Christliche Tatgesellschaft, [1935?]. 68 pp.

1856 BECKMANN, JOACHIM, ed.: *Kirchliches Jahrbuch für die evangelische Kirche in Deutschland 1933–1944. Begründet von Johannes Schneider. 60.–71. Jahrgang.* Gütersloh: Bertelsmann, 1949. In one vol.

DEUTSCHE EVANGELISCHE KIRCHE*
1857 GERSTENMAIER, EUGEN, ed.: *Kirche, Volk und Staat. Stimmen aus der Deutschen Evangelischen Kirche zur Oxforder Weltkirchenkonferenz.* In Verbindung mit Paul Althaus [and others] hrsg. Berlin: Furche Verlag, 1937. 311 pp.

1858 KATER, HORST: *Die Deutsche Evangelische Kirche in den Jahren 1933 und 1934. Eine rechts- und verfassungsgeschichtliche Untersuchung zu Gründung und Zerfall einer Kirche im nationalsozialistischen Staat.* Göttingen: Vandenhoeck & Ruprecht, 1970. 226 pp., bibl.

1859 MANKEL, WILHELM: *Die Deutsche Evangelische Kirche. Das neue Reichskirchenrecht.* Giessen: Roth, [1933]. 105 pp.]

1860 GEISSLER, BRUNO & MICHAELIS, OTTO, eds.: *An der Front. Evangelische Kämpfer des Deutschtums im Ausland.* Leipzig: Schloessmann, 1938. 199 pp., ports., bibls.

1861 GERLACH-PRAETORIUS, ANGELIKA: *Die Kirche vor der Eidesfrage. Die Diskussion um den Pfarrereid im 'Dritten Reich'.* Göttingen: Vandenhoeck & Ruprecht, 1967. 235 pp., bibl.

1862 [HAMBURG] WILHELMI, HEINRICH: *Die Hamburger Kirche in der national-sozialistischen Zeit 1933–1945.* Göttingen: Vandenhoeck & Ruprecht, 1968. 326 pp.

1863 [HUMBURG, PAUL] OBENDIEK, HARMANNUS: *D. Paul Humburg—Der Zeuge: Die Botschaft. Ein Wort des Gedenkens. Die Botschaft dargeboten aus seinen Schriften.* Wuppertal: Müller, 1947. 116 pp.

* Nazi organization of the evangelical church under the Reichsbischof.

1864 [KURHESSEN-WALDECK] SLENCZA, HANS: *Die evangelische Kirche von Kurhessen-Waldeck in den Jahren von 1933–1945.* Göttingen: Vandenhoeck & Ruprecht, 1977. 283 pp.

1865 NORDEN, GÜNTHER VAN: *Der deutsche Protestantismus im Jahr der nationalsozialistischen Machtergreifung.* Gütersloh: Mohn, 1979. 438 pp., bibl.

1866 PIPER, OTTO: *Recent developments in German Protestantism.* Introd.: H. G. Wood. London: Student Christian Movement Press, 1934. xvi + 159 pp.

1867 [SCHLESWIG-HOLSTEIN] KINDER, CHRISTIAN: *Neue Beiträge zur Geschichte der evangelischen Kirche in Schleswig-Holstein und im Reich 1924–1945.* Flensburg: Karfeld, 1966. 208 pp. [2nd ed.]

1868 STUDEMUND, WILHELM: *Die evangelische Kirche und das Führerprinzip.* Göttingen: Vandenhoeck & Ruprecht, 1934. 24 pp.

1869 THALMANN, RITA: *Protestantisme et nationalisme en Allemagne (de 1900 à 1945). D'après les itinéraires spirituels de Gustav Frenssen (1863–1945); Walter Flex (1887–1917); Jochen Klepper (1903–1942); Dietrich Bonhoeffer (1906–1945).* [Paris]: Klincksieck, 1976. 482 pp., maps, diagrs., tabs.

1870 WÜNSCH, GEORG: *Evangelische Ethik des Politischen.* Tübingen: Mohr, 1936. 669 pp.

Bekennende Kirche

1871 ASMUSSEN, HANS: *Aufsätze, Briefe, Reden 1927–1945.* Itzehoe/Berlin: 'Die Spur', 1963. 171 pp.

1872 BOLOGNA, SERGIO: *La chiesa confessante sotto il nazismo 1933–1936.* Milano: Feltrinelli, 1967. 268 pp., bibl.

1873 DIBELIUS, OTTO: *Ein Christ ist immer im Dienst. Erlebnisse und Erfahrungen in einer Zeitenwende.* Stuttgart: Kreuz Verlag, 1961. 332 pp., illus. [English version: *In the service of the Lord. Autobiography.* London: Faber & Faber, 1965.]

1874 DIBELIUS, OTTO & NIEMÖLLER, MARTIN: *Wir rufen Deutschland zu Gott.* Berlin: Warneck, 1937. 110 pp.

1875 GRÜBER, HEINRICH: *Erinnerungen aus sieben Jahrzehnten.* Köln: Kiepenheuer & Witsch, 1968. 429 pp., illus. (2. Aufl.).

1876 JANNASCH, W.: *Deutsche Kirchendokumente. Die Haltung der Bekennenden Kirche im Dritten Reich.* Hrsg.: Schweizerisches evangelisches Hilfswerk für die Bekennende Kirche in Deutschland mit Flüchtlingsdienst. Zollikon-Zürich: Evangelischer Verlag, 1946. 116 pp.

1877 LIEB, FRITZ: *Christ und Antichrist im Dritten Reich. Der Kampf der Deutschen Bekenntniskirche.* Paris: Éds. du Carrefour, 1936. 277 pp.

1878 NIEMÖLLER, WILHELM: *Aus dem Leben eines Bekenntnispfarrers.* Bielefeld: Bechauf, 1961. 287 pp.

1879 NIEMÖLLER, WILHELM: *Der Pfarrernotbund. Geschichte einer kämpfenden Bruderschaft.* Hamburg: Wittig, 1973. 269 pp.

1880 NIEMÖLLER, WILHELM: *Kampf und Zeugnis der Bekennenden Kirche.* Bielefeld: Bechauf, 1948. 527 pp., illus.

1881 NIEMÖLLER, WILHELM: *Die Bekennende Kirche sagt Hitler die Wahrheit. Die Geschichte der Denkschrift der vorläufigen Leitung von Mai 1936.* Bielefeld: Bechauf, 1954. 54 pp.

1882 NIESEL, WILHELM: *Kirche unter dem Wort. Der Kampf der Bekennenden Kirche der altpreussischen Union 1933–1945.* Göttingen: Vandenhoeck & Ruprecht, 1978. xiii + 340 pp., bibl. (Arbeiten zur Geschichte des Kirchenkampfes).

1883 [SILESIA] HORNIG, ERNST: *Die bekennende Kirche in Schlesien 1933–1945. Geschichte und Dokumente.* Göttingen: Vandenhoeck & Ruprecht, 1977. xxi + 381 pp., bibl.

SYNODS

1884 BECKMANN, JOACHIM: *Rheinische Bekenntnissynoden im Kirchenkampf. Eine Dokumentation aus den Jahren 1933–1945.* Neukirchen-Vluyn: Neukirchener Verlag, 1975. xii + 491 pp.

1885 NIEMÖLLER, GERHARD: *Die erste Bekenntnissynode der Deutschen Evangelischen Kirche zu Barmen.* Göttingen: Vandenhoeck & Ruprecht, 1959. (Arbeiten zur Geschichte des Kirchenkampfes).
Bd. 1: *Geschichte, Kritik und Bedeutung der Synode und ihre theologische Erklärung.* 269 pp., bibl.
Bd. 2: *Texte, Dokumente, Berichte.* 209 pp.

1886 NIEMÖLLER, WILHELM, ed.: *Die Preussensynode zu Dahlem. Die zweite Bekenntnissynode der Evangelischen Kirche der altpreussischen Union. Geschichte, Dokumente, Berichte.* Göttingen: Vandenhoeck & Ruprecht, 1975. xxv + 251 pp., bibl.

1887 NIEMÖLLER, WILHELM, ed.: *Die Synode zu Steglitz. Die dritte Bekenntnissynode der Evangelischen Kirche der Altpreussischen Union. Geschichte, Dokumente, Berichte.* Gottingen: Vandenhoeck & Ruprecht, 1970. 382 pp., tabs., bibl.

1888 NIEMÖLLER, WILHELM, ed.: *Die vierte Bekenntnissynode der Deutschen Evangelischen Kirche zu Bad Oeynhausen. Texte, Dokumente, Berichte.* Göttingen: Vandenhoeck & Ruprecht, 1960. 343 pp.

German Christians

1889 [BAVARIA] BAIER, HELMUT: *Die Deutschen Christen Bayerns im Rahmen des bayerischen Kirchenkampfes.* Nürnberg: Verein für bayerische Kirchengeschichte, 1968. xx + 601 pp., bibls.

1890 *Der Beitrag der Kirche im Kampf gegen den Bolschewismus. Gemeinschaftsarbeit im 2. Reichsberufswettkampf der deutschen Studenten*

1936/37. Weimar: Verlag Deutsche Christen, 1937. 98 pp. [By Ernst Daus and others. Bolshevism = Jews.]

1891 [BREMEN] HEINONEN, REIJO E.: *Anpassung und Identität. Theologie und Kirchenpolitik der Bremer Deutschen Christen 1933–45.* Göttingen: Vandenhoeck & Ruprecht, 1978. 302 pp. [From a dissertation, Tübingen 1972.]

1892 FABRICIUS, CAJUS: *Positive Christianity in the Third Reich.* Dresden: Püschel, 1937. 72 pp.

1893 *Gesangbuch der Kommenden Kirche.* Bremen: Verlag 'Kommende Kirche', [193–]. 233 pp., mus. scores.

1894 GÖTTE, KARL HEINZ: *Die Propaganda der Glaubensbewegung 'Deutsche Christen' und ihre Beurteilung in der deutschen Tagespresse. Ein Beitrag zur Publizistik im Dritten Reich.* Münster i. Westf.: [priv. pr.], 1957. 247 pp.

1895 GRABS, RUDOLF: *Paul de Lagarde und H. St. Chamberlain.* Weimar: Verlag Deutsche Christen, 1940. 88 pp. (Wegbereiter Deutschen Christentums).

1896 GRUNDMANN, WALTER: *Jesus der Galiläer und das Judentum.* Leipzig: Wigand, 1940. 246 pp. [German Christian view.]

1897 KUPTSCH, J.: *Nationalsozialismus und positives Christentum.* Weimar: Verlag Deutsche Christen, 1937. 168 pp.

1898 MEIER, KURT: *Die Deutschen Christen. Das Bild einer Bewegung im Kirchenkampf des Dritten Reiches.* Göttingen: Vandenhoeck & Ruprecht, 1964. xv + 381 pp., bibl.

1899 MÜLLER, LUDWIG: *Deutsche Gottesworte. Aus der Bergpredigt verdeutscht.* 3.–4. unveränd. Aufl. Weimar: Verlag Deutsche Christen, 1936. 42 pp. [Author was the Reich Bishop.]

1900 MÜLLER, LUDWIG: *Was ist positives Christentum?* Stuttgart: Der Tazzelwurm Verlag, 1939. 164 pp.

1901 NATIONALSOZIALISTISCHER PFARRERS-UND LEHRERKREIS DES WIERATALS/Th.: *Unsere Kampflieder.* 21.–40. Taus. Weimar: Verlag Deutsche Christen, 1933. 52 pp., mus. scores, illus.

1902 NICOLAISEN, CARSTEN: 'Die Stellung der "Deutschen Christen" zum Alten Testament'. [In] *Zur Geschichte des Kirchenkampfes II. See* 1956.

1903 WEIDEMANN, HEINZ: *So sieht die Kommende Kirche aus.* 4. erw. Aufl. Bremen: Verlag Kommende Kirche, 1941. 176 pp.

1904 ZABEL, JAMES A.: *Nazism and the pastors. A study of the ideas of three Deutsche Christen groups.* Missoula, Mont.: Scholars Press, 1976. 243 pp., bibl. (American Academy of Religion Dissertation Series).

The struggle within the Protestant Church

1905 DÜHM, ANDREAS: *Der Kampf um die deutsche Kirche. Eine Kirchengeschichte*

154

des Jahres 1933/34 dargestellt für das evangelische Volk. Gotha: Klotz, 1934. 361 pp. [By a German Christian.]

1906 MURTORINNE, EINO: *Erzbischof Eidem zum deutschen Kirchenkampf 1933–1934.* Helsinki: Finnische Gesellschaft für Missiologie und Ökumenik, 1968. 127 pp., port., bibl.

1907 GAMSJÄGER, HELMUT: *Die Evangelische Kirche in Österreich in den Jahren 1933 bis 1938 unter besonderer Berücksichtigung der deutschen Kirchenwirren.* Dissertation [pres. to] Universität Wien. 1967. 148 pp., bibl. Typescr.

1908 KAISER, MARCUS URS: *Deutscher Kirchenkampf und Schweizer Öffentlichkeit in den Jahren 1933 und 1934.* Zürich: Theologischer Verlag, 1972. 392 pp., bibl.

1909 MEIER, KURT: *Der evangelische Kirchenkampf.* Göttingen: Vandenhoeck & Ruprecht, 1976.
Bd. 1: *Der Kampf um die 'Reichskirche'.* xv + 648 pp.
Bd. 2: *Gescheiterte Neuordnungsversuche im Zeichen staatlicher 'Rechtshilfe'.* vii + 472 pp.

1910 *Der nationalsozialistische Pfarrer im Kampf um die Volkskirche. Bericht über die Gautagung der nationalsozialistischen Pfarrer und Vorträge der Gautagung.* Dresden: Deutsch-Christlicher Verlag, 1935. 47 pp.

1911 NYGREN, ANDERS: *The Church controversy in Germany. The position of the evangelical Church in the Third Empire.* Transl.: G. C. Richards. London: Student Christian Movement, 1934. 115 pp.

1912 STOEVESANDT, KARL: *Bekennende Gemeinden und deutschgläubige Bischofs-diktatur. Geschichte des Kirchenkampfes in Bremen 1933–1945.* Göttingen: Vandenhoeck & Ruprecht, 1961. 201 pp.

1913 STOLL, CHRISTIAN: *Dokumente zum Kirchenstreit.* München: Kaiser, 1934/35.
I. Teil: *Idee und gegenwärtige Erscheinung der Deutschen Kirche.* 2. verm. Aufl. 48 pp.
II. Teil: *Kirche in Not!* 39 pp.
III. Teil: *Der Kampf um das Bekenntnis.* 80 pp.
IV. Teil: *Zwischen den Synoden.* 43 pp.
V. Teil: *Der Weg der Evang.–Lutherischen Kirche in Bayern.* 42 pp.
VI. Teil: *Um das Reichskirchenregiment.* 53 pp.

1914 [WÜRTTEMBERG] SCHÄFER, GERHARD: *Die evangelische Landeskirche in Württemberg und der Nationalsozialismus. Eine Dokumentation zum Kirchenkampf.* Stuttgart: Calwer, 1971– Bibls.
Bd. 1: *Um das politische Engagement der Kirche 1932–1933.* Geleitw.: Wolfgang Metzger. Publ. 1971. 607 pp.
Bd. 2: *Um eine deutsche Reichskirche 1933.* Publ. 1972. 1120 pp.
Bd. 3: *Der Einbruch des Reichsbischofs in die Württembergische Landeskirche 1934.* Publ. 1974. 731 pp.
Bd. 4: *Die intakte Landeskirche 1933–1936.* Publ. 1977. xix + 960 pp.

Opposition, resistance and persecution

1915 [BARTH, KARL] PROLINGHEUER, HANS: *Der Fall Karl Barth 1934–1935. Chronographie einer Vertreibung.* Neukirchen-Vluyn: Neukirchener Verlag, 1977. xxiii + 410 pp., ports., bibl.

1916 [BECKMANN, JOACHIM] NIEMÖLLER, WILHELM: 'Aus der Polizeiakte des Bekenntnispfarrers Joachim Beckmann'. [In] *Zur Geschichte des Kirchenkampfes, I.* See 1956.

BONHOEFFER, DIETRICH

1917 BONHOEFFER, DIETRICH: *Gesammelte Schriften.* Hrsg.: Eberhard Bethge. München: Kaiser. Illus.
Bd. 2: *Kirchenkampf und Finkenwalde. Resolutionen, Aufsätze, Rundbriefe, 1933–1943.* Publ. 1959. 667 pp.
Bd. 3: *Theologie—Gemeinde. Vorlesungen, Briefe, Gespräche, 1927–1944.* Publ. 1960. 571 pp.

1918 BONHOEFFER, DIETRICH: *Letters, lectures and notes from the collected works.* Ed.: Edwin H. Robertson. [Transl. from the German.]
Vol. 1: *No rusty swords. 1928–1936.* New York: Harper & Row, 1965. 384 pp.
Vol. 2: *The way to freedom. 1935–1939.* London: Collins, 1966. 288 pp.
Vol. 3: *True patriotism. 1939–1945.* New York: Harper & Row, 1973. 256 pp.

1919 BONHOEFFER, DIETRICH: *Widerstand und Ergebung. Briefe und Aufzeichnungen aus der Haft.* Hrsg. Eberhard Bethge. München: Kaiser, 1970. 464 pp., maps. [New ed. First ed. 1951. English version: *Letters and papers from prison.* London: Student Christian Movement Press, 1973.]

1920 BETHGE, EBERHARD: *Dietrich Bonhoeffer. Theologe—Christ—Zeitgenosse.* München: Kaiser, 1967. 428 pp., illus., facsims. [Also: *Beiheft.* 30 pp., family tree.]

1921 BOSANQUET, MARY: *The life and death of Dietrich Bonhoeffer.* London: Hodder & Stoughton, 1969. 287 pp., illus., bibl. [First ed. 1968.]

1922 GODDARD, DONALD: *The last days of Dietrich Bonhoeffer.* New York: Harper & Row, 1976. 245 pp.

1923 PETERS, TIEMS RAINER: *Die Präsenz des Politischen in der Theologie Dietrich Bonhoeffers. Eine historische Untersuchung in systematischer Absicht.* München: Kaiser, 1976. 224 pp., bibl.

1924 [BONHOEFFER Family] LEIBHOLZ-BONHOEFFER, SABINE: *Vergangen—erlebt—überwunden. Schicksale der Familie Bonhoeffer.* 3. Aufl. Wuppertal-Barmen: Kiefel, 1969. 230 pp., illus.

1925 BUXTON, DOROTHY F., ed.: *I was in prison. Letters from German pastors.* Preface: Bishop of Liverpool [Albert A. David]. London: Student Christian Movement Press, 1938. 64 pp.

1926 [Danzig] Sodeikat, E.: 'Die Verfolgung und der Widerstand der Evangelischen Kirche in Danzig'. [In] *Zur Geschichte des Kirchenkampfes. See 1956.*

1927 [Dibelius, Otto] Gollert, Friedrich: *Dibelius vor Gericht.* München: Beck, 1959. 193 pp.

1928 [East Prussia] Linck, Hugo: *Der Kirchenkampf in Ostpreussen 1933 bis 1945. Geschichte und Dokumentation.* München: Gräfe & Unzer, 1968. 295 pp., facsims., bibl.

1929 [Elberfeld] Vorländer, Herwart: *Kirchenkampf in Elberfeld 1933–1945. Ein kritischer Beitrag zur Erforschung des Kirchenkampfes in Deutschland.* Göttingen: Vandenhoeck & Ruprecht, 1968. 696 pp., bibl.

1930 Frey, Arthur: *Cross and swastika. The ordeal of the German church.* Introd.: Karl Barth. Transl. from the German. London: Student Christian Movement Press, 1938. 224 pp. [German version: *Der Kampf der evangelischen Kirche in Deutschland und seine allgemeine Bedeutung.* Nijkerk (Holland): Callenbach, 1937.]

1931 Grüber, Heinrich: *Dona nobis pacem! Gesammelte Predigten und Aufsätze aus 20 Jahren.* Hrsg. von seinen Freunden. Zusammengest. und bearb.: Günter Wirth, Gottfried Kretschmar. Berlin: Union Verlag, 1956. 405 pp., illus. [Incl. sermons in Dachau concentration camp.]

1932 [Hahn, Hugo] Prater, Georg, ed.: *Kämpfer wider Willen. Erinnerungen des Landesbischofs von Sachsen, D. Hugo Hahn aus dem Kirchenkampf 1933–1945.* Metzingen: Brunnquell Verlag, 1969. 351 pp., ports.

1933 Klinger, Fritz, ed.: *Dokumente zum Abwehrkampf der deutschen evangelischen Pfarrerschaft gegen Verfolgung und Bedrückung 1933–1945.* Nürnberg: Mendelsohn, 1946. 125 pp.

1934 [Koechlin, Alphons] Bell, George Kennedy Allen & Koechlin, Alphons: *Briefwechsel 1933–1954.* Hrsg.: Andreas Lindt. Geleitw.: W. A. Visser't Hooft. Zürich: EVZ-Verlag, 1969. 448 pp. [Transl. from the English.]

1935 Lilje, Hans: *Im finstern Tal.* Nürnberg: Lätare-Verlag, 1947. 122 pp. [Prison experiences of a pastor.]

1936 [Lübeck] Reimers, Karl Friedrich: *Lübeck im Kirchenkampf des Dritten Reiches. Nationalsozialistisches Führerprinzip und evangelisch-lutherische Landeskirche von 1933–1945.* Göttingen: Vandenhoeck & Ruprecht, 1965. 390 pp., bibl.

1937 [Mecklenburg] Beste, Niklot: *Der Kirchenkampf in Mecklenburg von 1933 bis 1945. Geschichte, Dokumente, Erinnerungen.* Göttingen: Vandenhoeck & Ruprecht, 1975. 375 pp.

1938 [Nassau-Hessen] Lueken, Wilhelm: *Kampf. Behauptung und Gestalt der evangelischen Landeskirche Nassau-Hessen.* Göttingen: Vandenhoeck & Ruprecht, 1963. 201 pp., bibl.

NIEMÖLLER, MARTIN
1939 NIEMÖLLER, MARTIN: *Briefe aus der Gefangenschaft Moabit.* Hrsg.: Wilhelm Niemöller. Frankfurt a.M.: Lembeck, 1975. 348 pp.

1940 NIEMÖLLER, MARTIN: *Dennoch getrost. Die letzten Predigten des Pfarrers Martin Niemöller vor seiner Verhaftung, gehalten in den Jahren 1936 und 1937 in Berlin-Dahlem.* Hrsg.: Schweizerisches Evangelisches Hilfswerk für die Bekennende Kirche in Deutschland. Zollikon-Zürich: Evangelischer Verlag, 1939. 184 pp., port. [Danish version: Copenhagen: Gyldendal, 1939; English: *The Gestapo defied.* London: Hodge, 1941; USA: *God is my Führer.* New York: Philosophical Library & Alliance Book Corp'n, 1941 (preface: Thomas Mann).]

1941 NIEMÖLLER, MARTIN: *'... zu verkündigen ein gnädiges Jahr des Herrn!' Sechs Dachauer Predigten.* Zürich-Zollikon: Evangelischer Verlag, 1946. 63 pp. [English version: *Dachau sermons.* London: Latimer House, (1947).]

1942 MILLER, BASIL: *Martin Niemöller. Hero of the concentration camp.* Grand Rapids, Mich.: Zondervan, 1942. 160 pp.

1943 SCHMIDT, JÜRGEN: *Martin Niemöller im Kirchenkampf.* Hamburg: Leibniz, 1971. 541 pp., illus., bibl.

1944 NIEMÖLLER, WILHELM: *Die Evangelische Kirche im Dritten Reich. Handbuch des Kirchenkampfes.* Bielefeld: Bechauf, 1956. 408 pp.

1945 [PECHMANN, WILHELM Frhr. von] KANTZENBACH, FRIEDRICH WILHELM: *Widerstand und Solidarität der Christen in Deutschland 1933–1945. Eine Dokumentation zum Kirchenkampf aus den Papieren des D. Wilhelm Frhrs. von Pechmann.* Neustadt/Aisch: Degener, 1971. viii + 349 pp., port., bibl.

1946 [POSEN] HEINE, LUDWIG: *Geschichte des Kirchenkampfes in der Grenzmark Posen-Westpreussen 1930–1940.* Göttingen: Vandenhoeck & Ruprecht, 1961. 115 pp.

1947 RIEGER, JULIUS: *The silent Church. The problem of the German confessional witness.* London: Student Christian Movement Press, 1944. 96 pp., bibl. [Silence as a method of resistance.]

1948 RÜPPEL, ERICH GÜNTER: *Die Gemeinschaftsbewegung im Dritten Reich. Ein Beitrag zur Geschichte des Kirchenkampfes.* Göttingen: Vandenhoeck & Ruprecht, 1969. 258 pp., bibl.

1949 [SAXONY] FISCHER, JOACHIM: *Die sächsische Landeskirche im Kirchenkampf 1933–1937.* Göttingen: Vandenhoeck & Ruprecht, 1972. 267 pp.

1950 SCHMID, HEINRICH: *Apokalyptisches Wetterleuchten. Ein Beitrag der Evangelischen Kirche zum Kampf im 'Dritten Reich'.* München: Verlag der Evangelisch-Lutherischen Kirche in Bayern, 1947. 459 pp.

SCHNEIDER, PAUL
1951 ROBERTSON, E. H.: *Paul Schneider, the pastor of Buchenwald. A free translation*

of the story told by his widow, with many quotations from his diary and letters. London: Student Christian Movement Press, 1956, 128 pp., port.

1952 VOGEL, HEINRICH, ed.: *Der Prediger von Buchenwald. Das Martyrium Paul Schneiders, 29.8.1897–18.7.1939.* Berlin: Lettner, 1953. 239 pp.

1953 *Tutzinger Texte. Sonderband I: Kirche und Nationalsozialismus. Zur Geschichte des Kirchenkampfes.* Beiträge von Helmut Baier [and others]. München: Claudius Verlag, 1969. 286 pp., bibl.

WURM, THEOPHIL
1954 WURM, THEOPHIL: *Erinnerungen aus meinem Leben.* Stuttgart: Quell-Verlag, 1953. 220 pp., illus. [Incl. an account of Protestant resistance.]

1955 SCHÄFER, GERHARD & FISCHER, RICHARD, comps.: *Landesbischof D. Wurm und der nationalsozialistische Staat 1940–1945. Eine Dokumentation.* Stuttgart: Calwer, 1968. 507 pp., tab., bibl.

1956 *Zur Geschichte des Kirchenkampfes. Gesammelte Aufsätze.* Göttingen: Vandenhoeck & Ruprecht, 1965, 1971.
[I]: Publ. 1965. 324 pp. [Incl.: Kurt Meier: 'Kirche und Nationalsozialismus'; O. Söhngen: 'Hindenburgs Eingreifen in den Kirchenkampf'; J. Glenthøj; 'Hindenburg, Göring und die evangelischen Kirchenführer'. Eds.: Heinz Brunotte, Ernst Wolf.]
II: Publ. 1971. [Incl.: Kurt Meier: 'Die Religionspolitik der NSDAP in der Zeit der Weimarer Republik'; Friedrich Wilhelm Kantzenbach: ' "Theologische Blätter" ... eine theologische Zeitschrift im Dritten Reich'; Peter W. Ludlow: 'Bischof Berggrav ...'; Hartmut Ludwig; 'Karl Barths Dienst der Versöhnung'.]

e. The Roman Catholic Church

BAVARIA
1957 *Die kirchliche Lage in Bayern nach den Regierungspräsidentenberichten 1933–1943.* Mainz: Matthias-Grünewald-Verlag, 1966– (Veröffentlichungen der Kommission für Zeitgeschichte bei der Katholischen Akademie in Bayern).
I: *Regierungsbezirk Oberbayern.* Publ. 1966. 395 pp. [Ed.: Helmut Witetschek.]
II: *Regierungsbezirk Ober- und Mittelfranken.* Publ. 1967. xxxv + 527 pp. [Ed.: Helmut Witetschek.]
III: *Regierungsbezirk Schwaben.* Publ. 1971. xxiv + 285 pp. [Ed.: Helmut Witetschek.]
IV: *Regierungsbezirk Niederbayern und Oberpfalz 1933–1945.* Publ. 1973. xliv + 415 pp. [Ed.: Walter Ziegler.]
V: *Regierungsbezirk Pfalz 1933–1940.* Publ. 1978. 343 pp., bibl. [Ed.: Helmut Prantl.]

159

1958   VOLK, LUDWIG: *Der bayerische Episkopat und der Nationalsozialismus 1930–1934.* Mainz: Matthias-Grünewald-Verlag, 1966. xxii + 216 pp., bibl. (Veröffentlichungen der Kommission für Zeitgeschichte ...). [2nd ed.]

1959   BRAUER, THEODOR: *Der Katholik im neuen Reich. Seine Aufgabe und sein Anteil.* München: Kösel & Pustet, 1933. 78 pp.

1960   CHWALA, ADOLF: *Katholisches Hand- und Gebetbüchlein für den Arbeitsdienst.* Dülmen i.Westf.: Laumann, 1933. 136 pp.

1961   [COLOGNE] HEHL, ULRICH VON: *Katholische Kirche und Nationalsozialismus im Erzbistum Köln 1933–1945.* Mainz: Matthias-Grünewald-Verlag, 1977. xxviii + 269 pp., illus.

1962   COLLOTTI, ENZO: 'I cattolica tedeschi e il nacionalsocialismo'. [In] *Studi storici,* VI/1, gennaio–marzo 1965. Roma: Istituto Gramsci. Pp. 127–158.

1963   COPPENRATH, ALBERT: *Meine Kanzelvermeldungen und Erlebnisse im Dritten Reich.* Köln: Bachem, 1946. 160 pp.

1964   DEUERLEIN, ERNST: *Der deutsche Katholizismus 1933.* Osnabrück: Fromm, 1963. 186 pp., bibl.

1965   D'HARCOURT, ROBERT: *Catholiques d'Allemagne.* Paris: Plon, 1938. 356 pp. [English version: *The German Catholics.* London: Burns Oates & Washbourne, 1939.]

1966   *Jahrbuch des Reichsverbandes für die katholischen Auslanddeutschen.* Hrsg.: Emil Clemenz Scherer, Richard Mai.   Berlin: Germania.
Jhrg. 5: *1933/34.* Publ. 1934. xi + 334 pp.
Jhrg. 6: *1935.* Publ. 1935. xii + 360 pp.
[Vol. 7 appeared as *Jahrbuch der katholischen auslanddeutschen Mission* (Kevelaer: Butzon & Bercker). There were no further issues.]

1967   *Der Katholische Gedanke und die Neuordnung von Wirtschaft und Gesellschaft. Die Münchener Soziologische Frühjahrstagung des Katholischen Akademikerverbandes (10.–13. März 1933). Tagungsbericht und kritisches Nachwort: 'Die Geistigen Spannungen innerhalb der modernen katholischen Soziologie', von Alex. Emmerich.* Augsburg: Haas & Grabherr, 1933. 30 pp.

KATHOLISCH-NATIONALKIRCHLICHE BEWEGUNG
1968   DEMMEL, HANS JOSEF: *Was ist alt-katholisch?* 2. verm. Aufl. Karlsruhe: Willibrord, 1937. 30 pp. (Schriftenreihe der 'Katholisch-Nationalkirchlichen Bewegung').

1969   GRÖBER, CONRAD: *Nationalkirche? Ein aufklärendes Wort zur Wahrung des konfessionellen Friedens.* Freiburg i.Br.: Herder, 1934. 77 pp.

1970   KRAL, JOSEF: *Deutsche Katholiken und Nationalsozialismus. Versuch einer Synthese.* Abensberg/Niederbayern: Tagblatt-Verlag, 1934. 399 pp.

1971 LEWY, GUENTER: *The Catholic Church and Nazi Germany.* New York: McGraw-Hill, 1964. 416 pp., map, bibl. [German version: *Die katholische Kirche und das Dritte Reich.* München: Piper, 1965.]

1972 STASIEWSKI, BERNHARD, ed.: *Akten deutscher Bischöfe über die Lage der Kirche 1933–1945.* Mainz: Matthias-Grünewald-Verlag, 1968– continuing. Bibls. (Veröffentlichungen der Kommission für Zeitgeschichte ...). I: *1933–1934.* Publ. 1968. 969 + lii pp. II: *1934–1935.* Publ. 1976. xlvi + 505 pp.

1973 [WÜRTTEMBERG] DOETSCH, WILHELM JOSEF: *Württembergs Katholiken unterm Hakenkreuz 1930–1935.* Stuttgart: Kohlhammer, 1969. 223 pp., tab., bibl.

1974 ZAHN, GORDON C.: *German Catholics and Hitler's wars. A study in social control.* New York: Sheed & Ward, 1962. 232 pp., bibl. [Analysis of Catholic failure to oppose war.]

The Vatican and the Third Reich

1975 ALBRECHT, DIETER, ed.: *Der Notenwechsel zwischen dem Heiligen Stuhl und der deutschen Reichsregierung.* Mainz: Matthias-Grünewald-Verlag, 1965–1969. (Veröffentlichungen der Kommission für Zeitgeschichte ...). I: *Von der Ratifizierung des Reichskonkordats bis sur Enzyklika 'Mit brennender Sorge'.* Publ. 1965. 459 pp. II: *1937–1945.* Publ. 1969. xxvii + 227 pp., bibl.

1976 DAMMANN, W. H.: *Kaiser, König, Pontifex. Blutendes Deutschtum unter päpstlicher Machtpolitik.* München: Bereiter, 1937. 224 pp.

1977 DELZELL, CHARLES F., ed.: *The Papacy and totalitarianism between the two world wars.* New York: Wiley, 1974. vii + 179 pp., bibl. [Anthology. Pt. 2: 'The Papacy and the Jewish Question', pp. 63–126.]

1978 HÄRTLE, HEINRICH: *Der deutsche Arbeiter und die päpstliche Sozialpolitik.* Berlin: Hochmuth, 1937. 31 pp. [Anti-Catholic.]

1979 MACCARRONE, MICHELE, ed.: *Il nazionalsocialismo e la Santa Sede.* Roma: Ed. Studium, 1947. 270 pp.

1980 PATIS, WILHELM: *Beiträge zur Geschichte der deutsch-vatikanischen Beziehungen in den letzten Jahrzehnten.* Berlin: Nordland Verlag, 1942. 308 pp. [Incl.: 'Franz von Stockhammerns freimaurerischer Nachrichtendienst im ersten Weltkrieg—Die internationalen Zusammenhänge zwischen Freimaurerei und Judentum'.]

1981 RHODES, ANTHONY: *The Vatican in the age of the dictators, 1922–1945.* London: Hodder & Stoughton, 1973. 383 pp., illus., bibl.

POPE PIUS XI

'Mit brennender Sorge' (encyclical)
1982 PIUS XI: *Das Rundschreiben 'Mit brennender Sorge über die Lage der katholischen Kirche im Deutschen Reich'. Enzyklika vom 14. März 1937.* Luzern: Rex Verlag, 1937. 32 pp.

1983   HIRT, SIMON, ed.: *Mit brennender Sorge. Das päpstliche Rundschreiben gegen den Nationalsozialismus und seine Folgen in Deutschland.* Freiburg i.Br.: Herder, 1946. 101 pp.

Reichskonkordat
1984   BRACHER, KARL DIETRICH: *Nationalsozialistische Machtergreifung und Reichskonkordat. Ein Gutachten zur Frage des geschichtlichen Zusammenhanges und der politischen Verknüpfung von Reichskonkordat und nationalsozialistischer Revolution.* Wiesbaden: Hessische Landesregierung, 1956. 84 pp.

1985   GERMANN, HANS GEORG: *Fünf Jahre Reichskonkordat mit der römischen Kirche.* Berlin: Fritsch, [1938]. 104 pp., bibl.

1986   KRÜGER, KURT: *Kommentar zum Reichskonkordat nebst Einleitung und dem Texte der Länderkonkordate.* Berlin: Stubenrauch, 1938. 83 pp.

1987   KUPPER, ALFONS, ed.: *Staatliche Akten über die Reichskonkordatsverhandlungen 1933.* Mainz: Matthias-Grünewald-Verlag, 1969. xlv + 537 pp., tabs., bibl. (Veröffentlichungen der Kommission für Zeitgeschichte ...).

POPE PIUS XII
1988   *Actes et documents du Saint Siège, relatifs à la seconde guerre mondiale.* Eds.: Pierre Blet, Angelo Martini, Robert A. Graham, Burkhart Schneider. Città del Vaticano: Libr. Ed. Vaticana, 1965– continuing.
    1: *Le Saint Siège et la guerre en Europe. Mars 1939–août 1940.* Publ. 1965. xxvii + 552 pp.
    2: *Lettres de Pie XII aux évêques allemands 1939–1944.* Publ. 1966. xxiv + 452 pp. [German version: *Die Briefe Pius' XII. an die deutschen Bischöfe 1939–1944.* Mainz: Matthias-Grünewald-Verlag, 1966.]
    3: *Le Saint Siège et la situation religieuse en Pologne et dans les Pays Baltes, 1939–1945.* Publ. 1967. xxxi + 963 pp. In 2 vols.
    4: *Le Saint Siège et la guerre en Europe. Juin 1940–juin 1941.* Publ. 1967. xxiv + 622 pp.
    5: *Le Saint Siège et la Guerre Mondiale. Juillet 1941–octobre 1942.* Publ. 1969. xxvi + 794 pp.
    6: *Le Saint Siège et les victimes de la Guerre. Mars 1939–décembre 1940.* Publ. 1972. xxviii + 557 pp.
    7: *Le Saint Siège et la Guerre Mondiale. Novembre 1942–décembre 1943.* Publ. 1973. xxvii + 765 pp.
    8: *Le Saint Siège et les victimes de la Guerre. Janvier 1941–décembre 1942.* Publ. 1974. xxviii + 806 pp.
    9: *Le Saint Siège et les victimes de la Guerre. Janvier–décembre 1943.* Publ. 1975. xxviii + 686 pp.

1989   BEALES, A. C. F.: *The Pope and the Jews. The struggle of the Catholic Church against antisemitism during the war.* London: Sword of the Spirit, 1945. 38 pp.

1990   FALCONI, CARLO: *Il silenzio di Pio XII.* Milano: Sugar, 1965. 566 pp., illus., facsims., maps. [English version: *The silence of Pius XII*. London: Faber & Faber, 1970.]

1991 FRIEDLANDER, SAUL: *Pie XII et le IIIe Reich. Documents.* Postface: Alfred Grosser. Paris: Éds du Seuil, 1964. 255 pp., facsims. [English version: *Pius XII and the Third Reich*. London: Chatto & Windus, 1966: German version: *Pius XII und das Dritte Reich*. Reinbek b. Hamburg: Rowohlt, 1965.]

Hochhuth, Rolf
1992 HOCHHUTH, ROLF: *Der Stellvertreter. Schauspiel.* Vorw.: Erwin Piscator. Reinbek b. Hamburg: Rowohlt, 1963. 274 pp., port. [Première Berlin 1963. English version: *The Representative*. Transl. and pref.: Robert David Macdonald. London: Methuen, 1963.]

1993 BERG, JAN: *Hochhuths 'Stellvertreter' und die 'Stellvertreter'-Debatte. 'Vergangenheitsbewältigung' in Theater und Presse der sechziger Jahre.* Kronberg Ts.: Scriptor Verlag, 1977. 234 pp., bibl. (Hochschulschriften Literaturwissenschaft).

1994 LEVAI, JENÖ, comp.: *Hungarian Jewry and the Papacy. Pope Pius XII did not remain silent. Reports, documents and records from Church and State archives.* Prologue and epilogue: Robert M. W. Kempner. London: Sands, 1968. 131 pp., illus., facsims. [Translated from German version of original Hungarian. German version: *Geheime Reichssache*. Köln-Müngersdorf: Verlag Wort und Werk, 1966; French version: *L'Église ne s'est pas tue*. Paris: Éds. du Seuil, 1966.]

1995 MORLEY, JOHN FRANCIS: *Vatican diplomacy and the Jews during the Holocaust, 1939–1943.* Dissertation [pres. to] New York University. 1979. 601 pp.

1996 RASSINIER, PAUL: *L'opération 'Vicaire'. Le rôle de Pie XII devant l'histoire.* Paris: La Table ronde, 1965. 266 pp., facsims., tab.

1997 VISSER, B. J. J.: *Gewalt gegen Gewissen. Nationalsozialismus, Vatikan, Episkopat. Die Entlarvung einer Geschichtsfälschung.* Deutscher Bearb.: Philipp Schertl. Würzburg: Naumann, 1974. 246 pp. [Pius XII and the rescue of Jews.]

1998 WUESTENBERG, BRUNO & ZABKAR, JOSEPH, eds.: *Der Papst an die Deutschen.* Frankfurt a.M.: Scheffler, 1956. 331 pp., illus.

Nazi anti-Catholicism

1999 ALBRECHT, FRIEDRICH WILHELM: *Politischer Katholizismus und Weltkrieg.* Inaugural-Dissertation [pres. to] Heidelberg Universität. 1941. 79 pp.

2000 BUTZ, FRIEDRICH CARL: *Kampf um Gott. Roman.* München: Eher, 1939. 418 pp.

2001 JAM, Dr. (pseud. of Michael Ahle): *Die katholische Kirche als Gefahr für den Staat.* Leipzig: Nationale Verlagsgesellschaft, 1936. 321 pp., illus.

2002 ASSMUS, BURGHARD: *Jesuitenspiegel. Interessante Beiträge zur Naturgeschichte der Jesuiten*. Berlin-Friedenau: Bock, 1938. 157 pp., bibl.

2003 CARDON, GREGOR: *Sind Jesuiten Freimaurer?* Kevelaer: Butzon & Bercker, 1934. 100 pp. [Defence.]

2004 SCHULTZE-PFAELZER, GERHARD: *Das Jesuiten-Buch. Weltgeschichte eines falschen Priestertums*. Berlin: Bischoff, 1936. 313 pp.

2005 LUTZE, VIKTOR: *Reden an die S.A. Der politische Katholizismus*. München: Eher, 1935. 24 pp.

2006 REVETZLOW, KARL: *Handbuch der Romfrage*. Beuern (Hessen): Posern, 1935. 356 pp.

2007 ROSENBERG, ALFRED, ed.: *Handbuch der Romfrage. Unter Mitwirkung einer Arbeitsgemeinschaft von Forschern und Politikern. Bd. I: A–K*. München: Hoheneichen-Verlag, 1940. xv + 828 pp. [No others publ.]

2008 TEKLENBURG, G. H.: *Roms Germanenhass und Judaverehrung. Zugleich eine geharnischte Antwort an Kardinal Faulhaber*. Hamburg: Uhlenhorst, [1934?]. 40 pp.

2009 VOLK, RAINER: *Die Katholische Aktion in deutscher Sicht*, Stuttgart: Truckenmüller, 1937. 130 pp. [Attack on Catholic Action movement.]

Opposition, persecution and resistance

2010 ADOLPH, WALTER: *Geheime Aufzeichnungen aus dem nationalsozialistischen Kirchenkampf 1935–1943*. Bearb.: Ulrich von Hehl. Mainz: Matthias-Grünewald-Verlag, 1979. xlii + 304 pp., illus. (Veröffentlichungen der Kommission für Zeitgeschichte ...).

2011 *Der Berliner Katholikenprozess*. Prague: Dölling, 1937. 47 pp., illus. [Trial of Kaplan Rossaint and numerous Catholics and Communists before the People's Court.]

2012 KÜHN, HEINZ: *Blutzeugen des Bistums Berlin*. Berlin-Dahlem: Morus-Verlag, 1951. 190 pp., illus.

2013 BINDER, GERHART: *Irrtum und Widerstand. Die deutschen Katholiken in der Auseinandersetzung mit dem Nationalsozialismus*. Einführung: Felix Messerschmid. München: Pfeiffer, 1968. 455 pp., facsims., tabs., bibl.

2014 HUBER, HEINRICH: *Dokumente einer christlichen Widerstandsbewegung. Gegen die Entfernung der Kruzifixe aus den Schulen, 1941*. München: Schnell & Steiner, 1948. 83 pp. ('Das andere Deutschland ...').

2015 NOAKES, JEREMY: 'The Oldenburg crucifix struggle of November 1936: a case study of opposition in the Third Reich'. [In] Peter D. Stachura, ed.: *The shaping of the Nazi state*. Pp. 210–233. *See* 1157.

2016 DELP, ALFRED, (S.J.): *Im Angesicht des Todes. Geschrieben zwischen Verhaftung und Hinrichtung, 1944–1945*. Frankfurt a.M.: Knecht, 1947. 181 pp.

FAULHABER, MICHAEL VON, CARDINAL

2017 FAULHABER, MICHAEL von: *Akten Kardinal Michael von Faulhabers 1917–1945*. Bearb.: Ludwig Volk. Mainz: Matthias-Grünewald-Verlag, 1975– (Veröffentlichungen der Kommission für Zeitgeschichte ...). Bd. I: *1917–1934*. xcv + 952 pp., port.

2018 GODEFRIED, pseud.: *Blut und Boden, Ehre und Freiheit! Das Vermächtnis Wittekinds und seine Antwort auf die politischen Predigten des Kardinals Faulhaber*. Hannover: Engelhard, 1934. 154 pp.

GALEN, CLEMENS AUGUST VON, CARDINAL

2019 BIERBAUM, MAX: *Nicht Lob, nicht Furcht. Das Leben des Kardinals von Galen, nach unveröffentlichten Briefen und Dokumenten*. Münster: Verlag Regensberg, 1955. 221 pp., illus.

2020 SMITH, PATRICK, ed.: *The Bishop of Münster and the Nazis. The documents in the case*. Foreword: Richard Downey. London: Burns Oates, 1942. x + 53 pp.

2021 GRÖBER, [CONRAD]: *Hirtenrufe des Erzbischofs Gröber in die Zeit*. Hrsg.: Konrad Hofmann. Freiburg i.Br.: Herder, 1947. 159 pp.

2022 JANSEN, JAN: *Katholiken und Kommunisten im deutschen Freiheitskampf*. Strasbourg: Éds. Prométhée, 1938. 97 pp., illus.

2023 KEMPNER, BENEDICTA MARIA: *Priester vor Hitlers Tribunalen*. München: Rütten & Loening, 1966. 496 pp., ports., facsims., bibl.

2024 KLOIDT, FRANZ: *Verräter oder Märtyrer? Dokumente katholischer Blutzeugen der nationalsozialistischen Kirchenverfolgung geben Antwort*. Düsseldorf: Patmos Verlag, 1962. 235 pp. [Incl.: Erich Klausener, Bernhard Letterhaus, Edith Stein, Johannes Maria Verweyen.]

2025 [LICHTENBERG, BERNHARD] MANN, H. G.: *Prozess Bernhard Lichtenberg. Ein Leben in Dokumenten*. Berlin: Morus Verlag, 1977. 120 pp., facsims., bibl.

2026 [MAYER, RUPERT] GRITSCHNEDER, OTTO, ed.: *Pater Rupert Mayer vor dem Sondergericht. Dokumente der Verhandlung vor dem Sondergericht in München am 22. und 23. Juli 1937*. München: Pustet, 1965. 155 pp., port.

2027 *Michael. Katholische Volksschriften zu Tagesfragen*. Saarbrucken: [no impr.], 1934. 16 pp. each.
1) *Das Alte Testament, nicht ein nationales, sondern ein Menschheitsbuch.*
2) *Rasse und Religion.*
3) *Germanentum und Christentum.*
4) *Jesus kein Arier!*

2028 MICKLEM, NATHANIEL: *National Socialism and the Roman Catholic Church. Being an account of the conflict between the National Socialist Government of Germany and the Roman Catholic Church, 1933–1938.* London: Oxford University Press, 1939. xvi + 243 pp., illus.

2029 MUCKERMANN, FRIEDRICH: *Im Kampf zwischen zwei Epochen. Lebenserinnerungen.* Bearb.: Nikolaus Junk. Mainz: Matthias-Grünewald-Verlag, 1973. xviii + 665 pp., port. (Veröffentlichungen der Kommission für Zeitgeschichte ...). [Incl.: 'Im Kampf gegen Hitler', pp. 519–651.]

2030 *Nazi war against the Catholic Church.* Washington, D.C.: US National Catholic Welfare Conference [1942]. 144 pp.

2031 NEUHÄUSLER, JOHANN: *Kreuz und Hakenkreuz. Der Kampf des Nationalsozialismus gegen die katholische Kirche und der kirchliche Widerstand.* München: Verlag Katholische Kirche Bayerns, 1946. 384 + 440 pp., illus.

2032 [ORDENSDEVISENPROZESSE] HOFFMANN, E. & JANSSEN, H., eds.: *Die Wahrheit über die Ordensdevisenprozesse 1935/36.* Bielefeld: Verlag Hausknecht, 1967. 288 pp., tabs.

2033 *The persecution of the Catholic Church in the Third Reich. Facts and documents.* Transl. from the German. London: Burns Oates, 1940. 565 pp., illus. [Incl. material on Nazi substitutes for religion.]

2034 [PREYSING, KONRAD] BISCHÖFLICHES ORDINARIAT BERLIN: *Konrad Kardinal von Preysing, Bischof von Berlin. Zur Vollendung seines 70. Lebensjahres* hrsg. Berlin: Morus-Verlag, 1950. 172 pp., illus. [Incl. special emphasis on the Cardinal's resistance to the Nazis.]

2035 ROSSO, MARIO: *Violencia nazi contra la Iglesia.* Buenos Aires: Editorial Future S.R.L., 1961. 92 pp.

SITTLICHKEITSPROZESSE
2036 HOCKERTS, HANS GÜNTER: *Die Sittlichkeitsprozesse gegen katholische Ordensangehörige und Priester 1936–1937. Eine Studie zur nationalsozialistischen Herrschaftstechnik und zum Kirchenkampf.* Mainz: Matthias-Grünewald-Verlag, 1971. xxv + 224 pp., bibl. (Veröffentlichungen der Kommission für Zeitgeschichte ...).

2037 ROSE, FRANZ: *Mönche vor Gericht. Eine Darstellung entarteten Klosterlebens nach Dokumenten und Akten.* Berlin: Klieber, 1939. 313 pp., illus., facsims.

2038 [SPROLL, JOANNES BAPTISTA] KOPF, PAUL & MÜLLER, MAX, eds.: *Die Vertreibung von Bischof Joannes Baptista Sproll von Rottenberg 1938–1945. Dokumente zur Geschichte des kirchlichen Widerstands.* Mainz: Matthias-Gruñewald-Verlag, 1971. xxxv + 386 pp., bibl. (Veröffentlichungen der Kommission für Zeitgeschichte ...).

2039 [STORM, GERHARD] KLOIDT, FRANZ: *KZ-Häftling Nr. 32281. Blutzeuge Gerhard Storm.* Xanten: Gesthuysen, 1966. 69 pp., illus., facsims.

166

f. Heresies, anti-Christianity, neo-paganism

ACKERMANN, JOSEF: *Heinrich Himmler als Ideologe.* See 3241.

2040 BANGERT, OTTO: *Der irdische Gott. Ein deutsches Brevier.* München: Hoheneichen-Verlag, 1939. 156 pp.

2041 BENDISCIOLI, MARIO: *Neopaganesimo razzista.* Brescia: Morcelliana, 1938. 116 pp. [2nd rev. ed.]

2042 BERGMANN, ERNST: *Die natürliche Geistlehre. System einer deutsch-nordischen Weltsinndeutung.* Stuttgart: Truckenmüller, 1937. 389 pp.

2043 BISCHOFF, ERICH: *Los von Gott? Eine Zeitfrage.* Neu hrsg. von Artur Pleissner. 5. (Neu-)Aufl. Dresden: Deutscher Literaturverlag, 1936. 102 pp.

2044 DINTER, ARTUR: *War Jesus Jude? Ein Nachweis auf Grund der Geschichte Galiläas, der Zeugnis der Evangelien und Jesu eigener Lehre.* Leipzig: Verlag Deutsche Volkskirche, 1934. 30 pp.

2045 FAHNEMANN, FRANZ & EICHBERG, EMIL, eds.: *Deutsches Gebet in der Schule. Eine Sammlung.* Saarbrücken: Verlag Buchgewerbehaus, 1937. 53 pp.

2046 FRENSSEN, GUSTAV: *Der Glaube der Nordmark.* Stuttgart: Gutbrod, 1936. 145 pp.

2047 FRITSCH, THEODOR: *Der neue Glaube.* Leipzig: Hammer-Verlag, 1936. 200 pp. [3rd ed.]

2048 GAMM, HANS JOACHIM: *Der braune Kult. Das Dritte Reich und seine Ersatzreligion. Ein Beitrag zur politischen Bildung.* Hamburg: Rütten & Loening, 1962. 221 pp., illus., facsims., bibl.

2049 HAUPTMANN, HANS: *Bolschewismus in der Bibel.* Leipzig: Klein, 1937. 118 pp.

2050 HUTTEN, KURT: *Ein neues Evangelium? Zu der Forderung einer 'Völkischen Reformation' der Kirche.* Stuttgart: Quell-Verlag der Evangelischen Gesellschaft, 1936. 48 pp.

2051 KLAGGES, DIETRICH: *Das Urevangelium Jesu, der deutsche Glaube.* 4. Aufl. Leipzig: Armanen-Verlag, 1936. 232 pp.

2052 KÜNNETH, WALTER: *Der grosse Abfall. Eine geschichtstheologische Untersuchung der Begegnung zwischen Nationalsozialismus und Christentum.* Hamburg: Wittig, 1947. 319 pp.

2053 LÖHDE, WALTER, ed.: *Für Gewissens und Glaubens Freiheit. Das Christentum im Urteil grosser Dichter, Denker und Staatsmänner.* Berlin: Nordland-Verlag, 1934. 185 pp.

2054 LOHMANN, JOH[ANNES]: *Hitlerworte als Gleichnisse für Gottesworte.* Bamberg: Maar, 1934. 18 pp.

2055 LOTHER, HELMUT: *Neugermanische Religion und Christentum. Eine kirchengeschichtliche Vorlesung.* Gütersloh: 'Der Rufer' Evangelischer Verlag, 1934. 171 pp., bibls. at end of chapters.

LUDENDORFF, ERICH AND MATHILDE

2056 LUDENDORFF, ERICH, ed.: *Mathilde Ludendorff, ihr Werk und Wirken.* München: Ludendorff, 1937. 324 pp., illus., bibl.

2057 LUDENDORFF, MATHILDE: *Erlösung von Jesu Christo.* 60.–61. Taus. Pähl (Obb.): Verlag Hohe Warte, 1957. 315 pp. [First ed. 1931.]

2058 ASSER-KRAMER, GERTRUD: *Neue Wege zu Frieden und Freiheit. Eine Einführung in die Gotterkenntnis Mathilde Ludendorffs.* Pähl (Obb.): von Bebenburg, 1962. 78 pp.

2059 KOPP, HANS: *Der General und die Religion. Zu Erich Ludendorffs 100. Geburtstag.* Pähl (Obb.): von Bebenburg, 1965. 88 pp., port.

2060 PETERSMANN, WERNER: *Die Bibel* doch *Gottes Wort. Gegen die 'Entdeutschung' durch Hauses Ludendorff!* Hrsg.: Leitung der Reichsbewegung Deutsche Christen. Berlin: Koch [193–]. 15 pp.

2061 MARINOFF, IRENE: *The heresy of National Socialism.* Foreword: R. Downey. London: Burns Oates & Washbourne, 1941. 158 pp., bibl.

2062 MILLER, ALFRED: *Volkentartung unter dem Kreuz. Der abendländische Geistespolyp als Fluch der Welt.* Leipzig: Klein, 1933. 274 pp., bibl. [Also: 2. verm. Aufl. 1936. 318 pp., illus., bibl.]

2063 MÜLLER-REIMERDES, FRIEDERIKE: *Der christliche Hexenwahn. Gedanken zum religiösen Freiheitskampf der deutschen Frau.* Leipzig: Klein, 1935. 64 pp.

2064 MURAWSKI, FRIEDRICH: *Der Kaiser aus dem Jenseits. Bilder von Wesen und Wirken Jahwehs und seiner Kirche.* Berlin: Fritsch, 1939. 448 pp., bibl.

2065 ROSSNER, FERDINAND: *Rasse und Religion.* Hrsg.: Walter Kopp. Hannover: Schaper, 1942. 107 pp. (Schriftenreihe des rassenpolitischen Amtes der Gauleitung Süd-Hannover-Braunschweig).

2066 SCHAIRER, J. B.: *Volk—Blut—Gott. Ein Gruss des Evangeliums an die deutsche Freiheitsbewegung.* Berlin: Warneck, 1933. 224 pp.

2067 SCHNEIDER, GEORG: *Völkische Reformation. Eine Wegweisung zu christdeutscher Einheit.* Stuttgart: Kohlhammer, 1934. 171 pp. [Incl.: III c: 'Jesus und seine Botschaft im Spiegel der jüdischen Seele'; d: 'War Jesus ein Arier?'.]

2068 SCHWANER, WILHELM, ed.: *Germanen-Bibel. Aus heiligen Schriften germanischer Völker.* 6. vollst. umgearb. Aufl. Stuttgart: Deutsche Verlags-Anstalt, 1934. xvi + 562 pp., illus., mus. scores.

2069 TRAUE, GEORG: *Millionen arischer Menschen im Glaubenskampf! 40 artgemässe Zweifelsfragen an Bibel und Kirche: 40 bekenntnisgemässe Antworten.* Braunschweig: Wollermann [1934]. 160 pp. [Incl.: 'Religiöse Erlebnisse eines SA-Mannes in der Kampfzeit'.]

2070 VONDUNG, KLAUS: *Magie und Manipulation. Ideologischer Kult und politische*

Religion des Nationalsozialismus. Göttingen: Vandenhoeck & Ruprecht, 1971. 256 pp., bibl.

2071 WESSELSKY, ANTON: *Die germanische Kulturtragödie und Deutschlands Erwachen. Eine Rechenschaft über das Zeitalter biblischer Mentalität und über sein Ende durch arisch-deutsche Religion der That.* Wien: [priv. pr.], 1933. 438 pp.

2072 WEY, (Dr.) van der: *Het nieuw-Heidendom.* 3e verm. uitg. Amsterdam: Uitg. Geloofsverdediging, 1938. 74 pp.

2073 WILL, IRMGARD: *Der Bolschewismus eine Frucht des Christentums.* Leipzig: Klein, 1937. 87 pp.

Deutsche Glaubensbewegung

2074 BARTSCHE, HEINZ: *Die Wirklichkeit der Allgemeinen Deutschen Glaubensbewegung der Gegenwart.* Inaugural-Dissertation [pres. to] Universität Leipzig. Breslau: Ludwig, 1938. 125 pp., bibl.

2075 FETZ, FRIEDRICH FERDINAND OTTO: *Durch positives Christentum im Lichte des Nationalsozialismus zur deutschen Glaubensbewegung.* Hamburg: Rieckmann, 1935. 56 pp.

2076 GRABERT, HERBERT: *Der protestantische Auftrag des deutschen Volkes. Grundzüge der deutschen Glaubensgeschichte von Luther bis Hauer.* Stuttgart: Gutbrod, 1936. 287 pp.

HAUER, JAKOB WILHELM, LEADER OF THE GERMAN FAITH MOVEMENT
2077 HAUER, [JAKOB] WILHELM: *Deutsche Gottschau. Grundzüge eines deutschen Glaubens.* 2. unveränd. Aufl. Stuttgart: Gutbrod, 1934. 288 pp.

2078 HAUER, [JAKOB] WILHELM and others: *Germany's new religion. The German Faith Movement.* Transl. from the German. New York: Abingdon Press, 1937. 168 pp.

2079 HAUER, J. WILHELM, ed.: *Glaube und Blut. Beiträge zum Problem Religion und Rasse.* Hrsg. in Mitarb. von [Friedrich] Berger, Hans F. K. Günther, [Herbert] Reier, [Johanna] Thoms-Paetow. Karlsruhe: Boltze, 1938. 184 pp.

2080 BRONISCH-HOLTZE, ERNST: *Der Akademiker zwischen Christentum und deutscher Glaubensbewegung. Ein Wort zur Auseinandersetzung zwischen dem christlichen Glauben und der deutschen Glaubensbewegung, wie sie insbesondere durch Prof. J. W. Hauer vertreten wird.* Gütersloh: Bertelsmann, 1934. 44 pp.

Germanic festivals

2081 HAUER, J. WILHELM: *Fest und Feier aus deutscher Art.* Stuttgart: Gutbrod, 1936. 60 pp.

2082 KAHL, HANS-DIETRICH: *Das deutsche Weihnachtsfest. Werden, Wesen und Gestaltung.* Dresden: Wolfsangel, 1940. 32 pp.

2083 KLODWIG, RUDOLF: *Deutsches Sippenfeiern.* Breslau: Deutscher Verlag, 1937. 39 pp.

2084 KNIGGENDORF, WALTER: *Ehe ohne Priestersegen.* Dresden: Wolfsangel, 1939. 15 pp.

2085 LECHNER, L.: *Die Totenfeier. Beispiele mit Anweisungen und einer Skizze zur Feier-Ordnung.* Stuttgart: Bühler, 1938. 35 pp., diagr. [2nd ed.]

2086 NIGGEMANN, HANS, ed.: *Sonnenwende.* 5. gänzl. umgearb. Aufl. Hamburg: Hanseatische Verlagsanstalt, 1935. 64 pp., mus. scores.

H. WOMEN

2087 ARNIM, BRIGITTE VON: *Hella kämpft fürs Dritte Reich. Roman.* Leipzig: Payne, 1934. 147 pp., illus.

2088 BOEDEKER, ELISABETH & MEYER-PLATH, MARIA, eds.: *50 Jahre Habilitation in Deutschland. Eine Dokumentation über den Zeitraum von 1920–1970.* Göttingen: Schwartz, 1974. xii + 387 pp.

2089 BOGER-EICHLER, ELSE: *Von tapferen, heiteren und gelehrten Hausfrauen.* München: Lehmann, 1937. 166 pp., illus.

BRAUN, EVA
2090 CHARLIER, JEAN-MICHEL & LAUNAY, JACQUES de: *Eva Hitler geb. Braun. Die führenden Frauen des Dritten Reiches.* Stuttgart: Seewald, 1979. 270 pp., illus. [Transl. from the French.]

2091 GUN, NERIN E.: *Eva Braun-Hitler. Leben und Schicksal.* Velbert: Blick und Bild Verlag, 1968. 212 pp., illus., facsims. [English version: *Eva Braun: Hitler's mistress.* London: Frewin, 1968.]

2092 *Der deutsche Soldat und die Frau aus fremdem Volkstum.* Berlin: NS-Führungsstab des OKW, 1943. 31 pp. (Richthefte des Oberkommandos der Wehrmacht).

2093 DIEHL, GUIDA: *Die deutsche Frau und der Nationalsozialismus.* Eisenach: Neulandverlag, 1932. 120 pp.

2094 DRESLER, ADOLF: *Die Frau im Journalismus.* München: Knorr & Hirth, 1936. 135 pp., ports.

2095 FRAUENAMT DER DEUTSCHEN ARBEITSFRONT: *Tagewerk und Feierabend der schaffenden deutschen Frau.* Im Auftr. der Reichsfrauenführerin hrsg. und bearb. Leipzig: Beyer, 1936. 112 pp., illus., tabs. [Text in German, English, French, Italian.]

2096 *Ein Frauenbuch für Feierstunden.* Hrsg. und bearb. vom Frauenamt der Deutschen Arbeitsfront und des Deutschen Frauenwerks. Berlin: Siebert, 1936. 128 pp.

2097 *Die Frauenfrage in Deutschland, 1931–1950. Eine Bibliographie.* Berlin: Deutscher Akademikerinnenbund, 1950. ix + 210 pp.

2098 GENTZKOW, LIANE VON: *Das deutsche Mädchen. Von der Frühzeit bis zur Gegenwart.* Zeichnungen: Gerh. Ulrich. Braunschweig: Westermann, 1941. 193 pp.

2099 [GOEBBELS, MAGDA] MEISSNER, HANS-OTTO: *Magda Goebbels. Ein Lebensbild.* München: Blanvalet, 1978. 351 pp., illus., bibl.

2100 GOTTSCHEWSKI, LYDIA: *Männerbund und Frauenfrage. Die Frau im neuen Staat.* München: Lehmann, 1934. 88 pp.

2101 GRÜNIG, G. & ZELLMER, E.: *Arbeitsschutzvorschriften für die erwerbstätige Frau und Mutter. Zusammenstellung des amtlichen Wortlauts der einschlägigen Gesetze, Verordnungen und Erlasse.* Berlin: Heymann, 1942. 191 pp., tabs.

2102 HAARER, JOHANNA: *Die deutsche Mutter und ihr erstes Kind.* München: Lehmann, 1936. 257 pp., illus.

2103 HEISS, LISA: *Die grosse Kraft. Frauenschaffen für Deutschlands Weltgeltung.* Stuttgart: Union Deutsche Verlagsgesellschaft, 1939. 229 pp.

2104 KIRKPATRICK, CLIFFORD: *Nazi Germany: its women and family life.* Indianapolis, Ind.: Bobbs Merrill, 1938. 353 pp., illus.

2105 KÖHLER-IRRGANG, RUTH: *Die Sendung der Frau in der deutschen Geschichte.* Leipzig: von Hase & Koehler, 1940. 248 pp., ports.

2106 LÜCK, MARGRET: *Die Frau im Männerstaat. Die gesellschaftliche Stellung der Frau im Nationalsozialismus. Eine Analyse aus pädagogischer Sicht.* Frankfurt a.M.: Lang, 1979. 266 pp., bibl.

2107 LÜDERS, MARIE ELISABETH: *Volksdienst der Frau.* Berlin-Tempelhof: Bott, 1937. 107 pp.

2108 MACCIOCCHI, MARIA-ANTOINIETTA: *Jungfrauen, Mütter und ein Führer. Frauen im Faschismus.* Berlin: Wagenbach, 1976. 108 pp., illus., bibl. [Transl. from the French.]

2109 MASON, TIM: 'Zur Lage der Frauen in Deutschland 1930–1940'. [In] *Gesellschaft. Beiträge zur Marxschen Theorie.* Nr. 6. Frankfurt a.M.: Suhrkamp, 1976.

2110 MOERS, MARTHA: *Der Fraueneinsatz in der Industrie. Eine psychologische Untersuchung.* Berlin: Duncker & Humblot, 1943. 153 pp.

2111 *Mutter. Ein Buch der Liebe und der Heimat für Alle.* Mit 120 Bildern nach Originalaufnahmen von J. B. Malina. Berlin: Verlag 'Mutter und Volk', 1934. 239 pp., illus., bibl.

2112 *N. S. Frauenbuch.* Hrsg. im Auftr. der Obersten Leitung der P.O., N. S. Frauenschaft von Ellen Semmelroth und Renate von Stieda. München: Lehmann, 1934. 249 pp., illus.

2113　PESTALOZZA, HANNA VON: *Ich will dienen. Eine Frau erfährt und bekennt deutsche Schicksalsfülle.* Berlin: Runge, 1935. 175 pp.

2114　PUGEL, THEODOR: *Die arische Frau im Wandel der Jahrtausende. Kulturgeschichtlich geschildert.* Wien: Österreichische Verlagsanstalt, 1936. 260 pp., illus.

2115　SCHILLING, HEINAR: *Germanische Frauen.* Leipzig: von Hase & Koehler, 1942. 211 pp. [Written 1934/35.]

2116　SCHOLTZ-KLINK, GERTRUD: *Die Frau im Dritten Reich. Eine Dokumentation.* Tübingen: Grabert, 1978. 546 pp., illus.

2117　STEINBACH, ERIKA, ed.: *Deutsches Frauenliederbuch.* Geleitw.: Gertrud Scholtz-Klink. Erw. Ausg. Kassel: Bärenreiter-Verlag, 1936. 61 pp., mus. scores.

2118　STEPHENSON, JILL: 'Girls' higher education in Germany in the 1930s'. [In] *Journal of Contemporary History,* Vol. 10, No. 1, 1975. London: Sage. Pp. 41–69. [Author also writes under name Jill McIntyre.]

2119　STEPHENSON, JILL: *Women in Nazi society.* London: Croom Helm, 1975. 223 pp., bibl.

2120　STRUVE, CAROLA: *Frauenfreiheit und Volksfreiheit auf kameradschaftrechtlicher Grundlage.* Heidelberg: Bündischer Verlag, 1933. 173 pp., port., chart.

2121　THOMAS, KATHERINE: *Women in Nazi Germany.* London: Gollancz, 1943. 102 pp.

2122　TREMEL-EGGERT, KUNI: *Barb. Der Roman einer deutschen Frau.* 10. Aufl. München: Eher, 1935. 418 pp.

2123　UNVERRICHT, ELSBETH: *Unsere Zeit und wir. Das Buch der deutschen Frau.* Cauting b. München: Berg, [1933]. 485 pp., illus.

2124　WINKLER, DÖRTE: *Frauenarbeit im 'Dritten Reich'.* Hamburg: Hoffmann & Campe, 1977. 252 pp., tabs., bibl.

War service

2125　*Frauen helfen siegen. Bilddokumente vom Kriegseinsatz unserer Frauen und Mütter.* Geleitw.: Gertrud Scholtz-Klink. 131.–140. Taus. Berlin: Zeitgeschichte Verlag, 1942. 47 pp., illus.

2126　GERSDORFF, URSULA VON: *Frauen im Kriegsdienst 1914–1945.* Stuttgart: Deutsche Verlags-Anstalt, 1969. 572 + [24] pp., illus., tabs., plan, bibl.

2127　REICHSFRAUENFÜHRUNG: *Deutsches Frauenschaffen im Kriege. Jahrbuch der Reichsfrauenführung.* Hrsg.: Erika [Fillies]-Kirmsse. Dortmund: Westfalen Verlag, 1940, 1941. In 2 vols. [Before 1940 entitled: *Deutsches Frauenschaffen.*]

2128　SEIDEL, INA & GROSSER, HANNS: *Dienende Herzen. Kriegsbriefe von Nachrichtenhelferinnen des Heeres.* Berlin: Limpert, 1942. 173 pp.

2129 SONNEMANN, THEODOR: *Die Frau in der Landesverteidigung. Ihr Einsatz in der Industrie.* Oldenburg: Stalling, 1939. 179 pp.

J. YOUTH AND EDUCATION

1. GENERAL

2130 ALEXANDER, LUCIE: *Unser der Weg. Vom Kampf der Jugend unserer Tage.* Berlin: Rödiger, 1935. 157 pp.

2131 BRUCKNER, WINFRIED and others: *Damals war ich vierzehn. Berichte und Erinnerungen.* Wien: Jugend und Volk Verlag, 1978. 125 pp. [Cover: *Jugend im Dritten Reich.*]

2132 GRÜN, MAX von der: *Wie war das eigentlich? Kindheit und Jugend im Dritten Reich.* Mit einer Dokumentation von Christel Schütz. Nachw.: Malte Dahrendorf. Darmstadt: Luchterhand, 1979. 263 pp.

2133 HEINDL, HANS: *Die totale Revolution oder Die neue Jugend im Dritten Reich. Ein Bericht.* Augsburg: [priv. pr.], 1973. 62 pp.

2134 HOLSTEIN, CHRISTINE: *Kleine Kindermädel. Ein Kinderjahr im Dritten Reich.* Reutlingen: Ensslin & Laiblin, 1935. 112 pp., illus.

2135 KLOSE, WERNER: *Generation im Gleichschritt. Ein Dokumentarbericht.* Oldenburg: Stalling, 1964. 296 pp., illus., bibl.

2136 KÖRBER, HILDE: *Kindheit und Jugend 1942–1947. Briefe und Aufzeichnungen junger Menschen.* Berlin-Grunewald: 1948. 191 pp.

LAW RELATING TO YOUTH
2137 ROHLFING, THEODOR & SCHRAUT, RUDOLF: *Jugendschutzgesetz, (Gesetz über Kinderarbeit und über die Arbeitszeit der Jugendlichen), nebst Ausführungsverordnungen. Textausgabe mit amtlicher Begründung, nebst systematischer Einleitung, einschliesslich des Jugendschutzes im Kriege.* 3. durchges. Aufl. Berlin: de Gruyter, 1944. 208 pp.

2138 WEBLER, HEINRICH, comp.: *Deutsches Jugendrecht nach dem Stande vom 1. Juli 1941.* Berlin: Heymann, 1941. 216 pp.

2139 LOEWENBERG, PETER: 'The psychohistorical origins of the Nazi youth cohort'. [In] *American Historical Review*, Vol. 76, No. 5, Dec. 1971. Pp. 1457–1502, illus.

2140 OST, LEOPOLD: *Das Jugendwohnheim.* Berlin: Eher, 1944. 126 pp.

2141 ROTH, BERT, ed.: *Kampf. Lebensdokumente deutscher Jugend von 1914–1934.* Geleitw.: Reichsminister Dr. Wilhelm Frick. Leipzig: Reclam, 1934. 323 pp.

2142 SCHWARZBAUER, FRITZ: *Ehrendienst am Volk. Wegweiser durch den*

Arbeitsdienst, Wehrdienst, Luftschutzdienst, Leibeserziehungsdienst, Notdienst, SS-Absperr- und Sicherungsdienst. Berlin: Deutscher Betriebswirte Verlag, 1939. 119 pp.

2143 SIEMERING, HERTHA: *Deutschlands Jugend in Bevölkerung und Wirtschaft. Eine statistische Untersuchung.* Berlin: Junker & Dünnhaupt, 1937. 446 pp., bibl.

YOUTH HOSTELS

KOCHSKÄMPER, MAX: *Herbergen der neuen Jugend.* See 2649.

2144 RODATZ, JOHANNES: *Erziehung durch Erleben. Der Sinn des deutschen Jugendherbergswerkes.* Vorw.: Baldur von Schirach. 2. neubearb. Aufl. Berlin: Limpert, 1936. 58 pp.

2. EDUCATION AND INDOCTRINATION

2145 ASSEL, HANS-GÜNTHER: *Die Perversion der politischen Pädagogik im Nationalsozialismus.* München: Ehrenwirth, 1969. 156 pp., bibl. (Schriften der Pädagogischen Hochschulen Bayerns).

2146 BAEUMLER, ALFRED: *Politik und Erziehung. Reden und Aufsätze.* Berlin. Junker & Dünnhaupt, 1937. 174 pp.

2147 BENZE, RUDOLF: *Erziehung im grossdeutschen Reich. Eine Überschau über ihre Ziele, Wege und Einrichtungen.* 3. erw. Aufl. Frankfurt a.M.: Diesterweg, 1943. 183 pp., illus.

2148 D'HARCOURT, ROBERT: *L'évangile de la force. Le visage de la jeunesse du IIIe Reich.* Paris: Plon, 1936. 248 pp.

2149 DONATH, F. & ZIMMERMANN, K.: *Biologie, Nationalsozialismus und neue Erziehung.* 2. Aufl. Leipzig: Quelle & Meyer, [193–?]. 72 pp.

2150 GOTTFARSTEIN, J.: *L'école du meurtre.* Paris: La Presse française et étrangère, 1946. 367 pp., illus.

2151 IMMER, KARL: *Entchristlichung der Jugend. Eine Materialsammlung.* Wuppertal-Barmen: Verlag 'Unter dem Wort', 1936. 24 pp.

2152 KANDEL, I. L.: *The making of Nazis.* New York: Bureau of Publications, Teachers' College, Columbia University, 1935. 143 pp.

2153 KAUFMANN, GÜNTER: *Das kommende Deutschland. Die Erziehung der Jugend im Reich Adolf Hitlers.* 3. vollst. verb. and erw. Aufl. Berlin: Junker & Dünnhaupt, 1943. 376 pp., ports., tabs., diagrs.

2154 KRIECK, ERNST: *Menschenformung. Grundzüge der vergleichenden Erziehungswissenschaft.* 6. Aufl. Leipzig: Quelle & Meyer, 1944. 371 pp.

2155 KRIECK, ERNST: *National-politische Erziehung.* 5.–6. Aufl. Leipzig: Armanen-Verlag, 1933. 186 pp.

2156 LINGELBACH, KARL CHRISTOPH: *Erziehung und Erziehungstheorien im nationalsozialistischen Deutschland. Ursprünge und Wandlungen der 1933–1945 in Deutschland vorherrschenden erziehungstheoretischen*

Strömungen: ihre politischen Funktionen und ihr Verhältnis zur ausserschulischen Erziehungspraxis des 'Dritten Reiches'. Weinheim: Beltz, 1970. 341 pp., bibl. (notes & bibl. pp. 255–338).

2157   LÖPELMANN, MARTIN: *Wege und Ziele der Kindererziehung unserer Zeit.* Leipzig: Hesse & Becker, [1936]. 340 pp., illus.

2158   MÄNNEL, HANSJÖRG: *Politische Fibel. Richtlinien für die politisch-weltanschauliche Schulung.* Leipzig: Fritsch, 1934. 172 pp.

2159   *Sammelhefte ausgewählter Vorträge und Reden für die Schulung in nationalsozialistischer Weltanschauung und nationalsozialistischer Zielsetzung.* Berlin: Eher, 1939. 254 pp.

2160   SCHNAPPER, M. B.: *Youth betrayed.* Introd.: Ilse Trauman. New York: International Relief Ass'n, [1936]. 63 pp.

2161   SCHUH, WILLY: *Erziehung im Dienste der Rassenhygiene ('Eugenische Erziehung').* Inaugural-Dissertation [pres. to] Ludwig-Maximilians-Universität zu München. Friedberg/Augsburg: Baur, 1937. 154 + iv pp., bibl.

2162   SPONHOLZ, HANS: *Deutsches Denken. Beiträge für die weltanschauliche Erziehung.* 7. Aufl. Berlin: Siep, 1935. 125 pp.

2163   ZIMMER, GREGOR: *Education for death. The making of the Nazi.* New York: Oxford University Press, 1941. 209 pp.

Children's books

2164   ALEY, PETER: *Jugendliteratur im Dritten Reich. Dokumente und Kommentare.* Vorw.: Klaus Doderer. Gütersloh: Bertelsmann, 1967. 262 pp., diagrs. tabs., facsims., bibl.

ANTI-SEMITISM

2165   BAUER, ELVIRA: *'Trau' keinem Fuchs auf grüner Heid und keinem Jud bei seinem Eid'. Ein Bilderbuch für Gross und Klein.* Nürnberg: Stürmer Verlag, [193–]. [Approx. 60 pp.], illus. [Book of verses and caricatures.]

2166   HIEMER, ERNST: *Der Giftpilz. Ein Stürmerbuch für Jung und Alt.* Nürnberg: Der Stürmer-Verlag, 1938. [62 pp.], illus. [English version: *The poisoned mushroom.* With a foreword by the Bishop of Durham. London: Friends of Europe, 1938.]

2167   HIEMER, ERNST: *Der Pudelmopsdackelpinscher und andere besinnliche Erzählungen.* Bilder: Willi Hofmann. Nürnberg: Der Stürmer-Verlag, 1940. 95 pp., illus.

2168   BEIER-LINDHARDT, ERICH: *Ein Buch vom Führer für die deutsche Jugend.* Geleitw.: Baldur von Schirach. 7. neubearb. Aufl. Oldenburg: Stalling, 1943. 146 pp., illus.

2169   *Deutschland, Deutschland über Alles. Ein Jahrbuch für die deutsche Jugend und das deutsche Volk im Dritten Reich.* Leipzig: Koehler, 1933. 399 pp., illus., mus. scores, facsims.

2170 DÖRNER, CLAUS: *Das deutsche Jahr. Feiern der Jungen Nation.* München: Eher, 1939. 215 pp., illus., mus. scores, bibl.

2171 *Jungvolk-Jahrbuch.* Hrsg.: Reichsjugendführung. München: 1935–1940. 6 vols., illus., mus. scores.

2172 LANG, HANS, ed.: *Die Wissenskiste. Voigtländers Jugendlexikon.* Leipzig: Voigtländer, 1936. 339 pp., illus., maps, diagr.

2173 LÜKE, FRANZ: *Rassen-A.B.C.* Stuttgart: Kamp, 1935. 81 pp., illus., diagrs., tabs.

2174 METTENLEITER, FRITZ: *Alaf sig arna. Alles Heil dem Artbewussten. Jugendbuch für Rassen- und Vererbungslehre, Ahnen- und Bevölkerungskunde in Erlebnissen.* Stuttgart: Loewe, [193–]. 188 pp., illus.

2175 SCHRAMM, HEINZ: *Das Hitlerbuch der deutschen Jugend.* 4. Aufl. Hamburg: Hanseatische Verlagsanstalt, 1933. 110 pp.

3. NAZI YOUTH ORGANIZATIONS

Hitler Youth

2176 BADE, WILFRID: *Trommlerbub unterm Hakenkreuz.* 2. Aufl. Stuttgart: Loewe, [193–]. 99 pp., illus.

2177 BARTELMAS, EUGEN FRIEDER & NOETHLICHS, RICHARD, eds.: *Gott, Freiheit, Vaterland. Sprech-Chöre der Hitlerjugend.* Stuttgart: Union Deutsche Verlagsgesellschaft, [193–?]. 138 pp.

2178 BRANDENBURG, HANS-CHRISTIAN: *Die Geschichte der HJ. Wege und Irrwege einer Generation.* Köln: Verlag Wissenschaft und Politik, 1968. 347 pp., illus., diagrs., bibl.

2179 BRENNECKE, FRITZ, ed.: *The Nazi primer. Official handbook for schooling the Hitler Youth.* Transl. from the orig. German with a preface by Harwood L. Childs. Commentary: William E. Dodd. New York: Harper, 1938. xxxvii + 280 pp., illus., maps, diagrs., tabs., facsims. [German orig.: *Handbuch für die Schulungsarbeit in der HJ. Vom deutschen Volk und seinem Lebensraum.* Bearb.: Paul Gierlichs.]

2180 BROCKDORFF, DIETER: *Einer vom Jahrgang 18. Das Schicksal des Hitlerjungen Günther Fries.* Rastatt: Pabel, 1963. 255 pp., illus.

2181 DORNER, CLAUS, ed.: *Freude, Zucht, Glaube. Handbuch für die kulturelle Arbeit im Lager.* Im Auftr. der Reichsjugendführung der NSDAP. Potsdam: Voggenreiter, 1937. 248 pp., illus., mus. scores, bibl.

2182 FAHNDERL, WILHELM, ed.: *H.J. marschiert! Das neue Hitler-Jugend-Buch.* Berlin: Franke, [1933]. 383 pp., illus., facsims.

2183 *Jungarbeiter ahoi! 1000 Hitlerjungen erleben das Meer und Norwegen. Ein*

Fahrtbericht in Wort und Bild. Nordlandfahrt der DAF Gau Magdeburg-Anhalt und des Gebietes Mittelelbe der HJ vom 1. bis 12. Mai 1937. Magdeburg: Gau-Presseabt. der DAF ... [1937]. 32 pp., illus.

2184 *Jungen—euere Welt! Das Jahrbuch der Hitler-Jugend. 1.–5. Jhrg.* Hrsg.: Karl Lapper, [1938–1940 only], Wilhelm Utermann. München: 1938/42. 5 vols., illus., diagrs.

2185 KERUTT, HORST & WEGENER, WOLFRAM M.: *Die Fahne ist mehr als der Tod. Ein deutsches Fahnenbuch.* München: Eher, 1941. 141 pp., illus.

2186 KOCH, HANNSJOACHIM W.: *The Hitler Youth. Origins and development 1922–1945.* London: Macdonald and Jane's, 1975. xi + 340 pp., illus., maps, diagrs., bibl. [German version: *Geschichte der Hitlerjugend. Ihre Ursprünge und ihre Entwicklung 1922–1945.* Percha am Starnberger See: Schulz, 1975.]

LAWS RELATING TO HITLER YOUTH
2187 KLEMER, GERHARD: *Jugendstrafrecht und Hitler-Jugend. Stellung und Aufgaben der Hitler-Jugend in der Jugendstrafrechtspflege.* 2. ergänz. Aufl. Berlin: Deutscher Rechtsverlag, [1941]. 110 pp., bibl.

2188 TETZLAFF, WALTER: *Das Disziplinarrecht der Hitler-Jugend. Entwicklung, gegenwärtiger Stand, Ausgestaltung.* Berlin: Deutscher Rechtsverlag, 1944. 197 pp., bibl. (Schriften zum Jugendrecht ...).

2189 *Lieder für die Hitler-Jugend und den Bund Deutscher Mädels.* Hrsg. von der ehem. Stammführung des Deutschen Jungvolkes und der Hitler-Jugend. [Leipzig?]: St.-Georg-Verlag, 1933. 63 pp. [3rd ed. of: *Lieder der jungen Front.]*

2190 LINDENBERG, FRIEDRICH WOLFGANG: *Heil unserm Führer! Das Hitlerbuch eines Hitlerjungen.* Reutlingen: Ensslin & Laiblin, 1936. 112 pp., illus.

2191 DIE NORDISCHE GESELLSCHAFT: *Nordland Fibel.* Berlin: Limpert, 1938. 400 pp., illus., tabs., map. (Sonderausg. für den Dienstgebrauch der Hitlerjugend. Unverkäuflich).

NORKUS, HERBERT
2192 LITTMANN, ARNOLD: *Herbert Norkus und die Hitlerjungen vom Beusselkietz. Nach dem Tagebuch des Kameradschaftsführers Gerd Mondt und nach Mitteilungen der Familie.* Vorw.: Baldur von Schirach. Berlin: Steuben-Verlag, 1934. 155 pp., illus. [Norkus, a member of the Hitler Youth, was killed by Communists in 1932.]

2193 MONDT, GERHARD: *Tagebuch der Kameradschaft Norkus.* Berlin: Steuben-Verlag, 1936. 104 pp., illus.

2194 PAETEL, KARL O., ed.: *Die Hitlerjugend. Bund deutscher Arbeiterjugend.*

Flarchheim i.Th.: Verlag Die Kommenden, 1930. 56 pp. (Handbuch der deutschen Jugendbewegung).

2195 REICHSJUGENDFÜHRUNG DER NSDAP, Abt. I: *Aufbau, Gliederung und Anschriften der Hitler-Jugend. Amtliche Gliederungsübersicht der Reichsjugendführung der NSDAP. Stand vom 1. Januar 1934.* Geleitw.: Baldur von Schirach. Berlin: Hitler-Jugend-Bewegung, 1934. 224 pp., illus., map, tabs., diagrs.

2196 REICHSJUGENDFÜHRUNG DER NSDAP, Abt. I: *Bekleidung und Ausrüstung der Hitler-Jugend. Amtliche Bekleidungsvorschrift.* Geleitw.: Reichsjugendführer Baldur von Schirach. Berlin: Hitler-Jugend-Bewegung, 1934. 143 pp., illus., diagrs., tabs.

2197 REICHSJUGENDFÜHRUNG: *HJ im Dienst. Ausbildungsvorschrift für die Ertüchtigung der deutschen Jugend.* 6. Aufl. Berlin: Bernard & Graefe, 1940. 365 pp., illus.

' 2198 SCHENZINGER, KARL-ALOYS: *Der Hitlerjunge Quex. Roman.* Berlin: 'Zeitgeschichte' Verlag, 1932. 264 pp.

2199 SCHIRACH, BALDUR VON, ed.: *Blut und Ehre. Lieder der Hitler-Jugend.* Berlin: Deutscher Jugendverlag, 1933. 128 pp., mus. scores.

2200 SCHIRACH, BALDUR VON: *Die Hitler-Jugend. Idee und Gestalt.* Leipzig: Koehler & Amelang, 1934. 224 pp., diagrs., tabs.

2201 SCHROEDER, RICHARD ERNST: *The Hitler Youth as a paramilitary organisation.* Dissertation [pres. to] University of Chicago. 1975. 319 pp., bibl.

2202 SIEMSEN, HANS: *Die Geschichte des Hitlerjungen Adolf Soers.* Düsseldorf: Komet-Verlag, 1947. 223 pp.

2203 STACHURA, PETER D.: *Nazi youth in the Weimar Republic.* Introd.: Peter H. Merkl. Santa Barbara, Calif.: Clio Books, 1975. xix + 301 pp., tabs., bibl.

2204 STEPHENS, FREDERICK J.: *Hitler Youth. History, organisation, uniforms and insignia.* London: Almark, 1973. 88 pp., illus., bibl.

2205 WELLEMS, HUGO: *Die letzten 100 Tage. Ein Tagebuch vom Kampf der HJ in der Saar.* Berlin: Verlag für Soziale Ethik und Kunstpflege, [1935?]. 60 pp.

2206 WERNER, KURT: *Mit Baldur von Schirach auf Fahrt.* München: Eher, 1937. 142 pp., illus.

2207 ZENTNER, CHRISTIAN, ed.: *Hitler-Jugend.* Hamburg: Verlag für Geschichtliche Dokumentation, [197–]. 113 pp., illus.

PIMPFE

2208 ELSNER, GÜNTER & LERCHE, KARL-GUSTAV: *Vom Pimpf zum Flieger.* 3. Aufl. München: Eher, 1942. 236 pp.

2209 REICHSJUGENDFÜHRUNG: *Pimpf im Dienst. Ein Handbuch für das deutsche Jungvolk in der HJ.* Potsdam: Voggenreiter, 1934. 348 pp., illus., mus. scores.

2210 SENDKE, ERICH: *Peter wird Pimpf.* 4. Aufl. Langensalza: Beltz, [193–]. 87 pp.

2211 *Wir Jungen in der Zeit. Pimpfe gestalten ein Buch.* Stuttgart: Fleischhauer & Spohn, 1936. 68 pp., illus. [Incl. definition of 'Kitsch', p. 30.]

Bund Deutscher Mädel

2212 BÜRKNER, TRUDE: *Der Bund Deutscher Mädel in der Hitler-Jugend.* Berlin: Junker & Dünnhaupt, 1937. 28 pp. (Schriften der Deutschen Hochschule für Politik ...).

2213 DARGEL, MARGARETE: *Mädel im Kampf. Erlebnisse und Erzählungen.* Wolfenbüttel: Kallmeyer, 1937. 121 pp., illus.

2214 JAEGER, SERAPHINE, ed.: *BDM in Bamberg.* Bayreuth: Gauverlag Bayerische Ostmark, [1937?]. [60 pp.], illus.

2215 *Mädel—euere Welt! Das Jahrbuch der Deutschen Mädel.* Hrsg.: Hilde Munske. München: Eher, 1940/43. 4 vols., illus.

2216 REICHSJUGENDFÜHRUNG: *Wir deutschen Mädel. BDM Jahrbuch 1935.* Berlin: Deutscher Jugendverlag, [1934]. 269 pp., illus., maps, mus. scores.

2217 REICHSJUGENDFÜHRUNG: *Wir Mädel singen. Liederbuch des Bundes Deutscher Mädel.* 2. erw. Ausg. Wolfenbüttel: Kallmeyer, 1937. 208 pp., mus. scores.

2218 REICHSJUGENDFÜHRUNG: *Wir schaffen.* München: Eher, 1938/39. 2 vols., 216 pp. ea. [Preceded 2215.]

2219 WEBER-STUMPFOHL, HERTA: *Ostmarkmädel. Ein Erlebnisbuch aus den Anfangsjahren und der illegalen Kampfzeit des BDM. in der Ostmark.* Berlin: Junge Generation Verlag, 1939. 222 pp., illus., tabs. (21.–40. Tausend).

2220 WISSER, EVA MARIA: *Kämpfen und glauben. Aus dem Leben eines Hitlermädels.* Geleitw.: [Magda] Goebbels. Potsdam: Steuben-Verlag, 1933. 99 pp.

4. SCHOOLS AND TEACHERS

2221 ANRICH, ERNST: *Neue Schulgestaltung aus nationalsozialistischem Denken.* Mitw.: Eduard Anrich. Stuttgart: Kohlhammer, 1933. 106 pp.

2222 BECK, FRIEDRICH ALFRED: *Die Erziehung im Dritten Reich. Ein Beitrag zur Pädagogik der politisch-geistigen Persönlichkeit.* Dortmund: Crüwell, 1936. 152 pp.

2223 BELSTER, HANS & FIKENSCHER, F.: *Unterricht am Staatsjugendtag. Aufbauarbeit im Dritten Reich ...* 2. ergänz. Aufl. Ansbach: Brögel, 1935. 125 pp.

2224 DET, E. J. van: *Hitler-regime en onderwijs.* Amsterdam: De Arbeiderspers, 1933. 142 pp.

2225 *Education in Nazi Germany.* By two English investigators. Foreword: Norman Angell. London: The Kulturkampf Association, 1938. 72 pp. [Spanish version: 'La educación en la Alemania nazi'. In *Luminar*, Vol. IV, No. 1, 1940. Publ. in Mexico.]

2226 EILERS, ROLF: *Die nationalsozialistische Schulpolitik. Eine Studie zur Funktion der Erziehung im totalitären Staat.* Köln: Westdeutscher Verlag, 1963. 152 pp., bibl.

2227 FAHL, R. & KNOBLICH (Dr.): *Die Schule des Dritten Reiches als Mitkämpferin in der Erzeugungsschlacht.* Breslau: Handel, 1935. 84 pp., illus.

2228 FAULWASSER, ARTHUR & WITZMANN, CONRAD, eds.: *Die Schulentlassungsfeier im Dritten Reich. Gedanken für Reden, Gedichte, Sprechchöre und Kernsprüche.* Leipzig: Glaser, 1935. 47 pp.

2229 FLESSAU, KURT-INGO: *Schule der Diktatur. Lehrpläne und Schulbücher des Nationalsozialismus.* Vorw.: H.-J. Gamm. München: Ehrenwirth, 1977. 224 pp., bibl.

2230 FLETCHER, A. W.: *Education in Germany.* Cambridge: Heffer, 1934. 61 pp.

2231 GAMM, HANS-JOCHEN: *Führung und Verführung. Pädagogik des Nationalsozialismus.* München: List, 1964. 494 pp., tabs., diagrs., bibl.

2232 GIESE, GERHARDT: *Staat und Erziehung. Grundzüge einer politischen Pädagogik und Schulpolitik.* Hamburg: Hanseatische Verlagsanstalt, 1933. 302 pp.

2233 HELLWIG, GERHARD: *Nationalsozialistische Feiern im Rahmen eines Hitlerjahres für Schule und Volksgemeinschaft des Dritten Reiches.* 2. Aufl. Berlin: Neuer Berliner Buchbetrieb, 1934. 256 pp.

2234 KLEIN, HANNS K. E.: *Erziehung zur Revolution. Eine kritische Studie zur Überwindung des Klassenkampfes auf pädagogischem Gebiet.* München: Duncker & Humblot, 1934. 268 pp.

2235 LINDEGREN, ALINA M.: *Education in Germany.* Washington, D.C.: Government Printing Office, 1939. 145 pp., illus., bibl.

2236 MANN, ERIKA: *School for barbarians. Education under the Nazis.* Introd.: Thomas Mann. London: Drummond, 1939. 162 pp., illus.

2237 SCHALLER, HERMANN: *Die Schule im Staate Adolf Hitlers. Eine völkische Grundlegung.* Breslau: Korn, 1935. 238 pp.

2238 SCHMIEDCHEN, JOHANNES, comp.: *Führer durch den Nationalsozialismus. Zusammengest. und bearb. auf Grund der Erfahrungen im Unterricht und in der Schulungsarbeit.* Berlin: Kanzler, 1933. 135 pp., illus.

2239 STIPPEL, FRITZ: *Die Zerstörung der Person. Kritische Studie zur nationalsozialistischen Pädagogik.* Donauwörth: Auer, 1957. 228 pp.

2240 STURM, KARL FRIEDRICH: *Deutsche Erziehung im Werden. Von der pädagogischen Reformbewegung zur völkischen und politischen Erziehung.* Berlin: Zickfeldt, 1938. 164 pp.

2241 TÜRK, FRANZ, ed.: *Sprech-Chöre für die nationalsozialistische deutsche Schule.* 2. Aufl. Frankfurt a.M.: Diesterweg, 1936. 60 pp.

2242 UNION DES INSTITUTEURS ALLEMANDS EMIGRÉS: *La nouvelle Allemagne dans son nouveau manuel scolaire.* Paris: 1937. 91 pp.

2243 WIENER, PETER F.: *German with tears.* London: Cresset Press, 1942. 93 pp., illus.

2244 WILHELM, THEODOR: 'Scholars or soldiers? Aims and results of "Nazi" education'. Reprinted from *International Education Review*, Vol. VIII (1939), No. 2. Berlin: Duncker & Humblot. Pp. 81–102.

Teachers

2245 BÖLLING, RAINER: *Volksschullehrer und Politik. Der Deutsche Lehrerverein 1918–1933.* Göttingen: Vandenhoeck & Ruprecht, 1978. 306 pp.

2246 KRAUSE-VILMAR, D., ed.: *Lehrerschaft, Republik und Faschismus 1918–1933. Beiträge zur Geschichte der organisierten Lehrerschaft in der Weimarer Republik.* Köln: Pahl-Rugenstein, 1978. 279 pp.

2247 KÜPPERS, HEINRICH: *Der Katholische Lehrerverband in der Übergangszeit von der Weimarer Republik zur Hitler-Diktatur. Zugleich ein Beitrag zur Geschichte des Volksschullehrerstandes.* Mainz: Matthias-Grünewald-Verlag, 1975. xxviii + 201 pp., bibl. (Veröffentlichungen der Kommission für Zeitgeschichte ...).

2248 [NATIONALSOZIALISTISCHER LEHRERBUND] *Zehn Jahr NSLB. Zur Jubiläumstagung in Hof am 22. und 23. April 1939.* Hrsg.: Reichswaltung des NS-Lehrerbundes. Bearb.: Paul Georg Herrmann. München: Eher, [1939]. 176 pp., illus.

2249 DER REICHSMINISTER FÜR WISSENSCHAFT, ERZIEHUNG UND VOLKSBILDUNG: *Ordnung der Prüfung für das Lehramt an Höheren Schulen im Deutschen Reich.* 7. Aufl. Berlin: Eher, 1943. 56 pp.

Educational establishments

GRUNDSCHULE

2250 MAESSE, HERMANN: *Grundschularbeit. Grundsätze—Planung—Stoffbereitung.* Frankfurt a.M.: Diesterweg, 1938. 124 pp., bibl.

HÖHERE SCHULE

2251 LIEDLOFF, WERNER: *Die Entwicklung des höheren Schulwesens in Thüringen von der marxistischen Revolution 1918 bis zur nationalsozialistischen Erhebung 1933.* Leipzig: Roske, 1936. 88 pp., tabs., charts.

2252 NATIONALSOZIALISTISCHER LEHRERBUND, Gau Westfalen-Süd: *Auf dem Wege zur nationalsozialistischen deutschen Jugendschule (Sechsjährige höhere Schule).* Dortmund: Crüwell, [193–]. 88 pp.

2253 REICHS- UND PREUSSISCHES MINISTERIUM FÜR WISSENSCHAFT, ERZIEHUNG UND VOLKSBILDUNG: *Erziehung und Unterricht in der höheren Schule. Amtliche Ausgabe.* Berlin: Weidmann, 1938. 265 pp.

2254 WOHLFAHRT, ERICH: *Geist und Torheit auf Primanerbänken. Bericht über die sächsischen Massnahmen zur Begrenzung des Hochschulzuganges.* Hrsg.:

W. Hartnacke. Radebeul/Dresden: Kupky & Dietze, 1934. 162 pp., plans., tabs.

2255 WOLF, A.: *Higher education in Nazi Germany, or education for world-conquest.* London: Methuen, 1944. 115 pp., tabs.

KINDERGARTEN

2256 BENZING, RICHARD: *Grundlagen der körperlichen und geistigen Erziehung des Kleinkindes im nationalsozialistischen Kindergarten.* Berlin: Eher, 1941. 112 pp., illus.

MITTELSCHULE

2257 *Bestimmungen über Erziehung und Unterricht in der Mittelschule.* Berlin: Eher, 1939. 84 pp.

PARTY SCHOOLS

2258 ORLOW, DIETRICH: 'Die Adolf-Hitler-Schulen'. [In] *Vierteljahrshefte für Zeitgeschichte*, 13. Jhrg., 3. Heft, 1965. Pp. 272–283.

2259 SCHOLTZ, HARALD: *NS-Ausleseschulen. Internatsschulen als Herrschaftsmittel des Führerstaates.* Göttingen: Vandenhoeck & Ruprecht, 1973. 427 pp., tabs.

2260 UEBERHORST, HORST, ed.: *Elite für die Diktatur. Die nationalpolitischen Erziehungsanstalten 1933–1945. Ein Dokumentarbericht.* Düsseldorf: Droste, 1969. 441 pp., facsim., tabs., maps.

VOLKSSCHULE

2261 HIGELKE, KURT, ed.: *Neubau der Volksschularbeit. Plan, Stoff und Gestaltung nach den Richtlinien des Reichserziehungsministerium vom 15. Dezember 1939. Unter Mitarbeit von Fachleuten gestaltet.* 3. durchges. und erw. Aufl. Leipzig: Klinkhardt, 1942. 368 pp., illus., diagrs., tabs. [Incl.: 'Grundliste für Schülerbüchereien der Volksschulen', pp. 357–368.]

2262 NATIONALSOZIALISTISCHER LEHRERBUND, Gau Westfalen-Süd: *Die deutsche Jungvolksschule. Nationalsozialistische deutsche Volksschule. Versuch ihrer Gestaltung unter Zugrundelegung des Erziehungs- und Unterrichtsplanes des Nationalsozialistischen Lehrerbundes, Gau Westfalen-Süd.* 2. verm. und verb. Aufl. Dortmund: Crüwell, [193–]. 76 pp.

Handbooks for teachers

2263 EGGERS, CARL: *Stoffsammlung für Schule und Schulung. Handbuch zur Vermittlung nationalsozialistischer Weltanschauung.* Halle: Schroedel, 1935. 168 pp.

2264 *Die Erzieher Grossberlins 1935. Verzeichnis der Lehrkräfte, Lehranstalten, Schulbehörden und Parteidienststellen.* Hrsg.: Dr. Meinshausen. Berlin: Verlag 'Nationalsozialistische Erziehung', 1935. 493 pp., tabs.

2265 *Handbuch des Schulwesens.* Hrsg.: Präsident des Gauarbeitsamtes und Reichstreuhänder der Arbeit Niederdonau, Wien. Bearb. von Maria Neuberger nach dem Stand vom September 1944. Wien: Lang, [1944]. 664 pp.

2266 HEHLMANN, WILHELM: *Pädagogisches Wörterbuch*. 3., durchges. und ergänz. Aufl. Stuttgart: Kröner, 1942. 492 pp.

2267 *Jahrbuch der Lehrer der höheren Schulen (Kunzes Kalender)*. 42.–51. Jhrg. Hrsg.: [Karl] Kunze, Ed[uard] Simon [and others]. Breslau: Trewendt & Granier, 1935–1949.

2268 NS-LEHRERBUND, REICHSFACHGEBIET RASSENFRAGE, & RASSENPOLITISCHES AMT DER NSDAP: *Schrifttum über Familie, Volk und Rasse für die Hand des Lehrers und Schülers*. Berlin: Eher, 1938. 37 pp.

2269 *Pädagogischer Handkatalog. Ein Wegweiser durch das seit 1933 erschienene Schrifttum und durch das wichtigste Schrifttum der Vorjahre auf dem Gebiete des Erziehungs- und Schulwesens. Für Schulleiter und Lehrer an Volks-, Mittel- und Aufbauschulen und für Dozenten und Studierende auf den Hochschulen für Lehrerbildung*. 9. Ausg. Österwieck/Harz: Zickfeldt, 1937. 102 pp.

2270 SZLISKA, (Dr.-phil. Rektor): *Erziehung und Wehrwillen. Pädagogisch-methodisches Handbuch für Erzieher*. Mit Unterstützung und unter Förderung der Deutschen Gesellschaft für Wehrpolitik und Wehrwissenschaften hrsg. Stuttgart: Rath, [1937]. 540 pp.

2271 DIE VERWALTUNG DES REICHS- UND PREUSSISCHEN MINISTERIUMS FÜR WISSENSCHAFT, ERZIEHUNG UND VOLKSBILDUNG: *Handbuch der Erziehung. Jahrgang I*. Berlin: Weidmann, 1937. 627 pp.

School subjects

BIOLOGY, EUGENICS AND RACISM

2272 ADOLF HITLER-SCHULEN: *Sparta. Der Lebenskampf einer nordischen Herrenschicht*. Arbeitsheft der Adolf Hitler-Schulen, 1940. 129 pp., illus.

2273 BARETH, KARL & VOGEL, ALFRED: *Erblehre und Rassenkunde für die Grund- und Hauptschule*. 2. Aufl. Bühl-Baden: Verlag Konkordia, 1937. 106 pp., diagrs., bibl.

2274 DEPDOLLA, PHILIPP: *Erblehre—Rasse—Bevölkerungspolitik. Vornehmlich für den Unterricht in höheren Schulen bestimmt*. 2. Aufl. Berlin: Metzner, 1935. 134 pp., diagrs.

2275 DOBERS, ERNST: *Die Judenfrage. Stoff und Behandlung in der Schule*. 3. erweit. Aufl. Leipzig: Klinkhardt, 1939. 80 pp., tabs., bibl. (Neuland in der Deutschen Schule ...).

2276 DOBERS, ERNST & HIGELKE, KURT, eds.: *Rassenpolitische Unterrichtspraxis. Der Rassengedanke in der Unterrichtsgestaltung der Volksschulfächer. Unter Mitarbeit von Fachleuten* hrsg. 2. verb. und durchges. Aufl. Leipzig: Klinkhardt, 1939. 392 pp., bibl.

2277 GRAF, JAKOB: *Familienkunde und Rassenbiologie für Schüler*. 2. verb. Aufl. München: Lehmann, 1935. 150 pp., illus., diagrs., tabs.

2278 KEIPERT, HANS: *Die Behandlung der Judenfrage im Unterricht. Ein Versuch*. Langensalza: Beltz, 1937. 48 pp., bibl.

2279 STECHE, O[TTO] and others: *Lehrbuch der Biologie für Oberschulen und Gymnasien. 4. Band für die 6., 7. and 8. Klasse.* [By] O. Steche, E. Stengel, M. Wagner. 3. Aufl. Leipzig: Quelle & Meyer, 1943. 414 pp., illus., tabs., diagrs.

GEOGRAPHY AND 'HEIMATKUNDE'
DAUMANN, OTTO & SKRIEWE, PAUL: *Die Schlacht für Deutschland. Ein Blick in die Ernährungs- und Rohstofflage.* See 2378.

2280 EGGERS, W., ed.: *Grosser Schulatlas. Ein Kartenwerk über das deutsche Land, das deutsche Volk und die Welt.* 17. Aufl. Leipzig: List & von Bressensdorf, 1941. 76 pp.

2281 JANTZEN, WALTER: *E. von Seydlitzsche Erdkunde für höhere Schulen.* Breslau: Hirt. [Part 1 publ. 1940, remainder 1942.]
Teil 1: *Deutschland.* 127 pp.
Teil 2: *Europa.* 96 pp.
Teil 3: *Die Ostfeste.* 119 pp.
Teil 4: *Die Westfeste.* 103 pp.
Teil 5: *Das Deutsche Reich.* 151 pp.
Teil 6: *Erde und Mensch.* 127 pp.
Teil 7: *Die Grossmächte der Erde.* 127 pp.
Teil 8: *Das Reich des Führers.* 133 pp.

2282 JANTZEN, WALT(H)ER, ed.: *Die Geographie im Dienste der nationalpolitischen Erziehung. Ein Ergänzungsheft zu den Lehrbüchern der Erdkunde. In Verbindung mit den Mitarbeitern der E. von Seydlitzschen Geographie hrsg.* 2. durchges. Aufl. Breslau: Hirt, 1936. 55 pp., illus., maps.

2283 POHLMEYER, ADOLF & KRIETSCH, KARL, eds.: *Betriebswirtschaftslehre. A. Kurzausgabe.* Neu hrsg. 11. Aufl. Leipzig: Gloeckner, 1941. 127 pp., tabs.

2284 SCHNASS, FRANZ: *Nationalsozialistische Heimat- und Erdkunde, mit Einschluss der Geopolitik des vaterländischen Gesamtunterrichts.* Osterwieck/Harz: Zickfeldt, 1934. 200 pp., tab.

GERMAN LANGUAGE AND LITERATURE
2285 *Dein Volk ist alles! Sammlung deutscher Gedichte für das 5.–8. Schuljahr.* Dortmund: Crüwell, 1937. 303 pp., bibl.

2286 ECHELMEYER, M. and others, eds.: *Muttersprache. Ein deutsches Lesebuch für Mittelschulen. 2. Band für die Klassen IV und III.* 6. Aufl. Münster i.W.: Aschendorff, 1937. 400 pp., illus.

2287 GROSSMANN, PAUL, ed.: *Gedenke! Gedichte und Kernsprüche für die Volksschule und ihre Feiern.* 7. ergänz. Aufl. Frankfurt a.M.: Diesterweg, 1941. 96 pp.

2288 HASUBEK, PETER: *Das deutsche Lesebuch in der Zeit des Nationalsozialismus. Ein Beitrag zur Literaturpädagogik zwischen 1933 und 1945.* Hannover: Schroedel, 1972. 192 pp., bibl.

2289 HÜHNHÄUSER, [ALFRED] and others, eds.: *Beiträge zum neuen*

Deutschunterricht. Hrsg.: [Alfred] Hühnhäuser, [Alfred] Pudelko, Studienrat Jacoby. Frankfurt a.M.: Diesterweg, 1939. vii + 221 pp. (Deutsche Volkserziehung).

2290 NIEMER, GOTTHARD & ARNOLD, HERBERT, eds.: *Vom Glauben zur Tat. Nationalsozialistisches Gedankengut im deutschen Schrifttum.* Breslau: Handel, 1936. 112 pp.

2291 RAHN, FRITZ: *Aufsatzerziehung. Eine Handreichung für Deutschlehrer zur Erfüllung der Lehrplanforderungen.* 3. Aufl. Frankfurt a.M.: Diesterweg, 1939. 63 pp.

2292 SOMMER, PAUL: *Deutschlands Erwachen. 100 Aufsatzthemen und Entwürfe über die jüngste nationale Erhebung zum Gebrauche für die deutsche Schule und die Hitler-Jugend.* Leipzig: Beyer, 1933. 95 pp.

2293 STAHLMANN, HANS: *Volkhafte Sprachkunde.* 3. Aufl. Leipzig: Brandstetter, 1944. 255 pp.

HISTORY

2294 EBERHARDT, FRITZ, ed.: *Neuer deutscher Geschichts- und Kulturatlas.* 2. Aufl. Leipzig: List & von Bressensdorf, 1937. 90 pp.

2295 *L'enseignement de l'histoire contemporaine et les manuels scolaires allemands. À propos d'une tentative d'accord franco-allemand.* Paris: Costes, 1938. 104 pp. (Publications de la Société de l'Histoire de la Guerre).

2296 GOLTZ, FRIEDRICH Frhr. von der & STIEFENHOFER, THEODOR: *Unsterbliches Deutschland. Völkischer Durchbruch in der Geschichte.* Braunschweig: Westermann, 1938. 384 pp., maps.

2297 GRUNWALD, KARL & LUKAS, OTTO, eds.: *Von der Urzeit zur Gegenwart. Aufgabe und Stoff eines Geschichtsunterrichts auf rassischer Grundlage.* 3. Aufl. Frankfurt a.M.: Diesterweg, 1938. 191 pp., illus., maps.

2298 HANKE, GEORG: *Weltkrieg—Niedergang und Aufbruch der deutschen Nation. Ein Führer durch die neueste Geschichte von 1914–1933.* 2. Aufl. Langensalza: Beltz, 1933. 134 pp., bibl.

2299 REIN, RICHARD: *Rasse und Kultur unserer Urväter. Ein methodisch-schultechnisches Hilfsbuch für Unterricht und Vorträge in der Vorgeschichte.* Frankfurt a.M.: Diesterweg, 1936. 126 pp., illus., maps, bibl.

2300 VIERNON, ADOLF: *Zur Theorie und Praxis des nationalsozialistischen Geschichtsunterrichts.* Halle: Schroedel, 1935. 113 pp.

LANGUAGES

English

2301 ARNS, K., comp.: *British Fascism. Mosley's fascist movement in Britain. From: A. K. Chesterton, 'Portrait of a Leader'. Authorised edition.* Frankfurt a.M.: Diesterweg, 1938. 52 pp., port.

2302 HEERWAGEN, H., ed.: *Jews and Gentiles in English fiction.* Leipzig: Gloeckner, 1936. 48 pp.

2303 KRÜPER, ADOLF: *Die nationalpolitische Bedeutung des englischen Unterrichts.* Frankfurt a.M.: Diesterweg, 1935. 146 pp.

2304 SCHAD, GUSTAV, ed.: *Germany in the Third Reich, as seen by Anglo-Saxon writers.* 2. Aufl. Frankfurt a.M.: Diesterweg, 1937. 63 pp., illus.

French

2305 BECK, CHRISTOPH, ed.: *Culte des héros et fatalités natales d'après M. Barrès, Ch. Maurras, Ch. Péguy, etc.* Bamberg: Buchner, 1936. 20 + 72 pp.

2306 GOBINEAU, CLÉMENT SERPEILLE de: *Racisme, Marxisme, le problème juif.* Hrsg.: P.R. Sanftleben. Bielefeld: Velhagen & Klasing, 1936. 33 pp.

2307 REIN, WILHELM & BOTZENMAYER, KARL, eds.: *Rapprochement franco-allemand.* Bamberg: Buchner, 1937. 94 pp.

MATHEMATICS AND SCIENCE

2308 GERHARDT, HANS and others: *Naturlehre für Hauptschulen. Teil 1, Kl. 2.* [By] Hans Gerhardt, Albert Höfner, Heinrich Steinkopf. Leipzig: Klinkhardt, 1943. 132 pp., illus.

2309 SALKOWSKI, ERICH: *Neue Ziele und Wege des Geometrie-Unterrichts.* Frankfurt a.M.: Salle, 1936. 86 pp.

MUSIC

2310 DIESENROTH, E. and others, eds.: *Kein Schöneres Land. Musikbuch für höhere Mädchenschulen. 1. Bd.: Deutsches Volkslied.* Zusammenarb.: H. Martin, K. Rehberg, A. Strube. Berlin: Schulverlag, 1944. 223 pp., illus., mus. scores.

2311 GÖTTSCHING, R. and others, eds.: *Deutsche Musik in der höheren Schule. Musikbuch A für Jungen.* 3. Ausg. Hannover: Meyer, 1941. 303 pp., mus. scores.

2312 NATIONALSOZIALISTISCHER LEHRERBUND, Reichsleitung: *Singkamerad. Schulliederbuch der deutschen Jugend.* 7. Aufl. München: Eher, 1936. 267 pp., illus., mus. scores.

2313 STRUBE, ADOLF and others, eds.: *Lied im Volk. Musikbuch für höhere Jungenschulen. 1. Band: Deutsches Volkslied.* Zusammenarb.: K. Benkel, K. Walther. Leipzig: Merseburger, 1942. 240 pp., mus. scores.

POLITICAL AND CIVIC EDUCATION

2314 MAY, WERNER: *Politischer Katechismus für den jungen Deutschen in Schule und Beruf.* 4. Aufl. Breslau: Handel, [1935?]. 72 pp. [8th ed. entitled: *Kleine Nationalkunde für Schule und Beruf.* Publ. 1938.]

2315 NOACK, ERWIN: *Die Gesetzgebung des Dritten Reiches.* 2. erw. Aufl. Hrsg.: Otto Schwarz. Berlin: Heymann, 1938. viii + 175 pp.

2316 OBERPRÄSIDENT DER RHEINPROVINZ, Abt. für höheres Schulwesen: *Nationalpolitische Lehrgänge für Schüler. Denkschrift.* Frankfurt a.M.: Diesterweg, 1935. 226 pp., illus.

2317 SOTKE, FRITZ, ed.: *Deutsches Volk und deutscher Staat. Staatsbürgerkunde für junge Deutsche.* Leipzig: Gloeckner, 1934. 144 pp.

2318 SPRECKELSEN, OTTO, comp.: *Marschierende Jugend. Plöner Liederbuch.* Im Auftr. der Nationalpolitischen Erziehungsanstalt Schloss Plön von deutschen Jungen gesammelt. Neufassung 1938. Itzehoe i.Holst.: NS-Gauverlag Schleswig-Holstein, 1938. 128 pp., mus. scores.

2319 WAETZIG, ALFRED: *Volk, Nation, Staat. Ein Beitrag zur staatspolitischen Schulung unserer jungen Volksgenossen.* 5. ergänz. Aufl. Stuttgart: Holland & Josenhans, 1939. 150 pp.

RELIGIOUS INSTRUCTION

2320 KERN, HANS & SCHROEDER, HANS EGGERT, eds.: *Lesebuch zur Glaubensfrage.* Berlin-Lichterfelde: Widukind-Verlag (Boss), 1935.
I. Teil: *Abwehr des Jahwehglaubens.* 77 pp.
II. Teil: *Bekenntnis zur Göttlichkeit der Natur.* 89 pp.

2321 KRAUSE, REINHOLD: *Soll mein Kind den Religionsunterricht in der Schule besuchen?* Dresden: Wolfsangel, 1939. 15 pp.

2322 RÖNCK, HUGO, ed.: *Ein Reich—Ein Gott! Vom Wesen deutschen Christentums. Handbuch für den Religions- und Konfirmandenunterricht.* 2. Aufl. Weimar: Verlag Deutscher Christen, 1939, xxiv + 225 pp. [Incl.: 'Der Pharisäer', 'Der ewige Jude'.]

2323 ROSSLER, MAX: *Der katholische Religionsunterricht im nationalsozialistischen Staate. Inaugural-Dissertation.* Würzburg: Rita-Verlag, 1937. 42 pp.

2324 SCHAEFER, DINA: *Literarischer Religionsunterricht nach dem neuen Lehrplan.* Köln: Benziger, 1934. 325 pp., diagrs., tabs.

2325 SCHLEMMER, HANS: *Vererbungswissenschaft und Religionsunterricht.* Frankfurt a.M.: Diesterweg, 1934. 36 pp.

2326 TÖGEL, HERMANN & WOHLRAB, E. H.: *Germanisches Gottgefühl im christlichen Religionsunterricht. 12 Unterrichtsentwürfe.* Leipzig: Dürr, 1935. 174 pp.

WEHRERZIEHUNG

2327 JUSTROW, KARL: *Der technische Krieg.* Berlin: Claassen, 1938/39. Illus., graphs, diagrs., maps, tabs., bibls.
I. Bd.: *Im Spiegelbild der Kriegserfahrungen und der Weltpresse.* 2. Aufl. 128 pp.
II. Bd.: *Waffenwirkung und Kampfesweise im Zukunftskrieg.* 216 pp.

2328 LEONHARDT, WALTER: *Der chemische Krieg. Luftschutz und Gasschutz. Ein Lehr- und Experimentierbuch.* Frankfurt a.M.: Diesterweg, 1938. 158 pp., illus.

2329 LUYKEN, MAX: *Gedanken zur nationalsozialistischen Wehrerziehung. Der Auftrag der SA.* Hrsg.: Die oberste SA-Führung. Als Manuskript gedruckt. [193–]. 160 pp. (Nur für den Dienstgebrauch).

2330 STELLRECHT, HELMUT: *Die Wehrerziehung der deutschen Jugend.* Geleitw.: Oberbefehlshaber der Wehrmacht. ... von Blomberg. Vorw.: Reichsjugendführer Baldur von Schirach. Berlin: Mittler, 1936. 154 pp.

2331　*Wehrerziehung im mathematisch-naturwissenschaftlichen Unterricht.* Frankfurt a.M.: Diesterweg, 1937.

PRIMERS

2332　BONA, KURT: *Von deutscher Art. Ein Lesebuch für höhere Schulen. 5. Teil.* 3. Aufl. Frankfurt a.M.: Salle, 1942. 266 pp.

2333　BUCHHOLZ, KARL and others, eds.: *Deutsche Sendung. Lesebuch für Madchen. 2.Klasse.* 2. Aufl. Bielefeld: Velhagen & Klasing, 1940. 333 pp., illus., bibl.

2334　HACKENBERG, FRIEDRICH and others, eds.: *Die Selbstbefreiung des deutschen Geistes. Ein deutsches Lesebuch für die siebente Klasse.* Bearb.: Friedrich Hackenberg, Bernhard Schwarz, Ludwig Pohnert. 2. Aufl. Frankfurt a.M.: Diesterweg, 1941. 325 pp., illus.

2335　JÜNGER, ERNST: *Der Krieg als inneres Erlebnis.* Hrsg.: Richard Winter. Bielefeld: Velhagen & Klasing, 1937. 52 pp.

2336　LEERS, JOHANN VON: *Der Junge von der Feldherrnhalle. Ein Weg ins deutsche Morgenrot.* 10. Aufl. Stuttgart: Union Deutsche Verlagsgesellschaft, [194–]. 99 pp., illus.

2337　LOEFF, WOLFGANG: *Die Reiter von Deutsch-Südwest. Gegen Hereros und Engländer.* 2. Aufl. Leipzig: Teubner, 1938. 47 pp. (Serie Erbe und Verpflichtung).

2338　SCHAPER, KARL: *Der Osten ruft. Erzählung aus dem Werk des grossen Welsenherzogs.* Düsseldorf: Pflugschar-Verlag, 1937. 111 pp., illus.

2339　*Schriften zu Deutschlands Erneuerung.* Breslau: Handel, 1933–1940. Illus. [Pamphlets of 16 or 24 pp. each, intended for school use, numbered 1–140.]

5.　ARBEITSDIENST

2340　BERENDT, ERICH F., ed.: *Männer und Taten. Das Losungsbuch des Reichsarbeitsdienstes.* Im Auftr. der Reichsleitung des Reichsarbeitsdienstes bearb. und hrsg. Leipzig: 'Der nationale Aufbau' Verlagsgesellschaft, [193–]. 451 + 423 pp., illus. (of runes). [In 2 vols.]

2341　DECKER, WILL: *Der deutsche Weg. Ein Leitfaden zur staatspolitischen Erziehung der deutschen Jugend im Arbeitsdienst.* Leipzig: Koehler & Amelang, 1933. 120 pp.

2342　DEUTSCHER ARBEITSDIENST FÜR VOLK UND HEIMAT: *Arbeitsdienst-Liederbuch.* Berlin: Schmidt, [193–]. 92 pp., mus. scores.

2343　*Deutscher Jugenddienst. Ein Handbuch.* Potsdam: Voggenreiter, 1933. 388pp., illus., mus. scores.

2344　GENTZ, ERWIN, comp.: *Das Landjahr. Die gesetzlichen Grundlagen und wichtigsten Bestimmungen.* Eberswalde: Müller, 1936. 333 pp.

2345　GÖNNER, (Generalarbeitsführer) von, ed.: *Spaten und Ähren. Das Handbuch der deutschen Jugend im Reichsarbeitsdienst.* Bearb.: Paul Seipp, Wolfgang Scheibe. Heidelberg: Vowinckel, 1939. 288 pp., illus.

2346 GRAEFE, AXEL VON: *Shoulder spades! A tale of the German Labour Service.* Leipzig: Bibliographisches Institut, 1936. 85 pp., illus.

2347 GRAEFE, BODO, ed.: *Leitfaden für den Arbeitsdienst.* Berlin: Bernard & Graefe, 1934. 328 pp., illus.

2347a [HIERL, KONSTANTIN] MALLEBREIN, WOLFRAM: *Konstantin Hierl: Schöpfer und Gestalter des Reichsarbeitsdienstes.* Hannover: 1971. 120 pp., bibl.

2348 HOLLAND, KENNETH: *Youth in European labor camps. A report to the American Youth Commission.* Washington, D.C.: American Council on Education, 1939. xiii + 303 pp., illus., tabs., bibls.

2349 HUSSMANN, PETER: *Der deutsche Arbeitsdienst. Eine staatsrechtliche Untersuchung über Idee und Gestalt des Deutschen Arbeitsdienstes und seine Stellung in der Gesamtstaatsstruktur.* Berlin: Stilke, 1935. 118 pp., bibl.

2350 *Jahrbuch des Reichsarbeitsdienstes.* Hrsg.: [Hermann] Müller-Brandenburg. Berlin: Volk und Reich Verlag, 1936–1943. In 7 vols., illus., diagrs., maps. [No others issued.]

2351 KÖHLER, HENNING: *Arbeitsdienst in Deutschland. Pläne und Verwirklichungsformen bis zur Einführung der Arbeitsdienstpflicht im Jahre 1935.* Berlin: Duncker & Humblot, 1967. 281 pp., bibl.

2352 KRETZSCHMANN, HERMANN: *Bausteine zum Dritten Reich. Lehr- und Lesebuch des Reichsarbeitsdienstes.* 5. Aufl. Leipzig: 'Der nationale Aufbau' Verlag, 1933. 608 pp.

2353 PINETTE-DECKER, KASPAR: *Männer, Land und Spaten. Werden und Wesen des Deutschen Arbeitsdienstes. Ein Stück Zeitgeschichte.* 2. Aufl. Leipzig: Voigtländer, 1935. 270 pp.

2354 STAMM, KURT: *Der Reichsarbeitsdienst. Reichsarbeitsdienstgesetz mit Ergänzungen, Bestimmungen und Erläuterungen.* Berlin: Verlag für Recht und Verwaltung, 1940. 739 pp.

2355 STELLRECHT, HELMUT: *Der Deutsche Arbeitsdienst. Aufgaben, Organisation und Aufbau.* Geleitw.: Hermann Göring. Einführung: Constantin Hierl. Berlin: Mittler, 1933. xii + 158 pp., tabs.

2356 TSAY, JEH-SHENG: *Der Reichsarbeitsdienst. Geschichte, Aufgabe, Organisation und Verwaltung des deutschen Arbeitsdienstes einschliesslich des Arbeitsdienstes für die weibliche Jugend.* Würzburg-Aumühle: Triltsch, 1940. 229 pp., bibl.

Arbeitsmaiden

2357 ALBRECHT, GERTRUD: *Das Pflichtjahr.* Geleitw.: Obergauführerin: Erna Franz. Berlin: Junker & Dünnhaupt, 1942. 79 pp.

2358 ARNOLD, ILSE: *So schaffen wir! Mädeleinsatz im Pflichtjahr.* Stuttgart: Union Deutsche Verlagsgesellschaft, 1941. 107 pp.

2359 ESTORFF, GUSTAV VON: *Dass die Arbeit Freude werde! Ein Bildbericht von den Arbeitsmaiden.* Geleitw.: Konstantin Hierl. Vorw.: Herbert Schmeidler. Berlin: Zeitgeschichte-Verlag, 1938. 63 pp., illus.

2360 HAAS, HILDE, ed.: *Ich war Arbeitsmaid im Kriege. Vom Einfass des Reichsarbeitsdienstes der weiblichen Jugend nach Berichten von Arbeitsmaiden.* Leipzig: Heinig, 1941. 156 pp., illus.

2361 REICHSJUGENDFÜHRUNG: *Mädel im Dienst. Ein Handbuch.* Potsdam: Voggenreiter, 1934. 304 pp.

2362 SCHEIBE, IRENE: *Weibliche Landjugend im Grenzland Ostpommern.* Heidelberg: Vowinckel, 1937. 147 pp.

2363 SCHMIDT-VANDERHEYDEN, H.: *Arbeitsmaiden in Ostpommern. Ein Rückblick.* Moringen: [priv. pr.], 1975. 96 pp., illus., map, facsims.

6. VOCATIONAL TRAINING

2364 ARNHOLD, KARL: *Psychische Kräfte im Dienst der Berufserziehung und Leistungssteigerung.* Nach einem Vortrag ... auf der Tagung der Deutschen Allgemeinen Ärztlichen Gesellschaft für Psychotherapie, Wien 7. Sept. 1940, im Rahmen des Gesamtthemas Psyche und Leistung. Berlin: Lehrmittelzentrale der Deutschen Arbeitsfront, [1941]. 82 pp.

2365 BERNDT, ALFRED-INGEMAR & KRÄNZLEIN, KURT: *Vom Arbeitsplatz zum M.-G. Dreyse.* Geleitw.: [Werner v.] Fritsch. Berlin: Stollberg, 1935. 79 pp., illus.

2366 DENZER, HANS, ed.: *Deutsche Arbeitserziehung.* Hrsg. im Auftr. des deutschen Vereins für werktätige Erziehung zum Abschluss seiner nahezu 60 jährigen Tätigkeit. 2. Aufl. Leipzig: Wunderlich, 1936. 160pp.

2367 HORSTEN, FRANZ: *Die nationalsozialistische Leistungsauslese. Ihre Aufgaben im Bereich der nationalen Arbeit und praktische Vorschläge für ihre Durchführung.* Würzburg: Triltsch, 1938. 135 pp.

2368 JUNG, WILLI: *Deutsche Arbeiterjugend. Auslese, Förderung, Aufstieg.* Berlin: Deutscher Verlag, 1941. 64 pp., illus. [Also French transl.]

2369 MUMELTER, MARIA LUISE: *Magdalen vom Erberhof.* Leipzig: Schneider, 1935. 112 pp., illus.

2370 NEUMANN, GERD: *Die Indoktrination des Nationalsozialismus in die Berufserziehung: Untersuchung zur Arbeits- und Erziehungsideologie während der Epoche zwischen 1935–1945.* Hamburg: 1969. 321 pp., bibl.

2371 PERZL, IRMGARD: *Jungmädel auf dem Köllingshof.* Reutlingen: Ensslin & Laiblin, 1941. 166 pp.

Reichsberufswettkampf

2372 AXMANN, ARTUR: *Olympia der Arbeit. Arbeiterjugend im Reichsberufswettkampf.* Fotos: Georg L. Hahn-Hahn. Berlin: Junker & Dünnhaupt, 1936. 88 pp., illus.

2373 KAUFMANN, GÜNTER: *Der Reichsberufswettkampf. Die berufliche Aufrüstung der deutschen Jugend.* Berlin: Junker & Dünnhaupt, 1935. 72 pp.

Berufsschulen (training schools)

2374 BEYER, VALENTIN, ed.: *Das neue Deutschland. Bausteine für den nationalpolitischen Unterricht an den Wehrmacht-Fachschulen.* 4. Aufl. Berlin: Kameradschaft Verlagsgesellschaft, 1935. 200 pp. [7th ed. entitled: *Das neue Deutschland im Werden.*]

2375 BÖTTCHER, P.: *Der politische Deutsche. Rechenschaftsberichte über die staatspolitische Erziehungsarbeit in der Berufs- und Handwerkerschule 1933 und 1934.* Langensalza: Beltz, [1935]. 84 pp.

2376 BORST, (D.Ing.): *Meisterschule und totaler Krieg. Die Aufgaben der Berufsführerschule in Technik und Wirtschaft. Ein Vortrag.* 2. Aufl. Esslingen a.N.: Verlag der Burg-Bücherei, 1937. 52 pp.

2377 BÜHNEMANN, HERMANN *Entwurf eines Erziehungs- und Bildungsplanes der völkischen Landschule.* Langensalza: Beltz, 1935. 55 pp.

2378 DAUMANN, OTTO & SKRIEWE, PAUL: *Die Schlacht für Deutschland. Ein Blick in der Ernährungs- und Rohstofflage. Rüstzeug für den Unterricht an den Volks- Mittel- und höheren Schulen, sowie an Berufs- und Fortbildungsschulen des Reiches.* Halle: Schroedel, 1936. 184 pp., illus., maps, tabs.

2379 HOFFMANN, HERBERT: *Blut und Boden. Wirtschaft und Politik. Wirtschaftserdkunde. Deutschland, die europäischen Staaten, Afrika, Asien, Australien und Amerika.* 3. Aufl. Hrsg.: Arbeitsgemeinschaft der Fachschaft VI (Berufsschulen) im NSLB Gau Württemberg-Hohenzollern. Stuttgart: Holland & Josenhans, 1937. 96 pp.

2380 NATIONALSOZIALISTISCHER LEHRERBUND: *Grundfragen des deutschen Berufs- und Fachschulwesens. 1. Reichstagung der Reichsfachschaft VI im Amt für Erzieher (NSLB) in Alexisbad.* Langensalza: Beltz, [1937?]. 405 pp.

7. ADULT EDUCATION AND INDOCTRINATION

2381 HEINRICH, KARL: *Deutsches Arbeitertum. Der nationalpolitische Unterricht.* Frankfurt a.M.: Diesterweg, 1935. 50 pp.

2382 KEIM, HELMUT & URBACH, DIETRICH: 'Erwachsenenbildung in Deutschland 1933–1945'. [In] *Aus Politik und Zeitgeschichte,* 19. Feb. 1977. Bonn: Bundeszentrale für politische Bildung. Pp. 3–27.

2383 KEIM, HELMUT & URBACH, DIETRICH: *Volksbildung in Deutschland 1933–1945. Einführung und Dokumente.* Braunschweig: Westermann, 1976. 358 pp., tabs., facsims.

2384 PICHT, WERNER: *Das Schicksal der Volksbildung in Deutschland.* Berlin: Verlag Die Runde, 1936. 238 pp., bibl. [New ed.: Braunschweig: Westermann,

1950. Incl.: 'Nachwort: Die Aufgabe der Erwachsenenbildung nach dem II. Weltkrieg', pp. 217–250.]

2385 SOLLHEIM, FRITZ: *Erziehung im neuen Staat. Volkspädagogik.* Langensalza: Beltz, 1934. 125 pp.

2386 SURÉN, HANS: *Volkserziehung im Dritten Reich. Manneszucht und Charakterbildung.* Stuttgart: Franckh, 1934. 155 pp.

2387 TRENKTROG, WALTHER, ed.: *Das Schulungslager der Deutschen Landsmannschaft. Pfingsten 1934.* 4. Aufl. Berlin: Deutsche Landsmannschaft, 1935. 120 pp.

2388 *Volkshochschule Gross-Berlin. Arbeitsplan für 1933/34.* 31 pp.

2389 *Wege zur Reifeprüfung. 5. Teil: Naturwissenschaften, Biologie, Chemie, Physik.* Breslau: Hirt, 1943. 375 pp., illus., diagrs. (75. Sammelband der Schriftenreihe 'Soldatenbriefe zur Berufsförderung'). [Incl.: 'Die biologisch-rassischen Grundlagen der Volksgemeinschaft und der Staatsführung', pp. 63–176.]

8. UNIVERSITIES AND LEARNED INSTITUTES

2390 AKADEMISCHES AUSKUNFTSAMT: *Studium und Prüfungen in Berlin. Amtlicher Führer für die Universitäten, Technische Hochschule und Handelshochschule.* Berlin: Weidmann, 1935. 222 pp.

2391 DEUTSCHE AKADEMIE MÜNCHEN: *Die Wissenschaft im Lebenskampf des deutschen Volkes. Festschrift zum 50jährigen Bestehen der Deutschen Akademie* ... München: 1940. 149 pp.

2392 *Die deutsche Universität im Dritten Reich. Acht Beiträge.* [By] Helmut Kuhn, Joseph Pascher, Hans Maier, Wolfgang Kunkel, Otto B. Roegele, Fritz Leist, Friedrich G. Friedmann, Eric Voegelin. München: Piper, 1966. 282 pp. (Eine Vortragreihe der Universität München).

2393 *Freiburger Universitätsblätter*, 3. Jhrg., Heft 6, Nov. 1964. Freiburg i.Br.: Rombach. [Incl.: Constantin von Dietze: 'Pflicht im Widerstreit der Verpflichtungen'; Albrecht Goetz von Olenhusen: 'Die nationalsozialistische Rassenpolitik und die jüdischen Studenten an der Universität Freiburg i.Br. 1933–1945'.]

GÖTTINGEN UNIVERSITY

2394 SCHURMANN, A., ed.: *Volk und Hochschule im Umbruch. Zur 200-Jahrfeier der Georg-August-Universität zu Göttingen.* Oldenburg: Stalling, 1937. 295 pp.

2395 SELLE, GÖTZ von: *Die Georg-August-Universität zu Göttingen 1737–1937.* Göttingen: Vandenhoeck & Ruprecht, 1937. 398 pp.

2396 [HAMBURG UNIVERSITY] SCHEIDT, WALTER: *Die Träger der Kultur.* Berlin: Metzner, 1934. 131 pp., diagrs., tabs., bibl.

2397 HARMS, BERNHARD: *Universitäten, Professoren und Studenten in der Zeitwende. Vornehmlich vom Standpunkt der Staatswissenschaften.* Jena: Gustav Fischer, 1936. 58 pp.

2398 HARTMANN, HANS: *Forschung sprengt Deutschlands Ketten.* Stuttgart: Union Deutsche Verlagsgesellschaft, 1943. 200 pp. [Incl. lists of learned institutes and their work.]

2399 HARTSHORNE, EDWARD YARNALL: *The German universities and National Socialism.* London: Allen & Unwin, 1937. 184 pp., facsim., tabs.

HEIDELBERG UNIVERSITY

2400 BOLLMUSS, REINHARD: *Handelshochschule und Nationalsozialismus. Das Ende der Handelshochschule Mannheim und die Vorgeschichte der Errichtung einer Staats- und Wirtschaftswissenschaftlichen Fakultät an der Universität Heidelberg 1933/34.* Meisenheim am Glan: Hain, 1973. 165 pp., bibl.

2401 CARMON, ARYE: 'The impact of the Nazi racial decrees on the University of Heidelberg. A case study'. [In] *Yad Vashem Studies.* Vol. XI. Pp. 131–163, tabs. *See* 5673.

Heidelberg and the universities of America. See 6308.

2402 MONTEFIORE, L[EONARD] G.: *The spirit of the German universities.* [No imprint: 1936?]. 19 pp. [Heidelberg as an example.]

2403 [HOCHSCHULE FÜR POLITIK] WAGNER, JOSEF & BECK, [FRIEDRICH] ALFRED, eds.: *Hochschule für Politik der Nationalsozialistischen Deutschen Arbeiterpartei. Ein Leitfaden.* München: Lehmann, 1933. 221 pp.

2404 ISENBURG, C. D.: *Dass wir Menschen würden ... Erkenntnis und Tat.* Weimar: Lautenbach, 1938. 285 pp.

2405 [KAISER-WILHELM-GESELLSCHAFT] MAX-PLANCK-GESELLSCHAFT ZUR FÖRDERUNG DER WISSENSCHAFTEN: *40 Jahre Kaiser-Wilhelm-Gesellschaft zur Förderung der Wissenschaften 1911–1951.* Göttingen: 1951. 286 pp., illus.

2406 KÖNIG, RENÉ: *Vom Wesen der deutschen Universität.* Berlin: Verlag Die Runde, 1935. 211 pp.

2407 KRIECK, ERNST: *Wissenschaft, Weltanschauung, Hochschulreform.* Leipzig: Armanen-Verlag, 1934. 99 pp.

2408 LILGE, FREDERIC: *Abuse of learning. The failure of the German university.* New York: Macmillan, 1948. 184 pp.

2409 LOSEMANN, VOLKER: *Nationalsozialismus und Antike. Studien zur Entwicklung des Faches Alte Geschichte 1933–1945.* Hamburg: Hoffmann & Campe, 1977. 283 pp., bibl. (notes and bibl. pp. 183–272), summary in English. [Abridged version of a dissertation *Antike und Nationalsozialismus*, Marburg 1970.]

2410 MANNHARDT, JOHANN WILHELM: *Hochschulrevolution.* Hamburg: Hanseatische Verlagsanstalt, 1933. 113 pp.

2411 MARSHALL, BARBARA: *The political development of German university towns in the Weimar Republic. Göttingen and Münster 1918–1930*. Thesis [pres. to] University of London, 1972. xvi + 272 pp., tabs., bibl. [Incl. National Socialists in universities.]

2412 MÜLLER, KARL ALEXANDER VON: *Vom alten zum neuen Deutschland. Aufsätze und Reden 1914–1938*. Stuttgart: Deutsche Verlags-Anstalt, 1938. 336 pp.

2413 [MUNICH UNIVERSITY] FRANK, WALTER: *Deutsche Wissenschaft und Judenfrage. Rede zur Eröffnung der Forschungsabteilung Judenfrage des Reichsinstituts für Geschichte des neuen Deutschlands geh. am 19. November 1936 in der grossen Aula der Universität München*. Mit Ansprachen von Karl Alexander v. Müller und Professor Vahlen. Hamburg: Hanseatische Verlagsanstalt, 1937. 51 pp.

2414 *Nationalsozialismus und die deutsche Universität*. Veröffentlichung der Freien Universität Berlin. Berlin: de Gruyter, 1966. 223 pp. (Universitätstage 1966).

2415 SEELIGER, ROLF, ed.: *Doktorarbeiten im Dritten Reich. Dokumentation mit Stellungnahmen*. München: Seeliger, 1966. 85 pp. (Braune Universität).

2416 [TÜBINGEN UNIVERSITY] ADAM, UWE DIETRICH: *Hochschule und Nationalsozialismus. Die Universität Tübingen im Dritten Reich*. Anhang von Wilfried Setzler: 'Die Tübinger Studentenfrequenz im Dritten Reich'. Tübingen: Mohr (Siebeck), 1977. x + 240 pp.

Professors, scientists, scholars and researchers

2417 BEYERCHEN, ALAN D.: *Scientists under Hitler. Politics and the physics community in the Third Reich*. New Haven, Conn.: Yale University Press, 1977. xii + 287 pp., ports., bibl. [Incl. dismissal of Jewish scientists. German version: *Wissenschaftler unter Hitler* ... Köln: Kiepenheuer & Witsch, 1980.]

2418 BLEUEL, HANS PETER: *Deutschlands Bekenner. Professoren zwischen Kaiserreich und Diktatur*. Bern: Scherz, 1968. 255 pp., bibl.

2419 [COLOGNE UNIVERSITY] CORSTEN, HERMANN, comp.: *Das Schrifttum der zur Zeit an der Universität Köln wirkenden Dozenten*. Aus Anlass der Erinnerungsfeier an die vor 550 Jahren erfolgte Gründung der alten Universität Köln, im Auftr. von Rektor und Senat hrsg. Köln: Schroeder, 1938. 498 pp.

2420 HEIDEGGER, MARTIN: *Die Selbstbehauptung der deutschen Universität. Rede ...* Breslau: Korn, [1933]. 22 pp.

2420a HEISENBERG, ELISABETH: *Das politische Leben eines Unpolitischen. Erinnerungen an Werner Heisenberg*. München: Piper, 1980. 201 pp., illus. [The distinguished physicist, opponent of Philipp Lenard.]

2421 *Jahrbuch des Auslandamtes der deutschen Dozentenschaft. Vorträge und Berichte zwischenstaatlicher Tagungen*. Leipzig: Bibliographisches Institut, 1942/43. Illus., tabs., diagrs.

Heft I: *Bulgarisch-Deutsches Akademikertreffen in Leipzig 8.–14. Juni 1941.* Publ. 1942. 215 pp.
Heft II: *Deutsch-Schwedische Akademikertagung in Rostock 24.–30. November 1943.* Publ. 1943. 136 pp.

Kürschners deutscher Gelehrten-Kalender. See 7.

2422 LENARD, PHILIPP: *Deutsche Physik.* München: Lehmann, 1936. 4 vols., illus.

2423 LENARD, PHILIPP: *Grosse Naturforscher. Eine Geschichte der Naturforschung in Lebensbeschreibungen.* 3. verm. Aufl. München: Lehmann, 1937. 344 pp., illus.

2424 MICHALSKI, GABRIELLE: *Der Antisemitismus im deutschen akademischen Leben in der Zeit nach dem Ersten Weltkrieg.* Frankfurt a.M.: Lang, 1979. 246 pp.

2425 NOTGEMEINSCHAFT DEUTSCHER WISSENSCHAFTLER IM AUSLAND: *List of displaced German scholars.* London: 1936. 125 pp. [And: *Supplementary list.* 1937.]

NSD-DOZENTENBUND

2426 REICHSDOZENTENFÜHRUNG: *Erste Reichstagung der Wissenschaftlichen Akademien des NSD-Dozentenbundes, München 8.–10. Juni 1939.* München: Lehmann, 1940. 146 pp.

2427 *Werden und Wachsen des deutschen Volkes. Wiedergabe der auf der Hochschultagung des NSD-Dozentenbundes Gau Berlin am 24.–25. Februar 1938 gehaltenen Ansprachen und Vorträge.* Berlin: NSD-Dozentenbund, 1938. 117 pp.

2428 PINL, MAX & FURTMÜLLER, LUX: 'Mathematicians under Hitler'. [In] *Leo Baeck Institute Year Book, XVIII.* (1973). Pp. 129–182. *See 3536.*

SCHMITT, CARL

2429 SCHMITT, CARL: *Ex captivitate salus. Erfahrungen der Zeit 1945/47.* Köln: Greven, 1950. 94 pp.

2430 HOFMANN, HASSO: *Legitimität gegen Legalität. Der Weg der politischen Philosophie Carl Schmitts.* Neuwied: Luchterhand, 1964. 304 pp., bibl.

2431 STARK, J. & MÜLLER, WILHELM: *Jüdische und deutsche Physik. Vorträge zur Eröffnung des Kolloquiums für theoretische Physik an der Universität München.* Hrsg.: Wilhelm Müller. Leipzig: Heling, 1941. 55 pp.

2432 WEINREICH, MAX: *Hitler's professors. The part of scholarship in Germany's crimes against the Jewish people.* New York: Yiddish Scientific Institute, 1946. 291 pp.

Students

2433 BLEUEL, HANS PETER & KLINNERT, ERNST: *Deutsche Studenten auf dem Weg ins Dritte Reich. Ideologien—Programme—Aktionen 1918–1935.* Gütersloh: Mohn, 1967. 294 pp., tabs., bibl.

2434 DÜNING, HANS JOACLLIM: *Der SA-Student im Kampf um die Hochschule 1925–1935. Ein Beitrag zur Geschichte der deutschen Universität im 20. Jahrhundert.* Weimar: Böhlaus, 1936. 136 pp., bibl.

2435 FAUST, ANSELM: *Der Nationalsozialistische Deutsche Studentenbund. Studenten und Nationalsozialismus in der Weimarer Republik.* Düsseldorf: Schwann, 1973. 179 + 192 pp., tabs., bibl. [In 2 vols.]

2436 FREISLER, ROLAND: *Das Werden des Juristen im Dritten Reich. 1. Teil: Das Hochschulstudium.* Berlin: Junker & Dünnhaupt, 1933. 48 pp.

2437 *Für den deutschen Geist. Aktion der Studentenschaft der Universität Greifswald.* Greifswald: Universitäts- und Ratsbuchhandlung, 1933. 87 pp. [Burning of books.]

2438 GILES, GEOFFREY J.: 'The rise of the National Socialist Students' Association and the failure of political education in the Third Reich'. [In] Peter D. Stachura, ed.: *The shaping of the Nazi state.* Pp. 160–185. *See* 1157.

2439 JAENSCH, E.-R.: *Zur Neugestaltung des deutschen Studententums und der Hochschule.* Leipzig: Barth, 1937. 89 pp. (Beihefte zur *Zeitschrift für angewandte Psychologie und Charakterkunde* ... Nr. 1).

2440 KATER, MICHAEL H.: *Studentenschaft und Rechtsradikalismus in Deutschland 1918–1933. Eine sozialgeschichtliche Studie zur Bildungskrise in der Weimarer Republik.* Hamburg: Hoffmann & Campe, 1975. 361 pp., bibl. [2. Teil: 'Der Nationalsozialismus als Ausweg aus der Krise der Studentenschaft'.]

2441 KREPPEL, OTTO: *Nationalsozialistisches Studententum und Studentenrecht.* Königsberg: Gräfe & Unzer, 1937. 86 pp., bibl.

2442 KUBACH, F., ed.: *Studenten bauen auf: Der 3. Reichsberufswettkampf der deutschen Studenten 1937/38. Ein Rechenschaftsbericht.* Hrsg.: Deutsche Arbeitsfront Zentralbüro/Berufswettkampf aller schaffenden Deutschen. 113 pp., illus.

2443 PALLMANN, GERHARD, ed.: *Wohlauf Kameraden! Ein Liederbuch der jungen Mannschaft von Soldaten, Bauern, Arbeitern und Studenten.* Im Auftr. des NS. deutschen Studentenbundes, der Reichsschaft der Studierenden der deutschen Hoch- und Fachschulen [and others]. Kassel: Bärenreiter-Verlag, 1934. 138 pp., mus. scores.

2444 RÖDER, BRIGITTE VON: *Helga studiert. Erzählung aus fröhlich-ernster Studienzeit.* 2. Aufl. Stuttgart: Union Deutsche Verlagsgesellschaft, [193–]. 125 pp.

2445 SONDERGELD, WALTER & SEIDEL, WOLFGANG, eds.: *Allgemeine Grundlagen des Hochschulstudiums.* Hrsg. im Auftr. des Reichsstudentenwerks von Adolf Scheel. Berlin: Klokow, [1944]. [Approx. 500 pp.], tabs. [In 2 vols.]. (Handbuch der akademischen Berufsausbildung).

2446 STEINBERG, MICHAEL STEPHEN: *Sabers and Brown Shirts. The German students' path to National Socialism, 1918–1933.* Chicago, Ill.: Chicago University Press, 1977. 237 pp.

2447 STUCKART, WILHELM: *Nationalsozialistische Rechtserziehung.* Frankfurt a.M.: Diesterweg, 1935. 83 pp.

2448 WARLOSKI, RONALD: *Neudeutschland. German Catholic students, 1919–1939.* The Hague: Nijhoff, 1970. xxviii + 220 pp.

2449 WINTER, BOTHO: *Geschichte der Berliner Burschenschaft Teutonia, 1887–1937.* Lahr. i. Baden: Schauenburg, [1938?]. 116 pp., illus.

9. OPPRESSION AND RESISTANCE

2450 ALTENHOFER, LUDWIG: *Aktion Gruen. Ein Buch vom Widerstand der Jugend gegen die Diktatur.* Würzburg: Arena-Verlag, 1956. 216 pp.

2451 EBELING, HANS & HESPERS, DIETER, comps.: *Jugend contra Nationalsozialismus. 'Rundbriefe' und 'Sonderinformationen deutscher Jugend'.* 2. Aufl. Frechen: Bartmann, 1968. 246 pp., diagrs.

2452 JAHNKE, KARL-HEINZ: *Entscheidungen. Jugend im Widerstand 1933–1945.* Frankfurt a.M.: Röderberg, 1970. 251 pp., ports., facisms., bibl.

2453 KLÖNNE, ARNO: *Gegen den Strom. Bericht über den Jugendwiderstand im Dritten Reich.* Hannover: Goedel, 1957. 180 pp., illus.

2454 WOLF, FRIEDRICH: *Das Trojanische Pferd. Ein Stück vom Kampf der Jugend in Deutschland. Anhang: Regiekommentar.* Moskau: Verlagsgenossenschaft ausländischer Arbeiter in der UdSSR, 1937. 134 pp.

Catholic youth

2455 OERTEL, FERDINAND: *Jugend im Feuerofen. Aus der Chronik des Kampfes der katholischen Jugend im Dritten Reich.* Recklinghausen: Paulus Verlag, 1960. 192 pp., illus., facsims.

2456 ROTH, HEINRICH, comp.: *Katholische Jugend in der NS-Zeit, unter besonderer Berücksichtigung des Katholischen Jungmännerverbandes. Daten und Dokumente.* Düsseldorf: Verlag Haus Altenberg, 1959. 240 pp., bibl.

2457 SCHELLENBERGER, BARBARA: *Katholische Jugend und Drittes Reich. Eine Geschichte des Katholischen Jungmännerverbandes 1933–1939 unter besonderer Berücksichtigung der Rheinprovinz.* Mainz: Matthias-Grünewald-Verlag, 1975. xxvii + 202 pp., map, diagrs., bibl. (Veröffentlichungen der Kommission für Zeitgeschichte …). [Incl.: II: 'Massnahmen des nationalsozialistischen Regimes gegen die katholischen Jugendverbände 1933–1936', pp. 33–92; V: 'Die katholischen Jugendverbände unter nationalsozialistischer Herrschaft 1936–1939', pp. 163–175.]

2458 WALKER, LAWRENCE D.: *Hitler Youth and Catholic youth, 1933–1936. A study in totalitarian conquest.* Washington, D.C.: The Catholic University of America Press, 1970. x + 203 pp., bibl.

Protestant youth

2459 LERSNER, DIETER: *Die evangelischen Jugendverbände Württembergs und die Hitler-Jugend 1933–1934.* Göttingen: Vandenhoeck & Ruprecht, 1958. 72 pp.

2460 RIEDEL, HEINRICH: *Kampf um die Jugend. Evangelische Jugendarbeit 1933–1945.* München: Claudius Verlag, 1976. xxii + 381 pp., illus., facsims., diagrs.

Workers' movement

2461 *Geschichte der deutschen Arbeiterjugendbewegung 1904–1945.* Dortmund: Weltkreis-Verlag (under licence from Verlag Neues Leben, Berlin), 1973. 631 pp., illus., facsims., bibl. [By an authors' collective, headed by Karl Heinz Jahnke.]

2462 JAHNKE, KARL HEINZ: *Jungkommunisten im Widerstand gegen den Hitlerfaschismus.* Berlin [East]: Verlag Neues Leben, 1977. 430 pp., bibl.

Resistance at universities

2463 KROUG, WOLFGANG: *Sein zum Tode. Gedanke und Bewährung. Lebensbilder im Kampf gebliebener Mitglieder der Akademischen Vereinigung Marburg.* Godesberg: Voggenreiter, 1955. 135 pp. [Incl. Adolf Reichwein.]

2464 LEIST, FRITZ: 'Möglichkeiten und Grenzen des Widerstandes an der Universität'. [In] *Die deutsche Universität im Dritten Reich.* Pp. 175–214. See 2392.

Weisse Rose

2465 DROBISCH, KLAUS, ed.: *Wir schweigen nicht! Eine Dokumentation über den antifaschistischen Kampf Münchener Studenten 1942–1943. Mit einer biographischen Skizze der Geschwister Scholl.* Berlin [East]: Union Verlag, 1968. 190 pp., illus., facsims.

2466 FLEISCHHACK, ERNST: 'Die Widerstandsbewegung "Weisse Rose". Literaturbericht und Bibliographie'. [In] Bibliothek für Zeitgeschichte/ Weltkriegsbücherei: *Jahresbibliographie 1970.* Frankfurt a.M.: Bernard & Graefe. Pp. 459–507.

2467 HANSER, RICHARD: *Deutschland zuliebe. Leben und Sterben der Geschwister Scholl. Die Geschichte der Weissen Rose.* München: Kindler, 1980. 346 pp., illus. [Orig. American ed.: *A noble treason.* New York: Putnam, 1979.]

2468 HOCHMUTH, URSEL, ed.: *Candidates of humanity. Dokumentation zur Hamburger Weissen Rose anlässlich des 50. Geburtstages von Hans Leipelt.* Hamburg: Vereinigung der Antifaschistischen und Verfolgten des Naziregimes Hamburg (VAN), 1971. 74 pp., ports., facsims., bibl.

2469 HUBER, CLARA, ed.: *Kurt Huber zum Gedächtnis. Bildnis eines Menschen, Denkers und Forschers.* Dargestellt von seinen Freunden. Regensburg: Habbel, 1947. 172 pp., port. [Munich professor executed for his part in the 'Weisse Rose'.]

2470   NEUMANN, ALFRED: *Six of them.* Transl. from the German. New York: Macmillan, 1945. 327 pp. [Novel]

2471   PETRY, CHRISTIAN: *Studenten aufs Schafott. Die Weisse Rose und ihr Scheitern.* München: Piper, 1968. 258 pp., illus., bibl.

2472   SCHOLL, INGE: *Die Weisse Rose.* Frankfurt a.M.: Verlag der Frankfurter Hefte, 1952. 110 pp. [The story of the leaders of the Munich students' revolt, Hans and Sophie Scholl, told by their sister. English version: *Six against tyranny.* London: Murray, 1955. Also: *Students against tyranny. The resistance of the White Rose, Munich 1942–1943.* Middletown, Conn.: Wesleyan University Press, 1970.]

2473   VIELHABER, KLAUS and others, eds.: *Gewalt und Gewissen. Willi Graf und die 'Weisse Rose'. Eine Dokumentation.* Zusammenarb.: Hubert Hanisch, Anneliese Knoop-Graf. Freiburg i.Br.: Herder-Bücherei, 1964. 123 pp., illus., facsims.

K.   CULTURE

1.   GENERAL

2474   BIE, RICHARD & MÜHR, ALFRED: *Die Kulturwaffen des neuen Reiches. Briefe an Führer, Volk und Jugend.* Jena: Diederichs, 1933. 157 pp.

2475   BISCHOFF, RALPH F.: *Nazi conquest through German culture.* Cambridge, Mass.: Harvard University Press, 1942. x + 198 pp., tabs.

2476   BLUMENFELD, ERWIN: *Durch tausendjährige Zeit.* Frauenfeld: Huber, 1976. 425 pp.

2477   CORINO, KARL, ed.: *Intellektuelle im Bann des Nationalsozialismus.* Hamburg: Hoffmann & Campe, 1980. 224 pp.

2478   *Durch die weite Welt. Natur, Sport und Technik.* Stuttgart: Franckh, 1941. 302 pp., illus., maps.

2479   EURINGER, RICHARD: *Chronik einer deutschen Wandlung 1925–1935.* Hamburg: Hanseatische Verlagsanstalt, 1936. 304 pp.

2480   FLITNER, ANDREAS, ed.: *Deutsches Geistesleben und Nationalsozialismus. Eine Vortragsreihe der Universität Tübingen.* Nachw.: Hermann Diem. Tübingen: Wunderlich, 1965. 243 pp., bibl. after ea. chapter.

2481   HELLWIG, L. W.: *Persönlichkeiten der Gegenwart. Luftfahrt—Wissenschaft—Kunst.* Mitarb.: E. Ruckhaber. Berlin: Pape, 1940. 319 pp., ports.

2482   HILLER, KURT: *Köpfe und Tröpfe. Profile aus einem Vierteljahrhundert.* Hamburg: Rowohlt, 1950. 404 pp. [Ch. VII: 'Mausoleum der Märtyrer'— Theodor Lessing, Erich Mühsam, Paul Honigsheim, Werner Abel, Hans Litten, Carl von Ossietzky, Rudolf Olden, Theodor Wolff, Erik Reger.]

2483 KANTOROWICZ, ALFRED: *Deutsche Schicksale. Intellektuelle unter Hitler und Stalin.* Wien: Europa-Verlag, 1964. 256 pp.

2484 KOLBOW, KARL FRIEDRICH: *Die Kulturpflege der preussischen Provinzen.* Stuttgart: Kohlhammer, 1937. 124 pp., maps.

2485 KRIECK, ERNST: *Deutsche Kulturpolitik.* Leipzig: Armanen-Verlag, 1936. 132 pp.

2486 LANGE, CARL & DREYER, [ERNST] ADOLF, eds.: *Deutscher Geist. Kulturdokumente der Gegenwart.* Leipzig: Voigtländer, 1933/35. Illus.
1: *Der Ruf. 1933. Sonderausgabe für die Mitglieder des Volksverbandes der Bücherfreunde.* Publ. 1933. 323 pp.
2: *Gestaltung des Reiches. 1934.* Publ. 1935. 280 pp.

2487 LÜTZELER, HEINRICH & MARGA: *Unser Heim.* 3. Aufl. Bonn: Verlag der Buchgemeinde, [194–]. 272 pp., illus., plans. [Description of furniture, china, ornaments for the home and interior decorating in general.]

MADAJCZYK, CZESŁAW, ed.: *Inter arma non silent musae. The war and the culture 1939–1945. Part I: The culture of the Third Reich.* See 5192.

2488 *Die neue Gemeinschaft. Das Parteiarchiv für nationalsozialistische Feier- und Freizeitgestaltung.* Hrsg.: Hauptkulturamt in der Reichspropagandaleitung. Hauptschriftleiter: Hermann Liese. München: Eher, 1942. 720 pp.

REICHSKULTURKAMMER

2489 BIGOT, HERVÉ: *La chambre de culture allemande dans le régime totalitaire du IIIe Reich.* Paris: Domat-Montchrestien, 1937. 146 pp., bibl.

2490 DREYER, ERNST ADOLF, ed.: *Deutsche Kultur im neuen Reich. Wesen, Aufgabe und Ziel der Reichskulturkammer.* Unter Mitarbeit der Präsidenten und Präsidialratmitglieder der Kammern. Berlin: Schieffen Verlag, 1934. 139 pp.

2491 HINKEL, HANS, ed.: *Handbuch der Reichskulturkammer.* Bearb.: Günther Gentz. Berlin: Deutscher Verlag für Politik und Wirtschaft, 1937. 351 pp.

2492 MENZ, GERHARD: *Der Aufbau des Kulturstandes. Die Reichskulturkammergesetzgebung, ihre Grundlagen und ihre Erfolge.* München: Beck, 1938. 78 pp., bibl.

2493 SCHRIEBER, KARL-FRIEDRICH and others, eds.: *Das Recht der Reichskulturkammer.* [Eds.]: Karl-Friedrich Schrieber, Alfred Metten, Herbert Collatz. Geleitw.: Hans Hinkel. Einführung in das Reichskulturkammerrecht: Heinz Tackmann. Berlin: de Gruyter, 1943. 2 vols.

2494 RICHARD, LIONEL: *Le nazisme et la culture.* Paris: Maspéro, 1978, 393 pp.

2495 RISCHER, WALTER: *Die nationalsozialistische Kulturpolitik in Düsseldorf 1933–1945.* Düsseldorf: Triltsch, 1972. 214 pp., bibl.

2496 SCHNELL, RALF, ed.: *Kunst und Kultur im deutschen Faschismus.* Mit Beiträgen von Martin Damus [and others]. Stuttgart: Metzler, 1978. 350 pp.

2497 STEDING, CHRISTOPH: *Das Reich und die Krankheit der europäischen Kultur.* Hamburg: Hanseatische Verlagsanstalt, 1938. xlviii + 772 pp., facsims.

2498 STEINBERG, ROLF, ed.: *Nazi-Kitsch.* Darmstadt: Melzer, 1975. 83 pp., illus., facsims.

2499 ZINGEL, FRITZ: *Was die Welt den Deutschen verdankt.* 3. Aufl. Leipzig: Koehler & Amelang, 1937. 295 pp.

2500 ZIPPERLEN, H.: *Die Stunde des Gerichts. Eine Kulturbilanz über das Dritte Reich.* Stuttgart-Botnang: Kulturaufbau-Verlag, 1946. 103 pp.

Linguistics

2501 BÄHR, RUDOLF: *Grundlagen für Karl Kraus' Kritik an der Sprache im nationalsozialistischen Deutschland.* Köln: Böhlau, 1977. 156 pp., diagrs., facsim., tabs., bibl.

2502 BERNING, CORNELIA: *Vom 'Abstammungsnachweis' zum 'Zuchtwart'. Vokabular des Nationalsozialismus.* Vorw.: Werner Betz. Berlin: de Gruyter, 1964. 225 pp., bibl.

2503 BORK, SIEGFRIED: *Missbrauch der Sprache. Tendenzen nationalsozialistischer Sprachregelung.* Bern: Franckh, 1970. 139 pp., bibl.

2504 DAHLE, WENDULA: *Der Einsatz einer Wissenschaft. Eine sprachinhaltliche Analyse militärischer Terminologie in der Germanistik 1933–1945.* Bonn: Bouvier, 1969. 309 pp., bibl. (bibl., quotations, list of authors, pp. 111–306).

2505 KLEMPERER, VICTOR: *'LTI'. Die unbewältigte Sprache. Aus dem Notizbuch eines Philologen.* München: Deutscher Taschenbuch Verlag, 1969. 286 pp. [Earlier ed.: *LTI. Notizbuch eines Philologen.* Berlin: Aufbau-Verlag, 1949.]

2506 LÄMMERT, EBERHARD and others: *Germanistik—eine deutsche Wissenschaft.* Beiträge von Eberhard Lämmert, Walther Killy, Karl Otto Conrady, Peter von Polenz. 2. Aufl. Frankfurt a.M.: Suhrkamp, 1967. 164 pp.

2507 MACKENSEN, LUTZ: *Die deutsche Sprache unserer Zeit. Zur Sprachgeschichte des 20. Jahrhunderts.* Heidelberg: Quelle & Meyer, 1956. 198 pp.

2508 MÜLLER, KARL: *Unseres Führers Sprachkunst auf Grund seines Werkes 'Mein Kampf'.* Dresden: Verlag Völkische Literatur, 1935. 56 pp., ports.

2509 PAECHTER, HEINZ: *Nazi-Deutsch. A glossary of contemporary German usage. With appendices on government, military and economic institutions.* In association with Bertha Hellman, Hedwig Paechter, Karl. O. Paetel. New York: Ungar, 1944. 128 pp., tabs.

2510 SCHULTHEISS, TASSILO: *Sprachwissenschaft auf Schleichwegen.* Berlin: Verlag Deutsche Kultur-Wacht, 1936. 84 pp.

2511 SCHWELIEN, JOACHIM: *Jargon der Gewalt.* Frankfurt a.M.: Ner-Tamid Verlag, 1961. 30 pp. [Eichmann trial.]

2512 SEIDEL-SLOTTY, EUGEN & INGEBORG: *Sprachwandel im Dritten Reich. Eine kritische Untersuchung faschistischer Einflüsse.* Halle/Saale: VEB Verlag Sprache und Literatur, 1961. 174 pp.

2513 TEICHERT, FRIEDRICH: *Artfremd oder deutsch? Ein Wörterbuch als Führer durch den Fremdwörterwulst des öffentlichen Lebens.* Berlin: Dümmler, 1934. 61 pp.

2514 THIERFELDER, FRANZ: *Deutsch als Weltsprache. 1. Band: Die Grundlagen der deutschen Sprachgeltung in Europa.* Berlin: Kurzeja, 1938. 221 pp., maps, graphs, tabs., bibl.

See also 5710–5713.

Folklore

2515 *Deutsche Volkskunde im Schrifttum. Ein Leitfaden für die Schulungs- und Erziehungsarbeit der NSDAP.* Berlin: Eher, 1938. 152 pp.

2516 EICHBERG, HENNING and others: *Massenspiele, NS-Thingspiel, Arbeiterweihespiel und olympisches Zeremoniell.* [By] Henning Eichberg, Michael Dultz, Glen Gadberry, Günther Rühle. Stuttgart: Frommann & Holzboog, 1977. 271 pp., illus., bibl.

2517 EMMERICH, WOLFGANG: *Germanistische Volkstumsideologie. Genese und Kritik der Volksforschung im Dritten Reich.* Tübingen Schloss: Tübinger Vereinigung für Volkskunde, 1968. 368 pp., bibl. (pp. 303–353).

2518 ERICH, OSWALD A. & BEITL, RICHARD: *Wörterbuch der deutschen Volkskunde.* Mitarb.: Otto Bramm [and others]. Leipzig: Kröner, 1936. 864 pp., map, diagrs.

2519 GUNTERT, HERMANN: *Am Nornenquell. Nordische Dichtungen.* Leipzig: Armanen-Verlag, 1933. 160 pp.

2520 HORDT, PHILIPP: *Der Durchbruch der Volkheit und die Schule.* 3. Aufl. Leipzig: Armanen-Verlag, 1933. 98 pp.

2521 LANGENBUCHER, HELLMUTH: *Volkhafte Dichtung der Zeit.* Berlin: Junker & Dünnhaupt, 1941. 653 pp., illus.

2522 SAMBETH, HEINRICH M., ed.: *Deutsche Volkslieder.* Geleitw.: Hans Naumann. Bonn: Braun-Peretti, 1937. 60 pp.

2523 SCHOTT, GEORG: *Weissagung und Erfüllung im deutschen Volksmärchen.* München: Eher, 1936. 207 pp.

2524 SELCHOW, BOGISLAV von: *Das Namenbuch. Eine Sammlung sämtlicher deutscher, altdeutscher und in Deutschland gebräuchlicher Vornamen mit Angabe ihrer Abstammung und ihrer Deutung.* Leipzig: Koehler, 1934. 175 pp.

2. LITERATURE

2525 BOESCHENSTEIN, H.: *The German novel, 1939–1944.* Toronto: University of Toronto, 1949. 189 pp.

2526 DENKLER, HORST & PRÜMM, KARL, eds.: *Die deutsche Literatur im Dritten Reich. Themen—Traditionen—Wirkungen*. Stuttgart: Reclam, 1976. 556 pp.

2527 EPTING, KARL, ed.: *Poètes et penseurs*. Paris: Sorlot, 1941. 192 pp. (Cahiers de l'Institut Allemand, No. 1). [Comprising: Erich Rothacker: 'Schopenhauer et Nietzsche'; Kaspar Pinette: 'Rainer Maria Rilke'; Georg Rabuse: 'Hans Carossa'; Bruno Meder: 'Erwin Guido Kolbenheyer'; Wolfram Albrecht: 'La poésie ouvrière'; Gerhard Funke: 'La poésie allemande contemporaine'.]

2528 FABRICIUS, HANS: *Schiller als Kampfgenosse Hitlers. Nationalsozialismus in Schillers Dramen*. Berlin: Verlag Deutsche Kultur-Wacht, 1934. 128 pp.

2529 GEISSLER, ROLF: *Dekadenz und Heroismus. Zeitroman und völkisch-nationalsozialistische Literaturkritik*. Stuttgart: Deutsche Verlags-Anstalt, 1964. 168 pp. (Schriftenreihe der Vierteljahrshefte für Zeitgeschichte).

2530 GRAY, RONALD: *The German tradition in literature 1871–1945*. Cambridge: Cambridge University Press, 1965. 383 pp.

2531 KETELSEN, UWE-K.: *Völkisch-nationale und nationalsozialistische Literatur in Deutschland 1890–1945*. Stuttgart: Metzler, 1976. ix + 116 pp., bibls.

2532 LENNARTZ, FRANZ: *Die Dichter unserer Zeit. 275 Einzeldarstellungen zur deutschen Dichtung der Gegenwart*. 3. Aufl. Stuttgart: Kröner, 1940. 392 pp.

2533 LOEWY, ERNST: *Literatur unterm Hakenkreuz. Das Dritte Reich und seine Dichtung. Eine Dokumentation*. Vorw.: Hans-Jochen Gamm. Frankfurt a.M.: Europäische Verlagsanstalt, 1966. 365 pp. [Also new ed.: Fischer Bücherei, 1969.]

2534 MULOT, ARNO: *Die deutsche Dichtung unserer Zeit*. 2. Aufl. Stuttgart: Metzler, 1944. 578 pp.

2535 ORLOWSKY, H.: *Literatura w III Rzeszy*. Poznań: Wyd. Poznańskie, 1979. 457 pp., illus., facsims.

2536 PAUCKER, HENRI R.: *Neue Sachlichkeit. Literatur im 'Dritten Reich' und im Exil*. Stuttgart: Reclam, 1974. 318 pp., ports., bibl. [Anthology.]

2537 RAABE-STIFTUNG IN DER NS-KULTURGEMEINSCHAFT: *Das Jahrbuch der deutschen Dichtung 1936. Deutsche Frauendichtung der Gegenwart*. Berlin: Volkschaft-Verlag, 1937. 259 pp., ports.

REICHSSCHRIFTTUMSKAMMER

2538 IHDE, WILHELM, ed.: *Handbuch der Reichsschrifttumskammer*. Mitarb.: Günther Gentz. Leipzig: Verlag des Börsenvereins der Deutschen Buchhändler, 1942. 276 pp.

2539 REICHSSCHRIFTTUMSKAMMER: *Schriftsteller-Verzeichnis 1942*. Leipzig: Börsenverein der deutschen Buchhändler, 1942. 244 pp.

2540 RICHARD, LIONEL: *Nazisme et littérature*. Paris: Maspéro, 1971. 202 pp., bibl.

2541 RICHARDS, DONALD RAY: *The German best-seller in the 20th century. A complete bibliography and analysis, 1915–1940.* Berne: Lang, 1968. 275 pp., tabs.

STROTHMANN, DIETRICH: *Nationalsozialistische Literaturpolitik. Ein Beitrag zur Publizistik im Dritten Reich.* See 2801.

2542 VILMAR, A. F. C.: *Geschichte der deutschen National-Literatur.* 3. Aufl. bearb. und fortgesetzt von Johannes Rohr. Berlin: Safari Verlag, 1936. 446 pp.

2543 WERDER, PETER VON: *Literatur im Bann der Verstädterung. Eine kulturpolitische Untersuchung.* Leipzig: Schwarzhäupter, 1943. 163 pp.

2544 WULF, JOSEPH: *Literatur und Dichtung im Dritten Reich. Eine Dokumentation.* Gütersloh: Mohn, 1963. 471 pp., illus., facsims.

Writers

BARTELS, ADOLF
2545 BARTELS, ADOLF: *Einführung in das deutsche Schrifttum für deutsche Menschen. In 52 Briefe.* 2. verb. Aufl. Leipzig: Koehler & Amelang, 1933. 614 pp.

2546 BARTELS, ADOLF: *Geschichte der deutschen Literatur. Grosse Ausgabe in drei Bänden.* Leipzig: Haessel, 1924–1928. In 3 vols.

2547 BAUMANN, ERHARD: *Jüdische und völkische Literaturwissenschaft. Ein Vergleich zwischen Eduard Engel und Adolf Bartels.* München: Eher, 1936. 117 pp.

BENN, GOTTFRIED
2548 BENN, GOTTFRIED: *Briefe an F. W. Oelze 1932–1945.* Vorw.: F. W. Oelze. Wiesbaden: Limes Verlag, 1977. 478 pp. (Gottfried Benn: Briefe. 1. Band).

2549 BENN, GOTTFRIED: *Doppelleben—Zwei Selbstdarstellungen. 1. Teil: Lebensweg eines Intellektualisten (1934): 2. Teil: Doppelleben (1950).* Wiesbaden: Limes Verlag, 1950. 213 pp.

2550 ALTER, REINHARD: *Gottfried Benn. The artist and politics (1910–1934).* Bern: Lang, 1976. 149 pp., bibl.

2551 KAISER, HELMUT: *Mythos, Rausch und Reaktion. Der Weg Gottfried Benns und Ernst Jüngers.* Berlin: Aufbau-Verlag, 1962. 371 pp.

BINDING, RUDOLF G.
2552 BINDING, RUDOLF G.: *Erlebtes Leben.* Hamburg: Dulk, 1950. 287 pp.

2553 BARTHEL, LUDWIG FRIEDRICH, ed.: *Das war Binding. Ein Buch der Erinnerung.* Wien: Neff, 1955. 305 pp., illus.

BLUNCK, HANS FRIEDRICH
2554 DREYER, ERNST ADOLF: *Hans Friedrich Blunck. Sicht des Werkes.* Leipzig: Weibezahl, 1934. 187 pp., illus., bibl.

BRONNEN, ARNOLT
2555 BRONNEN, ARNOLT: *Gibt zu Protokoll. Beiträge zur Geschichte des modernen Schriftstellers.* Hamburg: Rowohlt, 1954. 494 pp.

2556 KLINGNER, EDWIN: *Arnolt Bronnen—Werk und Wirkung. Eine Personalbibliographie.* Hildesheim: Gerstenberg, 1974. xvi + 84 pp., illus.

CAROSSA, HANS
2557 CAROSSA, HANS: *Führung und Geist. Ein Lebensgedenkbuch.* Leipzig: Insel-Verlag, 1933. 190 pp.

2558 CAROSSA, HANS: *Ungleiche Welten.* Wiesbaden: Insel Verlag, 1951. 339 pp.

EHRHART, GEORG
2559 EHRHART, GEORG: *Leben—eine köstliche Sache. Erinnerungen.* Stuttgart: Deutsche Verlags-Anstalt, 1962. 359 pp.

FREYTAG, GEORG
2560 FREYTAG, GEORG: *Der Bodungersang. Eine Kampfdichtung.* 2. Aufl. Landsberg (Warthe): Pfeiffer, 1937. 63 pp. [Against 'Rom und Juda'.]

HUCH, RICARDA
2561 BAUM, MARIE: *Leuchtende Spur. Das Leben Ricarda Huchs.* 4. Aufl. Tübingen: Wunderlich, 1964. 519 pp., illus., bibl.

JOHST, HANNS
2562 JOHST, HANNS: *Ruf des Reiches—Echo des Volkes. Eine Ostfahrt.* München: Eher, 1940. 134 pp.

2563 CASPER, SIEGFRIED: *Hanns Johst spricht zu Dir. Eine Lebenslehre aus seinen Reden und Werken.* 2. Aufl. Berlin: Nordland Verlag, 1943. 148 pp.

2564 PFANNER, HELMUT: *Hanns Johst: Vom Expressionismus zum Nationalsozialismus.* The Hague: 1970. 326 pp., bibl.

JÜNGER, ERNST
2565 JÜNGER, ERNST: *Auf den Marmorklippen.* Hamburg: Hanseatische Verlagsanstalt, 1939/41. 157 pp. [Criticism of the Nazi regime disguised as an allegorical novel.]

2566 JÜNGER, ERNST: *Strahlungen.* Tübingen: Heliopolis-Verlag, 1949. 648 pp. [Diaries 1941–1945.]

2567 ARNOLD, HEINZ LUDWIG, ed.: *Wandlung und Wiederkehr. Festschrift zum 70. Geburtstag Ernst Jüngers.* Aachen: Verlag Text und Kritik, 1965. 245 pp., port., bibl.

KAPP, GOTTFRIED
2568 KAPP, LUISE: *... In Deinem Namen. Lebensbild des Dichters Gottfried Kapp.* Dülmen (Westf.): Laumann, 1960. 128 pp., illus., bibl.

KOLBENHEYER, ERWIN GUIDO
2569 KOLBENHEYER, E. G.: *Der Einzelne und die Gemeinschaft. Goethes Denkprinzipien und der biologische Naturalismus. Zwei Reden.* München: Langen-Müller, 1939. 27 pp.

2570 KOCH, FRANZ: *Erwin Guido Kolbenheyer.* Göttingen: Göttinger Verlagsanstalt, 1953. 188 pp.

2571 WANDREY, CONRAD: *Kolbenheyer. Der Dichter und der Philosoph.* München: Langen (Müller), 1934. 372 pp., port.

MÖLLER, EBERHARD WOLFGANG
2572 MÖLLER, EBERHARD, WOLFGANG: *Das Schloss in Ungarn. Roman.* Berlin: 'Zeitgeschichte' Verlag, 1935. 419 pp.

NABOR, FELIX
2573 NABOR, FELIX: *Shylock unter Bauern. Ein Roman aus deutscher Notzeit.* Berlin-Schöneberg: Verlag Deutsche Kultur-Wacht, 1934. 175 pp.

OTTWALD, ERNST
2574 OTTWALT, ERNST: *Schriften. Beiträge in 'Berliner Volkszeitung'* [and elsewhere]. Hrsg.: Andreas W. Mytze. Berlin: Europäische Ideen, 1976. 258 pp., facsims.

2575 MYTZE, ANDREAS W.: *Ottwalt. Leben und Werk des vergessenen revolutionären deutschen Schriftstellers. Im Anhang bisher unveröffentlichte Dokumente.* Berlin: Verlag Europäische Ideen, 1977. 176 pp., illus., facsims.

RECK-MALLECZEWEN, FRIEDRICH PERCYVAL
2576 RECK-MALLECZEWEN, FRIEDRICH: *Bockelson. Geschichte eines Massenwahns.* Wiesentheid: Droemersche Verlagsanstalt, 1946. 188 pp. [Indirect attack on Nazism under the guise of a study of the Anabaptist movement.]

2577 RECK-MALLECZEWEN, FRIEDRICH PERCYVAL: *Tagebuch eines Verzweifelten.* Lorch-Stuttgart: Bürger, 1950. 235 pp., port.

SALOMON, ERNST VON
2578 SALOMON, ERNST VON: *Die Geächteten.* Berlin: Rowohlt, 1935. 484 pp.

WIECHERT, ERNST
2579 REINER, GUIDO, ed.: *Ernst Wiechert im Dritten Reich. Eine Dokumentation. Mit einem Verzeichnis der Ernst-Wiechert-Manuskripte im Haus Königsberg (Ernst-Wiechert-Bibliographie 2. Teil).* Paris: [priv. pr.], 1974. 210 pp., ports., facsims., tabs., bibl.

Poetry

2580 ANACKER, HEINRICH: *Die Fanfare. Gedichte der deutschen Erhebung.* 9. Aufl. München: Eher, 1943. 116 pp.

2581 GROLL, GUNTER, ed.: *De profundis. Deutsche Lyrik in dieser Zeit. Eine Anthologie aus zwölf Jahren.* München: Desch, 1946. 473 pp. [Anti-Nazi poetry written and partly published in Germany between 1933 and 1945.]

2582 GROTHE, HUGO, ed.: 'Deutsches Lied im fremden Land. Eine Auslese auslanddeutscher Lyrik'. Sonderheft der Zeitschrift *Deutsche Kultur in der Welt.* Leipzig: Grothe, 1937. 80 pp., bibl.

2583 HOFFMANN, CHARLES W.: *Opposition poetry in Nazi Germany.* Berkeley, Calif.: University of California Press, 1962. 184 pp., bibl.

2584 KOENIGSWALD, HARALD VON: *Die Gewaltlosen. Dichtung im Widerstand gegen den Nationalsozialismus.* Herborn: Oranien Verlag, 1962. 94 pp., ports.

2585 LEHMANN-HAUPT, HELLMUT, ed.: *Neue deutsche Gedichte.* New York: Krause, 1946. 46 pp. (Dokumente des Anderen Deutschland, Bd. III). [Authors: Karl Rausch, Reinhold Schneider, Helga Grimm.]

2586 RÖSSNER, HANS: *Lyrik im neuen Deutschland.* Bonn: Klett, 1936. 70 pp.

2587 SCHLÖSSER, MANFRED, ed.: *An den Wind geschrieben. Lyrik der Freiheit. Gedichte der Jahre 1933–1945.* Mitarb.: Hans-Rolf Ropertz. Darmstadt: Agora, 1960. 369 pp. [Incl. biographical details of the poets represented.]

Innere Emigration

2588 KUNISCH, HERMANN, ed.: *Handbuch der deutschen Gegenwartsliteratur.* Mitw.: Hans Hennecke. München: Nymphenburger Verlagshandlung, 1965. 781 pp. [Incl.: Herbert Wiesner: 'Innere Emigration—die innerdeutsche Literatur im Widerstand'.]

2589 PAETEL, KARL O., ed.: *Deutsche innere Emigration. Anti-nationalsozialistische Zeugnisse aus Deutschland. Gesammelt und erläutert.* Mit Original-Beiträgen von Carl Zuckmayer und Dorothy Thompson. New York: Krause, 1946. 115 pp.

2590 SCHNELL, RALF: *Literarische Innere Emigration, 1933–1945.* Stuttgart: Metzler, 1976. 211 pp., bibl.

Books and publishing

AMT SCHRIFTTUMSPFLEGE

2591 AMT SCHRIFTTUMSPFLEGE: *400 Bücher für nationalsozialistische Büchereien.* 2. Aufl. München: Eher, [1937]. 32 pp.

2592 PAYR, BERNHARD: *Das Amt Schrifttumspflege. Seine Entwicklungsgeschichte und seine Organisation.* Vorwort: Reichsamtsleiter Hans Hagenmeyer. Berlin: Junker & Dünnhaupt, 1941. 40 pp.

2593 ANDRAE, FRIEDRICH, comp.: *Volksbücherei und Nationalsozialismus. Materialien zur Theorie und Politik des öffentlichen Büchereiwesens in Deutschland 1933–1945.* Wiesbaden: Harrassowitz, 1970. 200 pp., diagr., facsim., bibls.

2594 FLEISCHHACK, KURT: *Wege zum Wissen. Buch—Buchhandel—Bibliotheken—Schrifttumsverzeichnis.* 4. wenig veränd. Aufl. Leipzig: Verlag des Börsenvereins der deutschen Buchhändler, 1943. 96 pp.

2595 HESS, ALBERT, ed.: *Das Verkehrs- und Verkaufsrecht des deutschen Buchhandels. Ergänzt durch das Satzungsrecht des Börsenvereins der Deutschen Buchhändler zu Leipzig und sonstige für den Buchhandel wichtige Bestimmungen.* Leipzig: Verlag des Börsenvereins der Deutschen Buchhändler, 1938. [230 pp.]

2596 LORCH, WILLI, ed.: *Was soll ich lesen? Werktätige in allen Stellungen und aus allen Gauen Deutschlands empfehlen ihren Arbeitskameraden gute Bücher und die Dichter schreiben Briefe an ihre Leser in den Fabriken.* Stuttgart: Siegle, 1938. 128 pp., ports.

2597 METZNER, KURT O.: *Geordnete Buchbesprechung. Ein Handbuch für Presse und Verlag.* Leipzig: Verlag des Börsenvereins des deutschen Buchhandels, 1935. 99 pp.

2598 REICHSMINISTERIUM FÜR VOLKSAUFKLÄRUNG UND PROPAGANDA, Abt. Schrifttum: *Liste der für Jugendliche und Büchereien ungeeigneten Druckschriften.* Leipzig: Verlag des Börsenvereins der Deutschen Buchhändler, 1940. 77 pp.

2599 SCHNEIDER, LAMBERT, ed.: *Rechenschaft über vierzig Jahre Verlagsarbeit 1925–1965. Ein Almanach.* Heidelberg: Schneider, 1965. 191 pp., bibl. [Incl.: 'In den Katakomben 1933–1945', pp. 37–79.]

2600 SCHRIEWER, FRANZ: *Die deutsche Volksbücherei.* Jena: Diederichs, 1939. 153 pp., tabs., diagrs., bibl.

2601 ULLSTEIN, HERMAN: *The rise and fall of the House of Ullstein.* London: Nicholson & Watson, [1944]. 256 pp.

2602 VOLK UND REICH VERLAG: *Um Volk und Reich. Zehn Jahre Arbeit des Volk und Reich Verlages.* Berlin: Volk und Reich Verlag, 1935. 242 pp., illus.

2603 WARMUTH, LUDWIG, ed.: *RSK Taschenbuch für den deutschen Buchhandel.* Berlin: Elsner, 1937. 291 pp., ports., diagrs., tabs. [Also publ. in other years.]

2604 *Weimarer Blätter.* Ausgewählt und gestaltet von der Reichsschrifttumsstelle. Leipzig: 1937–
1937: *Festschrift zur Woche des Deutschen Buches.* 168 pp.
1938: *Festschrift zur ersten Grossdeutschen Buchwoche.* 165 pp.
1940: *Festschrift zur Grossdeutschen Buchwoche 1940.* 159 pp. [This, and the following Festschrift, were issued by: Werbe- und Beratungsamt für das deutsche Schrifttum beim Reichsministerium für Volksaufklärung und Propaganda.]
1941: *Festschrift zur Kriegsbuchwoche 1941.* 163 pp.

Banned and burned books

2605 *Deutsche Nationalbiographie. Ergänzung I: Verzeichnis der Schriften die 1933–1945 nicht angezeigt werden durften.* Bearb. und hrsg. von der Deutschen Bücherei in Leipzig. Leipzig: Verlag des Börsenvereins der deutschen Buchhändler, 1949. 433 pp.

2606 DREWS, RICHARD & KANTOROWICZ, ALFRED, eds.: *Verboten und verbrannt. Deutsche Literatur 12 Jahre unterdrückt.* Berlin: Ullstein, 1947. 215 pp.

2607 *Liste des schädlichen und unerwünschten Schrifttums. Stand vom 31. Dezember 1938.* Leipzig: Hedrich, [1939]. 181 pp. [Also lists for 1939, 1940, 1941.]

2608 REICHSFÜHRER-SS UND CHEF DER DEUTSCHEN POLIZEI IM REICHSMINISTERIUM DES INNERN: *Verzeichnis der für das Reichsgebiet verbotenen ausländischen*

Druckschriften nach dem Stande vom 1. Oktober 1936. [Berlin: 1936].
47 + 4 pp.

2609 SERKE, JÜRGEN: *Die verbrannten Dichter. Berichte, Texte, Bilder der Zeit.*
Weinheim: Beltz, 1977. 269 pp., illus., facsims., bibl.

3. THE ARTS

a. General

2610 BRENNER, HILDEGARD: *Ende einer bürgerlichen Kunst-Institution. Die politische
Formierung der Preussischen Akademie der Künste ab 1933.* Stuttgart:
Deutsche Verlags-Anstalt, 1972. 174 pp., bibl. (Schriftenreihe der
Vierteljahrshefte für Zeitgeschichte).

2611 BRENNER, HILDEGARD: *Die Kunstpolitik des Nationalsozialismus.* Reinbek bei
Hamburg: Rowohlt, 1963. 287 pp., illus., facsims., diagrs., bibl.

2612 CRISPOLTI, E. and others: *Arte e fascismo in Italia e in Germania.* Milano:
Feltrinelli, 1974. 181 pp., illus., facsims. [Co-authors include Berthold Hinz,
Z. Birolli.]

2613 DIEL, ALEX: *Die Kunsterziehung im Dritten Reich. Geschichte und Analyse.*
Inaugural-Dissertation [pres. to] Ludwig-Maximilians-Universität zu
München. 1969. 341 pp., illus., facsims., diagr., bibl. [Incl.: 'Die
theoretische Fixierung von Sozialdarwinismus, Rassenlehre und
Antisemitismus als Manifestation antihumanitären Denkens', pp. 14–16.]

2614 *Die dreissiger Jahre—Schauplatz Deutschland.* München: Haus der Kunst,
1977. 254 pp., illus.

2615 GRAEVENITZ, FRITZ VON: *Kunst und Soldatentum.* Stuttgart: Belser, 1940.
63 pp., illus.

2616 GUTHMANN, HEINRICH: *Zweierlei Kunst in Deutschland? Der Bund der
Verschworenen.* Berlin: Volkschaft-Verlag für Buch, Bühne und Film, 1935.
118 pp.

2617 MÜLLER-MEHLIS, REINHARD: *Die Kunst im Dritten Reich.* München: Heyne,
1976. 230 pp., illus., bibl.

2618 RODENS, FRANZ: *Vom Wesen deutscher Kunst.* Berlin: Eher, 1941. 88 pp.

2619 STENZEL, HERMANN: *Die Welt der deutschen Kunst. Entwicklung, Wesensart
und Inhalt des germanischen Kunstschaffens.* München: Oldenbourg, 1943.
286 pp., illus.

2620 WEIGERT, HANS: *Die Kunst von heute als Spiegel der Zeit.* Leipzig: Seemann,
1934. 144 pp., illus.

2621 WESTECKER, WILHELM: *Krieg und Kunst. Das Erlebnis des Weltkrieges und des
Grossdeutschen Freiheitskrieges.* Vorw.: Bruno Brehm. Wien: Sopper &
Bauer, 1944. 107 pp., illus.

b. Music

2622 BODE, ALFRED: *Die kulturpolitischen Aufgaben der Verwaltung im deutschen Musikleben. Ihre Bedeutung und Durchführung.* Düsseldorf: Nolte, 1937. x + 101 + ix pp.

2623 [BRUCKNER, ANTON] ZIMMERMANN, REINHOLD: *Um Anton Bruckners Vermächtnis. Ein Beitrag zur rassischen Erkenntnis germanischer Tonkunst.* Stuttgart: Bühler, 1939. 139 pp., port., bibl.

2624 BÜCKEN, ERNST: *Musik der Deutschen. Eine Kulturgeschichte der deutschen Musik.* Köln: Staufen-Verlag, 1941. 315 + xxiv pp., illus., mus. scores.

2625 *Deutsches Volk—singend Volk.* Hrsg. im Einvernehmen mit dem Deutschen Sängerbund. Berlin: Weller, 1937. 164 pp., illus.

2626 GEISSMAR, BERTA: *The baton and the jackboot. Recollections of musical life.* London: Hamish Hamilton, 1944. 404 pp., illus. [German version: *Musik im Schatten der Politik.* Zürich: Atlantis-Verlag, 1945. Secretary to Wilhelm Furtwängler and manager of the Berlin Philharmonic Orchestra before being forced into exile.]

2627 *Jahrbuch der deutschen Musik.* Im Auftr. der Abt. Musik des Reichsministeriums für Volksaufklärung und Propaganda. Leipzig: Breitkopf & Härtel, 1943/44. Illus.
1. Jhrg.: *1943.* Hrsg.: Hellmuth von Hase. 211 pp.
2. Jhrg.: *1944.* Hrsg.: Hellmuth von Hase, Albert Dreetz. 192 pp.

2628 JAIDE, WALTER: *Vom Tanz der jungen Mannschaft. Eine Grundlegung für den deutschen Tanz zugleich Erklärung und Deutung der Tanzformen für die praktische Arbeit.* Leipzig: Teubner, 1935. 45 pp., illus.

2629 KÜHN, WALTER: *Führung zur Musik. Voraussetzungen und Grundlagen einer einheitlichen völkischen Musikerziehung.* Lahr (Baden): Schauenburg, 1939. 368 pp., tabs., mus. scores.

2630 MOSER, H. J.: *Musik Lexikon.* Berlin-Schöneberg: Hesse, 1935. 1005 pp.

2631 MÜLLER-BLATTAU, JOSEF: *Geschichte der deutschen Musik. Mit zahlreichen Notenbeispielen.* Berlin: Vieweg, 1938. 318 pp., facsim., mus. scores.

2632 RAABE, PETER: *Die Musik im Dritten Reich. Kulturpolitische Reden und Aufsätze.* Regensburg: Bosse, 1935. 93 pp., port.

REICHSMUSIKKAMMER
2633 IHLERT, HEINZ: *Die Reichsmusikkammer. Ziele, Leistungen und Organisationen.* Berlin: Junker & Dünnhaupt, 1935. 40 pp., tabs.

2634 REICHSMUSIKKAMMER, Presseamt: *Kultur, Wirtschaft, Recht und die Zukunft des deutschen Musiklebens. Vorträge und Reden von der ersten Arbeitstagung der Reichsmusikkammer.* Beiträge von Richard Strauss und andere. Berlin: Parrhysius, 1934. 319 pp.

2635 REUSCH, FRITZ: *Musik und Musikerziehung im Dienste der Volksgemeinschaft.* Osterwieck: Zickfeldt, 1938. 67 pp.

2636 ROCK, CHRISTA MARIA & BRÜCKNER, HANS, eds.: *Judentum und Musik. Mit dem ABC jüdischer und nichtarischer Musikbeflissener.* 2. verb. und erw. Aufl. München: Brückner, 1936. 248 pp.

2637 SCHMIDT, H. W. & WEBER, A.: *Die Garbe. Vom Leben und Schaffen deutscher Musiker. Musikstunde für höhere Lehranstalten.* Köln: Tonger, 1942. 552 pp., illus.

2638 SCHRENK, OSWALD: *Berlin und die Musik. Zweihundert Jahre Musikleben einer Stadt: 1740–1940.* Berlin: Bote & Beck, 1940. 312 + 115 pp., illus., bibl.

2639 STUMME, WOLFGANG, ed.: *Musik im Volk. Gegenwartsfragen der deutschen Musik.* 2. neubearb. und stark erw. Aufl. Berlin: Vieweg, 1944. 405 pp.

WAGNER, RICHARD

2640 ANDREEVSKY, ALEXANDER: *Der Weg zum Gral. Richard Wagner's Kämpferleben.* Berlin: Bong, 1941. 338 pp.

2641 LANGE, WALTER: *Richard Wagners Sippe. Vom Urahn zum Enkel.* Leipzig: Beck, 1938. 109 pp., illus., facsims., maps.

2642 WESTERNHAGEN, CURT von: *Richard Wagners Kampf gegen seelische Fremdherrschaft.* München: Lehmann, 1935. 127 pp., port.

2643 WULF, JOSEPH: *Musik im Dritten Reich. Eine Dokumentation.* Gütersloh: Mohn, 1963. 446 pp., illus., facsims.

2644 ZIEGLER, HANS SEVERUS: *Entartete Musik. Eine Abrechnung.* 2. durchges. Aufl. Hrsg. und eingel.: Friedrich W. Herzog. Düsseldorf: Völkischer Verlag, 1939. 32 pp., illus.

c. Architecture and town planning

2645 *Bauten der Bewegung.* Band I der Buchreihe des Zentralblatts der Bauverwaltung, hrsg. im Preussischen Finanzministerium. Berlin: Ernst, 1938. 148 pp., illus., plans. [Incl. foreword: Julius Schulte-Frohlinde: 'Baukultur im Dritten Reich'.]

2646 DÜLFFER, JOST and others: *Hitlers Städte. Baupolitik im Dritten Reich. Eine Dokumentation.* [By] Jost Dülffer, Jochen Thies, Josef Henke. Köln: Böhlau, 1978. 320 pp., illus., facsims., plans, bibl. [Incl. material on Berlin, Munich, Hamburg, Nuremberg, Linz and Hitler's Kroll-Oper speech, 10 February 1939.]

2647 FEDER, GOTTFRIED & RECHENBERG, FRITZ: *Die neue Stadt. Versuch der Begründung einer neuen Stadtplanungskunst aus der sozialen Struktur der Bevölkerung.* Berlin: Springer, 1939. viii + 480 pp., illus., plans, tabs., bibl., diagrs. in folder.

211

2648   KAUFFMANN, FRITZ ALEXANDER: *Deutsches Wohnen*. Berlin: Deutscher Verlag, 1941. 52 pp., illus.

2649   KOCHSKÄMPER, MAX: *Herbergen der neuen Jugend*. Berlin: Bauwelt-Verlag, 1937. 96 pp., illus., plans.

2650   LANE, BARBARA MILLER: *Architecture and politics in Germany 1918–1945*. Cambridge, Mass.: Harvard University Press, 1968. 278 pp., illus., plans, bibl.

2651   LUDOWICI, J. W. L.: *Das deutsche Siedlungswerk*. 2. verm. Aufl. Heidelberg: Winter, 1937. 95 pp., illus., plans, diagrs.

2652   *A nation builds: contemporary German architecture*. New York: German Library of Information, 1940. 133 pp., illus.

2653   *Die neue Stadt. Gesichtspunkte, Organisationsformen und Gesetzesvorschläge für die Umgestaltung deutscher Grossstädte*. Vorw. und Einl.: A. Hugenberg. Berlin: Scherl, 1935. 97 pp., illus., plans, diagrs., bibl.

2654   PELTZ-DRECKMANN, UWE: *Nationalsozialistischer Siedlungsbau. Versuch einer Analyse der die Siedlungspolitik bestimmenden Faktoren am Beispiel des Nationalsozialismus*. München: Minerva Verlag, 1978. 472 pp., illus., plans, tabs.

2655   PETSCH, JOACHIM: *Baukunst und Stadtplanung im Dritten Reich. Herleitung, Bestandsaufnahme, Entwicklung, Nachfolge*. München: Hanser, 1976. 274 pp., illus.

2656   RITTICH, WERNER: *Architektur und Bauplastik der Gegenwart*. Berlin: Rembrandt-Verlag, 1938. 160 pp., illus.

2657   [SCHAROUN, HANS] JONES, PETER BLUNDELL: *Hans Scharoun: a monograph*. London: Gordon Fraser, 1978. 134 pp., illus. [A modernist architect of the 1920s, forced by the late 1930s to modify designs to suit Hitler's ideas on popular housing.]

2658   SCHOLZ, ROBERT: *Architektur und bildende Kunst 1933–1945*. Preuss. Oldendorf: Schütz, 1977. 239 pp., illus.

SPEER, ALBERT
2659   SPEER, ALBERT, ed.: *Neue deutsche Baukunst*. Hrsg. vom Generalbauinspektor für die Reichshauptstadt Albert Speer. Dargestellt von Rudolf Wolters. Prag: Bücherring Volk und Reich, 1941. 96 pp.

2660   SPEER, ALBERT, comp.: *Die neue Reichskanzlei*. 3. Aufl. München: Eher, [193–]. 131 pp., illus., diagrs., plans.

2661   HERDING, KLAUS & MITTIG, HANS-ERNST: *Kunst und Alltag im NS-System. Albert Speers Berliner Strassenlaternen*. Giessen: Anabas-Verlag, 1975. 92 pp., illus., bibl.

TAYLOR, ROBERT R.: *The word in stone. See* 594.

2662 Teut, Anna: *Architektur im Dritten Reich 1933–1945*. Frankfurt a.M.: Ullstein, 1967. 389 pp., illus., maps, diagrs., facsim., tabs., bibl.

d. Painting and sculpture

Barlach, Ernst

2663 Barlach, Ernst: *Die Briefe 1888–1938. Band II: 1925–1938*. Hrsg.: Friedrich Dross. München: Piper, 1968. 931 pp.

2664 Schurek, Paul: *Barlach. Eine Bildbiographie*. München: Kindler, 1961. 143 pp., illus., facsims.

2665 Beyerlein, Kurt: *Von drei Reichen. Briefe des Malers aus den Jahren 1941–1945*. Reinbek bei Hamburg: Parus Verlag, 1947. 227 pp.

2666 Breker, Arno: *Im Strahlungsfeld der Ereignisse. Leben und Wirken eines Künstlers. Porträts, Begegnungen, Schicksale*. Preuss. Oldendorf: Schütz, 1972. 399 pp., illus., facsims.

2667 *Deutsche Künstler und die SS*. Hrsg.: Der Reichsführer-SS, SS Hauptamt. Berlin: Limpert, [1943]. [96 pp.], illus. [Exhibition catalogue.]

'Entartete Kunst'

2668 Dresler, Adolf, ed.: *Deutsche Kunst und entartete 'Kunst'. Kunstwerk und Zerrbild als Spiegel der Weltanschauung*. München: Deutscher Volksverlag, 1938. 79 pp., illus.

2669 *Entartete Kunst. Bildersturm vor 25 Jahren. Haus der Kunst München—25. Oktober bis 16. Dezember 1962. Katalog*. Redaktion, Texte, Dokumentation: Jürgen Claus. München: Ausstellungsleitung München, 1962. 432 pp., illus.

2670 Hansen, Walter: *Judenkunst in Deutschland. Quellen und Studien zur Judenfrage auf dem Gebiet der bildenden Kunst. Ein Handbuch zur Geschichte und Entartung deutscher Kunst 1900–1933*. Berlin: Als Manuskript gedruckt, 1942. 314 pp. + 64 pp. illus.

2671 Roh, Franz: *'Entartete Kunst'. Kunstbarbarei im Dritten Reich*. Hannover: Fackelträger-Verlag, 1962. 330 pp., illus., bibl.

2672 Grundig, Hans: *Zwischen Karneval und Aschermittwoch. Erinnerungen eines Malers*. Berlin: Dietz, 1958. 428 pp., illus.

2673 Grundmann, Günther: *Deutsche Kunst im befreiten Schlesien*. 2. erw. Aufl. Breslau: Korn, 1944. 232 pp., illus.

2674 Hiepe, Richard: *Gewissen und Gestaltung. Deutsche Kunst im Widerstand*. Frankfurt a.M.: Röderberg, 1960. 63 pp., illus.

Hinkel, Hermann: *Zur Funktion des Bildes im deutschen Faschismus. See* 2963.

2675   HINZ, BERTHOLD: *Art in the Third Reich*. Transl. from the German. Oxford: Blackwell, 1980. 268 pp., illus., bibl. [Extensively rev. version of: *Die Malerei im deutschen Faschismus. Kunst und Konterrevolution*. München: Hauser, 1974.]

2676   [KARSCH, JOACHIM] SONNTAG, FRITZ, ed.: *Briefe des Bildhauers Joachim Karsch aus den Jahren 1933 bis 1945*. Berlin: Mann, 1948. 135 pp.

2677   KAUFFMANN, FRITZ ALEXANDER: *Die neue deutsche Malerei*. Berlin: Deutscher Verlag, 1941. 83 pp., illus.

2678   [KOLLWITZ, KÄTHE] KOLLWITZ, HANS, ed.: *Ich sah die Welt mit liebevollen Blicken. Ein Leben in Selbstzeugnissen*. Hannover: Fackelträger-Verlag, 1968. 405 pp., illus., bibl.

2679   *Kunst im Dritten Reich. Dokumente der Unterwerfung*. Frankfurt a.M.: Frankfurter Kunstverein, 1974. 227 pp., illus., tabs. [Exhibition.]

2680   LEHMANN-HAUPT, HELLMUT: *Art under a dictatorship*. New York: Oxford University Press, 1954. 227 pp., illus.

2681   NOLDE, EMIL: *Reisen, Ächtung, Befreiung, 1919–1946*. Köln: Dumont Schauberg, 1967. 183 pp., illus. [2nd ed.]

2682   NOWOJSKI, WALTER, ed.: *In dunkler Zeit. Künstlerschicksale zwischen 1933 und 1945*. Mit 12 Grafiken von Fritz Cremer. Berlin: Henschel, 1963. 144 pp. [Anthology.]

2683   [PANKOK, OTTO] PEROTTI, BERTO: *Begegnung mit Otto Pankok*. Düsseldorf: Fladung, 1959. 47 + 55 pp., illus. [Anti-Nazi artist, who also helped Jews.]

2684   ROGNER, KLAUS P., ed.: *Verlorene Werke der Malerei. In Deutschland in der Zeit von 1939 bis 1945 zerstörte und verschollene Gemälde aus Museen und Galerien*. Bearb.: Marianne Bernhard—beratender Mitarb.: Kurt Martin. München: Ackermann, 1965. 231 + 225 pp., illus.

2685   SCHOLZ, ROBERT: *Lebensfragen der bildenden Kunst*. München: Eher, 1937. 96 pp.

2686   SCHULTZE-NAUMBURG, PAUL: *Nordische Schönheit. Ihr Wunschbild im Leben und in der Kunst*. Berlin: Lehmann, 1937. 204 pp., illus.

2687   STAATLICHE MUSEEN, BERLIN: *Drei Jahre nationalsozialistischer Museumsarbeit. Erwerbungen 1933–1935. Ausstellung—Schlossmuseum 1936*. 328 pp., illus.

2688   STEINGRÄBER, ERICH, ed.: *Deutsche Kunst der 20er und 30er Jahre*. München: Bruckmann, 1979. 408 pp., illus., diagrs., bibl.

WEBER, A. PAUL
2689   *A. Paul Weber. Handzeichnungen—Lithographien—1930–1978. Retrospektive zum 85. Geburtstag...* Köln: Rheinland-Verlag, 1978. 347 pp., illus.

2690   SCHARTEL, WERNER, ed.: *Kunst im Widerstand. A. Paul Weber: Das antifaschistische Werk*. Berlin: Elefanten Press, 1977. 140 pp., illus.

2691 WERNER, BRUNO E.: *Die deutsche Plastik der Gegenwart.* Berlin: Rembrandt-Verlag, 1940. 209 pp., illus.

2692 WERNERT, E.: *L'art dans le IIIe Reich. Une tentative d'esthétique dirigée.* Paris: Hartmann, 1936. 144 pp., illus., tabs., diagrs., bibl. (Centre d'Études de Politique étrangère ...).

2693 WULF, JOSEPH: *Die bildenden Künste im Dritten Reich. Eine Dokumentation.* Gütersloh: Mohn, 1963. 413 pp., illus., facsims.

2694 *Zwischen Widerstand und Anpassung. Kunst in Deutschland 1933–1945.* Berlin: Akademie der Künste, 1978. 271 pp., illus. [Exhibition.]

e. Stage and screen

Theatre

2695 ANDERSEN, LALE: *Der Himmel hat viele Farben. Leben mit einem Lied.* Stuttgart: Deutsche Verlags-Anstalt, 1972. 411 pp. [Singer of 'Lili Marleen'.]

2696 BAYERISCHE VERSICHERUNGSKAMMER MÜNCHEN: *Satzung der Versorgungsanstalt der deutschen Bühnen vom 25. Februar 1938. Anhang: 1. Tarifordnung für die deutschen Theater* ... München: 1938. 40 pp.

2697 BIEDRZYNSKI, RICHARD: *Schauspieler, Regisseure, Intendanten.* Heidelberg: Hüthig, 1944. 116 + [90] + xxiii pp., illus., bibl.

2698 *Deutsches Bühnen-Jahrbuch. Theatergeschichtliches Jahr- und Adressbuch.* 44.–55. Jhrg. Berlin: Genossenschaft Deutscher Bühnen-Angehörigen, 1933/44. Publ. yearly, ports. tabs.

EICHBERG, HENNING and others: *Massenspiele, NS-Thingspiel, Arbeiterweihespiel und olympisches Zeremoniell. See* 2516.

2699 *Festspielbuch—Reichsfestspiele Heidelberg 1938.* Schirmherr: Reichsminister Dr. Goebbels. 120 pp., ports. [Incl. 'Spielplan', with cast lists, multilingual summaries, numerous portraits of stage personalities.]

2700 FRAUENFELD, A. B.: *Der Weg zur Bühne.* Berlin: Limpert, 1940. 290 pp.

2701 FRENZEL, ELISABETH: *Judengestalten auf der deutschen Bühne. Ein notwendiger Querschnitt durch 700 Jahre Rollengeschichte.* München: Deutscher Volksverlag, 1942. 272 pp., illus., bibl.

2702 GEIGER, HEINZ: *Widerstand und Mitschuld. Zum deutschen Drama von Brecht bis Weiss.* Düsseldorf: Bertelsmann, 1973. 202 pp., bibl.

2703 GERTH, WERNER: *Die Theaterkritik der liberalistischen Epoche im Vergleich zur nationalsozialistischen Kritik.* Inaugural-Dissertation [pres. to] Universität Leipzig. Borna-Leipzig: Noske, 1936. 105 pp., bibl.

2704 GRAFF, SIGMUND: *Von S.M. zu N.S. Erinnerungen eines Bühnenautors, 1900 bis 1945.* München: Verlag Welsermühl, 1963. 389 pp., illus.

HAUPTMANN, GERHART
2705 *Gerhart Hauptmann zum 80. Geburtstage am 15. November 1942.* Breslau: Schlesien-Verlag, [1942]. 167 pp., illus., facsims., family trees, bibl.

2706 POHL, GERHART: *Bin ich noch in meinem Haus? Die letzten Tage Gerhart Hauptmanns.* Berlin: Lettner, 1953. 114 pp., illus.

2707 HOFFMANN, H., ed.: *Theaterrecht—Bühne und Artistik. Zusammenfassende Darstellung des gesamten Theaterrechts unter Berücksichtigung der Anordnungen der Reichskulturkammer und Reichstheaterkammer sowie der Bestimmungen der Reichsgewerbeordnung nebst Text mit Anmerkungen.* Berlin: Vahlen, 1936. 159 pp.

2708 KETELSEN, UWE-KARSTEN: *Von heroischem Sein und völkischem Tod. Zur Dramatik des Dritten Reiches.* Bonn: Bouvier, 1970. 392 pp., bibl.

2709 KINDERMANN, HEINZ: *Die europäische Sendung des deutschen Theaters.* Wien: Verlag der Ringbuchhandlung, 1944. 57 pp. (Wiener wissenschaftliche Vorträge und Reden, hrsg. von der Universität Wien …).

2710 LÜTH, ERICH: *Hamburger Theater 1933–1945. Ein theatergeschichtlicher Versuch.* Hrsg.: Theatersammlung der Hamburgischen Universität. Einl.: Diedrich Diederichsen. Hamburg: Bueckschmitt, 1962. 95 pp. [Incl. persecution and attempted protection of Jewish artistes.]

2711 MÖLLER, EBERHARD WOLFGANG: *Rothschild siegt bei Waterloo. Ein Schauspiel.* Berlin: Langen & Müller, 1934. 132 pp.

2712 RÜHLE, GÜNTHER: *Zeit und Theater, Band 3: Diktatur und Exil 1933–1945.* Berlin: Propyläen Verlag, [1974]. 874 pp. [Incl. plays by Hanns Johst, Heinrich Zerkaulen, Friedrich Bethge, Erwin Guido Kolbenheyer, Eberhard Wolfgang Möller, Curt Langenbeck, Hans Rehberg, Ferdinand Bruckner, Ernst Toller, Gerhart Hauptmann, Günther Weisenborn.]

2713 SCHLÖSSER, RAINER: *Das Volk und seine Bühne. Bemerkungen zum Aufbau des deutschen Theaters.* Berlin: Langen & Müller, 1935. 83 pp.

2714 SCHLÖTERMANN, HEINZ: *Das deutsche Weltkriegsdrama 1919–1937. Eine wertkritische Analyse.* Würzburg: Triltsch, 1944. 158 pp., bibl. ('Das Nationaltheater', Schriftenreihe des Theaterwissenschaftlichen Instituts der Friedrich-Schiller-Universität Jena).

2715 STRÜCKER, WILHELM: *Der Antisemit. Ein deutsches Trauerspiel in drei Aufzügen. Für Freilichtbühne und Theater.* Radolfzell a. Bodensee: Dressler, 1935. 61 pp.

2716 WULF, JOSEPH: *Theater und Film im Dritten Reich. Eine Dokumentation.* Gütersloh: Mohn, 1964. 437 pp., illus., facsims.

Cinema

2717 ALBRECHT, GERD: *Nationalsozialistische Filmpolitik. Eine soziologische Untersuchung über die Spielfilme des Dritten Reichs.* Stuttgart: Enke, 1969. 562 pp., tabs., bibl., list of films.

2718 BAUER, ALFRED: *Deutscher Spielfilm-Almanach 1929–1950.* Berlin: Filmblätter-Verlag, 1950. xxix + 856 pp., mimeog.

2719 BECKER, WOLFGANG: *Film und Herrschaft. Organisationsprinzipien und Organisationsstrukturen der nationalsozialistischen Filmpropaganda.* Berlin: Spiess, 1973. 297 pp., bibl.

2720 BELACH, HELGA, comp.: *Wir tanzen um die Welt. Deutsche Revuefilme 1933–1945.* München: Hanser, 1979. 271 pp.

2721 CADARS, PIERRE & COURTADE, FRANCIS: *Le cinéma nazi.* [Paris?]: Losfeld, 1972. 397 pp., illus., bibl., list of films.

2722 COURIER DU CENTRE: *Les dessous du cinéma allemand.* Paris: Guillempt & de Lamothe, [1934?]. 82 pp., illus.

2723 GEORGE, J. R.: *Jud Süss. Roman.* Berlin: Ufa-Buchverlag, 1941. 196 pp., illus. (Mit 16 Bildern aus dem gleichnamigen Terra-Film).

2724 GUCKES, EMIL: *Der Tonfilm als Werbemittel in Deutschland.* Dissertation [pres. to] Leopold-Franzens-Universität zu Innsbruck. 1937. 170 pp., graphs, tabs., bibl.

2725 HAMMENHÖG, W.: *Pettersson & Bendel. Roman.* Leipzig: Zschäpe-Verlag, 1935. 448 pp. [Transl. from the Swedish. This book was made into an anti-Semitic film, although the original was intended to be comic rather than anti-Semitic.]

HARLAN, VEIT

2726 HARLAN, VEIT: *Im Schatten meiner Filme. Selbstbiographie.* Hrsg.: H. C. Opfermann. Gütersloh: Mohn, 1966. 290 pp., illus., facsims., list of films.

2727 PARDO, HERBERT & SCHIFFNER, SIEGFRIED: *Jud Süss. Historisches und juristisches Material zum Fall Veit Harlan.* Mitarb.: H. G. van Dam, Norbert Wollheim. Hamburg: Auerdruck, 1949. 70 pp.

2728 HOLLSTEIN, DOROTHEA: *Antisemitische Filmpropaganda. Die Darstellung des Juden im nationalsozialistischen Spielfilm.* München-Pullach: Verlag Dokumentation, 1971. 367 pp., tab., bibl., list of films with casts. [Incl. abridged script of 'Jud Süss'.]

2729 HULL, DAVID STEWART: *Film in the Third Reich. A study of the German cinema 1933–1945.* Berkeley, Calif.: University of California Press, 1969. 291 pp., illus., tabs., bibl. [Incl. detailed accounts of the films 'Jud Süss' and 'Der ewige Jude'.]

2730 KOCH, HEINRICH & BRAUNE, HEINRICH: *Von deutscher Filmkunst. Gehalt und Gestalt.* Berlin: Scherping, 1943. [108 pp.], illus.

2731 KRACAUER, SIEGFRIED: *From Caligari to Hitler: a psychological history of the German film.* Princeton, N.J.: Princeton University Press, 1974. xii + 361 pp., illus., bibl. [First publ. 1947.]

2732 LEISER, ERWIN: *'Deutschland, erwache!' Propaganda im Film des Dritten Reiches.* Reinbek b. Hamburg: Rowohlt, 1968. 155 pp., illus., facsim., bibl.,

217

list of films. [English version: *Nazi cinema*. London: Secker & Warburg, 1974.]

2733   MANVELL, ROGER & FRAENKEL, HEINRICH: *The German cinema*. London: Dent, 1971. xv + 159 pp., illus., bibl., list of films. [Incl. (Chs. 4, 5): 'The film in Nazi Germany'.]

2734   NEUMANN, CARL and others: *Film-'Kunst', Film-Kohn, Film-Korruption. Ein Streifzug durch vier Film-Jahrzehnte.* [By] Carl Neumann, Curt Belling, Hans-Walther Betz. Berlin: Scherping, 1937. 172 pp., illus., bibl.

RIEFENSTAHL, LENI. *See* Index.

2734a   SAKKARA, MICHELE, ed.: *Die grosse Zeit des deutschen Films. Zeitgeschichte im Bild.* Leoni am Starnberger See: Druffel, 1980. 184 pp., illus.

2735   SANDER, A. U.: *Jugend und Film.* Berlin: Eher, 1944. 160 pp., tabs., bibl., lists of films.

2736   SPIKER, JÜRGEN: *Film und Kapital. Der Weg der deutschen Filmwirtschaft zum nationalsozialistischen Einheitskonzern.* Berlin: Spiess, 1975. 315 pp., tabs.

2737   TOEPLITZ, JERZY: *Geschichte des Films. VI. Teil: 1934–1939.* München: Rogner & Bernhard, 1980. 463 pp., illus., bibl. [Transl. from the Polish. Incl.: 'Der Film im Zeichen des Hakenkreuzes', pp. 250–286.]

2738   WETZEL, KRAFT & HAGEMANN, PETER A.: *Liebe, Tod und Technik. Kino des Phantastischen 1933–1945* [and] *Wilfried Basse. Notizen zu einem fast vergessenen Klassiker des deutschen Dokumentarfilms.* Mit Beiträgen von Rudolf Arnheim, Gertrud T. Basse, Friedrich Terveen. Hrsg.: Stiftung Deutscher Kinemathek. Berlin: Spiess, 1977. 97 pp., illus., list of films.

4.   SCIENCE, TECHNOLOGY AND SCHOLARSHIP

2739   BAEUMLER, ALFRED: *Männerbund und Wissenschaft.* Berlin: Junker & Dünnhaupt, 1943. 169 pp.

2740   GREGORY, RICHARD: *Science in chains.* London: Macmillan, 1941. 32 pp.

2741   HOFER, WALTHER, ed.: *Wissenschaft im totalen Staat.* Mit Beiträgen von H. J. Lieber, Klaus Meyer, László Révész, Joseph M. Bochénski, Siegfried Müller-Markus, Hans Nachtsheim, Gerhard Möbus, Walther Hofer. München: Nymphenburger Verlagshandlung, 1964. 231 pp.

2742   JÜRGENS, ADOLF, ed.: *Ergebnisse deutscher Wissenschaft. Eine bibliographische Auswahl aus der deutschen wissenschaftlichen Literatur der Jahre 1933–1938.* Essen: Essener Verlagsanstalt, 1939. 782 pp.

2742a   MEHRTENS, HERBERT & RICHTER, STEFFEN, eds.: *Naturwissenschaft, Technik und NS-Ideologie. Beiträge zur Wissenschaftsgeschichte des Dritten Reichs.* Frankfurt a.M.: Suhrkamp, 1980. 298 pp., illus., diagrs., bibl.

2743   MÜLLER, GERHARD: *Ernst Krieck und die nationalsozialistische Wissenschaftsreform. Motive und Tendenzen einer Wissenschaftslehre und Hoch-*

schulreform im Dritten Reich. Weinheim/Basel: Beltz, 1978. xii + 615 pp. [From a thesis entitled *Die Wissenschaftslehre Ernst Kriecks*, Freiburg i.Br. 1974.]

2744 NEEDHAM, JOSEPH: *The Nazi attack on international science*. London: Watts, 1941. 47 pp., tabs.

2745 RHEINISCHE   FRIEDRICH-WILHELMS-UNIVERSITÄT: *Neuerscheinungen der deutschen wissenschaftlichen Literatur von 1939–1945. Teil II: Auswahl von wichtigen Lehrbüchern und Monographien aus den Gebieten der Geisteswissenschaften, der Technik und Landwirtschaft*. Bonn: Dummler, 1946. 131 pp.

2746 SALLER, KARL: *Die Rassenlehre des Nationalsozialismus in Wissenschaft und Propaganda*. Darmstadt: Progress-Verlag, 1961. 180 pp., bibl. [Author wrote on racial matters during the Third Reich.]

2747 SIMON, LESLIE A.: *German research in World War II. An analysis of the conduct of research*. New York: Wiley, 1947. 218 pp., illus.

Economics

2748 *Bericht über den Tag der Deutschen Wirtschaftswissenschaft 1938. Leistungssteigerung der deutschen Wirtschaft*. Stuttgart: Kohlhammer, 1938. 310 pp. (Schriften der Deutschen Wirtschaftswissenschaftlichen Gesellschaft).

2749 WISKEMANN, ERWIN: *Die neue Wirtschaftswissenschaft*. Berlin: Junker & Dünnhaupt, 1936. 86 pp.

History

2750 HEIBER, HELMUT: *Walter Frank und sein Reichsinstitut für Geschichte des neuen Deutschlands*. Stuttgart: Deutsche Verlags-Anstalt, 1966. 1273 pp., tabs., bibl.

2751 HOLTZMANN, WALTHER & RITTER, GERHARD: *Die deutsche Geschichtswissenschaft im Zweiten Weltkrieg. Bibliographie des historischen Schrifttums deutscher Autoren 1939–1945*. Hrsg. im Auftr. des Verbandes der Historiker Deutschlands und der Monumenta Germaniae Historica. Marburg/Lahn: Simon, 1951. 512 pp.

2752 WERNER, KARL FERDINAND: *Das NS-Geschichtsbild und die deutsche Geschichtswissenschaft*. Stuttgart: Kohlhammer, 1967. 123 pp.

Philosophy

2753 GRUNSKY, HANS ALFRED: *Der Einbruch des Judentums in die Philosophie*. Berlin: Junker & Dünnhaupt, 1937. 36 pp. (Schriften der Deutschen Hochschule für Politik).

2754 HAERING, THEODOR, ed.: *Das Deutsche in der deutschen Philosophie*. 2. Aufl. Stuttgart: Kohlhammer, 1942. viii + 487 pp.

2755 RIECKE, HEINZ: *Der Rassegedanke und die neuere Philosophie.* Leipzig: Klein, 1935. 32 pp.

2756 SCHWARZ, HERMANN: *Grundzüge einer Geschichte der artdeutschen Philosophie.* Berlin: Junker & Dünnhaupt, 1937. 80 pp. (Schriften der Deutschen Hochschule für Politik).

2757 TYROWICZ, STANISŁAW: *Swiatło wiedzy zdeprawowanej. Idee niemieckieh socjologii i filozofii, 1933–1945* [Light on a depraved science—German sociology and philosophy, 1933–1945]. Poznań: Instytut Zachodni, 1970. 185 pp., bibl., summary in German.

Physics *See* Index (Professors).

Psychology

2758 EICKSTEDT, EGON Frhr. von: *Grundlagen der Rassenpsychologie.* Stuttgart: Enke, 1936. 163 pp., tabs.

Technology

2759 HEISS, RUDOLF, ed.: *Die Sendung des Ingenieurs im neuen Staat.* Berlin: VDI-Verlag, 1934. 134 pp., diagr.

2760 LUDWIG, KARL-HEINZ: *Technik und Ingenieure im Dritten Reich.* Düsseldorf: Droste, 1974. 544 pp., tabs., bibl.

2761 NONNENBRUCH, FRITZ: *Politik, Technik und Geist.* München: Hoheneichen Verlag, 1939. 527 pp.

2762 SCHRÖTER, MANFRED: *Deutscher Geist in der Technik.* Köln: Schaffstein, 1935. 65 pp.

5. PRESS

2763 ABEL, KARL-DIETRICH: *Presselenkung im NS-Staat. Eine Studie zur Geschichte der Publizistik in der nationalsozialistischen Zeit.* Vorw.: Hans Herzfeld. Berlin: Colloquium Verlag, 1968. 172 pp., facsim., bibl.

2764 D'ALQUEN, GUNTER, ed.: *Auf Hieb und Stich. Stimmen zur Zeit am Wege einer deutschen Zeitung.* Berlin: Eher, 1937. 326 pp.

2765 DAMMERT, RUDOLF: *Zeitung—unser täglicher Hausgast.* Leipzig: Voigtländer, 1938. 80 pp.

2766 DOBERS, ERNST: *Die Zeitung im Dienste der Rassenkunde.* Leipzig: Klinkhardt, 1936. 48 pp., illus., tabs., graph. (Neuland in der Deutschen Schule).

ECKART, DIETRICH
2767 GILLESPIE, WILLIAM: *Dietrich Eckart. An introduction for the English-speaking student.* 2nd ed. Houston, Tex.: [priv. pr.], 1976. iv + 34 pp., illus., facsims., bibl.

2768 GRUEN, WILHELM: *Dietrich Eckart als Publizist. I. Teil: Einführung. Mit einer Ahnentafel bis 1285 und einer Dietrich Eckart-Bibliographie von 1868 bis 1938.* München: Hoheneichen-Verlag, 1941. 206 pp., port., bibl.

2769 PLEWNIA, MARGARETE: *Auf dem Weg zu Hitler. Der 'völkische' Publizist Dietrich Eckart*. Bremen: Schünemann, 1970. 155 pp., illus., facsims., bibl. (Studien zur Publizistik, Bremer Reihe: Deutsche Presseforschung).

2770 ROSENBERG, ALFRED, ed.: *Dietrich Eckart. Ein Vermächtnis*. 3. Aufl. München: Eher, 1935. 252 pp., port. [Copyright 1928. A sixth ed. appeared in 1940.]

2771 ECKHARDT, HEINZ-WERNER: *Die Frontzeitungen des deutschen Heeres, 1939–1945*. Wien: Braumüller, 1975. xi + 176 pp., map, tabs., diagr., bibl.

2772 EKSTEINS, MODRISS: *The limits of reason. The German democratic press and the collapse of Weimar democracy*. London: Oxford University Press, 1975. xi + 337 pp., bibl.

2773 GROSSER, ALFRED: *Hitler, la presse et la naissance d'une dictature*. Paris: Colin, 1959. 262 pp., illus., bibl.

2774 GÜNSCHE, KARL-LUDWIG: *Phasen der Gleichschaltung. Stichtags-Analysen deutscher Zeitungen 1933–1938*. Osnabrück: Fromm, 1970. 95 pp., bibl.

2775 HAGEMANN, JÜRGEN: *Die Presselenkung im Dritten Reich*. Bonn: Bouvier, 1970. 398 pp., bibl. (pp. 323–373). [Extensive notes after ea. ch.]

2776 HALE, ORON J.: *The captive press in the Third Reich*. Princeton, N.J.: Princeton University Press, 1964. 353 pp., illus., tabs., bibl.

2777 [HUGENBERG, ALFRED] LEOPOLD, JOHN A.: *Alfred Hugenberg. The radical nationalist campaign against the Weimar Republic*. New Haven, Conn.: Yale University Press, 1977. xvi + 298 pp., illus., bibl.

2778 *Jahrbuch für vorbildliche Anzeigenwerbung im nationalsozialistischen Staate*. Hrsg.: A[lfons] Brugger. Illus., facsims., diagrs.
1935/36. Dresden: Pietzsch, 1935. 252 pp.
1938/39. Die Anzeige in der Wirtschaftswerbung. Berlin: Gohlicke, 1938. 329 pp.
[No others published.]

2779 *Journalismus ist eine Mission. Bericht vom 1. Kongress der Union Nationaler Journalisten-Verband, Venedig 1942*. Wien: Palais Schönborn, [1942]. 210 pp. (Terramare Institut).

2780 KAISER, FRIEDHELM: *Die Zeitung als Mittel der Nationalerziehung*. Leipzig: Noske, 1934. 71 pp., facsims., bibl.

2781 KLUTENTRETER, WILLY: *Presse und Volksgemeinschaft. Eine soziologisch-zeitungswissenschaftliche Studie über das Verhältnis von Presse, Volk und Staat in Deutschland*. Inaugural-Dissertation [pres. to] Universität Köln. 1937. 68 pp., bibl.

2782 KOERNER, RALF RICHARD: *Die publizistische Behandlung der Österreichfrage und die Anschlussvorbereitungen der Tagespresse des Dritten Reiches 1933–1938*. Inaugural-Dissertation [pres. at] Münster. 1956. 396 pp.

2783 KOSZYCK, KURT: *Deutsche Presse 1914–1945. Geschichte der deutschen Presse, Teil III.* Berlin: Colloquium Verlag, 1972. 587 pp., bibl. (pp. 502–566).

LAWS ON THE PRESS

2784 BEYER, RUDOLF, ed.: *Hitlergesetze IV. Schriftleitergesetz, Wirtschaftswerbungsgesetz, mit den Durchführungsverordnungen. Rabattgesetze. Sämtliche Gesetze mit den amtlichen Begründungen. Textausgabe.* Leipzig: Reclam, 1933.

2785 REICHSVERBAND DER DEUTSCHEN ZEITUNGSVERLEGER: *Pressehandbuch. Gesetze, Anordnungen, Erlasse, Bekanntmachungen zusammengestellt und erläutert nach den Bedürfnissen der Praxis.* Berlin: 1938. [Approx. 500 pp.]

2786 SCHRIEBER, KARL-FRIEDRICH & WILLI, ANTON, eds.: *Presserecht. Sammlung der für die Reichspressekammer geltenden Gesetze und Verordnungen, der amtlichen Anordnungen und Bekanntmachungen der Reichskulturkammer und der Reichspressekammer.* Berlin: Junker & Dünnhaupt, 1936. 115 pp.

2787 LEHMANN, ERNST HERBERT: *Die Zeitschrift im Kriege.* Berlin-Charlottenburg: Lorentz, [1939]. 81 pp., facsims.

2788 LÜDDECKE, THEODOR: *Die Tageszeitung als Mittel der Staatsführung.* Hamburg: Hanseatische Verlagsanstalt, 1933. 216 pp.

2789 MOLL, HELGA: *Der Kampf um die Weimarer Republik 1932/33 in der Berliner demokratischen Presse. Für und wider das 'System'. 'Berliner Tageblatt', 'Vossische Zeitung', 'Germania' und 'Vorwärts'.* Dissertation [pres. at] Wien. 1962. 270 pp.

2790 MÜNSTER, HANS A.: *Geschichte der deutschen Presse in ihren Grundzügen dargestellt.* Leipzig: Bibliographisches Institut, 1941. 150 pp.

2791 MÜNSTER, HANS A.: *Zeitung und Politik. Eine Einführung in die Zeitungswissenschaft.* Leipzig: Noske, 1935. 160 pp.

2792 *Presse in Fesseln. Eine Schilderung des NS-Pressetrusts. Gemeinschaftsarbeit des Verlages auf Grund authentischen Materials.* Berlin: Verlag Archiv und Kartei, 1947. 275 pp., ports. facsims., tabs., bibl.

2793 [PRESSE-KAMERADSCHAFTSLAGER] *Das erste deutsche Presse-Kameradschaftslager, Ostern 1934 in Wiesbaden, von der Gauleitung Hessen-Nassau der NSDAP mit rund 200 Teilnehmern aus allen Sparten des Journalismus' und der Pressearbeit innerhalb der Bewegung durchgeführt.* 136 pp., illus., facsims.

2794 [REICHSPRESSESTELLE] DRESLER, ADOLF: *Die Reichspressestelle der NSDAP.* 2. verm. und verb. Aufl. Berlin: de Gruyter, 1937. 15 pp., ports.

2795 REICHSVERBAND DER DEUTSCHEN PRESSE and others: *Richtlinien für redaktionelle Hinweise in Tageszeitungen, Zeitschriften und Korrespondenzen.* Hrsg. in Zusammenwirkung mit dem Werberat der Deutschen Wirtschaft und der Reichspressekammer. [Berlin]: 1935. 28 pp.

2796 SÄNGER, FRITZ: *Politik der Täuschungen. Missbrauch der Presse im Dritten Reich. Weisungen, Informationen, Notizen, 1933–1939.* Wien: Europa Verlag, 1975. 430 pp.

2797 SÖSEMANN, BERND: *Das Ende der Weimarer Republik in der Kritik demokratischer Publizisten. Theodor Wolff, Ernst Feder, Julius Elban, Leopold Schwarzschild.* Berlin: Colloquium Verlag, 1976. 251 pp., bibl.

2798 STEGMÜLLER, FRANZ: *Das Recht der Meinungsäusserung im nationalsozialistischen Staat.* Dissertation [pres. to] Ludwigs-Universität Giessen. 1938. 193 pp., bibl.

2799 STÖCKER, HANS and others, eds.: *Zwischen den Zeilen. Ein Beitrag zur Geschichte des Widerstandes der deutschen bürgerlichen Presse gegen die Diktatur des Nationalsozialismus.* Unter Benutzung des Verlagsarchivs hrsg. von Hans Stöcker, Heinz Greeven, Peter Herbrand. Düsseldorf: Droste, 1948. 55 pp.

2800 STOREK, HENNING: *Dirigierte Öffentlichkeit. Die Zeitung als Herrschaftsmittel in den Anfangsjahren der nationalsozialistischen Regierung.* Opladen: Westdeutscher Verlag, 1972. 156 pp., bibl.

2801 STROTHMANN, DIETRICH: *Nationalsozialistische Literaturpolitik. Ein Beitrag zur Publizistik im Dritten Reich.* 2. verb. und mit einem Register ausgest. Aufl. Bonn: Bouvier, 1963. 507 pp., tabs., bibl.

2802 SÜNDERMANN, HELMUT: *Tagesparolen. Deutsche Presseweisungen 1939–1945. Hitlers Propaganda und Kriegsführung.* Aus dem Nachlass hrsg. von Gerd Sudholt. Leoni am Starnberger See: Druffel, 1973. 320 pp.

2803 SÜNDERMANN, HELMUT: *Der Weg zum deutschen Journalismus. Hinweise für die Berufswahl junger Nationalsozialisten.* Vorw.: Reichspressechef Reichsleiter [Otto] Dietrich. München: Eher, 1938. 35 pp., illus.

2804 WALCHNER, SIEGFRIED: *Die Neuordnung der deutschen Presse und ihre wirtschaftliche Organisation.* Dissertation [pres. to] Ludwigs-Universität zu Giessen. 1937. 71 pp., map, diagrs., graphs, tabs.

2805 WESTERNHAGEN, A. E.: *Zeitungs-Titanen. Ein Roman... Vielleicht mehr.* Dresden: Müller, 1938. 224 pp.

2806 WULF, JOSEPH: *Presse und Funk im Dritten Reich. Eine Dokumentation.* Gütersloh: Mohn, 1964. 390 pp., illus., facsims.

Religious press

2807 ALTMEYER, KARL ALOYS: *Katholische Presse unter NS-Diktatur. Die katholischen Zeitungen und Zeitschriften Deutschlands in den Jahren 1933 bis 1945. Dokumentation.* Berlin: Morus-Verlag, 1962. 204 pp., illus., tabs., diagrs., bibl.

2808 EBERLE, JOSEPH: *Erlebnisse und Bekenntnisse. Ein Kapitel Lebenserinnerungen des früheren Herausgebers der Zeitschriften 'Das Neue Reich' und 'Schönere Zukunft'.* Stuttgart: Schwabenverlag, 1947. 104 pp.

223

2809 GOTTO, KLAUS: *Die Wochenzeitung Junge Front/Michael. Eine Studie zum katholischen Selbstverständnis und zum Verhalten der jungen Kirche gegenüber dem Nationalsozialismus.* Mainz: Matthias-Grünewald-Verlag, 1970. xxiv + 250 pp., bibl. (Veröffentlichungen der Kommission für Zeitgeschichte ...).

2810 HOFMANN, JOSEF: *Journalist in Republik, Diktatur und Besatzungszeit. Erinnerungen 1916–1947.* Bearb.: Rudolf Morsey. Mainz: Matthias-Grünewald-Verlag, 1977. 236 pp., port. (Veröffentlichungen der Kommission für Zeitgeschichte ...).

2811 HÜSGEN, MANFRED: *Die Bistumsblätter in Niedersachsen während der nationalsozialistischen Zeit. Ein Beitrag zur Geschichte der katholischen Publizistik im Dritten Reich.* Hildesheim: Lax, 1975. vii + 380 pp., bibl.

2812 STOLL, GERHARD E.: *Die evangelische Zeitschriftenpresse im Jahre 1933.* Witten: Luther-Verlag, 1963. 300 pp., illus., facsims., bibl.

Individual journals

'DER ANGRIFF'
2812a BRAMSTED, ERNEST: 'Goebbels and his newspaper "Der Angriff"'. [In] Max Beloff, ed.: *On the track of tyranny.* Pp. 45–65. *See* 3208.

2813 KESSEMEIER, CARIN: *Der Leitartikler Goebbels in den NS-Organen 'Der Angriff' und 'Das Reich'.* Münster: Fahle, 1967. 348 pp., illus., facsims., tabs., bibl.

2814 RAHM, HANS-GEORG: *'Der Angriff' 1927–1930. Der nationalsozialistische Typ der Kampfzeitung.* Berlin: Eher, 1939. 228 pp., illus., bibl.

'BERLINER ILLUSTRIRTE ZEITUNG'
2815 LUFT, FRIEDRICH, ed.: *Facsimile Querschnitt durch die Berliner Illustrirte.* Mitarb.: Alexander von Baeyer. München: Scherz, 1965. 207 pp.

'BERLINER LOKALANZEIGER'
2816 SCHMALING, CHRISTIAN: *Der Berliner Lokal-Anzeiger als Beispiel einer Vorbereitung des Nationalsozialismus.* Inaugural-Dissertation [pres. to] Freie Universität Berlin. 1968. 175 pp., bibl.

'BERLINER TAGEBLATT'
2817 BOVERI, MARGRET: *Wir lügen alle. Eine Hauptstadtzeitung unter Hitler.* Olten: Walter, 1965. 744 pp.

'DEUTSCHE RUNDSCHAU'
2818 MAUERSBERGER, VOLKER: *Rudolf Pechel und die 'Deutsche Rundschau'. Eine Studie zur konservativ-revolutionäre Publizistik in der Weimarer Republik 1918–1933.* Bremen: Schünemann, 1971. 344 pp., facsim., bibl.

2819 MIRBT, KARL WOLFGANG: *Methoden publizistischen Widerstandes im Dritten Reich. Nachgewiesen an der 'Deutschen Rundschau' Rudolf Pechels.* Inaugural-Dissertation [pres. to] Freie Universität Berlin. 1958. 367 pp.

2820 PECHEL, RUDOLF: *Zwischen den Zeilen. Der Kampf einer Zeitschrift für Freiheit und Recht 1932–1942. Aufsätze.* Einf.: Werner Bergengruen. Wiesentheid (Ufr.): Doemersche Verlagsanstalt, 1948. 348 pp., illus.

'DEUTSCHE ZUKUNFT'

2821 RENKEN, GERD: *Die 'Deutsche Zukunft' und der Nationalsozialismus. Ein Beitrag zur Geschichte des geistigen Widerstandes in den Jahren 1933–1940.* Inaugural-Dissertation [pres. to] Freie Universität Berlin. 1970. 301 pp., facsims., bibl.

'FRANKFURTER ZEITUNG'

2822 HEINRICHSDORFF, WOLFF: *Die liberale Opposition in Deutschland seit dem 30. Januar 1933 (dargestellt an der Entwicklung der 'Frankfurter Zeitung'). Versuch einer Systematik der politischen Kritik.* Hamburg: Evert, 1937. 60 pp., bibl.

2823 TAUCHER, FRANZ: *Frankfurter Jahre.* Wien: Europaverlag, 1977. 212 pp.

2824 WERBER, RUDOLF: *Die 'Frankfurter Zeitung' und ihr Verhältnis zum Nationalsozialismus untersucht an Hand von Beispielen aus den Jahren 1932–1943. Ein Beitrag zur Methodik der publizistischen Camouflage im Dritten Reich.* Inaugural-Dissertation [pres. to] Friedrich-Wilhelms-Universität zu Bonn. 1965. 230 pp., bibl.

'HAMBURGER TAGEBLATT'

2825 *Ein Gedanke wird Tat. Vom Wachsen und Werden einer nationalsozialistischen Tageszeitung.* Hamburg: Hamburger Tageblatt, 1940. 82 pp., illus.

'HOCHLAND'

2826 ACKERMANN, KONRAD: *Der Widerstand der Monatsschrift Hochland gegen den Nationalsozialismus.* München: Kösel-Verlag, 1965. 211 pp., facsims., bibl.

'DAS INNERE REICH'

2827 MALLMANN, MARION: *'Das Innere Reich'. Analyse einer konservativen Kulturzeitschrift im Dritten Reich.* Bonn: Bouvier, 1978. 327 pp., bibl.

'KRACAUER ZEITUNG'

2828 *Almanach. Deutsches Wort im Osten. Ein Jahr Krakauer Zeitung.* Krakau: Zeitungsverlag Krakau-Warschau, 1941. 334 pp., illus.

'NATIONAL-ZEITUNG'

2829 *Mit der N.Z. durch die Welt.* Essen: National-Zeitung, 1937. 128 pp., illus., maps. (Jhrg. 8).

'NEUE PREUSSISCHE ZEITUNG'

2830 TREUDE, BURKHARD: *Konservative Presse und Nationalsozialismus. Inhaltsanalyse der 'Neuen Preussischen (Kreuz-) Zeitung' am Ende der Weimarer Republik.* Bochum: Brockmeyer, 1975. 195 pp., diagrs., facsims., bibl.

'NEUE RUNDSCHAU'

2831 LOERKE, OSKAR: *Literarische Aufsätze aus der 'Neuen Rundschau' 1909–1941.* Hrsg.: Reinhard Tgahrt. Heidelberg: Lambert Schneider, 1967. 474 pp.

2832 SCHWARZ, FALK: 'Literarisches Zeitgespräch im Dritten Reich, dargestellt an der Zeitschrift "Neue Rundschau" '. [In] *Archiv für Geschichte des Buchwesens,* Bd. XII. Frankfurt a.M.: Buchhändler-Vereinigung, 1972. Pp. 1282–1483, tabs., bibl.

'DAS REICH'
2833 MARTENS, ERIKA: *Zum Beispiel—Das Reich. Zur Phänomenologie der Presse im totalitären Regime.* Köln: Verlag Wissenschaft und Politik, 1972. 294 pp., bibl.

2834 MÜLLER, HANS DIETER, ed.: *Facsimile Querschnitt durch Das Reich.* Einl.: Harry Pross. München: Scherz, 1964. 207 pp.

'DAS SCHWARZE KORPS'
2835 HEIBER, HELMUT & KOTZE, HILDEGARD VON: *Facsimile Querschnitt durch Das Schwarze Korps.* München: Scherz, 1968. 207 pp., illus., facsims.

2836 MAURER, MONICA: *Pressepolitik und Pressekritik der SS-Zeitung 'Das Schwarze Korps'. Ein Beitrag zur Pressegeschichte im Dritten Reich.* München: 1967. 97 + 6 pp., bibl. Mimeog.

2837 SCHILLING, HEINAR: *Weltanschauliche Betrachtungen. Zwanzig Aufsätze aus dem 'Schwarzen Korps'.* Braunschweig: Vieweg, 1938. 168 pp.

'SIGNAL'
2838 DOLLINGER, HANS, ed.: *Facsimile Querschnitt durch Signal.* Einl.: Willi Boelcke. München: Scherz, 1969. 207 pp., illus., facsims.

2839 MAYER, S. L., ed.: *Signal. Hitler's wartime picture magazine.* London: Hamlyn, 1978/79. Illus., maps.
1: *Years of triumph—1940–42.* Publ. 1978. 192 pp.
2: *Years of retreat—1943–44.* Publ. 1979. 192 pp.

2839a OBERKOMMANDO DER WEHRMACHT: *Signale.* [Berlin: 1945?]. 278 pp., illus. [Anthology of articles and pictures.]

'DER STÜRMER'
2840 HAHN, FRED: *Lieber Stürmer. Leserbriefe an das NS-Kampfblatt 1924 bis 1945. Eine Dokumentation aus dem Leo-Baeck-Institut, New York.* Bearb. der deutschen Ausg. von Günther Wagenlehner. Stuttgart: Seewald, 1978. 263 pp., illus., facsims.

'VÖLKISCHER BEOBACHTER'
2841 FRIND, SIGRID: *Die Sprache als Propagandainstrument in der Publizistik des Dritten Reiches, untersucht an Hitlers 'Mein Kampf' und der Kriegsjahrgängen des 'Völkischen Beobachters'.* Inaugural-Dissertation [pres. to] Freie Universität Berlin. Berlin: Ernst-Reuter-Gesellschaft, 1964. 193 pp.

2842 KÖHLER, GERHARD: *Kunstanschauung und Kunstkritik in der nationalsozialistischen Presse. Die Kritik im Feuilleton des 'Völkischen Beobachters' 1920–1933.* Inaugural-Dissertation [pres. to] Ludwig-Maximilians-Universität zu München. München: Eher, 1937. 269 pp., graph, tabs.

2843 KOLLER, HELLMUT: *Die nationalsozialistische Wirtschaftsidee im 'Völkischen Beobachter'.* Inaugural-Dissertation [pres. to] Ludwig-Maximilians-Universität zu München. München: Eher, 1939. 175 + 8 pp., graph, facsims., tabs., bibl.

226

2844 NOLLER, SONJA & KOTZE, HILDEGARD VON, eds.: *Facsimile Querschnitt durch den Völkischen Beobachter*. München: Scherz, 1967. 207 pp., illus.

2845 SCHWARZ, ROBERT: *'Sozialismus' der Propaganda. Das Werben des 'Völkischen Beobachters' um die österreichische Arbeiterschaft 1938/39*. Einl.: Gerhard Botz: 'Ideologie und soziale Wirklichkeit des "nationalen Sozialismus" in der "Ostmark" '. Wien: Europaverlag, 1975. 159 pp., illus., facsims., bibl. (Ludwig Boltzmann Institut für Geschichte der Arbeiterbewegung).

2846 STRICKNER, HERBERT: *Die geschichtliche Entwicklung der Sportberichterstattung und des Sportteils im 'Völkischen Beobachter', 1920–1936*. Zeulenroda: Sporn, 1938. 108 pp., chart.

6. RADIO

2847 DEUTSCHES RUNDFUNKARCHIV: *Tondokumente zur Zeitgeschichte 1939–1945*. Zusammengest. und bearb. von Walter Roller. Frankfurt a.M.: 1975. ix + 294 pp.

2848 DILLER, ANSGAR: *Der Frankfurter Rundfunk 1923–1945 unter besonderer Berücksichtigung der Zeit des Nationalsozialismus*. Inaugural-Dissertation [pres. to] Johann Wolfgang Goethe-Universität zu Frankfurt a.M. 1975. 392 pp., bibl.

2849 GOEBBELS, JOSEPH: *Nationalsozialistischer Rundfunk*. München: Eher, 1935. 15 pp.

2850 GOEDECKE, HEINZ & KRUG, WILHELM: *Wir beginnen das Wunschkonzert für die Wehrmacht*. Geleitw.: Alfred-Ingemar Berndt. 2. Aufl. Berlin: Nibelungen-Verlag, 1940. 224 pp., illus., facsims.

2851 HADAMOVSKY, EUGEN: *Dein Rundfunk. Das Rundfunkbuch für alle Volksgenossen*. München: Eher, 1934. 123 pp.

2852 *Künstler des Rundfunks. Ein Nachschlagewerk für Funk, Theater, Film, Kleinkunst, Podium*. Berlin: Limpert, 1938. 668 pp., ports.

2853 LERG, WINFRIED B. & STEININGER, ROLF: *Rundfunk und Politik 1923 bis 1973. Beiträge zur Rundfunkforschung*. Berlin: Spiess, 1975. 484 pp., diagrs., tabs.

2854 POHLE, HEINZ: *Der Rundfunk als Instrument der Politik. Zur Geschichte des deutschen Rundfunks von 1923–1938*. Hamburg: Hans Bredow-Institut, 1955. 480 pp. (Wissenschaftliche Schriftenreihe für Rundfunk und Fernsehen).

2855 REICHS-RUNDFUNKGESELLSCHAFT: *Reichs-Rundfunk. Entwicklung, Aufbau und Bedeutung*. Berlin: Schröder, 1934. 96 pp., illus., facsims., diagrs., map, tab.

2856 [REICHSRUNDFUNKKAMMER] DRESSLER-ANDRESS, HORST: *Die Reichsrundfunkkammer. Ziele, Leistungen und Organisation*. Berlin: Junker & Dünnhaupt, 1935. 43 pp. (Schriften der Deutschen Hochschule für Politik).

2857 REICHSVERBAND DEUTSCHER RUNDFUNKTEILNEHMER (RDR): *Rundfunk im Aufbruch. Handbuch des deutschen Rundfunks 1934 mit Funkkalender*.

Geleitw.: Dr. Goebbels. Baden: Schauenburg & Lahr, [1933]. 208 pp., illus., diagrs.

2858 RHEIN, EDUARD: *Wunder der Wellen. Rundfunk und Fernsehen dargestellt für Jedermann.* 44.–58. Taus. Berlin: Deutscher Verlag, 1942. 301 pp., illus. [First ed. 1935.]

2859 RIMMELE, LILIAN-DORETTE: *Der Rundfunk in Norddeutschland 1933–1945. Ein Beitrag zur nationalsozialistischen Organisations-, Personal- und Kulturpolitik.* Hamburg: Lüdke, 1977. 241 + 66 pp., bibl.

2860 SENDER FREIES BERLIN: *Darauf kam die Gestapo nicht. Beiträge zum Widerstand im Rundfunk.* Berlin: Haude & Spener, 1966. 87 pp.

2861 THIERFELDER, FRANZ: *Sprachpolitik und Rundfunk.* Berlin: Schenck, 1941. 71 pp.

2862 WAGENFÜHR, KURT: *Rundfunk dem Hörer vorgestellt.* Technische Mitarb.: Gerhard Duvigneau. Leipzig: Voigtländer, 1938. 64 pp., illus., diagrs., map.

2863 WEINBRENNER, HANS-JOACHIM, ed.: *Handbuch des deutschen Rundfunks.* Heidelberg: Vowinckel, 1938/40. Illus., diagrs., tabs.
1938. 332 pp.
1939/40. 336 pp.

WULF, JOSEPH: *Presse und Funk im Dritten Reich. See* 2806.

7. SPORT AND ATHLETICS

2864 BERNETT, HAJO: *Nationalsozialistische Leibeserziehung. Eine Dokumentation ihrer Theorie und Organisation.* Schorndorf b. Stuttgart: Hofmann, 1966. 232 pp., front., bibl.

2865 BERNETT, HAJO: *Sportpolitik im Dritten Reich. Aus den Akten der Reichskanzlei.* Schorndorf b. Stuttgart: Hofmann, 1971. 132 pp., bibl.

2866 BREITMEYER, ARNO & HOFFMANN, P. G., eds.: *Sport und Staat.* Im Auftr. des Reichssportführers unter Mitw. von Alfred Baeumler hrsg. [Hamburg]: Hilfsfond für den Deutschen Sport, 1934. 156 pp., illus. (1. Band).

2867 DEUTSCHE ARBEITSFRONT: *Sportappell der Betriebe 1939. Männer-Ausschreibung, Sportordnung.* [Hamburg]: 1938. 39 pp., reprods. of official forms.

2868 FRIESE, GERNOT: *Anspruch und Wirklichkeit des Sports im Nationalsozialismus.* Ahrensburg b. Hamburg: Czwalina, 1974. 115 + xix pp., bibl.

2869 HAYMANN, LUDWIG: *Deutscher Faustkampf nicht pricefight* [sic]. *Boxen als Rasseproblem.* Vorw.: Max Schmeling. München: Eher, [193–]. 102 pp.

2870 HOFFMANN, HEINRICH, ed.: *Hitler bei dem Deutschen Turn- und Sportfest in Breslau 1938.* München: Hoffmann, 1938. 80 pp., illus.

2871 HOKE, R. J. & SCHMITH, O.: *Grundlagen und Methodik der Leichtathletik. Eine*

Einführung in die Leichtathletik für Studenten und Ärzte. Leipzig: Barth, 1937. 225 pp., illus., diagrs.

2872   JOCH, WINFRIED: *Politische Leibeserziehung und ihre Theorie im national-sozialistischen Deutschland. Voraussetzungen, Begründungszusammenhang, Dokumentation.* Bern: 1976. 249 pp., bibl.

2873   KUNZE, OSKAR, comp.: *Sammlung der Erlasse des Amtes für körperliche Erziehung im Reichsministerium für Wissenschaft, Erziehung und Volksbildung, 1942.* Berlin: Weidmann, 1943. 131 pp., tabs.

2874   LENNAR, ROLF: *Kamerad, auch Du! Ernstes und Heiteres um das SA.-Sportabzeichen.* 1939. 87 pp., illus. (Kampfschriften der Obersten SA.-Führung).

2875   [LEWALD, THEODOR] KRÜGER, ARND: *Theodor Lewald. Sportführer ins Dritte Reich.* Berlin: Bartels & Wernitz, 1975. 144 pp., bibl.

2876   MEUSEL, HEINRICH, ed.: *Körperliche Grundausbildung.* Im Auftr. des Reichssportführers und im Einvernehmen mit der Reichsjugendführung unter Mitw. von Sportlehrern der Reichsakademie für Leibesübungen und des Deutschen Reichsbundes für Leibesübungen. Berlin: Weidmann, 1937. 238 pp., illus., bibl.

2877   MOMSEN, MAX: *Leibeserziehung mit Einschluss des Geländesports.* Osterwieck/Harz: Zickfeldt, 1935. 67 pp.

2878   REICHSJUGENDFÜHRUNG: *Jungmädelsport.* Potsdam: Voggenreiter, 1944. 176 pp., illus. (Mädel im Dienst).

2879   SIMON, HANS and others: *Die Körperkultur in Deutschland von 1917 bis 1945.* [By] Hans Simon, Fritz Jahn, Helga Kluge, Hans Schnürpel, Lothar Skorning, Horst Weder, Günther Wonneberger. Berlin [East]: Sportverlag, 1964. 255 pp., illus. (Geschichte der Körperkultur in Deutschland, Band III).

2880   *Der Sport im Gelände.* Berlin: Bernard & Graefe, 1936. Illus., diagrs.
Teil I: *Das Trainingsbuch für den Erwerb des SA-Sport-Abzeichens.* 123 pp.
Teil II: *Das Handbuch für den Erwerb des SA-Sport-Abzeichens. Anhalt und Winke für den Geländesport-Lehrer.* Bearb. im Auftr. der SA-Sportabzeichen-Hauptstelle.

2881   TIRALA, [LOTHAR] GOTTLIEB: *Sport und Rasse.* Frankfurt a.M.: Bechhold, 1936. 207 pp., illus., diagrs.

2882   WETZEL, HEINZ: *Politische Leibeserziehung. Beiträge zur Formung ihres Bildes.* 2. Aufl. Berlin: Limpert, 1936. 84 pp.

Gymnastics

2883   BENNECKE, HANS-JOACHIM: *Das Dietwesen des Reichsbundes für Leibesübungen. Aufbau, Stellung und Sinngehalt der Leibesübungen innerhalb der Volkskultur des neuen Deutschlands. Inaugural-Dissertation.* Düsseldorf: Dissertations Verlag, 1938. 62 pp.

2884 BUBENDEY, FRIEDRICH: *Jahn. Erkenntnis und Erbe*. 2. Aufl. Berlin: Fritsch, 1943. 102 pp., port.

2885 DEUTSCHE TURNERSCHAFT: *Amtliches Jahrbuch*. 29. Jhrg. Berlin: Limpert, 1935. 247 pp., illus. (Vergangenheit, Gegenwart und Zukunft der Deutschen Turnerschaft).

2886 JAENSCH, WALTHER and others: *Körperformung, Rasse, Seele und Leibesübungen*. Berlin: Metzner, [1936]. Illus., bibls.
   1. Bd.: *Leibesübungen und Körperkonstitution*. 115 pp.
   2. Bd.: *Rasse, Seele und körperliche Erziehung*. 112 pp. [Incl.: Egon von Niederhöffer: 'Rasse, Seele und Leibesübungen', pp. 57–75, bibl.]

2887 MALITZ, BRUNO: *Die Leibesübungen in der nationalsozialistischen Idee*. 2. Aufl. München: Eher, 1934. 70 pp.

2888 MARBY, FRIEDRICH BERNHARD: *Rassische Gymnastik als Aufrassungsweg. 1. Buch*. Gegeben von dem Entdecker und Neuschöpfer der Runen-Gymnastik. Stuttgart: Marby, 1935. 153 pp., illus., diagrs.

2889 MÜNCH, KURT, ed.: *Deutschkunde über Volk, Staat, Leibesübungen. Hilfsbuch für die politische Erziehung in den Vereinen des Deutschen Reichsbundes für Leibesübungen*. 4. Aufl. Berlin: Limpert, 1934. 341 pp. [Also 5th ed. 1935.]

2890 MÜNCH, KURT, ed.: *Vereinsdietwart. Handbuch für die werktätige Arbeit der Dietwarte und Diethelfer in den Vereinen des Deutschen Reichsbundes für Leibesübungen*. Berlin: Limpert, 1936. 383 pp.

2891 [NEUENDORFF, EDMUND] UEBERHORST, H.: *Edmund Neuendorff. Turnführer ins Dritte Reich*. Berlin: Bartel & Wernitz, 1970. 78 pp.

2892 SURÉN, HANS: *Gymnastik der Deutschen—Rassenbewusste Selbsterziehung*. Stuttgart: Franckh, 1935– Illus., diagrs.
   1. Bd.: *Unseres Körpers Schönheit und gymnastische Schulung*. 47. neubearb. Aufl. Publ. 1938. 127 + 35 + 60 pp.
   2. Bd.: *Lehren für Berufstätige und Gesetze für Sport und Arbeit, Männer und Frauen*. 46. neubearb. Aufl. Publ. 1935. 175 pp.

2893 *Zwanzig Briefe an einen jungen Dietwart*. Berlin: Limpert, 1934. 84 pp.

Olympic Games

2894 *Berlin: Die Kampfstätte der XI. Olympischen Spiele 1936*. Hrsg.: Propaganda-Ausschuss für die XI. Olympischen Spiele Berlin 1936 und die IV. Olympischen Winterspiele Garmisch-Partenkirchen. Berlin: Ener, [1935?]. 51 pp., illus.

2895 BOROWIK, HANS: *Wer ist's bei den Olympischen Spielen 1936. Kurzbiographien von mehr als 1000 Teilnehmern*. Berlin: Reichssportverlag, 1936. 176 pp.

2896 THE COMMITTEE ON FAIR PLAY IN SPORTS: *Preserve the Olympic ideal. A statement of the case against American participation in the Olympic Games at Berlin*. New York: [1935]. 62 pp., illus., facsims.

2897 *Duitschland, het land der Olympische Spelen? Feiten en Beschouwingen*.

Amsterdam: Joachimstal, [for] Joodsche Perscommissie voor Bijzondere Berichtgeving, [1935]. 32 pp.

2898 EUKEN, WILHELM: *Die Olympischen Spiele 1936 in Berlin*. Berlin: Berliner Buchvertrieb, 1936. 87 pp., illus., plan.

2899 HARBOTT, RICHARD: *Olympia und die Olympischen Spiele von 776 v. Chr. bis heute*. 2. umgearb. Aufl. Berlin: Limpert, 1935. 237 pp., illus., tabs.

2900 KRAUSE, GERHARD & MINDT, ERICH: *Olympia 1936. Eine nationale Aufgabe*. Im Auftr. des Reichssportführers und des Propagandaausschusses für die Olympischen Spiele 1936 Berlin, bearb. Berlin: Reichssportverlag, 1935. 148 pp., illus.

2901 KRUEGER, ARND: *Die Olympischen Spiele 1936 und die Weltmeinung: ihre aussenpolitische Bedeutung, unter besonderer Berücksichtigung der USA*. Berlin: 1972. 255 pp., bibl.

2902 LIMBERG, HANS, ed.: *Berlin im Bild im Olympiajahr 1936 (mit Anhang: Potsdam). Mementoes of Berlin* ... Berlin: Weichert, [1936]. 94 pp., illus., maps. [Captions in English, French, Italian, Spanish, Polish.]

2903 MANDELL, RICHARD D.: *The Nazi Olympics*. London: Souvenir Press, 1971. 316 pp., illus., tabs., plans.

2904 NEUE LEIPZIGER ZEITUNG: *Der Kampf um die Goldmedaillen von Garmisch-Partenkirchen 1936*. Leipzig: Leipziger Verlagsdruckerei, 1936. 126 pp., illus.

2905 REICHSMINISTERIUM DES INNERN: *Das Reichs-Sportfeld. Eine Schöpfung des Dritten Reiches für die Olympischen Spiele und die deutschen Leibesübungen*. Berlin: Reichssportverlag, 1936. 191 pp., illus.

2906 REICHSSPORTVERLAG: *1936. Das Jahr der Olympischen Spiele*. Berlin: [1935]. 240 pp., illus., tabs. [Pocket diary.]

2907 SISKA, HEINZ: *Völkerkampf Olympia*. Berlin: Brunnen-Verlag, 1936. 139 pp., illus.

2908 SURÉN, HANS: *Mensch und Sonne. Arisch-olympischer Geist*. 11. umgearb. und erw. Aufl. der Neuausg. Berlin: Scherl, 1936. 258 pp., illus. [First ed. 1924.]

8. HUMOUR AND SATIRE

2909 BENZINGER, JOSEF: *Die bairische Bibel*. Holzschnitte: Hans Jörg Schuster. Erfurt: Richter, 1939. 192 pp., illus. [Humorous 'translation' into dialect verse, with anti-Semitic overtones.]

2910 BUHOFER, INES & HELBLING, HANNO, eds.: *Kanzeltausch. Predigt und Satire im Dritten Reich. Eine Anthologie*. Zürich: Theologischer Verlag, 1973. 159 pp., bibl.

2911 HELLING, HANS, ed.: *Der Tafelredner bei allen Festlichkeiten. Heitere und ernste Trinksprüche und Tischreden*. 8. Aufl. Dresden: Rudolph, 1937. 157 pp.

2912 *Juden stellen sich vor.* 24 Zeichnungen vom Stürmerzeichner Fips. Nürnberg: Stürmer Verlag, 1934.

2913 JUNG, HERMANN: *Gelächter über eine zerbrochene Welt. Karikaturen aus Zeitungen und Zeitschriften.* Düsseldorf: Völkischer Verlag, 1940. 167 pp., illus.

2914 KADNER, SIEGFRIED: *Rasse und Humor.* München: Lehmann, 1936. 236 pp., illus.

2915 KEMNITZ, HANNO von, comp.: *Der Pfaffenstrick. Satirische Gedichte vom Mittelalter bis zur Neuzeit mit Karikaturen von Hans Günther Strick.* München: Ludendorff, 1937. 94 pp., illus.

2916 [KLADDERADATSCH] SCHULZ, KLAUS: *'Kladderadatsch'. Ein bürgerliches Witzblatt von der Märzrevolution bis zum Nationalsozialismus, 1848–1944.* Bochum: Brockmeyer, 1975. 264 pp., tabs., facsims., bibl.

2917 KLAEHN, FRIEDRICH JOACHIM: *Sturm 138. Ernstes und viel Heiteres aus dem SA-Leben.* Leipzig: Schaufuss, 1934. 207 pp. [From 'Jahre des Kampfes'.]

2918 KÜMMEL, HERBERT: *Auch Spass muss sein—im Lager und auf Fahrt. Mit Zeichnungen und Melodien.* Berlin: Limpert, 1937. 71 pp., illus., mus. scores.

2919 MJOELNIR [pseud. of Hans Schweitzer] & GOEBBELS, [JOSEPH]: *Das Buch Isidor. Ein Zeitbild voll Lachen und Hass.* München: Eher, 1931. 165 pp., illus. [5th ed. Also: GOEBBELS, JOSEPH, ed.: *Knorke. Ein neues Buch Isidor für Zeitgenossen.* Mitw.: Mjoelnir, Knipperdolling, Dax, Jaromir, Orje. 2. Aufl. München: Eher, 1931. 155 pp., illus. Dr. Bernhard Weiss, the Police President of Berlin, was nicknamed 'Isidor' by the Nazis.]

2920 MUMM, MICHEL: *Verflucht und zugenäht. Satirische Zeitgedichte aus dem 'Schwarzen Korps'.* Berlin: Brunnen-Verlag, 1938. 127 pp., illus.

2921 RAABE-STIFTUNG MÜNCHEN: *Das Jahrbuch der deutschen Dichtung 1938. Vom deutschen Humor.* Einl.: Th[addäus] Abitz-Schultze. Stuttgart: Strecker & Schröder, 1938. 286 pp., illus.

2922 RATHKE, ROBERT: *Der Apfelkrieg. Ein heiteres Spiel vom ewigen Juden.* Leipzig: Glaser, [1933?]. 48 pp.

2923 RUMPELSTILZCHEN [pseud. of Adolf Stein]: *Sie wer'n lachen!* Berlin: Brunnen-Verlag, 1933/34. 309 pp.

2924 SIEBOLD, KARL, ed.: *Deutschland lacht. Volkhafter Humor.* München: Deutscher Volksverlag, 1943. 279 pp.

2925 [SIMPLICISSIMUS] SCHÜTZE, CHRISTIAN, ed.: *Facsimile Querschnitt durch den Simplicissimus.* Einl.: Golo Mann. Bern: Scherz, 1963. 207 pp.

2926 SPRINGER, CARL: *Auf geht's! Humor aus der Kampfzeit der nationalsozialistischen Bewegung. Nach Erlebnissen alter Kämpfer.* München: Eher, 1939. 156 pp., illus.

2927 WALDL [pseud. of Walter Hofmann]: *Lacht ihn tot! Ein tendenziöses Bilderbuch.* Dresden: Nationalsozialistischer Verlag für den Gau Sachsen, 1937. [56 pp.], illus.

2928 ZEHRING, ARNO: *Meckereien von Baldrian. Ein polemisches Verse- und Bilderbuch von gestern und heute.* Zeichnungen: A. O. Koeppen von Oehlschlägel. Stendal: [priv. pr., 193–]. 60 pp., illus.

Anti-Nazi humour

2929 GAMM, HANS-JOCHEN: *Der Flüsterwitz im Dritten Reich.* München: List, 1963. 223 pp.

2930 HARDEN, HARRY: *Als wir alle Nazis waren ... Notizen eines Zeitgenossen.* Ohringen: Residenz-Verlag, 1952/53. 138 pp., illus.

2931 HIRCHE, KURT: *Der 'braune' und der 'rote' Witz.* Düsseldorf: Econ-Verlag, 1964. 309 pp.

2932 HOFFMANN, OTTO, comp.: *Witze, Karikaturen und sonstige Ergötzlichkeiten aus dem Dritten Reich.* 2. erw. Aufl. Cassarate: Libreria Internazionale, 1935. . 58 pp., illus.

2933 LARSEN, EGON: *Wit as a weapon. The political joke in history.* London: Muller, 1980. 108 pp. [Incl. ch. on jokes against Hitler and Mussolini.]

2934 VANDREY, MAX: *Der politische Witz im Dritten Reich.* München: Goldmann, 1967. 151 pp.

2935 VOX POPULI, pseud.: *Geflüstertes. Die Hitlerei im Volksmund.* Heidelberg: Freiheit-Verlag, 1946. 149 pp., illus.

L. PROPAGANDA*

1. GENERAL

2936 BARTLETT, F. C.: *Political propaganda.* Cambridge: Cambridge University Press, 1940. x + 158 pp.

2937 BAUMANN, GERHARD: *Grundlagen und Praxis der internationalen Propaganda.* Essen: Essener Verlagsanstalt, 1941. 280 pp.

2938 BRAMSTED, ERNEST K.: *Goebbels and National Socialist propaganda 1925–1945.* [East Lansing, Mich.]: Michigan State University Press, 1965. 488 pp., bibl.

2939 CHAKOTIN, SERGE: *The rape of the masses. The psychology of totalitarian political propaganda.* London: Routledge, 1940. xviii + 299 pp., tabs.

2940 DELARUE, JACQUES: *Conquête du pouvoir et nazification de l'opinion publique.* Bruxelles: 1976. 77 pp.

* 'Propaganda' is necessarily scattered throughout this bibliography, but specific sections in which such material is to be found are Nazi Ideology, Culture, Foreign Relations, Youth, Militarism and works on Goebbels.

2941 DIETZ, HEINRICH: *Agitation, Massenhysterie in England. Propagandamethoden historisch gesehen.* Essen: Essener Verlagsanstalt, 1941. 188 pp.

2942 DOMIZLAFF, HANS: *Propagandamittel der Staatsidee.* Altona-Othmarschen: Als Manuskript gedruckt, 1932. 105 pp., illus. (of flags).

2943 HADAMOVSKY, EUGEN: *Propaganda und nationale Macht. Die Organisation der öffentlichen Meinung für die nationale Politik.* Oldenburg i.O.: Stalling, 1933. 151 pp. [Author was appointed Reichssenderleiter and Direktor der Reichsrundfunkgesellschaft. He had held comparable posts in the Party before 1933.]

2944 INSTITUTE FOR PROPAGANDA ANALYSIS: *Propaganda analysis.* New York: 1938/40. 3 vols.

2945 KURATORIUM FÜR STAATSBÜRGERLICHE BILDUNG HAMBURG: *Hitler, seine 'Bewegung' und die 'Volksgemeinschaft' im Bild der nationalsozialistischen Propaganda.* Erläuterung und Hinweise: Gerhard Schoebe. Hamburg: 1964. 100 pp., bibl.

2946 LAMBERT, RICHARD S.: *Propaganda.* London: Nelson, 1939. 162 pp., bibl. [First publ. 1938; reprinted 1945.]

2947 LUMLEY, FREDERICK E.: *The propaganda menace.* New York: Century Co., 1933. 454 pp.

2948 MÜNZENBERG, WILLI: *Propaganda als Waffe.* Paris: Éds. du Carrefour, 1937. 280 pp., facsims. [French version (same publishers): *La propagande hitlérienne. Instrument de guerre.* 1938.]

2949 PICK, FREDERICK WALTER: *The art of Dr. Goebbels.* London: Hale, 1942. 175 pp., illus.

2950 SINGTON, DERRICK & WEIDENFELD, ARTHUR: *The Goebbels experiment. A study of the Nazi propaganda machine.* London: Murray, 1942. 260 pp., illus., diagrs.

2951 STARK, G.: *Moderne politische Propaganda.* München: Eher, 1930. 24 pp. (Schriftenreihe der Reichspropaganda-Abt., hrsg. von Dr. Goebbels, 1. Heft).

2952 STEED, WICKHAM: *The fifth arm.* London: Constable, 1940. 162 pp.

2953 STURMINGER, ALFRED: *Politische Propaganda in der Weltgeschichte. Beispiele vom Altertum bis in die Gegenwart.* Salzburg: Verlag 'Das Bergland-Buch', 1938. 320 pp., illus.

2954 SYWOTTEK, JUTTA: *Mobilmachung für den totalen Krieg. Die propagandistische Vorbereitung der deutschen Bevölkerung auf den Zweiten Weltkrieg.* Opladen: Westdeutscher Verlag, 1976. 398 pp., bibl.

2955 TRAVAGLINI, THOMAS: ' "m.E. sogar ausmerzen". Der 20. Juli 1944 in der nationalsozialistischen Propaganda'. [In] *Aus Politik und Zeitgeschichte,* 20. Juli 1974. Bonn: Bundeszentrale für politische Bildung. Pp. 3–23.

2956 TUTAS, HERBERT E.: *NS-Propaganda und deutsches Exil 1933–1939*. Meisenheim/Glan: Hain, 1973. 194 pp. (Deutsches Exil).

2957 WANDERSCHECK, HERMANN: *Weltkrieg und Propaganda*. Berlin: Mittler, 1936. 260 pp., illus., bibl.

2958 WHITE, AMBER BLANCO: *The new propaganda*. London: Gollancz, 1939. 383 pp.

2959 ZEMAN, Z. A. B.: *Nazi Propaganda*. London: Oxford University Press, in association with the Wiener Library, 1964. 226 pp., illus., facsims., tabs., bibl. [Dutch version: *De propaganda van de Nazi's*. Hilversum: de Haan, 1966. Also in German.]

2. ART AND THE MEDIA

2960 FRANCASTEL, PIERRE: *L'histoire de l'art, instrument de la propagande germanique*. Paris: Librairie de Médicis, 1945. 264 pp., illus., bibl. (Centre d'Études européennes de l'Université de Strasbourg).

2961 GANDILLHON, RENÉ: *Inventaire des affiches de la Guerre de 1939–1945 conservées aux Archives de la Marne*. Châlons sur Marne: Archives de la Marne, 1949. 52 pp., illus.

2962 GORDON, MATTHEW: *News is a weapon*. Introd.: Elmer Davis. New York: Knopf, 1942. xi + 268 pp.

2963 HINKEL, HERMANN: *Zur Funktion des Bildes im deutschen Faschismus. Bildbeispiele, Analysen, didaktische Vorschläge*. Steinbach/Giessen: Anabas-Verlag (Kämpf), 1975. 144 pp., illus., facsims., bibl.

2964 *Morgen die ganze Welt. Deutsche Kurzwellensender im Dienste der NS-Propaganda. Geschichte des Kurzwellenrundfunks in Deutschland 1933–1939*. Berlin: Haude & Spener, 1970. 116 pp., illus., facsims., diagrs., tabs. [Comprising: H. Lubbers, W. Schwipps: 'Morgen die ganze Welt', pp. 13–63; G. Goebel, W. Buschbeck: 'Die grösste Anlage der Welt für Kurzwellenrundfunk', pp. 67–116.]

2964a *Propaganda und Gegenpropaganda in Film 1933–1945*. Beiträgen von Hans Barkhausen [and others]. Wien: Österreichisches Filmmuseum, 1972. 120 pp., bibl., list of films (Peter Konlecher, Peter Kubelka, comps.).

2965 SCHEEL, KLAUS: *Krieg über Ätherwellen. NS Rundfunk und Monopole 1933–1945*. Berlin [East]: VEB Deutscher Verlag, 1970. 316 pp., illus., facsims.

2966 TAYLOR, RICHARD: *Film propaganda. Soviet Russia and Nazi Germany*. London: Croom Helm, 1979. 265 pp., illus.

2967 THOMAE, OTTO: *Die Propaganda-Maschinerie. Bildende Kunst und Öffentlichkeitsarbeit im Dritten Reich*. Berlin: Mann, 1978. 579 pp., bibl. [Incl. documentation on awards of prizes, exhibitions, press notices.]

2968 WELCH, DAVID ALBERT: *Propaganda and the German cinema, 1933–1945*.

Thesis [pres. to] London School of Economics. [1980?]. 519 pp. (Ref. No. F 5746).

2969 ZEMAN, ZBYNEK: *Selling the war: art and propaganda in World War II.* London: Orbis Publ., 1978. 120 pp., illus., bibl.

3. NAZI PROPAGANDA WRITINGS

2970 DIPLOMATICUS, pseud.: *Diplomatie und Hakenkreuz. Kämpfe und Erlebnisse eines Journalisten.* Berlin: Buch- und Tiefdruckgesellschaft, 1934. 307 pp., illus., facsims. [Pre-1933 NS-propaganda in diplomatic circles.]

2971 *Die Fahne hoch!* Hrsg.: H. Gerstmayer. Berlin: Neues Verlagshaus für Volksliteratur, 1933/35. [Pamphlets on nationalist and National Socialist subjects, almost always 24 pp., illus. Mostly on Kampfzeit, several on individual SA-men.]

2972 FUCHS, HANS: *Heimkehr ins Dritte Reich. Die Weltreise des Kreuzers 'Köln' zwischen zwei Epochen der deutschen Geschichte.* Dresden: Güntzsch, 1934. 208 pp., illus.

2973 *Germany speaks.* By 21 leading members of Party and State. Preface: Joachim von Ribbentrop. London: Butterworth, 1938. 406 pp., port., tabs., diagr.

2974 GOEBBELS, JOSEPH: *Das erwachende Berlin.* München: Eher, 1934. 184 pp., illus.

2975 HEISS, FRIEDRICH: *Bei uns in Deutschland. Ein Bericht.* Berlin: Volk und Reich Verlag, 1941. 167 pp., illus., diagrs. [3rd rev. and enl. ed.]

2976 KRIES, WILHELM VON: *Nie bezwungenes Volk. Die Schattenseiten unserer besten Eigenschaften.* Berlin: Mittler, 1935. x + 103 pp.

2977 LANGE, FRIEDRICH: *Wir zwischen 25 Nachbarvölkern.* 2. Aufl. Berlin: Verlag der Deutschen Arbeitsfront, 1941. 292 + xxiv pp., illus., maps, diagrs., bibl.

2978 LEY, ROBERT: *Deutschland ist schöner geworden.* Hrsg.: Hans Dauer, Walter Kiehl. Berlin: Mehden, 1936. 275 pp., illus., facsims., tabs.

2979 MOLENAAR, HERBERT: *Der Freiheit entgegen! Ein deutsches Buch von Kampf und Liebe. 2. Teil von 'Schwert und Flamme', nationalsozialistische Kampfgedichte und Sprechchöre, Berlin 1933–34.* Leipzig: Schaufuss, 1934. 77 pp.

2980 *Nationalpolitsche Aufklärungsschriften, Nr. 1–18.* Berlin: Hochmuth, 1936/41. 32 pp. each.

2981 REICHSPROPAGANDALEITUNG DER NSDAP: *Rednerinformation.* München: Eher, 1932. Nos. 1–10. [Confidential speakers' notes. Continued as *Einziges parteiamtliches Aufklärungs- und Redner-Informationsmaterial* (looseleaf series) up to 1943.]

2982 *Schlageter-Kalender 1937. Ein nationales Jahrbuch für das deutsche Volk.* Begründet vom Gau Saarpfalz der NSDAP. Heidelberg-Saarbrücken: Westmark-Verlag, [1936]. 120 pp., illus., maps.

2983 SENNINGER, BRUNO: *Die öffentliche Unehrlichkeit und die nationalistische Bewegung.* München: Huber, 1933. 174 pp.

2984 STUHLFATH, WALTER: *Deutsches Schicksal. Ein raum- und volkspolitisches Erziehungsbuch.* 7. Aufl. Langensalza: Beltz, 1937. 64 pp., maps, bibl.

Themes of propaganda

COLLAPSE OF SECOND REICH

2985 GESSNER, LUDWIG: *Der Zusammenbruch des Zweiten Reiches. Seine politischen und militärischen Lehren.* München: Beck, 1937. 248 pp.

2986 ZARNOW, GOTTFRIED & DRAHN, ERNST: *Der 9. November 1918. Die Tragödie eines grossen Volkes.* Hamburg: Hanseatische Verlagsanstalt, 1933. 152 pp., bibl.

2987 ZIEGLER, WILHELM: *Volk ohne Führung. Das Ende des Zweiten Reiches.* Hamburg: Hanseatische Verlagsanstalt, 1938. 309 pp.

STAB IN THE BACK (Dolchstoss von hinten)

2988 PETZOLD, JOACHIM: *Die Dolchstosslegende. Eine Geschichtsfälschung im Dienst des deutschen Imperialismus und Militarismus.* 2. unveränd. Aufl. Berlin [East]: Akademie Verlag, 1963. 148 pp., tabs., bibl. (Deutsche Akademie der Wissenschaften zu Berlin).

2989 RUDOLPH, LUDWIG Ritter von: *Die Lüge die nicht stirbt. Die 'Dolchstosslegende' von 1918.* Nürnberg: Glock & Lutz, 1958. 146 pp.

2990 SCHRÖDER, HEINZ: *Das Ende der Dolchstosslegende. Geschichtliche Erkenntnis und politische Verantwortung.* Hamburg: Hammerich & Lesser, 1946. 80 pp.

MARXISM, COMMUNISM, BOLSHEVISM

2991 EHRT, ADOLF, ed.: *Der Weltbolschewismus. Ein internationales Gemeinschaftswerk über die bolschewistische Wühlarbeit und die Umsturzversuche der Komintern in allen Ländern.* Hrsg.: Anti-Komintern. Berlin: Nibelungen Verlag, 1936. 506 pp., illus., facsims., graph.

2992 EHRT, ADOLF & SCHWEICKERT, JULIUS: *Entfesselung der Unterwelt. Ein Querschnitt durch die Bolschewisierung Deutschlands.* Berlin: Eckart-Verlag, 1932. 320 pp., illus., facsims., diagrs.

2993 GOEBBELS, JOSEPH: *Der Bolschewismus in Theorie und Praxis.* München: Eher, 1936. 32 pp. [Address at Nuremberg Party Rally 1936. Also French, English, Dutch and further German eds., publ. Berlin: Müller.]

2994 KRÖGER, THEODOR: *Brest-Litowsk. Beginn und Folgen des bolschewistischen Weltbetrugs.* Berlin: Deutscher Verlag, 1937. 323 pp., illus.

2995 LEIBBRANDT, GOTTLIEB: *Bolschewismus und Abendland. Idee und Geschichte eines Kampfes gegen Europa.* Berlin: Junker & Dünnhaupt, 1939. 156 pp.

Munich Soviet ('Räterepublik')

2996 SCHRICKER, RUDOLF: *Rotmord über München.* Geleitw.: Manfred von Killinger. Berlin: 'Zeitgeschichte' Verlag, [n.d.]. 226 pp., illus., facsims.

2997 VIERA, JOSEF: *Kommune über München*. Leipzig: Schneider, 1934. 88 pp., illus., map.

2998 WEIGAND, WILHELM: *Die rote Flut. Der Münchener Revolutions- und Rätespuk 1918/1919*. München: Eher, 1935. 512 pp. [Novel.]

2999 ROSENBERG, ALFRED: *The final fight between Europe and Bolshevism*. München: Eher, 1936. 22 pp. [Address at Nuremberg Party Rally 1936. Also in French and Italian.]

3000 STADTLER, EDUARD: *Bolschewismus als Weltgefahr*. 2. unveränd. Aufl. Düsseldorf: Neuer Zeitverlag, 1936. 272 pp.

Soviet Union

3001 ANDREJEW, W.: *Hier spricht Russland. Selbstbekenntnisse der Sowjetpresse*. Leipzig: Noske, 1936. 280 pp., illus.

3002 DIEMER, HELMUT: *Der Geist des Judentums im sowjet-russischen Eherecht*. Giessen: Dittert, 1938. 137 pp., bibl.

3003 LAUBENHEIMER, A., ed.: *Und Du siehst die Sowjets richtig. Berichte von deutschen und ausländischen 'Spezialisten' aus der Sowjet-Union*. 3. unveränd. Aufl. Berlin: Nibelungen-Verlag, 1937. 400 pp., illus.

WORKERS

3004 DIERS, MARIE: *Freiheit und Brot! Der Roman einer Arbeiterfamilie*. Berlin: Nationaler Freiheitsverlag, 1933. 135 pp.

3005 LORENZ, OTTOKAR: *Die deutsche Arbeiterbewegung*. Fürstenwalde-Spree: Verlag für Militärgeschichte und Deutsches Schrifttum, [1938]. 44 pp.

3006 PLAGEMANN, WILHELM: *Der politische Weg des deutschen Arbeitertums*. Frankfurt a.M.: Diesterweg, 1933. 56 pp. (Das Reich im Werden, Geschichtliche Reihe, Heft 1). [Extracts from Heinz Marr, Oswald Spengler, Moeller v.d. Bruck, August Winnig, Ernst Jünger and 'Mein Kampf'.]

ECONOMIC THEMES

3007 FEDER, GOTTFRIED: *Der Staatsbankrott. Die Rettung*. 9.–10. Taus. (Unveränd. Neudruck des im Jahre 1919 erschienenen Erstdruckes). Diessen vor München: Huber, 1924. 24 pp.

3008 FEDER, GOTTFRIED & BUCKELEY, A.: *Der kommende Steuerstreik. Seine Gefahr, seine Unvermeidlichkeit, seine Wirkung*. Diessen vor München: Huber, 1921. 107 pp., tabs., bibl.

3009 HALLER, P.: *Der Zusammenbruch der deutschen Wirtschaft—Die kommende Inflation!* Neuaufl. von P[aul] Hochmuth. Berlin: Music, 1930. 40 pp.

3010 HOCHMUTH, P[AUL]: *Wie schütze ich mein Eigentum im kommenden Staatsbankrott?* Berlin: 1930. 36 pp.

3011 *Krieg dem Hunger!* vom $^+_+{}^+$. Berlin: Brunnen-Verlag (Bischoff), 1931. 142 pp. [Novel about the future.]

3012 EBNER, ALFRED & NEUSS, OSKAR, eds.: *Schütze Dich vor Luftgefahr.* Vorw.: H. Grimme. Berlin: Freiheitsverlag, 1935. 69 pp., illus.

3013 LEERS, JOHANN von: *Bomben auf Hamburg! Vision oder Möglichkeit.* Leipzig: Voigtländer, 1932. 127 pp.

3014 PRANDTL, W. and others: *Gaskampfstoffe und Gasvergiftungen. Wie schützen wir uns?* [By]: [W]. Prandtl, [H]. Gebele, [J]. Fessler. München: Gmelin, 1933. 117 pp., illus., tabs., bibl.

3015 REICHSLUFTSCHUTZBUND, Landesgruppe Ostpreussen: *Luftschutz-Fibel.* Berlin: Verlag 'Offene Worte', 1933. 103 pp., illus., diagrs.

3016 SCHÜTTEL, LOTHAR: *Luftkrieg bedroht Europa!* München: Lehmann, 1938. 182 pp., tabs., maps.

3017 WIRTH, FRITZ & MUNTSCH, OTTO: *Die Gefahren der Luft und ihre Bekämpfung im täglichen Leben, in der Technik und im Krieg.* 3. völlig neubearb. Aufl. Berlin: Reinshagen, 1940, 287 pp., illus., diagrs., tabs., bibl. [First ed. 1932.]

Defensive propaganda

3018 BÖMER, KARL: *Das Dritte Reich im Spiegel der Weltpresse. Historische Dokumente über den Kampf des Nationalsozialismus gegen die ausländische Lügenhetze.* Leipzig: Armanen-Verlag, 1934. 173 pp., illus., facsims.

3019 HANFSTAENGL, ERNST, comp.: *Hitler in der Karikatur der Welt—Tat gegen Tinte. Ein Bildsammelwerk.* Berlin: Verlag Braune Bücher, 1933. 174 pp., illus., bibl. [Reprinted: Darmstadt: Melzer, (1978?)). Also: *Tat gegen Tinte. Hitler in der Karikatur der Welt.* Neue Folge. Berlin: Verlag Braune Bücher, 1934.]

3020 IBRÜGGER, FRITZ: *Die Lüge geht um die Welt.* Essen: Essener Verlags-Anstalt, 1942. 168 pp.

3021 KEEDING, HANS: *Zeitungen und Politik.* Berlin: Hochmuth, [1934]. 32 pp. (Hinter den Kulissen der Welthetze gegen das Dritte Reich, Heft 1).

3022 KÖNIG, KARL: *Ausländer sehen Dich an! Ratschläge und Mahnungen für Deutsche in der Heimat und in der Fremde.* Leipzig: Schnurpfeil & Steinmetz, 1936. 71 pp., bibl.

TRACHTENBERG, JAKOW, ed.: *Die Greuelpropaganda ist eine Lügenpropaganda sagen die deutschen Juden selbst. See 3546.*

Illustration as propaganda

3023 HEISS, FRIEDRICH: *Deutschland zwischen Nacht und Tag.* Berlin: Volk und Reich Verlag, 1934. 279 pp., illus., maps, tabs.

3024 *Raubstaat England.* Hamburg-Bahrenfeld: Cigaretten Bilderdienst, 1941. 129 pp., illus., maps.

3025 *Das Reich Adolf Hitlers. Ein Bildbuch vom Werden Grossdeutschlands.* 3. Aufl. München: Eher, [194–]. [130 pp.], illus. [Eds.: Wilhelm Utermann, Hellmut Holthaus.]

3026   WEGENER, KURT & KELLER, WILHELM: *So kam es! Ein Bildbericht vom Kampf um Deutschland 1918–1934.* Berlin-Tempelhof: Braun, 1935. 128 pp., illus., diagrs.

4. PROPAGANDA IN WORLD WAR II

a. General

3027   BALFOUR, MICHAEL: *Propaganda in war, 1939–1945. Organisations, policies and publics in Britain and Germany.* London: Routledge & Kegan, 1979. xvii + 520 pp.

3028   BUCHBENDER, ORTWIN & SCHUH, HORST, eds.: *Heil Beil! Flugblattpropaganda im Zweiten Weltkrieg. Dokumentation und Analyse.* Stuttgart: Seewald, 1974. 216 pp., illus., facsims.

3029   CRUICKSHANK, CHARLES: *The fourth arm. Psychological warfare, 1938–1945.* London: Davis-Poynter, 1977. 200 pp.

3030   DARRACOTT, JOSEPH & LOFTUS, BELINDA: *Second World War posters.* London: Imperial War Museum, 1972. 72 pp., illus.

3031   LINEBARGER, PAUL: *Psychological warfare.* 2nd ed. Washington, D.C.: Combat Forces Press, 1954. 318 pp., illus., diagrs., facsims.

3032   RHODES, ANTHONY: *Propaganda. The art of persuasion: World War II.* Ed.: Victor Margolin. London: Angus & Robertson, 1976. 319 pp., illus.

3033   RUPP, LEILA J.: *Mobilizing women for war. German and American propaganda, 1939–1945.* Princeton, N.J.: Princeton University Press, 1978. xii + 243 pp., illus.

3034   SAVA, GEORGE: *War without guns. The psychological front.* London: Faber & Faber, 1942. 156 pp.

3035   SETH, RONALD: *The truth-benders: psychological warfare in the Second World War.* London: Frewin, 1969. 204 pp.

3036   SZUNYOGH, BELA: *Psychological warfare: an introduction to ideological propaganda and the techniques of psychological warfare.* New York: William-Frederick, 1955. 118 pp., map. [German version: *Der psychologische Krieg.* Leer/Ostfriesland: Rautenberg & Möckel, 1951.]

3037   WHITE, JOHN BAKER: *The big lie.* Maidstone, Kent: Mann, 1973. x + 235 pp., illus. ['The inside story of psychological warfare'. First publ.: London: Evans, 1955.]

b. The radio war

3038   ALLARD, PAUL: *'Ici Londres'.* Paris: Eds. de France, 1942. 110 pp.

3039   BENNETT, JEREMY: *British broadcasting and the Danish resistance movement, 1940–1945. A study of the wartime broadcasts of the BBC Danish Service.* Cambridge: Cambridge University Press, 1966. 266 pp., illus., bibl.

3040 BRIGGS, ASA: *The war of words.* London: Oxford University Press, 1970. xviii + 766 pp., illus., tabs., bibl. (The History of Broadcasting in the United Kingdom, Vol. III).

3041 BRINITZER, CARL: *Hier spricht London. Von einem der dabei war.* Hamburg: Hoffmann & Campe, 1969. 339 pp., illus., bibl.

3042 BROEK, H. J. van den: *Hier Radio Oranje: vijf jaar radio in oorlogstijd.* Voorw.: Jan Moedwil. Amsterdam: Vrij Nederland, 1947. xvi + 343 pp., illus.

3043 CHILDS, HARWOOD L. & WHITTON, JOHN B., eds.: *Propaganda by short wave.* Princeton, N.J.: Princeton University Press, 1942. 355 pp., tabs., diagrs.

3044 ETTLINGER, HAROLD: *The Axis on the air.* Indianapolis, Ind.: Bobbs Merrill, 1943. 318 pp.

3045 GRACHT, HANS: *Hier spricht der Feind! London und Paris 'enthüllen' ...* Berlin: Deutscher Verlag für Politik und Wirtschaft, 1940. 48 pp., illus.

3046 KRIS, ERNST & SPEIER, HANS: *German radio propaganda: report on home broadcasts during the war.* In ass'n with Sidney Axelrod [and others]. London: Oxford University Press, 1944. xiv + 529 pp., illus., graphs. (Studies of the Institute of World Affairs).

3047 LAUBENTHAL, HEINZ: *Mit dem Mikrophon am Feind. Erlebnisse an drei Fronten.* Dresden: Thienemann, 1942. 157 pp., illus. [Author gave radio reports of his flights with the Luftwaffe.]

3048 LAVELEYE, VICTOR de: *Ici Radio Belgique: les meilleurs commentaires.* Bruxelles: Goemaere, 1949. xviii + 388 pp., illus., facsims.

3049 LEAN, E. TANGYE: *Voices in the darkness. The story of the European radio war.* London: Secker & Warburg, 1943. 243 pp., illus., maps.

3050 MANN, THOMAS: *Deutsche Hörer! 55 Radiosendungen nach Deutschland.* 2. erw. Aufl. Stockholm: Bermann-Fischer, 1945. 132 pp. [First ed.: ... *25 Radiosendungen...* 1942.]

3051 *Les procès de la radio: Ferdonnet et Jean Hérold-Paquis. Compte-rendu sténographique.* Paris: Michel, 1947. (Ed.: Maurice Garçon).

3052 SCHNABEL, REIMUND: *Missbrauchte Mikrofone. Deutsche Rundfunkpropaganda im Zweiten Weltkrieg. Eine Dokumentation.* Wien: Europa Verlag, 1967. 506 pp., facsims., bibl.

3053 SCHWIPPS, WERNER: *Wortschlacht im Äther. Der deutsche Auslandsrundfunk im Zweiten Welkrieg. Geschichte des Kurzwellenrundfunks in Deutschland 1939–1945.* Berlin: Haude & Spener, 1971. 148 pp., illus.

c. Countercharges and quotations

3054 BÖHR, HANS: *Britische Propaganda.* Berlin: Eher, 1940. 87 pp.

3055 CHURCHILL, WINSTON: *Meine Bundesgenossen. Aussprüche aus zwei Jahrzehnten.* Berlin: Nibelungen Verlag, 1944. 110 pp., illus. [Quotations from Churchill's speeches and reproductions of cartoons against the Soviet Union. Also Danish version: *Min Forbundsfaelle.*]

3056 COOLE, W. W. & POTTER, M. F., eds.: *Thus spake Germany.* Forew.: Lord Vansittart. London: Routledge, 1941. xxxviii + 438 pp., illus., maps, bibl. [Anthology of extracts from German writings.]

3057 ERDMANN, JENS: *Calumny as an instrument of policy. Some historical notes.* Berlin: German Information Service, [194–]. 28 pp., bibl.

3058 FRITZSCHE, HANS: *Krieg den Kriegshetzern. Acht Wochen politische Zeitungs- und Rundfunksschau.* Vorw.: Reichsminister für Volksaufklärung und Propaganda. Berlin: Brunnen-Verlag, 1940. 160 pp., illus.

3059 KNOP, W. G., comp.: *Beware of the English! German propaganda exposes England.* Forew.: Stephen King-Hall. London: Hamish Hamilton, 1939. 303 pp., illus., facsims.

3060 *Kriegsschuld und Presse.* Gemeinschaftsarbeit deutscher Zeitungswissenschaftler im Auftr. der Reichsdozentenführung. Beiträge von Ernst Herbert Lehmann [and others]. Vorw.: Reichsdozentenführer Walter Schultze. Nürnberg: Willmy, 1944. vii + 171 pp., facsims. (Schriftenreihe des Instituts zur Erforschung und Förderung des internationalen Pressevereins der Union Nationaler Journalistenverbände).

3061 KRIES, WILHELM VON: *Strategie und Taktik der englischen Kriegspropaganda. Auf Grund von englischen Quellen dargestellt.* Berlin: Kries, 1940. 131 pp. [English version: *Strategy and tactics of the British war propaganda.* Berlin: Zonder, 1941.]

3062 MCKENZIE, VERNON: *Here lies Goebbels!* London: Michael Joseph, 1940. 319 pp.

3063 REIPERT, FRITZ: *In acht Kriegswochen 107 mal gelogen! Dokumente über Englands Nachrichtenpolitik im gegenwärtigen Kriege.* Berlin: Eher, [1940?]. 47 pp.

3064 [WALLOP, GERARD VERNON], Lord LYMINGTON: *Famine in England.* Excerpts by Alan Sidgwick. Copenhagen: 'Literaria', 1940. 63 pp., illus. [German version: *Hungersnot in England.* Berlin: Volk und Reich Verlag, 1940.]

3065 WANDERSCHECK, HERMANN: *Höllenmaschinen aus England. Hinter den Kulissen der Londoner Lügenhetze.* Berlin: Mittler, 1940. ix + 104 pp.

3066 WEISE, OTTO: *Franzosen gegen England. Französische Äusserungen.* Berlin: Junker & Dünnhaupt, 1940. 97 pp.

3067 *Wilt U de waarheid weten? Hitler—zooals men hem aan U getoend heeft, en zooals hij in Werkelijkheid is.* Im Auftr. des Reichskommissars für die besetzten Niederländischen Gebiete hrsg. von dem Hauptamt für Volksaufklärung und Propaganda. [Amsterdam: 1940?]. [44 pp.], illus., facsims.

d. Allied propaganda (general)

BLACK PROPAGANDA

3068 AUCKLAND, R. G., comp.: *Catalogue of British 'Black Propaganda' to Germany, 1941–1945*. St. Albans, Herts.: Psywar Society, 1978. 32 pp., illus.

DELMER, SEFTON: *Black boomerang. See* 1236.

3069 KIRCHNER, KLAUS: *Achtung! Feindpropaganda!* Erlangen: Verlag für zeitgeschichtliche Dokumente und Curiosa, [1976].
Mappe 4: [Comprising facsimile reproduction and] Klaus Kirchner: *Krankheit rettet. Psychologische Kriegführung.* 304 pp., illus., facsims., bibl.

3070 KIRCHNER, KLAUS: *Flugblätter aus England 1939/1940/1941. Bibliographie-Katalog.* Erlangen: Verlag D + C, 1978. 445 pp., facsims., tabs., bibl.

3071 KIRCHNER, KLAUS: *Flugblätter aus den USA 1943/44. Bibliographie-Katalog.* Erlangen: Verlag D + C, 1977. 224 pp., facsims., illus., diagrs., tabs., bibl.

3072 KÜHN, HEINZ: *Hitler oder Deutschland. Freiheitsbriefe an die deutsche Wehrmacht.* Ghent: 1944. 88 pp. [On behalf of Nationalkomitee Freies Deutschland.]

3073 LERNER, DANIEL: *Sykewar: psychological warfare against Germany. D-day to VE-day.* Forew.: Robert A. McClure. Supplementary essay: Richard H. S. Crossman. New York: Stewart, [1949]. xviii + 463 pp., illus., facsims., bibl. [Reprinted as: *Psychological warfare against Nazi Germany.* Cambridge, Mass.: MIT Press, 1971.]

3074 OECHSNER, FREDERICK and others: *This is the enemy.* By F. Oechsner, J. W. Grigg, J. M. Fleischer, G. M. Stadler, C. B. Conger. Boston: Little, Brown, 1942. 364 pp.

3075 SCURLA, HERBERT: *Die Dritte Front. Geistige Grundlagen des Propagandakrieges der Westmächte.* 2. Aufl. Berlin: Stubenrauch, 1940. 92 pp. (Schriftenreihe des Deutschen Akademischen Austauschdienstes).

3076 SUPREME HQ ALLIED EXPEDITIONARY FORCE, Psychological Warfare Division: *The Psychological Warfare Division, SHAEF. An account of its operations in the Western European Campaign, 1944–1945.* Bad Homburg: 1945. 264 pp., illus., diagrs., facsims.

3077 VANSITTART, ROBERT: *Black record. Germany past and present.* London: Hamish Hamilton, 1941. 57 pp.

e. German propaganda (general)

3078 AUCKLAND, R. G., comp.: *Catalogue of German leaflets to Allied troops in Italy, also Italian civilians and soldiers, 1943–1945.* St. Albans, Herts.: Psywar Society, 1975. 43 pp., graphs. (2nd ed.).

3079 AUCKLAND, R. G., comp.: *Catalogue of V 1 rocket propaganda leaflets, 1944–45.* London: Psywar Society, 1978. 59 pp., illus.

3080 BAILLIE-STEWART, NORMAN: *The officer in the Tower.* As told to John Murdoch. London: Frewin, 1967. 304 pp., illus., facsims. [Author was involved in propaganda for the Germans.]

3081 BAIRD, J. W.: *The mythical world of Nazi war propaganda, 1939–1945.* Minneapolis, Minn.: University of Minnesota Press, 1974. xii + 329 pp., illus., bibl.

3082 BOELCKE, WILLI A., ed.: *Kriegspropaganda 1939–1941. Geheime Minister-konferenzen im Reichspropagandaministerium.* Stuttgart: Deutsche Verlags-Anstalt, 1966. 794 pp.

BOELCKE, WILLI A., ed.: *'Wollt Ihr den totalen Krieg?' Die geheimen Goebbels-Konferenzen 1939–1943.* See 780.

3083 BUCHBENDER, ORTWIN: *Das tönende Erz. Deutsche Propaganda gegen die Rote Armee im Zweiten Weltkrieg.* Stuttgart: Seewald, 1978. 378 pp., illus., facsims., diagrs.

3084 COLE, J. A.: *Lord Haw-Haw and William Joyce. The full story.* London: Faber & Faber, 1964. 516 pp., illus., facsims.

3085 FARAGO, LADISLAS, ed.: *German psychological warfare.* Ed. for the Committee for National Morale. Ass't ed.: Lewis Frederick Gittler, with cooperation of Gordon W. Allport, Edwin G. Boring. Interpretative summary: Kimball Young. New York: Putnam, 1942. xxii + 302 pp., bibl. [First ed. 1941.]

3086 GANZER, KARL RICHARD: *Aufstand und Reich. Lebenskräfte deutscher Geschichte. Reden und Aufsätze.* München: Lehmann, 1940. 170 pp., bibl.

3087 GEORGE, ALEXANDER L.: *Propaganda analysis. A study of inferences made from Nazi propaganda in World War II.* Evanston, Ill.: Row, Peterson, 1959. xxii + 287 pp.

3088 HERZSTEIN, ROBERT EDWIN: *The war that Hitler won. The most infamous propaganda campaign in history.* New York: Putnam, 1978. 491 pp., illus., facsims., bibl.

3089 HEYSING, G.: *Adler gegen Falken. Sonderdienst der Luftwaffe im Krieg gegen die Sowjetunion.* Hamburg: Die Wildente, 1967. 176 pp., illus., maps. [Propaganda companies of the Luftwaffe.]

3090 KAUTTER, EBERHARD: *Sozialismus und Wehrwille in deutscher Vergangenheit und Gegenwart.* Berlin: Eher, 1944. 176 pp.

3091 LOTZ, WILHELM: *Schönheit der Arbeit in Deutschland.* Berlin: Deutscher Verlag, 1940. 62 pp., illus. [Also in French and English.]

3092 PLEYER, KLEO: *Volk im Feld.* Hamburg: Hanseatische Verlagsanstalt, 1943. 250 pp., port. (62. Taus.).

3093 REIPERT, FRITZ: *Warum wir diesen Krieg gewinnen! Hinter der kämpfenden Truppe: Das Bollwerk der Heimat.* Berlin: Rödiger, [1940?]. 47 pp., illus.

3094 RHEINBABEN, WERNER Frhr. von: *Der Grossdeutsche Befreiungskrieg. Vorgeschichte—Verlauf—Siegeszuversicht.* Berlin: Junker & Dünnhaupt, 1942. 123 pp.

3095 RICHTER, FRIEDRICH, ed.: *Bewährung. Ein Kriegsbuch der Heimat.* Chemnitz: Pickenhahn, 1944. 335 pp.

3096 RÜDIGER, KARL-HEINZ: *Der Krieg der Freimaurer gegen Deutschland.* [No pl. of publ.]: OKW Abt. Inland, 1944. 32 pp., bibl. (Tornisterschrift des OKW Abt. Inland. Nur für den Gebrauch innerhalb der Wehrmacht).

3097 SEIBOLD, KARL, ed.: *Rufe in das Volk 1919–1944. Ein Almanach.* München: Deutscher Volksverlag, 1944. 351 pp., ports.

3098 *Unsere Wehrmacht im Kriege. Farbaufnahmen der Propaganda-Kompanien.* Berlin: Bong, 1941. 143 pp., illus. [Ed.: Paul Friedrich Höhne; Text: Carl Albert Drewitz].

3099 *Der Untermensch stand auf …* Berlin: Nordland Verlag, [1942]. [46 pp.], illus. (Bearb.: SS Hauptamt Schulungsamt). [Atrocity propaganda.]

f. Hostile Nazi propaganda

Anti-Allied propaganda

3100 ALDAG, PETER: *Worüber berichten wir heute. Unsere Gegner und ihr Krieg. Berichte aus dem 'Zeitgeschehen' des Grossdeutschen Rundfunks in Zusammenarbeit mit der Anti-Komintern.* Berlin: Nordland Verlag, 1941. 111 pp.

3101 CORONA, H. C.: *England und USA. Schrittmacher des Bolschewismus.* Prag: Graphia, 1944. 130 pp., illus., facsims.

3102 DIEWERGE, WOLFGANG: *Das Kriegsziel der Weltplutokratie. Dokumentarische Veröffentlichung der amerikanischen Friedensgesellschaft Theodore Nathan Kaufmann 'Deutschland muss sterben' ('Germany must perish').* Berlin: Eher, 1941. 31 pp., map.

3103 DOEGEN, WILHELM: *Unsere Gegner damals und heute. Engländer und Franzosen mit ihren europäischen und fremdrassigen Hilfsvölkern in deren Heimat, an der Front und—in deutscher Gefangenschaft im Weltkriege und im jetzigen Kriege—Grossdeutschlands koloniale Sendung.* Mitarb.: Hans Henning Frhr. Grote, Franz Hübner, George Bullrich. Berlin-Lichterfelde: Hübner, 1941. 122 pp., illus., facsims., tabs.

3104 REIPERT, FRITZ: *Kriegsmethoden und Kriegsverbrechen. Dokumente über die Kriegsführung der Plutokratien.* Berlin: Rödiger, 1941. 174 pp.

3105 RIEBE, PETER A.: *Revolution der Weltherrschaft und Englands Enteignung durch die USA.* Oldenburg: Stalling, 1943. 336 pp.

France

3106 AUSWÄRTIGES AMT: *Die Geheimakten des französischen Generalstabes*

1939/41. Berlin: Deutscher Verlag, 1941. 393 pp., facsims. [Also in Romanian and Portuguese, etc.]

3107 HALM, EDMUND: *Die Alliance française. Der Weltbund des französischen Kulturimperialismus. Eine Untersuchung auf Grund authentischen Materials.* Berlin: Junker & Dünnhaupt, 1940. 60 pp.

3108 HOLM, REINHARD: *La démocratie française et son effondrement spirituel.* Bruxelles: Maison Internationale d'Édition, 1940. 73 pp.

3109 REITHINGER, A.: *Frankreichs biologischer und wirtschaftlicher Selbstmord im Kriege Englands gegen Deutschland.* Stuttgart: Deutsche Verlags-Anstalt, 1940. 47 pp., maps. tabs.

Great Britain

3110 ALDAG, PETER: *Das Judentum in England.* Berlin: Nordland Verlag, 1943. 554 pp., bibl.

3111 ALEXANDER, MICHAEL Graf: *Von Scotland Yard ausgewiesen. Ein Erlebnis-Bericht.* Berlin: Schlieffen, 1941. 184 pp.

3112 CLAM, ERNST: *Lord Cohn. Die Verjudung der englischen Oberschicht von D'Israeli bis Hore-Belisha.* Leipzig: v. Hase & Koehler, 1940. 117 pp., map, family tree.

3113 *Das ist England!* Berlin: Eher, 1940. 11 vols. of approx. 100 pp. each. (Schriftenreihe der NSDAP).

3114 DREYER, SIEGBERT: *England und die Freimaurerei.* Berlin: Junker & Dünnhaupt, 1940. 55 pp.

3115 *The eighth crusade: uncensored disclosures of a British staff officer.* 4th ed. Berlin: Internationaler Verlag, 1940. vii + 205 pp. [First ed. 1939.]

3116 EVERWIEN, MAX: *Bibel, Scheckbuch und Kanonen. Das Gesicht Englands.* 4.–8. Taus. Berlin: Claassen, 1939. 245 pp.

3117 FRANK, REINHARD: *La domination de l'Angleterre sur l'Inde.* Berlin: Office d'Information allemand, 1940. 88 pp., illus. [German version: *Englands Herrschaft in Indien.* Berlin: Deutsche Informationsstelle, 1940.]

3118 HARTMANN, HANS: *Cant. Die englische Art der Heuchelei.* Berlin: Junker & Dünnhaupt, 1940. 61 pp.

3119 HAUSHOFER, ALBRECHT: *Englands Einbruch in China.* Berlin: Junker & Dünnhaupt, 1940. 53 pp.

3120 HILTON, SUSAN: *Eine Irin erlebt England und den Seekrieg.* Deutsche Bearb.: Bernhard Löschenkohl. Hamburg: Falken-Verlag, 1942. 148 pp.

3121 *'Humanes England'? Eine Dokumenten-Sammlung.* Berlin: Deutscher Verlag, 1940. 125 pp., illus., tabs.

3122 *Informations-Schriften.* Berlin: Europa-Verlag, 1940/41. Pamphlets of approx. 20 pp. each. [Versions in English and French show the following publ. details respectively: *The 20th Century Series*. London: The European Publishers Ltd.: *Information universelle*. Paris: Éds. Européennes. Incl.: Nr. 18: 'Die Prophezeiung des Nostradamus'; Nr. 45: 'Zwiegespräch mit der GPU' (from Alja Rachmanova: *Die Fabrik des neuen Menschen*).]

3123 JOYCE, WILLIAM: *Dämmerung über England*. Berlin: Internationaler Verlag, 1940. 232 pp. [English version: *Twilight over England*. Same publs. 2nd. ed. publ. in The Hague: Uitg.-Maatsch. 'Oceanus', 1942. Incl.: Ch. VI: 'The Jews', pp. 94–124.]

3124 KIRCHNER, HELLMUT: *Erbeutung und Ausbeutung Südafrikas*. Berlin: Junker & Dünnhaupt, 1940. 61 pp., tabs., bibl.

3125 KRIES, WILHELM von: *British is best. Das System der englischen Selbstgerechtigkeit*. Berlin: Junker & Dünnhaupt, 1940. 56 pp.

3126 LIPPE, KURT B. Prinz zur: *Interpretation of the German-English conflict*. Speech delivered by Prince Kurt B. zur Lippe M.A. before various American societies ... and an accompanying article by John H. Rand: 'Lusitania—Churchill—Athenia'. San Bernardino, Calif.: [No impr.], 1939. 22 pp.

3127 MARCUS, HANS: *Religiöser Kommunismus in England*. Berlin: Eher, 1942. 63 pp., bibl. (Schriftenreihe der NSDAP).

3128 OTTO, KARL: *Das verlassene englische Pfund*. Leipzig: Gloeckner, 1940. 72 pp., tabs.

3129 PERSICH, WALTER: *Winston Churchill ganz 'privat'. Abenteurer, Lord und Verbrecher*. Berlin: Schaffer, 1942. 336 pp.

3130 REHBERG, HANS: *Suez. Eine französische Tragödie*. Berlin: [priv. pr., 1940]. 69 pp. [Radio play attacking England.]

3131 SCANLON, JOHN: *Karussell in Westminster (Very foreign affairs)*. Aus dem Englischen übertragen. Berlin: Internationaler Verlag, 1940. 186 pp. [Author was sympathetic to the Germans before the war.]

3132 SCHAEFFER, WOLFGANG, ed.: *Chamberlain—beschirmt und unbeschirmt. Ausländische Zeichner demaskieren Englands Premierminister*. Vorw.: Karl Bömer. Frankfurt a.M.: Beensen, 1940. 87 pp.

3133 SCHEEL, OTTO: *Opkomst und verval van het Britische Rijk*. Amsterdam: Uitg. Westland, 1943. 286 pp. [German orig.: *Aufstieg und Niedergang der englischen See- und Weltmacht*. Flensburg: 1941.]

3134 SCHINDLER, RICHARD: *England garantiert ...! Grossbritanniens Kriegsführung gegen die Neutralen*. Leipzig: von Hase & Koehler, 1939. 127 pp.

3135 SCHNEIDER, WALTHER, ed.: *England der Brandstifter Europas. Heinrich von Treitschke über die europafeindlichen Machenschaften des britischen Imperialismus*. Nürnberg: Willmy, 1941. 134 pp., ports.

3136 SEIFERT, HERMANN ERICH: *Der jüdische Kampf um Palästina. England als Handlanger des Weltjudentums*. Berlin: Kasper, 1943. 120 pp., maps, bibl. (2. überarb. und ergänz. Aufl. des unter dem Titel *Palästina: Judenstaat?*

unter dem pseud. Heinrich Hest erschienenen Buches).

3137 SPIESSER, FRITZ: *Das Konzentrationslager.* München: Eher, 1940. 154 pp.
[Condemns British concentration camps in the Boer War.]

3138 STACHE, RUD[OLF]: *Polen! Söldner von Englands Gnaden. Tatsachenbericht.*
Bremen: Burmester, [1939?]. 95 pp., illus., map.

3139 THIERFELDER, FRANZ: *Englischer Kulturimperialismus. Der British Council als
Werkzeug der geistigen Einkreisung Deutschlands.* Berlin: Junker &
Dünnhaupt, 1940. 67 pp.

3140 VASSÉ, JEAN GONTIER de: *Ich komme soeben aus England! Tagebuch des
französischen Dunkirchen-Kämpfers. Begegnung mit dem Verfasser von
Wilhelm Fanderl.* Berlin: Nibelungen-Verlag, 1941. 59 pp., illus., facsims.

3141 *Weltpirat England.* Berlin: Uhlmann, 1939/40. Pamphlets of 40 pp. each.
[Incl. Gibraltar, Ireland, India, Palestine.]

3142 WIRSING, GISELHER: *One hundred families rule the British Empire.* Berlin:
Deutscher Verlag, 1940. 96 + 16 pp., illus., bibl. [German version: *Hundert
Familien beherrschen das Empire.*]

3143 ZIEGLER, WILHELM, ed.: *Ein Dokumentenwerk über die englische Demokratie.*
Im Auftr. des Reichsministeriums für Volksaufklärung und Propaganda
hrsg. unter Mitw. des Amtes Wissenschaft und Facherziehung der
Reichsstudentenführung. Berlin: Deutscher Verlag, [1940?]. 336 pp., illus.,
tabs.

Soviet Union

3144 AUSWÄRTIGES AMT: *Bolschewistische Verbrechen gegen Kriegsrecht und
Menschenrecht. Dokumente.* Berlin: 1941/42.
1. Folge: Publ. 1941. 309 pp.
2. Folge: Publ. 1942. 286 pp.
[Also in French.]

3145 DIEL, LOUISE: *Himmelbett Moskau. Frauenerlebnisse im Sowjetparadies.*
Berlin: Nibelungen Verlag, 1941. 266 pp.

3146 DIEWERGE, WOLFGANG, ed.: *Deutsche Soldaten sehen die Sowjet-Union.
Feldpostbriefe aus dem Osten.* Berlin: Limpert, 1941. 63 pp., illus.

3147 JORGENSEN, AAGE: *Et Bezog i Ukraine. 2400 km's Rundrejs over Central- og
Østeuropa*
[and]
HÄGGQUIST, (Professor): *Massegravene i Vinnitza.*
København: 1943. 32 pp., illus. [Offprint from 'Globus'. Anti-Russian
propaganda on Ukrainian themes for use in occupied Denmark.]

3148 KLUG, KAJETAN: *Die grösste Sklaverei der Weltgeschichte. Tatsachenberichte
aus den Strafgebieten der G.P.U.* Berlin: Eher, 1943. 64 pp., illus., maps,
facsim. [First publ. 1941, ed. by Karl Neuscheler.]

KOMMOSS, RUDOLF: *Juden hinter Stalin. See* 486.

3149 *Ma chère Maman! Chers parents! Cher frère! Cher ami! Lettres de soldats slovaques écrites de Russie Soviétique.* [No impr.: 1942?]. 12 pp., facsims. [Also in German: *Teure Mutter!*]

3150 MARJAY, FRIEDRICH: *Europa oder Chaos? Ein Ungar über den Bolschewismus.* Nürnberg: Willmy, [1943]. 285 pp., illus., facsims., tabs.

3151 VINDEX, pseud.: *Die Politik des Ölflecks. Der Sowjetimperialismus im Zweiten Weltkrieg.* Berlin: Deutscher Verlag, 1944. 147 pp.

3152 [WINNIZA] *Amtliches Material zum Massenmord von Winniza.* Im Auftr. des Reichsministers für die besetzten Ostgebiete auf Grund urkundlichen Beweismaterials zusammengestellt, bearb. und hrsg. Berlin: Eher, 1944. 282 pp., illus., facsims., maps.

United States of America

3153 ALDAG, PETER: *Dollar-Imperialismus.* Berlin: Eher, 1942. 182 pp. (Schriftenreihe der NSDAP).

3154 EHLERS, ERICH: *Freimaurer arbeiten für Roosevelt. Freimaurerische Dokumente über die Zusammenarbeit zwischen Roosevelt und der Freimaurerei.* Berlin: Nordland-Verlag, 1943. 70 pp., facsims.

3155 HALTER, HEINZ: *Der Polyp von New York. Die Geschichte Tammany Halls. Korruption und Verbrechen im demokratischen Amerika nach Tatsachen berichtet.* Dresden: Müller, 1942. 215 pp.

3156 JENTSCH, GERHART: *La politique de violence des États-Unis. L'emploi de la violence organisée dans la politique extérieure des États-Unis. Enquête statistique.* Sceaux: [1943?]. 24 pp.

3157 LEERS, JOHANN von: *Kräfte hinter Roosevelt.* 2. Aufl. Berlin-Steglitz: Fritsche, 1941. 189 pp., bibl. [French version: *Forces occultes derrière Roosevelt.* Bruxelles: Maison Internationale d'Édition, (1941).]

3158 LENZ, FRIEDRICH: *Die Krisis des Kapitalismus in den Vereinigten Staaten.* Stuttgart: Kohlhammer, 1944. 131 pp., tabs.

3159 PASE, MARTIN: *Roosevelts Reden und Raten im Scheinwerfer der Presse und Karikatur.* Leipzig: Lühe, [194–]. 117 pp.

3160 SCHWARZBURG, ERICH: *Die jüdische Kriegshetze in den U.S.A.* 2. Aufl. Frankfurt a.M.: Welt-Dienst-Verlag, 1944. 42 pp.

3161 WIRSING, GISELHER: *Der masslose Kontinent. Roosevelts Kampf um die Weltherrschaft.* 2. Aufl. Jena: Diederichs, 1942. 473 pp., tabs., map, bibl.

3162 WREDE, FRANZ-OTTO: *Schmelztiegel Amerika.* 31.–40. Taus. Berlin: Eher, 1941. 136 pp., maps, bibl. (Schriftenreihe der NSDAP).

3163 WÜNSCHE, JULIUS: *Der Wirtschaftskampf der USA um Süd- und Mittelamerika.* Leipzig: Lutzeyer, 1942. 197 pp.

3164 WUNDERLICH, CURT: *U $ A. Dollarimperialismus und Wallstreetterror. Belegt durch Postwertzeichen.* Berlin: Staneck, 1943. 143 pp.

g. Favourable Nazi propaganda

Finland

3165 KNYPHAUSEN, ANTON: *Finnlands Freiheitskampf. Die Verteidigung Europas in den finnischen Wäldern.* Hamburg: Broschek, 1942. 196 pp.

3166 RUPPERT, ARTHUR, ed.: *Bauern und Helden. Ein Finnlandbuch.* Bearb.: Heinz Hünger, Anitra Karsten. 2. Aufl. Leipzig: Lühe, 1943. 304 pp., illus., maps, tabs.

3167 *Waffenbruder Finland. Ein Buch für die deutschen Soldaten in Finnland.* Geleitw.: Alfred Rosenberg, P. E. Svufvud. Helsinki: Frenckellin, 1942. 283 pp., illus.

France

3168 MATTICK, HEINZ: *Die treibenden Kräfte in der Geschichte Frankreichs.* Berlin: Mittler, 1942. 95 pp., illus., maps.

Hungary

3169 *Deutschland—Ungarn.* Breslau: Gauverlag NS-Schlesien, [1941]. 202 pp., illus., tabs.

Italy

3170 HERKOMMER, JUL[IUS]: *Libyen von Italien kolonisiert. Ein Beitrag zur vorbildlichen Kolonialpolitik Italiens in Nordafrika* ... Freiburg i.Br.: Bielefeld, 1941. 195 pp., illus., tabs., map, bibl.

3171 IPSER, KARL: *Deutschland—Italien. Denkstätten einer Völkergemeinschaft.* Leipzig: Hammer, 1940. 239 pp., illus., map, bibl.

Japan

3172 FÜRHOLZER, EDMUND: *Freundesland im Osten. Ein Nipponbuch in Bildern.* Berlin: Limpert, 1943. 303 pp., illus.

3173 STEEN, HANS: *Helden unter dem Sonnenbanner. Ein Tatsachenbericht.* Dresden: Müller, 1943. 151 pp.

Middle East

3174 SEIFERT, HERMANN ERICH: *Der Aufbruch in der arabischen Welt.* Berlin: Eher, 1940. 91 pp., illus., map.

Romania

3175 *Deutschland—Rumänien.* Hrsg. im Auftr. des Reichskommissars und Staatsrats Josef Wagner. Breslau: Gauverlag NS-Schlesien, Auslandsabt., [1940]. 128 pp., illus., maps, tabs. [Text in German and Romanian.]

3176 LAEVEN, HARALD: *Marschall Antonescu.* Essen: Essener Verlagsanstalt, 1943. 177 pp., illus.

Ukraine

3177   DOROSCHENKO, DMYTRO: *Die Ukraine und das Reich. Neun Jahrhundert deutsch-ukrainischer Beziehungen im Spiegel der deutschen Wissenschaft und Literatur.* Leipzig: Hirzel, 1942. 299 pp.

3178   MIRTSCHUK, J., ed.: *Handbuch der Ukraine.* Im Auftr. des Ukrainischen Wissenschaftlichen Instituts in Berlin. Leipzig: Harrassowitz, 1941. 416 pp.

V. THE CRIMINAL STATE

A. INSTRUMENTS OF REPRESSION

1. SA (STURMABTEILUNG)

3179 ANACKER, HEINRICH: *Die Trommel. S.A. Gedichte.* 5. Aufl. München: Eher, 1936. 129 pp.

3180 ANDERLAHN, HANNS: *Gegner erkannt! Kampferlebnisse der SA. im Jahre 1937.* 68 pp., illus. (Kampfschriften der Obersten SA.-Führung, Bd. 3).

3181 BADE, WILFRID: *Die SA erobert Berlin. Ein Tatsachenbericht.* 8. Aufl. München: Knorr & Hirth, 1943. 261 pp., illus.

3182 BAYER, ERNST, ed.: *Die SA. Geschichte, Arbeit, Zweck und Organisation der Sturmabteilungen des Führers und der Obersten SA.-Führung* ... Berlin: Junker & Dünnhaupt, 1938. 32 pp., diagr. (Schriften der Hochschule für Politik, II: Der organisatorische Aufbau des Dritten Reiches ...).

3183 BENNECKE, HEINRICH: *Hitler und die SA.* München: Olzog, 1962. 264 pp., maps, tabs., bibl.

3184 *Dienst-Taschenbuch für Sturmführer, Truppführer, Scharführer.* Bearb.: Friedrich Joachim Klaehn. Leipzig: Schaufuss, 1934. 128 pp.

3185 DOBERT, EITEL WOLF: *Convert to freedom.* Transl. from the German. New York: Putnam, 1940. 337 pp. [Autobiography of a converted storm-trooper.]

3186 EHRENREICH, BERND: *Marine-SA. Das Buch einer Formation.* Hamburg: Hanseatische Verlagsanstalt, 1935. 139 pp.

3186a ELMAYER-VESTENBRUGG, RUDOLF von, ed.: *SA.-Männer im feldgrauen Rock. Taten und Erlebnisse von SA.-Männern in den Kriegsjahren 1939–1940.* Leipzig: Koehler, 1942. 289 pp., illus., bibl.

3187 ENGELBRECHTEN, J. K. von: *Eine braune Armee entsteht. Die Geschichte der Berlin-Brandenburger SA.* Im Auftr. des Führers der SA-Gruppe Berlin-Brandenburg SA-Obergruppenführer Dietrich von Jagow bearb. München: Eher, 1937. 428 pp., illus.

3188 GERSTMAYER, HERMANN: *SA-Mann Peter Müller.* 4. Aufl. Berlin: Beltz, [1935]. 87 pp., illus. [Novel.]

3189 GLASER, WALDEMAR: *Ein Trupp SA. Vom Leben und Kämpfen für Deutschland.* Leipzig: Koehler & Voigtländer, 1941. 288 pp.

3190 *Halbmast. Ein Heldenbuch der SA und SS. 1. Folge.* Den Toten der *Nationalsozialistischen Deutschen Arbeiterpartei zum Gedächtnis.* Berlin: Verlag Braune Bücher, 1932. 95 pp., illus.

3191 *Handbuch der SA.* Hrsg. mit Genehmigung der Obersten SA-Führung. Berlin: Verlag 'Offene Worte', 1939. 397 pp., illus.

3192 HEINES, [EDMUND], comp.: *Schlesisches SA-Liederbuch. Ausg. B.* 4. Aufl. Breslau: Steinberg & Attikal, 1933. 112 pp., illus., mus. scores. [Heines was the first to be murdered on 30 June 1934.]

3193 HOFFMANN, HEINRICH: *Das braune Heer. 100 Bilddokumente: Leben, Kampf und Sieg der S.A. und S.S.* Berlin: Verlag Zeitgeschichte, 1932. 96 pp., illus.

3194 IBACH, KARL: *Kemna. Wuppertaler Lager der SA, 1933.* Wuppertal: Vorstand der VVN, 1948. 132 pp.

3195 KILLINGER, MANFRED VON: *Die SA in Wort und Bild.* Leipzig: Kittler, 1933. 96 pp., illus.

3196 KOCH, KARL W. H.: *Männer im Braunhemd. Vom Kampf und Sieg der SA.* Neue, bis zur Gegenwart fortgeführte Aufl., mit einem Ausklang von Kurt Massmann. Berlin: Stubenrauch, 1936. 359 pp., illus.

3197 LOHMANN, HEINZ: *SA. räumt auf! Aus der Kampfzeit der Bewegung. Aufzeichnungen.* Einmalige Ausg. Hamburg: Deutsche Hausbücherei, [1933]. 273 pp., facsims.

3198 PANTEL, GERHARD: *Befehl Deutschland. Ein Tagebuch vom Kampf um Berlin.* München: Eher, 1936. 114 pp.

3199 REISSE, HERMANN: *Sieg Heil SA!* Berlin: Nationaler Freiheitsverlag, 1933. 135 pp.

3200 RÖHM, ERNST: *Die Geschichte eines Hochverräters.* 7. Aufl. München: Eher, 1934. 367 pp., illus. [Autobiography. Copyright 1928.]

3201 *SA.* Hrsg. im Auftr. der Obersten SA Führung. München: Eher, 1938. 128 pp., illus. [Incl.: 'Ehrentafel der Ermordeten der Bewegung', 'Geschichte der SA', 'Horst Wessel'.]

3202 SNYCKERS, HANS: *Tagebuch eines Sturmführers.* München: Eher, 1940. 134 pp.

3203 STELZNER, FRITZ: *Schicksal SA. Die Deutung eines grossen Geschehens. Von einem der es selbst erlebte.* München: Eher, 1936. 209 pp.

3204 WELLER, TÜDEL: *Rabauken! Peter Mönkemann haut sich durch. Roman.* München: Eher, 1938. 342 pp.

3205 WERNER, ANDREAS: *SA und NSDAP. SA: 'Wehrverband', 'Parteitruppe' oder 'Revolutionsarmee'? Studien zur Geschichte der SA und der NSDAP 1920–1933.* Inaugural-Dissertation [pres. to] Friedrich-Alexander-Universität zu Erlangen-Nürnberg. 1964. 599 + xxxvii + xiv pp., diagrs., tabs., bibl.

WESSEL, HORST

3206 EWERS, HANNS HEINZ: *Horst Wessel. Ein deutsches Schicksal.* Stuttgart: Cotta, 1935. 295 pp., port.

3207 WESSEL, INGEBORG: *Mein Bruder Horst. Ein Vermächtnis.* München: Eher, 1934. 155 pp.

2. SS (SCHUTZSTAFFEL)

a. General

AHNENERBE

3208 EPSTEIN, FRITZ T.: 'War-time activities of the SS-Ahnenerbe'. [In] Max Beloff, ed.: *On the track of tyranny. Essays presented ... to Leonard G. Montefiore.* London: Vallentine, Mitchell, for the Wiener Library, [1959]. Pp. 77–95.

3209 KATER, MICHAEL H.: *Das 'Ahnenerbe'. Die Forschungs- und Lehrgemeinschaft in der SS. Organisationsgeschichte von 1935 bis 1945.* Inaugural-Dissertation [pres. to] Ruprecht-Karl-Universität in Heidelberg. 1966. 594 pp., diagrs., bibl. (notes and bibl., pp. 295–594).

3210 ARTZT, HEINZ: *Mörder in Uniform. Organisationen, die zu Vollstreckern nationalsozialistischer Verbrechen wurden.* Vorw.: Gert Bastian. München: Kindler, 1979. 205 pp., illus., facsims., diagr., bibl. [Mainly on SS and its departments.]

3211 BAYLE, F[RANÇOIS]: *Psychologie et éthique du national-socialisme. Étude anthropologique des dirigeants S.S.* Préface: Pierre Oudard. Paris: Presses Universitaires de France, 1953. 546 pp., illus.

3212 BOEHNERT, GUNNAR CHARLES: *A sociography of the SS officer corps, 1925–1939.* [Dissertation pres. to] University of London. 1978. v + 262 pp., tabs., bibl.

3213 BOGATSVO, JULES: *Les S.S. Techniciens de la mort.* Adaptation: André Bernard. Paris: de Vecchi, 1973. 262 pp., illus., facsims.

3214 BRISSAUD, ANDRÉ: *Les agents de Lucifer.* Paris: Perrin, 1975. 556 pp., facsims., illus., bibl.

3215 BUCHHEIM, HANS and others: *Anatomie des SS-Staates.* 2. Aufl. München: Deutscher Taschenbuch-Verlag, 1979. [First publ. 1965.]
Bd. 1: Hans Buchheim: *Die SS—Das Herrschaftsinstrument. Befehl und Gehorsam.* 323 pp.
Bd. 2: Martin Broszat: *Nationalsozialistische Konzentrationslager 1933–1945*; Hans-Adolf Jacobsen: *Kommissarbefehl und Massenexecutionen sowjetischer Kriegsgefangener*; Helmut Krausnick: *Judenverfolgung.* 370 pp.

3216 BUCHHEIM, HANS: *SS und Polizei im NS-Staat.* Duisdorf b. Bonn: Studiengesellschaft für Zeitprobleme, 1964. 224 pp., bibl.

3217 CYGANSKI, MIROSŁAW: *SS w ruchu narodowosocjalistycznym i w III Rzeszy* [SS in the National Socialist movement and in the Third Reich] *1925–1945*. Poznań: Instytut Zachodni, 1978. 446 pp., diagrs., summary in English.

3218 DICKS, HENRY V.: *Licensed mass murder. A socio-psychological study of some SS killers.* London: Chatto, Heinemann, for Sussex University Press, 1972. xiii + 283 pp.

3219 *Dienstaltersliste der Schutzstaffel der NSDAP. Stand vom 1. Dezember 1937.* Bearb. von der SS-Personalkanzlei. Berlin: 1937. 401 pp. [Other such lists were issued dealing with different periods and various ranks.]

3220 GEORG, ENNO: *Die wirtschaftlichen Unternehmungen der SS.* Stuttgart: Deutsche Verlags-Anstalt, 1963. 154 pp., tabs. (Schriftenreihe der Vierteljahrshefte für Zeitgeschichte).

3221 GRÜNBERG, KAROL: *SS—czarna gwardia Hitlera* [SS—Hitler's black guard]. Warszawa: Książka i Wiedza, 1975. 558 pp., diagrs., bibl.

3222 GRUNBERGER, RICHARD: *Hitler's SS.* London: Weidenfeld & Nicolson, 1970. 128 pp., illus., bibl.

3223 HÖHNE, HEINZ: *Der Orden unter dem Totenkopf. Die Geschichte der SS.* Gütersloh: Mohn, 1967. 600 pp., illus., tabs., bibl. [English version: *The Order of the Death's Head.* London: Secker & Warburg, 1969.]

LEBENSBORN

3224 HILLEL, MARC & HENRY, CLARISSA: *Au nom de la race.* Paris: Fayard, 1975. 271 pp., illus., facsims., bibl. [English version: *Children of the SS.* London: Hutchinson, 1976. German version: *Lebensborn. Im Namen der Rasse.* Wien: 1975.]

3225 HRABAR, ROMAN: *'Lebensborn', czyli żrodło życia* ['Lebensborn', source of life]. Katowice: Wyd. 'Śląsk', 1975. 221 pp., illus., facsims., bibl.

LEIBSTANDARTE

3226 LUCAS, JAMES & COOPER, MATTHEW: *Hitler's elite. Leibstandarte SS 1933–45.* London: Macdonald & Jane's, 1975. 160 pp., illus., maps, bibl.

3227 WEINGARTNER, JAMES JOSEPH, jr.: *The Leibstandarte Adolf Hitler 1933–1945. Thesis submitted to the University of Wisconsin, 1967.* Ann Arbor, Mich.: University Microfilms, 1978. 261 pp., bibl.

3228 PAETEL, KARL O.: 'Geschichte und Soziologie der SS'. [In] *Vierteljahrshefte für Zeitgeschichte*, Bd. 2, 1954. Stuttgart: Deutsche Verlags-Anstalt. Pp. 1–33.

3229 REICHSFÜHRUNG SS: *SS-Liederbuch.* 7. Aufl. München: Eher, [194–]. 255 pp., mus. scores.

3230 REITLINGER, GERALD: *The SS—alibi of a nation, 1922–1945.* Melbourne: Heinemann, 1956. 502 pp., illus., bibl. [British re-issue: *Alibi of a nation.* Arms & Armour, 1981. German version: *Die SS. Tragödie einer deutschen Epoche. Mit 243 Kurzbiographien.* München: Desch, 1957.]

3231 SCHICKEL, ALFRED: 'Wehrmacht und SS. Eine Untersuchung über ihre Stellung und Rolle in den Planungen der nationalsozialistischen Führer'. [In] *Geschichte in Wissenschaft und Unterricht*, Jhrg. 21, Heft 10, Okt. 1970. Stuttgart: Klett. Pp. 581–606.

3232 SCHNABEL, REIMUND: *Macht ohne Moral. Eine Dokumentation über die SS.* Frankfurt a.M.: Röderberg, 1957. 580 pp., illus., diagrs.

3233 *Uniforms of the SS.* London: Historical Research Unit, 1968–1972. 6 vols., illus., facsims., bibls.
Vol. I: Andrew Mollo: *Allgemeine SS, 1923–1945.* Publ. 1968. 74 pp.
Vol. II: Hugh Page Taylor: *Germanische-SS, 1940–1945.* Publ. 1969. 152 pp.
Vol. III: Andrew Mollo: *SS-Verfügungstruppe, 1933–1939.* With introd. and unit histories by H. P. Taylor. Publ. 1970. 99 pp.
Vol. IV: Andrew Mollo: *SS-Totenkopfverbände, 1933–1945.* Publ. 1971. 51 pp., tabs.
Vol. V: Andrew Mollo: *Sicherheitsdienst and Sicherheitspolizei, 1931–1945.* Publ. 1971. 54 pp., diagrs.
Vol. VI: Andrew Mollo: *Waffen-SS clothing and equipment, 1939–1945.* Publ. 1972. 133 pp., bibl.

3234 ZUMPE, L.: 'Die Textilbetriebe der SS im Konzentrationslager Ravensbrück. Eine Studie über ökonomische Funktion und wirtschaftliche Tätigkeit der SS'. [In] *Jahrbuch für Wirtschaftsgeschichte*, Teil I, 1969. Berlin [East]: Akademie Verlag. Pp. 11–40, tabs.

b. SS leaders

Heydrich, Reinhard

3235 ARONSON, SHLOMO: *Heydrich und die Anfänge des SD und der Gestapo 1931–1935.* Inaugural-Dissertation [pres. to] Freie Universität Berlin. 1967. 431 pp.

3236 DESCHNER, GÜNTHER: *Reinhard Heydrich. Statthalter der totalen Macht. Biographie.* Esslingen: Bechtle, 1977. 376 pp., illus., bibl.

3237 HEYDRICH, LINA: *Leben mit einem Kriegsverbrecher.* Kommentare: Werner Maser. Pfaffhofen: Ludwig, 1976. 211 pp., illus., facsims., bibl.

3238 PAILLARD, GEORGES & ROUGERIE, CLAUDE: *Reinhard Heydrich (protecteur de Bohême et Moravie). Le violiniste de la mort.* Paris: Fayard, 1973. 316 pp., bibl.

3239 WIGHTON, CHARLES: *Heydrich. Hitler's most evil henchman.* London: Odhams Press, 1962. 288 pp., illus.

Himmler, Heinrich

3240 HIMMLER, HEINRICH: *Geheimreden 1933 bis 1945 und andere Ansprachen.* Hrsg.: Bradley F. Smith, Agnes F. Peterson. Einf.: Joachim C. Fest. [Berlin]: Propyläen Verlag, 1974. 319 pp., illus.

3241 ACKERMANN, JOSEF: *Heinrich Himmler als Ideologe*. Göttingen: Musterschmidt, 1970. 317 pp., illus., bibl. [Incl.: IV: 'Die Endlösung der Judenfrage'; VI: 'Himmler und der Osten. Germanisierung, Entvölkerung, Versklavung'.]

3242 CALIC, EDUARD: *Himmler et son empire*. Paris: Stock, 1966. 682 pp., illus., bibl.

3243 *Festgabe für Heinrich Himmler zu seinem 40. Geburtstag*. Darmstadt: Wittich, 1941. 292 pp.

3244 FRISCHAUER, WILLI: *Himmler. The evil genius of the Third Reich*. London: Odhams Press, 1953. 270 pp., illus.

3245 HEIBER, HELMUT, ed.: *Reichsführer!... Briefe an und von Himmler*. Stuttgart: Deutsche Verlags-Anstalt, 1968. 318 pp., bibl.

KERSTEN, FELIX

3246 KERSTEN, FELIX: *Totenkopf und Treue. Heinrich Himmler ohne Uniform. Aus den Tagebuchblättern des finnischen Medizinalrats*. Hamburg: Mölich, 1952. 407 pp. [English version: *The Kersten memoirs, 1940–1945*. Introd.: H. R. Trevor-Roper. London: Hutchinson, 1956.]

3247 BESGEN, ACHIM: *Der stille Befehl. Medizinalrat Kersten, Himmler und das Dritte Reich*. München: Nymphenburger Verlagshandlung, 1960. 206 pp., bibl.

3248 KESSEL, JOSEPH; *The man with the miraculous hands*. Introd.: H. R. Trevor-Roper. Transl. from the French. New York: Farrar, Straus & Cudahy, 1961. 235 pp. [German version: *Medizinalrat Kersten. Der Mann mit den magischen Händen*. München: Nymphenburger Verlagshandlung, 1961.]

3249 MANVELL, ROGER & FRAENKEL, HEINRICH: *Heinrich Himmler*. London: Heinemann, 1965. 285 pp., illus., bibl.

3250 SMITH, BRADLEY F.: *Heinrich Himmler. A Nazi in the making, 1900–1926*. Stanford, Calif.: Hoover Institution Press, 1971. ix + 211 pp., illus., facsims., bibl.

3251 VOGELSANG, REINHARD: *Der Freundeskreis Himmler*. Göttingen: Musterschmidt, 1972. 182 pp., illus., tabs., bibl.

3252 WYKES, ALAN: *Himmler*. London: Pan Books, 1973. 159 pp., illus.

c. Nationalsozialistisches Kraftfahr Korps

3253 NATIONALSOZIALISTISCHES KRAFTFAHR-KORPS: *Verordnungsblatt der Korps-führung. Auszüge ... 15. Okt. 1934–25. März 1938 ... nach dem Stand vom 1. Mai 1938*. 220 pp., maps, reprods. of forms.

3254 OPPERMANN, (Gruppenführer): *Unter den Sturmstandern des NSKK. Blätter aus der Geschichte des Nationalsozialistischen Kraftfahr-Korps*. München: Eher, 1936. 280 pp.

3. POLICE

a. Sicherheitsdienst

3255 BOBERACH, HEINZ, ed.: *Berichte der SD und der Gestapo über Kirche und Kirchenvolk in Deutschland 1934–1944.* Mainz: Matthias-Grünewald-Verlag, 1971. xliii + 1021 pp., bibl. (Veröffentlichungen der Kommission für Zeitgeschichte ...).

3256 BOBERACH, HEINZ, ed.: *Meldungen aus dem Reich. Auswahl aus den geheimen Lageberichten des Sicherheitsdienststes der SS 1939–1944.* Berlin: Luchterhand, 1965. 551 pp.

3257 BROWDER, GEORGE C.: 'Die Anfänge des SD. Dokumente aus der Organisationsgeschichte des Sicherheitsdienstes des Reichsführers SS'. [In] *Vierteljahrshefte für Zeitgeschichte,* Jhrg. 27, Heft 2, April 1979. Pp. 299–324.

3258 MOSSE, GEORGE L., ed.: *Police forces in history.* London: Sage, 1975. vii + 333 pp. [Incl.: Peter Hoffmann: 'Maurice Bavaud's attempt to assassinate Hitler in 1938'; George C. Browder: 'The SD ...'; Otto Ohlendorf: 'The Sicherheitsdienst and public opinion in Nazi Germany.']

3259 RAMMER, ALWIN: *Der Sicherheitsdienst der SS. Zu seiner Funktion im faschistischen Machtapparat und im Besatzungsregime des sogenannten Generalgouvernements Polen.* Berlin [East]: Deutscher Militärverlag, 1970. 324 pp., map. diagrs., bibl.

3260 DER REICHSFÜHRER SS & DER CHEF DES SICHERHEITSHAUPTAMTES: *Erfassung führender Männer der Systemzeit. Geheim! Juni 1939.* [Approx. 600 pp., mimeog. Alphabetical and classified list of 553 anti-Nazis with brief data on allegiances and activities before and after 1933.]

b. Gestapo (Geheime Staatspolizei)

3261 ARONSON, SHLOMO: *Beginnings of the Gestapo system. The Bavarian model in 1933.* Jerusalem: Israel Universities Press, 1969. 76 pp., ports., tabs.

3262 BAXTER, RICHARD: *Women of the Gestapo.* London: Quality Press, 1943. 95 pp.

3263 BRAMSTEDT, E. K.: *Dictatorship and political police. The technique of control by fear.* London: Kegan Paul, Trench, Truner, 1945. 275 pp.

3264 BRISSAUD, ANDRÉ: *Histoire du Service Secret nazi.* Paris: Plon, 1972. 392 pp., illus., diagrs., bibl.

3265 CRANKSHAW, EDWARD: *Gestapo—instrument of tyranny.* London: Putnam, 1956. 275 pp. [German version: Berlin: Colloquium Verlag, 1959.]

3266 DELARUE, JACQUES: *Histoire de la Gestapo.* [Paris]: Fayard, 1962. 399 pp., bibl. [English version: *The history of the Gestapo.* London: MacDonald, 1964. German version: *Geschichte der Gestapo.* Düsseldorf: Droste, 1964.]

3267 DESROCHES, ALAIN: *La Gestapo. Atrocités et secrets de l'inquisition nazie.* Paris: de Vecchi, 1975. 869 pp., facsims., illus.

3268 DIELS, RUDOLF: *Lucifer ante portas. Zwischen Severing und Heydrich.* Zürich: Interverlag, [n.d.]. 326 pp. [Account of author's role as first head of the Gestapo and his break with the Nazi regime.]

3269 HAUTECLOQUE, XAVIER de: *Police politique hitlérienne.* Paris: Eds. de la Nouvelle Revue critique, 1935. 224 pp.

3270 KOEHLER, HANSJÜRGEN: *Inside the Gestapo. Hitler's shadow over the world.* London: Pallas Publ. Co., 1940. 287 pp.

3271 POIESZ, WILHELM: *Gefangener der Gestapo.* Limburg: Lahn, 1948. 172 pp.

3272 THÉVOZ, ROBERT and others: *Pommern 1934/35 im Spiegel von Gestapo-Lageberichten und Sachakten.* [By] Robert Thévoz, Hans Branig, Cecile Lowenthal-Hensel. Köln: Grote, 1974. (Die Geheime Staatspolizei in den preussischen Ostprovinzen, 1934–1936. Veröffentlichungen aus den Archiven Preussischer Kulturbesitz ...).
Bd. 1: *Darstellung.* 335 pp., bibl.
Bd. 2: *Quellen.* 441 pp.

c. Other police

3273 BEST, WERNER: *Die deutsche Polizei.* Darmstadt: Wittich, 1941. 110 pp., tabs.

3274 FRANK, [HANS] and others: *Grundfragen der deutschen Polizei. Bericht über die konstituierende Sitzung des Ausschusses für Polizeirecht der Akademie für Deutsches Recht am 11. Oktober 1936.* [Speeches by] [Hans] Frank, Heinrich Himmler, [Werner] Best, (Prof.) Höhn. Hamburg: Hanseatische Verlagsanstalt, 1937. 35 pp.

3275 GROSCH, A. & PETTERS, WALTER: *Strafgesetzbuch für das deutsche Reich mit Nebengesetzen und Erläuterungen, sowie einem Anhang über Grundsätze und wichtige Bestimmungen des Strafprozessrechts und über das Kriegsstrafrecht. Zum Gebrauch für Polizei-, Kriminal-, und Gendarmeriebeamte.* Berlin: Schweitzer, 1944. 359 pp.

3276 *Jahrbuch der deutschen Polizei 1936.* Hrsg.: Hans Kehrl. Leitspruch: Dr. Frick. Geleitw.: K. Daluege. Leipzig: Breitkopf & Härtel, 1936. 167 pp., illus., facsim., diagr., tabs. [No others publ.]

3277 KOSCHORKE, HELMUTH, comp.: *Jederzeit einsatzbereit. Ein Bildbericht von der neuen deutschen Polizei.* Geleitw.: Wilhelm Frick, Heinrich Himmler, [Kurt Daluege, Reinhard Heydrich]. Berlin: Andermann, 1939. [73 pp]., illus.

3278 KOSCHORKE, HELMUTH, ed.: *Die Polizei—einmal anders! Geschrieben von der deutschen Presse zum 'Tag der deutschen Polizei'.* Geleitw.: Reichsführer SS Heinrich Himmler. München: Eher, 1937. 235 pp.

3279 LIEPELT, ADOLF: *Über den Umfang und die Bedeutung der Polizeigewalt im nationalsozialistischen Staat.* Würzburg: Triltsch, 1938. 71 pp., bibl.

3280 [NEBE, ARTHUR] GISEVIUS, HANS BERND: *Wo ist Nebe? Erinnerungen an Hitlers Reichskriminaldirektor.* Zürich: Droemer, 1966. 320 pp., bibl.

3281 NEUFELDT, HANS-JOACHIM and others: *Zur Geschichte der Ordnungspolizei, 1936–1945.* [By] Hans-Joachim Neufeldt, Jürgen Huck, Georg Tessin. Koblenz: [Bundesarchiv], 1957. 144 + 110 pp., tabs.

3282 REICHSKRIMINALPOLIZEIAMT, Berlin: *Organisation und Meldedienst der Reichskriminalpolizei.* Geleitw.: Chef der Sicherheitspolizei ... Reinhard Heydrich. Bearb.: SS-Standartenführer Reichskriminaldirektor Nebe, Kriminalrat Fleischer ... Berlin: Jaedicke, 1939. 278 pp. (looseleaf), diagrs., reprods of official forms. [Incl. 'Rassenschande'.]

RICHTER, HANS: *Einsatz der Polizei. Bei den Polizeibataillonen in Ost, Nord und West. See* 5244.

3283 SCHEER, BERNHARD & BARTSCH, GEORG, eds.: *Das Polizeiverwaltungsgesetz. Ein Leitfaden. Zum Handgebrauch für Studium und Praxis.* Anhang: 'Das Polizeiverwaltungsgesetz nebst Ausführungsbestimmungen und ergänzenden Verordnungen'. Im Einverständnis mit dem Kameradschaftsbund Deutscher Polizeibeamten neubearb. Berlin: Freiheitsverlag, 1936. 141 pp.

3284 WEHNER, BERND: *Die polnischen Greueltaten. Kriminalpolizeiliche Ermittlungsergebnisse.* Mitarb.: Kriminalkommissar Discar. Berlin: Jaedicke, 1942. 192 pp., illus., facsims., diagrs. (Archiv des Reichssicherheitshauptamtes).

4. PRISONS

3285 ALT, KARL: *Todeskandidaten. Erlebnisse eines Seelsorgers im Gefängnis München-Stadelheim mit zahlreichen im Hitlerreich zum Tode verurteilten Männern und Frauen.* München: Gross, 1946. 96 pp., illus.

3286 BENCKISER, NIKOLAS: *Tage wie Schwestern. Ein Bericht.* Frankfurt a.M.: Knecht, 1958. 287 pp. [Experiences in Gestapo prisons in Budapest and Vienna.]

3287 [BRINKMANN, FERDINAND] BRINKMANN, ELISABETH: *Der letzte Gang. Ein Priesterleben im Dienst Todgeweihter. Erinnerungen an meinem Bruder.* Münster: Aschendorff, 1951. 103 pp., port. [Incl. members of the Resistance.]

3288 KÜHMAYER, IGNAZ CHRISTOPH: *Auferstehung.* Wien: Wiener Dom-Verlag, 1948. 203 pp. [Experiences of an Austrian priest in Nazi prisons.]

3289 LORANT, STEFAN: *I was Hitler's prisoner. Leaves from a prison diary.* Transl. from the German. Harmondsworth, Middx.: Penguin Books, 1935. 278 pp.

3290 LUX, ALBERT: *Von Goerings Kriegsflugstaffeln in Goerings Zuchthäuser. Selbsterlebnisse eines elsässischen Soldaten des Weltkrieges.* Strasbourg: Brandt, 1938. 307 pp., illus.

PLÖTZENSEE
3291 *Ehrenbuch der Opfer von Berlin-Plötzensee.* Berlin: VVN-Westberlin, 1974. 215 pp., illus., facsims., lists of victims. (Red.: Willy Park, Willi Desch).

3292 GOSTOMSKI, VICTOR & LOCH, WALTER: *Der Tod von Plötzensee. Erinnerungen—Ereignisse—Dokumente. 1942–1945.* Freising: Kyrios-Verlag, 1969. 254 pp., illus., facsims.

3293 POELSCHAU, HARALD: *Die letzten Stunden. Erinnerungen eines Gefängnispfarrers, aufgezeichnet von Alexander Stenbock-Fermor.* Berlin: Volk und Welt Verlag, 1949. 153 pp., illus. [Incl. Dutch, Norwegian and Czech members of the Resistance.]

3294 RINSER, LUISE: *Gefängnistagebuch.* München: Desch, 1946. 234 pp.

3295 SCHULZE, FIETE: *Briefe und Aufzeichnungen aus dem Gestapo-Gefängnis in Hamburg.* Mit einer einleitenden Skizze von Erich Weinert. Berlin [East]: Dietz, 1959. 143 pp., illus., facsims. (Institut für Marxismus-Leninismus beim ZK der SED).

3296 U.C.: *Frauen in Fesseln. Erinnerungen einer Berliner Gefängnisfürsorgerin aus den Jahren 1933–1945.* Aufgeschrieben von Erich Klausener. Berlin: Morus, 1962. 32 pp.

3297 VIALLET, FRANÇOIS-ALBERT (pseud. of Ch. H. Boskowits): *La cuisine du diable.* Paris: Éds. Hier et Aujourd'hui, 1945. [German version: BOSKOWITS, Ch. H.: *Des Teufels Küche.* Wien: Zsolnay, 1947. 190 pp. Experiences of an Austrian Resistance fighter in German prisons and Wuhlheide concentration camp.]

3298 WEISENBORN, GÜNTHER: *Memorial.* München: Desch, 1947. 278 pp. [Persecution and prison experiences of a writer.]

B. PERSECUTION AND RESISTANCE

1. GENERAL

3299 BERADT, CHARLOTTE: *Das Dritte Reich des Traums.* München: Nymphenburger Verlag, 1966. 151 pp.

3300 BERNARD, HENRI: *L'autre Allemagne. La résistance allemande à Hitler, 1933–1945.* [Bruxelles]: La Renaissance du Livre, [1975?]. 299 pp., ports., plan.

3301 BÜCHEL, REGINE: *Der deutsche Widerstand im Spiegel von Fachliteratur und Publizistik seit 1945.* München: Bernard & Graefe, 1975. vii + 215 pp., bibl. (Schriften der Bibliothek für Zeitgeschichte ...).

3302 BURGER, R.: *Les horreurs fascistes en Allemagne.* Paris: Bureau d'Éditions, 1934. 100 pp.

3303 DEVOTO, ANDREA: *Bibliografia dell'oppressione nazista. Fino al 1962.* Firenze: Olschki, 1964. 149 pp.

3304 FRAENKEL, HEINRICH: *The German people versus Hitler.* London: Allen & Unwin, 1940. 370 pp., bibl.

3305 GALLIN, MARY ALICE: *German resistance to ... Hitler. Ethical and religious factors.* Washington, D.C.: The Catholic University of America Press, 1961. 259 pp., bibl.

3306 HART, HERMANN: *Attila der Letzte. Adolf Hitler und sein Drittes Reich vor dem Gerichtshof des Weltgewissens. Spiegel der Selbsterkenntnisse und auch Urteile der freien Welt zwischen 1933 und 1943. Eine Quellen- und Dokumentensammlung.* Volkach vor Würzburg: Hart, 1957. 341 pp., illus. [Collection made in Germany during the Nazi period.]

3307 HEIDEN, KONRAD: *The new Inquisition.* Transl. from the German. New York: Modern Age Books, 1939. 188 pp.

3308 HEYER, KARL: *Der Staat als Werkzeug des Bösen. Der Nationalsozialismus und das Schicksal des deutschen Volkes.* Stuttgart: Verlag Freies Geistesleben, 1965. 204 pp. [Reprint of first ed. entitled *Wenn die Götter den Tempel verlassen . . .*, publ. Freiburg i.Br. 1947.]

3309 HOCHMUTH, URSEL, ed.: *Faschismus und Widerstand 1933–1945. Ein Verzeichnis deutschsprachiger Literatur.* Frankfurt a.M.: Röderberg, 1973. 197 pp.

3310 JÄGER, HERBERT: *Verbrechen unter totalitärer Herrschaft. Studien zur nationalsozialistischen Gewaltkriminalität.* Olten: Walter, 1967. 388 pp., bibl.

3311 KLINGER, MAX (pseud. of Curt Geyer): *Volk in Ketten. Deutschlands Weg ins Chaos.* Carlsbad: 'Graphia', 1934. 104 pp.

3312 KOPP, OTTO, ed.: *Widerstand und Erneuerung. Neue Berichte und Dokumente vom inneren Kampf gegen das Hitler-Regime.* Stuttgart: Seewald, 1966. 308 pp.

3313 LIEPMANN, HEINZ: *Das Vaterland. Ein Tatsachen-Roman aus dem heutigen Deutschland.* Amsterdam: van Kampen & Zoon, 1933. 295 pp. [English version: *Murder—made in Germany. A story of present-day Germany.* London: Hamish Hamilton, 1934.]

3314 PECHEL, RUDOLF: *Deutscher Widerstand.* Erlenbach-Zürich: Rentsch, 1947. 343 pp.

3315 PRITTIE, TERENCE: *Germans against Hitler.* Foreword: Hugh Trevor-Roper. London: Hutchinson, 1964. 291 pp., illus., bibl. [German version: *Deutsche gegen Hitler. Eine Darstellung des deutschen Widerstands gegen den Nationalsozialismus während der Herrschaft Hitlers.* Tübingen: Wunderlich, 1964.]

3316 ROBERTS, STEPHEN H.: *The house that Hitler built.* London: Methuen, 1937. 380 pp.

3317 RODE, WALTHER: *Deutschland ist Caliban.* Zürich: Europa Verlag, 1934. 191 pp.

3318 USIKOTA (pseud. of Carl Brinitzer): *Zulu in Germany. The travels of a Zulu reporter amongst the natives of Germany. His dispatches to the 'Zulu Post'.* London: Gollancz, 1938. 191 pp.

3319 VOLLMER, BERNHARD: *Volksopposition im Polizeistaat. Gestapo- und Regierungsberichte 1934–1936.* Stuttgart: Deutsche Verlags-Anstalt, 1957. 399 pp.

3320 WEISENBORN, GÜNTHER, ed.: *Der lautlose Aufstand. Bericht über die Widerstandsbewegung des deutschen Volkes 1933–1945.* Hamburg: Rowohlt, 1962. 341 pp., bibl.

THE WIENER LIBRARY: *Catalogue Series No. 7—Persecution and Resistance.* See 78.

3321 WISE, JAMES WATERMAN: *Swastika. The Nazi terror.* New York: Smith & Haas, 1933. 128 pp.

2. LOCAL AND REGIONAL

Bad Buchau

3322 MOHN, JOSEPH: *Der Leidensweg unter dem Hakenkreuz.* Hrsg. von der Stadt Bad Buchau. 1970. 197 pp., illus., map, family tree, bibl. [Incl. persecution of Jews, Catholics and gypsies, and also euthanasia.]

Baden

3323 SCHADT, JÖRG, ed.: *Verfolgung und Widerstand unter dem Nationalsozialismus in Baden. Die Lageberichte der Gestapo und des Generalstaatsanwalts Karlsruhe 1933–1940.* Hrsg.: Stadtarchiv Mannheim. Stuttgart: Kohlhammer, 1976. 354 pp., diagrs. [Incl. left-wing and church resistance; Stahlhelm; persecution of the Jews.]

Bavaria

3324 KNAB, OTTO MICHAEL: *Kleinstadt unterm Hakenkreuz. Groteske Erinnerungen aus Bayern.* Luzern: Räber, [1934]. 106 pp.

Berlin

3325 ANDREAS-FRIEDRICH, RUTH: *Berlin underground, 1938–1945.* New York: Holt, 1945. 312 pp. [German orig.: *Der Schattenmann. Tagebuchaufzeichnungen 1933–1945.* Berlin: Suhrkamp, 1947.]

3326 WERNER, KURT & BIERNAT, KARL HEINZ: *Die Köpenicker Blutwoche 1933.* Berlin [East]: Dietz, 1960. 103 pp. (Institut für Marxismus-Leninismus beim ZK der SED).

Cassel

3327 BELZ, WILLI: *Die Standhaften. Über den Widerstand in Kassel 1933–1945.* Ludwigsburg: Schromm, 1960. 140 pp., illus., facsims.

Cologne

3328 *Widerstand und Verfolgung in Köln 1933–1945.* Ausstellung—Historisches Archiv der Stadt Köln, 8. Februar bis 28. April 1974. 423 pp., illus., facsims. [Comps.: Franz Irsfeld, Bernd Wittschier.]

Danzig

3329 SODEIKAT, ERNST: 'Der Nationalsozialismus und die Danziger Opposition'. [In] *Vierteljahrshefte für Zeitgeschichte*, 14. Jhrg., 2. Heft, April 1966. Pp. 139–174.

Dortmund

3330 KLOTZBACH, KURT: *Gegen den Nationalsozialismus. Widerstand und Verfolgung in Dortmund 1930–1945. Eine historisch-politische Studie.* Hannover: Verlag für Literatur und Zeitgeschehen, 1969. 311 pp., tabs., bibl. (Schriftenreihe des Forschungsinstituts der Friedrich-Ebert-Stiftung ...).

Duisburg

3331 BLUDAU, KUNO: *Gestapo—geheim! Widerstand und Verfolgung in Duisburg 1933–1945.* Bonn-Bad Godesberg: Verlag Neue Gesellschaft, 1973. xix + 324 pp., facsims., bibl. (Schriftenreihe des Forschungsinstituts der Friedrich-Ebert-Stiftung ...).

Essen

3332 STEINBERG, HANS-JOSEF: *Widerstand und Verfolgung in Essen 1933–1945.* Hannover: Verlag für Literatur und Zeitgeschehen, 1969. 422 pp., facsims., tabs., bibl. (Schriftenreihe des Forschungsinstituts der Friedrich-Ebert-Stiftung ...).

Frankfurt am Main

3333 MAUSBACH-BROMBERGER, BARBARA: *Widerstand in Frankfurt a.M.: Gegen den Faschismus 1933–1945.* Frankfurt a.M.: Röderberg, 1976. 312 pp., illus., facsims.

Hamburg

3334 BUCK, HANS-ROBERT: *Der kommunistische Widerstand gegen den Nationalsozialismus in Hamburg 1933 bis 1945.* Augsburg: Blasaditsch, 1969. 223 pp., bibl. (Veröffentlichungen des Seminars für Geschichte Osteuropas ... an der Universität München). [Orig. pres. as inaugural-dissertation to Ludwig-Maximilian-University München.]

3335 *Dokumente des Widerstandes. Ein Beitrag zur Verständnis des illegalen Kampfes gegen die Nazidiktatur. Eine Artikelserie aus der 'Hamburger Volkszeitung' Juli–Oktober 1947.* [Hamburg: 1947]. 114 pp., illus. [26 articles about resistance on the Waterfront.]

3336 HOCHMUTH, URSEL & MEYER, GERTRUD: *Streiflichter aus dem Hamburger Widerstand 1933–1945. Berichte und Dokumente.* Unveränd. Nachdruck. Frankfurt a.M.: Röderberg, 1980. 650 pp., illus., facsims., bibl.

3337 MEYER, GERTRUD: *Nacht über Hamburg. Berichte und Dokumente.* Ergänzungsband zu: Hochmuth/Meyer: Streiflichter aus dem Hamburger Widerstand ... Frankfurt a.M.: Röderberg, 1971. 364 pp., illus., facsims., bibl.

3338 PULS, URSULA: *Die Bästlein-Jacob-Abshagen-Gruppe. Bericht über den antifaschistischen Widerstandskampf in Hamburg und an der Wasserkante während des Zweiten Weltkrieges.* Berlin [East]: Dietz, 1959. 227 pp., illus.

Hannoversch Münden

3339 SCHUMANN, WILHELM: *Ihr seid den dunklen Weg für uns gegangen ... Skizzen aus dem Widerstand in Hannoversch Münden 1933–1939.* Frankfurt a.M.: Röderberg, 1973. 127 pp., illus., facsims. [Incl. persecution of the Jews and the Evangelical Church.]

Hanover

3340 ZORN, GERDA: *Widerstand in Hannover. Gegen Reaktion und Faschismus 1920–1946.* Frankfurt a.M.: Röderberg, 1977. 276 pp., illus., tabs., facsims., bibl.

Krefeld

3341 BILLSTEIN, AUREL: *Der eine fällt, die andern rücken nach ... Dokumente des Widerstandes und der Verfolgung in Krefeld 1933–1945.* Zusammengest. im Auftr. der Vereinigung der Verfolgten des Naziregimes (VVN—Bund der Antifaschisten), des Bundes der Verfolgten des Naziregimes (BVN) und der Jüdischen Gemeinde Krefeld. Frankfurt a.M.: Röderberg, 1973. 343 pp., illus., facsims., bibl. [Resistance of left-wing groups; Churches; 'Sippenhaft'; deportation of Jews.]

Leipzig

3342 KRAUSE, ILSE: *Die Schumann-Engert-Kresse-Gruppe. Dokumente und Materialien des illegalen antifaschistischen Kampfes (Leipzig—1943 bis 1945).* Berlin [East]: Dietz, 1960. 150 pp., illus., maps, facsims. (Institut für Marxismus-Leninismus beim ZK der SED ...).

Mannheim

3343 SALM, FRITZ: *Im Schatten des Henkers. Vom Arbeiterwiderstand in Mannheim gegen faschistische Diktatur und Krieg.* Frankfurt a.M.: Röderberg, 1973. 301 pp., illus., facsims.

Marburg

3344 SCHNEIDER, ULRICH: *Marburg 1933–1945. Arbeiterbewegung und Bekennende Kirche gegen den Faschismus.* Frankfurt a.M.: Röderberg, 1980. 149 pp., illus., facsims., bibl.

Munich

3345 BRETSCHNEIDER, HEIKE: *Der Widerstand gegen den Nationalsozialismus in München 1933 bis 1945.* München: Stadtarchiv, 1968. 282 pp., facsims., bibl.

Neu-Isenburg

3346 REBENTISCH, DIETER & RAAB, ANGELIKA, eds.: *Neu-Isenburg zwischen Anpassung und Widerstand. Dokumente über Lebensbedingungen und politisches Verhalten 1933–1945.* Neu-Isenburg: Magistrat der Stadt, 1978. 343 pp., illus., tabs., facsims. [V: 'Oppositionelle Strömungen und Widerstandsakte'; VI: 'Die Verfolgung der Juden'.]

Nuremberg

3347 BEER, HELMUT: *Widerstand gegen den Nationalsozialismus in Nürnberg 1933–1945.* Nürnberg: Stadtarchiv, 1976. x + 398 pp., diagrs., bibl.

3348 SCHIRMER, HERMANN: *Das andere Nürnberg. Antifaschistischer Widerstand in der Stadt der Reichsparteitage.* Frankfurt a.M.: Röderberg, 1974. 255 pp., facsims.

Oberhausen

3349 EMIG, ERIK: *Jahre des Terrors. Der Nationalsozialismus in Oberhausen. Gedenkbuch für die Opfer des Faschismus.* Hrsg. im Auftr. der Stadt Oberhausen. 1967. 259 pp., bibl. [Incl.: 'Die Judenverfolgung. Die Opfer und ihre Schicksale', pp. 110–257.]

Ostfriesland

3350 POPPINGA, ONNO and others: *Ostfriesland. Biographien aus dem Widerstand.* [By] Onno Poppinga, Hans Martin Barth, Hiltraut Roth. Frankfurt a.M.: Syndikat, 1978. 186 pp., bibl.

Rhineland and Ruhr

3351 PEUKERT, DETLEV: *Ruhrarbeiter gegen den Faschismus. Dokumentation über den Widerstand im Ruhrgebiet 1933–1945.* Frankfurt a.M.: Röderberg, 1976. 312 pp., illus., facsims., bibl.

3352 VEREINIGUNG DER VERFOLGTEN DES NAZI-REGIMES, Landesvorstand: *Widerstand an Rhein und Ruhr 1933–1945.* Düsseldorf: 1969. 184 pp., facsims., tabs., bibl. (of illegal material, pp. 159–184).

Solingen

3353 SBOSNY, INGE & SCHABROD, KARL: *Widerstand in Solingen. Aus dem Leben antifaschistischer Kämpfer.* Frankfurt a.M.: Röderberg, 1975. 135 pp., illus., facsims., tabs.

Stuttgart

3354 BOHN, WILLI: *Stuttgart: Geheim! Ein dokumentarischer Bericht.* Frankfurt a.M.: Röderberg, 1969. 288 pp., illus., facsims., bibl.

Thuringia

3355 GLONDAJEWSKI, GERTRUD & SCHUMANN, HEINZ: *Die Neubauer-Poser-Gruppe. Dokumente und Materialien des illegalen antifaschistischen Kampfes (Thüringen 1939 bis 1945).* Berlin [East]: Dietz, 1957. 127 pp. (Institut für Marxismus-Leninismus beim ZK der SED).

3356 WERNER, GERHART: *Aufmachen! Gestapo! Über den Widerstand in Wuppertal 1933–1945.* Mit Beiträgen von Karl Ibach, Hermann Lutze, Willy Spicher. Wuppertal: Hammer, 1975. 62 pp., illus., facsims.

3. INDIVIDUAL ACCOUNTS AND CASES

3357 ANDERSCH, ALFRED: *Die Kirschen der Freiheit. Ein Bericht.* Frankfurt a.M.: Frankfurter Verlagsanstalt, 1952. 130 pp. [An anti-Nazi deserts from Hitler's army.]

3358 [BERNSTORFF, ALBRECHT] STUTTERHEIM, KURT von: *Die Majestät des Gewissens. In Memoriam Albrecht Bernstorff.* Vorw.: Theodor Heuss. Hamburg: Christian, 1962. 100 pp., illus., bibl. [Anti-Nazi diplomat who helped to rescue Jews.]

3359 *Den Unvergessenen. Opfer des Wahns 1933 bis 1945.* Heidelberg: Schneider, 1952. 176 pp. [Collection of essays in memory of individual victims of persecution.]

3360 DREXEL, JOSEPH: *Rückkehr unerwünscht. Joseph Drexels 'Reise nach Mauthausen' und der Widerstandskreis Ernst Niekisch.* Hrsg.: Wilhelm Raimund Beyer. Stuttgart: Deutsche Verlags-Anstalt, 1978. 331 pp.

3361 [EHLERS, HERMANN] BÖRNER, WEERT: *Hermann Ehlers.* Hannover: Niedersächsische Landeszentrale für politische Bildung, 1963. 191 pp., illus., facsims., bibl.

3362 [FECHENBACH, FELIX] *Das Felix Fechenbach Buch.* Hrsg. zu seinem Gedenken. Arbon: Eichenverlag, 1936. 435 pp., illus.

3363 [HAMMER, WALTER] HAMMER-KÖSTEREY, ERNA & SIEKER, HUGO, eds.: *Die bleibende Spur. Ein Gedenkbuch für Walter Hammer, 1888–1966.* Hamburg: Janssen, [1967?]. 296 pp., illus., facsims.

HAUSHOFER, ALBRECHT
3364 HAUSHOFER, ALBRECHT: *Moabiter Sonette.* Berlin: Blanvallet, 1946. 95 pp. [Poems written in prison.]

3365 LAACK-MICHEL, URSULA: *Albrecht Haushofer und der Nationalsozialismus. Ein Beitrag zur Zeitgeschichte.* Stuttgart: Klett, 1974. 407 pp., bibl.

3366 [JÄGERSTÄTTER, FRANZ] ZAHN, GORDON C.: *In solitary witness. The life and death of Franz Jägerstätter.* London: Chapman, 1966. 277 pp., illus., facsims., bibl. [First publ. 1964.]

3367 [KLEPPER, JOCHEN] THALMANN, RITA: *Jochen Klepper. Ein Leben zwischen Idyllen und Katastrophen.* München: Kaiser, 1977. 403 pp., illus., facsims., map.

3368 KOLBE, MAXIMILIAN: *Jedem ist der Weg gewiesen. Texte eines Märtyrers.* Ostfildern 1: Schwabenverlag, 1977. 130 pp., bibl.

3369 [KUCKHOFF, ADAM] KUCKHOFF, GRETA, ed.: *Adam Kuckhoff zum Gedenken. Novellen—Gedichte—Briefe.* Berlin: Aufbau-Verlag, 1947. 119 pp.

3370 LIPS, EVA: *What Hitler did to us. A personal record of the Third Reich.* Transl. from the German. Introd.: Dorothy Thompson. London: Michael Joseph, 1938. 319 pp. [Two German scientists driven into exile. In USA entitled *Savage symphony.*]

3371 LITTEN, IRMGARD: *Die Hölle sieht Dich an. Der Fall Litten.* Vorw.: Rudolf Olden. Paris: Éds. Nouvelles Internationales, 1940. 293 pp., port. [Author's unavailing fight for the release of her son, Hans Litten. English version: *A mother fights Hitler.* Forew.: Archbishop of York (William Temple). London: Allen & Unwin, 1940.]

3372 MÜLLER, JOSEF: *Bis zur letzten Konsequenz. Ein Leben für Frieden und Freiheit.* München: Süddeutscher Verlag, 1975. 384 pp., illus., bibl. [Incl. Flossenbürg and last days of war.]

3373 NEILSON, WILLIAM ALLEN, ed.: *We escaped. Twelve personal narratives of the flight to America.* New York: Macmillan, 1941. 258 pp.

3374 [OTTO, HANS] KUCKHOFF, ARMIN, ed.: *Hans Otto. Gedenkbuch für einen Schauspieler und Kämpfer.* Berlin: Henschel, 1948. 103 pp., illus., facsims.

3375 [SACK, KARL] BÖSCH, HERMANN: *Heeresrichter Dr. Karl Sack im Widerstand. Eine historisch-politische Studie.* München: Müller, 1967. 101 pp., bibl.

3376 [SCHMENKEL, FRITZ] NEUHAUS, WOLFGANG: *Kampf gegen 'Sternlauf'. Der Weg des deutschen Partisanen Fritz Schmenkel.* Berlin [East]: Deutscher Militärverlag, 1970. 481 pp., illus., facsims.

3377 [THADDEN, ELISABETH von] LÜHE, IRMGARD von der: *Elisabeth von Thadden. Ein Schicksal unserer Zeit.* Düsseldorf: Diederichs, 1966. 291 pp., bibl. [A conservative anti-Nazi headmistress.]

Kreisauer Kreis

3378 [HAUBACH, THEODOR & MIERENDORFF, CARLO] *Agora, Zeitschrift eines humanistischen Gymnasiums.* 2. Jhrg., Nr. 7/8, Sept. 1956. Darmstadt: Ludwig-Georg-Gymnasium. 108 pp. [Special number dedicated to two former pupils and containing extracts from their writings.]

3379 [MOLTKE, HELMUTH von] BALFOUR, MICHAEL & FRISBY, JULIAN: *Helmuth von Moltke. A leader against Hitler.* London: Macmillan, 1972. 388 pp., illus., facsims.

3380 [REICHWEIN, ADOLF] *Adolf Reichwein. Ein Lebensbild aus Briefen und Dokumenten.* Ausgew. von Rosemarie Reichwein. Mitw.: Hans Bohnenkamp. Hrsg. und kommentiert von Ursula Schulz. München: Müller, 1974. 375 pp., illus.

3381 [REICHWEIN, ADOLF] HENDERSON, JAMES L.: *Adolf Reichwein. Eine politisch-pädagogische Biographie.* Hrsg.: Helmut Lindemann. Stuttgart: Deutsche Verlags-Anstalt, 1958. 223 pp., port.

3382 ROON, GER van: *Neuordnung im Widerstand. Der Kreisauer Kreis innerhalb der deutschen Widerstandsbewegung.* München: Oldenbourg, 1967. 652 pp., illus., bibl. [English version: *German resistance to Hitler. Count von Moltke and the Kreisau circle.* London: van Nostrand Reinhold, 1971.]

3383 STELTZER, THEODOR: *Von deutscher Politik. Dokumente, Aufsätze und Vorträge.* Hrsg.: Friedrich Minssen. Frankfurt a.M.: Knecht, 1949. 169 pp. [Incl. the memorandum on German opposition against National Socialism, dated 15 July 1944; also the appended documents of the Kreisauer Kreis—von Moltke, Yorck von Wartenburg, Mierendorff and others—of whom the author was one of the few survivors.]

3384 [YORCK VON WARTENBURG] HERMLIN, STEPHAN: *Der Leutnant Yorck von Wartenburg.* Hohentwiel: Oberbadische Druckerei & Verlagsanstalt, 1946. 45 pp.

4. POLITICAL

a. General

3385 BALZER, KARL: *Sabotage gegen Deutschland. Der heimtückische Kampf gegen die deutschen Frontsoldaten.* Preussisch Oldendorf: Schütz, 1974. 336 pp., illus., bibl.

3386 BOVERI, MARGRET: *Der Verrat im 20. Jahrhundert. Für und gegen die Nation.* Hamburg: Rowohlt, 1956. In 2 vols. [English version: *Treason in the twentieth century.* London: MacDonald, 1961. 408 pp., bibl.]
Bd. I: *Das sichtbare Geschehen.*
Bd. II: *Das unsichtbare Geschehen.* [Incl. passages on resistance leaders, such as Goerdeler and von Hassell, and chapters on leaders of the military resistance, the Kreisauer Kreis and the Rote Kapelle.]

3387 BRACHER, KARL DIETRICH: 'Anfänge der deutschen Widerstandsbewegung'. [In] *Zur Geschichte und Problematik der Demokratie. Festgabe für Hans Herzfeld.* Berlin: Duncker & Humblot, 1958. Pp. 375–395.

3388 FURTWÄNGLER, FRANZ JOSEF: *Männer, die ich sah und kannte.* Hamburg: Auerdruck, 1951. 229 pp. [Incl. Admiral Canaris, Julius Leber, Helmuth von Moltke and Adam von Trott zu Solz.]

3389 GOLLWITZER, HELMUT and others, eds.: *Du hast mich heimgesucht bei Nacht. Abschiedsbriefe und Aufzeichnungen des Widerstandes 1933–1945.* Hrsg.: Helmut Gollwitzer, Käthe Kuhn, Reinhold Schneider. München: Kaiser, 1954. 467 pp. [English version: *Dying we live. The final messages and records of the Resistance.* New York: Pantheon, 1961.]

3390 HAMMER, WALTER: *Hohes Haus in Henkers Hand. Rückschau auf die Hitlerzeit, auf Leidensweg und Opfergang deutscher Parlamentarier.* 2. erw. und verb. Aufl. Frankfurt a.M.: Europäische Verlagsanstalt, 1956. 132 pp., illus.

3391 *Hitler calls this living!* By a member of the German Freedom Party. London: Sidgwick & Jackson, 1939. 226 pp.

3392 HOFFMANN, PETER: *Widerstand, Staatsstreich, Attentat. Der Kampf der Opposition gegen Hitler.* München: Piper, 1969. 988 pp., illus., diagrs., plans, bibl. (Notes, pp. 671–880). [English version: *The history of the German resistance, 1933–1945.* Cambridge, Mass.: MIT Press, 1977.]

3393 HOFFMANN, PETER: *Widerstand gegen Hitler. Probleme des Umsturzes.* München: Piper, 1979. 103 pp.

3394 JANSEN, JON & WEYL, STEFAN: *The silent war. The Underground Movement in Germany.* Forew.: Reinhold Niebuhr. Philadelphia, Pa.: Lippincott, 1943. 357 pp.

3395 KERN, ERICH: *Verrat an Deutschland. Spione und Saboteure gegen das eigene Vaterland.* Göttingen: Schütz, 1963. 318 pp., illus., bibl.

3396 KETTENACKER, LOTHAR, ed.: *Das 'Andere Deutschland' im Zweiten Weltkrieg. Emigration und Widerstand in internationaler Perspektive. The 'Other Germany' in the Second World War. Emigration and resistance in international perspective.* Stuttgart: Klett, 1977. 258 pp. (Veröffentlichungen des Deutschen Historischen Instituts London). [Text in German and English.]

3397 KOSTHORST, ERICH: *Die deutsche Opposition gegen Hitler zwischen Polen- und Frankreichfeldzug.* Bonn: Bundeszentrale für Heimatdienst, 1955. 188 pp., maps.

3398 KÜHN, HEINZ: *Widerstand und Emigration. Die Jahre 1928–1945.* Hamburg: Hoffmann & Campe, 1980. 357 pp., port.

3399 LEBER, ANNEDORE, ed.: *Das Gewissen steht auf. Lebensbilder aus dem deutschen Widerstand 1933–1945.* Hrsg. in Zusammenarb. mit Willy Brandt und Karl Dietrich Bracher. Berlin: Mosaik-Verlag, 1954. 237 pp., illus. [English version: *Conscience in revolt. 64 stories of resistance in Germany, 1933–1945.* Introd.: Robert Birley. London: Vallentine, Mitchell, 1957.]

3400 LEBER, ANNEDORE, ed.: *Das Gewissen entscheidet. Bereiche des deutschen Widerstandes von 1933–1945 in Lebensbildern.* In Zusammenarb. mit Willy Brandt und Karl Dietrich Bracher. Berlin: Annedore Leber, 1957. 303 pp., illus.

3401 LEERS, JOHANN VON: *Reichsverräter, Folge 1, 2, 3.* Buenos Aires: Dürer Verlag, 1954/56. In 3 vols. (Sonderhefte der Zeitschrift 'Der Weg'). [A denunciation of German resistance.]

3402 *Nation Europa*, Heft 7/8, Juli/Aug. 1978. [Special issue entitled]: 'Verrat und Widerstand im Dritten Reich: Referate und Arbeitsergebnisse des zeitgeschichtlichen Kongresses der Gesellschaft für Freie Publizistik vom 26.–28. Mai in Kassel'. Coburg. 128 pp., illus. [Neo-Fascist publication.]

3403 RAST, GERTRUD: *Allein bist Du nicht. Kämpfe und Schicksale in schwerer Zeit.*

Frankfurt a.M.: Röderberg, 1972. 110 pp. [Incl. Fuhlsbüttel and Wilhelmsburg concentration camps.]

3404 RITTER, GERHARD A. & ZIEBURA, GILBERT, eds.: *Faktoren der politischen Entscheidung. Festgabe für Ernst Fraenkel zum 65. Geburtstag.* Berlin: de Gruyter, 1963. 451 pp., port. [Incl.: Gerhard Schulz: 'Über Entscheidungen und Formen des politischen Widerstandes in Deutschland'.]

3405 ROON, GER van: *Widerstand im Dritten Reich. Ein Überblick.* München: Beck, 1979. 251 pp. [Rev. and enl. German version of *Verzet tegen Hitler*, 1968.]

3406 ROTHFELS, HANS: *Die deutsche Opposition gegen Hitler. Eine Würdigung.* Frankfurt a.M.: Fischer, 1958. 214 pp. [Rev. ed. of the work first publ. in English in the USA, 1948, and in German, 1951. English version: *The German opposition to Hitler. An assessment.* London: Wolff, 1961. 166 pp.]

3407 SCHEURIG, BODO, ed.: *Deutscher Widerstand 1938–1944. Fortschritt oder Reaktion?* München: Deutscher Taschenbuch Verlag, 1969. 330 pp., bibl.

3408 SCHMITTHENNER, WALTER & BUCHHEIM, HANS, eds.: *Der deutsche Widerstand gegen Hitler.* Vier historisch-kritische Studien von Hermann Graml, Hans Mommsen, Hans Joachim Reichhardt, Ernst Wolf. Köln: Kiepenheuer & Witsch, 1966. 287 pp. [English version: GRAML, HERMANN and others: *The German resistance to Hitler.* Introd.: F. L. Carsten. London: Batsford, 1970.]

SCHUTZHAFT

3409 GEIGENMÜLLER, OTTO: *Die politische Schutzhaft im nationalsozialistischen Deutschland.* Würzburg: Scheiner, 1937. 61 pp., bibl.

3410 SPOHR, WERNER: *Das Recht der Schutzhaft.* Berlin: Stilke, 1937. 125 pp.

3411 WESTDEUTSCHER RUNDFUNK: *Es gab nicht nur den 20. Juli ... Dokumente aus einer Sendereihe im Westdeutschen Fernsehen.* Köln: 1979. 113 pp., illus. [Incl.: Heinz Kühn: 'Zum Widerstand im Dritten Reich'.]

3412 ZENTNER, KURT: *Illustrierte Geschichte des Widerstandes in Deutschland und Europa, 1933–1945.* München: Südwest Verlag, 1966. 608 pp., illus., facsims., maps, bibl.

3413 ZENTRALVERBAND DEMOKRATISCHER WIDERSTANDSKÄMPFER UND VERFOLGTEN ORGANISATIONEN: *Das andere Deutschland. Zeugnisse 1958–1966.* Beuel b. Bonn: 1967. 219 pp. [ZDWV is a member of FILDIR (Fédération Internationale Libre des Déportés et Internés de la Résistance) Paris. Text in German and French. Summaries in German, Danish, Hebrew, Italian, Dutch, Norwegian.]

3414 ZORN, GERDA & MEYER, GERTRUD: *Frauen gegen Hitler. Berichte aus dem Widerstand 1933–1945.* Frankfurt a.M.: Röderberg, 1974. 151 pp., illus. [Incl. concentration camps.]

b. Left-wing

3415 ALTMANN, PETER and others: *Der deutsche antifaschistische Widerstand*

271

1933–1945 in Bildern und Dokumenten. [By] Peter Altmannn, Heinz Brüdigam, Barbara Mausbach-Bromberger, Max Oppenheimer. Frankfurt a.M.: Röderberg, 1975. 334 pp., illus., facsims., bibl. (Hrsg. im Auftr. des Präsidiums der VVN).

3416 *Antifaschistische Lehrer im Widerstandskampf.* Berlin [East]: Volk und Wissen Verlag, 1967. 166 pp., ports.

BLACK, ROBERT: *Fascism in Germany. How Hitler destroyed the world's most powerful labour movement.* See 1118.

3417 BOHN, WILLI: *Transportkolonne Otto.* Frankfurt a.M.: Röderberg, 1970. 143 pp., illus., map, facsims., tab.

3418 BUBER-NEUMANN, MARGARETE: *Als Gefangene bei Stalin und Hitler.* München: Verlag der Zwölf, 1949. 285 pp. [2nd rev. & enl. ed.: Stuttgart: Deutsche Verlags-Anstalt, 1958. 472 pp. English version: *Under two dictators.* London: Gollancz, 1949. Contains section on Ravensbrück.]

3419 *Deutsche Widerstandskämpfer 1933–1945. Biographien und Briefe.* Berlin [East]: Dietz, 1970. In 2 vols. (Institut für Marxismus-Leninismus beim ZK der SED). [Authors: Luise Kraushaar and others. Red.: Karl Heinz Biernat and others.]
Bd. I: 658 pp., ports., facsims.
Bd. II: 582 pp., ports., facsim.

3420 DUHNKE, HORST: *Die KPD von 1933 bis 1945.* Köln: Kiepenheuer & Witsch, 1972. 605 pp., bibl.

3421 ESTERS, HELMUT & PELGER, HANS: *Gewerkschafter im Widerstand.* Hannover: Verlag für Literatur und Zeitgeschehen, 1967. 180 pp., port., facsims. (Schriftenreihe des Forschungsinstituts der Friedrich-Ebert-Stiftung ...).

3422 FÄHNDERS, WALTER and others, eds.: *Sammlung antifaschistischer sozialistischer Erzählungen, 1933–1945.* Hrsg.: Walter Fähnders, Helga Karrenbrock, Martin Rector. Darmstadt: Luchterhand, 1974. 315 pp., bibl.

3423 *Faschismusanalyse und antifaschistischer Kampf der Kommunistischen Internationale und der KPD 1923–1945.* 2. Aufl. Heidelberg: Sendler, 1974. 362 pp.

3424 FRENZEL, MAX and others: *Gesprengte Fesseln. Ein Bericht über den antifaschistischen Widerstand und die Geschichte der illegalen Parteiorganisation der KPD im Zuchthaus Brandenburg-Görden von 1933 bis 1945.* 2. Aufl. [By] Max Frenzel, Wilhelm Thiele, Artur Mannbar. Berlin [East]: Militärverlag der DDR, 1976. 367 pp., illus., facsims.

3425 GERHARD, DIRK: *Antifaschisten. Proletarischer Widerstand 1933–1945.* Berlin: Wagenbach, 1976. 175 pp.

3426 GOGUEL, RUDI: *Antifaschistischer Widerstand und Klassenkampf. Die faschistische Diktatur 1933 bis 1945 und ihre Gegner. Bibliographie deutschsprachiger Literatur aus den Jahren 1945 bis 1973.* Mitarb.: Jutta

Grimann, Manfred Püschner, Ingrid Volz. Berlin [East]: Militärverlag der DDR, 1976. 567 pp.

3427 GRASMANN, PETER: *Sozialdemokraten gegen Hitler 1933–1945.* München: Olzog, 1976. 163 pp., illus., facsims., bibl. [Incl. resistance from exile.]

3428 GUTE, HERBERT: *Partisanen ohne Gewehre. Ein Tagebuch aus der Erinnerung.* Berlin [East]: Deutscher Militärverlag, 1970. 391 pp.

3429 HAAG, LINA: *Eine Handvoll Staub.* [Kühlenfels b. Pegnitz]: Nest-Verlag, 1947. 166 pp. [English version: *How long the night.* London: Gollancz, 1948.]

3430 [JACOB, BERTHOLD] WILLI, JOST NIKOLAUS: *Der Fall Jacob-Wesemann, 1935–1936. Ein Beitrag zur Geschichte der Schweiz in der Zwischenkriegszeit.* Bern: Lang, 1972. xxvi + 434 pp., bibl.

JAHNKE, KARL HEINZ: *Jungkommunisten im Widerstand gegen den Hitlerfaschismus. See 2462.*

3431 KENNAN, GEORGE & WEBER, HERMANN: 'Aus dem Kadermaterial der illegalen KPD 1943. Dokumentation'. [In] *Vierteljahrshefte für Zeitgeschichte,* 20. Jhrg., Heft 4, 1972. Pp. 422–446. [Saefkow group.]

3432 [KÖNIG, HEINRICH] WAGNER, JOHANNES VOLKER: *... nur Mut, sei Kämpfer! Heinrich König: Ein Leben für die Freiheit.* Bochum: Stadtarchiv (Brockmeyer), 1976. 231 pp., illus., bibl. [SPD member.]

3433 LIEPMANN, HEINZ: *'... wird mit dem Tode bestraft'.* Zürich: Europa Verlag, 1935. 246 pp. [English version: *Fires underground. A narrative of the secret struggle carried on by the illegal organizations in Germany under penalty of death.* London: Harrap, 1936.]

3434 MÜLLER, OTTO: *Hinter Gittern.* Stuttgart: Kulturaufbau-Verlag, 1947. 64 pp. [Poems of a Communist in prison.]

3435 OSTERROTH, FRANK & SCHUSTER, DIETER: *Chronik der deutschen Sozialdemokratie. Bd. II: Vom Beginn der Weimarer Republik bis zum Ende des Zweiten Weltkrieges.* 2., neu bearb. und erw. Aufl. ... Berlin: Dietz, 1975. 452 pp.

3436 PETERSEN, JAN: *Unsere Strasse. Eine Chronik geschrieben im Herzen des faschistischen Deutschland 1933–1934.* Berlin: Dietz, 1947. 243 pp. [English version: *Our street.* London: Gollancz, 1938.]

3437 SCHLOTTERBECK, FRIEDRICH: *Je dunkler die Nacht desto heller die Sterne. Erinnerungen eines deutschen Arbeiters 1933–1945.* Zürich: Europa Verlag, 1945. 254 pp. [English version: *The darker the night, the brighter the stars.* London: Gollancz, 1947.]

3438 THÄLMANN, ERNST: *Zwischen Erinnerung und Erwartung. Autobiographische Aufzeichnungen geschrieben in faschistischer Haft. Biographische Dokumentation mit einer Thälmann-Chronik.* Hrsg.: Kuratorium 'Gedenkstätte Ernst Thälmann' Hamburg. Frankfurt a.M.: Röderberg, 1977. 111 pp., illus., bibl.

3439 WALTER (pseud. of Walter Ulbricht): *'Kriegsschauplatz Innerdeutschland'*. Strasbourg: Éds. Prométhée, 1938. 93 pp.

3440 WEBER, HERMANN, ed.: *Der deutsche Kommunismus. Dokumente 1915–1945*. 3. Aufl. Köln: Kiepenheuer & Witsch, 1973. 463 pp. [Incl. 'Die KPD in der Illegalität und Emigration', pp. 317–421.]

3441 WOLF, LORE: *Ein Leben ist viel zu wenig*. Frankfurt a.M.: Röderberg, 1974. 183 pp.

3442 *Zur Geschichte der deutschen antifaschistischen Widerstandsbewegung 1933–1945. Eine Auswahl von Materialien, Berichten und Dokumenten*. Berlin [East]: Verlag des Ministeriums für Nationale Verteidigung, 1957. 420 pp., illus., facsims. [Many documents on the Nationalkomitee 'Freies Deutschland'.]

Rote Kapelle

3443 BIERNAT, KARL HEINZ & KRAUSHAAR, LUISE: *Die Schulze-Boysen/Harnack-Organisation im antifaschistischen Kampf*. Berlin [East]: Dietz, 1972. 184 pp., illus., facsims.

3444 BRÜNING, ELFRIED: *... damit Du weiterlebst. Roman*. Berlin: Verlag Neues Leben, 1949. 247 pp. [Based on the lives of resistance fighters Hans and Hilde Coppi, members of the Schulze-Boysen group.]

3445 FLICKE, W. F.: *Die rote Kapelle*. Hilden/Rhein: Vier-Brücken Verlag, 1949. 377 pp. [Secret radio transmission of this resistance group.]

3446 HARNACK, AXEL VON: *Ernst von Harnack, 1888 bis 1945. Ein Kämpfer für Deutschlands Zukunft*. Schwenningen: Neckar Verlag, 1951. 78 pp., port.

3447 HÖHNE, HEINZ: *Kennwort: Direktor. Die Geschichte der Roten Kapelle*. Frankfurt a.M.: Fischer, 1970. 335 pp., illus., map, facsims., bibl. [Incl. list of persons involved, pp. 280–285. English version: *Codeword: Direktor. The story of the Red Orchestra*. London: Secker & Warburg, 1971.]

3448 KUCKHOFF, GRETA: *Vom Rosenkranz zur Roten Kapelle. Ein Lebensbericht*. 2. Aufl. Berlin [East]: Verlag Neues Leben, 1973. 434 pp.

3449 PERRAULT, GILLES: *L'orchestre rouge*. [Paris]: Fayard, 1967. 576 pp., illus., facsims., bibl.

3450 ROEDER, M.: *Die rote Kapelle*. Hamburg: Siep, 1952. 36 pp. [The Nazi judge in charge of the Rote Kapelle trial.]

3451 SUDHOLT, GERT, ed.: *Das Geheimnis der Roten Kapelle. Das US Dokument 0/7708. Verrat und Verräter gegen Deutschland*. 2. Aufl. Leoni am Starnberger See: Druffel, 1979. 376 pp.

3452 TREPPER, LEOPOLD: *Die Wahrheit. Autobiographie*. München: Deutscher Taschenbuch Verlag, 1978. 439 pp., illus., facsims. [First German ed. 1975, orig. publ. as *Le grand jeu*. English version of first ed.: *The great game. The story of the Red Orchestra*. London: Michael Joseph, 1977.]

c. Pacifists

3453 *Das deutsche Volk klagt an. Hitlers Krieg gegen die Friedenskämpfer in Deutschland. Ein Tatsachenbuch.* Paris: Éds. du Carrefour, 1936. 318 pp., illus.

OSSIETZKY, CARL VON

3454 OSSIETZKY, CARL VON: *Rechenschaft. Publizistik aus den Jahren 1913–1933.* Berlin [East]: Aufbau-Verlag, 1970. 461 pp. [Ed.: Bruno Frei.]

3455 GLOTZ, PETER & LANGENBUCHER, WOLFGANG R., eds.: *Vorbilder für Deutsche. Korrektur einer Heldengalerie.* München: Piper, 1974. 371 pp., illus., bibls. [Incl.: Dieter Hildebrandt: 'Carl von Ossietzky, 1880–1938'; Ingeborg & Hans Bohrmann: 'Julius Leber, 1891–1945'.]

3456 GROSSMANN, KURT R.: *Ossietzky. Ein deutscher Patriot.* München: Kindler, 1963. 580 pp., port., bibl.

3457 JACOB, BERTHOLD: *Weltbürger Ossietzky. Ein Abriss seines Werkes zusammengestellt und mit einer Biographie Ossietzkys versehen.* Vorw.: Wickham Steed. Paris: Éds. du Carrefour, 1937. 120 pp.

3458 VINKE, HERMANN: *Carl von Ossietzky.* Hamburg: Dressler, 1978. 175 pp., illus., facsims.

3459 *Refugee.* Transl. by Clara Leiser. New York: Prentice Hall, 1940. 308 pp. [Factual account of the experiences of an 'Aryan' German pacifist under the Nazi regime.]

d. Freemasonry

3460 DEUTSCH-CHRISTLICHE ORDEN: *Im Ordensstammhaus der Grossen Landesloge der Freimaurer von Deutschland Deutsch-Christlichen Ordens.* Berlin: Grosse Landesloge, 1935. 26 pp., illus.

3461 STEFFENS, MANFRED: *Freimaurerei in Deutschland. Bilanz eines Vierteljahrtausends.* Flensburg: Wolff, 1964. 636 pp., bibl. [Ch. XI: 'Verbot und Exil', pp. 385–421.]

3462 STEINGRUBER, ALBERT: *Warum Vernichtung der Freimaurerei im Dritten Reich? Entlarvung der Freimaurerei und ihre furchtbaren Geheimverbrechen. Die Enthüllungen der Ziele der freimaurerischen Weltgesellschaft. Selbsterlebnisse unter Freimaurern mit Randbemerkungen Wilhelm II.* Radolfzell am Bodensee: Dressler, 1934. 140 pp.

e. Right-wing, monarchists and military

3463 ARETIN, ERWEIN von: *Krone und Ketten. Erinnerungen eines bayerischen Edelmannes.* Hrsg.: Karl Buchheim, Karl Otmar von Aretin. München: Süddeutscher Verlag, 1954. 438 pp. [Persecution of a monarchist, incl. his experiences in Dachau.]

3464 BAUM, WALTER: 'Marine, Nationalsozialismus und Widerstand'. [In] *Vierteljahrshefte für Zeitgeschichte.* 11. Jhrg. 1. Heft. 1963. Pp. 16–48.

3465 CHOLTITZ, [DIETRICH] von: ... *brennt Paris? Adolf Hitler! Tatsachenbericht des letzten deutschen Befehlshabers in Paris.* Mannheim: Weltbücherei Una, [1950]. 101 pp. [Account of how the author foiled Hitler's command to destroy Paris.]

3466 DONOHUE, JAMES: *Hitler's conservative opponents in Bavaria, 1930–1945. A study of Catholic, monarchist and separatist anti-Nazi activities.* Leiden: Brill, 1961. 348 pp., facsim., bibl.

3467 GERSDORFF, RUDOLF-CHRISTIAN Frhr. von: *Soldat im Untergang.* Frankfurt a.M.: Ullstein, 1977. 226 pp., illus., bibl. [Incl. extermination of Jews.]

3468 GROSCURTH, HELMUTH: *Tagebücher eines Abwehroffiziers 1938–1940. Mit weiteren Dokumenten zur Militäropposition gegen Hitler.* Hrsg.: Helmut Krausnick, Harold C. Deutsch. Mitarb.: Hildegard von Kotze. Stuttgart: Deutsche Verlags-Anstalt, 1970. 594 pp., port., bibl. [Anhang IV: 'Die Juden-Erschiessung in Bjelaja Zerkow in August 1941', pp. 534–542.]

3469 HAMMERSTEIN, KUNRAT Frhr. von: *Spähtrupp.* Stuttgart: Goverts, 1963. 311 pp.

3470 [KLEIST-SCHMENZIN, EWALD von] SCHEURIG, BODO: *Ewald von Kleist-Schmenzin. Ein Konservativer gegen Hitler.* Oldenburg: Stalling, 1968. 296 pp., bibl.

3471 RAUSCHNING, HERMANN: *Die konservative Revolution. Versuch und Bruch mit Hitler.* New York: Freedom Publ. Co., 1941. 301 pp.

3472 STEINHOFF, JOHANNES: *The last chance: the pilots' plot against Göring, 1944–1945.* Transl. from the German. London: Hutchinson, 1977. 204 pp., illus. [First publ.: München: List, 1974.]

3473 [TRESCHKOW, HENNING von] SCHEURIG, BODO: *Henning von Treschkow. Eine Biographie.* Oldenburg: Stalling, 1973. 250 pp., illus., bibl.

3474 *Die Vollmacht des Gewissens.* Hrsg.: Europäische Publikation. München: Rinn, 1956, 1965. [Symposium of German military resistance.]
[Bd. I]: Publ. 1956. 572 pp.
Bd. II: *Der militärische Widerstand gegen Hitler im Kriege.* Publ. 1965. 539 pp.

f. Conspiracies against Hitler

3475 DEUTSCH, HAROLD C.: *The conspiracy against Hitler in the twilight war.* Minneapolis, Minn.: University of Minnesota Press, 1968. x + 394 pp., bibl. [German version: *Das Komplott, oder Die Entmachung der Generale: Blomberg- und Fritsch-Krise: Hitlers Weg zum Krieg.* Eichstätt: Neue Diana Press, 1974.]

ELSER, JOHANN GEORG
3476 BOGAERT, ANDRÉ: *Un homme seul contre Hitler. 8 novembre 1939.* Paris: Laffont, 1974. 261 pp., illus.

3477 GRUCHMANN, LOTHAR, ed.: *Autobiographie eines Attentäters—Johann Georg Elser. Aussage zum Sprengstoffanschlag im Bürgerbräukeller, München am 8. November 1939.* Stuttgart: Deutsche Verlags-Anstalt, 1970. 166 pp.

3478 KOERBER, WALTHER and others: *Mord! Spionage! Attentat! Die Blutspur des englischen Geheimdienstes und der Münchener Bombenanschlag.* [By] Walther Koerber, Herrmann Wanderscheck, Hans Zugschwert. Berlin: Becker, 1940. 93 pp., illus., facsims.

3479 REED, DOUGLAS: *Fire and bomb. A comparison between the burning of the Reichstag and the bomb explosion at Munich.* London: Cape, 1940. 38 pp.

HOFFMANN, PETER: *Widerstand, Staatsstreich, Attentat.* [Incl. diagrs. of bombs used in assassination attempts.] *See* 3392.

3480 MASON, HERBERT MOLLOY: *To kill Hitler. The attempts on the life of Adolf Hitler.* London: Michael Joseph, 1979. 303 pp., illus., bibl.

3481 MOURIN, MAXIME: *Les complots contre Hitler, 1938–1945.* Paris: Payot, 1948. 216 pp.

3482 SCHLABRENDORFF, FABIAN von: *Offiziere gegen Hitler.* Völlig neue Bearb. des 1946 erschienenen Buches 'Offiziere gegen Hitler'. Nach einem Erlebnis-bericht von Fabian von Schlabrendorff, bearb. und hrsg. von Gero von S. Gaevernitz. Zürich: Europa Verlag, 1951. 228 pp., illus. [English version (of first ed.): *Revolt against Hitler. The personal account of Fabian von Schlabrendorff.* Ed.: Gero v.S. Gaevernitz. London: Eyre & Spottiswoode, 1948.]

3483 STEWART, DOUGLAS K.: 'The "Putsch" of September 1938. The first attempt of the Opposition, led by the German army, to arrest Hitler, before the violation of Czechoslovakia'. [In] *The Army Quarterly and Defence Journal,* Vol. LXXVII, No. 2, Jan. 1959. London: Clowes. Pp. 202–231.

20 July 1944

3484 BALZER, KARL: *Der 20. Juli und der Landesverrat. Eine Dokumentation über Verratshandlung im deutschen Widerstand.* Göttingen: Schütz, 1967. 325 pp., illus., maps, plans, bibl.

BECK, LUDWIG

3485 BECK, LUDWIG: *Studien.* Hrsg.: Hans Speidel. Stuttgart: Koehler, 1955. 302 pp.

3486 REYNOLDS, NICHOLAS: *Treason was no crime. Ludwig Beck, chief of the German General Staff.* Introd.: John Wheeler-Bennett. London: Kimber, 1976. 317 pp., illus., bibl.

3487 SCHRAMM, WILHELM von, ed.: *Beck und Goerdeler. Gemeinschaftsdokumente für den Frieden 1941–1944.* München: Müller, 1965. 285 pp., bibl.

3488 [BOLZ, EUGEN] MILLER, MAX: *Eugen Bolz—Staatsmann und Bekenner.*

Stuttgart: Schwaben-Verlag, 1951. 564 pp., illus. [Biography of the former State President of Württemberg, victim of the failure of the July Plot.]

CANARIS, ADMIRAL WILHELM

3489   ABSHAGEN, KARL HEINZ: *Canaris. Patriot und Weltbürger.* Stuttgart: Union Deutsche Verlagsgesellschaft, 1949. 409 pp., illus.

3490   BRISSAUD, ANDRÉ: *Canaris. The biography of Admiral Canaris, Chief of German Military Intelligence in the Second World War.* Transl. and ed.: Ian Colvin. London: Weidenfeld & Nicolson, 1973. xvii + 347 pp., bibl.

3491   HÖHNE, HEINZ: *Canaris. Patriot im Zwielicht.* München: Bertelsmann, 1976. 607 pp., illus., diagrs., facsims., bibl. [English version: *Canaris.* London: Secker & Warburg, 1979.]

———

3492   CÉSAR, JAROSLAV & ČERNÝ, BOHUMIL: *Akce Valkýra.* Praha: Naše Vojsko, Svaz Protifašistickych Bojovniků, 1966. 249 pp., illus., facsims., maps.

3493   DESROCHES, ALAIN: *Opération Walkyrie. Les patriotes allemands contre Hitler.* Paris: Nouvelles Éditions latines, 1966. 250 pp.

3494   EHLERS, DIETER: *Technik und Moral einer Verschwörung. 20. Juli 1944.* Frankfurt a.M.: Athenäum Verlag, 1964. 250 pp., bibl.

3495   FITZGIBBON, CONSTANTINE: *The shirt of Nessus.* London: Cassell, 1956. 288 pp., illus. [New ed. entitled: *To kill Hitler.* London: Storey, 1972. 288 pp., illus., bibl.]

3496   [GOERDELER, CARL] RITTER, GERHARD: *Carl Goerdeler und die deutsche Widerstandsbewegung.* Stuttgart: Deutsche Verlags-Anstalt, 1954. 630 pp., illus., facsim. [English version: *The German Resistance. Carl Goerdeler's struggle against tyranny.* London: Allen & Unwin, 1958.]

3497   HAGEN, HANS W.: *Zwischen Eid und Befehl. Tatzeugenbericht von den Ereignissen am 20. Juli 1944 in Berlin und 'Wolfsschanze'.* München: Türmer Verlag, 1958. 94 pp. [And: 4th enl. and illus. ed.]

3498   HAMMERSTEIN, KUNRAT Frhr. von: *Flucht. Aufzeichnungen nach dem 20. Juli.* Olten: Walter-Verlag, 1966. 212 pp., ports.

3499   HASSELL, ULRICH von: *Vom andern Deutschland. Aus den nachgelassenen Tagebüchern 1938–1944.* Zürich: Atlantis Verlag, 1946. 416 pp. [English version: *The von Hassell diaries, 1938–1944. The story of the forces against Hitler inside Germany, as recorded by Ambassador U. von Hassell.* Introd.: Allan Welsh Dulles. Garden City, N.Y.: County Life Press, 1947.]

3500   [HIMMLER, HEINRICH] 'Die Rede Himmlers vor den Gauleitern am 3. August 1944'. [In] *Vierteljahrshefte für Zeitgeschichte.* Jhrg. 1, Heft 4, 1953. Pp. 357–394.

3501   JACOBSEN, HANS-ADOLF, ed.: *July 20, 1944. The German opposition to Hitler as viewed by foreign historians. An anthology.* Bonn: Press and Information Office of the Federal Government, 1969. 338 pp.

3502 JEDLICKA, LUDWIG: *Der 20. Juli 1944 in Österreich.* 2. erw. Aufl. Wien: Herold, 1966. 179 pp., illus., facsims., bibl.

3503 [KALTENBRUNNER-BERICHTE] *Spiegelbild einer Verschwörung. Die Kaltenbrunner-Berichte an Bormann und Hitler über das Attentat vom 20. Juli 1944. Geheime Dokumente aus dem ehemaligen Reichssicherheitshauptamt.* Hrsg.: Archiv [Karl Heinrich] Peter für historische und zeitgeschichtliche Dokumentation. Stuttgart: Seewald, 1961. 587 pp.

3504 KIRST, HANS HELMUT: *Aufstand der Soldaten. Roman des 20. Juli 1944.* München: Heyne, 1975. 398 pp.

3505 [LEBER, JULIUS] BECK, DOROTHEA & SCHOELLER, WILFRIED F., eds.: *Julius Leber. Schriften, Reden, Briefe.* Vorw.: Willy Brandt. Denkrede: Golo Mann. München: Leber, 1976. 327 pp., ports., facsims. [A Social Democratic member of the Reichstag in the Weimar Republic, later a leader of the resistance movement, executed after the failure of the July plot.]

3506 MANVELL, ROGER & FRAENKEL, HEINRICH: *The July plot. The attempt in 1944 on Hitler's life and the men behind it.* London: Bodley Head, 1964. 272 pp., illus., bibl. [German version: *Der 20. Juli.* Vorw.: Wolf Graf von Baudissin. Frankfurt a.M.: Ullstein, 1964.]

3507 MELNIKOW, DANIIL: *20. Juli 1944. Legende und Wirklichkeit.* Berlin [East]: Deutscher Verlag der Wissenschaften, 1964. 295 pp., illus., facsims., bibl. [Transl. from the Russian.]

3508 MÜLLER, WOLFGANG: *Gegen eine neue Dolchstosslegende. Ein Erlebnisbericht zum 20. Juli 1944.* Hannover: Verlag 'Das Andere Deutschland', 1947. 128 pp.

3509 [OSTER, HANS] GRAML, HERMANN: 'Der Fall Oster'. [In] *Vierteljahrshefte für Zeitgeschichte,* 14. Jhrg., 1. Heft, 1966. Pp. 26–59.

3510 ROYCE, HANS, comp.: *20. Juli 1944.* Geänd. und vervollst. Bearb. der Sonderausg. der Wochenzeitung 'Das Parlament': 'Die Wahrheit über den 20. Juli 1944'. Bonn: Bundeszentrale für Heimatdienst, 1953. 216 pp. [Also 3rd ed.: *20. Juli 1944.* Neu bearb. und ergänz. von Erich Zimmermann, Hans-Adolf Jacobsen. Bonn: Bundeszentrale für Heimatdienst, (n.d.). 354 pp., illus., tabs., facsims., maps, bibl. English version: *Germans against Hitler. July 20, 1944.* Publ. by the Press and Information Office of the Federal German Government. Bonn: Berto-Verlag, 1960.]

3511 SCHRAMM, WILHELM VON: *Der 20. Juli in Paris.* Bad Wörishofen: Kindler & Schiermeyer, 1953. 412 pp., illus. [English version: *Conspiracy among Generals.* Transl. and ed.: R. T. Clark. London: Allen & Unwin, 1956.]

3512 [SCHULENBURG, FRITZ-DIETLOF Graf von der] KREBS, ALBERT: *Fritz-Dietlof Graf von der Schulenburg. Zwischen Staatsraison und Hochverrat.* Hamburg: Leibniz-Verlag, 1964. 338 pp., port., map, bibl.

3513 SCHULTZ, HANS JÜRGEN, ed.: *Der Zwanzigste Juli—Alternative zu Hitler.* Stuttgart: Kreuz Verlag, 1974. 206 pp.

3514 [SEYDLITZ-KURZBACH, WALTHER VON] MARTENS, HANS: *General von Seydlitz, 1942–1945. Analyse eines Konfliktes.* Berlin: Kloeden, 1971. 101 pp., port., bibl.

3515 [STAEHLE, WILHELM] ROON, GER van: *Wilhelm Staehle. Ein Leben auf der Grenze, 1877–1945.* München: Müller, 1969. 112 pp., ports., bibl.

STAUFFENBERG, CLAUS PHILIP SCHENK GRAF VON
3516 FINKER, KURT: *Stauffenberg und der 20. Juli 1944.* 2. erw. Aufl. Berlin: Union Verlag, 1971. 477 pp., illus.

3517 GRABER, GERRY: *Stauffenberg.* New York: Ballantine, 1973. 158 pp., illus.

3518 KRAMARZ, JOACHIM: *Claus Graf Stauffenberg. 15. November 1907–20. Juli 1944. Das Leben eines Offiziers.* Frankfurt a.M.: Bernard & Graefe, 1965. 245 pp., illus., facsims., bibl. [English version: *Stauffenberg. The life and death of an officer.* Introd.: H. R. Trevor-Roper. London: André Deutsch, 1967.]

3519 MÜLLER, CHRISTIAN: *Oberst. i.G. Stauffenberg. Eine Biographie.* Düsseldorf: Droste, [1970?]. 623 pp., port., notes (pp. 509–611).

3520 ZELLER, EBERHARD: 'Claus und Berthold Stauffenberg'. [In] *Vierteljahrshefte für Zeitgeschichte,* 12. Jhrg., 3. Heft, Juli 1964. Pp. 223–249.

3521 [STIEFF, HELMUTH] 'Ausgewählte Briefe von Generalmajor Helmuth Stieff'. [In] *Vierteljahrshefte für Zeitgeschichte,* Jhrg. 2, 3. Heft, 1954. Pp. 291–305.

TROTT ZU SOLZ, ADAM VON
3522 LINDGREN, HENRIK: 'Adam von Trotts Reisen nach Schweden 1942–1944. Ein Beitrag zur Frage der Auslandsverbindungen des deutschen Widerstandes'. [In] *Vierteljahrshefte für Zeitgeschichte,* 18. Jhrg., 3. Heft, 1970. Pp. 274–291. [Incl.: Letter and memorandum in English on resistance and conditions in Germany, pp. 283–291.]

3523 SYKES, CHRISTOPHER: *Troubled loyalty. A biography of Adam von Trott zu Solz.* London: Collins, 1968. 477 pp., illus., map.

3524 WEINBRENNER, HANS-JOACHIM, ed.: *Volksgerichtshof-Prozesse zum 20. Juli 1944. Transkripte von Tonbandfunden.* Frankfurt a.M.: Lautarchiv des Deutschen Rundfunks, 1961. 150 pp., mimeog.

3525 ZELLER, EBERHARD: *Geist der Freiheit. Der 20. Juli.* 2. durchges. und verm. Aufl. München: Rinn, 1954. 454 pp., bibl. [And 4th ed., entitled *Geist der Freiheit—Der 20. Juli in 1963.* English version (of 4th ed.): *The flame of freedom. The German struggle against Hitler.* London: Wolff, 1967. 471 pp., port., bibl.]

3526 *Zur Vorgeschichte der Verschwörung vom 20. Juli 1944.* Von einem Autorenkollektiv des Instituts für deutsche Militärgeschichte unter der

Leitung von Oberst W. Stern. Berlin [East]: Verlag des Ministeriums für Nationale Verteidigung, 1960. 111 pp., bibl.

5. THE JEWS IN GERMANY

a. General

3527 BOTTOME, PHYLLIS: *The mortal storm.* Harmondsworth, Middx.: Penguin Books, 1940. 256 pp. [First publ. 1937. Novel.]

3528 DROBISCH, KLAUS and others: *Juden unterm Hakenkreuz. Verfolgung und Ausrottung der deutschen Juden, 1933–1945.* [By] Klaus Drobisch, Rudi Goguel, Werner Müller, Horst Dohle. Frankfurt a.M.: Röderberg, 1973. 437 pp., bibl.

3529 FEUCHTWANGER, LION: *Die Geschwister Oppenheim. Roman.* Amsterdam: Querido, 1934. 433 pp. [English version: *The Oppermans.*]

3530 *Der gelbe Fleck. Die Ausrottung von 500,000 deutschen Juden.* Vorw.: Lion Feuchtwanger. Paris: Éds. du Carrefour, 1936. 278 pp., illus.

3531 GLASER, HERMANN & STRAUBE, HARALD, eds.: *Wohnungen des Todes. Jüdisches Schicksal im Dritten Reich. Dokumente und Texte.* Bamberg: Buchner, 1961. 186 pp.

3532 [JEWISH CENTRAL INFORMATION OFFICE]: *Dokumentensammlung über die Entrechtung, Ächtung und Vernichtung der Juden in Deutschland seit der Regierung Adolf Hitler.* Abgeschl.: 15. Okt. 1936. [Amsterdam: publ. anonymously]. 254 pp., illus.

3533 *The Jews in Germany. Facts and figures* [and] *The Jews in Germany.* By L. G. Montefiore. London: Anglo-Jewish Association, 1934/35. 20 + 23 pp. (Pamphlets 2 & 3).

3534 *Jews in Nazi Germany. A handbook of facts regarding their present situation.* New York: American Jewish Committee, 1935. 177 pp.

3535 KRAUS, KARL: *Die dritte Walpurgisnacht.* Hrsg.: Heinrich Fischer. Mit einem Essay 'Karl Kraus und die Zeitgeschichte' von Wilhelm Alff. München: Kösel, 1967. 365 pp. [Kraus's book written 1933.]

3536 LEO BAECK INSTITUTE: *Year Book I–XXV.* London: East and West Library (later Secker & Warburg), 1956–1980 (continuing).

3537 *De ontrechting der Joden in Duitschland. Documenten en Beschouwingen* [and] *De ontrechting der Joden in Duitschland.* Amsterdam: Joachimsthal, 1933/35. 64 + 28 pp. (Uitgeg. in opdracht van het Comité voor Bijzondere Joodsche Belangen).

3538 *La persécution des Juifs en Allemagne. Documentation internationale.* Genève: Union Suisse des Communautés Israélites, 1933/34. In 3 vols.

3539 SCHEFFLER, WOLFGANG: *Judenverfolgung im Dritten Reich 1933 bis 1945.*

3. erw. Ausg. Frankfurt a.M.: Colloquium Verlag, 1961. 246 pp., bibl. [Also new updated ed. 1964.]

3540 SCHLEUNES, KARL A.: *The twisted road to Auschwitz. Nazi policy towards German Jews, 1933–1939.* [Chicago, Ill.]: University of Illinois, 1970. 280 pp., bibl.

3541 SCHOENBERNER, GERHARD, ed.: *Wir haben es gesehen. Augenzeugenberichte über Terror und die Judenverfolgung im Dritten Reich.* Hamburg: Rütten & Loening, 1962. 429 pp., maps, facsims. [And new ed.: Gütersloh: Bertelsmann, 1964. Subtitle omits the words 'Terror und'.]

3542 SCHONFELD, MOSES & APPELMAN, HERMAN, eds.: *The mark of the swastika. Extracts from the British War Blue Book, together with the White Paper on the treatment of German nationals in Germany.* New York: AD Press, 1941. 217 pp. [Text in English and Yiddish.]

3543 SCHWARZ, STEFAN: *Sage nie, Du gehst den letzten Weg. Tatsachenroman um den Leidensweg einer jüdischen Familie.* München: Heyne, 1979. [First ed. 1971.]

3544 *Das Schwarzbuch. Tatsachen und Dokumente. Die Lage der Juden in Deutschland 1933.* Paris: Comité des Délégations juives, 1934. 536 pp.

3545 SEIDLER, FRITZ: *The bloodless pogrom.* London: Gollancz, 1934. 288 pp.

3546 TRACHTENBERG, JAKOW, ed.: *Die Greuelpropaganda ist eine Lügenpropaganda sagen die deutschen Juden selbst.* Berlin-Charlottenburg: Trachtenberg, 1933. 142 pp. [Quotations from papers and declarations by prominent Jews, evidently extorted under pressure. Text in German, English, French.]

3547 *Le Troisième Reich et les Juifs. Essai d'une documentation.* Antwerp: Comité pour la Défense des Droits des Juifs, 1933. 235 pp. [Also in Dutch.]

3548 VOGEL, ROLF: *Ein Stück von mir. Deutsche Juden in deutschen Armeen 1813–1976. Eine Dokumentation.* Mainz: von Hase & Koehler, 1977. 397 pp., illus., tabs. [3. Kap.: 'Das Dritte Reich'.]

3549 WARBURG, G[USTAV]: *Six years of Hitler. The Jews under the Nazi regime.* Forew.: Neville Laski. London: Allen & Unwin, 1939. 317 pp.

3550 *The Yellow Spot. The outlawing of half a million human beings: a collection of facts and documents relating to three years' persecution of German Jews, derived chiefly from National Socialist sources, very carefully assembled by a group of investigators.* Introd.: Bishop of Durham. London: Gollancz, 1936. 387 pp., illus., facsims., tabs.

b. Emigration

3551 HUTTENBACH, HENRY R.: *The emigration book of Worms. The character and dimension of the Jewish exodus from a small German Jewish community, 1933–1941.* Koblenz: Landesarchivverwaltung Rheinland-Pfalz, 1974. 118 pp., facsims., tabs. (Reprint from *Dokumentation zur Geschichte der jüdischen Bevölkerung in Rheinland-Pfalz* ... Bd. 7).

3552 LOWENTHAL, ERNST G., ed.: *Philo-Atlas. Handbuch für die jüdische Auswanderung.* Berlin: Philo (Jüdischer Buchverlag), 1938. 283 pp., maps, tabs.

3553 STRAUSS, HERBERT A.: 'Jewish emigration from Germany—Nazi policies and Jewish responses'. [In] *Leo Baeck Institute Year Book, Vol. XXV, 1980.* Pp. 313–361. See 3536.

3554 VOGEL, ROLF: *Ein Stempel hat gefehlt. Dokumente zur Emigration deutscher Juden.* München: Droemer Knaur, 1977. 367 pp., bibl.

c. Extermination

3555 ADLER, H. G.: *Der verwaltete Mensch. Studien zur Deportation der Juden aus Deutschland.* Tübingen: Mohr, 1974. xxxii + 1076 pp., bibl.

3556 BILLIG, JOSEPH: *La solution finale de la question juive. Essai sur ses principes dans le IIIe Reich et en France sous l'occupation. Les dossiers documentaires ... constitués par S. Klarsfeld.* Paris: Serge & Beate Klarsfeld, 1977. 207 pp., bibl. [German version: *Die Endlösung der Judenfrage* ... Paris: Centre de Documentation juive contemporaine, 1979. Simultaneously publ. in New York (Beate-Klarsfeld-Foundation) and Frankfurt a.M. (Jewish Young Leadership).]

3557 IRGUN OLEJ MERKAS EUROPA: *Die letzten Tage des deutschen Judentums. Berlin Ende 1942. Tatsachenbericht eines Augenzeugen.* Tel Aviv: 'Bitaon', 1943. 41 pp.

3558 RIESENBURGER, MARTIN: *Das Licht verlöschte nicht. Dokumente aus der Nacht des Nazismus.* Berlin [East]: Union Verlag, 1960. 87 pp.

d. Local and regional persecution

Aix-la-Chapelle (Aachen)

3559 KREUTZ, ANNELIE: *Die Verfolgung der Juden im Dritten Reich in Aachen.* Hausarbeit [pres. to] Pädagogische Hochschule Rheinland. 1976. 112 pp.

Baden-Württemberg

3560 SAUER, PAUL, ed.: *Dokumente über die Verfolgung der jüdischen Bürger in Baden-Württemberg durch das nationalsozialistische Regime 1933–1945.* Im Auftr. der Archivdirektion Stuttgart. Stuttgart: Kohlhammer, 1966. 2 vols., facsims.

3561 SAUER, PAUL: *Die Schicksale der jüdischen Bürger Baden-Württembergs während der nationalsozialistischen Verfolgungszeit 1933–1945. Statistische Ergebnisse der Erhebungen der Dokumentationsstelle bei der Archivdirektion Stuttgart und zusammenfassende Darstellung* [and] *Beiband: Die Opfer der nationalsozialistischen Judenverfolgung 1933–1945. Ein Gedenkbuch.* Stuttgart: Kohlhammer, 1969. 2 vols., illus., facsims., tabs., bibl.

Bavaria

3562 OPHIR, BARUCH ZVI and others: *Germany—Bavaria*. [By] Baruch Zvi Ophir, Shlomo Schmiedt, Chasia Turtel-Aberzhanska. Jerusalem: Yad Vashem, 1972. 683 + xl pp., illus., diagr., maps. tabs., bibls. after ea. ch. (Pinkas Hakehillot: Encyclopaedia of Jewish communities ...). [In Hebrew, summary in English. German version: Ophir, B. Z. & Wiesemann, Falk, eds.: *Die jüdischen Gemeinden in Bayern 1918–1938*. München: Oldenbourg, 1979.]

Berlin

3563 BAKER, LEONARD: *Days of sorrow and pain. Leo Baeck and the Berlin Jews.* New York: Macmillan, 1978. viii + 396 pp., illus., bibl. [Incl. Theresienstadt.]

3564 BALL-KADURI, K. J.: 'Berlin wird judenfrei—Die Juden in Berlin in den Jahren 1942/43'. Sonderdruck aus *Jahrbuch für die Geschichte Mittel- und Ostdeutschlands*, Bd. 22. Berlin: Colloquium Verlag, 1973. [Enl. and updated version of 'Berlin is "purged" of Jews. The Jews in Berlin 1943' in *Yad Vashem Studies*, No. V. Jerusalem: 1963. Pp. 271–316.]

Breslau

3565 TAUSK, WALTER: *Breslauer Tagebuch 1933–1940*. Frankfurt a.M.: Röderberg, 1977. 264 pp., illus., facsims.

3566 WALK, JOSEPH, ed.: *Als Jude in Breslau 1941. Aus den Tagebüchern von Studienrat a.D. Dr. Willy Israel Cohn.* [Jerusalem]: Verband ehemaliger Breslauer und Schlesier in Israel & Bar-Ilan University Institute for the Research of Diaspora Jewry, 1975. 90 + 5 pp., illus., facsims., family tree.

Brunswick

3567 *Brunsvicensia Judaica. Gedenkbuch für die jüdischen Mitbürger der Stadt Braunschweig 1933–1945.* Braunschweig: Waisenhaus Buchdruckerei Verlag, 1966. 237 pp., illus.

Chemnitz (Karl-Marx-Stadt)

3568 DIAMANT, ADOLF: *Chronik der Juden in Chemnitz—heute Karl-Marx-Stadt. Aufstieg und Untergang einer jüdischen Gemeinde in Sachsen.* Frankfurt a.M.: Weidlich, 1970. 183 pp., illus., facsims., diagrs., tabs., bibl. [Ch. X: 'Bis zum Judenboykott 1933'; XI: 'Die Kristallnacht'; XII: 'Die letzten Jahre und die Deportationen'; Anhang A: 'Berichte von den Konzentrationslagern'.]

Danzig

3569 LICHTENSTEIN, ERWIN: *Die Juden der Freien Stadt Danzig unter der Herrschaft des Nationalsozialismus.* Tübingen: Mohr, 1973. xiii + 242 pp., tabs., bibl. (Schriftenreihe wissenschaftlicher Abhandlungen des Leo Baeck Instituts ...).

Dortmund

3570 KNIPPING, ULRICH: *Die Geschichte der Juden in Dortmund während der Zeit des Dritten Reiches.* Dortmund: Historischer Verein, 1977. 255 pp., illus., facsims., tabs., bibl.

Dresden

3571 DIAMANT, ADOLF: *Chronik der Juden in Dresden. Von den ersten Juden bis zur Blüte der Gemeinde und deren Ausrottung.* Geleitw.: Robert M. W. Kempner. Darmstadt: Agora Verlag, 1973. xiv + 521 pp., illus., plans, tabs., bibl. [Ch. XII: 'Der Judenboykott'; XIII: 'Die Kristallnacht'; XIV: 'Die letzten Jahre der Israelitischen Religionsgemeinde'; XV: 'Die Deportationen'.]

Frankfurt am Main

3572 KOMMISSION ZUR ERFORSCHUNG DER GESCHICHTE DER FRANKFURTER JUDEN: *Dokumente zur Geschichte der Frankfurter Juden 1933–1945.* Frankfurt a.M.: Kramer, 1963. 553 pp., tabs.

Giessen

3573 KNAUSS, ERWIN: *Die jüdische Bevölkerung Giessens 1933–1945. Eine Dokumentation.* Wiesbaden: Kommission für die Geschichte der Juden in Hessen, 1974. 152 pp., facsims. [Incl. lists of victims and survivors, pp. 54–152.]

Hamburg

3574 *Gedenkbuch für die jüdischen Opfer des Nationalsozialismus in Hamburg.* Hamburg: Staatsarchiv der Freien und Hansestadt Hamburg, 1965. 104 pp.

Heidelberg

3575 LUDWIG, MAX (pseud. of Max Oppenheimer): *Aus dem Tagebuch des Herrn O. Dokumente und Berichte über die Deportationen und den Untergang der Heidelberger Juden.* Vorw.: Hermann Maas. Heidelberg: Lambert Schneider, 1965. 69 pp., illus., facsims., tabs.

Hessen

3576 NOAM, ERNST & KROPAT, WOLF-ARNO: *Juden vor Gericht 1933–1945. Dokumente aus hessischen Justizakten.* Vorw.: Johannes Strelitz. Wiesbaden: Kommission für die Geschichte der Juden in Hessen, 1975. 327 pp., bibl. (Schriften der Kommission ...: Justiz und Judenverfolgung ...).

Kirchen

3577 HUETTNER, AXEL: *Die jüdische Gemeinde von Kirchen (Efringen-Kirchen, Kreis Lörrach) 1736–1940. Beiträge zur geschichtlichen-, politischen-, wirtschaftlichen und religiösen Situation der Juden im Markgräferland.* 2. verb. Aufl. Grenzach/Heidelberg: [priv. pr.], 1978. 372 pp., illus., tabs., bibl.

Landau

3578　*Die Landauer Judengemeinde. Ein Abriss ihrer Geschichte.* Landau/Pfalz: Stadtverwaltung, 1969. 87 pp., illus., facsim., tabs. [Incl. Third Reich, pp. 43–83.]

Mainz

3579　KLEIN, ANTON, ed.: *Tagebuch einer jüdischen Gemeinde 1941/43.* Mainz: von Hase & Koehler, 1968. 112 pp., tabs., bibl. (Im Auftr. der Jüdischen Gemeinde Mainz hrsg. und kommentiert).

Mannheim

3580　FLIEDNER, HANS-JOACHIM: *Die Judenverfolgung in Mannheim 1933–1945.* Hrsg.: Stadtarchiv Mannheim. Stuttgart: Kohlhammer, 1971. Illus., facsims., bibl.
Bd. I: *Darstellung.*
Bd. II: *Dokumente.*

Memmingen / Bavaria

3581　LINN, DOROTHEE: *Das Schicksal der jüdischen Bevölkerung in Memmingen von 1933 bis 1945. Jahresbericht einer Primanerin.* Stuttgart: Klett, 1968. 96 pp., tabs. [First issued 1962, in 200 mimeog. copies only. Subject undertaken as part of 'Reifeprüfung'.]

Mergentheim

3582　FECHENBACH, HERMANN: *Die letzten Mergentheimer Juden* und *Die Geschichte der Familie Fechenbach.* Stuttgart: Kohlhammer, 1972. 216 pp., illus., facsims.

Münster in Westfalen

3583　BRILLING, BERNHARD & DIECKMANN, ULRICH, eds.: *Juden in Münster 1933–1945. Eine Gedenkschrift.* Münster i.W.: Gesellschaft für christlich-jüdische Zusammenarbeit, 1960. 31 pp.

Munich

3584　CAHNMANN, WERNER J.: 'Die Juden in München 1918–1943'. [In] *Zeitschrift für bayerische Landesgeschichte,* Bd. 42, Heft 2, 1979. Pp. 403–461. [Author was Syndikus of the Bavarian branch of the Central-Verein. Incl. activities of the Central-Verein, Bavarian anti-Semitism and Jewish reactions to it.]

3585　HANKE, PETER: *Zur Geschichte der Juden in München zwischen 1933 und 1945.* München: Stadtarchiv, 1967. 353 pp., illus., tabs., facsims., bibl.

3586　LAMM, HANS: *Von Juden in München. Ein Gedenkbuch.* 3. unveränd. Aufl. Darmstadt: Verlag Darmstädter Blätter, 1979. 406 pp., illus.

Nuremberg

3587　MÜLLER, ARND: *Geschichte der Juden in Nürnberg 1146–1945.* Nürnberg:

286

Stadtbibliothek, 1968. 381 pp., illus., facsims., tabs., bibl. [Ch. 10: 'Die Verfolgung der Nürnberger Juden seit 1933', pp. 211–274; 11: 'Die Vernichtung der Nürnberger Juden im Zweiten Weltkrieg', pp. 275–296.]

Rhenish Palatinate and Saar

3588 SIMMERT, JOHANNES, ed.: *Die nationalsozialistische Judenverfolgung in Rheinland-Pfalz 1933 bis 1945.*
[and]
HARRMANN, HANS-WALTER, ed.: *Das Schicksal der Juden im Saarland 1920 bis 1945.* Koblenz: Landesarchivverwaltung Rheinland-Pfalz, 1974. 491 pp., facsims., tabs., bibl. (Dokumentation zur Geschichte der jüdischen Bevölkerung in Rheinland-Pfalz und im Saarland ...).

Rhine-Ruhr

3589 DÜWELL, KURT: *Die Rheingebiete in der Judenpolitik des Nationalsozialismus vor 1942. Beitrag zu einer vergleichenden zeitgeschichtlichen Landeskunde.* Bonn: Röhrscheid, 1968. 328 pp., tabs., map, bibl.

3590 GORDON, SARAH ANN: *German opposition to Nazi anti-Semitism measures between 1933 and 1945, with particular reference to the Rhine-Ruhr area.* Dissertation [pres. to] State University of New York, Buffalo. 1979. 502 pp.

Stuttgart

3591 ZELZER, MARIA: *Weg und Schicksal der Stuttgarter Juden. Ein Gedenkbuch.* Hrsg.: Stadt Stuttgart. Stuttgart: Klett, [1964]. 588 pp., illus., facsims., tabs.

Ulm/Donau

3592 KEIL, HEINZ, ed.: *Dokumentation über die Verfolgungen der jüdischen Bürger von Ulm/Donau.* Ulm: Stadt Ulm, 1961. 423 pp., mimeog.

Württemberg and Hohenzollern

3593 HERRMANN, GERT-JULIUS: *Jüdische Jugend in der Verfolgung. Eine Studie über das Schicksal jüdischer Jugendlicher aus Württemberg und Hohenzollern.* Inaugural-Dissertation [pres. to] Eberhard-Karls-Universität zu Tübingen. 1967. 210 pp., map, tabs., bibl.

Zwickau

3594 DIAMANT, ADOLF: *Zur Chronik der Juden in Zwickau. Dem Gedenken einer kleinen jüdischen Gemeinde in Sachsen.* Frankfurt a.M.: [priv. pr.], 1971. 97 pp., illus., facsims., tabs., diagr. [Incl.: 'Unter der faschistischen Diktatur', pp. 44–57; 'Die Ausweisung der polnischen Juden', pp. 58–67; 'Von der Kristallnacht bis zur Liquidation', pp. 68–78.]

e. Individual accounts and cases

3595 DEUTSCHKRON, INGE: *Ich trug den gelben Stern.* Köln: Verlag Wissenschaft und Politik, 1978. 215 pp.

3596 EDEL, PETER: *Wenn es ans Leben geht. Meine Geschichte.* Berlin [East]: Verlag der Nation, 1979. 451 + 420 pp., illus. [In 2 vols. 'Mischling', writer and artist, slave labourer at Siemensstadt, survivor of Grossbeeren, Auschwitz, Ebensee and other camps. Also involved in 'Operation Bernhard'.]

3596a FRANKENTHAL, KAETE: *Der dreifache Fluch: Jüdin, Intellektuelle und Sozialistin.* Frankfurt a.M.: Campus Verlag, 1980. [Author was active in development of social medicine; member of Berlin City Council and Prussian Diet; forced to emigrate in 1933, ultimately to the USA.]

3597 FROMM, BELLA: *Blood and banquets. A Berlin social diary.* New York: Harper, 1942. 332 pp. [A Jewish journalist on the 'Vossische Zeitung'.]

3598 GRÜNFELD, FRITZ V.: *Das Leinenhaus Grünfeld. Erinnerungen und Dokumente.* Hrsg.: Stefi Jersch-Wenzel. Berlin: Duncker & Humblot, 1967. 237 pp., illus., tabs., facsims., bibl.

3599 HERZ, EMIL: *Denk ich an Deutschland in der Nacht. Die Geschichte des Hauses Steg.* Berlin: Druckhaus Tempelhof, 1951. 330 pp. [Head of Ullstein's book department.]

3600 HINDLS, ARNOLD: *Einer kehrte zurück. Bericht eines Deportierten.* Stuttgart: Deutsche Verlags-Anstalt, 1965. 178 pp., port. (Veröffentlichungen des Leo Baeck Instituts).

3601 HOFFMAN, RUTH: *Meine Freunde aus Davids Geschlecht.* Berlin: Chronos-Verlag, 1947. 144 pp. [And 2nd ed.: Berlin: Lettner, 1955. 243 pp. Anecdotes about the author's Jewish friends and their fates.]

3602 JOSEPH, ARTUR: *Meines Vaters Haus. Ein Dokument.* Vorrede: Heinrich Böll. Köln: Kiepenheuer & Witsch, 1979. 143 pp. [Reminiscences of a Cologne businessman, first publ. 1959.]

3603 KATZ, JOSEF: *One who came back. The diary of a Jewish survivor.* Transl. from the German. New York: Herzl Press & Bergen-Belsen Memorial Press, 1973. 277 pp. [Incl. Riga Ghetto, Kaiserwald and Stutthof concentration camps.]

3604 KLEIN, CATHERINE: *Escape from Berlin.* Transl. from the German. London: Gollancz, 1944. 149 pp. [Escape from deportation, with help of non-Jewish friends.]

3605 MARX, HUGO: *Die Flucht. Jüdisches Schicksal 1940.* Düsseldorf: Verlag 'Allgemeine Wochenzeitung der Juden in Deutschland', 1955. 194 pp. [Experiences of German Jewish couple fleeing from Brussels. Incl. help by non-Jews.]

3606 MEIER, MAURICE: *Refuge.* New York: Norton, 1962. 241 pp., illus., facsims. [Transl. from the German.]

3607 PINCUS, LILY: *Verloren—gewonnen. Mein Weg von Berlin nach London.* Nachw.: Bernd H. Stappert. Stuttgart: Deutsche Verlags-Anstalt, 1980. 206 pp.

3608 ROSENFELD, ELSBETH: *The four lives of Elsbeth Rosenfeld. As told by her to the BBC.* Forew.: James Parkes. London: Gollancz, 1964. 158 pp.

3609 SIEGELBERG, MARK: *Schutzhaftjude Nr. 13877*. Shanghai: The American Press 'Sygma', 1939. 253 pp.

3610 [SINASOHN, RAHEL RUTH] SINASOHN, MAX: *Rahel Ruth Sinasohn. Das Leben einer talentierten, charmanten, gläubigen Jüdin, 1891–1969*. [Publ. in Israel]. 93 pp., illus.

3611 STANLEY, ILSE: *I will lift up mine eyes*. London: Gollancz, 1954. 224 pp. [The experiences of a cantor's daughter.]

3612 VOGT, PAUL, comp.: *Aus Not und Rettung. Stimmen aus dem Dunkel dieser Zeit. Gehört und gesammelt*. Hrsg. für den Flüchtlingsdienst des Schweizerischen Evangelischen Hilfswerkes für die Bekennende Kirche in Deutschland. 3. Aufl. Zürich: Oprecht, 1944. 100 pp.

3613 [WARBURG Family] WENZEL-BURCHARD, GERTRUD: *Granny. Gerta Warburg und die Ihren. Hamburger Schicksale*. Hamburg: Christians, [1970?]. 237 pp., illus., facsims.

3614 ZERNIK, CHARLOTTE E.: *Im Sturm der Zeit. Ein persönliches Dokument*. Düsseldorf: Econ Verlag, 1977. 120 pp., illus.

f. Underground survival

3615 BEHREND, RAHEL: *Verfemt und verfolgt. Erlebnisse einer Jüdin in Nazi-Deutschland 1933–1944*. Zürich: Büchergilde Gutenberg, 1945. 328 pp. [German edition: BEHREND-ROSENFELD, ELSE R.: *Ich stand nicht allein*. Hamburg: Europäische Verlagsanstalt, 1949. Also 3rd ed. 1979. Illegal life underground with help of Christian and non-Aryan friends: incl. details of deportation of Jews from Munich.]

3616 CASTLE STANFORD, JULIAN (formerly Julius Schloss): *Reflections. The diary of a German-Jew in hiding*. Ed.: Rebecca Fromer. Oakland, Calif.: Institute for the Righteous Acts, Judah L. Magnes Memorial Museum, 1965. 108 pp., illus., facsim. [German version: *Tagebuch eines deutschen Juden im Untergrund 1938–1945*. Darmstadt: Verlag Darmstädter Blätter, 1979.]

3617 KÖNIG, JOEL (pseud. of Esra Ben Gershôm): *David. Aufzeichnungen eines Überlebenden*. Frankfurt a.M.: Fischer, 1979. 331 pp. [Member of 'Bund deutsch-jüdischer Jugend' who survived underground. First publ. 1967 under title *Den Netzen entronnen*.]

3618 KRAKAUER, MAX: *Lichter im Dunkel*. Stuttgart: Behrendt, 1947. 131 pp. [Underground life and survival of a Jewish couple.]

3619 ROSENTHAL, HANS: *Zwei Leben in Deutschland*. Bergisch Gladbach: Lübbe, 1980. 343 pp., illus., facsims., tabs. [Author survived underground hidden by Berlin workers in the 'Laubkolonie Dreieinigkeit'.]

3620 SCHOHL-BRAUMANN, HELA: *Sieger bleibt die Liebe. Geschichte einer jüdischen Familie im 'Dritten Reich'*. Dortmund: Ruhr-Donau Verlag, 1961. 64 pp.

3621 SCHWERSENZ, JIZCHAK & WOLFF, EDITH: *Jüdische Jugend im Untergrund. Eine zionistische Gruppe in Deutschland während des Zweiten Weltkrieges*.

Historische Einführung: Shaul Esh. Tel-Aviv: Bitaon, 1969. 100 pp., illus., facsims. [Special issue of *Bulletin des Leo Baeck Instituts*, 12. Jhrg., Nr. 45. Hebrew version publ. by Hakibbutz Hameuchad.]

3622 SENGER, VALENTIN: *Kaiserhofstrasse 12*. Darmstadt: Luchterhand, 1978. 247 pp. [Jewish family living openly throughout the war with false papers in Frankfurt a.M. English version: *The invisible Jew*. London: Sidgwick & Jackson, 1979.]

g. Economic persecution

3623 DAHM, VOLKER: 'Liquidation des jüdischen Buchhandels im Dritten Reich'. Beilage [of] *Börsenblatt für den deutschen Buchhandel*. Frankfurter Ausg., Nr. 33, 25. April 1975. Pp. B237–B244.

3624 GENSCHEL, HELMUT: *Die Verdrängung der Juden aus der Wirtschaft im Dritten Reich*. Göttingen: Musterschmidt, 1966. 337 pp., tabs., bibl.

3625 JEWISH CENTRAL INFORMATION OFFICE: *Wirtschaftsboykott*. Amsterdam: 1934. 30 pp., tabs. [On Nazi boycott against German Jews and Jewry's boycott against Germany.]

3626 KÖHRER, HELMUTH: *Entziehung, Beraubung, Rückerstattung. Vom Wandel der Beziehungen zwischen Juden und Nichtjuden durch Verfolgung und Restitution*. Baden-Baden: Juristischer Verlag, 1951. 205 pp.

3627 KRÜGER, ALF: *Die Lösung der Judenfrage in der deutschen Wirtschaft. Kommentar zur Judengesetzgebung*. Berlin: Limpert, 1940. 440 pp.

3628 LESTSCHINSKY, JACOB: *La situation économique des Juifs depuis la guerre mondiale (Europe orientale et centrale)*. Paris: Rousseau, 1934. 148 pp., tabs., bibl. [Chs. XII–XIV deal with the persecution of German Jewry under Hitler.]

3629 WEIS, GEORGE, ed.: *Einige Dokumente zur Rechtsstellung der Juden und zur Entziehung ihres Vermögens 1933–1945*. [Berlin: 1954]. 100 pp., facsim. (Schriftenreihe zum Berliner Rückerstattungsrecht).

3630 WORLD JEWISH CONGRESS, Economic Bureau: *The economic destruction of German Jewry by the Nazi regime, 1933–1937. A study*. New York: American Jewish Congress, 1937. 68 pp.

'Aryanization'

3631 BUCHMANN, ERICH: *Von der jüdischen Firma Simson zur nationalsozialistischen Industriestiftung Gustloff-Werke*. Erfurt: Bodung, 1944. 36 pp., illus., facsims., family tree.

FLICK, FRIEDRICH
3632 OGGER, GÜNTER: *Friedrich Flick der Grosse*. Bern: Scherz, 1971. 407 pp., bibl.

3633 THIELEKE, KARL-HEINZ, ed.: *Fall 5. Anklageplädoyer, ausgewählte Dokumente, Urteil des Flick-Prozesses. Mit einer Studie über die 'Arisierung' des Flick-*

Konzerns. Eingel.: Klaus Drobisch. Berlin [East]: VEB Deutscher Verlag der Wissenschaften, 1965. 501 pp., tabs.

3634 MARKMANN, WERNER & ENTERLEIN, PAUL: *Die Entjudung der deutschen Wirtschaft. Arisierungsverordnungen vom 26. April und 12. November 1938 erläutert.* Berlin: Gesbach, 1938. 195 pp.

3635 SCHOLL, ALBERT: *Die Entjudung des deutschen Grundbesitzes. Die Verordnung über den Einsatz des jüdischen Vermögens vom 3. Dezember 1938 nebst Durchführungsverordnung vom 16. Januar 1939 und den ministeriellen Durchführungsbestimmungen vom 6. Februar 1939 erläutert.* Berlin: Heymann, 1939. 79 pp.

h. Cultural and professional persecution

3636 KAZNELSON, SIEGMUND, ed.: *Juden im deutschen Kulturbereich. Ein Sammelwerk.* Geleitw.: Richard Willstätter. 2., stark erw. Ausg. Berlin: Jüdischer Verlag, 1959. xx + 1060 pp. [Incl. biographical notes on many of the persecuted; also list of non-Jews often believed to be Jewish.]

3637 [LEBER, ANNEDORE, ed.]: *Doch das Zeugnis lebt fort. Der jüdische Beitrag zu unserem Leben.* Berlin: Leber, 1965. 378 pp., illus., facsims.

Jurists

3638 ALBERT, ERWIN: *Verzeichnis jüdischer Verfasser juristischer Schriften.* 2., ergänz. Aufl. Stuttgart: Kohlhammer, 1937. 55 pp.

3639 GÖPPINGER, HORST: *Die Verfolgung Juristen jüdischer Abstammung durch den Nationalsozialismus.* Mitw.: Johann Georg Reissmüller. Geleitw.: Wolfgang Haussmann. Villingen/Schwarzw.: Ring-Verlag, 1963. 156 pp.

3640 [STEIN, SIGMUND] DICKINSON, JOHN K.: *German and Jew. The life and death of Sigmund Stein.* Chicago, Ill.: Quadrangle Books, 1967. 339 pp.

3641 *Verzeichnis nichtarischer Rechtsanwälte Deutschlands.* Berlin: Scherk [printer], 1934. [128 pp.]

Scientists and scholars

3642 [LESSING, THEODOR] CÍLEK, ROMAN: *Výstřely ve vile Edelweiss. Pokus o reportažní rekonstrukci.* Praha: Vyd. Časopisů Mno, 1966. 164 pp., illus. [On the assassination of Theodor Lessing.]

NOTGEMEINSCHAFT DEUTSCHER WISSENSCHAFTLER IM AUSLAND: *List of displaced German scholars. See 2425.*

3643 OSTROWSKI, SIEGFRIED: 'Vom Schicksal der jüdischen Ärzte im Dritten Reich'. [In] *Bulletin des Leo Baeck Instituts.*, 6. Jhrg., Nr. 24, 1963. Tel-Aviv: Bitaon. Pp. 313–351.

3643a *Why I left Germany.* By a German-Jewish scientist. London: Dent, 1934. 214 pp.

Writers, artists, etc.

3644 DAHM, VOLKER: *Das jüdische Buch im Dritten Reich. Teil 1: Die Ausschaltung der jüdischen Autoren, Verleger und Buchhändler.* Frankfurt a.M.: Buchhändler Vereinigung, 1979. 300 cols., illus., bibl., summaries in English, French, German. (Sonderdruck aus *Archiv für Geschichte des Buchwesens*, Bd. 20, Lfg. 1–2). [Comprising: 1: 'Das "jüdische" Buch als Volksfeind'; 2: 'Die Ausschaltung jüdischer Autoren, Verleger und Buchhändler durch Berufsverbot'; 3: 'Die Ausschaltung "jüdischen" Schrifttums durch Berufsverbot'. Part 2 forthcoming. Based on a dissertation, Munich 1976/77.]

3645 [KOLMAR, GERTRUD] LANGER, LAWRENCE L.: 'Survival through art. The career of Gertrud Kolmar'. [In] *Leo Baeck Institute Yearbook*, XXIII. London: Secker & Warburg, 1978. Pp. 247–258.

3646 MÜHSAM, ERICH: *Auswahl. Gedichte—Drama—Prosa.* Mit einem Nachruf von Erich Weinert. Zürich: Limmat, 1962. 514 pp., illus. (Hrsg.: Deutsche Akademie der Künste zu Berlin).

3647 *Verzeichnis jüdischer Autoren. Vorläufige Zusammenstellung des Amtes Schrifttumspflege bei dem Beauftragten des Führers für die gesamte geistige und weltanschauliche Erziehung der NSDAP und der Reichsstelle zur Förderung des deutschen Schrifttums.* Berlin: 1938/39. In 7 parts.

j. November 1938 pogrom

3648 DIAMANT, ADOLF: *Zerstörte Synagogen vom November 1938. Eine Bestandsaufnahme.* Frankfurt a.M.: [priv. pr.], 1978. xvi + 227 pp., illus.

3649 FRANKE, MANFRED: *Mordverläufe 9./10.XI.1938. Ein Protokoll von der Angst, von Misshandlung und Tod, vom Auffinden der Spuren und deren Wiederentdeckung. Roman.* Darmstadt: Luchterhand, 1973. 378 pp., bibl.

3650 GRAML, HERMANN: *Der 9. November 1938. 'Reichskristallnacht'.* Bonn: Bundeszentrale für Heimatdienst, 1953. 20 pp. [Documented report.]

GRYNSZPAN, HERSCHL

3651 DIEWERGE, WOLFGANG: *Anschlag gegen den Frieden. Ein Gelbbuch über Grünspan und seine Helfershelfer.* München: Eher, 1939. 179 pp., illus.

3652 DUMOULIN, PIERRE: *L'affaire Grynspan. Un attentat contre la France.* Paris: Jean-Renard, 1942. 161 pp., facsims.

3653 GRIMM, [FRIEDRICH]: *Der Grünspanprozess.* Nürnberg: [priv. pr.], 1942. 159 pp.

3654 KAUL, FRIEDRICH KARL: *Der Fall des Herschl Grynszpan.* Berlin [East]: Akademie-Verlag, 1965. 182 pp., illus., facsims.

3655 HEIDEN, KONRAD: *Tyskland y Fara. Novemberpogromen, 1938.* Stockholm: Tidens Förlag, 1939. 133 pp. [French version, transl. from the German: *Les vêpres Hitleriennes. Nuits sanglantes en Allemagne.* Paris: Sorlot, 1939. 189 pp.]

3656 KOCHAN, LIONEL: *Pogrom. November 10, 1938.* London: André Deutsch, 1957. 159 pp.

3657 *Der Pogrom.* Vorw.: Heinrich Mann. Zürich: Verlag für soziale Literatur, 1939. 221 pp. [Newspaper and eyewitness reports on pogroms in Germany and world reaction.]

3658 *Reichskristallnacht. Pogrom, 9/10 November 1938.* Amsterdam: De Bezije Bij, 1968. 47 pp., illus., facsims.

3659 ROSENKRANZ, HERBERT: *'Reichskristallnacht': 9. November 1938 in Österreich.* Wien: Europa Verlag, 1968. 72 pp.

3660 SHAMIR, HAIM: 'Die Kristallnacht, die Notlage der deutschen Juden und die Haltung Englands'. [In] Walter Grab, ed.: *Jahrbuch, Institut für Deutsche Geschichte, 1. Bd.* Pp. 171–214. *See* 35a.

3661 THALMANN, RITA & FEINERMANN, EMMANUEL: *La nuit de cristal.* Paris: Laffont, 1972. 243 pp., illus., facsims. [English version: *Crystal Night, 9–10 November 1938.* New York: Coward, McCann & Geoghegan, 1974.]

k. Attempts at adaptation and resistance

3662 ADLER-RUDEL, S.: *Jüdische Selbsthilfe unter dem Naziregime 1933–1939. Im Spiegel der Berichte der Reichsvertretung der Juden in Deutschland.* Vorw.: Robert Weltsch. Tübingen: Mohr, 1974. xv + 221 pp., tabs. (Schriftenreihe wissenschaftlicher Abhandlungen des Leo Baeck Instituts).

3663 BALL-KADURI, KURT JAKOB: *Das Leben der Juden in Deutschland im Jahre 1933. Ein Zeitbericht.* Frankfurt a.M.: Europäische Verlagsanstalt, 1963. 226 pp., bibl.

3664 BALL-KADURI, KURT JAKOB: *Vor der Katastrophe. Juden in Deutschland 1934–1939.* Tel Aviv: Olamenu, 1967. 302 pp., facsim., bibl.

3665 GOLDSCHMIDT, FRITZ: *Meine Arbeit bei der Vertretung der Interessen der jüdischen Ärzte in Deutschland seit dem Juli 1933.* Hrsg.: Stephan Leibfried, Florian Tennstedt. Bremen: 1979. iv + 179 pp., illus., facsims. (Arbeitsberichte zu verschütteten Alternativen in der Gesundheitspolitik). [Author's activities on behalf of the Central-Verein and his negotiations with the Nazi authorities.]

3666 HERMANN, KLAUS J.: *Das Dritte Reich und die deutschjüdischen Organisationen 1933–1934.* Köln: Heymann, 1969. 156 pp., facsims.

3667 *Ja-Sagen zum Judentum. Eine Aufsatzreihe der 'Jüdischen Rundschau' zur Lage der deutschen Juden.* Berlin: 'Jüdische Rundschau', 1933. 159 pp.

3668 LICHTENSTEIN, F[RANZ], ed.: *Chalutzim on the Continent 1942.* Publ. by Hechalutz B'Anglia, Organisation of Jewish Pioneers for Palestine, 1943. 48 pp. [Letters from Hachsharah centres in Germany prior to their dissolution and deportation of the inmates.]

3669 LOWENTHAL, E[RNST] G., ed.: *Bewährung im Untergang. Ein Gedenkbuch.* Im

Auftr. des Council of Jews from Germany, London. Stuttgart: Deutsche Verlags-Anstalt, 1965. 199 pp., ports.

3670 MARGALIOT, ABRAHAM: 'The struggle for survival of the Jewish community in Germany in the face of oppression'. [In] *Jewish resistance during the Holocaust. Proceedings of the Conference on Manifestations of Jewish Resistance.* Jerusalem: Yad Vashem, 1971. Pp. 100–122.

UPPER SILESIA

3671 FEINBERG, NATHAN: *The Jewish front against Hitler on the stage of the League of Nations. (Bernheim Petition).* Issued by Yad Washem. Jerusalem: Bialik, 1957. 186 pp. [The Jews of Upper Silesia were a protected minority under the League of Nations, as established by the Bernheim Petition, which obliged the German government to comply with their treaty obligations.]

3672 WEICHSELBAUM, WILLY: *Der Rechtsschutz der Juden in Deutsch-Oberschlesien nach dem Genfer Abkommen von 1922.* Dresden: Dittert, 1935. 59 pp., bibl.

3673 WEISSMANN, GEORG: 'Die Durchsetzung des jüdischen Minderheitsrechtes in Oberschlesien 1933–1937'.
[And]
MEYER, FRANZ: 'Einleitung zur Denkschrift von Georg Weissmann'. [In] *Leo Baeck Institut Bulletin*, 6. Jhrg., Nr. 22, 1963. Tel-Aviv: Bitaon. Pp. 154–198 [and] 148–153. [The orig. memorandum is in the Zionist Central Archives, Jerusalem.]

3674 WELTSCH, ROBERT: 'Tragt ihn mit Stolz, den gelben Fleck!'. Sonderabdruck aus der 'Jüdischen Rundschau', Berlin, vom 4. April 1933. [4 pp.]. [Boycott of 1 April 1933.]

Cultural life

WRITINGS

3675 *Bibliographie des jüdischen Buches.* Frankfurt a.M.: Sänger, 1934–   Mimeog. [Issued in quarterly numbers, at least up to beginning of 1937.]

3676 LEO BAECK INSTITUTE NEW YORK: *Bibliothek und Archiv. Katalog: Band I: Deutschsprachige jüdische Gemeinden, Zeitungen, Zeitschriften, Jahrbücher, Almanache und Kalender, unveröffentlichte Memoiren und Erinnerungsschriften.* Hrsg.: Max Kreutzberger. Mitarb.: Irmgard Foerg. Tübingen: Mohr, 1970. xli + 623 pp., illus., facsims. [Includes material on Jewish life in the Nazi period.]

3677 PREUSSISCHER LANDESVERBAND DER JÜDISCHEN GEMEINDEN: *Die Wanderbücherei. Ein besprechendes Bücherverzeichnis.* Berlin: Levy, 1937. 179 pp.

EDUCATION

3678 COLODNER, SOLOMON: *Jewish education in Germany under the Nazis.* [No place of publ. (USA)]: Jewish Education Committee Press, 1964. 139 pp., facsims., tabs., maps, bibl.

3679 FUCHS, RICHARD: 'The "Hochschule für die Wissenschaft des Judentums" in the period of Nazi rule. Personal recollections'. [In] *Leo Baeck Institute Year Book*, XII. London: 1967. Pp. 3–31, illus.

3680 SIMON, ERNST: *Aufbau im Untergang. Jüdische Erwachsenenbildung im nationalsozialistischen Deutschland als geistiger Widerstand.* Tübingen: Mohr, 1959. 109 pp. (Schriftenreihe Wissenschaftlicher Abhandlungen des Leo Baeck Institute of Jews from Germany). [Shortened English version: 'Jewish adult education in Nazi Germany as spiritual resistance'. [In] *Leo Baeck Institute Year Book*, I. London: 1956. Pp. 68–104.]

3681 WALK, JOSEPH: *The education of the Jewish child in Germany. The law and its execution.* Jerusalem: Yad Vashem, Leo Baeck Institute, 1975. xiii + 383 pp., map, tabs., bibl. [In Hebrew, summary in English.]

3682 ZENTRALWOHLFAHRTSSTELLE DER DEUTSCHEN JUDEN & ZENTRALSTELLE FÜR JÜDISCHE WIRTSCHAFTSHILFE: *Grundlagen für die Berufsausbildung von Juden in Deutschland.* [Berlin: 1934?]. 63 pp.

SPORT
3683 BERNETT, HAJO: *Der jüdische Sport im nationalsozialistischen Deutschland 1933–1938.* Schorndorf: Hofman, 1978. 182 pp., facsims., bibl. (Schriftenreihe des Bundesinstituts für Sportwissenschaft).

3684 YOGI MAYER, PAUL: 'Equality—Egality. Jews and sport in Germany'. [In] *Leo Baeck Institute Yearbook*, XXV. London: Secker & Warburg, 1980. Pp. 221–241, illus. [Incl. 1936 Olympics.]

Active Resistance

3685 ESCHWEGE, HELMUT: 'Resistance of German Jews against the Nazi regime'. [In] *Leo Baeck Institute Yearbook*, XV. London: East & West Library, 1970. Pp. 143–180, illus., facsims. [Incl. Baum group.]

GUSTLOFF ASSASSINATION
3686 DIEWERGE, WOLFGANG: *Ein Jude hat geschossen. Augenzeugenbericht vom Mordprozess David Frankfurter.* München: Eher, 1937. 123 pp.

3687 LUDWIG, EMIL: *David und Goliath. Geschichte eines politischen Mordes. Epilog: David Frankfurter 9 Jahre später.* Zürich: Posen, 1945. 139 pp. [English version: *The Davos murder.* London: Methuen, 1937.]

3688 PIKARSKI, MARGOT: *Jugend im Berliner Widerstand. Herbert Baum und Kampfgefährten.* Berlin [East]: Militärverlag der DDR, 1978. 235 pp., illus., facsims., bibl. [Baum and 21 members of his Jewish Communist resistance group were executed by the Nazis after 1942.]

3689 [REICHSBUND JÜDISCHER FRONTSOLDATEN] DUNKER, ULRICH: *Der Reichsbund jüdischer Frontsoldaten 1919–1938. Geschichte eines jüdischen Abwehrvereins.* Düsseldorf: Droste, 1977. 354 pp., facsims., bibl.

l. 'Non-Aryan' Christians

3690 BRUNOTTE, HEINZ: 'Die Kirchenmitgliedschaft der nichtarischen Christen im

Kirchenkampf' [In] *Zeitschrift für evangelisches Kirchenrecht*, 13. Bd., 1/2 Heft, 1967. Tübingen: Mohr. Pp. 140–174.

3691 DOUGLASS, PAUL F.: *God among the Germans*. Philadelphia, Pa.: University of Pennsylvania Press, 1935. xiii + 325 pp., bibl. [VI: 'The Christian Jew in the Third Reich', pp. 116–143.]

3692 [FISCHER, GERTY] ANDREN, GRETA: *Ein Brief Christi*. Stuttgart: Quell-Verlag, 1949. 126 pp. (Schriften des Institutum Judaicum Delitzschianum). [Memorial to a Viennese Jewess converted to Christianity, who was deported to the Ghetto of Kielce, where she died.]

3693 JASPER, GERHARD: *Die evangelische Kirche und die Judenchristen*. Göttingen: Vandenhoeck & Ruprecht, 1934. 28 pp.

3694 KERN, KARL PETER: *Die Judentaufe. Das Christentum im Lichte der Tatsachen*. Stuttgart: Bühler, 1937. 77 pp., tabs.

3695 KLEPPER, JOCHEN: *Unter dem Schatten Deiner Flügel. Aus den Tagebüchern der Jahre 1932–1942*. Stuttgart: Deutsche Verlags-Anstalt, 1956. 1172 pp. [A clergyman and writer who committed suicide with his converted Jewish wife and stepdaughter when the latter was to be deported.]

3696 [LEHMANN, ERNST JOSEF] FLIEDNER, HANS-JOACHIM: 'Jude-Christ. Aus dem Leben des Pfarrers Ernst Josef Lehmann'. [In] *Mannheimer Hefte*, Heft 1, 1967. Pp. 25–37, illus.

3697 NEUMANN, FRIEDRICH: *Die Judenfrage und der christliche Jude*. Leipzig: Prochaska, 1935. 46 pp.

3698 POLJAK, ABRAM: *Zertrümmertes Hakenkreuz. Hitler als Feldherr und Spiritist*. 5. Aufl. Stuttgart: Patmos Verlag, 1952. 60 pp. [Written 1938/48. Author was a leader of the Judenchristen.]

3699 [STEIN, EDITH] TERESIA RENATA de SPIRITU SANCTO, (Sister): *Edith Stein, Schwester Benedicta a Cruce, Philosophin und Karmelitin. Ein Lebensbild, gewonnen aus Erinnerungen und Briefen*. 9. Aufl. Basel: Herder Freiburg Verlag, 1963. 238 pp. [First ed. 1948.]

3700 WOLFF, RICHARD: *Wir nichtarische Christen. Drei Reden*. Berlin: Reichsverband christlich-deutscher Staatsbürger nichtarischer oder nicht rein arischer Abstammung, 1934. 44 pp.

m. 'Mischlinge' and mixed marriages

3701 FRICK, HANS: *Die blaue Stunde*. München: Steinhausen, 1979. 137 pp. [Author recalls his youth as son of a Jewish father and Gentile mother, in Frankfurt a.M. in the Nazi years.]

3702 KOEHN, ILSE: *Mischling second degree. My childhood in Nazi Germany*. London: Hamish Hamilton, 1977. 240 pp.

3703 NOLTING-HAUFF, W.: *'IMI's'. Chronik einer Verbannung*. Bremen: Trüjen, 1946. 293 pp. [IMI's = Jüdische Mischlinge I. Grades.]

3704 OLENHUSEN, ALBRECHT GÖTZ VON: 'Die "nichtarischen" Studenten an den deutschen Hochschulen. Zur nationalsozialistischen Rassenpolitik 1933–1945'. [In] *Vierteljahrshefte für Zeitgeschichte*, Bd. XIV, Heft 2, April 1966. Pp. 175–206.

3705 PAEPCKE, LOTTE: *Ich wurde vergessen. Bericht einer Jüdin die das Dritte Reich überlebte. Mit einem aktuellen Nachwort.* Freiburg i.Br.: Herder, 1979. 128 pp. [Also earlier reminiscences publ. in 1952 under title *Unter einem fremden Stern.* The experiences of the Jewish partner in a 'privileged mixed marriage'.]

3706 SCHULZ, HEINZ: *Die Rechtsstellung der jüdischen Mischlinge nach den Verordnungen zum Reichsbürger- und Blutschutzgesetz.* Dissertation [pres. to] Universität zu Göttingen. 1938. 98 pp.

6. EXILES

a. General

3706a *Biographisches Handbuch der deutschsprachigen Emigration nach 1933. Bd. I: Politik, Wirtschaft, öffentliches Leben.* Leitung und Bearb.: Werner Röder, Herbert A. Strauss. Mitw.: Dieter Marc Schneider, Louise Forsyth. München: Saur, 1980. lviii + 875 pp., bibl., list of name changes.

3707 ČERNÝ, BOHUMIL: *Most k novému zivotu. Nemečka emigrace v ČSR v letech 1933–1939* [The bridge to a new life. The German emigration in the Czechoslovak Republic in the years 1933–1939]. Praha: Nakl. Lidowá Demokracie, 1967. 188 pp., illus., facsims., tabs.

3708 GOLDNER, FRANZ: *Die österreichische Emigration, 1938 bis 1945.* Wien: Herold, 1972. 348 pp., bibl. [English version: *Austrian emigration, 1938–1945.* New York: Ungar, 1979.]

KÜHN, HEINZ: *Widerstand und Emigration. Die Jahre 1928–1945. See* 3398.

3709 LOEWY, ERNST, ed.: *Exil. Literarische und politische Texte aus dem deutschen Exil 1933–1945.* Mitarb.: Brigitte Grimm, Helga Nagel, Felix Schneider. Stuttgart: Metzler, 1979. 1277 pp., bio-bibl.

3710 MÜSSENER, HELMUT: *Exil in Schweden. Politische und kulturelle Emigration nach 1933.* München: Hanser, 1974. 603 pp., bibls.

b. Political

3711 BLOCH, ERNST: *Vom Hazard zur Katastrophe. Politische Aufsätze 1934–1939.* Nachw.: Oskar Negt. Frankfurt a.M.: Suhrkamp, 1972. 447 pp.

3712 BONTÉ, FLORIMOND: *Les antifaschistes allemands dans la résistance française.* Paris: Éds. Sociales, 1969. 391 pp., plan, facsims.

BRANDT, WILLY

3713 BRANDT, WILLY: *Draussen. Schriften während der Emigration.* Hrsg.: Günther

Struve. München: Kindler, 1966. 384 pp. [English version: *In exile: Essays, reflections and letters, 1933–1947.* Biographical introd.: Terence Prittie. London: Wolff, 1971.]

3714 LEHMANN, HANS GEORG: *In Acht und Bann. Politische Emigration, NS-Ausbürgerung und Wiedergutmachung am Beispiel Willy Brandt.* München: Beck, 1976. 387 pp., facsims., diagrs., bibl.

3715 BRÜNING, HEINRICH: *Briefe und Gespräche 1934–1945.* Hrsg.: Claire Nix. Mitarb.: Reginald Phelps, George Pettee. Stuttgart: Deutsche Verlags-Anstalt, 1974. 556 pp., port., bibl.

3716 EDINGER, LEWIS J.: *German exile politics. The Social Democratic Executive Committee in the Nazi era.* Berkeley, Calif.: University of California Press, 1956. 329 pp. [Unsuccessful attempts of exiled SPD leaders to foment and assist resistance in Germany. German version: *Sozialdemokratie und Nationalsozialismus. Der Parteivorstand der SPD im Exil von 1933–1945.* Hannover: Norddeutsche Verlagsanstalt, 1960.]

3717 HÜRTEN, HEINZ, ed.: *'Deutsche Briefe' 1934–1938. Ein Blatt der katholischen Emigration.* Mainz: Matthias-Grünewald-Verlag, 1969. In 2 vols. (Veröffentlichungen der Kommission für Zeitgeschichte ...).
Bd. I: *1934–1935.* 733 + li pp., bibl.
Bd. II: *1936–1938.* 1186 pp.

3718 LOEWENSTEIN, HUBERTUS Prinz zu: *On borrowed peace.* New York: Doubleday, Doran, 1942. 344 pp. [Attempts to organize resistance against Nazi Germany.]

3719 MAIMANN, HELENE: *Politik im Wartesaal. Österreichische Exilpolitik in Grossbritannien 1938–1945.* Wien: Böhlau, 1975. xv + 355 pp., illus., facsims., bibl. (Veröffentlichungen der Kommission für neuere Geschichte Österreichs ...).

3720 *Menschen in Exil. Eine Dokumentation der sudetendeutschen sozial-demokratischen Emigration von 1938 bis 1945.* Stuttgart: Seliger-Archiv, 1974. 404 pp., tab.

3721 NIELSEN, FREDERIC W.: *Emigrant für Deutschland in der Tschechoslowakei, in England und in Canada. Tagebuchaufzeichnungen, Aufrufe und Berichte aus den Jahren 1933–1943.* [And] *Zitate und Kommentare zu 'Emigrant für Deutschland'.* Darmstadt: Bläschke, 1977. 515 + 89 pp., bibl.

3722 RENN, LUDWIG (pseud. of Arnold Friedrich Vieth von Golssenau): *Vor grossen Wandlungen. Roman.* Zürich: Oprecht, 1936. 212 pp.

3723 RÖDER, WERNER: *Die deutschen sozialistischen Exilgruppen in Grossbritannien. Ein Beitrag zur Geschichte des Widerstandes gegen den Nationalsozialismus.* Hannover: Verlag für Literatur und Zeitgeschehen, 1969. 322 pp., diagrs., tabs., bibl. (Schriftenreihe des Forschungsinstituts der Friedrich-Ebert-Stiftung). [7. Kap.: 'Die Mitwirkung der deutschen Exilsozialisten am Kampf gegen das Hitlerregime'.]

3724 SCHAUL, DORA, ed.: *Résistance. Erinnerungen deutscher Antifaschisten.* [By] Otto Niebergall [and others]. 2. Aufl. Frankfurt a.M.: Röderberg, 1973. 477 pp. [Issued under licence from Institut für Marxismus-Leninismus beim ZK der SED.]

3725 SCHEER, MAXIMILIAN: *Blut und Ehre.* Unter Mitarbeit eines Kollektivs deutscher Antifaschisten. Vorw.: E. J. Gumbel. Hrsg.: Überparteilicher Deutscher Hilfsausschuss, Paris. Paris: Éds. du Carrefour, 1937. 243 pp., illus.

3726 SEGER, GERHART: *Reisetagebuch eines deutschen Emigranten.* Zürich: Europa-Verlag, 1936. 187 pp. [Account of lecture tours carried out for the purpose of raising opposition to Nazi Germany.]

3727 [STAMPFER, FRIEDRICH] MATTHIAS, ERICH & LINK, WERNER, eds.: *Mit dem Gesicht nach Deutschland. Eine Dokumentation über die sozialdemokratische Emigration.* Aus dem Nachlass Friedrich Stampfer ergänzt durch andere Überlieferungen. Hrsg. im Auftr. der Kommission für Geschichte des Parlamentarismus und der politischen Parteien. Düsseldorf: Droste, 1968. 758 pp., port., facsim., bibl.

3728 STRASSER, OTTO & STERN, MICHAEL: *Flight from terror.* New York: McBride, 1943. 361 pp. [Otto Strasser was leader of the Frei-Deutschland Bewegung.]

3729 TEUBNER, HANS: *Exilland Schweiz. Dokumentarischer Bericht über den Kampf emigrierter deutscher Kommunisten 1933–1945.* Frankfurt a.M.: Röderberg, 1975. 373 pp., illus., facsims. (Institut für Marxismus-Leninismus beim ZK der SED).

3730 TILLICH, PAUL: *An meine deutschen Freunde. Die politischen Reden Paul Tillichs während des Zweiten Weltkriegs über die 'Stimme Amerikas'.* Einl. und Anmerkungen: Karin Schäfer-Kretzler. Stuttgart: Evangelisches Verlagswerk, 1973. 367 pp., bibl. (Ergänzungs- und Nachlassbände zu den gesammelten Werken von Paul Tillich, Bd. III). [Incl.: 'Der Widerstand der norwegischen Kirche (27.4.1942)', 'Die Kriegsverbrecher und ihre Bestrafung (30.10.1942)', 'Der Widerstand gegen den Terror (26.7.1943)'.]

3731 TUTAS, HERBERT E.: *Nationalsozialismus und Exil. Die Politik des Dritten Reiches gegenüber der deutschen politischen Emigration 1933–1939.* München: Hanser, 1975. 354 pp., bibl. (bibl. and notes, pp. 286–354).

Nationalkomitee Freies Deutschland

3732 EINSIEDEL, HEINRICH Graf von: *Tagebuch der Versuchung.* Berlin: Pontes, 1950. 239 pp., illus. [Diary, 1942–1950, of the former Vice-President of the 'Nationalkomitee Freies Deutschland', Moscow. English version: *The shadow of Stalingrad. Being the diary of a temptation.* London: Wingate, 1953.]

3733 KÜGELGEN, ELSE & BERNT von, eds.: *Die Front war überall. Erlebnisse und Berichte vom Kampf des Nationalkomitees 'Freies Deutschland'.* Einl.: Walter Ulbricht. 3. überarb. erw. Aufl. der 1963 erschienenen 2. Aufl. Berlin [East]: Verlag der Nation, 1968. 447 pp., facsims., bibl.

3734 LEONHARD, WOLFGANG: *Die Revolution entlässt ihre Kinder.* Köln: Kiepenheuer & Witsch, 1955. 558 pp. [Ch. VI deals with author's experiences with the 'Nationalkomitee'.]

FRANCE

3735 PECH, KARLHEINZ: *An der Seite der Résistance. Zum Kampf der Bewegung 'Freies Deutschland' für den Westen in Frankreich, 1943–1945.* Frankfurt a.M.: Röderberg, 1974. 386 pp., facsims., bibl. [Publ. under licence from the Militärverlag der DDR.]

GREAT BRITAIN

3736 LANGE, DIETER: 'Dokumente der Freien Deutschen Bewegung in Grossbritannien'. [In] *Zeitschrift für Geschichtswissenschaft*, XIX. Jhrg., Nr. 9, 1972. Berlin [East]: Verlag der Wissenschaften. Pp. 1113–1158.

3737 *Deutsche, wohin? Protokoll der Gründungsversammlung des National-Komitees Freies Deutschland und des Deutschen Offiziersbundes.* Vorw.: Paul Merker, Arnold Vieth von Golssenau (Ludwig Renn). Mexiko: Lateinamerikanisches Komitee der Freien Deutschen, 1944. 138 pp.

3738 KIESSLING, WOLFGANG: *Alemania Libre in Mexiko.* Berlin [East]: Akademie-Verlag, 1974. In 2 vols.
Bd. 1: *Ein Beitrag zur Geschichte des antifaschistischen Exils 1941–1946.* 338 pp.
Bd. 2: *Texte und Dokumente zur Geschichte des antifaschistischen Exils 1941–1946.* 466 pp., illus., facsims., bibl.

SOVIET UNION

3739 HAHN, ASSI: *Ich spreche die Wahrheit. Sieben Jahre Kriegsgefangen in Russland.* Esslingen: Bechtle, 1951. 251 pp., ports. [Incl. eyewitness accounts of activities of the movement 'Freies Deutschland' in Soviet POW camps.]

3740 SCHEURIG, BODO: *Freies Deutschland. Das Nationalkomitee und der Bund Deutscher Offiziere in der Sowjetunion 1943–1945.* München: Nymphenburger Verlagsbuchhandlung, 1960. 269 pp., bibl.

3741 WEINERT, ERICH: *Stalingrad Diary.* Forew.: J. Dugdale. London: ING Publs., 1944. 48 pp. [President of the Free Germany National Committee in Moscow.]

3742 WOLFF, WILLY: *An der Seite der Roten Armee. Zum Wirken des Nationalkomitees 'Freies Deutschland' an der sowjetisch-deutschen Front 1943 bis 1945.* Berlin [East]: Militärverlag der DDR, 1975. 370 pp., bibl.

SWITZERLAND

3743 BERGMANN, KARL HEINZ: *Die Bewegung 'Freies Deutschland' in der Schweiz 1943–1945.* Mit einem Beitrag von Wolfgang Jean Stock: 'Schweizer Flüchtlingspolitik und exilierte deutsche Arbeiterbewegung 1933–1943'. [München]: Hanser, 1974. 271 pp., bibl.

Journalists and periodicals

3744 [AUFBAU] SCHABER, WILL, ed.: *Aufbau—Reconstruction. Dokumente einer Kultur im Exil*. Geleitw.: Hans Steinitz. New York: The Overlook Press, 1972. 415 pp., illus., facsims.

3745 BERGLUND, GISELA: *Deutsche Opposition gegen Hitler in Presse und Roman des Exils. Eine Darstellung und ein Vergleich mit der historischen Wirklichkeit.* Stockholm: Almqvist & Wiksell, 1972. 411 pp., bibl. (bibl. and notes, pp. 292–404). (Acta Universitatis Stockholmiensis).

3746 CAZDEN, ROBERT E.: *German exile literature in America, 1933–1950. A history of the free German press and book trade.* Chicago, Ill.: American Library Association, 1970. ix + 250 pp., tabs., bibls. [Orig. a dissertation, 1965, amended and rev.]

3747 *Deutsches Exil 1933–1945. Eine Schriftenreihe.* Hrsg.: Georg Heintz.
Bd. 1: *Index der 'Neuen Weltbühne' von 1933–39.* Wiesbaden: Lendle, 1972. 103 + [36] pp.
[Continuing].

3748 DOTZAUER, GERTRAUDE: *Die Zeitschriften der deutschen Emigration in der Tschechoslowakei, 1933–1938.* Dissertation [pres. to] Universität Wien. 1971. vii + 423 pp., bibl.

FEUCHTWANGER, LION: *Exil. See 3807.*

3749 HALFMANN, HORST, ed.: *Zeitschriften und Zeitungen des Exils, 1933–1945. Bestandsverzeichnis der Deutschen Bücherei.* Leipzig: 1969. 79 pp.

3750 HARDT, HANNO and others, eds.: *Presse im Exil. Beitrag zur Kommunikationsgeschichte des deutschen Exils 1933–1945.* München: Saur, 1979. 512 pp.

3751 [KISCH, EGON ERWIN] SIEGEL, CHRISTIAN ERNST: *Egon Erwin Kisch. Reportage und politischer Journalismus.* Bremen: Schünemann, 1973. 384 pp., bibl. [Incl.: 'Der antifaschistische Kampf im Exil', 'Die Haftberichte nach dem Reichstagsbrand'.]

3752 MAAS, LIESELOTTE: *Handbuch der deutschen Exilpresse 1933–1945.* Hrsg.: Eberhard Lämmer. München: Hanser, 1976/80. In 3 vols.

3753 PRASCHEK, HELMUT, ed.: *'Neue Deutsche Blätter', Prag 1933–1935. Bibliographie einer Zeitschrift.* Vorw.: Wieland Herzfelde. Berlin [East]: Aufbau-Verlag, 1973. 100 pp.

3754 DER REICHSFÜHRER-SS & DER CHEF DES SICHERHEITSHAUPTAMTES: *Leitheft Emigrantenpresse und Schrifttum. Geheim!* März 1937. 53 pp., typescr.

3755 SCHWARZSCHILD, LEOPOLD: *Die Lunte am Pulverfass. Aus dem 'Neuen Tagebuch' 1933–1940.* Hrsg.: Valerie Schwarzschild. Vorw.: Kurt Sontheimer. Hamburg: Wegner, 1965. 430 pp.

3756 WALTER, HANS-ALBERT: *Deutsche Exilliteratur 1933–1950. Bd. 4: Exilpresse.* Darmstadt: Luchterhand, 1978. xii + 842 pp.

3757 [WOLFF, THEODOR] KÖHLER, WOLFGANG: *Der Chef-Redakteur Theodor Wolff. Ein Leben in Europa 1868–1943.* Düsseldorf: Droste, 1978. 319 pp.

3758 [ZUKUNFT] *Deutscher Freiheitskalender 1940. Hrsg. für die Leser und Freunde der 'Zukunft'.* [Paris]: Brant, [1939]. 101 pp., illus.

Illegal pamphlets and periodicals

3759 GITTIG, HEINZ: *Illegale antifaschistische Tarnschriften 1933 bis 1945.* Frankfurt a.M.: Röderberg, 1971. 262 pp., facsims., tabs., diagr., bibls. [Bibliography of pamphlets pp. 110–237; list of titles pp. 251–261.]

3760 [SEGER, GERHART: *Oranienburg. Erster authentischer Bericht eines aus dem Konzentrationslager geflüchteten.* Prag.: 1934.] 80 pp. [of which 18 are 'cover' pages]. [Illegal pamphlet. Titlepage shows: *Volk und Führer, Heft 5—Das Gesetz zur Ordnung der nationalen Arbeit.* Leipzig-Plagwitz: Harmonie-Verlag.]

3761 [UNSERE ZEIT] BRECHT, BERTOLT: *Fünf Schwierigkeiten beim Schreiben der Wahrheit.* Paris: Schutzverband deutscher Schriftsteller, [193–]. 11 pp. (Diese Schrift verfasste Bertolt Brecht zur Verbreitung in Hitler-Deutschland. Sie wird als Sonderdruck der antifaschistischen Zeitschrift 'Unsere Zeit' hrsg.). [Cover title: *Satzungen des Reichsverbandes deutscher Schriftsteller (R.D.S.).*]

3762 [Wiener Library collection of illegal anti-Nazi pamphlets and periodicals, mostly with cover titles, 1933–1944. 192 items.]

c. Cultural

3763 *Exil und Innere Emigration.* Frankfurt a.M.: Athenäum Verlag.
[I]: *Third Wisconsin Workshop.* Hrsg.: Reinhold Grimm, Jost Hermand. Publ. 1972. 210 pp.
II: *Internationale Tagung in St. Louis.* Hrsg.: Peter Uwe Hohendahl, Egon Schwarz. Publ. 1973. 170 pp.

3764 FERMI, LAURA: *Illustrious immigrants. The intellectual migration from Europe, 1930–41.* Chicago, Ill.: University of Chicago Press, 1968. 440 pp., ports.

3764a *Kunst und Literatur im antifaschistischen Exil.* Frankfurt a.M.: Röderberg, [1978?]. 3 vols., continuing (to 6 vols.).
Bd. I: Werner Mittenzwei, comp.: *Exil in der Schweiz.* 448 pp.
Bd. II: Klaus Jarmatz and others: *Exil in der UdSSR.* 662 pp.
Bd. III: Wolfgang Kiessling: *Exil in Lateinamerika.* [In preparation, 1980.]

Literature (secondary works)

BERENDSOHN, WALTER A.

3765 BERENDSOHN, WALTER A., ed.: *Deutsche Literatur der Flüchtlinge aus dem Dritten Reich. Berichte: Der Stand der Forschung und ihre Hilfsmittel, I–IV.* Stockholm: Tyska Institutionen, 1967–1969.

3766 BERENDSOHN, WALTER A.: *Die humanistische Front. Einführung in die deutsche Emigranten-Literatur.*

1. Teil: *Von 1933 bis Kriegsausbruch 1939.* Zürich: Europa-Verlag, 1946. 204 pp.

2. Teil: *Vom Kriegsausbruch 1939 bis Ende 1946.* Worms: Heintz, 1976. 236 pp., facsims.

3767 AKERMAN, ANATOL, comp.: *Personen- und Sachverzeichnis zu 'Deutsche Literatur der Flüchtlinge aus dem Dritten Reich, Bericht I–IV', hrsg. von Professor Berendsohn.* Stockholm: Stockholmer Koordinationsstelle zur Erforschung der deutschsprachigen Exilliteratur, 1971. 41 pp., mimeog.

3768 STOCKHOLMER KOORDINATIONSSTELLE ZUR ERFORSCHUNG DER DEUTSCHSPRACHIGEN EXIL-LITERATUR: *Berichte I–VI.* Stockholm: Deutsches Institut der Universität Stockholm, 1970/73. In 6 vols. [Continuation of 3765 above.]

3769 BERTHOLD, WERNER: 'Der deutsche PEN-Club im Exil 1933–1940. Bericht aus ungedruckten Materialien der Deutschen Bibliothek'. [In] Günther Pflug and others, eds.: *Bibliothek—Buch—Geschichte.* Frankfurt a.M.: Klostermann, 1977. Pp. 531–557.

3770 DAHLKE, HANS: *Geschichtsroman und Literaturkritik im Exil.* Berlin [East]: Aufbau-Verlag, 1979. 451 pp., bibl. [First ed. 1976.]

3771 DURZAK, MANFRED, ed.: *Deutsche Exilliteratur 1933–1945.* Stuttgart: Reclam, 1979. 600 pp. [Incl. Kurt R. Grossmann on Czechoslovakia; Alfred Kantorowicz on Spain; Gabriele Tergit on Britain.]

3772 KAMLA, T. A.: *Confrontation with exile: studies in the German novel.* Bern: Lang, 1975. 182 pp., bibl.

3773 SCHÜTZ, ERHARD & VOGT, JOCHEN: *Einführung in die deutsche Literatur des 20. Jahrhunderts. Bd. 2: Weimar Republik, Faschismus und Exil.* Opladen: Westdeutscher Verlag, 1977. 329 pp., bibl. [Incl. 'Innere Emigration', pp. 263–275; 'Literatur im Exil', pp. 276–328.]

3774 SPALEK, JOHN M. and others, eds.: *Deutsche Exilliteratur seit 1933. Bd. I: Californien.* Bern: Francke, 1976.
Teil 1: Hrsg.: John M. Spalek, Joseph Strelka. 868 pp.
Teil 2: Hrsg.: John M. Spalek, Joseph Strelka, Sandra H. Hawrylchak. 216 pp.
[Bibliographical section.]

3775 STEPHAN, ALEXANDER: *Die deutsche Exilliteratur 1933–1945. Eine Einführung.* München: Beck, 1979. 376 pp., bibl.

3776 STERNFELD, WILHELM & TIEDEMANN, EVA: *Deutsche Exilliteratur 1933–1945. Eine Bio-Bibliographie.* Vorw.: Hanns W. Eppelsheimer. 2. verb. und stark erw. Aufl. Heidelberg: Lambert Schneider, 1970. 606 pp.

3777 WINKLER, MICHAEL, ed.: *Deutsche Literatur im Exil 1933–45. Texte und Dokumente.* Stuttgart: Reclam, 1977. 512 pp.

Theatre

3778 DURIEUX, TILLA: *Eine Tür steht offen. Erinnerungen.* Berlin: Herbig, 1954. 341 pp., illus.

3779 [JACOBS, MONTY] *Der Theaterkritiker Monty Jacobs, 1875–1945. Ein Beitrag zur Geschichte der neueren Theaterkritik.* Berlin: Colloquium Verlag, 1965. 211 pp., bibl.

3780 KORTNER, FRITZ: *Aller Tage abend.* München: Kindler, 1959. 570 pp., port.

3781 POLGAR, ALFRED: *Handbuch des Kritikers.* Zürich: Oprecht, [1938]. 120 pp.

RÜHLE, GÜNTHER: *Zeit und Theater. Band 3: Diktatur und Exil, 1933–1945.* See 2712.

3782 *Theater im Exil 1933–1945. Ausstellung, Filmretrospektive, Konferenz, 21.10.–18.11.1973.* Berlin [East]: Akademie der Künste, [1973]. 200 pp., ports., facsims., bibl.

3783 WÄCHTER, HANS-CHRISTOF: *Theater im Exil. Sozialgeschichte des deutschen Exiltheaters 1933–1945.* Mit einem Beitrag von Louis Naef: 'Theater der deutschen Schweiz'. München: Hanser, 1973. 298 pp., bibl.

Artists

3784 *Die dreissiger Jahre—Schauplatz Deutschland.* München: Haus der Kunst, 1977. 254 pp., illus. [Exhibition catalogue. Also: *Deutschland 1930–1939. Verbot, Anpassung, Exil.* Red.: Erika Billeter. Zürich: Kunsthaus Zürich, 1977. 55 pp. (Ergänzung zum Katalog …).]

HEARTFIELD, JOHN
3785 HEARTFIELD, JOHN: *Photomontages of the Nazi period.* London: Universe Books, 1977. 143 pp., illus.

3786 TÖTEBERG, MICHAEL: *John Heartfield in Selbstzeugnissen und Bilddokumentation.* Reinbek b. Hamburg: Rowohlt, 1978. 155 pp., illus., bibl.

3787 HEINE, THOMAS THEODOR: *Die Märchen.* Amsterdam: Querido Verlag, 1935. 64 pp., illus.

3788 MOPP (pseud. of Max Oppenheimer): *Menschen finden ihren Maler.* Zürich: Oprecht, [1938]. 63 pp.

Musicians

3789 SCHNABEL, ARTUR: *My life and music.* Ed.: Edward Crankshaw. London: Longmans, 1961. 223 pp., port.

3790 SCHOENBERG, ARNOLD: *Briefe.* Hrsg.: Erwin Stein. Mainz: Schott, 1958. 309 pp., facsim., mus. scores.

3791 [TAUBER, RICHARD] NAPIER-TAUBER, DIANA: *Richard Tauber.* Forew.: Charles B. Cochran. Glasgow: Art & Education Publs., 1949. 237 pp., illus.

3792 WAGNER, FRIEDELIND & COOPER, PAGE: *Heritage of fire. The story of Richard Wagner's grand-daughter.* 3rd ed. New York: Harper, 1945. 231 pp.

3793 WALTER, BRUNO: *Thema und Variationen. Erinnerungen und Gedanken.* Stockholm: Bermann-Fischer, 1947. 527 pp., illus., facsims.

Science and scholarship

3794 GUMBEL, E. J., ed.: *Freie Wissenschaft. Ein Sammelbuch aus der deutschen Emigration.* Strasbourg: Brant, 1938. 282 pp.

3795 HALPERIN, S. WILLIAM, ed.: *Some 20th-century historians.* Chicago, Ill.: Chicago University Press, 1961. 298 pp. [Incl. Veit Valentin and Erich Eyck.]

3796 PROSS, HELGE: *Die deutsche akademische Emigration nach den Vereinigten Staaten 1933–1941.* Einf.: Franz L. Neumann. Berlin: Duncker & Humblot, 1975. 69 pp.

3797 WIDMANN, HORST: *Exil und Bildungshilfe. Die deutschsprachige akademische Emigration in die Türkei nach 1933. Mit einer Bio-Bibliographie der emigrierten Hochschullehrer im Anhang.* Bern: Lang, 1973. 308 pp., plan, facsims.

d. Exile literature (primary)

Poetry

3798 BECHER, JOHANNES R.: *Ausgewählte Dichtung aus der Zeit der Verbannung 1933–1945.* Berlin [East]: Aufbau-Verlag, [195–?]. 281 pp.

3799 JENTZSCH, BERND, ed.: [Anthology]. München: Kindler, 1979. In 3 vols.
[1]: *Ich sah das Dunkel schon von ferne kommen. Erniedrigung und Vertreibung in poetischen Zeugnissen.* (Exil).
[2]: *Der Tod ist ein Meister aus Deutschland. Deportation und Vernichtung in poetischen Zeugnissen.* (KZ).
[3]: *Ich sah aus Deutschlands Asche keinen Phönix steigen. Rückkehr und Hoffnung in poetischen Zeugnissen.* (Befreiung).
[Incl. poems by Günther Anders, Gertrud Kolmar, Else Lasker-Schüler, Walter Mehring, Nelly Sachs, Friedrich Torberg and others.]

3800 MEHRING, WALTER: *Und Euch zum Trotz. Chansons, Balladen und Legenden.* Paris: Europäischer Merkur, 1934. 125 pp., illus. (by author).

3801 SACHS, NELLY: *Das Leiden Israels: Eli: In den Wohnungen des Todes: Sternverdunkelung.* Nachw.: Werner Weber. Frankfurt a.M.: Suhrkamp, 1965. 179 pp. [Poems of a refugee Jewish poetess in Sweden.]

3802 SAENGER, EDUARD: *Die fremden Jahre. Gedichte aus der Emigration.* Heidelberg: Lambert Schneider, 1959. 75 pp., port. (Veröffentlichungen der Deutschen Akademie für Sprache und Dichtung, Darmstadt).

3803 *Und sie bewegt sich doch. Freie deutsche Dichtung.* Vorw.: Oskar Kokoschka. London: Verlag 'Freie Deutsche Jugend', 1943. 64 pp.

3804 WEINERT, ERICH: *Rufe in die Nacht. Gedichte aus der Fremde, 1933–1943.* Berlin: Volk und Welt, 1947. 282 pp.

3805 WOLFSKEHL, KARL: *Sang aus dem Exil.* Heidelberg: Lambert Schneider, [1957?]. lxxix pp.

Fiction

3806 DÖBLIN, ALFRED: *Babylonische Wanderung oder Hochmut kommt vor dem Fall. Roman.* Amsterdam: Querido, 1934. 694 pp., illus.

3807 FEUCHTWANGER, LION: *Exil.* Amsterdam: Querido, 1939. [English version: *Paris Gazette.* New York: Viking Press, 1940. Pt. 3 of 'Der Wartesaal'. Depicts the atmosphere and difficulties in which an exile newspaper was produced.]

3808 FRANK, BRUNO: *Closed frontiers. A story of modern Europe.* Transl. from the German. London: Macmillan, 1937. 335 pp.

3809 KOESTLER, ARTHUR: *Arrival and departure.* New York: Macmillan, 1943. 180 pp.

3810 MERZ, KONRAD (pseud. of Kurt Lehmann): *Ein Mensch fällt aus Deutschland.* Anhang: 'Aus dem Tagebuch eines Berliner Studenten'. Nachw.: Ingeborg Drewit. Hamburg: Konkret Literatur Verlag, [1978?]. 173 pp. [First publ.: Amsterdam; Querido, 1936. Novel in diary/letter form.]

Drama

3811 BRECHT, BERTOLD: *The private life of the master race. A documentary play.* English version and an essay on the work of Brecht by E. R. Bentley. New York: Laughlin, 1944. 140 pp., port., bibl.

3812 WOLF, FRIEDRICH: *Doktor Mamlocks Ausweg. Tragödie der westlichen Demokratie.* Zürich: Oprecht & Helbing, 1935. 81 pp.

Letters, political and autobiographical writings

3813 KERR, ALFRED: *Die Diktatur des Hausknechts.* Bruxelles: Éds. Les Associés, 1934. 142 pp.

3814 KERR, ALFRED: *Ich kam nach England. Ein Tagebuch aus dem Nachlass.* Hrsg.: Walter Huder, Thomas Koebner. Bonn: Bouvier, 1979. 206 pp.

3815 KESTEN, HERMANN, ed.: *Deutsche Literatur im Exil. Briefe europäischer Autoren 1933–1949.* München: Desch, 1964. 380 pp.

3816 LANIA, LEO: *Welt im Umbruch. Biographie einer Generation.* Frankfurt a.M.: Forum Verlag, 1954. 359 pp.

3817 LINDT, PETER M.: *Schriftsteller im Exil. Zwei Jahre deutsche literarische Sendung am Rundfunk in New York.* Vorw.: George N. Shuster. New York: Willard, 1944. 192 pp.

3818 MANN, ERIKA: *The lights go down.* Transl.: Maurice Samuel. New York: Farrar & Rinehart, 1940. 282 pp.

3819 MANN, ERIKA & KLAUS: *Escape to life.* Boston, Mass.: Houghton Mifflin, 1939. 384 pp., illus. [Resistance through voluntary exile.]

MANN, HEINRICH
3820 MANN, HEINRICH: *Verteidigung der Kultur. Antifaschistische Streitschriften und Essays.* Hamburg: Claassen, 1960. 564 pp.

3821 PAWEK, KARL: *Heinrich Manns Kampf gegen den Faschismus im französischen Exil 1933–1940.* Hamburg: Hamburger Arbeitsstelle für deutsche Exilliteratur, 1972. 192 pp., bibl.

3822 MANN, KLAUS: *Der Wendepunkt. Ein Lebensbericht.* Frankfurt a.M.: S. Fischer, 1952. 543 pp. [English version: *The turning point. Thirty-five years in this century.* London: Gollancz, 1954. 285 pp.]

MANN, THOMAS
3823 MANN, THOMAS: *Ein Briefwechsel.* Zürich: Oprecht, 1937. 16 pp. [Letter to the Dean of the Faculty of Philosophy of Bonn University on being struck off the list of Hon. Doctors. English version: London: 'Friends of Europe', 1937. Forew.: J. B. Priestley.]

3824 BITTERLI, URS: *Thomas Manns politische Schriften zum Nationalsozialismus 1918–1939.* Aarau: Keller, 1964. 108 pp., bibl.

3825 HÜBINGER, PAUL EGON: *Thomas Mann, die Universität Bonn und die Zeitgeschichte. Drei Kapitel deutscher Vergangenheit aus dem Leben des Dichters, 1905–1955.* München: Oldenbourg, 1974. ix + 682 pp., bibl.

3826 MANN, ERIKA, ed.: *Thomas Mann Briefe.* Frankfurt a.M.: Fischer, 1962/65. In 3 vols.
Bd. I: *1889–1936.* Publ. 1962. 581 pp.
Bd. II: *1937–1947.* Publ. 1963. 765 pp.

3827 MEHRING, WALTER: *Briefe aus der Mitternacht 1937–1941.* Heidelberg: Lambert Schneider, 1971. 42 pp.

3828 MEHRING, WALTER: *Die verlorene Bibliothek. Autobiographie einer Kultur.* Hamburg: Rowohlt, 1952. 243 pp. [Also enl. and rev. ed.: Icking: Kreisselmeier, 1964.]

3829 ROUBICZEK, PAUL: *Über den Abgrund. Aufzeichnungen 1939/40.* Hrsg.: Jörg-Ulrich Fechner. Vorw.: Werner Heisenberg. Wien: Molden, 1978. 280 pp. [Wartime notes of a philosopher, a Jewish convert to Christianity, exiled in England.]

3830 ZUCKMAYER, CARL: *Second wind.* Transl. from the German. Introd.: Dorothy Thompson. London: Harrap, 1941. 239 pp.

3831 ZWEIG, ARNOLD: *Bilanz der deutschen Judenheit. Ein Versuch.* Amsterdam: Querido, 1934. 318 pp. [English version: *Insulted and exiled. The truth about German Jews.* London: Miles, 1937.]

VI. THE ROAD TO WAR

A. MILITARY POLICY

1. ARMED FORCES IN POLITICS

3832   BIRD, KEITH W.: *Weimar, the German Naval Officer Corps and the rise of Nationalsocialism.* Amsterdam: Grüner, 1977. lx + 313 pp.

3833   BREIT, GOTTHARD: *Das Staats- und Gesellschaftsbild deutscher Generale beider Weltkriege im Spiegel ihrer Memoiren.* Boppard a.Rh.: Boldt, 1973. viii + 237 pp., bibl.

3834   BUCHER, PETER: *Der Reichswehrprozess. Der Hochverrat der Ulmer Reichswehroffiziere 1929/30.* Boppard a.Rh.: Boldt, 1967. 524 pp., bibl.

3835   BUCHHEIT, GERT: *Soldatentum und Rebellion. Die Tragödie der deutschen Wehrmacht.* Rastatt/Baden: Grote, 1961. 509 pp., bibl.

3836   CARSTEN, F. L.: *The Reichswehr and Politics, 1918 to 1933.* Oxford: Oxford University Press, 1966. vii + 427 pp., bibl. [German version: *Reichswehr und Politik 1918–1933.* 2. Aufl. Köln: Kiepenheuer & Witsch, 1965.]

3837   COOPER, MATTHEW: *The German army 1933–1945. Its political and military failure.* London: Macdonald & Jane's, 1978. x + 598 pp., illus., maps, bibl.

3838   DONNEVERT, RICHARD, ed.: *Wehrmacht und Partei.* Leipzig: Barth, 1938. 188 pp., tabs. [Also 3rd ed. 1941.]

3839   DÜLFFER, JOST: *Weimar, Hitler und die Marine. Reichspolitik und Flottenbau.* Anhang: Jürgen Rohwer. Düsseldorf: Droste, 1973. 615 pp., tabs., bibl.

3840   FÖRTSCH, HERMANN: *Schuld und Verhängnis. Die Fritsch-Krise im Frühjahr 1938 als Wendepunkt in der Geschichte der nationalsozialistischen Zeit.* Stuttgart: Deutsche Verlags-Anstalt, 1951. 239 pp.

3841   FREDE, GÜNTHER & SCHÜDDEKOPF, OTTO-ERNST: *Wehrmacht und Politik 1933–1945. Dokumente mit verbindendem Text.* Braunschweig: Limbach, 1953. 62 pp.

3842   FRIED, HANS ERNST: *The guilt of the German army.* New York: Macmillan, 1942. 426 pp. [How German militarism paved the way for National Socialism.]

3843   MÜLLER, KLAUS-JÜRGEN: *Das Heer und Hitler. Armee und national-sozialistisches Regime 1933–1940.* Stuttgart: Deutsche Verlags-Anstalt, 1969. 711 pp., bibl.

3844 RODEN, HANS, ed.: *Deutsche Soldaten. Vom Frontheer und Freikorps über die Reichswehr zur neuen Wehrmacht.* Geleitw.: Gen.-Leut. a.D. Frhr. von Watter. Schlussw.: Major Foertsch. Mitarb.: Deutsche Gesellschaft für Wehrpolitik und Wehrwissenschaften [and] Schlageter-Gedächtnis-Museum. Berlin: Franke (Breitkopf & Härtel), 1935. 267 pp., illus., facsims. [Incl. casualty lists of Freikorps, Reichswehr, Wehrmacht 1918–1935.]

3845 SCHÜTZLE, KURT: *Reichswehr wider die Nation. Zur Rolle der Reichswehr bei der Vorbereitung und Errichtung der faschistischen Diktatur in Deutschland, 1929–1933.* Berlin [East]: Deutscher Militärverlag, 1963. 243 + 7 pp., facsims., bibl.

3846 SIEWERT, CURT: *Schuldig? Die Generale unter Hitler. Stellung und Einfluss der hohen militärischen Führer im nationalsozialistischen Staat. Das Mass ihrer Verantwortung und Schuld.* Bad Nauheim: Podzun, 1968. 190 pp., illus.

3847 TAYLOR, TELFORD: *Sword and swastika. Generals and Nazis in the Third Reich.* New York: Simon & Schuster, 1952. xii + 431 pp., illus., maps, bibl.

3848 WHEELER-BENNETT, JOHN W.: *The Nemesis of power. The German army in politics, 1918–1945.* London: Macmillan, 1953. 829 pp., illus., tabs., bibl.

2. MILITARISM AND PREPARATION FOR WAR

3849 BALDWIN, HANSON W.: *The caissons roll. A military survey of Europe.* New York: Knopf, [193–]. xvi + 323 + ix pp., map, tabs.

3850 BURDICK, CHARLES BURTON: *German military planning for the war in the West, 1935–1940.* Michigan City: University Microfilms, 1955. 299 pp.

3851 ERCKNER, S.: *Exerzierplatz Deutschland.* Einl.: B. Langevin, L. Lévy-Bruhl, M. Prenant. Paris: Rosner, 1934. 188 pp. (Schriftenreihe des Instituts zum Studium des Faschismus).

3852 FRIED, HANS ERNEST: 'German militarism: substitute for revolution'. [In] *Political Science Quarterly*, Vol. LVIII, No.4, December 1943. New York: Academy of Political Science. Pp. 481–513. [Author also known as John H. E. Fried.]

3853 FRIEDRICH, G. & LANG, F., eds.: *Vom Reichstagsbrand zur Entfachung des Weltkriegsbrandes. Zum 5. Jahrestag des Reichstagsbrandprozesses.* Paris: Éds. Prométhée, 1938. 102 pp.

3854 GÖRNER, ALEXANDER: *Hitlers preussisches Engagement. Von der Feldherrnhalle bis Stalingrad. Zur Genealogie des Zweiten Weltkrieges.* Bellnhausen über Gladenbach/Hessen: Verlag des Instituts für Genealogie und Politik, 1966. 111 pp., illus., bibl.

3855 HENRI, ERNST: *Hitler over Europe.* London: Dent, 1934. 307 pp. [German version: *Feldzug gegen Moskau.* Paris: Éds. du Carrefour, 1937. Spanish version: *El plan de Hitler.* Buenos Aires: Eds. Mañana, 1934.]

3856 IRVING, DAVID: *The war path. Hitler's Germany, 1933–1939.* London: Michael

Joseph, 1978. xxv + 301 pp., illus., facsims., map. [German version: *Hitlers Weg zum Krieg*. München: Herbig, 1979.]

3857   JONES, F. ELWYN: *Hitler's drive to the East*. London: Gollancz, 1937. 126 pp.

3858   KACZMARCK, JAN: *Paz belífera. Alemania 1919–1939*. Santiago de Chile: Imprente Universitaria, 1943. 183 pp.

3859   MENDELSSOHN, PETER de: *The Nuremberg documents. Some aspects of German war policy 1939–1945*. London: Allen & Unwin, 1946. 291 pp. [Concentrates on period 1937–1941. Austrian ed. entitled: *Sein Kampf*; German ed.: *Die Nürnberger Dokumente*; US ed.: *Design for aggression*.]

3860   MILES, pseud.: *Deutschlands Kriegsbereitschaft und Kriegsaussichten? Im Spiegel der deutschen Fachliteratur*. Zürich: Europa Verlag, 1939. 149 pp., tabs.

3861   OLAF, MICHAEL: *La casa que hace las guerras*. Rio de Janeiro: TOR, [1938?]. 189 pp.

3862   ROBERTSON, E. M.: *Hitler's prewar policy and military plans, 1933–1939*. London: Longmans, Green, 1963. xiii + 207 pp., bibl.

3863   WOLLENBERG, ERICH: *Hitler, le militarisme allemand et la paix européenne*. 3e ed. Introd.: Jean-Philippe Lepêtre. [Casablanca]: Kaganski, 1945. 244 pp.

Military indoctrination

3864   BANSE, EWALD: *Wehrwissenschaft. Einführung in eine neue nationale Wissenschaft*. 2. verb. Aufl. Leipzig: Armanen-Verlag, 1933. 59 pp., bibl. [First ed. 1932.]

3865   CIGARETTEN-BILDERDIENST DRESDEN: *Die deutsche Wehrmacht*. Dresden: 1936. [60 pp.], illus.

3866   FOLKERTS, HAYO & POTURZYN, FISCHER von: *Luftfahrt-Fibel für die deutsche Jugend*. Leipzig: Dürr, [193–]. 72 pp., illus., map.

3867   GRUBER, WALTER, ed.: *Volk ans Gewehr! Das Buch vom neuen Deutschland*. Geleitw.: Bruno Loerzer. 3. neu bearb. Aufl. Berlin: Nibelungen-Verlag, 1935. 408 pp., illus.

3868   HUNDEIKER, EGON: *Rasse, Volk, Soldatentum*. München: Lehmann, 1937. 162 pp., illus.

3869   LEHMANN, OTT: *Soldaten von morgen. Vom Jungvolk zum Waffenträger*. Berlin. Stalling, 1937. 174 pp., illus., diagr.

3870   MESSERSCHMIDT, MANFRED: *Die Wehrmacht im NS-Staat: Zeit der Indoktrination*. Einführung: Johann Adolf Graf Kielmansegg. Hamburg: Decker, 1969. 519 pp., bibl.

3871   METZSCH, HORST von: *Krieg als Saat. Aus des Verfassers wehrpolitischen Vorlesungen an der Deutschen Hochschule für Politik*. Breslau: Hirt, 1934. 62 pp.

3872 MULOT, ARNO: *Der Soldat in der deutschen Dichtung unserer Zeit.* Stuttgart: Metzler, 1938. 88 pp.

3873 NIEDERMAYER, OSKAR Ritter von: *Wehrpolitik. Eine Einführung und Begriffsbestimmung.* Leipzig: Barth, 1939. 206 pp., maps, bibl.

3874 PONGS, HERMANN: *Krieg als Volksschicksal im deutschen Schrifttum. Ein Beitrag zur Literaturgeschichte der Gegenwart.* Stuttgart: Metzler, 1934. 91 pp.

3875 SCHWERTFEGER, BERNHARD & VOLKMANN, ERICH OTTO, eds.: *Die deutsche Soldatenkunde.* Leipzig: Bibliographisches Institut, 1937. 2 vols., illus., facsims., mus. scores, bibl. [Incl. 'Bilderatlas der deutschen Soldatenkunde'.]

3876 STUHLMANN, FRIEDRICH, ed.: *Wehr-Lexikon. Was jeder Deutsche von der Wehr wissen muss.* Berlin: Heymann, 1936. 422 pp., tabs.

3877 *Waffenträger der Nation. Ein Buch der deutschen Wehrmacht für das deutsche Volk.* Hrsg.: Reichskriegsministerium. Berlin: Riegler, 1935. 145 pp., illus.

B. FOREIGN RELATIONS

1. REFERENCE WORKS

3878 *Akten zur deutschen auswärtigen Politik, 1918–1945.* Aus dem Archiv des Auswärtigen Amts.
Serie C. *1933–1937: Das Dritte Reich: Die ersten Jahre.* Göttingen: Vandenhoeck & Ruprecht, 1971– continuing. 10 vols. [Bd. 1–5, covering 1.1.1933–31.10.1936.]
Serie D. *1937–1941* [*1937–1945* up to Bd. 11]. Baden-Baden: Imprimerie Nationale, 1951/57. [From Bd. 12]: Göttingen: Vandenhoeck & Ruprecht, 1969–1970. 15 vols. [Bd. 1–13. Various publishers in period 1961–1964.]
Serie E. *1941–1945.* Göttingen: Vandenhoeck & Ruprecht, 1969– continuing. 6 vols. [Bd. 1–6, covering 12.12.1941–30.9.43.]
[English versions: *Documents on German foreign policy 1918–1945. Series C 1933–1937). The Third Reich: first phase.* London: HMSO, 1957–. And *Series D.* London: HMSO, 1949–1964. Also publ. Washington, D.C.: Government Printing Office, simultaneously with London publications.]

3879 DEUTSCHES AUSLANDSWISSENSCHAFTLICHES INSTITUT: *Europa-Bibliographie.* In Verbindung mit der Universitätsbibliothek Leipzig hrsg. von Fritz Prinzhorn. Leipzig: Harrassowitz, 1941–1944.
1: *Nordischer Raum. Bd. 1: 1939/40; Bd. 2: 1941/42.*
2: *Schweiz. Bd. 1: 1939/41; Bd. 2: 1942/43.*
3: *Die westlichen Länder des europäischen Südostens 1937/1941.*
4: *Frankreich. Bd. 1: 1939/1942.*
5: *Bulgarien. Bd. 1: 1939/1942.*
6: *Grossdeutschland, Reichsgau Sudetenland, Protektorat Böhmen und Mähren, Nord-Frankreich. Bd. 1: 1941/42.*
7: *Nordwesteuropäischer Raum: Niederlande, Belgien.*
8: *Ostland. Bd. 1: 1939/42.*

3880 *Documents on international affairs.* Issued under auspices of Royal Institute of International Affairs. London: Oxford University Press, 1951/54.
1939–1946: Vol. I: *March–September 1939.* Publ. 1951. 575 pp.
Vol. II: *Hitler's Europe.* Ed.: Margaret Carlyle. Publ. 1954. 362 pp.

3881 *Documents secrets du Ministère des Affaires étrangères d'Allemagne.* Traduit du russe par Madeleine et Michel Eristov. Paris: Dupont, 1946.
1: *Turquie.* 130 pp.
2: *Hongrie.* 140 pp.
3: *Espagne.* 165 pp.
[Also in English: Moscow: Foreign Languages Publ. House, 1948.]

3882 *Foreign affairs bibliography. A selected and annotated list of books on international relations.* New York: Harper, for Council on Foreign Relations, 1945, 1955.
1932–1942. Ed.: Robert Gale Woolbert. Publ. 1945. xxi + 705 pp.
1942–1952. Ed.: Henry L. Roberts. Ass'ts: Jean Gunther, Janis A. Kreslins. Publ. 1955. xxii + 727 pp.

3883 *Jahrbuch der Weltpolitik.* Hrsg.: F.A. Six. Berlin: Junker & Dünnhaupt, 1942/44. 3 vols., maps. (Deutsches Auslandswissenschaftliches Institut).

3884 *Jahrbuch für auswärtige Politik.* Hrsg.: Fritz Berber [from 1942 Friedrich Berber]. Berlin: Gross, 1938/43. 6 vols., bibls. [No others publ. in Third Reich.]

3885 KENT, GEORGE O., ed.: *A catalog of files and microfilms of the German Foreign Ministry archives 1920–1945.* Stanford, Calif.: The Hoover Institution on War, Revolution, and Peace, 1962/72. 4 vols.

3886 KRASKE, ERICH, ed.: *Handbuch des Auswärtigen Dienstes.* Auf Veranlassung des Auswärtigen Amts bearb. Halle/Saale: Niemeyer, 1939. 715 pp., tabs.

3887 MICHALKA, WOLFGANG, ed.: *Das Dritte Reich. Dokumente zur Innen- und Aussenpolitik.* München: Deutscher Taschenbuch Verlag, 1980/81.
Bd. 1: *Volksgemeinschaft und Revisionspolitik.*
Bd. 2: *Weltmachtanspruch und nationaler Zusammenbruch.*

3888 *Survey of international affairs.* London: Oxford University Press, under auspices of Royal Institute of International Affairs, 1933–1953. Maps.
1933–1936. By Arnold J. Toynbee. Publ. 1933/37. 6 vols.
1937: Vol. I. Publ. 1938. 674 pp.
Vol. II: The international repercussions of the war in Spain, 1936/7. Publ. 1938. 434 pp.
1938: Vol. I. Publ. 1941. 735 pp.
Vol. II: The crisis over Czechoslovakia, January to September 1938. By R. G. D. Laffan and others. Publ. 1951. 475 pp., tabs.
Vol. III. Ed.: Veronica M. Toynbee. Publ. 1953. 622 pp.

3889 *Survey of international affairs, 1939–1946.* London: Oxford University Press, under auspices of Royal Institute of International Affairs, 1952/58.

The world in March 1939. Eds.: Arnold Toynbee, Frank T. Ashton-Gwatkin. Publ. 1952. 546 pp., maps, tabs.

The eve of war. Eds.: Arnold Toynbee, Veronica M. Toynbee [who also edit the remaining vols]. Publ. 1958. 744 pp.

The initial triumph of the Axis. Publ. 1958. 742 pp.

Hitler's Europe. Publ. 1954. 730 pp.

The war and the neutrals. Publ. 1956. 378 pp.

The realignment of Europe. Publ. 1955. 619 pp., maps, tabs. [Incl. postwar planning.]

2. GENERAL

3890   BAUMONT, MAURICE: *La faillite de la paix, 1918–1939.* 3e éd. Paris: Presses Universitaires de France, 1951. 949 pp.

BEHN, JOACHIM: *Auswirkung der Rassegesetzgebung auf das zwischenstaatliche Recht. See* 1350.

3891   BEN ELISSAR, ELIAHU: *La diplomatie du IIIe Reich et les Juifs, 1933–1939.* Paris: Julliard, 1969. 521 pp., bibl.

3892   BERBER, FRIEDRICH, ed.: *Europäische Politik 1933–1938. Im Spiegel der Prager Akten.* 3. erw. Aufl. Essen: Essener Verlagsanstalt, 1942. 139 pp. (Veröffentlichungen des Deutschen Instituts für Aussenpolitische Forschung).

3893   BERNUS, PIERRE: *Le dossier de l'agression allemande. Les prédecesseurs de Hitler; Les étapes de la destruction du Traité de Versailles; De Munich à l'offensive contre Pologne; Les négociations finales; Livre bleu anglais, Livre blanc allemand, Livre jaune français.* Paris: Payot, 1940. 237 pp.

3894   BLOCH, CHARLES: *Hitler und die europäischen Mächte 1933/34. Kontinuität oder Bruch.* Frankfurt a.M.: Europäische Verlagsanstalt, 1966. 97 pp., bibl.

3895   BLUCHER, WIPERT VON: *Gesandter zwischen Diktatur und Demokratie. Erinnerungen aus den Jahren 1933–1944.* Wiesbaden: Limes Verlag, 1951. 414 pp.

BROWNING, CHRISTOPHER R.: *The Final Solution and the German Foreign Office. See* 5678.

3896   CARR, WILLIAM: *Arms, autarky and aggression. A study in German foreign policy, 1933–1939.* New York: Norton, 1973. 136 pp., bibl.

3897   DIRKSEN, HERBERT VON: *Moskau, Tokio, London. Erinnerungen und Betrachtungen zu 20 Jahren deutscher Aussenpolitik, 1919–1939.* Stuttgart: Kohlhammer, 1949. 279 pp., illus.

3898   DOLLMANN, EUGEN: *The interpreter. Memoirs.* Transl. from the German. London: Hutchinson, 1967. 352 pp., illus. [German orig.: *Dolmetscher der Diktatoren.* Bayreuth: Hestia-Verlag, 1963.]

3899   ERCKNER, S.: *Die grosse Lüge. Hitlers Verschwörung gegen den Frieden.* Paris:

Éds. du Carrefour, 1936. 256 pp. [Abridged English version: *Hitler's conspiracy against peace*.]

3900 FORNDRAN, ERHARD and others, eds.: *Innen- und Aussenpolitik unter nationalsozialistischer Bedrohung. Determinanten internationaler Beziehungen in historischen Fall-Studien.* [Eds.]: Erhard Forndran, Frank Golczewski, Dieter Riesenberger. Opladen: Westdeutscher Verlag, 1977. 361 pp., tabs.

3901 FREYTAGH-LORINGHOVEN, AXEL Frhr. von: *Deutschlands Aussenpolitik 1933–1940.* 7. Aufl. Berlin: Stollberg, 1940. 288 pp.

3902 *Friedensplan der Deutschen Regierung vom 31. März 1936.* Berlin: Müller, [1936]. 15 pp. [Also in English.]

3903 FUNKE, MANFRED, ed.: *Hitler-Deutschland und die Mächte. Materialien zur Aussenpolitik des Dritten Reiches.* Düsseldorf: Droste, 1976. 848 pp., diagr., tab.

3904 GILBERT, MARTIN & GOTT, RICHARD: *The appeasers.* London: Weidenfeld & Nicolson, 1963. 380 pp., illus. [German version: *Der gescheiterte Frieden: Europa 1933–1939.* Stuttgart: Kohlhammer, 1964.]

3905 GRAY, EDMUND: *The road to war, 1918–1939.* London: Chatto & Windus, 1970. 110 pp., illus.

3906 HADAMOVSKY, EUGEN: *Hitler kämpft um den Frieden Europas. Ein Tagebuch von Adolf Hitler's Kampf für Frieden und Gleichberechtigung.* 6. Aufl. München: Eher, 1938. 271 pp.

3907 HIDEN, JOHN: *Germany and Europe, 1919–1939.* London: Longman, 1977. vii + 183 pp., bibl.

3908 HILDEBRAND, KLAUS: *Deutsche Aussenpolitik 1933–1945. Kalkül oder Dogma?* Stuttgart: Kohlhammer, 1971. 186 pp., bibl. [English version: *The foreign policy of the Third Reich.* London: Batsford, 1973.]

3909 HILLGRUBER, ANDREAS, ed.: *Staatsmänner und Diplomaten bei Hitler. Vertrauliche Aufzeichnungen über Unterredungen mit Vertretern des Auslandes.* Frankfurt a.M.: Bernard & Graefe, 1967. In 2 vols.
1. Teil: *1939–1941.* 699 pp., illus.
2. Teil: *1942–1944.* 568 pp.

3910 HITLER, ADOLF: *National Socialism and world relations.* Speech delivered in the German Reichstag on January 30th, 1937. Berlin: Müller, 1937. 46 pp. (Anglo-German Information Service).

3911 HOLLDACK, HEINZ, ed.: *Was wirklich geschah. Die diplomatischen Hintergründe der deutschen Kriegspolitik. Darstellung und Dokumente.* München: Nymphenburger Verlagshandlung, 1949. 547 pp.

3912 JACOBSEN, HANS-ADOLF: *Nationalsozialistische Aussenpolitik 1933–1938.* Frankfurt a.M.: Metzner, 1968. xx + 944 pp., illus., tabs., diagrs., bibl.

3913 JANOWSKY, OSCAR I. & FAGEN, MELVIN M.: *International aspects of German racial policies.* Pref.: James Brown Scott. Postscript: Josiah C. Wedgwood. New York: Oxford University Press, 1937. xxi + 266 pp., tab. [I: 'Precedents for international action to safeguard human rights'.]

3914 KLOTZ, HELMUT: *Die Aussenpolitik der Nationalsozialisten.* Berlin: AP-Korrespondenz, 1931. 31 pp. [Anti-Nazi.]

3915 KORDT, ERICH & ABSHAGEN, KARL HEINZ, eds.: *Wahn und Wirklichkeit. Die Aussenpolitik des Dritten Reiches. Versuch einer Darstellung.* Stuttgart: Union Deutsche Verlagsgesellschaft, 1947. 419 pp.

3916 KUHN, AXEL: *Hitlers aussenpolitisches Programm. Entstehung und Entwicklung 1919–1939.* Stuttgart: Klett, 1970. 286 pp., bibl.

3917 LIEDTKE, HEINZ: *Kellogg-Pakt und völkischer Staat.* Inaugural-Dissertation [pres. to] Universität Köln. Würzburg: 1936. 42 pp., bibl.

RIBBENTROP, JOACHIM VON

3918 RIBBENTROP, JOACHIM VON: *Zwischen London und Moskau. Erinnerungen und letzte Aufzeichnungen.* Aus dem Nachlass hrsg. von Annelies von Ribbentrop. Leoni am Starnberger See: Druffel, 1953. 336 pp., illus. [English version: *The Ribbentrop memoirs.* Introd.: Alan Bullock. London: Weidenfeld & Nicolson, 1954.]

3919 MICHALKA, WOLFGANG: *Ribbentrop und die deutsche Weltpolitik 1933–1940. Aussenpolitische Konzeptionen und Entscheidungsprozesse im Dritten Reich.* München: Fink, 1980. 371 pp. (Veröffentlichungen des Historischen Instituts der Universität Mannheim). [Based on a dissertation, Mannheim 1976.]

3920 SCHLESINGER, MORITZ: *Erinnerungen eines Aussenseiters im diplomatischen Dienst.* Aus dem Nachlass hrsg. und eingel. von Hubert Schneider. Köln: Verlag Wissenschaft und Politik, 1977. 315 pp.

3921 SCHMIDT, PAUL: *Statist auf diplomatischer Bühne 1923–1945. Erlebnisse des Chefdolmetschers im Auswärtigen Amt mit den Staatsmännern Europas.* [136.–137. Taus.] Bonn: Athenäum-Verlag, 1954. 607 pp., bibl. [English version: *Hitler's interpreter.* London: Heinemann, 1951.]

3922 SCHUBERT, GÜNTER: *Anfänge nationalsozialistischer Aussenpolitik.* Köln: Verlag Wissenschaft und Politik, 1963. 251 pp., bibl.

3923 SEABURY, PAUL: *The Wilhelmstrasse. A study of German diplomats under the Nazi regime.* Berkeley, Calif.: University of California, 1954. 217 pp., bibl.

3924 STOAKES, GEOFFREY: 'The evolution of Hitler's ideas on foreign policy 1919–1925'. [In] Stachura, Peter D., ed.: *The shaping of the Nazi State. See* 1157.

3925 SUCHE, JOACHIM: *Der Meerenvertrag von Montreux, vom 20. Juli 1936 und seine Vorgeschichte (seit 1918).* München: Duncker & Humblot, 1936. 73 pp., bibl.

3926 USHAKOV, V. B.: [*Foreign policy of Hitlerite Germany*]. Moskva: Izd. IMO, 1961. 270 pp., bibl. [In Russian.]

3927 USCHAKOW, W. B.: *Deutschlands Aussenpolitik 1917–1945. Ein historischer Abriss.* Berlin [East]: VEB Deutscher Verlag der Wissenschaften, 1964. 471 pp., bibl.

3928 WACHE, WALTER: *System der Pakte. Die politischen Verträge der Nachkriegszeit.* Berlin: Volk und Reich Verlag, 1938. 425 pp., maps, diagrs.

3929 WEINBERG, GERHARD L.: *The foreign policy of Hitler's Germany: diplomatic revolution in Europe 1933–36.* Chicago, Ill.: University of Chicago Press, 1971. xi + 397 pp., maps, bibl.

3930 [WEIZSÄCKER, ERNST von] *Die Weizsäcker-Papiere 1933–1950.* Hrsg.: Leonidas E. Hill. Frankfurt a.M.: Ullstein (Propyläen), 1974. 684 pp.

3931 WOLLSTEIN, GÜNTER: *Vom Weimarer Revisionismus zu Hitler. Das Deutsche Reich und die Grossmächte in der Anfangsphase der nationalsozialistischen Herrschaft in Deutschland.* Bonn: Voggenreiter, 1973. 325 pp., bibl.

3. EXPANSIONISM

a. First steps

Repudiation of the Versailles peace treaty

3932 BACH, AUGUST, ed.: *Das Ende der Kriegsschuldlüge. Die feierliche Zurückziehung der deutschen Unterschrift unter das Schuldbekenntnis von Versailles durch den Führer und Reichskanzler in der Reichstagsrede am 30. Januar 1937.* Berlin: Quaderverlag, 1937. 282 pp.

3933 BERBER, FRITZ, ed.: *Das Diktat von Versailles. Entstehung—Inhalt—Zerfall. Eine Darstellung in Dokumenten.* Vorw.: Joachim von Ribbentrop. Essen: Essener Verlagsanstalt, 1939. xlvi + 1672 pp., tabs. In 2 vols. (Veröffentlichungen des Deutschen Instituts für Aussenpolitische Forschung).

3934 BITTER, F. W. & ZELLE, A.: *Bolschewismus im Versailler Diktat.* Hrsg.: Handelskammer Hamburg und Bremen. 1933. 99 pp.

3935 GRIMM, FRIEDRICH: *Versailles.* 2. geänd. Aufl. Köln: Schaffstein, 1934. 63 pp.

3936 JESSOP, T. E.: *The Treaty of Versailles—was it just?* London: Nelson, 1942. 167 pp., map, bibl.

3937 JORDAN, W. M.: *Great Britain, France and the German Problem, 1918–1939. A study of Anglo-French relations in the making and maintenance of the Versailles settlement.* London: Oxford University Press, under the auspices of the Royal Institute of International Affairs, 1943. xi + 235 pp.

3938 KAPP, ROLF: *Versailles, the root of the war.* Berlin: Greve, 1941. 44 pp., maps.

3939 KRIEGK, OTTO: *Das Ende von Versailles. Die Aussenpolitik des Dritten Reiches.* Oldenburg: Stalling, 1934. 154 pp.

3940 LEDERER, IVO J., ed.: *The Versailles settlement. Was it foredoomed to failure?* Boston, Mass.: Heath, 1966. 116 pp., bibl.

3941 MANNHART (pseud.): *Verrat um Gotteslohn? Schulddokumente neuzeitlicher Konfessionspolitik.* 3. erw. Aufl. Dresden-Blasewitz: Knöpke, 1938. 128 pp., bibl. [Earlier ed. subtitled: *Hintergründe des Diktates von Versailles.* München: Deutscher Druck, 1937.]

3942 MÜLLER-BRANDENBURG, [HERMANN]: *Das Diktat von Versailles und sein Sterben.* Leipzig: Der Nationale Aufbau, 1937. 123 pp.

3943 SCHWENDEMANN, KARL: *Versailles nach 15 Jahren. Der Stand der Revision des Versailler Diktats.* Berlin: Zentralverlag, 1935. 229 pp., illus.

3944 ZIEGLER, WILHELM: *Der Endkampf in Versailles.* 20. Taus. Hamburg: Hanseatische Verlagsanstalt, 1940/41. 89 pp.

Germany and the League of Nations

3945 BARROS, JAMES: *Betrayal from within. Joseph Avenol, Secretary-General of the League of Nations, 1933–1940.* New Haven, Conn.: Yale University Press, 1969. 289 pp. + xii pp., ports., bibl.

3946 KÖRBER, ROBERT: *Die Stellung des Deutschen zum Völkerbund.* Leipzig: Weicher, 1928. 40 pp., bibl. (Der völkische Sprechabend).

3947 KRIEGK, OTTO: *Hinter Genf steht Moskau.* Leipzig: Nibelungen-Verlag, 1936. 137 pp., illus.

3948 MICHAELIS, HERBERT: *Der Völkerbund im Dienste von Versailles.* Berlin: Junker & Dünnhaupt, 1941. 70 pp. (Schriften des Deutschen Instituts für Aussenpolitische Forschung).

3949 TRUCKENBRODT, WALTER: *Deutschland und der Völkerbund. Die Behandlung reichsdeutscher Angelegenheiten im Völkerbundsrat von 1920 bis 1939.* Essen: Essener Verlagsanstalt, 1941. 220 pp. (Veröffentlichungen des Deutschen Instituts für Aussenpolitische Forschung).

3950 [UPPER SILESIA] GEMISCHTE KOMMISSION FÜR OBER-SCHLESIEN: *Amtliche Sammlung der Stellungnahmen des Präsidenten der Gemischten Kommission für Ober-Schlesien auf dem Gebiete des Minderheitenrechtes auf Grund der Vorschriften des III. Teils des deutsch-polnischen Genfer Abkommens vom 15. Mai 1922 in der Zeit vom 15. Juni 1922 bis 15. Juni 1937. Bd. II.* Berlin: de Gruyter, 1937. 591 pp. [Text in Polish and German.]

Failure of disarmament

3951 LEAGUE OF NATIONS, Conference for the reduction and limitation of armaments: *Preliminary report on the work of the Conference.* Prepared by ... Arthur Henderson. Geneva: 1936. 205 pp. (League of Nations Publications, IX, Disarmament, 1936. IX.3. Off. No. Conf. D 171(1)).

3952 LEAGUE OF NATIONS, Conference for the reduction and limitation of armaments: *National control of the manufacture of and trade in arms. Information as to present position collected by the Secretariat in accordance with the resolution adopted on May 31st, 1937, by the Bureau of the Conference.* Geneva: 1938. 241 pp., tabs. (League of Nations Publications IX, Disarmament, 1938. IX.1. Off. No. Conf. D 184).

3953 LLOYD, LORNA & SIMS, NICHOLAS A.: *British writing on disarmament from 1914 to 1978: a bibliography.* London: Pinter, 1979. 171 pp.

3954 LOOSLI-USTERI, CARL: *Geschichte der Konferenz für die Herabsetzung und die Begrenzung der Rüstungen 1932–1934. Ein politischer Weltspiegel.* Zürich: Polygraphischer Verlag, 1940. 867 pp.

3955 MORGAN, J. H.: *Assize of arms. Being the story of the disarmament of Germany and her rearmament, 1919–1939.* London: Methuen, 1945. 291 pp., illus.

3956 OERTZEN, F. W. von: *Das ist die Abrüstung. Der Hohn der Abrüstungs-Artikel von Versailles.* Oldenburg i.O.: Stalling, 1931. 260 pp., map.

3957 SCHWENDEMANN, K.: *Abrüstung und Sicherheit. Handbuch der Sicherheitsfrage und der Abrüstungskonferenz. Mit einer Sammlung der wichtigsten Dokumente.* Berlin: Weidmann, 1932/35.
Bd. I: 2. Aufl. [Publ. 1933, first ed. 1932]. x + 881 pp.
Bd. II: Publ. 1935. xix + 799 pp.

3958 WHEELER-BENNETT, JOHN W.: *The pipe dream of peace. The story of the collapse of disarmament.* New York: Morrow, 1935. 302 pp.

German demand for equal rights (Gleichberechtigung)

3959 BRUNS, VIKTOR: *Germany's equality of rights as a legal problem.* Paper read at the First Plenary Meeting of the Academy of German Law on Nov. 5th 1933. Berlin: Heymann, 1935. 34 pp.

3960 DEUTSCHE GESELLSCHAFT FÜR WEHRPOLITIK UND WEHRWISSENSCHAFTEN: *Wehrfreiheit.* Jahrbuch der Deutschen Gesellschaft für Wehrpolitik und Wehrwissenschaften 1935. Hamburg: Hanseatische Verlagsanstalt, 1935. 116 pp. [Also appeared in other years.]

3961 EGGERS, KURT: *Von der Freiheit des Krieges.* Berlin: Nordland Verlag, [1940]. 63 pp.

3962 GRIMM, FRIEDRICH: *Wir sind im Recht! Deutschlands Kampf um Wehrfreiheit und Gleichberechtigung.* Berlin: Junker & Dünnhaupt, 1935. 31 pp. (Schriften der Deutschen Hochschule für Politik).

3963 SCHMIDT, RICHARD & GRABOWSKY, ADOLF, eds.: *Deutschlands Kampf um Gleichberechtigung. Tatsachen und Probleme der Verhandlungen über Abrüstung und Gleichberechtigung 1933/1934.* Berlin: Heymann, 1934. 298 pp. [Also in English under title *Disarmament and equal rights.*]

3964 WEBERSTEDT, HANS, ed.: *Deutschland fordert Gleichberechtigung. Eine Sammlung von Aufsätzen und Rundfunkreden über die Fragen der Gleichberechtigung, Sicherheit und Abrüstung.* Leipzig: Armanen-Verlag, 1933. 93 pp.

b. Rearmament

3965 BERNHARDT, WALTER: *Die deutsche Aufrüstung 1934–1939. Militärische und politische Konzeptionen und ihre Einschätzung durch die Alliierten.* Vorw.: Michael Freund. Frankfurt a.M.: Bernard & Graefe, 1969. 179 pp., tabs., bibl.

3966 CASTELLAN, GEORGES: *Le réarmement clandestin du Reich 1930–1935. Vu par le Deuxième Bureau de l'État-Major français.* Préface: Général Weygand. Paris: Plon, 1954. 590 pp., map, tabs.

3967 KLOTZ, HELMUT: *Germany's secret armaments.* London: Jarrolds, 1934. 190 pp.

3968 LEHMANN-RUSSBUELDT, OTTO: *Aggression. The origin of Germany's war machine.* Appendix: Hans Aktuhn, on Germany's secret air rearmament, 1919–1933. Pref.: Rennie Smith. Transl. from the German. London: Hutchinson, 1942. 63 pp. (A Fight for Freedom publication).

3969 MEINCK, GERHARD: *Hitler und die deutsche Aufrüstung 1933–1937.* Wiesbaden: Steiner, 1959. 246 pp., tabs., bibl. (Veröffentlichungen des Instituts für europäische Geschichte Mainz).

3970 MÜLLER, A.: *Hitlers motorisierte Stossarmee. Heeres- und Wirtschafts-Motorisierung im Dritten Reich.* Mit einem Anhang über die Militarisierung der entmilitarisierten Zone. Paris: Éds. du Carrefour, 1936. 220 pp., illus., tabs.

3971 STERNBERG, FRITZ: *Die deutsche Kriegsstärke. Wie lange kann Hitler Krieg führen?* Paris: Brant, 1938. 351 pp., diagrs., tabs. [English version: *Germany and a lightning war.* London: Faber & Faber, 1938.]

3972 VOORST TOT VOORST, J. J. G. Baron van: *De Duitse herbewapening.* Den Haag: Moorman, 1936. 108 pp., illus., tabs., bibl.

3973 WOODMAN, DOROTHY, ed.: *Hitler rearms. An exposure of Germany's war plans.* Introd.: Earl of Listowel. London: The Bodley Head, 1934. 336 pp., illus. [French version: *Au seuil de la guerre. Documents sur le réarmement de l'Allemagne Hitlérienne.* Paris: Éds. du Carrefour, 1934.]

Conscription

3974 FOERTSCH, [HERMANN]: *Wehrpflicht-Fibel.* 3. Aufl. Berlin: Verlag 'Offene Worte', [1935]. 106 pp., illus., tabs.

3975 HESSE, KURT: *Soldatendienst im neuen Reich.* Berlin: Ullstein, [193-]. 158 pp., illus.

3976 MÜLLER-LOEBNITZ, W., ed.: *Vom Wesen und Wert der allgemeinen Wehrpflicht.* Hrsg.: Deutsche Gesellschaft für Wehrpolitik und Wehrwissenschaften. Berlin: Riegler, 1936. 196 pp., ports., tabs., bibl.

Westwall (Siegfried Line)

3977 BIERMANN, OTTO and others: *Deutsche Gemeinschaftsarbeit. Geschichte, Idee und Bau des Westwalls.* Geleitw.: Robert Ley. Stuttgart: Deutsche Volksbücher, [1940?]. 96 pp., illus., maps, tabs.

3978 FLACK, WERNER: *Wir bauen den Westwall. Ein Fronterlebnis deutscher Jugend im Frieden.* Oldenburg: Stalling, 1939. 206 pp.

c. Methods of expansionism

Subversion, infiltration, espionage and propaganda

BISCHOFF, RALPH F.: *Nazi conquest through German culture. See* 2475.

3979 *Das Braune Netz. Wie Hitlers Agenten im Auslande arbeiten und den Krieg vorbereiten.* Paris: Eds. du Carrefour, 1935. 375 pp., illus., facsims. [English version: *The Brown Network.* Introd.: William Francis Hare. New York: Knight, 1936.]

3980 BUCHHEIT, GERT: *Der deutsche Geheimdienst. Geschichte der militärischen Abwehr.* München: List, 1966. 494 pp., bibl.

3981 CLASSEN, WILHELM: *Aussengeltung des Reiches. Arbeiten zur auswärtigen Kulturpolitik.* Heidelberg: Winter, 1938. 65 pp.

3982 GARBUTT, REGINALD: *Germany. The truth.* London: Rich & Cowan, 1939. 256 pp. [For six years chief organiser of foreign propaganda and espionage under Himmler.]

3983 GUNZENHÄUSER, MAX: *Geschichte des geheimen Nachrichtendienstes 'Spionage, Sabotage und Abwehr'. Literaturbericht und Bibliographie.* Frankfurt a.M.: Bernard & Graefe, 1968. viii + 434 pp. (Schriften der Bibliothek für Zeitgeschichte).

3984 HAGEN, WALTER: *Die geheime Front. Organisation, Personen und Aktionen des deutschen Geheimdienstes.* Linz: Nibelungen-Verlag, 1950. 514 pp., bibl.

3985 LENNHOFF, EUGENE: *Agents of hell. Himmler's Fifth Column.* London: Hutchinson, 1940. 157 pp.

3986 MURPHY, RAYMOND E. & others, comps.: *National socialism. Basic principles, their application by the Nazi Party's foreign organization and the use of Germans abroad for Nazi aims.* Prepared in the Special Unit of the division of European affairs by R. E. Murphy, Francis B. Stevens, Howard Trivers, Joseph M. Roland. Washington, D.C.: Government Printing Office, 1943. 510 pp., facsims., diagrs.

3987 REILE, OSCAR: *Geheime Westfront. Die Abwehr 1935–1945.* München: Welsermühl, 1962. 490 pp., illus., map.

3988 SCHRAMM, WILHELM von: *Der Geheimdienst in Europa 1937–1945.* München: Langen, Müller, 1974. 406 pp., facsims., bibl.

3989 SPIVAK, JOHN L.: *Secret armies. The new technique of Nazi warfare.* New York: Modern Age Books, 1939. 160 pp., facsims.

Encouragement of foreign nationalist movements

3990 BÄHRENS, KURT: *Die flämische Bewegung. Europäisches Problem oder innerbelgische Frage.* Berlin: Verlag Volk und Reich, 1935. 136 pp., maps, diagrs., tabs., bibl.

3991 HAAS, WERNER: *Europa will leben. Die nationale Erneuerungsbewegungen in Wort und Bild.* Geleitw.: Edmund Marhefka. Berlin: Batschari, 1936. 378 pp.

3992 KELLER, HANS K. E. L., ed.: *Der Kampf um die Völkerordnung. Forschungs- und Werbebericht der Akademie für die Rechte der Völker (Nationalistische Akademie) und der Internationalen Arbeitsgemeinschaft der Nationalisten (Nationalistische Aktion).* Berlin: Vahlen, 1939. 298 pp., illus.

3993 KELLER, HANS K. E. L.: *Warum nationalistische Internationale?* Zürich: Nauck, 1936. Pp. 17–35. [Speech given at 2nd International Congress of Nationalists, London, July 1936.]

3994 KROGMANN, WILLY: *Breiz da Vreiziz! (Die Bretagne den Bretonen!). Zeugnisse zum Freiheitskampf der Bretonen.* Halle/Saale: Niemeyer, 1940. 103 pp., illus., maps, diagrs. (Schriftenreihe der Deutschen Gesellschaft für keltische Studien). [Introds. in German, text in French.]

3995 SCHRICKER, RUDOLF: *Volk in Ketten. Das Erbe von Trianon.* Berlin: Batschari, 1935. 97 pp., illus., maps, diagr., facsims.

3996 ZECK, HANS F.: *Die flämische Frage. Ein germanisches Volk kämpft um sein Lebensrecht.* Leipzig: Goldmann, 1938. 142 pp., tabs., maps, bibl.

German minorities abroad (Volksdeutsche)

AUSLANDSORGANISATION DER NSDAP

3997 *Grossdeutschland und Auslands-Deutschtum. VI. Reichstagung der Auslands- organisation der NSDAP ... 1938 in Stuttgart.* Berlin: Gauverlag der A.-O. der NSDAP, [1938]. [84 pp.], illus.

3998 *Jahrbuch der Auslands-Organisation der NSDAP.* Berlin: Gauverlag der A.-O. der NSDAP, 1938/42. 4 vols., illus., diagrs., tabs.

––––––––––

3999 BECK, ROBERT: *Schwebendes Volkstum im Gesinnungswandel. Eine sozialpsychologische Untersuchung.* Stuttgart: Kohlhammer, 1938. 75 pp., diagrs., bibl. (Schriftenreihe der Stadt der Auslandsdeutschen).

4000 *Bücher berichten von Deutschen im Grenzland und Ausland. Bestandsverzeichnis einer Leihbücherei.* Zusammengest. und hrsg. von 'Volksdeutscher Sonder-Buchdienst des Deutschen Ausland-Instituts und Volksbund für das Deutschtum in Ausland Stuttgart'. 2. Aufl. mit Nachtrag. Stuttgart: 1936. 78 pp.

DEUTSCHES AUSLAND-INSTITUT

4001 DEUTSCHES AUSLAND-INSTITUT: *Bibliographisches Handbuch des Ausland- deutschtums.* Stuttgart: Ausland und Heimat-Verlag, [issued annually].

4002 *Jahrbuch für auslandsdeutsche Sippenkunde.* Stuttgart: Weinbrenner, 1936/37. Tabs., diagrs., maps. [Vols. 1 and 2. In subsequent years the name was changed to *Sippenkunde des Deutschtums im Ausland*, then *Jahrbuch der Hauptstelle für Sippenkunde* ..., etc.]

4003 RITTER, ERNST: *Das Deutsche Ausland-Institut in Stuttgart 1917–1945. Ein Beispiel deutscher Volkstumsarbeit zwischen den Weltkriegen.* Wiesbaden: Steiner, 1976. vi + 168 pp., bibl. [Abridged dissertation.]

4004 *Deutsches Grenzland. Jahrbuch des Instituts für Grenz- und Auslands-Studien.* Hrsg.: Max Hildebert Boehm, Karl C. von Loesch. Berlin: Deutsche Buchvertriebsstelle, 1936/40. 5 vols., illus.

4005 FITTBOGEN, GOTTFRIED: *Was jeder Deutsche vom Grenz- und Auslandsdeutschtum wissen muss.* 8. Aufl. München: Oldenbourg, 1937. 245 pp., tabs., maps. [First ed. 1924.]

4006 KIRN, PAUL: *Politische Geschichte der deutschen Grenzen.* 4. verb. Aufl. Mannheim: Bibliographisches Institut, 1958. 191 pp.

4007 KLEIN, KARL KURT: *Literaturgeschichte des Deutschtums im Ausland.* Leipzig: Bibliographisches Institut, 1939. 474 pp.

4008 LANGE, FRIEDRICH: *Grenzen zwischen Deutschen und Deutschen.* München: Eher, 1933. 128 pp., illus.

4009 MCKALE, DONALD M.: *The swastika outside Germany.* [Kent, Ohio]: Kent State University Press, 1977. xvi + 288 pp., bibl.

4010 OTTO, HEINZ, ed.: *Deutsche schaffen in aller Welt. Ein Bildband deutscher Leistung im Auslande.* Geleitw.: E. W. Bohle. II. Aufl. Mit Beiträgen von R. Csaki, K. Ströhn. Berlin: Kasper [in ass'n with] Gauverlag der A.-O. der NSDAP 'Seefahrt und Ausland', 1942. 400 pp., illus.

4011 SCHUMACHER, RUPERT VON: *Volk vor den Grenzen. Schicksal und Sinn des Aussendeutschtums in der gesamtdeutschen Verflechtung.* Stuttgart: Union Deutsche Verlagsgesellschaft, [1936]. 276 pp., illus., maps, tabs., bibl. (2. Aufl.).

4012 VERBAND DEUTSCHER VEREINE IM AUSLAND: *Wir Deutsche in der Welt.* Berlin: Stollberg, 1935/42. 7 vols., illus., tabs.

VOLKSBUND FÜR DAS DEUTSCHTUM IN AUSLAND
4013 VOLKSBUND FÜR DAS DEUTSCHTUM IN AUSLAND: *Jahrbücher.* Berlin: Verlag Grenze und Ausland, 1935/38. Illus., mus. scores.
1935: *Andreas Hofer.* 118 pp.
1936: *Prinz Eugen.* 119 pp.
1937: *Hermann Blumenau.* 127 pp.
1938: *Peter Rosegger.* 119 pp.

4014 JACOBSEN, HANS-ADOLF, ed.: *Hans Steinacher. Bundesleiter des VDA 1933–1937. Erinnerungen und Dokumente.* Boppard a.Rh.: Boldt, 1970. 68 + 623 pp., illus., facsims., tabs., diagr. (Schriften des Bundesarchivs).

4015   STILLICH, OSKAR: *Fort mit dem VDA aus den Schulen! Vortrag.* Begleitw.: Paul Oestreich. Breslau: Verlag fürs deutsche Volk, [1930]. 35 pp.

4015a WÄCHTLER, FRITZ, ed.: *Deutsche fern der Heimat.* München: Deutscher Volksverlag, 1938. 200 pp., illus.

Lebensraum

4016   DICKINSON, ROBERT E.: *The German Lebensraum.* Harmondsworth, Middx.: Penguin Books, 1943. 223 pp., maps, diagrs., tabs., bibl.

4017   DIETZEL, K. H. and others, eds.: *Lebensraumfragen europäischer Völker.* Hrsg.: K. H. Dietzel, O. Schmeider, H. Schmitthenner. Leipzig: Quelle & Meyer, 1941. Illus., maps, tabs.
Bd. I: *Europa.* xii + 735 pp.
Bd. II: *Europas koloniale Ergänzungsräume.* vii + 571 pp.

4018   GRUCHMANN, LOTHAR: *Nationalsozialistische Grossraumordnung. Die Konstruktion einer 'deutschen Monroe-Doctrine'.* Stuttgart: Deutsche Verlagsanstalt, 1962. (Schriftenreihe der Vierteljahrshefte für Zeitgeschichte).

4019   SCHWERTFEGER, BERNHARD: *Im Kampf um den Lebensraum. 70 Jahre deutschen Ringens 1870–1940.* Potsdam: Rütten & Loening, 1941. xvi + 373 pp.

Geopolitics

4020   DORPALEN, ANDREAS: *The world of General Haushofer. Geopolitics in action.* Introd.: Herman Beukema. New York: Farrar & Rinehart, 1942. 337 pp., port., maps.

4021   GYORGY, ANDREW: *Geopolitics. The new German science.* Berkeley, Calif.: University of California Press, 1944. vi pp. + pp. 141–303, diagr., bibl.

4022   HARBECK, KARL-HEINZ: *The 'Zeitschrift für Geopolitik', 1924–1944.* Inaugural-Dissertation [pres. to] Christian Albrecht University in Kiel. 1963. 313 pp.

4023   HAUSHOFER, KARL & FOCHLER-HAUKE, GUSTAV, eds.: *Probleme der Weltpolitik in Wort und Bild.* 2 Teile in einem Bande. Völlig erneuerte und stark erw. Neuaufl. von 'Welt in Gärung'. Leipzig: Breitkopf & Härtel, 1939. 412 pp., illus., maps, tabs.

4024   SIEWERT, WULF: *Der Atlantik. Geopolitik eines Weltmeeres.* 2. Aufl. Leipzig: Teubner, 1943. 96 pp., maps.

4025   STRAUSZ-HUPÉ, ROBERT: *Geopolitics. The struggle for space and power.* New York: Putnam, 1942. xiii + 274 pp., maps.

Colonies

4026   AMERY, L. S.: *The German colonial claim.* London: Chambers, 1939. 198 pp., maps.

4027   BARAVALLE, ROBERT: *Deutschland braucht seine Kolonien. Ein Ruf an alle*

Deutschen und eine Forderung an die Welt. Graz: Stocker, 1939. 96 pp., tabs., diagrs., maps, bibl.

4028 BAUER, H. H.: *Kolonien im Dritten Reich.* Köln-Deutz: Gauverlag Westdeutscher Beobachter, 1936. 273 + 262 pp., illus. [In 2 vols.]

4029 BENNETT, BENJAMIN: *Hitler over Africa.* London: Laurie, 1939. 195 pp.

4030 BRÜSCH, KARL, ed.: *Afrika braucht Gross-Deutschland.* Berlin-Wilmersdorf: Süsserott, [1939]. 192 pp., illus., tabs.

4031 *Das Deutsche Koloniale Jahrbuch.* Neue Folge von Süsserotts illustrierten Kolonial-Kalender. Berlin: Süsserott. Illus.
1939: *Kolonien—Grossdeutschlands Anspruch.* Bearb.: Karl Brüsch. 192 pp.
1941: *Kolonien—ein Kraftfeld Grossdeutschlands.* Bearb.: Hans Bender. 208 pp.

4032 GILWICKI, CONSTANTIN VON: *Die Enteignung des deutschen Kolonialbesitzes.* Hamburg: Broschek, [1938]. 101 pp. [Transl. from the Polish.]

4033 GRIMM, HANS: *Suchen und hoffen 1928–1934.* Lippoldsberg: Klosterhaus, 1972. 338 pp., illus., facsims., map.

4034 HILDEBRAND, KLAUS: *Vom Reich zum Weltreich. Hitler, NSDAP und koloniale Frage 1919–1945.* München: Fink, 1969. 955 pp., bibl. (Veröffentlichungen des Historischen Instituts der Universität Mannheim).

4035 JADFARD, RENÉ: *La France et les revendications coloniales allemandes.* Paris: Querelle, 1938. 123 pp., bibl.

4036 JOHANNSEN, KURT & KRAFT, H. H.: *Germany's colonial problem. The necessity for redistributing the world's raw material resources. Facts and arguments supporting Germany's claim to the return of her colonies.* London: Thornton Butterworth, 1937. 96 pp., tabs., map.

4037 *Koloniales Schrifttum in Deutschland.* München: Eher, 1941. 109 pp.

4038 KUM'A N'DUMBE III, ALEXANDRE: 'Pläne zu einer nationalsozialistischen Kolonialherrschaft in Afrika'. [In] Wolfgang Benz & Hermann Graml, eds.: *Aspekte deutscher Aussenpolitik im 20. Jahrhundert.* Stuttgart: Deutsche Verlags-Anstalt, 1976. Pp. 165–192.

4039 MAROGER, GILBERT: *L'Europe et la question coloniale. Revendications coloniales allemandes: aspirations coloniales polonaises.* Préface: Sébastien Charléty. Paris: Sirey, 1938. 464 pp., tabs., bibl.

4040 ROYAL INSTITUTE OF INTERNATIONAL AFFAIRS: *Germany's claim to colonies.* London: 1938. 75 pp., map, tabs.

4041 SCHEIDL, FRANZ J.: *Deutschlands Kampf um seine Kolonien. Eine gemeinverständliche urkundliche Darstellung.* Wien: Deutscher Verlag für Jugend und Volk, 1939. 306 pp., tabs.

4042 SCHMITT-EGNER, PETER: *Kolonialismus und Faschismus. Eine Studie zur historischen und begrifflichen Genesis faschistischer Bewusstseinsformen am deutschen Beispiel.* Giessen: Achenbach, 1965. 224 pp. [From a dissertation, Frankfurt a.M.]

4043 SCHMOKEL, WOLFE W.: *Dream of Empire: German colonialism, 1919–1945.* New Haven, Conn.: Yale University Press, 1964. 204 pp., bibl. [German version: *Der Traum vom Reich.* Gütersloh: Mohn, 1967.]

4044 SCHNEE, HEINRICH: *German colonization past and future. The truth about the German colonies.* Introd.: William Harbutt Dawson. London: Allen & Unwin, 1926. 176 pp., illus. [Author was President of Bund der Auslandsdeutschen and later President of the Reichskolonialbund; he also held many other posts relating to colonies.]

4045 SCHOEN, LUDWIG: *Das koloniale Deutschland. Deutsche Schutzgebiete unter Mandatsherrschaft.* 8. neubearb. Aufl. Berlin: Freiheitsverlag, 1938. 180 pp.

4046 WOLFF, GÜNTER, ed.: *Beiträge zur Kolonialforschung.* Hrsg. im Auftr. der Deutschen-Forschungsgemeinschaft. Berlin: Reimer, 1942. 194 + 219 pp., illus., diagrs., graphs, tabs., bibls., summaries in French and Italian. [In 2 vols.]

4047 WRIGHT, S. FOWLER: *Should we surrender colonies?* London: Reader's Library, [1939]. 251 pp., map.

d. First Successes

Return of the Saar

4048 BALK, THEODOR: *Hier spricht die Saar. Ein Land wird interviewt.* Zürich: Ring-Verlag, 1934. 176 pp.

4049 GRABOWSKY, ADOLF & SANTE, GEORG WILHELM, eds.: *Die Grundlagen des Saarkampfes. Handbuch zur Volksabstimmung.* Vorw.: Franz von Papen. Berlin: Heymann, 1934. 394 pp., maps, graphs.

4050 GRIMM, FRIEDRICH: *Frankreich an der Saar. Der Kampf um die Saar im Lichte der historischen französischen Rheinpolitik.* Hamburg: Hanseatische Verlagsanstalt, 1934. 135 pp., illus., bibl.

4051 HOFFMANN, HEINRICH: *Hitler holt die Saar heim.* Geleitw.: Josef Bürckel. Berlin: Zeitgeschichte Verlag, 1938. [60 pp.], illus.

4052 JACOB, ALFRED HELMUT: *Das Ende des Separatismus in Deutschland. Dargestellt am Abwehrkampf der deutschen Publizistik in der Pfalz und an der Saar 1919 bis 1935. Ein Beitrag zur deutschen Wehrpolitik der Gegenwart.* Berlin: Curtius, 1940. 120 pp., bibl.

4053 JACOBY, FRITZ: *Die nationalsozialistische Herrschaftsübernahme an der Saar. Die innenpolitischen Probleme der Rückgliederung des Saargebietes bis 1935.* Saarbrücken: Thinnes & Nolte, 1973. 275 pp., bibl. (Veröffentlichungen der Kommission für saarländische Landesgeschichte und Volksforschung).

4054 LAMBERT, MARGARET: *The Saar.* London: Faber & Faber, 1934. 332 pp., map.

4055   REYNOLDS, B. T.: *The Saar and the Franco-German problem.* London: Arnold, 1934. 279 pp., illus., tabs., maps.

4056   ZENNER, MARIA: *Parteien und Politik im Saargebiet unter dem Völkerbunds-regime 1920–1935.* Inaugural-Dissertation [pres. at] Köln. Saarbrücken: Thinnes & Nolte, 1966. 434 pp., tabs., map, bibl. (Veröffentlichungen der Kommission für saarländische Landesgeschichte und Volksforschung).

March into the Rhineland

4057   BRAUBACH, MAX: *Der Einmarsch deutscher Truppen in die entmilitarisierte Zone am Rhein in März 1936. Ein Beitrag zur Vorgeschichte des Zweiten Weltkrieges.* Köln: Westdeutscher Verlag, 1956. 40 pp. (Arbeits-gemeinschaft für Forschung des Landes Nordrhein-Westfalen).

4058   EMMERSON, JAMES THOMAS: *The Rhineland crisis, 7 March 1936. A study in multilateral diplomacy.* London: Temple Smith, in ass'n with London School of Economics and Political Science, 1977. 383 pp., maps, bibl.

4059   RAUMER, KURT: *Der Rhein in deutschem Schicksal. Reden und Aufsätze zur Westfrage.* Berlin: Stilke, 1936. 109 pp.

C.   RELATIONS WITH AXIS STATES

1.   ITALY

4060   ALFIERI, DINO: *Dictators face to face.* London: Elek, 1954. 307 pp. [Transl. from the Italian.]

4061   ANFUSO, FILIPPO: *Rom-Berlin in diplomatischem Spiegel.* Essen: Pohl, 1951. 361 pp. [Transl. from the Italian.]

4062   CIANO, GALEAZZO: *L'Europa verso la catastrofe. 184 colloqui con Mussolini, Hitler, Franco, Chamberlain* [and others]. Gennaio: Mondadori, 1947. 722 pp. [English version: *Ciano's diplomatic papers. Record of conversations during 1936–1942 with Hitler, Mussolini, Franco, Goering, Ribbentrop and other statesmen.* Ed.: Malcolm Muggeridge. London: Odhams, 1948. 490 pp.]

4063   DEAKIN, F. W.: *The brutal friendship. Mussolini, Hitler and the fall of Italian fascism.* London: Weidenfeld & Nicolson, 1962. 896 pp., bibl.

4064   DZELEPY, [E.-N.]: *L'alliance des fascismes.* Paris: Baudinière, 1935. 220 pp.

4065   HOFFMANN, HEINRICH: *Hitler in Italien.* München: 1938. 96 pp., illus.

4066   HUDAL, ALOIS: *Die deutsche Kulturarbeit in Italien.* Münster: Aschendorff, 1934. 320 pp., illus., tabs.

4067   MICHAELIS, MEIR: *Mussolini and the Jews. German-Italian relations and the Jewish question in Italy, 1922–1945.* Oxford: Clarendon Press, for Institute of Jewish Affairs, 1978. xii + 472 pp., bibl.

4068 MINISTERO DEGLI AFFARI ESTERI: *I documenti diplomatici italiani.* Roma: Libreria dello Stato, 1953– continuing
7a serie: *1922–1935.*
8a serie: *1935–1939.*
9a serie: *1939–1943.*

4069 PETITFRÈRE, RAY: *Le faux ménage: Hitler-Mussolini.* Namur: Godenne, 1965. 580 pp., illus., facsims., diagrs., bibl.

4070 RINTELEN, ENNO VON: *Mussolini als Bundesgenosse. Erinnerungen des deutschen Militärattaches in Rom 1936–1943.* Tübingen: Wunderlich, 1951. 265 pp., bibl.

4071 SCHREIBER, GERHARD: *Revisionismus und Weltmachtstreben. Marineführung und deutsch-italienische Beziehungen 1919–1944.* Stuttgart: Deutsche Verlags-Anstalt, 1978. 428 pp. (Schriftenreihe des militärgeschichtlichen Forschungsamtes).

The early phase

4072 CASSELS, ALAN: *Mussolini's early diplomacy.* Princeton, N.J.: Princeton University Press, 1970. xvii + 425 pp., map, bibl. [Incl.: 'Mussolini and German nationalism', pp. 146–174.]

4073 DE FELICE, RENZO: *Mussolini e Hitler—i rapporti segreti, 1922–1933. Con documenti inediti.* Firenze: Le Monnier, 1975. 315 pp.

4074 HOEPKE, KLAUS-PETER: *Die deutsche Rechte und der italienische Faschismus. Ein Beitrag zum Selbstverständnis und zur Politik von Gruppen und Verbänden der deutschen Rechten.* Hrsg.: Kommission für Geschichte des Parlamentarismus und der politischen Parteien. Düsseldorf: Droste, 1968. 348 pp., bibl.

4075 *Inchiesta su Hitler.* Roma: 'Nuova Europa', [1932]. 117 pp., illus. [Letters appearing in 'Antieuropa', replying to a letter by Anton Hilckmann.]

4076 *Les lettres secrètes échangées par Hitler et Mussolini.* Introd.: André François-Poncet. Paris: Éds. du Pavois, 1946. 190 pp.

South Tyrol

4077 ALCOCK, ANTONY EVELYN: *The history of the South Tyrol question.* London: Michael Joseph, for Graduate Institute of International Studies, Geneva, 1970. xxi + 535 pp., maps, graphs, tabs., bibl.

4078 LATOUR, CONRAD F.: *Südtirol und die Achse Berlin-Rom 1938–1945.* Stuttgart: Deutsche Verlagsanstalt, 1962. 158 pp., bibl. (Schriftenreihe der Vierteljahrshefte für Zeitgeschichte).

4079 LUTZENDORF, FELIX: *Völkerwanderung 1940. Ein Bericht aus dem Osten.* Berlin: Fischer, 1940. 107 pp. [Incl. South Tyrol.]

SCHECHTMAN, JOSEPH B.: *European population transfers 1939–1945.* See 5217.

4080 *Die farbige Front. Hinter den Kulissen der Weltpolitik.* Leipzig: List, 1936. 639 pp., map. [11th–15th ed. On the Ethiopian war.]

4081 FUNKE, MANFRED: *Sanktionen und Kanonen. Hitler, Mussolini und der internationale Abessinienkonflikt 1934–1936.* Düsseldorf: Droste, 1970. viii + 220 pp., bibl.

4082 SCHMIEDER, OSKAR & WILHELMY, HERBERT: *Die faschistische Kolonisation in Nordafrika.* Leipzig: Quelle & Meyer, 1939. 201 pp., illus., map.

2. THE AXIS PACTS

4083 DRECHSLER, KARL, ed.: *Das Bündnis der Rivalen. Der Pakt Berlin–Tokio. Neue Dokumente zur Ost- und Südostasienpolitik des faschistischen deutschen Imperialismus im Zweiten Weltkrieg.* Berlin [East]: Deutscher Verlag der Wissenschaften, 1978. 178 pp.

4084 DÜSSEL, CARL: *Europa und die Achse. Die kontinentaleuropäische Frage als Kehrseite britischer Politik.* 2. Aufl. Essen: Essener Verlagsanstalt, 1940. 125 pp.

4085 GALÉRA, KARL SIEGMAR Baron von: *Die Achse Berlin–Rom. Entstehung— Wesen—Bedeutung.* Leipzig: Conrad, 1939. 304 pp., ports., bibl.

4086 ISSRAELJAN, V. & KUTAKOV, L.: *Diplomacy of aggression. Berlin–Rome–Tokyo Axis, its rise and fall.* Transl. from the Russian. Moscow: Progress Publs., 1970. 438 pp.

4087 PETERSEN, JENS: *Hitler–Mussolini. Die Entstehung der Achse Berlin–Rom, 1933–1936.* Tübingen: Niemeyer, 1973. xxvi + 559 pp., bibl. (Bibliothek des Deutschen Historischen Instituts in Rom).

4088 TOSCANA, MARIO: *Le origini diplomatiche del Patto d'Acciaio.* 2a ed. rived. ed ampl. Firenze: Sansoni, 1956. 414 pp. [English version: *The origins of the Pact of Steel.* Baltimore, Md.: Johns Hopkins University Press, 1967.]

4089 WISKEMANN, ELIZABETH: *The Rome–Berlin Axis. A history of the relations between Hitler and Mussolini.* London: Oxford University Press, 1949. 376 pp., illus. [New, rev. ed.: London: Collins, 1966. 446 pp., illus., bibl.]

3. JAPAN

4090 CORDES, ERNST: *Das jüngste Kaiserreich. Schlafendes/Wachendes Mandschukuo.* Frankfurt a.M.: Societäts-Verlag, 1936. 225 pp., illus., map.

4091 HAUSHOFER, KARL: *Japan baut sein Reich.* Berlin: Zeitgeschichte-Verlag, 1941. 330 pp., illus., maps, diagrs., bibl.

4092 LUFFT, HERMANN: *Japans strategische Stellung.* Berlin: Junker & Dünnhaupt, 1940. 300 pp., tabs.

4093 MARTIN, BERND: *Deutschland und Japan im Zweiten Weltkrieg. Vom Angriff auf Pearl Harbor bis zur deutschen Kapitulation.* Göttingen: Musterschmidt, 1969. 326 pp., illus., facsims., maps, tabs., bibl.

4094 MESKILL, JOHANNA MENZEL: *Hitler and Japan: the hollow alliance.* New York: Atherton Press, 1966. 245 pp., bibl.

4095 PRESSEISEN, ERNST L.: *Germany and Japan. A study in totalitarian diplomacy 1933–1941.* The Hague: Nijhoff, 1958. 368 pp.

4096 PUSTAU, ED. VON & OKANOUYE-KUROTA, (Dr.): *Japan und Deutschland, die beiden Welträtsel. Politische, wirtschaftliche und kulturelle Entwicklung.* Deutsche Ausg. Berlin: Deutscher Verlag für Politik und Wirtschaft, 1936. 223 pp., illus., maps, diagrs., graphs, tabs.

4097 URACH, Fürst A.: *Ostasien. Kampf um das kommende Grossreich.* Berlin: Steinigen, 1940. 191 pp., illus., maps.

4098 SOMMER, THEO: *Deutschland und Japan zwischen den Mächten 1935–1940. Von Antikominternpakt zum Dreimächtepakt. Eine Studie zur diplomatischen Vorgeschichte des Zweiten Weltkrieges.* Tübingen: Mohr, 1962. 540 pp., bibl.

4099 STOYE, JOHANNES: *Japan. Gefahr oder Vorbild.* Leipzig: Quelle & Meyer, 1936. 331 pp., map, diagrs., tabs., bibl.

D. RELATIONS WITH EUROPEAN STATES

1. GROSSDEUTSCHLAND (GREATER GERMANY)

4100 BORKENAU, F.: *The new German empire.* Harmondsworth, Middx.: Penguin Books, 1939. 216 pp., tabs.

4101 DOOLAARD, A. den: *Het hakenkruis over Europa. Een grote reportage.* Amsterdam: Querido, 1938. 182 pp., maps, facsims.

4102 *Des Führers Wehrmacht half Grossdeutschland schaffen. Berichte deutscher Soldaten von der Befreiung der Ostmark und des Sudetenlandes.* Hrsg.: Oberkommando der Wehrmacht. Berlin: Andermann, 1939. 226 pp., illus.

4103 HADAMOVSKY, EUGEN: *Weltgeschichte im Sturmschritte. Das Grossdeutsche Jahr 1938.* 2. Aufl. München: Eher, 1939. 345 pp., map.

4104 HELBOK, ADOLF & LEHMANN, EMIL: *Heimgekehrte Grenzlande im Südosten. Ostmark, Sudetengau, Reichsprotektorat Böhmen und Mähren. Ein Handbuch...* Mitarb.: Friedrich Ranzi. Leipzig: Reclam, 1939. 480 pp., illus., maps.

4105 HOFFMANN, HEINRICH: *Hitler baut Gross-Deutschland.* Berlin: Verlag 'Zeitgeschichte', 1938. 32 pp., illus.

4106 PLASSMANN, J. O. & TRATHNIGG, G., eds.: *Deutsches Land kehrte heim. Ostmark und Sudetenland als germanischer Volksboden.* Berlin: Ahnenerbe-Stiftung-Verlag, 1939. 147 pp., illus., maps, facsims., tabs., mus. scores.

4107 PLEYER, WILHELM: *Deutschland ist grösser! Gedichte eines Grenzlanddeutschen.* 2. Aufl. Weimar: Duncker, [193–]. 47 pp.

4108 REIMANN, G.: *Germany—world empire or world revolution.* London: Secker & Warburg, 1938. 302 pp.

4109 SÜNDERMANN, HELMUT: *Die Grenzen fallen. Von der Ostmark zum Sudetenland.* München: Eher, 1939. 250 pp.

2. AUSTRIA

Up to 1938

4110 EICHSTÄDT, ULRICH: *Von Dollfuss zu Hitler. Geschichte des Anschlusses Österreichs 1933–1938.* Wiesbaden: Steiner, 1955. x + 558 pp.

4111 GEHL, JÜRGEN: *Austria, Germany, and the Anschluss, 1931–1938.* Forew.: Alan Bullock. London: Oxford University Press, 1963. 212 pp., maps, bibl.

KOERNER, RALF RICHARD: *Die publizistische Behandlung der Österreichfrage und die Anschlussvorbereitungen der Tagespresse des Dritten Reiches, 1933–1938. See* 2782.

4112 LUŽA, RADOMÍR: *Austro-German relations in the Anschluss era.* Princeton, N.J.: Princeton University Press, 1975. xvi + 438 pp., graph. [German version: *Österreich und die grosse deutsche Idee in der NS-Zeit.* Wien: Böhlau, 1977.]

4113 ROSS, DIETER: *Hitler und Dollfuss. Die deutsche Österreich-Politik 1933–1934.* Hamburg: Leibniz, 1966. 341 pp., bibl.

The Churches and National Socialism

4114 FATTINGER, JOSEF: *Kirche in Ketten. Die Predigt des Blutes und der Tränen. Zeitgemässe Beispielsammlung aus den Jahren 1938 bis 1945.* Innsbruck: Rauch, 1949. 749 pp.

4115 FRIED, JAKOB: *Nationalsozialismus und katholische Kirche in Österreich.* Wien: Wiener Dom-Verlag, 1947. 248 pp.

GAMSJÄGER, HELMUT: *Die Evangelische Kirche in Österreich in den Jahren 1933 bis 1938 ... See* 1907.

4116 GERMANICUS, pseud.: *Der Dolchstoss gegen die deutschen Bischöfe. Bischof Hudal und der Nationalsozialismus.* Prag: Grunov, 1937. 23 pp.

4117 REIMANN, VIKTOR: *Innitzer. Kardinal zwischen Hitler und Rom.* Wien: Molden, 1967. 380 pp., facsims.

Nazi subversion in Austria

4118 *Das Braunbuch. Hakenkreuz gegen Österreich.* Hrsg.: Bundeskanzleramt, Büro des Bundesministers für Sicherheitswesen. Wien: Österreichische Staatsdruckerei, 1933. 43 pp., illus., facsims.

4119 CARSTEN, F. L.: *Fascist movements in Austria: From Schönerer to Hitler.* London: Sage, 1977. 356 pp., bibl.

4120 JAGSCHITZ, GERHARD & BAUBIN, ALFRED: *Der Putsch. Die Nationalsozialisten 1934 in Österreich.* Graz: Verlag Styria, 1976. 260 pp., illus., facsims., bibl.

4121 SCHILLING, ALEXANDER: *Dr. Walter Riehl und die Geschichte des Nationalsozialismus. Anhang: Hitler in Österreich.* Leipzig: Forum Verlag, 1933. 380 pp.

4122 SCHOPPER, HANS: *Presse im Kampf. Geschichte der Presse während der Kampfjahre der NSDAP (1933–1938) in Österreich.* München: Rohrer, 1942. 430 pp., illus.

4123 SPRINGENSCHMID, KARL: *Österreichische Geschichten aus der ersten Zeit des 'illegalen' Kampfes.* 6. Aufl. Brunn: Rohrer, 1942. 129 pp. [First ed. 1935.]

The Anschluss

4124 BROOK-SHEPHERD, GORDON: *Anschluss. The rape of Austria.* London: Macmillan, 1963. 222 pp., illus.

4125 DEUTSCHE BANK: *Das Land Österreich im deutschen Wirtschaftsraum.* Berlin: 1938. 47 pp., map, tabs.

4126 GALÉRA, KARL SIEGMAR Baron von: *Österreichs Rückkehr ins Deutsche Reich. Von Kaiser Karl zu Adolf Hitler.* Leipzig: Nationale Verlags-Gesellschaft, 1938. 318 pp.

4127 HARTMANN, MITZI: *Austria still lives.* London: Michael Joseph, 1938. 295 pp.

4128 HOFFMANN, HEINRICH: *Hitler in seiner Heimat. Reichsbilderbericht.* Berlin: Verlag 'Zeitgeschichte', 1938. [60 pp.], illus.

4129 INGRIM, ROBERT: *Der Griff nach Österreich.* Zürich: Europa Verlag, 1938. 179 pp., map.

4130 KÖRBER, ROBERT: *Rassesieg in Wien, der Grenzfeste des Reiches.* Wien: Braumüller, 1939. 308 pp., illus., facsims., bibl.

4131 *Reich und Ostmark. Eine Vortragsreihe der österreichischen Verwaltungs-Akademien über Aufbau, Verwaltung und Aufgaben des Grossdeutschen Reiches!* Berlin: Spaeth & Linde, 1938. 191 pp., tabs.

4132 REICHSAUSSCHUSS FÜR FREMDENVERKEHR IN BERLIN: *Österreich, Deutschlands Ostmark, ruft! Bilder aus der Heimat Adolf Hitlers.* Wien: Reisezeitung der Deutschen Ostmark, 1938. 199 pp., illus.

4133 ROSAR, WOLFGANG: *Deutsche Gemeinschaft. Seyss-Inquart und der Anschluss.* Wien: Europa Verlag, 1971. 441 pp., illus., diagr., bibl.

4134 SCHAUSBERGER, NORBERT: *Der Griff nach Österreich. Der Anschluss.* Wien: Jugend und Volk, 1978. 666 pp., tabs., bibl.

4135 SCHUSCHNIGG, KURT: *Austrian requiem.* Transl. from the German. New York: Putnams, 1946. 314 pp.

4136 SCHUSCHNIGG, KURT: *Im Kampf gegen Hitler. Die Überwindung der Anschlussidee.* Wien: Molden, 1969. 472 pp. [English version: *The brutal takeover. The Austrian ex-Chancellor's account of the Anschluss of Austria by Hitler.* New York: Atheneum, 1971.]

4137 SÜNDERMANN, HELMUT: *Wie deutsch bleibt Österreich? Antwort an Schuschnigg.* Leoni am Starnberger See: Druffel, 1970. 236 pp., map.

4138 WAGNER, DIETER & TOMKOWITZ, GERHARD: *Ein Reich, ein Volk, ein Führer. The Nazi annexation of Austria, 1938.* London: Longman, 1971. 255 pp., illus., maps, bibl. [Abridged transl. of German orig.: München: Piper, 1968.]

4139 *Wien 1938.* Wien: Verein für Geschichte der Stadt Wien, 1978. 326 pp. [General ed.: Felix Czeike. Incl. the situation of the Jews. Anthology.]

3. BALKAN AND DANUBIAN STATES

4140 BAHR, RICHARD: *Deutsches Schicksal im Südosten.* Hamburg: Hanseatische Verlagsanstalt, 1936. 245 pp., map, bibl.

4141 RÖTTNER, HELMUT: *England greift nach Südost-Europa. Wirtschaftlicher Tatbestand und Folgerungen.* Wien: Luser, 1939. 157 pp., tabs., bibl.

4142 DAMMERT, RUDOLF: *Deutschlands Nachbarn im Südosten. Völker und Mächte im Donauraum.* Leipzig: Voigtlander, 1938. 390 pp., maps, bibl.

4143 *Deutschland und Südosteuropa. Die natürlichen, völkischen, kulturellen und wirtschaftlichen Beziehungen des Deutschtums mit den Völkern im Südosten.* Eine Gemeinschaftsarbeit der Gaudozentenführung im Gau Steiermark und des Südostdeutschen Institutes Graz. Graz: Steierische Verlagsanstalt, 1942. 134 pp., illus., maps, diagr., tabs.

4144 FABRY, PHILIPP W.: *Balken-Wirren 1940–1941. Diplomatische und militärische Vorbereitung des deutschen Donauüberganges.* Darmstadt: Wehr und Wissen Verlagsgesellschaft, 1966. 195 pp., bibl.

4145 FODOR, M. W.: *South of Hitler.* 2nd ed. London: Allen & Unwin, 1938. 321 pp., illus.

4146 GRUENBERG, L.: *Die deutsche Südostgrenze.* Leipzig: Teubner, 1941. 199 pp., maps, tabs., bibl. (Veröffentlichungen des Deutschen Auslandswissenschaftlichen Instituts).

4147 HERRSCHAFT, HANS: *Das Banat. Ein deutsches Siedlungsgebiet in Südosteuropa.* 2. verb. und ergänz. Aufl. Berlin: Verlag Grenze und Ausland, 1942. 338 pp., illus., tabs., bibl.

4148 HOFFMANN, WALTER: *Lebensraum oder Imperialismus. Eine wirtschafts-politische Studie Südosteuropas.* Berlin: Deutsche Informationsstelle, 1940. 139 pp., illus., map, tabs., bibl. (England ohne Maske).

4149 HOLLINGWORTH, CLARE: *There's a German just behind me.* London: Secker &

Warburg, 1942. 300 pp., map. [Description of conditions in the Balkans at the point of becoming German satellites.]

4150 JANEFF, JANKO: *Südosteuropa und der deutsche Geist*. Herrsching: Deutscher Hort Verlag, 1938. 96 pp.

MUNZ, MAX: *Die Verantwortlichkeit für die Judenverfolgungen im Ausland ...* See 5783.

4151 OLSHAUSEN, KLAUS: *Zwischenspiel auf dem Balkan. Die deutsche Politik gegenüber Jugoslawien und Griechenland von März bis Juli 1947*. Stuttgart: Deutsche Verlags-Anstalt, 1973. 375 pp., tabs., maps, bibl.

4152 ORLOW, DIETRICH: *The Nazis in the Balkans. A case study of totalitarian politics*. Pittsburgh, Pa.: University of Pittsburgh Press, 1968. 235 pp., tabs., bibl.

4153 SCHNEEFUSS, WALTER: *Deutschtum in Südost-Europa*. Leipzig: Goldmann, 1939. 145 pp.

4154 VAGO, BELA: *The shadow of the swastika. The rise of fascism and antisemitism in the Danube Basin, 1936–1939*. London: Saxon House, for the Institute of Jewish Affairs, 1975. 431 pp., tabs.

4155 WARD, BARBARA and others: *Hitler's route to Bagdad*. Prepared for ... the Fabian Society. By Barbara Ward, Barbara Buckmaster, Clare Hollingworth, Vandeleur Robinson, Lilo Linke. Introd.: Leonard Woolf. Maps: J. F. Horrabin. London: Allen & Unwin, 1939. 356 pp., maps, tabs. [On Yugoslavia, Bulgaria, Greece, Turkey.]

Bulgaria

4156 *Jahrbuch der deutsch-bulgarischen Gesellschaft*. Hrsg.: Ewald von Massow. Schriftl.: Kurt Haucker. Leipzig: Meiner, 1938/41. 3 vols., illus.

Greece

4157 CRUICKSHANK, CHARLES: *Greece 1940–1941*. London: Davis-Poynter, 1976. 206 pp.

4158 PANTEL, HANS-HENNING: *Griechenland zwischen Hammer und Amboss*. Leipzig: Goldmann, 1942. 118 pp., bibl.

4159 SCHRAMM-VON THADDEN, EHRENGARD: *Griechenland und die Grossmächte im Zweiten Weltkrieg*. Wiesbaden: Steiner, 1955. 244 pp., illus. (Veröffentlichungen des Instituts für Europäische Geschichte Mainz).

Hungary

4160 ÁDÁM, MAGDA and others: *Allianz Hitler–Horthy–Mussolini. Dokumente zur ungarischen Aussenpolitik, 1933–1944*. Einleitende Studie und Vorbereitung der Akten von Magda Ádám, Gyula Juhász, Lajos Kerekes. Redigiert von Lajos Kerekes. Budapest: Akadémiai Kiadó, 1966. 409 pp. [Transl. from the Hungarian.]

4161   FENYO, MARIO D.: *Hitler, Horthy, and Hungary. German–Hungarian relations, 1941–1944*. New Haven, Conn.: Yale University Press, 1972. 279 pp., bibl.

4162   GRATZ, GUSTAV: *Deutschungarische Probleme*. [Budapest]: Neues Sonntagsblatt, [1938]. 261 pp., tabs.

HORTHY, MIKLÓS
4163   SCHMIDT-PAULI, EDGAR VON: *Nikolaus von Horthy. Admiral, Volksheld und Reichsverweser*. Hamburg: Toth, 1942. 344 pp., illus., facsims. [First ed. 1936.]

4164   SZÍNAI, MIKLÓS & SZŰCS, LÁSZLÓ, eds.: *Horthy Miklós titkos iratai* [The secret papers of Nicolas Horthy]. Budapest: Kossuth Könyvkiadó, 1963. 533 pp., facsims., bibl. [2nd ed.]

4165   KERTESZ, STEPHEN D.: *Diplomacy in a whirlpool. Hungary between Nazi Germany and Soviet Russia*. Notre Dame, Ind.: University of Notre Dame Press, 1953. 271 pp.

4166   LACKO, M.: *Arrow-Cross men, National Socialists, 1935–1944*. Budapest: Akadémiai Kiadó, 1969. 112 pp.

4167   WEIDLEIN, JOHANN, ed.: *Geschichte der Ungarndeutschen 1930–1950*. Schorndorf: [priv. pr.], 1958. 408 pp.

Romania

4168   BECKER, JAKOB: *Bessarabien und sein Deutschtum*. Württemberg: Krug, 1966. 226 pp., facsim., maps, tabs., bibl.

4169   CERNEA, RADU: *Adevarul despre Germania național-socialistă* [The truth about National Socialist Germany]. Bucureşti: [no impr.], 1936. 208 pp.

4170   HARTL, HANS: *Das Schicksal des Deutschtums in Rumanien (1938–1945–1953)*. Würzburg: Holzner, 1958. 177 pp. (Beihefte zum Jahrbuch der Albertus-Universität Königsberg/Pr.).

4171   HILLGRUBER, ANDREAS: *Hitler, König Carol und Marschall Antonescu. Die deutsch-rumänischen Beziehungen 1938–1944*. Wiesbaden: Steiner, 1954. 382 pp., illus., bibl. (Veröffentlichungen des Institutes für europäische Geschichte Mainz).

4172   HÜGEL, KASPAR: *Das Banater deutsche Schulwesen in Rumänien von 1918 bis 1944*. München: Verlag des Südostdeutschen Kulturwerkes, 1968. 177 pp., map, bibl.

4173   INSTITUT FÜR STATISTIK UND BEVÖLKERUNGSPOLITIK DER DEUTSCHEN VOLKSGRUPPE IN RUMÄNIEN: *Die deutschen Siedlungen in Rumänien nach der Bestandsaufnahme vom 3. November 1940. Mit einer Karte …* Hermannstadt: Krafft & Drotleff, 1941. 64 pp., tabs., map.

4174   MIEGE, WOLFGANG: *Das Dritte Reich und die deutsche Volksgruppe in Rumänien 1933–38. Ein Beitrag zur nationalsozialistischen Volkstumspolitik*. Bern: Lang, 1972. 346 pp. (Europäische Hochschulschriften).

4175 SIMION, A: 'Les conditions politiques du Diktat de Vienne (30 Août 1940)'. [In] *Revue roumaine d'Histoire*. Tome XI, No. 3, 1972. Bucarest: Académie de la République Socialiste de Roumanie. Pp. 447–472.

Yugoslavia

4176 BURCHARD, WERNER and others: *Volkheitskundliche Untersuchung im deutschen Siedlungsgebiet in der südslawischen Batschka*. Reichssiegerarbeit der Sparte 'Rasse und Gesundheitswesen' im Reichsberufswettkampf der deutschen Studenten 1936/37—Mannschaft der Fachgruppe Medizin der Studentenführung Universität Halle. Mannschaftsführer: Werner Burchard. München: Lehmann, 1938. 188 pp., illus., diagrs., plans, tabs., family trees.

4177 REISTER, HEINRICH & EGGER, LEOPOLD: *Das grosse Angebot*. Hrsg.: Landespropagandaamt der deutschen Volksgruppe in Jugoslawien. Novisad-Neusatz: Druckerei und Verlags-AG, 1941. 112 pp., illus.

4178 SOMMER, F.: *Fern vom Land der Ahnen. Geschichte der deutschen evangelischen Gemeinde Schutzberg in Bosnien 1895–1942* [and] *Notvolle Heimkehr. Das Schicksal der Bosniendeutschen 1942–1960*. Mülheim, Ruhr: [priv. pr.], 1960. 180 pp., illus., tabs.

4179 WUESCHT, JOHANN: *Jugoslawien und das Dritte Reich. Eine dokumentierte Geschichte der deutsch-jugoslawischen Beziehungen von 1933 bis 1945*. Stuttgart: Seewald, 1969. 359 pp., maps, tabs., bibls.

4. BALTIC STATES

4180 *Estländischer deutscher Jugendkalender*. Tallin: Wassermann, 1938. 191 pp., illus., map, tabs., mus. scores.

4181 GALÉRA, KARL SIEGMAR Baron von: *Deutsche unter Fremdherrschaft. Die Geschichte der geraubten und unerlösten deutschen Gebiete. 1. Buch: Polen und die baltischen Nachfolgestaaten im Kampf gegen deutsches Volkstum.* Leipzig: Nationale Verlagsgesellschaft, 1933. 344 pp., illus., tabs.

4182 MYLLYNIEMI, SEPPO: *Die baltische Krise 1938–1941*. Aus dem Finnischen übersetzt. Stuttgart: Deutsche Verlags-Anstalt, 1979. 167 pp., map, bibl. (Institut für Zeitgeschichte München).

4183 OERTZEN, F. W. von: *Baltenland. Eine Geschichte der deutschen Sendung im Baltikum*. München: Bruckmann, 1939. 337 pp., maps.

4184 REI, AUGUST, comp.: *Nazi–Soviet conspiracy and the Baltic states. Diplomatic documents and other evidence*. London: Boreas Publ. Co., 1948. 61 pp., (Issued under authority of the Estonian National Council and the Estonian Information Centre).

4185 [RIGA] *Deutsche Kulturleistungen in Riga. Dokumente*. Danzig: Kafemann, 1939. 112 pp., illus., facsims. (Hrsg.: Ostland-Institut in Danzig).

4186 THALHEIM, KARL C. & ZIEGFELD, A. HILLEN, eds.: *Der deutsche Osten. Seine*

Geschichte, sein Wesen und seine Aufgabe. Berlin: Propyläen-Verlag, 1936. 624 pp., illus., maps, facsims., tabs.

4187 ZIEGLER, MATTHES, comp.: *Der Deutsche im Baltikum. Für die Jugend zusammengestellt*. Langensalza: Beltz, 1934. 120 pp., illus.

5. CZECHOSLOVAKIA

Up to 1938

4188 BRUEGEL, J[OHANN] W[OLFGANG]: *Czechoslovakia before Munich. The German minority problem and British appeasement policy*. London: Cambridge University Press, 1973. xiii + 334 pp., map, tabs., bibl.

4189 BRÜGEL, JOHANN WOLFGANG: *Tschechen und Deutsche 1918–1938*. München: Nymphenburger Verlagshandlung, 1967. 662 pp., tabs., bibl.

4190 CÉSAR, JAROSLAV & ČERNÝ, BOHUMIL: *Politika německých buržoazních stran v Československu v letech 1918–1938* [History of the policy of the German bourgeois parties in Czechoslovakia, 1918–1938]. Praha: Nakl. Československé Akademie Věd, 1962. Illus., facsims., tabs., summaries in German.
Dil I: *1918–1929*. 512 pp.
Dil II: *1930–1938*. 584 pp., bibl.

4191 ENGLIŠ, KAREL: *'German Socialism' as programme of the Sudete German Party. A critical analysis*. Transl. from the Czech. Prague: 'Orbis', 1938. 93 pp., tabs. (Czechoslovak Sources and Documents).

4192 FOCHLER-HAUKE, GUSTAV: *Deutscher Volksboden und deutsches Volkstum in der Tschechoslowakei. Eine geographische-geopolitische Zusammenschau*. Heidelberg: Vowinckel, 1937. 324 pp., maps, bibl.

4193 HISTORICUS, pseud.: *Il problema dell'Europa Centrale*. Roma: Istituto Nazionale di Cultura Fascista, 1938. 127 pp., maps, tab. [On the Sudeten problem.]

4194 HÖSS, KONSTANTIN, comp.: *Die SdP [Sudetendeutsche Partei] im Parlament. Ein Jahresbericht 1935/36*. Im ... Auftr. der SdP und der KdP zusammengest. Karlsbad: Frank, 1937. 335 pp., illus., diagrs., tabs., list of party newspapers.

4195 KOUTEK, JAROSLAV: *Nacistická Pátá Kolona v ČSR* [The Nazi Fifth Column in Czechoslovakia]. Praha: Svaz Protifašistickych bojovniků, 1962. 254 pp., illus.

4196 KRÁL, VÁCLAV, ed.: *Die Deutschen in der Tschechoslowakei 1933–1947. Dokumentensammlung*. Praha: Nakl. Československé Akademie Věd, 1964. 663 pp. (Acta Occupationis Bohemiae et Moraviae).

4197 KREBS, HANS: *Kampf in Böhmen*. Berlin: Volk und Reich Verlag, 1937. 232 pp., illus., maps, facsims.

4198   LEONCINI, FRANCESCO: *La questione dei Sudeti, 1918–1938*. Padova: Liviana, 1976. 512 pp., map, bibl. (Universita degli Studi di Padova).

4199   PLEYER, WILHELM: *Der Puchner. Ein Grenzlandschicksal. Roman*. München: Langen & Müller, 1934. 363 pp.

4200   SMELSER, RONALD M.: *The Sudeten problem, 1933–1938. Volkstumspolitik and the formulation of Nazi foreign policy*. Folkestone, Kent: Dawson, 1975. x + 324 pp., diagr., bibl. [German version: *Das Sudetenproblem und das Dritte Reich 1933–1938*. München: Oldenbourg, 1979.]

4201   VORBACH, KURT: *200 000 Sudetendeutsche zuviel! Der tschechische Vernichtungskampf gegen 3.5 Millionen Sudetendeutsche und seine volkspolitischen Auswirkungen*. München: Deutscher Volksverlag, 1936. 384 pp., illus., maps, tabs., bibl.

4202   WELISCH, SOPHIE ANN: *The Sudeten German question in the League of Nations*. Dissertation [pres. to] Fordham University, New York. [Publ. as microfilm by] University of Michigan: 1969. 254 pp., map, bibl.

4203   WISKEMANN, ELIZABETH: *Czechs and Germans. A study of the struggle in the historic provinces of Bohemia and Moravia*. London: Oxford University Press, under auspices of the Royal Institute of International Affairs, 1938. 299 pp., maps, bibl.

4204   WOLMAR, WOLFGANG WOLFRAM VON: *Prag und das Reich. 600 Jahre Kampf deutscher Studenten*. Dresden: Müller, 1943. 611 pp., illus., facsims.

Annexation

4205   BENEŠ, VOJTA & GINSBURG, R. A.: *Ten million prisoners (Protectorate Bohemia and Moravia)*. Chicago, Ill.: Czech-American National Alliance, 1940. 180 pp., port.

4206   DELFINER, HENRY: *Vienna broadcasts to Slovakia, 1938–1939. A case study in subversion*. New York: Columbia University Press, 1974. 142 pp., bibl.

4207   BODENSIECK, HEINRICH: 'Das Dritte Reich und die Lage der Tschechoslowakei nach München'. [In] *Vierteljahrshefte für Zeitgeschichte*, Heft 3, Juli 1961. Pp. 249–261.

4208   DEUTSCHE BANK: *Das Protektorat Böhmen und Mähren im deutschen Wirtschaftsraum*. Berlin: 1939. 79 pp., map, tabs., bibl.

4209   HENLEIN, KONRAD: *Heim ins Reich. Reden aus den Jahren 1937 und 1938*. Hrsg.: Ernst Tscherne. Reichenberg: NS Gauverlag Sudetenland, 1939. 131 pp., port.

4210   HOFFMANN, HEINRICH, ed.: *Hitler befreit Sudetenland*. Geleitw.: Konrad Henlein. Berlin: Zeitgeschichte-Verlag, 1938. [60 pp.], illus.

4211   KOGEL, (Hauptmann): *Einmarsch ins Sudetenland*. Flensburg: Flensburger Nachrichten Grenzverlag, 1938. 31 pp., illus., maps.

See also 4483–4499.

6. EIRE

4212 Bauer, Robert: *Irland im Schatten Englands. Ein Kapitel britischer Ausrottungspolitik.* Berlin: Junker & Dünnhaupt, 1940. 52 pp., tabs., bibl.

4213 Fromme, Franz: *Irlands Kampf um die Freiheit. Darstellung und Beispiel einer völkischen Bewegung bis in die neueste Zeit.* Berlin: Siemens, 1933. 179 pp., illus., map, bibl.

4214 Share, Bernard: *The emergency. Neutral Ireland, 1939–1945.* Dublin: Gill & Macmillan, 1978. xiii + 146 pp., illus., bibl.

7. FRANCE

4215 Bothmer, Hermann von: *Germanisches Bauerntum in Nordfrankreich.* Goslar: Blut und Boden Verlag, 1939. 91 pp., illus., maps, tabs., bibl.

4216 Buschmann, Roland: *Hinter der Maginot-Linie. Das französische Volk Opfer systematischer Irreführung.* Berlin: Limpert, 1939. 95 pp., illus. (71.–110. Taus.).

4217 Cameron, Elizabeth R.: *Prologue to appeasement. A study in French foreign policy.* Washington, D.C.: American Council on Public Affairs, 1942. ix + 228 pp., illus., bibl.

4218 Carré, Jean-Marie: *Les écrivains français et le mirage allemand, 1800–1940.* Paris: Boivin, 1947. 223 pp.

4219 Centre de Documentation Juive Contemporaine: *Catalogues.* Paris: 1964/68. No. 1: *La France de l'Affaire Dreyfus à nos jours.* Publ. 1964. 266 pp. [Incl.: 'La France sous l'occupation', pp. 71–183.] No. 2: *La France—Le Troisième Reich—Israél.* Publ. 1968. 254 pp.

4220 Centre National de la Recherche Scientifique: *Les relations franco-allemandes 1933–1939. Strasbourg 7–10 Octobre 1975.* Paris: 1976. 424 pp. [Symposium.]

4221 Dobert, Eitel Wolf: *Ein Nazi entdeckt Frankreich. Aus Tagebuchblättern.* Bern: Gotthelf-Verlag, 1932. 174 pp. [French version: *Un Nazi découvre la France.* Neuchâtel: Delachaux & Niestle, 1933.]

4222 *Documents diplomatiques français, 1932–1939.* [Ed. by] Ministère des Affaires étrangères, Commission de Publication des Documents relatifs aux Origines de la Guerre 1939–1945. Paris: Imprimerie Nationale, 1963– continuing. Série 1: *1932–1935.* Série 2: *1936–1939.*

4223 Engelmayer, Otto: *Die Deutschlandideologie der Franzosen. Ihre geistesgeschichtlichen Grundlagen.* Berlin: Junker & Dünnhaupt, 1936. 142 pp.

4224 François-Poncet, André: *Souvenirs d'une ambassade à Berlin. Septembre 1931–Octobre 1938.* Paris: Flammarion, 1946. 356 pp. [English version:

The fateful years. London: Gollancz, 1949. German version: *Als Botschafter in Berlin 1931–1938*. Mainz: Kupferberg, 1947.]

4225 GALLO, MAX: *Cinquième colonne, 1930–1940. Et ce fut la défaite* ... [Paris]: Plon, 1970. 333 pp., illus., facsims., diagr.

4226 GRIMM, FRIEDRICH: *Frankreich-Berichte 1934 bis 1944*. Hrsg. vom Kreis seiner Freunde. Bodman: Hohenstaufen-Verlag, 1972. 306 pp.

4227 GRIMM, FREDERIC, ed.: *Hitler et la France*. Préface: J. von Ribbentrop. Paris: Plon, 1938. 182 pp. [Extracts from speeches and French reactions to them.]

4228 HOFFMANN, HEINRICH: *Deutschland in Paris. Ein Bildbuch*. München: Hoffmann [and] Paris: Pavillon Allemand (Exposition Internationale), 1937. 128 pp., illus.

4229 HOGGAN, DAVID L.: *Frankreichs Widerstand gegen den Zweiten Weltkrieg. Die französische Aussenpolitik von 1934 bis 1939*. Tübingen: Verlag der deutschen Hochschullehrer-Zeitung, 1963. 520 pp., bibl. (Veröffentlichungen des Instituts für deutsche Nachkriegsgeschichte). [Nazi apologetics.]

4230 KIMMEL, ADOLF: *Der Aufstieg des Nationalsozialismus im Spiegel der französischen Presse 1930–1933*. Bonn: Bouvier, 1969. 218 pp., bibl.

4231 KLING, HERMANN: *Zweitausend Jahre Kampf um den Rhein. Ein Überblick über die deutsch-französischen Beziehungen bis zur Gegenwart*. Stuttgart: Holland & Josenhans, 1935. 474 pp., illus., maps, diagrs., bibl.

4232 MANGOLD, EWALD K. B.: *Frankreich und der Rassengedanke. Eine politische Kernfrage Europas*. München: Lehmann, 1937. 152 pp., bibl.

4233 MAURRAS, CHARLES: *Devant l'Allemagne éternelle. Gaulois, Germains, Latins. Chronique d'une résistance*. Paris: Éds. 'À l'Étoile', 1937. ix + 399 pp.

4234 MAYER, NORBERT: *Ungewisses Frankreich. Frankreichs Presse zum deutsch-französischen Problem seit 1933*. München: Hugendubel, 1936. 215 pp., illus., bibl.

4235 MICAUD, CHARLES A.: *The French right and Nazi Germany, 1933–1939. A study of public opinion*. Durham, N.C.: Duke University Press, 1943. 255 pp.

4236 *L'Ordre Nouveau. Mission ou démission de la France. Réponse à Hitler*. Paris: Fustier, 1936. 64 pp.

4237 SCHRAMM, WILHELM VON: *... ...sprich von Frieden, wenn Du den Krieg willst. Die psychologischen Offensiven Hitlers gegen die Franzosen 1933 bis 1939. Ein Bericht*. Mainz: von Hase & Koehler, 1973. 208 pp., bibl.

Alsace-Lorraine

4238 BARON, HEINRICH: *Mit Karl Roos—dem Blutzeugen des deutschen Elsass—die letzten Tage in der Todeszelle. Bericht*. Strassburg: Strassburger Monatshefte, 1940. 46 pp., illus.

4239 *Das deutsche Elsass. Ausstellung der Bayerischen Staatsbibliothek*. München: 1941. 162 + 12 pp., illus., facsims., bibls.

French Empire

4240 SCHMITZ-KAIRO, PAUL: *Frankreich in Nord-Afrika*. Leipzig: Goldmann, 1938. 128 pp., maps.

4241 SEMJONOW, JURI: *Glanz und Elend des französischen Kolonialreiches*. Berlin: Deutscher Verlag, 1942. 569 pp., illus., maps, tab.

4242 SORIA, GEORGES: *Un grave danger: l'infiltration allemande au Maroc*. Préface: Léon Archimbaud. Paris: 'Paix et Liberté', [1937?]. 28 pp., map.

8. GREAT BRITAIN

4243 AIGNER, DIETRICH: *Das Ringen um England. Das deutsch-britische Verhältnis. Die öffentliche Meinung 1933–1939. Tragödie zweier Völker*. München: Bechtle, 1969. 444 + 219 pp., diagrs., tabs., bibls.

4244 ANGLO-GERMAN ACADEMIC BUREAU: *Report on the activities ... during the first decade of its existence*. Issued on the ... 10th anniversary, 16th March 1938. London: 1938. 29 pp.

4245 BERBER, FRIEDRICH, ed.: *Deutschland–England 1933–1939. Die Dokumente des deutschen Friedenswillens*. 3. Aufl. Essen: Essener Verlagsanstalt, 1942. 235 pp. (Veröffentlichungen des Deutschen Instituts für Aussenpolitische Forschung). [First ed. 1940.]

4246 COWLING, MAURICE: *The impact of Hitler. British politics and British policy 1933–1940*. London: Cambridge University Press, 1975. 561 pp., port.

4247 DEISSMANN, ERNST: *Deutsche Arbeit in England auf dem Gebiet der kulturellen Beziehungen. Jahresbericht des Deutschen Akademischen Austauschdienstes*. London: 1933. 49 pp.

4248 *Documents on British foreign policy, 1919–1939*. London: HMSO, 1947–
Series 2: *1929–1938*. Eds.: Rohan Butler, J. P. T. Bury, M. E. Lambert.
Series 3: *1938–1939*. Eds.: E. L. Woodward, Rohan Butler [and others].
[Complete in 10 vols.]

4249 EDEN, ANTHONY; *The Eden memoirs*. London: Cassell, 1960/65.
I: *Full circle*. Publ. 1960. 619 pp., maps.
II: *Facing the dictators*. Publ. 1962. 159 pp.
III: *The reckoning*. Publ. 1965. 623 pp.

4250 GANNON, FRANKLIN REID: *The British press and Germany, 1936–1939*. Oxford: Clarendon Press, 1971. x + 314 pp., bibl.

4251 GEYR VON SCHWEPPENBURG, LEO DIETRICH Frhr.: *The critical years*. Introd.: Leslie Hore-Belisha. London: Allen Wingate, 1952. viii + 207 pp., illus. [German orig.: *Erinnerungen eines Militärattachés. London 1933–1937*. Stuttgart: Deutsche Verlags-Anstalt, 1949.]

4252 GILBERT, MARTIN: *The roots of appeasement*. London: Weidenfeld & Nicolson, 1966. 254 pp., maps, bibl.

4253 GOLDING, LOUIS: *A letter to Adolf Hitler*. London: Leonard & Virginia Woolf, 1932. 28 pp.

4254 GOLDMAN, AARON L.: 'The Link and the Anglo-German Review'. [In] *The South Atlantic Quarterly*. Vol. LXXI, No. 3, Summer 1972. Durham, N.C.: Duke University Press. Pp. 424–433.

4255 GRANZOW, BRIGITTE: *A mirror of Nazism. British opinion and the emergence of Hitler, 1929–1933*. Introd.: Bernard Crick. London: Gollancz, 1964. 248 pp.

4256 GRIFFITHS, RICHARD: *Fellow travellers of the Right. British enthusiasts for Nazi Germany, 1933–1939*. London: Constable, 1980.

4257 GRIMM, HANS: *Englische Rede. Wie ich den Engländer sehe*. Deutscher und englischer Wortlaut. Gütersloh: Bertelsmann, 1938. 55 pp.

4258 HARASZTI, ÉVA: *Treaty-breakers or 'Realpolitiker'? The Anglo-German naval agreement of June 1935*. Boppard a. Rh.: Boldt, 1974. 276 pp., tabs., bibl.

4259 HAUSER, OSWALD: *England und das Dritte Reich. Eine dokumentierte Geschichte der englisch–deutschen Beziehungen von 1933 bis 1939 auf Grund unveröffentlichter Akten aus dem britischen Staatsarchiv. 1. Band: 1933–1936*. Stuttgart: Seewald, 1972. 317 pp., bibl.

HENDERSON, NEVILE
4260 HENDERSON, NEVILE: *Failure of a mission. Berlin 1937–1939*. London: Hodder & Stoughton, 1940. 318 pp. [French version: *Deux ans avec Hitler*. Paris: Flammarion, 1940.]

4261 STRAUCH, RUDI: *Sir Nevile Henderson. Britischer Botschafter in Berlin von 1937 bis 1939. Ein Beitrag zur diplomatischen Vorgeschichte des Zweiten Weltkrieges*. Bonn: Röhrscheid, 1959. 384 pp., bibl.

4262 HENKE, JOSEF: *England in Hitlers politischen Kalkül 1935–1939*. Boppard a.Rh.: Boldt, 1973. 346 pp., bibl. (Schriften des Bundesarchivs).

4263 HILLSON, NORMAN: *I speak of Germany. A plea for Anglo-German friendship*. London: Routledge, 1937. 300 pp., illus.

4264 INDORF, HANS: *Fair Play und der 'englische Sportgeist'*. Hamburg: Friederichsen, de Gruyter, 1938. 78 pp., bibl.

4265 KEANE, RICHARD, ed.: *Germany—what next? Being an examination of the German menace in so far as it affects Great Britain*. By L. S. Amery [and others]. Harmondsworth, Middx.: Penguin Books, 1939. 248 pp.

4266 KENNEDY, JOHN F.: *Why England slept*. London: Hutchinson, 1940. 40 pp., bibl.

4267 KRIEGER, HEINZ: *England und die Judenfrage in Geschichte und Gegenwart.* Frankfurt a.M.: Diesterweg, 1938. 115 pp., bibl.

4268 LEHMANN, MAX: *Die Erziehung zum Deutschenhass in der englischen Schule. Deutschland in den englischen Schulgeschichtsbüchern.* Berlin: Junker & Dünnhaupt, 1942. 139 pp., bibl. (Schriften des Deutschen Instituts für Aussenpolitische Forschung).

4269 LESSLE, MANFRED: *Englands Weg zum Appeasement 1932–1936. Ein Beitrag zur Vorkriegsgeschichte Englands, dargestellt unter besonderer Berücksichtigung der Presse.* Dissertation [pres. to] Universität Heidelberg. 1969. 278 pp., bibl.

4270 LONDONDERRY, Marquess of (Charles S. H. Vane-Tempest-Stewart): *Ourselves and Germany.* London: Hale, 1938. 185 pp., ports. [Also: Harmondsworth, Middx.: Penguin Books, 1938. Incl. a new preface, a second postscript (on Munich Pact) and appendix.]

4271 MESSERSCHMIDT, ERNST AUGUST: *Propaganda und Einsatz der englischen Linksgruppen auf dem Gebiet der Aussenpolitik der Gegenwart.* Dissertation [pres. to] Hansische Universität Hamburg. 1939. 224 pp., bibl.

4272 MEYERS, REINHARD P. F. W.: *The attitude of the British Cabinet and senior advisers, concerned with decision-making, towards the resurgence of Nazi Germany, with particular reference to the period ending with the Munich crisis.* Thesis [pres. to] University of Reading. 1972. 409 pp., diagrs., tabs., bibl.

4273 REVENTLOW, ERNST Graf zu: *Der Vampir des Festlandes. Eine Darstellung der englischen Politik nach ihren Treibkräften, Mitteln und Wirkungen.* 13. bis zur Gegenwart fortgeführte Aufl. Berlin: Mittler, 1939. 226 pp. [Swedish version: *Den Engelske jämviktspolitiken.* Stockholm: Svea Rikes, 1939.]

4274 ROGGE, HEINRICH: *Hitlers Versuche zur Verständigung mit England.* Berlin: Junker & Dünnhaupt, 1940. 93 pp. (3. unveränd. Aufl. Schriften des Deutschen Instituts für Aussenpolitische Forschung).

4275 SCHULZE, KURT & LEWINGTON, H. E.: *Der Fuehrer des Deutschen Reiches. A short account of his life and work.* London: Harrap, 1935. 80 pp., illus. [For use in British schools.]

4276 SETON-WATSON, R. W.: *Britain and the dictators. A survey of post-war British policy.* London: Cambridge University Press, 1938. 460 pp.

4277 THOST, HANS W.: *Als Nationalsozialist in England.* München: Eher, 1939. 382 pp.

4278 TÖNNIES, NORBERT: *Der Krieg vor dem Kriege. Englands Propaganda bis zum 3. September 1939.* Essen: Essener Verlagsanstalt, 1940. 310 pp.

4279 VANSITTART, ROBERT: *The mist procession. Autobiography.* London: Hutchinson, 1958. 568 pp., port.

4280 WOOTTON, GRAHAM: *The official history of the British Legion.* London:

MacDonald & Evans, 1956. 348 pp., illus., facsims. [Incl. British Legion contacts with the Third Reich and suggestions for policing a Sudeten plebiscite.]

Secret contacts

4281 DAHLERUS, BIRGER: *The last attempt.* Introd.: Norman Birkett. London: Hutchinson, 1947. 134 pp., illus., facsims., maps. [Transl. from the Swedish. German version: *Der letzte Versuch. London–Berlin Sommer 1939.*]

4282 DOUGLAS-HAMILTON, JAMES: *Motive for a mission. The story behind Rudolf Hess's flight to Britain.* Forew.: Alan Bullock. Edinburgh: Mainstream Publ., 1979. 329 pp., illus., bibl. [First ed. 1971. A considerable part of the work deals with Albrecht Haushofer and British wartime contacts with Germans.]

4283 GRAHAM-MURRAY, JAMES: *The sword and the umbrella.* Isle of Man: Gibbs & Phillips, 1964. 252 pp., illus., bibl.

4284 KIRKPATRICK, IVONE: *The inner circle. Memoirs.* London: Macmillan, 1959. x + 275 pp., illus. [Incl. interrogation of Rudolf Hess.]

4285 RIBBENTROP, ANNELIES VON: *Die Kriegsschuld des Widerstandes. Aus britischen Geheimdokumenten 1938/39.* Aus dem Nachlass hrsg. von Rudolf von Ribbentrop. Leoni am Starnberger See: Druffel, 1975. 414 pp., bibl. (2. Aufl.).

4286 YOUNG, A. P.: *The 'X' documents.* Ed.: Sidney Aster. London: André Deutsch, 1974. 253 pp., bibl.

See also 3484–3526.

British Empire and Commonwealth

AUSTRALIA
4287 LODEWYCKX, AUGUSTIN: *Die Deutschen in der australischen Wirtschaft.* Stuttgart: Enke, 1938. 62 pp., tabs., bibl.

CANADA
4288 KIRKCONNELL, WATSON: *Canada, Europe and Hitler.* Toronto: Oxford University Press, 1939. vii + 213 pp.

4289 LEHMANN, HEINZ: *Das Deutschtum in Westkanada.* Berlin: Junker & Dünnhaupt, 1939. 414 pp., map, diagr., tabs. (Veröffentlichungen der Hochschule für Politik).

INDIA
4290 BARTZ, KARL: *Englands Weg nach Indien. Schicksalsstunden des britischen Weltreiches.* Berlin: Ullstein, 1936. 314 pp., illus.

4291 CHOWDHURI, EMRAN HUSAIN: *Der indische Arbeiter unter britischer Herrschaft.* Würzburg-Aumühle: Triltsch, 1939. 125 pp.

4292 MARK, DIETER: *Blutrache gegen England! Die Fahne des Propheten über Nordwestindien.* Berlin: Deutscher Verlag für Politik und Wirtschaft, 1940. 62 pp.

4293 SCHMIDT, WERNER: *Der Kulturanteil des Deutschtums am Aufbau des Burenvolkes.* Hannover: Hahn, 1938. 303 pp., illus., facsims., map, tabs., bibl. (Sonderveröffentlichung II der Geographischen Gesellschaft zu Hannover).

4294 SOUTH WEST AFRICA COMMISSION: *Report.* Pretoria: Union of South Africa, 1936. 102 pp., tabs. [On Nazi activity in the area.]

9. LOW COUNTRIES

4295 GERMAN LIBRARY OF INFORMATION: *Allied intrigue in the Low Countries. Further documents concerning the Anglo-French policy of extending the war. Full text of White Book No. 5.* New York: 1940. xxxix + 94 pp., facsims., map. [German orig.: Auswärtiges Amt: *Die Generalstabbesprechungen Englands und Frankreichs mit Belgien und die Niederlanden.* Berlin: Deutscher Verlag, 1940.]

4296 LOHSE, GÜNTER: *Die gebrochene Neutralität. Belgiens und Hollands Entscheidung für England.* Essen: Essener Verlagsanstalt, 1943. 268 pp., bibl.

4297 PETRI-KÖLN, FRANZ: *Die Niederlande (Holland und Belgien) und das Reich. Volkstum, Geschichte, Gegenwart.* Bonn: Röhrscheid, 1940. 56 pp., maps.

Belgium

4298 *Belgium. The official account of what happened, 1939–1940.* London: Evans, for Belgian Ministry of Foreign Affairs, 1941. 110 + x pp., maps, facsims.

4299 DEHOTTAY, PETER: *Die Kriegsschuld der belgischen Presse.* Berlin: Junker & Dünnhaupt, 1942. 87 pp.

4300 *Documents diplomatiques belges, 1920–1940. La politique de sécurité extérieure.* Publ. par Ch. de Visscher, F. Vanlangenhove. Bruxelles: Palais des Académies, 1964/66. 6 vols.

4301 PESCH, LUDWIG: *Volk und Nation in der Geistesgeschichte Belgiens.* Berlin: Volk und Reich Verlag, 1941. 135 pp., bibl.

4302 STRIEFLER, ERNST: *Gottfried Kurth. Ein deutsch-belgisches Grenzlandschicksal.* Leipzig: Hirzel, 1941. 84 pp.

4303 WIBALD, pseud.: *Eupen-Malmedy, St. Vith.* Langensalza: Beltz, 1937. 60 pp., illus., map, bibl. (Der Deutsche im Grenzlande).

4304 WULLUS-RUDIGER, J.-A.: *La Belgique et la crise européenne 1914–1945.* Paris: Berger-Levrault, 1944/45. 523 + 256 pp., map. [In 2 vols.]

4305 WULLUS-RUDIGER, J.-A. (under name Armand Wullus): *Les origines internationales du drame Belge de 1940.* Bruxelles: Vanderlinden, 1950. xiv + 402 pp., map.

4306   *Die Deutsch-Niederländische Gesellschaft im Jahre 1938.* Berlin: [1939?]. 155 pp., illus., tabs.

4306a HAIGHTON, ALFRED A.: *Waarheen voert Mussert?* Oisterwijk: Uitg. 'Oisterwijk', [1937]. 266 pp. [Anton Mussert, was leader of the Nationaal-Socialist Beweging.]

4307   KOOY, G. A.: *Het échec van een 'volkse' beweging. Nazificatie en denazificatie in Nederland 1931–1945.* Assen: van Gorcum, 1964. 359 pp., maps, tabs., bibl.

4308   LAURENS, ANNE: *L'affaire King Kong. Cinquième colonne aux Pays-Bas.* Paris: Michel, 1969. 223 pp., illus., bibl.

4309   MANNING, A. F. & KERSTEN, A. E., eds.: *Documenten betreffende de buitenlandse politiek van Nederland 1919–1945. Periode C: 1940–1945.* 's-Gravenhage: Nijhoff, 1976– continuing. Bibls., lists of documents in English. (Rijksgeschiedkundige Publicatiën).
Deel I: *10. Mei–31. Okt. 1940.* Publ. 1976. xcv + 594 pp.
Deel II: *1. Nov. 1940–31. Mei 1941.* Publ. 1977. lxxxv + 635 pp.

4310   OSZWALD, R. P., ed.: *Deutsch-niederländische Symphonie.* Wolfshagen-Scharbeutz: Westphal, 1944. 360 pp., illus., bibl. [2nd enl. ed.; first ed. 1937. On Raf Verhulst.]

4311   SCHWÄGERL, ANTON: *Das Auslanddeutschtum im niederländischen Kolonial-bereich unter Berücksichtigung der geographischen und sozialen Verhält-nisse.* Weimar: Böhlau, 1937. ix + 355 pp., map, tabs., bibl.

10. MEMEL

4312   BROCK, PAUL: *Die auf den Morgen warten ...! Roman.* München: Eher, 1939. 333 pp. [On Memel Germans.]

4313   KALIJARVI, THORSTEN V.: *The Memel Statute. Its origin, legal nature and observation to the present day.* London: Hale, 1937. 255 pp., bibl.

4314   LEERS, JOHANN VON: *Memelland.* München: Eher, 1932. 31 pp. (Grossdeutsche Forderungen).

4315   PLIEG, ERNST ALBRECHT: *Das Memelland 1920–1939. Deutsche Autonomie-bestrebung im litauischen Gesamtstaat.* Würzburg: Holzner, 1962. 268 pp., bibl.

4316   PREGEL, REINHOLD: *Das Schicksal des Memelgebietes.* 2. Aufl. Langensalza: Beltz, 1936. 100 pp., illus., map.

11. POLAND

4317   BREYER, RICHARD: *Das Deutsche Reich und Polen 1932–1937. Aussenpolitik und Volksgruppenfragen.* Würzburg: Holzner, 1955. 372 pp.

4318 BROSZAT, MARTIN: *Zweihundert Jahre deutsche Polenpolitik.* München: Ehrenwirth, 1963. 269 pp., map.

4319 GOLCZEWSKI, FRANK: *Das Deutschlandbild der Polen 1918–1939. Eine Untersuchung der Historiographie und der Publizistik.* Düsseldorf: Droste, 1974. 316 pp., bibl.

4320 LIPSKI, JÓZEF: *Diplomat in Berlin, 1933–1939. Papers and memoirs.* Ed.: Wacław Jędrzejewicz. New York: Columbia University Press, 1968. 679 pp., illus., facsim., bibl.

4321 MINISTRY FOR FOREIGN AFFAIRS, Republic of Poland: *Official documents concerning Polish–German and Polish–Soviet relations 1933–1939.* Published by authority of the Polish Government. London: Hutchinson, [1939]. 222 pp.

4322 PETER, EGON, ed.: *Raubstaat Polen.* Berlin: Nibelungen-Verlag, 1939. 159 pp., facsim., illus., maps.

4323 POZNANSKI, CZESLAW: *The flaming border.* Pref.: Adam Ciolkosz. London: Hutchinson, [1943]. 92 pp.

4324 WOJCIECHOWSKI, MARIAN: *Die polnisch-deutschen Beziehungen 1933–1938.* Leiden: Brill, 1971. 583 pp., bibl. [Polish orig.: *Stosunki polsko-niemieckie 1933–1938.*]

See also 4509–4518.

German minority

4325 BIERSCHENK, THEODOR: *Die deutsche Volksgruppe in Polen 1934–1939.* Kitzingen: Holzner, 1954. 405 pp., map, bibl.

4326 CYGAŃSKI, MIROSŁAW: *Mniejszość niemiecka w Polsce Centralnej w latach 1919–1939* [German minorities in Central Poland, 1919–1939]. Łodz: Wyd. Łodskie, 1962. 184 pp.

4327 DWINGER, EDWIN ERICH: *Der Tod in Polen. Die volksdeutsche Passion.* Jena: Diederichs, 1940. 172 pp.

4328 HARTMANN, HANS: *Höllenmarsch der Volksdeutschen in Polen September 1939. Auf Grund ärztlicher Dokumente dargestellt.* Berlin: Verlag Neues Volk, 1940. 106 pp., facsims.

4329 KAUDER, VIKTOR, ed.: *Das Deutschtum in Polen.* Leipzig: Hirzel, 1939. 546 pp., illus., maps.

4330 KRIEGER, ARNOLD: *Empörung in Thorn. Ein weichseldeutscher Roman.* München: Eher, 1942. 367 pp.

4331 LESNIEWSKI, ANDRZEJ, ed.: *Irredenta und Provokationen. Zur Geschichte der deutschen Minderheit in Polen.* Poznań: Wyd. Zachodnie, 1960. 71 pp., illus., facsims. [French version: *La Ve colonne allemande en Pologne.*]

4332 *Looking East. Germany beyond the Vistula.* Berlin: Terramare Office, 1933. 81 pp., illus., map.

346

4333 LÜCK, KURT, ed.: *Deutscher Gestalter und Ordner im Osten.* 2. erw. Aufl. Leipzig: Hirzel, 1942. xii + 364 pp., illus., facsims. (Forschungen zur deutsch-polnischen Nachbarschaft im ostmitteleuropäischen Raum).

4334 LÜCK, KURT, ed.: *Volksdeutsche Soldaten unter Polens Fahnen. Tatsachenberichte von der anderen Front aus dem Feldzug der 18 Tage.* In Verbindung mit der 'Zentrale für die Gräber der ermordeten Volksdeutschen beim Reichsstatthalter im Reichsgau Wartheland'. 2. ergänz. Aufl. Berlin: Verlag Grenze und Ausland, 1940. 161 pp.

4335 NASARSKI, PETER E.: *Deutsche Jugendbewegung und Jugendarbeit in Polen 1919–1939.* Würzburg: Holzner, 1957. 134 pp., bibl.

4336 THE POLISH MINISTRY OF INFORMATION: *The German fifth column in Poland.* London: Hutchinson, [1939?]. 157 pp., illus., facsims.

4337 POSPIESZALSKI, KAROL MARIAN: *The case of 58,000 'Volksdeutsche'. An investigation into Nazi claims concerning losses of the German minority in Poland before and during September 1939.* Poznań: Wyd. Instytutu Zachodni, 1959. 218 pp., facsim., tabs. [Text in Polish, English, German.]

4338 SCHADEWALDT, HANS, comp.: *Polish acts of atrocity against the German minority in Poland. Compilation founded on documentary evidence and published for the German Foreign Office.* 2nd ed. with important addenda. Berlin: Volk und Reich Verlag [and] German Library of Information, 1940. 259 pp., illus., facsims.

Danzig and the Polish Corridor

4339 BASSAREK, ARTUR: *Danzigs Befreiung. Ein Tatsachenbericht mit Bildern.* Danzig: Kafemann, 1939. 39 pp., illus.

4340 BURCKHARDT, CARL J.: *Meine Danziger Mission, 1937–1939.* München: Callwey, 1960. 366 pp., maps, facsims.

4341 DENNE, LUDWIG: *Das Danzig-Problem in der deutschen Aussenpolitik 1934–39.* Bonn: Röhrscheid, 1959. 322 pp.

4342 GÄRTNER, MARGARETE, comp.: *Zeugnisse der Wahrheit. Danzig und der Korridor im Urteil des Auslandes.* Einl.: Albert Brackmann. Berlin: Volk und Reich Verlag, 1939. 79 pp. [Also publ. in English under title *Danzig and the Corridor.*]

4343 HEISS, FRIEDRICH and others, eds.: *Deutschland und der Korridor.* Zusammenarb.: Günter Lohse, Waldemar Wucher. Berlin: Volk und Reich Verlag, 1939. 311 pp., illus., diagrs., maps, tabs. [First ed. (by F. Heiss and A. Hillen Ziegfeld) 1933.]

4344 KIMMICH, CHRISTOPH M.: *The Free City. Danzig and German foreign policy, 1919–1934.* New Haven, Conn.: Yale University Press, 1968. 196 pp., maps, bibl.

4345 LEVINE, HERBERT S.: *Hitler's Free City. A history of the Nazi Party in Danzig, 1925–1939.* Chicago, Ill.: University of Chicago Press, 1973. xii + 223 pp., bibl.

4346 MACHRAY, ROBERT: *East Prussia. Menace to Poland and peace.* London: Allen & Unwin, 1943. 112 pp., maps, tabs.

4347 SENAT DANZIG, Abt. für Volksaufklärung und Propaganda: *12 Monate nationalsozialistische Aufbauarbeit in 'Freistadt Danzig'.* Danzig: 1934. 64 pp.

4348 STRASBURGER, HENRYK: *Sprawa Gdańska* [The question of Danzig]. Warszawa: Wyd. Klubu Społeczno-Politycznego, 1937. 112 pp., tabs.

4349 ZELLE, ARNOLD: *50 Korridorthesen. Abrechnung mit Polen.* Berlin: Volk und Reich Verlag, 1939. 95 pp., maps, diagrs., tabs., bibl. [First ed. 1933 under title *100 Korridorthesen.*]

Upper Silesia

4350 GRÜNBERG, KAROL: *Nazi-Front Schlesien. Niemieckie organizacje polityczne w Województwie Śląskim w latach 1933–1939* [German political organisations in the Woiwode of Silesia 1933–1939]. Katowice: Śląsk, 1963. 231 pp., bibl., summaries in English, Russian, German.

4351 POPIOŁEK, KASIMIERZ & SOBAŃSKI, WACŁAW, eds.: *The last attempt to Germanize Opole Silesia.* Poznań: Western Press Agency, 1959. 82 + 35 pp., maps. [Also publ. in German.]

4352 ROSE, WILLIAM JOHN: *The drama of Upper Silesia. A regional study.* Brattleboro, Vt.: Daye, 1935. 349 pp., bibl.

12. PORTUGAL

4353 ZAPP, MANFRED: *Portugal als autoritärer Staat.* Berlin: Deutscher Verlag für Politik und Wirtschaft, 1937. 88 pp., illus., tabs.

13. SCANDINAVIA

4354 HERRMANN, ERNST: *Wikinger unserer Zeit. Nansen, Amundsen, Sven Hedin.* Berlin: Holle, 1937. 427 pp., illus., maps, facsims., bibl.

4355 MALINA, J. B., ed.: *Der germanische Norden und wir. Dänemark—Norwegen—Schweden.* Berlin: Franke, 1934. 279 pp., illus.

4356 SINGER, KURT: *Duel for the Northland. The war of enemy agents in Scandinavia.* New York: McBride, 1943. x + 212 pp.

Denmark

4357 JOESTEN, JOACHIM: *Rats in the larder. The story of Nazi influence in Denmark.* New York: Putnam, 1939. 270 pp. [British title: *Denmark's day of doom.*]

4358 KOHL, LOUIS von: *Das dänische Schicksal. Zwischen Löwen und Herzen.* Berlin: Volk und Reich Verlag, 1936. 125 pp.

SCHLESWIG-HOLSTEIN

4359 JESSEN, FRANZ de: *Manuel historique de la question du Slesvig, 1906–1938.* Copenhagen: Reitzel, 1939. 901 pp., maps, tabs.

4360 SCHLESWIG-HOLSTEINER BUND: *Schleswig und Versailles*. Kiel: Verlag Heimat und Erbe, 1936. 39 pp.

4361 TÄGIL, SVEN: *Deutschland und die deutsche Minderheit in Nordschleswig. Eine Studie zur deutschen Grenzpolitik 1933–1939*. Stockholm: Svenska Bokförlaget, 1970. 205 pp., bibl.

Finland

4362 ÜBERSCHÄR, GERD R.: *Hitler und Finnland 1939–41. Die deutsch-finnischen Beziehungen während des Hitler-Stalin-Paktes*. Wiesbaden: Steiner, 1978. 372 pp., illus.

Iceland

4363 JÓNASSON, MATTHÍAS: *Island. Schicksal eines germanischen Stammes*. Berlin: Holle, 1943. 335 pp., illus., tabs., graph, map, bibl.

Norway

4364 BOEHM, HERMANN: *Norwegen zwischen England und Deutschland. Die Zeit vor und während des Zweiten Weltkrieges*. Lippoldsberg: Klosterhaus-Verlag, 1956. 194 pp.

4365 HORN, MARTIN: *Norwegen zwischen Krieg und Frieden*. Innsbruck: Gauverlag Tirol-Vorarlberg, 1941. 171 pp., illus., maps, tabs., bibl.

4366 KOHT, HALVDAN: *Norway—neutral and invaded*. London: Hutchinson, 1941. 224 pp., ports.

Sweden

4367 BUTT, WOLFGANG: *Mobilmachung des Elfenbeinturms. Reaktionen auf den Faschismus in der schwedischen Literatur 1933–1939*. Neumünster: Wachholtz, 1977. 278 pp., illus., bibl.

4368 CARLGREN, WILHELM M.: *Svensk utrikespolitik 1939–1945*. Stockholm: Allmänna Förlaget, 1973. 612 pp., illus., bibl.

4369 CARLSSON, HOLGER: *Nazismen i Sverige. Ett varningsord*. Stockholm: Federativs, 1942. 224 pp., bibl.

4370 GRÖNBERG, ERIK: *Jag var Gestapos agent*. Stockholm: Bokförlaget Natur och Kultur, 1944. 223 pp.

4371 MALL, KURT: *Der Nationalsozialismus in Schweden im Spiegel seiner Kampfpresse*. Inaugural-Dissertation [pres. to] Ruprecht-Karls-Universität zu Heidelberg. 1936. 112 pp.

14. SPAIN

4372 BURDICK, CHARLES B.: *Germany's military strategy and Spain in World War II*. Syracuse, N.Y.: Syracuse University Press, 1968. 228 pp., illus., maps, bibl.

4373 DANKELMANN, OTFRIED: *Franco zwischen Hitler und den Westmächten*. Berlin [East]: VEB, 1970. 322 pp., illus., maps, tabs., bibl.

4374 DETWILER, DONALD S.: *Hitler, Franco und Gibraltar. Die Frage des spanischen Eintritts in den Zweiten Weltkrieg.* Wiesbaden: Steiner, 1962. 185 pp., illus., map, bibl. (Veröffentlichungen des Instituts für europäische Geschichte Mainz).

4375 DZELEPY, E. N.: *Franco, Hitler et les Alliés.* Bruxelles: Éds. Politiques, 1961. 207 pp.

4376 GARRIGA, RAMON: *Las relaciones secretas entre Franco y Hitler.* Buenos Aires: Alvarez, 1965. 391 pp.

4377 NIEMEIER, GEORG: *Die deutschen Kolonien in Südspanien. Beiträge zur Kulturgeographie der untergegangenen Deutschtumsinseln in der Sierra Morena und in Niederandalusien.* Hamburg: Behre, 1937. 126 pp., illus., plans, tabs. (Studien des Ibero-Amerikanischen Instituts Hamburg).

4378 PAPELEUX, LÉON: *L'Amiral Canaris entre Franco et Hitler. Le rôle de Canaris dans les relations germano-espagnoles, 1915–1944.* Préface: Henri Bernard. [Tournai]: Casterman, 1977. 222 pp., maps, tabs., bibl.

4379 PUZZO, DANTE A.: *Spain and the Great Powers, 1936–1941.* New York: Columbia University Press, 1962. 296 pp., bibl.

4380 RUHL, KLAUS-JÖRG: *Spanien im Zweiten Weltkrieg. Franco, die Falange und das 'Dritte Reich'.* Hamburg: Hoffmann & Campe, 1975. 414 pp., bibl., summary in English.

4381 SCHLEYER, FELIX: *Diplomat im roten Madrid.* Berlin: Herbig, 1938. 230 pp., illus.

Spanish Civil War

4382 ABENDROTH, HANS-HENNING: *Hitler in der spanischen Arena. Die deutsch-spanischen Beziehungen im Spannungsfeld der europäischen Interessenpolitik vom Ausbruch des Bürgerkriegs bis zum Ausbruch des Weltkrieges 1936–1939.* Paderborn: Schöningh, 1973. 411 pp., bibl.

4383 ANTI-KOMINTERN: *Das Rotbuch über Spanien. Bilder, Dokumente, Zeugenaussagen.* Berlin: Nibelungen-Verlag, 1937. 317 pp., illus., facsims., maps.

4384 BEUMELBERG, WERNER: *Kampf um Spanien. Die Geschichte der Legion Condor.* Bearb. im Auftr. des Reichsluftfahrtministeriums. Oldenburg: Stalling, 1939. 311 pp., illus., maps.

4385 EINHORN, MARION: *Die ökonomischen Hintergründe der faschistischen deutschen Intervention in Spanien 1936–1939.* Berlin [East]: Akademie-Verlag, 1962. 239 pp., tabs., bibl.

HARPER, GLENN T.: *German economic policy in Spain during the Spanish Civil War, 1936–1939.* See 1656.

4386 LENT, ALFRED: *Wir kämpften für Spanien. Erlebnisse eines deutschen Freiwilligen im spanischen Bürgerkrieg.* Oldenburg: Stalling, 1939. 255 pp., illus.

4387 MAIER, KLAUS A.: *Guernica 26.4.1937. Die deutsche Intervention in Spanien und der 'Fall Guernica'*. Freiburg: Rombach, 1975. 166 pp., map, tabs., bibl. (Hrsg.: Militärgeschichtliches Forschungsamt).

4388 MERKES, MANFRED: *Die deutsche Politik im spanischen Bürgerkrieg 1936–1939.* 2. neubearb. und erw. Aufl. Bonn: Rohrscheid, 1969. 477 pp., tabs., bibl.

4389 MIKUSCH, DAGOBERT VON: *Franco befreit Spanien.* Leipzig: List, 1939. 322 pp., illus., maps.

4390 *The Nazi conspiracy in Spain, by the editor of 'The Brown Book of the Hitler terror'.* Transl. from the German ms. by Émile Burns. London: Gollancz, 1937. 256 pp., facsims.

4391 *El Nazismo al desnudo. Su intervención y ayuda a los fasciosos españoles puesta al descubierto por sus propios documentos.* [Barcelona]: Comité Nacional de la C.N.T., 1938. 422 pp., illus., facsims., tabs.

4392 *Schwarz-Rot-Buch. Dokumente über den Hitlerimperialismus.* Hrsg. von der Gruppe der 'Deutsch-Anarcho-Syndikalisten'. Barcelona: Asy-Verlag, 1937. 335 pp., illus., facsims.

4393 SEVILLANO CARBAJAL, VIRGILIO: *La Espana ...¿ de quién? Ingleses, Franceses y Alemanes en este país.* Madrid: Sánchez, 1936. 238 pp., maps, tabs.

4394 SPIELHAGEN, FRANZ: *Spione und Verschwörer in Spanien. Nach offiziellen nationalsozialistischen Dokumenten.* Paris: Éds. du Carrefour, 1936. 176 + [30] pp., illus., facsims. [French version: O. K. Simon: *Hitler en Espagne.* Paris: Denoël, 1938.]

4395 VINAS, ANGEL: *La Alemania nazi y el 18 de Julio.* Madrid: Alianza Editorial, 1974. 558 pp., illus., tabs., bibl.

15. SOVIET UNION

4396 ALLARD, SVEN: *Stalin und Hitler. Die sowjetrussische Aussenpolitik 1930–1941.* Bern: Francke, 1974. 314 pp., bibl. (Erw. deutsche Fassung von *Stalin och Hitler*, 1970).

4397 CARR, EDWARD HALLETT: *German–Soviet relations between the two world wars, 1919–1939.* Baltimore, Md.: Johns Hopkins Press, 1951. 146 pp

4398 DEGRAS, JANE, ed.: *Soviet documents on foreign policy.* London: Oxford University Press, under auspices of Royal Institute of International Affairs, 1951/53.
Vol. I: *1917–1924.* Publ. 1951. xxi + 501 pp.
Vol. II: *1925–1932.* Publ. 1952. xxi + 560 pp.
Vol. III: *1933–1941.* Publ. 1953. xxii + 500 pp.

4399 DUROSELLE, JEAN-BAPTISTE, ed.: *Les relations germano-soviétiques de 1933 à 1939. Recueil d'études.* Préface: Pierre Renouvin. Paris: Colin, 1954. 279 pp. (Cahiers de la Fondation nationale des Sciences politiques).

4400 FABRY, PHILIPP W.: *Die Sowjetunion und das Dritte Reich. Eine dokumentierte*

Geschichte der deutsch-sowjetischen Beziehungen von 1933 bis 1941. Prolegomena: Ernst Deuerlein. Stuttgart: Seewald, 1971. 485 pp., illus., maps, tabs., facsims., bibl.

4401 *Der Faschismus in Deutschland.* Moskau: Verlagsgenossenschaft Ausländischer Arbeiter in der UdSSR, 1934. 282 pp. [Speeches from: XIII Plenum des EKKI, Dezember 1933.]

4402 GREIFE, HERMANN: *Sowjetforschung. Versuch einer nationalsozialistischen Grundlegung der Erforschung des Marxismus und der Sowjet-Union.* Berlin: Nibelungen-Verlag, 1936. 71 pp. (Schriften des Instituts zur wissenschaftlichen Erforschung der Sowjet-Union).

4403 HENRI, ERNST: *Hitler over Russia? The coming fight between the Fascist and Socialist armies.* Transl.: Michael Davidson. London: Dent, 1936. 340 pp.

4404 HIGGINS, TRUMBULL: *Hitler and Russia. The Third Reich in a two-front war, 1937–1943.* New York: Macmillan, 1966. 310 pp., maps., bibl.

4405 HILGER, GUSTAV: *Wir und der Kreml. Deutsch-sowjetische Beziehungen 1918–1941. Erinnerungen eines deutschen Diplomaten.* Frankfurt a.M.: Metzner, 1955. 322 pp. [English version (with Alfred G. Meyer): *The incompatible allies.* New York: Macmillan, 1953.]

4406 *Hitlerdeutschland und Sowjetunion. Die Wahrheit über den russisch-deutschen Vertrag.* Wien: Bund der Freunde der Sowjetunion, 1933. 15 pp. [Anti-Nazi.]

4407 KRUMMACHER, F. A. & LANGE, HELMUT: *Krieg und Frieden. Geschichte der deutsch-sowjetischen Beziehungen von Brest-Litowsk zum Unternehmen Barbarossa.* München: Bechtle, 1970. 564 pp.

4408 LAQUEUR, WALTER: *Russia and Germany. A century of conflict.* London: Weidenfeld & Nicolson, 1965. 367 pp., map, bibl. [German version: *Deutschland und Russland.* Berlin: Propyläen Verlag, 1966.]

4409 MCSHERRY, JAMES E.: *Stalin, Hitler and Europe.* Cleveland, Ohio: World Publ. Co., 1968/70. Bibls.
Vol. I: *The origins of World War II, 1933–1939.* 308 pp.
Vol. II: *The imbalance of power, 1939–1941.* 357 pp.

4410 NICLAUSS, KARLHEINZ: *Die Sowjetunion und Hitlers Machtergreifung. Eine Studie über die deutsch-russischen Beziehungen der Jahre 1929 bis 1935.* Bonn: Röhrscheid, 1966. 208 pp., bibl.

4411 NIEDERMAYER, OSKAR VON & SEMJONOW, JURI: *Sowjet-Russland. Eine geopolitische Problemstellung.* Geleitw.: Karl Haushofer. Berlin-Grunewald: Vowinckel, 1934. 151 pp., tabs., maps.

4412 STEPHAN, JOHN J.: *The Russian Fascists. Tragedy and farce in exile, 1925–1945.* London: Hamish Hamilton, 1978. xxii + 450 pp., illus.

4413 TESKE, HERMANN, ed.: *General Ernst Köstring. Der militärische Mittler zwischen dem Deutschen Reich und der Sowjetunion, 1921–1941.* Frankfurt a.M.: Mittler, 1965. 334 pp. (Hrsg.: Bundesarchiv/Militärarchiv).

4414 WEINGARTNER, THOMAS: *Stalin und der Aufstieg Hitlers. Die Deutschlandpolitik der Sowjetunion und der Kommunistischen Internationale 1929–1934.* Berlin: de Gruyter, 1970. 302 pp., bibl.

The Nazi–Soviet Pact

4415 BRÜGEL, JOSEF, ed.: *Stalin und Hitler. Pakt gegen Europa.* Wien: Europa Verlag, 1973. 349 pp., bibl.

4416 CARROLL, EBER MALCOLM & EPSTEIN, FRITZ THEODOR, eds.: *Das nationalsozialistische Deutschland und die Sowjetunion 1939–1941. Akten aus dem Archiv des deutschen Auswärtigen Amts.* [Washington, D.C.]: Department of State, 1948. xliv + 416 + 13 pp., illus.

4417 DEEG, PETER: *Für und wider den Russen-Pakt. Vor 50 Jahren.* Nürnberg: Der Stürmer, 1940. 84 pp.

4418 FABRY, PHILIPP W.: *Der Hitler-Stalin-Pakt 1939–1941. Ein Beitrag zur Methode sowjetischer Aussenpolitik.* Darmstadt: Fundus-Verlag, 1962. 535 pp.

4419 LEACH, BARRY A.: *German strategy against Russia 1939–1941.* Oxford: Clarendon Press, 1973. 308 pp., illus., maps, tabs., bibl.

4420 ROSSI, A.: *Deux ans d'alliance germano-soviétique. Août 1939–juin 1941.* Paris: Fayard, 1949. 225 pp., illus., facsims. [English version: *The Russo-German alliance.* London: Chapman & Hall, 1950.]

4421 SEIDL, ALFRED, ed.: *Die Beziehungen zwischen Deutschland und der Sowjetunion 1939–1941. Dokumente des Auswärtigen Amtes.* Tübingen: Laupp, 1949. 414 pp.

4422 SONTAG, RAYMOND JAMES & BEDDIE, JAMES STUART, eds.: *Nazi–Soviet relations, 1939–1941.* Introd.: James Reston. New York: Didier, 1948. 362 pp., illus., bibl.

4423 TOSCANO, M.: *L'Italia e gli accordi tedesco-sovietici dell'Agosto 1939.* Firenze: Sansoni, 1952. 96 pp.

4424 TRUCHANOVSKY, V. G.: *Istoria meshdunarodnich otnosheny vneshney politiky SSSR. Tom II: 1939–1945* [History of the international relations of the USSR]. Moskva: Izd. IMO, 1962. 683 pp., map.

German minority

4425 HUMMEL, THEODOR: *100 Jahre Erbhofrecht der deutschen Kolonisten in Russland.* Berlin: Reichsnährstand Verlags-Gesellschaft, 1936. 253 pp., illus., tabs., maps.

4426 SERAPHIM, ERNST: *Führende Deutsche im Zarenreich.* Berlin: Junker & Dünnhaupt, 1942. 455 pp., ports., bibl.

Ukraine

4427 ILNYTSKYJ, ROMAN: *Deutschland und die Ukraine 1934–1945. Tatsachen europäischer Ostpolitik. Ein Vorbericht.* 2. Aufl. München: Osteuropa-Institut, 1958. 2 vols.

4428 SCHMIDT, AXEL: *Ukraine. Land der Zukunft.* Berlin: Hobbing, 1939. 203 pp.

4429 UKRAINISCHE AKTION: *In Polen nichts neues.* Berlin: 1939. 30 pp., illus.

16. SWITZERLAND

4430 BÖSCHENSTEIN, HERMANN: *Vor unsern Augen. Aufzeichnungen über das Jahrzehnt 1935–1945.* Bern: Stämfli, 1978. 334 pp. [On the Third Reich and World War II.]

4431 BONJOUR, EDGAR: *Geschichte der schweizerischen Neutralität. Vier Jahrhundert eidgenössischer Aussenpolitik.* Basel: Helbing & Lichtenhahn, 1970/76. Facsims. (4. durchges. Aufl.).
Bd. III: *1930–1939.* Publ. 1970. 431 pp.
Bd. IV–VI: *1939–1945.* Publ. 1970/71. 3 vols.
Bd. VII–IX: *1939–1945. Dokumente.* Publ. 1974/76. 3 vols.

4432 DREIFUSS, ERIC: *Die Schweiz und das Dritte Reich. Vier deutsch-schweizerische Zeitungen im Zeitalter des Faschismus 1933–1939.* Vorw.: Willy Bretscher. Frauenfeld: Huber, 1971. 251 pp., tabs., bibl.

4433 BOURGEOIS, DANIEL: *Le Troisième Reich et la Suisse, 1933–1941.* Neuchâtel: Eds. de la Baconnière, 1974. xvii + 463 pp., illus., facsims., maps, bibl.

HÄSLER, ALFRED A.: *Das Boot ist voll ... Die Schweiz und die Flüchtlinge 1933–1945.* See 6386.

4434 PADEL, GERD H.: *Die politische Presse der deutschen Schweiz und der Aufstieg des Dritten Reiches 1933–1939. Ein Beitrag zur Geschichte der geistigen Landesverteidigung.* [Zürich?]: Gut, 1951. 185 pp., bibl. (Abdruck der ... der Universität Zürich vorgelegten Dissertationen).

4435 SCHWARZ, URS: *The eye of the hurricane. Switzerland in World War II.* Boulder, Colo.: Westview Press, 1980. xv + 169 pp., bibl.

4436 WEBER, KARL: *Die Schweiz im Nervenkrieg. Aufgabe und Haltung der Schweizer Presse in der Krisen- und Kriegszeit 1933–1945.* Bern: Lang, 1948. 316 pp.

Nazi subversion and propaganda

4437 [BOERLIN, ERNST]: *Bericht des Bundesrates an die Bundesversammlung über die antidemokratische Tätigkeit von Schweizern und Ausländer im Zusammenhang mit dem Kriegsgeschehen 1939–1945 (Motion Boerlin). I. Teil (vom 28. Dezember 1945).* 144 pp., diagrs., tabs. [Also publ. in French.]

4438 BOLLIGER, HANS: *Der Deutschschweizer und das Deutsche Reich.* Konstanz: 'Bodensee-Rundschau', 1937. 62 pp.

4439 *Deutsches Schaffen. Jahrbuch der Gemeinschaft Zürich der Deutschen Kolonie in der Schweiz 1941/42.* Zürich: Nationalsozialistische Deutsche Arbeiter-Partei Auslandsorganisation, 1942. 196 pp., illus., diagrs., bibl.

4440 FERNIS, HANS GEORG: *Ewig nimmer gegen's Reich. Schweizer Bekenntnisse aus sechs Jahrhunderten.* Berlin: Verlag Grenze und Ausland, 1942. 121 pp., bibl.

4441 HUMBEL, KURT: *Nationalsozialistische Propaganda in der Schweiz 1931–1939. Einige Hauptaspekte der Mittel, Technik, Inhalte, Methoden und Wirkungen der deutschen Propaganda gegenüber Auslandsdeutschen und Deutschschweizern sowie behördliche Abwehrmassnahmen.* 2. unveränd. Aufl. Bern: Haupt, 1977. 295 pp., bibl.

4442 LACHMANN, GÜNTER: *Der Nationalsozialismus in der Schweiz 1931–1945. Ein Beitrag zur Geschichte der Auslandsorganisation der NSDAP.* Inaugural-Dissertation [pres. to] Freie Universität Berlin. 1962. 114 pp. [Part 3: The Gustloff murder and Frankfurter trial, pp. 55–73.]

4443 WAEGER, GERHART: *Die Sündenböcke der Schweiz. Die Zweihundert im Urteil der geschichtlichen Dokumente 1940–1946.* 2. Aufl. Olten: Walter, 1971. 288 pp., bibl.

4444 WYL, HANS VON: *Ein Schweizer erlebt Deutschland. Tatsachenbericht...* Zürich: Europa Verlag, 1938. 269 pp.

4445 ZANDER, ALFRED: *Eidgenossenschaft und Reich. Ein Schweizer über das Verhältnis der Eidgenossenschaft zum Reich.* Berlin: Verlag Grenze und Ausland, 1942. 140 pp., illus. (3. überarb. Aufl.).

E. ORIGINS OF WORLD WAR II

1. THE CONTEMPORARY VIEW

4446 AGERO, JUAN: *'Asi fue posible ...' Antecedentes de la segunda crisis europea en el siglo XX.* 2a ed. Madrid: Rubinos, 1941. 160 pp.

4447 CAMPBELL, MALCOLM: *Drifting to war.* London: Hutchinson, 1936, 190 pp.

4448 CHAMPEAUX, GEORGES: *La croisade des démocraties.* Paris: Centre d'Études de l'Agence Inter-France, 1941/43.
1: *Formation de la coterie de la guerre.* 318 + xxv pp.
2: *De l'affaire tchéque au revirement de la Cité.* 389 + xxii pp.

4449 *Events leading up to World War II. Chronological history of certain major international events leading up to and during World War II, with the ostensible reasons advanced for their occurrence, 1931–1944.* Washington, D.C.: Government Printing Office, 1944. 421 pp. (78th Congress, 2d. Session, House Document No. 541).

4450 HAINES, C. GROVE & HOFFMANN, ROSS J. S.: *The origins and background of the Second World War.* London: Oxford University Press, 1943. 659 pp., maps, bibl.

4451 KRIEGK, OTTO: *Wer treibt England in den Krieg? Die Kriegshetzer Duff Cooper,*

Eden, Churchill und ihr Einfluss auf die englische Politik. Berlin: Nibelungen-Verlag, 1939. 137 pp.

4452 MINISTÈRE DES AFFAIRES ÉTRANGÈRES DE L'URSS: *Documents et matériaux se rapportant à la veille de la deuxième guerre mondiale.* Moscou: Éds. en Langues étrangères, 1948. Facsims.
Tome 1: *Novembre 1937–1938.* 325 pp.
Tome 2: *Archives Dirksen (1938–1939).* 255 pp.
[German version: *Dokumente und Materialien aus der Vorgeschichte des Zweiten Weltkrieges.* Publ. 1948/49.]

4453 SCHWARZ, KARL, ed.: *Der Krieg, seine Vorgeschichte und seine Entwicklung bis zum 1. Februar 1940.* [Introd. essay]: 'Europa oder Versailles' [and Appendix]: 'Die historischen Gründe für Polens Niederbruch, und Die unmittelbaren Ursachen des deutsch-polnischen Krieges' [by] Johann von Leers [and] Wilhelm Koppe. 3. Aufl. Berlin: Stubenrauch, 1940. 408 pp., maps, tabs.

4454 WEGERER, ALFRED VON: *The origins of World War II. A brief survey of the beginnings of the present war, on the basis of official documents.* New York: Smith, 1941. viii + 128 pp., bibl. [Nazi viewpoint.]

4455 ZIEGLER, WILHELM: *Wie kam es zum Kriege 1939?* Leipzig: Reclam, 1939. 77 pp., bibl.

2. POSTWAR VIEWS AND CONTROVERSIES

4456 BAUMONT, MAURICE: *Les origines de la Deuxième Guerre Mondiale.* Paris: Payot, 1969. 363 pp. [English version: *The origins of the Second World War.* Ferguson, N. H.: Yale University Press, 1978.]

4457 BLAEDEL, NIC: *Forbrydelse og Dumhed. Hitler-Krigens Forspil i europaeisk Storpolitik.* Forord: Erik Seidenfaden. København: Hagerup, 1947. 625 pp., port. [First ed. 1945.]

4458 CALVOCORESSI, PETER & WINT, GUY: *Total war. Causes and courses of the Second World War.* London: Allen Lane, 1972. xiii + 959 pp., illus., facsims., maps, bibl.

4459 D'ARGILE, RENÉ and others: *Das Geheimnis um die Ursachen des Zweiten Weltkrieges.* Wiesbaden: Priester, 1958. 216 pp. [Transl. from the French; apologetics by French fascists.]

4460 GANTENBEIN, JAMES W., ed.: *Documentary background of World War II: 1931 to 1941.* New York: Columbia University Press, 1948. 1122 pp.

4461 *Geschichtsfälscher. Aus Geheimdokumenten über die Vorgeschichte des Zweiten Weltkrieges.* Berlin [East]: Dietz, 1952. 71 pp. [3rd ed.]

4462 HÄRTLE, HEINRICH: *Amerikas Krieg gegen Deutschland. Wilson gegen Wilhelm II—Roosevelt gegen Hitler.* Göttingen: Schütz, 1968. 322 pp., illus. [Apologetics.]

4463 HANSEN, ULRICH: *Die Vorgeschichte des Zweiten Weltkrieges in kommunistischer Sicht.* Bonn: Bundesministerium für gesamtdeutsche Fragen, 1965. 119 pp., facsims., bibl.

4464 HOFER, WALTHER: *Die Entfesselung des Zweiten Weltkrieges. Eine Studie über die internationalen Beziehungen im Sommer 1939.* Mit Dokumenten. Frankfurt a.M.: Fischer, 1964. 518 pp., bibl. [Rev. ed. with rebuttal of Hoggan and Taylor theses. First ed. 1954.]

4465 HOFER, WALTHER: *War premeditated 1939.* London: Thames & Hudson, 1953. 227 pp.

HOGGAN, DAVID L.

4466 HOGGAN, DAVID L.: *Der unnötige Krieg 1939–1945. 'Germany must perish'.* Tübingen: Grabert, 1974. xiv + 627 pp., ports. (Veröffentlichungen des Instituts für deutsche Nachkriegsgeschichte). [Transl. from the English.]

4467 BARNES, HARRY E.: *Die deutsche Kriegsschuldfrage. Eine Rechtfertigung David L. Hoggans.* Tübingen: Verlag der Deutschen Hochschullehrer-Zeitung, 1964. 133 pp., illus.

4468 GLASER, KURT: *Der Zweite Weltkrieg und die Kriegsschuldfrage (Die Hoggan-Kontroverse).* Würzburg: Marienburg-Verlag, 1965. 167 pp.

4469 IRVING, DAVID, ed.: *Breach of security. The German secret intelligence file on events leading to the Second World War.* Introd.: D. C. Watt. London: Kimber, 1968. 216 pp., illus.

4470 MOSLEY, LEONARD: *On borrowed time. How World War II began.* London: Weidenfeld & Nicolson, 1969. 509 pp., illus., maps, bibl.

4471 NICOLL, PETER H.: *Englands Krieg gegen Deutschland. Die Ursachen, Methoden und Folgen des Zweiten Weltkriegs.* Tübingen: Verlag der Deutschen Hochschullehrer-Zeitung, 1963. 588 pp., illus., bibl. (Veröffentlichungen des Instituts für deutsche Nachkriegsgeschichte).

4472 PANKRATOWA, A. M.: *Deutschland, Russland und die Westmächte. Aus der diplomatischen Vorgeschichte des Zweiten Weltkrieges.* Berlin: Volk und Welt, 1947. 96 pp. [Abridged extract from: W. P. Potjomkin, ed.: *Geschichte der Diplomatie, Band 3.* Moscow: Verlag für fremdsprachige Literatur, 1947.]

4473 RIBBENTROP, ANNELIES VON: *'Verschwörung gegen den Frieden'. Studien zur Vorgeschichte des Zweiten Weltkrieges.* Leoni am Starnberger See: Druffel, 1962. 540 pp., illus., bibl.

4474 ROBERTSON, E. M., ed.: *The origins of the Second World War. Historical interpretations.* London: Macmillan, 1971. vi + 312 pp., bibl.

4475 SALVEMINI, GAETANO: *Prelude to World War II.* London: Gollancz, 1953. 519 pp.

4476 SCHMIDT, ROYAL J.: *Versailles and the Ruhr: seedbed of World War II*. The Hague: Nijhoff, 1968. 310 pp., ports., maps, bibl.

TAYLOR, ALAN JOHN PERCIVALE
4477 TAYLOR, A. J. P.: *The origins of the Second World War*. Harmondsworth, Middx.: Penguin Books, 1974. 357 pp. [First ed. 1961 (London: Hamish Hamilton). Reprinted, with a foreword 'Second thoughts', 1963.]

4478 BARNES, HARRY ELMER: *Blasting the historical blackout in Britain. Professor A. J. P. Taylor's 'The origins of the Second World War': its nature, reliability, shortcomings and implications*. [No impr.: 196–]. 42 pp. [Apologetics.]

4479 TCHERNOFF, J.: *Les démagogies contre les démocraties. Préliminaires et causes de la deuxième grande guerre*. Paris: Pichon & Durand-Auzias, 1947. 440 pp.

4480 TOSCANA, MARIO: *Pagine di storia diplomatica contemporanea. 2: Origini e vicende della Seconda Guerra Mondiale*. Milano: Giuffrè, 1963. 578 pp.

4481 [VANSITTART, ROBERT] COLVIN, IAN: *Vansittart in office. An historical survey of the origins of the Second World War, based on the papers of Sir Robert Vansittart, Permanent Under-Secretary of State for Foreign Affairs, 1930–1938*. London: Gollancz, 1965. 360 pp., port., bibl.

4482 WALENDY, UDO: *Wahrheit für Deutschland. Die Schuldfrage des Zweiten Weltkrieges*. Vlotho/Weser: Verlag für Volkstum und Zeitgeschichtsforschung, 1964. 399 pp., port., bibl. [Apologetics.]

3. THE MUNICH PACT

4483 BENEŠ, EDVARD: *Mnichovské dny. Paměti* [The days of Munich. Recollections]. Praha: Svoboda, 1968. 555 pp., illus., facsims.

4484 CELOVSKY, BORIS: *Das Münchener Abkommen 1938*. Hrsg.: Institut für Zeitgeschichte München. Stuttgart: Deutsche Verlags-Anstalt, 1958. 518 pp. (Quellen und Darstellungen zur Zeitgeschichte, Bd.3).

4485 HAJEK, J. S.: *Signal auf Krieg. München 1938*. Berlin [East]: Rütten & Loening, 1960. 243 pp., illus., facsims., bibl.

4486 KILLANIN, MICHAEL MORRIS (Lord), ed.: *Four days—25–29 September, 1938*. London: Heinemann, [1938?]. 242 pp.

4487 KOKOŠKA, JAROSLAV: *Plán 'Grün'. Reportáżni kronika zářijovych událostí toků 1938* [Plan 'Grün'. Reportage-chronicle of the events of September 1938]. Praha: Naše vojsko & Edice Svazu protifašistických bojovníků, 1968. 237 pp., illus., facsim.

4488 KRÁL, VÁCLAV: *Plán Zet* [Plan Z]. Praha: Naše Vojsko, 1973. 236 pp.

4489 MORAVEC, EMANUEL: *Das Ende der Benesch-Republik. Die tschechoslowakische Krise 1938*. 5. Aufl. Prag: Orbis-Verlag, 1942. 402 pp. [Transl. from the Czech.]

4490 NOGUÈRES, HENRI: *Munich ou la drôle de paix—29 Septembre 1938.* Paris: Laffont, 1963. 427 pp., illus., maps. [English version: *Munich, or the phoney peace.* London: Weidenfeld & Nicolson, 1965.]

4491 PITT-RIVERS, GEORGE LANE-FOX: *The Czech conspiracy. A phase in the world-war plot.* London: Boswell, 1938. 93 pp., illus., maps, graphs.

4492 RIPKA, HUBERT: *Munich: before and after. A fully documented Czechoslovak account of the crises of September 1938 and March 1939 with a detailed analysis of the repercussions of the Munich Agreement on the situation of Europe as a whole and of Central Europe in particular together with an essay on the reconstruction of a free Europe.* Transl. from the manuscript. London: Gollancz, 1939. 523 pp. (Left Book Club edition).

4493 ROBBINS, KEITH: *Munich 1938.* London: Cassell, 1968. 398 pp., illus., map, bibl.

4494 RONNEFARTH, HELMUT K. G.: *Die Sudetenkrise in der internationalen Politik. Entstehung, Verlauf, Auswirkung.* Wiesbaden: Steiner, 1961. xii + 775 + 358 pp., ports., maps, bibl. [In 2 vols.]

4495 THE SLOVAK COUNCIL: *Shall millions die for 'This Czechoslovakia ...'? Memorandum, London, June 1938.* Geneva: 1938. 61 pp., maps. [Introd.: F. Jehlicka, Victor Dvorchak.]

4496 STANISŁAWSKA, STEFANIA: *Polska a Monachium* [Poland and Munich]. Warszawa: Książka i Wiedza, 1967. 467 pp., facsims., bibl., summaries in Russian and English.

4497 TAYLOR, TELFORD: *Munich. The price of peace.* London: Hodder & Stoughton, 1979. 1084 pp., bibl.

4498 TEICHOVA, ALICE: *An economic background to Munich. International business and Czechoslovakia, 1918–1938.* London: Cambridge University Press, 1974. xx + 422 pp., tabs., diagrs., bibl.

4499 WHEELER-BENNETT, JOHN W.: *Munich. Prologue to tragedy.* London: Macmillan, 1948. 507 pp.

4. THE LAST YEAR OF PEACE

4500 BONNET, GEORGES: *De Munich à la guerre. Défense de la paix.* Nouvelle éd. rev. et augm. [Paris]: Plon, 1967. 585 pp. [German version: *Vor der Katastrophe.* Köln: Greven, 1953.]

4501 DAHLEM, FRANZ: *Am Vorabend des Zweiten Weltkrieges. Erinnerungen. 1938 bis August 1939.* Berlin [East]: Dietz, 1977/79. 494 + 472 pp. [In two vols. A Communist political emigré tells of Communist reactions to international politics, and of the other emigrés he met in Moscow and various European states.]

4502 GAFENCO, GRÉGOIRE: *Derniers jours de l'Europe. Un voyage diplomatique en 1939.* Éd. revue et augm. Paris: Egloff, 1946. 316 pp. [English version: *The last days of Europe.* London: Muller, 1947.]

4503   MINISTÈRE DES AFFAIRES ÉTRANGÈRES: *Documents diplomatiques 1938–1939. Pièces relatives aux événements et aux négociations qui ont précédé l'ouverture des hostilités* ... Paris: Imprimerie Nationale, 1939. 359 pp. [Also publ. in English and German.]

4504   NAMIER, L. B.: *Diplomatic prelude 1938–1939.* London: Macmillan, 1948. 503 pp.

4505   SCHUMAN, FREDERICK L.: *Night over Europe. The diplomacy of Nemesis, 1939–1940.* New York: Knopf, 1941. xv + 600 + xiv pp.

4506   *Weltgeschichte der Gegenwart in Dokumenten. Geschichte des Zweiten Weltkrieges in Dokumenten.* Hrsg.: Michael Freund. Freiburg i.Br.: Herder & Alber, 1953/56.
I: *Der Weg zum Kriege 1938–1939.* Publ. 1953 xii + 474 pp.
II: *An der Schwelle des Krieges 1939.* Publ. 1955. xvi + 503 pp.
III: *Der Ausbruch des Krieges 1939.* Publ. 1956. ix + 440 pp.

4507   WERNER, MAX: *Der Aufmarsch zum Zweiten Weltkrieg.* Strassburg: Brant, 1938. 356 pp.

4508   WISKEMANN, ELIZABETH: *Undeclared war.* 2nd ed. London: Macmillan, 1967. 332 pp. [First ed. 1939.]

5. THE POLISH CRISIS: SEPTEMBER 1939

4509   AURICH, PETER: *Der deutsch-polnische September 1939.* München: Olzog, 1970. 147 pp., illus., facsims., map, bibl.

4510   AUSWÄRTIGES AMT: *Dokumente zur Vorgeschichte des Krieges.* Berlin: Heymann, 1939. xxvii + 488 pp.

4511   BALL, ADRIAN: *Le dernier jour du vieux monde—3 Septembre 1939.* Paris: Laffont, 1963. 297 pp., illus. [Transl. from the English.]

4512   CIENCIALA, ANNA M.: *Poland and the Western powers 1938–1939. A study in the interdependence of Eastern and Western Europe.* London: Routledge & Kegan Paul, 1968. 310 pp., port., maps, bibl.

4512a   FLEMING, NICHOLAS: *August 1939. The last days of peace.* London: Davis, 1979. xiv + 242 pp., illus., map, bibl.

4513   MINISTRY OF INFORMATION: *How Hitler made the war. The inner story as told in Foreign Office telegrams and documents, abridged from the Blue Book and Sir Nevile Henderson's Final Report.* London: HMSO, 1939. 43 pp.

4514   PEIS, GÜNTER: *The man who started the war.* London: Odhams, 1960. 223 pp. [Alfred Naujocks, a Colonel in the SS, was in charge of the pretended Polish attack on the transmitter at Gleiwitz, used as justification for the attack on Poland. Later he was involved in the Venlo Incident and in faking banknotes.]

4515   SCHÄFER, E. PHILIPP: *13 Tage Weltgeschichte. Wie es zum Zweiten Weltkrieg kam.* Düsseldorf: Econ-Verlag, 1964. 376 pp., illus., facsims., bibl.

4516   SPIRU, BASIL, ed.: *September 1939*. Berlin [East]: Rütten & Loening, 1959. 161 pp., maps.

4517   WEHRT, [RUDOLF] van: *War over Europe. August/September 1939. The inside story*. Berlin: Steiniger, [1939]. 103 pp., illus.

4518   ZENTNER, CHRISTIAN: *Der Kriegsausbruch—1. September 1939. Daten, Bilder, Dokumente*. Frankfurt a.M.: Ullstein, 1979. 240 pp., illus.

F.   RELATIONS WITH THE WESTERN HEMISPHERE

1.   GENERAL

4519   ARCINIEGAS, GERMÁN: *Los Alemanes en la conquista de América*. Buenos Aires: Losada, 1941. 268 pp., bibl.

4520   CHASE, ALLAN: *Falange. The Axis secret army in the Americas*. New York: Putnam, 1943. x + 278 pp., illus., facsims.

4521   DELL, ROBERT: *Germany unmasked*. London: Hopkinson, 1934. 271 pp. [Appendix: 'Decree regarding the tasks of the Reich Ministry of National Enlightenment and Propaganda, and General instructions for German propaganda relative to action in North and South America', pp. 153–271. Text in German and English.]

4522   FRYE, ALTON: *Nazi Germany and the American hemisphere, 1933–1941*. New Haven, Conn.: Yale University Press, 1967. 229 pp.

4523   SCHMIEDER, O., ed.: *Gegenwartsprobleme der Neuen Welt. Teil I: Nordamerika*. Leipzig: Quelle & Meyer, 1943. xi + 802 pp., illus., diagrs., maps. [German postwar plans for USA and Canada.]

2.   UNITED STATES OF AMERICA

4524   *Comment Roosevelt est entré en guerre. Documents secrets relatifs à la politique belliciste du Président des États-Unis. Tome I*. Berlin: Commission des Archives du Ministère des Affaires étrangères, 1943. 117 pp., facsims. [Also in German.]

4525   COMPTON, JAMES V.: *The swastika and the eagle. Hitler, the United States and the origin of World War II*. Boston, Mass.: Houghton Mifflin, 1967. 297 pp., illus., bibl.

4526   DEDEKE, DIETER: *Das Dritte Reich und die Vereinigten Staaten von Amerika, 1933–1937. Ein Beitrag zur Geschichte der deutsch-amerikanischen Beziehungen*. Inaugural-Dissertation [pres. to] Freie Universität Berlin. 1969. 345 pp., bibl.

4527   DIECKHOFF, HANS HEINRICH: *Zur Vorgeschichte des Roosevelt-Krieges*. Berlin: Junker & Dünnhaupt, 1943. 190 pp. (Schriftenreihe des Deutschen Instituts für Aussenpolitische Forschung und des Hamburger Instituts für Auswärtige Politik).

DODD, WILLIAM E. jr. & MARTHA, eds.: *Ambassador Dodd's diary, 1933–1938.* *See* 1238.

4528 *Foreign relations of the United States. Diplomatic papers.* Ed.: Department of State, Historical Office. Washington, D.C.: Government Printing Office, 1947–70. [Each year is covered by several volumes. European relations are included in Vol. 2 of each year 1932–1941; Vols. 2 and 3 of 1942 and 1943; in 1944 the relevant vols. are 3 and 4, in 1945 3–5, in 1946 1–5.]

4529 FRIEDLÄNDER, SAUL: *Hitler et les États-Unis, 1939–1941.* Genève: Droz, 1963. 298 pp., bibl. [Also issued in German under title *Auftakt zum Untergang.*]

4530 HALFELD, ADOLF: *USA greift in die Welt.* Hamburg: Broschek, 1941. 252 pp., tabs. (5. Aufl.).

4531 HASS, GERHART: *Von München bis Pearl Harbor. Zur Geschichte der deutsch-amerikanischen Beziehungen 1938–1941.* Berlin [East]: Akademie-Verlag, 1965. 278 pp., tabs., bibl. (Deutsche Akademie der Wissenschaften zu Berlin).

4532 KRAINZ, OTHMAR: *Juda entdeckt Amerika.* Hrsg.: Gertrud Niegisch. Bad Fürth b. München: Deutscher Hort-Verlag, 1938. 224 pp., bibl.

4533 LUCKWALDT, FRIEDRICH: *Der Aufstieg der Vereinigten Staaten zur Weltmacht. Eine Geschichte ihrer Aussenpolitik.* Berlin: de Gruyter, 1935. 176 pp., maps, bibl.

4534 LUFFT, HERMANN: *Von Washington bis Roosevelt. Geschichte der amerikanischen Aussenpolitik.* Berlin: Junker & Dünnhaupt, 1944. xvi + 530 pp., maps, graphs, tabs.

4535 NEUMANN, ERWIN: *Die Neutralität der Vereinigten Staaten.* Berlin: Junker & Dünnhaupt, 1939. 126 pp., bibl. (Veröffentlichungen der Hochschule für Politik).

4536 OFFNER, ARNOLD A.: *American appeasement. United States foreign policy and Germany, 1933–1938.* Cambridge, Mass.: Harvard University Press, 1969. 328 pp., bibl.

4537 SCHRÖDER, HANS JÜRGEN: *Deutschland und die Vereinigten Staaten 1933–1939. Wirtschaft und Politik in der Entwicklung des deutsch-amerikanischen Gegensatzes.* Wiesbaden: Steiner, 1970. 338 pp., bibl. (Veröffentlichungen des Instituts für europäische Geschichte Mainz).

4538 SHAFIR, SHLOMO: *The impact of the Jewish crisis on American-German relations.* Dissertation [pres. to] Georgetown University, Washington, D.C. 1971. 1033 pp., bibl. [In 2 vols.]

4539 SUTTON, ANTONY C.: *Wall Street and the rise of Hitler.* Seal Beach, Calif.: '76 Press, 1976. 220 pp., tabs., diagrs., bibl.

4540 TREFOUSSE, H. L.: *Germany and American neutrality, 1939–1941.* New York: Bookman Associates, 1951. 247 pp., illus.

4541 AMERIKADEUTSCHER VOLKSBUND: *Kämpfendes Deutschtum. Jahrbuch.* Illus.
1. Jhrg. 1937. Hrsg.: Walter Kappe. New York: Deutscher Weckruf und Beobachter, [1936]. [80 pp.].
2. Jhrg. 1938. Hrsg.: Severin Winterscheidt. New York: AV Publ., [1937]. [52 pp.].

4542 DIAMOND, SANDER A.: *The Nazi movement in the United States, 1924–1941.* Ithaca, N.Y.: Cornell University Press, 1974. 380 pp., illus., tab., bibl.

4543 DIES, MARTIN: *The Trojan Horse in America.* New York: Dodd, Mead & Co., 1940. 366 pp.

4544 HAWGOOD, JOHN A.: *The tragedy of German-America. The Germans in the United States of America during the nineteenth century and after.* New York: Putnam, 1940. xviii + 334 pp., bibl.

4545 HOUSE OF REPRESENTATIVES, Special Committee on Un-American Activities: *Investigation of un-American propaganda activities in the United States. (Chairman: Martin Dies). Hearings, reports and appendices + Index.* Washington, D.C.: Government Printing Office, 1938–1943. 24 vols.

4546 KIPPHAN, KLAUS: *Deutsche Propaganda in den Vereinigten Staaten 1933–1941.* Heidelberg: Winter, 1971. 223 pp., bibl. [Orig. a dissertation, pres. 1969.]

4547 SMITH, ARTHUR L.: *The Deutschtum of Nazi Germany and the United States.* The Hague: Nijhoff, 1965. 172 pp., bibl.

4548 TIMPE, GEORG, ed.: *Katholisches Deutschtum in den Vereinigten Staaten von Amerika. Ein Querschnitt.* Freiburg i. Br.: Herder, 1937. xii + 247 pp., illus., facsims., list of periodicals. (Hrsg.: Reichsverband für die katholischen Auslanddeutschen und St. Bonifaciuswerk).

4549 TURROU, LEON G.: *The Nazi spy conspiracy in America.* As told to David G. Wittels. London: Harrap, 1939. 276 pp., illus.

VIERECK, GEORGE SYLVESTER
4550 GERTZ, ELMER: *Odyssey of a barbarian. The biography of George Sylvester Viereck.* Buffalo, N.Y.: Prometheus Books, 1979. 305 pp. [German-American poet and novelist, propagandist for Germany from World War I onward, Hitler's apologist in America.]

4551 JOHNSON, NIEL M.: *George Sylvester Viereck: German-American propagandist.* Urbana, Ill.: University of Chicago Press, 1972. 282 pp., ports., facsims., bibl.

3. LATIN AMERICA

4552 ARTUCCIO, HUGO FERNANDEZ: *The Nazi underground in South America.* New York: Farrar & Rinehart, 1942. 311 pp.

4553 *Der deutsche Faschismus in Lateinamerika 1933–1943.* Berlin [East]: Humboldt-University, 1966. 204 pp., tabs.

4554 EDSCHMID, KASIMIR (pseud. of Eduard Schmid): *Destin allemand*. Introd. et trad.: J. Benoist-Mechin. Paris: Plon, 1934. 458 pp. [German title: *Deutsches Schicksal*. Novel on settlers in South America.]

4555 POMMERIN, REINER: *Das Dritte Reich und Lateinamerika. Die deutsche Politik gegenüber Süd- und Mittelamerika, 1939–1942.* Düsseldorf: Droste, 1977. 377 pp., bibl. [From a dissertation, pres. to Cologne University 1976.]

4556 REICHSSTELLE FÜR DAS AUSWANDERUNGSWESEN: *Deutsche Vereine, Schulen, Kirchengemeinden und sonstige Anstalten und Einrichtungen in Südamerika.* Berlin: Reichsverlagsamt, 1935. 52 pp.

Argentina

4557 BUSSEMEYER, PETER: *Argentinisches Tageblatt. 50 Jahre Werden und Aufstieg einer ausländischen Zeitung.* Buenos Aires: 1939. 174 pp., illus.

4558 COMITE CONTRA EL RACISMO Y EL ANTISEMITISMO DE LA ARGENTINA: *Informe confidencial de las actividades nazis en la Argentina.* Buenos Aires: 1941. 79 pp., illus., maps, facsims.

4559 DEPARTMENT OF STATE: *Consultation among the American Republics with respect to the Argentine situation.* Washington, D.C.: Government Printing Office, 1946. 86 pp., tabs. (Publication 2473).

4560 DEUTSCHER VOLKSBUND FÜR ARGENTINIEN: *Jahrbuch 1937.* Buenos Aires: [1936]. 184 pp., illus., tabs., maps. (Jhrg. 13).

EBEL, ARNOLD: *Die diplomatischen Beziehungen des Dritten Reiches zu Argentinien unter besonderer Berücksichtigung der Handelspolitik 1933–1939. See* 1647.

4561 KEIPER, WILHELM, ed.: *Der Deutsche in Argentinien. Für Jugend und Volk.* 3. Aufl. (völlig umgestaltete Neuausg.). Langensalza: Beltz, 1938. 106 pp., illus., map. [First ed. 1929.]

4562 MENDOZA, JUAN C. de: *La Argentina y la Swastica.* Buenos Aires: Ed. Victoria, 1941. 188 pp.

4563 SANTANDER, SILVANO: *Tecnica de una traición. Juan D. Peron y Eva Duarte, agentes del nazismo en la Argentina.* Buenos Aires: Ed. Antygna, 1955. 127 pp., illus., facsims.

Bolivia

4564 KÜBLER, FRITZ: *Deutsche in Bolivien.* Stuttgart: Strecker & Schroder, 1936. 91 pp., illus.

Brazil

4565 DA SILVA PY, AURELIO: *A 5ª Coluna no Brasil. A conspiração nazi no Rio Grande do Sul.* 3ª Ed. Pôrto Alegre: Ed. La Livraria do Globo, 1942. 406 pp., illus., facsims., tabs.

4566 HARMS-BALTZER, KÄTE: *Die Nationalisierung der deutschen Einwanderer und ihrer Nachkommen in Brasilien als Problem der deutsch-brasilianischen*

Beziehungen 1930–1938. Berlin: Colloquium Verlag, 1970. 244 pp., bibl.

4567 HUNSCHE, KARL-HEINRICH: *Der brasilianische Integralismus. Geschichte und Wesen der faschistischen Bewegung Brasiliens*. Stuttgart: Kohlhammer, 1938. 247 pp., port., diagrs., bibl.

4568 KÖNIGK, GEORG: *Die Politik Brasiliens während des Weltkrieges und die Stellung des brasilianischen Deutschtums*. Hamburg: Christians, 1935. 66 pp.

4569 OBERACKER, KARLHEINRICH: *Die volkspolitische Lage des Deutschtums in Rio Grande do Sul (Südbrasilien)*. Jena: Fischer, [193–]. 101 pp., map, tabs., bibl. (Schriften des Instituts für Grenz- und Auslanddeutschtum an der Universität Marburg).

4570 REIFSCHNEIDER, GEORG: *Der Auswanderer. Deutscher Arbeiter als weisser Sklave auf Brasiliens Kaffeeplantagen. Seine abenteuerliche Flucht und Heimkehr*. Köln-Lindenthal: Stauf, 1937. 195 pp., illus.

Chile

4571 ECKEHARD, pseud.: *Cuatro años de gobierno de Hitler*. Santiago: Ed. Zig-Zag, [1938?]. 239 pp., illus., graphs, tabs. [German propaganda.]

4572 HADAMOVSKY, E[UGEN]: *La paz de Europa*. Santiago: Ed. Zig-Zag, [1936?]. 160 pp.

Mexico

4573 VOLLAND, KLAUS: *Das Dritte Reich und Mexiko. Studien zur Entwicklung des deutsch-mexikanischen Verhältnisses 1933–1942 unter besonderer Berücksichtigung der Ölpolitik*. Frankfurt a.M.: Lang, 1976. 364 pp., tabs., bibl.

Uruguay

4574 ARTUCCIO, HUGO FERNANDEZ: *Nazis en el Uruguay*. Montevideo: 1940. 146 pp.

4575 *Los Nazis y la justicia uruguaya*. Vistas fiscales …: Luis A. Bouza, Ernesto Mautone. Sentencias …: Hamlet Reyes, Julio C. de Gregorio, Ricardo Jalabert. Montevideo: Claudio García, 1941. 160 pp.

G. MIDDLE EAST

4576 BJÖRKMAN, WALTHER and others: *Arabische Führergestalten*. [By] Walther Björkman, Reinhard Hüber, Ernst Klingmüller, Dagobert von Mikusch, Hans Heinrich Schaeder. Heidelberg: Vowinckel, 1944. 159 pp.

4577 CLAUSS, LUDWIG FERDINAND: *Semiten der Wüste unter sich. Miterlebnis eines Rassenforschers*. Berlin: Büchergilde Gutenberg, 1937. 154 pp., illus.

4578 FAMCHON, YVES & LERUTH, MAURICE: *L'Allemagne et le Moyen-Orient. Analyse d'une pénétration économique contemporaine*. Préface: M. Jules-Julien. Paris: Éds. des Relations internationales, 1957. 206 pp., tabs., bibl.

4579   ROGGE, JOHN O.: *The official German report. Nazi penetration 1924–1942. Pan-Arabism 1939–today.* New York: Yoseloff, 1961. 478 pp.

4580   SCHATTENFROH, FRANZ: *Britenfaust und Judengeist. Eine Reise durch Ägypten und Palästina im Schatten des Krieges.* Berlin: Verlag für Wirtschaft und Kultur, 1940. 103 pp., illus., map.

4581   SCHMITZ-[KAIRO], PAUL: *All-Islam! Weltmacht von morgen.* Leipzig: Goldmann, 1937. 260 pp., illus.

4582   SCHMITZ-KAIRO, PAUL: *Die arabische Revolution.* Leipzig: Goldmann, 1942. 221 pp.

4583   SCHRÖDER, BERND PHILLIP: *Deutschland und der Mittlere Osten im Zweiten Weltkrieg.* Göttingen: Musterschmidt, 1975. 310 pp., illus., maps., bibl.

4584   TILLMANN, HEINZ: *Deutschlands Araberpolitik im Zweiten Weltkrieg.* Berlin [East]: Deutscher Verlag der Wissenschaften, 1965. 473 pp., bibl. (Schriftenreihe des Instituts für allgemeine Geschichte an der Martin Luther-Universität Halle-Wittenberg).

4585   TZSCHIRNER, GEORGE: *Kraftfeld Arabien und Europas Krieg.* Dresden: Heyne, 1939. 292 pp., maps.

4586   VERNIER, BERNARD: *La politique islamique de l'Allemagne.* Paris: Hartmann, 1939. 117 pp.

4587   WALLACH, JEHUDA L., ed.: *Germany and the Middle East, 1835–1939. International symposium, April 1975.* Tel Aviv: Tel Aviv University (Institute of German History), 1975. 211 pp., tabs.

4588   WEGENER, WALTHER: *Syrien, Irak, Iran.* Leipzig: Goldmann, 1943. 302 pp., illus., maps.

Egypt

4589   KRAMER, THOMAS W.: *Deutsch-ägyptische Beziehungen in Vergangenheit und Gegenwart.* Tübingen: Erdmann, 1974. 339 pp., bibl. (Wissenschaftlich-publizistische Buchreihe des Instituts für Auslandsbeziehungen Stuttgart).

Palestine

AMIN-AL-HUSSEINI, MUFTI OF JERUSALEM
4590   FISCHER-WETH, KURT: *Amin-al-Husseini, Grossmufti von Palästina.* Berlin-Friedenau: Titz, 1943. 95 pp., illus.

4591   PEARLMAN, MAURICE: *Mufti of Jerusalem. The story of Haj Amin el Husseini.* London: Gollancz, 1947. 91 pp., illus.

4592   SCHECHTMAN, JOSEPH B.: *The Mufti and the Fuehrer. The rise and fall of Haj Amin el-Husseini.* New York: Yoseloff, 1965. 336 pp., port.

4593   WIESENTHAL, S[IMON]: *Grossmufti—Grossachse der Achse. Tatsachenbericht.* Salzburg: Ried, 1947. 63 pp., illus., facsims.

4594 KANAAN, HAVIV: [*The Nazi Fifth Column in Palestine, 1933–1948*]. Tel Aviv: Hakibbutz Hameuchad, 1968. 146 pp., illus., facsims., tabs., bibl. [In Hebrew.]

4595 WIRSING, GISELHER: *Engländer, Juden, Araber in Palästina.* 5. umgearb. Aufl. Jena: Diederichs, 1942. 285 pp., illus., tabs., maps. [First ed. 1939.]

4596 YISRAELI, DAVID: *The Palestine problem in German politics, 1889–1945.* Ramat-Gan: Bar-Ilan University, 1974. 334 pp., summary in English. [In Hebrew.]

Saudi Arabia

4597 MIKUSCH, DAGOBERT VON: *König Ibn Sa'ud. Das Werden eines Staates.* Berlin: Volksverband der Bücherfreunde Wegweiser-Verlag, 1942. 417 pp., map, family tree, bibl.

Syria

4598 SCHULTZ-ESTEVES, CHRISTOPH: *Syriens Freiheitskampf.* Leipzig: Goldmann, 1939. 144 pp.

Turkey

4599 BETHGE, MARTIN: *Im Lande Ismet Inönüs. Beobachtungen und Streiflichter aus der Türkei.* Berlin: Deutscher Verlag, 1944. 235 pp.

4600 ÖNDER, ZEHRA: *Die türkische Aussenpolitik im Zweiten Weltkrieg.* München: Oldenbourg, 1977. 313 pp., tabs., bibl. [From a dissertation pres. to Freie Universität Berlin.]

H. FAR EAST

4601 DRECHSLER, KARL: *Deutschland—China—Japan 1933–1939. Das Dilemma der deutschen Fernostpolitik.* Berlin [East]: Akademie Verlag, 1964. 180 pp., bibl. (Deutsche Akademie der Wissenschaften zu Berlin).

4602 HAUSHOFER, KARL: *Deutsche Kulturpolitik im indopazifischen Raum.* Biographischer Anhang: Hans Roemer. Hamburg: Hoffmann & Campe, 1939. 287 pp., illus., maps.

4603 KUCK, FRITZ: *Deutsche in Fern-Ost.* Leipzig: Lühe, 1938. 45 pp., tabs.

4604 ROSS, COLIN: *Das neue Asien.* 3. Aufl. Leipzig: Brockhaus, 1940. 287 pp., illus., maps.

4605 STRUNK, ROLAND & RIKLI, MARTIN: *Achtung! Asien marschiert! Ein Tatsachenbericht.* Berlin: Drei Masken Verlag, 1934. 221 pp., illus., maps.

China

4606 ABEGG, LILY: *Chinas Erneuerung. Der Raum als Waffe.* Frankfurt a.M.: Societäts-Verlag, 1940. 481 pp., illus., map.

4607 AMANN, GUSTAV: *Chiang Kaichek und die Regierung der Kuomintang in China.* Heidelberg: Vowinckel, 1936. viii + 240 pp., illus., facsims., maps, tabs.

4608　Liang, Hsi Huey: *The Sino-German connection. Alexander von Falkenhausen between China and Germany, 1900–1941.* Assen: van Gorcum, 1978. xv + 229 pp.

4609　Peck, Joachim: *Kolonialismus ohne Kolonien. Der deutsche Imperialismus und China 1937.* Berlin [East]: Akademie-Verlag, 1961. 188 pp.

India

4610　Ganpuley, N. G.: *Netaji in Germany. A little-known chapter.* With a special chapter: 'Background with a lifesketch', by M. R. Vyas. Bombay: Bharatija Vidya Bhavas, 1964. 200 pp., illus., facsims., bibl. [On Subhas Chandra Bose. 2nd ed. Transl. from the German.]

4611　Schnabel, Reimund: *Tiger und Schakal. Deutsche Indienpolitik 1941–1943. Ein Dokumentarbericht.* Wien: Europa Verlag, 1968. 329 pp., port., facsims. (pp. 91–316), map.

Japan *see* **Index**

VII. WORLD WAR II

A. REFERENCE BOOKS

4612 BAYLISS, GWYN M.: *Bibliographic guide to the two world wars. An annotated survey of English-language reference materials.* London: Bowker, 1977. xv + 578 pp.

4613 *Encyclopédie de la guerre 1939–1945.* Sous la direction de Marcel Baudot, Henri Bernard, Hendrik Brugmans, Michael R. D. Foot, Hans-Adolf Jacobsen. Tournai: Casterman, 1977. 439 pp., maps, bibl.

4614 ENSER, A. G. S.: *A select bibliography of the Second World War: books in English, 1939–1974.* London: Deutsch, 1977. 592 pp.

Guides to German records. See 50.

4615 MASON, DAVID: *Who's Who in World War II.* London: Weidenfeld & Nicolson, 1978. 363 pp., illus., maps.

4616 MAYER, S. L. & KOENIG, W. J.: *The two world wars. A guide to manuscript collections in the United Kingdom.* London: Bowker, 1976. xii + 317 pp.

4617 O'NEILL, JAMES E. & KRAUSKOPF, ROBERT, eds.: *World War II. An account of its documents.* Washington, D.C.: Howard University Press, 1976. xix + 269 pp., illus., facsims., bibl.

4618 *Saggio bibliografico sulla seconda guerra mondiale.* Roma: Ministero della Difesa, Stato Maggiore Esercito, Ufficio Storico, 1949. 209 pp.

4619 ZENTNER, CHRISTIAN, ed.: *Lexikon des Zweiten Weltkrieges. Mit einer Chronik der Ereignisse von 1939–1945 und ausgewählten Dokumenten.* München: Südwest Verlag, 1977. 312 pp., illus.

4620 ZIEGLER, JANET, comp.: *World War II: books in English 1945–65.* Stanford, Calif.: Hoover Institution Press, 1971. xvii + 194 pp.

B. GENERAL HISTORIES

4621 ASSMANN, KURT: *Deutsche Schicksalsjahre. Historische Bilder aus dem Zweiten Weltkrieg und seiner Vorgeschichte.* Wiesbaden: Eberhard Brockhaus, 1950. 568 pp., maps, tabs.

4622 BERGSCHICKER, HEINZ: *Der Zweite Weltkrieg. Eine Chronik in Bildern.* Berlin [East]: Deutscher Militärverlag, 1964. 472 pp., illus.

4623 *Bulletin—Arbeitskreis 'Zweiter Weltkrieg'.* Berlin [East]: Deutsche Akademie der Wissenschaften, 1969– continuing.

4624 BUTLER, JAMES RAMSEY MONTAGU, ed.: *History of the Second World War.*
London: HMSO, 1956– continuing.
Series 1: *Grand Strategy*
1: Norman Henry Gibbs: *Rearmament.* Publ. 1976.
2. J. R. M. Butler: *September 1939–June 1941.* Publ. 1957.
3: J. M. A. Gwyer (I) & J. R. M. Butler (II): *June 1941–August 1942.* Publ.
1964.
4: Michael Howard: *August 1942–September 1943.* Publ. 1972.
5: John Ehrman: *August 1943–September 1944.* Publ. 1956.
6: John Ehrman: *October 1944–August 1945.*
Series 3: *Victory in the West*
1: L. F. Ellis [and others]: *The Battle of Normandy.* Publ. 1962.
2: L. F. Ellis & A. E. Warhurst: *The defeat of Germany.* Publ. 1968.

4625 *Cahiers d'histoire de la deuxième guerre mondiale.* [Issued by] Centre national
d'Histoire des deux Guerres Mondiales. Bruxelles: de Méyère, 1967–
continuing.

4626 COLLIER, RICHARD: *1940. The world in flames.* London: Hamish Hamilton,
1979. 258 pp., illus., bibl. (pp. 233–249).

4627 DAHMS, HELLMUTH GÜNTHER: *Geschichte des Zweiten Weltkrieges.* Tübingen:
Wunderlich, 1965. 918 + 28 pp., maps. [New enl. ed.]

4628 *Des victoires de Hitler au triomphe de la démocratie et du socialisme. Origines
et bilan de la Deuxième Guerre Mondiale (1939–1945). Compte rendu des
travaux du colloque scientifique organisé par l'Institut Maurice Thorez
(Paris, 17–19 Octobre 1969).* Paris: Éds. Sociales, 1970. 446 pp.

4629 DESCHNER, GÜNTHER, ed.: *Der Zweite Weltkrieg. Bilder, Daten, Dokumente.*
Gütersloh: Bertelsmann, 1968. 687 pp., illus., maps.

4630 *Geschichte des Zweiten Weltkrieges.* 2. erw. Aufl. Würzburg: Ploetz, 1960.
171 + 929 pp., maps. [Ed.: Karl Ploetz.]

4631 HILLGRUBER, ANDREAS, ed.: *Probleme des Zweiten Weltkrieges.* Köln:
Kiepenheuer & Witsch, 1967. 455 pp., bibl.

4632 JACOBSEN, HANS-ADOLF: *1939–1945. Der Zweite Weltkrieg in Chronik und
Dokumenten.* 5. vollständig überarb. und erw. Aufl. Darmstadt: Wehr und
Wissen Verlagsgesellschaft, 1961. 764 pp., diagrs., graphs, maps, tabs., bibl.

4633 JACOBSEN, HANS-ADOLF & ROHWER, JÜRGEN, eds.: *Entscheidungsschlachten des
Zweiten Weltkrieges.* Im Auftr. des Arbeitskreises für Wehrforschung hrsg.
Frankfurt a.M.: Bernard & Graefe, 1960. xx + 580 + 68 pp., illus., tabs.,
maps, bibl.

4634 LAUNAY, JACQUES de: *Les grandes décisions de la Deuxième Guerre Mondiale.*
Nyon, Suisse: G. V. Service, 1973/75. Illus.
I: *1939–1941.* Publ. 1973. 422 pp.
II: *1942–1943.* Publ. 1974. 348 pp.
III: *1944–1945.* Publ. 1975. 530 pp., tabs.

4634a *Revue d'Histoire de la Deuxième Guerre Mondiale.* Paris: Presses Universitaires de France. [For index, *see* 81.]

4635 SALIS, J. R. VON: *Weltchronik 1939–1945.* Zürich: Füssli, 1966. 556 pp., maps.

4636 STEGEMANN, WILLI: *Der neue Weltkrieg.* Zürich: Verlag Berichthaus, 1942/44. Maps.
1. Bd.: *1939–40.* Publ. 1942. 197 pp.
2. Bd.: *1940–41.* Publ. 1942. 199 pp.
3. Bd.: *1941–42.* Publ. 1943. 218 pp.
4. Bd.: *1942–43.* Publ. 1944. 224 pp.

4637 TAYLOR, A. J. P.: *The Second World War. An illustrated history.* New York: Putnam, 1975. 234 pp., illus., maps.

4638 TIPPELSKIRCH, KURT VON: *Geschichte des Zweiten Weltkrieges.* 2. neu bearb. Aufl. Bonn: Athenäum-Verlag, 1956. 636 pp.

4639 WERNER, MAX: *Battle for the world. The strategy and diplomacy of the Second World War.* New York: Modern Age Books, 1941. 403 pp., maps.

4640 WRIGHT, GORDON: *The ordeal of total war, 1939–1945.* New York: Harper & Row, 1968. 314 pp., illus., maps, bibl.

C. GERMANY IN WORLD WAR II

1. GENERAL

4641 AMBELANG, HERMANN & SCHULZ, WALTER, eds.: *Mit unsern Fahnen ist der Sieg.* 2. Aufl. Berlin: Weidmann, 1942. 445 pp.

4642 BADE, WILFRID & HAACKE, WILMONT, eds.: *Das heldische Jahr. Front und Heimat berichten den Krieg. 97 Kriegsfeuilletons.* Vorw.: Reichspressechef Dr. Dietrich. Berlin: Zeitgeschichte-Verlag, [1940]. 448 pp.

4643 *Der deutsche Imperialismus und der Zweite Weltkrieg. Materialien der wissenschaftlichen Konferenz der Kommission der Historiker der DDR und der UdSSR ... 1959.* Berlin [East]: Rütten & Loening, 1960/61.
Bd. 1: *Hauptreferate und Dokumente der Konferenz.* Red.: Stefan Doernberg, Gerhart Hass. Publ. 1960. 343 pp.
Bd. 2: *Beiträge zum Thema 'Die Vorbereitung des Zweiten Weltkrieges durch den deutschen Imperialismus'.* Red.: Günter Paulus, Wolfgang Ruge. Publ. 1961. 794 pp., bibl.

4644 *Deutschland im Zweiten Weltkrieg.* Von einem Autorenkollektiv unter Leitung von Wolfgang Schumann [and others]. Köln: Pahl-Rugenstein, 1974–continuing. Illus., maps.
1: *Vorbereitung, Entfesselung und Verlauf des Krieges bis zum 22. Juni 1941.* Leitung: Gerhart Hass. Publ. 1974.
2: *Vom Überfall auf die Sowjetunion bis zur sowjetischen Gegenoffensive bei Stalingrad (Juni 1941–November 1942).* Leitung: Karl Brechsker [and others]. Publ. 1975.

4645 FARAGO, LADISLAS, ed.: *The Axis grand strategy. Blueprints for the total war.* New York: Farrar & Rinehart, 1942. ix + 164 pp., map.

4646 KARSAI, ELEK: *A Berchtesgadeni sasfészektöl a Berlin bunkeri* ... [From the Eagle's Nest in Berchtesgaden to the Bunker of Berlin. Chapters from the history of World War II. 4th ed.]. Budapest: Tancsics, 1965. 630 pp., illus., facsims., maps, bibl.

4647 KÜHNER, OTTO-HEINRICH: *Wahn und Untergang 1939–1945.* Stuttgart: Deutsche Verlags-Anstalt, 1957. 311 pp., bibl. [From a Süddeutscher Rundfunk programme.]

4648 LANGE, HORST: *Tagebücher aus dem Zweiten Weltkrieg.* Mainz: von Hase & Koehler, 1980. 346 pp.

4649 NECKER, WILHELM: *Nazi Germany can't win. An exposure of Germany's strategic aims and weaknesses.* Transl. from the German. London: Lindsay Drummond, 1939. xii + 364 pp., maps.

4650 ROHDEN, PETER RICHARD: *Seemacht und Landmacht. Die Gesetze ihrer Politik und ihrer Kriegsführung.* Leipzig: Goldmann, 1942. 186 pp.

4651 SERRIGNY, [BERNARD]: *L'Allemagne face à la guerre totale.* Paris: Grasset, 1940. 245 pp., tabs.

4652 SÜNDERMANN, HELMUT: *Die Entscheidungen reifen, Berichte und Bekenntnisse aus grosser Zeit.* München: Eher, [1943?]. 117 pp. [Articles from May 1939 to February 1943].

4653 ZIFF, WILLIAM B.: *The coming battle of Germany.* London: Hamish Hamilton, 1942. 207 pp., tabs., bibl.

2. THE HOME FRONT

4654 ANDERMAN, W. Th.: *Bis der Vorhang fiel. Berichtet nach Aufzeichnungen aus den Jahren 1940 bis 1945.* Dortmund: Schwalbenberg, 1947. 414 pp.

BERLIN
4655 FINDAHL, THEO: *Letzter Akt—Berlin 1939–1945.* Hamburg: Hammerich & Lesser, 1946. 224 pp. [Transl. from the Norwegian].

4656 FLANNERY, HARRY W.: *Assignment to Berlin.* New York: Knopf, 1942. 439 pp., tabs.

4657 BERNSEE, HANS: *Aufgaben der Volkswohlfahrt im Kriege.* Berlin: Eher, 1941. 115 pp.

4658 BOOR, LISA de: *Tagebuchblätter aus den Jahren 1938–1945.* München: Biederstein-Verlag, 1963. 245 pp.

DECKEN, S. EBERHARD von der: *Die Front gegen den Hunger. See 1666.*

4659 DEUEL, WALLACE R.: *People under Hitler.* New York: Harcourt, Brace, 1942. 392 pp.

4660 DRÖGE, FRANZ: *Der zerredete Widerstand. Zur Soziologie und Publizistik des Gerüchts im Zweiten Weltkrieg.* Düsseldorf: Bertelsmann, 1970. 258 pp., graphs, tabs., bibl.

4661 HEDIN, SVEN: *Sven Hedin's German diary, 1935–1942.* Transl. by Joan Bulman. Dublin: Euphorion Books, 1961. 282 pp.

4661a MISSALLA, HEINRICH: *Für Volk und Vaterland. Die kirchliche Kriegshilfe im Zweiten Weltkrieg.* Königstein/Ts.: Athenäum Verlag, 1978. 215 pp.

4662 NAVARRO, FRANCISCO: *¡Alemania por dentro!* Mexico: Ed. Minerva, [1942?]. 299 pp., illus., maps. [2nd ed.]

4663 [NUREMBERG] NADLER, FRITZ: *Eine Stadt im Schatten Streichers. Bisher unveröffentlichte Tagebuchblätter. Dokumente und Bilder vom Kriegsjahr 1943.* Nürnberg: Fränkische Verlagsanstalt und Buchdruckerei, 1969. 204 pp., illus., facsims.

4664 REICHSKURATORIUM FÜR DAS DEUTSCHE FACHSCHRIFTTUM: *Fachbücher für Kriegswichtige Berufe.* Leipzig: Börsenverein der Deutschen Buchhändler, 1942. 270 pp.

4665 RIEMER, KARL HEINZ: *Zensurpost aus dem III. Reich. Die Überwachung des II. Weltkrieges durch deutsche Dientststellen.* Düsseldorf: Poststempelgilde 'Rhein-Donau', 1966. vii + 82 pp., illus.

4666 SEYDEWITZ, MAX: *Civil life in wartime Germany. The story of the home front.* New York: Viking Press, 1945. 448 pp.

4667 STEINERT, MARLIS G.: *Hitlers Krieg und die Deutschen. Stimmung und Haltung der deutschen Bevölkerung im Zweiten Weltkrieg.* Düsseldorf: Econ Verlag, 1970. 646 pp., bibl. (Veröffentlichung des Institut universitaire de Hautes Etudes internationales, Genf). [Incl.: 'Die Vernichtung "lebensunwertes Lebens", die Euthanasie Aktion', pp. 152–161; 'Die Verfolgung der Juden', pp. 236–262.]

4668 WENDEL, ELSE: *Hausfrau at war. A German woman's account of life in Hitler's Reich.* In collaboration with Eileen Winncroft. London: Odhams Press, 1957. 255 pp., illus.

4669 WOLFF-MÖNCKEBERG, MATHILDE: *On the other side. To my children: from Germany 1940–1945.* Transl. and ed.: Ruth Evans. London: Owen, 1979. 172 pp., illus. [Family letters describing civilian life in Hamburg during the war.]

See also 2125–2129.

Young people

4670 GRANZOW, KLAUS: *Tagebuch eines Hitler-Jungen, 1943–1945.* Bremen: Schünemann, 1965. 184 pp.

4671 *Kriegsbücherei der deutschen Jugend.* Berlin: Steiniger, 1941/44. 156 issues of 32 pp. ea., illus.

4672 REICHSJUGENDFÜHRUNG: *Die Werkarbeit im Kriegseinsatz der Hitler-Jugend. Anweisung für DJ., HJ., JM., BDM.-Werk 'Glaube und Schönheit'.* Berlin: 1942. 180 pp.

4673 SCHÄTZ, LUDWIG: *Schüler-Soldaten. Die Geschichte der Luftwaffenhelfer im Zweiten Weltkrieg.* Geleitw.: Gerhard Hümmelchen. Darmstadt: Thesen Verlag, 1974. 160 pp., illus., facsims., tabs., bibl. [2nd ed.]

4674 *Unser Kriegs-Liederbuch.* Hrsg.: Reichsjugendführung. 3. Aufl. München: Eher, [1939?]. 95 pp., port.

3. WAR ECONOMY

4675 CUNIO, HERMANN: *Kriegswirtschaftsstrafrecht. Mit Erläuterungen.* Bad Oeynhausen: Lutzeyer, [194–]. 207 pp.

4676 EICHHOLTZ, DIETRICH: *Geschichte der deutschen Kriegswirtschaft 1939–1945.* Berlin [East]: Akademie-Verlag, 1969. 408 pp., tabs., bibl.

4677 KREIDLER, EUGEN: *Die Eisenbahnen im Machtbereich der Achsenmächte während des Zweiten Weltkriegs. Einsatz und Leistung für die Wehrmacht und Kriegswirtschaft.* Göttingen: Musterschmidt, 1975. 440 pp., illus., maps.

4678 LORWIN, LEWIS L.: *National planning in selected countries.* Washington, D.C.: National Resources Planning Board, 1941. 173 pp., diagrs., tabs.

4679 MILWARD, ALAN S.: *The German economy at war.* London: Athlone Press, 1965. vi + 214 pp., map.

4680 SCHREIBER, PETER WOLFRAM, pseud.: *IG Farben. Die unschuldigen Kriegsplaner. Profit aus Krisen, Kriegen und KZs. Geschichte eines deutschen Monopols.* Stuttgart: Verlag Neuer Weg, 1978. 283 pp., illus., facsims. [By a group of authors, members of Kommunistische Studentengruppen.]

4681 STEINWEG, GÜNTHER: *Die deutsche Handelsflotte im Zweiten Weltkrieg. Aufgaben und Schicksal.* Göttingen: Schwartz, 1954. viii + 178 pp., illus.

THOMAS, GEORG: *Geschichte der deutschen Wehr- und Rüstungswirtschaft, 1918–1945. See* 1775.

4682 WAGENFÜHR, ROLF: *Die deutsche Industrie im Kriege 1939–1945.* 2. Aufl. Berlin: Duncker & Humblot, 1963. 216 pp., tabs., bibl.

Weapons and matériel (including prewar period)

4683 [BRAUN, WERNHER von] BERGAUST, ERIK: *Wernher von Braun. Ein unglaubliches Leben.* Düsseldorf: Econ Verlag, 1976. 637 pp., illus., bibl. [The rocket scientist, 'father' of the V 1 and V 2, taken to US after World War II to work for NASA.]

4684 GARLIŃSKI, JÓSEF: *Hitler's last weapons. The underground and war against V 1 and V 2.* London: Friedmann, 1978. xviii + 244 pp., illus.

4685 Goudsmit, Samuel A.: *Alsos. The failure in German science (The search for the German atom bomb)*. London: Sigma Books, 1947. 259 pp., illus., facsims.

4686 Hanslian, Rudolf, ed.: *Der chemische Krieg. I. Bd.: Militärischer Teil*. Bearb.: E. Baum [and others]. 3. völlig neubearb. Aufl. in 2 Bden. Berlin: Mittler, 1937. xv + 779 pp., illus., diagrs., bibl. [First ed. 1927].

4687 Irving, David: *The mare's nest*. London: Kimber, 1964. 320 pp., illus., facsims., maps, tabs. [On Peenemunde.]

4688 Leeb, Emil: *Aus der Rüstung des Dritten Reiches. Das Heereswaffenamt 1938–1945. Ein authentischer Bericht des letzten Chef des Heereswaffenamtes*. Berlin: Mittler, 1958. 68 pp.

4689 Lusar, Rudolf: *Die deutsche Waffen und Geheimwaffen des Zweiten Weltkrieges und ihre Weiterentwicklung*. 2. Aufl. München: Lehmann, 1958. 239 pp., illus.

4690 Pachtner, Fritz: *Waffen. Ein Buch vom Schaffen und Kämpfen im Waffenbau*. Leipzig: Goldmann, 1942. 320 pp., illus.

4691 Pottgiesser, Hans: *Die Deutsche Reichsbahn im Ostfeldzug 1939–1944*. II. erw. Aufl. Neckargemünd: Vowinckel, 1975. 152 pp., illus., facsims., maps, bibl. [First ed. 1960].

4692 Rohde, Horst: *Das deutsche Wehrmachtstransportwesen im Zweiten Weltkrieg. Entstehung—Organisation—Aufgaben*. Stuttgart: Deutsche Verlags-Anstalt, 1971. 439 pp., tabs., bibl.

4693 Seydewitz, Max & Doberer, Kurt: *Todesstrahlen und andere neue Kriegswaffen*. London: Malik-Verlag, 1936. 187 pp.

Speer, Albert

4694 Boelcke, Willi A., ed.: *Deutschlands Rüstung im Zweiten Weltkrieg. Hitlers Konferenzen mit Albert Speer 1942–1945*. Frankfurt a.M.: Verlagsgesellschaft Athenaion, 1969. 495 pp., illus., graphs, tabs.

4695 Janssen, Gregor: *Das Ministerium Speer. Deutschlands Rüstung im Krieg*. Berlin: Ullstein, 1968. 446 pp., tabs., diagr., bibl.

D. GERMAN ARMED FORCES, INCLUDING PREWAR PERIOD

1. GENERAL

4696 Absolon, Rudolf: *Wehrgesetz und Wehrdienst 1935–1945. Das Personalwesen in der Wehrmacht*. Boppard a.Rh.: Boldt, 1960. 430 pp., tabs. (Schriften des Bundesarchivs).

4697 Absolon, Rudolf: *Die Wehrmacht im Dritten Reich*. Boppard a.Rh.: Boldt, 1969– continuing. (Schriften des Bundesarchivs).
Bde. I, II: *30. Januar 1933–2. August 1934. Mit einem Rückblick auf das*

Militärwesen in Preussen, im Kaiserreich und in der Weimarer Republik. Publ. 1969, 1971. 445 + xiv + 601 pp., chronologies (pp. 267–412 & 323–508 respectively).
Bd. III: *3. August 1934–4. Februar 1938.* Publ. 1975. xviii + 533 pp.
Bd. IV: *5. Februar 1938–31. August 1939.* Publ. 1979. xix + 412 pp.

4698　BÄHR, WALTER & HANS W., eds.: *Kriegsbriefe gefallener Studenten, 1939–1945.* Tübingen: Wunderlich, 1952. 471 pp.

4699　BENARY, ALBERT: *Melder, Funker, Störungssucher. Ein Buch vom Nachrichtenmann.* Berlin: Schneider, 1940. 135 pp., illus., maps.

4700　BLEY, WULF, comp.: *Kampf gegen den Westen. Neue Erlebnisberichte von der Land-, Luft- und Seefront.* Leipzig: von Hase & Koehler, 1940. 107 pp.

4701　DEUTSCHE GESELLSCHAFT FÜR WEHRPOLITIK UND WEHRWISSENSCHAFTEN: *Heer, Flotte und Luftwaffe. Wehrpolitisches Taschenbuch.* Berlin: Riegler, 1939. 86 pp., illus.

4702　DIETZ, HEINRICH: *Das Wehrgesetz vom 21. Mai 1935 und seine Ausführung im Frieden und Krieg. Erläuterungswerk.* Leipzig: Wordel, 1943. 584 pp.

4703　DÖRKEN, GEORG & SCHERER, WERNER, eds.: *Das Militärstrafgesetzbuch und die Kriegssonderstrafrechtsverordnung. Mit Erläuterungen.* 3. Aufl. Berlin: Vahlen, 1942. 180 pp.

4704　FRANKE, HERMANN, ed.: *Handbuch der neuzeitlichen Wehrwissenschaften.* Hrsg. im Auftr. der Deutschen Gesellschaft für Wehrpolitik und Wehrwissenschaften. Berlin: de Gruyter, 1936–
I: *Wehrpolitik und Kriegsführung.* 749 pp.
II: *Das Heer.* 804 pp.
III: 1. *Die Kriegsmarine.* 415 pp.
　　2. *Die Luftwaffe.* 415 pp.

4705　HELD, WALTER, ed.: *Verbände und Truppen der deutschen Wehrmacht und Waffen-SS im Zweiten Weltkrieg. Eine Bibliographie der deutschsprachigen Nachkriegsliteratur.* Osnabrück: Biblio Verlag, 1978. xxiii + 649 pp.

4706　LANGE, (Major i. Generalstab) von, ed.: *Gegen Bomber, Bunker, Panzer. Kampf und Sieg an allen Fronten.* Berlin: Scherl, 1942. 320 pp.

4707　MOLLO, ANDREW: *German uniforms of World War II.* London: Macdonald & Jane's, 1976. 160 pp., illus.

4708　SCHREINER, ALBERT: *Vom totalen Krieg zur totalen Niederlage Hitlers. Eine kritische Auseinandersetzung mit der Wehrmachtsideologie des Dritten Reiches.* Paris: Éds. Prométhée, 1939. 264 pp.

4709　SCHWELING, OTTO PETER: *Die deutsche Militärjustiz in der Zeit des Nationalsozialismus.* Bearb., eingel. und hrsg. von Erich Schwinge. 2. Aufl. Marburg: Elwert, 1978. xvii + 407 pp., tabs.

4710　SEEMEN, GERHARD VON: *Die Ritterkreuzträger 1939–1945.* Anhang über die Verleihungsbestimmung: Rudolf Absolon. Bad Nauheim: Podzun, 1955. 323 pp.

4711　SIMONEIT, MAX: *Die Anwendung psychologischer Prüfungen in der deutschen Wehrmacht (Deutsche Wehrmachtpsychologie von 1927–1942).* [No pl.]: US Army, Europe, Historical Division, 1948. 66 pp., typescr.

4712　TESSIN, GEORG: *Formationsgeschichte der Wehrmacht 1933–1939. Stäbe und Truppenteile des Heeres und der Luftwaffe.* Boppard a.Rh.: Boldt, 1959. 266 pp. (Schriften des Bundesarchivs).

4713　TESSIN, GEORG: *Verbände und Truppen der deutschen Wehrmacht und Waffen SS im Zweiten Weltkrieg 1939–1945.* Bearb. auf Grund der Unterlagen des Bundesarchiv-Militärarchivs. Hrsg. mit Unterstützung des Bundesarchivs und des Arbeitskreises für Wehrforschung. Frankfurt a.M.: Mittler (later vols.: Osnabrück: Biblio Verlag), 1965– continuing. [13th vol. publ. 1976.]

4714　TUMLER, FRANZ: *Der Soldateneid. Eine Erzählung.* München: Langen & Müller, 1939. 181 pp.

4715　WIEST, HUGO: *Heer, Kriegsmarine, Luft-Waffe. Ein Volksbuch über Aufbau und Organisation der Wehrmacht.* Oldenburg: Stalling, 1935. 175 pp., tabs.

2.　HANDBOOKS AND INSTRUCTIONS FOR PERSONNEL

4716　ALTRICHTER, FRIEDRICH: *Der Reserveoffizier. Ein Handbuch für den Offizier und Offizieranwärter des Beurlaubtenstandes aller Waffen.* 15. neubearb. Aufl. Berlin: Mittler, 1943. 280 pp., illus., diagrs.

4717　ALTRICHTER, FRIEDRICH: *Der soldatische Führer.* Oldenburg: Stalling, 1938. 165 pp.

4718　ALTRICHTER, FRIEDRICH: *Das Wesen der soldatischen Erziehung.* Oldenburg: Stalling, 1935. 223 pp., bibl.

4719　BERGHAHN, VOLKER R.: 'NSDAP und "geistige Führung" der Wehrmacht 1939–1943'. [In] *Vierteljahrshefte für Zeitgeschichte,* Heft 1, 1969. Pp. 17–71.

4720　FOERTSCH, HERMANN: *Der Offizier der neuen Wehrmacht. Eine Pflichtenlehre.* 2. Aufl. Berlin: Eisenschmidt, 1936. 94 pp.

4721　GRAFF, SIGMUND: *Über das Soldatische.* Berlin: Nibelungen Verlag, 1943. 131 pp.

4722　HUBE, (Oberstleutnant), ed.: *Der Infanterist. Handbuch für Selbstunterricht und Ausbildung des jungen Soldaten der Infanterie.* Neuausg. 6.–7. vollk. veränd. Aufl. Berlin: Verlag 'Offene Worte', 1934/35. Illus., maps, diagrs.
Bd. I: *Für Kasernenstube und Unterrichtsraum.* 563 pp.
Bd. II: *Für Kasernenhof, Schiessstand und Gelände.* 389 pp.

4723　LEHMENT, JOACHIM: *Kriegsmarine und politische Führung.* Berlin: Junker & Dünnhaupt, 1937. 131 pp.

4724　PINTSCHOVIUS, KARL: *Die seelische Widerstandskraft im modernen Kriege.* Oldenburg: Stalling, 1936. 192 pp., bibl.

4725　REIBERT, W., ed.: *Der Dienstunterricht im Heere*. Ausg. für den Gewehr- und 1. M.G.-Schützen. 8. neubearb. Aufl. Berlin: Mittler, 1936. 333 pp., illus., diagrs. [Also: Ausg. für den Schützen der Schützenkompanie. 11., neubearb. Aufl. Neudruck, 1939. 325 pp., illus., maps, facsims., diagrs.]

4726　ROTH, ARMIN: *Wehrmacht und Weltanschauung. Grundfragen für Erziehungsarbeit in der Wehrmacht*. Geleitw.: Reichsminister und Oberbefehlshaber der Luftwaffe Reichsmarschall Göring. Berlin: Mittler, 1940. 108 pp.

4727　SCHERKE, FELIX & VITZTHUM, URSULA Gräfin: *Bibliographie der geistigen Kriegsführung*. Berlin: Bernard & Graefe, 1938. 98 pp.

4728　SORGE, SIEGFRIED: *Der Marineoffizier als Führer und Erzieher*. 4. Aufl. Berlin: Mittler, 1943. viii + 172 pp. [First ed. 1936.]

4729　VOLKMANN-LEANDER, BERNHARD VON: *Soldaten oder Militärs? Ein Buch zum Nachdenken*. 3. Aufl. München: Lehmann, 1936. 175 pp., port.

4730　ZIEGLER, MATTHES: *Soldatenglaube—Soldatenehre. Ein deutsches Brevier für Hitler-Soldaten*. Berlin: Nordland-Verlag, 1940. 70 pp. [Incl. SS recruits' oath, p. 51.]

3.　STRATEGY

4731　ERFURTH, WALDEMAR: *Die Überraschung im Kriege*. Berlin: Mittler, 1938. 147 pp., maps. (Nach Beiträgen des Verfassers in der 'Militärwissenschaftlichen Rundschau' 1937 (5, 6), 1938 (1–3)). [English version: *Surprise*. Harrisburg, Pa.: Military Service Publ., 1943.]

4732　ERFURTH, WALDEMAR: *Der Vernichtungssieg. Eine Studie über das Zusammenwirken getrennter Heeresteile*. Berlin: Mittler, 1939. vii + 105 pp., maps.

4733　FÖRSTER, GERHARD: *Totaler Krieg und Blitzkrieg. Die Theorie des totalen Krieges und des Blitzkrieges in der Militärdoktrin des faschistischen Deutschland am Vorabend des Zweiten Weltkrieges*. Berlin [East]: Deutscher Militärverlag, 1967. 255 pp., tabs., bibl.

4734　FOERTSCH, HERMANN: *Kriegskunst heute und morgen*. Berlin: Andermann, 1939. 258 pp.

4735　KUCH, RUDOLF: *Wehr-Schach (DRGM). Kurze Einführung in seine Regeln und Spielmethode mit Kampf-Aufgaben und Lösungen*. Frankfurt a.M.: Kichler, 1938. 48 pp., illus.

4736　LEEB, WILHELM Ritter von: *Die Abwehr*. Berlin: Mittler, 1938. 109 pp., maps. [English version: *Defence*. Harrisburg, Pa.: Military Service Publ., 1943.]

4737　LUDENDORFF, ERICH: *Der totale Krieg*. München: Ludendorff, 1940. 210 pp.

4738　ROMMEL, ERWIN: *Aufgaben für Zug und Kompagnie. Gefechtsaufgaben, Gefechtsschiessen, Geländebesprechung. Ihre Anlage und Leitung*. 4. neubearb. Aufl. Berlin: Mittler, 1940. 82 pp., illus., diagrs.

4739 STERNBERG, FRITZ: *Germany and a lightning war. Transl. from the German.* London: Faber & Faber, 1938. 345 pp., diagrs., tabs., graphs.

4. MILITARY LEADERS

a. General

4740 BEZIMENSKY, L[EV] A[LEKSANDROVICH]: *Germanskie generaly—ce Gitlerom i bez nevo* [German generals with and without Hitler. 2nd rev. and enl. ed.]. Moskva: Misl, 1964. 532 pp., illus., facsims., tabs., maps.

4741 BRETT-SMITH, RICHARD: *Hitler's generals.* London: Osprey, 1976. viii + 306 pp., ports., map, bibl.

4742 DEMETER, KARL: *Das deutsche Offizierkorps in Gesellschaft und Staat 1650–1945.* 3. unveränd. Aufl. Frankfurt a.M.: Bernard & Graefe, 1964. 321 pp., tabs. [English version: *The German officer-corps in society and state, 1650–1945.* Introd.: Michael Howard. London: Weidenfeld & Nicolson, 1965.]

4743 ERFURTH, WALDEMAR: *Die Geschichte des deutschen Generalstabes von 1918 bis 1945.* Göttingen: Musterschmidt, 1957. 326 pp., diagrs., tabs., bibl.

4744 GREINER, HELMUTH: *Die oberste Wehrmachtführung 1939–1945.* Wiesbaden: Limes Verlag, 1951. 444 pp., maps.

4745 HALDER, FRANZ: *Kriegstagebuch. Tägliche Aufzeichnungen des Chefs des Generalstabes des Heeres 1939–1942.* Hrsg.: Arbeitskreis für Wehrforschung Stuttgart. Stuttgart: Kohlhammer, 1962/64. Illus., maps, tabs. (Bearb.: Hans-Adolf Jacobsen).
Bd. I: *Vom Polenfeldzug bis zum Ende der Westoffensive (14.8.1939–30.6.1940).* Publ. 1962. 391 pp.
Bd. II: *Von der geplanten Landung in England bis zum Beginn des Ostfeldzuges (1.7.1940–21.6.1941).* Publ. 1963. 503 pp.
Bd. III: *Der Russlandfeldzug bis zum Marsch auf Stalingrad (22.6.1941–24.9.1942).* Publ. 1964. 589 pp.

4746 HART, W. E.: *Hitler's generals.* New York: Doubleday, Doran, 1944. xx + 222 pp., ports.

4747 HILLGRUBER, ANDREAS, ed.: *Von El Alamein bis Stalingrad. Aus dem Kriegstagebuch des Oberkommandos der Wehrmacht (Wehrmachtführungsstab).* Neuausg. München: Deutscher Taschenbuch Verlag, 1964. 303 pp.

4748 HUMBLE, RICHARD: *Hitler's generals.* London: Barker, 1973. 167 pp., illus.

4749 IRVING, DAVID: *Hitler und seine Feldherren.* Frankfurt a.M.: Ullstein, 1975. x + 885 pp., illus., bibl. [English version: *Hitler's war.* New York: Viking Press, 1977. Incl. material not in the German version.]

4750 LEYEN, FERDINAND Prinz von der: *Rückblick zum Mauerwald. Vier Kriegsjahre im Oberkommando des Heeres.* 2. Aufl. München: Biederstein, 1966. 183 pp.

4751 LIDDELL HART, B[ASIL] H[ENRY]: *The other side of the hill. Germany's generals, their rise and fall, with their own account of military events, 1939–1945.* London: Cassell, 1951. 487 pp. [Rev. and enl. ed. German version: *Deutsche Generale des Zweiten Weltkriegs. Aussagen, Aufzeichnungen und Gespräche.* Düsseldorf: Econ Verlag, 1964.]

4752 MARTIENSSEN, ANTHONY: *Hitler and his admirals.* London: Secker & Warburg, 1948. 275 pp.

4753 MÖLL, OTTO E.: *Die deutschen Generalfeldmarschälle 1935–1945.* Bearb.: Wolfgang W. Marek. Rastatt/Bad.: Pabel, 1961. 272 pp., illus., maps, tab., bibl.

4754 MÜLLER-HILLEBRAND, BURKHART: *The organizational problems of the Army High Command and their solutions, 1938–1945.* [No pl.]: US Army, Europe, Historical Division, 1953. 86 pp., mimeog.

4755 MURAWSKI, ERICH: *Der deutsche Wehrmachtbericht 1939–1945. Ein Beitrag zur Untersuchung der geistigen Kriegsführung. Mit einer Dokumentation der Wehrmachtberichte von 1.7.1944 bis zum 9.5.1945.* Boppard a.Rh.: Boldt, 1962. 768 pp. (Schriften des Bundesarchivs).

4756 NIELSEN, ANDREAS: *The German Air Force General Staff.* Introd.: Telford Taylor. New York: Arno Press, 1968. 265 + xiii + [6] pp., diagrs. (USAF Historical Studies). [Reprint of 1959 ed.]

4757 RICHARDSON, WILLIAM & FREIDIN, SEYMOUR, eds.: *The fatal decisions.* [Essays by] Werner Kreipe, Günther Blumentritt, Fritz Bayerlein, Kurt Zeitzler, Bodo Zimmermann, Hasso von Manteuffel. Commentary: Siegfried Westphal. Introd.: Cyril Falls. Transl. from the German by Constantine Fitzgibbon. London: Michael Joseph, 1956. xii + 261 pp., ports., maps.

4758 RIESS, CURT: *The self-betrayed. Glory and doom of the German generals.* New York: Putnam, 1942. xvi + 402 pp., maps, bibl.

4759 SCHAUB, KONRADJOACHIM: *Die Berichte des Oberkommandos der Wehrmacht vom 1. September 1939 bis zum Waffenstillstand in Frankreich.* Nach amtlichen Material zusammengest. und bearb. Berlin: Deutsche Verlagsgesellschaft, 1940. 333 pp.

4760 SCHRAMM, PERCY ERNST, ed.: *Kriegstagebuch des Oberkommandos der Wehrmacht (Wehrmachtführungsstab).* Im Auftr. des Arbeitskreises für Wehrforschung hrsg. Frankfurt a.M.: Bernard & Graefe, 1961– Tabs., maps.
Bd. I: Jacobsen, Hans-Adolf, comp.: *1. August 1940–31. Dezember 1941.* Publ. 1965. 1285 pp.
Bd. II: Hillgruber, Andreas, comp.: *1. Januar 1942–31. Dezember 1942.* Publ. 1963. 2 vols., 1464 pp.
Bd. III: Hubatsch, Walther, comp.: *1. Januar 1943–31. Dezember 1943.* Publ. 1963. 2 vols., 1661 pp.

Bd. IV: Schramm, Percy Ernst, comp.: *1. Januar 1944–22. Mai 1945*. Publ. 1961. 2 vols., 1940 pp.
Nachtrag
Bd. IV, 1 B, 9. Abschn., I. Teil: Hillgruber, Andreas, comp.: *Der Krieg in Finnland, Norwegen und Dänemark vom 1. Januar–31. März 1944*.

4761 SIEGLER, FRITZ von, comp.: *Die höheren Dienststellen der deutschen Wehrmacht 1933–1945*. Im Auftr. des Instituts für Zeitgeschichte zusammengest. und erläutert. München: Institut für Zeitgeschichte, 1953. 155 pp., diagrs., tabs.

4762 WARLIMONT, WALTER: *Im Hauptquartier der deutschen Wehrmacht 1939–1945. Grundlagen, Formen, Gestalten*. Frankfurt a.M.: Bernard & Graefe, 1962. 570 pp., illus., facsims., tabs., bibl.

b. Individuals

4763 [BAADE, E.-G.] PLEHWE, FRIEDRICH-KARL von: *Reiter, Streiter und Rebell. Das ungewöhnliche Leben des General E.-G. Baade*. [Bensberg]: Schäuble, 1976. 286 pp., illus.

4764 [BAYERLEIN, FRITZ] KOLLATZ, KARL: *Generalleutnant Fritz Bayerlein. Rommels Stabschef in Afrika—Kommandeur der Panzerlehrdivision*. Rastatt/Bad.: Pabel, [1962?]. 78 pp., maps.

4765 [GOERING, HERMANN] LEE, ASHER: *Goering. Air leader*. London: Duckworth, 1972. 256 pp., illus., bibl.

GUDERIAN, HEINZ
4766 GUDERIAN, HEINZ: *Erinnerungen eines Soldaten*. 4. Aufl. Neckargemünd: Vowinckel, 1960. 464 pp., illus., maps. [First ed. 1951.]

4767 MACKSEY, KENNETH: *Guderian, Panzer general*. London: Macdonald & Jane's, 1975. xii + 226 pp., illus., maps, bibl.

HALDER, FRANZ
4768 BOR, PETER: *Gespräche mit Halder*. Wiesbaden: Limes Verlag, 1950. 267 pp., illus., maps.

4769 SCHALL-RIAUCOUR, HEIDEMARIE Gräfin: *Aufstand und Gehorsam. Offizierstum und Generalstab im Umbruch. Leben und Wirken von Generaloberst Franz Halder, Generalstabschef 1938–1942*. Vorw.: Adolf Heusinger. Wiesbaden: Limes Verlag, 1972. 351 pp., facsim., illus., bibl.

4770 [HOEPNER, ERICH] CHALES de BEAULIEU, WALTER: *Generaloberst Erich Hoepner. Militärisches Porträt eines Panzer-Führers*. Neckargemünd: Vowinckel, 1969. 260 pp., maps.

4771 HOSSBACH, FRIEDRICH: *Zwischen Wehrmacht und Hitler 1934–1938*. Wolfenbüttel: Wolfenbüttler Verlagsanstalt, 1949. 224 pp. [Writer of the Hossbach Memorandum, a record of a secret conference between Hitler and his military leaders on 5 November 1937, in which Hitler declared that, given the impossibility of total autarky, Germany had a right to Lebensraum: he then set out the timetable for expansion and war. A translation may be found in L. Snyder: *Encyclopedia of the Third Reich*, see 1.]

4772 [KEITEL, WILHELM] GÖRLITZ, WALTER, ed.: *Generalfeldmarschall Keitel. Verbrecher oder Offizier? Erinnerungen, Briefe, Dokumente des Chefs OKW.* Göttingen: Musterschmidt, 1961. 447 pp., illus.

4773 KESSELRING, ALBERT: *Gedanken zum Zweiten Weltkrieg.* Bonn: Athenäum Verlag, 1955. 201 pp., maps.

4774 KESSELRING, ALBERT: *Memoirs.* London: Kimber, 1974. 319 pp., illus., map. [German orig.: *Soldat bis zum letzten Tag.* Bonn: Athenäum Verlag, 1953.]

4775 LEEB, WILHELM Ritter von: *Tagebuchaufzeichnungen und Lagebeurteilungen aus zwei Weltkriegen.* Aus dem Nachlass hrsg. und mit einem Lebensabriss versehen von Georg Meyer. Stuttgart: Deutsche Verlags-Anstalt, 1976. 500 pp., port., bibl. (Beiträge zur Militär- und Kriegsgeschichte, hrsg. vom Militärgeschichtlichen Forschungsamt).

4776 MANSTEIN, ERICH VON: *Aus einem Soldatenleben 1887–1939.* Bonn: Athenäum Verlag, 1958. 359 pp., illus.

4777 RAEDER, ERICH: *Mein Leben.* Tübingen: Schlichtenmayer, 1956/57. 2 vols., illus.
Bis zum Flottenabkommen mit England 1935. Publ. 1956. 317 pp., facsims.
Von 1935 bis Spandau 1955. Publ. 1957. 347 pp.
[English version: *My life.* Annapolis, Md.: US Naval Institute, 1960.]

4778 RÖHRICHT, EDGAR: *Pflicht und Gewissen. Erinnerungen eines deutschen Generals 1932 bis 1944.* Stuttgart: Kohlhammer, 1965. 236 pp.

ROMMEL, ERWIN
4779 ROMMEL, ERWIN: *Krieg ohne Hass.* Hrsg.: Lucie-Marie Rommel, Fritz Bayerlein. 3. Aufl. Heidenheim: Verlag Heidenheimer Zeitung, 1950. 401 pp. [English version: *The Rommel papers.* Ed.: B. H. Liddell Hart. London: Collins, 1953.]

4780 DOUGLAS-HOME, CHARLES: *Rommel.* Introd.: Lord Chalfont. London: Weidenfeld & Nicolson, 1973. 224 pp., illus.

4781 IRVING, DAVID: *The trail of the fox. The life of Fieldmarshal Erwin Rommel.* London: Weidenfeld & Nicolson, 1977. 448 pp., illus. [German version: *Erwin Rommel. Biographie.* Hamburg: Hoffmann & Campe, 1978.]

4782 LEWIN, RONALD: *Rommel as military commander.* London: Batsford, 1968. 262 pp., illus., maps, tabs., bibl.

4783 [RUNDSTEDT, GERD VON] BLUMENTRITT, GÜNTHER: *Von Rundstedt. The soldier and the man.* London: Odhams Press, 1952. 288 pp., port.

4784 SPEIDEL, HANS: *Aus unserer Zeit.* 2. Aufl. Berlin: Propylaen, 1977. 512 pp., illus.

TROTHA, ADOLF VON
4785 TROTHA, ADOLF von: *Seegeltung—Weltgeltung. Gedanken eines Admirals.* Hrsg.: Reichsbund Deutscher Seegeltung. Berlin: Mittler, 1940. 139 pp., illus.

4786 BARGEN, BENDIX von, ed.: *Admiral von Trotha. Persönliches, Briefe, Reden und Aufzeichnungen 1920–1937.* Berlin: Warneck, 1938. 207 pp., illus.

UDET, ERNST
4787 UDET, ERNST: *Mein Fliegerleben.* Berlin: Ullstein, 1935. 183 pp., illus.

4788 ISHOVEN, ARMAND van: *The fall of an eagle.* Ed.: Ch. Bower. London: Kimber, 1980. 208 pp. [On Udet; describes his work for the Luftwaffe.]

4789 ZUCKMAYER, CARL: *Des Teufels General.* London: Harrap, 1962. 314 pp., port. [Play based on death of Udet.]

4790 WAGNER, EDUARD: *Der Generalquartiermeister. Briefe und Tagebuchaufzeichnungen des Generalquartiermeisters des Heeres General der Artillerie Eduard Wagner.* Hrsg.: Elisabeth Wagner. München: Olzog, 1963. 318 pp.

4791 WESTPHAL, SIEGFRIED: *Erinnerungen.* 2. Aufl. Mainz: von Hase & Koehler, 1975. 499 pp., illus.

5. ARMY

a. General

4792 BENOIST-MECHIN, J.: *Histoire de l'armée allemande depuis l'Armistice.* Paris: Michel, 1936/38. Maps.
I: *De l'armée impériale à la Reichswehr.* Publ. 1936.
II: *De la Reichswehr à l'armée nationale, 1919–1936.* Publ. 1938.
[Also: new ed. covering 1918–1945. Paris: Michel, 1954. Further ed. (10 vols. announced) covering 1918–1946. Paris: Michel, 1964– Latest German version: *Geschichte der deutschen Militärmacht.* Oldenburg: Stalling, 1965– (10 vols. announced).]

4793 GROTE, HANS HENNING Frhr.: *Unvergleichliche deutsche Infanterie. Schicksale einer Waffe.* Hamburg: Hanseatische Verlagsanstalt, [1940]. 238 pp.

4794 HARTLAUB, FELIX: *Von unten gesehen. Impressionen und Aufzeichnungen des Obergefreiten Felix Hartlaub.* Hrsg.: Geno Hartlaub. Stuttgart: Koehler, 1950. 156 pp.

4795 *Herzhafter Soldaten-Kalender.* Weimar: Gesellschaft der Bibliophilen, 1944. [108 pp.], illus.

4796 *Im Angriff und im Biwak. Soldaten erzählen Soldatengeschichten.* Berlin: Eher,

1943. 94 pp., illus. (VB-Feldpost 2. Folge. Ges. und hrsg. von VB-Schriftleiter Utermann).

4797   *Jahrbuch des deutschen Heeres.* Leipzig: Breitkopf & Härtel, 1936/42. 7 vols., illus., maps. [Publ. annually.]

4798   KEILIG, WOLF: *Das deutsche Heer 1939–1945.* Bad Nauheim: Podzun, 1956– 3 looseleaf vols., approx. 500 pp. ea., maps, diagrs., tabs. [Unit lists and details.]

4799   KEILIG, WOLF, ed.: *Rangliste des deutschen Heeres 1944/45. Dienstalterslisten T und S der Generale und Stabsoffiziere des Heeres* ... Bad Nauheim: Podzun, 1955. 408 pp., tabs.

4800   HEUSINGER, ADOLF: *Befehl in Widerstreit. Schicksalsstunden der deutschen Armee 1923–1945.* 14.–18. Taus. Tübingen: Wunderlich, Leins, 1950. 396 pp., map.

4801   MANSTEIN, ERICH von and others: *Die deutsche Infanterie 1939–1945. Eine Dokumentation in Bildern.* Bad Nauheim: Podzun, 1967. 332 pp., illus.

4802   MANZ, (Major), ed.: *Bewaffnete Alpenheimat. Ein Buch vom Ersatzheer im Alpenraum.* Im Auftr. des Stellvertretenden Generalkommandos XVIII AK. Innsbruck: Gauverlag Tirol-Vorarlberg, 1941. 285 pp., illus.

4803   MENGE-GENSER, M. von: *Das Auge der Armee. Kampf und Sieg eines Fernaufklärers.* Nach den Tagebuchblättern des Oberleutnants M. von Menge-Genser. Berlin: Menge, 1943. 146 pp., illus., facsim.

4804   MÜLLER-HILLEBRAND, BURKHART: *Das Heer 1933–1945. Entwicklung des organisatorischen Aufbaues.* Darmstadt: Mittler, 1954– Maps, tabs., graphs.
Bd. I: *Das Heer bis zum Kriegsbeginn.* Geleitw.: Franz Halder.
Bd. II: *Die Blitzfeldzüge 1939–1941. Das Heer im Kriege bis zum Beginn des Feldzuges gegen die Sowjetunion im Juni 1941.*
Bd. III: *Der Zweifrontenkrieg. Das Heer vom Beginn des Feldzuges gegen die Sowjetunion bis zum Kriegsende.* Frankfurt: Mittler & John, 1969.

4805   NECKER, WILHELM: *The German army of today.* London: Lindsay Drummond, [194–]. 205 pp., illus., diagrs. (by John Heartfield), tabs.

4806   ONDARZA, (Hauptmann) von: *Taschenbuch der leichten Artillerie.* 10. Aufl. Berlin: Verlag 'Offene Worte', 1939/40. 232 pp., illus.

Paratroops

4807   GROTH, HERMAN & KADE, LUDWIG: *So wurde man Fallschirmjäger.* Berlin: Nibelungen Verlag, 1943. 94 pp., illus.

4808   HOVE, ALKMAR von: *Achtung! Fallschirmjäger. Eine Idee bricht sich Bahn.* Leoni am Starnberger See: Druffel, 1954. 231 pp., illus., maps.

4809   MIKSCHE, F. O.: *Paratroops, the history, organization and tactical use of airborne formations.* Preface: [Basil Henry] Liddell Hart. London: Faber & Faber, 1943. 167 pp., diagrs., maps, tabs. [French version: *Blitzkrieg. Étude sur la tactique allemande de 1937 à 1943.* Trad. et rév.: Lt.-Col. Pagès. Harmondsworth, Middx.: Eds. Pingouin, 1944. 207 pp.]

4810 PERAU, JOSEF: *Priester im Heere Hitlers. Erinnerungen 1940–1945.* Essen: Ludgerus, 1962. 272 pp., illus., maps.

Pioneers

4811 ROSSMANN, KARL: *Kampf der Pioniere.* Berlin: Eher, 1944. 54 pp., illus., mus. score.

4812 ZENTRALARCHIV DER PIONIERE: *Deutsche Pioniere 1939–1945. Eine Dokumentation in Bildern.* 2. überarb. Aufl. Neckargemünd: Vowinckel, 1976. 239 pp., illus., diagrs., map.

4813 PRÜLLER, WILHELM: *Diary of a German soldier.* Ed.: H. C. Robbins Landon, Sebastien Leitner. Pref.: Correlli Barnett. London: Faber & Faber, 1963. 200 pp., port.

4814 ROSINSKI, HERBERT: *The German army.* Ed.: Gordon A. Craig. London: Pall Mall Press, 1966. 322 pp.

4815 *Sammlung von Heeresverwaltungs-Verfügungen (früher Glashagen). Erlasse aus dem Gebiete des Kassen-, Haushalts-, Besoldungs-, Verpflegungs-, Bekleidungs-, Unterkunfts-, Bau- und Krankenwesens mit ausführlichem Sachverzeichnis.* Mit Genehmigung des Oberkommandos des Heeres zusammengest. von H. Jacob ... Berlin: Bernard & Graefe, 1936– 13 vols.

Tanks

4816 BAUER, EDDY: *La guerre des blindés. Les opérations de la deuxième guerre mondiale sur les fronts d'Europe et d'Afrique.* Préface: Jean Valluy. 2e éd. entièrement refondue. Paris: Payot, 1962. 2 vols. 813 pp., maps.
Tome I: *Flux et reflux des Panzer.*
Tome II: *L'écrasement du IIIe Reich.*

4817 BERNDT, ALFRED-INGEMAR: *Panzerjäger brechen durch! Erlebnisse einer Kompanie im grossdeutschen Freiheitskampf 1939/40.* München: Eher, 1940. 251 pp., map.

4818 CHAMBERLAIN, PETER & DOYLE, HILARY L.: *Encyclopedia of German tanks of World War II: a complete illustrated directory of German battle tanks ... 1933–1945.* Technical ed.: Thomas L. Jents. London: Arms & Armour Press, 1978. 272 pp., illus.

4819 GUDERIAN, HEINZ: *Achtung—Panzer! Die Entwicklung der Panzerwaffe, ihre Kampftaktik und ihre operative Möglichkeiten.* Stuttgart: Union Deutsche Verlagsgesellschaft, 1937. 212 pp., illus., maps, bibl.

4820 GUDERIAN, HEINZ, ed.: *Mit den Panzern in Ost und West. I: Erlebnisberichte von Mitkämpfern aus den Feldzügen in Polen und Frankreich 1939/40.* Berlin: Volk und Reich Verlag, 1942. 340 pp., illus., maps.

4821 GUDERIAN, HEINZ: *Panzer-Marsch.* München: Schildt, 1956. 244 pp., illus.

4822 NEHRING, [WALTHER K.]: *Die Geschichte der deutschen Panzerwaffe 1916–1945.* Stuttgart: Motorbuch Verlag, 1974. 328 + 65 pp., tabs., maps, bibl. [Author was Generalstabschef des Panzerkorps Guderian and later Oberbefehlshaber der I. Panzerarmee.]

b. Waffen SS

4823 BAADE, FRITZ and others, eds.: *Unsere Ehre heisst Treue. Kriegstagebuch des Kommandostabes Reichsführer SS. Tätigkeitsbericht der 1. und 2. SS-Inf.-Brigade, der 1. SS-Kav.-Brigade und von Sonderkommandos der SS.* Wien: Europa Verlag, 1965. 253 pp., maps, diagrs., facsims.

4824 BUTLER, R.: *The Black Angels. The story of the Waffen SS.* London: Hamlyn, 1978. 276 pp., illus.

4825 DUPRAT, FRANÇOIS: *Les campagnes de la Waffen SS.* Paris: Les sept couleurs, 1973. 2 vols., 309 + 247 pp., maps.

4826 KRÄTSCHMER, ERNST-GÜNTHER: *Die Ritterkreuzträger der Waffen-SS.* Göttingen: Plesse, 1955. 439 pp., illus.

4827 LEHMANN, RUDOLF: *Die Leibstandarte. Bd. I.* Nach Vorarb. durch Karl-Heinz Schulz. Osnabrück: Munin, 1977. 504 pp., illus., maps.

4828 PANZERMEYER (pseud. of Kurt Meyer): *Grenadiere.* München: Schild-Verlag, 1956. 415 pp., illus., maps.

4829 SKORZENY, OTTO: *Lebe gefährlich* [and] *Wir kämpften—wir verloren.* Siegburg-Niederpleis: Ring Verlag (Cramer), 1962. 268 + 268 pp., illus., map. (Kriegsberichte der Waffen SS). [Leader of the daring rescue of Mussolini from the Gran Sasso. Other exploits were the kidnap of Admiral Horthy and infiltrating the advancing Americans.]

4830 STEIN, GEORGE H.: *The Waffen SS. Hitler's elite guard at war, 1939–1945.* Ithaca, N.Y.: Cornell University Press, 1966. 330 pp., illus., maps, bibl. [Ch. X: 'The tarnished shield: Waffen SS criminality', pp. 250–281.]

4831 SYDNOR, CHARLES W. jr.: *Soldiers of destruction. The SS Death's Head Division 1933–1945.* Princeton, N.J.: Princeton University Press, 1977. xvi + 371 pp., illus., maps.

4832 WEIDINGER, OTTO: *Division Das Reich. Der Weg der SS-Panzer-Division der Waffen-SS.* Osnabrück: Munin, 1967/69. Illus., diagrs., maps, plans, facsims.
Bd. I: *1934–1939.* Publ. 1967. 352 pp.
Bd. II: *1940–1941.* Publ. 1969. 559 pp.

4833 WEIDINGER, OTTO: *Kameraden bis zum Ende. Der Weg des SS-Panzer-grenadier-Regiments 4 'DF' 1939–1945. Die Geschichte einer deutsch-*

österreichischen Kampfgemeinschaft. Göttingen: Plesse, 1962. 459 pp., illus., maps, diagrs.

4834 *Wenn alle Brüder schweigen. Grosser Bildband über die Waffen-SS.* Osnabrück: Munin, 1973. 544 pp., illus., facsims., maps.

c. Foreign contingents

4835 CHAEPPI, BENNO H.: *Germanischer Freiwilliger im Osten.* Geleitw.: Stabsführer der Germanischen Leitstelle. Nürnberg: Willmy, 1943. 76 pp., illus.

4836 GOSZTONY, PETER: *Hitlers fremde Heere. Das Schicksal der nichtdeutschen Armeen im Ostfeldzug.* Düsseldorf: Econ Verlag, 1976. 545 pp., illus., bibl.

4837 *Historia.* [Special issue entitled]: *L'internationale SS. 600,000 étrangers, Français, Belges, Suisses, etc.* Paris: Tallandier, 1973. 192 pp., illus. (Hors Série).

4838 HOFFMANN, JOACHIM: *Die Ostlegionen 1941–1943. Turkotataren, Kaukasier und Wolgafinnen im deutschen Heer.* Freiburg i.Br.: Rombach, 1976. 197 pp., tab. (Hrsg.: Militärgeschichtliches Forschungsamt).

4839 MABIRE, JEAN: *Les SS françaises: la Brigade Frankreich.* Paris: Fayard, 1973. 460 pp., illus., facsims.

4840 [PANNWITZ, Helmuth von] KERN, ERICH: *General von Pannwitz und seine Kosaken.* Göttingen: Plesse, 1963. 208 pp., illus., maps, facsims.

4841 REIPERT, FRITZ, comp.: *SS für ein Grossgermanien. Der Anteil des neuen Norwegen.* [Oslo]: Der höhere SS-Obergruppenführer und General der Polizei Rediess, [1942]. 169 pp., illus.

4842 SAINT-LOUP, MARC AUGIER: *Legion der Aufrechten. Frankreichs Freiwillige an der Ostfront.* Leoni am Starnberger See: Druffel, 1977. 356 pp.

4843 STRASSNER, PETER: *Europäische Freiwillige. Die Geschichte der 5. SS-Panzerdivision Wiking.* 2. verb. Aufl. Osnabrück: Munin, 1971. 448 pp., illus., facsims., maps, tabs., bibl. [First ed. 1968.]

VLASOV, ANDREI ANDREIEVICH
4844 DVINOV, B.: *Vlasovskoe dvizhenie v svete dokumentov ...* [The Vlasov movement in the light of documents. With an appendix of secret documents]. [New York: priv. pr.], 1950. 121 pp., facsims.

4845 DWINGER, EDWIN ERICH: *General Wlassow. Eine Tragödie unserer Zeit.* Frankfurt a.M.: Dikreiter, 1951. 416 pp.

4846 STRIK-STRIKFELDT, WILFRIED: *Gegen Stalin und Hitler. General Wlassow und die russische Freiheitsbewegung.* Mainz: von Hase & Koehler, 1970. 287 pp., illus., diagrs., bibl.

4847 ZEE, SYTZE van der: *Voor Führer, volk en vaderland sneuvelde ... De SS in Nederland, Nederland in de SS.* Den Haag: Kruseman, 1975. 248 pp., illus., facsims., bibl.

6. LUFTWAFFE AND AIR WAR

a. Early years (including civil air force)

4848 GEYER, H.: *Deutschlands Luftfahrt und Luftwaffe. Entwicklung, Leistung, Gliederung, Aufgaben, Berufe.* Berlin: de Gruyter, 1937. 145 pp., tabs.

4849 ['HINDENBURG'] LEHMANN, ERNST A.: *Auf Luftpatrouille und Weltfahrt.* Leipzig: Schmidt & Günther, 1936. 408 pp., illus., tab. [Contains much material on the 'Hindenburg' airship. The author, her captain, was killed in the crash the following year.]

4850 HOMZE, EDWARD L.: *Arming the Luftwaffe. The Reich Air Ministry and German aircraft industry, 1919–1939.* Lincoln, Nebr.: University of Nebraska Press, 1976. xv + 296 pp., illus., diagrs., tabs.

4851 *Jahrbuch der Deutschen Akademie der Luftfahrtforschung.* Berlin: 1938/39. Illus.
1937/38: 321 pp.
1938/39: 247 pp.
Ergänzungsband 1938. München: Oldenbourg. 403 pp.

4852 LEHMANN-RUSSBUELDT, OTTO: *Germany's air force.* Introd.: Wickham Steed. London: Allen & Unwin, 1935. 160 pp., tabs., bibl.

4853 LONGOLIUS, FRITZ: *Flugzeugbau für Deutschland. Die Luftfahrtindustrie im Lebenskampf des deutschen Volkes.* Berlin: Wiking Verlag, [1939]. 87 pp., illus., diagrs.

4854 PICKERT, WOLFGANG: *Unsere Flakartillerie. Einführung in ihre Grundlagen für Soldaten und Laien.* Berlin: Mittler, 1937. 27 pp., illus., diagrs.

4855 REICHSLUFTFAHRTMINISTERIUM: *Katalog der Zentralluftfahrtbücherei.* Leipzig: Leiner, 1940. 404 pp.

4856 STAMER, Fr.: *Deutscher Segelflug. Vaterländische Tat und fliegerische Jugendbewegung. Werden, Wesen und Aufgaben.* Leipzig: Bibliographisches Institut, 1937. 40 pp., illus., diagrs.

4857 THIEDE, F. & SCHMAHL, E.: *Die fliegende Nation.* Berlin: Union Deutsche Verlagsgesellschaft, 1933. 141 pp., illus., diagrs.

4858 UHSE, BODO: *Lieutenant Bertram. A novel of the Nazi Luftwaffe.* Transl. from the German. New York: Simon & Schuster, 1944. 430 pp. [Incl. air intervention in the Spanish Civil War.]

4859 VÖLKER, KARL-HEINZ: *Die deutsche Luftwaffe 1933–1939. Aufbau, Führung und Rüstung der Luftwaffe sowie die Entwicklung der deutschen Luftkriegstheorie.* Stuttgart: Deutsche Verlags-Anstalt, 1967. 334 pp., maps, diagrs., tabs., bibl.

4860 WOODMAN, DOROTHY: *Hitlers Luftflotte startbereit. Enthüllungen über den tatsächlichen Stand der Hitlerschen Luftrüstungen.* Paris: Éds. du Carrefour, 1935. 177 pp., illus., maps, facsims., tabs. [Continuation of *Hitler rearms, see 3973.*]

b. War years

4861 ADERS, GEBHARD: *History of the German night fighter force, 1917–1945.* London: Macdonald & Jane's, 1979. 221 pp.

4862 BARTZ, KARL: *Als der Himmel brannte. Der Weg der deutschen Luftwaffe.* Hannover: Sponnholtz, 1955. 268 pp.

4863 BAUMBACH, WERNER: *Zu spät? Ein Beitrag zur Geschichte des Zweiten Weltkrieges.* Buenos Aires: Dürer Verlag, 1949. 396 pp. [Apologist on the Luftwaffe.]

4864 BEKKER, CAJUS: *Angriffshöhe 400. Ein Kriegstagebuch der deutschen Luftwaffe.* Oldenburg: Stalling, 1964. 484 pp., illus., facsims., maps, tabs., bibl.

4865 BONGARTZ, HEINZ: *Luftmacht Deutschland. Aufstieg, Kampf und Sieg— Werden und Aufstieg der deutschen Luftwaffe—Der Luftkrieg in Polen.* 2. veränd. Aufl. Essen: Essener Verlagsanstalt, 1941. 264 pp., illus.

4866 FEUCHTER, GEORG W.: *Geschichte des Luftkrieges. Entwicklung und Zukunft.* Bonn: Athenäum-Verlag, 1954. 441 pp.

4867 FEUERSTEIN, ERWIN: *Mit und ohne Ritterkreuz. Die Erfolgreichsten der deutschen Luftwaffe.* Stuttgart: Motorbuch Verlag, 1974. 184 pp., tabs., bibl.

4868 GREY, C. G.: *The Luftwaffe.* London: Faber & Faber, 1944. 251 pp., illus., diagrs.

4869 *Jahrbuch der deutschen Luftwaffe.* Geleitw.: [Hermann] Göring. Leipzig: Breitkopf & Härtel 1937/1942. 5 vols., illus. [Jhrg. 3 ed. by Dr. Kurbs, remainder by Dr. Eichelbaum.]

4870 KEHRBERG, ARNO: *Nationalsozialistische Fliegerkorps. Die Vorschule der deutschen Flieger.* Vorw.: Fr. Christiansen. Berlin: Schuhmacher, 1942. 227 pp., illus.

4871 KENS, KARLHEINZ & NOWARRA, HEINZ J.: *Die deutschen Flugzeuge 1933–1945. Deutschlands Luftfahrt—Entwicklungen bis zum Ende des Zweiten Weltkrieges.* 2. verb. und durch einen Nachtrag ergänzte Aufl. München: Lehmann, 1964. 940 pp., illus.

4872 LEE, ASHER: *The German air force.* London: Duckworth, 1946. 284 pp., illus., maps.

4873 LESKE, GOTTFRIED: *I was a Nazi flier.* Ed.: Curt Riess. New York: Dial Press, 1941. 351 pp.

MILCH, ERHARD

4874 IRVING, DAVID: *Die Tragödie der deutschen Luftwaffe. Aus den Akten und Erinnerungen von Feldmarschall Milch.* Aus dem Englischen. Frankfurt a.M.: Ullstein, 1971. 487 pp., illus., facsims. (3. Aufl.).

4875 OSTERKAMP, THEO & BACHÉR, FRITZ: *Tragödie der Luftwaffe? Kritische Begegnung mit dem gleichnamigen Werk von Irving/Milch.* Neckargemünd: Vowinckel, 1971. 172 pp., plans.

4876 Forell, Fritz von, ed.: *Mölders und seine Männer.* Graz: Steirische Verlagsanstalt, 1941. 206 pp., illus. (151.–210. Taus.).

4877 Forell, Fritz von: *Werner Mölders: Flug zur Sonne. Die Geschichte des grossen Jagdfliegers.* Leoni am Starnberger See: Druffel, 1976. 223 pp., illus., facsims. [2nd ed. Previous ed.: *Mölders—Mensch und Flieger.* Salzburg: Sirius-Verlag, 1951.]

4878 Müllenbach, Herbert: *Und setzet Ihr nicht das Leben ein. Ruhmesblätter der deutschen Luftwaffe.* 4. Aufl. Gütersloh: Bertelsmann, 1941. 280 pp., illus.

4879 Overy, R. J.: *The air war, 1939–1945.* London: Europa Publs., 1980. xii + 263 pp., illus., tabs., bibl.

4880 Price, Alfred: *Luftwaffe. Birth, life and death of an air force.* London: Macdonald, 1970. 160 pp.

4881 Reitsch, Hanna: *Fliegen—Mein Leben.* Stuttgart: Deutsche Verlags-Anstalt, 1952. 310 pp., illus. (4. Aufl.).

4882 Rieckhoff, H. J.: *Trumpf oder Bluff? 12 Jahre deutsche Luftwaffe.* Genf: Interavia, 1945. 296 pp., diagrs., maps.

4883 Suchenwirth, Richard: *Historical turning-points in the German Air Force war effort.* Introd.: Telford Taylor. New York: Arno Press, 1968. 143 + 13 + [6] pp. [Reprint of USAF Historical Division edition, 1959.]

4884 Supf, Peter: *Luftwaffe von Sieg zu Sieg. Von Norwegen bis Kreta. Nach Frontberichten und eigenen Erlebnissen.* Mit einer kurzen militärischen Übersicht von Gen.-Leut. W. Haehnelt. Berlin: Deutscher Verlag, 1941. 221 pp., illus., maps, tab.

4885 Toliver, Raymond F. & Constable, Trevor J.: *Das waren die deutschen Jagdfliegerasse 1939–1945.* Stuttgart: Motorbuch Verlag, 1975. 416 pp., illus., tabs. [5th ed. Appeared originally in English, 1968 under title *Horrido!*]

c. Battle of Britain

4886 Banaszczyk, Eugeniusz: *W Bitwie o Anglię* [In the Battle of Britain]. Warszawa: Książka i Wiedza, 1973. 199 pp., illus., map.

4887 Eichelbaum, (Major), ed.: *Immer am Feind. Deutsche Luftwaffe gegen England. Tatsachenbericht in Wort und Bild.* Berlin: Adler-Bücherei (Scherl), 1940. 128 pp., illus.

4888 Jullian, Marcel: *The Battle of Britain, July–September 1940.* Transl. from the French. London: Cape, 1967. 295 pp., illus., facsims., maps, bibl.

4889 Kohl, Hermann: *Wir fliegen gegen England. Einsatz der Luftwaffe 1939/40.* Reutlingen: Ensslin & Laiblin, 1940. 143 pp., illus., map.

4890   OBERKOMMANDO DER WEHRMACHT : *Fahrten und Flüge gegen England. Berichte und Bilder.* Berlin: Zeitgeschichte Verlag, 1941. 208 pp., illus., maps.

4891   SPAIGHT, J. M.: *The Battle of Britain, 1940.* Forew.: Viscount Trenchard. London: Bles, 1941. 231 pp., illus.

4892   TOWNSEND, PETER: *Duel of eagles.* London: Weidenfeld & Nicolson, 1971. xvii + 455 pp., illus., map, diagrs. [First ed. in France 1969 under title *Un duel d'aigles*: first English ed. 1970.]

4893   WEBER, THEO: *Die Luftschlacht um England.* Fraunfeld: Flugwehr und Technik, 1956. 205 pp., illus., diagrs., graphs, maps, tabs.

d.   Air attacks against Germany

4894   AUSWÄRTIGES AMT: *Dokumente über die Alleinschuld Englands am Bombenkrieg gegen die Zivilbevölkerung.* Berlin: Deutscher Verlag, 1943. 183 pp., tabs.

4895   [BERLIN] GIRBIG, WERNER: *...im Anflug auf die Reichshauptstadt. Die Dokumentation der Bombenangriffe auf Berlin—stellvertretend für alle deutschen Städte.* Stuttgart: Motorbuch Verlag, 1970. 247 pp., illus., plans, diagrs., tabs., facsims., bibl.

4896   BONACINA, GIORGIO: *Comando Bombardieri, Operazione Europa. L'offensiva aerea strategica degli alleati nella seconda guerra mondiale.* Milano: Longanesi, 1975. 446 pp., illus., tabs., bibl.

4897   BUNDESMINISTER FÜR VERTRIEBENE, FLÜCHTLINGE UND KRIEGSGESCHÄDIGTE: *Dokumente deutscher Kriegsschäden. Evakuierte, Kriegssachgeschädigte, Währungsgeschädigte. Die geschichtliche und rechtliche Entwicklung.* Bonn: 1958/67. Illus.
Bd. 1: xv + 504 pp.
Bd. 2: 1. *Soziale und rechtliche Hilfsmassnahmen für die luftkriegsbetroffene Bevölkerung ...* xvi + 716 pp., maps.
    2. *Die Lage des deutschen Volkes und die allgemeinen Rechtsprobleme der Opfer des Luftkrieges von 1945–1948.* xii + 384 pp.
Bd. 3: *Die kriegssachgeschädigte Wirtschaft, Industrie, Handel und Gewerbe, Landwirtschaft.* xv + 973 pp.
Bd. 4: 1. *Massnahmen im Wohnungsbau ... sowie Rechtsprobleme ...* xvi + 591 pp., map.
    2. *Kriegs- und Nachkriegsschicksal der Reichshauptstadt.* xix + 1139 pp.
Bd. 5: *Bibliographie.* Zusammenst.: Ewald Willim. viii + 420 pp.
Beiheft 1: *Aus den Tagen des Luftkrieges und des Wiederaufbaus. Erlebnis- und Erfahrungsberichte.* 461 pp.
Beiheft 2: *Der Luftkrieg im Spiegel der neutralen Presse.* xi + 496 pp.
[General ed.: Peter Paul Nahm (for Bd. 1 with Edgar von Wietersheim).]

COLOGNE
4898   TAYLOR, ERIC: *1000 Bomber auf Köln. Operation Millenium 1942. Ein Bild/*

Text Band. Düsseldorf: Droste, 1979. 178 pp., illus., maps. [Transl. from the English.]

4899 WINKELKEMPER, TONI: *Der Grossangriff an Köln. Englands Luftkrieg gegen Zivilbevölkerung. Ein Beispiel.* Berlin: Eher, 1942. 64 pp.

DRESDEN
4900 BERGANDER, GÖTZ: *Dresden im Luftkrieg.* Köln: Böhlau, 1977. xv + 341 pp., illus., maps, bibl.

4901 IRVING, DAVID: *The destruction of Dresden.* Forew.: Robert Saundby. London: Kimber, 1963. 255 pp., illus., maps, diagrs. [German version: *Der Untergang Dresdens.* Gütersloh: Mohn, 1964.]

4902 EULER, HELMUTH: *Als Deutschlands Dämme brachen.* 3. Aufl. Stuttgart: Motorbuch Verlag, 1975. 224 pp., illus., tabs., facsims., bibl.

4903 EVANGELISCHER BUND: *Zerstörte Kirchen—lebende Gemeinde. Tatsachen und Zeugnisse zum Luftkrieg.* Berlin: Heliand-Verlag, 1944. 150 pp., illus.

4904 HABERMACHER, GERHARD: *Reuter fälscht die Luftkriegsschuld.* Mitw.: Walther Koerber. Nürnberg: Willmy, 1944. 136 pp.

HAMBURG
4905 BRUNSWIG, HANS: *Feuersturm über Hamburg. Die Luftangriffe auf Hamburg im Zweiten Weltkrieg und ihre Folgen.* Stuttgart: Motorbuch Verlag, 1978. 472 pp., illus., facsims., maps.

4906 MIDDLEBROOK, MARTIN: *The battle of Hamburg. Allied bomber forces against a German city in 1943.* London: Allen Lane, 1980. 424 pp., illus., maps, bibl.

4907 HAMPE, ERICH, ed.: *Der zivile Luftschutz im Zweiten Weltkrieg. Dokumentation und Erfahrungsberichte über Aufbau und Einsatz.* Frankfurt a.M.: Bernard & Graefe, 1963. xvi + 627 pp., tabs.

4908 HASTINGS, MAX: *Bomber Command.* London: Michael Joseph, 1979. 399 pp. [Critical of Bomber Command, incl. material on bombing of Germany.]

4909 KIRCHNER, WILHELM: *Feldballon und Luftsperren.* Berlin: Mittler, 1939. 96 pp., illus.

4910 KOCH, HORST-ADALBERT: *Flak. Die Geschichte der deutschen Flakartillerie 1935–1945.* Bad Nauheim: Podzun, 1954. 243 pp., illus.

4911 KOHLHAUSEN, H.: *Der Kampf des deutschen Kunstschutzes um die Erhaltung europäischer Kulturwerte (Massnahmen gegen den angelsächsischen Bombenterror).* Prag: Graphia-Verlag, 1944. 20 + [32] pp., illus.

4912 KUROWSKI, FRANZ: *Der Luftkrieg über Deutschland.* Düsseldorf: Econ Verlag, 1977. 424 pp.

4913 [NUREMBERG] MIDDLEBROOK, MARTIN: *The Nuremberg raid, 30–31 March 1944.* London: Allen Lane, 1973. 369 pp., illus.

4914 [OFFENBACH a.M.] LUX, EUGEN: *Die Luftangriffe auf Offenbach am Main 1939–1945. Eine Dokumentation.* Offenbach a.M: Offenbacher Geschichtsverein, 1971. 147 pp., illus., facsims., plans, tabs., bibl.

4915 POLLARD, A. O.: *Bombers over the Reich.* London: Hutchinson, 1941. viii + 208 pp., illus., tabs.

4916 RUMPF, HANS: *Das war der Bombenkrieg. Deutsche Städte im Feuersturm. Ein Dokumentarbericht.* Oldenburg: Stalling, 1961. 208 pp., illus.

4917 [STUTTGART] *Chronik der Stadt Stuttgart, 4: Stuttgart im Luftkrieg 1939–1945. Mit Dokumentenanhang.* [By] Heinz Bardua. Stuttgart: Klett, 1967. Illus.

4918 *Target: Germany. The US Army Air Force's official story of the VIII Bomber Command's first year over Europe.* London: HMSO, 1944. 119 pp., illus., maps, diagrs.

4919 WEBSTER, CHARLES & NOBLE, FRANKLAND: *The strategic air offensive against Germany, 1939–1945.* London: HMSO, 1961. 4 vols. (History of the Second World War, UK series).

7. NAVY

a. Prewar

4920 BENSEL, ROLF: *Die deutsche Flottenpolitik von 1933 bis 1939. Eine Studie über die Rolle des Flottenbaus in Hitlers Aussenpolitik.* Berlin: Mittler, 1958. 77 pp., tabs., bibl. (Beiheft 3 der 'Marine Rundschau').

4921 BUCHARTZ, MAX & ZELLER, EDGAR: *Matrosen, Soldaten, Kameraden. Ein Bildbuch von der Reichsmarine.* Hamburg: Deutsche Hausbücherei, 1933. 127 pp., illus., facsim.

4922 DÖNITZ, KARL: *Die U-Bootswaffe.* 2. Aufl. Berlin: Mittler, 1939. 65 pp.

b. War at sea

'ALTMARK'
4923 FOLEY, THOMAS: *I was an 'Altmark' prisoner. The first authentic account of the 'Graf Spee's' activities, life aboard the raider and life aboard the hellship 'Altmark'...* London: Aldor, 1940. 127 pp.

4924 FRISCH, FRIEDRICH: *Der Überfall auf die 'Altmark'.* Berlin: Deutsche Informationsstelle, 1940. 64 pp., illus.

4925 BEKKER, CAJUS: *Kampf und Untergang der Kriegsmarine. Ein Dokumentarbericht aufgezeichnet nach zahlreichen Dokumenten ...* Rastatt/Bad.: Pabel, 1961. 184 pp.

4926 BEKKER, C. D.: *Swastika at sea. The struggle and destruction of the German navy, 1939–1945.* London: Kimber, 1954. 207 pp., illus.

4927 ['BISMARCK'] BERTHOLD, WILL: *The sinking of the Bismarck.* London: Longmans Green, 1958. 190 pp., illus.

4928 CANT, GILBERT: *The war at sea.* New York: Day, 1942. 340 pp., illus., maps, tabs.

4929 DÖNITZ, KARL: *Deutsche Strategie zur See im Zweiten Weltkrieg. Die Antworten des Grossadmirals auf 40 Fragen.* Frankfurt a.M.: Bernard & Graefe, 1970. 230 pp. [First ed. in Paris, 1969, under title *La guerre en 40 questions.*]

4930 *Führer conferences on naval affairs, 1939–1945. With an index.* London: The Admiralty, 1947. 7 vols.

4931 GEMZEL, CARL-AXEL: *Raeder, Hitler und Skandinavien. Der Kampf für einen maritimen Operationsplan.* Lund, Sweden: Gleerup, 1965. 390 pp., facsims., maps, bibl.

4932 GEMZEL, CARL AXEL: *Organization, conflict, and innovation. A study of German naval strategic planning, 1888–1940.* Stockholm: Scandinavian University Books, 1973. 448 pp., bibl., diagr.

4933 GIESE, FRIEDRICH: *Die Kriegsmarine im grossdeutschen Freiheitskampf.* Berlin: Limpert, 1940. 103 pp.

4934 GIESE, FRITZ: *Die deutsche Marine 1920 bis 1945.* Frankfurt a.M.: Bernard & Graefe, 1956. 150 pp.

'GRAF SPEE'
4935 MINISTRY OF FOREIGN AFFAIRS, the Oriental Republic of Uruguay: *Uruguayan Blue Book. The documents relating to the sinking of the 'Admiral Graf Spee' and the internment of the merchant vessel 'Tacoma'.* London: Hutchinson, [1940]. 95 pp.

4936 POPE, DUDLEY: *The Battle of the River Plate.* Rev. ed. London: Pan Books, 1974. xv + 220 pp., illus., plans. [First ed.: London: Kimber, 1956. US title: *Graf Spee—the life and death of a raider.*]

4937 MACINTYRE, DONALD: *The naval war against Hitler.* London: Batsford, 1971. 376 pp., illus., maps, diagrs., bibl.

MEDITERRANEAN
4938 ANSEL, WALTER: *Hitler and the Middle Sea.* Durham, N.C.: Duke University Press, 1972. 514 pp., maps, bibl.

4939 BAUM, WALTHER & WEICHOLD, EBERHARD: *Der Krieg der 'Achsenmächte' im Mittelmeerraum. Die Strategie der Diktatoren.* Göttingen: Musterschmidt, 1973. 478 pp., illus., maps, bibl.

4940 COMITÉ D'HISTOIRE DE LA DEUXIÈME GUERRE MONDIALE: *La guerre en Méditerranée, 1939–1945. Actes du Colloque international … Paris … 1969.* Paris: Éds. du Centre national de la Recherche scientifique, 1971. 792 pp., plans.

4941 THOMAS, DAVID A.: *Crete: the battle at sea.* London: André Deutsch, 1972. 224 pp., illus., maps, bibl.

4942 MEIER, FRIEDRICH: *Kriegsmarine am Feind. Ein Bildbericht über den deutschen Freiheitskampf zur See.* Berlin: Klinghammer, 1941. 240 pp.

4943 *Nauticus. Jahrbuch für Deutschlands Seeinteressen.* Berlin: Mittler, 1936/44. 8 vols., illus., maps, diagrs., tabs.

4944 PORTEN, EDWARD P. von der: *The German navy in World War II.* New York: Crowell, 1969. 274 pp., illus., maps, tabs., bibl.

4945 ROHWER, J. & HÜMMELCHEN, G.: *Chronik des Seekriegs 1939–1945.* Hrsg.: Arbeitskreis für Wehrforschung & Bibliothek für Zeitgeschichte. Oldenburg: Stalling, 1968. 655 pp.

4946 RUGE, FRIEDRICH: *Der Seekrieg 1939–1945.* 3. erw. Aufl. Stuttgart: Koehler, 1962. xi + 324 pp.

4947 SALEWSKI, MICHAEL: *Die deutsche Seekriegsleitung 1935–1945.* Frankfurt a.M.: Bernard & Graefe, 1970/75. Illus., maps.
Bd. I: *1935–1941.* Publ. 1970. 595 + xiii pp., bibl.
Bd. II: *1942–1945.* Publ. 1975.
Bd. III: *Denkschriften und Lagebetrachtungen 1938–1944.* Publ. 1973. 411 pp.

4948 ['SCHARNHORST'] WATTS, A. J.: *The loss of the 'Scharnhorst'.* London: Ian Allen, 1970. 84 pp., illus., tabs., diagrs.

4949 THOMAZI, A.: *Le tragique destin des cuirassés allemands.* Paris: Plon, 1946. 118 pp., maps.

4950 ['TIRPITZ'] WOODWARD, DAVID: *The 'Tirpitz'. The story, including the destruction of the 'Scharnhorst', of the campaign against the German battleship.* London: Kimber, 1953. 221 pp., illus.

4951 WAGNER, GERHARD, ed.: *Lagevorträge der Oberbefehlshaber der Kriegsmarine vor Hitler, 1939–1945.* München: Lehmann, 1972. 716 pp., maps, tabs., bibl.

U-boats

4952 ['ATHENIA'] HALFELD, ADOLF: *Der 'Athenia' Fall.* Berlin: Deutsche Informationsstelle, 1940. 40 pp., map, facsims.

4953 BUCHHEIM, LOTHAR-GÜNTHER: *U-Boot Krieg.* Mit einem Essay von Michael Salewski. München: Piper, 1976. [150 pp. approx.], illus. [English verson: *U-boat war.* London: Collins, 1978.]

4954 BUSCH, HARALD: *So war der U-Boot-Krieg.* Bielefeld: Deutscher Heimat-Verlag, 1954. 471 pp., illus. [2nd enl. ed.]

4955 FREYER, PAUL HERBERT: *Der Tod auf allen Meeren. Ein Tatsachenbericht zur Geschichte des faschistischen U-Boot-Krieges.* Berlin [East]: Deutscher Militärverlag, 1970. 390 pp., illus., tabs., map, bibl.

4956 HARTMANN, WERNER: *Feind im Fadenkreuz. U-Boot auf Jagd im Atlantik.* Nacherzählt von Gerhart Weise. Vorw.: Karl Dönitz. Berlin: Jahr, 1943. 232 + [62] pp., illus.

4957 PRIEN, GÜNTHER: *Mein Weg nach Scapa Flow.* Berlin: Deutscher Verlag, 1940. 190 pp., illus. [Author sank the 'Royal Oak' in October 1939.]

4958 FRANK, WOLFGANG: *Prien greift an. Nach Aufzeichnungen des Verfassers an Bord und dem beim Befehlshaber der Unterseeboot vorliegenden dienstlichen Kriegstagebuch des Korvettenkapitäns Günther Prien.* Hamburg: Köhler, 1942. 281 pp., illus., facsims.

4959 FRANK, WOLFGANG: *Der Stier von Scapa Flow. Leben und Taten des U-Boot-Kommandanten Günther Prien.* Oldenburg: Stalling, 1958. 292 pp., illus., map.

4960 RINK, HERMANN: *'Seal' setze weisse Flagge. Wie das grösste englische U-Boot erbeutet wurde.* Berlin: Steiniger, [194–]. 32 pp., illus. (Kriegsbücherei der deutschen Jugend).

E. CAMPAIGNS OF WORLD WAR II

1. POLAND

4961 APPELIUS, MARIO: *Una guerra di 30 giorni. La tragedia della Polonia.* Milano: Sperling & Kupfer, 1940. 277 pp., illus.

4962 BETHELL, NICHOLAS: *The war Hitler won. September 1939.* London: Allen Lane, 1972. viii + 472 pp., illus., facsims., maps, bibl.

4963 BOCHOW, MARTIN: *So siegte Grossdeutschland. Ein Bildbericht aus den weltgeschichtlichen Septembertagen des Jahres 1939. Das neue Gedenkbuch für alle Deutschen.* Berlin: Büchergilde Gutenberg, 1940. 147 pp., illus.

4964 DECKER, WILL, ed.: *Mit dem Spaten durch Polen. Der Reichsarbeitsdienst im polnischen Feldzug.* Leipzig: von Hase & Koehler, 1939. 122 pp., illus.

4965 DIETRICH, OTTO and others: *Auf den Strassen des Sieges. Erlebnisse mit dem Führer in Polen.* Ein Gemeinschaftsbuch von Otto Dietrich, Helmut Sündermann, Wilfrid Bade, Gunter D'Alquen, Heinz Lorenz. München: Eher, 1940. 207 pp., illus.

4966 EICHELBAUM, H., ed.: *Schlag auf Schlag. Die deutsche Luftwaffe in Polen. Ein Tatsachenbericht in Bild und Wort.* Berlin: Reif, 1939. 126 pp., illus., map.

4967 *The German invasion of Poland. Polish Black Book containing documents, authenticated reports and photographs.* Pref.: Archbishop of York. London: Hutchinson, by authority of Polish Ministry of Information, 1940. 128 pp., illus., map, facsim.

4968 HADAMOVSKY, EUGEN: *Blitzmarsch nach Warschau. Frontberichte eines politischen Soldaten.* München: Eher, 1941. 261 pp., map.

4969 KESSELRING, [ALBERT], ed.: *Unsere Flieger über Polen. Vier Frontoffiziere berichten.* Berlin: Deutscher Verlag, 1939. 154 pp., illus.

4970 KORWIN-RHODES, MARTA: *The mask of warriors. The siege of Warsaw, September 1939.* New York: Libra Publs., 1964. 191 pp.

4971 KUCZYNSKI, BOGUSLAW: *El terror viene del cielo.* La Plata: Calomino, 1941. 199 pp.

4972 MORDAL, JACQUES: *La guerre a commencé en Pologne.* Paris: Presses de la Cité, 1968. 318 pp., maps, illus., bibl.

4973 OBERKOMMANDO DER WEHRMACHT & AUFKLÄRUNGSDIENST DER SA: *Der Sieg in Polen.* Geleitw.: General Keitel. Berlin: Andermann, 1939. 174 pp., illus., maps, tabs.

4974 RUDNICKI, K. S.: *The last of the war horses.* London: Bachman & Turner, 1974. 255 pp., illus., maps.

4975 SCHAUFF, RUDOLF: *Der polnische Feldzug. England! Dein Werk!* Berlin: 'Die Wehrmacht', 1939. 61 pp., illus., maps.

4976 SCHLECHT, HEIN & RIECKE, HEINZ, eds.: *Dichter auf den Schlachtfeldern in Polen.* Leipzig: Poeschl & Trepte, [1940?]. 99 pp.

4977 VOGEL, RUDOLF: *Grenzerjunge im Blitzkrieg. Eine Erzählung aus dem Polenfeldzug.* Stuttgart: Union Deutsche Verlagsgesellschaft, 1940. 188 pp., illus.

2. THE PHONY WAR

4978 JOHANN, A. E.: *Zwischen Westwall und Maginotlinie. Der Kampf im Niemandsland.* Berlin: Deutscher Verlag, 1939. 196 pp., illus.

4979 MICHEL, HENRI: *La Drôle de Guerre.* [Paris]: Hachette, 1971. 319 pp., tabs., bibl.

4980 NAEGELEN, MARCEL-EDMOND: *L'attente sous les armes, ou La drôle de guerre.* Paris: Martineau, 1970. 279 pp., maps, tabs., bibl.

3. SCANDINAVIA

4981 BATHE, ROLF: *Der Kampf um die Nordsee. Chronik des Luft- und Seekrieges im Winter 1939/40 und des norwegischen Feldzuges.* Oldenburg: Stalling, 1941. 310 pp., illus., maps.

4982 CURTIS, MONICA: *Norway and the war, September 1939–December 1940.* London: Oxford University Press, 1941. 154 pp.

4983 ENGSTRAND, STUART: *Printemps norvégien 1940.* London: Secker & Warburg, 1944. 422 pp. [Novel.]

4984 GERMAN LIBRARY OF INFORMATION: *Britain's designs on Norway. Documents concerning the Anglo-French policy of extending the war. Full text of the White Book No. 4.* New York: 1940. xxxiii + 150 pp., facsims. [French version: *Le coup de main tenté par l'Angleterre contre la Norvège.* Berlin: Müller, 1940.]

4985 HASE, GEORG VON, ed.: *Die Kriegsmarine erobert Norwegens Fjorde. Erlebnisberichte von Mitkämpfern.* Im Auftr. des Oberkommandos der Kriegsmarine hrsg. 78.–121. Taus. Leipzig: von Hase & Koehler, 1940. 436 pp., illus., maps.

HILLGRUBER, ANDREAS, comp.: *Der Krieg in Finnland, Norwegen und Dänemark, 1. Januar–31. März 1940. See* 4760.

4986 HUBATSCH, WALTHER: *'Weserübung'. Die deutsche Besetzung von Dänemark und Norwegen 1940. Nach amtlichen Unterlagen dargestellt.* Anhang: 'Dokumente zum Norwegenfeldzug 1940'. 2. völlig neu bearb. Aufl. Göttingen: Musterschmidt, 1960. xix + 586 pp., illus., maps.

4987 LEHMKUHL, HERMAN K.: *Hitler attacks Norway.* Forew.: Edward Evans. London: Hodder & Stoughton, for Royal Norwegian Government Information Office, 1943. 99 pp., illus.

4988 LINDBECK-LARSEN, ODD: *Krigen i Norge 1940.* Oslo: Gyldendal Norsk Forlag, 1965. 188 pp., illus., maps.

NARVIK
4989 BUSCH, FRITZ OTTO: *Narvik. Vom Heldenkampf deutscher Zerstörer.* 4. Aufl. Gütersloh: Bertelsmann, 1940. 408 pp., illus., maps.

4990 FANTUR, WERNER: *Narvik—Sieg des Glaubens.* Berlin: Junker & Dünnhaupt, 1941. 174 pp., illus., maps.

4. THE WESTERN FRONT, 1940

a. Attack on the Low Countries

4991 BOVENE, G. A. van, ed.: *Wij waren voort ... Historische feiten en uitspreken vlak vooren en na den 10 den Mei 1940.* Batavia-Centrum: Kloff, 1940. 296 pp., illus.

4992 DEUTSCHE INFORMATIONSSTELLE: *Dokumente britisch–französischer Grausamkeit. Die britische und französische Kriegsführung in den Niederlanden, Belgien und Nordfrankreich im Mai 1940.* Berlin: Volk und Reich Verlag, 1940. 427 pp., illus., facsims. (Hrsg. im Auftr. des Auswärtigen Amtes).

4993 FRANK, FRIEDRICH and others: *Unser Kampf in Holland, Belgien und Flandern vom 10. Mai bis 4. Juni 1940.* München: Bruckmann, 1941. 172 pp., illus., maps.

4994 KLEFFENS, E. N. van: *The rape of the Netherlands.* London: Hodder & Stoughton, 1940. 253 pp., map. [German version: *Der Einfall in die Niederlande.* New York: Europa Verlag, 1941.]

4995 *Luxembourg and the German invasion. Before the war and after.* Pref.: Joseph Bech. London: Hutchinson, by authority of the Government of Luxembourg, 1942. 64 pp., illus.

4996 SCHÄRER, MARTIN R.: *Deutsche Annexionspolitik im Westen. Die Wieder-*

eingliederung Eupen-Malmedys im Zweiten Weltkrieg. 2. verb., um eine Einleitung ... verm. Aufl. Bern: Lang, 1978. 378 + [18] pp., illus., bibl. (Europäische Hochschulschriften ...).

4997 TERKUHLE, E.: *Ik denk aan Rotterdam.* Batavia-Centrum: Kloff, [1941]. 31 pp. [The surprise air raid on Rotterdam heralded the German takeover.]

4998 VERVOOREN, F & KENTIE, W. O., comps.: *Nederland in den oorlog! Historisch document met reproducties van officieele stukken.* 2e 10-duiz. Utrecht: Bruna & Zoon, 1940. 70 pp., illus., facsims., maps, tabs. [Facsims. of placards, ration cards, press items, etc., covering invasion period.]

b. The Six Weeks' War

4999 BEER, WILLY and others: *Unser Kampf in Frankreich. 5.–25. Juni 1940.* München: Bruckmann, 1941. 220 pp., illus., maps.

5000 DEIGHTON, LEN: *Blitzkrieg. From the rise of Hitler to the fall of Dunkirk.* London: Cape, 1979. 307 pp., bibl. [May/June 1940, with a background account of Hitler's rise.]

5001 DRAPER, THEODORE: *The six weeks war. France, May 10–June 25, 1940.* New York: Viking Press, 1944. 346 pp., maps, tabs. [Incl. text of Franco-German armistice.]

FALL GELB

5002 JACOBSEN, HANS-ADOLF: *Fall Gelb. Der Kampf um den deutschen Operationsplan zur Westoffensive 1940.* Wiesbaden: Steiner, 1957. 337 pp., maps. (Veröffentlichungen des Instituts für Europäische Geschichte Mainz).

5003 VETSCH, CHRISTIAN: *Aufmarsch gegen die Schweiz. Der deutsche 'Fall Gelb'— Irreführung der Schweizer Armee 1939/40.* Olten: Walter, 1973. 224 pp., plans, facsims., bibl.

5004 *Der grosse Befehl. Der Sieg im Westen in 100 Bilddokumenten.* Hrsg.: Oberkommando der Wehrmacht. Berlin: Zeitgeschichte-Verlag, 1941. [102 pp.], illus.

5005 JACOBSEN, HANS-ADOLF, ed.: *Dokumente zur Vorgeschichte des Westfeldzuges, 1939–1940.* Göttingen: Musterschmidt, 1956. 225 pp., tabs.

5006 JACOBSEN, HANS-ADOLF, ed.: *Dokumente zum Westfeldzug 1940.* Göttingen: Musterschmidt, 1960. 340 pp., maps.

5007 JACOBSEN, HANS-ADOLF & MÜLLER, K. J.: *Dünkirchen. Ein Beitrag zur Geschichte des Westfeldzuges 1940.* Neckargemünd: Vowinckel, 1958. 239 pp., illus., maps.

5008 LABUSQUIÈRE, JEAN: *Vérité sur les combattants. Grandes batailles de mai et juin 1940.* Documentation de Pierre Léty. Lyon: Lardanchet, 1941. 109 pp., maps.

5009 LAUNAY, MICHEL: *L'armistice de 1940*. Vendôme: Presses Universitaires de France, 1972. 95 pp., map, bibl.

5010 MURAWSKI, ERICH: *Der Durchbruch im Westen. Chronik des holländischen, belgischen und französischen Zusammenbruchs*. 61.–100. Taus. Oldenburg: Stalling, 1940. 343 pp., illus., maps, tabs.

5011 ORDIONI, PIERRE: *Commandos et cinquième colonne en mai 1940. La bataille de Longwy*. Paris: Nouvelles Éds. Latines, 1970. 350 pp.

5012 SCHÄFER, J.: *Entscheidung im Westen. Der Feldzug der 6 Wochen. Die Berichte des OKW vom 10. Mai bis 25. Juni 1940 mit den täglichen militärischen und politischen Erläuterungen der Kölnischen Zeitung*. 40.–50. Taus. Köln: Du Mont Schauberg, 1940. 220 pp., maps, tabs.

5013 TAYLOR, TELFORD: *The march of conquest. The German victories in Western Europe 1940*. London: Hulton, 1959. 460 pp., illus., maps, bibl.

5014 TSCHIMPKE, ALFRED: *Die Gespenster-Division*. 3. Aufl. München: Eher, 1941. 196 pp. [First ed. 1940, subtitled *Mit der Panzerwaffe durch Belgien und Frankreich*.]

5015 WEISS, WILHELM, ed.: *Triumph der Kriegskunst. Das Kriegsjahr 1940 in der Darstellung des 'Völkischen Beobachters'*. Mit Beiträgen von Generalfeldmarschall Kesselring [and others]. München: Eher, 1942. 253 pp., map. [2nd ed.]

5. 'SEELÖWE' ('OPERATION SEA-LION')

5016 CLARKE, COMER: *England under Hitler*. London: New English Library, 1972. 143 pp. [First ed. 1963. German plans for administration of Britain; also incl. occupation of the Channel Islands.]

5017 FLEMING, PETER: *Invasion 1940. An account of the German preparations and the British countermeasures*. London: Hart Davis, 1957. 323 pp., illus.

5018 *German occupied Great Britain. Ordinances of the military authorities*. [Lancing, Sx.: Foord, 197–]. 94 pp. [Reprint of documents first printed in Leipzig 1941.]

5019 KLEE, KARL: *Das Unternehmen 'Seelöwe'. Die geplante deutsche Landung in England 1940*. Göttingen: Musterschmidt, 1958/59.
Bd. 1: Publ. 1958. 300 pp., maps, diagrs., tabs .
Bd. 2: *Dokumente*. Publ. 1959. 457 pp.

5020 LAMPE, DAVID: *The last ditch*. London: Cassell, 1968. 219 pp., illus., maps, tabs., diagrs. [Incl.: 'Sonderfahndungsliste', pp. 173–201 (reduced facsimile).]

5021 NECKER, WILHELM: *Hitler's war machine and the invasion of Britain*. London: Drummond, [1941?]. 281 pp., diagrs., maps.

5022 WHEATLEY, RONALD: *Operation Sea Lion. German plans for the invasion of England 1939–1942*. Oxford: Clarendon Press, 1958. 201 pp., illus., maps.

5023　*Wir fahren gegen Engelland!* Berlin: Deutscher Verlag, [1940] 47 pp., illus., map.

6.　NORTH AFRICA

DEUTSCHES AFRIKAKORPS

5024　LEWIN, RONALD: *The life and death of the Afrika Korps. A biography.* London: Batsford, 1977. 207 pp., illus., maps, bibl.

5025　LUFTWAFFEN-KRIEGSBERICHTER-KOMPANIE: *Balkenkreuz über Wüstensand. Farbbilderwerk vom Deutschen Afrikakorps.* Geleitw.: Generalfeldmarschall Rommel. Oldenburg: Stalling, 1943. 159 pp., illus., map.

5026　*Marsch und Kampf des Deutschen Afrikakorps. Bd. I.* Hrsg.: Generalkommando. München: Röhrig, 1943. 214 pp., illus.

5027　VERBAND EHEMALIGER ANGEHÖRIGER DEUTSCHES AFRIKAKORPS: *Schicksal Nord Afrika.* Hrsg. in Verbindung mit dem Rommel-Sozialwerk. Döffingen Kreis Böblingen/Württ.: Europa-Contact Verlag, 1954. 328 pp., illus., facsims., maps.

5028　HAUPT, WERNER & BINGHAM, J. K. W.: *Der Afrika Feldzug 1941–1943.* Dorheim/H.: Podzun, 1968. 160 pp., illus., maps.

5029　MACKSEY, KENNETH: *Crucible of power. The fight for Tunisia, 1942–1943.* London: Hutchinson, 1969. xiv + 325 pp., illus., maps, bibl.

5030　SCHMIDT, HEINZ WERNER: *With Rommel in the desert.* London: Harrap, 1951. 240 pp., illus.

5031　WAGNER, OTTO: *S Cizineckou Legií proti Rommelovi* [With the Foreign Legion against Rommel]. Praha: Naše Vojsko, 1970. 196 pp., illus., facsims. [Czech emigré and Free French soldiers.]

7.　BALKANS

5032　BATHE, ROLF & GLODSCHEY, ERICH: *Der Kampf um den Balkan. Chronik des jugoslawischen und griechischen Feldzugs.* Oldenburg: Stalling, 1942. 316 pp., illus., maps.

5033　BAUER, HELMUT: *Ein Vielvölkerstaat zerbricht. Werden und Vergehen Jugoslawiens.* 2. erg. und verb. Aufl. Leipzig: Lühe, 1941. 132 pp., maps, bibl.

5034　*Blesková válka na Balkáné* [Blitzkrieg in the Balkans]. Praha: Orbis, 1941. 61 pp., illus.

5035　CREVELD, MARTIN L. van: *Hitler's strategy 1940–1941. The Balkan clue.* London: Cambridge University Press, 1973. x + 248 pp., maps, bibl.

5036　*Dokumente zum Konflikt mit Jugoslawien und Griechenland.* Berlin: Eher, 1941. 198 pp.

5037 MACKENZIE, COMPTON: *Wind of freedom. The history of the invasion of Greece by the Axis powers, 1940–1941.* London: Chatto & Windus, 1943. 275 pp., illus., map.

5038 OVEN, WILFRED VON & HAHN-BUTRY, JÜRGEN: *Panzer am Balkan. Erlebnisbericht der Panzergruppe von Kleist.* Im Auftrag der Panzergruppe hrsg. von der Panzer-Propaganda-Kompanie. Berlin: Limpert, 1941. 228 pp., illus., map, facsim.

5039 PAPAGOS, ALEXANDER: *The Battle of Greece, 1940–1941.* Transl. into English. Athens: Scazikis 'Alpha', 1949. 406 pp., illus., maps.

8. SOVIET UNION

a. Up to the Battle of Stalingrad

5040 ANDERLE, ALFRED & BASLER, WERNER, eds.: *Juni 1941. Beiträge zur Geschichte des hitlerfaschistischen Überfalls auf die Sowjetunion.* Berlin [East]: Rütten & Loening, 1961. 368 pp. (Veröffentlichungen des Instituts für Geschichte der Völker der UdSSR an der ... Universität Halle-Wittenberg ...). [Incl. resistance in Poland and Czechoslovakia; also 'Nationalkomitee Freies Deutschland'.]

5041 ANTIKOMINTERN: *Warum Krieg mit Stalin? Das Rotbuch der Anti-Komintern.* Berlin: Nibelungen-Verlag, 1941. 128 pp., illus., tabs.

5042 BESYMENSKI, LEW: *Sonderakte 'Barbarossa'. Dokumente, Darstellung, Deutung.* Stuttgart: Deutsche Verlags-Anstalt, 1968. 351 pp., tabs., bibl.

5043 CECIL, ROBERT: *Hitler's decision to invade Russia, 1941.* London: Davis-Poynter, 1975. 192 pp., map, bibl.

5044 *Front am Polarkreis. Das Buch eines Lappland-Korps. Deutsche Soldaten im finnischen Urwald.* Berlin: Limpert, 1943. 163 pp., illus., maps, diagr.

5045 GERCKE, FRITZ: *Nach Hause geschrieben. Aus dem Feldzug 1941 gegen Sowjet-Russland.* Berlin: Zander, 1941. 160 pp., illus., mus. score.

5046 GOITSCH, HEINRICH & RAHS, HANS: *Die Wahrheit über den Ostfeldzug. Dokumente englischer Lügen und Irrtümer mit einer Chronik des Ostfeldzuges.* Düsseldorf: Völkischer Verlag, 1942. 114 pp.

5047 HELMDACH, ERICH: *Überfall? Der sowjetisch-deutsche Aufmarsch 1941.* 3. Aufl. Neckargemünd: Vowinckel, 1976. 132 pp., map, bibl.

5048 LOOK, HANS & FISCHER, HANS, comps.: *Arbeitsmänner zwischen Bug und Volga. Erlebnisberichte und Bilder vom Einsatz des jüngsten Jahrganges an der Ostfront.* Berlin: Eher, 1942. 104 pp.

5049 NIEDERLEIN, FRITZ, ed.: *Sieg über Raum und Zeit.* Berlin: Limpert, 1943. 432 pp., illus., maps.

5050 MILDNER, FRIEDRICH, ed.: *Flak vor! Mit unseren Panzern vom Bug bis vor die*

Tore Moskaus. Bearb.: Gerhard Kirsch, Joachim Schulz-Werner. Berlin: Limpert, 1943. 387 pp., illus.

5051 PETROV, VLADIMIR: *'June 22nd, 1941'. Soviet historians and the German invasion.* Columbia, S.C.: University of South Carolina Press, 1968. 322 pp.

5052 RIEKER, KARL-HEINRICH: *Ein Mann verliert einen Weltkrieg. Die entscheidenden Monate des deutsch-russischen Krieges 1942/43.* Frankfurt a.M.: Fridericus-Verlag, 1955. 307 pp.

5053 STOLTE, HEINZ: *Zwei Jahre Witebsk. Am 10. Juli 1941 wurde die Stadt Witebsk von deutschen Truppen eingenommen.* [No pl.]: Panzer-Propaganda 697, 1943. 24 pp., illus.

5054 TIEKE, WILHELM: *Der Kaukasus und das Öl. Der deutsch-sowjetische Krieg in Kaukasien 1942/43.* Osnabrück: Munin, 1970. 504 pp., illus., maps, bibl.

5055 TOLSTOY, ALEXEI: *My country. Articles and stories of the Great Patriotic War of the Soviet Union.* Transl. from the Russian. London: Hutchinson, 1943. 117 pp.

Leningrad

5056 GOURE, LEON: *The siege of Leningrad.* Stanford, Calif.: Stanford University Press, 1962. 363 pp., illus., maps, bibl.

5057 PAWLOW, DMITRIJ W.: *Die Blockade von Leningrad 1941.* Fraunfeld: Huber, 1967. 230 pp., illus., map, tabs. [Transl. from the Russian.]

Moscow

5058 *Die Niederlage der Hitlerarmee vor Moskau. Eine Sammlung von Dokumenten und Aufsätzen.* Moskau: Verlag für Fremdsprachige Literatur, 1943. 97 pp., maps, illus.

5059 REINHARD, KLAUS: *Die Wende vor Moskau. Das Scheitern der Strategie Hitlers im Winter 1941/42.* Stuttgart: Deutsche Verlags-Anstalt, 1972. 355 pp., tabs., maps, bibl.

5060 SETH, RONALD: *Operation Barbarossa. The battle for Moscow.* London: Blond, 1964. 191 pp., maps, bibl.

5061 TURNEY, ALFRED W.: *Disaster at Moscow. Von Bock's campaigns 1941–1942.* Albuquerque, N.Mex.: University of New Mexico Press, 1970. 228 pp., illus., maps, diagrs., bibl.

b. Stalingrad

5062 KERR, WALTER: *Das Geheimnis Stalingrad. Hintergründe einer Entscheidungsschlacht.* Düsseldorf: Econ Verlag, 1977. 388 pp. [English version: *The secret of Stalingrad.* London: Macdonald and Jane's, 1978, x + 274 pp., illus., maps, bibl.]

5063 ROHDEN, HANS-DETLEF HERHUDT von: *Die Luftwaffe ringt um Stalingrad.* Wiesbaden: Limes Verlag, 1950. 148 pp.

5064 SEYDLITZ, WALTHER VON: *Stalingrad. Konflikt und Konsequens. Erinnerungen.* Einl.: Bodo Scheurig. Oldenburg: Stalling, 1977. 387 pp., map.

5065 WIEDER, JOACHIM: *Stalingrad und die Verantwortung der Soldaten.* Geleitw.: Helmut Gollwitzer. München: Nymphenburger Verlagshandlung, 1962. 334 pp., map, bibl. [Incl. documents (in Supplement).]

c. General

5066 CARELL, PAUL: *Hitler's war on Russia.* Transl. from the German by Ewald Osers. London: Harrap, 1964/70. Illus.
[1]: *The story of the German defeat in the East.* Publ. 1964. 640 pp.
2: *Scorched earth.* Publ. 1970. 556 pp.
[German orig.: 1. *Unternehmen Barbarossa*; 2. *Verbrannte Erde*; 3. *Der Russlandkrieg fotografiert von Soldaten. Der Bildband.* Berlin: Ullstein, 1963/67.]

5067 CLARK, ALAN: *Barbarossa. The Russian–German conflict 1941–1945.* London: Hutchinson, 1965. 444 pp., illus., maps, bibl.

5068 DOERR, HANS: *Der Feldzug nach Stalingrad. Versuch eines operativen Überblicks.* Darmstadt: Mittler, 1955. 139 pp., maps, bibl.

5069 EHRENBURG, ILYA: *The war 1941–45.* London: MacGibbon & Kee, 1964. 198 pp., illus. (*Men, years—life.* Vol. V). [Transl. from the Russian.]

5070 FISCHER, ALEXANDER: *Sowjetische Deutschlandpolitik im Zweiten Weltkrieg 1941–1945.* Stuttgart: Deutsche Verlagsanstalt, 1975. 252 pp., bibl. (Hrsg. vom Institut für Zeitgeschichte).

5071 *Great Patriotic War of the Soviet Union 1941–1945. A general outline.* Moscow: Progress Publs., 1974. 269 pp., illus., maps. [Abridged transl. of the Russian ed. of 1970.]

5072 INSTITUT FÜR MARXISMUS-LENINISMUS BEIM ZENTRALKOMITEE DER KOMMUNISTI-SCHEN PARTEI DER SOWJETUNION: *Geschichte des Grossen Vaterländischen Krieges der Sowjetunion.* Berlin [East]: Deutscher Militärverlag, 1962/65. 6 vols., illus., facsims., tabs., & maps in separate folder.

5073 MIDDELDORF, EIKE: *Taktik im Russlandfeldzug. Erfahrungen und Folgerungen.* Darmstadt: Mittler, 1956. 239 pp., diagrs.

5074 MRÁZKOVÁ, DANIELA & REMES, VLADIMÍR, eds.: *The Russian war, 1941–1945.* Text: A. J. P. Taylor. London: Cape, 1978. 143 pp., illus. [Czech orig.: *Fotografovali Válku.* German version: *Von Moskau nach Berlin.* Oldenburg: Stalling, 1979. Russian photographs.]

5075 SEATON, ALBERT: *The Russo-German war, 1941–1945.* London: Barker, 1971. xix + 628 pp., maps, tabs., bibl.

5076 UEBE, KLAUS: *Russian reactions to German airpower in World War II.* Introd.: Telford Taylor. New York: Arno Press, 1968. 146 + xviii + [6] pp., illus., diagrs., maps, bibl. (USAF Historical Studies). [Reprinted from 1964 ed., publ. by USAF Historical Division, ed. Harry R. Fletcher.]

5077 UHLIG, HEINRICH: 'Das Einwirken Hitlers auf Planung und Führung des Ostfeldzuges'. [In] *Aus Politik und Zeitgeschichte*, 16., 23. März 1960. Bonn: Bundeszentrale für Heimatdienst. Pp. 161–198.

5078 WERTH, ALEXANDER: *Russia at war, 1941–1945*. London: Barrie & Rockliff, 1964. 1100 pp., maps, bibl. [Incl. Nazi crimes in Ukraine and other parts of Soviet Union; extermination of Jews; partisans; Majdanek concentration camp. German version: *Russland im Krieg 1941–1945*. München: Droemer Knaur, 1965.]

9. ITALY

5079 CAVAGLIONE, PINO LEVI: *Guerriglia nel castelli Romani*. Roma: Einaudi, 1945. 165 pp.

5080 CONNELL, CHARLES: *Monte Cassino. The historic battle*. Foreword: W. Anders. London: Elek, 1963. 206 pp., illus., maps.

5081 KUROWSKI, FRANZ: *Das Tor zur Festung-Europa. Abwehr und Rückzugskämpfe des XIV. Panzerkorps auf Sizilien, Sommer 1943*. Neckargemünd: Vowinckel, 1966. 168 pp., maps, bibl.

5082 LINKLATER, ERIC: *The campaign in Italy*. London: HMSO, 1951. 480 pp., illus., maps. (The Second World War, 1939–1945).

5083 SCHRÖDER, JOSEF: *Italiens Kriegsaustritt 1943. Die deutschen Gegenmassnahmen im italienischen Raum: Fall 'Alarich' und 'Achse'*. Göttingen: Musterschmidt, 1969. 412 pp., illus., maps, diagrs., tabs., bibl.

10. DEFEAT IN THE EAST AND SOUTH

5084 ANDERS, WLADYSLAW: *Hitler's defeat in Russia*. Forew.: Truman Smith. Chicago, Ill.: Regnery, 1953. xv + 267 pp.

5085 FRIESSNER, HANS: *Verratene Schlachten. Die Tragödie der deutschen Wehrmacht in Rumänien und Ungarn*. Hamburg: Holsten, 1956. 267 pp., illus., maps.

5086 GOSZTONY, PETER: *Endkampf an der Donau 1944/45*. Wien: Molden, 1969. 356 pp., illus., maps, bibl.

5087 GUILLAUME, A.: *Warum siegte die Rote Armee?* Geleitw.: Walter Bedell Smith. Baden-Baden: Verlag für Kunst und Wissenschaft, 1950. 296 pp., illus., maps.

5088 HNILICKA, KARL: *Das Ende auf dem Balkan 1944/45. Die militärische Räumung Jugoslawiens durch die deutsche Wehrmacht*. Göttingen: Musterschmidt, 1970. 404 pp., illus., maps, bibl.

5089 KISSEL, HANS: *Die Katastrophe in Rumänien 1944*. Darmstadt: Wehr und Wissen Verlagsgesellschaft, 1964. 287 pp., maps.

5090 KLINK, ERNST: *Das Gesetz des Handelns. Die Operation 'Zitadelle' 1943*. Stuttgart: Deutsche Verlags-Anstalt, 1966. 355 pp., tabs., maps, bibl.

5091 STUHLPFARRER, KARL: *Die Operationszonen 'Alpenvorland' und 'Adriatisches Küstenland' 1943–1945*. Wien: Hollinek, 1969. 179 pp., tabs., bibl. (Publikationen des Österreichischen Institut für Zeitgeschichte...).

Austria

5092 RAUCHENSTEINER, MANFRIED: *Krieg in Österreich 1945*. Wien: Österreichischer Bundesverlag für Unterricht, Wissenschaft und Kunst, 1970. 388 pp., illus., maps, plans, tabs., bibl. (Schriften des Heeresgeschichtlichen Museums in Wien).

5093 ROSSIWALL, THEO: *Die letzten Tage. Die militärische Besetzung Österreichs 1945*. Wien: Kremayr & Scherian, 1969. 351 pp., illus., plans, facsims., bibl.

5094 SCHÄRF, ADOLF: *April 1945 in Wien*. Wien: Deutsch, 1948. 127 pp.

5095 WEIBEL-ALTMEYER, HEINZ: *Hitlers Alpenfestung. Ein Dokumentarbericht*. [Klagenfurt]: Kaiser, 1971. 291 pp. [First ed. 1966].

11. DEFEAT IN THE WEST

ARDENNES OFFENSIVE

5096 ELSTOB, PETER: *Hitler's last offensive*. London: Secker & Warburg, 1971. xvi + 413 pp., diagr., maps, bibl.

5097 JUNG, HERMANN: *Die Ardennen-Offensive 1944/45. Ein Beispiel für die Kriegsführung Hitlers*. Göttingen: Musterschmidt, 1971. 406 pp., illus., maps, tabs., bibl.

5098 NOBÉCOURT, JACQUES: *Le dernier coup de dès de Hitler. La bataille des Ardennes*. Paris: Laffont, 1962. 438 pp., illus., maps, bibl. [English version: *Hitler's last gamble*. London: Chatto & Windus, 1967.]

5099 ARON, ROBERT: *De Gaulle before Paris. The liberation of France, June–August 1944*. Transl. from the French. London: Putnam, 1962. 312 pp.

5100 ARON, ROBERT: *De Gaulle triumphant. The liberation of France, August 1944–May 1945*. Transl. from the French. London: Putnam, 1964. 360 pp., bibl.

ATLANTIC WALL

5101 PARTRIDGE, COLIN: *Hitler's Atlantic Wall*. Castel, Guernsey: D.I. Publs., 1976. 144 pp., illus.

5102 VENNEMANN, WOLFGANG: *Les forteresses de l'Atlantique contre l'Angleterre*. [Paris]: 1943. 72 pp., illus., maps, tabs. [Cover title: *De Vauban à Todt*.]

5103 BENNETT, RALPH: *Ultra in the West. The Normandy campaign, 1944/45*. London: Hutchinson, 1979. 305 pp.

5104 CARELL, PAUL: *Sie kommen. Der deutsche Bericht über die Invasion und die*

80tägige Schlacht um Frankreich. Frankfurt a.M.: Ullstein, 1964. 246 pp., maps.

5105 PIEKALKIEWICZ, JANUSZ: *Invasion: Frankreich 1944.* München: Südwest Verlag, 1979. 320 pp., illus.

5106 RUGE, FRIEDRICH: *Rommel und die Invasion. Erinnerungen.* Stuttgart: Koehler, 1959. 286 pp., illus., maps.

5107 SCHRAMM, PERCY ERNST, ed.: *Die Invasion 1944. Aus dem Kriegstagebuch des Oberkommandos der Wehrmacht (Wehrmachtführungsstab).* München: Deutscher Taschenbuch Verlag, 1963. 293 pp.

5108 SHULMAN, MILTON: *Defeat in the West.* Introd.: Ian Jacob. London: Secker & Warburg, 1947. 336 pp., illus., maps, bibl. [German version: *Die Niederlage im Westen.* Einf.: Gerhard Ritter. Gütersloh: Bertelsmann, 1949.]

5109 SPEIDEL, HANS: *Invasion 1944. Ein Beitrag zu Rommels und des Reiches Schicksal.* Tübingen: Wunderlich, 1952. 202 pp.

5110 THOMPSON, R. W.: *The Battle for the Rhineland.* London: Hutchinson, 1958. 241 pp., maps.

Victory in the West, Series 3. See 4624.

5111 WESTPHAL, SIEGFRIED: *Heer in Fesseln. Aus den Papieren des Stabschefs von Rommel, Kesselring und Rundstedt.* Bonn: Athenäum-Verlag, 1950. 332 pp., illus., maps. [English version: *The German army in the West.* London: Cassell, 1951.]

12. DEFEAT IN GERMANY

5112 BERNADOTTE, Count FOLKE: *The curtain falls. Last days of the Third Reich.* Transl. from the Swedish. New York: Knopf, 1945. 155 pp., illus. [German version: *Das Ende. Meine Verhandlungen in Deutschland im Frühjahr 1945 und ihre politischen Folgen.* Zürich: Europa Verlag, 1945. Incl. Swedish rescue action for Danish, Norwegian and Jewish prisoners of the Nazis.]

5113 BLOND, GEORGES: *The death of Hitler's Germany.* Transl. from the French. New York: Macmillan, 1954. 302 pp., maps, bibl. [French orig.: *L'agonie de l'Allemagne.* Paris: Fayard, 1952.]

5114 CHUIKOV, VASILI I: *The end of the Third Reich.* Transl. from the Russian. Introd.: Alastair Horne. London: McGibbon & Kee, 1967. 261 pp., maps. [Reprinted: Moscow: Progress Publs., 1978.]

5115 [DOENITZ GOVERNMENT] STEINERT, MARLIS G.: *Die 23 Tage der Regierung Dönitz.* Düsseldorf: Econ-Verlag, 1967. 426 pp., bibl. [English version: *Capitulation 1945.* London: Constable, 1969.]

5116 DOLLINGER, HANS, ed.: *Die letzten hundert Tage. Das Ende des Zweiten Weltkrieges in Europa und Asien.* Wissenschaftliche Beratung: Hans-Adolf Jacobsen. München: Desch, 1965. 431 pp., illus., facsims., maps, tabs., bibl.

5117 FÖRSTER, GERHARD & LAKOWSKI, RICHARD, comps.: *1945. Das Jahr der endgültigen Niederlage der faschistischen Wehrmacht. Dokumente.* Berlin [East]: Militärverlag der DDR, 1975. 462 pp.

5118 KOLLER, KARL: *Der letzte Monat. Die Tagebuchaufzeichnungen des ehemaligen Chefs des Generalstabes der deutschen Luftwaffe von 14. April bis zum 27. Mai 1945.* Mannheim: Wohlgemüth, 1949. 138 pp.

5119 LAUNAY, JACQUES de: *Les derniers jours de fascisme en Europe.* Paris: Albatros, 1974. 321 pp.

RESISTANCE BY GERMANS

5120 KISSEL, HANS: *Der deutsche Volkssturm 1944/1945. Eine territoriale Miliz im Rahmen der Landesverteidigung.* Frankfurt a.M.: Mittler, 1962. 173 pp., illus., map, bibl.

5121 MINOTT, RODNEY G.: *The fortress that never was. The myth of Hitler's Bavarian stronghold.* New York: Holt, Rinehart & Winston, 1964. 208 pp., illus., maps.

5122 WHITING, CHARLES: *Werewolf. The story of the Nazi resistance movement, 1944–1945.* London: Cooper, 1972. 208 pp., illus.

5123 TOLAND, JOHN: *The last 100 days.* London: Barker, 1966. 622 pp., illus., maps, bibl.

Berlin

5124 BOVERI, MARGRET: *Tage des Überlebens. Berlin 1945.* München: Piper, 1968. 337 pp., facsim.

5125 DAVID, PAUL: *Am Königsplatz. Die letzten Tage der Schweizerischen Gesandtschaft in Berlin.* Zürich: Thomas, 1948. 166 pp.

5126 JERK, WIKING: *Endkampf um Berlin.* 2. Aufl. Buenos Aires: Dürer-Verlag, [1947]. 172 pp.

5127 KUBY, ERICH: *Die Russen in Berlin 1945.* München: Scherz, 1965. 426 pp., illus.

5128 SCHENCK, ERNST-GÜNTHER: *Ich sah Berlin sterben. Als Arzt in der Reichskanzlei.* Herford: Nicolai, 1970. 190 pp.

5129 STRAWSON, JOHN: *The battle for Berlin.* London: Batsford, 1974. 182 pp., illus.

5130 TULLY, ANDREW: *Berlin. Story of a battle.* New York: Simon & Schuster, 1963. 304 pp., illus., maps, bibl.

See also 721–725.

Other towns and regions

BAYREUTH

5131 MEYER, WERNER: *Götterdämmerung. April 1945 in Bayreuth.* Percha am Starnberger See: Schulz, 1975. 208 pp.

5132 SCHWARZWÄLDER, HERBERT: *Bremen und Nordwestdeutschland am Kriegsende 1945. I: Die Vorbereitung um den Endkampf.* Bremen: Schünemann, 1972. 205 pp., illus., facsims., plans, bibl.

5133 HORNIG, ERNST: *Breslau 1945. Erlebnisse in der eingeschlossenen Stadt.* Geleitw.: Joachim Konrad. München: Korn, 1975. 287 pp., bibl.

5134 WAGNER, DIETER: *München '45 zwischen Ende und Anfang.* München: Süddeutscher Verlag, 1970. 174 pp., illus., facsim., maps, bibl.

5135 HARTUNG, HUGO: *Schlesien 1944/45. Aufzeichnungen und Tagebücher.* München: Deutscher Taschenbuch Verlag, 1976. 158 pp.

5136 MAIER, REINHOLD: *Ende und Wende. Das schwäbische Schicksal 1944–1946. Briefe und Tagebuchaufzeichnungen.* Tübingen: Wunderlich, 1948. 415 pp.

German prisoners of war

5137 ANDERS, WILHELM, ed.: *Verbrechen der Sieger. Das Schicksal der deutschen Kriegsgefangenen in Osteuropa.* 2. Aufl. Leoni am Starnberger See: Druffel, 1976. 398 pp., bibl.

5138 MASCHKE, ERICH: *Die deutschen Kriegsgefangenen des Zweiten Weltkrieges. Eine Zusammenfassung.* In Verbindung mit Kurt W. Böhme [and others]. München: Gieseking, 1974. x + 446 pp., illus., tabs. (Zur Geschichte der deutschen Kriegsgefangenen des II. Weltkrieges).

5139 SULLIVAN, MATTHEW BARRY: *Thresholds of peace. Four hundred thousand German prisoners and the people of Britain, 1944–1948.* London: Hamish Hamilton, 1979. xi + 420 pp., illus., bibl.

5140 WOLFF, HELMUT: *Die deutschen Kriegsgefangenen in britischer Hand. Ein Überblick.* München: Gieseking, 1974. xvi + 605 pp. (Zur Geschichte der deutschen Kriegsgefangenen des II. Weltkrieges).

F. ESPIONAGE AND SABOTAGE

5141 ACCOCE, PIERRE & QUET, PIERRE: *La guerre a été gagnée en Suisse: L'affaire Roessler.* Paris: Perrin, 1966. 318 pp., illus., facsims., bibl. [English version: *The Lucy ring.* London: Allen, 1967.]

5142 BEST, S. PAYNE: *The Venlo incident.* London: Hutchinson, [1950?]. 260 pp., illus., plan, facsims. [Incl. imprisonment in various concentration camps.]

5143 BROCKDORFF, WERNER: *Geheimkommandos des Zweiten Weltkrieges. Geschichte und Einsätze der Brandenburger, der englischen Commands [sic] und SAS-Einheiten, der amerikanischen Rangers und sowjetischer Geheimdienste.* München: Welsermühl, 1967. 446 pp., illus., bibl.

5144 EPPLER, JOHN: *Operation Condor. Rommel's spy.* Transl. by S. Seago. London: Macdonald & Jane's, 1977. 250 pp., illus.

5145 GARLIŃSKI, JÓZEF: *Intercept. Secrets of the Enigma war.* Introd.: R. V. Jones. London: Dent, 1979. 219 pp. [Appendix by Tadeusz Lisicki. On the Polish breaking of the Ultra code.]

5146 GRACHT, HANS: *Die fünfte Kolonne.* Berlin: Mölich, 1941. 47 pp.

5147 GUILLAUME, GILBERT: *Mes missions face à l'Abwehr. Contre-espionnage, 1938–1945.* Paris: Plon, 1971. 248 pp.

GUISAN, HENRI
5148 GUISAN, HENRI: *Bericht an die Bundesversammlung über den Aktivdienst 1939–1945.* Bern: Rösch, Vogt, 1946. 273 pp.

5149 KIMCHE, JON: *Spying for peace. General Guisan and Swiss neutrality.* London: Weidenfeld & Nicolson, 1961. 168 pp., map. [German version: *General Guisans Zweifrontenkrieg.* Frankfurt a.M.: Ullstein, 1967.]

5150 HINSLEY, FRANCIS HARRY: and others: *British intelligence in the Second World War. Its influence on strategy and operations. Vol. I.* London: HMSO, 1979. (History of the Second World War).

5151 KAHN, DAVID: *Hitler's spies. German military intelligence in WW2.* London: Hodder & Stoughton, 1978. xiii + 671 pp., illus., maps. [From a dissertation.]

5152 MORAVEC, FRANTISEK: *Master of spies. The memoirs.* Preface: J. C. Masterman. London: The Bodley Head, 1975. 251 pp., map.

OPERATION BERNHARD
5153 BURGER, A.: *Padělal jsem dolary* [I have forged dollars]. Praha: [priv. pr.], 1948. 88 pp., illus., facsims. [Eyewitness account of Nazi counterfeiting operations, written down by Jindrich Lion.]

5154 PIRIE, ANTHONY: *Operation Bernhard. The greatest forgery of all time.* London: Cassell, 1961. 236 pp., illus., bibl.

5155 RÁDO, SÁNDOR: *Deckname Dora.* Stuttgart: Deutsche Verlags-Anstalt, [1971?]. 441 pp. [Orig. Hungarian title: *Dora jelenti ...*]

5156 REILE, OSCAR: *Macht und Ohnmacht der Geheimdienste. Der Einfluss der Geheimdienste der USA, Englands, der UdSSR, Frankreichs und Deutschlands auf die politischen und militärischen Ereignisse im Zweiten Weltkrieg.* München: Welsermühl, 1968. 331 pp., bibl. [Incl. Canaris and Rote Kapelle.]

5157 RÉMY (pseud. of Gilbert Renault): *Mémoires d'un agent de la France Libre, Juin 1940–Juin 1942.* Paris: Solar, 1947. 552 pp., illus. [English version: *Memoirs of a secret agent of Free France. Vol. I: June 1940–June 1942: The silent company.* New York: McGraw-Hill, 1948.]

5158 ROWAN, RICHARD WILMER: *Terror in our time. The Secret Service of surprise attack.* New York: Longmans, Green, 1941. 438 pp., maps.

5159 SEID, ALFRED: *Der englische Geheimdienst.* Berlin: Junker & Dünnhaupt, 1940. 44 pp., tab.

5160 SLADE, (Marquis) de: *The frustrated Axis.* Witten: [priv. pr., 197–]. xvi + 142 pp., port. [Attempts to subvert British prisoners of war.]

SPECIAL OPERATIONS EXECUTIVE

5160a COOKRIDGE, E. H.: *Inside SOE. The story of special operations in Western Europe, 1940–1945.* London: Barker, 1966. 640 pp., illus., bibl.

5161 FOOT, M. R. D.: *SOE in France. An account of the work of the British Special Operations Executive in France 1940–1944.* London: HMSO, 1966. 550 pp., illus., tabs., bibl. (History of the Second World War).

5162 GARLINSKI, JOZEF: *Poland, SOE and the Allies.* Transl. from the Polish. London: Allen & Unwin, 1969. 248 pp., illus., maps, tabs., bibl.

5163 WHITING, CHARLES: *The battle for Twelveland. An account of Anglo-American intelligence operations within Nazi Germany, 1939–1945.* London: Cooper, 1975. xiv + 240 pp., illus.

G. GERMAN WAR AIMS: EUROPE AND BEYOND

5164 DAITZ, WERNER: *Lebensraum und gerechte Weltordnung. Grundlagen einer Anti-Atlantik Charta. Ausgewählte Aufsätze.* Amsterdam: De Amsterdamsche Keurkamer, 1943. 225 pp.

5165 DEIST, WILHELM, MESSERSCHMIDT, MANFRED and others: *Ursachen und Voraussetzungen der deutschen Kriegspolitik.* Stuttgart: Deutsche Verlags-Anstalt, 1979. 764 pp.

5166 ESTRADA, JOSÉ JOAQUIN: *¿ Por qué lucha Alemania?* Madrid: Rubinos, 1941. 166 pp.

5167 HASS, GERHART & SCHUMANN, WOLFGANG, eds.: *Anatomie der Aggression. Neue Dokumente zu den Kriegszielen des faschistischen deutschen Imperialismus im Zweiten Weltkrieg.* Berlin [East]: VEB Deutscher Verlag der Wissenschaften, 1972. 238 pp., illus., facsims. [Incl. economic exploitation and forced labour.]

5168 HITLER, ADOLF: *My New Order.* Ed. with a commentary by Raoul de Roussey de Sales. Introd.: Raymond Gram Swing. New York: Reynal & Hitchcock, 1941. 1008 pp. [Extracts from speeches.]

5169 JORDAN, RUDOLF: *Vom Sinn dieses Krieges.* Berlin: Eher, 1942. 95 pp.

5170 KOPP, WALTER, ed.: *Rassenpolitik im Kriege. Eine Gemeinschaftsarbeit aus Forschung und Praxis.* Hannover: Schaper, 1941. 121 pp.

5171 KRÜGER, KARL: *Kolonialanspruch und kontinentale Wirtschaftsplanung.* Dresden: Meinhold, 1940. 29 pp., bibl.

5172 PERSONALAMT DES HEERES: *Wofür kämpfen wir?* Berlin: 1944. 144 pp.

5173 RICH, NORMAN: *Hitler's war aims.* London: André Deutsch, 1973/74. Illus., maps, bibls.
[I]: *Ideology, the Nazi state and the course of expansion.* xliii + 352 pp.
II: *The establishment of the New Order.* xv + 548 pp. [1: 'The Jews'.]

5174 STOECKER, HELMUTH, ed.: *Drang nach Afrika. Die koloniale Expansionspolitik und Herrschaft des deutschen Imperialismus in Afrika von den Anfängen bis zum Ende des Zweiten Weltkrieges.* Mitw.: Jolanda Ballhaus [and others]. Berlin [East]: Akademie-Verlag, 1977. 370 pp., maps, bibl.

H. OCCUPATION, PERSECUTION AND RESISTANCE

1. THE NEW ORDER IN EUROPE

a. General

5175 BACKE, HERBERT: *Um die Nahrungsfreiheit Europas. Weltwirtschaft oder Grossraum.* Leipzig: Goldmann, 1942. 274 pp., illus., maps, charts.

5176 BROCKDORFF, WERNER: *Kollaboration oder Widerstand. Die Zusammenarbeit mit den Deutschen in den besetzten Ländern während des Zweiten Weltkrieges und deren schreckliche Folgen.* München: Welsermühl, 1968. 355 pp., illus., facsim., bibl.

5177 COLLOTTI, ENZO, ed.: *L'occupazione nazista in Europa.* Roma: Ed. Riuniti, 1964. 617 pp. (Istituto nazionale per la storia del movimento di liberazione in Italia).

5178 DELAISI, FRANCIS: *La révolution européenne.* Bruxelles: Éds. Toison d'Or, 1942. 290 pp.

5179 EINZIG, PAUL: *Europe in chains.* Harmondsworth, Middx.: Penguin Books, 1940. 128 pp.

5180 *Europa als Lebenskampfgemeinschaft. Europäische Vorlesungen gehalten auf einem europäischen Studenten- und Frontkämpfertreffen veranstaltet von der Reichsstudentenführung.* Berlin: Der akademische Kulturaustausch, [194–]. 147 pp. [Also in French.]

FOREIGN LABOUR

5181 DIDIER, FRIEDRICH: *Europa arbeitet in Deutschland. Sauckel mobilisiert die Leistungsreserven.* Berlin: Eher, 1943. 128 pp., illus.

5182 DIDIER, FRIEDRICH, ed.: *Handbuch für die Dienststellen des General-bevollmächtigten für den Arbeitseinsatz und die interessierten Reichsstellen im Grossdeutschen Reich und in den besetzten Gebieten. Band I.* [Berlin]:

Generalbevollmächtigter für den Arbeitseinsatz, 1944. 300 pp. [Comprising: Vollmachten, Verlautbarung, Verordnungen, Organisation des GBA.]

5183 HOMZE, EDWARD L: *Foreign labor in Nazi Germany*. Princeton. N.J.: Princeton University Press, 1967. 350 pp., tabs., bibl.

5184 INTERNATIONAL LABOUR OFFICE: *The exploitation of foreign labour by Germany*. Montreal: 1945. 286 pp.

5185 FREYMOND, JEAN: *Le IIIe Reich et la réorganisation économique de l'Europe, 1940–1942. Origines et projets*. Leiden: Sijthoff, 1974. xxii + 302 pp., tabs., bibl. (Institut universitaire de Hautes Études internationales).

5186 FRIED, FERDINAND: *Wende der Weltwirtschaft*. Leipzig: Goldmann, 1940. 402 pp., maps, tabs.

5187 GANZER, KARL RICHARD: *Das Reich als europäische Ordnungsmacht*. 150. Taus. Hamburg: Hanseatische Verlagsanstalt, 1941. 137 pp.

5188 GROSSMANN, VLADIMIR: *The Pan-Germanic web: remaking Europe*. Toronto: Macmillan, 1944. viii + 179 pp.

5189 KAMENETSKY, IGOR: *Secret Nazi plans for Eastern Europe. A study of Lebensraum policies*, New York: Bookman Associates, 1961. 263 pp., tabs., bibl.

5190 KASTEN, HELMUT: *Die Neuordnung der Währung in den besetzten Gebieten und die Tätigkeit der Reichskreditkassen während des Krieges 1939–40*. Berlin: Bank-Verlag, 1941. 142 pp.

5191 LEMKIN, RAPHAEL: *Axis rule in occupied Europe. Laws of occupation—analysis of government—proposals for redress*. Washington, D.C.: Carnegie Endowment of International Peace, 1944. 674 pp., bibl.

5192 MADAJCZYK, CZESŁAW, ed.: *Inter arma non silent musae. The war and the culture, 1939–1945*. Warszawa: Państwowy Instytut Wyd., 1977. 656 pp. [Pt. I: 'The culture of the Third Reich'; Pt. II: 'The cultural life of the Nazi-occupied countries', pp. 41–442. Essays in German, English, French, Russian.]

5193 NISPEN TOT SEVENAER, C. M. O. van: *L'occupation allemande pendant la dernière guerre mondiale. Considérations sur le caractère du pouvoir de la puissance occupante et de ses mesures selon les principes généraux du droit et selon la 4ème convention de La Haye*. 's-Gravenhage: Nijhoff, 1946. 324 pp.

5194 SCHULZ, RAIMUND: *Le grand espace économique européen*. Préface: René Bétourné. Paris: La Vie industrielle, 1942. 182 pp., illus., tabs.

5195 SIX, FRANZ ALFRED: *Europa. Tradition und Zukunft*. Hamburg: Hanseatische Verlagsanstalt, 1944. 157 pp. [Collection of speeches and articles written 1938–1943.]

5196   WISE, MAURICE K.: *Requisition in France and Italy. The treatment of national private property and services*. New York: Columbia University Press, 1944. 207 pp., bibl.

5197   ZIMMERMANN, WALTER, ed.: *Deutschland und der Norden. Gemeinsame Wege zur Kontinentalwirtschaft*. Hrsg. im Auftr. der Nordischen Gesellschaft ... unter Mitw. von Karl Detlev Buck [and others]. Lübeck: Reichskontor der Nordischen Gesellschaft, 1941. 224 pp., tabs.

5198   ZOON, WILHELM: *Neuordnung im Osten. Bauernpolitik als deutsche Aufgabe*. 2. Aufl. Berlin: Deutsche Landbuchhandlung, 1940. 159 pp.

b.   Looting of art treasures

FRANCE

5199   CASSOU, JEAN, ed.: *Le pillage par les Allemands des oeuvres d'art et des bibliothèques appartenants à des Juifs en France. Recueil de documents. Précédé d'une introduction sur la doctrine esthétique du national-socialisme et l'organisation des beaux-arts sous le IIIe Reich*, par Jacques Sabile. Paris: Eds. du Centre, 1947. 267 pp., illus., facsims. (Centre de Documentation Juive Contemporaine).

5200   TREUE, WILHELM, ed.: 'Zum nationalsozialistischen Kunstraub in Frankreich. Der "Bargatzky-Bericht". Dokumentation'. [In] *Vierteljahrshefte für Zeitgeschichte*. 13. Jhrg., 3. Heft, Juli 1965. Pp. 285–337.

5201   VALLAND, ROSE: *Le front de l'art. Défense des collections françaises, 1939–1945*. Paris: Plon, 1961. 262 pp., illus., facsims.

5202   HOWE, THOMAS CARR, jr.: *Salt mines and castles. The discovery and restitution of looted European art*. Indianapolis, Ind.: Bobbs-Merrill, 1946. 334 pp., illus.

5203   MIHAN, GEORGE: *Looted treasure. Germany's raid on art*. London: Alliance Press, [194–]. 93 pp., illus.

5204   [POLAND] *The Nazi Kultur in Poland*. London: HMSO, 1945. 220 pp., maps, illus. [Nazi spoliation and destruction of Polish cultural treasures.]

5205   ROXAN, DAVID & WANSTALL, KEN: *The jackdaw of Linz. The story of Hitler's art thefts*. London: Cassell, 1964. 195 pp., illus., maps.

c.   Population movements

5206   BOSSE, HEINRICH, comp.: *Der Führer ruft. Erlebnisbericht aus den Tagen der grossen Umsiedlung im Osten*. Berlin: Zeitgeschichte Verlag, 1941. 277 pp., illus., map, mus. scores.

5207   FRUMKIN, GREGORY: *Population changes in Europe since 1939. A study of population changes in Europe since World War II, as shown by the balance sheets of 24 European countries*. London: Allen & Unwin, 1951. 191 pp. [Incl. statistics of Jewish losses.]

5208 GÖTZ, KARL: *Die grosse Heimkehr*. Stuttgart: Spemann, 1942. 247 pp.

5209 HECKER, HELLMUTH: *Die Umsiedlungsverträge des Deutschen Reiches während des Zweiten Weltkrieges*. Hamburg: Metzner, 1971. 223 pp., bibl. (Werkhefte der Forschungsstelle für Völkerrecht).

5210 KERMISZ, JOSEF, ed: *'Akcje' i 'Wysiedlenia'* ['Action' and 'Resettlement']. Warszawa: 1946. 472 pp. (Dokumenty i materialy do Dziejow Okupacji niemieckiej w Polsce, Tom II). [German mass displacements and genocide of populations in Eastern Europe.]

5211 KOEHL, ROBERT L.: *RKFDV: German resettlement and population policy, 1939–1945. A history of the Reich Commission for the Strengthening of Germandom*. Cambridge, Mass.: Harvard University Press, 1957. 263 pp.

5212 KULISCHER, EUGENE, M.: *The displacement of population in Europe*. Montreal: International Labour Office, 1943. 171 pp., maps. [Incl. expulsion and deportation of Jews; mobilization of foreign labour by Germany.]

5213 LESNIEWSKI, ANDRZEJ, ed.: *1939–1950. Population movements between the Oder and Bug Rivers*. Poznań: Wyd. Zachodnie, 1961. 108 pp., maps, tabs. (Zachodnia Agencja Prasowa). [Incl. memorandum of Erich Wetzel on the German plan for the East, 1942. Text in English and German.]

5214 LOEBER, DIETRICH A., ed: *Diktierte Option. Die Umsiedlung der Deutsch-Balten aus Estland und Lettland, 1939–1941. Dokumentation*. Neumünster: Wachholtz, 1972. 787 pp., illus., facsims. (Sonderforschungsbereich 'Skandinavien- und Ostseeforschung' an der Universität Kiel).

5215 ŁUCZAK, CZESŁAW, comp.: *Wysiedlenia ludności polskiej na tzw. ziemiach wcielonych do Rzeszy, 1939–1945* [The transfer of the Polish population from the so-called territories incorporated in the Reich]. Poznań: Instytut Zachodni, 1969. 134 pp., illus., facsims., tabs., bibl. (Documenta Occupationis Teutonicae, VIII). [Text of documents in German.]

5216 *Der Menscheneinsatz. Grundsätze, Anordnungen und Richtlinien*. Hrsg.: Hauptabt. I des Reichskommissariats für die Festigung deutschen Volkstums. Berlin: Reichsdruckerei, 1940. 237 pp., tabs. (Vertraulich! Nur für den inneren Dienstgebrauch. Der Reichsführer SS—Reichskommissar für die Festigung deutschen Volkstums).

5217 SCHECHTMAN, JOSEPH B.: *European population transfers, 1939–1945*. New York: Oxford University Press, 1946. 532 pp., tabs., maps, bibl.

5218 SOBCZAK, JANUSZ: *Hitlerowskie przesiedlenia ludności niemieckiej w dobie II Wojny Światowej* [Nazi resettlements of the German population during World War II]. Poznań: Instytut Zachodni, 1966. 370 pp., tabs., bibl., summaries in Russian and English.

5219 SOMMER, HELLMUT: *135 000 gewannen das Vaterland. Die Heimkehr der Deutschen aus Wolhynien, Galizien und dem Narewgebiet*. Berlin: Nibelungen-Verlag, 1940. 62 pp., illus.

415

2. PERSECUTION AND RESISTANCE

a. General

5220 BERNARD, HENRI: *Histoire de la résistance européenne. La 'quatrième force' de la guerre 39–45.* Préface: Colin Gubbins. Verviers, Belgique: Gérard, 1968. 283 pp., illus., facsims., maps, bibl.

5221 BOURNE, G. H.: *Starvation in Europe.* London: Allen & Unwin, 1943. 140 pp., illus.

THE CHURCHES

5222 CASTONIER, ELISABETH: *The eternal front.* London: Clarke, [n.d.]. 125 pp. [Resistance of the Churches in Austria, Czechoslovakia, Poland, Holland, Belgium, Denmark, Norway, France.]

5223 MARTIN, HUGH and others: *Christian counter-attack. Europe's Churches against Nazism.* [By] Hugh Martin, Douglas Newton, H. M. Waddams, R. R. Williams. New York: Scribner, 1944. 125 pp.

5224 SETH, RONALD: *For my name's sake. A brief account of the struggle of the Roman Catholic Church against the Nazis in Western Europe and against Communist persecution in Eastern Europe.* London: Bles, 1958. 246 pp. [Ch. VI: 'Dachau'.]

5225 CROWTHER, J. G.: *Science in liberated Europe.* London: Pilot Press, 1949. 336 pp., maps, diagrs., tabs. [Incl. persecution of scientists and resistance in France, Denmark, Holland, Czechoslovakia.]

5226 ENANDER, BO & ARNHEIM, FRANZ: *Sa härskade Herrefolket* [The rule of the Herrenvolk]. Stockholm: Bonniers, 1945. 163 pp., illus.

5227 ETNASI, FERNANDO: *La resistenza in Europa.* Pref.: Arrigo Boldrini. Progettazione grafica: Giuseppe Montanucci. Roma: Grafica Editoriale, 1970/72. Illus., facsims.
I: *Albania, Austria, Belgio, Bulgaria, Cecoslovacchia, Danimarca, Francia, Germania, Grecia, Italia.* Publ. 1970. 468 pp.
II: *Jugoslavia, Lussemburgo, Norvegia, Olanda, Polonia, Romania, Ungheria, Unione Sovietica.* Publ. 1972. 475 pp.

5228 FOOT, M. R. D.: *Resistance. An analysis of European resistance to Nazism, 1940/45.* London: Methuen, 1976. xix + 346 pp., maps., bibl.

5229 HAWES, STEPHEN & WHITE, RALPH, eds.: *Resistance in Europe, 1939–1945.* Based on the proceedings of a symposium held at the University of Salford, March 1973. London: Allen Lane, 1975. 235 pp., bibl. [Incl.: Józef Garliński: 'The underground movement in Auschwitz', pp. 55–76.]

5230 HEALEY, DENIS, ed.: *The curtain falls. The story of the socialists in Eastern Europe.* Foreword: Aneurin Bevan. London: Lincolns-Prager, 1951. 99 pp., map. [Incl. resistance movements in Poland, Hungary and the Nazi occupation of Czechoslovakia.]

5231 HOHENDORF, GERD and others, eds.: *Lehrer im antifaschistischen Widerstandskampf der Völker. Studien und Materialien 1. Folge.* Berlin [East]: Volk und Wissen Volkseigener Verlag, 1974. 399 pp.

5232 *International Conference on the history of the Resistance movements* ... Oxford: Pergamon Press, 1960/64. Text in French and English.
First International Conference ... held at Liège–Bruxelles–Breendonk, 14–17 September 1958. Publ. 1960. 410 pp., maps.
Second International Conference ... held at Milan, 26–29 March 1961. Publ. 1964. 663 pp.

5232a KRAUS, RENÉ: *Europe in revolt.* New York: Macmillan, 1942. 563 pp. [Incl. chs. on extermination of the Jews and forced labour.]

5233 MACKSEY, KENNETH: *The partisans of Europe in the Second World War.* New York: Stein & Day, 1975. 271 pp., illus., maps, bibl.

5234 MALVEZZI, PIERO & PIRELLI, GIOVANNI, eds.: *Lettere di condannati a morte della resistenza europea.* Pref.: Thomas Mann. Torino: Einaudi, 1963. 813 pp. [Enl. and newly rev. ed. First ed. 1954. German version: *Und die Flamme soll Euch nicht versengen.* Zürich: Steinberg, 1955. 554 pp.]

5235 MICHEL, HENRI: *The shadow war. Resistance in Europe 1939–1945.* Transl. from the French. London: André Deutsch, 1972. 416 pp., map, bibl. [Orig. French title: *La guerre de l'ombre.*]

UNDERGROUND PRESS

5236 BROME, VINCENT: *Europe's free press. The underground newspapers of occupied lands described as far as the censor permits. (France, Belgium, the Netherlands, Luxembourg, Germany, Czechoslovakia, Poland, Yugoslavia, Norway).* London: Feature Books, [194–]. 128 pp.

5237 MUZZY, ADRIENNE FLORENCE: 'A list of clandestine periodicals of World War II'. [In] *Ulrich's Periodicals Directory,* 5th ed. (postwar). New York: Bowker, 1947. Pp. 329–347.

5238 WOODMAN, DOROTHY: *Europe rises. The story of resistance in occupied Europe.* London: Gollancz, 1943. 154 pp.

b. SS and police as occupying forces

5239 BEAU, GEORGES & GAUBUSSEAU, LEOPOLD: *R.5. Les S.S. en Limousin, Périgord, Quercy.* Paris: Presses de la Cité, 1969. 509 pp., illus., facsims., maps, diagrs., tabs.

5240 *Einsatzgruppen in Polen. Einsatzgruppen der Sicherheitspolizei, Selbstschutz und andere Formationen in der Zeit vom 1. September 1939 bis Frühjahr 1940.* Ludwigsburg: Zentrale Stelle der Landesjustizverwaltungen, 1962/63. 221 + 199 pp., diagrs., tabs., mimeog. [In 2 vols.]

5241 KOSCHORKE, HELMUTH: *Polizeireiter in Polen.* 21.–40. Taus. Berlin: Schneider, 1940. 59 pp., illus. [Boys' book.]

5242 KRAUSNICK, HELMUT & WILHELM, HANS-HEINRICH: *Die Truppe des Weltanschauungskrieges. Die Einsatzgruppen der Sicherheitspolizei und des SD 1938–1942*. Hrsg.: Institut für Zeitgeschichte. Stuttgart: Deutsche Verlags-Anstalt, 1980. 640 pp.

5243 NAWROCKI, STANISŁAW: *Policja hitlerowska w tzw. Kraju Warty w latach 1939–1945* [The Nazi police in the Warthegau ...]. Poznań: Instytut Zachodni, 1970. 297 pp., illus., facsims., bibl., summaries in Russian and English. (Badania nad okupacją niemiecką w Polsce, X).

5244 RICHTER, HANS: *Einsatz der Polizei. Bei den Polizeibataillonen in Ost, Nord und West*. Berlin: Eher, 1941. 106 pp., illus.

5245 *SS im Einsatz. Eine Dokumentation über die Verbrechen der SS*. Berlin [East]: Kongress Verlag, 1957. 626 pp., illus.

5246 *De SS in Nederland. Documenten uit SS-archiven 1935–1945*. [Introd. and ed.]: N.K.C.A. in't Veld. 's-Gravenhage: Nijhoff, 1976. x + 1714 pp., diagr., bibl., summary in English (pp. 1501–1643). (Rijksinstituut voor Oorlogsdocumentatie, Bronnenpublicaties, Documenten). [In two vols., text of documents in German.]

3. INDIVIDUAL COUNTRIES

a. Austria

Occupation, 1938–1945

5247 *Austria: Basic handbook. Pt. I: Geographical, political and social; Pt. II: Administration*. London: Foreign Office & Ministry of Economic Warfare, [1944]. In 2 vols., maps.

5248 BOTZ, GERHARD: *Die Eingliederung Österreichs in das Deutsche Reich. Planung und Verwirklichung des politisch-administrativen Anschlusses, 1938–1940*. Wien: Europaverlag, 1972. 192 pp., map, diagr. (Schriftenreihe des Ludwig-Boltzmann-Instituts für Geschichte der Arbeiterbewegung).

5249 BOTZ, GERHARD: *Wien vom 'Anschluss' zum Krieg. Nationalsozialistische Machtübernahme und politisch-soziale Umgestaltung am Beispiel der Stadt Wien 1938/39*. Einleitender Beitrag: Karl R. Stadler. Wien: Jugend und Volk, 1978. 646 pp., tabs., diagrs.

5250 CHAILLET, PIERRE: *L'Autriche souffrante*. Paris: Blond & Gay, 1939. 128 pp.

5251 *Kalender der Volks-Zeitung 1939*. Wien: Ostmärkische Zeitungsverlagsgesellschaft, [1938]. 159 pp., illus., diagrs. [Incl.: 'Die neue deutsche Ehegesetzgebung'; 'Die wichtigsten deutschen Rangabzeichen'.]

5252 KLUSACEK, CHRISTINE: *Österreichs Wissenschaftler und Künstler unter dem NS-Regime*. Wien: Europa Verlag, 1966. 56 pp., facsims., bibl.

5253 LENK, RUDOLF: *Oberdonau—Die Heimat des Führers*. Hrsg.: Gauamt für Kommunalpolitik, Gau Oberdonau. München: Bruckmann, 1940. 120 pp., illus., maps.

5254 MAASS, WALTER B.: *Country without a name. Austria under Nazi rule, 1938–1945.* New York: Ungar, 1979. x + 178 pp., illus., maps, bibl.

5255 REBHANN, FRITZ M.: *Wien war die Schule.* Wien: Herold, 1978. 208 pp.

5256 SCHAUSBERGER, NORBERT: *Rüstung in Österreich 1938–1945. Eine Studie über die Wechselwirkung von Wirtschaft, Politik und Kriegsführung.* Wien: Hollinek, 1970. 228 pp., tabs., bibl. (Publikationen des österreichischen Instituts für Zeitgeschichte und des Instituts für Zeitgeschichte der Universität Wien).

5257 STADLER, KARL: *Österreich 1938–1945. Im Spiegel der NS-Akten.* Wien: Herold, 1966. 427 pp., bibl.

Persecution and resistance

5258 DOKUMENTATIONSARCHIV DES ÖSTERREICHISCHEN WIDERSTANDES: *Kataloge.* Wien: 1963/75. Nrs. 1–10, mimeog.

5259 FREI, BRUNO: *Der kleine Widerstand.* Wien: Sensen-Verlag, 1978. iv + 143 pp., facsims., bibl.

5260 HINDELS, JOSEF: *Österreichs Gewerkschaften im Widerstand 1934–1945.* Wien: Europaverlag, 1976. 434 pp., bibl.

5261 KONRAD, HELMUT: *Widerstand an Donau und Moldau. KPÖ und KSC zur Zeit des Hitler-Stalin-Paktes.* Wien: Europaverlag, 1978. 351 pp., facsims.

5262 MOLDEN, OTTO: *Der Ruf des Gewissens. Der österreichische Freiheitskampf 1938–1945. Beiträge zur Geschichte der österreichischen Widerstands-bewegung.* Wien: Herold, 1958. 370 pp., illus.

5263 NEUGEBAUER, WOLFGANG, ed.: *Widerstand und Verfolgung im Burgenland 1934–1945. Eine Dokumentation. Auswahl.* Mitarb.: Erica Fischer [and others]. Wien: Österreichischer Bundesverlag, 1979. 486 pp., illus., facsims.

5264 NIEDERMEYER, ALBERT: *Wahn, Wissenschaft und Wahrheit. Lebenserinne-rungen eines Arztes.* Innsbruck: Tyrolia-Verlag, 1956. 535 pp. [Incl. Nazi oppression in Austria and Sachsenhausen concentration camp.]

5265 RIEGER, HANS: *Das Urteil wird jetzt vollstreckt.* Wien: Europa Verlag, 1977. 131 pp. [First ed. 1967 under title *Verurteilt zum Tod.*]

5266 SPIEGEL, TILLY: *Frauen und Mädchen im österreichischen Widerstand.* Wien: Europa Verlag, 1967. 76 pp.

5267 SPIEGEL, TILLY: *Österreicher in der belgischen und französischen Résistance.* Wien: Europa Verlag, 1969. 80 pp., facsims.

5268 TIDL, MARIE: *Die Roten Studenten. Dokumente und Erinnerungen 1938–1945.* Vorw.: Karl R. Stadler. Wien: Europaverlag, 1976. vii + 300 pp., port., facsims., mus. score. (Ludwig-Boltzmann-Institut für Geschichte der Arbeiterbewegung).

5269 [VIENNA] NEUGEBAUER, WOLFGANG, comp.: *Widerstand und Verfolgung in Wien 1934–1945.* Hrsg.: Dokumentationsarchiv des österreichischen

Widerstandes. Wien: Österreichischer Bundesverlag für Unterricht, Wissenschaft und Kunst, 1975. 3 vols., illus., facsims.

5270 VOGL, FRIEDRICH: *Widerstand im Waffenrock. Österreichische Frei-heitskämpfer in der deutschen Wehrmacht 1938–1945.* Geleitw.: Bundes-präsident Rudolf Kirschschläger. Vorw.: Herbert Steiner. Wien: Europa-verlag, 1977. xiv + 258 pp., illus., facsims., maps. (Ludwig-Boltzmann-Institut für Geschichte der Arbeiterbewegung).

b. Balkan and Danubian states

5271 HERCOVA, LISA: *Im Dienst der Partisanen. Aufzeichnungen aus dem Balkan.* Zürich: Europa Verlag, 1945. 160 pp.

5272 HILLGRUBER, ANDREAS: *Südost-Europa im Zweiten Weltkrieg. Literaturbericht und Bibliographie.* Frankfurt a.M.: Bernard & Graefe, 1962. 150 pp. (Schriften der Bibliothek für Zeitgeschichte).

5273 LEIBROCK, OTTO: *Der Südosten, Grossdeutschland und das neue Europa.* Berlin: Volk und Reich Verlag, 1941. 354 pp.

5274 LOVERDO, COSTA de: *Les Maquis rouges des Balkans, 1941–1945. (Grèce, Yougoslavie, Albanie).* Paris: Stock, 1967. 388 pp., illus., maps, bibl.

Albania

5275 AMERY, JULIAN: *Sons of the eagle. A study in guerilla war.* London: Macmillan, 1948. 354 pp., illus., maps.

5276 ASH, WILLIAM: *Pickaxe and rifle.* London: Baker, 1974. 270 pp., illus., bibl. [Chs. 3–7 cover the war years.]

5277 TILMAN, H. W.: *When men and mountains meet.* Cambridge: Cambridge University Press, 1946. 232 pp., illus., maps. [Resistance in Italy and Albania.]

Bulgaria

5278 MILLER, MARSHALL LEE: *Bulgaria during the Second World War.* Stanford, Calif.: Stanford University Press, 1975. xii + 290 pp., bibl.

5279 *The struggle of the Bulgarian people against Fascism.* Sofia: 1946. 113 pp., port., facsims., tabs., map.

Greece

5280 ARGENTI, PHILIP P.: *The occupation of Chios by the Germans and the administration of the island. Described in contemporary documents.* Cambridge: Cambridge University Press, 1966. 375 pp., map, illus., facsims., tabs.

5281 BYFORD-JONES, W.: *The Greek trilogy. Resistance—liberation—revolution.* London: Hutchinson, 1945. 270 pp., illus.

5282 HOURMOUZIOS, S. L., ed.: *Starvation in Greece.* London: Harrison, 1943. 48 pp., illus.

5283 KEDROS, ANDRÉ: *La résistance grecque, 1940–1944*. Paris: Laffont, 1966. 543 pp., illus., maps, tabs., bibl.

5284 TSATSOS, JEANNE: *The sword's fierce edge. A journal of the occupation of Greece, 1941–1944*. Auth. English transl. Nashville, Tenn.: Vanderbilt University Press, 1969. vii + 131 pp., illus.

5285 TSOUDEROS, EMMANUEL: *Axis crimes in Greece. Greek White Paper*. London: Ketcher, Hudson & Kearns (ptrs.), 1942. 13 pp.

5286 WASON, BETTY: *Miracle in Hellas. The Greeks fight on*. London: Museum Press, 1943. 239 pp., illus.

5287 WOODHOUSE, C. M.: *The struggle for Greece, 1941–1949*. London: Hart-Davis, MacGibbon, 1976. xii + 324 pp., illus., maps.

Hungary

5288 [ENDRE, LÁSZLÓ] LÉVAI, JENÖ: *Endre Láśzló. A háborús bünösök Magyar listavezetöje* [... The foremost Hungarian war criminal]. Budapest: Müller, 1945. 112 pp.

5289 FENYÖ, MIKSA: *Az elsodort ország. Naplójegyzetek 1944–1945-böl* [The country that was swept away. Notes from a diary from 1944–1945]. Budapest: Révai, 1946. 637 pp.

5290 GYENES, ISTVÁN: *Élet a föld alatt* [Life underground]. Budapest: Gábor, 1945. 96 pp. [The battle of Budapest.]

5291 KOVACS, ÉTIENNE & FLORIAN, JEAN, eds.: *Champions hongrois de la liberté contre le fascisme. Aperçus sur l'histoire du Mouvement Partisan Hongrois*. Budapest: Éd. 'Athenaeum', 1946. 67 pp.

5292 LÉVAI, JENÖ: *Horogkereszt, Kaszáskereszt, Nyilaskereszt* [Swastika, Sickle-Cross, Arrow-Cross]. Budapest: Müller, 1945. 124 pp.

5293 MILLOK, SÁNDOR: *A kínok útja. Budapesttöl–Mauthausenig. Elmény-regény* [The road of torture. From Budapest to Mauthausen. An autobiographical novel]. Budapest: Károly, 1945. 168 pp., facsim.

5294 NADANYI, PAUL: *The 'Free Hungary' movement*. New York: The Amerikai Magyar Nepszava, 1942. 63 pp. (2nd rev. ptg.).

Romania

5295 PASCU, St. and others, eds.: *Independenţa României*. Bucureşti: Academiei Republicii Socialiste România, 1977. 526 pp., illus. [Incl. resistance, pp. 443–466.]

5296 POPESCU-PUTURI, ION and others: *La contribution de la Roumanie à la victoire sur le fascisme. Études*. Bucarest: Académie de la République socialiste de Roumanie, 1965. 158 pp., bibl. (Bibliotheca Historica Romaniae).

5297 POPESCU-PUTURI, ION and others: *La Roumanie pendant la deuxième guerre mondiale. Études*. Bucarest: Académie de la République populaire roumaine, 1964. 142 pp. (Bibliotheca Historica Romaniae).

5298 *România in războiul antihitlerist* [Romania in the anti-Hitlerite struggle]. *23 August 1944–9 Mai 1945.* [Bucarest]: Editura Militară, 1966. 812 pp., illus., facsims., maps, tabs., bibl. (Institutul de Studii Istorice și Social-Politice de pe Lingă CC al PCR).

Yugoslavia

5299 ADAMIC, LOUIS: *The eagle and the roots.* New York: Doubleday, 1952. 531 pp., maps.

5300 CSOKOR, FRANZ THEODOR: *Als Zivilist im Balkankrieg.* Wien: Ullstein, 1947. 291 pp. [Mainly about Yugoslavia.]

5301 ČOLOKOVIĆ, RODOLJUB: *Winning freedom.* London: Lincolns-Prager, 1962. 430 pp., maps. [Shortened version of original 'Sketches from the war of liberation' in Serbian.]

5302 DEAKIN, F. W.: *The embattled mountain.* London: Oxford University Press, 1972. xvii + 284 pp., illus., maps. [First ed. 1971.]

5303 DJILAS, MILOVAN: *Wartime.* Transl. by Michael B. Petrovich. London: Secker & Warburg, 1977. 470 pp., illus., map.

5304 JUKIC, ILIJA: *The fall of Yugoslavia.* Transl. by Dorian Cooke. New York: Harcourt Brace Jovanovich, 1974. 315 pp., bibl.

5305 MARJANOVIC, JOVAN & MORACA, PERO: [*Our war of liberation and the people's revolution, 1941–1945.*] Beograd: Prosveta, 1958. 331 pp., illus., maps. [In Serbian.]

5306 PETROVITCH, SVETISLAV-SVETA: *Free Yugoslavia calling.* New York: Greystone Press, 1941. 356 pp.

5307 [STEPINAC, DRALOIZIJE (ALOYSIUS)] *The case of Archbishop Stepinac.* Washington, D.C.: Embassy of the Federal People's Republic of Yugoslavia, 1947. 96 pp., illus., facsims.

5308 STRUGAR, VLADO: *Der jugoslawische Volksbefreiungskrieg 1941 bis 1945.* Berlin [East]: Deutscher Militärverlag, 1969. 338 pp., illus. [Transl. from the Serbocroat.]

5309 *Les systèmes d'occupation en Yougoslavie, 1941–1945. Rapports au 3e Congrès International sur l'Histoire de la Résistance européenne à Karlovy Vary, les 2–4 Septembre 1963.* Belgrade: Institut pour l'Étude du Mouvement ouvrier, 1963. 564 pp. [Text in English, French and Russian.]

5310 [TITO (JOSIP BROZ)] AUTY, PHYLLIS: *Tito. A biography.* London: Longman, 1970. 343 pp., illus., maps, bibl.

5311 TOMASEVICH, JOZO: *The Chetniks. War and revolution in Yugoslavia, 1941–1945.* Stanford, Calif.: Stanford University Press, 1975. x + 508 pp., map, bibl.

CROATIA

5312 DRESLER, ADOLF: *Kroatien.* 2. Aufl. Essen: Essener Verlagsanstalt, 1944. 171 pp.

5313 HORY, LADISLAUS & BROSZAT, MARTIN: *Der kroatische Ustascha-Staat 1941–1945*. 2. Aufl. Stuttgart: Deutsche Verlags-Anstalt, 1965. 183 pp., map. (Institut für Zeitgeschichte, München).

5314 KOVAČIĆ, MATIJA, comp.: *Greueltaten und Verwüstungen der Aufrührer im unabhängigen Staate Kroatien in den ersten Lebensmonaten des kroatischen Nationalstaates*. Bearb. und hrsg. im Auftr. des Ministeriums des Aüsseren auf Grund von Beweismaterial. Zagreb: Verlag des Kroatischen Bibliographischen Instituts, 1942. 144 pp., illus., facsims. [Also in Croatian: MINISTARSTVA VANSKIH POSLOVA: *Odmetnička zvjerstva i pustošenja ...*]

5315 SATTLER, WILHELM: *Die deutsche Volksgruppe im unabhängigen Staat Kroatien. Ein Buch vom Deutschtum in Slawonien, Syrmien und Bosnien.* Graz: Steirische Verlagsanstalt, 1943. 114 pp., map.

c. Channel Islands

5316 CRUICKSHANK, CHARLES: *The German occupation of the Channel Islands*. London: Oxford University Press, 1975. xii + 370 pp., illus., maps, diagrs., bibl. [Incl. deportation, pp. 206–230.]

5317 FALLA, FRANK W.: *The silent war*. London: Frewin, 1967. 223 pp., illus., facsims. [Resistance in Guernsey.]

5318 SINEL, L. P., comp.: *The German occupation of Jersey. A diary of events from June 1940 to June 1945.* London: Corgi Books, 1969. 318 pp., illus., tabs.

d. Czechoslovakia

Occupation

5319 BELINA, JOSEF: *Czech labour under Nazi rule*. Preface: D. R. Grenfell. London: Lincolns-Prager, 1943. 63 pp.

5320 BEUER, GUSTAV: *Berlin or Prague? The Germans of Czechoslovakia at the crossroads.* London: Lofox, [1942]. 80 pp., bibl.

5321 BRANDES, DETLEF: *Die Tschechen unter deutschem Protektorat*. Hrsg. vom Vorstand des Collegium Carolinum, Forschungsstelle für die böhmischen Länder. München: Oldenbourg, 1969/75.
Teil I: *Besatzungspolitik, Kollaboration und Widerstand im Protektorat Böhmen und Mähren bis Heydrichs Tod, 1939–1942*. Publ. 1969. 372 pp., bibl. (bibl. and notes, pp. 271–353).
Teil II: *Besatzungspolitik, Kollaboration und Widerstand im Protektorat Böhmen und Mähren von Heydrichs Tod bis zum Prager Aufstand, 1942–1945*. Publ. 1975. 205 pp., map, bibl.

5322 BRÜGEL, JOHANN WOLFGANG: *Tschechen und Deutsche 1939–1946*. München: Nymphenburger Verlagshandlung, 1974. 325 pp., bibl.

5323 ČERNY, FRANTIŠEK, ed.: *Theater. Divadlo. Vzpomínky českých divadelníkủ na německou okupaci a Druhou Světovou Válku* [Theatre. Reminiscences of

423

Czech theatre people on the Nazi occupation and the Second World War].
Praha: Orbis, 1965. 442 pp., illus., facsims.

5324 FEIERABEND, LADISLAV KAREL: *Ve vládě Protektorátu* [In the government of the Protectorate]. New York: Universum Press, 1962. 171 pp.

5325 [FRANK, KARL HERMANN] FRANK, ERNST: *Karl Hermann Frank. Staatsminister im Protektorat.* Heusenstamm: Orion-Heimretter-Verlag, 1971. 182 pp., illus., facsims., maps, diagrs. bibl. [Actually issued in 1970. Incl.: 10: 'Heydrich übernimmt die Führung'; 13: 'Theresienstadt'.]

5326 JACOBY, GERHARD: *Racial state. The German nationalities policy in the Protectorate of Bohemia-Moravia.* New York: Institute of Jewish Affairs of AMJ and WJC, 1944. 355 pp., maps, tabs., bibl.

5327 KENNAN, GEORGE F.: *From Prague after Munich. Diplomatic papers, 1938–1940.* Princeton, N.J.: Princeton University Press, 1968. 266 pp., illus., maps, tabs.

5328 *Liste des schädlichen und unerwünschten Schrifttums im Protektorat Böhmen und Mähren. Stand vom 3. März 1944. Sämtliche, in der vorliegenden Liste angeführten Bücher sind, gleich ob in Originalfassung oder übersetzt, vom Umlauf auszuschliessen.* Hrsg.: Ministerium für Volksaufklärung. 225 pp.

5329 LORENZ, MAX & SCHINNERER, ERICH, eds.: *Das deutsche Strafrecht im Reichsgau Sudetenland und im Protektorat Böhmen und Mähren.* Prag: Calve, 1940/41. 354 pp. [Also: *Ergänzungsband—Okt. 1940–Nov. 1941.* 60 pp.]

5330 NAUDE, HORST: *Erlebnisse und Erkenntnisse. Als politischer Beamter im Protektorat Böhmen und Mähren 1939–1945.* München: Fides-Verlagsgesellschaft, 1975. 216 pp., bibl. (Veröffentlichung des Sudetendeutschen Archivs).

5331 UMBREIT, HANS: *Deutsche Militärverwaltungen 1938–39. Die militärische Besetzung der Tschechoslowakei und Polens.* Stuttgart: Deutsche Verlags-Anstalt, 1977. 296 pp., maps, bibl.

Czechoslovak exiles

5332 BROD, TOMAN & ČEJKA, EDUARD: *Na zapadni frontě ...* [On the Western Front. The history of the Czechoslovakian military units in the West in the years of World War II.] Praha: Naše Vojsko svaz Protifašistických Bojovniko, 1963. 610 pp., illus., tabs., maps, bibl. [2nd enl. ed.]

5333 MASARYK, JAN: *Speaking to my country.* Forew.: Anthony Eden. London: Lincolns-Prager, 1944, 150 pp.

5334 OTÁHALOVÁ, LIBUŠE & ČERVINKOVÁ, MILADA, eds.: *Dokumenty z historie Československé politiky 1939–1943.* Praha: Academia Nkl. Československé Akademie Věd, 1966. 815 pp. (Acta occupationis Bohemiae et Moraviae). [In two vols., text in Czech and German. Concerning Czech emigrés in the West, their relationships with Western countries and the Czechoslovak Resistance, the Protectorate Government, etc.]

5335 URBAN, RUDOLF: *Tajné fony III. sekce. Z archivu Ministerstva Zahraničí Republiky Česko-Slovenske* [Secret funds of the Third Section. From the archives of the Ministry for Foreign Affairs of the Czechoslovak Republic]. Praha: Orbis, 1943. 240 pp., illus., facsims., tabs. [Nazi propaganda against the emigré Czechs.]

Persecution and resistance

5336 DOLEŽAL, JIŘÍ & KŘEN, JAN: *Czechoslovakia's fight. Documents on the resistance movement of the Czechoslovak people, 1938–1945.* Prague: Czechoslovak Academy of Sciences, 1964. 156 + 49 pp., illus., facsims., maps, tabs. (Committee on the History of the Czechoslovak Resistance Movement).

5337 FUČIK, JULIUS: *Reportáž psaná na oprátce* [Reportage with the noose around one's neck]. Praha: Svoboda, 1950. 133 pp., illus. [Record of life in Nazi prisons. German version: *Reportage unter dem Strang geschrieben.* Berlin: Dietz, 1947. English version: *Notes from the gallows.* Pref.: Samuel Sillen. Note: Augustina Fuchik. New York: New Century Publs., 1948.]

5338 HABRINA, RAIMUND, ed.: *Žalm Moravy* [Psalm of Moravia]. Praha: 'Mír', 1948. 100 pp., illus. [Prisons and concentration camps in Moravia during German occupation.]

HEYDRICH, REINHARD
5339 BURGESS, ALAN: *Seven men at daybreak.* London: Evans, 1960. 231 pp., illus., maps.

5340 CZECHOSLOVAK MINISTRY OF FOREIGN AFFAIRS: *Memorandum of the Czech government on the reign of terror in Bohemia and Moravia under the regime of Reinhard Heydrich.* London: 1942. 101 pp.

5341 IVANOV, MIROSLAV: *L'attentat contre Heydrich. 27 mai 1942.* Paris: Laffont, 1972, 317 pp., illus., plan, facsims. [English version: *Target: Heydrich.* New York: Macmillan, 1974.]

5342 STRÖBINGER, RUDOLF: *Das Attentat von Prag.* Landshut: Verlag Politisches Archiv, 1976. 270 pp., bibl.

LIDICE
5343 BALINT, NICHOLAS G., ed.: *Liddice lives forever.* New York: Europa Books, 1942. 96 pp., illus.

5344 HUTAK, J. B.: *With blood and with iron. The Lidice story.* London: Hale, 1957. 160 pp., illus.

5345 KROPÁČ, FRANTIŠEK: *Zločin v Lidicich. Román-skutečnost* [The Lidice crime. Memoirs]. Praha: Společnost pro Obnovu Lidic, 1946. 268 pp., illus.

5346 MASTNY, VOJTECH: *The Czechs under Nazi rule. The failure of national resistance, 1939–1942.* New York: Columbia University Press, 1971. xiii + 274 pp., maps, diagr., tabs., bibl.

5347　Moulis, Miloslav: *Mládež proti okupantům* [Youth against the occupiers]. Praha: Svoboda, 1966. 272 pp., illus., facsims., bibl.

Prague Uprising

5348　Bartošek, Karel: *Pražské povstání 1945* [The Prague uprising, 1945]. Praha: Svaz Protifašistických Bojovníků, 1960. 257 pp., illus. [German version: *Der Prager Aufstand 1945*. Berlin [East]: Deutscher Militärverlag, 1965. English version: *The Prague uprising*. Prague: Artia, 1965.]

5349　Fraschka, Günter: *Prag die blutige Stadt. Der Aufstand vom 5. Mai 1945*. Rastatt/Baden: Pabel, 1960. 190 pp.

5350　*Rudé Právo, 1939–1945*. [Prague]: Svoboda, 1971. 688 pp., illus., facsims., bibl. (Ústav marxismu-leninismu UV KSČ).

Students

5351　Comité National Tchécoslovaque: *Mémorandum relatif aux persécutions de l'enseignement universitaire et à la suppression de l'activité scientifique en Bohême et en Moravie*. Paris: 1940. 30 pp.

5352　*Persekuce českého studentsva za okupace. 28. řijen 1939: Německý útok na české vysokoškoláky: Uzavření českých vysokých škol* [Persecution of Czech students during the Occupation. 28 October 1939: the German attack on Czech university students: closure of the Czech universities]. Praha: Ministerstvo Vnitra, 1946. 155 pp., illus., facsims. [Eds.: František Kropáč, Vlastimil Louda.]

5353　Zatloukal, Jaroslav: *Svědectví kounicových kolejí* [Testimony of Kaunitz College]. Brno: Melantrich, 1946. 118 pp. [Describes how the college was turned into a Gestapo prison and lists prisoners and those executed there.]

Slovakia

5354　Dress, Hans: *Slowakei und faschistische Neuordnung Europas 1939–1941*. Berlin [East]: Akademie-Verlag, 1972. 199 pp., tabs., bibl. (Schriften des Zentralinstituts für Geschichte).

5355　Durica, Milan Stanislao: *La Slovacchia e le sue relazione politiche con la Germania 1938–1945. I: Dagli accordi di Monaco all'inizio della Seconda Guerra Mondiale (ottobre 1938–settembre 1939). Con 85 documenti inediti*. Padova: Marsilio, 1964. 274 pp., illus., bibl. [Documents in orig. languages.]

5356　Mikus, Joseph A.: *Slovakia. A political history, 1918–1950*. Rev. and imp. ed. Transl. from the French. Milwaukee, Wis.: Marquette University Press, 1963. 392 pp., tabs., bibl.

5357　Steinbühl, Josef: *Mein Leben. Kampf eines katholischen Pfarrers für den Glauben und das Deutschtum in der Slowakei*. Stuttgart: Hilfsbund Karpatendeutscher Katholiken, 1975. 160 pp., illus., maps, facsims.

5358 [TISO, JOZEF] *Pred súdom národa* [Before the nation's court]. *Proces a Dr. Jozef Tiso, Dr. Ferdinand Durčanský a Alexander Mach.* Bratislava: Poverínictvo informácií, 1947. 5 vols.

UPRISING

5359 HUSAK, GUSTAV: *Svedectvo o Slovenskom národnom povstaní* [Testimony of the Slovak national uprising]. [Bratislava]: Vyd. politickej literatúry, 1964. 617 pp., illus.

5360 PREČAN, VILÉM, comp.: *Slovenské národné povstanie. Dokumenty* [Slovak national uprising. Documents]. Bratislava: Vyd. politickej literatúry, 1965. 1218 + 68 pp., facsims., tabs., bibl.

5361 VENOHR, WOLFGANG: *Aufstand für die Tschechoslowakei. Der slowakische Freiheitskampf von 1944.* Hamburg: Wegner, 1969. 372 pp., illus., maps, bibl.

e. Eastern Europe

5362 FERVERS, KURT: *Zeitenwende im Osten. Schicksal und Gestalt des Ostraums.* Düsseldorf: Völkischer Verlag, 1942. 191 + 32 pp., illus.

5363 [OBERLÄNDER, THEODOR] DROZDZYNSKI, ALEKSANDER & ZABOROWSKI, JAN: *Theodor Oberländer. A study in German east policies.* Transl. from the Polish. Poznań: Wyd. Zachodni, 1960. 324 pp., illus., facsims., maps.

5364 *Osteuropa historisch-politisch gesehen.* Potsdam: Rütten & Loening, 1942. 387 pp.
Teil I: Paul Rohrbach: *Osteuropa.*
Teil II: Axel Schmidt: *Polen.*

5365 OSTEUROPAINSTITUT IN BRESLAU: *Jahrbuch.* Breslau: Schlesien-Verlag, 1941/43.
1940: Hrsg: Georg Behaghel. 266 pp., diagrs., tabs.
1941: Hrsg.: Hans-Jürgen Seraphim. 269 pp., tabs.
1942: Hrsg.: Hans-Jürgen Seraphim. 355 pp., illus., maps, tabs.
[No others publ.]

5366 ROHLFING, THEODOR and others, eds.: *Die Neuordnung des Rechts in den Ostgebieten. Sammlung der Reichsgesetze, der Verordnungen der Militärbefehlshaber, der Reichsstatthalter Danzig West-Preussen und Wartheland, des Generalgouverneurs für das Gouvernement Polen mit kurzen Anmerkungen.* [Ed. by] Theodor Rohlfing, Rudolf Schraut, Dr. Münstermann. Berlin: de Gruyter, 1940. 191 pp. [Also 4 supplements, publ. 1941/42.]

5367 VEGESACK, SIEGFRIED VON: *Als Dolmetscher im Osten. Ein Erlebnisbericht aus den Jahren 1942–43.* Hannover-Döhren: Hirscheydt, 1965. 265 pp., illus.

Baltic states

5368 CZOLLEK, ROSWITHA: *Faschismus und Okkupation. Wirtschaftspolitische Zielsetzung und Praxis des faschistischen deutschen Besatzungsregimes in den baltischen Sowjetrepubliken während des Zweiten Weltkrieges.* Berlin

[East]: Akademie-Verlag, 1974. 224 pp., bibl. (Akademie der Wissenschaften der DDR, Schriften des Zentralinstituts für Geschichte).

5369 KALME, ALBERT: *Total terror. An exposé of genocide in the Baltics*. New York: Appleton-Century-Crofts, 1951. 310 pp., illus., facsims.

5370 MYLLYNIEMI, SEPPO: *Die Neuordnung der baltischen Länder 1941–1944. Zum nationalsozialistischen Inhalt der deutschen Besatzungspolitik*. Helsinki: Societas Historica Finlandiae, 1973. 308 pp., diagrs., bibl.

5371 ORAS, ANTS: *Baltic eclipse*. London: Gollancz, 1948. 305 pp. [Fate under Russians and Germans.]

ESTONIA
5372 LUMI, R.: [*The avengers*]. Tallinn: Kirjastus 'Eesti Raamat', 1967. 261 pp., illus., facsims., maps. [In Estonian.]

5373 *People, be watchful!* Tallinn: Estonian State Publ. House, 1962. 274 pp., illus., facsims. [Compiled by Raul Kruus, on the basis of documents and press reports.]

LATVIA
5374 *Latvia in 1939–1942. Background, Bolshevik and Nazi occupation. Hopes for the future*. Washington, D.C.: Press Bureau of the Latvian Legation, 1942. 137 pp., bibl.

5375 *Latvia under German occupation 1941–1943*. Washington, D.C.: Press Bureau of the Latvian Legation, 1943. 112 pp., bibl.

5376 LATVIJAS PSR MINISTRU PADOMES ARHIVU PARVALDE and others: *Mēs apsūdzam* [We accuse]. Rigā: Izd. 'Liesma', 1965. 273 pp., illus., tabs., facsims., maps. [Incl. extermination of Jews and Salaspils concentration camp.]

LITHUANIA
5377 PAPLAUSKAS, J.: [*The dawn is breaking*]. Vilnius: Valstybiné Grožines Literatūre Leidykla, 1963. 212 pp., ports. [In Lithuanian.]

5378 PELEKIS, K.: *Genocide. Lithuania's threefold tragedy*. Ed. by Rumsaitis. Germany [no other pl. given]: 'Venta', 1949. 286 pp., illus., facsims., tabs., bibl.

5379 VARDYS, STANLEY V., ed.: *Lithuania under the Soviets. Portrait of a nation, 1940–1965*. London: Praeger, 1965. 299 pp., tabs., bibl. [Incl. resistance against Nazis.]

Danzig

5380 DIEWERGE, WOLFGANG: *Der neue Reichsgau Danzig-Westpreussen. Ein Arbeitsbericht vom Aufbauwerk im deutschen Osten*. Berlin: Junker & Dünnhaupt, 1940. 102 pp., maps.

5381 LEONHARDT, HANS L.: *Nazi conquest of Danzig*. Chicago, Ill.: University of Chicago Press, 1942. xvi + 363 pp., illus., tabs., bibl. [Incl. the fate of the trade unions, persecution of the Jews, C. J. Burckhardt's report, etc.]

f. Poland

Occupation and German administration

5382 BAEDEKER, KARL: *Das Generalgouvernement. Reisehandbuch.* Leipzig: Baedeker, 1943. 264 pp., maps, tabs.

5383 DU PREL, MAX Frhr.: *Das Generalgouvernement.* Würzburg: Triltsch, 1942. 404 pp., illus. [German propaganda with passages on the Jewish situation and ghettoes.]

FRANK, HANS

5384 *Das Diensttagebuch des deutschen Generalgouverneurs in Polen 1939–1945.* Hrsg.: Werner Prag, Wolfgang Jacobmeyer. Stuttgart: Deutsche Verlags-Anstalt, 1975. 1026 pp. (Quellen und Darstellungen zur Zeitgeschichte). [Incl: 'Spitzenbeamte in der Zivilverwaltung ... Kurzbiographien', pp. 945–956.]

5385 PIOTROWSKI, STANISŁAW: *Hans Frank's diary.* Warszawa: Państwowe Wyd. Naukowe, 1961. 320 pp. [Shortened version of orig. Polish work.]

5386 GAUWEILER, HELMUT, ed.: *Deutsches Vorfeld im Osten. Bildbuch über das Generalgouvernement.* Bearb. im Einvernehmen mit der Hauptabt. Propaganda in der Regierung des Generalgouvernements. Krakau: Buchverlag Ost, 1941. 207 pp., illus., facsims.

5387 GÜRTLER, PAUL: *Nationalsozialismus und evangelische Kirchen im Warthegau. Trennung von Staat und Kirche im nationalsozialistischen Weltanschauungsstaat.* Göttingen: Vandenhoeck & Ruprecht, 1958. 359 pp., map, bibl.

5388 NAWROCKI, STANISŁAW: *Hitlerowska okupacja Wielkopolski w okresie zarządu wojskowego, Wzresień–Październik 1939 r.* [Nazi occupation of Great Poland at the time of the army command, Sept.–Oct. 1939]. Poznań: Instytut Zachodni, 1966. 288 pp., bibl., summaries in Russian and English. (Badania nad Okupacją Niemiecką w Polsce).

5389 POPIOŁEK, KAZIMIERZ: *Silesia in German eyes, 1939–1945.* Katowice: Wyd. 'Śląsk', 1964. 328 pp., facsims., tabs. (Śląski Instytut Naukowy). [Transl. from the Polish.]

5390 POSPIESZALSKI, KAROL MARIAN, ed.: *Hitlerowskie 'Prawo' okupacyjne w Polsce* [Nazi occupation 'law' in Poland]. Poznań: Instytut Zachodni, 1952/58. 2 vols. (Documenta Occupationis teutonicae). [Pt. I: Warthegau; Pt. II: Generalgouvernement.]

UMBREIT, HANS: *Deutsche Militärverwaltungen, 1938–39. See* 5331.

WARSAW

5391 BLÄTTLER, FRANZ: *Warschau 1942. Tatsachenbericht eines Motorfahrers der zweiten schweizerischen Ärztemission 1942 in Polen.* Zürich: Micha, [194–]. 123 pp., illus.

5392 GOLLERT, FRIEDRICH: *Zwei Jahre Aufbauarbeit im Distrikt Warschau.* Im

Auftr. des Gouverneurs des Distrikts Warschau SA-Gruppenführer Dr. Ludwig Fischer. Warschau: 1941. 200 pp., illus. [Incl. euphemistic description of Warsaw Ghetto. Also: *Warschau unter deutscher Herrschaft.* Krakau: Burg-Verlag, 1942.]

5393 WEH, ALBERT, ed.: *Das Recht des Generalgouvernements. Nach Sachgebieten geordnet mit Erläuterungen und einem ausführlichen Sachverzeichnis.* 3. völlig neu bearb. Aufl. Krakau: Burgverlag, Verlag des Instituts für Deutsche Ostarbeit, 1941. 2 looseleaf vols. [Also: *Übersicht über das Recht des Generalgouvernements. Stand: 1.1.1943.* 80 pp.]

Persecution and resistance

5394 *Acta Poloniae Historica, 4.* [Ed. by] Instytut Historii Polskiej Akademii Nauk. Warszawa: Wyd. Polskiej Akademii Nauk, 1961. 277 pp. [Incl.: Henryk Zielinski: 'La question de "l'État indépendent de Haute-Silésie" ...', pp. 34–57; Lucjan Dobroszycki & Marek Getter: 'The Gestapo and the Polish Resistance movement (on the example of the Radom District)', pp. 85–118, diagrs., tab.]

5395 *Armia Krajowa w dokumentach* [Home Army in documents], *1939–1945.* Londyn: Studium Polski Podziemnej (Polish Underground Movement— 1939–1945—Study Trust), 1970– Maps, facsims., summaries in English.
Tom I: [Sept. 1939–June 1941]. Publ. 1970. xxvii + 584 pp.
Tom II: [June 1941–April 1943]. Publ. 1973. xxxv + 554 pp., illus.

5396 BARTOSZEWSKI, WLADYSLAW: *Warsaw death ring, 1939–1944.* [Warsaw]: Interpress Publs., 1968. 450 pp., illus., facsims., map, tabs.

5397 BOR-KOMOROWSKI, T.: *The secret army.* London: Gollancz, 1950. 407 pp., port. [Polish Underground and Warsaw uprising.]

5398 CYPRIAN, TADEUSZ & SAWICKI, JERZY: *Nazi rule in Poland, 1939–1945.* Warsaw: Polonia Publ. House, 1961. 262 pp., illus. [Polish orig.: *Nie oszczedzac Polski!* Warszawa: Wyd. Iskry, 1960.]

5399 *German crimes in Poland.* Warsaw: Central Commission for investigation of German crimes in Poland, 1946/47. Illus., maps, plans, diagrs.
I: [By] Sophie Cyzńska & Bogumil Kupść [and others]. Publ. 1946. 271 pp. [Incl. chs. on camps in general, Auschwitz, Treblinka, Chelmno, executions in Warsaw, Warsaw Rising (1944), Soviet prisoners of war.]
II: Publ. 1947. 168 pp. [Incl. chs. on Hans Frank's diary, mass executions, deportations from Zamość; Belzec, Sobibor, Stutthof, Warsaw Ghetto, experimental operations in Ravensbrück, euthanasia, German propaganda against Poland.]

5400 *The German New Order in Poland.* London: Hutchinson, for the Polish Ministry of Information, [1941?]. 585 pp., illus., facsims., maps. [American ed.: *The Black Book of Poland.* 2nd impr. New York: Putnam, (1942).]

5401 GINTER, MARIA: *Life in both hands.* Illus. by the author's own paintings.

London: Hodder & Stoughton, 1964. 253 pp. [Personal story of a heroine of the Polish resistance.]

5402 [GOETH, AMON LEOPOLD] *Proces ludobojcy Amona Leopolda Goetha przed Najwyzszym Trybunalem Narodowym* [The case of the murderer A. L. Goeth before the People's High Court]. Warszawa: 1947. 510 pp.

5403 [GREISER, ARTUR] *Proces Artura Greisera przed Najwyzszym Trybunalem Narodowym.* Warszawa: Glowny Polski Instytut Wyd., 1946. 418 pp. (Glowna Komisja Badania Zbrodni Niemieckich w Polsce). [Trial of the Gauleiter of Danzig for crimes in Poland.]

5404 [HAHN, LUDWIG] KUR, TADEUSZ: *Sprawie dliwosc poblazliwa. Proces kata Warszawy Ludwiga Hahna w Hamburgu* [Justice with indulgence. The trial in Hamburg of the Hangman of Warsaw, Ludwig Hahn]. Warszawa: Wyd. Ministerstwa Obrony Narodowej, 1975. 607 pp., illus., facsims.

5405 JACOBMEYER, WOLFGANG: *Heimat und Exil. Die Anfänge der polnischen Untergrundbewegung im Zweiten Weltkrieg.* Hamburg: Leibniz-Verlag, 1973. 369 pp., tabs., bibl. (notes and bibl. pp. 255–362). (Hamburger Beiträge zur Zeitgeschichte).

5406 JUCHNIEWICZ, MIECZYSŁAW: *Les Polonais dans la Résistance européenne, 1939–1945.* Varsovie: Éds. Interpress, 1972. 195 pp., illus. (Conseil de Protection des Monuments de la Lutte et du Martyre).

5407 KARSKI, JAN: *Story of a secret state.* Boston, Mass.: Houghton Mifflin, 1944. 391 pp. [The Polish Underground. Incl. Ch. XXIX: 'Warsaw Ghetto'; Ch. XXX: 'Death Camp of Belzec'.]

5408 [KOCH, ERICH] ORLOWSKI, SLAWOMIR & OSTROWICZ, RADOSLAW: *Erich Koch: przed Polskim sadem* [... before the Polish tribunal]. Warszawa: Wyd. Ministerstwa Obrony Narodowej, 1959. 291 pp., illus., facsims.

LODZ
5409 KESSELRING, MARIETTA von: *Erlebnisse einer zur SS Sekretärin Gezwungenen. Tatsachenbericht.* Zürich: Micha, 1945. 148 pp. [Experiences of SS atrocities against Poles and Jews in Lodz.]

5410 *Zbrodnie hitlerowskie Łódz i województwie Łódzkim* [Nazi crimes in Lodz and the Voivode of Lodz]. Lódz: Polskie Towarzystwo Historyczne, Oddzial w Lódzi, 1972. 527 pp., tabs., maps. (Red.: Ryszard Rosin).

5411 POLISH MINISTRY OF FOREIGN AFFAIRS: *The German Occupation of Poland. Extract of Note addressed to the Governments of the Allied and Neutral Powers on May 3, 1941.* London: 1941. 187 pp.

5412 ROGOWSKI, MARIAN: *Gewonnen gegen Hitler.* Aus dem Polnischen ... München: Rogner & Bernhard, 1973. 266 pp., illus., facsims.

5413 SAWAJNER, JOSEF: *W podziemiach tajnej drukarni* [Underground secret printing press]. Krakow: Wierzchowski, 1947. 79 pp., illus.

5414 SEGAL, SIMON: *The New Order in Poland*. New York: Knopf, 1942. 286 pp. [British ed.: *Nazi Rule in Poland*. London: Hale, 1943.]

5415 WARFIELD, HANIA & GAITHER: *Call us to witness. A Polish chronicle*. New York: Ziff-Davis, 1945. 434 pp. [German occupation up to 1942; incl. genocide of Poles, Russians and Jews.]

5416 WROŃSKI, TADEUSZ: *Kronika okupowanego Krakowa* [Chronicle of occupied Krakow]. Krakow: Wyd. Literackie, 1974. 562 pp., illus., facsims., bibl.

Cultural persecution and resistance

5417 BOJARSKA, BARBARA: *Eksterminacja intelligencji polskieh na Pomorzu Gdańskim. Wrzesień–Grudzień 1939*. [Extermination of the Polish intelligentsia in the Gdansk Pomerania district, Sept.–Dec. 1939]. Poznań: Instytut Zachodni, 1972. 186 pp., bibl., summary in English. (Badania nad Okupacją Niemiecką w Polsce).

5418 KLESSMANN, CHRISTOPH: *Die Selbstbehauptung einer nation. National-sozialistische Kulturpolitik und polnische Widerstandsbewegung im General-gouvernement 1939–1945*. Düsseldorf: Bertelsmann, 1971. 277 pp., bibl.

5419 KOWALENKO, WŁADISŁAW: *Tajny uniwersytet ziem zachodnich w latach 1940–1944*. Poznań: Drukarnia Sw. Wojciecha, 1946. 94 pp. [History of the underground existence of Poznan University, officially closed by German order.]

5420 KRASUSKI, JOZEF: *Tajne szkolnictwo polskie w okresie okupacji hitlerowskiej 1939–1945* [Clandestine Polish educational system during the Nazi occupation, 1939–1945]. Warszawa: Państwowe Wyd. Naukowe, 1971. 369 pp., tabs., bibl., summaries in Russian and English.

Catholic Church

5421 BROSZAT, MARTIN: *Verfolgung polnischer katholischer Geistlicher 1939–1945*. München: 1959. 87 pp. (Gutachten des Instituts für Zeitgeschichte).

5422 HLOND, AUGUST: *The persecution of the Catholic Church in German-occupied Poland. Reports presented by Cardinal Hlond, Primate of Poland, to Pope Pius XII, Vatican broadcasts and other reliable evidence*. Pref.: Cardinal Hinsley. London: Burns, Oates, 1941. 123 pp., map, illus., facsims.

5423 JACEWICZ, WIKTOR & WOŚ, JAN: *Martyrologium polskiego duchowieństwa rzymskokatolickiego pod okupacja hitlerowska w latach 1939–1945* [Martyrology of the Polish Roman Catholic clergy during the Nazi occupation, 1939–1945]. Warszawa: Akademia Teologii Katolickiej, 1977–continuing. In 3 vols., maps. [Part of series: Kościół katolicki na ziemiach polski w czasis II Wojny Światowej.]

5424 SZILING, JAN: *Polityka okupanta hitlerowskiego wobec kościoła katolickiego 1939–1945* [The Nazi occupation policy towards the Catholic Church 1939–1945]. Poznań: Instytut Zachodni, 1970. 306 pp., tabs., bibl., summary in English.

Warsaw Uprising, 1944

5425 BARTELSKI, LESŁAW M.: *Powstanie warszawskie.* Warszawa: Iskry, 1967. 282 pp., illus., map, facsim.

5426 BRUCE, GEORGE: *The Warsaw Uprising. 1 August–2 October 1944.* London: Hart-Davis, 1972. 224 pp., maps, illus., bibl.

5427 CIECHANOWSKI, JAN M.: *The Warsaw Rising of 1944.* Cambridge: Cambridge University Press, 1974. xi + 332 pp., map, bibl. [Abridged and rev. version of 1968 dissertation: *The political and ideological background of the Warsaw Rising, 1944.*]

5428 KLIMASZEWSKI, TADEUSZ: *Verbrennungskommando Warschau.* Berlin [East]: Verlag Volk und Welt, 1962. 196 pp. [Polish version: Warszawa: 'Czytelnik', 1959.]

5429 ORSKA, IRENA: *Silent is the Vistula. The story of the Warsaw Uprising.* Transl. from the Polish. New York: Longmans, Green, 1946. 275 pp.

g. Soviet Union

Occupation (general)

5430 DALLIN, ALEXANDER: *The German occupation of the USSR in World War II: a bibliography.* Assistance: Conrad F. Latour. New York: Department of State, 1955. 74 pp. (External Research Paper, 122).

5431 DALLIN, ALEXANDER: *German rule in Russia, 1941–1945. A study of occupation policies.* London: Macmillan, 1957. 695 pp. [German version: *Deutsche Herrschaft in Russland, 1941–1945.* Düsseldorf: Droste, 1958.]

5432 INSTITUT MARXISMA-LENINISMA PRI ZK KPSS: [*The German fascist occupation regime, 1941–1944*]. Moskva: Politicheskoi Literatury, 1965. 387 pp. [In Russian.]

5433 REITLINGER, GERALD: *The house built on sand. The conflicts of German policy in Russia, 1939–1945.* London: Weidenfeld & Nicolson, 1960. 459 pp., maps, bibl. [German version: *Ein Haus auf Sand gebaut. Hitlers Gewaltpolitik in Russland 1941–1944.* Hamburg: Rütten & Loening, 1962.]

5434 RÖDER, WERNER, ed.: *Sonderfahndungsliste UdSSR. Faksimile der 'Sonderfahndungsliste UdSSR' des Chefs der Sicherheitspolizei und des SD ... Beiband mit einem Kommentar ...* Erlangen: Verlag D + C, 1976. 316 + 80 pp., ports., facsims.

Persecution and resistance

5435 ARMSTRONG, JOHN A., ed.: *Soviet partisans in World War II.* Forew.: Philip E. Mosely. Madison, Wis.: University of Wisconsin Press, 1964. 792 pp., maps, bibl.

5436 BISTROVA, V. E., comp.: [*Heroes of the Resistance. The underground struggle of Soviet patriots behind the lines of the German fascist occupiers during the years of the Great Patriotic War.* 2nd ed.] Moskva: Izd. Politicheskoi Literatury, 1968. 557 pp., illus., facsims. [In Russian. First ed. 1965.]

5437 BORSHCHAGOVSKY, ALEXANDER: *The match of death.* Transl. from the Russian. Moscow: Foreign Languages Publ. House, 1961. 221 pp., port.

5438 COOPER, MATTHEW: *The phantom war. The German struggle against Soviet partisans, 1941–1944.* London: Macdonald & Jane's, 1979. ix + 217 pp., illus., bibl.

5439 EHRENBURG, ILYA: *We come as judges.* [London]: Soviet War News, 1945. 63 pp., illus. [Articles on German war crimes in Russia.]

5440 HESSE, ERICH: *Der sowjetrussische Partisanenkrieg 1941 bis 1944 im Spiegel deutscher Kampfanweisungen und Befehle.* Göttingen: Musterschmidt, 1969. 292 pp., illus., facsims., maps, diagrs., tabs., bibl.

5441 HOWELL, EDGAR M.: *The Soviet partisan movement, 1941–1944.* Washington, D.C.: Department of the Army, 1956. 217 pp., maps, diagrs., bibl.

5442 MOLOTOV, V. M.: *Note submitted, concerning the monstrous crimes, atrocities and acts of violence perpetrated by the German fascist invaders in the occupied Soviet areas and the responsibility of the German government and military command for these crimes.* Moscow: Foreign Languages Publ. House, 1942. 144 pp., illus. [Cover title: *We shall not forgive!* A number of other, similar, notes were issued during 1942.]

5443 *The People's verdict. A full report of the proceedings at the Krasnodar and Kharkov German atrocity trials.* London: Hutchinson [1944?]. 124 pp., illus.

5444 PONOMARENKO, (Lt.-Gen.) and others: *Behind the front line. Being an account of the military activities, exploits, adventures and day to day life of the Soviet guerillas operating behind the German lines, from the Finnish–Karelian front to the Crimea.* London: Hutchinson, [194–]. 160 pp.

5445 *Soviet government statements on Nazi atrocities.* London: Hutchinson, [194–]. 320 pp.

5446 ZENTRALE STELLE DER LANDESJUSTIZVERWALTUNGEN: *Abschlussbericht— Executionen des Sonderkommandos 4a der Einsatzgruppe C und der mit diesem Kommando eingesetzten Einheiten während des Russland-Feldzuges in der Zeit vom 22.6.1941 bis zum Sommer 1943.* Ludwigsburg: 1964. 350 pp., mimeog. (Nr. 11(4) AR-Z 269/60).

5447 ZENTRALE STELLE DER LANDESJUSTIZVERWALTUNGEN: *NS-Verbrechen anlässlich des Partisanenkampfes in der UdSSR 1941–1944.* Ludwigsburg: 1969. 80 pp., diagrs., mimeog.

h. France

Occupation (general)

5448 AMBRIÈRE, FRANCIS and others: *Vie et mort des Français, 1939–1945.* [Paris]: Hachette, 1971. 611 pp., illus., facsims., bibl.

5449 ARON, RAYMOND: *De l'armistice à l'insurrection nationale.* 3e éd. Paris: Gallimard, 1945. 369 pp.

CENTRE DE DOCUMENTATION JUIVE CONTEMPORAINE: *Catalogues. See* 4219.

COLLABORATION

5450 ALLARD, PAUL: *Der Krieg der Lüge. Wie man uns das Hirn vernebelte.* Leipzig: List, 1941. 254 pp., illus.

5451 DELPERRIE de BAYAC, J.: *Histoire de la Milice, 1918–1945.* Paris: Fayard, 1969. 684 pp., illus.

5452 JAMET, CLAUDE, ed.: *Le rendez-vous manqué de 1944. Vingt ans après, 16 anciens résistants, vichyistes et collaborationistes confrontent leurs points de vue dans un débat organisé* ... Paris: Éds. France-Empire, 1964. 317 pp., illus.

5453 ORY, PASCAL: *Les collaborateurs, 1940–1945.* Paris: Éds. du Seuil, 1976. 316 pp., bibl.

5454 HÉRACLÈS, PHILIPPE, comp.: *La loi nazie en France.* Préface et commentaires de Robert Aron. Paris: Authier, 1974. 348 pp.

5455 HUDDLESTON, SISLEY: *France. The tragic years, 1939–1947. An eyewitness account of war, occupation and liberation.* Boston, Mass.: Western Islands, 1965. 297 pp.

5456 JÄCKEL, EBERHARD: *Frankreich in Hitlers Europa. Die deutsche Frankreichpolitik im Zweiten Weltkrieg.* Stuttgart: Deutsche Verlags-Anstalt, 1966. 396 pp., bibl.

5457 MILWARD, ALAN S.: *The New Order and the French economy.* Oxford: Clarendon Press, 1970. viii + 320 pp., maps, graphs, tabs., bibl.

PARIS

5458 BASALDUA, PEDRO de: *Con los Alemanes en París. Paginas de un diario.* Buenos Aires: Ekin, 1943. 226 pp.

5459 THORNTON, WILLIS: *The liberation of Paris.* London: Hart-Davis, 1963. 231 pp., illus., bibl.

5460 WALTER, GÉRARD: *La vie à Paris sous l'Occupation, 1940–1944.* 2e éd., rev. et augm. Paris: Colin, 1960. 254 pp., illus., bibl., list of Parisian journals.

PROPAGANDA

5461 EPTING, KARL: *État et santé.* Paris: Sorlot, 1942. 141 pp. (Cahiers de l'Institut Allemand). [Incl.: 'Le problème de la race et la législation raciale allemande', by Eugen Fischer.]

5462 FRIEDRICH, (Dr.): *Un journaliste allemand vous parle* ... Paris: Éds. Le Pont, [1941/43]. 24 pamphlets. [Incl.: 'Du vrai et du faux socialisme', 'Aux travailleurs de France'.]

5463 NOBÉCOURT, R. G.: *Les secrets de la propagande en France occupée*. Paris: Fayard, 1962. 530 pp.

5464 POLONSKI, JACQUES: *La presse, la propagande et l'opinion publique sous l'occupation*. Paris: Centre de Documentation juive contemporaine, 1946. 157 pp.

5465 RENAUDOT, FRANÇOISE: *Les Français et l'Occupation*. Préface: Georgette Elgey. Paris: Laffont, 1976. 254 pp., illus., facsims. [Incl. persecution of the Jews.]

5466 VANINO, MAURICE: *Le temps de la honte. De Rethondes à l'Ile d'Yeu*. Paris: Éds. Créator, 1952. 357 pp. [Incl.: 'Les Juifs', pp. 220–256; 'Les Églises', pp. 257–297.]

Alsace-Lorraine

5467 BROGLY, MÉDARD: *La grande épreuve. L'Alsace sous l'Occupation allemande, 1940–1944*. Paris: Éds. du Cerf, 1945. 150 pp. [Transl. from clandestine wartime publications in German.]

5468 KETTENACKER, LOTHAR: *Nationalsozialistische Volkstumspolitik im Elsass*. Stuttgart: Deutsche Verlags-Anstalt, 1973. 388 pp., bibl.

5469 MEISSNER, OTTO: *Elsass und Lothringen deutsches Land*. Berlin: Stollberg, 1942. 321 pp., illus., map. (3. Aufl.).

5470 MEY, EUGÈNE: *Le drame de l'Alsace, 1939–1945*. Paris: Berger-Levrault, 1949. 248 pp.

5471 *Zwei Jahre nationalsozialistischer Aufbau in Elsass*. [Strassburg]: Oberrheinischer Gauverlag, [1942]. [64 pp.], illus.

Persecution and resistance

5472 BIDAULT, GEORGES: *D'une résistance à l'autre*. Paris: Éds. du Siècle, 1965. 382 pp. [Part I: 1940–1945, pp. 21–110. English version: *Resistance. The political autobiography of Georges Bidault*. London: Weidenfeld & Nicolson, 1967.]

5473 BLUMENSON, MARTIN: *The Vildé affair. Beginnings of the French Resistance*. London: Hale, 1978. 287 pp., illus.

CATHOLIC CHURCH

5474 DUQUESNE, JACQUES: *Les catholiques français sous l'occupation*. Paris: Grasset, 1966. 477 pp., bibl.

5475 PELISSIER, JEAN: *Si la Gestapo avait su! Un prêtre à l'Opéra de Munich et dans la Haute Couture*. Paris: Bonne Presse, 1945. 156 pp. [Incl. lists of deported and executed French priests.]

5476 SALIÈGE, [JULES]: *Un évêque français sous l'Occupation. Extraits des messages*. Paris: Éds. Ouvrières, 1945. 165 pp.

5477 VERGNET, PAUL: *Les catholiques dans la Résistance. La libération nationale.* Paris: Éds. des Saints Pères, 1946. 312 pp.

5478 CHURCHILL, PETER: *The spirit in the cage.* London: Hodder & Stoughton, 1954. 251 pp. [A British agent working with the Maquis.]

5479 COLLIER, RICHARD: *Ten thousand eyes.* London: Collins, 1958. 320 pp., illus. [Resistance against Todt organization.]

5480 DEBU-BRIDEL, JACQUES, ed.: *La Résistance intellectuelle—Jean Guéhenno; François Mauriac; Henri Moureu; les professeurs Robert Debré, Pierre Biquard et Étienne Bernard; René Capitant; Edith Thomas; Claude Morgan; Jacques Debû-Bridel; René Tavernier; Joë Nordmann; Édouard Pignon; Louis Daquin; Pierre Villon.* Paris: Julliard, 1970. 263 pp.

5481 DURAND, PAUL: *La SNCF pendant la guerre. Sa résistance à l'occupant.* Préface: Louis Armand; Avant-propos: André Ségalat. Paris: Presses Universitaires de France, 1968. 668 pp., tabs., bibl.

5482 GASCAR, PIERRE: *Histoire de la captivité des Français en Allemagne, 1939–1945.* [Paris]: Gallimard, 1967. 317 pp., bibl.

GESTAPO IN FRANCE
5483 AZIZ, PHILIPPE: *Au service de l'ennemi. La Gestapo française en province.* [Paris]: Fayard, 1972. 186 pp. [Districts of Bourges, St.-Étienne, Marseilles.]

5484 HASQUENOPH, MARCEL: *La Gestapo en France.* Paris: de Vecchi, 1975. 504 pp.

5485 KENNARD, COLERIDGE: *Gestapo. France, 1943–1945.* London: Richards, 1947. 206 pp.

5486 RUFFIN, RAYMOND: *La résistance normande face à la Gestapo.* Paris: Presses de la Cité, 1977. 254 pp., illus., maps, tabs., facsims.

5487 TERROINE, ÉMILE F.: *Dans les géoles de la Gestapo. Souvenirs de la prison de Montluc.* Lyon: 1944. 150 pp.

5488 LUTHER, HANS: *Der französische Widerstand gegen die deutsche Besatzungsmacht und seine Bekämpfung.* Tübingen: Institut für Besatzungsfragen in Tübingen zu den deutschen Besatzungen im 2. Weltkrieg, 1957. 297 pp.

5489 MICHEL, HENRI: *Bibliographie critique de la Résistance.* [Paris]: Institut Pédagogique National, 1964. 223 pp., bibl.

5490 NOGUÈRES, HENRI and others: *Histoire de la Résistance en France de 1940 à 1945.* En collaboration: M. Degliame-Fouché, J.-L. Vigier. Paris: Laffont, 1967– continuing. Illus., facsims., bibls.
[I]: *La première année. Juin 1940–Juin 1941.* 510 pp.
[II]: *L'armée de l'ombre. Juillet 1941–Octobre 1942.* 733 pp.
[III]: *Et du Nord au Midi ... Novembre 1942–Septembre 1943.* 717 pp.

5491 KRUUSE, JENS: *Madness at Oradour. 10 June 1944 ... and after*. Transl. from the Danish. London: Secker & Warburg, 1969. 179 pp. [First ed. as: *Som vanvid*. Copenhagen: 1967.]

5492 POITEVIN, PIERRE: *Dans l'enfer d'Oradour. Le plus monstrueux crime de la guerre*. Paris: Société des Journaux et Publications du Centre, 1944. 222 pp., illus., facsim., tabs.

5493 PEARSON, MICHAEL: *Tears of glory. The betrayal of Vercors, 1944*. London: Macmillan, 1978. 254 pp., map.

5494 RÉMY, pseud.: *La ligne de démarcation*. Paris: Perrin, 1964/70. Vols. I–XVIII, illus., facsims., maps.

UNDERGROUND PRESS AND LITERATURE

5495 BELLANGER, CLAUDE: *Presse clandestine, 1940–1944*. Paris: Colin, 1961. 264 pp., illus., facsims., bibl.

5496 BIBLIOTHÈQUE NATIONALE: *Catalogue des périodiques clandestins diffusés en France de 1939 à 1945. Suivi d'un catalogue des périodiques clandestins diffusés à l'étranger*. Paris: 1954. 282 pp.

5497 VEILLON, DOMINIQUE: *'Le Franc-tireur'. Un journal clandestin, un mouvement de Résistance, 1940–1944*. Paris: Flammarion, 1977. 428 pp., illus., facsims., bibl.

5498 VERCORS, pseud.: *Le silence de la mer. Récit. Écrit en France—publié à Londres*. London: 1943. 46 pp. (Les Cahiers du Silence). [Ostracism as an attempted means of resistance.]

Vichy France

5499 BRUSSAUD, ANDRÉ: *La dernière année de Vichy, 1943–1944*. Préface: Robert Aron. Paris: Perrin, 1965. 580 pp., bibl.

5500 DELPERRIE de BAYAC, JACQUES: *Le royaume du Maréchal. Histoire de la zone libre*. Paris: Laffont, 1975. 413 pp., illus., bibl.

5501 *France during the German occupation, 1940–1944. A collection of 292 statements on the government of Maréchal Pétain and Pierre Laval*. Transl. from the French. Stanford, Calif.: Stanford University, for Hoover Institution on War, Revolution, and Peace, [1957]. 3 vols. [Incl. German persecution of the Jews.]

5502 KEDWARD, H. R.: *Resistance in Vichy France. A study of ideas and motivation in the Southern Zone, 1940–1942*. Oxford: Oxford University Press, 1978. ix + 311 pp., maps, bibl.

5503 NEUGEBAUER, KARL-VOLKER: *Die deutsche Militärkontrolle im unbesetzten Frankreich und in Französisch Nordwestafrika, 1940–1942*. Hrsg.: Militärgeschichtliches Forschungsamt. Boppard a.Rh.: Boldt, 1980. 186 pp.

5504 *Pétain et les Allemands. Mémorandum d'Abetz sur les rapports franco-allemands.* [Paris]: Gaucher, 1948. 200 pp., illus.

j. Italy

5505 ANFUSO, FILIPPO: *Da Palazzo Venezia al Lago di Garda, 1936–1945.* III ed. con aggiunta di documenti di Roma–Berlino–Salò. Bologna: Cappelli, 1957. 509 pp., illus., facsims. [Incl. Italian and German resistance movements.]

5506 BATTAGLIA, ROBERTO: *Storia della resistenza italiana.* Torino: Einaudi, 1970. 682 pp., maps, bibl. [2nd rev. ed. 1953.]

5507 BERGWITZ, HUBERTUS: *Die Partisanenrepublik Ossola. Vom 10. September bis zum 23. Oktober 1944.* Vorw.: Edgar Rosen. Hannover: Verlag für Literatur und Zeitgeschehen, 1972. 165 pp., bibl. (Veröffentlichungen des Institutes für Sozialgeschichte Braunschweig).

5508 BORRELLI, ARMANDO & BENEDETTI, E. ANACLETO, eds.: *Uomini e tedeschi. Scritti e disegni di deportati.* Milano: Casa di Arosio, per gli orfani di guerra e dei deportati, 1947. 408 pp., illus. [Eyewitness reports on Italians interned in German camps after the Italian capitulation.]

5509 COLLOTTI, ENZO: *L'amministrazione tedesca dell'Italia occupata, 1943–1945. Studio e documenti.* Milano: Lerici, 1963. 607 pp., tabs., illus. (Istituto Nazionale per la Storia del Movimento di Liberazione in Italia). [Documents in Italian and German.]

5510 CONTI, LAURA, ed.: *La resistenza in Italia, 25 luglio 1943–23 aprile 1945. Saggio bibliografico.* Milano: Feltrinelli, 1961. 404 pp., map.

5511 MALVEZZI, PIERO & PIRELLI, GIOVANNI: *Lettere di condannati a morte della resistenza italiana, 8 settembre 1943–25 aprile 1945.* A cura di Piero Malvezzi, Giovanni Agnoletti. Torino: Einaudi, 1952. 315 pp.

5512 RAMATI, ALEXANDER: *While the Pope kept silent. Assisi and the Nazi occupation.* As told by Padre Rufino Niccacci. London: Allen & Unwin, 1978. 181 pp., map.

ROME

5513 PERRONE CAPANO, RENATO: *La resistenza in Roma.* Napoli: Macchiaroli, 1963. 2 vols., illus., facsims., bibl.

5514 TROISIO, ARMANDO: *Roma sotto il terrore nazi-fascista, 8 settembre 1943–4 giugno 1944. Documentario.* Roma: Mondini, 1944. 206 pp. [Incl. persecution of Jews.]

5515 WYSS, M. de: *Rome under the terror.* London: Halle, 1945. 218 pp., illus.

k. Low Countries

Belgium

Occupation (general)

5516 BAUDUIN, FERNAND: *L'économie belge sous l'Occupation, 1940–1944.* Bruxelles: Bruylant, 1945. 435 pp.

5517　DELANDSHEERE, PAUL & OOMS, ALPHONSE: *La Belgique sous les Nazis*. Bruxelles: L'Édition universelle, [1945?]. 4 vols.

5518　JACQUEMYNS, G.: *La société belge sous l'Occupation allemande, 1940–1944*. Brussels: Nicholson & Watson, 1950. 3 vols. [Vol. 1: 'Mode de vie. Comportement moral et social'; Vol. 3: 'Les travailleurs déportés et leurs familles'.]

5519　LECLEF, (Chanoine), ed.: *Le Cardinal van Roey et l'Occupation allemande en Belgique. Actes et documents*. Bruxelles: Goemaere, 1945. 360 pp.

5520　SELLESLAGH, F.: *L'emploi de la main d'oeuvre belge sous l'Occupation, 1940*. Bruxelles: Centre de Recherche et d'Études historiques de la Seconde Guerre Mondiale, 1970. 117 pp., tabs.

5521　SOMERHAUSEN, ANNE: *Written in darkness. A Belgian woman's record of the Occupation, 1940–1945*. New York: Knopf, 1946. 340 pp. [Incl. aid to Jews.]

5522　WEBER, WOLFRAM: *Die innere Sicherheit im besetzten Belgien und Nordfrankreich 1940–1944. Ein Beitrag zur Geschichte der Besatzungsverwaltungen*. Vorw.: Jacques Willebrod. Düsseldorf: Droste, 1978. 198 pp. [From a dissertation (Cologne).]

Persecution and resistance

5523　GOFFIN, ROBERT: *Passeports pour l'au-delà. Récit de l'underground belge*. New York: Éds. de la Maison française, 1944. 373 pp. [English version: *The White Brigade*. New York: Doubleday, Doran, 1944. Documentary novel about the Belgian Underground and Breendonck concentration camp.]

5524　GORIS, JAN-ALBERT: *Belgium in bondage*. Introd.: James Hilton. New York: Fischer, 1943. 259 pp.

5525　GOTOVITCH, JOSÉ, ed.: 'Les rapports de la Sicherheitspolizei sur la Résistance belge en 1943. Documents'. [In] *Cahiers d'Histoire de la Deuxième Guerre Mondiale*. Pp. 182–237. *See* 4625.

MALMÉDY

5526　BERTHOLD, WILL: *Mitgefangen—Mitgehangen—Malmedy. Roman nach Tatsachen*. München: Kindler, 1957. 399 pp.

5527　GREIL, LOTHAR: *Oberst der Waffen-SS Joachim Peipler und der Malmedy-Prozess*. München-Lochhausen: Schild-Verlag, 1977. 111 pp., illus.

UNDERGROUND PRESS

5528　BELGIAN MINISTRY OF INFORMATION: *The underground press in Belgium*. London: 1944. 60 + 49 pp., facsims.

5529　DUJARDIN, JEAN and others: *Inventaire de la presse clandestine, 1940–1944, conservée en Belgique*. Par Jean Dujardin, Lucia Rymenans, José Gotovitch. Bruxelles: Centre national d'Histoire des deux Guerres mondiales, 1966. 192 pp., facsims., tabs. (Archives générales du Royaume). [Text in French and Flemish.]

5530   WAR CRIMES COMMISSION: *War crimes committed* ... Liège: Thone, 1945/48.
Series of pamphlets, illus., maps, facsim. (Kingdom of Belgium—Ministry of
Justice). [Issued in French and English.]
... *during the invasion of the national territory, May 1940.* [Incl. destruction of
the library of the University of Louvain, massacres at Vinkt.]
... *during the occupation of Belgium, 1940–1945.* [Incl. crimes against hostages,
Breendonck concentration camp.]
... *during the liberation of the national territory, September 1944.*
... *during von Rundstedt's counter-offensive in the Ardennes, December
1944–January 1945.*

Holland

Occupation (general)
COLLABORATION
5531   HOOF, HENRI van: *Duivels met dubbele tongen. De Nederlandsche tragedie van
1921–1941 in Romanvorm verteld.* Amsterdam: Volksche Uitg. Westland,
1944. 231 pp., illus. [Collaborationist.]

ZEE, SYTZE van der: *Voor Führer, volk en vaderland sneuvelde* ... *De SS in
Nederland, Nederland in de SS. See 4347.*

5532   *Documentatie. Status en werkzaamheid van organisaties en instellingen uit de
tijd der Duitse bezetting van Nederland.* Samengesteld ten behoeve van de
Bijzondere Rechtspleging ... [Amsterdam]: Buijten & Schipperheijn, [194–].
381 pp.

5533   JONG, L[OUIS] de: *Het Koninkrijk der Nederlanden in de Tweede Wereldoorlog.*
's-Gravenhage: Nijhoff, 1969– continuing. 13 vols. (Rijksinstituut voor
Oorlogsdocumentatie).

5534   KWIET, KONRAD: *Reichskommissariat Niederlande. Versuch und Scheitern
nationalsozialistischer Neuordnung.* Stuttgart: Deutsche Verlags-Anstalt,
1968. 172 pp., bibl.

5535   MAASS, WALTER B.: *The Netherlands at war, 1940–1945.* London: Abelard-
Schuman, 1970. 264 pp., illus., maps, bibl.

5536   OORTHUYS, CAS: *1944–45—het laatste jaar. Een verslag in foto's over
onderdrukking en bevrijding.* Amsterdam: Uitg. Contact, 1970. 104 pp.,
illus.

PROPAGANDA
5537   DU PREL, MAX Frhr., ed.: *Die Niederlande im Umbruch der Zeiten. Alte und
neue Beziehungen zum Reich.* Im Auftr. des Reichskommissars für die
besetzten Niederländischen Gebiete Reichsminister Seyss-Inquart. Mitw.:
Willi Janke. Würzburg: Triltsch, 1941. 395 pp., illus., facsims., diagrs.,
maps, tabs.

5538   HOFFMANN, GABRIELE: *NS-Propaganda in den Niederlanden. Organisation und*

Lenkung der Publizistik unter deutscher Besatzung 1940–1945. München-Pullach: Verlag Dokumentation, 1972. 296 pp., bibl.

5539 HÜTTIG, W.: *De tegenstanders der rassenidee en hun strijdmethode.* Nederlandsche Bewirkung ... Amsterdam: Uitg. Westland, 1942. 44 pp.

5540 WARMBRUNN, WERNER: *The Dutch under German occupation, 1940–1945.* Stanford, Calif.: Stanford University Press, 1963. 338 pp., map, bibl.

Persecution and resistance
5541 BOEREE, Th. A.: *Kroniek van Ede gedurende de Bezettingstijd. Met grepen uit het leven der partisanen.* Ede: Frouws, [194–]. 320 pp.

5542 BOLHUIS, J. J. van and others, eds.: *Onderdrukking en verzet. Nederland in oorlogstijd.* Arnhem: van Loghum Slaterus, [1947/55]. 4 vols., illus., facsims., tabs., maps.

CHURCHES
5543 STOKMAN, S., ed.: *Het verzet van de nederlandsche Bisschoppen tegen nationaal-socialisme en duitsche tyrannie. Herderlijke brieven, instructies en andere documenten.* Utrecht: Uitg. Het Spectrum, 1945. 320 pp.

5544 TOUW, H. C.: *Het verzet der Hervormde Kerk.* 's-Gravenhage: Boekcentrum, 1946. 683 + 393 pp., in 2 vols.

5545 VISSER'T HOOFT, W. A., comp.: *Holländische Kirchendokumente. Der Kampf der holländischen Kirche um die Geltung der göttlichen Gebote im Staatsleben. Dokumente.* Zollikon-Zürich: Evangelischer Verlag, 1944. 118 pp. [Also in English: London: Student Christian Movement, 1944.]

5546 VISSER'T HOOFT, W. A.: *Memoirs.* London: SCM Press, 1973. x + 379 pp., illus. [Incl. the Church struggle in Germany, relations with the German resistance and peace-feelers, extermination of the European Jews.]

5547 FORD, HERBERT: *Flee the captor.* Nashville, Tenn.: Southern Publ. Ass'n, 1966. 373 pp., illus., facsims. [Dutch-Paris Underground and its leader, John Henry Weidner.]

5548 FRIES, K. de: *'In deze bajes ...'* [In these cells]. *Een jaar Oranje-Hotel.* Utrecht: de Haan, 1947. 239 pp.

5549 JONG, L[OUIS] de & STOPPELMAN, JOSEPH W. F.: *The lion rampant. The story of Holland's resistance to the Nazis.* New York: Querido, 1943. 386 pp.

5550 *Malnutrition and starvation in Western Netherlands, September 1944–July 1945.* The Hague: General State Printing Office, 1948. 2 vols., illus., diagrs., tabs. [Editorial Committee: G. C. E. Burger and others.]

5551 MARTENS, ALLARD & DUNLOP, DAPHNE: *The silent war. Glimpses of the Dutch Underground and views on the Battle of Arnhem.* London: Hodder & Stoughton, 1961. 318 pp., illus., maps, bibl.

5552 PATER, J. C. H. de: *Het schoolverzet*. 's-Gravenhage: Nijhoff, 1969. 530 pp., summary in English. (Ministerie van Onderwijs en Wetenschappen: Rijksinstituut voor Oorlogsdocumentatie).

5553 RANDWIJK, H. M. van: *In de schaduw van gisteren. Kroniek van het verzet 1940–1945*. Ingeleid: J.A.H.J.S. Bruins Slot. 8.druk. Den Haag: Bakker, 1970. 324 pp., facsims. [First ed. 1967.]

5554 RIJKSINSTITUUT VOOR OORLOGSDOCUMENTATIE: *Het proces Christiansen*. 's-Gravenhage: Nijhoff, 1950. 256 pp. [War crimes in Holland, incl. shooting of hostages and destruction of village of Putten with deportation of male population.]

5555 RIJKSINSTITUUT VOOR OORLOGSDOCUMENTATIE: *Het proces Rauter*. 's-Gravenhage: Nijhoff, 1952. 640 pp., summary in English. [Trial of SS general for war crimes in Holland.]

STUDENTS
5556 BLASE, F. W., ed.: *Studenten onder de bezetting*. Amsterdam: Kirchner, 1946. vii + 277 pp., illus. [Forew.: G. van der Leeuw.]

5557 *Delft. Gedenkboek van het verzet der Delftsche studenten en docenten gedurende de jaren 1940–1945*. Uitg.: Delftsche Studenten Raad in opdracht van de Delftsche Contactgroep. Delft: 1947. 222 pp., ports.

UNDERGROUND PRESS AND LITERATURE
5558 JONG, DIRK de: *Het vrije boek in onvrije tijd. Bibliografie van illegale en clandestiene belletrie*. Leiden: Sijthoff, 1958. 340 pp., illus.

5559 WINKEL, L. E.: *De ondergrondse pers, 1940–1945*. 's-Gravenhage: Nijhoff, 1954. 414 pp., illus., facsims., summary in English.

5560 VRIES, Ph. de: *1941–1945. Geschiedenis van het verzet der artsen in Nederland*. Haarlem: Willink, 1949. 385 pp.

WORKERS
5561 BOUMAN, P. J.: *De April–Mei stakingen van 1943*. 's-Gravenhage: Nijhoff, 1950. 483 pp., maps.

5562 RÜTER, A. J. C.: *Rijden en staken. De Nederlandse spoorwegen in oorlogstijd*. 's-Gravenhage: Nijhoff, 1960. 478 pp., tabs., summary in English. (Rijksinstituut voor Oorlogsdocumentatie).

5563 SIJES, B. A.: *De Februari-Staking, 25–26 Februari 1941*. 's-Gravenhage: Nijhoff, 1954. 237 pp., illus., summary in English. (Ministerie van Onderwijs, Kunsten en Wetenschappen: Rijksinstituut voor Oorlogsdocumentatie).

5564 STOKMAN, S.: *De katholieke arbeidersbeweging in oorlogstijd*. Utrecht: Uitg. Het Spectrum, 1946. 167 pp.

Luxembourg

5565   CERF, PAUL: *Longtemps j'aurai mémoire*. [Luxembourg]: Éds du Letzeburger Land, 1974. 227 pp., illus., facsims., bibl.

5566   EWERT, EUGEN: *Die Luxemburger im Reich*. Luxemburg: Verlagsanstalt Moselland, [1943]. 55 pp.

5567   KOCH-KENT, HENRI: *Sie boten Trotz. Luxemburger im Freiheitskampf, 1939–1945*. Luxemburg: [priv. pr.], 1974. 412 pp., maps, bibl.

5568   KOCH-KENT, HENRI & HOHENGARTEN, ANDRÉ: *Luxemburger als Freiwild*. Luxemburg: [priv. pr.], 1972. 40 pp., tabs., bibl. [Incl. list of names (pp. 11–26) publ. in *Deutsches Fahndungsbuch*, 6. Jhrg., Nr. 265. Berlin: Reichskriminalpolizeiamt, 1. Okt. 1943.]

5569   WEBER, PAUL: *Geschichte Luxemburgs im Zweiten Weltkrieg*. 2. erw. Aufl. Luxembourg: Buck, 1958. 156 pp.

l. Scandinavia

Denmark

Occupation (general)

5570   ALKIL, NIELS: *Besaettelsestidens Fakta. Dokumentarisk Haandbog met Henblik paa Lovene af 1945 om landsskadelig Virksomhed*. København: Schultz, 1945. 2 vols.

5571   *Best-Sagen. Københavns byrets cøste landrets og højesterets domme*. København: Gads, 1950. 64 pp. [Trial of Karl Rudolf Werner Best, Hermann v. Hanneken, Günther Pancke and Otto Richard Bovensiepen.]

5572   FOLKETING: [Memorandum, reports and supplements covering the occupation submitted to Parliament by various official commissions]. København: Schultz, 1945/54. 38 vols. [In Danish.]

5573   GUDME, STEN: *Denmark—Hitler's 'Model Protectorate'*. Transl. from the Danish. London: Gollancz, 1942. 165 pp.

5574   HALLER, VIRGINIA: *Neumond über Kopenhagen*. München: Bergstadtverlag, 1961. 262 pp. [A German in occupied Denmark.]

5575   OUTZE, BØRGE, ed.: *Denmark during the German occupation*. Copenhagen: Scandinavian Publ. Co., 1946. 155 pp., illus., maps. [Incl. an account of Stutthof concentration camp by Helge Larsen.]

5576   PETROW, RICHARD: *The bitter years. The invasion and occupation of Denmark and Norway, April 1940–May 1945*. London: Hodder & Stoughton, 1974. 403 pp., illus., maps, bibl.

5577   POULSEN, HENNING: *Besaettelsesmagten og de Danske nazister. Det politiske forhold mellem Tyske myndigheder og nazistiske kredse i Danmark, 1940–43*. [Copenhagen?]: Gyldendal, 1970. 498 pp., bibl., summary in German.

5578 THOMSEN, ERICH: *Deutsche Besatzungspolitik in Dänemark, 1940–1945.* Düsseldorf: Bertelsmann, 1971. 277 pp., bibl.

Resistance

5579 BARFOD, JØRGEN H.: *The Museum of Denmark's fight for freedom, 1940–1945. A short guide.* Copenhagen: The National Museum, 1975. 40 pp., illus.

BENNETT, JEREMY: *British broadcasting and the Danish resistance movement. See* 3039.

5580 BORCHSENIUS, PAUL: *L'Église, âme de la Résistance.* Genève: Ed. Labor et Fides, [1944]. 99 pp. [Transl. from the Danish.]

5581 BUSCHARDT, LEO and others, eds.: *Den illegale presse, 1940–45. En antologi.* [Eds.]: Leo Buschardt, Albert Fabritius, Morten Ruge, Helge Tønnesen. [Copenhagen]: Gyldendal, 1965. 564 pp.

5582 FLERON, KATE: *Kvinder i Modstandskampen.* København: Busck, 1945. 205 pp.

5583 HAESTRUP, JØRGEN: *Secret alliance. A study of the Danish resistance movement, 1940–45.* Odense: Odense University Press, 1976/77. 3 vols. [Danish orig.: *Hemmelig alliance.* København: Thaning & Appels, 1959.]

5584 THOMAS, JOHN ORAM: *The giant killers. The story of the Danish resistance movement, 1940–1945.* London: Joseph, 1975. 320 pp., illus., maps.

Norway

Occupation, persecution and resistance

5585 ASTRUP, HELEN & JACOT, B. L.: *Oslo intrigue. A woman's memoir of the Norwegian resistance.* New York: McGraw-Hill, 1954. 237 pp.

5586 BRANDT, WILLY: *Norwegens Freiheitskampf, 1940–1945.* Hamburg: Auerdruck, 1948. 143 pp.

5587 CHRISTENSEN, SYNNÖVE: *Ich bin eine norwegische Frau. Tatsachenbericht.* Zürich: Humanitas-Verlag, 1944. 298 pp.

CHURCH

5588 *Ande mot vald. Norges kyrka och skola, 1940–1942.* Stockholm: Federativs, 1942. 96 pp.

5589 BERGGRAV, EIVIND (Bishop of Oslo): *With God in the darkness, and other papers illustrating the Norwegian church conflict.* Eds.: G. K. A. Bell, H. M. Waddams. London: Hodder & Stoughton, 1943. 109 pp., port.

COLLABORATION

5590 FEN, AKE: *Nazis in Norway.* Harmondsworth, Middx.: Penguin Books, 1943. 157 pp., map.

5591 LOOCK, HANS-DIETRICH: *Quisling, Rosenberg und Terboven. Zur Vorgeschichte und Geschichte der nationalsozialistischen Revolution in Norwegen.* Stuttgart: Deutsche Verlags-Anstalt, 1970. 587 pp., bibl.

5592 [QUISLING, VIDKUN] VOGT, BENJAMIN: *Mennesket og forraederen Vidkun Quisling* [Traitor or patriot ...]. Oslo: Aschehoug, 1965. 182 pp.

5593 *Statistikk over Landssvik, 1940–1945.* Oslo: Statistisk Sentralbyrå, 1954. 64 pp., tabs., summary in English. (Norges offisielle Statistikk, XI. 179).

5594 FROGNER, CARSTEN: *Die unsichtbare Front.* Zürich: Europa Verlag, 1944. 200 pp. [Resistance, incl. section on Grini concentration camp.]

5595 GVELSVIK, TORE: *Norwegian resistance, 1940–1945.* Transl. from the Norwegian. London: Hurst, 1979. x + 224 pp., illus.

LOFOTEN ISLANDS

5596 MIKES, G[EORGE]: *The epic of Lofoten.* London: Hutchinson, [194–]. 79 pp., illus. [Lofoten Islanders' resistance to the Nazis and assistance during the British raid.]

5597 *Secret German documents seized during the raid on the Lofoten Islands on the 4th March 1941, embodying instructions to the army on the control of the press and on collaboration with the Gestapo in dealing with Norwegian nationals.* London: HMSO, 1941. 28 pp. (Cmd. 6270, Norway No. 1, 1941. Corrected reprint).

5598 LUIHN, HANS: *De illegale avisene. Den frie, hemmelige pressen i Norge under okkupasjonen.* Oslo: Universitetsforlaget, 1960. 3 vols.

5599 *Milorg D 13 i kamp. Episoder fra det hemmelige militoere motstandsarbeid i Oslo og omegn under okkupasjonen nedtegnet etter Milorgrapporter og personlige beretninger.* Oslo: Mortensen, 1961. 286 pp., illus.

5600 [MOEN, PETTER] SCHAPER, EDZARD, ed.: *Peter Moen's diary.* London: Faber & Faber, 1951. 146 pp. [Transl. from the Norwegian. German version: *Petter Moens Tagebuch.* Frankfurt a.M.: Fischer, 1959. Moen was a leader of the Norwegian resistance.]

PETROW, RICHARD: *The bitter years. The invasion and occupation of Denmark and Norway. See* 5576.

5601 UNDSET, SIGRID: *Return to the future.* Transl. from the Norwegian. New York: Knopf, 1942. 251 pp.

VIII. WAR CRIMES

A. GENERAL

5602 ARONEANU, EUGÈNE: *Le crime contre l'humanité.* Préface: André Boissarie. Paris: Dalloz, 1961. 322 pp., port.

5603 BILLIG, J.: *L'Allemagne et le génocide. Plans et réalisations nazis.* Préface: François de Menthon. Paris: Eds. du Centre, 1950. 110 pp.

5604 DESCHNER, KARLHEINZ, ed.: *Das Jahrhundert der Barbarei.* München: Desch, 1966. 529 pp., bibls. [Incl.: H. G. Adler: 'Pogrome und Konzentrationslager. Die Judenverfolgung im 20. Jahrhundert', pp. 243–315; Karlheinz Deschner: 'Die Politik der Päpste', pp. 316–370.]

5605 GLOWNA KOMISJA BADANIA ZBRODNI HITLEROWSKI W POLSCE, Ministerstwo Sprawiedliwości: *Stan i perspektywy badań w zakresie zbrodni hitlerowskich. Materiały z konferencji naukowez w dniach 27–28 kwietnia 1970r. Tom I* [Position of research in the sphere of Nazi crimes. Material from an academic conference, 27–28 April, 1970. Vol. I]. Warszawa: 1973. 417 pp., tabs. [For official use only. Incl. large section on concentration and extermination camps.]

5606 HASSEL, SVEN: *The legion of the damned.* Transl. from the Danish. London: Allen & Unwin, 1957. 239 pp. [Experiences in a Nazi penal regiment.]

JÄGER, HERBERT: *Verbrechen unter totalitärer Herrschaft. Studien zur nationalsozialistischen Gewaltkriminalität. See* 3310.

5607 *The Pohl case. Trials of war criminals, Vol. 5.* [Pohl was head of WVHA = SS Wirtschafts- und Verwaltungshauptamt, in charge of concentration camps, medical experiments, extermination of Jews, 'Euthanasia' and slave labour.] *See* 5636.

5608 ROUSSET, DAVID: *Le pître ne rit pas.* Paris: Éds. du Pavois, 1948. 263 pp. [German war crimes in France, Eastern Europe and concentration camps.]

5609 *The RuSHA case. Trials of war criminals, Vols. 4, 5.* [Kidnapping and/or extermination of children, robbery and expropriation, extermination of Jews. RuSHA = Rasse- und Siedlungshauptamt.] *See* 5636.

5610 RUSSELL OF LIVERPOOL, EDWARD (Lord): *The scourge of the swastika. A short history of Nazi war crimes.* London: Cassell, 1954. 259 pp., illus. [Ch. I: 'Hitler's instruments of tyranny'; Ch. VI: 'Concentration camps'; Ch. VII: 'The "Final Solution" of the Jewish question'. Also: London: Corgi Books, 1954. German version: *Geissel der Menschheit.* Berlin: Volk und Welt Verlag, 1955.]

5611 UTHOFF, HAYO: *Rollenkonforme Verbrechen unter einem totalitären System.* Einf.: Ferdinand A. Hermens. Berlin: Duncker & Humblot, 1975. 329 pp., bibl.

5612 [WIESENTHAL, SIMON] *Essays über Naziverbrechen Simon Wiesenthal gewidmet.* Amsterdam: Wiesenthal Fonds, 1973. 295 pp. [Incl.: Lau Mazirel: 'Die Verfolgung der "Zigeuner" im Dritten Reich', pp. 124–176, bibl.; Harry Pross: 'Anmerkungen zur Sprache der Diktatur in Deutschland'.]

5613 ZORN, GERDA: *Nach Ostland geht unser Ritt. Deutsche Eroberungspolitik zwischen Germanisierung und Völkermord.* Vorw.: Herbert Wehner. Berlin: Dietz, 1980. 192 pp., map, bibl. [3. Teil: 'Von der Expansion zum Völkermord'.]

B. WAR CRIMES TRIALS

1. GENERAL

5614 DAM, H. G. van & GIORDANO, RALPH, eds.: *KZ-Verbrechen vor deutschen Gerichten. Dokumente aus den Prozessen gegen Sommer (KZ Buchenwald): Sorge, Schubert (KZ Sachsenhausen): Unkelbach (Ghetto in Czenstochau)* [and Vol. 2]: *Einsatzkommando Tilsit. Der Prozess zu Ulm.* Frankfurt a.M.: Europäische Verlagsanstalt, 1962/66. 2 vols.

5615 JASPERS, KARL: *Die Schuldfrage. Für Völkermord gibt es keine Verjährung.* München: Piper, 1979. 201 pp. [Written 1945–1968.]

5616 *Justiz und NS-Verbrechen. Sammlung deutscher Strafurteile wegen nationalsozialistischer Tötungsverbrechen 1945–1966.* (Bearb.: Adelheid L. Rüter-Ehlermann, H. H. Fuchs, C. F. Rüter. Amsterdam: University Press, 1968/80. Bd. I–XXI (in progress).

5617 KEMPNER, ROBERT M.: *Das Dritte Reich im Kreuzverhör.* Königstein/Ts.: Athenäum/Droste, 1980. 300 pp.

5618 KEMPNER, ROBERT M. W.: *SS im Kreuzverhör.* München: Rütten & Loening, 1964. 304 pp.

5619 LEWIS, JOHN R., comp.: *Uncertain judgment: a bibliography of war crimes trials.* Santa Barbara, Calif.: ABC-Clio Press, 1979. xxxiii + 251 pp.

5620 MEYROWITZ, HENRI: *La répression par les tribunaux allemands des crimes contre l'humanité et de l'appartenance à une organisation criminelle, en application de la loi No 10 du Conseil de Contrôle allié.* Paris: Pichon & Durand-Auzias, 1960. 514 pp., bibl. [Incl. denazification.]

5621 NEUMANN, INGE S., comp.: *European war crimes trials. A bibliography.* Additional material furnished by the Wiener Library, London, ed. by Robert A. Rosenbaum. New York: Carnegie Endowment for International Peace, 1951. 113 pp.

5622 OPPITZ, ULRICH DIETER: *Strafverfahren und Strafvollstreckung bei NS-*

Gewaltverbrechen. Dargest. an Hand von 542 rechtskräftigen Urteilen deutscher Gerichte aus der Zeit von 1945–1975. 2., erw. Aufl. Ulm: Oppitz, 1979. 380 + xxiv pp., diagrs., facsims., tabs., bibl.

5623 RÜCKERL, ADALBERT, ed.: *NS-Prozesse. Nach 25 Jahren Strafverfolgung: Möglichkeiten—Grenzen—Ergebnisse.* Mit Beiträgen von Adalbert Rückerl [and others]. Vorw.: Rudolf Schieler. Karlsruhe: Müller, 1971. 205 + [16] pp., tabs., facsims. [Incl.: Manfred Blank: 'Die Ermordung der Juden im "Generalgouvernement" Polen'; Alfred Streim: 'Die Verbrechen der Einsatzgruppen'; Günter Kimmel: 'Tötungsverbrechen in nationalsozialistischen Konzentrationslagern'.]

5624 RÜCKERL, ADALBERT: *Die Strafverfolgung von NS-Verbrechen 1945–1978. Eine Dokumentation.* Heidelberg: Müller, 1979. 148 pp. [English version: *The investigation of Nazi crimes, 1945–1978.* Same publishing details. Report by the head of the Federal Bureau for the Prosecution of Nazi Crimes.]

See also 5719–5728.

2. NUREMBERG TRIALS

5625 CYPRIAN, TADEUSZ & SAWICKI, JERZY: *Nuremberg in retrospect. People and issues of the trial.* Warsaw: Western Press Agency, 1967. 245 pp., bibl.

5626 DEUTSCHES RUNDFUNKARCHIV: *Tondokumente zur Zeitgeschichte: Nürnberger Prozess (1945–1946).* Frankfurt a.M.: 1971. 63 pp.

5627 HAENSEL, CARL: *Das Gericht vertagt sich. Tagebuch eines Verteidigers bei den Nürnberger Prozessen.* München: Limes-Verlag, 1980. 347 pp., illus.

5628 HARRIS, WHITNEY R.: *Tyranny on trial. The evidence at Nuremberg.* Introd.: Robert H. Jackson. Dallas, Tex.: Southern Methodist University Press, 1954. 608 pp., illus.

5629 HEYDECKER, JOE & LEEB, JOHANNES: *Der Nürnberger Prozess. Neue Dokumente, Erkenntnisse und Analysen.* Köln: Kiepenheuer & Witsch, 1979. 582 pp., illus. [English orig.: Westport, Conn.: Greenwood Press, 1977.]

5630 INTERNATIONAL MILITARY TRIBUNAL: *Trial of the major war criminals.* Nuremberg: 1949. 42 vols. [Also publ. in German. Vols. 25–42 comprise 'Documents in evidence': although extensive, the documentation by no means covers all the documents collected for trial purposes; the Institut für Zeitgeschichte, Munich, has a complete indexed set, and partial collections are to be found in the Imperial War Museum, London, and elsewhere.]

5631 MASER, WERNER: *Nürnberg. Tribunal der Sieger.* Düsseldorf: Econ Verlag, 1977. 700 pp., illus., bibl. [English version: *Trial of a nation.* London: Penguin Books, 1977.]

5632 NEAVE, AIREY: *Nuremberg: a personal record of the trial of the major war criminals in 1945–6.* London: Hodder & Stoughton, 1978. 348 pp., illus.

5633 POLEWOI, BORIS: *Nürnberger Tagebuch.* Berlin [East]: Verlag Volk und Welt, 1974. 309 pp. [4th ed., transl. from the Russian. First German ed. 1971.]

5634 SMITH, BRADLEY F.: *Reaching judgment at Nuremberg.* London: André Deutsch, 1977. xviii + 349 pp., ports., bibl.

5635 STEINIGER, P. A.: *Der Nürnberger Prozess. Aus den Protokollen, Dokumenten und Materialien des Prozesses gegen die Hauptkriegsverbrecher vor dem Internationalen Militärgerichtshof.* Berlin [East]: Rütten & Loening, 1957. 2 vols.

5636 *Trials of War Criminals before the Nuernberg Military Tribunals under Control Council Law No. 10.* Washington, D.C.: US Gov't Printing Office, 1949/52.
Vol. 1: *The Medical case.*
Vol. 2: *The Medical case. The Milch case.*
Vol. 3: *The Justice case.*
Vol. 4: *The Einsatzgruppen case. The RuSHA case.*
Vol. 5: *The RuSHA case. The Pohl case.*
Vol. 6: *The Flick case.*
Vol. 7: *The I. G. Farben case.*
Vol. 8: *The I. G. Farben case.*
Vol. 9: *The Krupp case.*
Vol. 10: *The High Command case.*
Vol. 11: *The High Command case. The Hostage case.*
Vol. 12: *The Ministries case.*
Vol. 13: *The Ministries case.*
Vol. 14: *The Ministries case.*
Vol. 15: *Procedure, practice and administration.*
[Selection publ. in German: Berlin: Deutscher Verlag der Wissenschaft, 1961/70.]

The accused

5637 [DOENITZ, KARL] THOMPSON, H. K. & STRUTZ, HENRY, eds.: *Doenitz at Nuremberg. A reappraisal. War crimes and the military professional.* New York: Amber Publ. Corp., 1976. xxxii + 198 pp., ports. [An American apologetic view.]

5638 DAVIDSON, EUGENE: *The trial of the Germans. An account of the 22 defendants before the International Military Tribunal at Nuremberg.* New York: Macmillan, 1966. 636 pp., illus., bibl.

5639 FRITZSCHE, HANS: *Hier spricht Hans Fritzsche.* Zürich: Interverlag, 1948. 307 pp.

5640 HÄRTLE, HEINRICH: *Freispruch für Deutschland. Unsere Soldaten vor dem Nürnberger Tribunal.* 2. Aufl. Göttingen: Schütz, 1965. 345 pp., illus., bibl.

HESS, RUDOLF
5641 BIRD, EUGENE K.: *Hess. Der 'Stellvertreter des Führers' Englandflug und britische Gefangenschaft Nürnberg und Spandau.* München: Desch, 1974. 310 pp., illus., facsim. [Orig. English title: *The loneliest man in the world.*]

5642 SCHWARZWÄLLER, WULF: *Rudolf Hess, 'Der Stellvertreter des Führers'—Der Mann in Spandau.* Wien: Molden, 1974. 303 pp., illus., bibl.

5642a KELLEY, DOUGLAS M.: *Twenty-two cells in Nuremberg. A psychiatrist examines the Nazi criminals.* New York: Greenberg, 1947. 245 pp.

5643 [MANSTEIN, FRITZ ERICH VON LEWINSKI] PAGET, R. T.: *Manstein. His campaigns and his trial.* Forew.: Lord Hankey. London: Collins, 1951. xv + 239 pp., maps.

5644 SPEER, ALBERT: *Spandauer Tagebücher.* Frankfurt a.M.: Ullstein (Propylaen), 1975. 671 pp., illus., facsims. [English version: *Spandau: the secret diaries.* London: Collins, 1976.]

5645 VERCEL, MICHEL C.: *Les rescapés de Nuremberg. Les 'Seigneurs de la guerre' après le verdict.* Avec la collaboration pour la documentation de Laurence Bastit. Paris: Michel, 1966. 250 pp., illus., facsim., bibl.

5646 ZIEGLER, HANS SEVERUS, ed.: *Grosse Prüfung. Letzte Briefe und letzte Worte todtgeweihter.* Nachw.: Hans-Ulrich Rudel. Hannover: National-Verlag, 1972. 158 pp., ports., facsims.

C. THE HOLOCAUST

1. HISTORIES, DOCUMENTATIONS, BIBLIOGRAPHIES

5647 BAUER, YEHUDA and others, eds.: *Guide to unpublished materials of the Holocaust period. Vols. I–V.* Jerusalem: Hebrew University, Institute of Contemporary Jewry, 1970/79. 5 vols. [Vols. I and II ed. by J. Robinson and Y. Bauer. Vol. V devoted to Yad Vashem Archives.]

5648 *Encyclopaedia of the Jewish Diaspora. A memorial library of countries and communities.* Jerusalem: Encyclopaedia of the Jewish Diaspora Co., 1953/67. 9 vols. [In Hebrew or Yiddish; in some cases with summaries or tables of contents in English.]

5649 *Encyclopaedia Judaica.* Eds.: Cecil Roth, Geoffrey Wigoder [and others]. Jerusalem: 1971/72. 16 vols., illus., facsims., diagrs., maps, mus. scores, tabs. [Index vol. (Vol. I) publ. 1972, remainder 1971. Incl. material on the Nazi period, concentration camps, racial laws, the Wannsee protocol, etc.]

5650 FRIEDMAN, PHILIP & GAR, JOSEPH: *Bibliography of Yiddish books on the Catastrophe and heroism.* New York: Yad Washem and Yivo Institute for Jewish Research, Joint Documentary Projects, 1962. 330 pp.

5651 GUTTMANN, T.: *Dokumentenwerk über die jüdische Geschichte in der Zeit des Nazismus. Ehrenbuch für das Volk Israel.* Jerusalem: 'Awir Jacob', 1943/45. 2 vols.
  I: Publ. 1943. [Incl.: Leipzig, Sachsenhausen, Buchenwald, Dachau, Lublin, Burgenland, Vienna.]
  II: Publ. 1945. [Incl.: Romania, Bulgaria, Poland, Holland, Vienna, Breslau, Buchenwald.]

5652 INTERNATIONAL TRACING SERVICE (Comité international de la Croix-Rouge):

Vorläufiges Verzeichnis der Konzentrationslager und deren Aussen-
kommandos sowie anderer Haftstätten unter dem Reichsführer-SS in
Deutschland und deutschbesetzten Gebieten (1933–1945). Arolsen: 1969.
50 + 612 pp. [Incl. dates of foundation and closing or relief of each camp,
with number of persons held, purpose of forced labour and many other
details; also incl. ghettoes. Also: *Catalogue of camps and prisons in
Germany* ... Arolsen: 1949/51. 2 vols.]

5653 KIBBUTZ LOHAMEI HAGHETTAOT: *Extermination and resistance. Historical
records and source material.* Israel: Ghetto Fighters' House, 1958. 196 pp.,
illus. [Also in Hebrew.]

5654 KOSSOY, EDWARD: *Handbuch zum Entschädigungsverfahren.* Mitarb.:
Eberhard Hammitzsch. Vorw.: Klaus Werner. München: Oldenbourg,
1958. 223 pp., maps, tabs., reprods. of official forms, bibl. [Incl.:
'Haftlingsnummern in Konzentrationslagern', pp. 90–117, tabs.; 'Juden-
kennzeichen', pp. 120–131 (with dates of enforcement); 'Verzeichnis der
Ghettos, Zwangsarbeitslager und Konzentrationslager', pp. 150–182 (with
map references for each).]

5655 PIEKARZ, MENDEL: [*The Holocaust and its aftermath. Hebrew books published in
the years 1933–1972*]. Jerusalem: Yad Vashem, 1974. vii + 920 pp. [In
Hebrew; 2 vols.]

5656 PIEKARZ, MENDEL: [*The Holocaust and its aftermath as seen through Hebrew
periodicals. A bibliography*]. Jerusalem: Yad Vashem, 1978. 492 pp. [In
Hebrew.]

5657 ROBINSON, JACOB & FRIEDMAN, PHILIP: *Guide to Jewish history under Nazi
impact.* New York: Yad Washem and Yivo Institute for Jewish Research,
Joint Documentary Projects, 1960. 425 pp. (Bibliographical series, I).

5658 ROBINSON, JACOB & FRIEDMAN, (Mrs. Philip): *The Holocaust and after. Sources
and literature in English.* Jerusalem: Israel Universities Press, 1973. 353 pp.
(Yad Vashem ... and Yivo ...—Joint Documentary Projects, Bibliographical
series, 12).

5659 ROBINSON, JACOB & SACHS, HENRY, eds.: *The Holocaust. The Nuremberg
evidence. Part 1: Documents. Digest, Index and chronological tables.*
Jerusalem: Yad Vashem and Yivo Institute for Jewish Research, 1976.
370 pp.

5660 WIENER LIBRARY: *List of Nuremberg documents dealing with the persecution of
Jews.* London: 1967. 231 pp., typescr.

2. GENERAL STUDIES COVERING 1933–1945

5661 ADAM, UWE DIETRICH: *Judenpolitik im Dritten Reich.* Königstein/Ts.:
Athenäum Verlag, 1979. 382 pp. [First publ. 1972.]

5662 DAWIDOWICZ, LUCY S.: *The war against the Jews, 1933–1945.* New York:
Holt, Rinehart & Winston, 1975. xviii + 460 pp., maps, tab., bibl. [German
version: *Der Krieg gegen die Juden 1933–1945.* München: Kindler, 1979.]

5663 EISENBACH, ARTUR: *Hitlerowska polityka zaglady Żydow* [Hitler's policy towards the Jews]. Warszawa: Książka i Wiedza, 1961. 700 pp., facsims., bibl., summary in English.

5664 FRIEDMAN, PHILIP: 'The Jewish badge and the yellow star in the Nazi era'. [In] *Historia Judaica*, Vol. XVII, No. 1, April 1955. Pp. 41–72.

5665 FRIEDMAN, PHILIP: 'The Karaites under Nazi rule' [In] *On the track of tyranny*. Pp. 97–117. *See* 3208.

5666 *Hitler's ten-year war on the Jews*. New York: Institute of Jewish Affairs, 1943. 311 pp.

5667 LEVIN, NORA: *The Holocaust. The destruction of European Jewry, 1933–1945*. New York: Crowell, 1968. 768 pp., illus., tabs.

5668 POLIAKOV, LÉON: *Bréviaire de la haine. (Le IIIe Reich et les Juifs)*. Préface: François Mauriac. Paris: Calmann-Lévy, 1951. 385 pp., illus. [English version: *Harvest of hate*. Introd.: Lord Russell of Liverpool. Forewords: François Mauriac, Reinhold Niebuhr. London: Elek Books, 1956. Also: New York: Syracuse University Press, 1954.]

5669 SCHOENBERNER, GERHARD: *Der gelbe Stern. Die Judenverfolgung in Europa 1933–1945*. Hamburg: Rütten & Loening, 1960. 223 pp., illus., map, facsims., bibl. [English version: *The yellow star. The persecution of the Jews in Europe, 1933–1945*. London: Corgi Books, 1969. Also: New York: Bantam, 1973. The work consists mainly of illustrations.]

5670 *Le Statut des Juifs en France, en Allemagne et en Italie. Textes et analyse des dispositions en vigueur* ... Lyons: Express-Documents, [194–]. 132 pp. [Legislation, 1932–1941.]

5671 STEINBERG, LUCIEN: *La révolte des Justes. Les Juifs contre Hitler, 1933–1945*. Paris: Fayard, 1970. 605 pp., bibl. [Incl.: 'Réseaux juifs à Berlin', 'Partisans juifs en Italie et dans les Balkans', 'Soulèvements des ghettos et révoltes des camps de la mort', 'Les Juifs dans la Résistance française'. English version: *Not as a lamb. The Jews against Hitler*. Farnborough, Hants: Saxon House, 1974.]

5672 TENENBAUM, JOSEPH: *Race and Reich. The story of an epoch*. New York: Twayne, 1956. 554 pp. [Incl.: Appendix 1: 'Gypsy genocide'. Also in Hebrew: Jerusalem: Yad Vashem, 1960.]

5673 *Yad Vashem Studies on the European Jewish catastrophe and resistance*. Jerusalem: 1957/79 continuing. 13 vols. + Index to Vols. I–VI. [Eds.: I–IV: Shaul Esh (with Benzion Dinur, Vol. I); V–VI: Nathan Eck & Aryeh Leon Kubovy; VII–XIII: Livia Rothkirchen. Publ. in English and Hebrew.]

5674 *Yivo Annual of Jewish social science, Vol. VIII*. Ed.: Koppel S. Pinson. New York: Yiddish Scientific Institute, 1953. [This particular issue is devoted entirely to the Jewish catastrophe of 1933–1945.]

3. EUROPE, 1939–1945

a. General

5675 AINSZTEIN, REUBEN: *Jewish resistance in Nazi-occupied Eastern Europe, with a historical survey of the Jew as fighter and soldier in the Diaspora.* London: Elek Books, 1974. xxviii + 970 pp., bibl. [Incl. Jewish partisans, the fighting city-ghettoes, the Warsaw Ghetto Revolt, revolts in the death-camps.]

5676 *Blackbook of localities whose Jewish population was exterminated by the Nazis.* Jerusalem: Yad Vashem, 1965. 439 pp.

5677 BROSZAT, MARTIN: 'Hitler and the genesis of the "Final Solution". An assessment of David Irving's theses'. [In] *Yad Vashem Studies*, XIII, 1979. pp. 73–125. *See* 5673.

5678 BROWNING, CHRISTOPHER R.: *The Final Solution and the German Foreign Office. A study of Referat D III of Abteilung Deutschland, 1940–1943.* New York: Holmes & Meier, 1979. 276 pp., map, bibl. [Incl.: 'The evolution of the German Jewish policy and the background', 'Referat Deutschland', 'Jewish policy and the German Foreign Office 1933–1940'.]

5679 BUND DER VERFOLGTEN DES NAZIREGIMES: *Das 'Wannsee-Protokoll' zur Endlösung der Judenfrage, und einige Fragen an die, die es angeht.* Düsseldorf: Bundesvorstand des BVN, 1952. 26 pp.

5680 CENTRE DE DOCUMENTATION JUIVE CONTEMPORAINE: *Persécution des Juifs en France et dans les autres pays de l'Ouest, présentée par la France à Nuremberg. Recueil de documents.* Publié sous la direction d'Henri de Monneray. Préface: René Cassin; introd.: Edgar Faure. Paris: Éds. du Centre, 1947. 423 pp., illus.

5681 CENTRE DE DOCUMENTATION JUIVE CONTEMPORAINE: *La persécution des Juifs dans les pays de l'Est, présentée par la France à Nuremberg. Recueil de documents.* Publié sous la direction d'Henri de Monneray. Paris: Éds. du Centre, 1949. 359 pp., illus.

5682 ECK, NATHAN: [*The holocaust of the Jewish people in Europe*]. [Jerusalem]: Yad Vashem, 1975. 451 pp., maps, tabs., bibl. [In Hebrew.]

5683 EISENBACH, ARTUR: *Hitlerowska polityka eksterminacji Żydow w latach 1939–1945—Jako jeden z przejawow imperializmu niemieckiego.* Warszawa: Żydowski Instytut Historyczny, 1953. 432 pp. [Documented survey of Nazi persecution and extermination of the Jews.]

5684 GILBERT, MARTIN: *Final journey. The fate of the Jews in Nazi Europe.* London: Allen & Unwin, 1979. 224 pp., illus. [Largely composed of eyewitness accounts.]

5685 GREEN, GERALD: *Holocaust.* London: Corgi Books (Transworld Publs.), 1978. 408 pp.

5686 HERSEY, JOHN: *Here to stay.* London: Hamish Hamilton, 1962. 295 pp. [Incl. Vilna, pp. 133–145; Auschwitz, pp. 176–218.]

5687 HILBERG, RAUL, ed.: *The destruction of the European Jews.* Chicago, Ill.: Quadrangle Books, 1961. 788 pp. [Also 1967 ed. with new postscript by author.]

5688 HILLGRUBER, ANDREAS: 'Die "Endlösung" und das deutsche Ostimperium als Kernstück des rassenideologischen Programms des Nationalsozialismus'. [In] *Vierteljahrshefte für Zeitgeschichte,* 20. Jhrg., 2. Heft, April 1972. Pp. 133–153.

5689 [*The Jewish partisans*]. Merhavia: 'Sifriat Poalim' Worker's Book Guild (Hashomer Hatzair), 1958. 2 vols., illus., maps, bibl., list of the fallen. [In Hebrew. Incl. sections on Jewish undergrounds in Belgium, France, Greece, Holland, Hungary, Poland, Czechoslovakia, Yugoslavia, and in the ghettoes of Bialystock, Kovno, Vilna, Minsk.]

5690 *Jewish resistance during the Holocaust. Proceedings of the Conference on Manifestations of Jewish Resistance, Jerusalem, April 7–11 1968.* Jerusalem: Yad Vashem, 1971. 562 pp., bibls. after some papers. [Hebrew orig.: Jerusalem: 1970. Ed. Meir Grubsztein.]

5691 *Les Juifs en Europe, 1939–1945. Rapports présentés à la Première Conférence européenne des Commissions historiques et des Centres de Documentation Juifs.* Paris: Éds. du Centre, 1949. 252 pp., tabs. (Centre de Documentation juive contemporaine).

5692 KORMAN, GERD, ed.: *Hunter and hunted. Human history of the Holocaust.* New York: Viking Press, 1973. 320 pp., bibl.

5693 KOWALSKI, ISAAC: *A secret press in Nazi Europe. The story of a Jewish united partisan organization.* New York: Central Guide Publ., 1969. 416 pp., illus., facsims., maps, mus. scores, bibl.

5694 KRAUS, OTA & KULKA, ERICH: *Massenmord und Profit. Die faschistische Ausrottungspolitik und ihre ökonomische Hintergründe.* Berlin [East]: Dietz, 1963. 438 pp., illus., tabs., facsims., bibl.

5695 LESTSCHINSKY, JACOB: *Crisis, catastrophe and survival. A Jewish balance sheet, 1914–1948.* New York: Institute of Jewish Affairs, 1948. 108 pp.

5696 LEVAI, JENÖ: *Zsidósors Európában* [Jewish fate in Europe]. Budapest: Magyar Téka, 1948. 335 pp., illus., facsims., maps.

5697 MANVELL, ROGER & FRAENKEL, HEINRICH: *The incomparable crime. Mass extermination in the twentieth century. The legacy of guilt.* London: Heinemann, 1967. 339 pp., facsims., plan, bibl.

5698 REITLINGER, GERALD: *The Final Solution.* London: Sphere Books, 1971. 667 pp., bibl. [First ed. 1953; 2nd rev. and augm. ed. 1968. German version: *Die Endlösung. Hitlers Versuch der Ausrottung der Juden Europas 1939–1945.* 3. durchges. und verb. Aufl. Berlin: Colloquium Verlag, 1960.]

5699 RUTHERFORD, WARD: *Genocide.* New York: Ballantyne Books, 1973. 160 pp., illus., facsims., bibl.

5700   SCHWARZ, LEO W.: *The root and the bough. Epic of an enduring people.* New York: Rinehart, 1949. 362 pp. [Jewish resistance in Warsaw, Vilna, Treblinka; Jewish partisans in Poland and France; ghettoes and concentration camps.]

5701   SHABBETAI, K.: *As sheep to the slaughter?* Forew.: Gideon Hausner. Bet Dagan: Keshev Press, 1962. 75 pp. [Transl. from the Hebrew. German version: *Wie Schafe zur Schlachtbank?* Keshev Press, 1965.]

5702   SHALIT, LEVI: *Azoi zeinen mir gestorben* [Thus we died]. Munich: 1947. 332 pp., illus. [In Yiddish. Publ. under licence of the 'Jewish Newspaper', 12 May 1947.]

5703   SUHL, YURI, ed.: *They fought back. The story of the Jewish resistance in Nazi Europe.* New York: Crown Publ., 1967. 327 pp., illus., maps. [Sponsored by the American Federation of Polish Jews.]

5704   SYRKIN, MARIE: *Blessed is the match. The story of Jewish resistance.* London: Gollancz, 1948. 254 pp.

5705   TRUNK, ISAIAH: *Jewish responses to Nazi persecution. Collective and individual behaviour in extremis.* New York: Stein & Day, 1979. xii + 371 pp., illus., maps. [Transl. from the Yiddish.]

5706   VAGO, BELA & MOSSE, GEORGE L., eds.: *Jews and non-Jews in Eastern Europe, 1918–1945.* New York: Wiley, 1974. xvii + 334 pp.

5707   WUCHER, ALBERT: *Eichmanns gab es viele. Ein Dokumentarbericht über die Endlösung der Judenfrage.* München: Knaur, 1961. 286 pp., bibl.

5708   YAHIL, LENI: 'Madagascar—phantom of a solution for the Jewish question'. [In] Bela Vago and George L. Mosse, eds.: *Jews and non-Jews in Eastern Europe.* Pp. 315–334. *See* 5706.

5709   ZIMMELS, H. J.: *The echo of the Nazi Holocaust in Rabbinic literature.* London: [priv. pr.], 1975. xxiii + 372 pp. [Responsa illustrating how Jews lived while confronting extermination.]

Nazi vocabulary of extermination

5710   BLUMENTHAL, NACHMAN: *Slowa niewinne* [Innocent words]. Kraków: Centralna Żydowska Komisja Historyczna w Polsce, 1947. 271 pp. [Vol. I. Glossary of Nazi vocabulary which was used to disguise the extermination campaign.]

5711   ESH, SHAUL: 'Words and their meanings. Twenty-five examples of Nazi idiom.' [In] *Yad Vashem Studies, V.* Pp. 133–167. *See* 5673.

5712   STERNBERGER, DOLF and others: *Aus dem Wörterbuch des Unmenschen.* [By] Dolf Sternberger, Gerhard Storz, W. E. Süskind. Hamburg: Claassen, 1957. 134 pp.

5713   WULF, JOSEPH: *Aus dem Lexikon der Mörder. 'Sonderbehandlung' und verwandte Worte in nationalsozialistischen Dokumenten.* Gütersloh: Mohn, 1963. 111 pp.

b. Eichmann, Adolf

5714 ASCHENAUER, RUDOLF, ed.: *Ich, Adolf Eichmann. Ein historischer Zeugenbericht.* Leoni am Starnberger See: Druffel, 1980. 450 pp., illus. [The publishers state that this is a report by Adolf Eichmann made in 1955 and removed to safety hours before his capture.]

5715 CENTRE DE DOCUMENTATION JUIVE CONTEMPORAINE: *Le dossier Eichmann et 'la solution finale de la question juive'.* Préfaces: Edgar Faure, François de Menthon, Robert Kempner. Introd.: Joseph Billig. Paris: Éds. du Centre, 1960. 221 pp., facsims.

5716 KEMPNER, ROBERT M. W.: *Eichmann und Komplizen.* Zürich: Europa Verlag, 1961. 452 pp., bibl.

5717 OPPENHEIMER, MAX, ed.: *Eichmann und die Eichmänner. Dokumentarische Hinweise auf den Personenkreis der Helfer und Helfershelfer bei der 'Endlösung'.* Ludwigsburg: Schromm, 1961. 189 pp., illus., map.

5718 REYNOLDS, QUENTIN and others: *Minister of death. The Adolf Eichmann story.* [By] Quentin Reynolds, Ephraim Katz, Zwi Aldouby. New York: Viking Press, 1960. 246 pp.

Eichmann trial

ARENDT, HANNAH

5719 ARENDT, HANNAH: *Eichmann in Jerusalem. A report on the banality of evil.* New York: Viking Press, 1963. 275 pp., bibl. [Rev. and enl. ed. 1964. German version: *Eichmann in Jerusalem. Ein Bericht von der Banalität des Bösen.* Von der Autorin durchges. und ergänz. Ausg. München: Piper, 1964.]

5720 *Aus Politik und Zeitgeschichte,* 4. Nov. 1964. Bonn: Bundeszentrale für politische Bildung. 47 pp. [Comprising: Paul Arnsberg: 'War Eichmann ein Dämon?'; Wolfgang Scheffler: 'Hannah Arendt und der Mensch im totalitären Staat'; Hannah Arendt: 'Vorrede zur deutschen Ausgabe'.]

5721 ROBINSON, JACOB: *And the Crooked shall be made straight. The Eichmann trial, the Jewish catastrophe and Hannah Arendt's narrative.* New York: Macmillan, 1965. 406 pp., bibl.

5722 BRAHAM, RANDOLPH L.: *The Eichmann case: a source book.* New York: World Federation of Hungarian Jews, 1969. 186 pp. [Bibliography.]

5723 GRÜBER, HEINRICH: *Zeuge pro Israel.* Berlin: Käthe Vogt, 1963. 103 pp.

5724 HAUSNER, GIDEON: *Justice in Jerusalem.* London: Nelson, 1967. 528 pp., illus. [German version: *Die Vernichtung der Juden, das grösste Verbrechen der Geschichte.* 2. Aufl. München: Kindler, 1979.]

5725 PAPADATOS, PIERRE A.: *Le procès Eichmann.* Genève: Droz, 1964. 125 pp., bibl. [English version: Papadatos, Peter: *The Eichmann trial.* New York: Praeger, 1964.]

5726 RUSSELL OF LIVERPOOL, EDWARD (Lord): *The trial of Adolf Eichmann*. London: Heinemann, 1962. 324 pp.

5727 SCHMORAK, DOV B.: *Der Prozess Eichmann. Dargestellt an Hand der in Nürnberg und Jerusalem vorgelegten Dokumente sowie der Gerichts-protokolle*. Wien: Deutsch, 1964. 437 pp., illus.

5728 WIESENTHAL, SIMON: *Ich jagte Eichmann. Tatsachenbericht*. Gütersloh: Mohn, 1961. 255 pp.

c. Individual accounts

5729 ARTOM, EMANUELE: *Diari. Gennaio 1940–febbraio 1944*. [Eds.]: Paola De Benedetti, Eloisa Ravenna. Milano: Centro di Documentazione Ebraica Contemporanea, 1966. 142 pp., port., facsims., map.

5730 BIRENBAUM, HALINA: *Hope is the last to die. A personal documentation of Nazi terror*. Transl. from the Polish. Foreword: Ludwik Kryzanowski. New York: Twayne, 1971. 246 pp. [First ed. 1967 in Warsaw. Incl. Warsaw Ghetto, Auschwitz, Majdanek, Ravensbrück, Neustadt-Glewe.]

5731 BODER, DAVID P.: *I did not interview the dead*. Urbana, Ill.: University of Illinois Press, 1949. 220 pp. [Verbatim narratives of 8 displaced persons, mainly Jews.]

5732 DOBSCHINER, JOHANNA-RUTH: *Selected to live*. London: Pickering & Inglis, 1970. 255 pp., illus., facsims. [Orig. publ. 1968 in Holland.]

5733 FRANK, ANNE: *Het achterhuis. Dagboekbrieven van 12 Juni 1942–1 Augustus 1944*. [Forew.]: Anne Romein-Verschoor. Amsterdam: Uitg. Contact, 1947. 253 pp. [German version: *Das Tagebuch der Anne Frank* ... Heidelberg: Schneider, 1950. Also: 11. durchges. Aufl., 1979. Also paperback ed.: 46. Aufl. Frankfurt a.M.: Fischer, 1979. English version: *The diary of a young girl*. Forew.: Storm Jameson. London: Constellation Books, 1952. Illus. Also transls. in over 50 other languages.]

5734 FRIEDLÄNDER, SAUL: *Wenn die Erinnerung kommt* ... Aus dem Französischen. Stuttgart: Deutsche Verlags-Anstalt, 1978. 192 pp. [First ed. under title: *Quand vient le souvenir*. Paris: Eds. du Seuil, 1978. The son of an assimilated family from Prague who had emigrated to France, the author was saved by being brought up in Occupied France as a Catholic child.]

5735 HEIMAN, LEO: *I was a Soviet guerilla*. London: Brown and Watson, 1959. 192 pp. [Experiences of a Polish Jew.]

5736 HEYMAN, ÉVA: *The diary of Éva Heyman*. Introd. and notes: Judah Marton. Transl. from the Hebrew. Jerusalem: Yad Vashem, 1974. 124 pp., illus.

5737 [HUPPERT, HILDE] ZWEIG, ARNOLD: *Fahrt zum Acheron*. Berlin: VVN-Verlag, 1951. 121 pp. [Hilde Huppert's experiences of persecution, ghettoes and concentration camps, rewritten by Zweig.]

5738 *Im Feuer vergangen. Tagebücher aus dem Ghetto*. Vorw.: Arnold Zweig. 2. Aufl. Berlin [East]: Rütten & Loening, 1959. 609 pp. [Diaries from the ghettoes of Warsaw, Cracow and Lemberg by Leon Weliczker, Gusta Dawidsohn-Draengerowa, Janina Hescheles, Noemi Szac-Wajnkranc and Dorka Goldkorn.]

5739 KLIEGER, BERNARD: *Der Weg den wir gingen. Reportage einer höllischen Reise.* 8. deutsche Ausg. Bruxelles-Ixelles: Codac Juifs, 1962. 215 pp., illus., tab., facsims. [Incl. Auschwitz.]

5740 KLONICKI (KLONYMUS), ARYEH: *The diary of Adam's father.* Ed.: Meir Chovev. Tel Aviv: Beit Lohamei Hagettaot & Hakibbutz Hameuchad, 1970. 87 + [16] pp., illus., map, facsims. [Also in Hebrew.]

5741 LIND, JAKOV: *Counting my steps. An autobiography.* London: Cape, 1970. 223 pp.

5742 LITTNER, JAKOB: *Aufzeichnungen aus einem Erdloch.* München: Klugem, 1948. 148 pp. [Experiences of a Polish Jew in Munich and Poland.]

5743 LOMBROSO, SILVIA: *Si puo stampare* [This can be printed]. *Pagine vissute, 1938–1945.* Roma: Casa ed. 'Dalmatia', [1945]. 231 pp. [A Jewess under Fascism and the Nazis.]

5744 MATTHIES, KURT: *Ich hörte die Lerchen singen. Ein Tagebuch aus dem Osten, 1941/45.* 2. Aufl. München: Kösel, 1956. 281 pp.

5745 MINCO, MARGA: *Das bittere Kraut. Eine kleine Chronik.* Hamburg: Rowohlt, 1959. 74 pp. [The only survivor of a Dutch Jewish family. English version: *Bitter herbs. A little chronicle.* London: Oxford University Press, 1960.]

5746 PAWLOWICZ, SALA (with KLOSE, KEVIN): *I will survive.* New York: Norton, 1962. 286 pp.

5747 PISAR, SAMUEL: *Of blood and hope.* London: Cassell, 1980. 316 pp. [Author, born in Bialystok, spent three years as a young boy in Auschwitz.]

5748 ROSEN, DONIA: *The forest, my friend.* Transl.: Mordechai S. Chertoff. New York: Bergen Belsen Memorial Press, 1971. 117 pp., facsim.

5749 RUBINOWICZ, DAWID: [*The diary of the boy Dawid Rubinowicz.* Transl. from Polish with added chapter by Sarah Nishmit]. [Tel Aviv]: Hakibbutz Hameuchad & Ghetto Fighters' House, 1964. 82 pp., illus., facsims. [In Hebrew. German version: *Das Tagebuch des David Rubinowicz.* Frankfurt a.M.: Fischer, 1960. Polish orig.: *Pamietnik Dawida Rubinowicza.* Warszawa: Książka i Wiedza, 1960. Also gramophone record: CLP 73336. Freiburg: Christophorus, (196–).]

5750 SAMUELS, GERTRUDE: *Mottele. A partisan odyssey.* New York: Harper & Row, 1976. ix + 179 pp.

5751 SANDBERG, MOSHE: *My longest year. In the Hungarian labour service and in the Nazi camps.* Ed. with historical survey by Livia Rothkirchen. Jerusalem: Yad Vashem, 1968. xxxiv + 114 pp., illus. [Transl. from the Hebrew; orig. publ. 1966. Incl. Dachau.]

5752 SPANIER, GINETTE: *Long road to freedom. The story of her life under the German occupation*. London: Hale, 1976. 172 pp., map. [First publ. under title: *It isn't all mink*. London: Fontana Books, 1961. A French Jewess.]

5753 SYRKIN, MARIE: 'Diaries of the Holocaust'. [In] Murray Mindlin & Chaim Bermant, eds.: *Explorations*. London: Barrie & Rockliff, in ass'n with Institute of Contemporary History and Wiener Library, 1967. Pp. 73–96.

5754 SZENDE, STEFAN: *Den siste Juden fran Polen* [The last Jew from Poland]. Stockholm: Bonniers, 1944. 316 pp. [English version: *The promise Hitler kept*. London: Gollancz, 1945. German version: *Der letzte Jude aus Polen*. Zürich: Europa Verlag, 1945. Eyewitness report of extermination of Jews by a Jew who escaped in 1943.]

5755 THORNE, LEON: *Out of the ashes. The story of a survivor*. New York: Rosebern Press, 1961. 203 pp. [Ghettoes of Lemberg, Drohobycz, Sambor; and labour camps Janover and Hyrawka.]

5756 WEINSTOCK, EARL & WILNER, HERBERT: *The seven years*. London: Faber & Faber, 1959. 230 pp. [Autobiography of a Romanian Jew.]

d. Individual countries

Austria

5757 BUNDESMINISTERIUM FÜR INNERES, Gruppe Staatspolizei, Abt. 2C: *NS-Gesetzgebung gegen die jüdische Bevölkerung Österreichs*. [Wien: 1964?]. 151 pp., mimeog. [In 2 vols.]

5758 FRAENKEL, JOSEF, ed.: *The Jews of Austria. Essays on their life, history and destruction*. London: Vallentine, Mitchell, 1967. 584 pp., tabs., bibl. [Part IV: 'Destruction', pp. 469–546.]

5759 GOLD, HUGO: *Gedenkbuch der untergegangenen Judengemeinden des Burgenlandes*. Tel Aviv: Olamenu, 1970. 148 pp., illus., plan, tabs., bibl.

5760 GOLD, HUGO: *Geschichte der Juden in Wien. Ein Gedenkbuch*. Tel Aviv: Olamenu, 1966. 158 pp., illus., tabs., facsims., bibl.

5761 MENDELSSOHN, PETER de: *Across the dark river. Novel*. London: Hutchinson, 1939. 384 pp.

5762 ROSENKRANZ, HERBERT: *Verfolgung und Selbstbehauptung. Die Juden in Österreich 1938–1945*. Wien: Herold, 1978. 400 pp.

5763 *Studia Judaica Austriaca, Bd. V: Der Gelbe Stern in Österreich. Katalog und Einführung zu einer Dokumentation*. Eisenstadt: Roetzer, 1977. 134 pp., illus., facsims.

5764 WEINZIERL, ERIKA: *Zu wenig Gerechte. Österreicher und Judenverfolgung 1938–1945*. Graz: Verlag Styria, 1969. 208 pp., bibl.

Baltic states

ESTONIA

5765 DWORZECKI, M[ARC]: *Jewish camps in Estonia, 1942–1944*. Jerusalem: Yad

Vashem, 1970. 402 + xxii pp., illus., facsims., tabs., bibl. [In Hebrew, summary in English.]

LATVIA

5766 *The Jews in Latvia.* Tel Aviv: Association of Latvian and Esthonian Jews in Israel, 1971. 384 pp., tabs., bibl. [Eds.: M. Bode and others.]

5767 KAUFMANN, MAX: *Die Vernichtung der Juden Lettlands.* München: [priv. pr.], 1947. 542 pp., illus.

LITHUANIA

5768 ARAD, YITZHAK: 'The "Final Solution" in Lithuania in the light of German documentation'. [In] *Yad Vashem Studies, XI.* Pp. 234–272, tabs. See 5673.

5769 BLUMENTHAL, N[ACHMANN], ed.: *Mir.* Jerusalem: Encyclopaedia of the Jewish Diaspora, 1962. 767 + 62 pp., illus., facsims., map. [In Hebrew with an English summary.]

5770 GEFEN, ABA: *Unholy alliance.* Jerusalem: Yuval Tal, 1973. 277 pp., illus.

5771 GUTVERSTEHEN, JOSEPH: '[Lithuanian Jewry. Unique material of the first weeks of the Holocaust in Lithuania, 1941]'. [In] *Hagut Ivrit Be'Eyropa*, [Studies of Jewish themes by contemporary Jewish scholars]. Tel Aviv: Brit-Ivrith-Olamit, 1969. Pp. 157–187. [In Hebrew.]

5772 LEVIN, DOV: *They fought back. Lithuanian Jewry's armed resistance to the Nazis, 1941–1945.* Jerusalem: Yad Vashem, 1974. viii + 267 pp., illus., facsims., maps, tabs., bibl. [In Hebrew, summary in English.]

Belgium

5773 ALBINSKY, J.: *8 ans au service du peuple.* Bruxelles: Solidarité Juive, 1947. 30 pp.

5774 GARFINKELS, BETTY: *Les Belges face à la persécution raciale 1940–1944.* Sous la direction de Max Gottschalk. Bruxelles: Éds. de l'Institut de Sociologie de l'Université Libre de Bruxelles, 1965. 104 pp., illus., bibl. (Centre national des hautes études juives).

5775 MINISTÈRE DE LA SANTÉ PUBLIQUE ET DE LA FAMILLE: *Liste alphabétique des personnes arrêtées par l'autorité occupante en tant qu'Israélites ou Tziganes et déportées par les convois partis du camp de rassemblement de Malines entre le 4 août 1942 et le 31 juillet 1944.* Bruxelles: 1971. 6 vols., mimeog. [In French and Flemish. With 7-page annex: 'Tableau recapitulatif des Israélites et Tziganes déportés du camp de rassemblement de Malines vers les camps d'extermination de Haute Silésie'.]

5776 MINISTÈRE DE LA SANTÉ PUBLIQUE ET DE LA FAMILLE: *Liste des Israélites domiciliés en Belgique en Mai 1940, internés dans des camps de travail forcé du Nord de la France, employés par des firmes effectuant des travaux pour l'organisation Todt, transférés dans les camps de rassemblement de Malines, de Drancy, au camp de concentration de Breendonk et dans des prisons belges. Déportés, évadés, libérés et décédés.* [Bruxelles: 197–]. 560 pp., mimeog.

5777 PERELMAN, FELA: *Dans le ventre de la baleine*. Bruxelles: La Renaissance du Livre, 1947. 196 pp., illus.

5778 SCHMIDT, EPHRAIM: *L'histoire des Juifs à Anvers (Antwerpen)*. Préface: Nico Gunzburg. [Antwerp: Ontwikkeling, 1969?]. xxi + 291 + 51 pp., illus., facsims., tabs., bibls. [Incl.: 'Les Juifs à Anvers durant la deuxième guerre mondiale', pp. 141–230.]

5779 STEINBERG, LUCIEN: *Le comité de défense des Juifs en Belgique, 1942–1944*. Préface: Henri Bernard. Bruxelles: Éds. de l'Université de Bruxelles, 1973. 198 pp., tabs., bibl. (Centre national des hautes études juives).

Bulgaria

5780 CHARY, FREDERICK B.: *The Bulgarian Jews and the Final Solution, 1940–1944*. Pittsburgh, Pa.: University of Pittsburgh Press, 1972. xiv + 246 pp., tabs., bibl.

5781 *Evrei zaginali v antifashistkata borba* [Jews who perished in the struggle against Fascism]. [Sofia?: Central Consistory of Jews in the People's Republic of Bulgaria], 1958. 367 pp., illus.

5782 *Godishnik* [Annual]. Sofia: Social, Cultural and Educational Association of Jews in the People's Republic of Bulgaria, Central Boards, 1966/77. Vols. I–XII continuing. [Published in Bulgarian and English.]

5783 MUNZ, MAX: *Die Verantwortlichkeit für die Judenverfolgungen im Ausland während der nationalsozialistischen Herrschaft. Ein Beitrag zur Klärung des Begriffes der 'Veranlassung' ... seines Verhältnisses zur Staatssouveranität und seiner Anwendung auf die Einwirkung des nationalsozialistischen Deutschlands auf nichtdeutsche Staaten 1933–1945 hinsichtlich der Rechtsstellung und Behandlung der Juden unter besonderer Berücksichtigung der Judenverfolgungen in Bulgarien, Rumänien und Ungarn*. Inaugural-Dissertation. Frankfurt a.M.: 1958. 251 pp.

Czechoslovakia

5784 FEDER, RICHARD: *Zidovská tragedie—Dejství posledni* [Jewish tragedy—last act]. Kolin: 1947. 175 pp., illus. [Persecution in the 'Protectorate' and Terezin.]

5785 JÜDISCHE KULTUSGEMEINDE IN PRAG: *Tätigkeitsbericht 1941*. Überreicht bei der Zentralstelle für jüdische Auswanderung Prag. [76 pp], illus., diagrs., tabs.

5786 JURÁŠEK, STANISLAV: *Předpisy o židovském majetku a další předpisy židů se týkající. Dodatek* [Regulations relating to Jewish property and other regulations concerning Jews. Supplement]. Praha: [priv. pr.], 1940/41. 100 + 95 pp. [In 2 vols.]

5787 KRAKAU, KNUD: *Willkür und Recht. Zur nationalsozialistischen Regelung der Staatsangehörigkeit—besonders der Juden—im sogenannten 'Protektorat Böhmen and Mähren'*. Hamburg: Hamburger Gesellschaft für Völkerrecht und auswärtige Politik, 1966. 81 pp. (Werkhefte der Forschungsstelle für Völkerrecht ... der Universität Hamburg).

5788 WEIL, JIŘI: *Život s hvězdou* [Life with the star]. Praha: Mlada Fronta, 1964. 158 pp.

SLOVAKIA

5789 GRÜNHUT, ARON: *Katastrophenzeit des slowakischen Judentums. Aufstieg und Niedergang der Juden von Pressburg.* Tel-Aviv: [priv. pr.], 1972. 203 + [48] pp., illus., facsims.]

5790 JELINEK, Y.: 'The Vatican, the Catholic Church, the Catholics and the persecution of the Jews during World War II: the case of Slovakia'. [In] Bela Vago and George L. Mosse, eds.: *Jews and non-Jews in Eastern Europe.* Pp. 221–255. *See* 5706.

5791 KAMENEC, IVAN: 'Vznik a vývoj židovských pracovných táborov a stredísk na Slovensku v rokoch 1942–1944' [The origin and evolution of Jewish labour camps and centres in Slovakia, 1942–1944]. [In] *Nove Obzory,* 8, 1966. 38 pp., illus., tabs., summaries in German and Russian.

5792 LIPSCHER, LADISLAV: *Die Juden im slowakischen Staat 1939–1945.* München: Oldenbourg, 1979. 210 pp.

5793 ROTHKIRCHEN, LIVIA: *The destruction of Slovak Jewry. A documentary history.* Jerusalem: Yad Vashem, [n.d.]. 257 + lxxv pp., facsims. [In Hebrew, introd. in English.]

5794 *The tragedy of Slovak Jewry. Photographs and documents.* Bratislava: Centre of CUJCR, 1949. 142 pp., illus., facsims. [Text in Hebrew and English. Documentary ed.: F. Steiner.]

5795 VASEK, ANTON: *Die Lösung der Judenfrage in der Slowakei. Systematische Übersicht der antijüdischen Gesetzgebung.* Bratislava-Pressburg: 'Globus'-Verlag, 1942. 161 pp.

Denmark

5796 MELCHIOR, MARCUS: *Darkness over Denmark.* London: New English Library, 1973. 192 pp. [First ed. 1968.]

5797 OPPENHEIM, RALPH: *The door of death.* London: Harvill, 1948. 239 pp. [Documentary novel about the fate of a Danish-Jewish family.]

See also 6379–6381.

France

5798 *Activité des organisations juives en France sous l'occupation.* Paris: Eds. du Centre, 1947. 245 pp., illus., maps, diagrs., facsims., tabs. (Centre de Documentation Juive Contemporaine).

BILLIG, JOSEPH: *Die Endlösung der Judenfrage. Studie über ihre Grundsätze im III. Reich und in Frankreich während der Besatzung. See* 3556.

5799 BILLIG, JOSEPH: *L'Institut d'Étude des Questions Juives, officine française des autorités nazies en France. Inventaire commenté de la collection de documents provenant des archives de l'Institut conservés au CDJC.* Paris: Centre de Documentation Juive Contemporaine, 1974. 217 pp., bibl.

463

5800 BILLIG, JOSEPH: *Le Commissariat Général aux Questions Juives, 1941–1944.* Paris: Éds. du Centre, 1955/60. 3 vols., facsims., tabs.

5801 *Cahiers clandestins du Témoignage Chrétien.* Paris: Éds. du Témoignage Chrétien, 1946. 362 pp., illus. [Deals largely with Nazi persecution of the Jews.]

5802 *The deportation of German and Austrian Jews from France 1942–1944.* Paris: La Solidarité, 1980. [Lists German and Austrian Jews deported from France with details of transports. Text in French, German, English.]

5803 DIAMANT, DAVID: *Les Juifs dans la Résistance française, 1940–1944. Avec armes ou sans armes.* Préface: Albert Ouzoulias (Colonel André). Postface: Charles Lederman. Paris: Éds. Le Pavillon, 1971. 365 pp., illus., facsims., diagrs., bibl. (of French and Yiddish clandestine publs.).

5804 ÉTAT FRANÇAIS: *Statut des Juifs, français et étrangers, en France occupée, France non-occupée et aux colonies et Pays de Protectorats ... Législation française et ordonnances allemandes ...* Cahors: [194–]. 15 pp. (Extrait du 'Recueil des Lois Usuelles').

5805 GHEZ, PAUL: *Six mois sous la botte.* Tunis: S.A.P.I., 1943. 163 pp. [Persecution of Jews during German occupation of Tunisia.]

5806 GREEN, WARREN: 'The fate of Oriental Jews in Vichy France'. [In] *Wiener Library Bulletin*, Vol. xxxii, new series 49/50, 1979. Pp. 40–50. [On the exemption from racial laws of Karaites, Gruzinians, Jugutis and other ethnic groups.]

5807 KLARSFELD, SERGE, ed.: *Die Endlösung der Judenfrage in Frankreich. Deutsche Dokumente 1941–1944.* Paris: Klarsfeld, 1977. 244 pp.

5808 KLARSFELD, SERGE, ed.: *Le mémorial de la déportation des Juifs de France. Listes alphabétiques par convois des Juifs déportés de France. Historique des convois de déportation. Statistiques de la déportation des Juifs de France. Listes alphabétiques par camps de Juifs décédés pendant leur internement en France. Listes alphabétiques de Juifs exécutés ou abattus sommairement en France.* Paris: Klarsfeld, 1978. [600 pp., approx.], illus., facsims., tabs.

5809 LÉVY, CLAUDE & TILLARD, PAUL: *La grande rafle du Vel d'Hiv. 16 juillet 1942.* [Introd.]: Joseph Kessel. Paris: Laffont, 1967. 267 pp., illus., facsims., bibl.

5810 NODOT, RENÉ: *Les enfants ne partiront pas! Témoignages sur la déportation des Juifs—Lyon et région 1942–1943.* Préface: Gaston Jaubert (Col. Jonage dans la Résistance). Lyon: Imprimerie Nouvelle Lyonnaise, 1970. 36 pp.

5811 ODIC, CHARLES: *'Stepchildren' of France.* Transl. from the French. New York: Roy, 1945. 181 pp. [Persecution and deportation of Jews.]

5812 POLIAKOV, L[ÉON]: *L'Étoile jaune.* Préface: Justin Godart. Paris: Éds. du Centre, 1949. 93 pp. (Centre de Documentation Juive Contemporaine). [Incl. reaction of French population.]

5813 RUTKOWSKI, ADAM: *La lutte des Juifs en France à l'époque de l'occupation,*

1940–1944. Introd.: Georges Wellers. Paris: Centre de Documentation Juive Contemporaine, 1975. 349 pp., bibl.

5814 STEINBERG, LUCIEN: *Les autorités allemandes en France occupée. Inventaire commenté de la collection de documents conservés au CDJC provenant des archives de l'Ambassade d'Allemagne, de l'Administration Militaire Allemande et de la Gestapo en France.* Avant-propos: Isaac Schneersohn; Préface: Jacques Delarue. Paris: Centre de Documentation Juive Contemporaine, 1966. 355 pp.

5814a SZAJKOWSKI, ZOSA: *Analytical Franco-Jewish gazetteer 1939–1945. With an introduction to some problems in writing the history of the Jews in France during World War II.* New York: publ. with the assistance of the American Academy for Jewish Research and others, 1966. 349 pp., map.

5815 UNITED RESTITUTION ORGANIZATION: *Judenverfolgung in Frankreich. Dokumente über die Verantwortlichkeit des Reiches für die Juden-massnahmen im besetzten und unbesetzten Frankreich, insbesondere auch Algerien, Marokko, Tunis.* Frankfurt a.M.: 1959. 170 pp.

5816 WELLERS, GEORGES: *L'étoile jaune à l'heure de Vichy. De Drancy à Auschwitz.* Paris: Fayard, 1973. v + 452 pp., bibl. [Also incl. Compiègne concentration camp.]

Greece

5817 GALANTÉ, ABRAHAM: *Appendice à l'histoire des Juifs de Rhodes, Chio, Cos, etc.* et *Fin tragique des communautés juives de Rhodes et de Cos, oeuvre de brigandage hitlerien.* Istanbul: Kagit ve Basim Işleri, 1948. 76 pp.

5817a KABELI, ISAAC: 'The resistance of the Greek Jews'. [In] *Yivo Annual of Jewish Social Science, VIII.* Pp. 281–288. See 5674.

5818 MOLHO, MICHAEL & NEHAMA, JOSEPH, eds.: *In Memoriam. Hommage aux victimes juives des nazis en Grèce.* 2e éd. rev. et augm. par Joseph Nehama. Thessalonique: Communauté Israélite de Thessalonique, 1973. 469 pp., illus., facsims., tabs. [First ed. 1948. Also in Hebrew, with English summary: *The destruction of Greek Jewry 1941–1944.* Jerusalem: Yad Vashem, 1965.]

5819 NOVITCH, MIRIAM, ed.: *Le passage des barbares. Contribution à l'histoire de la déportation et de la résistance des Juifs grecs.* [Nice: 1971]. 141 pp., illus., bibl.

Holland

5820 HARARI, JACOB: *Die Ausrottung der Juden im besetzten Holland. Ein Tatsachenbericht.* Tel-Aviv: Irgun Olej Merkas Europa, 1944. 100 pp.

5821 JONG, LOUIS de: 'Jews and non-Jews in Nazi-occupied Holland' [In] *On the track of tyranny.* Pp. 139–155. See 3208.

5822 JOODS HISTORISCH MUSEUM AMSTERDAM: *Documenten van de Jodenvervolging in Nederland 1940–1945.* Amsterdam: Polak & van Gennep, 1965. 175 pp., illus., facsims.

5823 KEMPNER, ROBERT M. W.: *Edith Stein und Anne Frank. Zwei von hunderttausend. Die Enthüllungen über die NS-Verbrechen in Holland vor dem Schwurgericht in München. Die Ermordung der 'nicht-arischen' Mönche und Nonnen.* Freiburg i.Br.: Herder, 1968. 189 pp., ports., facsims., tabs.

5824 KOCHBA, ADINA, comp. & KALINOV, RINA, ed.: [*Underground of the Zionist youth in occupied Holland*]. Tel Aviv: Hakibbutz Hameuchad, 1969. 312 pp., illus., facsims., tabs., bibl. [In Hebrew.]

5825 KORT, M. de: *Verhandeling over de verordning betreffende het Joodsche grondbezit. (No. 154/1941).* Amsterdam: Holdert, 1941. 136 pp.

5826 PRESSER, J[ACOB]: *Ondergang. De vervolging en verdelging van het Nederlandse Jodendom 1940–1945.* 's-Gravenhage: Nijhoff, 1965. 2 vols., illus., facsims., maps, tabs. [English version: *Ashes in the wind. The destruction of Dutch Jewry.* London: Souvenir Press, 1968. 556 pp.]

5827 SIJES, B. A.: *Studies over jodenvervolging.* Assen: van Gorcum, 1974. viii + 184 pp.

5828 WANDER, (Dr.): *Die Anmeldepflicht jüdischer oder jüdisch beeinflusster Unternehmen in den Niederlanden. Kommentar zur Verordnung des Reichskommissars für die besetzten niederländischen Gebiete über die Anmeldung von Unternehmen, vom 22.10.1940.* Amsterdam: De Amsterdamsche Keurkamer, 1940. 115 pp. [Also in Dutch.]

5829 WEINREB, F.: *Collaboratie en verzet 1940–1945. Een poging tot ontmythologisering.* Red.: Renate Rubinstein. Amsterdam: Meulenhoff, 1969. 1926 pp. in 3 vols.
1.: *Het land der blinden.* Voorwoord: J. Presser.
2.: *Van Windekind naar Westerbork.*
3.: *Eindspel.* Nabeschouwing: A. Nuis.

Hungary

5830 BRAHAM, RANDOLPH L., ed.: *The destruction of Hungarian Jewry. A documentary account.* New York: Pro Arte (for the World Federation of Hungarian Jews), 1963. 2 vols., tabs., facsims., biographical index, bibl.

5831 BRAHAM, RANDOLPH L., ed.: *The Hungarian Jewish catastrophe. A selected and annotated bibliography.* New York: Yad Vashem ... and Yivo Institute of Jewish Research, 1962. 86 pp. (Joint Documentary Projects).

5832 BRAHAM, RANDOLPH L.: 'The Rightists, Horthy and the Germans: factors underlying the destruction of Hungarian Jewry'. [In] Bela Vago & George L. Mosse, eds.: *Jews and non-Jews in Eastern Europe.* Pp. 137–156. *See* 5706.

5833 DEAK, ANDREJA: *Razzia in Novisad, und andere Geschehnisse während des Zweiten Weltkrieges in Ungarn und Jugoslawien.* Zürich: Classen, 1967. 222 pp.

5834 LAMBERT, GILLES: *Opération Hazalah. Budapest 1944: Les jeunes sionistes face aux nazis et aux Juifs de Hongrie.* [Paris]: Hachette, 1972. 189 pp., bibl.

5835 LEVAI, JENÖ: *Eichmann in Hungary. Documents.* Budapest: Pannonia Press, 1961. 294 pp., illus., facsims., tabs.

5836 LEVAI, JENÖ: *Fekete Könyv. A Magyar Zsidosag szenvedeseiröl.* Budapest: Officina nyomda, [1946]. 320 pp. [English version: Eugene Levai: *Black Book on the martyrdom of Hungarian Jewry.* Ed.: Lawrence P. Davis. Zürich: Central European Times [and] Vienna: Panorama Publ. Co., 1948. 135 pp., illus.]

5837 PALASTI, LASZLO: *A Bori halálút regénye.* Budapest: Gábor, 1945. 94 pp. [The death march to Bor.]

SENESH, HANNAH

5838 *Hannah Senesh. Her life and diary.* London: Vallentine, Mitchell, 1971. 257 pp. [First ed. in Hebrew, 1945.]

5839 MASTERS, ANTHONY: *The summer that bled. The biography of Hannah Senesh.* London: Michael Joseph, 1972. 349 pp., illus., bibl.

5840 [TRANSYLVANIA] CARMILLY-WEINBERGER, MOSHE, ed.: *Memorial volume for the Jews of Cluj-Kolozsvár.* New York: 1970. 313 + 155 pp., illus. [In Hungarian, English and Hebrew. Hungarian section includes: S. Sámuel: 'Utunk Auschwitzba' [Our way to Auschwitz] and 'Zsidó ejtöerynyösök' [Jewish parachutists]. English section includes: M. Carmilly-Weinberger: 'The tragedy of Transylvanian Jewry'. Transylvania was allotted to Hungary under the Vienna Award of 1940.]

5841 UNITED RESTITUTION ORGANIZATION: *Judenverfolgung in Ungarn. Dokumentensammlung.* Frankfurt a.M.: 1959. 235 pp., facsims., maps.

5842 *Vádirat a nácizmus ellen. Dokumentumok a magyarországi zsidóüldözés történetéhez* [An accusation against Nazism. Documents on the history of the persecution of the Jews in Hungary]. [Ed. by]: Ilona Beneschofsky, Elek Karsai. Budapest: A Magyar Izraeliták Országos Képviselete Kiadasa, 1958/67. Illus., facsims.

1: *1944 március 19–1944 május 15. A német megszállástol a deportálás megkezdéséig* [19 Mar.–15 May 1944. From the German occupation to the start of the deportations]. Publ. 1958. 379 pp.

2: *1944 május 15–1944 junius 30. A Budapesti zsidóság összeköltöztetése* [15 May–30 June 1944. The concentration of the Jews in Budapest]. Publ. 1960. 401 pp.

3: *1944 május 26–1944 óktober 15. A Budapesti zsidóság deportálásának felfüggesztése* [26 May–15 Oct. 1944. The suspension of the deportation of the Jews in Budapest]. Publ. 1967. 720 pp. [Elek Karsai sole ed.]

WALLENBERG, RAOUL. *See* Index.

Italy

5843 CENTRO DI DOCUMENTAZIONE EBRAICA CONTEMPORANEA, MILANO: *Ebrei in Italia: deportazione, resistenza.* Firenze: Giuntina, 1975. 61 pp., facsims., tab. [First ed. 1974.]

5844	De Felice, Renzo: *Storia degli ebrei italiani sotto il fascismo*. Prefazione: Delio Cantimori. [Torino]: Einaudi, 1961. 697 pp., illus., facsims. [VIII: 'L'ultimo atto della tragedia: lo sterminio nazista'.]

Kappler, Herbert

5845	Aschenauer, Rudolf: *Der Fall Herbert Kappler. Ein Plädoyer für Recht, Wahrheit und Verstehen*. München: Damm Verlag, 1968. 74 pp., bibl. [Also supplement: *Um Wahrheit und Gerechtigkeit im Fall Herbert Kappler*. München: Damm Verlag, 1969. 20 pp.]

5846	Tagliacozzo, Michael: 'Le responsabilità di Kappler nella tragedia degli ebrei di Roma'. [In] *La Rassegna Mensile di Israel*, XXXVI, 7–9, Luglio–Settembre 1970. Milano. Pp. 389–414.

5847	*Quaderni del Centro di Studi sulla Deportazione e l'Internamento, 1–9*. Roma: Associazione Nazionale ex Internati, 1964/77 continuing. 9 vols., tabs., bibls. [Vol. 5 includes summaries in English, French and German; Vol. 6 incl. extermination of Gypsies; Vol. 7 incl. liberation of Fallingbostel concentration camp.]

5848	[Rome] Debenedetti, Giacomo: *16 Ottobre 1943*. Roma: Ed. del Secolo, 1945. 83 pp. [Deportation of Jews from Rome.]

Sereni, Enzo

5849	Carpi, Daniel and others, eds.: *Scritti in memoria di Enzo Sereni. Saggi sull'ebraismo romano*. [Eds.]: Daniel Carpi, Attilio Milano, Umberto Nahon. Gerusalemme: Fondazione Sally Mayer, Scuola Superiore di Studi Ebraici, Milano, 1970. 392 + 320 pp., illus., plans, facsims., tabs. [In Italian and Hebrew, with summaries in Italian of Hebrew articles. Incl. biographical material on Enzo Sereni.]

5850	Urquhart, Clara & Brent, Peter Ludwig: *Enzo Sereni. A hero of our times*. London: Hale, 1967. 176 pp., port.

Trieste

5851	Gherardi Bon, Silva: *La persecuzione antiebraica a Trieste, 1938–1945*. Udine: Del Bianco, 1972. 269 pp., illus., facsims., bibl.

5852	Kostoris, Sergio: *La risiera di Trieste. Un crimine comune non militare*. Roma: Barulli, 1974. 72 pp.

Norway

5853	Friedmann, T[uvia], ed.: *Dokumentensammlung über 'Die Deportierung der Juden aus Norwegen nach Auschwitz'*. Ramat Gan: Stadtverwaltung, 1963. 101 pp., illus., charts, facsims.

5854	*Nordiska Röster. Mot judeförföljelse och vald. Dokument och kommentarer*. [Stockholm?]: Judisk Tidskrift, 1943. 48 pp.

Poland

5855	Baltzan, P.: [*The world which was destroyed*]. [No imprint: 1967/68?]. 3 vols., illus., tabs., map, facsims. [In Hebrew.]

I: 327 pp.

II: [*In the chains of destiny*]. 322 pp.

III: [*From servitude to freedom*]. 335 pp.

5856 [Baranov] Blumenthal, Nachman, ed.: *Yiskor Baranow. A memorial to the Jewish community of Baranow.* Jerusalem: Yad Vashem—The Baranow Association, 1964. 236 + xvi pp., illus., facsims. [In Yiddish, Hebrew and English.]

5857 Berenstein, T. and others: *Eksterminacja Żydow na Ziemiach Polskich okresie okupacja hitlerowskiej. Zbior dokumentow.* [By] T. Berenstein, A. Eisenbach, A. Rutkowski. Warszawa: Żydowski Instytut Historczny, 1957. 379 pp., bibl.

5858 *Biuletyn glownej komisji badania zbrodni hitlerowskich w Polsce, XXVI.* Warszawa: Wyd. Prawnicze, 1975. 263 pp., illus., facsims., tabs. [This issue is devoted entirely to persecution of the Jews.]

5859 *The Black Book of Polish Jewry. An account of the martyrdom of Polish Jewry under the Nazi occupation.* Eds.: Jacob Apenszlak, Jacob Kenner, Isaac Lewin, Moses Polakiewicz. [New York]: American Federation for Polish Jews, with Association of Jewish Refugees and Immigrants from Poland, 1943. 343 pp., illus.

5860 Chersztein, M[ieczysław]: *Geopfertes Volk. Der Untergang des polnischen Judentums.* Stuttgart: 1946. 122 pp. [Ghettoes of Vilna, Cracow, Lodz, Warsaw, Sandomir, Stanislaw; Jews in the USSR; extermination camps of Belzec, Treblinka, Majdanek; concentration camps.]

5861 Datner, Szymon and others: *Genocide, 1939–1945.* [By] Szymon Datner, Janusz Gumkowski, Kazimierz Leszczyński. Ed.: Jan Jalbrzykowski. Warszawa: Wyd. Zachodni, 1962. 334 pp., facsims., tabs.

5862 Dawidowicz, David: *Synagogues in Poland and their destruction.* Jerusalem: Mosad Harav Kook & Yad Vashem, 1960. 96 + 7 pp., illus., map, bibl. [In Hebrew, summary in English.]

5863 Eisenbach, Artur: *Operation Reinhard. Mass extermination of the Jewish population in Poland.* Poznań: 1962. 47 pp.

5864 Falstein, Louis, ed.: *The martyrdom of Jewish physicians in Poland.* Studies by Dr. Leon Wulman and Dr. Joseph Tenenbaum. Research and documentation by Dr. Leopold Lazarowitz and Dr. Simon Malowist. New York: Exposition Press, for Medical Alliance—Association of Jewish Physicians from Poland, 1963. 500 pp., illus., facsims., bibl. [Incl. list of physicians who perished, pp. 303–497.]

5865 Feigenboim, M. J.: *'Podliasche in Umkum'. Notizen fun Churban.* Munich: Zentrale historische Kommission beim Zentralkomitee der befreiten Juden in der amerikanischen Zone in Deutschland, 1948. 355 pp. [In Yiddish.]

5866 Friedmann, T., ed.: *Bericht des SS- und Polizeiführers über die Vernichtung der Juden Galiziens* [and] *Tagebuch von SS-Hauptscharf. F. Landau über* seine *Tätigkeit in Drohobycz 1941–44. Dokumentensammlung.* Haifa: Historisches Institut in Haifa für Erforschung der Nazi-Kriegsverbrechen, 1959. 21 pp., illus., mimeog.

5867 HOHENSTEIN, ALEXANDER: *Wartheländisches Tagebuch aus den Jahren 1941/42.* Stuttgart: Deutsche Verlags-Anstalt, 1961. 320 pp.

5868 [GLOBOCNIK, ODILO] PIOTROWSKI, STANISLAW: *Misja Odyla Globocnika. Sprawozdania o wynikach finansowych zaglady żydow w Polsce.* Warszawa: Państwowe Instytut Wyd., 1949. 111 pp. [The expropriation of Polish Jews; incl. 'Aktion Reinhardt'.]

5869 KANTOROWICZ, N.: [*The Jewish resistance movement in Poland, 1941–1945*]. New York: Sharon Books, 1967. 35 + 460 pp., maps, bibl. [In Yiddish.]

5870 KULKIELKO, RENYA: *Escape from the pit.* New York: Sharon Books, 1947. 189 pp. [Extermination of Jews; Warsaw Ghetto; Jewish resistance.]

5871 NIRENSTAJN, ALBERTO: *Ricorda cosi ti ha fatto Amalek.* Turino: Einaudi, 1958. 439 pp. [English version: Albert Nirenstein: *A tower from the enemy. Contributions to a history of Jewish resistance in Poland.* New York: Orion Press, 1958.]

5872 PAT, JACOB: *Ashes and fire.* New York: International Universities Press, 1947. 254 pp. [Yiddish orig.: *Ash un fajer. Yiber de hurves fun Poilen.* New York: 'CYCO' Bicher-Farlag, 1946. Incl. Jewish partisans.]

5873 POLISH MINISTRY OF FOREIGN AFFAIRS: *The mass extermination of Jews in German-occupied Poland. Note addressed to the Governments of the united nations on December 10th, 1942 and other documents.* London: Hutchinson, [1942]. 16 pp.

5874 [REINEFARTH, HEINZ] LESZCZYŃSKI, KAZIMIERZ: *Heinz Reinefarth.* Warszawa: Wyd. Zachodni, 1961. 99 pp.

5875 RINGELBLUM, EMANUEL: *Polish–Jewish relations during the Second World War.* Eds.: Joseph Kermish, Shmuel Krakowski. Introd.: Joseph Kermish. Jerusalem: Yad Vashem, 1974. xxxix + 330 pp., port. [Transl. from the Polish: written 1943.]

5876 SPERBER, MANÈS: ... *than a tear in the sea.* Introd.: André Malraux. Transl. by Constantine Fitzgibbon. New York: Bergen Belsen Memorial Press, 1967. 89 + xxi pp.

5877 [STRYJ] FRIEDMANN, T[UVIA], ed.: *Schupo-Kriegsverbrecher von Stryj vor dem Wiener Volksgericht. Dokumentensammlung.* Haifa: Verband der ehemaligen Einwohner von Stryj in Israel, 1957. xii + 54 pp., facsims., mimeog.

5878 TENENBAUM, JOSEPH: *Underground. The story of a people.* New York: Philosophical Library, 1952. 532 pp., illus. [Liquidation of ghettoes; Jewish resistance in ghettoes; concentration camps of Poland.]

5879 [WEISSMANDEL, MICHAEL DOV] *From the boundary. Memories of the years*

1942–1945, of the great, just and famous Rabbi Michael Dov Weissmandel, who gave his life for the sake of Israel. Brooklyn, N.Y.: 'Emunah', 1960. 352 + 25 pp., facsims.

5880 [WOLKOVISK] EINHORN, MOSES, ed.: *Wolkovisker Yizkor Book.* New York: [priv. pr.], 1949. 2 vols., illus. [In Yiddish; summary in English, pp. 902–990.]

5881 YAD VASHEM: *Poland: I: The communities of Lodz and its region.* Jerusalem: 1976. xv + 285 pp., illus., map, bibl. (Pinkas Hakehillot—Encyclopaedia of Jewish Communities). [Eds.: Danuta Dąbrowska, Abraham Wein. In Hebrew, introd. in English.]

Romania

5882 [BUKOVINA] GOLD, HUGO, ed.: *Geschichte der Juden in der Bukowina, II. Ein Sammelwerk.* Tel Aviv: Olamenu, 1962. 228 pp., illus.

5883 CARP, MATATIAS: *Cartea neagra. Suferinţele evreilor din România, 1940–1944.* [The black book. The sufferings of the Jews in Romania, 1940–1944.] Pref.: Alexandru Safran. Bucureşti: Ed. 'Dacia Taiana', 1946/48. Illus.
I: *Legionarii şi rebeliumea.* Publ. 1946. 379 pp., tabs.
II: *Pogromul dela Iaşi.* Publ. 1948. 168 pp.
III: *Transnistria.* Publ. 1947. 476 pp., facsims., map, tabs.
[Vol. III also in Yiddish: Buenos Aires: Ed. 'Besaraber Iden', 1950.]

5884 ROHWER, JÜRGEN, ed.: *Die Versenkung der jüdischen Flüchtlingstransporter Struma und Mefkure im Schwarzen Meer (Februar 1942, August 1944). Historische Untersuchung.* Frankfurt a.M.: Bernard & Graefe, 1965. 153 pp., maps, tabs., bibl. (Schriften der Bibliothek für Zeitgeschichte, Weltkriegsbücherei/Stuttgart).

TRANSNISTRIA

5885 FISHER, JULIUS S.: *Transnistria: the forgotten cemetery.* South Brunswick: Yoseloff, 1969. 161 pp., tabs., bibl.

5886 SCHECHTMAN, JOSEPH B.: 'The Transnistria Reservation'. [In] *Yivo Annual of Jewish Social Science, VIII.* Pp. 178–196. *See* 5674.

5887 UNITED RESTITUTION ORGANIZATION: *Judenverfolgung in Rumänien. Dokumentensammlung.* Frankfurt a.M.: 1959. 3 vols., mimeog.

5888 YAD VASHEM: *Romania: I.* Jerusalem: 1969. 552 pp., illus., facsims., bibl. (Pinkas Hakehillot—Encyclopaedia of Jewish Communities). [In Hebrew.]

Soviet Union

5889 AINSZTEIN, REUVEN: 'La contribution des Juifs russes à l'effort de guerre' [In] *Dispersion et Unité*, No. 7, Hiver 1966. Jerusalem: World Zionist Organization. Pp. 175–196.

5890 ARONSON, GREGOR and others, eds.: *Russian Jewry, 1917–1967.* Eds.: Gregor Aronson, Jacob Frumkin, Alexis Goldenweiser, Joseph Lewitan. New

York: Yoseloff, 1969. 613 pp., bibl. [Transl. from the Russian. German occupation, pp. 88–170.]

BABI YAR

5891 ANATOLI (KUZNETSOV), A.: *Babi Yar. A document in the form of a novel.* London: Cape, 1970. 477 pp., maps. (Uncensored and expanded version. First publ. in censored form in *Yunost*, 1966). [Transl. from the Russian. The censored version was transl. and publ.: London: MacGibbon & Kee, 1967; German version: Berlin (East): Verlag Volk und Welt, 1968.]

5892 ST. GEORGE, GEORGE: *The road to Babyi-Yar.* London: Spearman, 1967. 191 pp., illus., facsims., map.

5893 GRANATSTEIN, YEHIEL & KAHANOVICH, MOSHE: *Biographical dictionary of Jewish resistance. I: Jewish partisans and underground fighters in western Soviet territory.* Forew.: Nachman Blumenthal. Jerusalem: Yad Vashem, 1965/68. 214 + 16 + 288 pp., ports., maps. [2 vols., in Hebrew, summary in English.]

5894 [KUBE, WILHELM] HEIBER, HELMUT, ed.: 'Aus den Akten des Gauleiters Kube. Dokumentation'. [In] *Vierteljahrshefte für Zeitgeschichte*, 4. Jhrg., 1. Heft, Januar 1956. Pp. 67–92.

5895 WALLACH, JEHUDA L.: 'Feldmarschall Erich von Manstein und die deutsche Judenausrottung in Russland'. [In] *Institut für deutsche Geschichte, Jahrbuch 4, 1975.* Pp. 457–478. *See* 35a.

5896 WEST, BENJAMIN, ed.: [*The destruction of Russian Jewry by the Nazis, 1941–1943*]. Tel Aviv: Hozaat Archeon Haavodah-Hamakhlekah Ickheker Yahadut Russia, 1963. 291 pp., illus., facsims. [In Hebrew.]

Yugoslavia

DEAK, ANDREJA: *Razzia in Novisad, und andere Geschehnisse während des Zweiten Weltkriegs in Ungarn und Jugoslawien. See* 5833.

5897 DEAK, ANDRAS: *Sarga karszalag* [The yellow armband]. Ujvidek: Testveriseg-Egyseg, 1954. 399 pp. [In Hungarian. Underground life of a Jewish family in Yugoslavia.]

5898 *Jevrejski Almanah* [Jewish Almanach]. Belgrade: Federation of Jewish Communities in Yugoslavia. [Summaries in English.]
1954 [Contains short accounts of Jewish members of Yugoslav resistance.]
1955/56 [Contains articles on Nazi extermination of Jews.]
1959/60 [Incl.: Ber Mark: 'Resistance of Polish Jewry during Hitler's occupation from 1939–1944'; Aleksander Stanojlovic: 'The tragedy of the Banat Jewry during the Second World War'.]

5899 JEWISH HISTORICAL MUSEUM, BELGRADE: *Zbornik—Jewish studies. Studies and facts and figures on participation of Jews in the People's Liberation War.* Belgrade: Federation of Jewish Communities in Yugoslavia, 1973/75. Illus., facsims., bibls. [In Serbo-Croat, summaries in English.]

2: 316 pp. [Incl. Rab concentration camp.]

3: 302 pp. [Incl. Banjica concentration camp.]

5900 [*Jews of Bitolj—victims of Fascism*]. Bitolj: 1958. [In Macedonian. Memorial publication on the 15th anniversary of the deportation of the Jewish community, with list of families deported.]

5901 LÖWENTHAL, ZDENKO, ed.: *The crimes of the Fascist occupants and their collaborators against Jews in Yugoslavia*. Belgrade: Federation of Jewish Communities of Yugoslavia, 1957. 245 pp., illus. + 42 pp. in English, containing foreword, summary and text relating to photo-documentation. [Based on documents collected by the Yugoslav State Commission for Investigation of War Crimes.]

5902 SAVEZ JEVREJSKIH OPŠTINA JUGOSLAVIJE (Federation of Jewish Communities in Yugoslavia): *Spomenica, 1919–1969* [Memorial Book]. Beograd: [1969]. 246 pp., illus., facsims., diagrs., tabs., bibl., summary in English.

e. Ghettoes

5903 ALBORT, SCHMUEL: *Dos Getto in Flammen*. Munich: Feld, 1948. 208 pp. (Publ. by the Association of Lithuanian Jews in Germany). [In Yiddish.]

5904 BARKAI, MEYER, ed.: *The fighting ghettoes*. Transl. from the Hebrew. Philadelphia, Pa.: Lippincott, 1962. 407 pp., maps.

5905 BORWICZ, MICHAL M. and others, eds.: *Dokumenty zbrodni i meczenstwa* [Documents of crime and suffering]. [Eds.]: Michal M. Borwicz, Nella Rost, Jozef Wulf. [Cracow: Jewish Historical Commission in Cracow], 1945. 214 pp. [Ghettoes and concentration camps.]

5906 FRIEDMAN, PHILIP: 'Two saviours who failed. Moses Merin of Sosnowiec and Jacob Gens of Vilna'. [In] *Commentary*, Vol. 26, No. 6, Dec. 1958. New York. Pp. 479–491. [First publ. in Hebrew, 1954.]

5907 FUKS, MARIAN: *Z diariusza muzycznego. Sylwetki, eseje, szkice* [From a musical diary. Silhouettes, essays, sketches]. Warszawa: Żydowski Instytut Historyczny w Polsce, 1977. 398 pp., illus., English summaries after some articles. [Incl.: martyrology and ghetto in musical compositions; musical life in the ghettoes of Warsaw, Cracow and Lodz; numerous accounts of Jewish and Polish musicians.]

5908 GRÉGOIRE, O.: *Le Ghetto en flammes. La lutte des Juifs contre les Nazis*. Paris: Zeluck, 1945. 205 pp.

5909 MARK, BERNARD: *Życie i walka mlodzieży w gettach w okresie okupacji hitlerowskiej, 1939–1944* [The life and struggle of the youth in the ghettoes in German-occupied territory]. Warszawa: Iskry, 1961. 94 pp.

5910 NESHAMIT, SARA: [*The ghetto struggle*]. Jerusalem: [Ministry of Education and Culture], 1968. 200 pp., illus., facsims., tabs., plan. [In Hebrew.]

5911 OLICKI, L., ed.: [*Between life and death. Literary activities in the ghettoes and camps*]. Warsaw: 'Yiddish Buch', 1955. 149 pp., facsims. [In Yiddish.]

5912 TENNENBAUM-BACKER, NINA: [*A man and a fighter. Mordekhai Tennenbaum-Tamaroff, hero of the ghettoes*]. Jerusalem: Yad Vashem, 1974. 282 pp., illus., facsims., plan, bibl. [In Hebrew.]

5913 TRUNK, ISAIAH: *Judenrat. The Jewish councils in Eastern Europe under Nazi occupation.* Introd.: Jacob Robinson. New York: Macmillan, 1972. xxxv + 664 pp., illus., maps, tabs.

5914 TUSHNET, LEONARD: *The pavement of Hell.* New York: St. Martin's Press, 1972. xi + 210 pp., ports. [Lodz, Warsaw, Vilna.]

Individual ghettoes

BIALYSTOK
5915 BLUMENTHAL, NACHMAN: [*Conduct and actions of a Judenrat. Documents from the Bialystock Ghetto*]. Jerusalem: Yad Vashem, 1962. 561 + 50 pp., summary in English. [In Hebrew. Documents in Yiddish.]

5916 MARK, BERL: *Den oifstand in Bialistoker Getto.* Warszawa: Żydowski Instytut Historyczny w Polsce, 1950. 508 pp., illus. [In Yiddish. Polish version: *Ruch oporu w Getcie Bialistokim. Samoobrona zaglada powstanie.* 1952. 283 pp. Documented story of resistance in the ghetto.]

5917 [BRZEZIN] ALPERIN, A. & SUMMER, N., eds.: *Brzezin memorial book.* New York: Brzeziner Book Committee, 1961. 288 pp., illus., facsims., tabs.

CRACOW
5918 PANKIEWICZ, TADEUSZ: *Apteka w getcie Krakowskim* [Pharmacy in the Cracow Ghetto]. Kraków: Świat i Wiedza, 1947. 150 pp.

5919 *W 3-cia rocnice zaglady Ghetta w Krakowie (13.III.1943–13.III.1946).* [The 3rd anniversary of the destruction of Cracow Ghetto]. Kraków: 1946. 197 pp. (Wojewodzka Żydowska Komisja Historyczna).

CZĘSTOCHOWA
5920 *Częstochowa.* Jerusalem: Encyclopaedia of the Jewish Diaspora, 1967. 839 pp., plan, illus., facsims., tabs. [In Hebrew and Yiddish.]

5921 ORENSTEIN, BENJAMIN: *Churban Czenstochow* [The destruction of Czenstochow]. [Bamberg]: Zentral Farwaltung fun der Czenstochower Landmanszaft in der amerikaner Zone in Dajczland, 1948. 463 pp., illus., facsims., tabs. [In Yiddish.]

KOVNO
5922 BROWN, ZVIE & LEVIN, DOV: *The story of an Underground. The resistance of the Jews of Kovno (Lithuania) in the Second World War.* Jerusalem: Yad Vashem, 1962. 422 + xvii pp., illus., facsims., maps, summary in English. [In Hebrew.]

5923 GARFUNKEL, L.: [*The destruction of Kovno's Jewry*]. Jerusalem: Yad Vashem, 1959. 330 pp., illus., chart. [In Hebrew.]

5924 LURIE, ESTHER: *A living witness. Kovno Ghetto scenes and types. Drawings and watercolours with accompanying text*. Tel Aviv: 1958. [30 pp., approx.]

5925 [LACHWA] MICHAEL, H. A. and others, eds.: *[First Ghetto to revolt—Lachwa]*. Jerusalem: The Encyclopaedia of the Jewish Diaspora, 1957. 500 pp., illus., facsims., maps, bibl. [In Hebrew.]

LODZ (LITZMANNSTADT)

5926 DĄBROWSKA, DANUTA & DOBROSZYCKI, LUCIAN, eds.: *Kronika getta Łódzkiego. Z oryginału do druku przygotowali, wstępem i przypisami zaopatrzyli* [Chronicle of Lodz Ghetto. Ed. from the original with introd. and notes]. Łódz: Wyd. Łodzkie, 1965/66. Illus., map, facsims., tabs.
1: *Styczeń 1941–maj 1942* [January 1941–May 1942]. Publ. 1965. 632 pp.
2: *Czerwiec–grudzień 1942* [June–December 1942]. Publ. 1966. 607 pp. [Incl. 'Tageschronik, August–Dezember 1942', in German, pp. 454–604.]

5927 GUMKOWSKI, JANUSZ and others, eds.: *Briefe aus Litzmannstadt*. Hrsg.: Janusz Gumkowski, Adam Rutkowski, Arnfrid Astel. Köln: Middelhauve, 1967. 134 pp., bibl. [Transl. from the Polish.]

5928 HERSHKOVITCH, BENDET: 'The Ghetto in Litzmannstadt (Lodz)'. [In] *Yivo Annual of Jewish Social Science, V*. New York: 1950. Pp. 85–122.

5929 KLUGMAN, ALEKSANDER, ed.: *The last journey of the Jews of Lodz*. Photographs: Henryk Ross. Tel Aviv: Kibel, [1950]. 84 pp., illus., facsims., map. [Text in English, German, Yiddish, Polish, French, Hebrew.]

5930 [RUMKOWSKI, MORDECHAI CHAIM] BLOOM, SOLOMON F.: 'Dictator of the Lodz Ghetto. The strange history of Mordechai Chaim Rumkowski'. [In] *Commentary*, Vol. 7, No. 2, Feb. 1949. Pp. 111–122.

5931 TRUNK, ISAIAH: *Ghetto Lodz. A historical and sociological study, including documents, maps, and tables*. New York: Yad Vashem/Yivo Institute for Jewish Research, Joint Documentary Projects, 1962. 528 pp., maps, tabs. [In Yiddish with English summary.]

5932 WULF, JOSEF: *Lodz. Das letzte Ghetto auf polnischem Boden*. Bonn: Bundeszentrale für Heimatdienst, 1962. 84 pp.

LUBLIN

5933 BLUMENTHAL, NACHMAN: *Documents from Lublin Ghetto. Judenrat without direction*. Jerusalem: Yad Vashem, 1967. 395 + 312 + 30 pp., illus., facsims. [In Hebrew, transl. from the Polish. Introd. in English. Protocols of the Judenrat reproduced in Polish, pp. 1–312.]

5934 FRIEDMAN, PHILIP: 'The Lublin Reservation and the Madagascar plan. Two aspects of Nazi Jewish policy during the Second World War'. [In] *Yivo Annual of Jewish Social Science, VIII*. Pp. 151–177. *See* 5674.

5935 MOLDAWER, S.: 'The road to Lublin'. [In] *Contemporary Jewish Record*. March/April 1940. New York. Pp. 119–133. [Deportation of German Jews.]

5936 ROSENFELD, ELSE & LUCKNER, GERTRUD, eds.: *Lebenszeichen aus Piaski. Briefe Deportierter aus dem Distrikt Lublin, 1940–1943.* Nachw.: Albrecht Goes. München: Biederstein, 1968. 183 pp., tabs.

LWÓW (LEMBERG)
5937 FRENKEL, MIECZYSŁAW R.: *To jest moderstwo* [This is murder]. Katowice: Wyd. 'Śląsk', 1958. 319 pp.

5938 WELLS (WELICZKER), LEON: *The Janowska road.* New York: Macmillan, 1963. 305 pp., maps. [German version: *Ein Sohn Hiobs.* München: Hanser, 1963.]

MINSK

5939 GRINSTIN, JACOB: [*Survivor of Jubilee Square. Account of the Minsk Ghetto by a partisan*]. Tel Aviv: Hakibbutz Hameuchad, 1968. 207 pp., illus. [In Hebrew, transl. from the Yiddish.]

5940 LOEWENSTEIN, KARL: *Minsk. Im Lager der deutschen Juden.* Bonn: Bundeszentrale für Heimatdienst, 1961. 58 pp.

5941 SMOLIAR, HERSH: *Resistance in Minsk.* Oakland, Calif.: Judah L. Magnes Memorial Museum, 1966. 109 pp., ports. [Orig. publ. in the Soviet Union in Yiddish and Russian.]

5942 [RIGA] LEVINSTEIN, MEIR: [*The Holocaust in Riga*]. Tel Aviv: Beit Edot Mordechai Ahielewicz & Sifriot Poalim, 1975. 152 pp., illus. [In Hebrew.]

5943 [SHAVLI (SHAULEN)] YERUSHALMI, ELIEZER: [*Pinkas Shavli. A diary from a Lithuanian Ghetto, 1941–1944*]. Jerusalem: Yad Vashem, 1958. 420 pp., illus. [In Hebrew.]

STANISLAU
5944 FREUNDLICH, ELISABETH: 'Massaker in Stanislau 1941'. [In] *Institut für deutsche Geschichte, Jahrbuch 4.* Pp. 423–455. *See* 35a.

5945 FRIEDMANN, T[UVIA], ed.: *Schupo und Gestapo Kriegsverbrecher von Stanislau vor dem Wiener Volksgericht. Dokumentensammlung.* Haifa: Historisches Institut für Erforschung der Nazikriegsverbrechen, 1957. 83 pp., mimeog.

TEREZIN (THERESIENSTADT)
5946 ADLER, H. G.: *Theresienstadt 1941–1945. Das Antlitz einer Zwangsgemeinschaft. Geschichte, Soziologie, Psychologie.* Tübingen: Mohr, 1955. 773 pp.

5947 ADLER, H. G.: *Die verheimlichte Wahrheit. Theresienstädter Dokumente.* Tübingen: Mohr, 1958. 372 pp., illus., maps.

5948 BOR, JOSEF: *The Terezin requiem.* London: Heinemann, 1963. 83 pp. [Transl. from the Czech. German version: *Theresienstädter Requiem.* Gütersloh: Mohn, 1966.]

5949 FRANKOVÁ, ANITA & HYNDRÁKOVÁ, ANNA: 'Die jüdische Selbstverwaltung im Ghetto von Terezin (Theresienstadt) 1941–1945. Ihre Organisation,

Tätigkeit und Rechtsbefugnis'. [In] *Judaica Bohemiae*. VIII, 1. Praha: Státní Židovské Muzeum, 1972. Pp. 36–54.

5950 GOLDSCHMIDT, ARTHUR: *Geschichte der evangelischen Gemeinde Theresienstadt, 1942–1945*. Tübingen: Furche, 1948. 36 pp. [Congregation of baptized Jews.]

5951 GREEN, GERALD: *The artists of Terezin*. New York: Hawthorn Books, 1969. 191 pp., illus.

5952 ... *I never saw another butterfly* ... *Children's drawings and poems from Theresienstadt concentration camp 1942–1944*. New York: McGraw-Hill, [1964]. 80 pp., illus. [Transl. from the Czech. German version: *'Hier leben keine Schmetterlinge ...'*. Prag: Staatliches Jüdisches Museum, 1959.]

5953 JACOBSEN, JACOB: *Terezin. The daily life, 1943–1945*. Annex: 'The Russians in Terezin', by David Cohen. London: Jewish Central Information Office, 1946. 23 pp.

5954 LEDERER, ZDENEK: *Ghetto Theresienstadt*. London: Goldston, 1953. 275 pp., tabs., bibl.

5955 MURMELSTEIN, B.: *Terezin. Il ghetto-modello di Eichmann*. [Bologna]: Cappelli, 1961. 239 pp., diagrs.

5956 OPPENHEIM, RALPH: *An der Grenze des Lebens. Theresienstädter Tagebuch*. Hamburg: Rütten & Loening, 1961. 251 pp., illus., facsims.

5957 STARKE, KÄTHE: *Der Führer schenkt den Juden eine Stadt. Bilder, Impressionen, Reportagen, Dokumente*. Berlin: Haude & Spener, 1975. 260 pp., illus., facsims., plan, tabs.

5958 *Terezin-Ghetto. List of saved persons and Introduction*. Prague: Repatriation Dept. of the Ministry of Protection of Labour and Social Welfare, 1945. 541 pp.

5959 *Totenbuch Theresienstadt. I: Deportierte aus Österreich*. Wien: Jüdisches Komitee für Theresienstadt, 1971. 159 pp.

VILNA

5960 BALBERYSZSKI, M.: *Likwidacja Getta Wilenskiego* [Liquidation of the Vilna Ghetto]. Warszawa: Centralna Żydowska Komisja Historyczna, 1946. 40 pp.

5961 DVORJETSKI, MARC: *La victoire du ghetto*. Paris: Éds. France-Empire, 1962. 319 pp. [Transl. from the Yiddish.]

5962 KALMANOVITCH, ZELIG: 'A diary of the Nazi Ghetto in Vilna'. [In] *Yivo Annual of Jewish Social Science*, VIII. Pp. 9–81. See 5674.

5963 KRUK, HERMAN: *Tagbukh fun vilner getto. Diary of the Vilna Ghetto*. Notes and explanations: Mordecai W. Bernstein. New York: Yivo Institute for Jewish Research, 1961. xlv + 620 pp., port., facsims.

5964 RUDASHEVSKI, ITZAK: [*The diary of a Vilna boy, June 1941–April 1943*]. Tel

Aviv: Hakibbutz Hameuchad, 1968. 126 pp., illus., facsim. [In Hebrew, transl. from the Yiddish. English version: *The diary of the Vilna Ghetto, June 1941–April 1943*. Revisions and additions: Percy Matenko. (Tel Aviv): Ghetto Fighters' House & Hakibbutz Hameuchad, 1973.]

5965 SUZKEWER, ABRAHAM: *Kol-Nidre. Poem*. Aus dem Jüdischen übertragen von Leon Bernstein. Basel: Verlag 'Jüdische Rundschau', [194–]. 32 pp.

5966 SUTZKEVER, A.: [*From the Vilna Ghetto*]. Moscow: Farlag 'Der Emas', 1946. 254 pp., illus., facsims. [In Yiddish.]

5967 [VITTEL] KATZNELSON, YITZHAK: *Vittel diary, 22.5.43–16.9.43*. [Tel Aviv]: Ghetto Fighters' House, 1964. 276 pp., port. [Transl. from the Hebrew.]

f. Warsaw Ghetto

5968 AVNON, ARIEH, ed.: *The 'Gordonia' press in the Warsaw Ghetto underground*. Transl. from the Polish. Historical introd.: Joseph Kermish. Haulda: Gordonia-Maccabi Hatzair Archives, 1966. 256 pp., port., facsims. [Text in Hebrew and Yiddish, summary in English.]

5969 BERG, MARY: *Warsaw Ghetto. A diary*. New York: Fischer, 1945. 253 pp.

5970 BERNSTEIN, J. and others: *Ghetto. Berichte aus dem Warschauer Ghetto 1939–1945*. Vorw.: Rudolf Hirsch. Berlin: Union Verlag, 1966. 506 pp. [First ed. in Yiddish: Warsaw: 'Idisz Buch', 1955/62.]

5971 CZERNIAKOW, ADAM: *Warsaw Ghetto diary, 6.9.39–23.7.1942*. Eds.: Nachman Blumenthal, Nathan Eck, Joseph Kermish, Aryeh Tartakower. Jerusalem: Yad Vashem, 1968. 395 + 264 + xxi pp., illus., facsims., tabs., map, bibl. [In Hebrew, introd. in English; diary reproduced in Polish, 264 pp.]

5972 DONAT, ALEXANDER: *The Holocaust kingdom*. London: Secker & Warburg, 1965. 361 pp., maps.

5973 KAPLAN, CHAIM A.: *Scroll of agony. The Warsaw diary of Chaim A. Kaplan*. Transl. and ed.: Abraham I. Katsh. London: Hamish Hamilton, 1966. 329 pp., maps.

KORCZAK, JANUSZ
5974 HYAMS, JOSEPH: *A field of buttercups*. London: Müller, 1969. 219 pp., port.

5975 JAWORSKI, MAREK: *Janusz Korczak*. Warsaw: Interpress, 1978. 221 pp., illus., bibl. [In English.]

5976 OLCZAK, HANNA (Hanna Mortkowicz-Olczakowa): *Mister Doctor. The life of Janusz Korczak*. London: Davies, 1965. 227 pp., port. [Transl. from the Polish. German version: *Janusz Korczak. Biographie*. Weimar: Kiepenheuer, 1961.]

5977 *Maladie de famine. Recherches cliniques sur la famine exécutées dans la Ghetto de Varsovie en 1942*. Warsaw: American Joint Distribution Committee, 1946. 264 pp.

5978   MALVEZZI, PIERO: *Le voci del ghetto. Antologia della stampa clandestina ebraica a Varsavia, 1941–1942*. Bari: Laterza, 1970. 501 pp., tabs. [Incl. lists of writers and scholars working in the ghetto.]

5979   MEED, VLADKA: *On both sides of the wall. Memoirs from the Warsaw Ghetto*. Introd.: Elie Wiesel. [Tel Aviv]: Beit Lohamei Hagettaot (Ghetto Fighters' House) & Hakibbutz Hameuchad, 1972. 343 pp., illus., facsims. [First ed. in Yiddish: New York: 1948. Hebrew ed. 1968. Full name of author: Feigele Peltel-Miedzyrzecki.]

5980   RINGELBLUM, EMANUEL: *Notizen fun Warschaver Getto*. Warszawa: 'Idisz Buch', 1952. 352 pp. [Also 1961 ed. under title *Ketuvim fun getto. Bd. I: Tagbuch fun warschaver getto, 1939–1942*. English version (of 1952 ed.): *Notes from the Warsaw Ghetto. The journal of Emanuel Ringelblum*. Ed.: Jacob Sloan. New York: McGraw-Hill, 1958. German version: *Ghetto Warschau. Tagebücher aus dem Chaos*. Introd.: Arieh Tartakower. Stuttgart: Seewald, 1967.]

5981   SAKOWSKA, RUTA: *Ludzie z dzielnicy zamknietej. Żydzi w Warszawie w okresie hitlerowskiej okupacji* [People in the Quarter. Jews in Warsaw during the Nazi occupation (Oct. 1939–March 1943)]. Warszawa: Państwowe Wyd. Naukowe, 1975. 398 pp., illus., map, tabs., bibl.

5982   TRUNK, ISAIAH: 'Epidemics and mortality in the Warsaw Ghetto, 1939–1942'. [In] *Yivo Annual of Jewish Social Science*, VIII. Pp. 82–122. *See* 5674.

5983   ZIEMIAN, JOSEPH: *The cigarette sellers of Three Crosses Square*. Transl. from the Polish. London: Vallentine, Mitchell, 1970. 162 pp., illus. [Also in Hebrew: Jerusalem: 1963.]

5984   ZYLBERBERG, MICHAEL: *A Warsaw diary, 1939–1945*. London: Vallentine, Mitchell, 1969. 220 pp., illus., facsims., tabs., bibl. [Author survived by means of false papers.]

Uprising

5985   ANDRZEJEWSKI, JERZY: *Warschauer Karwoche*. München: Langen & Müller, 1964. 177 pp. [Transl. from the Polish. Orig. title: *Wielki tydzien*. Written 1943 in Warsaw.]

5986   BLUMENTHAL, NACHMAN & KERMISH, JOSEPH: *Resistance and revolt in the Warsaw Ghetto. A documentary history*. Jerusalem: Yad Vashem, 1965. 495 + xlviii pp., map. [In Hebrew, summary in English.]

5987   BORWICZ, MICHEL, ed.: *L'insurrection du Ghetto de Varsovie*. Paris: Julliard, 1966. 251 pp., illus., plan, bibl.

5988   FRIEDMAN, PHILIP, ed: *Martyrs and fighters. The epic of the Warsaw Ghetto*. New York: Praeger, 1954. 325 pp., illus.

5989 GOLDSTEIN, BERNARD: *The stars bear witness*. Transl. and ed.: Leonard Shatzkin. New York: Viking Press, 1949. 295 pp.

5990 HERSEY, JOHN: *The wall. A novel.* London: Hamish Hamilton, 1951. 632 pp. [German version: *Der Wall.* Reinbek b. Hamburg: Rowohlt, 1956.]

5991 *Judenlos unter Hitler. Die Ausrottung der Juden in Warschau und ihr heldenhafter Widerstand.* Schweiz: Verlag Sch. SAG, 1944. 75 pp.

5992 KERMISZ, JOSEF: *Powstanie w getcie Warszawskim, 19.4–16.5.1943* [The uprising in the Warsaw Ghetto ...]. Łodz: Centralna Żydowska Komisja Historyczna, 1946. 120 pp. [Yiddish version: *Der oifsztand in Warshewer Getto. 19ter April–16ter Mai 1943.* Buenos Aires: Zentral-farband fun pojlische jidn in Argentine, 1948.]

5993 LITAI, CHAIM LAZAR: *Muranowska 7. The Warsaw Ghetto rising.* Transl. from the Hebrew. Tel Aviv: Massada-P.E.C. Press, 1966. 341 pp., illus.

5994 MARK, BER: *Der Oifstand in Warszewer Getto.* Warszawa: 'Idisz Buch', 1955. 435 pp., illus. [Rev. ed. from the Polish. New, completed ed. and collection of documents: *Powstanie w getcie warszawskim.* Warszawa: 'Idisz Buch', 1963. German version: Bernard Mark: *Der Aufstand im Warschauer Ghetto. Entstehung und Verlauf.* Berlin (East): Dietz, 1957. Also 3rd enl. ed. 1959.]

5995 NOVITCH, MIRIAM: *La révolte du Ghetto de Varsovie. Documents inédits de la presse clandestine.* [Paris]: Presses du Temps présent, 1968. 142 pp., illus., facsims., bibl.

5996 SHOSKES, HENRY: *No traveller returns.* Ed. with a prologue and epilogue by Curt Riess. New York: Doubleday, Doran, 1945. 267 pp.

STROOP, JÜRGEN (and STROOP REPORT)
5997 *La bataille du Ghetto de Varsovie. Vue et racontée par les Allemands.* Paris: Éds. du Centre, 1946. 88 pp. (Centre de Documentation Juive Contemporaine).

5998 MOCZARSKI, KAZIMIERZ: *Gespräche mit dem Henker. Das Leben des SS-Gruppenführers und Generalleutnants der Polizei Jürgen Stroop aufgezeichnet im Mokotów-Gefängnis zu Warschau.* Mit Beiträgen: Andrzej Szczypiorski: 'Über Kazimierz Moczarski'; Erich Kuby: 'Ein ganz gewöhnlicher Deutscher'. Düsseldorf: Droste, 1978. 426 pp., illus., facsims. [Transl. from the Polish.]

5999 *The report of Jürgen Stroop concerning the uprising in the Ghetto of Warsaw and the liquidation of the Jewish residential area.* Introd. and notes: B. Mark. Warsaw: Jewish Historical Institute, 1958. 124 pp. + appendix of facsims., illus. [Also new English version: *The Stroop report.* London: Secker & Warburg, 1980.]

6000 WIRTH, ANDRZEJ, ed.: *Der Stroop-Bericht. Es gibt keinen jüdischen Wohnbezirk in Warschau mehr!* Warsaw: 1960. Facsim. ed with illus.

6001 WULF, JOSEF: *Das Dritte Reich und seine Vollstrecker. Die Liquidation von*

500,000 Juden im Ghetto Warschau. Berlin-Grunewald: Arani, 1961. 383 pp., illus., facsims.

D. CONCENTRATION CAMPS

General

6002 ANTONI, E.: KZ. *Von Dachau bis Auschwitz. Faschistische Konzentrationslager 1933–1943.* Frankfurt a.M.: Röderberg, 1979. 144 pp., illus.

6003 BERNADAC, CHRISTIAN: *Les médecins de l'impossible.* Paris: Éds. France-Empire, 1968. 444 pp., bibl. [Incl.: Natzweiler, Oranienburg, Mauthausen, Ebensee, Melk, Gusen, Dachau, Schörzingen, Allach, Ravensbrück, Salaspils, Neuengamme, Buchenwald, Gross-Rosen, Nordhausen, Auschwitz, Bergen-Belsen.]

6004 BETTELHEIM, BRUNO: *The informed heart. The human condition in modern mass society.* [London]: Thames & Hudson, 1961. 309 pp. [Study of pyschological effects of life in a concentration camp. German version: *Aufstand gegen die Masse.* München: Szczesny, 1964.]

6005 BILLIG, JOSEPH: *Les camps de concentration dans l'économie du Reich hitlérien.* Préface: Jacques Droz. Paris: Presses Universitaires de France, 1973. 346 pp., illus., tabs., bibl. (Centre de Documentation Juive Contemporaine).

6006 BILLINGER, KARL: *Schutzhäftling 880. Aus einem deutschen Konzentrationslager.* Paris: Éds du Carrefour, 1935. 196 pp. [Enl. English version: *All quiet in Germany.* London: Gollancz, 1935. 288 pp. Novel.]

6007 BORNSTEIN, ERNST ISRAEL: *Die lange Nacht. Ein Bericht aus sieben Lagern.* [Introd.]: Max Mikorey. Frankfurt a.M.: Europäische Verlagsanstalt, 1967. 243 pp., diagr. [Grünheide, Markstadt, Gross-Rosen, Flossenbürg, Leonberg. Mühldorf.]

6008 [BREWDA, ALINA] MINNEY, R. J.: *I shall fear no evil. The story of Dr. Alina Brewda.* London: Kimber, 1966. 223 pp., port. [Warsaw Ghetto, Majdanek, Auschwitz, Ravensbrück.]

6009 BUBENÍČKOVÁ, RÚŽENÁ and others: *Tábory utrpeni a smrti* [The camps of suffering and death]. [By] Rúžená Bubeníčková, Ludmila Kubátová, Irene Malá. [Prague]: Svoboda, 1969. 489 pp., illus., facsims., maps, plans, tabs., summary in German.

6010 CARROUGES, MICHEL: *Le Père Jacques.* Paris: Éds. du Seuil, 1958. 321 pp., illus., bibl. [Mauthausen, Neue Breme, Gusen.]

6011 COHEN, ELIE A.: *Human behavior in the concentration camp.* New York: Norton, 1953. 295 pp. [Dutch orig.: *Het Duitse concentratie kamp. Een medische en psychologische studie.* Amsterdam: 1952. A documented study of medical experiments and the psychology both of the SS and their victims.]

6012 DALUEGE, KURT & LIEBERMANN VON SONNENBERG, [ERICH]: *Nationalsozi-*

alistischer Kampf gegen das Verbrechertum. München: Eher, 1935. 138 pp., illus., diagr., tabs. [The sending of 'incorrigible' criminals to concentration camps, where they often held positions of authority.]

6013 DE MARTINO, GAETANO: *Dal carcere di San Vittore ai 'Lager' tedeschi sotto la Sferza nazifascista*. Milano: Ed. 'Alaya', 1945. 161 pp.

6014 DES PRES, TERENCE: *The survivor. An anatomy of life in the death camps*. New York: Oxford University Press, 1976. vii + 218 pp.

6015 DEVOTO, A[NDREA]: 'Psicologia e psicopatologia dei Lager nazisti'. [In] *Rivista di Psicologia Sociale*. XI, 2, 1962. Cagliari: Istituto di Psicologia dell'Università di Cagliari. Pp. 163–186, bibl.

6016 FARAMUS, ANTHONY CHARLES: *The Faramus story. Being the experience of A. C. Faramus*. Presented by Frank Owen. Forew.: Eddie Chapman. London: Wingate, 1954. 178 pp. [Political prisoner from Jersey in Buchenwald and Mauthausen.]

6017 *Fašistické koncentrační tábory a věznice území Československa za druhé světové války* [Fascist concentration camps and prisons in the territory of Czechoslovakia during World War II]. Praha: Svaz Protifašistických Bojovníků, 1964. 36 pp., tabs.

6018 FOSMARK, JOHANNES, ed.: *Danske i tyske koncentrationsleire* [Danes in German concentration camps]. København: Nordisk Forlag, 1945. 231 pp., illus.

GERSTEIN, KURT
6019 FRANZ, HELMUT: *Kurt Gerstein. Aussenseiter des Widerstandes der Kirche gegen Hitler*. Zürich: EVZ-Verlag, 1964. 112 pp., illus., facsims.

6020 FRIEDLÄNDER, SAUL: *Kurt Gerstein ou l'ambigüité du bien*. Postface: Léon Poliakov. Tournai: Casterman, 1967. 203 pp., illus., facsims. [English version: *Counterfeit Nazi. The ambiguity of good*. London: Weidenfeld & Nicolson, 1967.]

6021 HEGER, HEINZ: *Die Männer mit dem rosa Winkel. Der Bericht eines Homosexuellen über seine KZ-Haft von 1939–1945*. Hamburg: Merlin-Verlag, 1972. 169 pp., illus. [Sachsenhausen and Flossenbürg. English version: *The men with the pink triangle*. London: Gay Men's Press, forthcoming.]

6022 HILLER, KURT: *Leben gegen die Zeit. Bd. I: Logos*. Reinbek b. Hamburg: Rowohlt, 1969. 421 pp., port. [Incl.: 'Kazett', pp. 226–294; Brandenburg and Oranienburg camps.]

6023 HOFFMANN, BEDRICH: *A kdo vás zabiji? Zivot a utrpení kněžstva v koncentračnich taborech*. [And who will kill you? The experiences and sufferings of priests in concentration camps]. Přerov: Společenské Podniky, 1946. 590 pp., illus.

6024 [INTERNATIONAL RED CROSS]: *Documents sur l'activité du Comité international* de la Croix-Rouge en faveur des civils détenus dans les camps de concentration en Allemagne, 1939–1945. Genève: 1946. 156 pp.

6025 KA-TZETNIK 135633, pseud.: *House of dolls*. Transl. from the Hebrew. London: Muller, 1956. 239 pp. [Novel based on the diary of a Jewess forced into prostitution in a Nazi labour camp.]

6026 KAUTSKY, BENEDIKT: *Teufel und Verdammte. Erfahrungen und Erkenntnisse aus sieben Jahren in deutschen Konzentrationslagern*. Zürich: Büchergilde Gutenberg, 1946. 328 pp.

6027 KIEDRZŃSKA, WANDA, ed.: *Materialy do bibliografii hitlerowskich obozów koncentracyjnych* [Bibliography of material on Nazi concentration camps]. *Literatura międzynarodowa 1934–1962*. Warszawa: Państwowe Wyd. Naukowe, 1964. 109 pp., summary in English (of introd.). (Instytut Historii Polskiej Akademii Nauk).

6028 KLAUSNER, ISRAEL: [*Extermination camps in Poland*. Introd.: Isaac Gruenbaum]. Jerusalem: Mass, [1947]. 267 pp., illus. [In Hebrew.]

6029 KOGON, EUGEN: *Der SS-Staat. Das System der deutschen Konzentrationslager*. 6. Aufl. München: Heyne, 1979. 427 pp. [First ed. 1946. English version: *The theory and practice of hell. The German concentration camps and the system behind them*. London: Secker & Warburg, 1950. French version: *L'état SS*. Paris: Éds. du Seuil, 1970. First French ed. 1947 (two chapters omitted) under title: *L'enfer organisé*.]

6030 *Konzentrationslager. Ein Appell an das Gewissen der Welt. Ein Buch der Greuel. Die Opfer klagen an*. Carlsbad: 'Graphia', 1936. 254 pp. (Sozialdemokratische Schriftenreihe 'Probleme des Sozialismus'). [Dachau, Brandenburg, Papenburg, Königstein, Lichtenburg, Colditz, Sachsenburg, Moringen, Hohnstein, Reichenbach, Sonnenburg.]

6031 KRAUS, OTA, & KULKA, ERICH: *Noc a mlha* [Night and fog]. Praha: Naše Vojsko-SPB, 1958. 431 pp., illus., map showing camps. [Sequel to *Továrna na smrt*, see 6074. Incl. slave labour.]

6032 LANGBEIN, HERMANN: *Die Stärkeren. Ein Bericht*. Wien: Stern, 1949. 215 pp. [A Communist's experiences in Gurs, Le Vernet, Dachau, Auschwitz.]

6033 LANGHOFF, WOLFGANG: *Die Moorsoldaten. 13 Monate Konzentrationslager. Unpolitischer Tatsachenbericht*. Zürich: Schweizer Spiegel Verlag, 1935. 327 pp., illus.

6034 MALÁ, IRENA & KUBÁTOVÁ, LUDMILA: *Pochody smrti* [Death marches]. Praha: Nakl. Politické Literatury, 1965. 331 pp., illus., facsims., maps, tabs., summaries in Russian, English, French.

6035 MARSHALL, BRUCE: *The White Rabbit. From the story told by Wing-Commander F. F. E. Yeo-Thomas*. London: Evans, 1952. 262 pp., port. [An organizer of the French resistance; incl. sections on Buchenwald, Gleina, Rehmsdorf.]

6036 NANSEN, ODD: *Day after day*. Transl. from the Norwegian. London: Putnam, 1949. 600 pp., port. [Diary of Fridtjof Nansen's son, in Grini, Veidal,

Sachsenhausen, Neuengamme. American ed.: *From day to day*. New York: Putnam, 1949.]

6037 PASCOLI, PIETRO: *I deportati. Pagine di vita vissuta*. 2a ed. Firenze: La Nuova Italia Ed., 1960. 217 pp., bibl.

6038 PIASENTE, PARIDE, ed.: *Italian servicemen interned in Nazi camps. Notes for the study of a less known aspect of the Second World War*. Roma: Associazione Nazionale ex-Internati, [1972]. 38 pp.

6039 PINGEL, FALK: *Häftlinge unter SS-Herrschaft. Widerstand, Selbstbehauptung und Vernichtung im Konzentrationslager*. Hamburg: Hoffmann & Campe, 1978. 336 pp. [Orig. a dissertation, Bielefeld 1976, entitled *Selbstbehauptung, Widerstand und Vernichtung*.]

6040 ROUSSET, DAVID: *L'univers concentrationnaire*. Paris: Eds. du Pavois, 1946. 187 pp. [English version: *A world apart*. London: Secker & Warburg, 1951. American ed.: *The other kingdom*. New York: Reynal & Hitchcock, 1947.]

6041 RÜCKERL, ADALBERT, ed.: *Nationalsozialistische Vernichtungslager im Spiegel deutscher Strafprozesse. Belzec, Sobibor, Treblinka, Chelmno*. Vorw.: Martin Broszat. München: Deutscher Taschenbuch Verlag, 1977. 358 pp., diagr., map, bibl.

6042 SALUS, GRETE: *Eine Frau erzählt*. Bonn: Bundeszentrale für Heimatdienst, 1958. 99 pp. [Jewish survivor of Auschwitz, Oederan, Theresienstadt.]

6043 SALVESEN, SYLVIA: *Forgive—but do not forget*. Transl. from the Norwegian. Rev. and ed. by Lord Russell of Liverpool. London: Hutchinson, 1958. 234 pp. [A member of the Norwegian resistance in Grini and Ravensbrück.]

6044 SCHÄTZLE, JULIUS: *Stationen zur Hölle. Konzentrationslager in Baden und Württemberg 1933–1945*. Hrsg. im Auftr. der Lagergemeinschaft Heuberg-Kuhberg-Welzheim. 2. verb. Aufl. Frankfurt a.M.: Röderberg, 1980. 81 pp., illus., map.

6045 *Simone et ses compagnons presentés par leurs camarades de prisons et de camps*. Paris: Éds. de Minuit, 1947. 193 pp., illus. [French martyrs of the Resistance in Fresnes, Ravensbrück, Theresienstadt.]

6046 STRIGLER, MORDCHAI: *In die fabrikn fun toit* [In the factories of death]. Buenos Aires: Zentral-farband fun pojlishe Jidn in Argentine, 1948. 429 pp. [In Yiddish.]

6047 *Studien zur Geschichte der Konzentrationslager*. Stuttgart: Deutsche Verlags-Anstalt, 1970. 202 pp., tabs., bibls. after some articles. (Schriftenreihe der *Vierteljahrshefte für Zeitgeschichte*). [Incl. Fuhlsbüttel, Neuengamme, Mauthausen, Ravensbrück, Bergen-Belsen, Dora-Mittelbau.]

6048 *Les témoins qui se firent égorger*. [Paris?]: Éds. Défense de France, 1946. 217 pp., illus.

6049 UNION FÜR RECHT UND FREIHEIT, PRAG: *Deutsche Frauenschicksale*. London: Malik, 1937. 254 pp. [Women in Nazi prisons and concentration camps, incl. Moringen, Hohnstein.]

6050 UNIVERSITÉ DE STRASBOURG: *De l'Université aux camps de concentration. Témoignages strasbourgeois.* Paris: Éds. 'Les Belles Lettres', 1947. 549 pp.

6051 VERMEHREN, ISA: *Reise durch den letzten Akt. Ein Bericht. 10.2.44 bis 29.6.45.* Hamburg: Wegner, 1948. 233 pp. [A 'Sippenhäftling' in Ravensbrück, Buchenwald, Dachau.]

6052 WALLNER, PETER: *By order of the Gestapo. A record of life in Dachau and Buchenwald concentration camps.* Transl. from the German. London: Murray, 1941. 279 pp.

6053 WEINSTOCK, ROLF: *'Das wahre Gesicht Hitlerdeutschlands'. Häftling Nr. 59.000 erzählt von dem Schicksal der 10.000 Juden aus Baden, aus der Pfalz und aus dem Saargebiet in den Höllen von Dachau, Gurs-Drancy, Auschwitz, Jawischowitz, Buchenwald.* Singen (Hohentwiel): Volksverlag, 1948. 185 pp., illus.

6054 WEISS, RESKA: *Journey through hell. A woman's account of her experiences at the hands of the Nazis.* London: Vallentine, Mitchell, 1961. 255 pp., map. [Incl. Auschwitz and Neumark concentration camps, and ghettoes of Riga, Ponovez and Shavli.]

6055 WIESEL, ELIE: *La nuit.* Paris: Éds. de Minuit, 1958. 179 pp. [Hungarian-Jewish boy in Auschwitz, Buna, Buchenwald. English version: *Night.* Forew.: François Mauriac. London: MacGibbon & Kee, 1960.]

6056 WOLFF, JEANETTE: *Sadismus oder Wahnsinn. Erlebnisse in den deutschen Konzentrationslagern im Osten.* Dresden: Sachsenverlag, [1946]. 64 pp. [Riga Ghetto; labour camps of Salaspils, Jungfernhof, Schlüsselmühle, Korben; concentration camps of Kaiserwald and Stutthof.]

6057 WORMSER, OLGA & MICHEL, HENRI, eds.: *Tragédie de la déportation, 1940–1945. Témoignages de survivants des camps de concentration allemands.* Paris: Hachette, 1945. 511 pp.

6058 WORMSER-MIGOT, OLGA: *Le système concentrationnaire nazi, 1933–1945.* Paris: Presses Universitaires de France, 1968. 660 + vii pp., tabs., bibl. (Publications de la Faculté des Lettres et Sciences humaines de Paris-Sorbonne).

Amersfoort

6059 GUNNING, C. P.: *Op de Schoolbanken in het P.D.A. Wat ik heb ervaren en geleerd in het concentratie-kamp te Amersfoort, Januari–April 1942.* Amsterdam: Elsevier, 1946. 212 pp.

6060 HUNSCHE, J. F.: *P.D.A. (Polizeiliches Durchgangslager Amersfoort). Herinneringen van een gijzelaar, waarin met toestemming van de Vereeniging 'De Amsterdamsche Gijzelaars P.D.A. 1942' opgenomen het kort verslag van het verblijf van 85 Amsterdamsche gijzelaars in het 'Polizeiliches Durchgangslager' Amersfoort 30 Jan.–20 Apr. 1942.* Voorw.: H. R. Hoetink, A. N. J. den Hollander, J. M. Romein. [Amsterdam: 1945?]. 160 pp., illus., plan.

485

Auschwitz

6061 ADLER, H. G. and others, eds.: *Auschwitz. Zeugnisse und Berichte.* [Eds.]: H. G. Adler, Hermann Langbein, Ella Lingens-Reiner. Köln: Europäische Verlags-Anstalt, 1979. 316 pp. [First ed. 1962.]

6062 BEZWINSKA, JADWIGA & CZECH, DANUTA, eds.: *KL Auschwitz as seen by the SS—Höss, Broad, Kremer.* Oświęcim: Państwowe Muzeum, 1972. 331 pp., illus., plans, facsims., bibl. [Transl. from the German by Constantine Fitzgibbon and Krystyna Michalik. Comprising: 'Commandant of Auschwitz, Rudolf Höss', 'Reminiscences of Pery Broad', 'Diary of Johann Kremer'. Also: *Amidst a nightmare of crime. Manuscripts of members of Sonderkommando.* 1973. 207 pp.]

6063 CASTLE, JOHN: *The password is courage.* London: Souvenir Press, 1954. 224 pp. [Sergeant-Major Coward, a POW in Auschwitz.]

6064 DEMANT, EBRO, ed.: *Auschwitz—'direkt von der Rampe weg ...'. Kaduk, Erber, Klehr: drei Täter geben zu Protokoll.* Einf.: Axel Eggebrecht. Reinbek b. Hamburg: Rowohlt, 1979. 143 pp., bibl.

6065 FÉNELON, FANIA & ROUTIER, MARCELLE: *The musicians of Auschwitz.* London: Michael Joseph, 1977. 262 pp. [German version: *Das Mädchenorchester in Auschwitz.* Frankfurt a.M.: Röderberg, 1976. French orig.: *Sursis pour l'orchestre.* Paris: Stock, 1976.]

FRANKFURT TRIAL

6066 LANGBEIN, HERMANN: *Der Auschwitz-Prozess. Eine Dokumentation.* Wien: Europa Verlag, 1965. 2 vols.

6067 NAUMANN, BERND: *Auschwitz. Bericht über die Strafsache gegen Mulka und andere vor dem Schwurgericht Frankfurt.* Frankfurt a.M.: Athenäum Verlag, 1965. 552 pp., illus., tabs., diagrs. [English version: *Auschwitz.* Introd.: Hannah Arendt. London: Pall Mall Press, 1966.]

6068 GARLIŃSKI, JÓZEF: *Fighting Auschwitz: the resistance movement in the concentration camp.* London: Friedmann, 1975. xi + 327 pp., illus., plans, tabs., maps, bibl. [First ed. in Polish: Odnova: London, 1974.]

6069 HÖSS, RUDOLF: *Kommandant in Auschwitz. Autobiographische Aufzeichnungen.* Hrsg.: Martin Broszat. Ungek. 4. Aufl. Stuttgart: Deutscher Taschenbuch Verlag, 1978. 188 pp. [English version: *Commandant of Auschwitz. The autobiography of Rudolf Hoess.* Introd.: Lord Russell of Liverpool. London: Weidenfeld & Nicolson, 1959. First ed.: Warsaw: 1951.]

6070 INTERNATIONAL AUSCHWITZ COMMITTEE: *Anthology.* Warsaw: 1970/71. 7 vols.
I: *Inhuman medicine.* xii + 274 + 261 pp. [In 2 vols: Pt. I incl. Dr. Johann P. Kremer.]
II: *In hell they preserved human dignity.* 212 + 227 + 222 pp. [In 3 vols: Pt. 2 incl. gypsies, Pt. 3 children.]
III: *It did not end in 'forty-five.* 211 + 262 pp. [In 2 vols.]

6071   KA-TZETNIK 135633, pseud.: *Piepel.* London: Blond, 1961. 284 pp. [Transl. from the Hebrew. A young Jewish boy in Auschwitz.]

6072   KIELAR, WIESLAW: *Anus Mundi. Fünf Jahre Auschwitz.* Frankfurt a.M.: Fischer, 1979. 416 pp., plans. [English version: London: Allen Lane, 1981. Orig. Polish ed.: Krakow: Wyd. Literackie, 1972.]

6073   KOSSAK, ZOFIA: *Z otchlani* [From the abyss]. Poznań: Naglowski, 1947. 259 pp. [Birkenau. French version: *Du fond de l'abîme, Seigneur ...* Paris: Michel, 1951.]

6074   KRAUS, OTA & KULKA, ERICH: *Továrna na smrt* [Factory of death]. Praha: Orbis, 1956. 217 pp., illus. [Full documented story of Auschwitz. German version: *Die Todesfabrik.* Berlin (East): Kongress-Verlag, 1957. English version: *The death factory. Document on Auschwitz.* Oxford: Pergamon Press, 1966. 284 pp., maps, illus., tabs., facsims., bibl. Also Hebrew version: Jerusalem: 1960.]

6075   LANGBEIN, HERMANN: *Menschen in Auschwitz.* Wien: Europa Verlag, 1972. 607 pp., bibl.

6076   LENGYEL, OLGA: *Five chimneys. The story of Auschwitz.* Chicago, Ill.: Ziff-Davies, 1947. 213 pp.

6077   LEVI, PRIMO: *Se questo è un uomo?* Torino: De Silva, 1947, 197 pp. [Italian Jew in Auschwitz. English version: *If this is a man.* London: Orion Press, 1959. German version: *Ist das ein Mensch? Erinnerungen an Auschwitz.* Frankfurt a.M.: Fischer, 1979. Enl. ed.; first ed. 1961.]

6078   LUKOWSKI, JERZY: *Bibliografia obozu koncentracyjnego Oświęcim-Brzezinka* [Bibliography of the concentration camp Auschwitz-Birkenau] *1945–1965.* Warszawa: Międzynarodowy Komitet Oświęcimski, Sekretariat Generalny, 1968/70. 5 vols.
    I: Publ. 1968. 155 pp.
    II: *Procesy zbrodniarzy hitlerowskich—członków administracji i abrojnej obozu* [Trial of the hitlerite criminals—administration members and armed garrison of the camps]. Publ. 1968. 387 pp.
    III: Publ. 1968. 201 pp. [In subsequent vols. the dates of the works listed were extended.]
    IV: *1966–1967* [together with additional materials from the years 1945–1965]. Publ. 1969. 249 pp.
    V: *1968–1969.* Publ. 1970. 234 pp.

6079   MÜLLER, FILIP: *Auschwitz inferno. The testimony of a Sonderkommando.* Forew.: Yehuda Bauer. Literary collaboration: Helmut Freitag. Ed. and transl.: Susanne Flatauer. London: Routledge & Kegan Paul, 1979. xii + 180 pp., illus., plans. [German version: *Sonderbehandlung. Drei Jahre in den Krematorien und Gaskammern von Auschwitz.* Deutsche Bearb.: Helmut Freitag. München: Steinhausen, 1979. 287 pp., diagrs.]

6080   NEDERLANDSCHE ROODE KRUIS: *Auschwitz.* 's-Gravenhage: 1947/53. 6 vols.
    I: *Het dodenboek van Auschwitz.* Publ. 1947. 20 pp.

II: *De deportatietransporten van Juli 1942, tot en met 24 Augustus, 1942.* Publ. 1948. 52 pp.

III: *De deportatietransporten in de zg. Cosel-periode.* Publ. 1952. 97 pp.

IV: *De deportatietransporten in 1943.* Publ. 1953. 70 pp.

V: *De deportatietransporten in 1944.* Publ. 1953. 38 pp., mimeog.

VI: *De afvoertransporten uit Auschwitz et omgeving naar het Noorden en het Westen, en de grote evacuatietransporten.* Publ. 1952. 125 pp., charts, mimeog.

6081 PAŃSTWOWE MUZEUM W OŚWIĘCIMIU: *From the history of KL-Auschwitz.* Oswięcim: 1967/76. Illus., facsims. [Transl. from the Polish.]
I: Publ. 1967. 225 pp.
II: Publ. 1976. 299 pp., maps. [On medical conditions.]

6082 PAŃSTWOWE MUZEUM W OŚWIĘCIMIU: *Hefte von Auschwitz—Zeszyty Oswięcimskie.* [Institute of Party History], 1957/71. 15 vols., illus., facsims., summaries in English, French, German, Russian. [Publ. in Polish and German. German titles include: 5: *Erinnerungen*; 13: *Tagebuch des SS Arztes Johann Paul Kremer*; Sonderheft 1 [*sic*—should be Sonderheft 2]: *Handschriften von Mitgliedern des Sonderkommandos.* For English versions of some of this material, *see* 6062.]

6083 PAŃSTWOWE MUZEUM W OŚWIĘCIMIU: *Oboz koncentracny Oświęcim w tworczosci artystycznej.* [Ed.]: Kazimierz Smoleń. Oświęcim: 1960/61. 2 vols.

6084 PERL, GISELA: *I was a doctor in Auschwitz.* New York: International Universities Press, 1948. 189 pp.

6085 SZMAGLEWSKA, SEWERYNA: *Dymy nad Birkenau.* Warszawa: 'Czytelnik', 1967. 371 pp., plans. [English version: *Smoke over Birkenau.* New York: Holt, 1947.]

6086 ZYWULSKA, KRYSTYNA: *Přežila jsem Osvětím* [I survived Auschwitz]. Praha: Naše vojsko-SPB, 1957. 229 pp. [English version: *I came back.* London: Dobson, 1951. A Polish 'Aryan's' experiences.]

Belzec

6087 REDER, RUDOLF: *Belzec.* Krakow: Centralna Żydowska Komisja Historyczna przy C. K. Żydow Polskich, 1946. 65 pp., illus. [Publications of the Regional Jewish Historical Commission in Cracow.]

6088 TREGENZA, MICHAEL: 'Belzec death camp'. [In] *Wiener Library Bulletin*, 1977, XXX, n.s. 41/42. Pp. 8–25. illus., plans.

Bergen-Belsen

6089 *The Belsen Trial. Trial of Josef Kramer and 44 others.* Ed.: Raymond Phillips. Forew.: Lord Jowitt. London: Hodge, 1949. 749 pp., illus.

6090 [GRESE, IRMA] LUSTGARTEN, EDGAR: 'Irma Grese'. [In] *The business of murder.* London: Harrap, 1968. Pp. 77–105.

6091 HERZBERG, ABEL J.: *Twee stroomenland. Dagboek uit Bergen-Belsen.* Arnhem: van Loghum Slaterus, 1950. 285 pp.

6092 KOLB, EBERHARD: *Bergen Belsen. Geschichte des 'Aufenthaltslagers' 1943–1945.* Hannover: Verlag für Literatur und Zeitgeschehen, 1962. 344 pp., tabs., maps, diagrs., bibl.

6093 LEVY-HASS, HANNA: *Vielleicht war das alles erst der Anfang. Tagebuch aus dem KZ Bergen-Belsen 1944–1945.* Hrsg.: Eike Geisel. Berlin: Rotbuch Verlag, 1979. 110 pp.

6094 SINGTON, DERRICK: *Belsen uncovered.* London: Duckworth, 1946. 208 pp., illus. [German version: *Die Türe öffnen sich. Authentischer Bericht über das englische Hilfswerk für Belsen mit amtlichen Photos und einen Rückblick* von Rudolf Küstermeier. Hamburg: Kulturverlag, 1948.]

6095 [VERWEYEN, JOHANNES MARIA] KAMPS, KARL: *Johannes Maria Verweyen. Gottsucher, Mahner und Bekenner.* Wiesbaden: Credo-Verlag, 1955. 114 pp., port. [Religious philosopher who died in Belsen in 1945.]

Breendonck

6096 CONSEIL D'ADMINISTRATION DU MÉMORIAL NATIONAL DU FORT DE BREENDONK: *Un témoin. Le fort de Breendonk.* Bruxelles: 1961. 113 pp., illus., facsims., map.

6097 MARBAIX, EDGAR: *Breendonck-la-Mort.* Bruxelles: de Myttenaere, 1944. 104 pp.

Buchenwald

6098 ANTELME, ROBERT: *Die Gattung Mensch.* Berlin: Aufbau-Verlag, 1949. 350 pp.

6099 *Les enfants de Buchenwald.* Genève: Union O.S.E., 1946. 85 pp., illus.

6100 JULITTE, PIERRE: *L'arbre de Goethe.* Préface: Joseph Kessel. Paris: Presses de la Cité, 1965. 373 pp., maps.

6101 *Konzentrationslager Buchenwald. Band I: Bericht des Internationalen Lagerkomitees.* Weimar: Thüringer Volksverlag, 1949. 215 pp., illus. [No others issued.]

6102 KOPP, GUIDO: *Ich aber habe leben müssen ... Die Passion eines Menschen des 20. Jahrhunderts.* Salzburg: Ried, 1946. 370 pp.

6103 KÜHN, GÜNTER & WEBER, WOLFGANG: *Stärker als die Wölfe. Ein Bericht über die illegale militärische Organisation im ehemaligen Konzentrationslager Buchenwald und den bewaffneten Aufstand.* Berlin [East]: Militärverlag der DDR, 1977. 324 pp., illus., plans, bibl.

6104 MOULIS, MILOSLAV: *To byl Buchenwald* [In the claws of Buchenwald]. Praha: Naše Vojsko-S.P.B., 1957. 122 pp., illus., diagrs. [History and structure of the camp. Also: 2nd enl. ed. 1959. 204 pp.]

6105 STEINWENDER, LEONHARD: *Christus im Konzentrationslager. Wege der Gnade und des Opfers.* Salzburg: Müller, 1946. 134 pp. [A Catholic priest in Buchenwald.]

6106 THOMAS, JACK: *No banners. The story of Alfred and Henry Newton.* London: Allen, 1955. 346 pp., illus., facsims.

6107 WIECHERT, ERNST: *Häftling Nr. 7188. Tagebuchnotizen und Briefe.* Hrsg.: Gerhard Kamin. München: Desch, 1966. 128 pp., facsim.

Chelmno

6108 BEDNARZ, WLADYSLAW: *Das Vernichtungslager zu Chelmno am Ner.* Vorw.: Waclaw Barcikowski. Wortgetreu übersetzt. Schwerin: Die Oberste Kommission für die Untersuchung der deutschen Verbrechen in Polen, 1949. 203 pp., mimeog. [Polish orig.: *Oboz stracen w Chelmnie nad Nerem.* Warszawa: Państwowe Instytut Wyd., 1946. 74 pp., illus.]

6109 LESZCZYŃSKI, JULIAN: 'Od formuły obozu zagłady—Höppner-Chelmno n/Nerem—de "Endlösung" ' [From the formation of the concentration camp to the 'Endlösung'—Höppner of Chelmno on the Ner]. [In] *Biuletyn Zydowskiego Instytutu Historycznego,* 1977, 1/101. Pp. 41–61, facsims.

6110 POSPIESZALSKI, KAROL MARIAN: 'Niemiecki nadleśniczy o zagładzie Żydów w Chelmnie nad Nerem' [German foresters on the extermination of Jews at Chelmno on the Ner]. [In] *Przegladu Zachodniego,* XVIII, 3, 1962. Poznań: Instytut Zachodni. Pp. 85–104. [Text in Polish and German.]

Compiègne

6111 BERNHARD, JEAN-JACQUES: *Le camp de la mort lente.* Paris: Michel, 1944. 246 pp. [Compiègne 1941/42. English version: *The camp of slow death.* London: Gollancz, 1945.]

Dachau

6112 BEIMLER, HANS: *Im Mörderlager Dachau. Vier Wochen in den Händen der braunen Banditen.* Moskau: Verlagsgenossenschaft ausländischer Arbeiter in der UdSSR, 1933. 69 pp. [English version: New York: 1933. French version: Paris: 1933.]

6113 BERBEN, PAUL: *Dachau, 1933–1945. The official history.* London: Norfolk Press, 1975. xv + 300 pp., illus., maps, plans, facsims., tabs., bibl. [Belgian orig.: *Histoire du camp de concentration de Dachau, 1933–1945.* Publ. 1968.]

6114 *Dachau. The Nazi hell. From the notes of a former prisoner at the notorious Nazi concentration camp.* Arranged by G. R. Kay. Transl. from the German. London: Aldor, 1939. 216 pp. [Also abridged version: *Dachau.* London: Wells Gardner, Darton, 1942. 158 pp.]

6115 GROSS, K. A.: *Zweitausend Tage Dachau. Erlebnisse eines Christenmenschen unter Herrenmenschen und Herdenmenschen. Berichte und Tagebücher des Häftlings Nr. 16921.* München: Neubau Verlag, [194–]. 344 pp.

6116 JOOS, JOSEPH: *Leben auf Widerruf. Begegnungen und Beobachtungen im*

Konzentrationslager Dachau 1941–1945. Olten: Walter, 1946. 260 pp., illus.

6117 KUPFER-KOBERWITZ, EDGAR: *Die Mächtigen und die Hilflosen. Als Häftling in Dachau.* Stuttgart: Vorwerk, 1957/60. [Based on secret diary notes.]
Bd. I: *Wie es begann* [1941–1942]. Publ. 1957. 430 pp.
Bd. II: *Wie es endete* [1943–1945]. Publ. 1960. 263 pp.

6118 MUSIOL, TEODOR: *Dachau, 1933–1945.* Katowice: Wyd. 'Śląsk' [for] Instytut Śląski w Opolu, 1971. 469 + [110] pp., illus., facsims., maps, tabs., bibl., summaries in English, Russian, French, German. [2nd rev. and enl. ed.]

6119 OVERDUIN, J.: *Der Himmel in der Hölle von Dachau.* Aus dem Holländischen übersetzt. Zürich: Zwingli-Verlag, 1947. 406 pp., illus. [Incl. Amersfoort concentration camp and prisons in Arnhem, Essen, Würzburg, Nuremberg.]

6120 ROST, NICO: *Goethe in Dachau. Literatur und Wirklichkeit.* München: Weismann, [194–]. 314 pp. [Transl. from the Dutch. Diary pages testifying to the power of spiritual values even in a concentration camp.]

6121 SELZER, MICHAEL: *Deliverance day. The last hours of Dachau.* London: Sphere Books, 1980. 251 pp., bibl.

6122 *Die Toten von Dachau. Deutsche und Österreicher. Ein Gedenk- und Nachschlagewerk.* München: Staatskommissariat für rassisch, religiös und politisch Verfolgte in Bayern, 1947. 104 pp.

PRIESTS AND PASTORS

6123 BERNARD, JEAN: *Pfarrerblock 25487. Ein Bericht.* Hrsg.: Charles Reinert, Gebhard Stillfried. München: Pustet, 1962. 171 pp.

6124 [BRANDSMA, TITUS] REES, JOSEPH: *Titus Brandsma. A modern martyr.* London: Sidgwick & Jackson, 1971. 192 pp., illus., facsim. [Incl. Amersfoort concentration camp. Dutch theologian, a victim of the Gestapo.]

6125 CARLS, HANS: *Dachau. Erinnerungen eines katholischen Geistlichen aus der Zeit seiner Gefangenschaft 1941–1945.* Köln: Bachem, 1946. 218 pp., illus., map, bibl. [Incl. lists of priests, 'Ehrenhäftlinge', etc.]

6126 MÜNCH, MAURUS: *Unter 2579 Priestern in Dachau. Zum Gedenken an den 25. Jahrestag der Befreiung in der Osterzeit 1945.* 2. erw. Aufl. Trier: Zimmer, 1972. 189 pp.

6127 SCHNABEL, REIMUND: *Die Frommen in der Hölle. Geistliche in Dachau.* Frankfurt a.M.: Röderberg, 1966. 333 pp., illus., facsims., tabs., diagrs., bibl.

Dora

6128 CABALA, ADAM: *Arsenal grobow* [Arsenal of tombs]. Kraków: Wyd. Literackie, 1968. 272 + [32] pp., illus., facsims.

6129 MICHEL, JEAN & NUCÉRA, LOUIS: *Dora. Dans l'enfer du camp de concentration ou les savants nazis préparaient la conquête de l'espace.* [Paris]: Lattès, 1975. 439 pp.

6130 RASSINIER, PAUL: *Le mensonge d'Ulysse.* 4e éd. Paris: La Librairie française, 1955. 330 pp. [Attack on concentration camp literature by a former prisoner at Dora. German version: *Die Lüge des Odysseus.* Wiesbaden: Priester, 1959. Spanish version: *La mentira de Ulises.* Barcelona: Acervo, 1962. Italian version: *La menzogna di Ulisse.* Discorso introduttivo: Prof. Anton Domingl, Monaco. Milano: Le Rune, 1966.]

Drancy

6131 DARVILLE, JACQUES & SIMON, WICHENE: *Drancy la Juive ou La deuxième Inquisition.* Préface: Tristan Bernard. Cachan (Seine): Breger, [1945]. 127 pp., illus.

6132 WELLERS, GEORGES: *De Drancy à Auschwitz.* Paris: Éds. du Centre, 1946. 231 pp., illus. (Centre de Documentation Juive Contemporaine).

Flossenbürg

6133 WALLEITNER, HUGO: *Zebra. Ein Tatsachenbericht aus dem Konzentrationslager Flossenbürg.* Bad Ischl: [priv. pr., 1948?]. 191 pp., illus.

Gross-Rosen

6134 MOŁDAWA, MIECZYSŁAW: *Gross-Rosen, Obóz koncentracyjny na Śląsku* [... Concentration camp in Silesia]. Warszawa: Wyd. 'Polonia', 1967. 182 pp., illus., maps, tabs., diagrs.

Gurs

6135 CADIER, HENRI: *Le calvaire d'Israél et la solidarité chrétienne.* Genève: Éds. Labor et Fides, 1945. 144 pp., illus.

6136 ISOLANI, GERTRUD: *Stadt ohne Männer. Roman.* 2. Aufl. Basel: Buchverlag Basler Zeitung, 1979. 336 pp. [The women's concentration camp, where the author was interned.]

6137 KREHBIEL-DARMSTÄDTER, MARIA: *Briefe aus Gurs und Limonest, 1940–1943.* Ausgew., erläut. und hrsg.: Walter Schmitthenner. Heidelberg: Lambert Schneider, 1970. 383 pp., port.

6138 SCHRAMM, HANNA: *Menschen in Gurs. Erinnerungen an ein französisches Internierungslager 1940–1941.* Barbara Vormeier: 'Dokumentarischer Beitrag zur französischen Emigrantenpolitik 1933–1944'. Worms: Heintz, 1977. xii + 404 pp., illus., facsims., tabs., bibl. [Document section, pp. 275–384.]

Gusen

6139 BOUARD, M. de: 'Le kommando de Gusen'. [In] *Revue d'Histoire de la Deuxième Guerre Mondiale,* 12e année, No 45, Janvier 1962. Pp. 45–70, graph. *See* 4634a.

Hoh(e)nstein

6140 *Mord im Lager Hohenstein. Berichte aus dem Dritten Reich.* Moskau: Verlagsgenossenschaft ausländischer Arbeiter in der UdSSR, 1933. 87 pp., illus. [Concentration camp for communists run by SA from 1933 to 1934.]

6141 *Von der Jugendburg Hohnstein zum 'Schutzhaft-Lager Hohnstein'.* Bearb.: Franz Hackel. Berlin-Potsdam: VVN Verlag, 1949. 51 pp.

Husum

6142 JORAND, P.: *Husum ... Ici on extermine! ... (Les camps de la mort).* Nancy: Vagner, 1946. 39 pp.

Ilava

6143 SANDOR, ELO: *Ilava.* Brno: Mir, 1947. 45 pp. [In Slovak.]

Janow (Lemberg)

6144 BORWICZ, MICHAL MAKSYMILIAN (BORUCHOWICZ): *Uniwersytet zbirow* [University of criminals]. Krakow: Centralna Żydowska Komisja, 1946. 104 pp., illus. [SS at Janow.]

Jasenovac

6145 *Sećanja Jevreja na logor Jasenovac* [Memories of Jews from the concentration camp Jasenovac]. Beograd: Savez jevrejskih opština Jugoslavije, 1972. 285 pp., illus., facsims., plans.

Majdanek (Lublin)

6146 *Communiqué de la Commission extraordinaire polono-soviétique chargée d'établir les forfaits commis par les Allemands au camp de destruction de Maidanek à Lublin.* Moscow: Éds. en Langues étrangères, 1944. 28 pp. [German version: *Die Hölle von Maidanek. Bericht der Ausserordentlichen Polnisch-Sowjetrussischen Kommission zur Untersuchung der von den Deutschen im Vernichtungslager Maidanek in der Stadt Lublin vergangenen Verbrechen.* Zürich: Verlag der Partei der Arbeit, 1945. 46 pp., illus. Also issued in English.]

6147 GRYŃ, EDWARD & MURAWSKA, ZOFIA: *Majdanek concentration camp.* Lublin: Wyd. Lubelskie, 1966. 65 pp., illus., facsims., maps. (Państwowe Muzeum na Majdanku). [Transl. from the Polish.]

6148 LICHTENSTEIN, HEINER: *Majdanek. Reportage eines Prozesses.* Nachwort: Simon Wiesenthal. Frankfurt a.M.: Europäische Verlagsanstalt, 1979. 188 pp., maps.

6149 SIMONOV, KONSTANTIN: *Ich sah das Vernichtungslager.* Verlag der sowjetischen Militärverwaltung in Deutschland, [1945?]. 200 pp., illus.

Mauthausen

6150 BARTOLAI, SANTE: *Da Fossoli a Mauthausen. Memorie di un sacerdote nei campe di concentramento nazisti.* Modena: Istituto storico della Resistenza, 1966. 108 pp.

6151 BAUM, BRUNO: *Die letzten Tage von Mauthausen.* Berlin [East]: Deutscher Militärverlag, 1965. 155 pp., illus., tabs., bibl.

6152   BERNADAC, CHRISTIAN: *Mauthausen*. Paris: Éds. France-Empire, 1974/75.
I: *Les 186 marches*. Publ. 1974. 379 pp., tabs.
II: *Le neuvième cercle*. Publ. 1975. 381 pp.

6153   CHOUMOFF, P. S.: *Les chambres de gaz de Mauthausen. La vérité historique rétablie ... à la demande de l'Amicale de Mauthausen*. Paris: Amicale des Déportés et Familles des Disparus du Camp de Concentration de Mauthausen, 1972. 95 pp., illus., facsims., plans, tabs.

6154   LE CHÊNE, EVELYN: *Mauthausen. The history of a death camp*. London: Methuen, 1971. 296 pp., illus., facsims., tabs., bibl. [Incl. list of staff members, pp. 260–284.]

6155   MARŠÁLEK, HANS: *Die Geschichte des Konzentrationslagers Mauthausen. Dokumentation*. Wien: Österreichische Lagergemeinschaft Mauthausen, 1974. x + 319 pp., illus., facsims., tabs., bibl.

6156   PAPPALETTERA, VINCENZO & LUIGI: *La parola agli aguzzini. Le SS e i kapo de Mauthausen svelano le leggi del Lager*. 3a ed. [Milano]: Mondadori, 1970. 252 pp., illus., map, diagrs., bibl. [First ed. 1969.]

6157   SACHAROW, VALENTIN: *Aufstand in Mauthausen*. Berlin [East]: Verlag Volk und Welt, 1961. 241 pp., illus., map of camp.

6158   WENGER, WILLO: *Fern und ewig leuchtet Frieden. Ein Erlebnis aus dem Zeitgeschehen nach Berichten sowie nach Aufzeichnungen eines zum Tode Verurteilten*. Zürich: Europa Verlag, 1947. 337 pp.

Natzweiler

6159   ALLAINMAT, HENRY: *Auschwitz en France. La verité sur le seul camp d'extermination nazi en France—Le Struthof*. Paris: Presses de la Cité, 1974. 243 pp., illus., facsims., tab., list of victims.

6160   VORLÄNDER, HERWART, ed.: *Nationalsozialistische Konzentrationslager im Dienst der totalen Kriegsführung. Sieben württembergische Aussenkommandos des KZ Natzweiler/Elsass*. Stuttgart: Kohlhammer, 1978. xix + 270 + 35 pp., illus., plans, tabs., facsims. (Veröffentlichungen der Kommission für geschichtliche Landeskunde in Baden-Württemberg).

6161   WEBB, ANTHONY M., ed.: *The Natzweiler trial*. Forew.: Hartley Shawcross. London: Hodge, 1949. 233 pp.

Neuengamme

6162   AMICALE INTERNATIONALE DE NEUENGAMME: *Bibliographie der über Neuengamme erschienenen Bücher und Zeitschriften ...* Hamburg: 1959. [Part I: Books and articles, 7 pp.; Part 2: Documents and reports, 7 pp.; Part 3: List of transports, 6 pp.]

6163   GOGUEL, RUDI: *'Cap Arcona'. Report über den Untergang der Häftlingsflotte in der Lübecker Bucht am 3. Mai 1945*. Frankfurt a.M.: Röderberg, 1972. 156 pp., illus., facsims., plans, bibl.

6164   KERN, PAUL and others: *Les jours de notre mémoire, 1940–1945. Neuengamme*.

Quatre survivants témoignent. [By] Paul Kern, Marcel Angles, Maurice Choquet, Pierre Brunet. Paris: Éds. La Pensée Universelle, 1975. 250 pp., illus.

6165 LAGERGEMEINSCHAFT NEUENGAMME: *So ging es zu Ende ... Neuengamme. Dokumente und Berichte.* Hamburg: Kristeller, 1960. 102 pp., illus., facsims., bibl.

6166 MEIER, HEINRICH CHRISTIAN: *So war es. Das Leben im KZ Neuengamme.* Hamburg: Phönix-Verlag Christen, 1946. 126 pp.

6167 POEL, ALB[ERT] van de: *Neuengamme. Getuigenis over het ongemaskerde Nationaal-Socialisme van een duitsch concentratiekamp.* Heerlen: Winants, [1945]. 134 pp. [German version: *Ich sah hinter den Vorhang. Ein Holländer erlebt Neuengamme.* Hamburg: Mölich, 1948.]

6168 *Totenbuch Neuengamme.* Hrsg.: Freundeskreis. Wiesbaden: Saaten-Verlag, [196–]. 573 pp., tabs., bibl. [Text in German, French, Flemish, Czech, Danish, Greek, Italian, Serbo-Croat, Dutch, Polish, Spanish, Russian, Hungarian, English.]

Novaky

6169 KAMENEC, IVAN: 'Židovský koncentračný a pracovný tábor y Novákoch' [Jewish concentration and labour camp in Novaky]. [In] *Horna Nitra,* III, 1966. [Bratislava?]: Stredoslovenské Vyd. Pp. 51–67, illus., tabs.

Oranienburg—Sachsenhausen

6170 BALLHORN, FRANZ: *Die Kelter Gottes. Tagebuch eines jungen Christen 1940–1945.* Münster: Verlag Regensburg, 1980. 132 pp. [Orig. publ. 1946.]

6171 CIEŚLAK, TADEUSZ: *Oranienburg-Sachsenhausen: hitlerowskie obozy koncentracyjne [... the Nazi concentration camps], 1933–1945.* Warszawa: Księżka i Wiedza, 1972. 261 pp., plan, tab.

6172 SCHAFER, (SA Sturmbannführer, Standarte 208, Lagerkommandant) [WERNER]: *Konzentrationslager Oranienburg. Das Anti-Braunbuch über das erste deutsche Konzentrationslager.* Berlin: Buch- und Tiefdruck Gesellschaft, [1935]. 246 pp., illus., facsims., tabs. [Reply to Gerhart Seger: *Orianienburg. See 3760.*]

6173 SEGER, GERHART: *A nation terrorized.* Forew.: Heinrich Mann. Chicago, Ill.: Teolly & Lee, 1935. 204 pp.

6174 UTSCH, BERT: *Gestapo-Häftling 52478 aus dem KZ Oranienburg-Sachsenhausen.* Vorw.: Bert Irving. Ottobeuren: [priv. pr.], 1945. 154 pp., illus.

Sachsenhausen

6175 GWIAZDOMORSKI, JAN: *Wspomnienia z Sachsenhausen. Dzieje uwiezienia profesorów Uniwersytetu Jagiellońskiego* [Reminiscences of Sachsenhausen. Events during the imprisonment of professors of Jagiellon University], *6.XI.1939–9.II.1940.* Kraków: Wyd. Literackie, 1969. 280 pp., illus., plans, facsims.

6176 KOMITEE DER ANTIFASCHISTISCHEN WIDERSTANDSKÄMPFER IN DER DDR: *Sachsenhausen*. Berlin [East]: Kongress-Verlag, [1962]. 186 pp., illus. [Text in German, Russian, French, English.]

6177 *Todeslager Sachsenhausen. Ein Dokumentarbericht vom Sachsenhausen-Prozess*. Berlin: SWA-Verlag, 1948. 215 pp.

Papenburg

6178 HINRICHS, KLAUS: *Staatliches Konzentrationslager VII. Eine 'Erziehungsanstalt' im Dritten Reich*. London: Malik, 1936. 436 pp.

Potulice

6179 JASTRZĘBSKI, WLODZIMIERZ: *Potulice. Hitlerowski obóz przesiedleńczy i pracy, luty 1941 r.–styczeń 1945 r.* [Potulice. The Hitlerite deportation and forced labour camp, Feb. 1941–Jan. 1945]. Bydgoszcz: Państwowe Wyd. Naukowe, 1967. 95 pp., illus., plan, tabs., bibl.

Radom

6180 WAKS, SHAMMAI: *Grief is my song*. Los Angeles, Calif.: [priv. pr.], 1968. 104 pp., ports. [In Yiddish, with English preface; some poems in English and Polish. Incl. account of forced labour on armaments in Camp Radom, pp. 81–87.]

Ravensbrück

6181 AMICALE DE RAVENSBRÜCK & ASSOCIATION DES DÉPORTÉES ET INTERNÉES DE LA RÉSISTANCE: *Les Françaises à Ravensbrück*. Paris: Gallimard, 1965. 347 pp., tabs., illus.

6182 BORSUM, LISE: *Kvindehelvedet Ravensbrück* [Women's hell—Ravensbrück]. København: Christensen, 1947. 291 pp.

6183 DOBACZEWSKA, WANDA: *Kobiety z Ravensbrück* (Women of Ravensbrück]. Warszawa: 'Czytelnik', 1946. 169 pp.

6184 DUFOURNIER, DENISE: *La maison des mortes. Ravensbrück*. Préface: Maurice Schumann. Paris: Hachette, 1945. 220 pp. [English version; *The women's camp of death*. London: Allen & Unwin, 1948.]

6185 HERMANN, NANDA: *Der gesegnete Abgrund. Schutzhäftling Nr. 6582 im Frauenkonzentrationslager Ravensbrück*. Nürnberg: Glock & Lutz, 1948. 216 pp., illus. [Authoress was the secretary of Pater Friedrich Muckermann, S.J.]

6186 [JESENSKA, MILENA] BUBER-NEUMANN, MARGARETE: *Milena. Kafkas Freundin*. München: Heyne, 1979. 221 pp. [First ed. 1963. Milena died in Ravensbrück in 1944.]

6187 LA GUARDIA GLUCK, GEMMA: *My story*. ed.: S. L. Shneiderman. New York: McKay, 1961. 116 pp.

6188 MAUREL, MICHELINE: *Un camp très ordinaire*. Préface: François Mauriac.

Paris: Éds. de Minuit, [1957]. 191 pp. [Neubrandenburg, a branch of Ravensbrück. English version: *Ravensbrück*. London: Blond, 1958.]

6189 SAINT-CLAIR, SIMONE: *Ravensbrück. L'enfer des femmes*. [Paris]: Fayard, 1972. 266 pp. [New ed., amended and enl. First ed. 1945.]

'Red Cross'

6190 MILENTIJEVICH, ZORAN: *Jevreji zatochenitsi logora Tsrveni Krst* [Jewish inmates of the camp 'Red Cross']. Nish: Narodni m'zej Nish, 1978. 36 pp., illus., facsims., tabs., bibl., summaries in English, French and Russian. [In Serbian.]

Rees

6191 KRIMP, H. M.: *Razzia, December 1944. Waar bleven onze mannen—'Kamp Rees'*. Overveen: Secretariaat Comite 'Nasorg Kamp Rees', 1947. 53 pp., illus., facsims., mimeog.

Rudolstadt

6192 BARTHEL, KARL: *Die Welt ohne Erbarmen. Bilder und Skizzen aus dem K.Z. Rudolstadt*. Griefenverlag, 1946. 162 pp.

Salaspils

6193 SAUSNITISA, K., ed.: [*In the death camp of Salaspils. Collected reminiscences*]. Riga: Latviskoe Gosudarstvennoe Isd., 1964. 386 pp., illus. [In Russian.]

Skarzysko-Kamienna

6194 FREY, HANS, comp. *Die Hölle von Kamienna*. Berlin-Potsdam: VVN Verlag, 1949. 96 pp., illus.

Sobibor

6195 NOVITCH, MIRIAM: *Sobibor. Martyre et révolte. Documents et témoignages*. Paris: Centre de Publ. Asie Orientale, 1978. 170 pp., illus., bibl.

6196 SZMAJZNER, STANISLAW: *Inferno em Sobibor. A tragédia de um adolescente judeu*. Rio de Janeiro: Bloch, 1968. 307 pp., plans.

Stutthof

6197 DUNN-WASOWICZ, KRZYSZTOF: *Stutthof*. Warszawa: Państwowe Instytut Wyd., 1946. 103 pp.

Terezin Fortress

6198 ALBRECHTOVÁ, GERA: *Čas proti láske. Dennik jednejznás* [Time against love. Diary of one of us]. Bratislava: Obzor, 1966. 177 pp.

6199 *Terezin*. Praha: Naše Vojsko [for] Svaz Protifašistickych Bojovnikù, 1966. [44 pp.], illus. [Text in Czech, Russian, English, German, French, by Táňa Kulišová. Incl. section on Theresienstadt Ghetto.]

Treblinka

6200 AUERBACH, RACHEL: [*On the fields of Treblinka—A report*]. Lodz: Centralna Żydowska Komisja Historyczna, 1947. 109 pp., illus. [In Yiddish.]

6201 GROSSMAN, WASSILI: *Die Hölle von Treblinka*. London: I.N.G. Publications, 1945. 24 pp. [Spanish version: *El infierno de Treblinka*. Buenos Aires: Congreso Judío Mundial (Ejecutivo Sudamericano), 1968.]

6202 NOVITCH, MIRIAM: *La vérité sur Treblinka*. Paris: Presses du Temps Présent, 1967. 134 pp., illus., bibl.

6203 STEINER, JEAN-FRANÇOIS: *Treblinka*. Préface: Simone de Beauvoir. Paris: Fayard, 1966. 395 pp.

6204 WIERNIK, YANKEL: *A year in Treblinka. An inmate who escaped tells the day-to-day facts of one year of his torturous experience*. New York: American Representation of the General Jewish Workers' Union of Poland, [1945]. 46 pp.

Vernet (Le Vernet)

6205 FREI, BRUNO: *Die Männer von Vernet. Ein Tatsachenbericht*. Berlin [East]: Deutscher Militärverlag, 1961. 324 pp.

6206 KOESTLER, ARTHUR: *Scum of the earth*. London: Jonathan Cape, 1941. 255 pp.

Vught (Scheveningen)

6207 DOORN, BOUD van: *Vught. Dertien maanden in het concentratiekamp*. Laren: Schoonderbeek, 1945. 156 pp. [With drawings by Peter Zwart.]

6208 *Vught. Poort van de Hel! Oorlogsherinneringen van 'n Jood*. Hilversum: 'Aldus', 1945. 77 pp.

6209 ZANTEN, GERTH van: *Vught. Het kampen en de mensen*. Amsterdam: Het Nederlandsche Roode Kruis. [197–]. 63 pp., illus., facsims.

Westerbork

6210 MECHANICUS, PHILIP: *In dépot. Dagboek uit Westerbork*. Ingel.: J. Presser. Amsterdam: Polak & van Gennep, 1964. 303 pp. [English version: *Waiting for death. A diary*. London: Calder & Boyars, 1968.]

6211 NIEROP, IS. van & COSTER, LOUIS: *Westerbork. Het leven en werken in het kamp*. 's-Gravenhage: Haagsche Drukkerij en Uitg., 1945. 31 pp.

6212 PRESSER, JACOB: *De nacht der Girondijnen*. Amsterdam: Commissie voor de Propaganda van het Nederlandse Boek, 1957. 84 pp. [Novel about Westerbork. English version: *Breaking point*. Cleveland, Ohio: The World Publ. Co., 1958; German version: *Die Nacht der Girondisten*. Reinbek b. Hamburg: Rowohlt, 1959.]

E. MEDICAL CRIMES

1. GENERAL

'The Medical Case'. *Trials of war criminals ... Vols. 1, 2. See* 5636.

6213 MITSCHERLICH, ALEXANDER & MIELKE, FRED: *Das Diktat der Menschen-
verachtung. Eine Dokumentation.* Heidelberg: Lambert Schneider, 1947.
175 pp. [English version: *Doctors of infamy. The story of the Nazi medical
crimes.* New York: Schuman, 1949. Incl. statements by Andrew C. Ivy,
Telford Taylor and Leo Alexander.]

6214 MITSCHERLICH, ALEXANDER & MIELKE, FRED, eds.: *Medizin ohne Menschlichkeit.
Dokumente des Nürnberger Ärzteprozesses.* Frankfurt a.M.: Fischer
Bücherei, 1960. 296 pp., illus., tabs. [New ed. of *Wissenschaft ohne
Menschlichkeit ...,* 1949, with new introd. English version: *The death
doctors.* London: Elek Books, 1962.]

6215 *Przeglad Lekarski* [Medical Review]. [Special issues on]: 'Oświęcim' [dedicated
to the problems in the field of medicine under Nazi occupation]. Kraków:
1961– Illus., facsims., tabs., graphs, bibls. (Series II).
Rok XVII, 1961, Nr. 1a. 96 pp.
Rok XVIII, 1962. 95 pp.
Rok XIX, 1963. Nr. 1a. 137 pp.
Rok XXI, 1965, Nr. 1. 190 pp.
Rok XXVII, 1971, Nr. 1. 187 pp.

6216 TERNON, YVES & HELMAN, SOCRATE: *Histoire de la médecine SS* ou *Le mythe du
racisme biologique.* Paris: Casterman, 1969. 223 pp., tabs., bibl.

6217 TERNON, YVES & HELMAN, SOCRATE: *Les médecins allemands et le national-
socialisme. Les métamorphoses du Darwinisme.* Tournai: Casterman, 1973.
218 pp., bibl.

2. 'EUTHANASIA'

6218 [BODELSCHWINGH, (Pastor) FRIEDRICH von] PERGANDE, KURT: *Der Einsame von
Bethel. Vater Bodelschwingh und die Geschichte seines Werkes.* Stuttgart:
Der Quell Verlag, 1958. 364 pp., illus. [Incl. the opposition to the Nazis
by the founder's son—Fr. von Bodelschwingh jr.—concerning the
extermination of 'lives not worth living'.]

6218a GRUCHMANN, LOTHAR: 'Euthanasie und Justiz im Dritten Reich'. [In]
Vierteljahrshefte für Zeitgeschichte, 20. Jhrg., 3. Heft, Juli 1972.
Pp. 235–279.

HADAMAR
6219 *The Hadamar trial. Trial of Alfons Klein* [and six others]. Ed.: Earl W. Kittner.
London: Hodge, 1949. 250 pp. ['Euthanasia' of Russian and Polish slave
labourers with tuberculosis.]

6220 HERMANN, ALFRED: *Die Mordkiste von Hadamar. Eine Erzählung aufgrund authentischer Dokumente und wahrer Begebenheiten.* Dortmund: Ruhr-Donau Verlag, 1961. 46 pp., illus., facsims., bibl.

6221 HASE, HANS CHRISTOPH VON, ed.: *Evangelische Dokumente zur Ermordung der 'unheilbar Kranken' unter der nationalsozialistischen Herrschaft in den Jahren 1939–1945.* Hrsg. im Auftr. von 'Innere Mission und Hilfswerk der Evangelischen Kirche in Deutschland'. Stuttgart: [1964]. 128 pp., bibl.

6222 HONOLKA, BERT: *Die Kreuzelschreiber. Ärzte ohne Gewissen. Euthanasie im Dritten Reich.* Hamburg: Rütten & Loening, 1961. 157 pp.

6223 MENGES, JAN: *'Euthanasie' in het Derde Rijk.* Akademisch proefschrift [pres. to] Universiteit van Amsterdam. Haarlem: Bohn, 1972. ix + 188 pp., tab., bibl., summaries in German, English, French.

6224 NOWAK, KURT: *'Euthanasie' und Sterilisierung im Dritten Reich. Die Konfrontation der evangelischen und katholischen Kirche mit dem 'Gesetz zur Verhütung erbkranken Nachwuchses' und der 'Euthanasie' Aktion.* 2. Aufl. Göttingen: Vandenhoeck & Ruprecht, 1980. 221 pp. [Enl. version of a dissertation, Leipzig 1971.]

6225 PLATEN-HALLERMUND, ALICE: *Die Tötung Geisteskranker in Deutschland. Aus der Deutschen Ärztekommission beim amerikanischen Militärgericht (Leiter Dr. Alexander Mitscherlich).* Frankfurt a.M.: Verlag der Frankfurter Hefte, 1948. 131 pp.

6226 SCHMIDT, GERHARD: *Selektion in der Heilanstalt 1939–1945.* Geleitw.: Karl Jaspers. Stuttgart: Evangelisches Verlagswerk, 1965. 151 pp.

6227 SERENY, GITTA: *Into that darkness. From mercy killing to mass murder.* London: André Deutsch, 1974. 379 pp., illus., maps, bibl.

3. MEDICAL EXPERIMENTS

6228 BAYLE, FRANÇOIS: *Croix gammée contre caducée. Les expériences humaines en Allemagne pendant la deuxième guerre mondiale.* Neustadt (Pfalz): Imprimerie Nationale, 1950. 1521 pp., illus. [A fully documented account.]

6229 BERNADAC, CHRISTIAN: *Les médecins maudits. Les expériences médicales humaines dans les camps de concentration.* Paris: Éds. France-Empire, 1967. 288 pp., bibl.

6230 *Inter-Allied conferences on war medicine, 1942–1945.* Convened by the Royal Society of Medicine. Hon. Ed.: Henry Letheby Tidy. London: Staples Press, 1947. 531 pp., illus. [Incl. medical experiments and XII: 'German concentration camps: conditions of liberated and displaced persons'.]

6231 MENKES, G. and others: *Cobayes humaines. Enquête de trois médecins suisses dans les bagnes nazis.* [By] G. Menkes, R. Hermann, A. Miège. Genève: Éds. Trois Collines, 1946. 99 pp., illus.

6232 URIS, LEON: *QBVII*. London: Corgi Books, 1972. 447 pp. [First ed. 1971. Novel about medical experiments on Jews in concentration camps.]

Individual camps

AUSCHWITZ

6233 KAUL, F. K.: *Ärzte in Auschwitz*. Mit Unterstützung von Winfried Matthäus im Rahmen der Arbeit des Instituts für zeitgenössische Rechtsgeschichte bei der Juristischen Fakultät der Humboldt-Universität zu Berlin. Berlin [East]: VEB Verlag Volk und Gesundheit, 1968. 337 pp., illus., tabs., graph.

6234 NYISZLI, MIKLOS: 'SS Obersturmführer Docteur Mengele. Journal d'un médecin déporté au crematorium d'Auschwitz' [In] *Les Temps Modernes*, VI, Nos. 65/66, Mars–Avril 1951. Paris. [Transl. from the Hungarian.]

6235 TRUCK, BETTY & ROBERT-PAUL: *Médecins de la honte. La vérité sur les expériences médicales pratiquées à Auschwitz*. Paris: Presses de la Cité, 1975. 188 pp., illus., tab., bibl.

BUCHENWALD

6236 POLLER, WALTER: *Arztschreiber in Buchenwald. Bericht des Häftlings 996 aus Block 39*. Hamburg: Phönix-Verlag Christen, 1947. 236 pp., illus. [English version: *Medical Block, Buchenwald. The personal testimony of Inmate 996, Block 36*. London: Corgi Books, 1965. Second German ed.: Offenbach a.M.: Verlag Das Segel, 1960.]

RAVENSBRÜCK

6237 *Beyond human endurance. The Ravensbrück women tell their stories*. Warsaw: Interpress Publ., 1970. 181 pp., illus. [Transl. from the Polish.]

6238 MACHLEJD, WANDA, ed.: *Experimental operations on prisoners of Ravensbrück concentration camp*. Poznań: Wyd. Zachodnie, 1960. 58 pp.

SACHSENHAUSEN

6239 SZALET, LEON: *Experiment 'E'. A report from an extermination laboratory*. New York: Didier, 1945. 284 pp.

SKARZYSKO-KAMIENNA

6240 BAUMINGER, ROZA: *Przy pikrynie i trotylu*. Kraków: 1946. 62 pp. [Medical experiments in a Jewish slave labour camp in Poland.]

F. FORCED LABOUR

6241 BILLSTEIN, AUREL: *Fremdarbeiter in unserer Stadt 1939–1945. Kriegsgefangene und deportierte 'fremdvölkische Arbeitskräfte' am Beispiel Krefelds*. Frankfurt a.M.: Röderberg, 1980. 195 pp., tabs., bibl.

6242 EVRARD, JACQUES: *La déportation des travailleurs français dans le IIIe Reich*. Paris: Fayard, 1972. 460 pp., illus., facsims., bibl.

6243 FERENCZ, BENJAMIN B.: *Less than slaves. Jewish forced labor and the quest for compensation*. Forew.: Telford Taylor. Cambridge, Mass.: Harvard University Press, 1979. 249 pp. [Incl. I.G. Farben, Krupps, Siemens.]

[FLICK, FRIEDRICH] OGGER, GÜNTER: *Friedrich Flick der Grosse.* See 3632.

6244 [I.G. FARBEN] DUBOIS, JOSIAH E. & JOHNSON, EDWARD: *Generals in grey suits. The directors of the 'I.G. Farben' cartel—their conspiracy and trial at Nuremberg.* London: The Bodley Head, 1953. 373 pp. [Much of the book deals with I.G. Farben's use of slave labour.]

6245 KANNAPIN, HANS-ECKHARDT: *Wirtschaft unter Zwang. Anmerkungen und Analysen zur rechtlichen und politischen Verantwortung der deutschen Wirtschaft unter der Herrschaft des Nationalsozialismus im Zweiten Weltkrieg, besonders im Hinblick auf den Einsatz und die Behandlung von ausländischen Arbeitskräften und Konzentrationslagerhäftlingen in deutschen Industrie- und Rüstungsbetrieben.* Köln: Deutsche Industrieverlag, 1966. 334 pp., tabs., bibl.

6246 LANGE, HORST: *REIMAHG—Unternehmen des Todes. Der Aufbau der deutschen faschistischen Luftwaffe—Rolle des Gustloff-Konzerns— Verbrechen an ausländischen Zwangsarbeitern im unterirdischen Flugzeugswerk 'Reimahg' bei Kahla, 1944/1945.* Jena: Rat des Kreises, 1969. 164 pp., illus., diagrs., plans, tabs., facsim., bibl.

6247 ŁUCZAK, CZESŁAW, comp.: *Położenie polskich robotników przy musowych w Rzeszy, 1939–1945* [The situation of Polish forced labour workers in the Reich, 1939–1945]. Poznań: Instytut Zachodni, 1975. cvi + 355 pp., facsims., tabs., summaries in Russian, English, German. [Text of documents in German.]

6248 PASZOWSKI, K.: *Pruszkow 1944.* Poznań: Spoldzielna Wyd. 'Czytelnik', 1944/45. 34 pp. [Pruszkow transit camp for Poles, most of whom were sent on to Germany for forced labour.]

6249 SIJES, B. A.: *De arbeidsinzet. De gedwongen arbeid van Nederlanders in Duitsland, 1940–1945.* 's-Gravenhage: Nijhoff, 1966. 730 pp., illus., facsims., tabs., diagrs., bibl., summary in English. (Rijksinstituut voor Oorlogsdocumentatie).

6250 UNITED NATIONS RELIEF AND REHABILITATION ADMINISTRATION (UNRRA): *Foreign workers in Germany. A report based on official German sources.* 2nd ed., rev. to November 1, 1944. UNRRA, European Regional Office, Displaced Persons Division, December 1944. 84 pp., mimeog.

6251 VOS, JEAN de: *I was Hitler's slave.* As related to Richard Baxter. London: Quality Press, 1942. 122 pp. [A Belgian worker.]

6252 WEISSMANN KLEIN, GERDA: *All but my life.* New York: Hill & Wang, 1957. 246 pp. [A young Polish girl in Nazi slave labour camps.]

6253 ZENTRALE STELLE DER LANDESJUSTIZVERWALTUNGEN: *Sonderbehandlung der in den deutschen Gebieten eingesetzten Zivilarbeiter und Kriegsgefangenen wegen Verstosses gegen die ihnen auferlegten Lebensführungsregeln.* Ludwigsburg: [196–]. [53 pp.], mimeog.

6254 ZSADANYI, OSZKAR: *Mindenki szolgája. Feljegyzések az Oroszországi es*

502

Ukrajnai munkaszolgálatosok kálvásriájáról [Notes on the calvary of the labour-battalions in Russia and the Ukraine]. Budapest: Molnár, 1945. 152 pp.

G. CHILDREN

6255 BRINGMANN, FRITZ: *Kindermord am Bullenhuserdamm. SS-Verbrechen in Hamburg 45: Menschenversuch an Kindern.* Hrsg.: Arbeitsgemeinschaft Neuengamme für die BRD, Hamburg. Frankfurt a.M.: Röderberg, 1978. 64 pp., illus., facsims., bibl.

6256 *Children in bondage. A survey of child life in the occupied countries of Europe and in Finland.* Conducted by the 'Save the Children' Fund. London: Longmans, Green, 1942. 136 pp., tabs.

6257 DEUTSCHKRON, INGE, ed.: *... denn ihrer war die Hölle. Kinder in Ghettos und Lagern.* Köln: Verlag Wissenschaft und Politik, 1979. 157 pp., illus. (children's drawings). [First ed. 1965.]

6258 GEVE, THOMAS: *Youth in chains.* Jerusalem: Mass, 1958. 262 pp., diagrs. [Memoirs of a childhood in concentration camps.]

6259 HOŘEC, JAROMÍR, ed.: *Deníky dětí Deníky a zápisky z koncentračnich ta borů* [Children's diaries from concentration camps and ghettoes]. Praha: Naše Vojsko-SPB, 1961. 269 pp., illus.

6260 JERUSCHALMI, ELIESER: *Das jüdische Märtyrerkind, nach Tagebuchaufzeichnungen aus dem Ghetto von Schaulen 1941/44.* Darmstadt-Eberstadt: Ökumenische Marienschwesterschaft, 1960. 64 pp., illus. [Transl. from the Hebrew.]

6261 KÜCHLER-SILBERMAN, LENA: *One hundred children.* New York: Doubleday, 1961. 288 pp. [Children rescued in Poland and brought to Israel. Hebrew orig.: Jerusalem: Yad Vashem, 1959. 460 pp., illus.]

6262 KUPER, JACK: *Child of the Holocaust.* London: Routledge & Kegan Paul, 1967. 283 pp.

6263 LOWRIE, DONALD A.: *The hunted children.* New York: Norton, 1963. 256 pp., illus.

6264 NEUMANN, ROBERT: *Children of Vienna.* London: Gollancz, 1946. 159 pp. [German version: *Die Kinder von Wien. Roman.* Einf.: Christine Nöstlinger. Weinheim: Beltz & Gelberg, 1979. First German ed. 1948.]

6265 PAPANEK, ERNST & LINN, EDWARD: *Out of the fire.* New York: Morrow, 1975. 299 pp.

6266 SOSNOWSKI, KIRYŁ: *The tragedy of children under Nazi rule.* Poznań: Zachodnia Agencja Prasowa, 1962. 470 pp., illus., facsims., diagrs., map, tabs., bibl. [Ed.: Wanda Machlejd. Polish title: *Dziecko w systemie hitlerowskim.*]

6267   *Velpke Baby Home trial. Trial of Heinrich Gericke* [and seven others]. Ed.:
George Brand. London: Hodge, 1950. 356 pp. [Home for babies of slave
workers, where most of them died of calculated neglect.]

6268   *Verbrechen an polnischen Kindern 1939–1945. Eine Dokumentation.* Anhang:
'Dokumente deutscher Verwaltung im besetzten Polen'. Hrsg.:
Hauptkommission zur Untersuchung der Naziverbrechen in Polen.
München: Pustet, 1973. 239 pp., illus., facsims., bibl. [Polish orig.: Glowna
Komisja Badania Zbrodni Hitlerowskich w Polsce: *Zbrodnie hitlerowskie na
dzieciach i mlodziezy polskei* ... Warszawa: Wyd. Prawnicze, 1969. Also:
Czesław Pilichowski: *Zbrodnie hitlerowskie* ... Warszawa: (Council for the
Preservation of Monuments to Resistance and Martyrdom), 1972. Incl.
'Sippenhaft'.]

H.   GYPSIES

6269   ADLER, MARTA: *My life with the Gypsies.* London: Souvenir Press, 1960.
204 pp., port. [Nazi persecution, Chs. 11, 12.]

6270   DÖRING, HANS-JOACHIM: *Die Zigeuner im nationalsozialistischen Staat.*
Hamburg: Kriminalistik Verlag, 1964. 231 pp., bibl. (Kriminologische
Schriftenreihe aus der Deutschen Kriminologischen Gesellschaft).

6271   FINGER, OTTO: *Studien an zwei asozialen Zigeunermischlinge-Sippen. Ein
Beitrag zur Asozialen- und Zigeunerfrage.* 2. Aufl. Giessen: Christ, 1937.
67 pp. (Schriftenreihe des Instituts für Erb- und Rassenpflege, Giessen).

6272   JUSTIN, EVA: *Lebensschicksale artfremd erzogener Zigeunerkinder und ihrer
Nachkommen.* Berlin: Schoetz, 1944. 142 pp., tabs.

6273   KENRICK, DONALD & PUXON, GRATTON: *The destiny of Europe's Gypsies.*
London: Chatto–Heinemann, for Sussex University Press, 1972. 256 pp.,
tabs., bibl. [Part II: 'The Nazi period, 1933–1945', pp. 59–84.]

6274   NOVITCH, MYRIAM: *Le génocide des Tziganes sous le régime nazi.* [Paris?]:
Comité pour l'Érection du Monument en Mémoire des Tziganes assassinés à
Auschwitz, [1965?]. 29 pp., illus., facsim., bibl. [Italian version: 'Il genocidio
degli Zigani sotto il regime nazista'. (In) *Quaderni del Centro di Studi sulla
Deportazione e l'Internamente*, Vol. 2, 1965. Roma: Associazione Nazionale
ex Internati.]

6275   SIJES, B. A. and others: *Vervolging van Zigeuners in Nederland, 1940–1945.*
's-Gravenhage: Nijhoff, 1979. 189 pp., tabs., bibl., summary in English.
(Rijksinstituut voor Oorlogsdocumentatie).

6276   STEINMETZ, SELMA: *Österreichs Zigeuner im NS-Staat.* Wien: Europa Verlag,
1966. 64 pp., tabs., bibl. (Schriftenreihe des Dokumentationsarchivs des
österreichischen Widerstandes).

J. HOSTAGES

6277 ARSENIJEVIC, DRAGO: *Otages volontaires des SS.* Paris: Eds. France-Empire, 1974. 363 pp., illus., bibl.

6278 *Geisel- und Partisanentötungen im Zweiten Weltkrieg. Hinweise zur rechtlichen Beurteilung.* Ludwigsburg: Zentrale Stelle der Landesjustizverwaltungen, 1968. 135 pp., bibl., mimeog.

HOSTAGE TRIAL

6279 *The Hostage case. Trials of war criminals ... Vol. 11.* [Murder, deportation and robbery by Germans.] *See* 5636.

6280 ZÖLLER, MARTIN & LESZCZYNSKI, KAZIMIERZ: *Fall 7. Das Urteil im Geiselmordprozess. Gefällt am 19. Februar 1948 vom Militärgerichtshof V der Vereinigten Staaten von Amerika.* Mit einer Einleitung und einer Chronik über den Volksbefreiungskampf in Jugoslawien, Griechenland und Albanien. Berlin [East]: Deutscher Verlag der Wissenschaften, 1965. 250 pp., bibl.

6281 RIJSHOUWER, J. A. H. & WERMESKERKEN, H. van: *Vier jaar Indisch gijzelaar. Buchenwald, Haaren, St. Michielsgestel, Vught, Amersfoort.* 's-Gravenhage: van Hoeve, 1946. 341 pp.

6282 ROEST, PHILIP: *Wij gijzelden. Reportages uit het Kamp 'Beekvliet' te St. Michielsgestel.* 's-Gravenhage: Boucher, 1946. 193 pp., illus.

ROME

6283 ASCARELLI, ATTILIO: *Le Fosse Ardeatine.* [Roma]: Canesi, 1965. 204 pp., illus., facsims. [New ed., first ed. 1945. Nazi murder of hostages in Rome.]

6284 KATZ, ROBERT: *Death in Rome.* London: Cape, 1967. 324 pp., maps, bibl. [Also publ. as *Black Sabbath. A journey through a crime against humanity.* Toronto: Macmillan, 1969.]

K. PRISONERS OF WAR

6285 AITKEN, LESLIE: *Massacre on the road to Dunkirk. Wormhout 1940.* London: Kimber, 1977. 189 pp., illus., maps.

6286 DATNER, SZYMON: *Crimes against POWs. Responsibility of the Wehrmacht.* Warszawa: Zachodnia Agencja Prasowa, 1964. 382 pp., illus., facsims., bibl. [Polish orig.: *Zbrodnie Wehrmachtu na jeńcach wojennch armii regularnych w II Wojniej Światowej.* Warszawa: Wyd. Ministerstwa Obrony Narodowej, 1961.]

6287 JOFFÉ, CONSTANTIN: *Les enterrés vivants du Stalag XVII A.* New York: Éds. de la Maison française, [194–]. 220 pp. [Incl. persecution of Jewish POWs.]

6288 SMITH, SYDNEY: *Wings Day, the man who led the RAF's epic battle in German captivity.* London: Collins, 1968. 252 pp., illus. [Incl. Sachsenhausen, Dachau, Flossenbürg.]

6289 STREIT, CHRISTIAN: *Keine Kameraden. Die Wehrmacht und die sowjetischen Kriegsgefangenen 1941–1945.* Stuttgart: Deutsche Verlags-Anstalt, 1978. 445 pp., facsim., bibl. (Hrsg.: Institut für Zeitgeschichte). [From a dissertation (1977) entitled *Die sowjetischen Kriegsgefangenen als Opfer des nationalsozialistischen Vernichtungskrieg.*]

6290 TROFIMENKO, G.: *Ich war in Deutschland gefangen.* Zürich: Verlag der Partei der Arbeit, 1945. 85 pp., illus. [A Soviet officer in German slave labour camps.]

6291 WILENSKY, M., comp.: *War behind barbed wire. Reminiscences of Buchenwald ex-prisoners of war.* Moscow: Foreign Languages Publ. House, 1959. 155 pp. [Transl. from the Russian.]

L. RESPONSES TO PERSECUTION

1. EXTERNAL PROTESTS AND REACTIONS

6292 ANTI-ISM LEAGUE OF AMERICA: *The anti-Nazi forum.* [New York: 1939]. 64 pp.

6293 BALTHAZAR, DESIDER and others: *Die Gefährdung des Christentums durch Rassenwahn und Judenverfolgung.* Luzern: Vita Nova Verlag, 1935. 70 pp.

6294 BEZIRKSVEREINIGUNG ZÜRICH FÜR DEN VÖLKERBUND: *Stellungnahme gegen Rassenverfolgung. Öffentliche Kundgebung.* Zürich: 1935. 46 pp.

6295 BLACK, WILLIAM HARMAN: *If I were a Jew.* New York: Real Book Co., 1938. 294 pp. [An American denounces the Third Reich after visit to Germany.]

6296 BOARD OF DEPUTIES OF BRITISH JEWS & ANGLO-JEWISH ASSOCIATION: *Disabilities of the Jews in Germany. Report of the protest meeting at the Queen's Hall, 27 June 1933.* London: 1933. 28 pp.

6297 BOARD OF DEPUTIES OF BRITISH JEWS & ANGLO-JEWISH ASSOCIATION (Joint Foreign Committee): *The persecution of the Jews in Germany.* London: April 1933. 51 pp. [Also: *Supplementary Bulletins*, Nos. 1 & 2, May, June 1933.]

6298 BOEGNER, MARC and others: *Discours de protestation contre les atteintes portées en Allemagne à la dignité de la personne humaine, à la liberté de conscience chrétienne et laïque, et aux droits humains et civiques des Israélites.* Préfaces: M. le Chanoine Desgranges, Maurice Dormann. Discours de Marc Boegner, Marcel Déat, Justin Godart, Jacques Hadamard, Paul Reynaud, Julien Weil. Paris: Éds. 'Pour la dignité humaine', 1937. 52 pp.

BOYCOTT CAMPAIGN
6299 JOSEPHUS, pseud.: *Der deutsch-jüdische Krieg.* Wien: [priv. pr.], 1935. 294 pp.

6300 LIBERMAN, KOPEL: 'Le boycottage économique de l'Allemagne'. [In] *Défense économique*, Janvier 1934. Bruxelles. 31 pp.

6301 NON-SECTARIAN ANTI-NAZI LEAGUE TO CHAMPION HUMAN RIGHTS: *Nazis against the world. The counter-boycott is the only defensive weapon against Hitlerism's world threat to civilization. Selected speeches from world leaders of public opinion.* New York: [1934]. 134 pp.

6302 TENENBAUM, JOSEPH: *American investments and business interests in Germany.* New York: Joint Boycott Council, [1939?]. 39 pp.

6303 COMITÉ FRANÇAIS POUR LA PROTECTION DES INTELLECTUELS JUIFS PERSÉCUTÉS: *Protestation de la France contre les persécutions antisémites.* Paris: Lipschutz, 1933. 64 pp., illus. [Report of meeting, 10 May 1933.]

6304 ERRERA, ALFRED: 'La Belgique devant l'Allemagne antisémite'. [In] *Le Flambeau*, May 1934. Bruxelles: Sopel. 39 pp.

6305 FEIN, HELEN: *Accounting for genocide. National responses and Jewish victimization during the Holocaust.* New York: Free Press, 1979. xxi + 468 pp.

6306 *Gdy nienawiść szaleje ... Głosy duchowieństwa chrześcijańskiego* [When fury rages ... Voices of the Christian clergy]. Warszawa: Hoesick, [1937?]. 99 pp.

6307 HARAND, IRENE: *'Sein Kampf'. Antwort an Hitler.* Wien: [priv. pr.], 1935. 347 pp., port. [English version: *His struggle. An answer to Hitler.* Chicago, Ill.: Artcraft Press, 1937; French version: *Son combat. Réponse à Hitler.* Bruxelles/Vienne: 'Gerechtigkeit', 1936.]

6308 *Heidelberg and the universities of America.* New York: Viking Press, 1936. 61 pp., tab. [Refusal of American universities to send representatives to jubilee celebrations of Heidelberg University, because of persecution of 'non-Aryan' and politically suspect staff there.]

6309 HUTCHINSON, PAUL and others: *Naziism vs. civilization. Addresses delivered at a mass meeting held at the Chicago Stadium, December 3rd, 1933, under the auspices of Chicago Committee for the Defense of Human Rights against Naziism.* Chicago, Ill.: [1933]. 30 pp.

6310 JACOB, BERTHOLD and others: *Warum schweigt die Welt?* Paris: Éds. du Phénix, 1936. 64 pp.

6311 *The Jewish Review, VI,* Sept.–Dec. 1933. Eds.: Norman Bentwich, Harry Sacher. London: The Soncino Press. 119 pp., tabs. [Issue on Jews in Germany.]

6312 [LEAGUE OF NATIONS] *La question des Juifs allemands devant la Société des Nations. Au Conseil de la Société des Nations à Genève—Au Congrès de l'Union des Associations pour la Société des Nations à Montreux—A la Conference Internationale du Travail à Genève. Documents divers.* Paris: Rousseau, 1933. 161 pp.

6313 MCDONALD, JAMES G.: *Letter of resignation addressed to the Secretary General of the League of Nations. With an annex containing an analysis of the measures in Germany against 'non-Aryans' and of their effects in creating refugees.* London: 1935. x + 34 pp., tab. [Also publ. in French.]

507

6314 MANN, THOMAS: *Sieben Manifeste zur jüdischen Frage 1936–1948*. Hrsg.: Walter A. Berendsohn. Darmstadt: Melzer, 1966. 97 pp., bibl.

6315 PARLIAMENTARY DEBATES, House of Commons, Vol. 385, No. 17, Dec. 17, 1942: *Jews (German barbarities): United Nations declaration*. London: HMSO.

6316 PINCHUK, BEN-CION: 'Soviet media on the fate of Jews in Nazi-occupied territory, 1939–1941'. [In] *Yad Vashem Studies, Vol. XI*. Pp. 221–233. *See* 5673.

6317 SCHWEIZERISCHES EVANGELISCHES HILFSWERK FÜR DIE BEKENNENDE KIRCHE IN DEUTSCHLAND: *Juden—Christen—Judenkristen. Ein Ruf an die Christenheit*. Zollikon: Verlag der Evangelischen Buchhandlung, 1939. 52 pp.

6318 SHAMIR, HAIM: [*Before the Holocaust. Jews in the Third Reich and Western European public opinion, 1933–1939*]. Tel Aviv: Beit Edot Mordechai Anilevitch, Sifriat Poalim & University of Tel Aviv, 1974. 367 pp., bibl. [In Hebrew.]

6319 SHARF, ANDREW: *The British press and Jews under Nazi rule*. London: Oxford University Press, under auspices of Institute of Race Relations, 1964. 228 pp., bibl.

6320 SINGER, CHARLES: *The Christian approach to Jews*. Slightly enlarged from a memorandum prepared for the International Missionary Council. Forew.: Bishop of Chichester [G. K. A. Bell]. Pref.: H. W. Fox. London: Allen & Unwin, 1937. 30 pp.

6321 SNOEK, JOHAN M.: *The Grey Book. A collection of protests against anti-semitism and the persecution of Jews issued by non-Roman Catholic Churches and church leaders during Hitler's rule*. Introd.: Uriel Tal. Assen: van Gorcum, 1969. 315 pp., bibl.

6322 STEIN, JOSHUA BERTON: *Britain and the Jews of Europe, 1933–1939. Dissertation presented to ... Saint Louis University, 1971*. Ann Arbor, Mich.: University Microfilms, 1978. viii + 386 pp., bibl.

6323 *The voice of religion. The views of Christian religious leaders on the persecution of the Jews in Germany by the National-Socialists*. 2nd printing. New York: American Jewish Committee, 1933. 31 pp.

6324 *Vrede over Israel*. Amsterdam: Ten Have, [1935]. 36 pp. [Speeches at a protest meeting in Amsterdam.]

6325 WORLD ALLIANCE FOR COMBATING ANTI-SEMITISM: *J'accuse!* London: [193–]. 55 pp., illus.

2. ATTEMPTS AT RELIEF AND RESCUE

6326 ADLER, H. G.: *Der Kampf gegen die 'Endlösung der Judenfrage'*. Bonn: Bundeszentrale für Heimatdienst, 1958. 119 pp.

6327 BAUMINGER, ARIEH L.: *Roll of honour*. Jerusalem: Yad Vashem, 1970. 95 pp., illus., facsim., bibls. after each article.

6328 DRUKS, HERBERT: *The failure to rescue*. New York: Speller, 1977. 108 pp., bibl.

6329 [EVIAN CONFERENCE] *Proceedings of the Intergovernmental Committee, Evian, July 6th to 15th, 1938. Verbatim record of the plenary meetings of the Committee. Resolutions and reports.* 57 pp., tabs.

6330 FRIEDMAN, PHILIP: *Their brothers' keepers*. New York: Crown Publs., 1957. 224 pp. [Christians who helped the oppressed escape from Germany and Occupied Europe.]

6331 GUTMAN, YISRAEL & ZUROFF, EPHRAIM, eds.: *Rescue attempts during the Holocaust. Proceedings of the Second Yad Vashem International Historical Conference, Jerusalem, April 8–11, 1974*. Jerusalem: Yad Vashem, 1977. 679 pp., facsims.

6332 HIAS (Hebrew Sheltering and Immigrant Aid Society): *Rescue through emigration 1941*. [New York: 1941]. 62 pp., illus., facsims.

6333 LAQUEUR, WALTER: *The terrible secret. An investigation into the suppression of information about Hitler's 'Final Solution'*. London: Weidenfeld & Nicolson, 1980. 262 pp.

6334 MORSE, ARTHUR D.: *While six million died*. London: Secker & Warburg, 1968. 420 pp., bibl.

6335 SABILLE, JACQUES: *Lueurs dans la tourmente. Épisodes de la lutte pour la défense de Juifs persécutés en Europe du Nord pendant la guerre de Hitler*. Préface: Justin Godart. Paris: Éds. du Centre, 1956. 171 pp., illus. [Holland and Scandinavia.]

6336 THOMAS, GORDON & MORGAN-WITTS, MAX: *Voyage of the damned*. London: Hodder & Stoughton, 1974. 317 pp., illus., maps, bibl. [The refugee ship 'St. Louis'.]

Protestant Churches

GRÜBER, HEINRICH (BÜRO GRÜBER)
6337 GRÜBER, HEINRICH: *Erinnerungen aus sieben Jahrzehnten*. 2. Aufl. Köln: Kiepenheuer & Witsch, 1968. 429 pp., illus.

6338 WECKERLING, RUDOLF, ed.: *Durchkreuzter Hass. Vom Abenteuer des Friedens. Bericht und Selbstdarstellungen*. Berlin: Vogt, 1961. 255 pp. [Incl. Laura Livingstone: 'Aus Deutschlands dunklen Tagen'; Rudolf Schade: 'Pontifex—nicht Partisan'. Both essays are accounts of Pastor Grüber's rescue work.]

6339 HOWARD, ELIZABETH F.: *Across barriers*. Introd.: Henry W. Nevinson. 6th ed. Chigwell: Chigwell Press, 1946. 118 pp. [The work of Quakers in prewar Nazi Germany.]

6340 LUDLOW, PETER: 'The refugee problem in the 1930s: the failures and successes of Protestant relief programmes'. [In] *The English Historical Review, XC,* July 1975, No. CCCLVI. [London]: Longmans. Pp. 564–603.

6341 SCHWEIZERISCHES EVANGELISCHES HILFSWERK FÜR DIE BEKENNENDE KIRCHE IN DEUTSCHLAND: *Soll ich meines Bruders Hüter sein? Weitere Dokumente zur Juden- und Flüchtlingsnot unserer Tage.* Zollikon-Zürich: Evangelischer Verlag, 1944. 108 pp.

Catholic Church

BEALES, A. C. F.: *The Pope and the Jews. See* 1989.

6342 METZLER, G.: *Heimführen werde Ich Euch von überall her. Aufzeichnungen am Rande des Zeitgeschehens.* Wien: Herder, 1959. 214 pp. [Centre of assistance for Catholic 'non-Aryans'. Incl. help for unconverted Jews.]

6343 REUTTER, LUTZ-EUGEN: *Katholische Kirche als Fluchthelfer im Dritten Reich. Die Betreuung von Auswanderern durch den St. Raphaels-Verein.* Recklinghausen-Hamburg: Paulus Verlag (Bitter), 1971. 305 pp., tabs., bibl. (bibl. and notes, pp. 205–305).

3. INDIVIDUAL COUNTRIES

Australia

6344 MACHOVER, J. M.: *Towards a rescue. The story of Australian Jewry's stand for the Jewish cause, 1940–1948.* Sydney, N.S.W.: Australian Jewish Historical Society, 1971. 76 pp., illus.

Bulgaria

6345 *Saving of the Jews in Bulgaria, 1941–1945.* Sofia: State Publishing House 'Septembvri', 1977. [128 pp.], illus., facsims. [By Albert Cohen, Anri Assa.]

Canada

6346 ABELLA, IRVING & TROPER, HAROLD: ' "The line must be drawn somewhere". Canada and Jewish refugees, 1933–1939'. [In] *Canadian Historical* Review, 60, No. 2, 1979. Toronto. Pp. 178–209, bibl.

France

6347 HALLIE, PHILIP: *Lest innocent blood be shed. The story of the village of Le Chambon and how goodness happened there.* London: Michael Joseph, 1979. 291 pp. [How the inhabitants of a Protestant village in Southern France rescued Jewish and non-Jewish refugees between 1940 and 1944. American ed.: New York: Harper & Row, 1979.]

6348 LEBOUCHER, FERNANDE: *The incredible mission of Father Benoît.* Transl. from the French. London: Kimber, 1969. 192 pp. [Father Marie-Benoît smuggled endangered Jews from France into Italy.]

Germany

6349 DAENE, WILHELM: *Ein Werkmeister erzählt. Bericht eines Mannes und einer*

Frau über ihre engagierte Hilfe bei der Rettung von Menschenleben jüdischer Mitbürger in der Zeit der Naziherrschaft. Berlin-Tempelhof: Gustav-Heinemann-Oberschule, 1979. 40 pp., mimeog.

6350 GROSSMANN, KURT R.: *Die unbesungenen Helden. Menschen in Deutschlands dunklen Tagen.* 2. Aufl. Berlin-Grunewald: Arani, 1961. 415 pp., bibl. [First ed. 1957.]

6351 HORBACH, MICHAEL: *Out of the night.* London: Vallentine, Mitchell, 1967. x + 261 pp. [German orig.: *Wenige. Zeugnisse der Menschlichkeit 1933–1945.* München: Kindler, 1964.]

6352 LEUNER, H[EINZ] D[AVID]: *When compassion was a crime. Germany's silent heroes, 1935–45.* London: Wolff, 1966. 164 pp., bibl. [German version: *Als Mitleid ein Verbrechen war. Deutschlands stille Helden ...* Wiesbaden: Limes Verlag, 1966.]

6353 REWALD, ILSE: *Berliner, die uns halfen, die Hitlerdiktatur zu überleben.* Berlin: Landeszentrale für politische Bildungsarbeit, Gedenk- und Bildungsstätte Stauffenbergerstr., 1975. 24 pp., facsims., bibl. [Incl. reprint of 'Wannsee-Protokoll'.]

6354 TUTAEV, DAVID: *The Consul of Florence.* London: Secker & Warburg, 1966. 303 pp., port. [Gerhard Wolf, German consul, saved Jews during the German occupation of Italy. He also prevented military damage to the city and its art treasures.]

6355 ZASSENHAUS, HILTGUNT: *Ein Baum blüht in November. Bericht aus den Jahren des Zweiten Weltkriegs.* Hamburg: Hoffmann & Campe, 1974. 293 pp. [A young German girl who helped Norwegian deportees. English version: *Walls.* London: Blond & Briggs, 1974.]

Great Britain

6356 [BALDWIN, STANLEY (Earl Baldwin of Bewdley)] *Appel de Lord Baldwin.* Paris: Race et Racisme, 1939. 43 pp., illus. (Série: Les pogromes en Allemagne) [A BBC broadcast of 8 December 1938.]

6357 *Conference for the relief of German Jewry. Reports and resolutions.* London: Joint Foreign Committee, 1933. 40 pp.

6358 GOLLANCZ, VICTOR: *'Let my people go'. Some practical proposals for dealing with Hitler's massacre of the Jews and an appeal to the British public.* London: Gollancz, 1943. 32 pp.

6359 [MONTEFIORE, LEONARD G.] STEIN, LEONARD & ARONSFELD, C. C., eds.: *Leonard G. Montefiore, 1889–1961. In Memoriam.* London: Vallentine, Mitchell, for the Wiener Library, 1964. 109 pp., port. [Helped to rescue and educate Jewish children from Central Europe.]

6360 *Nazi massacres of the Jews and others. Some practical proposals for immediate rescue made by the Archbishop of Canterbury* [William Temple] *and Lord Rochester in speeches on March 23rd, 1943, in the House of Lords.* London: Gollancz, 1943. 16 pp.

6361   PARLIAMENTARY DEBATES, House of Lords, Vol. 110, No. 95, 27th July 1938. *Refugee problems. Motion by Bishop of Chichester* [G. K. A. Bell]. London: HMSO. Cols. 1210–1252.

6362   RATHBONE, ELEANOR F.: *Rescue the perishing. A summary of the position regarding the Nazi massacres of Jewish and other victims and of proposals for their rescue. An appeal, a programme and a challenge.* London: National Committee for Rescue from Nazi Terror, 1943. 24 pp.

6363   WASSERSTEIN, BERNARD: *Britain and the Jews of Europe, 1939–1945.* London: Institute of Jewish Affairs, 1979. viii + 389 pp., bibl.

Holland

6364   ADER-APPELS, J. A.: *Een Groninger pastorie in de storm.* Amsterdam: Kirschner, 1949. 366 pp. [Jews hidden from the Nazis by a Dutch clergyman and his wife.]

6365   BOOM, CORRIE ten & SHERRILL, JOHN & ELIZABETH: *The hiding place.* London: Hodder & Stoughton, 1973. 221 pp. [Incl. Ravensbrück.]

CASTLE STANFORD, JULIUS: *Reflections ... See* 3616

Hungary

6366   BISS, ANDREAS: *Der Stopp der Endlösung. Kampf gegen Himmler und Eichmann in Budapest.* Stuttgart: Seewald, 1966. 358 pp., facsims. [English version: *A million Jews to save. Check to the Final Solution.* London: Hutchinson, 1973.]

BRAND, JOEL
6366a   ELON, AMOS: *Timetable. The story of Joel Brand.* London: Hutchinson, 1981. [Documentary novel.]

6367   WEISSBERG, ALEX: *Die Geschichte von Joel Brand.* Köln: Kiepenheuer & Witsch, 1956. 319 pp. + supplement of documents. [English version: *Advocate for the dead. The story of Joel Brand.* London: André Deutsch, 1958. Attempted 'deal' with Nazis to save the lives of some Hungarian Jews.]

KASZTNER, RESZÖ
6368   *Der Kastner-Bericht über Eichmanns Menschenhandel in Ungarn.* Vorw.: Carlo Schmid. München: Kindler, 1961. 368 pp.

6369   ROSENFELD, SHALOM: [*Criminal file 124. The Grünwald–Kastner trial*]. Tel Aviv: Karni, 1955. 470 pp. [In Hebrew.]

6370   LEVAI, JENÖ: *Fehér könyv. Külföldi akciók magyar zsidók mentésére* [White Book. Foreign intervention for the rescue of Hungarian Jewry]. Budapest: Officina, 1946. 174 pp.

Italy

6371 POLIAKOV, LÉON & SABILLE, JACQUES: *Jews under the Italian occupation.* Forew.: Justin Godart. Paris: Éds. du Centre, 1955. 208 pp. [Collection of documents showing Italian resistance to Nazi racial policies. French orig.: Léon Poliakov: *La condition des Juifs en France sous l'occupation italienne.* 1946.]

Poland

6372 BARTOSZEWSKI, WŁADYSŁAW & LEWINÓWNA, ZOFIA, eds.: *Ten jest z ojczyzny mojej. Polacy z pomoca żydom 1939–1945* [This is my fellow countryman. Poles who helped the Jews 1939–1945]. Kraków: Wyd. Znak, 1966. 634 pp., plans, summary in English. [English version: *Righteous among nations. How Poles helped the Jews, 1939–1945.* London: Earlscourt Publs., 1969.]

6373 DATNER, SZYMON: *Las sprawiedliwych* [The forest of the righteous]. Warszawa: Książka i Wiedza, 1968. 115 pp. [Incl. list of Poles executed for helping Jews.]

6374 DAVID, JANINA: *A square of sky, The recollections of a childhood.* London: Hutchinson, 1964. 221 pp. [Saved by nuns who pretended she was a Gentile.]

6375 IRANEK-OSMECKI, KAZIMIERZ: *He who saves one life.* Forew.: Joseph L. Lichten. New York: Crown Publs., 1971. xvi + 336 pp. [Polish orig.: *Kto ratuje jedno życie ... Polacy i Żydzi, 1939–1945* ... London: Orbis, 1968.]

Romania

6376 LAVI, TH.: 'The background to the rescue of Romanian Jewry during the period of the Holocaust'. [In] Bela Vago & George L. Mosse, eds.: *Jews and non-Jews in Eastern Europe.* Pp. 177–186. See 5706.

Scandinavia

6377 VALENTIN, HUGO: 'Rescue and relief activities on behalf of Jewish victims of Nazism in Scandinavia'. [In] *Yivo Annual of Jewish Social Science, VIII.* Pp. 224–251. *See* 5674.

6378 YAHIL, LENI: 'Scandinavian countries to the rescue of concentration camp prisoners'. [In] *Yad Vashem Studies, VI.* Pp. 181–220, facsims. *See* 5673.

Denmark

6379 BERTELSEN, AAGE: *Oktober '43. Oplevelser og tilstande under jodeforfolgelsen i Danmark.* Aarhus: Jydsk Centraltrykkeri's Forlag, 1952. 142 pp. [German version: *Oktober 1943. Ereignisse und Erlebnisse während der Judenverfolgung in Dänemark.* Einl.: Scholem Asch. München: Ner-Tamid-Verlag, 1960. English version: *October '43.* New York: Putnam, 1954. Rescue of Jews from deportation by Danish resistance.]

6380 KLAER, ERLING: *Med Gestapo i kølvandet.* København: Frimodt, 1945. 126 pp. [Author took part in rescue action for Danish Jews and continued with other refugees, finally captured by the Gestapo and sent to Neuengamme.]

6381   YAHIL, LENI: *Test of a democracy. The rescue of Danish Jewry in World War II.*
Jerusalem: Magnes Press, the Hebrew University, Yad Vashem, 1966.
316 + 16 pp., bibl., summary in English. (Publications of the Institute for the
European Jewish Catastrophe). [In Hebrew. English version: *The rescue of
Danish Jewry. Test of a democracy.* Philadelphia, Pa.: Jewish Publication
Society of America, 1969. 536 pp., tabs., bibls. (bibls. and notes,
pp. 422–530).]

Sweden

BERNADOTTE, Count FOLKE: *The curtain falls. Last days of the Third Reich. See*
5112.

WALLENBERG, RAOUL
6382   LEVAI, JENÖ: *Raoul Wallenberg. Regényes élete, hösi küzdelmei, rejtélyes
eltünesenek titka* [Raoul Wallenberg. His romantic life, heroic struggles and
the story of his mysterious disappearance]. Budapest: Magyar Téka, 1948.
327 pp., illus. [Also: *Raoul Wallenberg hjälten in Budapest. Autentisk
skildring av Kungl. Svenska Beskickningens i Budapest. Räddningsaktion
1944–1945.* Stockholm: Saxon & Lindstrom, 1948.]

6383   WULF, JOSEF: *Raoul Wallenberg.* Berlin: Colloquium Verlag, 1958. 95 pp.,
bibl.

Spain and Portugal

6384   LESHEM, PEREZ (Fritz Lichtenstein): 'Rescue efforts in the Iberian peninsula'.
[In] *Leo Baeck Institute Year Book XIV.* Pp. 231–256, illus., facsims. *See*
3536.

Switzerland

6385   BAUER, YEHUDA: ' "Onkel Saly"—die Verhandlungen des Saly Mayer zur
Rettung der Juden 1944/45'. [In] *Vierteljahrshefte für Zeitgeschichte,*
25. Jhrg., 2. Heft, April 1977. Pp. 188–219.

6386   HÄSLER, ALFRED A.: *Das Boot ist voll ... Die Schweiz und die Flüchtlinge
1933–1945.* Zürich: Fretz & Wasmuth, 1967. 364 pp., illus., facsims. [Incl.:
'Der J-Stempel taucht auf', 'Fanal Krystallnacht', 'Beginn der
Todestransporte', 'Bericht aus Gurs', 'Die Tragödie Jochen Kleppers', 'Das
offenbare Sterben', 'Bericht aus Polen'.]

6387   SUTRO, NETTIE: *Jugend auf der Flucht 1933–1948. Fünfzehn Jahre im Spiegel
des Schweizer Hilfswerks für Emigrantenkinder.* Vorw.: Albert Schweitzer.
Zürich: Europa Verlag, 1952. 286 pp., bibl.

United States of America

6388   BAUER, YEHUDA: *My brother's keeper. A history of the Jewish Joint Distribution
Committee, 1929–1939.* Philadelphia, Pa.: Jewish Publication Society of
America, 1974. xi + 350 pp., tabs., bibl. [3: 'Germany 1933–1938'; 5:
'Prelude to the Holocaust'; 6: 'The beginning of the end'.]

6389   COHEN, NAOMI W.: *Not free to desist. The American Jewish Committee,
1906–1966.* Introd.: Salo W. Baron. Philadelphia, Pa.: Jewish Publication

Society of America, 1972. xiii + 652 pp. ['The Nazi fury', pp. 154–192; 'The years of the Holocaust', pp. 227–264.]

6390 DUGGAN, STEPHEN & DRURY, BETTY: *The rescue of science and learning. The story of the Emergency Committee in aid of Displaced Foreign Scholars.* New York: Macmillan, 1948. 214 pp.

6391 FEINGOLD, HENRY L.: *The politics of rescue. The Roosevelt administration and the Holocaust, 1938–1945.* New Brunswick, N.J.: Rutgers State University, 1970. xiii + 394 pp., bibl.

6392 GENIZI, HAIM: 'American non-sectarian refugee relief organisations, 1933–1945'. [In] *Yad Vashem Studies, XI.* Pp. 164–220. *See* 5673.

6393 KOHANSKI, ALEXANDER S., ed.: *American Jewish Conference. Its organization* and *Proceedings of the First Session, Aug. 29–Sept. 2, 1943, New York.* New York: 1944. 407 pp., tabs. [Incl.: 'Symposium on rescue of European Jewry'.]

IX. AFTER THE FALL OF THE THIRD REICH

A. WARTIME PLANNING

6394 BACKER, JOHN H.: *The decision to divide Germany. American foreign policy in transition.* Durham, N.C.: Duke University Press, 1978. viii + 212 pp.

6395 *Handbook for military government in Germany prior to defeat or surrender. (Incorporating revision 1–20 Dec. 1944).* [London?: 1945]. [350 pp. approx.]

6396 HILLER, KURT, ed.: *After Nazism—democracy? A symposium by four Germans.* London: Drummond, 1945. 204 pp. [Other contributors: Walter D. Schultz, Hans Jaeger, Eugen Brehm.]

6397 *Research and Postwar Planning Bibliography, Nos. I–XXII.* New York: Interallied Information Centre (April–Sept. 1942), United Nations Information Office (December 1942–August 1945). 4 vols., mimeog.

6398 ROYAL INSTITUTE OF INTERNATIONAL AFFAIRS: *The problems of Germany. An interim report by a Chatham House study group.* London: Oxford University Press, 1943. 92 pp.

6399 SHARP, TONY: *The wartime alliance and the zonal division of Germany.* Oxford: Clarendon Press, 1975. ix + 220 pp.

B. ESCAPED WAR CRIMINALS

6400 BESIMENSKY, L[EV] A[LEKSANDROVICH]: *[On the trail of Martin Bormann. 2nd ed.].* Moskva: Izd. Politicheskoi Literatury, 1965. 190 pp., illus., facsim. [In Russian. German version: *Auf den Spuren von Martin Bormann.* Berlin [East]: Dietz, 1965.]

6401 BLUM, HOWARD: *Wanted! The search for Nazis in America.* New York: Quadrangle/New York Times Book Co., 1977. 256 pp.

6402 BROCKDORFF, WERNER: *Flucht vor Nürnberg. Pläne und Organisation der Fluchtwege der NS-Prominenz im 'Römischen Weg'.* München-Wels: Welsermühl, 1969. 286 pp., illus., bibl.

6403 FRIEDMANN, TUVIA: *The hunter.* Ed. and transl. by David C. Gross. London: Gibbs & Phillips, 1961. 299 pp.

6404 LEVY, ALAN: *Wanted: Nazi criminals at large.* New York: Berkly, 1962. 175 pp., illus., bibl.

6405 PINTER, ISTVAN & SZABO, LASZLO, eds.: *Criminals at large. Documents.* Budapest: Pannonia Press, 1961. 330 pp. + 16 pp. illus. & facsims.

6406 PLAUEN, E. O.: *Der Galgentanz, eine Morität unseres Jahrhunderts. La danza de la horca.* Buenos Aires: Dürer SRL, 1952. 69 pp., illus. (Sonderheft der Zeitschrift 'Der Weg'). [Cartoons by 'Erik'. Text and cartoons reprinted from 'Das Reich', Berlin 1940/44. Text in German and Spanish.]

6407 STEVENSON, WILLIAM: *The Bormann brotherhood.* London: Barker, 1973. xviii + 344 pp.

6408 SZABÓ, LADISLAO: *Hitler está vivo. Nuevo Berchtesgaden en el Antártico.* Buenos Aires: Ed. El Tabano, 1947. 167 pp., illus., maps.

6409 WIESENTHAL, SIMON: *The murderers among us.* Ed., with a profile of the author, by Joseph Wechsberg. London: Heinemann, 1967. 312 pp., illus., facsims. [Incl. Erich Raja. German version: *Doch die Mörder leben.* München: Droesner, 1967.]

C. EXPULSION OF GERMANS

6410 BÖDDEKER, GÜNTER: *Die Flüchtlinge. Die Vertreibung der Deutschen im Osten.* München: Herbig, 1980. 383 pp., illus., maps, bibl.

6411 BRUSTAT-NAVAL, FRITZ: *Unternehmen Rettung. Letztes Schiff nach Westen.* Herford: Koehler, 1970. 262 pp., illus., facsim., maps, tabs., bibl.

6412 SCHEIDER, THEODOR and others, eds.: *Dokumentation der Vertreibung der Deutschen aus Ost-Mitteleuropa.* Hrsg.: Theodor Scheider, Werner Conze, Adolf Diestelkamp, Rudolf Laun, Peter Rassow, Hans Rothfels. Bonn: Bundesministerium für Vertriebene, Flüchtlinge und Kriegsgeschädigte, 1954/61. 11 vols.
I, 1, 2: *Die Vertreibung der deutschen Bevölkerung aus den Gebieten östlich der Oder-Neisse.* [English version: *The expulsion of the German population from the territories east of the Oder-Neisse line. A selection from Vols. I, 1 and I, 2.*]
I, 3: *Polnische Gesetze und Verordnungen 1944–1955.*
II: *Das Schicksal der Deutschen in Ungarn.*
III: *Das Schicksal der Deutschen in Rumänien.* [English version: *The expulsions of the Germans from Eastern-Central Europe. A selection from Vols. II and III.*]
IV, 1, 2: *Die Vertreibung der deutschen Bevölkerung aus der Tschechoslowakei.* [English version: *The expulsion of the German population from Czechoslovakia. A selection from Vols. IV, 1 and IV, 2.*]
V: *Das Schicksal der Deutschen in Jugoslawien.*

6413 SCHIMITZEK, STANISLAW: *Truth or conjecture? German civilian war losses in the East.* Warszawa: Zachodnia Agencja Prasowa, 1966. 381 pp., maps, facsims., tabs., bibl.

6414 ZAYAS, ALFRED M. de: *Nemesis at Potsdam. The Anglo-Americans and the expulsion of the Germans. Background, execution, consequences.* Forew.:

Robert Murphy. London: Routledge & Kegan Paul, 1977. 268 pp., illus.

6415 ZIEMER, GERHARD: *Deutscher Exodus. Vertreibung und Eingliederung von 15 Millionen Ostdeutschen.* Stuttgart: Seewald, 1973. 246 pp., illus.

D. THE SURVIVORS OF PERSECUTION

1. VICTIMS' ORGANIZATIONS

6416 AXIS VICTIMS LEAGUE: *Round table conferences 1–5.* New York: 1943/45. 4 vols. (An association for restitution and compensation of rights and interests to Axis victims).

6417 BUND DER VERFOLGTEN DES NAZIREGIMES: *Ein Jahr BVN.* Düsseldorf-Gerresheim: 1950. 34 pp.

6418 VEREINIGUNG DER VERFOLGTEN DES NAZIREGIMES: *Bericht von der Delegierten-Konferenz zur Gründung der VVN in der sowjetischen Besatzungszone Deutschlands am 22.–23. Februar 1947 in Berlin.* 83 pp., illus.

2. DISPLACED PERSONS

6419 ALLIED EXPEDITIONARY FORCE: *Displaced Persons registration instructions.* [No place]: June 1944. 299 pp.

6420 *The Displaced Persons. Analytic bibliography. Report of a Special Sub-committee on the Judiciary, House of Representatives.* Washington, D.C.: Government Printing Office, 1950. 82 pp.

6421 INSTITUT FÜR BESATZUNGSFRAGEN: *DP-Problem. Eine Studie über die ausländischen Flüchtlinge in Deutschland.* Tübingen: Mohr (Siebeck), 1950. 201 pp.

6422 *Memo to America: The DP story. The final report of the US Displaced Persons Commission.* Washington, D.C.: Government Printing Office, 1952. 376 pp.

6423 ROBINSON, NEHEMIAH: *Convention relating to the status of stateless persons. Its history and interpretation. A commentary.* New York: Institute of Jewish Affairs, 1955. iv + 161 pp.

6424 UNITED NATIONS RELIEF AND REHABILITATION ADMINISTRATION: *Displaced Persons operation in Europe and the Middle East.* London: UNRRA European Regional Office, Division of Operational Analysis, 1946. 69 pp., tabs., mimeog. (Restricted).

6425 VERNANT, JACQUES: *The refugee in the post-war world. Bibliography.* London: Allen & Unwin, 1953. 827 pp.

3. THE JEWS

6426 AMERICAN INSTITUTE OF INTERNATIONAL INFORMATION: *Report on a remnant of*

Nazi victims—The Jews of Germany. New York: [1948]. 29 pp. [And Supplement: Fred M. Hechinger: *Germany's Nazi legacies.*]

6427 BAUER, YEHUDA: *Flight and rescue: Brichah.* New York: Random House, 1970. x + 369 pp., maps, bibl.

6428 *Central Committee of Liberated Jews in the British Zone, Germany 1945–1947.* [No place]: 1947. 103 pp. [Text in English and German.]

6429 EFROS, ISRAEL: *Heimlose Jidn. A besuch in di jidische lagern in Deitshland.* Buenos Aires: Zentral-farband fun pojlishe Jidn in Argentine, 1947. 249 pp., illus.

6430 GOLLANCZ, VICTOR: *'Nowhere to lay their heads'. The Jewish tragedy in Europe and its solution.* London: Gollancz, 1945. 31 pp.

6431 HARDMAN, LESLIE H.: *The survivors. The story of the Belsen remnant.* Told by Leslie H. Hardman, written by Cecily Goodman. Forew.: Lord Russell of Liverpool. London: Vallentine, Mitchell, 1958. 113 pp., illus. [A Jewish chaplain in Belsen, two days after its liberation.]

6432 JEWISH RELIEF UNIT, LEGAL ADVISER, BAOR: *Legal aspects of Jewish rehabilitation in Germany. Studies and documents.* [No place]: 1946/47. 5 vols.

6433 JÜDISCHE GEMEINDE BERLIN; *Verzeichnis der nach der Befreiung durch die Alliierten in Berlin registrierten Juden, I–III.* Berlin: 1945. 85 + 66 + 64 pp. [In 3 vols.]

6434 LYNX, J. J., ed.: *The future of the Jews. A symposium.* London: Drummond, 1945. 195 pp., [Incl. Otto Lehmann-Russbueldt: 'Should and could the Jews return to Germany?'.]

6435 MAOR, HARRY: *Über den Wiederaufbau der jüdischen Gemeinden in Deutschland seit 1945.* Inaugural-Dissertation [pres. to] Johannes Gutenberg-Universität zu Mainz. 1961. 235 pp., tabs., facsims., lists of congregations.

6436 MENKE, JOHANNES: *Die soziale Integration jüdischer Flüchtlinge des ehemaligen Regierungslagers 'Föhrenwald' in ... Düsseldorf, Frankfurt und München. Nach im Sommer 1959 ... durchgeführten sozialhygienischen Feldstudien über die ehemaligen Lagerinsassen.* Bielefeld: Bergelsmann, 1960. 104 pp., illus., tabs.

6437 RABINOWITZ, DOROTHY: *New lives. Survivors of the Holocaust living in America.* New York: Knopf, 1977. viii + 242 pp.

6437a SYKES, CHRISTOPHER: *Cross roads to Israel.* London: Collins, 1965. 479 pp., illus., bibl. [Incl. immigration from Europe, Anglo-American Conference, etc. Covers period 1917–1948.]

6438 WIESENTHAL, SIMON: *Die Sonnenblume. Von Schuld und Vergebung.* Hamburg: Hoffmann & Campe, 1970. 246 pp. [On whether Jews can forgive those who carried out the Holocaust. English version: *The sunflower. With a symposium.* London: Allen, 1970.]

6439 WILDER-OKLADEK, F.: *The return movement of Jews to Austria after the Second World War. With special consideration of the return from Israel.* The Hague: Nijhoff, 1969. 130 pp., diagrs., tabs., bibl.

4. CHILDREN

6440 BROSSE, THERESE: *War-handicapped children. Report on the European situation.* Paris: UNESCO, 1950. 142 pp.

6441 COLLIS, ROBERT: *The ultimate value.* London: Methuen, 1951. 181 pp., illus. [The rescue of two children from Bergen-Belsen and their mental and physical rehabilitation under the author's care.]

6442 LEMPP, REINHART: *Extrembelastung im Kindes- und Jugendalter, Über psychosoziale Spätfolgen nach nationalsozialistischer Verfolgung im Kindes- und Jugendalter anhand von Aktengutachten.* Bern: Huber, 1979. 158 pp.

6443 MACARDLE, DOROTHY: *Children of Europe. A study of the children of liberated countries. Their war-time experiences, their reactions and their needs. With a note on Germany.* London: Gollancz, 1949. 349 pp., illus. (by Kalman Landau).

6444 WOLFFHEIM, NELLY: 'Kinder aus Konzentrationslagern. Mitteilungen über die Nachwirkungen des KZ-Aufenthaltes auf Kinder und Jugendliche'. [In] *Psychoanalyse und Kindergarten* ... Hrsg.: Gerd Biermann. München: Reinhardt, 1966.

5. LASTING EFFECTS OF PERSECUTION

6445 BAEYER, WALTER Ritter von and others: *Psychiatrie der Verfolgten. Psychopathologische und gutachtliche Erfahrungen an Opfern der nationalsozialistischen Verfolgung und vergleichbarer Extrembelastungen.* [By] Walter Ritter von Baeyer, Heinz Häfner, Karl Peter Kisker. Berlin: Springer, 1964. 397 pp., tabs., diagrs., bibl.

6446 EISSLER, K. R.: 'Die Ermordung von wievielen seiner Kinder muss ein Mensch symptomfrei ertragen können um eine normale Konstitution zu haben?'. [In] *Psyche.* 17. Jhrg., 5. Heft., Aug. 1963. Stuttgart: Klett, Pp. 241–291.

6447 EPSTEIN, HELEN: *Children of the Holocaust. Conversations with sons and daughters of survivors.* New York: Putnam, 1979. 348 pp., bibl.

6448 HELWEG-LARSEN, PER and others: *Famine disease in German concentration camps—Complications and sequels with special reference to tuberculosis, mental disorders and social consequences.* Copenhagen: Munkagaard, 1952. 460 pp., bibl. (Acta Psychiatrica et Neurologica Scandinavica).

INTERNATIONAL AUSCHWITZ COMMITTEE: *Anthology, III.* See 6070.

6449 MICHEL, MAX: *Gesundheitschäden durch Verfolgung und Gefangenschaft und ihre Spätfolgen ... Referate und Ergebnisse der Internationalen Sozialmedizinischen Konferenz über die Pathologie der ehemaligen*

Deportierten und Internierten, 5.–7. Juni 1954 in Kopenhagen ... Frankfurt a.M.: Röderberg, 1955. 382 pp.

6450   NIEDERLAND, WILLIAM G.: *Folgen der Verfolgung: Das Überlebenden-Syndrom. Seelenmord.* Frankfurt a.M.: Suhrkamp, 1980. 244 pp., bibl. [12 individual cases.]

6451   WORLD VETERANS FEDERATION: *International conference on the later effects of imprisonment and deportation.* With the participation of the Netherlands Government, the International Committee of the Red Cross ... and the World Council for the Welfare of the Blind. The Hague, November 20–25, 1961. 189 pp., tabs.

E.   REPARATIONS AND RESTITUTION

6452   ALLIED CONTROL AUTHORITY: *The plan for reparations and the level of post-war German economy. In accordance with the Berlin Protocol.* Berlin: Control Commission for Germany (British Element), 1946. 35 pp., tabs. [Incl.: 'Report of the Tripartite Conference of Berlin, 1945'. (Potsdam Conference).]

6453   BLESSIN, GEORG & GIESSLER, HANS: *Bundesentschädigungsschlussgesetz. Kommentar zu der Neufassung des BEG.* München: Beck, 1967. 1162 pp. [Also Nachtrag, 1969.]

6454   CONFERENCE ON JEWISH MATERIAL CLAIMS AGAINST GERMANY: *Twenty years later. Activities ... 1952–1972.* New York: [1972?]. 152 pp., tabs.

6455   DAM, H. G. VAN and others: *Wiedergutmachungsgesetze und Durchführungsverordnungen.* [By] H. G. van Dam, Martin Hirsch, Rolf Loewenberg. Berlin: Vahlen, 1966. 400 pp., tabs., diagrs.

6456   HASENACK, WILHELM: *Dismantling in the Ruhr Valley. A menace to European recovery (ERP).* Cologne: Westdeutscher Verlag, 1949. 100 pp.

6457   RATCHFORD, B. U. & ROSS, WILLIAM D.: *Berlin reparations assignment. Round One of the German peace settlement.* Chapel Hill, N.C.: University of North Carolina Press, 1947. 259 pp.

6458   REICHELT, W.-O., comp.: *Die Demontageliste. Eine vollständige Übersicht über die Reparationsbetriebe sowie die amtlichen Erklärungen der Militärbefehlshaber der britischen und USA-Zone.* Hamburg: Drei Türme Verlag, 1947. 47 pp. [Incl. lists of factories involved.]

6459   ROBINSON, NEHEMIAH: *Indemnification and reparations. Jewish aspects.* New York: Institute of Jewish Affairs of the American Jewish Congress and World Jewish Congress, 1944. 302 pp., bibl.

6460   SCHWARZ, WALTER: *Rückerstattung nach den Gesetzen der Alliierten Mächte.* München: Beck, 1974. xxv + 394 pp., tabs. (Die Wiedergutmachung nationalsozialistischen Unrechts durch die Bundesrepublik Deutschland, Bd. 1).

F. OCCUPATION AND REHABILITATION OF GERMANY

6461 BALFOUR, MICHAEL: 'Four-power control in Germany and Austria, 1945–1946. I: Germany'. [In] *Survey of International Affairs, 1939–1946*. Pp. 1–265. *See* 3889.

BUNDESMINISTER FÜR VERTRIEBENE ...: *Dokumente deutscher Kriegsschäden* ... *See* 4897.

6462 CONSTANTINE of BAVARIA, Prince: *After the flood*. Transl. from the German. London: Weidenfeld & Nicolson, 1954. 215 pp.

DENAZIFICATION

6463 FITZGIBBON, CONSTANTINE: *Denazification*. London: Michael Joseph, 1969. 222 pp.

6464 NIETHAMMER, LUTZ: *Entnazifizierung in Bayern. Säuberung und Rehabilitierung unter amerikanischer Besatzung*. Frankfurt a.M.: Fischer, 1972. 710 pp., bibl.

6465 SALOMON, ERNST VON: *Der Fragebogen*. Reinbek b. Hamburg: Rowohlt, 1951. 808 pp. [English version: *The answers to the 131 questions in the Allied Military Government 'Fragebogen'*. London: Putnam, 1954.]

6466 EBSWORTH, RAYMOND: *Restoring democracy in Germany. The British contribution*. Forew.: Robert Birley. London: Stevens, 1960. 222 pp.

6467 FRIEDMAN, W.: *The Allied Military Government of Germany*. London: Stevens, under auspices of London Institute of World Affairs, 1947. 362 pp., tabs., bibl.

6468 *Germany reports*. Introd.: Konrad Adenauer. 3rd ed., brought completely up to date. [Bonn]: Press and Information Office of the Federal Government, 1961. 917 pp., illus., diagrs., tabs., maps. [Reports on all aspects of Western Germany from the collapse onward.]

6469 GOLLANCZ, VICTOR: *Leaving them to their fate. The ethics of starvation*. London: Gollancz, 1946. 48 pp.

6470 MANN, ANTHONY: *Comeback. Germany, 1945–1952*. London: Macmillan, 1980. 229 pp., illus., maps.

6471 MERRITT, ANNA J. & RICHARD L., eds.: *Public opinion in Occupied Germany. The OMGUS surveys 1945–1949*. Forew.: Frederick W. Williams. Urbana, Ill.: University of Illinois Press, 1970. 328 pp., graphs.

6472 NETTL, J. P.: *The Eastern Zone and Soviet policy in Germany, 1945–1950*. London: Oxford University Press, 1951. 324 pp., tabs., charts.

RE-EDUCATION

6473 FAULK, HENRY: *Group captives. The re-education of German prisoners of war in Britain, 1945–1948*. London: Chatto & Windus, 1977. 233 pp., tabs., graphs.

6474　HOCKING, WILLIAM ERNEST: *Experiment in education—what we can learn from teaching Germany*. London: Allen & Unwin, 1954. 303 pp. [Denazification and re-education in the US Zone.]

6475　RICHTER, WERNER: *Re-educating Germany*. Transl. from the German. Chicago, Ill.: University of Chicago Press, 1945. 227 pp.

6476　RESSING, KARL-HEINZ: *Briefe aus der Quarantäne. Ein junger Deutscher an seine Freunde in Frankreich*. Hamburg: von Hugo, 1946. 103 pp.

6477　SANDULESCU, JACQUES: *Hunger's rogues. On the Black Market in Europe, 1948*. New York: Harcourt, Brace, Jovanovich, 1974. 280 pp. [Chiefly on Germany.]

6478　TÜNGEL, RICHARD & BERNDORFF, HANS RUDOLF: *Auf dem Bauche sollst Du kriechen ... Deutschland unter den Besatzungsmächten*. Hamburg: Wegner, 1958. 428 pp.

G.　GERMAN VIEWS OF THE THIRD REICH

1.　GENERAL

6479　BRÜDIGAM, HEINZ: *Wahrheit und Fälschung. Das Dritte Reich und seine Gegner in der Literatur seit 1945. Versuch eines kritischen Überblicks*. Frankfurt a.M.: Röderberg, 1959. 93 pp.

EDUCATION OF CHILDREN

6480　GLASER, HERMANN & STRAUBE, HARALD: *Nationalsozialismus und Demokratie. Ein Arbeitsbuch zur Staatsbürgerlichen Bildung*. München: Bayerischer Schulbuch-Verlag, 1961. 128 pp., illus., maps.

6481　HAGEMANN, ERNST: *Der Nationalsozialismus. Ein didaktischer Entwurf*. [Hanover]: Niedersächsische Landeszentrale für Politische Bildung, 1965. 148 pp., bibl. (... Für die Hand les Lehrers).

6482　MEYERS, PETER & RIESENBERGER, DIETER, eds.: *Der Nationalsozialismus in der historisch-politischen Bildung*. Göttingen: Vandenhoeck & Ruprecht, 1979. 218 pp.

6483　FUTTERKNECHT, FRANZ: *Das Dritte Reich im deutschen Roman der Nachkriegszeit. Untersuchungen zur Faschismustheorie und Faschismusbewältigung*. 2. Aufl. Bonn: Grundmann, 1980. 342 pp.

HITLER, ADOLF

6484　BOSSMANN, DIETER, ed.: *'Was ich über Adolf Hitler gehört habe ...'. Folgen eines Tabus: Auszüge aus Schüler-Aufsätzen von heute*. Frankfurt a.M.: Fischer, 1977. 359 pp.

6485　FEST, JOACHIM C. & HERRENDOERFER, CHRISTIAN: *Hitler, eine Karriere*. Frankfurt a.M.: Ullstein, 1977. 189 pp., illus. (Bildband zum grossen Dokumentarfilm).

6486 [FEST, JOACHIM C.] BERLIN, J. and others, eds.: *Was verschweigt Fest? Analysen und Dokumente zum Hitler-Film von J. C. Fest.* Köln: Pahl-Rugenstein, 1978. 217 pp., illus.

6487 KALOW, GERT: *The shadow of Hitler: a critique of political consciousness.* Transl. from the German. London: Rapp & Whiting, 1968. xii + 144 pp. [German orig.: *Hitler—das deutsche Trauma.* München: Piper, 1974.]

6488 KEMPOWSKI, WALTER, comp.: *Haben Sie Hitler gesehen? Deutsche Antworten.* Nachw.: Sebastian Haffner. München: Hanser, 1973. 118 pp.

6489 KEMPOWSKI, WALTER: *Haben Sie davon gewusst? Deutsche Antworten.* Nachw.: Eugen Kogon. Hamburg: Knaus, 1979. 148 pp., map [of KZ's.]

6490 LANG, DANIEL: *A backward look. Germans remember.* New York: McGraw-Hill, 1979. 112 pp., illus.

6491 SCHALL, PAUL: *Politik—die Schwäche der Deutschen.* Stuttgart: Fink, 1963. 78 pp. [4: 'Die unbewältigte Vergangenheit'.]

6492 VOGT, HANNAH: *Schuld oder Verhängnis? Zwölf Fragen an Deutschlands jüngste Vergangenheit.* Frankfurt a.M.: Diesterweg, 1961. 251 pp., illus., maps, facsims. [English version: *The burden of guilt. A short history of Germany, 1914–1945.* Transl.: Herbert Strauss. Introd.: Gordon A. Craig. London: Oxford University Press, 1965.]

6493 WAGENER, HANS, ed.: *Gegenwartsliteratur und Drittes Reich. Deutsche Autoren in der Auseinandersetzung mit der Vergangenheit.* Stuttgart: Reclam, 1977. 342 pp., bibl.

6494 ZMARZLIK, HANS-GÜNTER: *Wieviel Zukunft hat unsere Vergangenheit? Aufsätze und Überlegungen eines Historikers vom Jahrgang 1922.* München: Piper, 1970. 281 pp., bibl.

2. APOLOGISTS

6495 GRABERT, HERBERT: *Hochschullehrer klagen an. Von der Demontage deutscher Wissenschaft.* 2. vergr. Aufl. Göttingen: Göttinger Verlagsanstalt, 1952. 93 pp.

6496 HÄRTLE, HEINRICH: *Die Kriegsschuld der Sieger. Churchills, Roosevelts und Stalins Verbrechen gegen die Menschlichkeit.* Göttingen: Schütz, 1966. 341 pp., illus., facsims., map, bibl.

6497 KERN, ERICH, pseud. of Erich Knud Kernmayr: *Opfergang eines Volkes. Der totale Krieg.* Göttingen: Schütz, 1962. 389 pp., illus., bibl.

6498 LUTZ, HERMANN: *'Verbrecher-Volk' im Herzen Europas? Die Wahrheit in der Geschichte ist unteilbar wie Deutschland.* Tübingen: Schlichtenmayer, 1959. 304 pp., illus., facsims., bibl.

6499 Roth, Heinz: *Wieso waren wir Väter Verbrecher? Auf der Suche nach der Wahrheit.* 3. unveränd. Aufl. Odenhausen/Lumda: [priv. pr.], 1972. 171 pp., bibl.

6500 Sündermann, Helmut: *Das Dritte Reich. Eine Richtigstellung in Umrissen.* Erw. Neuaufl. Leoni a. Starnberger See: Druffel, 1964. 252 pp.

H. AFTER THE HOLOCAUST
1. POSTWAR GERMANY

6501 Bier, Jean-Paul: *Auschwitz et les nouvelles littératures allemandes.* Bruxelles: Éds. de l'Université de Bruxelles, 1979. 232 pp. (Centre national des Hautes Études Juives).

6502 Hammerstein, Franz von & Törne, Volker von: *10 Jahre Aktion Sühnezeichen.* Berlin: Lettner, 1968. 64 pp.

'Holocaust' (film)

6503 Härtle, Heinrich: *Was 'Holocaust' verschweigt. Deutsche Verteidigung gegen Kollektivschuld-Lügen.* Leoni am Starnberger See: Druffel, 1979. 94 pp.

6504 Märthesheimer, Peter & Frenzel, Ivo, eds.: *Im Kreuzfeuer: Der Fernsehfilm 'Holocaust'. Eine Nation ist betroffen.* Mitarb.: Hellmuth Auerbach, Walter H. Pehle. Frankfurt a.M.: Fischer, 1979. 332 pp., illus., tabs., bibl.

6505 Zentner, Christian: *Anmerkungen zu 'Holocaust'. Die Geschichte der Juden im Dritten Reich.* München: Delphin Verlag, 1979. 144 pp., illus., bibl.

6506 Schlink, Basilea: *Israel—mein Volk.* Darmstadt-Eberstadt: Ökumenische Marienschwesterschaft, 1958. 142 pp. [Head of a non-sectarian order dedicated to atonement for Germany's crimes against the Jews.]

6507 Stohr, Martin and others, eds.: *Erinnern, nicht vergessen. Zugänge zum Holocaust.* Hrsg. … im Auftr. der Arbeitsgemeinschaft Juden und Christen beim Deutschen Evangelischen Kirchentag. München: Kaiser, 1979. 178 pp., facsims.

See also 3559–3594: many local and regional histories also include chapters on the fate of their Jewish communities

2. DENIAL

6508 Algazy, Joseph: *The summary of the 'Final Solution' and the literature denying the Holocaust.* In appendices: 'The "Korherr File" and selected excerpts from the "Anti-Holocaust" literature'. Treatise [pres. to] Tel Aviv University. 1979. 9 + 190 pp., tabs., facsims., bibl., summary in English. [In Hebrew.]

6509 Arndt, Ino & Scheffler, Wolfgang: 'Organisierter Massenmord an Juden in nationalsozialistischen Vernichtungslagern. Ein Beitrag zur Richtigstellung apologetischer Literatur'. [In] *Vierteljahrshefte für Zeitgeschichte*, 24. Jhrg., Heft 2, 1976. Pp. 105–135.

6510 BUTZ, ARTHUR R.: *The hoax of the twentieth century.* Richmond, Sy.: Historical Review Press, [1975]. 315 pp., illus., maps, tabs., bibl. [German version: *Der Jahrhundertbetrug.* Same publs., 1977. Transl.: Elspeth Schade, Udo Walendy.]

6511 CHRISTOPHERSON, THIES: *Die Auschwitz-Lüge. Ein Erlebnisbericht.* 5. unveränd. Aufl. Mohrkirch: Kritik-Verlag, 1973. 62 pp. [English version: *Auschwitz.* Richmond, Sy.: Historical Review Press, [197–]. 'There were no gas chambers! Only fumigation chambers for delousing clothes'.]

6512 HARWOOD, RICHARD: *Six million lost and found.* Richmond, Sy.: Historical Review Press, [197–]. 28 pp. [Orig. title: *Did six million really die?* German title: *Starben wirklich sechs Millionen?*]

6513 KLARSFELD, SERGE, ed.: *The Holocaust and the neo-Nazi mythomania.* [Comprising]: Joseph Billig: 'The launching of the "Final Solution"'; Georges Wellers: 'The existence of gas chambers, the number of victims and the Korherr report'. New York: Beate Klarsfeld Foundation, 1978. xvii + 215 pp., port., facsims., tabs. [Richard Korherr compiled statistics of 'resettled' Jews for Himmler.]

RASSINIER, PAUL: *Le mensonge d'Ulysse. See* 6130.

6514 ROSENTHAL, LUDWIG: *'Endlösung der Judenfrage': Massenmord oder 'Gaskammerlüge'? Eine Auswertung der Beweisaufnahme im Prozess gegen Hauptkriegsverbrecher vor dem Internationalen Militärgerichtshof Nürnberg von 14. Nov. 1945 bis 1. Okt. 1946.* Darmstadt: Verlag Darmstädter Blätter, 1979. 145 pp., illus. [Against the apologists.]

6515 SCHEIDL, FRANZ J.: *Die Wahrheit über die Millionenvergasung von Juden.* Wien: [priv. pr., 196–]. 256 pp. (Geschichte der Verfemung Deutschlands).

6516 SUZMAN, ARTHUR & DIAMOND, DENIS: *Six million did die. The truth shall prevail.* Johannesburg: South African Jewish Board of Deputies, 1977. 117 pp., illus., map.

6517 WALENDY, UDO: *Forged 'war crime' photos malign German people!* Transl. from the German. Vlotho/Weser: Verlag für Volkstum und Zeitgeschichtsforschung, 1979. 80 pp., illus. [Also: *Forged war crimes.* Richmond, Sy.: Historical Review Press, 197–.]

3. RELIGIOUS AFTERMATH

6518 *Auschwitz als Herausforderung für Juden und Christen.* Heidelberg: Lambert Schneider, 1980. 661 pp., bibl. [Hrsg.: Günther B. Ginzel. Incl.: 'Kirchliche Dokumente zum Verhältnis von Juden und Christen', 'Theologie nach Auschwitz'.]

6519 *Beten nach Auschwitz. Texte und Modelle für Gottesdienst und Gemeindefeiern zum Gedenken an den Holocaust (Buss- und Bettag)*. Stuttgart: Radius-Verlag, 1980. 64 pp.

6520 Brenner, Reeve Robert: *The faith and doubt of Holocaust survivors.* New York: Free Press (Macmillan), 1980. xiii + 266 pp., bibl.

6521 Fleischner, Eva, ed.: *Auschwitz: beginning of a new era? Reflections on the Holocaust.* New York: The Catholic Church of St. John the Divine, 1974. xviii + 468 pp.

Gutteridge, Richard: *Open thy mouth for the dumb! See* 1817.

6522 Knopp, Josephine, ed.: *International theological symposium on the Holocaust, Oct. 15–17, 1978.* Philadelphia, Pa.: National Institute on the Holocaust, 1979. v + 134 pp. [Also: *International Conference on the lessons of the Holocaust, Oct. 18–20, 1978.* v + 228 pp.]

6523 Oesterreicher, Johannes: *Auschwitz, der Christ und das Konzil.* Meitingen b. Augsburg: Kyrios Verlag, 1964. 51 pp. [On Vatican II.]

527

INDEX

Aachen—*See* Aix-la Chapelle
Abegg, Lily, 4606
Abel, Heinz, 1566
Abel, Karl-Dietrich, 2763
Abel, Theodore, 129, 137
Abel, Werner, 2482
Abella, Irving, 6346
Abendroth, Hans-Henning, 4382
Abetz, Otto, 5504
Abitz-Schultze, Thaddäus, 2921
Abshagen, Karl Heinz, 1188, 3338, 3489, 3915
Absolon, Rudolf, 4696, 4697, 4710
Abwehr—*See* Secret Service
Abyssinia, 4080, 4081
Accoce, Pierre, 5141
Achenbach, O. R., 927
Achilles-Delmas, F., 700
Ackermann, Josef, 3241
Ackermann, Konrad, 2826
Action française, 325
Ádám, Magda, 4160
Adam, Uwe Dietrich, 2416, 5661
Adamic, Louis, 5299
Adenauer, Konrad, 6468
Ader-Appels, J. A., 6364
Aders, Gerhard, 4861
Adler, Dr., 1574
Adler, H. G., 3555, 5604, 5946, 5947, 6061, 6326
Adler, Marta, 6269
Adler-Rudel, S., 3662
'Adolf-Hitler-Schulen', 2258, 2272
Adolph, Walter, 2010
Agero, Juan, 4446
Agnoletti, Giovanni, 5511
Agnoli, Johannes, 1185
agriculture, 555, 556, 1663–1681, 2227, 2378, 2745—*See also* Peasantry
laws relating to, 1663, 1689
Agthe, M., 490
Ahle, Michael, 2001
'Ahnenerbe', 3208, 3209
Aigner, Dietrich, 4243
Ainsztein, Reuben, 5675, 5889

air force, German, civil, 4848, 4849, 4851, 4853, 4855–4857
military—*See* Luftwaffe
air-raid defence, German, 2328, 4854
Aitken, Leslie, 6285
Aix-la-Chapelle, 940, 3559
Akademie für die Rechte der Völker, 3992
Akademisches Auskunftsamt, 2390
Akerman, Anatol, 3767
'Aktion Grün', 2450
'Aktion Reinhardt', 5863, 5868
'Aktion Sühnezeichen', 6502
Aktuhn, Hans, 3968
Albani, Johannes, 1776
Albania, 5227, 5274–5277, 6280
Albert, Erwin, 3638
Albinsky, J., 5773
Albort, Schmuel, 5903
Albrecht, Dieter, 1975
Albrecht, Friedrich Wilhelm, 1999
Albrecht, Gerd, 2717
Albrecht, Gertrud, 2357
Albrecht, Karl Heinz, 970
Albrecht, Wolfram, 2527
Albrechtová, Gera, 6198
Alcock, Antony Evelyn, 4077
Aldag, Peter, 3100, 3110, 3153
Aldouby, Zwi, 5718
Aleff, Eberhard, 1129
Alexander, Leo, 6213
Alexander, Lucie, 2130
Alexander, Michael Graf, 3111
Aley, Peter, 2164
Alff, Wilhelm, 3535
Alfieri, Dino, 4060
Algazy, Joseph, 6508
Algeria, Jews of, 5815
Alkil, Niels, 5570
Allach concentration camp, 6003
Allainmat, Henry, 6159
Allard, Paul, 3038, 5450
Allard. Sven, 4396
Alldeutscher Verband, 160
Alleau, René, 279
Allen, William Sheridan, 917, 1024

Allgemeiner Deutscher Beamtenbund, 1010
Alliance chrétienne arienne, 245
Alliance Israélite Universelle, 251
Allied Control Authority, 6452
Allied Expeditionary Force, 6419
Allport, Gordon W., 3085
Alperin, A., 5917
Alsace-Lorraine, 4238, 4239, 5467–5471, 6160
Alt, Karl, 3285
Altenhofer, Ludwig, 2450
Altensteig, G., 850
Alter, Reinhard, 2550
Altgelt, Ingeborg, 1454
Althaus, Paul, 1857
Altmann, Peter, 3415
'Altmark', 4923, 4924
Altmeyer, Karl Aloys, 2807
Altrichter, Friedrich, 4716–4718
Aman, Bruno, 438
Amann, Gustav, 4607
Ambelang, Hermann, 4641
Ambrière, Francis, 5448
Ambrosi, Dominique, 605
Ameln, Heinz, 1735
American Federation of Polish Jews, 5703
American Historical Association, 50, 55
American Institute of International Information, 6426
American Jewish Committee, 3534, 6323, 6389
American Jewish Conference, 6393
American Jewish Joint Distribution Committee, 5977, 6388
Amerikadeutscher Volksbund, 4541
Amersfoort concentration camp, 6059, 6060, 6119, 6124, 6281
Amery, Julian, 5275
Amery, L. S., 4026, 4265
Amin-al-Husseini (Ex-Mufti), 4590–4593
Ammann-Aarau, Hektor, 1176
Amt Schrifttumspflege, 2591, 2592, 3647
An die Dunkelmänner unserer Zeit, 1849, 1850, 1853
Anacker, Heinrich, 2580, 3179
Anatoli (Kuznetzow), A., 5891
Anderbrügge, Klaus, 562
'Andere Deutschland, Das', 2585, 3300, 3396, 3413
Anderlahn, Hanns, 3180
Anderle, Alfred, 5040
Anderman, W. Th., 4654

Anders, Günther, 3799
Anders, Wilhelm, 5137
Anders, Wladyslaw, 5080, 5084
Andersch, Alfred, 3357
Andersen, Hanns, 465
Andersen, Lale, 2695
Andics, Hellmut, 203
Andrae, Friedrich, 2593
Andreas-Friedrich, Ruth, 3325
Andreevsky, Alexander, 2640
Andrejew, W., 3001
Andren, Greta, 3692
Andrews, Wayne, 262
Andrzejewski, Jerzy, 5985
Anfuso, Filippo, 4061, 5505
Angebert, Jean-Michel, 280
Angell, Norman, 2225
Anger, Walter, 43
Angles, Marcel, 6164
Anglo-American Conference, 6437a
Anglo-German Academic Bureau, 4244
Anglo-German naval treaty 1935, 4258
'Anglo-German Review', 4254
Anglo-Jewish Association, 3533, 6296, 6297
'Angriff, Der', 782, 2812a–2815
animal welfare, 1467, 1468, 1490
Anrich, Eduard, 2221
Anrich, Ernst, 2221
Ansbacher, H. L., 513
Ansel, Walter, 4938
Antelme, Robert, 6098
'Anti Europa', 308, 4075
Anti-Ism League of America, 6292
Antikomintern, 478, 484, 1084, 2991, 3100, 4098, 4383, 5041
Anti-Nazi, Der, 1011
'Antisemitische Korrespondenz', 223
anti-Semitism: general, 78, 150, 151, 203, 205, 207
anti-Semitism, German: general, 59, 78, 151, 204, 206, 282, 416–437, 2165–2167, 2424
    economic, 448, 451, 455, 456, 547, 2573
    political, 208–214, 547, 557, 1014—*See also* 'Jewish world conspiracy'
    racial, 215–224, 438–446, 2173
    religious and moral: general, 151 225–237, 441, 444, 459–467, 1259, 2560
        Jewish criminality, 450, 465–467, 573
    social and cultural, 238–249, 447–458, 478, 481, 482, 547, 588, 590–592,

2413, 2431, 2547, 2636, 2670, 2701, 2710, 2715, 2723, 2725–2729, 2734, 2753, 3002

Antonescu, Ion, 3176, 4171

Antoni, E., 6002

Antonius, Peter, 281

Antwerp, Jews of, 5778

Apenszlak, Jacob, 5859

'Appeasement', 1644, 1655, 3904, 4188, 4217, 4252, 4269, 4536

Appelius, Mario, 4961

Appelman, Herman, 3542

Appuhn, Charles, 728

Arabs—See Middle East

Arad, Yitzhak, 5768

Arbeitsdienst—See Reichsarbeitsdienst

Arbeitskreis für Wehrforschung, 4633, 4713, 4745, 4760, 4945

Arbeitskreis 'Zweiter Weltkrieg', 4623

Arbeitsmaiden—See Reichsarbeitsdienst (women)

Arbeitsrecht—See workers, laws relating to

Archimbaud, Léon, 4242

architecture, National Socialist, 594, 2645–2662

Archiv, Das, 16

Archiv Peter, 3503

Archiv für Wohlfahrtspflege, 1441

Arciniegas, Germán, 4519

Ardennes offensive, 5096–5098, 5530

Arendt, Hannah, 150, 5719–5721, 6067

Arendt, Paul, 936

Aretin, Erwein von, 3463

Aretin, Karl Otmar von, 877, 3463

Aretz, Jürgen, 1696a

Argenti, Philip P., 5280

Argentina: general, 4559, 4562, 4563
German economic relations with, 1646, 1647
'Volksdeutsche', 4558, 4560, 4561

'Argentinisches Tageblatt', 4557

Armand, Louis, 5481

armed forces, German: general, 2850, 3072, 3231, 3865, 3870, 3877, 4102, 4696–4960
generals, 3485–3487, 3511, 3514, 3833, 3840, 3846, 3847, 4740, 4741, 4743–4753, 4757, 4758, 4763–4791 4799, 5636
laws relating to, 1459, 4696, 4702, 4703, 4815
military justice—See under courts of law

officer corps, 3467–3469, 3473, 3512, 3516–3521, 3832–3834, 4716, 4717, 4720, 4728, 4742, 4756, 4799, 4803
in politics, 3832–3848
resistance, 3464, 3465, 3467–3469, 3472–3475, 3482–3487, 3489–3495, 3497, 3504, 3506–3521, 3524–3526 5270
strategic theories, 4731–4739, 4859
training and indoctrination of, 4716–4730
in World War II, 4698–4700, 4703, 4705–4708, 4710, 4713, 4719, 6286, 6289—See also Oberkommando der Wehrmacht

'Armia krajowa' (Home Army), 5395, 5397, 5405, 5407

Armstrong, John A., 5435

army, German: general, 3843, 3844, 4697, 4700, 4701, 4704, 4706, 4712, 4714, 4715, 4722, 4725, 4792–4822
foreign contingents, 4835–4847
paratroops, 4807–4809
pioneers, 4811, 4812
tanks, 4706, 4766, 4767, 4770, 4816–4822, 4832, 4833, 4843, 5014, 5038, 5050, 5081

Arnaud, René, 1272

Arndt, Ino, 6509

Arnheim, Franz, 5226

Arnheim, Rudolf, 2738

Arnhem, Battle of, 5551

Arnhold, Karl, 1697, 1722, 2364

Arnim, Brigitte von, 2087

Arnim, Herbert von, 1263

Arnim, Max, 3

Arnold, Heinz Ludwig, 2567

Arnold, Herbert, 2290

Arnold, Ilse, 2358

Arnot, R. Page, 1590

Arns, K., 2301

Arnsberg, Paul, 5720

Aron, Raymond, 5449

Aron, Robert, 5099, 5100, 5454, 5499

Aroneanu, Eugene, 5602

Aronsfeld, C. C., 6359

Aronson, Gregor, 5890

Aronson, Shlomo, 3235, 3261

Arsenijevic, Drago, 6277

art, looted, 5199–5205

artists, anti-Nazi, 2663–2665, 2672, 2674, 2676, 2678, 2681–2683, 2689, 2690
exiled, 3784–3788

arts in the Third Reich: general, 2496, 2610–2621, 2673, 5199
visual arts, 593, 2658, 2663–2694, 4911
See also painters, sculpture, music, literature, etc.
Artom, Emanuele, 5729
Artuccio, Hugo Fernandez, 4552, 4574
Artzt, Heinz, 3210
'Aryanization', 3631–3635
'Aryans', 193–199, 389, 442, 446, 1824, 2027, 2067, 2069, 2071, 2114, 2908
Arzt, Heinz, 1313
Ascarelli, Attilio, 6283
Asch, Scholem, 6379
Aschenauer, Rudolf, 5714, 5845
Ash, William, 5276
Ashton-Gwatkin, Frank T., 3889
Asmussen, Hans, 1871
Assa, Anri, 6345
Assel, Hans-Günther, 2145
Asser-Kramer, Gertrud, 2058
Assisi, 5512
Assmann, Kurt, 4621
Assmus, Burghard, 2002
Association des Déportées et Internées de la Résistance, 6181
Association of Lithuanian Jews in Germany, 5903
Astel, Arnfrid, 5927
Aster, Sidney, 4286
Astrup, Helen, 5585
'Athenia', 3126, 4952
athletics—*See* sport
Atkins, H. G., 587
'Atlantic Wall', 5101, 5102
Attanasio, Salvator, 1179
Aubin, Hermann, 1171
Auckland, R. G., 3068, 3078, 3079
Auerbach, Hellmuth, 6504
Auerbach, Rachel, 6200
'Aufartung' (incl. 'Aufnordung', 'Aufrassung'), 188, 241, 411, 1492, 2888
'*Aufbau*', 3744
Aurich, Peter, 4509
'Ausbürgerung', 1357, 3714
Auschwitz-Birkenau concentration camp: general, 3596, 5229, 5399, 5686, 5730, 5739, 5747, 5816, 5840, 5853, 6002, 6003, 6008, 6032, 6042, 6053–6055, 6061–6086, 6132, 6215, 6501, 6511, 6518, 6519, 6521, 6523
medical experiments in, 6233–6235
museum, 6081–6083

Auslandsorganisation der N.S.D.A.P., 3997, 3998, 4442
Ausschuss für Deutsche Einheit, 854
Australia, 4287, 6344
Austria: general, 344, 1108, 2845, 4113, 5092–5094, 6461
'Anschluss', 683, 1510, 1639, 2872, 4110–4112, 4124–4139, 5249
Church, Catholic, 4115, 4117, 5222
Church, Evangelical, 1907
exiles from, 3708, 3719
N.S.D.A.P., 4118–4123
Austria, occupied: general, 1294, 1331, 1389, 1488, 1684, 5247–5257
Communist Party, 5261
intellectuals, 5252
Jews, 210, 1443, 3659, 4139, 5757, 5764, 6439
persecution, 5263–5265, 5269, 6276
resistance, 3297, 3502, 5227, 5258–5263, 5266–5270
See also Ostmark
Auswärtiges Amt, 3106, 3144, 3881, 3886, 3921, 4295, 4338, 4421, 4510, 4894, 4992, 5678
archives, 3878, 3885, 4416
Autarky in Third Reich, 516, 1581–1589, 1639, 3896
'Autobahnen', 1760–1764
Auty, Phyllis, 5310
Avenol, Joseph, 3945
Avnon, Arieh, 5968
awards in Third Reich, 1296–1299, 4710, 4826
Axelrod, Sidney, 3046
Axis, The, 4060–4082, 4520, 4677, 5191, 5285
Axis Pacts, 4083–4089
Axis Victims' League, 6416
Axmann, Artur, 2372
Aziz, Philippe, 5483

Baade, E.-G., 4763
Baade, Fritz, 4823
Babi Yar, 5891, 5892
Bach, August, 3932
Bach, Hans, 1682
Bacher, Fritz, 4875
Backe, Herbert, 1495, 1663, 5175
Backer, John H., 6394
Bad Buchau, 3322
Bade, Wilfrid, 894, 1130, 2176, 3181, 4642, 4965

Baden, 140, 941, 3323, 6053
Baden-Württemberg, 3560, 3561, 6044
Baeck, Leo, 1834, 3563
Baedeker, Karl, 5382
Bähr, Hans W., 4698
Bähr, Rudolf, 2501
Bähr, Walter, 4698
Bährens, Kurt, 3990
Baer, E. Fritz, 1666
Bässler, Hans, 1487
Bästlein, Bernhard, 3338
Bäumler, Alfred, 814, 2146, 2739, 2866
Baeyer, Alexander von, 2815
Baeyer, Walter von, 414, 6445
Bagel-Bohlan, Anja E., 1765
Bahne, Siegfried, 1113
Bahnsen, Uwe, 723
Bahr, Richard, 4140
Bahrdt, Hans Paul, 238
Baier, Helmut, 1889, 1953
Baillie-Stewart, Norman, 3080
Baird, J. W., 3081
Bajer, Hans, 938
Baker, Leonard, 3563
Bakker, G., 355
Balberyszski, M., 5960
Baldwin, Hanson W., 3849
Baldwin, Stanley (Earl Baldwin of Bewdley), 6356
Balfour, Michael, 3027, 3379, 6461
Balint, Nicholas G., 5343
Balk, Theodor, 4048
Balkan and Danubian States: general, 4140–4155
    Germans, expulsion of, 6412
    Jews of, 5671
    Third Reich and, 1648–1652, 4144, 4149, 4151, 4152
    in World War II, 5032–5039, 5088, 5271–5274
    See also individual countries
Ball, Adrian, 4511
Ball-Kaduri, Kurt Y(J)akob, 3564, 3663, 3664
Ballhaus, Jolanda, 5174
Ballhorn, Franz, 6170
Balthazar, Desider, 6293
Baltic States: general, 1988, 4182–4184, 5368–5371
    'Volksdeutsche', 4181, 4183, 4185–4187, 5214
    See also individual countries
Baltzan, P., 5855

Balzer, Karl, 3385, 3484
Bamberg, 2214
Banaszczyk, Eugeniusz, 4886
Banaszkiewicz, Jakub, 130
Banat, 4147, 4172, 5898
Bang, Paul, 493
Bangert, Otto, 524, 2040
Banjica concentration camp, 5899
Bank für Deutsche Industrie-Obligationen, 1668
'Banker, The', 1496
Bannister, Sybil, 1225
Banse, Ewald, 340, 356, 3864
Barabbino, Carlo, 362
Baranov, 5856
Baravalle, Robert, 4027
'Barbarossa'—See World War II: Campaigns in Soviet Union, German
Barcikowski, Wacław, 6108
Bardua, Heinz, 4917
Bareth, Karl, 2273
Barfod, Jørgen, 5579
Bargatzky-Bericht, 5200
Bargen, Bendix von, 4786
Barkai, Avraham, 524a
Barkai, Meyer, 5904
Barkhausen, Hans, 2964a
Barlach, Ernst, 2663, 2664
Barnes, Harry Elmer, 4467, 4478
Barnett, Correlli, 4813
Baron, Heinrich, 4238
Baron, Salo W., 6389
Barrès, M., 2305
Barrès, Philippe, 1025
Barros, James, 3945
Barsam, Richard Meran, 125
Bartelmas, Eugen Frieder, 2177
Bartels, Adolf, 183, 215, 447, 499, 2545–2547
Bartelski, Lesław, 5425
Barth, Hans Martin, 3350
Barth, Karl, 1915, 1930, 1956
Barth, Karl (Dr. rer. pol.), 1559
Barthel, Karl, 6192
Barthel, Ludwig Friedrich, 2553
Barthel, Max, 1189
Bartlett, F. C., 2936
Bartlett, Vernon, 1226
Bartling, K., 1627
Bartolai, Sante, 6150
Bartošek, Karel, 5348
Bartoszewski, Władysław, 5396, 6372
Bartsch, Georg, 3283
Bartsche, Heinz, 2074

Bartz, Karl, 4290, 4862
Basaldua, Pedro de, 5458
Basch, Antonin, 1648
Basil, Fritz, 1168
Basle Centre for Economic and Social Research, 1506
Basler, Werner, 5040
Bassarek, Artur, 4339
Basse, Gertrud T., 2738
Basse, Wilfried, 2738
Bassenge, Friedrich, 596
Bastian, Gert, 3210
Bastit, Laurence, 5645
Bathe, Rolf, 4981, 5032
Battaglia, Roberto, 5506
Battle of Britain, 4886–4893
Baubin, Alfred, 4120
Baudissin, Wolf Graf von, 3506
Baudot, Marcel, 4613
Bauduin, Fernand, 5516
Bauer, Alfred, 2718
Bauer, Eddy, 4816
Bauer, Elvira, 2165
Bauer, Franz, 171
Bauer, Günther, 1790
Bauer, H. H., 4028
Bauer, Hans, 808
Bauer, Helmut, 5033
Bauer, Robert, 4212
Bauer, Wilhelm, 17
Bauer, Yehuda, 5647, 6079, 6385, 6388, 6427
Baum, Bruno, 6151
Baum, E., 4686
Baum, Herbert, 3688
Baum, Marie, 2561
Baum, Walter, 3464, 4939
Baum group, 3685, 3688
Baumann, Erhard, 2547
Baumann, Gerhard, 2937
Baumbach, Werner, 4863
Baumböck, Karl, 481
Baumecker, Otto, 1684
Baumgärtner, Raimund, 1847
Baumgart, Winfried, 57
Bauminger, Arieh L., 6327
Bauminger, Roza, 6240
Baumont, Maurice, 3890, 4456
Baur, Erwin, 400
Bausch, Hans, 1144
Bavaria: general, 131, 1059, 1173, 1581, 3324, 5121
  churches, 1889, 1913, 1957, 1958

Jews, 1173, 3562, 3584
  and N.S.D.A.P., 117, 683, 942–944
  postwar, 6464
  resistance, 3463, 3466
  See also Munich, Franconia
Bavaud, Maurice, 3258
Baxter, Richard, 3262, 6251
Bayer, Ernst, 3182
Bayerische Versicherungskammer München, 2696
Bayerischer Landesverband für Wanderdienst, 1264
Bayerisches Staatsministerium des Innern, 1264
Bayerisches Staatsministerium für Unterricht und Kultus, 1173
Bayerlein, Fritz, 4757, 4764, 4779
Bayle, François, 3211, 6228
Bayles, William D., 606
Bayliss, Gwyn M., 4612
Baynes, Norman H., 741
Bayreuth, 5131
Beales, A. C. F., 1989
'Beamtenrecht'—See bureaucracy, laws relating to
Beau, Georges, 5239
Beauvoir, Simone de, 6203
Bech, Joseph, 4995
Becher, Johannes R., 3798
Beck, Christoph, 2305
Beck, Dorothea, 3505
Beck, Friedrich Alfred, 309, 972, 2222, 2403
Beck, Ludwig, 3485–3487
Beck, R., 1055
Beck, Robert, 3999
Becker, Heinz, 1358
Becker, Jakob, 4168
Becker, Wolfgang, 2719
Beckmann, Joachim, 1856, 1884, 1916
Beddie, James Stuart, 4422
Bednarz, Władysław, 6108
Beek, Gottfried zur, pseud., 297
Beer, Helmut, 3347
Beer, Willy, 4999
Behaghel, Georg, 5365
Behn, Joachim, 1350
Behrend, Hans, 1590
Behrend, Rahel (Behrend-Rosenfeld, Else R.), 3615
Beier-Lindhardt, Erich, 2168
Beimler, Hans, 6112
Beitl, Richard, 2518

'Bekennende Kirche'—See Church, Confessional
Bekker, Cajus D., 4864, 4925, 4926
Belach, Helga, 2720
Belgian Ministry of Foreign Affairs, 4298
Belgian Ministry of Information, 5528
Belgium: general, 683, 3879, 4298–4305, 6304
  Flemish movement, 3990, 3996
  invasion of, 4992, 4993, 5010, 5014
Belgium, occupied: general, 4837, 5516–5522
  churches, persecution and resistance of, 5222, 5519
  Jews of, 5689, 5773–5779
  persecution and resistance, 5227, 5267, 5523–5530
  underground press, 5236, 5528, 5529
  workers, 5518, 5520, 6251
Belina, Josef, 5319
Bell, George Kennedy Allen (Bishop of Chichester), 1934, 5589, 6320, 6361
Bellanger, Claude, 5495
Belling, Curt, 2734
Beloff, Max, 3208
Below, Nicolaus von, 705
Belster, Hans, 2223
Belz, Willi, 3327
Belzec extermination camp, 5399, 5407, 5860, 6041, 6087, 6088
Ben Elissar, Eliahu, 3891
Ben Gershom, Esra, 3617
Benary, Albert, 4699
Benckiser, Nikolas, 3286
Bender, Hans, 4031
Bender, Roger James, 1296, 1299
Bendiscioli, Mario, 1791, 2041
Benedetti, E. Anacleto, 5508
Benedicta a Cruce, Sister—See Stein, Edith
Beneš, Edvard, 4483, 4489
Beneš, Vojta, 4205
Beneschofsky, Ilona, 5842
Benkel, K., 2313
Benn, Gottfried, 2548–2551
Bennecke, Hans-Joachim, 2883
Bennecke, Heinrich, 252, 1101, 3183
Bennett, Benjamin, 4029
Bennett, Jeremy, 3039
Bennett, Ralph, 5103
Benoist-Méchin, J., 4554, 4792
Benoît, Father, 6348

Bensel, Rolf, 4920
Bentin, Lutz-Arwed, 533
Bentley, E. R., 3811
Bentwich, Norman, 6311
Benz, Wolfgang, 36, 4038
Benze, Rudolf, 2147
Benzing, Richard, 2256
Benzinger, Josef, 2909
Beradt, Charlotte, 3299
Berben, Paul, 6113
Berber, Friedrich, 3884, 3892, 4245
Berber, Fritz, 3884, 3933
Berchtold, Josef, 634
Berendsohn, Walter A., 3765–3768, 6314
Berendt, Erich F., 2340
Berensmann, Wilhelm, 363
Berenstein, T., 5857
Berg, Jan, 1993
Berg, Mary, 5969
Berg, Rudolf, pseud.—See Klagges, Dietrich
Bergander, Götz, 4900
Bergaust, Erik, 4683
Bergen-Belsen concentration camp, 6003, 6047, 6089–6095, 6431, 6441
Bergengruen, Werner, 2820
Berger, Alexander, 1826
Berger, Erich, 945
Berger, Friedrich, 2079
Berggrav, Eivind (Bishop), 1956, 5589
Berghahn, Volker R., 1124, 4719
Berglund, Gisela, 3745
Bergmann, Alexander, 1487
Bergmann, Ernst, 163, 577, 2042
Bergmann, Karl Heinz, 3743
Bergschicker, Heinz, 4622
Bergwitz, Hubertus, 5507
Berle, Adolf A., 120
Berlin: general, 1161, 1432, 1441, 2638, 2646, 2894, 2902, 6457
  and education, 2264, 2388
  Handelshochschule, 2390
  Jews of, 455, 473, 3557, 3563, 3564, 3607, 3619, 3688, 5671, 6353, 6433
  'Kampfjahre', 945–947, 1162, 2789, 2974, 3181, 3187, 3198
  persecution and resistance, 2011, 2012, 2034, 3325, 3326
  Staatliche Museen, 2687
  university, 2390, 2427
  in World War II, 4655, 4656, 4895, 4897, 5124–5130
Berlin, J., 6486

Berliner Akademie für ärztliche Fort-
bildung, 1432
'*Berliner Illustrirte Zeitung*', 2815
'*Berliner Lokalanzeiger*', 2816
'*Berliner Tageblatt*', 2789, 2817
'*Berliner Volkszeitung*', 2574
Bernadac, Christian, 1827, 6003, 6152,
6229
Bernadotte, Count Folk, 5112
Bernard, André, 3213
Bernard, Etienne, 5480
Bernard, Henri, 3300, 4378, 4613, 5220,
5779
Bernard, Jean, 6123
Bernard, Jean-Jacques, 6111
Bernard, Tristan, 6131
Berndorff, Hans Rudolph, 1050, 6478
Berndt, Alfred-Ingemar, 16, 121, 1131,
1582, 2365, 2850, 4817
Bernett, Hajo, 2864, 2865, 3683
Bernhard, Marianne, 2684
Bernhardi, Dietrich, 200
Bernhardt, Walter, 3965
Bernheim Petition, 3671, 3672
Berning, Cornelia, 2502
Bernsee, Hans, 4657
Bernstein, Herman, 298
Bernstein, J., 5970
Bernstein, Leon, 5965
Bernstein, Mordecai W., 5963
Bernstorff, Albrecht, 3358
Bernus, Pierre, 3893
Bertelsen, Aage, 6379
Berthold, Werner, 3769
Berthold, Will, 4927, 5526
'Berufsschulen', 2374–2380
Berufswettkampf aller schaffenden Deut-
schen, 2442
Besgen, Achim, 3247
Bessarabia, 4168
Besson, Waldemar, 975, 1144
Best, Karl Rudolf Werner, 1342, 3273,
3274, 5571
Best, S. Payne, 5142
Beste, Niklot, 1937
Bes(z)ymenski, Lew, 721, 833, 4740,
5042, 6400
Bethell, Nicholas, 4962
Bethge, Eberhard, 1917, 1919, 1920
Bethge, Friedrich, 2712
Bethge, Hermann, 649
Bethge, Martin, 4599
Bétourné, René, 5194

Bettelheim, Bruno, 6004
Betze, Hans-Walther, 2734
Betz, Werner, 2502
Beucler, André, 622
Beuer, Gustav, 5320
Beukema, Herman, 4020
Beumelberg, Werner, 4384
Beuth, W., 1698
Bevan, Aneurin, 5230
Beyer, Justus, 563
Beyer, Rudolf, 1490, 1540, 1560, 1707,
2784
Beyer, Valentin, 2374
Beyer, Wilhelm Raimund, 3360
Beyerchen, Alan D., 2417
Beyerlein, Kurt, 2665
Bezirksvereinigung Zürich. . ., 6294
Bezwinska, Jadwiga, 6062
Biallas, Hans, 1723, 1736
Bialystock Ghetto, 5689, 5915, 5916
Bible, the, 193, 2049, 2060, 2069, 2071,
2909, 3116
revision of, 440, 2068
See also New Testament and Old
Testament
Bibliographie des jüdischen Buches, 3675
Bibliographie zur Zeitgeschichte, 63
Bibliothek für Zeitgeschichte, 65, 66, 4945
Bibliothèque Nationale (Paris), 5496
Bidault, Georges, 5472
Bie, Richard, 2474
Biedrzynski, Richard, 2697
Bielefeld, 948
Bier, Jean-Paul, 6501
Bierbaum, Max, 2019
Biermann, Otto, 3977
Biernat, Karl Heinz, 3326, 3419, 3443
Bierschenk, Theodor, 4325
Bigot, Hervé, 2489
Billeter, Erika, 3784
Billig, Joseph, 3556, 5603, 5715, 5799,
5800, 6005, 6513
Billinger, Karl, 650, 6006
Billstein, Aurel, 3341, 6241
Binder, Gerhart, 2013
Binding, Karl, 187
Binding, Rudolf G., 2552, 2553
Bingham, J. K. W., 5028
Binion, Rudolph, 701
Biquard, Pierre, 5480
Bird, Eugene K., 5641
Bird, Keith W., 3832
Birenbaum, Halina, 5730

536

Birkenfeld, Wolfgang, 1594, 1775
Birkett, Norman, 4281
Birley, Robert, 3399, 6466
Birolli, Z., 2612
Bischöfliches Ordinariat, Berlin, 2034
Bischoff, Erich, 2043
Bischoff, Ralph F., 2475
Bischoff, Willi, 1041
Bise, Pierre, 1227
'Bismarck', 4927
Bismarck, Otto von, 169, 170, 182
Biss, Andreas, 6366
Bissinger, Edgar, 1616
Bistrova, V. E., 5436
Bitolj, 5900
Bitter, F. W., 3934
Bitterli, Urs, 3824
Biuletyn głownej komisji badania zbrodni hitlerowskich w Polsce, XXVI, 5858
Björkman, Walther, 4576
Blaas, Siegfried, 364
Black, Robert, 1118
Black, William Harman, 6295
Blaedel, Nic, 4457
Blaese, Ernst, 1379
Blättler, Franz, 5391
Blaich, Fritz, 1497
Blank, Manfred, 5623
Blanke, Bernhard, 1185, 1422
Blankenburg, Paul, 1058, 1498
Blase, F. W., 5556
Blau, Bruno, 1351
Bleichert, Gaston Adolf von, 1542
Blessin, Georg, 6453
Blessinger, Karl, 590
Blet, Pierre, 1988
Bleuel, Hans Peter, 597, 2418, 2433
Bley, Wulf, 481, 757, 4700
'Blitzkrieg', 3971, 4733, 4739, 4804, 4809, 4968, 4977, 4999–5001, 5004, 5006, 5010–5015, 5034
Bloch, Charles, 1102, 1103, 3894
Bloch, Ernst, 1012, 3711
Block, Martin, 492
Blomberg, Werner von, 2330, 3475
Blond, Georges, 5113
Blood-Ryan, H. W., 793, 856
Bloom, Solomon F., 5930
Blucher, Wipert von, 3895
Bludau, Kuno, 1567, 3331
Blüher, Hans, 420, 459, 1811
Blum, Howard, 6401
Blume, Heinrich, 500

Blumenfeld, Erwin, 2476
Blumenson, Martin, 5473
Blumenthal, Nachman, 5710, 5769, 5856, 5893, 5915, 5933, 5971, 5986
Blumentritt, Günther, 4757, 4783
Blunck, Hans Friedrich, 365, 1172, 2554
Board of Deputies of British Jews, 6296, 6297
Boberach, Heinz, 1413, 3255, 3256
Boberski, Günther, 1442
Bocheński, Joseph M., 2741
Bochow, Martin, 4963
Bock, Fedor von, 5061
Bock, Gerhard, 3
Bockelmann, Wilhelm, 557
Bockhoff, E. H., 482, 1323
Bode, Alfred, 2622
Bode, M., 5766
Bodelschwingh, Friedrich von, 6218
Bodelschwingh, Friedrich von, jr., 6218
Bodensieck, Heinrich, 4207
Boder, David, 5731
Boeckel, Otto, 224
Böddeker, Günter, 6410
Bödeker, Elisabeth, 2088
Boegner, Marc, 6298
Boehm, Hermann, 4364
Boehm, Max Hildebert, 4004
Böhme, Kurt W., 5138
Boehnert, Gunnar Charles, 3212
Böhnke, Wilfried, 968
Böhr, Hans, 3054
Boelcke, Willi A., 780, 2838, 3082, 4694
Böll, Heinrich, 3602
Bölling, Rainer, 2245
Bömer, Karl, 3018, 3132
Böök, Fredrik, 1228
Boepple, Ernst, 742
Boeree, Th. A., 5541
Boerlin, Ernst, 4437
Börner, Weert, 3361
Börsenverein der deutschen Buchhändler, 2595
Bösch, Hermann, 3375
Boeschenstein, Hermann, 2525, 4430
Boesler, Felix, 1541
Böttcher, P., 2375
Böttner, Helmut, 4141
Bogaert, André, 3476
Bogatsvo, Jules, 3213
Boger-Eichler, Else, 2089
Bohle, E. W., 4010

Bohley, Erich, 1561
Bohn, Willi, 3354, 3417
Bohnenkamp, Hans, 3380
Bohrmann, Hans, 3455
Bohrmann, Ingeborg, 3455
Boissarie, André, 5602
Bojano, Filippo, 1026
Bojarska, Barbara, 5417
Boldrini, Arrigo, 5227
Boldt, Gerhard, 722
Bolhuis, J. J. van, 5542
Bolitho, Gordon, 1229
Bolivia, 4564
Boller, Hans-Hermann, 1746
Bolliger, Hans, 4438
Bollmus(s), Reinhard, 1265, 2400
Bologna, Sergio, 1872
Bolshevism—See Communism
Bolz, Eugen, 3488
Bona, Kurt, 2332
Bonacina, Giorgio, 4896
Bondy, Louis W., 872
Bongartz, Heinz, 4865
Bonhoeffer, Dietrich, 1834, 1869,
    1917–1923
Bonhoeffer family, 1924
Bonjour, Edgar, 4431
Bonn University, 3823, 3825
Bonnet, Georges, 4500
Bonnin, Georges, 976
Bonté, Florimond, 3712
Boockmann, Hartmut, 34
Boog, Horst, 181
book trade, 2594, 2595, 2603
books: banning and burning of, 2437,
    2598, 2605–2609, 5328
    childrens', 2164–2175
    officially approved, 73, 74, 2591–2593,
        2596, 2597, 2600, 2603, 2604
Boom, Corrie ten, 6365
Boor, Lisa de, 4658
Bor, 5837
Bor, Josef, 5948
Bor, Peter, 4768
Bor-Komorowski, T., 5397
Borch, Herbert von, 1301
Borchsenius, Paul, 5580
Boring, Edwin G., 3085
Bork, Siegfried, 2503
Borkenau, F., 4100
Bormann, Martin, 738, 755, 832–836,
    3503, 6400, 6407
Bornstein, Ernst Israel, 6007

Borovička, V. P., 143
Borowik, Hans, 2895
Borowski, Peter, 651
Borrelli, Armando, 5508
Borresholm, Boris von, 781
Borshchagovsky, Alexander, 5437
Borst, Dr., 2376
Borsum, Lise, 6182
Borwicz, Michal Maksymilian (Boru-
    chowicz), 5905, 5987, 6144
Bosanquet, Mary, 1921
Boskowitz, Ch. H., 3297
Bosl, Karl, 4
Bosse, Heinrich, 5206
Bossmann, Dieter, 6484
Bothmer, Hermann von, 4215
Bottome, Phyllis, 3527
Botz, Gerhard, 1443, 2845, 5248, 5249
Botzenmayer, Karl, 2307
Bouard, M. de, 6139
Bouhler, Philipp, 26, 71, 623
Bouman, P. J., 5561
Bourgeois, Daniel, 4433
bourgeoisie, German—See middle classes
Bourges, district of, 5483
Bourne, G. H., 5221
Bouza, Luis A., 4575
Bovene, G. A. van, 4991
Bovensiepen, Otto Richard, 5571
Boveri, Margret, 2817, 3386, 5124
Bower, Ch., 4788
boycott, Jewish, anti-Nazi, 3625,
    6299–6302
boycotts, National Socialist, 1013, 3568,
    3571, 3625, 3674
Boyens, Armin, 1828
Bracher, Karl Dietrich, 933, 1027, 1056,
    1132, 1984, 3387, 3399, 3400
Brackmann, Albert, 4342
Brady, Robert A., 310
Bräutigam, Otto, 1190
Brafmann, Jacob, 283
Braham, Randolph L., 5722, 5830–5832
Bramm, Otto, 2518
Bramsted, Ernest K., 782, 2812a, 2938,
    3263
Brand, George, 6267
Brand, Joel, 6366a, 6367
Brandenburg, 683
Brandenburg concentration camp, 6022,
    6030
Brandenburg, Hans, 1172
Brandenburg, Hans-Christian, 2178

Brandenburger, Kurt, 1595
Brandes, Detlef, 5321
Brandsma, Titus, 6124
Brandt, Karl, 1664
Brandt, Otto, 34
Brandt, Willy, 3399, 3400, 3505, 3713, 3714, 5586
Branig, Hans, 3272
Branting, Georg, 1108
Bratislava, 5789
Braubach, Max, 4057
Brauer, Theodor, 1959
Braun, Eva, 721, 2090, 2091
Braun, Franz, 357
Braun, Magnus von, 1191
Braun, Otto, 1028
Braun, Wernher von, 4683
Braunbuch über Reichstagbrand und Hitler Terror, 1082, 4390
Braunbuch II. Dimitroff contra Göring . . ., 1090, 1098
Braune, Heinrich, 2730
braune Netz, Das, 3979
Brausse, Hans Bernhard, 514
Brazil, 4565, 4567
  'Volksdeutsche', 4566, 4568–4570
Brechsker, Karl, 4644
Brecht, Arnold, 1029
Brecht, Bertold, 2702, 3761, 3811
Bredow, Klaus, 1104
Breendonck concentration camp, 5523, 5530, 5776, 6096, 6097
Brehm, Bruno, 1133, 2621
Brehm, Eugen, 6396
Breit, Gotthard, 3833
Breiting, Richard, 624
Breitling, Richard, 175
Breitling, Rupert, 366
Breitmeyer, Arno, 2866
Breitscheid, Rudolf, 1000
Breker, Arno, 2666
Bremen, 1891, 1912, 5132
Brennan, J. H., 141
Brennecke, Fritz, 2179
Brenner, Hildegard, 2610, 2611
Brenner, Reeve Robert, 6520
Brent, Peter Ludwig, 5850
Brentano, Bernard, 1192
Breslau: Jews of, 3565, 3566, 5651
  in World War II, 3566, 5133
Bretscher, Willy, 4432
Bretschneider, Heike, 3345
Brett-Smith, Richard, 4741

Breuning, Klaus, 1777
Brewda, Alina, 6008
Brewitz, Walther, 416, 448
Breyer, Richard, 4317
Briggs, Asa, 3040
Brigneau, François, 907
Brilling, Bernhard, 3583
Briman, Aron, 225, 226
Bringmann, Fritz, 6255
Brinitzer, Carl, 3041, 3318
Brinkmann, Elisabeth, 3287
Brinkmann, Ferdinand, 3287
Brinkmann, Jürgen, 1297
Brinkmann, Rudolf, 1499
Brissaud, André, 3214, 3264, 3490
Bristler, Eduard, 564
British Broadcasting Corporation (BBC), 3039, 3041, 6356
British Legion, 4280
Broad, Pery, 6062
Brock, Paul, 4312
Brockdorff, Dieter, 2180
Brockdorff, Werner, 5143, 5176, 6402
Brockhaus (encyclopaedia), 18
Brod, Toman, 5332
Brodersen, Uwe, 1324
Broek, H. J. van den, 3042
Brogly, Médard, 5467
Brome, Vincent, 5236
Bronder, Dietrich, 151
Bronisch-Holtze, Ernst, 2080
Bronnen, Arnolt, 2555, 2556
Brook-Shepherd, Gordon, 4124
Brosse, Jacques, 702
Brosse, Thérèse, 6440
Broszat, Martin, 36, 131, 311, 515, 1173, 1345, 3215, 4318, 5313, 5421, 5677, 6041, 6069
Browder, George C., 3257, 3258
Brown, Zvie, 5922
Browning, Christopher R., 5678
Bruce, George, 5426
Bruckner, Anton, 2623
Bruckner, Ferdinand, 2712
Bruckner, Winfried, 2131
Brückmann, Wilhelm, 1444
Brückner, Hans, 2636
Brückner, Wilhelm, 674
Brüdigam, Heinz, 1057, 3415, 6479
Brügel, Johann Wolfgang, 4188, 4189, 5322
Brügel, Josef, 4415
Brüning, Elfried, 3444

Brüning, Heinrich, 922, 1030, 1052, 3715
Brüsch, Karl, 4030, 4031
Brugger, Alfons, 2778
Brugmans, Hendrik, 4613
Brugsch, Theodor, 1430
Bruins Slot, J.A.H.J.S., 5553
Brune, Horst, 1382
Brunet, Pierre, 6164
Brunotte, Heinz, 1956, 3690
Bruns, Viktor, 3959
Brunschvig, Georges, 307
Brunswick, 949, 950, 3567
Brunswig, Hans, 4905
Brussaud, André, 5499
Brustat-Naval, Fritz, 6411
Brzezin, 5917
Bubendey, Friedrich, 2884
Bubeničková, Ružená, 6009
Buber, Martin, 1820
Buber-Neumann, Margarete, 3418, 6186
Buch der deutschen Gaue, Das, 1174
Buchartz, Max, 4921
Buchbender, Ortwin, 3028, 3083
Buchenwald concentration camp:
    general, 1220, 1951, 1952, 5614, 5651,
        6003, 6016, 6035, 6051–6053, 6055,
        6098–6107, 6281, 6291
    Internationales Lagerkomitee, 6101
    medical experiments at, 6236
Bucher, Peter, 3834
Buchheim, Hans, 1792, 3215, 3216, 3408
Buchheim, Karl, 3463
Buchheim, Lothar-Günther, 4953
Buchheit, Gert, 706, 1404, 3835, 3980
Buchholz, Dr., 1574
Buchholz, Karl, 2333
Buchmann, Erich, 3631
Buchner, Franz, 942
Buchner, Hans, 525, 526, 938
Buchrucker, Major, 420, 895
Buck, Hans-Robert, 3334
Buck, Karl Detlev, 5197
Buckeley, A., 3008
Buckmaster, Barbara, 4155
Budapest: general, 3286, 5290, 5293
    Jews in, 5834, 5842, 6382
Büchel, Regine, 3301
Bücken, Ernst, 2624
Bühler, Theodor, 1445
Bühnemann, Hermann, 2377
Bürckel, Josef, 4051
Bürkner, Trude, 2212
Büro Grüber, 6337, 6338

Buhofer, Ines, 2910
Bukovina, 5882
Bulgaria: general, 2421, 3879, 4155, 4156
    Jews of, 5651, 5780–5783, 6345
    resistance, 5227, 5278, 5279
Bullock, Alan, 652, 775, 1159, 3918,
    4111, 4282
Bullrich, Georg, 3103
Bulman, Joan, 4661
Bumke, Erwin, 1409
Buna slave labour camp, 6055
Bund deutsch-jüdischer Jugend, 3617
Bund Deutscher Mädel, 2189, 2212–2220,
    4672
    Jungmädel, 2878
Bund Deutscher Offiziere, 3737, 3740
Bund nationalsozialistischer deutscher
    Juristen, 1397
Bund Neues Deutschland, 1500
Bund der Verfolgten des Naziregimes
    (BVN), 3341, 5679, 6417
Bundesarchiv, 62a, 4713
Bundeskanzleramt, 4118
Bundesminister für Vertriebene . . . , 4897
Bundesministerium für Inneres (Austria),
    5757
Burchard, Werner, 4176
Burckhardt, Carl J., 4340, 5381
Burden, Hamilton T., 120
Burdick, Charles Burton, 3850, 4372
bureaucracy, before 1933, 1010
bureaucracy, National Socialist, 923, 1073,
    1280, 1301–1322, 1333
    communal, 1304, 1308, 1482, 1487
    laws relating to, 1317–1322
    legal, 1305, 1309, 1315, 1334
    in World War II, 5384, 5636
Burgdörfer, Friedrich, 367, 401, 494,
    1469
Burgelin, Henri, 91
Burgenland: Jews of, 5651, 5759
Burger, A., 5153
Burger, G. C. E., 5550
Burger, R., 3302
Burgess, Alan, 5339
Burns, Emile, 4390
Bury, J. P. T., 4248
Busch, Eberhard, 1812
Busch, Fritz Otto, 4989
Busch, Harald, 4954
Buschardt, Leo, 5581
Buschbeck, W., 2964
Buschmann, Roland, 4216

Bussemeyer, Peter, 4557
Butler, Ewan, 794
Butler, James Ramsay Montagu, 4624
Butler, R., 4824
Butler, Rohan D'O, 152, 4248
Butt, Wolfgang, 4367
Butz, Arthur R., 6510
Butz, Friedrich Carl, 2000
Buxton, Dorothy F., 1925
Byford-Jones, W., 5281
Bytwerk, Randall Lee, 873

Cabala, Adam, 6128
cabaret in Third Reich, 2695, 2852
Cadars, Pierre, 2721
Cadberry, Glen, 2516
Cadier, Henri, 6135
Cahiers d'histoire de la deuxième guerre mondiale, 4625
Cahnmann, Werner J., 3584
Calic, Eduard, 624, 1083, 1085, 3242
Calleo, David, 253
Callmann, Rudolf, 1013
Calvocoressi, Peter, 4458
Cameron, Elizabeth R., 4217
Campbell, Malcolm 4447
Canada: general, 4288, 4523
  refugees, 3721, 6346
  'Volksdeutsche', 4289
Canaris, Wilhelm, 3388, 3489–3491, 4378, 5156
Cant, Gilbert, 4928
Cantimori, Delio, 5844
'Cap Arcona', 6163
capital punishment in Third Reich:
  general, 1401, 3285, 3287
  political, 1406a, 2463, 2467, 3291–3293, 3433, 5265, 5353
Capitant, René, 5480
Caplan, Jane, 1302
Cardon, Gregor, 2003
Carell, Paul, 5066, 5104
Carlebach, Emil, 1031
Carlgren, Wilhelm M., 4368
Carls, Hans, 6125
Carlsson, Holger, 4369
Carlyle, Margaret, 3880
Carlyle, Thomas, 284
Carmilly-Weinberger, Moshe, 5840
Carmon, Arye, 2401
Carol, King of Romania, 4171
Carossa, Hans, 2527, 2557, 2558
Carp, Matatias, 5883

Carpi, Daniel, 5849
Carr, Edward Hallett, 4397
Carr, William, 653, 3896
Carr-Saunders, A. M., 378
Carré, Jean-Marie, 4218
Carroll, Berenice A., 1766
Carroll, Eber Malcolm, 4416
Carrouges, Michel, 6010
Carsten, F. L., 896, 3408, 3836, 4119
Cartier, Raymond, 707
Casper, Siegfried, 2563
Cassel, 3327
Cassels, Alan, 4072
Cassin, René, 5680
Cassou, Jean, 5199
Castellan, Georges, 3966
Castle, John, 6063
Castle Stanford, Julian, 3616
Castonier, Elisabeth, 5222
castration, 1491, 1492
Cathars, 280
Catholics: exiled, 3717, 3718
  and National Socialism, 318, 631, 1696a, 2455–2458
  See also Church, Catholic
Cavaglione, Pino Levi, 5079
Cazden, Robert E., 3746
Cecil, Robert, 331, 5043
Čejka, Eduard, 5332
Celovsky, Boris, 4484
censorship in Third Reich, 4665
Central Committee of Liberated Jews in the British Zone . . . , 6428
Centralverein deutscher Staatsbürger jüdischer Glaubens, 1014, 3584, 3665
Centre de Documentation juive contemporaine, 4219, 5199, 5464, 5680, 5681, 5691, 5715
Centre national de la Recherche scientifique, 4220
Centro di Documentazione Ebraica Contemporanea, Milano, 5843
Cerf, Paul, 5565
Cernea, Radu, 4169
Černy, Bohumil, 85, 3492, 3707, 4190
Černy, František, 5323
Cerruti, Elisabetta, 1230
Červinková, Milada, 5334
César, Jaroslav, 85, 3492, 4190
Chaeppi, Benno H., 4835
Chaillet, Pierre, 5250
Chakotin, Serge, 2939
Chales de Beaulieu, Walter, 4770

Chalfont, Lord (Alun Arthur Gwynne Jones), 4780
Chamberlain, Houston Stewart, 183, 285, 286, 1895
Chamberlain, Neville, 3132, 4062
Chamberlain, Peter, 4818
Champeaux, Georges, 4448
Chandler, Albert R., 332
Channel Islands, 5016, 5316–5318
Chapman, Eddie, 6016
Chappat, Colonel, 729
Charléty, Sébastien, 4039
Charlier, Jean-Michel, 2090
Chary, Frederick B., 5780
Chase, Allen, 4520
Châteaubriant, Alphonse de, 1231
Chelmno extermination camp, 5399, 6041, 6108–6110
Chemnitz, 3568
Chen, Yoau-Ting, 1314
Chersztein, Mieczysław, 5860
Chertoff, Mordechai S., 5748
Chesi, Valentin, 1747
Chesterton, A. K., 2301
Chetniks, 5311
children, European: crimes against, 5609, 5747, 5952, 5964, 5974, 6070, 6071, 6099, 6255–6268, 6441, 6442, 6444
postwar, 6440–6444
Childs, Harwood L., 2179, 3043
Chile, 4571, 4572
China, 3119, 4601, 4606–4609
Chios, Island of, 5280, 5&7
Choltitz, Dietrich von, 346
Choquet, Maurice, 6164
Choumoff, P. S., 6153
Chovev, Meir, 5740
Chowdhuri, Emran Husain, 4291
Christensen, Synnöve, 5587
Christians: and Jews, 1811–1825, 6317, 6518
'non-Aryan', 1820, 3690–3700, 3829, 5823, 5950, 6317, 6342
Christiansen, Fr., 4870
Christiansen, Friedrich Christian, 5554
Christopherson, Thies, 6511
Chuikov, Vasili I., 5114
Church, Catholic: general, 1957–1974
and the Jews: 1781, 1787, 1813, 1814, 1989, 2008, 6342, 6343, 6348, 6374
National Socialist attacks on, 1786, 1976, 1978, 1999–2009
Church, Catholic in Germany: and the

Jews, 1813, 1814, 2008
in the 'Kampfzeit', 1777, 1781, 1783, 1787
persecution and resistance of, 1259, 1827, 1833, 1834, 1840, 1844, 2010–2039, 3322, 3466—See also under churches, Christian
and religious instruction, 2323
Church, Catholic in occupied Europe: persecution and resistance of, 5224, 5823—See also individual countries
Churches, Christian and the Jews, 6306, 6320, 6323
Churches, Christian in Germany: general, 1776–1810, 3255, 4661a
and euthanasia, 411, 6218, 6221, 6224
and National Socialism, 308, 318, 1782, 1785, 1786, 1807, 2151, 4114–4117
persecution and resistance of, 1259, 1826–1854, 3323, 3341, 5546, 6019
Churches, Christian in occupied Europe: persecution and resistance of, 5222–5224, 5475—See also Concentration camps
Churches, Protestant: and the Jews, 6317, 6321, 6339–6341
Churches, Protestant in Germany: general, 1778, 1855–1870, 4810
and the Jews, 1812, 1815, 1817, 1819–1822, 3690, 3693, 6337, 6338
in the 'Kampfzeit', 1778–1780
Churches, Protestant in Germany: individual denominations
Baptist, 1855
Confessional: general, 1871–1883
persecution and resistance of, 1826, 1833, 1834, 1840, 1844, 1915–1956, 3339, 3344
synods, 1884–1888, 1913
German Christians, 1889–1905, 1910, 2060, 2322
interdenominational struggle, 1889, 1898, 1905–1914
Churchill, Peter, 5478
Churchill, Winston Spencer, 3055, 3126, 3129, 4451, 6496
Chwala, Adolf, 1960
Ciano, Galeazzo, 4062
Ciechanowski, Jan M., 5427
Cienciala, Anna M., 4512
Cieślak, Tadeusz, 6171
Cigaretten-Bilderdienst, 648, 894, 3024, 3865

Cilek, Roman, 3642
Ciller, A., 254
cinema, National Socialist, 2716–2738, 2852
Ciolek-Kümper, Jutta, 961
Ciolkosz, Adam, 4323
citizenship, deprivation of—*See* 'Ausbürgerung'
Claassen, Oswald, 201
Clam, Ernst, 3112
Clark, Alan, 5067
Clark, R. T., 1032, 3511
Clarke, Comer, 5016
Class, Heinrich, 161
class structure, 1184, 1185
'class struggle', 558, 560, 1005, 1065, 2234
Classen, Wilhelm, 3981
Claus, Jürgen, 2669
Clauss, Ludwig Ferdinand, 368, 369, 4577
Claussen, Wilhelm, 1525
Clemens, Manfred, 255
Cluj-Kolozsvár, Jews of, 5840
Coblenz, 1166
Coblitz, Wilhelm, 1342
Coburg, 951
Cohen, Albert, 6345
Cohen, David, 5953
Cohen, Elie A., 6011
Cohen, Naomi W., 6389
Cohn, Heinz, 1352
Cohn, Norman, 299
Cohn, Willy Israel, 3566
Colditz concentration camp, 6030
Cole, J. A., 1232, 3084
collaborators in occupied Europe, 1299, 4306a, 5176, 5321, 5450–5453, 5531, 5590–5593, 5829
Collatz, Herbert, 2493
Collegium Carolinum: Vorstand, 5321
Collier, Richard, 4626, 5479
Collins, Sarah Mabel, 1233
Collis, Robert, 6441
Collotti, Enzo, 1134, 1962, 5177, 5509
Colodner, Solomon, 3678
Cologne: general, 1961, 3328, 4898, 4899
Jews of, 1355, 3602
university, 2419
Čoloković, Rodoljub, 5301
colonialism, National Socialist, 386, 495, 496, 498, 3103, 4017, 4026–4047, 5171, 5174
coloured races, 493–498

Colvin, Ian, 3490, 4481
Combes de Patris, B., 729
Comisión Investigadora de Actividades Anti-Argentina, 1646
Comisión Investigadora de Actividades Antinacionales, 1662
Comité voor Bijzondere Joodsche Belangen, 3537
Comité pour la Défense des Droits des Juifs, 3547
Comite contra el Racismo y el Antisemitismo de la Argentina, 4558
Comité des Délégations juives, 3544
Comité Français pour la Protection des Intellectuels Juifs Persécutés, 6303
Comité d'Histoire de la Deuxième Guerre Mondiale, 4940
Comité international de la Croix-Rouge, 5652, 6024, 6451
Comité National Tchécoslovaque, 5351
commandos in World War II, 5011, 5143
Commissariat Général aux Questions Juives, 5800
Committee of Fair Play in Sports, 2896
Committee for National Morale, 3085
Committee on Un-American Activities, 4545
communal administration, National Socialist, 1266–1271
communism, 157, 481–491, 1890, 2991–3003, 3101, 3127, 4402
'Communist Manifesto', 559
Communist Party (KPD), 884, 885, 996, 1113, 1705, 3420, 3438–3440, 4501
persecution and resistance of, 1408, 2011, 2022, 3334, 3423, 3424, 3431, 3434, 3688, 3722–3725, 3729, 6032, 6140
Compiègne concentration camp, 5816, 6111
Compton, James V., 4525
concentration camps: general, 3215, 5142, 5605, 5607, 5608, 5610, 5623, 5649, 5652, 5654, 5675, 5700, 5737, 5751, 5905, 6002–6058, 6257–6259, 6378, 6444, 6448, 6489, 6509
allied soldiers and, 6035, 6063, 6094, 6288, 6290, 6291
Jews in, 3568, 5604, 5649, 5675, 5700, 5730, 5733, 5751, 5765, 5860, 5878, 6004, 6007, 6019, 6020, 6025, 6042, 6046, 6053–6056, 6071, 6077, 6087, 6088, 6108–6110, 6131, 6132, 6135,

543

6137, 6144, 6145, 6180, 6186, 6190, 6195, 6196, 6200–6204, 6206, 6208, 6210–6212, 6240, 6386
medical experiments in, 5399, 5607, 6011, 6228–6232—*See also under* individual camps
priests and pastors in, 1826, 1827, 1931, 1941, 1942, 1951, 1952, 6010, 6023, 6105, 6123–6127, 6150
resistance in, 5229, 5671, 5675, 5878, 6039, 6068, 6103, 6157, 6195, 6291
various nationalities in:
    Austrians, 6122, 6155
    Belgians, 5523, 5775, 5776, 6096, 6097
    Czechs, 5153, 5338, 6009, 6017, 6143, 6186
    Dutch, 5733, 6059, 6060, 6080, 6091, 6120, 6124, 6167, 6191, 6207–6212, 6365
    French, 6010, 6045, 6050, 6065, 6111, 6129–6132, 6153, 6154, 6164, 6180, 6181, 6184, 6188, 6189
    Italians, 5508, 6013, 6038, 6077, 6150
    Poles, 6073, 6085, 6086, 6175, 6179, 6183, 6197, 6252—*See also under* Jews in
    Scandinavians, 5594, 6018, 6036, 6043
    women in, 3414, 5730, 5737, 6008, 6025, 6042, 6043, 6045, 6049, 6051, 6054, 6056, 6065, 6073, 6076, 6084–6086, 6093, 6136–6138, 6181–6189, 6198, 6237, 6238, 6252
Conference of Jewish Material Claims against Germany, 6454
Conference on Manifestations of Jewish Resistance, 3670
Conger, C. B., 3074
Connell, Charles, 5080
Conrady, Karl Otto, 2506
conscription in Third Reich, 3974–3976
Conseil d'Administration du Mémorial National du Fort de Breendonk, 6096
Constable, Trevor J., 4885
Constantine of Bavaria, Prince, 6462
Conti, L., 874
Conti, Laura, 5510
Conway, J. S., 1829
Conze, Werner, 878, 6412
Cooke, Dorian, 5304

Cookridge, E. H., 5160a
Coole, W. W., 3056
Cooper, Matthew, 3226, 3837, 5438
Cooper, Page, 3792
cooperatives, German, 1567, 1568
Coppenrath, Albert, 1963
Coppi, Hans, 3444
Coppi, Hilde, 3444
Coppock, J. B. M., 1592
Cordes, Ernst, 4090
Corino, Karl, 2477
Corona, H. C., 3101
Corsten, Hermann, 2419
Cos, Jews of, 5817
Coster, Louis, 6211
Council of Jews from Germany, London, 3669
'*Courrier du Centre*', 2722
Courtade, Francis, 2721
courts of law, National Socialist, 1400–1412
    military, 1400–1403, 4709
Coward, Charles, 6063
Cowling, Maurice, 4246
Cracow, 5416
Cracow Ghetto, 5738, 5860, 5907, 5918, 5919
craftsmen, 893, 1721, 1746–1759, 2375
Craig, Gordon A., 32, 4814, 6492
Crankshaw, Edward, 3265, 3789
Cremer, Fritz, 2682
Crete, 4884, 4941
Creveld, Martin L. van, 5035
Crick, Bernard, 4255
criminality, National Socialist theories on, 1479, 1492—*See also under* anti-semitism
Crinis, Max de, 1437
Crispolti, E., 2612
Croatia, 1299, 5312–5315
    Ministry of Foreign Affairs, 5314
Cross, Colin, 657
Crossman, Richard N. S., 3073
Crowther, J. G., 5225
crucifix struggle, 2014, 2015
Cruickshank, Charles, 3029, 4157, 5316
Csaki, R., 4010
Csokor, Franz Theodor, 5300
culture: general, 23, 2474–2500, 2859
    and economics, 528
    and politics, 584, 586
    and war, 5192
Cunningham, Charles, 1234

Cunio, Hermann, 4675
currency control, 1542–1547, 1641, 1654
Curtis, Monica, 4982
Custos, Dr., 501
Cygański, Mirosław, 3217, 4326
Cyprian, Tadeusz, 5398, 5625
Cyzńska, Sophie, 5399
Czech, Danuta, 6062
Czech-Jochberg, Erich, 625
Czechoslovakia: general, 683, 3238, 3483, 3879, 3888, 5230
    annexation of, 4205–4211, 5230
    Churches, resistance of, 5222
    exiles from, 5031, 5332–5335
    exiles from Third Reich in, 3707, 3721, 3748, 3771
    Jews in, 5689, 5784–5788
    Ministry for Foreign Affairs, 5335, 5340
    occupation of, 5319–5361
    persecution and resistance, 3293, 5040, 5225, 5227, 5236, 5321, 5334, 5336–5353, 6017
    Sudetenland: general, 3879, 4193, 4197–4204, 4280
        annexation of, 4102, 4104, 4106–4109
        laws, National Socialist, relating to, 1331, 1389, 1684, 5329
        Sozialdemokratische Partei, 3720
    'Volksdeutsche', 4188–4204, 5320, 5322, 5326, 5357, 6412
    youth, persecution and resistance of, 5347, 5351, 5352
    See also Munich Pact, Slovakia
Czeike, Felix, 4139
Czerniakow, Adam, 5971
Czenstochau (Częstochowa) Ghetto, 5614, 5920, 5921
Czichon, Eberhard, 985
Czollek, Roswitha, 5368

Daab, Friedrich, 174
Dabrowska, Danuta, 5881, 5926
Dachau concentration camp, 1255, 1931, 1941, 3463, 5224, 5651, 5751, 6002, 6003, 6030, 6032, 6051–6053, 6112–6127, 6288
Daene, Wilhelm, 6349
Dahlberg, Gunnar, 370
Dahle, Wendula, 2504
Dahlem, Franz, 4501
Dahlerus, Birger, 4281
Dahlke, Hans, 3770
Dahm, Volker, 3623, 3644

Dahms, Hellmuth Günther, 4627
Dahrendorf, Malte, 2132
Daim, Wilfried, 292
Daisenberger, J. A., 232
Daitz, Werner, 1583, 5164
Dallin, Alexander, 5430, 5431
D'Alquen, Gunter, 2764, 4965
Daluege, Kurt, 3276, 3277, 6012
Dam, H. G. van, 2727, 5614, 6455
Dammann, W. H., 1976
Dammert, Rudolf, 2765, 4142
Damus, Martin, 2496
Dankelmann, Otfried, 4373
Dankworth, Herbert, 263
Danubian States—See Balkan and Danubian States
Danzig: general, 838, 1299, 1684, 3329, 4339–4349, 5366, 5380, 5381
    Jews of, 3569, 5381
    persecution and resistance, 1926, 5417
    and the Polish Corridor, 4342, 4343, 4349
    senate, 4347
    and Third Reich, 4339, 4341, 4343–4349, 5381
Daquin, Louis, 5480
Darcy, Paul, 1235
Dargel, Margarete, 2213
D'Argile, René, 4459
Darmstadt, 952
Darracott, Joseph, 3030
Darré, R. Walther, 338, 392, 547–549, 553, 556, 759–761, 1665
Darville, Jacques, 6131
Da Silva Py, Aurelio, 4565
Datner, Szymon, 5861, 6286, 6373
Dauer, Hans, 2978
Daumann, Otto, 2378
Dauphin-Meunier, A., 1501
Daus, Ernst, 1890
David, Albert A. (Bishop of Liverpool), 1925
David, F., 312
David, Janina, 6374
David, Paul, 5125
Davidson, Eugene, 654, 826, 5638
Davidson, Michael, 4403
Davis, Brian Leigh, 1174a
Davis, Elmer, 2962
Davis, Lawrence P., 5836
Dawid, Heinz, 1353
Dawidowicz, David, 5862
Dawidowicz, Lucy S., 5662

Dawidsohn-Draengerowa, Gusta, 5738
Dawson, William Harbutt, 4044
Dax, pseud., 2919
Day, Harry Melville Arbuthnot ('Wings'), 6288
Deak, Andreja (Andras), 5833, 5897
Deakin, F. W., 4063, 5302
Déat, Marcel, 6298
Debenedetti, Giacomo, 5848
De Benedetti, Paola, 5729
Debré, Robert, 5480
Debû-Bridel, Jacques, 5480
Decken, S. Eberhard von der, 1666
Decker, Will, 2341, 4964
Deckert, Josef, 227
decorations—*See* awards
Dedeke, Dieter, 4526
Deeg, Peter, 449, 1354, 4417
De Felice, Renzo, 4073, 5844
Degener, Herbert A. L., 12
Degliame-Fouché, M., 5490
Degras, Jane, 4398
Dehen, Peter, 17
Dehlinger, A., 1325
Dehottay, Peter, 4299
Deighton, Len, 5000
Dein Volk ist alles!, 2285
Deissmann, Ernst, 4247
Deist, Wilhelm, 5165
Deisz, Robert, 1359
Delaisi, Francis, 5178
Delandsheere, Paul, 5517
Delarue, Jacques, 2940, 3266, 5814
Delfiner, Henry, 4206
Delft, 5557
Delius, Rudolf von, 578
Dell, Robert, 4521
Delmer, Sefton, 879, 1236
Delp, Alfred, 1833, 1834, 2016
Delperrie de Bayac, J., 5451, 5500
Delzell, Charles P., 1977
Demant, Ebro, 6064
De Martino, Gaetano, 6013
Demeter, Karl, 4742
Demmel, Hans Josef, 1968
Den Unvergessenen, 3359
Denckler, Werner, 1699
Denkler, Horst, 2526
Denmark: general, 4357, 4358, 4986
  Folketing, 5572
  See also Schleswig-Holstein
Denmark, occupied: general, 3147, 4760, 5570–5578

Jews in, 5796, 5797, 6379–6381
  resistance, 3039, 5112, 5225, 5227, 5579–5584, 6379
  by Churches, 5222, 5580
  underground press, 5581
Denne, Ludwig, 4341
Denzer, Hans, 2366
Department of Overseas Trade, London, 1502
Depdolla, Philipp, 2274
Desch, Willi, 3291
Deschner, Günther, 289, 3236, 4629
Deschner, Karlheinz, 5604
Desgranges, (Chanoine), 6298
Des Pres, Terence, 6014
Desroches, Alain, 3267, 3493
Det, E. J. van, 2224
Detwiler, Donald S., 715, 4375
Deuel, Wallace R., 4649
Deuerlein, Ernst, 897, 977, 1964, 4400
Deutsch, Harold C., 3468, 3475
Deutsch-christliche Orden, 509, 3460
Deutsch-Niederländische Gesellschaft, 4306
Deutsche Akademie der Luftfahrt-forschung, 4851
Deutsche Akademie München, 2391
'Deutsche-Anarcho-Syndikalister, Der', 4392
Deutsche Arbeitsdienst für Volk und Heimat, 2342
Deutsche Arbeitsfront, 1122, 1446, 1453, 1625, 1722–1734, 1737, 1752, 2183, 2867
  Frauenamt, 2095, 2096
  Zentralbüro, 1724, 1728, 2442
Deutsche Bank, 4125, 4208
Deutsche Bibliothek, 58, 3769
Deutsche Bücherei, 2605, 3749
Deutsche Christen, 1889–1905, 1910, 2060, 2322
Deutsche christliche Studentenbewegung, 1848
Deutsche-Forschungsgemeinschaft, 4046
Deutsche Führerlexikon 1934/1935, Das, 607
Deutsche Gesellschaft für Wehrpolitik und Wehrwissenschaften, 2270, 3844, 3960, 3976, 4701, 4704
Deutsche Glaubensbewegung, 2074–2080
Deutsche Hochschule für Politik, 44, 320, 3871
Deutsche Informationsstelle, 4992

Deutsche Koloniale Jahrbuch, Das, 4031
Deutsche Landsmannschaft, 2387
Deutsche Rechtsfront, 1384, 1385
'*Deutsche Rundschau*', 2818–2820
Deutsche Turnerschaft, 2885
deutsche Universität im Dritten Reich, Die, 2392
'*Deutsche Verkehrs-Zeitung*', 1290
Deutsche Volksgruppe in Jugoslavien: Landespropagandaamt, 4177
'*Deutsche Zukunft*', 2821
Deutscher Evangelischer Kirchentag, 6507
Deutscher Industrie- und Handelstag, 1617
Deutscher Jugenddienst . . . , 2343
Deutscher Lehrerverein, 2245
Deutscher Metallarbeiter-Verband, 1001
(Deutscher) Reichsbund für Leibesübungen, 2876, 2883, 2889, 2890
Deutscher Sängerbund, 2625
Deutscher Verein für werktätige Erziehung, 2366
Deutscher Volksbund für Argentinien, 4560
Deutsches Afrikakorps, 5024–5027
Deutsches Ausland-Institut, 4000–4003
Deutsches Auslandswissenschaftliches Institut, 44, 375, 3879
Deutsches Bücherverzeichnis . . . , 67
Deutsches Bühnen-Jahrbuch, 2698
Deutsches Frauenwerk, 2096
Deutsches Handwerksinstitut . . . , 1749
Deutches Institut für Bankwissenschaft und Bankwesen, 1503
Deutsches Jungvolk, 2189
Deutsches Reichsarchiv, 1154
Deutsches Rundfunkarchiv, 2847, 5626
Deutsches Volksbildungswerk, 1737
Deutschkron, Inge, 3595, 6257
Deutschland, Deutschland über Alles. Ein Jahrbuch . . . , 2169
Deutschnationaler Handlungs-gehilfen-Verband, 1004
Deutschvölkischer Schutz-und-Trutz-Bund, 216, 217
Devi, Savitri, 655
Devoto, Andrea, 3303, 6015
Dewey, John, 264
D'Harcourt, Robert, 755, 1965, 2148
Diamant, Adolf, 3568, 3571, 3594, 3648
Diamant, David, 5803

Diamond, Denis, 6516
Diamond, Sander A., 4542
Dibelius, Otto, 1873, 1874, 1927
Dichgans, Hans, 1569
Dickinson, John K., 3640
Dickinson, Robert E., 4016
Dicks, Henry V., 804, 3218
Didier, Friedrich, 5181, 5182
Diebow, Hans, 417, 626
Dieckhoff, Heinrich, 4527
Dieckmann, Ulrich, 3583
Diederichsen, Diedrich, 2710
Diehl, Guida, 2093
Diehl, James M., 880
Diehl-Thiele, Peter, 112
Diehn, Otto, 1830
Diel, Alex, 2613
Diel, Louise, 3145
Diels, Rudolf, 3268
Diem, Hermann, 2480
Diemer, Helmut, 3002
Diers, Marie, 3004
Dies, Martin, 4543, 4545
Diesenroth, E., 2310
Diestelkamp, Adolf, 6412
Dietrich, Otto, 516, 627, 656, 2803, 4642, 4965
Dietz, Heinrich, 2941, 4702
Dietz, Rolf, 1708
Dietze, Constantin von, 2393
Dietzel, K. H., 4017
Diewerge, Wolfgang, 3102, 3146, 3651, 3686, 5380
Diller, Ansgar, 2848
Dimitrov(ff), Georgi, 1090–1092, 1094
Dinklage, Ludwig, 1628
Dinter, Artur, 218, 420, 2044
Dinur, Benzion, 5673
Diplomaticus, *pseud.*, 2970
Dirksen, Herbert von, 3897, 4452
disarmament: general, 3951–3954, 3956–3958
  German, 3955, 3963, 3964
Discar, Kriminalkommissar, 3284
displaced persons, 5731, 6230, 6419–6425
  populations, 4079, 5206–5219
Ditmas, E. M. R., 82
Dittrich, Zdenek Radslav, 926
Ditz, Berthold, 965
Diwald, Hellmut, 32a
Djilas, Milovan, 5303
Dobaczewska, Wanda, 6183
Doberer, Kurt, 4693

Dobers, Ernst, 2275, 2276, 2766
Dobert, Eitel Wolf, 3185, 4221
Dobroszycki, Luci(j)an, 5394, 5926
Dobschiner, Johanna-Ruth, 5732
Documents on German foreign policy, 3878
Dodd, Martha, 1237, 1238
Dodd, William E., 1237, 1238, 2179
Dodd, William E., jr., 1238
Doderer, Klaus, 2164
Dodkins, C. M., 1299
Döblin, Alfred, 3806
Doegen, Wilhelm, 3103
Doeleke, Werner, 273
Dönitz, Karl, 762, 763, 4922, 4929, 4956, 5115, 5637
Döring, Dörte, 1629
Döring, Hans-Joachim, 6270
Dörken, Georg, 4703
Doernberg, Stefan, 4643
Dörner, Claus, 2170, 2181
Doerr, Hans, 5068
Doetsch, Wilhelm Josef, 1973
Dohle, Horst, 3528
Dokumentationsarchiv des österreichischen Widerstandes, 5258, 5269
'Dolchstosslegende', 2988–2990
Doležal, Jiři, 5336
Dollfuss, Engelbert, 1108, 4110, 4113
Dollinger, Hans, 2838, 5116
Dollmann, Eugen, 3898
Domarus, Max, 743
Dombrowski, Hanns, 1298
Domes, F. J., 365
domestic servants, 'Aryan', 1364
Domingl, Anton, 6130
Domizlaff, Hans, 2942
Domke, Wolf, 1684
Dommaschk, Heinz, 1667
Dommisch, Hans, 1058
Domröse, Ortwin, 1059
Domvile, Barry, 1249
Domville-Fife, Charles W., 1239
Donat, Alexander, 5972
Donath, F., 2149
Donay, Eduard, 1175
Donnevert, Richard, 3838
Donohue, James, 3466
Doolard, A., 4101
Doorn, Boud van, 6207
Dora concentration camp, 6047, 6128–6130
Dormann, Maurice, 6298

Dorn, Karl, 1596
Doroschenko, Dmytro, 3177
Dorpalen, Andreas, 1076, 4020
Dortmund, 1175, 3330, 3570
Dose, F. M., 418
Dotzauer, Gertraude, 3748
Doucet, F. W., 1134a
Douglas-Hamilton, James, 4282
Douglas-Home, Charles, 4780
Douglass, Paul F., 3691
Downey, Richard, 2020, 2061
Doyle, Hlary L., 4818
Dräger, Heinrich, 537
Drahn, Ernst, 2986
Drancy concentration camp, 5776, 5816, 6053, 6131, 6132
Draper, Theodore, 5001
Drascher, Wahrhold, 393
Drechsler, Karl, 4083, 4601
Dreetz, Albert, 2627
Dreifuss, Eric, 4432
Drescher, Leo, 1668
Dresden, 3571, 4900, 4901
Dresler, Adolf, 46, 764, 2094, 2668, 2794, 5312
Dress, Hans, 5354
Dressler-Andress, Horst, 2856
Drewit, Ingeborg, 3810
Drewitz, Carl Albert, 3098
Drews, Richard, 2606
Drews, Wolfgang, 1193
Drexel, Joseph, 3360
Drexler, Anton, 86
Dreyer, Ernst Adolf, 2486, 2490, 2554
Dreyer, Max, 1498
Dreyer, Siegbert, 3114
Driesmans, Heinrich, 188
Drobisch, Klaus, 1831, 2465, 3528, 3633
Dröge, Franz, 4660
Drohobycz Ghetto, 5755, 5866
Dross, Friedrich, 2663
Droz, Jacques, 6005
Drozdzynski, Aleksander, 5363
Druks, Herbert, 6328
Drumont, Eduard, 287
Drury, Betty, 6390
Dryssen, Carl, 341
Dubail, René, 1504
Dubitscher, F., 1470
Dubois, Josiah E., 6244
Dühm, Andreas, 1905
Dühring, Eugen, 183, 219
Dülfer, Jost, 2646, 3839

Düning, Hans Joachim, 2434
Dürr, Dagobert, 945
Düssel, Carl, 4084
Düsseldorf, 1163, 1447, 2495, 6436
Duesterberg, Theodor, 1125
Düwell, Kurt, 3589
Duff Cooper, Alfred, 4451
Dufournier, Denise, 6184
Dugdale, E. S., 727
Dugdale, J., 3741
Duggan, Stephen, 6390
Duhnke, Horst, 3420
Duisburg, 3331
Dujardin, Jean, 5529
Dukart, Joachim, 592
Dulles, Allen Welsh, 3499
Dultz, Michael, 2516
Dumoulin, Pierre, 3652
Duncan-Jones, A. S., 1832
Dunker, Ulrich, 3689
Dunkirk, 3140, 5000, 5007, 6285
Dunlop, Daphne, 5551
Dunn-Wasowicz, Krzysztof, 6197
Duprat, François, 4825
Du Prel, Max Frhr., 5383, 5537
Duquesne, Jacques, 5474
Durand, Paul, 5481
Durčanský, Ferdinand, 5358
Durch die weite Welt . . . , 2478
Durica, Milan Stanislao, 5355
Durieux, Tilla, 3778
Duroselle, Jean-Baptiste, 4399
Durzak, Manfred, 3771
Dussauze, Véronique, 1272
Dutch, Oswald, 608, 857
Duvigneau, Gerhard, 2862
Dvinov, B., 4844
Dvorchak, Victor, 4495
Dvorjetski (Dworzecki), Marc, 5765, 5961
Dwinger, Edwin Erich, 609, 4327, 4845
Dzelepy, E.-N., 898, 4064, 4375

East Indies, Dutch: 'Volksdeutsche', 4311
East Prussia, 1164, 1928, 4346
Eastern Europe: general, 1356a, 4835,
    5189, 5198, 5206, 5213, 5362–5367
  expulsion of Germans, 6410–6415
  persecution and resistance, 3241, 5210,
    5230, 5242, 5608, 5681, 5706
  See also individual countries
Ebel, Arnold, 1647
Ebel, Horst, 529

Ebeling, Carl-Otto, 1303
Ebeling, Hans, 2451
Ebenbock, Fritz, 1732
Ebensee concentration camp, 3596, 6003
Ebenstein, William, 1240
Eberhardt, Fritz, 2294
Eberle, Joseph, 2808
Ebermayer, Erich, 783, 1194
Ebner, Alfred, 3012
Ebsworth, Raymond, 6466
Echelmeyer, M., 2286
Echterhölter, Rudolf, 1326
Eck, Nathan, 5673, 5682, 5971
Eckart, Dietrich, 183, 483, 2767–2770
Eckehard, pseud., 4571
Ecker, Jakob, pseud.—See Briman, Aron
Eckhardt, Heinz-Werner, 2771
Eckhardt, Walther, 1319
economics in Third Reich, 2748, 2749
economy, German: general, 23, 523–
    536, 1185, 1187, 1495–1538, 1570–
    1578, 2843
  war, 2376, 4675–4682, 4897, 6245
  See also finance, industry, etc.
Ede, 5541
Edel, Peter, 3596
Eden, Anthony, 4249, 4451, 5333
Edinger, Lewis J., 3716
Edmondson, Nelson, 164
Edschmid, Kasimir, pseud., 4554
education and indoctrination: general,
    2145–2163, 2381–2389, 2515
  adult, 1737, 2381–2390
  vocational,   1627,   1722,   1757,
    2364–2380
  See also schools, teachers
Education in Nazi Germany, 2225
Efros, Israel, 6429
Eggebrecht, Axel, 1161, 6064
Egger, Leopold, 4177
Eggers, Carl, 2263
Eggers, Kurt, 1033, 3961
Eggers, W., 2280
Egypt, 4580, 4589
Ehlers, Dieter, 3494
Ehlers, Erich, 3154
Ehlers, Hermann, 3361
Ehrenberg, Hans, 1835
Ehrenburg, Ilya, 5069, 5439
'Ehrenhäftlinge', 6125
Ehrenreich, Bernd, 3186
Ehrhart, Georg, 2559
Ehrle, Gertrud, 1833

Ehrman, John, 4624
Ehrt, Adolf, 881, 1084, 2991, 2992
Eichberg, Emil, 2045
Eichberg, Henning, 2516
Eichelbaum, H., 4869, 4887, 4966
Eichenauer, Richard, 591, 592, 1683
Eichholtz, Dietrich, 1767, 4676
Eichler, Max, 19
Eichler, Paul, 409
Eichmann, Adolf, 5714–5728, 5835, 6366, 6368
  trial, 2511, 5719–5728
Eichstädt, Ulrich, 4110
Eicke, Rudolf, 1630
Eickstedt, Econ Frhr. von, 371, 2758
Eidem, Erling, 1906
Eilemann, Johannes, 598
Eilers, Rolf, 2226
Einhart, *pseud*., 161
Einhorn, Marion, 4385
Einhorn, Moses, 5880
'Einsatzgruppen', 5240, 5242, 5245, 5446, 5614, 5623, 5636
Einsiedel, Heinrich Graf von, 3732
Einzig, Paul, 1505, 5179
Eire, Republic of, 3141, 4212–4214
Eisenbach, Artur, 5663, 5683, 5857, 5863
Eisenhart Rothe, Johann Friedrich Ernst von, 899
Eisenmenger, Johann Andreas, 228
Eissler, K. R., 6446
Ekkehard, E., 245
Eksteins, Modriss, 2772
Elban, Julius, 2797
Elberfeld, 1929
elections and plebiscites: general, 42, 890, 1070, 1294, 4049
  Landtag, 140, 961, 962
  Reichstag, 997, 1053, 1294
Elgey, Georgette, 5465
Ellerbek, Ellegaard, 189
Elliot Smith, Sir Grafton, 390
Elliott, W. Y., 1278
Ellis, L. F., 4624
Elmayer-Vestenbrugg, Rudolf, 3186a
Elon, Amos, 6366a
Elser, Johann Georg, 688, 3476–3479
Elsner, Günter, 2208
Elstob, Peter, 5096
Eltzbacher, Paul, 250
Emessen, T. R., 795
Emig, Erik, 3349

emigration from Third Reich, 3396, 3398, 3440
  Jewish, 1352, 2425, 3551–3554, 6340, 6341, 6343
Emmerich, Alex., 1967
Emmerich, Wolfgang, 1700, 2517
Emmerson, James Thomas, 4058
'Enabling Law', 1062, 1068
Enander, Bo, 5226
Encyclopaedia of the Jewish Diaspora, 5648
Encyclopaedia Judaica, 5649
Endre, Lászlo, 5288
Engel, Eduard, 2547
Engel, Major, 712
Engel, Wilhelm, 1778
Engelbrechten, J. K., 1162, 3187
Engelhardt, E. Frhr. von, 472
Engelmayer, Otto, 4223
Engert, Otto, 3342
Engliš, Karel, 4191
Engstrand, Stuart, 4983
Enlind, K. Arvid, 697
Enser, A. G. S., 4614
'Entartete Kunst', 2668–2671
'Entartete Musik', 2644
Enterlein, Paul, 3634
Epp, Franz Ritter von, 837
Eppelsheimer, Hanns W., 3776
Eppler, John, 5144
Epstein, Fritz Theodor, 55, 3208, 4416
Epstein, Helen, 6447
Epting, Karl, 2527, 5461
Erbe, Hans, 1548
Erbe, René, 1506
'Erbhofrecht'—See peasantry: inheritance laws
Erckner, S., 3851, 3899
Erd, Herbert, 843
Erdmann, Jens, 3057
Erdmann, Karl Dietrich, 35
Erfurth, Waldemar, 4731, 4732, 4743
Erich, Oswald A., 2518
Eristov, Madeleine, 3881
Eristov, Michel, 3881
'Ermächtigungsgesetz'—See 'Enabling Law'
Ermarth, Fritz, 1507
Errera, Alfred, 6304
'Ersatz', 1594–1597
Eschenburg, Theodor, 933
Eschwege, Helmut, 3685
Esenwein-Rothe, Ingeborg, 1570

Esh, Shaul, 3621, 5673, 5711
Espe, Walter M., 900
espionage: general, 3983, 5141–5163,
  allied, 5145, 5150, 5156, 5157, 5159,
    5163
  industrial, 1609
  National Socialist, 3982, 3984, 5144,
    5151, 5156
Essen, 3332
Esser, Hermann, 419
Esters, Helmut, 3421
Estonia, 4180, 5214, 5372, 5373, 5765
Estonian Information Centre, 4184
Estonian National Council, 4184
Estorff, Gustav von, 2359
Estrada, José Joaquin, 5166
État Français, 5804
Etnasi, Fernando, 5227
Ettlinger, Harold, 3044
Eucken, Rudolf, 162
eugenics, 187–192, 276, 400–415, 1434,
  1469–1494, 2161, 2174, 3224, 3225
  laws relating to, 1473, 1484, 1488, 1489
  See also under school subjects
Euken, Wilhelm, 2898
Euler, Helmuth, 4902
Eupen-Malmédy, 4303, 4996, 5526, 5527
Euringer, Richard, 2479
Europäische Publikation, 3474
'Euthanasia', 411, 414, 415, 3322, 4667,
  5399, 5607, 6218–6227
Evangelischer Bund, 4903
Evans, Edward, 4987
Evans, Ruth, 4669
Everwien, Max, 502, 3116
Évian Conference, 6329
Evrard, Jacques, 6242
Ewers, Hanns Heinz, 3206
Ewert, Eugen, 5566
exhibitions, National Socialist:
  'Das deutsche Elsass', 4239
  'Die dreissiger Jahre . . .' , 3784
  'Kunst in Deutschland 1933–1945',
    2694
  'Kunst im Dritten Reich', 2679
  'Schaffendes Volk', 1531
exiles, Russian, 4412
exiles from the Third Reich: general, 2956,
  3461, 3706a–3710
  cultural, 2712, 3709, 3710, 3763–3831
  political, 1192, 1197, 1200, 1204a, 1207,
    3709–3743, 4501
  resistance of, 3427, 3712, 3716, 3718,

3721, 3723–3743, 3745, 3747, 3748,
3751, 3759–3762—*See also* under
literature
Eyck, Erich, 882, 3795
Eymer, Heinrich, 1491

Fabian Society, 4155
Fabricius, Cajus, 1892
Fabricius, Hans, 2528
Fabritius, Albert, 5581
Fabry, Philipp W., 658, 4144, 4400,
  4418
Fähnders, Walter, 3422
Fagen, Melvin M., 3913
Fahl, R., 2227
Fahnderl, Wilhelm, 901, 2182
Fahne hoch! Die, 2971
Fahnemann, Franz, 2045
Fahrenkrog, Ralph L., 372
Falconi, Carlo, 1990
Falkenhausen, Alexander von, 4608
'Fall Gelb', 5002, 5003
Falla, Frank W., 5317
Fallingbostel concentration camp, 5847
Falls, Cyril, 4757
Falstein, Louis, 5864
Famchon, Yves, 4578
Fantur, Werner, 4990
Far East: general, 4601–4605—*See also*
  individual countries
Farago, Ladislas, 3085, 4645
Faramus, Anthony Charles, 6016
Farquharson, Alexander, 1241
Farquharson, J. E., 1669
Fascism, Italian, 138, 157, 159, 308, 325,
  335, 337, 2612, 4072–4076
Fassbender, Siegfried, 527
Fattinger, Josef, 4114
Faulhaber, Michael von (Cardinal), 1813,
  1814, 2008, 2017, 2018
Faulk, Henry, 6473
Faulwasser, Arthur, 2228
Faure, Edgar, 5680, 5715
Faust, Anselm, 2435
Fauth, Gerhard, 877
Favez, Jean-Claude, 1102
Fechenbach, Felix, 3362
Fechenbach, Hermann, 3582
Fechner, Jörg-Ulrich, 3829
Feder, Ernst, 2797
Feder, Gottfried, 313, 314, 338, 420, 538,
  539, 2647, 3007, 3008
Feder, Richard, 5784

Federal German Government: Press and Information Office, 3510
Fédération Internationale Libre des Déportés et Internés de la Résistance (FILDIR), 3413
'Federgeld', 537
Fehst, Herman, 484
Feierabend, Ladislav Karel, 5324
Feigenboim, M. J., 5865
Fein, Helen, 6305
Feinberg, Nathan, 3671
Feinermann, Emmanuel, 3661
Feingold, Henry L., 6391
Felden, Klemens, 204
Feldmann, I. G., 404
Felix, Gilbert, 708
'Feme'-murders, 884
Fen, Ake, 5590
Fénelon, Fania, 6065
Fenyo, Mario D., 4161
Fenyö, Miksa, 5289
Ferdonnet, Paul, 3051
Ferencz, Benjamin B., 6243
Fermi, Laura, 3764
Fernis, Hans Georg, 4440
Fervers, Kurt, 473, 5362
Fessler, J., 3014
Fest, Joachim C., 610, 659, 3240, 6485, 6486
festivals, National Socialist, 180, 1693, 1704, 1797, 2488, 2516, 2669
'Festung-Europa', 5081
Fetz, Friedrich Ferdinand Otto, 2075
Feuchter, Georg W., 4866
Feuchtwanger, Lion, 1090, 3529, 3530, 3807
Feuerstein, Erwin, 4867
Fichte, Johann Gottlieb, 162–164
Fichte Society, 164
Fiehler, Karl, 1267
'Fifth Column', 3985, 4195, 4225, 4308, 4331, 4336, 4565, 4594, 5011, 5146
Figge, Reinhard, 991
Fikenscher, F., 2223
Fillies-Kirmsse, Erika, 2127
Final Solution—*See* Holocaust, Jews, European; Jews, German; and under individual countries
finance, National Socialist, 537–543, 1539–1565, 1654, 1655
  laws relating to, 1540, 1544, 1545, 1547, 1548, 1641
  See also currency control; and taxation

Finckh, Ludwig, 1471
Findahl, Theo, 4655
Finger, Otto, 6271
Finker, Kurt, 3516
Finland, 683, 3165, 3166, 4362
  in World War II, 3167, 4760, 5044, 6256
Fips, 2912
Fischer, Alexander, 5070
Fischer, Conan J., 132
Fischer, Curt, 992
Fischer, Erica, 5263
Fischer, Eugen, 400, 421, 5461
Fischer, Franz, 1779
Fischer, Gerty, 3692
Fischer, Hans, 5048
Fischer, Heinrich, 3535
Fischer, Joachim, 1949
Fischer, Ludwig, 115, 5392
Fischer, Richard, 1955
Fischer, Werner, 1151
Fischer-Weth, Kurt, 4590
Fischli, Bruno, 265
Fisher, Julius S., 5885
Fittbogen, Gottfried, 4005
Fitzgerald, Edward, 1155
FitzGibbon, Constantine, 3495, 4757, 5876, 6062, 6463
Flack, Werner, 3978
flags, National Socialist, 1300, 2185
Flannery, Harry W., 4656
Flatauer, Susanne, 6079
Flechtheim, Ossip K., 933
Fleischer, J. M., 3074
Fleischer, Kriminalrat, 3282
Fleischhack, Ernst, 2466
Fleischhack, Kurt, 2594
Fleischhauer, Ulrich, 305
Fleischner, Eva, 6521
Fleming, Gerald, 858
Fleming, Nicholas, 4512a
Fleming, Peter, 5017
Flemming, Jens, 62a
Fleron, Kate, 5582
Flessau, Kurt-Ingo, 2229
Flessner, Vollmar, 565, 1631
Fletcher, A. W., 2230
Fletcher, Harry R., 5076
Flex, Walter, 1869
Flick, Friedrich, 3632, 3633
Flick trial, 3633, 5636
Flicke, W. F., 3445
Fliedner, Hans-Joachim, 3580, 3696

Flitner, Andreas, 2480
Florence, 6354
Florian, Jean, 5291
Flossenbürg concentration camp, 3372, 6007, 6021, 6133, 6288
Flügge, C. A., 1855
Fochler-Hauke, Gustav, 579, 4023, 4192
Fodor, M. W., 4145
Föhrenwald displaced persons camp, 6436
Foerg, Irmgard, 3676
Förster, Albert, 838, 839
Foerster, Friedrich Wilhelm, 165
Förster, Gerhard, 4733, 5117
Förtsch, Hermann, 3840, 3844, 3974, 4720, 4734
Foley, Thomas, 4923
Folkerts, Hayo, 3866
folklore, 452, 2515–2524
food production—See agriculture
Foot, Michael R. D., 4613, 5161, 5228
forced labour: general, 5167, 5232a, 5607, 5652, 6031, 6056, 6179, 6219, 6220, 6241–6254, 6267
of Belgians, 5518, 6251
of Channel Islanders, 5316
of Dutch, 5554, 6249
of French, 5776, 6242
of Jews, 3596, 5776, 6056, 6180, 6240, 6243—See also ghettoes
of Poles, 6247, 6248, 6252
of Soviet citizens, 6254, 6290
Ford, Herbert, 5547
Foreign affairs bibliography, 3882
foreign labour in Third Reich, 5181–5184, 5212
foreign opinion of Third Reich, 1064, 1225–1262, 2304, 2901, 3018, 3020–3022, 3306, 3657, 4235, 4243, 4250, 4255, 4256, 4280, 4538
foreign policy, National Socialist, general: 1631, 1634, 3878–3931
See also under Hitler, Adolf; and individual countries
foreigners in Third Reich, 15, 1356, 1356a, 3289
Forell, Fritz von, 4876, 4877
Forndran, Erhard, 3900
Forstmann, Albrecht, 1632
Forstmeier, Friedrich, 1768
Forsyth, Louise, 3706a
Fosmark, Johannes, 6018
Fosse Ardeatine, 6283, 6284
Fossoli concentration camp, 6150

Four-Year-Plans—See under Autarky
Fox, H. W., 6320
Fraenkel, Ernst, 933, 3404
Fraenkel, Heinrich, 679, 786, 800, 807, 1066, 2733, 3249, 3304, 3506, 5697
Fraenkel, Josef, 5758
'Franc-tireur, Le', 5497
Francastel, Pierre, 2960
France: armistice (1940), 5001, 5009
Breton movement, 3994
Empire, 4240–4242, 5503, 5804, 5805, 5815
exiles in, 3712, 3725, 3735, 6138
Fascism in, 4459, 4837, 4839, 4842
Jews in, 6298, 6303
racism, 4232, 5670
radio in World War II, 3045
and Third Reich, 1653, 2295, 2307, 3879, 3937, 4035, 4055, 4216–4242
France, occupied: general, 4219, 5448–5471, 5522
Churches, persecution and resistance of, 5222, 5466, 5474–5477
and Jews, 3556, 5465, 5466, 5501, 5670, 5671, 5680, 5689, 5700, 5734, 5752, 5798–5804, 5807–5815, 6347, 6348, 6371
looting by National Socialists, 5196, 5199–5201
militia, 5451
persecution and resistance, 3712, 3735, 5255, 5227, 5239, 5267, 5472–5498, 5608, 5671, 5803, 6035, 6045
press, 5464
underground press, 5236, 5495–5497, 5801
See also under World War II
France, Vichy: general, 5452, 5499–5504
Jews in, 5670, 5804, 5806, 5815, 5816
resistance, 5502
Franco, Francisco, 4062, 4373–4376, 4378, 4380, 4389
François, Jean, 1106
François-Poncet, André, 738, 4076, 4224
Franconia, 953, 954, 957
Frank, Anne, 5733, 5823
Frank, Bruno, 3808
Frank, Ernst, 5325
Frank, Friedrich, 4993
Frank, Hans: Governor of Poland, 764–766, 5384, 5385, 5399
Minister of Justice, 115, 482, 517, 566,

599, 1323, 1327, 1342, 1370, 1371, 3274
Frank, Karl Hermann, 5325
Frank, Reinhard, 3117
Frank, Walter, 260, 315, 422, 837, 2413, 2750
Frank, Wolfgang, 4958, 4959
Franke, Hermann, 1579, 4704
Franke, Manfred, 3649
Frankenthal, Kaete, 3596a
Frankfurt, a.M., 2848, 3333, 3572, 3622, 3701, 6436
Frankfurt trial, 6066, 6067
Frankfurter, David, 3686, 3687, 4442
'Frankfurter Zeitung', 2822–2824
Franková, Anita, 5949
Franz, Erna, 2357
Franz, Günther, 4
Franz, Helmut, 6019
Franz, Walther, 1164
Franz-Willing, Georg, 902, 903, 978
Franzel, Emil, 316
Fraschka, Günter, 1401, 5349
Frauendienst, Werner, 34
Frauenfeld, A. B., 2700
Frede, Günther, 3841
Free Corps, 100, 166, 167, 3844
Free French, 5031, 5157
'Free Hungary' movement, 5294
Freemasons: defensive literature, 2003, 3460, 3461
    National Socialist attacks against, 472, 499–512, 557, 1980, 3096, 3114, 3154, 3462
Frei, Bruno, 144, 561, 3454, 5259, 6205
'Frei Deutschland' movement, 3728
'Freiburger Universitätsblätter', 2393
Freidin, Symour, 4757
Freikorps—See Free Corps
Freimut, Bernardin, 229
Freisler, Roland, 1305, 1372–1375, 1404, 1405, 1408, 1417, 2436
Freitag, Helmut, 6079
Freitag, Hermann, 1328
Frenkel, Mieczysław, R., 5937
Frenssen, Gustav, 1869, 2046
Frenzel, Elisabeth, 2701
Frenzel, Ivo, 6504
Frenzel, Max, 3424
Frettlöh, C., 1751
Freund, Michael, 1135, 3965, 4506
Freundlich, Elisabeth, 5944
Frey, Arthur, 1930

Frey, Hans, 6194
Freyer, Paul Herbert, 4995
Freymond, Jean, 5185
Freytag, Georg, 2560
Freytagh-Loringhoven, Axel Frhr. von, 3901
Frick, Hans, 3701
Frick, Wilhelm, 767–769, 992, 1060, 1268, 2141, 3276, 3277
Fried, Ferdinand, 1633, 5186
Fried, Hans Ernst (John H. E.), 3842, 3852
Fried, Jakob, 4115
Fried, Milton, 1771
Friedensplan der deutschen Regierung ... 1936, 3902
Friedländer, Kurt, 1368
Friedla(e)nder, Saul, 423, 1991, 4529, 5734, 6020
Friedman, Philip, 5650, 5657, 5664, 5665, 5906, 5934, 5988, 6330
Friedman, Mrs. Philip, 5658
Friedman, W., 6467
Friedmann, Friedrich G., 2392
Friedmann, Tuvia, 5853, 5866, 5877, 5945, 6403
Friedrich, Dr., 5462
Friedrich, G., 3853
Friedrich, H., 904
Friedrich, Robert, 1447
Friedrichs, Axel, 44
Friedrichs, Karlernst, 1584
Fries, Günther, 2180
Fries, K. de, 5548
Friese, Gernot, 2868
Friessner, Hans, 5085
Frind, Sigrid, 2841
Frisby, Julian, 3379
Frisch, Friedrich, 4924
Frischauer, Willi, 796, 824, 3244
Fritsch, Theodor, 239, 240, 304, 456, 2047
Fritsch, Werner von, 1137, 2365, 3475, 3840
Fritscher, Gotthold, 592
Fritzsche, H. Rolf, 1515
Fritzsche, Hans, 3058, 5639
Fröhlich, Elke, 131, 1173
Frogner, Carsten, 5594
Fromer, Rebecca, 3616
Fromm, Bella, 3597
Fromm, Erich, 133
Fromme, Franz, 4213
Frommolt, G., 1431

Frumkin, Gregory, 5207
Frumkin, Jacob, 5890
Frye, Alton, 4522
Frymann, Daniel, 168
Fuchs, Eduard, 205
Fuchs, H. H., 5616
Fuchs, Hans, 2972
Fuchs, Richard, 3679
Fuc(h)ik, Augustina, 5337
Fič(h)ik, Julius, 5337
Führer conferences on naval affairs, 1939–1945, 4930
'Führerhauptquartier', 753, 756
'Führerprinzip', 513–523, 865, 1868, 1936, 2376
Führer-Reden zum Winterhilfswerk . . ., 1464
Fürholzer, Edmund, 3172
Fuhlsbüttel concentration camp, 3403, 6047
Fuhrmann, E., 1329
Fuks, Marian, 5907
Funk, Walther, 770, 771, 1654
Funke, Gerhard, 2527
Funke, Manfred, 3903, 4081
Furtmüller, Lux, 2428
Furtwängler, Franz Josef, 3388
Furtwängler, Wilhelm, 2626
Futterknecht, Franz, 6483

Gaeb, Wilhelm, 1384
Gärtner, Margarete, 4342
Gaevernitz, Gero v. S., 3482
Gafenco, Grégoire, 4502
Gahlmann, Franz, 113
Gail, F. W., 1472
Galanté, Abraham, 5817
Galen, Clemens August von (Cardinal), 2019, 2020
Galera, Karl Siegmar Baron von, 20, 4085, 4126, 4181
Galicia, 5219, 5866
Galkin, A. A., 87
Gallin, Mary Alice, 3305
Gallo, Max, 1107, 4225
Gamm, Hans Joachim (Hans-Jochen), 2048, 2231, 2533, 2929
Gamsjäger, Helmut, 1907
Gandhillon, René, 2961
Gannon, Franklin Reid, 4250
Ganpuley, N. C., 4610
Gantenbein, James W., 4460
Ganzer, Karl Richard, 3086, 5187

Gar, Joseph, 5650
Garbutt, Reginald, 3982
Garçon, Maurice, 3051
Gardon, A., 287
Garfinkels, Betty, 5774
Garfunkel, L., 5923
Garliński, Jósef, 4684, 5145, 5162, 5229, 6068
Garmisch-Partenkirchen, 2894, 2904
Garriga, Ramon, 4376
Gascar, Pierre, 5482
Gasman, Daniel, 275
Gassert, G., 1508
Gau- und Kreisverzeichnis der NSDAP, 88
Gaubusseau, Léopold, 5239
Gauch, Hermann, 551
Gauleiters, 611, 838, 839, 841, 845, 860, 871–873, 875, 876, 963, 972, 1788, 3500, 5403
Gaulle, Charles de, 5099, 5100
Gaupresseamt der NSDAP, 934
Gauss, Paul, 1176
Gauweiler, Helmut, 5386
Gazelles, Henri, 1793
Gebele, H., 3014
Gebhardt, Bruno, 35
Gefen, Aba, 5770
Gehl, Jürgen, 4111
Gehl, Walter, 1136
Geigenmüller, Otto, 3409
Geiger, Heinz, 2702
Geis, Robert Raphael, 1834
Geisel, Eike, 6093
Geisler, W., 359
Geissler, Bruno, 1860
Geissler, Rolf, 2529
Geissmar, Berta, 2626
gelbe Fleck, Der, 3530
'Gemeindepolitik'—*See* communal administration
Gemischte Kommission für Oberschlesien, 3950
Gemzel, Carl-Axel, 4931, 4932
General-Gouvernement—*See under* Poland, occupied
Genizi, Haim, 6392
Genoud, François, 738
Gens, Jacob, 5906
Genschel, Helmut, 3624
Gentz, Erwin, 2344
Gentz, Günther, 2491, 2538
Gentzkow, Liane von, 2098

geopolitics, 355–361, 2284, 4020–4025, 4411
Georg, Enno, 3220
George, Alexander L., 3087
George, J. R., 2723
Gerbeth, O., 1293
Gercke, Fritz, 5045
Gerhard, Dirk, 3425
Gerhard, H. W., 1002
Gerhardt, Hans, 2308
Gerhardt, Johannes, 1448
Gericke, Heinrich, 6267
Gerlach, Wolfgang, 1815
Gerlach-Praetorius, Angelika, 1861
Gerlich, Fritz, 1020
German Faith movement—*See* 'Deutsche Glaubensbewegung'
German Freedom Party, 3391
German Historical Institute, London, 61, 3396
German Library of Information, 4295, 4984
German minorities—*See* 'Volksdeutsche'
'*Germania*', 2789
Germania Judaica, 59
Germanic festivals, 2081–2086
Germanicus, *pseud.*, 1509, 4116
Germann, Hans Georg, 1985
Germany, post-war: general, 78, 6394–6523
    black market, 6477
    denazification, 5620, 6463–6465, 6474
    dismantling of industry, 6456, 6458
    division of, 6394, 6399
    and Holocaust, 6501–6523
    Jews, 6426, 6427–6429, 6431–6436
    military government, 6395, 6399, 6458, 6465, 6467
    Nazi apologetics, 1145, 4229, 4462, 4482, 6495–6500
    occupation of, 6461, 6462, 6467, 6471, 6472, 6478
    planning for, 3889, 6394–6399
    re-education, 6473–6475
    rehabilitation of, 6466, 6468, 6470
    restitution and reparations, 3626, 3714, 6452–6460
    and Third Reich, 6479–6494
    zones of occupation, 6399, 6464, 6466, 6472, 6474
Germany speaks, 2973
Gersdorff, Rudolf-Christian Frhr. von, 3467

Gersdorff, Ursula von, 2126
Gerson, Werner, 142
Gerstein, Kurt, 6019, 6020
Gerstenhauer, M. R., 373
Gerstenmaier, Eugen, 1857
Gerstmayer, Hermann, 2971, 3188
Gerth, Werner, 2703
Gertz, Elmer, 4550
Gervasi, Frank, 660
Gervinus, Fritz, 934
Gesamtverband deutscher antikommunistischer Vereinigungen—*See* Antikomintern
'*Geschichte und Gesellschaft*', 1634
Gessner, Dieter, 1034
Gessner, Ludwig, 2985
Gestapo: general, 3233, 3235, 3261–3272, 3286, 3295, 3331, 3356, 6174
    in occupied Europe, 5240, 5242, 5353, 5394, 5483–5487, 5525, 5597, 5814, 5945, 6124, 6380
    reports, 1844, 3255, 3272, 3319, 3323
Getter, Marek, 5394
Geutebruck, Richard W., 1531
Geve, Thomas, 6258
Geyer, Curt, 169, 3311
Geyer, H., 4848
Geyr von Schweppenburg, Leo Dietrich Frhr., 4251
Gherardi Bon, Silva, 5851
ghettoes: general, 5383, 5652, 5654, 5671, 5675, 5700, 5737, 5878, 5903–5914, 6257, 6259—*See also* individual towns
Ghez, Paul, 5805
Gibbs, Norman Henry, 4624
Gibbs, Philip, 1242
Gibraltar, 3141
Gien, R., 1003
Gierlichs, Paul, 2179
Gies, Horst, 549
Giese, Friedrich, 4933
Giese, Fritz, 4934
Giese, Gerhardt, 2232
Giesler, Hermann, 661
Giessen, 3573
Giessler, Hans, 6453
Gilbert, Felix, 708
Gilbert, G. M., 804
Gilbert, Martin, 3904, 4252, 5684
Giles, Geoffrey J., 2438
Gillespie, William, 2767

Gilman, Sander L., 588
Gilwicki, Constantin von, 4032
Gimbel, A., 958
Ginsburg, R. A., 4205
Ginter, Maria, 5401
Ginzel, Günther B., 6518
Giordano, Ralph, 5614
Girbig, Werner, 4895
Gisevius, Hans-Bernd, 662, 1137, 3280
Gittig, Heinz, 3759
Gittler, Lewis Frederick, 3085
Glaser, Hermann, 266, 3531, 6480
Glaser, Kurt, 4468
Glaser, Waldemar, 3189
'Gleichberechtigung', 3906, 3959–3964
'Gleichschaltung', 941, 957, 1111–1128,
    1414, 1629, 2774
Gleina concentration camp, 6035
Glenthøj, J., 1956
Globke, Hans, 1363
Globocnik, Odilo, 5868
Glodschey, Erich, 5032
Glöckler, Otto, 1387
Glondajewski, Gertrud, 3355
Glotz, Peter, 3455
Glowna komisja badania zbrodni hitler-
    owski w Polsce, 5605, 6268
Glum, Friedrich, 89, 267
Gmelin, Hermann, 840
Gobineau, Clément Serpeille de, 2306
Gobineau, Comte Joseph-Arthur de,
    288–290
Godart, Justin, 5812, 6298, 6335, 6371
Goddard, Donald, 1922
Godefried, *pseud.*, 2018
'*Godishnik*' (annual), 5782
Goebbels, Joseph: general, 338, 648,
    772–790, 2699
    diaries, 775–777
    journalist and author, 773, 778, 779,
        946, 1582, 2812a, 2813, 2919, 2974
    and propaganda, 780, 785, 789, 2849,
        2857, 2938, 2949–2951, 3058, 3062
    speeches, 772–774, 2993
Goebbels, Magda, 2099, 2220
Goebbels family, 721
Goebel, G., 2964
Goedecke, Heinz, 2850
Göhring, Martin, 170, 1138
Goeltzer, Kurt, 626
Gönner, (Generalarbeitsführer) von,
    2345
Göppinger, Horst, 3639

Goerdeler, Carl Friedrich, 3386, 3487,
    3496
Görgen, Hans-Peter, 1163
Göring, Carin, 802
Göring, Emmy, 797
Goering, Hermann: general, 516, 648,
    791–802, 1956, 2355, 3290, 4062
    and the 'Luftwaffe', 794, 799, 801,
        3472, 4726, 4765, 4869
Görlitz, Walter, 663, 4772
Görlitzer, Arthur, 351
Görner, Alexander, 3854
Görres, Ida Friederike, 1208
Goes, Albrecht, 5936
Goeth, Amon Leopold, 5402
Götte, Karl Heinz, 1894
Göttingen, 2411
    university, 2394, 2395, 2411
Göttsching, R., 2311
Götz, Karl, 5208
Goetz von Olenhusen, Albrecht, 2393
Goffin, Robert, 5523
Goguel, Rudi, 3426, 3528, 6163
Goitsch, Heinrich, 5046
Golczewski, Frank, 3900, 4319
Gold, Hugo, 5759, 5760, 5882
Goldenweiser, Alexis, 5890
Golding, Louis, 4253
Goldkorn, Dorka, 5738
Goldman, Aaron L., 4254
Goldner, Franz, 3708
Goldschmidt, Arthur, 5950
Goldschmidt, Fritz, 3665
Goldstein, Bernard, 5989
Goldstein, Julius, 220
Goldston, Robert, 1139
Gollancz, Victor, 6358, 6430, 6469
Gollert, Friedrich, 1927, 5392
Gollwitzer, Helmut, 3389, 5065
Goltz, Friedrich Frhr. von der, 2296
Goltz, Rüdiger, Graf von der, 599, 1375,
    1405
Gooch, G. P., 1241
Goodman, Cecily, 6431
Goote, Thor, 905
Gordon, Harold J., jr., 979
Gordon, Matthew, 2962
Gordon, Sarah Ann, 3590
Goris, Jan-Albert, 5524
Gorzny, Willi, 68
Gosset, Pierre, 664
Gosset, Renée, 664
Gossweiler, Kurt, 986, 1151

Gostomski, Victor, 3292
Gosztony, Peter, 4836, 5086
Gotovitch, José, 5525, 5529
Gott, Richard, 3904
Gottfarstein, J., 2150
Gottfeld, Erich, 1352
Gotto, Klaus, 2809
Gottschalk, Max, 5774
Gottschewski, Lydia, 2100
Goudsmit, Samuel A., 4685
Goure, Leon, 5056
Government, National Socialist: general, 72, 758, 999—*See also* bureaucracy, ministries, etc.
Grab, Walter, 35a
Graber, Gerry, 3517
Grabert, Herbert, 2076, 6495
Grabowsky, Adolf, 3963, 4049
Grabs, Rudolf, 1895
Gracht, Hans, 3045, 5146
Graefe, Axel von, 2346
Graefe, Bodo, 2347
Graevenitz, Fritz von, 2615
Graf, Christoph, 1085
Graf, Jakob, 402, 2277
Graf, Otto, 1175
Graf, Willi, 2473
'Graf Spee', 4923, 4935, 4936
Graff, Sigmund, 2704, 4721
Graham, J. Gibson, 804
Graham, Robert A., 1988
Graham-Murray, James, 4283
Graml, Hermann, 36, 3408, 3509, 3650, 4038
Granatstein, Yehiel, 5893
Granzow, Brigitte, 4255
Granzow, Klaus, 4670
Grasmann, Peter, 3427
Gratz, Gustav, 4162
Grau, Fritz, 1372
Gray, Edmund, 3905
Gray, Ronald, 2530
Great Britain: and Czechoslovakia, 4188
and disarmament, 3953
and Europe, 4084
exiles in, 3719, 3721, 3723, 3736, 3771, 3814, 3829
and France, 3937
German economic relations with, 1654, 1655, 1659
German prisoners-of-war in, 5139, 5140
and India, 3117, 3141, 4290–4292
'invasion' of, 4745, 5016–5023

and Jews, National Socialist persecution of, 3660, 6296, 6297, 6311, 6315, 6319, 6322, 6356–6363
National Socialist propaganda concerning, 474, 4267
and Palestine—*See* Palestine
radio in World War II, 3027, 3038, 3039, 3041, 3045
and Spain, 4393
and Third Reich: general, 4243–4280, 4777
secret contacts with, 4281–4286
Great Patriotic War of the Soviet Union, 5071
Grebing, Helga, 90
Greece: general, 4151, 4155, 4157–4159
invasion and occupation of, 5032, 5036, 5037, 5039
Greece, occupied: Jews of, 5689, 5817–5819
persecution and resistance, 5227, 5274, 5280–5287, 6280
Green, Gerald, 5685, 5951
Green, Warren, 5806
Greeven, Heinz, 2799
Grégoire, O., 5908
Gregorio, Julio C. de, 4575
Gregory, Richard, 2740
Greife, Hermann, 4402
Greifelt, Kurt, 1618
Greiff, Walter, 1619
Greifswald University, 2437
Greil, Lothar, 5527
Greiner, Helmuth, 4744
Greiner, Josef, 665
Greiser, Artur, 5403
Grenfell, D. R., 5319
Grese, Irma, 6090
'Greuelpropaganda', 3546
Grey, C. G., 4868
Griesmayr, Gottfried, 374
Grieser, Utho, 1282
Griessdorf, Harry, 333
Grieswelle, Detlef, 628
Griffith, E. S., 1507
Griffiths, Richard, 4256
Grigg, J. W., 3074
Grimann, Jutta, 3426
Grimm, Brigitte, 3709
Grimm, Friedrich, 1096, 1195, 3653, 3935, 3962, 4050, 4226, 4227
Grimm, Hans, 352, 1196, 4033, 4257
Grimm, Helga, 2585

Grimm, Reinhold, 3763
Grimme, H., 3012
Grini concentration camp, 5594, 6036, 6043
Grinstin, Jacob, 5939
Gritschneder, Otto, 2026
Gritzbach, Erich, 798
Grobe, Alfred, 19
Groeber, Conrad (Archbishop), 1969, 2021
Grönberg, Erik, 4370
Groener, Wilhelm, 1000
Grohé, Josef, 841
Groll, Gunter, 2581
Grosch, A., 3275
Groschuff, Hans, 1571
Groscurth, Helmuth, 3468
Gross, David C., 6403
Gross, Hermann, 1649
Gross, K. A., 6115
Gross, Walter, 460
Grossbeeren concentration camp, 3596
Grossdeutschland: general, 44, 1131, 1154, 1348, 2604, 2621, 3025, 3094, 3879, 4100–4109, 4963, 5273
  administration of, 1264, 1348, 4131, 5182
  and colonies, 3103, 4030, 4031
  constitution, 1346
  economy, 1525, 1535, 1650
  and education, 2147
  laws, 1319, 1338, 1354, 1442, 1459, 1684
  prophetic visions of, 175, 281, 344
  'Volksdeutsche', 3997
  in World War II, 2621, 3094, 3103, 4933, 5182
Gross-Rosen concentration camp, 6003, 6007, 6134
Grosser, Alfred, 91, 2773
Grosser, Hanns, 2128
Grossman, Wassili, 6201
Grossmann, Kurt A., 3456, 3771, 6350
Grossmann, Paul, 2287
Grossmann, Vladimir, 5188
Grote, Hans Henning Frhr. von, 843, 906, 947, 3103, 4793
Groth, Herman, 4807
Groth, Karl, 1549
Grothe, Hugo, 2582
Gruber, Kurt, 1169
Gruber, Walter, 1061, 3867
Grubsztein, Meir, 5690

Gruchmann, Lothar, 36, 3477, 4018, 6218a
Grüber, Heinrich, 1875, 1931, 5723, 6337, 6338
Grün, Max von der, 2132
Gruen, Wilhelm, 2768
Gruenbaum, Isaac, 6028
Grünberg, Hans Bernhard von, 528
Grünberg, Karol, 3221, 4350
Gruenberg, L., 4146
Grünfeld, Fritz V., 3598
Grünheide concentration camp, 6007
Grünhut, Aron, 5789
Grünig, G., 2101
Grünspan, Herschl—See Grynszpan
Grünwald, Malkiel, 6369
Grunberger, Richard, 1177, 3222
Grundig, Hans, 2672
Grundmann, Günther, 2673
Grundmann, Herbert, 35
Grundmann, Walter, 1816, 1848, 1896
Grunfeld, Frederic V., 1178
Grunsky, Hans Alfred, 2753
Grunwald, Karl, 2297
Gryń, Edward, 6147
Grynszpan, Herschl, 3651–3654
Guardini, Romano, 1835
Gubbins, Collin, 5220
Guckes, Emil, 2724
Guderian, Heinz, 4766, 4767, 4819–4822
Gudme, Sten, 5573
Guéhenno, Jean, 5480
Günsche, Karl-Ludwig, 2774
Günther, Adolf, 375
Günther, Hans F. K., 338, 376, 377, 394, 439, 550, 666, 1486, 2079
Guernica, 4387
Guernsey, 5317
Gürtler, Paul, 5387
Gürtner, Franz, 1373–1375
Gütt, Arthur, 1360, 1423, 1491
Guides to German Records, 50
Guillaume, A., 5087
Guillaume, Gilbert, 5147
Guillebaud, C. W., 1449, 1510
Guilleminault, Gilbert, 907
Guisan, Henri, 5148, 5149
Gumbel, E. J., 3725, 3794
Gumkowski, Janusz, 5861, 5927
Gun, Nerin E., 2091
Gunning, C. P., 6059
Guntert, Hermann, 2519
Gunther, Jean, 3882

Gunzburg, Nico, 5778
Gunzenhäuser, Max, 3983
Gurian, Waldemar, 1794
Gurland, A. R. L., 1572
Gurs concentration camp, 6032, 6053, 6135–6138, 6386
Gusen concentration camp, 6003, 6010, 6139
Gustloff, Wilhelm: assassination, 3686, 3687, 4442
Gustloff-Werke, 3631, 6246
Gute, Herbert, 3428
Guthmann, Heinrich, 2616
Gutman, Yisrael, 6331
Gutteridge, Richard, 1817
Guttmann, T., 5651
Gutverstehen, Joseph, 5771
Gvelsvik, Tore, 5595
Gwiazdomorski, Jan, 6175
Gwyer, J. M. A., 4624
Gyenes, István, 5290
Gymnastics, National Socialist, 2870, 2876, 2883–2893
Gyorgy, Andrew, 4021
Gypsies: general, 492, 1264, 6269–6276
    persecution of, 3322, 5612, 5672, 5775, 5847, 6070, 6269, 6270, 6273–6276

Haacke, Wilmont, 4642
Haag, Lina, 3429
Haake, Heinz, 908
Haaren concentration camp, 6281
Haarer, Johanna, 2102
Haas, Hilde, 2360
Haas, Werner, 3991
Haase, Carl, 60
Habermacher, Gerhard, 4904
Habrina, Raimund, 5338
Hackel, Franz, 6141
Hackenberg, Friedrich, 2334
Hacker, Friedrich, 703
Hackett, Francis, 730
Hadamar case, 6219, 6220
Hadamard, Jacques, 6298
Hadamovsky, Eugen, 1701, 2851, 2943, 3906, 4103, 4572, 4968
Haddon, A. O., 378
Haeckel, Ernst, 275
Haecker, Theodor, 1835
Häfner, Heinz, 6445
Häggquist, Professor, 3147
Haehnelt, W., 4884
Haensel, Carl, 5627

Haering, Theodor, 2754
Härtle, Heinrich, 396, 1978, 4462, 5640, 6496, 6503
Häsler, Alfred A., 6386
Haestrup, Jørgen, 5583
Haffner, Sebastian, 667, 1243, 6488
Hagemann, Ernst, 6481
Hagemann, Jürgen, 2775
Hagemann, Peter A., 2738
Hagen, Hans W., 3497
Hagen, Louis, 783, 1140
Hagen, Walter, 3984
Hagenmeyer, Hans, 2592
Hahn, Assi, 3739
Hahn, Fred, 2840
Hahn, Hugo, 1932
Hahn, Ludwig, 5404
Hahn-Butry, Jürgen, 5038
Haidn, E., 115
Haighton, Alfred A., 4306a
Haines, C. Grove, 4450
Haiser, Franz, 190, 395
Hajek, J. S., 4485
Halbach, Fritz, 440
Halban, Leon, 1795
Halder, Franz, 709, 4745, 4768, 4769, 4804
Hale, Oron J., 2776
Halfeld, Adolf, 4530, 4952
Halfmann, Horst, 3749
Halle University, 4176
Haller, P., 3009
Haller, Virginia, 5574
Hallgarten, George W. F., 909
Hallie, Philip, 6347
Halm, Edmund, 3107
Halperin, S. William, 3795
Halter, Heinz, 3155
Hambloch, Ernest, 1635
Hambrecht, Rainer, 953
Hamburg: general, 955–957, 1204, 2646, 4669
    air-raids on, 3013, 4905, 4906
    Church, Protestant, 1862
    Jews of, 2710, 3574, 3613
    law courts, 1414, 1415
    persecution and resistance, 3295, 3334–3338, 6255
    theatre, 2710
    university, 2396, 2468, 2710
Hamburger, L., 1573
Hamburger Nationalklub von 1919, 746

560

'*Hamburger Tageblatt*', 2825
'*Hamburger Volkszeitung*', 3335
Hamburgisches Welt-Wirtschafts-Archiv, 1639
Hamel, Iris, 1004
Hameln-Pyrmont (Kreis), 1693
Hamilton, Alastair, 268
Hammelbeck, Oskar, 1834
Hammenhög, W., 2725
Hammer, Walter, 3363, 3390
Hammer, Wolfgang, 668
Hammer-Kösterey, Erna, 3363
Hammerstein, Franz von, 6502
Hammerstein, Kunrat Frhr. von, 3469, 3498
Hammitzsch, Eberhard, 5654
Hampe, Erich, 4907
Hamsher, William, 827
Hamšik, Dušan, 669
Handbuch der deutschen Geschichte, 34, 35
Handbuch der Judenfrage, 239
Handbuch der Justizverwaltung, 1330
Handelskammer Hamburg und Bremen, 3934
'Handwerk'—*See* Craftsmen
Hanefeld, Kurt, 1675
Hanfstaengel, Ernst ('Putzi'), 629, 937, 1197, 3019
Hanisch, Hubert, 2473
Hanke, Georg, 2298
Hanke, Peter, 3585
Hankey, Lord, 5643
Hanneken, Hermann von, 5571
Hannover, 3340
Hannover, Heinrich, 910
Hannover-Drück, Elisabeth, 910
Hannoversch Münden, 3339
Hansen, Ulrich, 4463
Hansen, Walter, 2670
Hanser, Richard, 630, 2467
Hanslian, Rudolf, 4686
Hanussen, Erik Jan, 143, 144
Harand, Irene, 6307
Harari, Jacob, 5820
Haraszti, Eva, 4258
Harbeck, Karl-Heinz, 4022
Harbott, Richard, 2899
Hardach, Gerd, 1042
Harden, Harry, 2930
Hardman, Leslie H., 6431
Hardt, Hanno, 3750
Hare, William Francis, 3979

Harlan, Veit, 2726, 2727
Harms, Bernhard, 2397
Harms-Baltzer, Käte, 4566
Harnack, Axel von, 3446
Harnack, Ernst von, 3443, 3446
Harper, Glenn T., 1656
Harrer, Karl, 86
Harris, M. A., 1543
Harris, Whitney R., 5628
Harrmann, Hans-Walter, 3588
Hart, Hermann, 3306
Hart, W. E., 4746
Hartenstein, Hans, 1547
Hartinger, J. F., 631
Hartl, Hans, 4170
Hartlaub, Felix, 4794
Hartlaub, Geno, 4794
Hartmann, Hans, 2398, 3118, 4328
Hartmann, Mitzi, 4127
Hartmann, Werner, 4956
Hartnacke, W., 2254
Hartner, Herwig, 441
Hartshorne, Edward Yarnall, 2399
Hartung, Hugo, 5135
Hartz, Gustav, 544
Harwood, Richard, 6512
Hase, Georg von, 4985
Hase, Hans Christoph von, 6221
Hase, Hellmuth von, 2627
Hasenack, Wilhelm, 6456
Hasquenoph, Marcel, 5484
Hass, Gerhart, 4531, 4643, 4644, 5167
Hassel, Sven, 5606
Hasselbach, Ulrich von, 911
Hasselbach, W. von, 1670
Hasselbacher, Friedrich, 503
Hassell, Ulrich von, 3386, 3499
Hassinger, Hugo, 358
Hastings, Max, 4908
Hasubek, Peter, 2288
Haubach, Theodor, 3378
Haucker, Kurt, 4156
Hauer, Jakob Wilhelm, 2077–2081
Haupt, Werner, 5028
Hauptamt für Volksaufklärung und Propaganda, 3067
Hauptarchiv der NSDAP, 51
Hauptparteileitung der NSDAP, 26
Hauptmann, Gerhart, 2705, 2706, 2712
Hauptmann, Hans, 420, 2049
Hauser, Oswald, 4259
Hauser, Otto, 403, 424

Haushofer, Albrecht, 3119, 3364, 3365, 4282
Haushofer, Karl, 358–360, 4020, 4023, 4091, 4411, 4602
Hausner, Gideon, 5701, 5724
Haussmann, Wolfgang, 3639
Hautecloque, Xavier de, 3269
Hawes, Stephen, 5229
Hawgood, John A., 4544
Hawrylchak, Sandra H., 3774
Haymann, Ludwig, 2869
Healey, Denis, 5230
health services, National Socialist, 1423, 1428–1441, 1450
Heartfield, John, 3785, 3786, 4805
Heberle, Rudolf, 134, 135, 883
Hechalutz B'Anglia, 3668
Hechinger, Fred M., 6426
Hecker, Hellmuth, 5209
Hedin, Sven, 1244, 4354, 4661
Hedrich, Kurt, 495
Heer, Friedrich, 230, 718
Heer, Hannes, 1005
Heerwagen, H., 2302
Heger, Heinz, 6021
Hegner, H. S., 1284
Hehl, Ulrich von, 1961, 2010
Hehlmann, Wilhelm, 2266
Heiber, Helmut, 36, 670, 713, 774, 775, 784, 2750, 2835, 3245, 5894
Heidegger, Martin, 2420
Heidelberg, 2699, 3575
   University, 2400–2402, 6308
Heiden, Konrad, 92, 671, 912, 913, 3307, 3655
Heiligenthal, R., 1273
Heims, Heinrich, 753
Heiman, Leo, 5735
'Heimatkunde', 2280, 2284
Heindel, Rudolf, 529
Heindl, Hans, 2133
Heine, Ludwig, 1946
Heine, Thomas Theodor, 3787
Heinemann, John L., 812
Heinemann, W., 1450
Heines, Edmund, 3192
Heinonen, Reijo E., 1891
Heinrich, Karl, 2381
Heinrichsdorff, Wolff, 2822
Heintz, Georg, 3747
Heinz, Friedrich Wilhelm, 342
Heinz, Grete, 51
Heinz, Heinz A., 672

Heisenberg, Elisabeth, 2420a
Heisenberg, Werner, 2420a, 3829
Heiss, Friedrich, 1511, 2975, 3023, 4343
Heiss, Lisa, 2103
Heiss, Rudolf, 2759
Helbling, Hanno, 2910
Helbok, Adolf, 4104
Held, Walter, 4705
Helling, Hans, 2911
Hellman, Bertha, 2509
Hellwig, Gerhard, 2233
Hellwig, L. W., 2481
Helman, Socrate, 6216, 6217
Helmdach, Erich, 5047
Helmreich, Ernst Christian, 1796
Helweg-Larsen, Per, 6448
Helzel, Alfred, 1512
Henderson, Arthur, 3951
Henderson, James. L., 3381
Henderson, Nevile, 4260, 4261, 4513
Henke, Josef, 2646, 4262
Henkel, Heinrich, 1388
Henlein, Konrad, 4209, 4210
Hennecke, Hans, 2588
Hennemann, Gerhard, 600
Hennig, Eike, 136, 1141
Hennig, Richard, 361
Henning, Friedrich-Wilhelm, 1497
Henningsen, Hans, 853, 963
Henri, Ernst, 3855, 4403
Henry, Clarissa, 3224
Henson, H. H. (Bishop of Durham), 2166, 3550
Hentschel, Volker, 1035
Hentschel, Willibald, 191
Hepp, Karl, 958
Héraclès, Philippe, 5454
Herbrand, Peter, 2799
Hercova, Lisa, 5271
Herder (Lexikon), 21
Herding, Klaus, 2661
Herkommer, Julius, 3170
Herling, H., 1424
Hermand, Jost, 3763
Hermann, Alfred, 6220
Hermann, Klaus J., 3666
Hermann, Nanda, 6185
Hermann, R., 6231
Hermanns, Will, 940
Hermant, Max, 317
Hermens, Ferdinand A., 5611
Hermlin, Stephan, 3384
Herne, 1165

562

Hérold-Paquis, Jean, 3051
Herrendoerfer, Christian, 6485
'Herrenklub', 898
'Herrenvolk'—*See* master race
Herrmann, Ernst, 4354
Herrmann, Gert-Julius, 3593
Herrmann, Gotthilf, 1797, 1798
Herrschaft, Hans, 4147
Hersey, John, 5686, 5990
Hershkovitch, Bendet, 5928
Herz, Emil, 3599
Herzberg, Abel J., 6091
Herzfeld, Hans, 1027, 1846, 2763, 3387
Herzfelder, Wieland, 3753
Herzhafter-Soldaten-Kalender, 4795
Herzog, Friedrich W., 2644
Herzstein, Robert Edwin, 3088
Hescheles, Janina, 5738
Hespers, Dieter, 2451
Hess, Albert, 2595
Hess, Rudolf, 803–807, 4282, 4284, 5641, 5642
Hesse, Erich, 5440
Hesse, Kurt, 1769, 3975
Hessen, 140, 952, 958, 959, 1938
  'Bauernbewegung', 224
  Jews, 3576
Hessenland, Max, 1602
Hest, Heinrich, *pseud.*, 3136
Heston, Leonard L., 696
Heston, Renate, 696
Heuber, Wilhelm, 566
Heusinger, Adolf, 4769, 4800
Heuss, Theodor, 632, 1062, 3358
Heydecker, Joe J., 1142, 5629
Heydrich, Lina, 3237
Heydrich, Reinhard, 3235–3239, 3268, 3277, 3282
  in Czechoslovakia, 5321, 5325, 5339–5342
Heyen, Franz Josef, 1166
Heyer, Karl, 3308
Heyman, Eva, 5736
Heysing, G., 3089
HIAS (Hebrew Sheltering and Immigrant Aid Society), 6332
Hiden, John, 3907
Hielscher, Friedrich, 1198
Hiemer, Ernst, 2166, 2167
Hiemisch, Max, 948
Hiepe, Richard, 2674
Hierl, C(K)onstantin, 343, 842, 843, 1199, 2355, 2359

Higelke, Kurt, 2261, 2276
Higgins, Mary Boyd, 258
Higgins, Trumbull, 4404
Hilberath, Leo, 1304
Hilberg, Raul, 5687
Hildebrand, Klaus, 1143, 3908, 4034
Hildebrandt, Dieter, 3455
Hildebrandt, Friedrich, 552
Hildebrandt, Otto, 461
Hildebrandt, Wilhelm, 1424
Hilfrich, Carl, 1597
Hilger, Gustav, 4405
Hilger, Rudolf, 908
Hill, L., 1304
Hill, Leonidas E., 3930
Hillel, Marc, 3224
Hiller, Kurt, 2482, 6022, 6396
Hillermeier, Heinz, 1406a
Hillgruber, Andreas, 710, 1036, 3909, 4171, 4631, 4747, 4760, 5272, 5688
Hillson, Norman, 4263
Hilton, James, 5524
Hilton, Susan, 3120
Himmler, Heinrich: general, 149, 993, 1282, 3240–3252, 3500, 3982, 3985
  Reichsführer-SS, 2608, 2667, 3245, 3260, 3274, 3277, 3278, 3754, 5216, 5652, 6366, 6513
Hindels, Josef, 5261
Hindenburg, Paul von Beneckendorff und von, 1076–1081, 1956
'Hindenburg' (airship), 4849
Hindls, Arnold, 3600
Hinkel, Hans, 453, 757, 844, 2491, 2493
Hinkel, Hermann, 2963
Hinkler, Paul, 994
Hinrichs, Klaus, 6178
Hinsley, Arthur (Cardinal), 5422
Hinsley, Francis Harry, 5150
Hinz, Berthold, 2612, 2675
Hippel, Fritz von, 1274, 1416
Hippius, Rudolf, 404
Hirche, Kurt, 2931
Hirsch, Martin, 6455
Hirsch, Rudolf, 5970
Hirt, Simon, 1983
Hirth, Frédéric, 633
Historicus, *pseud.*, 4193
historiography in Third Reich, 2750–2752
Historische Kommission bei der Bayerischen Akademie der Wissenschaften, 9

Hitler, Adolf: general, 555, 621–756, 1053, 2773, 4275, 5000, 5253, 6408
and architecture, 661, 2657
and armed forces, 707, 909, 3839, 3843, 3846, 3969, 4740, 4749, 4752, 4771
and colonies, 4034
and conservatives, 642, 3466, 3470, 3471
conspiracies against, 3258, 3392, 3475–3526
foreign opinion on, 639, 3019, 4075, 4539
foreign policy: general, 3854–3858, 3862, 3863, 3894, 3899, 3906, 3909, 3910, 3916, 3924, 4362, 4920
and France, 683, 4227, 4237
German post-war opinion on, 695, 6484–6488
and Great Britain, 4262, 4274
and Hungary, 4160, 4161
and industrialists, 673, 909, 985, 988, 989, 1599
and Italy, 683, 4062, 4063, 4069, 4073, 4076, 4081, 4087, 4089, 4160
and Jews, 483, 749, 5173, 5663, 5677, 5698
'Lagebesprechungen', 713, 714
last days of, 721–725, 4646
medical history of, 696–699
as military leader, 676, 705–717, 2802, 4694, 4930, 4931, 4938, 4951, 5035, 5059, 5077, 5096–5098
and N.S.D.A.P., 96, 97, 516, 621, 676, 908, 916, 995, 3183
psychology of, 700–704, 754
and religion, 230, 280, 718–720, 3698
as a revolutionary, 105a, 159, 338, 677, 687
and Romania, 4171
and the Soviet Union, 683, 4396, 4415, 5043—See also Hitler–Stalin Pact
and Spain, 4373–4376, 4378, 4382
speeches, 628, 686, 741–752, 2646, 3910, 3932, 5168
and sport, 2870
table talk, 715, 753–756
testaments, 738, 740
and United States, 4525, 4529
war aims, 691, 5173
in World War I, 640
as a writer, 686, 726–740, 752, 2508
youth of, 635, 636, 638, 643, 644, 4121
Hitler family, 644, 689

Hitler spricht. . . ., 22
Hitler–Stalin Pact, 4362, 4415–4424, 5261
Hitler Youth: general, 934, 1468, 2176–2211, 2292, 2458, 2459, 4670, 4672
laws relating to, 2187, 2188
Pimpfe, 2208–2211
'Hitlergruss', 865
Hlond, August, 5422
Hnilicka, Karl, 5088
Hoche, Alfred, 187
Hoche, Werner, 1063, 1331, 1338
Hochhuth, Rolf, 777, 1992, 1993
'Hochland', 2826
Hochmuth, Paul, 3009, 3010
Hochmuth, Ursel, 2468, 3309, 3336, 3337
Hochschule für Politik, 2403
Hochschule für die Wissenschaft des Judentums, 3679
Hochschulen für Lehrerbildung, 2269
Hochstetter, Franz, 540
Hockerts, Hans Günter, 2036
Hocking, William Ernest, 6474
Hodes, Franz, 3
Hoecke, Paul, 481
Höfner, Albert, 2308
Hoegner, Wilhelm, 884, 1037, 1200
Höhn, Professor, 3274
Höhne, Heinz, 3223, 3447, 3491
Höhne, Paul Friedrich, 3098
Hoepke, Klaus-Peter, 4074
Hoepner, Erich, 4770
Hoernle, Edwin, 1690
Hörster-Philipps, Ulrike, 673
Höss, Konstantin, 4194
Höss, Rudolf, 6062, 6069
Hoetink, H. R., 6060
Hövel, Paul, 1513
Hofer, Walther, 34, 1085, 2741, 4464, 4465
Hoffman, Ruth, 3601
Hoffmann, Bedrich, 6023
Hoffmann, Bruno, 1355
Hoffmann, Charles W., 2583
Hoffmann, E., 2032
Hoffmann, Erich, 1433
Hoffmann, Gabriele, 5538
Hoffmann, H., 2707
Hoffmann, Hanns Hubert, 4
Hoffmann, Heinrich, 121, 634, 674, 894, 914, 915, 2870, 3193, 4051, 4065, 4105, 4128, 4210, 4228
Hoffmann, Herbert, 2379

Hoffmann, Joachim, 4838
Hoffmann, Otto, 2932
Hoffmann, P. G., 2866
Hoffmann, Peter, 675, 3258, 3392, 3393
Hoffmann, Ross J. S., 4450
Hoffmann, Walter, 4148
Hofmann, Hasso, 2430
Hofmann, Josef, 2810
Hofmann, Konrad, 2021
Hofmann, Walter, 2927
Hofmann, Willi, 2167
Hogben, Lancelot, 370
Hoggan, David L., 4229, 4464, 4466–4468
Hohendahl, Peter Uwe, 3763
Hohendorf, Gerd, 5231
Hohengarten, André, 5568
Hohenstein, Alexander, 5867
Hohlfeld, Johann, 45
Hohnstein concentration camp, 6030, 6049, 6140, 6141
Hoke, R. J., 2871
Holborn, Hajo, 1038
Holland: general, 3879, 4306–4311, 6451
   invasion of, 4991–4994, 4997, 4998, 5010
   and Jews, 6324, 6335
   radio, 3042
Holland, occupied: general, 821, 4847 5531–5540
   Jews in, 5651, 5689, 5745, 5820–5829, 6364, 6365
   persecution and resistance, 3293, 5225, 5227, 5246, 5541–5564, 6275
      of Churches, 5222, 5543–5546, 6364
      underground press and literature, 5236, 5558, 5559
   propaganda, National Socialist, 5537–5539
   students, 5556, 5557
   workers, 5561–5564, 6249
Holland, Kenneth, 2348
Hollander, A. N. J. den, 6060
Holldack, Heinz, 3911
Hollingworth, Clare, 4149, 4155
Hollstein, Dorothea, 2728
Holm, Reinhard, 3108
Holocaust: general, 1822, 1995, 3241, 5078, 5232a, 5376, 5546, 5607, 5609, 5610, 5647–5663, 5666–5713, 6305, 6315, 6316, 6326, 6331, 6333, 6334, 6353, 6362, 6366–6369, 6386, 6389,
6391, 6437, 6438—See also Eichmann, Adolf, and under individual countries
   denial of, 6508–6517
   German officers and, 3467, 3468
   individual Jewish accounts of, 5729–5756
'Holocaust' (film), 6503–6505
Holstein, Christine, 2134
Holthaus, Hellmut, 3025
Holting-Hauff, W., 3703
Holtz, Achim, 1702
Holtzmann, Walther, 2751
Homann, Fritz, 1759
Homann, Rudolf, 1849
Hombourger, René, 785
homosexuality in Third Reich, 1428, 6021—See also June 30, 1934
Homze, Edward L., 4850, 5183
Honigsheim, Paul, 2482
Honolka, Bert, 6222
Hoof, Henri van, 5531
Hoover Institution on War, Revolution and Peace, 51
Hopfinger, K. B., 1611
Horbach, Michael, 6351
Hordt, Philipp, 2520
Hore-Belisha, Leslie, 3112, 4251
Hořec, Jaromír, 6259
Horn, Martin, 4365
Horn, Wolfgang, 518, 915a
Horne, Alastair, 5114
Hornig, Ernst, 1883, 5133
Horrabin, J. F., 4155
Horsten, Franz, 2367
Horthy, Miklós, 4160, 4161, 4163, 4164, 4829, 5832
Hory, Ladislaus, 5313
Hossbach, Friedrich, 4771
hostages, crimes against, 5530, 5554, 5636, 6060, 6277–6284
Hotzel, Curt, 947
Hourmouzios, S. L., 5282
Hove, Alkmar von, 4808
Howard, Edmund, 195
Howard, Elizabeth F., 6339
Howard, Michael, 4624, 4742.
Howe, Ellic, 145
Howe, Thomas Carr, jr., 5202
Howell, Edgar M., 5441
Hrabar, Roman, 3225
Hubatsch, Walther, 711, 1077, 4760, 4986
Hube, (Oberstleutnant), 4722
Huber, Clara, 2469

Huber, Engelbert, 504
Huber, Ernst, 1346
Huber, Heinrich, 2014
Huber, Heinz, 1144
Huber, Kurt, 2469
Hubmann, Hans, 1201
Huch, Ricarda, 2561
Huck, Jürgen, 3281
Hudal, Alois (Bishop), 318, 4066, 4116
Huddleston, Sisley, 5455
Huder, Walter, 3814
Hübbenet, Anatol von, 1738
Hüber, Reinhard, 4576
Hübinger, Paul Egon, 3825
Hübner, Franz, 3103
Hügel, Kaspar, 4172
Hühnhäuser, Alfred, 2289
Hümmelchen, Gerhard, 4673, 4945
Hünger, Heinz, 3166
Hürten, Heinz, 3717
Hüsgen, Manfred, 2811
Hüttenberger, Peter, 611
Hüttig, W., 5539
Huettner, Axel, 3577
Huffeld, Hans, 1099
Hugenberg, Alfred, 2653, 2777
Hull, David Stewart, 2729
Humbel, Kurt, 4441
Humbert, Manuel, 731
Humble, Richard, 4748
Humburg, Paul, 1863
Hummel, Theodor, 4425
humour, anti-Nazi, 2929–2935
    National Socialist, 2909–2928
Hundeiker, Egon, 3868
Hungary: general: 4160–4167, 5085, 5288, 5289
    Arrow Cross movement, 4166, 5292
    Jews, 1994, 5689, 5751, 5783, 5830–5842, 6055, 6366–6370
    persecution and resistance, 5227, 5230, 5290–5294
    and Third Reich, 3169, 3881, 4160–4162, 4165
    'Volksdeutsche', 4167, 6042
Hunke, Heinrich, 1514
Hunsche, J. F., 6060
Hunsche, Karl-Heinrich, 4567
Huppert, Hilde, 5737
Husak, Gustav, 5359
Hussmann, Peter, 2349
Husum concentration camp, 6142
Hutak, J. B., 5344

Hutchinson, Paul, 6309
Hutin, Serge, 280
Hutten, Kurt, 2050
Huttenbach, Henry R., 3551
Hutton, J. Bernhard, 805
Huxley, Julian, 378
Hyams, Joseph, 5974
Hyndráková, Anna, 5949
Hyrawka Jewish Labour camp, 5755

Ibach, Karl, 3194, 3356
Ibn Sa'ud, King, 4597
Ibrügger, Fritz, 3020
Iceland, 4363
IG Farben, 4680, 5636, 6243, 6244
Ihde, Wilhelm, 2538
Ihlert, Heinz, 2633
Ilava concentration camp, 6143
illegal publications—See press
Ilnytskyj, Roman, 4427
Immer, Karl, 2151
Imperial War Museum, London, 5630
India, 3117, 3141, 4290–4292, 4610, 4611
Indorf, Hans, 4264
industry: general, 1566, 1569–1615, 1721, 2110, 2129, 4682, 6245
    chemical, 1591, 1596
    energy, 1593, 1594
    metal, 1588, 1603, 1608, 1610
    pharmaceutical, 1592
    textile, 1597, 1607
    tourist, 1601
Informations-Schriften, 3122
Ingrim, Robert, 4129
'Innere Emigration', 2588–2590, 3763, 3773
'Innere Reich, Das', 2827
Innitzer, Theodor (Cardinal), 4117
Inönü, Ismet, 4599
Institut für Besatzungsfragen, Tübingen, 6421
Institut für deutsche Geschichte, Tel Aviv, 35a
Institut zur Erforschung der Judenfrage, 484
Institut zur Erforschung des jüdischen Einflusses auf das deutsche kirchliche Leben, 1816, 1818
Institut d'Études des Questions Juives, 5799

Institut für Grenz- und Auslands-Studien, 4004
Institut für Konjunkturforschung, 1520, 1600
Institut Marxisma-Leninisma pri ZK KPSS, 5072, 5432
Institut für Marxismus-Leninismus beim ZK der SED, 1703
Institut Maurice Thorez, 4628
Institut für Osteuropäische Wirtschaft an der Universität Königsberg, 435
Institut für Statistik... der deutschen Volksgruppe in Rumänien, 4173
Institut zum Studium der Judenfrage, 425, 428, 478
Institut für Zeitgeschichte, München, 36, 64, 1173, 4484, 4761, 5070, 5242, 5313, 5421, 5630, 6289
Institute of Jewish Affairs, New York, 5666, 6423, 6459
Institute for Propaganda Analysis, New York, 2944
Institute of Race Relations, London, 6319
Instytut Historii Polskiej Akademii Nauk, 5394
Inter Nationes, Bonn, 76
Internationaal van der Lubbe-Comité, 1095
International Auschwitz Committee, 6070
International Central Bureau Joy and Work, Berlin, 1739, 1740
International Conferences on ... the Resistance movements, 5232, 5309
International Labour Office, 5184
International Military Tribunal, 53, 5630, 5635, 6514
International Tracing Service, 5652
International Who's Who, The, 6
Internationale Arbeitsgemeinschaft der Nationalisten, 3992
Ipsen, Hanspeter, 1332
Ipser, Karl, 3171
Iran, 4588
Iranek-Osmecki, Kazimierz, 6375
Iraq, 4588
Irgun Olej Merkas Europa, 3557
Irsfeld, Franz, 3328
Irving, Bert, 6174
Irving, David, 3856, 4469, 4687, 4749, 4781, 4874, 4875, 4901, 5677
Irwahn, Fritz, 1704
Isenburg, C. D., 2404
Ishoven, Armand van, 4788
Isolani, Gertrud, 6136

Israel—*See* Palestine
Issraeljan, V., 4086
Italy: general, 138, 3078, 3170, 3171, 5037, 5507
Empire, 3170, 4080–4082
German occupation of, 5083, 5509, 5512, 5514, 5515, 6038
and Jews, 4067, 5514, 5670, 5671, 5743, 5843–5850, 6371
persecution and resistance, 5079, 5227, 5277, 5505–5515, 5843
requisitioning by Germans, 5196
and Third Reich, 4060–4071, 4085, 4087, 4089, 5505
See also the Axis and under World War II
Ivanov, Miroslav, 5341
Ivy, Andrew C., 6213
Iwanow-Moskwin, Nikolai, 485

Jacewicz, Wiktor, 5423
Jackson, Robert H., 5628
Jacob, Alfred Helmut, 4052
Jacob, Berthold, 3338, 3430, 3457, 6310
Jacob, H., 4815
Jacob, Ian, 5018
Jacobmeyer, Wolfgang, 5384, 5405
Jacobs, Monty, 3779
Jacobsen, Hans-Adolf, 3215, 3501, 3510, 3912, 4014, 4613, 4632, 4633, 4745, 4760, 5002, 5005–5007, 5116
Jacobsen, Jacob, 5953
Jacoby, Fritz, 4053
Jacoby, Gerhard, 5326
Jacoby, (Studienrat), 2289
Jacot, B. L., 5585
Jacquemyns, G., 5518
Jadfard, René, 4035
Jäckel, Eberhard, 632, 738a, 5456
Jäger, August, 567
Jaeger, Hans, 6396
Jäger, Herbert, 3310
Jäger, Jörg-Johannes, 1603
Jaeger, Seraphine, 2214
Jägerstätter, Franz, 3366
Jaensch, E.-R., 2439
Jaensch, Walther, 2886
Järte, Otto, 1064
Jagiellon University, 6175
Jagow, Dietrich von, 3187
Jagschitz, Gerhard, 4120
Jagusch, Heinrich, 1726
Jahn, Friedrich Ludwig, 171, 2884

Jahn, Fritz, 2879
Jahncke, Kurt, 16
Jahnke, Karl-Heinz, 2452, 2461, 2462
Jahrbuch des Auslandsamtes der deutschen Dozentenschaft. . . ., 2421
Jahrbuch für auslandsdeutsche Sippenkunde, 4002
Jahrbuch des Deutschen Handwerks 1935, 1748
Jahrbuch des deutschen Heeres, 4797
Jahrbuch der deutschen Musik, 2627
Jahrbuch der deutschen Wirtschaft 1937, 1515
Jahrbuch für nationalsozialistische Wirtschaft, 1516
Jaide, Walter, 2628
Jalabert, Ricardo, 4575
Jalbrzykowski, Jan, 5861
Jam, Dr., *pseud.*, 2001
Jameson, Storm, 5733
Jamet, Claude, 5452
Jamrowski, Otto, 23
Janeff, Janko, 4150
Janke, Willi, 5537
Jankuhn, Herbert, 34
Jannasch, W., 1876
Janover (Janow) Jewish labour camp, 5755, 6144
Janowsky, Oscar I., 3913
Jansen, Jan, 2022, 3394
Jansen, Quirin, 940
Janssen, Gregor, 4695
Janssen, H., 2032
Janssen, Karl-Heinz, 721
Jantzen, Walter, 2281, 2282
Japan: general, 3172, 3173, 4090–4099
   and Third Reich, 4083, 4086, 4093–4096, 4098, 4602
   See also the Axis
Jarmatz, Klaus, 3764a
Jaromir, *pseud.*, 2919
Jasenovac concentration camp, 6145
Jasper, Gerhard, 3693
Jasper, Gotthard, 1039
Jaspers, Karl, 5615, 6226
Jastrzebski, Wlodzimierz, 6179
Jaubert, Gaston (Col. Jonage), 5810
Jawischowitz concentration camp, 6053
Jaworski, Marek, 5975
Jedlicka, Ludwig, 3502
Jędrzejewicz, Wacław, 4320
Jehlicka, F., 4495
Jehovah's Witnesses, 1799, 1800

Jelinek, Y., 5790
Jellinek, K., 404
Jena: Friedrich-Schiller-Universität Historisches Institut, 33
Jenks, William A., 635
Jents, Thomas L., 4818
Jentsch, Gerhart, 3156
Jentzsch, Bernd, 3799
Jerk, Wiking, 5126
Jersch-Wenzel, Stefi, 3598
Jersey, 5318, 6016
Jeruschalmi, Elieser, 6260
Jesenska, Milena, 6186
Jess, Friedrich, 405
Jessen, Franz de, 4359
Jessop, T. E., 3936
Jesuits, 507, 557, 2002–2004
Jetzinger, Franz, 636
Jevrejski Almanah, 5898
Jewish badge—*See* yellow badge
Jewish Central Information Office, 3532, 3625
Jewish Historical Museum, Belgrade, 5899
Jewish Relief Unit, BAOR, 6432
Jewish survivors, 6426–6439
'Jewish world conspiracy', 250, 251, 297–307, 472–491, 501, 1799, 1890
Jews, European, persecution of: general, 32a, 3215, 5170, 5604, 5660–5664—
   See also Holocaust, individual countries, ghettoes and concentration camps
   deportations and expulsions of: general, 3799, 5112, 5212, 5853
      from Austria, 1443, 3692, 5802, 5959
      from Belgium, 5775, 5776
      from France, 5802, 5808, 5810, 5811
      from Holland, 6080
      from Hungary, 5842
      from Italy, 5843, 5848
      from Yugoslavia, 5900
   health damage to, 5977, 5982, 6445–6451
   intellectuals, 5907, 5951, 5978
   physicians, 3596a, 3643, 3665, 5864, 5977
   protests and reactions, 2896, 2897, 6292–6325
   rescue and relief efforts: general, 2683, 3358, 3604, 3605, 3615–3619, 5112, 5521, 5734, 5810, 6261, 6326–6393
      failure to rescue, 6328, 6329, 6333, 6334, 6346, 6363, 6367, 6386, 6391

resistance of, 5653, 5671, 5673, 5675, 5690, 5703, 5704, 5893—*See also* ghettoes, individual countries and partisans, Jewish
restitution and reparations, 6243, 6453–6455, 6459
spoliation of, 3626, 3629, 3631–3635, 5199, 5786, 5825, 5828, 5868
statistics on, 15, 5207, 5695
Jews, foreign in Third Reich, 1356, 3594
Jews, German: cultural life in Third Reich, general, 3675–3684
   education, 3677–3682
   sport, 3683, 3684
and National Socialist foreign policy, 3891, 4067, 5678, 5783
persecution of, general, 1842, 3322, 3323, 3339, 3346, 3349, 3527–3706, 4538, 4667, 5661—*See also* individual towns and regions
   cultural, 2417, 3623, 3636–3647
   deportations and expulsions, 3341, 3555, 3568, 3571, 3575, 3600, 3615, 3668, 5935
   economic, 3623–3635
   extermination, 3555–3558, 3587
   'J-Stempel', 6386
rescue of, 6349–6354
resistance of, 3671, 3672, 3680, 3685–3689, 5671
self-help attempts, 3662–3674
Joch, Winfried, 2872
Jochmann, Werner, 746, 753, 955
Jodl, Alfred, 715
Joesten, Joachim, 4357
Jöstlein, Hans, 1727
Joffe, Constantin, 6287
Johann, A. E., 4978
Johannsen, Kurt, 4036
Johanny, Carl, 116
Johe, Werner, 1414
John, Evan, 732
Johnson, Edward, 6244
Johnson, Niel M., 4551
Johnston, M. K., 804
Johst, Hanns, 319, 2562–2564, 2712
Joly, Maurice, 300
Jonak von Freyenwald, Hans, 301, 306, 426, 1799
Jonasson, Matthías, 4363
Jonca, Karol, 1819
Jones, D. Ellis, 804
Jones, F. Elwyn, 3857

Jones, Peter Blundell, 2657
Jones, R. V., 5145
Jones, Thomas, 1245
Jones, Walter J., 568
Jong, Dirk de, 5558
Jong, Louis de, 5533, 5549, 5821
Joods Historisch Museum, Amsterdam, 5822
Joodsche Perscommissie voor Bijzondere Berichtgeving, 2897
Joos, Joseph, 6116
Jorand, P., 6142
Jordan, Rudolf, 845, 1788, 5169
Jordan, W. M., 3937
Jorgensen, Aage, 3147
Joseph, Artur, 3602
Josephus, *pseud.*, 6299
Jowitt, Lord (William Allen Jowitt), 6089
Joyce, William, 3084, 3123
Juchniewicz, Mieczysław, 5406
'Jud Süss', 2723, 2727–2729
Juden stellen sich vor, 2912
'Judenrat', 5913, 5915, 5933
Judenspiegel . . ., 225, 226
judges, National Socialist, 1388, 1389, 1395, 1396, 1410
Jüdische Gemeinde Berlin, 6433
'*Jüdische Rundschau*', 3667, 3674
Jünger, Ernst, 173, 349, 2335, 2551, 2565–2567, 3006
Jünger, Friedrich Georg, 1202
Jünger, Wolfgang, 1604
Jürgens, Adolf, 2742
Juhász, Gyula, 4160
Jukic, Ilija, 5304
Jules-Julien, M., 4578
Julitte, Pierre, 6100
Jullian, Marcel, 4888
July 20 Plot (1944), 1137, 1408, 2955, 3484–3526
June 30 (1934), 1101–1112, 3192
Jung, Hermann, 2913, 5097
Jung, Rudolf, 172
Jung, Willi, 2368
'*Junge Front/Michael*', 2809
Junge, Max, 16
Jungermann, Wilhelm, 1605
Jungfernhof labour camp, 6056
'Jungkonservative', 887
Jungnickel, Max, 420
Jungvolk-Jahrbuch, 2171
Junk, Nikolaus, 2029
'Junker', 1551

Junker, Detlef, 1789
Jurášek, Stanislav, 5786
jurists: Jewish, 450, 3638–3641
    National Socialist, 1096, 1195,
    1384–1399, 1410, 2436, 2447, 3375,
    3450, 3653, 5636
Just, Leo, 34
Just, Oskar, 553
justice, perversion of, 1344, 1413–1422
Justin, Eva, 6272
Justinian, *pseud.*, 1093
Justrow, Karl, 2327
Justus, Dr., *pseud.—See* Briman, Aron
Juvet, René, 1246

Kabeli, Isaac, 5817a
Kaczmarch, Jan, 3858
Kade, Ludwig, 4807
Kadner, Siegfried, 2914
Kadritzke, Niels, 1185, 1517
Kaemmel, Ernst, 1571
Kahanovich, Moshe, 5893
Kahl, Hans-Dietrich, 2082
Kahl-Furthmann, G., 859
Kahn, David, 5151
Kahn, Siegbert, 221
Kaindl, Raimund Friedrich, 344
Kaisenberg, Georg, 1111
Kaiser, Friedhelm, 2780
Kaiser, Helmut, 2551
Kaiser, Klaus, 949
Kaiser, Marcus Urs, 1908
Kaiser-Wilhelm-Gesellschaft, 2405
Kaiserwald concentration camp, 3603,
    6056
Kalbe, Ernstgert, 1094
Kalender der Volkszeitung 1939, 5251
Kalijarvi, Thorsten V., 4313
Kalinov, Rina, 5824
Kallenbach, Hans, 637
Kalmanovitch, Zelig, 5962
Kalme, Albert, 5369
Kalow, Gert, 6487
Kaltenbrunner-Berichte, 3503
Kamenec, Ivan, 5791, 6169
Kamenetsky, Igor, 5189
Kamin, Gerhard, 6107
Kamla, T. A., 3772
Kampffmeyer, G., 188
Kampfgemeinschaft revolutionärer
    Nationalsozialisten, 895
Kampmann, Theoderich, 1835
Kamps, Karl, 6095

Kanaan, Haviv, 4594
Kandel, I. L., 2152
Kannapin, Hans-Eckhardt, 6245
Kantorowicz, Alfred, 2483, 2606, 3771
Kantorowicz, N., 5869
Kantzenbach, Friedrich Wilhelm, 1945,
    1956
Kaplan, Chaim A., 5973
Kapp, Gottfried, 2568
Kapp, Luise, 2568
Kapp, Rolf, 3938
Kappe, Walter, 4541
Kappler, Herbert, 5845, 5846
Karaites, 5665, 5806
Karl, Georg, 427
Karlsruhe, 3323
Karoli, Richard, 1574
Karrenbrock, Helga, 3422
Karsai, Elek, 4646, 5842
Karsch, Joachim, 2676
Karski, Jan, 5407
Karsten, Anitra, 3166
Kasten, Helmut, 5190
Kasztner, Reszö, 6368, 6369
Kater, Horst, 1858
Kater, Michael H., 1800, 2440, 3209
Katholisch-Nationalkirchliche Bewegung,
    1968, 1969
Katholische Aktion, 2009
Katholischer Akademieverband, 1967
Katholischer Jungmännerverband, 2456,
    2457
Katholischer Lehrerverband, 2247
Katsh, Abraham I., 5973
Katz, Ephraim, 5718
Katz, Josef, 3603
Katz, Robert, 6284
Ka-Tzetnik 135633, *pseud.*, 6025, 6071
Katznelson, Yitzhak, 5967
Kauder, Viktor, 4329
Kauffmann, Fritz Alexander, 2648, 2677
Kaufmann, Günter, 2153, 2373
Kaufmann, Max, 5767
Kaufmann, Theodore Nathan, 3102
Kaul, Friedrich-Karl, 1410, 3654, 6233
Kautsky, Benedikt, 6026
Kautter, Eberhard, 345, 3090
Kay, G. R., 6114
Kaznelson, Siegmund, 3636
Keane, Richard, 4265
Kedros, André, 5283
Kedward, H. R., 5502
Keeding, Hans, 3021

Kehr, Helen, 78, 84
Kehrberg, Arno, 4870
Kehrl, Hans, 1203, 3276
Keil, Heinz, 3592
Keilig, Wolf, 4798, 4799
Keim, Helmut, 2382, 2383
Keiper, Wilhelm, 4561
Keipert, Hans, 2278
Keitel, Wilhelm, 4772, 4973
Keiter, Friedrich, 379
Kele, Max H., 1006
Keller, Hans K. E. L., 3992, 3993
Keller, J., 465
Keller, Wilhelm, 3026
Kelley, Douglas McG., 804, 5642
Kellog pact, 3917
Kemna concentration camp, 3194
Kemnitz, Hanno von, 2915
Kempner, Benedicta Maria, 2023
Kempner, Robert M. W., 1015, 1413, 1994, 3571, 5617, 5618, 5715, 5716, 5823
Kempowski, Walter, 6488, 6489
Kennan, George F., 3431, 5327
Kennard, Coleridge, 5485
Kennedy, John F., 4266
Kenner, Jacob, 5859
Kenrick, Donald, 6273
Kens, Karlheinz, 4871
Kent, George C., 3885
Kent, Madeleine, 1247
Kentie, W. O., 4998
Kerekes, Lajos, 4160
Kermish, Joseph (Kermisz, Josef), 5210, 5875, 5968, 5971, 5986, 5992
Kern, Erich, 676, 3395, 4840, 6497
Kern, Hans, 2320
Kern, Karl Peter, 3694
Kern, Paul, 6164
Kernholt, Otto, 206, 451
Kernmayr, Erich Knud—*See* Kern, Erich
Kerr, Alfred, 3813, 3814
Kerr, Walter, 5062
Kerrl, Hans, 1269
Kershaw, Ian, 676a, 1173
Kersten, A. E., 4309
Kersten, Felix, 3246–3248
Kertesz, Stephen D., 4165
Kerutt, Horst, 2185
Kessel, Joseph, 3248, 5809, 6100
Kesselring, Albert, 4773, 4774, 4969, 5015, 5111
Kesselring, Marietta von, 5409

Kessemeier, Carin, 2813
Kessler, Heinrich, 186
Kesten, Hermann, 3815
Ketelsen, Uwe-Karsten, 595, 2531, 2708
Kettenacker, Lothar, 3396, 5468
Ketter, Friedrich, 1434
Keyserling, Graf Hermann, 338
Kharkov, 5443
Kibbutz Lohamei Haghettaot, 5653
Kiedrzynska, Wanda, 6027
Kiehl, Walter, 808, 811, 2978
Kielar, Wieslaw, 6072
Kielce Ghetto, 3692
Kielmansegg, Johann Adolf Graf, 3870
Kienast, E., 5
Kiessling, Wolfgang, 3738, 3764a
Killanin, Michael Morris (Lord), 4486
Killinger, Manfred von, 846, 2996, 3195
Killy, Walther, 2506
Kimche, Jon, 5149
Kimenkowski, Ewald, 1078
Kimmel, Adolf, 4230
Kimmel, Günter, 5623
Kimmich, Christopher M., 4344
Kinder, Christian, 1867
Kindermann, Heinz, 2709
King, Joseph, 1040
King-Hall, Stephen, 3059
Kipphan, Klaus, 4546
Kirchen, 3577
Kirchheimer, Otto, 1572
Kirchliche Hochschule Berlin, 1836
'*Kirchlicher Anzeiger*', 1850
Kirchner, Hellmut, 3069–3071
Kirchner, Klaus, 3069–3071
Kirchner, Wilhelm, 4909
Kirdorf, Emil, 989
Kirkconnell, Watson, 4288
Kirkpatrick, Clifford, 2104
Kirkpatrick, Ivone, 4284
Kirn, Paul, 4006
Kirsch, Gerhard, 5050
Kirschenmann, Dietrich, 569
Kirschschläger, Rudolf, 5270
Kirst, Hans Helmut, 3504
Kisch, Egon Erwin, 144, 3751
Kisker, Karl Peter, 6445
Kissel, Hans, 5089, 5120
Kissenkoetter, Udo, 862
'Kitsch', 2211, 2498
Kittel, Gerhard, 421, 1820, 1821
Kittner, Earl W., 6219
Kjellen, Rudolf, 358, 359

'*Kladderadatsch*', 2916
Klaehn, Friedrich Joachim, 2917, 3184
Klaer, Erling, 6380
Klagges, Dietrich, 320, 530, 847, 2051
Klare, Kurt, 1424, 1435
Klarsfeld, Serge & Beate, 3556, 5807, 5808, 6513
Klausener, Erich, 2024, 3296
Klausner, Israel, 6028
Klee, Karl, 5019
Kleffens, E. N. van, 4994
Klein, Alfons, 6219
Klein, Anton, 3579
Klein, Burton H., 1770
Klein, Catherine, 3604
Klein, Hanns K. E., 2234
Klein, Karl Kurt, 4007
Kleist, Peter, 1145
Kleist-Schmenzin, Ewald von, 3470
Klemer, Gerhard, 2187
Klemperer, Klemens von, 173
Klemperer, Victor, 2505
Klenner, Jochen, 117
Klepper, Jochen, 1869, 3367, 3695, 6386
Klessmann, Christoph, 5418
Klieger, Bernard, 5739
Klimaszewski, Tadeusz, 5248
Kling, Hermann, 4231
Klinger, Fritz, 1933
Klinger, Max, *pseud—See* Geyer, Curt
Klingler, Günther, 1685
Klingmüller, Ernst, 4576
Klingner, Edwin, 2556
Klink, Ernst, 5090
Klinnert, Ernst, 2433
Klodwig, Rudolf, 2083
Klönne, Arno, 2453
Klöss, Erhard, 41a, 747
Kloidt, Franz, 2024, 2039
Klonicki (Klonymus), Aryeh, 5740
Klose, Kevin, 5746
Klose, Werner, 2135
Klotz, Helmut, 3914, 3967
Klotz, Leopold, 1780
Klotzbach, Kurt, 1705, 3330
Klütz, Alfred, 1417
Klug, Kajetan, 3148
Kluge, Helga, 2879
Klugman, Aleksander, 5929
Kluic, Stevo, 1248
Kluke, Paul, 916, 1612
Klusacek, Christine, 5252
Klutentreter, Willy, 2781

Knab, Otto Michael, 3324
Knauerhase, Ramon, 1518
Knauss, Erwin, 3573
Knickerbocker, H. R., 885
Kniggendorf, Walter, 2084
Knipperdolling, *pseud.*, 2919
Knipping, Ulrich, 3570
Knoblich, (Dr.), 2227
Knöpfel, Hans Erwin, 1385
Knoop-Graf, Anneliese, 2473
Knop, W. G. F., 1509, 3059
Knopp, Josephine, 6522
Knost, Friedrich A., 1361, 1487
Knyphausen, Anton, 3165
Koch, Erich, 93, 848, 5408
Koch, Franz, 2570
Koch, Hans, 1779
Koch, Hannsjoachim W., 2186
Koch, Heinrich, 2730
Koch, Horst-Adalbert, 4910
Koch, Karl W. H., 3196
Koch, Paul, 193
Koch-Kent, Henri, 5567, 5568
Kochan, Lionel, 3656
Kochanowski, Erich, 481
Kochba, Adina, 5824
Kochskaemper, Max, 2649
Kockskemper, Wilhelm, 462
Koebner, Thomas, 3814
Koechlin, Alphons, 1934
Koehl, Robert L., 5211
Köhler, Gerhard, 2842
Koehler, Hansjürgen, 3270
Köhler, Henning, 2351
Köhler, Wolfgang, 3757
Köhler-Irrgang, Ruth, 2105
Koehn, Ilse, 3702
Köhn-Behrens, Charlotte, 380
Köhne, Renate, 62a
Köhrer, Helmuth, 3626
Kölble, Josef, 1333, 1519
'*Kölnische Zeitung*', 5012
König, Heinrich, 3432
König, Joel, *pseud.*, 3617
König, Karl, 3022
König, René, 2406
Koenig, W. J., 4616
Königk, Georg, 4568
Königstein concentration camp, 6030
Koenigswald, Harold von, 2584
Könitzer, Willi, 428
Koepp, Friedrich, 363
Koeppen von Oehlschlägel, A. O., 2928

Körber, Hilde, 2136
Körber, Robert, 3946, 4130
Koerber, Walther, 3478, 4904
Koerner, Ralf Richard, 2782
Körner, Ruth, 83
Koestler, Arthur, 3809, 6206
Köstring, Ernst, 4413
Kötschau, Karl, 1435
Kofler, J. A., 1781
Kogel, (Hauptmann), 4211
Kogon, Eugen, 933, 6029, 6489
Kohanski, Alexander S., 6393
Kohl, Hermann, 4889
Kohl, Louis von, 4358
Kohlhausen, H., 4911
Koht, Halvdan, 4366
Kokoschka, Oskar, 3803
Kokoška, Jaroslav, 4487
Kolb, Eberhard, 6092
Kolbe, Dieter, 1409
Kolbe, Maximilian, 3368
Kolbenheyer, Erwin Guido, 183, 321, 2527, 2569–2571, 2712
Kolbow, Karl Friedrich, 2484
Kollatz, Karl, 4764
Koller, Hellmut, 2843
Koller, Karl, 5118
Kollwitz, Hans, 2678
Kollwitz, Käthe, 2678
Kolmar, Gertrud, 3645, 3799
Koloniales Schrifttum in Deutschland, 4037
Komitee der Antifaschistischen Widerstandskämpfer in der DDR, 6176
Kommission zur Erforschung der Geschichte der Frankfurter Juden, 3572
Kommission für Geschichte des Parlamentarismus. . . ., 890, 1124, 3727, 4074
Kommoss, Rudolf, 486
Konjunktur-Statistisches Handbuch, 1520
Konlecher, Peter, 2964a
Konrad, Franz, 1275
Konrad, Helmut, 5261
Kooy, G. A., 4307
Kopf, Paul, 2038
Kopp, Guido, 6102
Kopp, Hans, 2059
Kopp, Otto, 3312
Kopp, Walter, 2065, 5170
Koppe, Wilhelm, 4453
Koppel, Helga, 1149
Korben Labour camp, 6056

Korczak, Janusz, 5974–5976
Kordt, Erich, 3915
'Korherr file', 6508, 6513
Kormann, Gert, 5692
Kornev, N., 613
Kort, M. de, 5825
Kortner, Fritz, 3780
Korwin-Rhodes, Marta, 4970
Koschorke, Helmuth, 3277, 3278, 5241
Kossak, Zofia, 6073
Kossoy, Edward, 5654
Kosthorst, Erich, 3397
Kostoris, Sergio, 5852
Koszyck, Kurt, 2783
Kotz, Alfred, 519
Kotze, Hildegard von, 712, 748, 2835, 2844, 3468
Koutek, Jaroslav, 4195
Kovaćić, Matija, 5314
Kovacs, Etienne, 5291
Kovno Ghetto, 5689, 5922–5924
Kowalenko, Władisław, 5419
Kowalski, Isaac, 5693
Kracauer, Siegfried, 2731
'*Kracauer Zeitung*', 2828
Kränzlein, Kurt, 2365
Krätschmer, Ernst-Günther, 4826
Krafft, Herbert, 1605
Kraft, H. H., 4036
'Kraft durch Freude', 1731, 1735–1745
KdF-Wagen-Fabrik, 1725
Krainz, Othmar, 4532
Krakau, Knud, 5787
Krakauer, Max, 3618
Krakowski, Shmuel, 5875
Kral, Josef, 1970
Král, Václav, 4196, 4488
Kramarz, Joachim, 3518
Kramer, Josef, 6089
Kramer, Thomas W., 4589
Krannhals, Paul, 580
Kraske, Erich, 3886
Krasnodar, 5443
Krasuski, Jozef, 5420
Kraus, J., 1623
Kraus, Karl, 2501, 3535
Kraus, Ota, 5694, 6031, 6074
Kraus, René, 5232a
Kraus Periodicals, 69
Krause, A. B., 1521
Krause, Erich, 1164
Krause, Gerhard, 2900
Krause, Ilse, 3342

Krause, Reinhold, 2321
Krause-Vilmar, D., 2246
Kraushaar, Luise, 3419, 3443
Krauskopf, Robert, 4617
Krausnick, Helmut, 748, 933, 1147, 3215, 3468, 5242
Krebs, Albert, 917, 3512
Krebs, Hans, 721, 4197
Krebs, Richard, 1222
Krefeld, 3341, 6241
Krehbiel-Darmstädter, Maria, 6137
Kreidler, Eugen, 4677
Kreipe, Werner, 4757
Kreisauer Kreis, 3378–3384, 3386
Kremer, Johann Paul, 6062, 6070, 6082
Kremmler, H., 1585
Kren, Jan, 5336
Kreppel, Otto, 2441
Kreslins, Janis A., 3882
Kresse, Kurt, 3342
Kretschmar, Georg, 1801
Kretschmar, Gottfried, 1931
Kretzschmann, Hermann, 2352
Kreutz, Annelie, 3559
Kreutzberger, Max, 3676
'Kreuz-Zeitung', 2830
Krieck, Ernst, 2154, 2155, 2407, 2485, 2743
Krieg dem Hunger!, 3011
Krieger, Arnold, 4330
Krieger, Heinz, 4267
Kriegk, Otto, 3939, 3947, 4451
Kriegsbücherei der deutschen Jugend, 4671
'Kriegsschuldlüge', 3932
Kries, Wilhelm von, 2976, 3061, 3125
Krietsch, Karl, 2283
Krimp, H. M., 6191
Kris, Ernst, 3046
'Kristallnacht'—See November 1938 pogrom
Kröger, Hans, 1065
Kröger, Theodor, 2994
Krogmann, Carl Vincent, 1204
Krogman, Willy, 3994
Krohn, Marie-Elisabeth, 1451
Kronenberg, Kurt, 1473
Kropáč, František, 5345, 5352
Kropat, Wolf-Arno, 3576
Krose, Hermann, 1802
Kroug, Wolfgang, 2463
Kruck, Alfred, 160
Krüger, Alf, 956, 3627
Krüger, Arnd, 2875, 2901

Krüger, Karl, 5171
Krueger, Kurt, 697, 1986
Krüger, Oskar, 1119
Krüper, Adolf, 2303
Krug, Karl, 1372
Krug, Wilhelm, 2850
Krugmann, R. W., 1650
Kruk, Herman, 5963
Krummacher, F. A., 748, 4407
Krupp firm, 5636, 6243
Krutsch, Hermann, 1561
Kruus, Raul, 5373
Kruuse, Jens, 5491
Kryzanowski, Ludwik, 5730
Kubach, F., 2442
Kubátová, Ludmila, 6009, 6034
Kube, Wilhelm, 849, 850, 1041, 5894
Kubelka, Peter, 2964a
Kubizek, August, 638
Kubovy, Aryeh Leon, 5673
Kuby, Erich, 5127, 5998
Kuch, Rudolf, 4735
Kucher, Walter, 496
Kuck, Fritz, 4603
Kuckhoff, Adam, 3369
Kuckhoff, Armin, 3374
Kuckhoff, Greta, 3369, 3448
Kuczynski, Boguslaw, 4971
Kuczynski, Jürgen, 1706
Kübler, Fritz, 4564
Küchler-Silberman, Lena, 6261
Kügelgen, Bernt von, 3733
Kügelgen, Else von, 3733
Kühling, Karl, 967
Kühmayer, Ignaz Christoph, 3288
Kühn, Günter, 6103
Kühn, Heinz, 2012, 3072, 3398, 3411
Kühn, Walter, 2629
Kühne, Lotar, 1390
Kühne, Rudolf, 1545
Kühner, Otto-Heinrich, 4647
Kühnl, Reinhard, 47, 863, 1042
Kümmel, Herbert, 2918
Künneth, Walter, 1851, 1852, 2052
Küppers, Heinrich, 2247
Kürschners deutscher Gelehrten-Kalender, 7
Kürschners deutscher Literatur-Kalender, 8
Küstermeier, Rudolf, 6094
Kuhn, Axel, 738a, 3916
Kuhn, Heinz, 1204a
Kuhn, Helmut, 2392
Kuhn, Käthe, 3389
Kulischer, Eugene M., 5212

574

Kulišová, Taňa, 6199
Kulka, Erich, 5694, 6031, 6074
Kum'a N'Dumbe III, Alexandre, 4038
Kulkielko, Renya, 5870
Kummer, Rudolf, 487
Kunisch, Hermann, 2588
Kunkel, Wolfgang, 2392
Kuntze, Paul H., 346
Kunze, Karl, 2267
Kunze, Oskar, 2873
Kuper, Jack, 6262
Kupfer-Koberwitz, Edgar, 6117
Kupper, Alfons, 1987
Kupść, Bogumil, 5399
Kuptsch, J., 1897
Kur, Tadeusz, 5404
Kuratorium 'Gedenkstätte Ernst Thälmann', 3438
Kuratorium für Staatsbürgerliche Bildung, Hamburg, 2945
Kurbs, (Dr.), 4869
Kurella, Alfred, 1092
Kurhessen-Waldeck, 1864
Kurmark, 960
Kurowski, Franz, 4912, 5081
Kursell, Otto von, 937, 982
Kurth, Gottfried, 4302
Kurth, Paul, 442
Kutakov, L., 4086
Kuznetsov, A., 5891
Kwiet, Konrad, 5534
Kyffhäuser Bund, 1127, 1128
Kyffhäuser-Verband der Vereine Deutscher Studenten, 363
Kynass, Fritz, 452

Laack-Michel, Ursula, 3365
Laatsman, W., 1837
Labusquière, Jean, 5008
Lachmann, Günter, 4442
Lachwa Ghetto, 5925
Lacko, M., 4166
Lador-Lederer, J. Josef, 1636
Lämmert, Eberhard, 2506, 3752
'Länder', 1111, 1112
Laeven, Harald, 3176
Laffan, R.G.D., 3888
Lagarde, Paul de, 174–176, 183, 1895
La Guardia Gluck, Gemma, 6187
Lakowski, Richard, 5117
Laloire, Marcel, 1276
Lambert, Gabriel, 1146

Lambert, Gilles, 5834
Lambert, Margaret, 4054, 4248
Lambert, Richard S., 2946
Lamm, Hans, 3586
Lammers, H.-H., 1277
Lampe, David, 5020
Lampe, Friedrich Wilhelm, 614
Lampe, Hans, 1288
Landau, 3578
Landau, F., 5866
Landau, Kalman, 6443
Landjahr—See Reichsarbeitsdienst
Landsberg Fortress, 637
Lane, Barbara Miller, 322, 2650
Lang, Daniel, 6490
Lang, F., 3853
Lang, Hans, 2172
Lang, Jochen von, 834
Lang, Johann, 1568
Lang, Serge, 815
Langbein, Hermann, 6032, 6061, 6066, 6075
Lange, Carl, 2486
Lange, Dieter, 3736
Lange, Eitel, 799
Lange, Friedrich, 2977, 4008
Lange, Helmut, 4407
Lange, Horst, 4648, 6246
Lange, Karl, 353, 733
Lange, (Major i. Generalstab) von, 4706
Lange, Walter, 2641
Langen, F. E. Frhr. von, 231
Langenbeck, Curt, 2712
Langenbucher, Hellmuth, 2521
Langenbucher, Wolfgang, 3455
Langer, Lawrence, L., 3645
Langer, Walter C., 703
Langer, William L., 703
Langevin, B., 3851
Langeweyde, Wolf Sluyterman von, 581
Langgässer, Elisabeth, 1205
Langhoff, Wolfgang, 6033
Lania, Leo, 3816
Lanz von Liebenfels, Georg (Jorg), 291, 292
Lapper, Karl, 2184
Laqueur, Walter, 4408, 6333
Larsen, Egon, 2933
Larsen, Helge, 5575
Lasker-Schüler, Else, 3799
Laski, Harold J., 310
Laski, Neville, 3549

Latin America: general, 3163, 3764a, 4519–4522, 4552, 4553, 4555
'Volksdeutsche', 4554, 4556
See also individual countries
Latour, Conrad F., 4078, 5430
Latvia: general, 5214, 5374–5376
Jews of, 5766, 5767
Latvijas PSR Ministru Padomes Arhivu Parvalde, 5376
Laubenheimer, A., 3003
Laubenthal, Heinz, 3047
Laun, Rudolf, 6412
Launay, Jacques de, 2090, 4634, 5119
Launay, Michel, 5009
Laurens, Anne, 4308
Laurie, A. P., 1249
Laval, Pierre, 5501
Laveleye, Victor de, 3048
Lavi, Th., 6376
Law(s), National Socialist: general, 1263, 1323–1422, 2315
administrative, 1342, 1343, 1347
citizenship, 565, 1328, 1357, 1363, 1366, 1482, 1487, 5787
constitutional, 569, 1345–1348
criminal, 1364, 1367, 1370–1383, 2187, 3275, 5329
economic, 1329, 1368, 1529, 1568, 1571, 1609, 1620, 1624, 1641—See also under finance
international, 564, 1323, 1350, 1362
and 'New Order', 5366, 5454
and politics, 565, 573, 576, 1332, 1339, 1414
racial, 1060, 1339, 1349–1369, 2401, 3627, 3706, 5461, 5649, 5670, 5757, 5795, 5804, 5806
'Reform' of, 1336, 1371, 1373–1375, 1378, 1405
and religion, 1339
war-time, 1322, 1329, 1618, 1708, 3275, 4675, 4702, 4703
See also under workers, youth, etc.
Lawaczeck, Franz, 545
Lawrence, David Herbert, 293
Layton, Walter, 1509
Lazarowitz, Leopold, 5864
Lea Valley Books, 70
Leach, Barry A., 4419
League of Nations: general, 281, 3671–3673, 3945–3950, 4202
disarmament conferences, 3951, 3952, 3954, 3957

and Jews, 6312, 6313
Lean, E. Tangye, 3049
learned institutions, German—See universities
Leasor, James, 806
'Lebensborn', 3224, 3225
'Lebensraum', 352–354, 1176, 2179, 4016–4019, 4148, 4771, 5164, 5189
'Lebensunwertes Leben', 187, 415, 1494, 4667, 6218—See also euthanasia
Leber, Annedore, 3399, 3400, 3637
Leber, Julius, 3388, 3455, 3505
Leboucher, Fernande, 6348
Lebovics, Herman, 256
Le Chêne, Evelyn, 6154
Lechner, L., 2085
Leclef, (Chanoine), 5519
Ledeen, Michael A., 324
Lederer, Ivo J., 3940
Lederer, Zdenek, 5954
Lederman, Charles, 5803
Lee, Asher, 4765, 4872
Leeb, Emil, 4688
Leeb, Johannes, 1142, 5629
Leeb, Wilhelm Ritter von, 4736, 4775
Leers, Johann von, 153, 429, 466, 554, 570, 918, 1749, 2336, 3013, 3157, 3401, 4314, 4453
Leeuw, G. van der, 5556
Legion Condor, 4384
Le Grix, François, 677
Lehmann, (Dr.), 1373
Lehmann, Emil, 4104
Lehmann, Ernst A., 4849
Lehmann, Ernst Herbert, 2787, 3060
Lehmann, Ernst Josef, 3696
Lehmann, Hans Georg, 3714
Lehmann, Heinrich, 1621
Lehmann, Heinz, 4289
Lehmann, J. F., 269
Lehmann, Kurt, 3810
Lehmann, Max, 4268
Lehmann, Ott, 3869
Lehmann, Rudolf, 4827
Lehmann, Walter, 1474
Lehmann-Haupt, Hellmut, 2585, 2680
Lehmann-Russbueldt, Otto, 3968, 4852, 6434
Lehment, Joachim, 4723
Lehmkuhl, Herman K., 4987
Leibbrandt, Georg, 491
Leibbrandt, Gottlieb, 2995
Leibfried, Stephan, 1434a, 3665

Leibholz-Bonhoeffer, Sabine, 1924
Leibrock, Otto, 5273
Leider, K., 404
Leipelt, Hans, 2468
Leipzig, 1723, 2595, 2605, 3342, 5651
  Universitätsbibliothek, 3879
Leiser, Clara, 3459
Leiser, Erwin, 2732
Leist, Fritz, 2392, 2464
Leistritz, Hans Karl, 24, 571
Leitner, Sebastian, 4813
Lemkin, Raphael, 5191
Lemmer, Ernst, 1206
Lempp, Reinhart, 6442
Lenard, Philipp, 2420a, 2422, 2423
Lengyel, Olga, 6076
Leningrad, 5056, 5057
Lenk, Rudolf, 5253
Lennar, Rolf, 2874
Lennartz, Franz, 2532
Lennhoff, Eugene, 3985
Lent, Alfred, 4386
Lenz, Fritz, 400, 406
Lenz, Friedrich, 3158
Lenz, Wilhelm, 61
Leo Baeck Institute, New York, 2840,
  3676
  Veröffentlichungen, 79
  Year Book, London, 3536
Leonberg concentration camp, 6007
Leoncini, Francesco, 4198
Leonhard, Wolfgang, 3734
Leonhardt, Hans L., 5381
Leonhardt, Walter, 2328
Leonhardt, Werner, 1293
Leopold, John A., 2777
Lepêtre, Jean-Philippe, 3863
Lerche, Karl-Gustav, 2208
Lerg, Winifried B., 2853
Lerner, Daniel, 3073
Lersner, Dieter, 2459
Leruth, Maurice, 4578
Leshem, Perez, 6384
Leske, Gottfried, 4873
Lesniewski, Andrzej, 4331, 5213
Lessing, Theodor, 2482, 3642
Lessle, Manfred, 4269
Lestschinsky, Jacob, 3628, 5695
Leszczyński, Julian, 6109
Leszczyński, Kazimierz, 5861, 5874, 6280
Letterhaus, Bernhard, 2024
Léty, Pierre, 5008
Leuner, Heinz David, 6352

Lévai, Jenö (Eugene), 1994, 5288, 5292,
  5696, 5835, 5836, 6370, 6382
Levi, Primo, 6077
Levin, Dov, 5772, 5922
Levin, Nora, 5667
Levine, Herbert S., 4345
Levinstein, Meir, 5942
Levy, Alan, 6404
Lévy, Claude, 5809
Lévy-Bruhl, L., 3851
Levy-Hass, Hanna, 6093
Lewald, Theodor, 2875
Lewin, Isaac, 5859
Lewin, Ronald, 4782, 5024
Lewington, H. E., 4275
Lewinówna, Zofia, 6372
Lewis, David, 678
Lewis, John R., 5619
Lewis, Percy Wyndham, 639
Lewitan, Joseph, 5890
Lewy, Guenter, 1971
Lexer, Erich, 1491
Lexikon der deutschen Geschichte, 37
Ley, Robert, 26, 338, 808–811, 1735,
  1741, 2978, 3977
Leyen, Ferdinand Prinz von der, 4750
L'Houet, A., 241
Liang, Hsi Huey, 4608
Liberman, Kopel, 6300
Libya, 3170
Lichten, Joseph L., 6375
Lichtenberg, Bernhard, 2025
Lichtenburg concentration camp, 6030
Lichtenstein, Erwin, 3569
Lichtenstein, Franz, 3668
Lichtenstein, Fritz, 6384
Lichtenstein, Heiner, 6148
Liddell Hart, Basil Henry, 4751, 4779,
  4809
Lidice, 5343–5345
Lieb, Fritz, 1877
Lieber, H. J., 2741
Liebermann von Sonnenberg, Erich, 6012
Liedtke, Heinz, 3917
Liedloff, Werner, 2251
Liepelt, Adolf, 3279
Liepmann, Heinz, 3313, 3433
Lilge, Frederic, 2408
Lilje, Hans, 1935
Limbeck, Hans, 1522, 2902
Limonest concentration camp, 6137
Linck, Hugo, 1928
Lind, Jakov, 5741

Lindbeck-Larsen, Odd, 4988
Lindegren, Alina M., 2235
Lindemann, Christa, 1475
Lindemann, Helmut, 3381
Linden, Herbert, 1360
Linden, Walther, 1823
Lindenberg, Christoph, 94
Lindenberg, Friedrich Wolfgang, 2190
Lindgren, Henrik, 3522
Lindt, Andreas, 1934
Lindt, Peter M., 3817
Linebarger, Paul, 3031
Lingelbach, Karl Christoph, 2156
Lingens-Reiner, Ella, 6061
Lingg, Anton, 95
linguistics, National Socialist, 2501–2514, 2841, 2861, 5612, 5710–5713
'Link, The,' 4254
Link, Heinrich, 529
Link, Werner, 3727
Link, Wilhelm, 529
Linke, Lilo, 4155
Linklater, Eric, 5082
Linn, Dorothea, 3581
Linn, Edward, 6265
Linz, 2646, 5205
Lion, Jindrich, 5153
Lippe, 961, 962
Lippe, Karpel, 226
Lippe, Kurt B. Prinz zur, 3126
Lippert, Julius, 851, 852
Lips, Eva, 3370
Lipscher, Ladislav, 5792
Lipski, Józef, 4320
Lisicki, Tadeusz, 5145
Liskowsky, Oskar, 453
Lissner, Jacob, 1356
List, Guido von, 189
Liste des schädlichen und unerwünschten Schrifttums 1938–1941, 2607
Listowel, Earl of (William Francis Hare), 3973
Litai, Chaim Lazar, 5993
literature, German: general, 2525–2609, 3773, 4007
fiction, 2525, 2529, 2541, 2565, 2572, 2573, 2578
Jewish, 3644, 3647, 3675–3677
National Socialist, 339, 2519, 2521, 2531–2537, 2586, 3872
National Socialist theories on, 499, 587–589, 2543, 2801
nationalist, 349–351, 2531, 2578

poetry, 2527, 2580–2587
See also theatre
literature, German, exile: general, 2536, 3754, 3764a–3777, 3798–3831
fiction, 3722, 3745, 3770, 3772, 3806–3810
poetry, 3798–3805
political, 3709, 3711, 3713, 3715, 3726, 3728, 3741, 3744, 3759–3762, 3813, 3819–3822, 3831
theatre, 2712, 3778–3783, 3811, 3812
Lithuania, 5377–5379
Jews of, 5768–5772
Littell, Franklin H., 1822
Litten, Hans, 2482, 3371
Litten, Irmgard, 3371
Littlejohn, David, 1299
Littmann, Arnold, 2192
Littner, Jakob, 5742
Litzmannstadt—See Lodz
Livingstone, Laura, 6338
Livre Blanc austro-allemand sur les assassinats des 30 Juin et 25 Juillet 1934 . . ., 1108
Lloyd, Lorna, 3953
Loch, Walter, 3292
Locke, Hubert G., 1822
Lodewickx, Augustin, 4287
Lodz: city and region, 5409, 5410, 5881
ghetto, 1198, 5860, 5907, 5914, 5926–5932
Loeber, Dietrich A., 5214
Löbsack, Wilhelm, 838, 839
Loeff, Wolfgang, 2337
Löhde, Walter, 2053
Löpelmann, Martin, 2157
Loeper, Wilhelm Friedrich, 853
Loerke, Oskar, 2831
Loerzer, Bruno, 3867
Loesch, Karl C. von, 4004
Löschenkohl, Bernhard, 3120
Lösener, Bernhard, 1361
Löwe, Heinrich Georg F., sen., 237
Loewenberg, Peter, 2139
Loewenberg, Rolf, 6455
Loewenfeld, Philipp, 1016
Loewenstein, Prince Hubertus, 919, 1207, 3718
Loewenstein, Karl, 5940
Löwenthal, Zdenko, 5901
Loewy, Ernst, 2533, 3709
Lofoten Islands, 5596, 5597

Loftus, Belinda, 3030
Lohalm, Uwe, 216
Lohmann, Heinz, 3197
Lohmann, Johannes, 2054
Lohse, Günter, 4296, 4343
Lombroso, Silvia, 5743
London Institute of World Affairs, 6467
Londonderry, Marquess of (Charles S. H. Vane-Tempest-Stewart), 4270
Long, Olivier, 1659
Longolius, Fritz, 4853
Loock, Hans-Dietrich, 5591
Look, Hans, 5048
Loosli-Usteri, Carl, 3954
Lorant, Stefan, 3289
Lorch, Willi, 2596
Lord Haw-Haw—See Joyce, William
Lorenz, Heinz, 4965
Lorenz, Max, 5329
Lorenz, Ottokar, 558, 3005
Lorwin, Lewis L., 4678
Losemann, Volker, 2409
Lother, Helmut, 2055
Lotz, Wilhelm, 3091
Louda, Vlastimil, 5352
Lougee, Robert W., 176
Louvain University, 5530
Loverdo, Costa de, 5274
Low Countries, 4295–4297—See also Belgium and Holland
Lowenthal, Ernst C., 3552, 3669
Lowenthal-Hensel, Cecile, 3272
Lower Saxony, 963, 964, 2811
Lowrie, Donald A., 6263
Lubbe, Marinus van der, 1095, 1098
Lubbers, H., 2964
Lubinski, Georg, 1368
Lublin Ghetto, 5651, 5933–5936
Lucas, James, 3226
Luckner, Gertrud, 5936
Luckwaldt, Friedrich, 4533
Łuczak, Czesław, 5215, 6247
Ludecke, Kurt G. W., 1109
Ludendorff, Erich, 505, 980, 2056, 2059, 2060, 4737
Ludendorff, Mathilde, 2056–2058, 2060
Ludlow, Peter W., 1956, 6340
Ludowici, J. W. L., 2651
Ludwig, Emil, 3687
Ludwig, Hartmut, 1956
Ludwig, Karl-Heinz, 2760
Ludwig, Max, pseud., 3575
Lübeck, 1936

'Christenprozess', 1840
Lübke, Anton, 1606
Lück, Kurt, 4333, 4334
Lück, Margret, 2106
Lüddecke, Theodor, 1710, 2788
Lüders, Marie-Elisabeth, 2107
Lüders, Martin, 1079
Lüdtke, Gerhard, 7
Lueger, Karl, 294
Lühe, Irmgard von der, 3377
Lüke, Franz, 2173
Lueken, Wilhelm, 1938
Lüth, Erich, 2710
Lütke, Heinz, 261
Lützeler, Felix, 506
Lützeler, Franz-Karl, 1686
Lützeler, Heinrich, 2487
Lützeler, Marga, 2487
Lufft, Hermann, 4092, 4534
Luft, Friedrich, 2815
Luftwaffe: general, 3866, 3968, 4701, 4704, 4712, 4715, 4848–4885
general staff, 4756, 5118
in World War II, 3047, 3089, 3472, 4787–4789, 4861–4885, 4966, 4969, 4971, 5063, 5076, 6246—See also World War II: air war
Luftwaffen-Kriegsberichter-Kompanie, 5025
Luihn, Hans, 5598
Lukács, Georg, 154
Lukas, Otto, 2297
Lukowski, Jerzy, 6078
Lumi, R., 5372
Lumley, Frederick E., 2947
Lurie, Esther, 5924
Lurie, Samuel, 1550
Lusar, Rudolf, 4689
Lustgarten, Edgar, 6090
Luther, Hans, 886, 5488
Luther, Martin, 155, 270, 271, 1823, 1852, 1854, 2076
Lutz, Hermann, 6498
Lutze, Hermann, 3356
Lutzke, Viktor, 2005
Lutzendorf, Felix, 4079
Lutzhöft, Hans-Jürgen, 381
Lux, Albert, 3290
Lux, Eugen, 4914
Luxembourg, 4995, 5227, 5236, 5565–5569
Luyken, Max, 2329
Luža, Radomír, 4112

Lvovsky, Z., 645
Lwow (Lemberg) Ghetto, 5738, 5755, 5937, 5938
Lymington, Lord, 3064
Lynx, J. J., 6434
Lyons, 5812

Maas, Hermann, 3575
Maass, Liselotte, 3752
Maass, Walter B., 5254, 5535
Mabire, Jean, 4839
Macardle, Dorothy, 6443
Maccarrone, Michele, 1979
Macciocchi, Maria-Antoinietta, 2108
McClure, Robert A., 3073
McDonald, James G., 6313
Macdonald, Robert David, 1992
MacFarland, Charles S., 1803
McGovern, James, 835
McGovern, William Montgomery, 155
Mach, Alexander, 5358
Machlejd, Wanda, 6238, 6266
Machover, J. M., 6344
Machray, Robert, 4346
'Machtergreifung'—See Weimar Republic, fall of
MacIntyre, Donald, 4937
McKale, Donald M., 96, 4009
Mackensen, Lutz, 2507
MacKenzie, Compton, 5037
McKenzie, Vernon, 3062
Macksey, Kenneth, 4767, 5029, 5233
McLachlan, D., 790
MacOrlan, Pierre, 645
McRandle, James H., 97
McSherry, James E., 4409
Madaczyk, Czesław, 5192
Madagascar Plan, 446, 5708, 5934
Mädel — euere Welt!, 2215
Männel, Hansjörg, 2158
Männer im Dritten Reich, 615
Märker, Friedrich, 382
Märthesheimer, Peter, 6504
Maesse, Hermann, 2250
Maginot Line, 4216, 4978
Magnus, G., 1452
Mahnke, Karl Georg, 1476
Mai, Richard, 1966
Maier, Hans, 2392
Maier, Klaus A., 4387
Maier, Reinhold, 5136
Maier-Hartmann, Fritz, 46
Maimann, Helene, 3719

Mainz, 1166, 3579
Maiwald, E. W., 1531
Majdanek concentration camp, 5078, 5730, 5860, 6008, 6146–6149
Majer, Diemut, 1356a
Malá, Irene, 6009, 6034
Malina, J. B., 2111, 4355
Malines concentration camp, 5775, 5776
Malitz, Bruno, 2887
Mall, Kurt, 4371
Mallebrein, Wolfram, 2347a
Mallmann, Marion, 2827
Malowist, Simon, 5864
Malraux, André, 5876
Maltitz, Horst von, 920
Malvezzi, Piero, 5234, 5511, 5978
Mandel, Ernest, 931
Mandell, Richard D., 2903
Mangold, Ewald K. B., 4232
Manheim, Ralph, 727, 1038
Mankel, Wilhelm, 1859
Mankiewicz, H., 323
Mann, Anthony, 6470
Mann, Erika, 2236, 3818, 3819, 3826
Mann, Golo, 38, 328, 624, 2925, 3505
Mann, Gunter, 276
Mann, Heinrich, 731, 3657, 3820, 3821, 6173
Mann, Klaus, 3819, 3822
Mann, Thomas, 338, 1940, 2236, 3050, 3823–3826, 5234, 6314
Mannbar, Artur, 3424
Mannewitz, Rudolf, 1425
Mannhardt, Johann Wilhelm, 2410
Mannhart, pseud., 3941
Mannheim, 1167, 3343
    Handelshochschule, 2400
    Stadtarchiv, 3323, 3580
Manning, A. F., 4309
Manstein, Fritz Erich von Lewinski, 4776, 4801, 5643, 5895
Mantau-Sadila, Hans Heinz, 616, 758
Manteuffel, Hasso von, 4757
Manvell, Roger, 679, 786, 800, 807, 1066, 2733, 3249, 3506, 5697
Manz, Hergo, 4802
Maor, Harry, 6435
Maquis—See under partisans
Marbaix, Edgar, 6097
Marburg, 2463, 3344
Marby, Friedrich Bernhard, 2888
Marcus, Hans, 3127
Marek, Wolfgang W., 4753

Margaliot, Abraham, 3670
Margolin, Victor, 3032
Marhefka, Edmund, 3991
Marinoff, Irene, 2061
Marjanovic, Jovan, 5305
Marjay, Friedrich, 3150
Mark, Bernard (Ber, Berl), 5898, 5909,
    5916, 5994, 5999
Mark, Dieter, 4292
Markgraf, Bruno, 1852
Markmann, Werner, 3634
Markow, Sergej von, 301
Markstadt concentration camp, 6007
Markus, Gertrud, 1151
Marley, Lord (Dudley Leigh Aman),
    1082
Maroger, Gilbert, 4039
Marr, Heinz, 3006
Marrenbach, Otto, 1728
marriage in Third Reich, 411, 1363,
    1486–1489, 2084
Maršalek, Hans, 6155
Marschner, Heinz, 1637
Marseilles, 5483
Marshall, Barbara, 2411
Marshall, Bruce, 6035
Martens, Allard, 5551
Martens, Erika, 2833
Martens, Hans, 3514
Martienssen, Anthony, 4752
Martin, Benno, 1282
Martin, Bernd, 4093
Martin, H., 2310
Martin, Hugh, 5223
Martin, James Stewart, 1638
Martin, Kurt, 2684
Martini, Angelo, 1988
Marton, Judah, 5736
Marx, Fritz Morstein, 1278
Marx, Hugo, 3605
Marxism—See Communism; and under
    National Socialism
Masaryk, Jan, 5333
Maschke, Erich, 5138
Maschmann, Melita, 1208
Maser, Werner, 680, 680a, 734, 739, 921,
    3237, 5631
Mason, David, 4615
Mason, Herbert Molloy, 3480
Mason, John Brown, 1838
Mason, Timothy, 1711, 2109
Massfeller, Franz, 1360
Massing, Paul W., 208

Massmann, Kurt, 3196
Massow, Ewald von, 4156
'master race', 331, 392–399, 2272
Masterman, J. C., 5152
Masters, Anthony, 5839
Mastny, Vojtech, 5346
Matenko, Percy, 5964
Mathematics in Third Reich, 2428
Matthäus, Winfried, 1410, 6233
Matthias, Erich, 925, 933, 1114, 3727
Matthies, Kurt, 5744
Mattick, Heinz, 3168
Mattig, Michael, 80
Matzerath, Horst, 1270
Matzler, Fritz, 592
Mau, Hermann, 1147
Mauersberger, Volker, 2818
Maull, Otto, 358
Maur, Helmut V., 1712
Maurel, Micheline, 6188
Maurer, Emil, 531
Maurer, Ilse, 922
Maurer, Monica, 2836
Mauriac, François, 5480, 5668, 6055,
    6188
Maurras, Charles, 2305, 4233
Maus, Ingeborg, 576
Mausbach-Bromberger, Barbara, 3333,
    3415
Mauthausen concentration camp, 3360,
    5293, 6003, 6010, 6016, 6047,
    6150–6158
Mautone, Ernesto, 4575
Max-Planck-Gesellschaft zur Förderung
    der Wissenschaften, 2405
May, Werner, 2314
Mayer, Norbert, 4234
Mayer, Rupert, 2026
Mayer, S. L., 2839, 4616
Mayer, Saly, 6385
Mayer, Ulrich, 974
mayors, National Socialist, 851, 852, 1204,
    1266, 1267
Mazirel, Lau, 5612
Mazor, Michel, 98
Mechanicus, Philip, 6210
Mecklenburg, 965, 1937
medals—See awards
Meder, Bruno, 2527
medical care—See health services,
    National Socialist
medical crimes: general, 5636, 6213–
    6217

6255—*See also* Euthanasia and under concentration camps
Medicus, Franz Albrecht, 1287
Mediterranean, 4938–4941
Meed, Vladka, 5979
'Mefkure', 5884
Mehring, Walter, 3799, 3800, 3827, 3828
Mehringer, Helmut, 520
Mehrmann, Johann, 415
Mehrtens, Herbert, 2742a
Meier, Friedrich, 4942
Meier, Heinrich Christian, 6166
Meier, Kurt, 1782, 1898, 1909, 1956
Meier, Maurice, 3606
Meier, Paul, 559
Meier-Benneckenstein, Paul, 44, 351, 1279
Mein Kampf, 353, 726–736, 2508, 2841, 3006
Meinck, Gerhard, 3969
Meinck, Jürgen, 1067
Meinecke, Friedrich, 1209
Meiner, M., 302
Meinshausen, (Dr.), 2264
Meissner, Hans-Otto, 783, 1043, 2099
Meissner, Otto, 1210, 1343, 5469
Meister, Anton, 454
Meister, Wilhelm, *pseud.*, 217
Melchior, Marcus, 5796
Melk concentration camp, 6003
Melnikow, Daniil, 3507
Memel, 1684, 4312–4316
Memmingen/Bav., 3581
Mende, Franz, 1453
Mendelssohm, Peter de, 3859, 5761
Mendoza, Juan C. de, 4562
Menge-Genser, M. von, 4803
Mengele, Josef, 6234
Menges, Jan, 6223
Menke, Johannes, 6436
Menkes, G., 6231
Mennecke, Kurt, 1455
Menschell, Wolfgang, 1376
Mensens, Christoph, 1561
Menthon, François de, 5603, 5715
Menz, Gerhard, 2492
Menze, Ernst August, 266
merchant marine, German, 1628, 4681
Mergentheim, 3582
Merin, Moses, 5906
Merkel, Hans, 532, 1691
Merker, Paul, 1148, 3737
Merkes, Manfred, 4388

Merkl, Peter H., 137, 2203
Merritt, Anna J., 6471
Merritt, Richard L., 6471
Mertes, Alois, 996
Merz, Konrad, *pseud.*, 3810
Meskill, Johanna Menzel, 4094
Messerschmid, Felix, 2013
Messerschmidt, Ernst August, 4271
Messerschmidt, Hermann, 347
Messerschmidt, Manfred, 3870, 5165
Metten, Alfred, 2493
Mettenleiter, Fritz, 2174
Metzger, Wolfgang, 1914
Metzler, G., 6342
Metzner, Kurt O., 2597
Metzsch, Horst von, 3871
Meusch, H., 1750
Meusel, Heinrich, 2876
Mexico, 3737, 3738, 4573
Mey, Eugène, 5470
Meyer, Adolf, 640
Meyer, Alfred G., 4405
Meyer, Arnold Oskar, 34
Meyer, Franz, 3673
Meyer, Georg, 4775
Meyer, Gertrud, 3336, 3337, 3414
Meyer, Henry Cord, 39
Meyer, Herbert, 572
Meyer, Klaus, 2741
Meyer, Konrad, 354
Meyer, Kurt, 4828
Meyer, Otto, 1334
Meyer, Werner, 5131
Meyer-Christian, Wolf, 474
Meyer-Plath, Maria, 2088
Meyerhoff, Hermann, 1165
Meyers Lexikon, 25
Meyers, Peter, 6482
Meyers, Reinhard P. F. W., 4272
Meyrowitz, Henri, 5620
Micaud, Charles A., 4235
'Michael. . .', 2027
Michael, H. A., 5925
Michaelis, Herbert, 34, 45, 49, 3948
Michaelis, Meir, 4067
Michaelis, Otto, 1860
Michalik, Krystyna, 6062
Michalka, Wolfgang, 3887 3919
Michalski, Gabrielle, 2424
Michel, Ernst, 1713
Michel, Henri, 4979, 5235, 5489, 6057
Michel, Jean, 6129
Michel, Max, 6449

582

Micklem, Nathaniel, 2028
Mickwitz, Eugen von, 1639
Middeldorf, Eike, 5073
middle classes, German, 136, 204, 256, 534, 893, 950, 1021
Middle East: general, 3174, 4576–4588
and Third Reich, 4578, 4579, 4583, 4584, 4586, 4587
See also individual countries
Middlebrook, Martin, 4906, 4913
Miège, A., 6231
Miege, Wolfgang, 4174
Mielke, Fred, 6213, 6214
Mielke, Robert, 1692
Mierendorff, Carlo, 3378, 3383
Mihan, George, 5203
Mikes, George, 5596
Mikorey, Max, 6007
Miksche, F. O., 4809
Mikus, Joseph A., 5356
Mikusch, Dagobert von, 4389, 4576, 4597
Milano, Attilio, 5849
Milch, Erhard, 4874, 4875, 5636
Mildner, Friedrich, 5050
Milentijevich, Zoran, 6190
Miles, *pseud.*, 3860
Miles Ecclesiae, *pseud.*, 1804
military indoctrination, 3864–3877
military training schools, National Socialist, 2374
Miller, Alfred, 2062
Miller, Basil, 1942
Miller, Marshall Lee, 5278
Miller, Max, 3488
Millok, Sándor, 5293
Milorg D 13 i kamp, 5599
Miltenberg, Weigand von, 641
Milward, Alan S., 4679, 5457
Milward, Hans S., 830
Minco, Marga, 5745
Minderrassigkeit—*See* Untermenschentum
Mindt, Erich, 2900
Ministère des Affaires étrangères (France), 4222, 4503
Ministère de la Santé Publique et de la Famille (Belgium), 5775, 5776
Ministero degli Affari Esteri (Italy), 4068
Minney, R. J., 6008
Minott, Rodney G., 5121
Minsk Ghetto, 5689, 5939–5941
Minssen, Friedrich, 3383

Mirbt, Karl Wolfgang, 2819
Mirtschuk, J., 3178
Misch, Carl, 1357
'Mischlinge', 15, 1353, 3596, 3701–3704, 3706, 5940
IMIs, 3703
Missalla, Heinrich, 4661a
Missbach, Artur, 1607
Missong, Alfred, 308
Mit brennender Sorge, 1975, 1982, 1983
Mitscherlich, Alexander, 6213, 6214, 6225
Mittenzwei, Werner, 3764a
Mittig, Hans-Ernst, 2661
mixed marriages, 1365, 3695, 3701, 3705
Mjoelnir, *pseud.*, 2919
Moczarski, Kazimierz, 5998
Model, (Dr.), 24
Möbus, Gerhard, 2741
Moedwil, Jan, 3042
Mölders, Werner, 4876, 4877
Möll, Otto E., 4753
Möller, Eberhard Wolfgang, 2572, 2711, 2712
Moeller van den Bruck, Arthur, 173, 177–179, 338, 3006
Moen, Petter, 5600
Mönckmeier, Otto, 1516, 1574
Moenius, Georg, 308
Mönning, Richard, 62
Mörbitz, H., 1402
Moers, Martha, 2118
Mohler, Armin, 257
Mohn, Joseph, 3322
Mołdawa, Mieczysław, 6134
Moldawer, S., 5935
Molden, Otto, 5262
Molenaar, Herbert, 2979
Molho, Michael, 5818
Moll, Helga, 2789
Mollo, Andrew, 3233, 4707
Molotov, Vyacheslav Mikhailovich, 5442
Moltke, Graf Helmuth James von, 1833, 3379, 3382, 3383, 3388
Mommsen, Hans, 1086, 1306, 3408
Mommsen, Wolfgang Justin, 34
Momsen, Max, 2877
monarchists, 3463, 3466
'*Monatschrift für Geschichte und Wissenschaft des Judentums*,' 79
Mondt, Gerd, 2192, 2193
Monneray, Henri de, 5680, 5681

Montanucci, Giuseppe, 5227
Monte Cassino, 5080
Montefiore, Leonard, 2402, 3208, 3533, 6359
Montluc prison, 5487
Montreux treaty 1936, 3925
Mopp, *pseud*., 3788
Moraca, Pero, 5305
Moravec, Emanuel, 4489
Moravec, Frantisek, 5152
Mordal, Jacques, 4972
Morgan, Claude, 5480
Morgan, J. H., 3955
Morgan-Witts, Max, 6336
Moringen concentration camp, 6030, 6049
Morley, John Francis, 1995
Morocco, 4242, 5815
Morse, Arthur D., 6334
Morsey, Rudolf, 933, 1030, 1068, 1114, 1115, 2810
Morvilliers, Roger, 735
Moscow, 5058–5061
Moseley, Philip E., 5435
Moser, H. J., 2630
Mosley, Leonard, 801, 4470
Mosley, Oswald, 2301
Mosse, George L., 180, 222, 272, 324, 1179, 3258, 5706
Mosse, Werner E., 238
Moulis, Miloslav, 5347, 6104
Moureu, Henri, 5480
Mourin, Maxime, 3481
Mowrer, Edgar Ansel, 1250
Mrázková, Daniela, 5074
Muchow, Reinhold, 546
Muckermann, Friedrich, 2029, 6185
Muckermann, Hermann, 407
Mühldorf concentration camp, 6007
Mühr, Alfred, 1021, 2474
Mühsam, Erich, 2482, 3646
Müllenbach, Herbert, 4878
Müller, A., 3970
Müller, Arnd, 3587
Müller, Artur, 1144
Müller, Christian, 3519
Müller, (Dr.), 923
Müller, Filip, 6079
Müller, Georg-Wilhelm, 778
Müller, Gerhard, 2743
Müller, Hans Dieter, 2834
Müller, Heinz, 1319
Müller, Josef, 223, 1180, 3372
Müller, Karl, 2508

Müller, Karl Alexander von, 175, 2412, 2413
Müller, Karl Valentin, 1714
Müller, Klaus-Jürgen, 3843, 5007
Müller, Ludwig, 1899, 1900
Müller, Max, 2038
Müller, Otto, 3434
Müller, Werner, 3528
Müller, Wilhelm, 2431
Müller, Willi, 1362, 1729
Müller, Wolfgang, 1125, 3508
Müller-Blattau, Joseph, 592, 2631
Müller-Brandenburg, Hermann, 2350, 3942
Müller von Hausen, Ludwig, 297
Müller-Hillebrand, Burkhart, 4754, 4804
Müller-Kronach, Paul, 488
Müller-Loebnitz, W., 3976
Müller-Markus, Siegfried, 2741
Müller-Mehlis, Reinhard, 2617
Müller-Partenkirchen, Fritz, 1693
Müller-Reimerdes, Friederike, 2063
Müller-Rüdersdorf, -?-, 849
Münch, Ingo von, 1324
Münch, Kurt, 2889, 2890
Münch, Maurus, 6126
Müncheberg, Friedrich, 1730
Münchmeyer, Ludwig, 489
Münster i. W., 2411, 3583
Münster, Hans A., 2790, 2791
Münstermann, (Dr.), 5366
Münz, Ludwig, 1280
Münzenberg, Willi, 617, 2948
Mürer, Niels, J., 1251
Müssener, Helmut, 3710
Muggeridge, Malcolm, 4062
Muhlen, Norbert, 819
Mulka, Robert Karl Ludwig, 6067
Mulot, Arno, 2534, 3872
Mumelter, Maria Luise, 2369
Mumm, Michel, 2920
Munich: general, 1168, 1168a, 2646, 3345, 5134
 Jews of, 3584–3586, 3615, 5742, 6436
 'Putsch' (1923), 622, 846, 884, 927, 976–981
 trial, 982–984
 Soviet republic of, 2996–2998
 University, 2413, 2431, 2465–2467, 2469–2472
Munich Pact, 1137, 3893, 4270, 4272, 4483–4499
Munk, Frank, 1181

584

Munske, Hilde, 2215
Muntsch, Otto, 3017
Munz, Max, 5783
Murawska, Zofia, 6147
Murawski, Erich, 4755, 5010
Murawski, Friedrich, 2064
Murdoch, John, 3080
Murmelstein, B., 5955
Murphy, James, 727
Murphy, Raymond E., 3986
Murphy, Robert, 6414
Murtorinne, Eino, 1906
music, 590–592, 2622–2644
musicians, exiled, 3789–3793
Musiol, Teodor, 6118
Mussert, Anton Adriaan, 4306a
Mussolini, Benito: general, 4062, 4067, 4072, 4073, 4076, 4160, 4829
and Third Reich, 4063, 4069, 4070, 4081, 4087, 4089
Muth, Karl, 1835
Muzzy, Adrienne, 5237
Myllyniemi, Seppo, 4182, 5370
Mythus des 20. Jahrhunderts, Der, 330–333, 1847–1854
Mytze, Andreas W., 2574, 2575

Naab, Ingbert (Pater), 1020
Nabor, Felix, 2573
Nachtsheim, Hans, 2741
Nadanyi, Paul, 5294
Nadler, Fritz, 4663
Naef, Louis, 3783
Naegelen, Marcel-Edmond, 4980
Nagel, Helga, 3709
Nagel, Jakob, 1288, 1290
Nahm, Peter Paul, 4897
Nahon, Umberto, 5849
Namier, L. S., 4504
Nansen, Fridtjof, 4354
Nansen, Odd, 6036
Napier-Tauber, Diana, 3791
Narvik, 4989, 4990
Nasarski, Peter, E., 4335
Nassen, Paul, 1120
Nathan, Otto, 1771
'*Nation Europa*', 3402
National Archives (U.S.), 52, 56
'National Bolshevism', 889
nationalism, German, 160–186, 195, 215, 247, 340–351, 881, 889, 891, 1869, 2169, 2983, 4072

nationalist movements, European, 3990–3996
Nationalistische Akademie, 3992
Nationalistische Aktion, 3992
Nationalkomitee 'Freies Deutschland', 1831, 3072, 3442, 3732–3743, 5040
Nationalpolitische Aufklärungsschriften, 2980
National Socialism, ideology of: general, 308–604
and anti Semitism, 416–491
cultural theories, 577–595
economic theories, 312, 334, 524–543, 989, 1281
and ethics, 596–604, 3211
legal theories, 562–576
and liberalism, 323
and Marxism, 547, 557–561
racist theories, 362–415
and sex, 597
and workers, 543–546, 1002, 1006–1008
National Socialism, pre-1933: opposition to, 931, 1000, 1010–1023
Nationalsozialismus in Staat, Gemeinde und Wirtschaft, 1281
N.S.B.O. (NS-Betriebszellenorganisationen), 1733
Nationalsozialistische Bibliographie, 71
N.S.D.A.P. (Nationalsozialistische Deutsche Arbeiterpartei): general, 85–149, 647, 676, 726, 3190, 3205
and agriculture, 555, 1669
and armed forces, 3838, 3847, 4719
Dienststellen, 29
factionalism in, 96, 102, 862–870
finances (pre-1933), 985–990
Gau- und Kreisverzeichnis, 88
Gaupresseamt, 934
genesis of, 894, 901, 911, 927, 955, 959
'Kampfzeit', 621, 623, 625, 627, 759, 776, 778, 841, 846, 853, 855, 861–866, 894–1023, 2069, 2192, 2917, 2919, 2926, 2971, 3026, 3197, 3832—*See also* S.A. and under Churches
laws relating to, 113, 115, 119
in legislatures (pre-1933), 991–1000
Partei-Kanzlei, 27
party statistics, 105
and police, 956
Rechsleitung etc.—*See under* Reichs-...
sociological studies of, 129–140
songbooks, 936–939, 1683, 3192

and state, 112–119, 922
NS.-Frauenschaft, 2112
NS.-Kulturgemeinde, 1763
NS.-Volkswohlfahrt, 1454–1457
NSD.-Dozentenbund, 2426, 2427
Nationalsozialistischer Deutscher Front-
soldatenbund (NSDFB)—See Stahlhelm
NSD.-Studentenbund, 2435, 2438, 2443
NS.-Hago, 1575
NS.-Kraftfahr-Korps (NSKK), 3253, 3254
NS.-Lehrerbund (NSLB): general, 859,
2248, 2252, 2262, 2312, 2379, 2380
Reichsfachgebiet Rassenfrage, 2268
NS.-Pfarrers- und Lehrerkreis des
Wieratals/Th., 1901
NS.-Pressetrust, 2792
NS.-Rechtswahrerbund, 1391
Reichsgruppe Hochschullehrer, 450
Nationalsozialistisches Handbuch, 26
National Socialists, post-World War II:
escapes of, 6401–6405, 6409
'National-Zeitung', 2829
nature cures in Third Reich, 1435, 1436
Natzweiler concentration camp, 6003,
6159–6161
Naude, Horst, 5330
Naudh, H., *pseud.*, 209
Naujocks, Alfred, 4514
Naumann, Bernd, 6067
Naumann, Hans, 2522
Nauticus, 4943
Navarro, Francisco, 4662
navy, German: general, 3464, 3832, 3839,
4071, 4701, 4704, 4715, 4723, 4728,
4752, 4920–4922
in World War II, 4777, 4785, 4786,
4923–4960, 4985, 4989
Nawrocki, Stanislaw, 5243, 5388
Nazi conspiracy and aggression, 53
Nazi war against the Catholic Church,
2030
Neave, Airey, 805, 5632
Nebe, Arthur, 3280, 3282
Necker, Wilhelm, 4649, 4805, 5021
Nederlandsche Roode Kruis, 6080
Needham, Joseph, 2744
Neef, Hermann, 1307
Neesze, Gottfried, 118
Negt, Oskar, 3711
Nehama, Joseph, 5818
Nehring, Walther K., 4882
Neilson, William Allen, 3373
Nelson, Walter Henry, 1613

neo-paganism, 2033, 2040–2086
Neresoff, Wladislaw, 1523
Nettl, J. P., 6472
Neubauer, Theodor, 3355
Neuberger, Maria, 2265
Neubert, Reinhard, 1392
Neubrandenburg sub-camp, 6188
Neuburger, Otto, 72
Neue Breme concentration camp, 6010
'Neue Deutsche Blätter', 3753
neue Glaube, Der . . ., 1805
'Neue Leipziger Zeitung', 2904
'Neue politische Literatur', 80
'Neue Preussische Zeitung', 2830
'Neue Rundschau', 2831, 2832
'Neue Weltbühne', 3747
Neuendorff, Edmund, 2891
Neuengamme concentration camp, 6003,
6036, 6047, 6162–6168, 6380
Arbeitsgemeinschaft für die BRD, 6255
'Neues Reich', 2808
'Neues Tagebuch', 3755
Neufeldt, Hans- Joachim, 3281
Neugebauer, Karl-Volker, 5503
Neugebauer, Wolfgang, 5263, 5269
Neuhäusler, Johann, 2031
Neuhaus, Wolfgang, 3376
Neu-Isenburg, 3346
Neuman, H. J., 822
Neumann, Alfred, 2470
Neumann, Carl, 2734
Neumann, Erwin, 4535
Neumann, Franz, 99, 1572
Neumann, Franz L., 3796
Neumann, Friedrich, 3697
Neumann, Gerd, 2370
Neumann, Inge S., 5621
Neumann, Robert, 1149, 6264
Neumann, Sigmund, 173
Neumark concentration camp, 6054
Neurath, Constantin von, 812
Neurohr, Jean F., 156
Neuscheler, Karl, 3148
Neuss, Oskar, 3012
Neustadt-Glewe concentration camp,
5730
Nevinson Henry W., 6339
'New Order': general, 4236, 5168, 5173,
5175–5219
in Eastern Europe, 5189, 5198, 5366,
5370—See also under Poland
economic, 770, 5167, 5185, 5186, 5190,
5194, 5197

in Poland, 5400, 5414
in Slovakia, 5354
in Western Europe, 5196, 5457, 5534
See also persecution and resistance.
New Testament, 1851, 1896, 1899, 2027, 2044, 2057, 2066, 2067, 2322
Newton, Alfred, 6106
Newton, Douglas, 5223
Newton, Henry, 6106
Ney, E. L., 100
Nibelungenlied, 274
Niccacci, Padre Rufino, 5512
Nicholls, Anthony J., 924, 925
Niclauss, Karlheinz, 4410
Nicolai, Helmut, 541
Nicolaisen, Carsten, 1801, 1902
Nicolas, M.-P., 397
Nicoll, Peter H., 4471
Niebergall, Otto, 3724
Niebuhr, Reinhold, 3394, 5668
Niederhöffer, Egon, 2886
Niederland, William G., 6450
Niederlein, Fritz, 5049
Niedermayer, Oskar Ritter von, 3873, 4411
Niedermeyer, Albert, 5264
Niegisch, Gertrud, 4532
Niehoff, Karena, 781
Niekisch, Ernst, 256, 1017, 1211, 3360
Nielsen, Andreas, 4756
Nielsen, Frederic W., 3721
Niemeier, Georg, 4377
Niemer, Gotthard, 2290
Niemöller, Gerhard, 1885
Niemöller, Martin, 1874, 1939–1943
Niemöller, Wilhelm, 1878–1881, 1886–1888, 1916, 1939, 1944
Nierop, Is. van, 6211
Nies, Erich, 1212
Niesel, Wilhelm, 1882
Niethammer, Lutz, 6464
Nietzsche, Friedrich, 154, 262, 396–399, 2527
Niggemann, Hans, 2086
'Night and fog' 1408, 6031
'Night of the long knives'—*See* Röhm-Putsch
Nilus, Sergej A., 301
Nirenstein, Albert (Nirenstajn, Alberto), 5871
Nischk, Kurt, 1308
Nishikawa, Masao, 54
Nishmit (Neshamit), Sarah, 5749, 5910

Nispen tot Sevenaer, C.M.O., 5193
Nix, Claire, 3715
Noack, Erwin, 2315
Noakes, Jeremy, 48, 964, 2015
Noam, Ernst, 3576
Nobécourt, Jacques, 5098
Nobécourt, R. J., 5463
Noble, Frankland, 4919
Nodot, René, 5810
Nöstlinger, Christine, 6264
Nötges, Jakob, 1783
Noethlichs, Richard, 2177
Noguères, Henri, 4490, 5490
Nohlen, Dieter, 42
Nolde, Emil, 2681
Noller, Sonja, 2844
Nolte, Ernst, 101, 325
Nolting-Hauff, W., 3763
Nonnenbruch, Fritz, 1524, 2761
Non-Sectarian Anti-Nazi League, 6301
Norden, Albert, 1551
Norden, Günther van, 1865
Nordhausen concentration camp, 6003
Nordics, 198, 365, 368, 381, 383, 548, 553, 586, 1851, 2042, 2272, 2519, 2686, 3879
Nordische Gesellschaft, 2191, 5197
Nordmann, H., 209
Nordmann, Joë, 5480
Norkus, Herbert, 2192, 2193
Normandy, 4624, 5103–5107, 5109, 5486
Norway: general, 4364–4366
invasion of, 4366, 4760, 4884, 4981–4990
Norway, occupied: general, 4760, 5576, 5585–5601, 6355
Jews of, 5853, 5854
persecution and resistance, 3293, 5112, 5227, 5236, 5585–5589, 5594–5600, 6043
of Church, 3730, 5222, 5588, 5589
Notgemeinschaft deutscher Wissenschaftler im Ausland, 2425
Nottbeck, Berend von, 1211
Nova, Fritz, 521
Novaky concentration camp, 6169
November 1938 Pogrom, 3568, 3571, 3594, 3648–3661, 6386
Novisad, 5833
Novitch, Miriam, 5819, 5995, 6195, 6202, 6274
Nowak, Kurt, 6224

Nowarra, Heinz J., 4871
Nowojski, Walter, 2682
Nucéra, Louis, 6129
Nüse, Karl-Heinz, 1403
Nuis, A., 5829
Nuremberg: general, 1282, 2646, 3347,
   3348, 3587, 4663, 4913
   laws, 1358–1364, 1488, 6224
   party rallies in, 120–128, 2993, 2999
Nuremberg Trials: general, 53, 5607,
   5609, 5619, 5625–5636, 5659, 6244,
   6279, 6280
   trial of the major war criminals, 827,
   1142, 5625, 5626, 5628–5635, 5660,
   6514
Nygren, Anders, 1911
Nyiszli, Miklos, 6234
Nyomarkay, Joseph, 102

Obendiek, Harmannus, 1863
Oberacker, Karlheinrich, 4569
Oberammergau passion play, 232
Oberdonau, Gau, 5253
Oberharz, 966
Oberhausen, 3349
Oberkommando: des Heeres, 4750, 4754
   der Kriegsmarine, 4985
   der Wehrmacht, 31, 2839a, 4102, 4890,
   4973, 5004, 5012
   'Richthefte', 2092
   war diaries and documents, 711, 715,
   4747, 4759, 4760, 4772, 5107
Oberländer, Theodor, 854, 5363
Oberlindober, Hanns, 855
Oberpräsident der Rheinprovinz, 2316
Oberschelp, Reinhard, 68
Obst, Erich, 358
Obwurzer, Herbert von, 1586
occultism, 141–149, 279–282, 3122
'Odal-Verfassung', 551, 554
Odic, Charles, 5811
O'Donnell, James P., 723
Oechsner, Frederick, 3074
Oechsner, Hans, 1694
Oederan concentration camp, 6042
Ökumenische Marienschwesterschaft,
   6506
Oelfken, Tami, 1213
Oelze, F. W., 2548
Önder, Zehra, 4600
Oertel, Ferdinand, 2455
Oertzen, F. W. von, 3956, 4183
Oertzen, K. L. von, 348

Oesterreicher, Johannes, 6523
Österreichische Verwaltungs-Akademien,
   4131
Oestreich, Paul, 771, 4015
Offenbach a.M., 4914
Offers, Bernhard, 1487
Offner, Arnold A., 4536
Ogger, Günter, 3632
Ohlendorf, Otto, 3258
Ohnesorge, Wilhelm, 1289, 1290
Okanouye-Kurota, (Dr.), 4096
Olaf, Michael, 3861
Olczak (Mortkowicz-Olczakowa), Hanna,
   5976
Olczewski, Helmuth, 1377
Old Testament, 440, 464, 481, 483, 488,
   1902, 2027, 2064, 2320
Olden, Rudolf, 681, 2482, 3371
Oldenburg, 2015
Olenhusen, Albrecht Götz von, 3704
Olicki, L., 5911
Olshausen, Klaus, 4151
Olympic Games: general, 2516, 2894–
   2908, 3684
Olympic Games 1936: propaganda-
   Ausschuss, 2894, 2900
   Winter Games, 2894, 2904
Ondarza, Leon Herbert von, 4806
O'Neill, James E., 4617
Ooms, Alphonse, 5517
Oorthuys, Cas, 5536
Operation Bernhard, 3596, 4514, 5153,
   5154
'Operation Reinhard'—See 'Aktion
   Reinhard'
Opfermann, H. C., 2726
Ophir, Baruch Zvi, 3562
Opitz, Reinhard, 1552
Oppenheim, Ralph, 5797, 5956
Oppenheimer, Max, 3415, 3575, 3788,
   5717
Oppenheimer-Bluhm, Hilde, 1715
Oppermann, Theodor, 3254
Oppitz, Ulrich Dieter, 5622
opposition—See resistance
Oradour-sur-Glane, 5491, 5492
Oranienburg-Sachsenhausen concentra-
   tion camp, 3760, 5264, 5614, 5651,
   6003, 6021, 6022, 6036, 6170–6177,
   6288
   medical experiments at, 6239
Oras, Ante, 5371
Orb, Heinrich, 1150

'Ordensdevisenprozesse', 2032
orders—*See* awards
Ordioni, Pierre, 5011
Orenstein, Benjamin, 5921
Orje, *pseud.*, 2919
Orlow, Dietrich, 103, 2258, 4152
Orlowski, Slawomir, 5408
Orlowsky, H., 2535
Ormesson, Wladimir d', 898
Orska, Irena, 5429
Ory, Pascal, 5453
Oslo, 5599
Osman-Bey, (Major), 251
Osnabrück, 967
Ossietzky, Carl von, 2482, 3454–3458
Ossola, 5507
Ost, Leopold, 2140
Ostendorf, Edwin, 1165
Oster, Hans, 3509
Osterkamp, Theo, 4875
Osterroth, Frank, 3435
Osteuropainstitut in Breslau, 5365
Ostfriesland, 3350
'Osthilfe', 1668
Ostland-Institut, Danzig, 4185
Ostmark, 2219, 4102, 4104, 4106, 4109,
   4131, 4132, 4802
Ostrowicz, Radoslaw, 5408
Ostrowski, Siegfried, 3643
Oszwald, R. P., 4310
Otáhalová, Libuše, 5334
Otruba, Gustav, 1497
Otto, Hans, 3374
Otto, Heinz, 4010
Otto, Karl, 3128
Ottwalt, Ernst, 1018, 2574, 2575
Oudard, Pierre, 3211
Outze, Børge, 5575
Ouzoulias, Albert, (Colonel André), 5803
Oven, Wilfred von, 787, 5038
Overduin, J., 6119
Overy, R. J., 4879
Owen, Frank, 6016

Pachtner, Fritz, 4690
Pacifists, German, 3453–3459
Padel, Gerd H., 4434
Paechter, Hedwig, 2509
Paechter, Heinz, 2509
Paepcke, Lotte, 3705
Paetel, Karl O., 2194, 2509, 2589, 3228
Pätzold, Kurt, 1151
Pagès (Lt.-Col.) 4809

Paget, R. T., 5643
Paillard, Georges, 3238
painters, National Socialist, 2675, 2677
Palasti, Laszlo, 5837
Palestine, 3136, 3141, 4580, 4590–4596,
   6261, 6437a
Pallmann, Gerhard, 1683, 2443
Pancke, Günther, 5571
Pankiewicz, Tadeusz, 5918
Pankok, Otto, 2683
Pankratowa, A. M., 4472
Pannwitz, Helmuth von, 4840
Państwowe Muzeum w Oświęcimiu,
   6081–6083
Pantel, Gerhard, 3198
Pantel, Hans-Henning, 4158
Panzer-Propaganda-Kompanie, 5038
Panzermeyer, *pseud.*, 4828
papacy—*See* Vatican
Papadatos, Pierre A. (Peter), 5725
Papagos, Alexander, 5039
Papanek, Ernst, 6265
Papeleux, Léon, 4378
Papen, Franz von, 856, 857, 926, 998,
   1044, 1214, 4049
Papenburg concentration camp, 6030,
   6178
Paplauskas, J., 5377
Pappalettera, Luigi, 6156
Pappalettera, Vincenzo, 6156
Pardo, Herbert, 2727
Paris, 3511, 5458, 5460
   liberation of, 3465, 5459
Park, Willy, 3291
Parkes, James, 207, 233, 3608
parliament, British: House of Commons,
   6315
   House of Lords, 6360, 6361
parties, political, German, 33, 77, 883,
   1113–1117
partisans: general, 5233, 6278
   in the Balkans, 5271, 5274, 5275, 5314
   in France, 5478
   in Holland, 5541
   in Hungary, 5291
   in Italy, 5079, 5507
   Jewish, 5671, 5675, 5689, 5693, 5700,
      5735, 5750, 5772, 5872, 5893, 5939
   Soviet, 5078, 5435–5438, 5440, 5441,
      5444, 5447, 5735
Partridge, Colin, 5101
Pascal, Roy, 1252
Pascher, Joseph, 2392

Pascoli, Pietro, 6037
Pascu, St., 5295
Pase, Martin, 3159
Passarge, Karl, 1640
Passarge, Siegfried, 283, 420, 443
Paszowski, K., 6248
Pat, Jacob, 5872
Pater, J. C. H. de, 5552
Paterna, Erich, 1151
Patis, Wilhelm, 1980
Paucker, Henri R., 2536
Paul, Alexander, 1477
Paul, Otto Ernst, 1525
Paulsen, Peter, 202
Paulus, Günter, 4643
Paumgarten, Karl, 430
Pawek, Karl, 3821
Pawlas, Karl R., 1412
Pawlikowski, Konstantin Ritter de
    Cholewa, 234
Pawlow, Dmitrij W., 5057
Pawlowicz, Sala, 5746
Payne, Robert, 682
Payr, Bernhard, 2592
Pearlman, Maurice, 4591
Pearson, Michael, 5493
peasantry, German: general, 135, 136,
    224, 241, 547–555, 1180, 1682–1696
    inheritance laws for, 1684–1688
Pech, Karlheinz, 3735
Pechel, Rudolf, 1030, 2818–2820, 3314
Pechmann, Wilhelm Frhr. von, 1945
Peck, Joachim, 4609
Peenemünde, 4687
Peeters, Fl. J. P., 1839
Péguy, Charles, 2305
Pehle, Walter H., 6504
Peipler, Joachim, 5527
Peis, Günter, 4514
Pelekis, K., 5378
Pelger, Hans, 3421
Pélissier, Jean, 5475
Pelke, Else, 1840
Peltel-Miedzyrzecki, Feigele, 5979
Peltz-Dreckmann, Uwe, 2654
PEN-Club, German, 3769
people's court—See 'Volksgericht'
Perau, Josef, 4810
Perelman, Fela, 5777
Pergande, Kurt, 6218
Perl, Gisela, 6084
Peron, Juan D., 4563
Peron (Duarte), Eva, 4563

Perotti, Berto, 2683
Perrault, Gilles, 3449
Perrone Capano, Renato, 5513
Perroux, François, 326
persecution of the Catholic Church in the
    Third Reich, The, 2033
persecution, National Socialist: lasting
    effects of, 6445–6451
persecution and resistance in Third Reich:
    general, 78, 1198, 3299–3321, 3357–
    3414, 3730, 4285, 4660, 5227, 5505,
    5546
    cultural—literature, 2565, 2568, 2576,
        2581, 2583–2585, 2587–2590, 3298
        press, 2799, 2819, 2820,, 2822–2824,
        2826
    local and regional, 3322–3356, 3590,
    military, 3386, 3464, 3465, 3467–
        3469, 3472–3475, 3482, 3483—See
        also July 20, 1944
    political—left-wing, 3323, 3335, 3338,
        3341–3344, 3351, 3354, 3355,
        3415–3452, 3505, 3716, 3722
        right-wing, 3463, 3466, 3470, 3471,
        3487, 3496, 3499
    See also Jews, German; and pacifists
persecution and resistance in occupied
    Europe: general, 78, 3412, 5220–5246,
    5406
    underground press, 5236, 5237, 5693
    See also individual countries and regions
Persich, Walter, 3129
Personalamt des Heeres, 5172
Perzl, Irmgard, 2371
Pesch, Ludwig, 4301
Pestalozza, Hanna von, 2113
Pétain, Henri Philippe, 5500, 5501, 5504
Peter, Egon, 4322
Peters, Bernhard, 1824
Peters, Karl, 1378
Peters, Tiems Rainer, 1923
Petersen, Carl, 383
Petersen, Gita, 858
Petersen, Jan, 3436
Petersen, Jens, 4087
Petersmann, Werner, 2060
Peterson, Agnes F., 51, 3240
Peterson, Edward N., 1282a
Petitfrère, Ray, 683, 4069
Petri-Köln, Franz, 4297
Petroff, Irma, 1045
Petroff, Peter, 1045
Petrov, Vladimir, 5051

Petrovich, Michael B., 5303
Petrovitch, Svetislav-Sveta, 5306
Petrow, Richard, 5576
Petry, Christian, 2471
Petsch, Joachim, 2655
Pettee, George, 3715
Petters, Walter, 3275
Petwaidig, Walter, 1152
Petzina, Dietmar, 36, 1497, 1526, 1587
Petzold, Joachim, 887, 2988
Peukert, Detlev, 3351
Pfanner, Helmut F., 2564
Pfarrernotbund, 1879
Pfeifer, Eva, 642
Pflug, Hans, 1182
Pfürtner, Stephanus, 1840
Pfundtner, Hans, 769, 1277
Phelps, Reginald H., 749, 3715
Philipp, Hans, 1022
Phillips, N. R., 804
Phillips, Raymond, 6089
philosophy, study of, in Third Reich,
  2753–2757
Phister, Bernhard, 1458
'phony war', 4978–4980
physicians: National Socialist, 874, 5128,
  5636, 6070, 6082, 6213–6217, 6222,
  6225, 6228–6240
  in occupied Europe, 5264, 5560, 6008,
    6084, 6234
  in Third Reich, 1430 1432–1434a,
    1438, 1440, 2871
physics in Third Reich, 2417, 2420a, 2422,
  2431
Piasente, Paride, 6038
Piaski, 5936
Piatier, André, 1546
Pichl, Eduard, 211
Picht, Werner, 2384
Pick, Frederick Walter, 2949
Picker, Henry, 756
Pickert, Wolfgang, 4854
Piekalkiewicz, Janusz, 5105
Piekarz, Mendel, 5655, 5656
Pietrowsky, Stanislaw, 766
Pietrusky, F., 1437
Pietzsch, Albert, 1579
Pignon, Edouard, 5480
Pikarski, Margot, 3688
Pikart, Eberhard, 1062
Pilichowski, Czesław, 6268
Pinchuk, Ben-Cion, 6316
Pincus, Lily, 3607

Pinette (-Decker), Kaspar, 2353, 2527
Pingel, Falk, 6039
Pingel, Henner, 952
Pinl, Max, 2428
Pinson, Koppel S., 5674
Pinter, Istvan, 6405
Pintschovius, Karl, 4724
Piotrowski, Stanislaw, 766, 5385, 5868
Piper, Otto, 1866
Pirelli, Giovanni, 5234, 5511
Pirie, Anthony, 5154
Pisar, Samuel, 5747
Piscator, Erwin, 1992
Pitt-Rivers, George Lane-Fox, 4491
Pius XI, Pope, 1982, 1983
Pius XII, Pope, 1988–1998, 5422
  and the Jews, 1989, 1990, 1992–1997
Plagemann, Wilhelm, 3006
Plassmann, J. O., 4106
Platen-Hallermund, Alice, 6225
Plauen, E. O., 6406
plebiscites—See elections
Plehwe, Friedrich-Karl von, 4763
Pleiger, Paul, 1608
Pleissner, Artur, 2043
Plesse, Sigurd, 966
Plewnia, Margarete, 2769
Pleyer, Kleo, 3092
Pleyer, Wilhelm, 4107, 4199
Plieg, Ernst Albrecht, 4315
Plischke, Kurt, 444
Ploetz, Alfred, 273
Ploetz, Karl, 4630
Plötzensee Prison, 3291, 3292
Plumb, J. H., 690
Poehl, G. V., 490
Poel, Albert van de, 6167
Poelschau, Harald, 3293
Poesche, Theodor, 194
Pötsch, Walter, 431, 467
Poetzsch-Heffter, Fritz, 1069
Pohl, Gerhart, 2706
Pohl, Johann, 463
Pohl, Oswald, 5607, 5636
Pohle, Heinz, 2854
Pohlmeyer, Adolf, 2283
Pohnert, Ludwig, 2334
Poiesz, Wilhelm, 3271
Poitevin, Pierre, 5492
Polakiewicz, Moses, 5859
Poland: general, 4496, 5162, 5364
  Ministry for Foreign Affairs, 4321
  and Soviet Union, 4321

and Third Reich, 683, 4317–4324, 4509–4518
'Volksdeutsche', 4181, 4325–4338, 4977, 5219, 6412
See also under World War II: campaigns
Poland, occupied: general, 5331, 5382–5429
  Church, Catholic, 1988, 5222, 5421–5424
  Church, Evangelical, 5387
  Generalgouvernement, 1356a, 3259, 5366, 5382, 5383, 5386, 5390, 5393, 5418, 5623
  Jews: general, 5383, 5415, 5623, 5651, 5689, 5700, 5735, 5742, 5754, 5855–5881, 6372–6375—See also ghettoes
    resistance of, 5869–5871, 5878, 5898, 5968, 5985–6001
  persecution and resistance: general, 5040, 5227, 5230, 5240, 5241, 5394–5429, 6268
    cultural, 5204, 5417–5420, 6175
  population transfers, 5215
  Reichsgau Wartheland (Warthegau), 4334, 5243, 5366, 5387, 5390, 5867
  spoliation of, 5204
  underground press, 5236, 5413
  workers, 6247, 6248, 6267
Polenz, Peter von, 2506
Polewoi, Boris, 5633
Polgar, Alfred, 3781
Poliakov, Léon, 195, 327, 1310, 5668, 5812, 6020, 6371
police, National Socialist, 3216, 3255–3284, 5241, 5243, 5244
Polish Corridor—See Danzig
Polish Ministry of Foreign Affairs (Exiled), 5411, 5873
Polish Ministry of Information (Exiled), 4336, 4967
Poljak, Abram, 3698
Pollard, A. O., 4915
Poller, Walter, 6236
Polonski, Jacques, 5464
Pomerania, 860, 2362, 2363, 3272, 5417
Pommerin, Reiner, 4555
Pongs, Hermann, 3874
Ponomarenko, (Lt.-Gen.), 5444
Ponovez Ghetto, 6054
Pool, James, 987
Pool, Suzanne, 987
Poole, Kenyon E., 1553
Pope, Dudley, 4936

Popescu-Puturi, Ion, 5296, 5297
Popiołek, Kasimierz, 4351, 5389
Popitz, Johannes, 533
Poppinga, Onno, 3350
population policy, National Socialist, 409, 767, 1476, 1479, 1481, 1488, 1489, 1559, 2174, 5251
Porten, Edward P. von der, 4944
Portugal, 4353, 6384
Posen, 1946
Poser, Magnus, 3355
Pospieszalski, Karol Marian, 4337, 5390, 6110
Posse, H. E., 1515
Possony, Stefan Th., 1772
Potempa case, 916
Potjomkin, W. P., 4472
Potsdam ceremonies 1933, 934, 1099, 1100
  Conference (1945), 6414, 6452
Potter, M. F., 3056
Pottgiesser, Hans, 4691
Potthoff, Heinrich, 1116
Potulice concentration camp, 6179
Poturzyn, Fischer von, 3866
Poulsen, Henning, 5577
Poznan University, 5419
Poznanski, Czeslaw, 4323
Prag, Werner, 5384
Prague, 5321, 5348, 5349
  Jüdische Kultusgemeinde, 5785
  University, 4204
Prandtl, W., 3014
Prange, Gordon W., 750
Prantl, Helmut, 1957
Praschek, Helmut, 3753
Prater, Georg, 1932
Prečan, Vilém, 5360
Pregel, Reinhold, 4316
Preis, Erwin, 1732
Preis, Kurt, 1168a
Preiss, Heinz, 871, 954
Prenant, M., 3851
press, German: general, 1734, 2763–2846, 4052
  exile, 3744–3750, 3807
  laws relating to, 2784–2786
  literature and the arts in, 2597, 2801, 2831, 2832, 2842
  pre-1933, 454, 949, 981, 2772, 2773, 2777, 2783, 2789, 2810, 2814, 2816, 2818, 2830, 2842, 2846
  religious journals, 2807–2812

religious questions in, 1855, 1894
resistance of, 2799, 2820–2824, 2826
war years, 2771, 2783, 2787, 2802, 2824, 2828, 2838–2839a
press and pamphlets, illegal, 3759–3762, 5236
Pressburg—*See* Bratislava
Presse-Kameradschaftslager, 2793
Presseisen, Ernst, L., 4095
Presser, Jacob, 5826, 5829, 6210, 6212
Preussische Akademie der Künste, 2610
Preussischer Landesverband der jüdischen Gemeinden, 3677
Preussisches Finanzministerium, 2645
Preussisches Justizministerium, 1381
Preussisches Medizinalbeamtenverein, 1479
Preussisches Ministerium des Innern, 30
Preussisches Staatsministerium, 28
Preysing, Konrad von (Cardinal), 2034
Price, Alfred, 4880
Pridham, Geoffrey, 48, 943
Prien, Günther, 4957–4959
Priester, Hans E., 1527
Priestley, J. B., 3823
Prinzhorn, Fritz, 3879
Prion, W., 1554
prisoners-of-war: allied, 6241, 6253, 6286, 6287
British, 5160, 6063, 6285, 6288
French, 5482
German, 513, 3739–3741, 5137–5140, 6473
Jewish, 6287
Soviet, 3215, 5399, 6289–6291
prisons, National Socialist: general, 3285–3298, 5652, 6119
Gestapo, 3286, 3295, 5353
in occupied Europe, 3286, 5337, 5338, 5353, 6045, 6119
priests and pastors in, 1919, 1925, 1935, 1938, 3288
resistance fighters in, 3287, 3291–3293, 3364, 3424, 5337, 6045
women in, 3285, 3294, 3296, 6045, 6049
Pritchard, John, 1087
Pritt, D. N., 1090
Prittie, Terrence, 3315, 3713
professors, university, German, 2397, 2417–2432, 2463, 2464, 2469
Prolingheuer, Hans, 1915

propaganda: general, 2936, 2937, 2939, 2942–2944, 2946, 2947, 2951–2953, 2957, 2958, 2969
British, 4278
National Socialist: general, 2938–2940, 2943, 2945, 2948, 2954–2956, 2959, 2970–3026, 4441
and air war warnings, 3012–3017
anti-British, 4264, 4273, 4291
anti-Communist, 2991–3003
and the arts, 2960, 2963, 2967, 2969, 2979
and the cinema, 2719, 2728, 2732, 2964a, 2966, 2968
economic, 3007–3011
racial, 3103, 5461
and radio, 2943, 2964, 2965, 3045–3047, 4206
and workers, 2845, 3004–3006
See also Weimar Republic, fall of
in World War II: general, 2961, 2962, 2969, 3027–3037
allied 3045, 3057, 3069, 3073, 3075, 3076, 3730
British, 2941, 3039–3401, 3045, 3054, 3056, 3061, 3068, 3070, 3077
National Socialist: general, 2949, 2950, 2954, 2955, 2957, 2965, 2969, 3027, 3033, 3047, 3052, 3053, 3078–3099
anti-allied, 3100–3105, 4295, 4992
anti-British, 3024, 3055, 3059, 3061, 3063, 3065, 3066, 3101, 3103, 3105, 3110–3143, 4212, 4268, 4292, 4580, 4595, 4975, 4984, 5046
anti-Polish, 3138, 3284, 4322, 4327–4330, 4333, 4334, 4338, 5399
anti-Semitic, 3002, 3102, 3110, 3112, 3123, 3136, 3160, 4532, 4580, 4595
anti-Soviet Union, 3144–3152
anti-United States, 3101, 3102, 3105, 3153–3164, 4527
and armed forces, 3047, 3089, 3092, 3096, 3098, 5038
atrocity stories, 3099, 3104, 3121, 3144, 3147, 3152, 3284—*See also* Poland: 'Volksdeutsche'
and France, 3103, 3106–3109, 3168, 5462–5464

radio warfare: general 3038–3058
   National Socialist, 3044–3047, 3052, 3053, 3058, 3084, 3100
   United States, 3033, 3071
Pross, Harry, 2834, 5612
Pross, Helga, 3796
prostitution in Third Reich, wartime, 1428
Protectorate of Bohemia and Moravia
  —See Czechoslovakia
Protocols of Zion, 297–307, 472
   Berne trial, 305–307
Prüller, Wilhelm, 4813
Prümm, Karl, 349, 2526
Prussia, 28, 683, 1055, 1283, 1320, 1331, 1338, 2484
   Landtag, 994, 996, 998
Prussianism, 341, 350
Pruszkow transit camp, 6248
'*Przeglad Lekarski*' (Medical Review), 6215
psychological warfare—See propaganda in World War II
publishers, German, 269, 2597, 2599, 2601, 2602
Pudelko, Alfred, 2289
Pudor, Heinrich, 384, 455
Pünder, Hermann, 1215
Püschel, Wilhelm, 1418
Püschner, Manfred, 3426
Pugel, Theodor, 2114
Puls, Ursula, 3338
Pulzer, Peter G. J., 210
Purpus, H., 1751
Pustau, Ed. von, 4096
Putten, 5554
Puxon, Gratton, 6273
Puzzo, Dante A., 4379

'*Quaderni del Centro di Studi sulla Deportazione e l'Internamente*', 5847, 6274
Quakers, 6339
Quet, Pierre, 5141
Quint, Herbert A., 663
Quisling, Vidkun, 5591, 5592
Quitmann, Walter, 1622

Raab, Angelika, 3346
Raabe, Peter, 2632
Raabe-Stiftung . . ., 2537, 2921

Raas, Emil, 307
Rab concentration camp, 5899
Rabinowitz, Dorothy, 6437
Rabitsch, Hugo, 643
Rabuse, Georg, 2527
Rachmanova, Alja, 3122
racist theories, National Socialist: general, 150, 159, 362–415, 528, 1714, 2174, 2613, 3704, 3828, 4232, 5539, 5688, 6216, 6293
   and agriculture, 548, 553
   and art, 388
   and culture, 379, 586, 590–592, 2299, 2393
   and finance, 541
   and health, 1424, 1426, 1427, 1431, 1434, 1478
   and humour, 2914
   international aspects of, 1350, 3913
   legal aspects of, 562, 564, 565, 570, 572–574
   and literature, 387, 588, 589, 2547
   and philosophy, 2755, 2756
   in the press, 2766
   and psychology, 2758
   religious aspects, 1814, 2027, 2050, 2065, 2079
   and science, 2389, 2401, 2413, 2746
   and sport, 2869, 2881, 2886, 2888, 2892
   See also Eugenics, 'Aryans', 'Nordics' and under school subjects
Radel, J.-Lucien, 157
Radin, Paul, 385
radio in Third Reich: general, 1790, 2806, 2847–2863, 3524
   cultural aspects of, 2850, 2852, 2859
   and politics, 2853, 2854
   resistance in, 2860
   See also under propaganda
Rádo, Sándor, 5155
Radom concentration camp, 6180
Raeder, Erich, 4777, 4931
Rahm, Hans-Georg, 2814
Rahn, Fritz, 2291
Rahs, Hans, 5046
Railways—See under World War II
Raisenberg, Georg, 1343
Raja (Rajakowitsch), Erich, 6409
Ramati, Alexander, 5512
Rammer, Alwin, 3259
Randwijk, H. M. van, 5553
Ranzi, Friedrich, 4104
Rappard, William E., 1659

Rasch, Harold, 1320, 1547
Rasehorn, Theo, 1413
Rasputin, Grigorij, 487
'Rassenhygiene'—*See* Eugenics
Rassenpolitisches Amt der N.S.D.A.P., 2268
'Rassenschande', 444, 1358, 1364, 1415, 3282
Rassinier, Paul, 1996, 6130
Rassow, Peter, 6412
Rast, Gertrud, 3403
Ratchford, B. U., 6457
Rathbone, Eleanor P., 6362
Rathenau, Walther, 338
Rathke, Robert, 2922
Rauchensteiner, Manfried, 5092
Raumer, Kurt, 4059
Raupach, Hans, 878
Rausch, Karl, 2585
Rauschning, Hermann, 328, 3471
Rauter, Hans Albin, 5555
Ravenna, Eloisa, 5729
Ravensbrück concentration camp, 3234, 3418, 5399, 5730, 6003, 6008, 6043, 6045, 6047, 6051, 6181–6189, 6365
  Amicale de, 6181
  medical experiments at, 6237, 6238
Ravenscroft, Trevor, 146
raw materials, German, 1602–1608, 1615, 1680, 2378—*See also* 'Ersatz'
Rawlins, E. C. Donaldson, 1502
rearmament, German, 1594, 1768, 1775, 3896, 3955, 3965–3978, 4624, 4850, 4853, 4860, 4865, 5256
Rebentisch, Dieter, 3346
Rebhann, Fritz M., 5255
Rechenberg, Fritz, 2647
Reck-Malleczewen, Friedrich Percyval, 2576, 2577
Rector, Martin, 3422
Red Cross—*See* Comité International de la Croix-Rouge
'Red Cross' concentration camp, 6190
'Red Orchestra'—*See* 'Rote Kapelle'
Reder, Rudolf, 6087
Rediess, Wilhelm, 4841
Reed, Douglas, 870, 1088, 3479
Rees concentration camp, 6191
Rees, J. R., 804
Rees, Joseph, 6124
Reger, Erik, 2482
Rehberg, Hans, 2712, 3130
Rehberg, K., 2310

Rehberger, Horst, 941
Rehmsdorf concentration camp, 6035
Rehwaldt, Hermann, 147
Rei, August, 4184
Reibert, W., 4725
'*Reich, Das*', 2813, 2833, 2834, 6406
Reich, Albert, 927
Reich, Wilhelm, 258
Reichardt, Fritz, 1671
Reichelt, W.-O., 6458
Reichenbach concentration camp, 6030
Reichhardt, Hans Joachim, 3408
Reichle, Hermann, 1528, 1676
Reichmann, Eva G., 242
Reichsakademie für Leibesübungen, 2876
Reichsamt für wehrwirtschaftliche Planung, 1773
'*Reichsanzeiger*', 1357
'Reichsarbeitsdienst', 1960, 2142, 2340–2356, 4964, 5048
  laws relating to, 2344, 2354
  for women, 2356–2363
Reichsarbeitsrat, 1716
Reichsausschuss für Fremdenverkehr in Berlin, 4132
Reichsbank, 886, 1555
'Reichsberufswettkampf', 1890, 2372, 2373, 2442, 4176
Reichsbetriebsgemeinschaft Handel in der DAF, 1625
Reichsbund der deutschen Beamten, 1311, 1555
Reichsbund Deutscher Seegeltung, 4785
Reichsbund jüdischer Frontsoldaten, 3689
Reichsdienststrafhof, 1312
Reichsdozentenführung, 2426, 3060
Reichsfachschaft deutscher Werbefach-leute (NSRDW), 1622
Reichsfinanzministerium, 1529
Reichsfrauenführerin—*See* Scholtz-Klink, Gertrud
Reichsfrauenführung, 2127
Reichsfremdenverkehrsverband, 1601
Reichsführer SS—*See* Himmler, Heinrich
Reichsführung SS, 3229
Reichsgericht, 1409–1411
'*Reichsgesetzblatt*', 1325
Reichsgruppe Industrie, 1598
Reichshandwerkertag, 1752
Reichshandwerksmeister, 1755
Reichsinstitut für Geschichte des neuen Deutschlands, 211, 2413, 2750
Reichsjugendführung, 2171, 2181,

2195–2197, 2209, 2216–2218, 2361, 2876, 2878, 4672, 4674
Reichsjustizministerium, 1305, 1309, 1330, 1335, 1380
Reichskanzlei, 722, 723, 1284, 2660, 2865, 5128
'Reichskirche', 1909, 1913, 1914
Reichskolonialbund, 4044
Reichskommissar für die Preisbildung, 1569
Reichskommissariat für die Festigung deutschen Volkstums, 5211, 5216
Reichskonkordat, 1975, 1984–1987
Reichskreditkassen, 5190
Reichskriegerbund—See Kyffhäuser Bund
Reichskriegsgericht, 1400
Reichskriegsministerium, 3877
Reichskriminalpolizeiamt, 3282
Reichskulturkammer, 2489–2493, 2707, 2786
Reichskuratorium für das deutsche Fachschrifttum, 4664
Reichsleitung der NSDAP, 29, 1317
Reichsluftfahrtministerium, 4384, 4855
Reichsluftschutzbund, Landesgruppe Ostpreussen, 3015
'Reichsmeldeordnung', 1285, 1286
Reichsminister für die besetzten Ostgebiete, 3152
'Reichsministerialblatt der landwirtschaftlichen Verwaltung', 1672
Reichsministerium des Innern, 30, 769, 1070, 1287, 2608, 2905
Reichsministerium für die kirchlichen Angelegenheiten, 1801
Reichsministerium für Volksaufklärung und Propaganda, 73, 74, 2598, 2604, 2627, 3082, 3143, 4521, 5328
Reichsmusikkammer, 2633, 2634
Reichsnährstand, 29, 1673–1676
Reichsorganisationsleiter der NSDAP, 88, 104, 105
Reichsparteitage, 121, 123, 124
Reichspost, 1288–1290
Reichspressekammer, 2786, 2795
Reichspressestelle der NSDAP, 2794
Reichs- und preussisches Ministerium für Wissenschaft, Erziehung und Volksbildung, 2249, 2253, 2261, 2271, 2873
Reichspropagandaleitung:
Hauptkulturamt, 2488
der NSDAP, 1465, 2981

Reichspropagandaministerium — See Reichsministerium für Volksaufklärung . . .
Reichsrat, 999
Reichs-Rechtsanwaltskammer, 1386
Reichs-Rundfunkgesellschaft, 2855, 2943
Reichsrundfunkkammer, 2856
Reichsschaft der Studierenden der deutschen Hoch- und Fachschulen, 2443
Reichsschrifttumkammer, 2538, 2539
Reichsschrifttumsstelle, 2604
Reichssicherheitshauptamt, 3503
Reichssportführer, 2866, 2876, 2900
Reichssportverlag, 2906
Reichsstatthalter, 1313, 1314
Reichsstelle für den Aussenhandel, 1641
Reichsstelle für das Auswanderungswesen, 4556
Reichsstelle zur Förderung des deutschen Schrifttums, 3647
Reichsstudentenführung, 3143, 5180
Reichsstudentenwerk, 2445
Reichstag, 5, 10, 991–993, 995–997, 999, 1000, 3390, 3910, 3932
Reichstag Fire, 1063, 1066, 1082–1089 1103, 1137, 3479, 3751
trial, 1090–1098, 3853
Reichstheaterkammer, 2707
Reichstreuhänder der Arbeit, Niederdonau, Wien, 2265
Reichsverband christlich-deutscher Staatsbürger nicht-arischer oder nicht rein arischer Abstammung, 3700
Reichsverband der deutschen Presse, 2795
Reichsverband der deutschen Zeitungsverleger, 2785
Reichsverband Deutscher Rundfunkteilnehmer, (RDR), 2857
Reichsverband für die katholischen Auslandsdeutschen, 1966, 4548
Reichsvertretung der Juden in Deutschland, 3662
Reichswehr, 100, 1000, 1101, 3834, 3836, 3844, 3845, 4792—See also Wehrmacht and Army, German
Reichswirtschaftskammer, 1530, 1579
Reichswirtschaftsrat, 1716
Reichwein, Adolf, 2463, 3380, 3381
Reichwein, Rosemarie, 3380
Reier, Herbert, 2079
Reif, Adelbert, 828
Reifschneider, Georg, 4570
Reile, Oscar, 3987, 5156

Reimann, Guenter, 1642, 4108
Reimann, Viktor, 788, 4117
Reimers, Karl Friedrich, 1071, 1936
Rein, Richard, 2299
Rein, Wilhelm, 2307
Reinefarth, Heinz, 5874
Reiner, Guido, 2579
Reinert, Charles, 6123
Reinhard, Klaus, 5059
Reinhardt, Fritz, 542, 1121, 1556, 1562
Reipert, Fritz, 16, 3063, 3093, 3104, 4841
Reismann, Otto, 1763
Reisse, Hermann, 3199
Reismüller, Johann Georg, 3639
Reister, Heinrich, 4177
Reithinger, A., 3109
Reitlinger, Gerald, 3230, 5433, 5698
Reitsch, Hanna, 4881
Remes, Vladimír, 5074
Rémy, *pseud*., 5157, 5494
Renaudot, Françoise, 5465
Renault, Gilbert—*See* Rémy, *pseud*.
Renken, Gerd, 2821
Renn, Ludwig, *pseud.—See* Vieth von
  Golssenau, Arnold Friedrich
Renouvin, Pierre, 4399
Renteln, Adr. von, 1586
Repkow, Eike von, *pseud*., 1015
*Research and Postwar Planning
  Bibliography*, 6397
Ressing, Karl-Heinz, 6476
Reston, James, 4422
Retcliffe, Sir John, *pseud*., 302
Reuling, Robert, 119
Reusch, Fritz, 2635
Reuss zur Lippe, Marie-Adelheid
  Prinzessin, 759
Reuter, Fritz, 1319, 1492
Reutter, Lutz-Eugen, 6343
Reventlow, Graf Ernst zu, 181, 329, 420,
  432, 1153, 4273
Revermann, Klaus, 1046
Révész, Lászlo, 2741
Revetzlow, Karl, 2006
Revolution, German (1918), 44,
  2985–2990, 2996–2998
  National Socialist (1933), 44, 105a, 544,
    677, 955, 1038, 1040, 1041, 1049,
    1072, 1074, 1084, 1115, 1984, 3205
'*Revue d'Histoire de la Deuxième Guerre
  Mondiale*', 81, 4634a
Rewald, Ilse, 6353
Reyes, Hamlet, 4575

Reynaud, Paul, 6298
Reynolds, B. T., 4055
Reynolds, Nicholas, 3486
Reynolds, Quentin, 5718
Rhein, Eduard, 2858
Rheinbaben, Werner Frhr. von, 3094
Rheinische Friedrichs-Wilhelm-Univer-
  sität, 2745
Rheinländer, Paul, 1588
Rhenish Palatinate, 3588, 6053
Rhineland, 683, 2457, 3352, 3589, 3590,
  3970, 4057–4059, 5110
Rhodes, Jews of, 5817
Rhodes, Anthony, 1981, 3032
Rhodes, James M., 105a
Ribbentrop, Annelies von, 3918, 4285,
  4473
Ribbentrop, Joachim von, 1131, 2973,
  3918, 3919, 3933, 4062, 4227
Ribbentrop, Rudolf von, 4285
Rich, Norman, 5173
Richard, Lionel, 2494, 2540
Richards, Donald Ray, 2541
Richards, G. C. 1911
Richardson, William, 4757
Richter, Alfred, 618
Richter, Bodo, 1489
Richter, Friedrich, 3095
Richter, Hans, 5244
Richter, Steffen, 2742a
Richter, Werner, 6475
Riebe, Peter A., 3105
Riecke, Heinz, 475, 2755, 4976
Rieckhoff, H. J., 4882
Riedel, Heinrich, 2460
Riedel, Matthias, 1608
Riedler, Anton, 1709
Riefenstahl, Leni, 126
Rieger, Hans, 5265
Rieger, Julius, 1947
Riehl, Walter, 4121
Rieker, Karl-Heinrich, 5052
Riemer, Karl Heinz, 4665
Riesenberger, Dieter, 3900, 6482
Riesenburger, Martin, 3558
Riess, Curt, 4758, 4873, 5996
Rietzsch, Otto, 1372
Riga, 4185
  ghetto, 3603, 5942, 6054, 6056
Rijshouwer, J. A. H., 6281
Rijksinstituut voor Oorlogsdocumentatie,
  5246, 5533, 5552, 5554, 5555, 5562,
  5563, 6249, 6275

Rikli, Martin, 4605
Rilke, Rainer Maria, 2527
Rimmele, Lilian-Dorette, 2859
Ringelblum, Emanuel, 5875, 5980
Ringler, Arnulf, 1283
Rink, Hermann, 4960
Rinser, Luise, 3294
Rintelen, Enno von, 4070
Rintelen, Franz von, 857
Ripka, Hubert, 4492
Rischer, Walter, 2495
Ristow, Erich, 1493
Ritter, Ernst, 4003
Ritter, Gerhard, 2751, 3404, 3496, 5108
Rittershaus, Ernst, 408
Rittich, Werner, 2656
ritual murder, 227, 237, 468–471
Robbins, Keith, 4493
Robbins Landon, H. C., 4813
Roberts, Helmuth, 534
Roberts, Henry L., 3882
Roberts, Stephen H., 3316
Robertson, E. M., 3862, 4474
Robertson, Edwin H., 1918, 1951
Robinson, Hans, 1415
Robinson, Jacob, 5647, 5657–5659, 5721,
  5913
Robinson, Nehemiah, 6423, 6459
Robinson, Vandeleur, 4155
Rochester, Lord, (Ernest Henry Lamb),
  6360
Rock, Christa Maria, 2636
Rodatz, Johannes, 2144
Rode, Walther, 3317
Roden, Hans, 3844
Rodens, Franz, 2618
Rodenwaldt, Ernst, 386
Roderich-Stoltheim, E., *pseud.* (Theodor
  Fritsch), 456
Röder, Brigitte von, 2444
Roeder, M., 3450
Röder, Werner, 3706a, 3723, 5434
Roegele, Otto B., 2392
Roegels, Fritz Carl, 947
Röhl, J. C. G., 182
Röhm, Ernst, 837, 1106, 1221, 3200
Röhm-Putsch, 1059, 1066, 1101–1110
Röhricht, Edgar, 4778
Röhrs, Hans-Dietrich, 698, 699
Roemer, Hans, 4602
Rönck, Hugo, 2322
Röschel, Alfred, 1379
Rössler, Hellmuth, 4

Rössner, Hans, 2586
Roest, Philip, 6282
Roetter, Friedrich, 1419
Roey, Joseph van, 5519
Rogge, Heinrich, 4274
Rogge, John O., 4579
Rogner, Klaus P., 2684
Rogowski, Marian, 5412
Roh, Franz, 2671
Rohde, Horst, 4692
Rohden, Hans-Detlef Herhudt von, 5063
Rohden, Peter Richard, 4650
Rohlfing, Theodor, 2137, 5366
Rohling, August, 235
Rohr, Johannes, 2542
Rohrbach, Paul, 5364
Rohwer, Jürgen, 3839, 4633, 4945, 5884
Roland, Joseph M., 3986
Roller, Walter, 2847
Roloff, Ernst-August, 950
Roman Catholic—*See* Catholic
Romania: general, 3175, 3176, 4168–
  4175, 5085, 5089, 5295–5298
  Jews of, 5651, 5756, 5783, 5840,
  5882–5888, 6376
  resistance in, 5227, 5295, 5296, 5298
  'Volksdeutsche', 4168, 4170, 4172–
  4174, 6412
Rome, 5513–5515, 5846, 5848, 6283,
  6284
Romein, J. M., 6060
Romein-Verschoor, Anne, 5733
Rommel, Erwin, 4738, 4764, 4779–4782,
  5025, 5030, 5031, 5106, 5109, 5111,
  5144
Rommel, Lucie-Marie, 4779
Rommel-Sozialwerk, 5027
Ronge, Paul, 1394
Ronnefarth, Helmut K. C., 4494
Ronnefeld, Bodo, 1601
Roon, Ger van, 3382, 3405, 3515
Roos, Karl, 4238
Roosevelt, Franklin Delano, 3154, 3157,
  3159, 3161, 4462, 4524, 4527, 4534,
  6391, 6496
Ropertz, Hanz-Rolf, 2587
Rosar, Wolfgang, 4133
Rose, Franz, 476, 2037
Rose, William John, 4352
Rosen, Donia, 5748
Rosen, Edgar, 5507
Rosen, J., 1183
Rosenbaum, Robert A., 5621

598

Rosenberg, Alfred: ideologist and writer, 282, 286, 330–333, 338, 433, 491, 507, 543, 1847–1854, 2007
minister and propagandist, 124, 813–815, 1265, 2770, 2999, 3167, 5591
Rosenfeld, Elsbeth, 3608
Rosenfeld, Else, 5936
Rosenfeld, Shalom, 6369
Rosenkranz, Herbert, 3659, 5762
Rosenthal, Alfred, 398
Rosenthal, Hans, 3619
Rosenthal, Julius, 648
Rosenthal, Ludwig, 6514
Rosicrucians, 508
Rosin, Rijzard, 5410
Rosinski, Herbert, 4814
'Rosma', Orientalische Cigaretten-Compagnie. 615
Ross, Colin, 4604
Ross, Dieter, 4113
Ross, Henryk, 5929
Ross, William D., 6457
Rossaint, Josef, 2011
Rossi, A., 4420
Rossiwall, Theo, 5093
Rossler, Max, 2323
Rossmann, Karl, 4811
Rossner, Ferdinand, 2065
Rosso, Mario, 2035
Rost, Nella, 5905
Rost, Nico, 6120
Rosten, Curt, 106, 1047
Rostosky, Friedrich, 1687
'Rote Kapelle', 3386, 3443–3452, 5156
Roth, Alfred, 420
Roth, Armin, 4726
Roth, Bert, 2141
Roth, Cecil, 5649
Roth, Heinrich, 2456
Roth, Heinz, 6499
Roth, Hiltraut, 3350
Rothacker, Erich, 2527
Rothe, Carl, 1774
Rothenberger, Curt, 1395
Rothfels, Hans, 737, 933, 3406, 6412
Rothkirchen, Livia, 5673, 5751, 5793
Rothschild Family, 448, 455, 2711
Rotterdam, 4997
Roubiczek, Paul, 3829
Rougerie, Claude, 3238
Rousset, David, 5608, 6040
Roussy de Sales, Raoul de, 5168

Routier, Marcelle, 6065
Rowan, Richard Wilmer, 5158
Roxan, David, 5205
Royal Institute of International Affairs, 82, 207, 741, 1543, 3880, 3888, 3889, 3937, 4040, 4203, 4398, 6398
'Royal Oak', 4957, 4959
Royce, Hans, 3510
Rshewskaja, Jelena, 724
Rubinowicz, Dawid, 5749
Rubinstein, Renate, 5829
Rudashevski, Itzak, 5964
'Rudé Právo', 5350
Rudel, Hans-Ulrich, 5646
Rudnicki, K. S., 4974
Rudolf, E. V. von, 477
Rudolph, Hermann, 1810
Rudolph, Ludwig Ritter von, 2989
Rudolstadt concentration camp, 6192
Rückerl, Adalbert, 5623, 5624, 6041
Rüdiger, Karl-Heinz, 3096 ;
Rüdin, Ernst, 1491
Rühle, Gerd von, 573, 849, 960, 1154
Rühle, Günther, 2516, 2712
Rüppel, Erich Günter, 1948
Rüter, A. J. C., 5562
Rüter, C. F., 5616
Rüter-Ehlermann, Adelheid L., 5616
Ruether, Rosemary Radford, 236
Rüthers, Bernd, 1337
Ruffin, Raymond, 5486
Ruge, Friedrich, 4946, 5106
Ruge, Ludwig, 1216
Ruge, Morten, 5581
Ruge, Wolfgang, 4643
Ruhl, Klaus-Jörg, 4380
Ruhmeshalle der SA . . ., 934
Ruhr, 968, 1615, 3351, 3352, 3590, 4476, 6456
Rumkowski, Mordechai Chaim, 5930
Rumpelstilzchen, pseud., 2923
Rumpf, Hans, 4916
Rumsaitis, -?-, 5378
Rundstedt, Gerd von, 4783, 5111, 5530
Runge, Friedrich Wilhelm, 1695
Rupp, Gordon, 271
Rupp, Leila J., 322, 3033
Ruppert, Arthur, 3166
Ruppert, Fritz, 1459
Rupprecht, Adolf, 1117
RuSHA—See under SS
Russel of Liverpool, Lord (Edward), 1208, 5610, 5668, 5726, 6043, 6069, 6431

Rutherford, Ward, 5699
Rutkowski, Adam, 5813, 5857, 5927
Ruttker, Falk, 574, 1491
Ryder, A. J., 40
Rymenans, Lucia, 5529
Ryszka, Franciszek, 1291

S.A.: general, 100, 934, 1103, 2005, 2329, 3179–3207
    Aufklärungsdienst, 4973
    concentration camps of, 3194, 6140
    in 'Kampfzeit', 132, 901, 905, 934, 995, 2069, 2434, 2446, 2917, 2971, 3181, 3187, 3188, 3190, 3193, 3197–3201, 3205
    Marine, 3186
    Oberste SA-Führung, 1162, 2329, 3182, 3191, 3201
    -Sport-Abzeichen, 2874, 2880
    in World War II, 3186a, 3189
    See also Röhm Putsch
S.S.: general, 934, 2667, 3208–3260, 4730, 5409, 5618, 6255
    and concentration camps, 3215, 5607, 6011, 6039, 6062, 6144, 6156
    economic activities, 3220, 3234, 5607
    Hauptamt Schulungsamt, 3099
    in 'Kampfzeit', 3190, 3193
    Leibstandarte, 3226, 3227, 4287
    in occupied Europe, 4847, 5239, 5242, 5245, 5246, 5532, 5866, 6144
    -Personalkanzlei, 3219
    Rasse- und Siedlungshauptamt (RuSHA), 5609, 5636
    Sicherheitsdienst (SD), 3233, 3235, 3255–3260, 5242, 5434
    -Waffen—*See* Waffen-SS
Saage, Richard, 535
Saalfeld, Lerke von, 274
Saar territory, 1547, 2205, 3588, 4048–4056, 6053
Sabille, Jacques, 5199, 6335, 6371
sabotage and subversion, National Socialist, 3979–3989, 4356, 4370, 4437–4445, 5142, 5145, 5146, 5153, 5154, 5160—*See also* 'Fifth Column'
Sacharow, Valentin, 6157
Sacher, Harry, 6311
Sachs, Henry, 5659
Sachs, Nelly, 3799, 3801
Sachsenburg concentration camp, 6030
Sachsenhausen concentration camp—*See*

Oranienburg-Sachsenhausen
Sack, Karl, 1096, 3375
Sadila-Mantau, Hans Heinz—*See* Mantau-Sadila
Saefkow, Anton, 3431
Sänger, Eduard, 3802
Sänger, Fritz, 2796
Safran, Alexandru, 5883
Saggio bibliografico sulla seconda guerra mondiale, 4618
Sagitz, Walter, 75
Sahner, Heinz, 135
Saint-Clair, Simone, 6189
St.-Étienne, District of, 5483
St. George, George, 5892
'St. Louis', 6336
Saint-Loup, Marc Augier, 4842
St. Michielsgestel, 6281, 6282
St. Raphaels-Verein, 6343
Sakkara, Michele, 2734a
Sakowska, Ruta, 5981
Salaspils labour camp, 5376, 6003, 6056, 6193
Salburg, Edith Gräfin, 240
Salewski, Michael, 4947, 4953
Saliège, Jules (Cardinal), 5476
Salin, Edgar, 256, 886
Salis, J. R. von, 4635
Salkowski, Erich, 2309
Saller, Karl, 2746
Salm, Fritz, 3343
Salomon, Ernst von, 166, 2578, 6465
Salus, Grete, 6042
Salvemini, Gaetano, 4475
Salvesen, Sylvia, 6043
Sambeth, Heinrich M., 2522
Sambor Ghetto, 5755
Sammelhefte ausgewählter Vorträge und Reden . . ., 2159
Samuel, Maurice, 3818
Samuel, S., 5840
Samuels, Gertrude, 5750
Sandberg, Moshe, 5751
Sander, A. U., 2735
Sandomir Ghetto, 5860
Sandor, Elo, 6143
Sandulescu, Jacques, 6477
Sandvoss, E., 399
Sanftleben, P. R., 2306
Santander, Silvano, 4563
Sante, Georg Wilhelm, 4049
Santoro, Cesare, 1253

Sartorius, Carl, 1347
satire, National Socialist—*See* Humour
Sattler, Wilhelm, 5315
Sauckel, Fritz, 816, 5181
Saudi Arabia, 4597
Sauer, Franz, 1321, 1335
Sauer, Paul, 1170, 3560, 3561
Sauer, Wilhelm, 1336, 1676
Sauer, Wolfgang, 1056
Saundby, Robert, 4901
Sausnitisa, K., 6193
Sava, George, 3034
Save the Children Fund, 6256
Sawajner, Josef, 5413
Sawicki, Jerzy, 5398, 5625
Saxony, 996, 1169, 1932, 1949, 2254
  Jews of, 3568, 3594
Sbosny, Inge, 3353
Scandinavia, 4354–4356, 4931, 6335,
  6377, 6378—*See also* individual
  countries
Scanlon, John, 3131
Scelle, Georges, 564
Schaber, Will, 3744
Schabrod, Karl, 3353
Schacht, Hjalmar Horace Greeley,
  817–820, 1048, 1217, 1557, 1579, 1630
Schack, Hans, 1411
Schad, Gustav, 2304
Schade, Elspeth, 6510
Schade, Rudolf, 6338
Schadewaldt, Hans, 4338
Schadt, Jörg, 3323
Schaeder, Hans Heinrich, 4576
Schaefer, Dina, 2324
Schäfer, E. Philipp, 4515
Schäfer, Gerhard, 1914, 1955
Schäfer, Gert, 99
Schäfer, Hermann, 1512
Schäfer, J., 5012
Schäfer, Wolfgang, 107
Schäfer-Kretzler, Karin, 3730
Schaeffer, Wolfgang, 3132
Schärer, Martin R., 4996
Schärf, Adolf, 5094
Schätz, Ludwig, 4673
Schätzle, Julius, 6044
Schafer, Werner, 6172
Schaffner, Jakob, 1744
Schairer, J. B., 2066
Schall, Paul, 6491
Schall-Riaucour, Heidemarie Gräfin,
  4769

Schaller, Hermann, 2237
Schaper, Edzard, 5600
Schaper, Karl, 2338
'Scharnhorst', 4948, 4950
Scharoun, Hans, 2657
Schartel, Werner, 2690
Schattenfroh, Franz, 445, 4580
Schaub, Konradjoachim, 4759
Schauff, Rudolf, 4975
Schaukal, Richard von, 420
Schaul, Dora, 3724
Schaumburg-Lippe, Friedrich Christian
  Prinz zu, 789, 1218, 1717
Schausberger, Norbert, 4134, 5256
Schechtman, Joseph B., 4592, 5217,
  5886
Scheel, Adolf, 2445
Scheel, Günter, 49
Scheel, Klaus, 2965
Scheel, Otto, 3133
Scheele, Godfrey, 888
Scheer, Bernhard, 3283
Scheer, Maximilian, 3725
Scheffler, Wolfgang, 3539, 5720,
  6509
Scheibe, Irene, 2362
Scheibe, Wolfgang, 2345
Scheider, Theodor, 6412
Scheidl, Franz J., 4041, 6515
Scheidt, Walter, 2396
Schellenberg, Walter, 858
Schellenberger, Barbara, 2457
Schemann, Ludwig, 290, 387
Schemm, Hans, 859
Schenck, Ernst-Günther, 5128
Schenk, Ernst von, 815
Schenzinger, Karlaloys, 2198
Scherer, Emil Clemens, 1966
Scherer, Werner, 4703
Scherke, Felix, 4727
Schertl, Philipp, 1997
Scheunemann, Walther, 334
Scheurig, Bodo, 3407, 3470, 3473, 3740,
  5064
Scheveningen concentration camp—*See*
  Vught
Schick, Hans, 508
Schickedanz, Arno, 457
Schickel, Alfred, 3231
Schiedemair, Rolf, 1348
Schieder, Wolfgang, 138
Schieferl, Franz Xaver, 228
Schieler, Rudolf, 5623

Schier, Waldemar, 1576
Schiffner, Siegfried, 2727
Schild, Hermann, 1195
Schildt, Gerhard, 1007
Schiller, Friedrich, 2528
Schilling, Alexander, 4121
Schilling, Heinar, 2115, 2837
Schilling, Victor, 1426
Schimitzek, Stanislaw, 6413
Schindler, Richard, 3134
Schinnerer, Erich, 5329
Schirach, Baldur von, 619, 823, 824, 2144,
    2168, 2192, 2195, 2196, 2199, 2200,
    2206, 2330
Schirach, Henriette von, 824
Schirmer, Hermann, 3348
Schirmeister, M. A. von, 773
Schjelderup, Kristian, 1841
Schlabrendorff, Fabian von, 3482
Schlag nach!, 31
Schlageter-Gedächtnis-Museum, 3844
Schlageter-Kalender 1937, 2982
Schlange-Schöningen, Hans, 1155
Schlecht, Hein, 4976
Schlegel, Werner, 1049
Schlegelberger, Franz, 1338
Schleicher, Kurt von, 1050, 1051
Schlemmer, Hans, 2325
Schlempp, Hans, 1285
Schlesinger, Moritz, 3920
Schleswig-Holstein, 134,   135,   1867,
    4359–4361
Schleunes, Karl A., 3540
Schley, Arnold, 616, 906
Schleyer, Felix, 4381
Schlink, Basilea, 6506
Schlösser, Manfred, 2587
Schlösser, Rainer, 2713
Schlötermann, Heinz, 2714
Schloss, Julius, 3616
Schlotterbeck, Friedrich, 3437
Schlüsselmühle labour camp, 6056
Schmahl, Eugen, 224, 4857
Schmaling, Christian, 2816
Schmeer, Karlheinz, 1292
Schmeider, O., 4017
Schmeil, Otto, 409
Schmeling, Max, 2869
Schmelzeisen, G. K., 575
Schmenkel, Fritz, 3376
Schmid, Carlo, 6368
Schmid, Eduard, 4554
Schmid, Heinrich, 1950

Schmidt, Axel, 4428, 5364
Schmidt, Ephraim, 5778
Schmidt, Gerhard, 6226
Schmidt, H. W., 2637
Schmidt, Heinz Werner, 5030
Schmidt, Ingrid, 80
Schmidt, Jürgen, 1943
Schmidt, Paul, 1589
Schmidt, Paul (interpreter), 3921
Schmidt, Peter, 841
Schmidt, Richard, 3963
Schmidt, Royal J., 4476
Schmidt, Werner, 4293
Schmidt-Kehl, L., 1434
Schmidt-Klevenow, Kurt, 1365
Schmidt-Pauli, Edgar von, 620, 4163
Schmidt-Vanderheyden, H., 2363
Schmiedchen, Johannes, 2238
Schmiedel, Erich, 529
Schmieder, Oskar, 4082, 4523
Schmiedt, Shlomo, 3562
Schmith, O., 2871
Schmitt, Carl, 533, 576, 2429, 2430
Schmitt, Walther, 560
Schmitt-Egner, Peter, 4042
Schmitthenner, H., 4017
Schmitthenner, Walter, 3408, 6137
Schmitz-Kairo, Paul, 4240, 4581, 4582
Schmokel, Wolfe W., 4043
Schmorak, Dov B., 5727
Schnabel, Artur, 3789
Schnabel, Reimund, 3052, 3232, 4611,
    6127
Schnapper, M. B., 2160
Schnass, Franz, 2284
Schnauber, Cornelius, 588, 752
Schnee, Heinrich, 212, 4044
Schneefuss, Walter, 4153
Schneersohn, Isaac, 5814
Schneider, Burkhart, 1988
Schneider, Dieter Marc, 3706a
Schneider, Felix, 3709
Schneider, Georg, 2067
Schneider, Hubert, 3920
Schneider, Johannes, 1856
Schneider, Lambert, 2599
Schneider, Paul, 1951, 1952
Schneider, Reinhold, 2585, 3389
Schneider, Richard, 1315
Schneider, Robert, 509, 512
Schneider, Ulrich, 3344
Schneider, Walther, 3135
Schneider, Wolfgang, 1634

Schnell, Fritz, 410
Schnell, Ralf, 2496, 2590
Schnürpel, Hans, 2879
Schoebe, Gerhard, 2945
Schoeller, Wilfried F., 3505
Schön, Eberhart, 959
Schön, Ludwig, 4045
Schoenbaum, David, 1184
Schoenberg, Arnold, 3790
Schoenberner, Gerhard, 3541, 5669
Schöne, Friedrich, 1304
Schöner, Hellmut, 981
'Schönere Zukunft', 2808
Schönerer, Georg, 211, 212
Schönichen, Walther, 1467
Schönleben, Eduard, 831
Schörzingen concentration camp, 6003
Schohl-Braumann, Hela, 3620
Scholder, Klaus, 1784
Scholl, Albert, 3635
Scholl, Hans, 2465, 2467, 2472
Scholl, Inge, 2472
Scholl, Sophie, 2465, 2467, 2472
Scholtis, August, 1219
Scholtz, Harald, 2259
Scholtz-Klink, Gertrud, 2095, 2116, 2117, 2125
Scholz, Robert, 2658, 2685
Schonfeld, Moses, 3542
schools: general, 2221–2244, 2250–2262, 2520
 ceremonies, 2228, 2233, 2287
 individual types of:
  Aufbauschule, 2269
  Grundschule, 2250, 2273
  Hauptschule, 2273
  Höhere Schule, 2249, 2251–2255, 2267, 2274, 2279, 2281, 2310, 2311, 2313, 2316, 2332, 2378
  Kindergarten, 2256
  Mittelschule, 2257, 2269, 2286, 2378
  N.S.D.A.P. Foundations, 2258–2260
  training—See Berufsschulen
  Volksschule, 2245, 2247, 2261, 2262, 2269, 2285, 2287, 2378
 subjects: biology, 2149, 2277, 2279
  English, 2301–2304
  eugenics, 2272–2274, 2325
  French, 2305–2307
  geography, 2280–2284
  German language and literature, 2285–2293
  history, 2294–2300
  Jewish question, 2275, 2278, 2302, 2306
  mathematics and science, 2308, 2309, 2331
  music, 2310–2313, 2637
  politics and civics, 2314–2319
  primers, 2261, 2332–2339
  racism, 2273, 2274, 2276–2278
  religion, 2320–2326
  'Wehrerziehung', 2327–2331
  See also teachers
Schoon, Carl H., 1439
Schopper, Hans, 4122
Schorn, Hubert, 1339, 1396
Schott, Erdmann, 1806
Schott, Georg, 684, 2523
Schottky, Johannes, 1427
Schraepler, Ernst, 49
Schramm, Ferdinand, 1753
Schramm, Hanna, 6138
Schramm, Heinz, 2175
Schramm, Helmut, 468
Schramm, Percy Ernst, 715, 4760, 5107
Schramm, Wilhelm von, 3487, 3511, 3988, 4237
Schramm-von Thadden, Ehrengard, 4159
Schraut, Rudolf, 1397, 1754, 2137, 5366
Schreiber, Gerhard, 4071
Schreiber, Manfred, 1643
Schreiber, Peter Wolfram, pseud., 4680
Schreiner, Albert, 4708
Schreiner, Helmuth, 1785
Schrenk, Oswald, 2638
Schricker, Rudolf, 2996, 3995
Schrieber, Karl-Friedrich, 2493, 2786
Schriewer, Franz, 2600
Schriften zu Deutschlands Erneuerung, 2339
Schrifttum über Deutschland 1918–1963 . . ., 76
Schröder, Arno, 962, 973
Schröder, Bernd Philipp, 4583
Schroeder, Hans Eggert, 2320
Schröder, Hans-Jürgen, 1660, 4537
Schröder, Heinz, 2990
Schröder, Josef, 5083
Schroeder, Richard Ernst, 2201
Schroer, Hermann, 237
Schroeter, Manfred, 2762
Schubert, Günter, 3922
Schubert, Wilhelm Karl Ferdinand, 5614
Schuder, Kurt, 1762
Schüddekopf, Otto Ernst, 889, 3841

Schüler, Felix, 1755
Schüler, Winfried, 247
Schürmann, Artur, 1677
Schütt, Ed., 1479
Schüttel, Lothar, 3016
Schütz, Christel, 2132
Schütz, Erhard, 3773
Schütze, Christian, 2925
Schütze, (Dr.), 1315
Schützle, Kurt, 3845
Schuh, Horst, 3028
Schuh, Willy, 2161
Schulchan Aruch, 237
Schulenburg, Fritz-Dietlof Graf von der, 3512
Schulte-Frohlinde, Julius, 2645
Schultheiss, Tassilo, 2510
Schultz, Gerhard, 1383
Schultz, Hans Jürgen, 3513
Schultz, (Prof.), 308
Schultz, Walter D., 6396
Schultz, Wolfgang, 582
Schultz-Esteves, Christoph, 4598
Schultze, Rainer-Olaf, 42
Schultze, Walter, 3060
Schultze-Naumburg, Paul, 388, 2686
Schultze-Pfaelzer, Gerhard, 1080, 1407, 2004
Schulz, Ernst, 464
Schulz, F. O. H., 478
Schulz, Gerhard, 335, 922, 1056, 3404
Schulz, Heinz, 3706
Schulz, Karl-Heinz, 4827
Schulz, Klaus, 2916
Schulz, Raimund, 5194
Schulz, Ursula, 3380
Schulz, Walter, 4641
Schulz-Kress, H. von, 1618
Schulz-Werner, Joachim, 5050
Schulze, Fiete, 3295
Schulze, Georg, 1286
Schulze, Kurt, 4275
Schulze, Martin, 971
Schulze-Boysen, Harald (Harro), 3443, 3444
Schulze-Manitius, Hans, 1480
Schumacher, Martin, 890
Schumacher, Rupert von, 4011
Schuman, Frederick L., 685, 750, 4505
Schumann, Georg, 3342
Schumann, Hans-Gert, 1122
Schumann, Heinz, 3355
Schumann, Maurice, 6184

Schumann, Wilhelm, 3339
Schumann, Wolfgang, 1767, 4644, 5167
Schuon, Karl Theodor, 139
Schuon-Wiehl, Anneliese K., 139
Schurek, Paul, 2664
Schurmann, A., 2394
Schuschnigg, Kurt, 4135–4137
Schuster, Dieter, 3435
Schuster, Hans Jürg, 2909
'Schutzhaft', 3409, 3410, 3609, 6006, 6141, 6185
Schwägerl, Anton, 4311
Schwaner, Wilhelm, 2068
Schwartz-Bostunitsch, Gregor, 479, 510
Schwarz, Albert, 34
Schwarz, Bernhard, 2334
Schwarz, Falk, 2832
Schwarz, Hans, 177, 178
Schwarz, Hermann, 336, 2756
Schwarz, Karl, 4453
Schwarz, Leo W., 5700
Schwarz, Max, 10
Schwarz, Otto, 2315
Schwarz, Robert, 2845
Schwarz, Stefan, 3543
Schwarz, Urs, 4435
Schwarz, Walter, 1609, 6460
Schwarz-Rot-Buch, 4392
Schwarzbauer, Fritz, 2142
Schwarzburg, Erich, 3160
Schwarze Front, 173, 881
'Schwarze Korps, Das', 2835–2837, 2920
Schwarzschild, Leopold, 2797, 3755
Schwarzschild, Valerie, 3755
Schwarzwälder, Herbert, 5132
Schwarzwäller, Wulf, 5642
Schwede-Coburg, Franz, 860, 951
Schwedhelm, Karl, 183
Schweikert, Julius, 2992
Schweitzer, Albert, 6387
Schweitzer, Arthur, 1577
Schweitzer, Hans, 2919
Schweizer Hilfswerk für Emigrantenkinder, 6387
Schweizerisches evangelisches Hilfswerk für die Bekennende Kirche in Deutschland . . ., 1876, 1940, 3612, 6317, 6341
Schwelien, Joachim, 2511
Schweling, Otto Peter, 4709
Schwendemann, Karl, 3943, 3957
Schwerber, Peter, 583

Schwerin von Krosigk, Lutz Graf, 825, 1558
Schwersenz, Jizchak, 3621
Schwertfeger, Bernhard, 3875, 4019
Schwierskott, Hans-Joachim, 179
Schwinge, Erich, 4709
Schwipps, Werner, 2964, 3053
science and learning in Third Reich: general, 1060, 2391, 2407–2409, 2415, 2423, 2432, 2481, 2739–2747, 4685, 5252, 6129—See also individual disciplines and under racist theories, National Socialist
scientists and scholars: exiled, 3370, 3794–3797, 6390
   Jewish, 2417, 2425, 3642, 3643a
   persecution and resistance of, 2420a, 2425, 2463, 2464, 2469, 5225, 6308
Scott, James Brown, 3913
sculpture in Third Reich, 2666, 2676, 2691
Scurla, Herbert, 3075
Seabury, Paul, 3923
Seago, S., 5144
Seaton, Albert, 5075
Sebottendorff, Rudolf von, 148
secret service, National Socialist, 858, 3980, 3982–3985, 3987–3989
secret societies, 279, 282, 502, 506, 508—See also Freemasons
Seebach, Werner Frhr. von, 1366
Seeliger, Rolf, 2415
'Seelöwe'—See Great Britain, invasion of
Seemen, Gerhard von, 4710
Segal, Simon, 5414
Ségalat, André, 5481
Segel, Benjamin, 303
Segelken, Hans, 1398
Seger, Gerhart, 3726, 3760, 6172, 6173
Seibold, Karl, 3097
Seid, Alfred, 5159
Seidel, Ina, 2128
Seidel, Wolfgang, 2445
Seidel-Slotty, Eugen, 2512
Seidel-Slotty, Ingeborg, 2512
Seidenfaden, Erik, 4457
Seidl, Alfred, 4421
Seidler, Franz, 1428
Seidler, Fritz, 3545
Seifert, Herman Erich, 434, 3136, 3174
Seillière, Ernest, 284, 293
Seipel, Wilhelm, 224
Seipp, Paul, 2345

Selchow, Bogislav von, 2524
Seldte, Franz, 860a, 1460
Sell, Manfred, 497
Selle, Götz von, 2395
Selleslagh, F., 5520
Selzer, Michael, 6121
Selzner, Claus, 1723
Semigothäisches Genealogisches Taschenbuch . . ., 243
Semi-Kürschner . . ., 244, 245
Semjonow, Juri, 4241, 4411
Semmelroth, Ellen, 2112
Semmler, Rudolf, 790
Sender Freies Berlin, 2860
Sendke, Erich, 2210
Senesh, Hannah, 5838, 5839
Senger, Valentin, 3622
Senn, Wilhelm Maria, 1786
Senninger, Bruno, 2983
Seraphim, Ernst, 4426
Seraphim, Hans-Jürgen, 5365
Seraphim, Peter-Heinz, 435
Sereni, Enzo, 5849, 5850
Sereny, Gitta, 6227
Serke, Jürgen, 2609
Serrigny, Bernard, 4651
Sesselmann, Marc, 914
Seth, Ronald, 3035, 5060, 5224
Seton-Watson, R. W., 4276
Setzler, Wilfried, 2416
Sevillano Carbajal, Virgilio, 4393
Seydewitz, Max, 4666, 4693
Seydlitz-Kurzbach, Walther von, 3514, 5064
Seyss-Inquart, Arthur, 821, 822, 3067, 4133, 5537
Shabbetai, K., 5701
Shafir, Shlomo, 4538
Shalit, Levi, 5702
Shamir, Haim, 3660, 6318
Share, Bernard, 4214
Sharf, Andrew, 6319
Sharp, Tony, 6399
Shatzkin, Leonard, 5989
Shavli (Shaulen) Ghetto, 5943, 6054, 6260
Shawcross, Hartley, 6161
Sherrill, Elizabeth, 6365
Sherrill, John, 6365
Shirer, William L., 1156, 1254
Shneiderman, S. L., 6187
Shoskes, Henry, 5996
Shulman, Milton 5108
Shuster, George N., 1842, 3817

Sibyll, Claus, 834
Sicherheitsdienst—*See under* SS
Sicily, 5081
Sidgwick, Alan, 3064
Sidgwick, Christopher, 1255
Siebarth, Werner, 686
Siebert, Fr., 192
Siebertz, Paul, 511
Siebold, Karl, 2924
Siegel, Christian Ernst, 3751
Siegelberg, Mark, 3609
Siegele-Wenschkewitz, Leonore, 1807, 1821
Siegfried Line, 3977, 3978, 4978
Siegler, Fritz von, 4761
Sieker, Hugo, 3363
Siemens, firm of, 6243
Siemens, Hermann Werner, 1481
Siemensstadt, 3596
Siemering, Hertha, 2143
Siemsen, Hans, 2202
Siewert, Curt, 3846
Siewert, Wulf, 4024
Sigg, Marianne, 1367
Sigilla Veri, 245
'*Signal*' 2838–2839a
Sijes, B. A., 5563, 5827, 6249, 6275
Silesia, 1819, 1883, 2673, 5135, 5389, 6134
  Upper, 3671–3673, 3950, 4350–4352, 5394
Sillen, Samuel, 5337
Simion, A., 4175
Simmel, Oskar, 1834
Simmert, Johannes, 3588
Simon, Eduard, 2267
Simon, Ernst, 3680
Simon, Hans, 2879
Simon, Leslie A., 2747
Simon, O. K., 4394
Simon, Paul, 1835
Simon, Wichene, 6131
Simoneit, Max, 4711
Simonov, Konstantin, 6149
'*Simplicissimus*', 2925
Simpson, Amos E., 820
Sims, Nicholas A., 3953
Simson, firm of, 3631
Sinasohn, Max, 3610
Sinasohn, Rahel Ruth, 3610
Sinclair, Upton, 697
Sinel, L. P., 5318
Singer, Charles, 6320

Singer, J., 1399
Singer, Kurt, 4356
Sington, Derrick, 2950, 6094
'Sippenhaft', 3341, 6051, 6268
'Sippenkunde (-forschung)', 1470, 1471, 1473, 1482, 1483, 2083, 2174, 2277, 4002, 6271
Siska, Heinz, 2907
Sittlichkeitsprozesse, 2036, 2037
Six, Franz Alfred, 44, 3883, 5195
Skalnik, Kurt, 294
Skarzysko-Kamienna concentration camp, 6194, 6240
Skorning, Lothar, 2879
Skorzeny, Otto, 4829
Skriewe, Paul, 2378
Slade, Marquis de, 5160
slavery, National Socialist theories on, 395
Slencza, Hans, 1864
Sloan, Jacob, 5980
Slovak Council, 4495
Slovakia: general, 1299, 3149, 4206, 5354–5358
  Jewish labour camps in, 5791
  Jews of, 5789–5795
  uprising, 5359–5361
Smelser, Ronald M., 4200
Smith, Arthur L., 4547
Smith, Bradley F., 614, 3240, 3250, 5634
Smith, Patrick, 2020
Smith, Rennie, 3968
Smith, Sydney, 6288
Smith, Truman, 5084
Smith, Walter Bedell, 5087
Smolen, Kazimierz, 6083
Smoliar, Hersh, 5941
Snoek, Johan M., 6321
Snowden, Viscount (Philip), 1040
Snyckers, Hans, 3202
Snyder, Louis L., 1, 184, 4771
Sobański, Wacław, 4351
Sobczak, Janusz, 5218
Sobibor extermination camp, 5399, 6041, 6195, 6196
Social Darwinism, 273, 275, 276, 2613, 6217
Social Democratic Party (SPD): general, 557, 1116, 1705, 3435, 3727
  in Weimar Republic, 1005, 1008, 1009, 1019
  persecution and resistance of, 1117, 1204a, 3427, 3432, 3716, 3723

social welfare in Third Reich, 1423, 1428–1466, 4657
  laws relating to, 1368, 1442, 1444, 1452, 1457, 1459, 1691, 1707, 2101, 2137, 2138
sociology in Third Reich, 404, 2757
Sodeikat, E., 1926, 3329
Sodenstern, Hans von, 947
Söhngen, O., 1956
Sörgel, Werner, 1610
Soers, Adolf, 2202
Sösemann, Bernd, 2797
Sohn-Rethel, Alfred, 1185
Soldan, Georg, 928
Solingen, 3353
Sollheim, Fritz, 2385
Sombart, Werner, 256
Somerhausen, Anne, 5521
Sommer, F., 4178
Sommer, Hellmut, 5219
Sommer, Martin, 5614
Sommer, Paul, 2292
Sommer, Theo, 4098
Sommerfeldt, Martin H., 802
'Sonderbehandlung', 5713, 6079, 6253
Sonderegger, René, 1110
'Sonderfahndungsliste', 5020, 5434, 5568
Sondergeld, Walter, 2445
'Sondergericht', 1412, 2026
'Sondertreuhänder der Arbeit', 1712
Sonnemann, Theodor, 2129
Sonnenburg concentration camp, 6030
Sonntag, Fritz, 2676
Sontag, Raymond James, 4422
Sontheimer, Kurt, 891, 933, 3755
Sorb, (Commandant), 716
Sorge, Gustav Hermann, 5614
Sorge, Siegfried, 4728
Soria, Georges, 4242
Sosnowiec Ghetto, 5906
Sosnowski, Kiryl, 6266
Sotke, Fritz, 2317
South Africa, 3124, 3137, 4293
South East Europe—See Balkan and Dannubian states
South Tyrol, 4077–4079
South-West Africa, German, 2337, 4294
South West Africa Commission, 4294
Soviet Union: general, 4396–4429
  exiles in, 3734, 3741, 3742, 3764a
  exiles from, 4412
  and Hungary, 4165

Ministry of Foreign Affairs, 4452
  and Poland—See under Poland
  prisoners-of-war in, 3739–3742
  and Third Reich, 4184, 4396, 4397, 4399–4410, 4413, 4414, 4472—See also Hitler-Stalin pact
  and 'Volksdeutsche', 4425, 4426
  See also under World War II
Soviet Union: Occupied Territories of:
  general 5430–5447
  Jews in, 5860, 5889–5896
  persecution and resistance in, 5227, 5435–5447, 6254
  See also Ukraine
Spaight, J. M., 4891
Spain: general, 3881
  civil war, 1656, 3888, 4382–4395, 4858
  exiles in, 3771, 6384
  and Third Reich, 1656, 4372–4395
  and 'Volksdeutsche', 4377
  and World War II, 4372, 4374, 4375, 4378–4380
Spandau prison, 4777, 5641, 5642, 5644
Spanier, Ginette, 5752
Spann, Othmar, 256
Special Operations Executive (SOE), 5160a–5162
Speer, Albert, 702, 826–828, 2659–2661, 4694, 4695, 5644
Speidel, Hans, 3485, 4784, 5109
Speier, Hans, 3046
Spender, Stephen 268
Spengler, Oswald, 173, 256, 259, 338, 3006
Sperber, Manès, 929, 5876
Spicher, Willy, 3356
Spiegel, Tilly, 5266, 5267
'Spiegel, Der', 714
Spielhagen, Franz, 4394
Spiesser, Fritz, 3137
Spiker, Jürgen, 2736
Spiru, Basil, 4516
Spitz, H., 1756
Spivak, John L., 3989
Spohr, Werner, 3410
Sponholz, Hans, 2162
sport and athletics in Third Reich, 2142, 2478, 2846, 2864–2882
Spreckelsen, Otto, 2318
Sprenger, Jakob, 224
Springenschmidt, Karl, 4123
Springer, Carl, 2926

Sproll, Joannes Baptista, 2038
Stache, Rudolf, 3138
Stachura, Peter D., 864, 930, 997, 1157, 2203
Stadler, G. M., 3074
Stadler, Karl R., 5249, 5257, 5268
Stadlinger, Friedrich, 1757
Stadtler, Eduard, 3000
Staehle, Wilhelm, 3515
Staff, Ilse, 1420
Stahlberg, Wolfgang, 363
Stahlhelm, 100, 860a, 934, 1124–1126, 3323
Stahlmann, Hans, 2293
Stalin, Josef, 486, 4396, 4414, 6496–See also Hitler–Stalin pact
Stalingrad, 3741, 4644, 4745, 4747, 5062–5065
Stamer, Fr., 4856
Stamm, Kurt, 2354
Stampfer, Friedrich, 3727
Stang, Walter, 593
Stanislaw(u) Ghetto, 5860, 5944, 5945
Stanislawska, Stefania, 4496
Stanley, Ilse, 3611
Stanojlovic, Aleksander, 5898
Stapel, Wilhelm, 185, 186, 420, 458, 588, 1808
Stappert, Bernd H., 3607
Starcke, Gerhard, 1723, 1733, 1734
Stark, G., 2951
Stark, Gary D., 269
Stark, J., 2431
Starke, Käthe, 5957
Stasiewski, Bernhard, 1972
Statistisches Handbuch von Deutschland 1928–1944, 13
Statistisches Reichsamt, 14, 15, 1380, 1461
Staude, Heinrich, 358
Stauf von der March, Ottokar, 420, 469
Stauff, Philipp, 244–246
Stauffenberg, Berthold von, 3520
Stauffenberg, Claus Philip Schenk Graf von, 3516–3520
Steche, Otto, 2279
Steding, Christoph, 2497
Steed, Wickham, 919, 1256, 2952, 3457, 4852
Steen, Hans, 3173
Steffen, Franz, 1787
Steffens, Heinz, 1624
Steffens, Manfred, 3461

Steg family, 3599
Stegemann, Willi, 4636
Stegmüller, Franz, 2798
Steiermark: Gaudozentenführung, 4143
Stein, Adolf, 2923
Stein, Edith, 2024, 3699, 5823
Stein, Erwin, 3790
Stein, George H., 4830
Stein, Joshua Berton, 6322
Stein, Leon, 248
Stein, Leonard, 6359
Stein, Sigmund, 3640
Steinacher, Hans, 4014
Steinbach, Erika, 2117
Steinberg, Hans-Josef, 3332
Steinberg, Lucien, 5671, 5779, 5814
Steinberg, Michael Stephen, 2446
Steinberg, Rolf, 2498
Steinbock-Fermor, Alexander, 3293
Steinbömer, Gustav, 584
Steinbrick, Otto, 308
Steinbühl, Josef, 5357
Steiner, F., 5794
Steiner, Herbert, 5270
Steiner, Jean-François, 6203
Steiner, Johannes, 1020
Steinert, Marlis G., 4667, 5115
Steingräber, Erich, 2688
Steingruber, Albert, 3462
Steinhoff, Johannes, 3472
Steiniger, P. A., 5635
Steininger, Rolf, 2853
Steinitz, Hans, 3744
Steinkopf, Heinrich, 2308
Steinmetz, Selma, 6276
Steinweg, Günther, 4681
Steinwender, Leonhard, 6105
Stellrecht, Helmut, 687, 2330, 2355
Steltzer, Theodor, 3383
Stelzner, Fritz, 3203
Stenzel, Hermann, 2619
Stephan, Alexander, 3775
Stephan, John J., 4412
Stephan, Karl, 1085
Stephens, Frederick J., 2204
Stephenson, Jill, 2118, 2119
Stepinac, Draloizije (Aloysius), 5307
sterilization in Third Reich, 411, 1490–1494, 6224
Sterling, Eleonore, 213
Stern, Fritz, 892
Stern, J. P., 688
Stern, Michael, 3728

Stern, W., 3526
Sternberg, Fritz, 3971, 4739
Sternberger, Dolf, 5712
Sternfeld, Wilhelm, 3776
Stetten-Erb, Herbert Frhr. von, 842
Steuernagel, Friedrich, 1758
Stevens, Francis B., 3986
Stevenson, William, 6407
Steward, John S., 1844
Stewart, Douglas K., 3483
Stieda, Renate von, 2112
Stiefenhofer, Theodor, 2296
Stieff, Helmuth, 3521
Stierlin, Helm, 689
Stillfried, Gebhard, 6123
Stillich, Oskar, 4015
'Stimme Amerikas', 3730
Stippel, Fritz, 2239
Stirk, S. D., 350
Stoakes, Geoffrey, 1157, 3924
Stock, Richard Wilhelm, 436
Stock, Wolfgang Jean, 1037, 3743
Stock Exchange, National Socialist attacks
    on, 542
Stockhammern, Franz von, 1980
Stockholmer Koordinationsstelle zur
    Erforschung der deutschsprachigen
    Exilliteratur, 3767, 3768
Stockhorst, Erich, 11
Stoddard, Lothrop, 295, 1257
Stoecker, Adolf, 260
Stöcker, Hans, 2799
Stoecker, Helmuth, 5174
Stöckmann, Albert, 1340
Störmer, Hellmuth, 1457
Stoevesandt, Karl, 1912
Stohr, Martin, 6507
Stojanoff, Petr, 1097
Stokman, S., 5543, 5564
Stoll, Christian, 1913
Stoll, Gerhard E., 2812
Stollreiter, Heinrich, 1757
Stollweis, Michael, 1341
Stolte, Heinz, 5053
Stone, Norman, 690
Stonner, Anton, 585
Stoppelman, Joseph W. F., 5549
Storek, Henning, 2800
Storm, Gerhard, 2039
Storz, Gerhard, 5712
Stoye, Johannes, 4099
Strasbourg university, 6050
Strasburger, Henryk, 4348

Strasser, Gregor, 861–865
Strasser, Otto, 561, 697, 866–870, 1110,
    3728
Strassner, Peter, 4843
Straube, Harald, 3531
Strauch, Rudi, 4261
Strauss, Harald, 6480
Strauss, Herbert A., 3553, 3706a, 6492
Strauss, Richard, 2634
Strausz-Hupé, Robert, 4025
Strawson, John, 717, 5129
Streicher, Julius, 449, 465, 640, 871–873,
    1354, 4663
Streim, Alfred, 5623
Streit, Christian, 6289
Strelitz, Johannes, 3576
Strelka, Joseph, 3774
Strength through joy—See 'Kraft durch
    Freude'
Strick, Hans Günther, 2915
Strickner, Herbert, 2846
Striefler, Ernst, 4302
Strigler, Mordchai, 6046
Strik-Strikfeldt, Wilfried, 4846
Strobl, Gustav, 1825
Ströbinger, Rudolf, 5342
Ströhn, K., 4010
Stroop, Jürgen, 5997–6001,
Stroothenke, Wolfgang, 411
Strothmann, Dietrich, 2801
Strube, Adolf, 2310, 2313
Strücker, Wilhelm, 2715
Strugar, Vlado, 5308
'Struma', 5884
Strunk, Roland, 4605
Struthof concentration camp, 6159
Strutz, Henry, 5637
Struve, Carola, 2120
Struve, Günther, 3713
Stryj, 5877
Stuckart, Wilhelm, 1348, 1363, 2447
Studemund, Wilhelm, 1868
students, university: general, 1060, 1848,
    1890, 2397, 2416, 2433–2449, 4698,
    5180
  laws relating to, 2441
  'non-Aryan', 2393, 3704
  resistance of, 2464–2468, 2470–
    2473
'Stürmer, Der', 470, 2840, 2912
Stuhlfath, Walter, 2984
Stuhlmann, Friedrich, 3876
Stuhlpfarrer, Karl, 5091

Stumme, Wolfgang, 2639
Sturm 22/97, 939
Sturm, Karl Friedrich, 2240
Sturminger, Alfred, 2953
Stutterheim, Kurt von, 3358
Stuttgart, 3354, 3591, 4917
  Archivdirektion, 3560, 3561
Stutthof concentration camp, 3603, 5399,
  5575, 6056, 6197
Subhas Chandra Bose, 4610
Suche, Joachim, 3925
Suchenwirth, Richard, 4883
Sudeten problem—See Czechoslovakia
Sudetendeutsche Partei, 4191, 4194
Sudholt, Gert, 740, 2802, 3451
Südostdeutsches Institut, Graz, 4143
Sündermann, Helmut, 2802, 2803, 4109,
  4137, 4652, 4965, 6500
Süskind, W. E., 5712
Suhl, Yuri, 5703
Sullivan, Matthew Barry, 5139
Supf, Peter, 4884
Supreme HQ Allied Expeditionary Force
  (SHAEF), 3076
Surén, Hans, 2386, 2892, 2908
Survey of International Affairs, 82
Sutro, Nettie, 6387
Sutton, Antony C., 4539
Suzkewer, Abraham, 5965, 5966
Suzman, Arthur, 6516
Svufvud, P. E., 3167
Swabia, 1957, 5136
Swastika, 200–202, 1778, 5292
Swatek, Dieter, 1578
Sweden: general, 4367–4371
  exiles in, 3710, 3801
  National Socialism in, 4369, 4371
  rescue actions by, 5112, 6382, 6383
  and Third Reich, 1657, 2421, 4367,
    4370
Swing, Raymond Gram, 5168
Switzerland: general, 3879, 4430–4445,
  5141, 5148, 5149, 5391
  and the Jews, 6294, 6317
  and refugees, 3729, 3743. 3764a,
    3783, 6385–6387
  and Third Reich, 1658, 3430,
    4432–4434, 4445, 4837, 5003, 5125
  and 'Volksdeutsche', 4438, 4439, 4441,
    4442
Sydnor, Charles W., 4831
Sykes, Christopher, 3523, 6437a
Sylt, Island of, 969

synagogues, destruction of, 3648, 5862
Syria, 4588, 4598
Syrkin, Marie, 5704, 5753
Sywottek, Jutta, 2954
Szabó, Ladislao (Laszlo), 6405, 6408
Szac-Wajnkranc, Noemi, 5738
Szajkowski, Zosa, 5814a
Szalet, Leon, 6239
Szczypiorski, Andrzej, 5998
Szende, Stefan, 5754
Sziling, Jan, 5424
Színai, Miklós, 4164
Szliska, Jakob, 2270
Szmaglewska, Seweryna, 6085
Szmajzner, Stanislaw, 6196
Szúcs, László, 4164
Szunyogh, Bela, 3036

Tackmann, Heinz, 2493
Taddey, Gerhard, 37
Tägil, Sven, 4361
Tagliacozzo, Michael, 5846
Tal, Uriel, 6321
Talmud, 225, 226, 228, 229, 231, 234,
  235, 241, 463, 481
Tartakower, Aryeh, 5971, 5980
'Tat, Die', 256, 338
Tauber, Richard, 3791
Taucher, Franz, 2823
Tausk, Walter, 3565
Tautz, Johannes, 148a
Taverner, Eric, 1258
Tavernier, René, 5480
taxation in Third Reich, 1559–1562, 1571
Taylor, Alan John Percivale, 4464, 4477,
  4478, 4637, 5074
Taylor, Eric, 4898
Taylor, Hugh Page, 3233
Taylor, Richard, 2966
Taylor, Robert, R., 594
Taylor, Telford, 737, 3847, 4497, 4756,
  4883, 5013, 5076, 6213, 6243
Tchernoff, J., 4479
teachers: general, 2245–2249
  handbooks for, 2263–2271
  resistance of, 3377, 3416, 5231
  in Weimar Republic, 2245–2247
  See also Nationalsozialistischer Lehrer-
    bund (NSLB)
technology in Third Reich, 545, 583,
  2327, 2376, 2478, 2742a, 2759–2762
Teichert, Friedrich, 2513

Teichova, Alice, 4498
Teklenburg, G. H., 2008
Telschow, Otto, 963
Témoignage Chrétien, 5801
Temple, William (Archbishop), 3371, 4967, 6360
Tenenbaum, Joseph, 5672, 5864, 5878, 6302
Tennenbaum-Backer, Nina, 5912
Tennenbaum-Tamaroff, Mordekhai, 5912
Tennstedt, Florian, 1434a, 3665
Teppe, Karl, 1295
Terboven, Josef, 5591
Teresia Renata de Spiritu Sancto (Sister), 3699
Terezin Fortress (concentration camp), 6198, 6199
  See also Theresienstadt
Tergit, Gabriele, 3771
Terkuhle, E., 4997
Ternon, Yves, 6216, 6217
Terroine, Emile F., 5487
Terveen, Friedrich, 2738
Teschemacher, Hermann, 1579
Teschitz, Karl, 1809
Teske, Hermann, 4413
Tessan, François de, 1259
Tessin, Georg, 3281, 4712, 4713
Tetzlaff, Walter, 2188
Teubner, Hans, 3729
Teut, Anna, 2662
Teutonia, Berliner Burschenschaft, 2449
Tgahrt, Reinhard, 2831
Thadden, Elisabeth von, 3377
Thälmann, Ernst, 3438
Thalheim, Karl C., 1532, 4186
Thalmann, Rita, 1869, 3367, 3661
Thape, Ernst, 1220
theatre, German: general, 265, 2695–2716, 3778–3781
  laws relating to, 2696, 2707
  National Socialist, 595, 2516, 2697–2700, 2703, 2704, 2708–2716, 2852
Thelwall, C. M. C., 1502
theosophy, 1810
Theresienstadt Ghetto, 3563, 5325, 5784, 5946–5959, 6042, 6045, 6199
Thevoz, Robert, 3272
Thiede, F., 4857
Thiele, Wilhelm, 3424
Thieleke, Karl-Heinz, 3633
Thier, Erich, 158

Thierack, Otto Georg, 1395
Thierfelder, Franz, 2514, 2861, 3139
Thies, Jochen, 691, 2646
Third Reich. Studies by 27 leading historians . . ., The, 1158
Thoene, Albrecht W., 389
Thomae, Otto, 2967
Thomas, David A., 4941
Thomas, Edith, 5480
Thomas, Georg, 1775
Thomas, Gordon, 6336
Thomas, Jack, 6106
Thomas, John Oram, 5584
Thomas, Katherine, 2121
Thomazi, A., 4949
Thompson, Dorothy, 2589, 3370, 3830
Thompson, H. K., 5637
Thompson, R. W., 5110
Thoms-Paetow, Johanna, 2079
Thomsen, Erich, 5578
Thorne, Leon, 5755
Thornton, M. J., 108
Thornton, Willis, 5459
Thost, Hans W., 4277
Thule Gesellschaft . . ., 148, 279
Thuringia, 970, 971, 1293, 2251, 3355
Thyssen, Fritz, 988, 989
Tidl, Marie, 5268
Tidy, Henry Letheby, 6230
Tiedemann, Eva, 3776
Tieke, Wilhelm, 5054
Tillard, Paul, 5809
Tillich, Paul, 3730
Tillmann, Heinz, 4584
Tilman, H. W., 5277
Tilton, Timothy Alan, 1696
Timeroumenos, *pseud.*, 1421
Timm, Herbert, 1718
Timpe, Georg, 4548
Timpke, Henning, 957
Tingsten, Herbert, 337
Tippelskirch, Kurt von, 4638
Tirala, Lothar Gottlieb, 390, 2881
'Tirpitz', 4950
Tiso, Josef, 5358
Tito (Josip Broz), 5310
Tjören, A., 446
Tobias, Fritz, 1089
Todt, Friedrich Wilhelm (Fritz), 829–831, 1763, 5102, 5479, 5776
Tögel, Hermann, 2326
Tønnesen, Helge, 5581
Tönnies, Norbert, 4278

611

Toeplitz, Jerzy, 2737
Törne, Volker von, 6502
Töteberg, Michael, 3786
Toland, John, 692, 5123
Toliver, Raymond F., 4885
Toller, Ernst, 1021, 2712
Tolstoy, Alexei, 5055
Tomasevich, Jozo, 5311
Tomkowitz, Gerhard, 4138
Topf, Erwin, 1678
Torberg, Friedrich, 3799
Tormin, Walter, 1129
Tornow, Werner, 1679
Torrès, Henry, 1421
Toscano, Mario, 4088, 4423, 4480
'total war', 2376, 2954, 4458, 4640, 4645,
    4651, 4708, 4733, 4737
Totok, Wilhelm, 68
Tourly, Robert, 645
Touw, H. C., 5544
town planning in Third Reich, 2647, 2653,
    2655, 2661
Townsend, Peter, 4892
Toynbee, Arnold J., 3888, 3889
Toynbee, Veronica M., 3888, 3889
Trachtenberg, Jakow, 1098, 3546
trade in Third Reich: general, 1616–
    1622
    foreign, 1579, 1603, 1618, 1627–
    1645—See also under individual
    countries
    laws relating to, 1618, 1620, 1621,
    1624, 1641
    retail, 893, 1623–1626
    wholesale, 1618
trade unions: Austrian, 5260
    Catholic, 1696a
    'Christlich-Soziale', 1705
    Socialist: and National Socialism, 312,
    546, 1001, 1003–1005, 1120, 1705
    persecution and resistance of,
    1118–1123, 3421, 3743, 5381
    'Volksdeutsche', 254
Trandafilovitch, Ivan, 1651
Transnistria, 5883, 5885, 5886
Transylvania, 5840
Trathnigg, G., 4106
Traue, Georg, 2069
Trauman, Ilse, 2160
Travaglini, Thomas, 2955
treason in Third Reich: laws relating to,
    1382, 1383, 1544
Trebitsch, Arthur, 296

Treblinka extermination camp, 5399,
    5700, 5860, 6041, 6200–6204
Trefousse, H. L., 4540
Tregenza, Michael, 6088
Treitschke, Heinrich von, 183, 214, 3135
Tremel-Eggert, Kuni, 2122
Trenchard, Viscount (Hugh Montague),
    4891
Trenktrog, Walther, 2387
Trepper, Leopold, 3452
Treschkow, Henning von, 3473
Treude, Burkhard, 2830
Treue, Wilhelm, 34, 5200
Treviranus, Gottfried Reinhold, 1052
Trevor-Roper, Hugh R., 638, 711, 725,
    738, 754, 777, 832, 1178, 3246, 3248,
    3315, 3518
Trier (Trèves), 1166
Trieste: Jews of, 5851, 5852
'Triumph des Willens', 125, 126
Trivers, Howard, 3986
Trofimenko, G., 6290
Troisio, Armando, 5514
Troper, Harold, 6346
Trossman, K., 719
Trotha, Adolf von, 4785, 4786
Trotha, Thilo von, 813
Trotsky, Leon, 931
Trott zu Solz, Adam von, 3388, 3522,
    3523
Truchanovsky, V. G., 4424
Truck, Betty, 6235
Truck, Robert-Paul, 6235
Truckenbrodt, Walter, 3949
Trumpp, Thomas, 62a, 998
Trunk, Isaiah, 5705, 5913, 5931, 5982
Trurnit, Hansgeorg, 428
Tsatsos, Jeanne, 5284
Tsay, Jeh-Sheng, 2356
Tscherne, Ernst, 4209
Tschimpke, Alfred, 5014
Tschirschky, Fritz Günter von, 1221
Tsouderos, Emanuel, 5285
Tübingen university, 1821, 2416
Tüngel, Richard, 6478
Türk, Franz, 2241
Tully, Andrew, 5130
Tumler, Franz, 4714
Tunisia, 5029, 5805, 5815
Turkey, 3799, 3881, 4155, 4599, 4600
Turner, Henry Ashby, jr., 646, 989, 1159
Turney, Alfred W., 5061
Turrou, Leon G., 4549

Turtel-Aberzhanska, Chasia, 3562
Tushnet, Leonard, 5914
Tutaev, David, 6354
Tutas, Herbert E., 2956, 3731
Tutzinger Texte . . ., 1953
Tyrell, Albrecht, 647, 932
Tyrowicz, Stanisław, 2757
Tzschirner, George, 4585

U. C., 3296
Udet, Ernst, 4787–4789
Uebe, Klaus, 5076
Ueberhorst, Horst, 2260, 2891
Überparteilicher Hilfsausschuss, Paris, 3725
Überschär, Gerd R., 4362
Uhlig, Heinrich, 1626, 5077
Uhse, Bodo, 4858
Ukraine, 3147, 3177, 4427, 4428, 5078, 6254
'Ukrainische Aktion', 4429
Ukrainisches Wissenschaftliches Institut, Berlin, 3178
Ulbricht, Walter, 3439, 3733
Ullmann, Hans Peter, 77
Ullstein, firm of, 3599
Ullstein, Herman, 2601
Ulm/Donau, 3592
Ulmenstein, Frhr. von, 1483
Ulrich, Gerhard, 2098
'Ultra' code, 5145
Umbreit, Hans, 5331
'Unbewältigte Vergangenheit', 6491
Und sie bewegt sich doch, 3803
Undset, Sigrid, 5601
unemployment in Germany, 1120, 1121, 1707, 1718, 1721
Unger, Aryeh, 109
Unger, Erich, 351
Unger-Winkelried, Emil, 480, 1008
uniforms, 1174a, 2196, 2204, 3233, 4707
Union des Instituteurs allemands émigrés, 2242
Union Nationaler Journalisten-Verband, 2779, 3060
Union für Recht und Freiheit, Prag, 6049
Union Suisse des Communautés israélites, 3538
United Nations Relief and Rehabilitation Administration (UNRRA), 6250, 6424
United Restitution Organization, 5815, 5841, 5887
United States: general, 4519–4551

air force, 4918
Department of State, 4559
Displaced Persons Commission, 6422
exiles in, 3373, 3744, 3746, 3764, 3774, 3796, 3817
foreign policy of, 4528, 4533, 4534, 4536, 6394
House of Representatives, 6420
and Jews, 6292, 6295, 6301, 6302, 6308, 6309, 6437
National Socialist escapees in, 6401
National Socialist subversion and propaganda in, 4542, 4543, 4545, 4546, 4549–4551
Office of Chief of Council for Prosecution of Axis Criminality, 53
rescue actions of, 6388–6393
Tariff Commission, 1661
and Third Reich, 1659–1661, 2901, 4525, 4526, 4529, 4531, 4536–4540, 4546, 4547
and 'Volksdeutsche', 4541, 4544, 4547, 4548, 4550, 4551
universities, German: general, 354, 2390–2444—*See also under* individual cities resistance at, 2463–2473
Unkelbach, Wilhelm, 5614
Unruh, Friedrich Franz von, 110
'Unsere Zeit', 3761
'Untermenschentum', 295, 467, 477, 3099
Unverricht, Elsbeth, 2123
Urach, Fürst A., 4097
Urbach, Dietrich, 2382, 2383
Urban, Rudolf, 5335
Uris, Leon, 6232
Urquhart, Clara, 5850
Ursachen und Folgen, 49
Uruguay, 1662, 4574, 4575
Ministry of Foreign Affairs, 4935
Usadel, Georg, 41, 601
Ushakov, V. B. (Uschakow, W. B.), 3926, 3927
Usikota, *pseud.—See* Brinitzer, Carl
Ustashi, 5313
Utermann, Wilhelm, 2184, 3025, 4796
Uthoff, Hayo, 5611
Utikal, Gerhard, 471
Utsch, Bert, 6174
Uweson, Ulf, 637

V1 and V2 rockets, 3079, 4683, 4684
Vago, Bela, 4154, 5706

Vahlen, (Professor), 2413
Valentin, Hugo, 6377
Valentin, Veit, 4la, 3795
Valland, Rose, 5201
Valluy, Jean, 4816
Valtin, Jean, *pseud*., 1222
van der Lubbe, Marinus, 1095, 1098
Vandrey, Max, 2934
Vanino, Maurice, 5466
Vanlangenhove, F., 4300
Vansittart, Lord (Robert Gilbert), 3056, 3077, 4279, 4481
Vardys, Stanley V., 5379
Vasek, Anton, 5795
Vassé, Jean Gontier de, 3140
Vassilier, Stefan, 1652
Vatican policy: general, 5604
   on Jews, 1977, 1989, 5790–*See also under* Pope Pius XII
   and Third Reich, 1975–1998
   and World War II, 1988, 1989
'Vatican II', 6523
Vegesack, Siegfried von, 5367
Veidal concentration camp, 6036
Veillon, Dominique, 5497
Vel d'Hiv, 5809
Veld, N.K.C.A. in't, 5246
Velpke baby home, 6267
Venlo incident, 4514, 5142
Vennemann, Wolfgang, 5102
Venohr, Wolfgang, 5361
Verband deutscher Vereine im Ausland, 4012
Verband ehemaliger Angehöriger Deutsches Afrikakorps, 5027
Verband der Historiker Deutschlands, 2751
Vercel, Michel C., 5645
Vercors, 5493
Vercors, *pseud*., 5498
Vereinigung der Verfolgten des Naziregimes (VVN), 3341, 3352, 3415, 6418
Vergnet, Paul, 5477
Verhulst, Raf, 4310
Vermehren, Isa, 6051
Vermeil, Edmond, 338, 720, 1260
Vernant, Jacques, 6425
Vernekohl, Wilhelm, 1030
Vernet, (Le), concentration camp, 6032, 6205, 6206
Vernier, Bernard, 4586
Versailles Treaty: general, 44, 503, 3937, 3948, 3956, 4360, 4453, 4476

repudiation of, 3887, 3893, 3931–3944, 4071
Verschuer, Otmar Frhr. von, 412, 1440
Verspohl, Hermann, 1364
Vervooren, F., 4998
Verwaltungsrecht—*See* law, administrative
Verweyen, Johannes Maria, 2024, 6095
Vesters, J. A., 1845
Vetsch, Christian, 5003
Vetter, Hans, 1468
Vetter, Lili, 1223
Viallet, François-Albert, *pseud*., 3297
Viefhaus, Erwin, 1203
Vielhaber, Klaus, 2473
Vienna: general, 3286, 4139, 5249, 5255, 5269, 6264
   Jews of, 5651, 5760
Viera, Josef, 2997
Viereck, George Sylvester, 4550, 4551
Viereck, Peter, 277
Viernon, Adolf, 2300
Viernstein, Th., 1479
'*Vierteljahrshefte für Zeitgeschichte*', 63, 83
Vieth von Golssenau, Arnold Friedrich, 3722, 3737
Vigier, J.-L., 5490
Vildé affair, 5473
Villon, Pierre, 5480
Vilmar, A. F. C., 2542
Vilna Ghetto, 5686, 5689, 5700, 5860, 5906, 5914, 5960–5966
Vinas, Angel, 4395
Vindex, *pseud*., 3151
Vinke, Hermann, 3458
Vinkt (Belgium), 5530
Vinnitza (Winniza), 3147, 3152
Visscher, Ch. de, 4300
Visser, B. J. J., 1997
Visser't Hooft, W. A., 1934, 5545, 5546
Vittel Ghetto, 5967
Vitzthum, Ursula Gräfin, 4727
Vlasov, Andrei Andreievich, 4844–4846
vocational training—*See* education, vocational
Voegelin, Eric, 2392
Völker, Hans, 1489
Völker, Karl-Heinz, 4859
'Völkisch' movement, 224, 247, 363, 373, 588, 589, 1787
'*Völkischer Beobachter*', 2841–2846, 5015
Vogel, Alfred, 2273
Vogel, Bernhard, 42

Vogel, Heinrich, 1952
Vogel, Rolf, 3548, 3554
Vogel, Rudolf, 4977
Vogels, Werner, 1688
Vogelsang, Reinhard, 3251
Vogelsang, Thilo, 36, 63, 1051, 1160
Voggenreiter, Ludwig, 984
Vogl, Friedrich, 5270
Vogt, Benjamin, 5592
Vogt, Hannah, 6492
Vogt, Jochen, 3773
Vogt, Paul, 3612
Voigt, Harald, 969
Volk, Ludwig, 1958, 2017
Volk, Rainer, 2009
Volk und Reich Verlag, 2602
Volkmann, Erich Otto, 3875
Volkmann, Hans-Erich, 1532a, 1768
Volkmann-Leander, Bernhard von, 4729
Volksabstimmungen—See elections
Volksbücherei, 2593, 2600
Volksbund für das Deutschtum im Ausland, 4013–4015, 4044
'Volksdeutsche': general, 1299, 1966, 3997–4015a, 4079, 4361—See also under individual countries
'Volksgemeinschaft', 2233, 2389, 2635, 2781, 2945, 3887
'Volksgericht', 1404–1408, 2011, 3524
Volkshochschule, 2388
'Volksschädlinge', 1417
Volkssturm, 5120
Volkswagen, 1611–1613
Volland, Klaus, 4573
Vollbehr, Ernst, 1764
Vollmer, Bernhard, 3319
Volz, Hans, 44, 111, 1162
Volz, Ingrid, 3426
Vondung, Klaus, 589, 2070
Voorst tot Voorst, J. J. G. Baron van, 3972
Vorbach, Kurt, 4201
Vorländer, Herwart, 1929, 6160
Vormeier, Barbara, 6138
'Vorwärts', 2789
Vos, Jean de, 6251
'Vossische Zeitung', 2789, 3597
Vox Populi, pseud., 2935
Vries, Ph. de, 5560
Vries de Heekelingen, H. de, 339
Vught (Scheveningen) concentration camp, 6207–6209, 6281
Vyas, M. R., 4610

Wache, Walter, 437, 3928
Waddams, H. M., 5223, 5589
Wächter, Hans-Christoff, 3783
Wächtler, Fritz, 4015a
Waeger, Gerhart, 4443
Waetzig, Alfred, 2319
Waffen-SS: general, 3233 4705, 4713, 4823–4834, 4843, 5527
from France, 4837, 4839, 4842
from Low Countries, 4837, 4847
from Norway, 4841
from Switzerland, 4837
Waffenträger der Nation, 3877
Wagemann, Ernst, 1519, 1533, 1534, 1563
Wagener, Hans, 6493
Wagener, Otto, 536, 646
Wagenführ, Horst, 1535
Wagenführ, Kurt, 2862
Wagenführ, Rolf, 4682
Wagenlehner, Günther, 2840
Wagner, Adolf, 1266
Wagner, Albrecht, 1344
Wagner, Dieter, 4138, 5134
Wagner, Eduard, 4790
Wagner, Elisabeth, 4790
Wagner, Friedelind, 3792
Wagner, G. S., 790
Wagner, Gerhard, 4951
Wagner, Gerhard (NS physician), 874
Wagner, Johannes, 1487
Wagner, Johannes Volker, 3432
Wagner, Josef(ph), 875, 972, 2403, 3175
Wagner, Ludwig, 693
Wagner, Otto, 5031
Wagner, Richard 246–248, 2640–2642
Wagner, Walter, 1408
Wahl, Karl, 876
Waite, Robert G. L., 167, 703, 704
Waks, Shammai, 6180
Walchner, Siegfried, 2804
Waldl, pseud., 2927
Waldmann, Guido, 592
Walendy, Udo, 4482, 6510, 6517
Walk, Joseph, 3566, 3681
Walker, A. S., 1300
Walker, Lawrence D., 2458
Walker, Malvin, 2
Wallach, Jehuda L., 4587, 5895
Wallbach, Gerhard, 1368
Walleitner, Hugo, 6133
Wallenberg, Raoul, 6382, 6383
Wallner, Peter, 6052

Walter, *pseud.—See* Ulbricht, Walter
Walter, Bruno, 3793
Walter, Friedrich, 1167
Walter, Gérard, 5460
Walter, Hans-Albert, 3756
Walter van der Bleek, Kurt L., 188
Walther, Herbert, 694
Walther, K., 2313
Walther, Karl August, 1186
Wander, (Dr.), 5828
Wanderscheck, Hermann, 2957, 3065, 3478
Wandrey, Conrad, 2571
Wannsee Protocol, 5649, 5679, 6353
Wanstall, Ken, 5205
war crimes: general, 5602–5613
    deportations, 5399—*See also under* Jews
    genocide, 5210, 5369, 5415, 5603, 5613—*See also* Holocaust
    trials: in German courts, 5404, 5614–5616, 5620, 5622–5624, 6041, 6064, 6066, 6067, 6078, 6148
        in Europe, 5402, 5403, 5443, 5527, 5554, 5555, 5571, 5607, 5609, 5617–5619, 5621, 5877, 5945, 6089, 6161, 6177, 6219, 6267
    See also Nuremberg trials
War Crimes Commission (Belgium), 5530
war criminals, 3730, 4830, 5402–5404, 5407, 5443, 5637, 5638, 5640–5644, 5646, 5845, 5846, 5998, 6062, 6069, 6400–6409
war preparations, National Socialist:
    general, 3849–3863
    economic, 1760–1775
Warburg, Gerta, 3613
Warburg, Gustav, 3549
Warburg, Sidney, 990
Warburg family, 3613
Ward, Barbara, 4155
Ward Price, G., 1261
'Warenhaus', 526, 1623, 1626
warfare, chemical, 2328, 3014, 4686
Warfield, Gaither & Hania, 5415
Warhurst, A. E., 4624
Warlimont, Walter, 4762
Warloski, Ronald, 2448
Warmbrunn, Werner, 5540
Warmuth, Ludwig, 2603
Warsaw: general, 5391, 5392, 5396, 5399, 5404
    uprising (1944), 5397, 5399, 5425–5429

Warsaw Ghetto, 5392, 5399, 5407, 5730, 5738, 5860, 5870, 5907, 5914, 5968–5984, 6008
    uprising (1943), 5675, 5700, 5985–6001
Warthegau—*See* Poland, occupied: Reichsgau Wartheland
Wason, Betty, 5286
Wasserstein, Bernard, 6363
Watt, D. C., 727, 4469
Watter, Frhr. von, 3844
Watts, A. J., 4948
weapons and matériel, 4683–4685, 4689, 4693
Webb, Anthony M., 6161
Webb, James, 282
Weber, A., 2637
Weber, A. Paul, 846, 1017, 1785, 2689, 2690
Weber, Adolf, 1536
Weber, Alexander, 140
Weber, August, 1000
Weber, Eugen, 159
Weber, Hermann, 3431, 3440
Weber, Karl, 4436
Weber, Paul, 5569
Weber, Robert, 1484
Weber, Theo, 4893
Weber, Werner, 3801
Weber, Wolfgang, 6103
Weber, Wolfram, 5522
Weber-Stumpfohl, Herta, 2219
Weberstedt, Hans, 3964
Webler, Heinrich, 2138
Webster, Charles, 4919
Wechsberg, Joseph, 6409
Weckerling, Rudolf, 6338
Wedel, Hasso von, 16
Weder, Horst, 2879
Wedgwood, Josiah C., 3913
'Weg, Der', 3401, 6406
Wegener, Kurt, 3026
Wegener, Walther, 4588
Wegener, Wolfram M., 2185
Wegerer, Alfred von, 4454
Weh, Albert, 5393
Wehner, Bernd, 3284
Wehner, Herbert, 5613
Wehrmacht—*See* armed forces, German
Wehrt, Rudolf van, 4517
'Wehrwirtschaft', 1514, 1772, 1773, 1775
'Wehrwissenschaften', 3864, 3960, 4704
Weibel-Altmeier, Heinz, 5095

Weichold, Eberhard, 4939
Weichselbaum, Willy, 3672
Weidemann, Heinz, 1903
Weidemann, Johannes, 1269, 1271
Weidenfeld, Arthur, 2950
Weidinger, Otto, 4832, 4833
Weidlein, Johann, 4167
Weidmüller, Ludwig, 1568
Weidner, John Henry, 5547
Weigand, Wilhelm, 2998
Weigert, Hans, 2620
Weil, Jiri, 5788
Weil, Julien, 6298
Weimar Republic: general, 34, 35, 36, 44,
    45, 49, 62a, 78, 877–1054, 1074, 1076
  economy of, 62a, 878, 886, 893
  education in, 2246, 2247, 2251
  fall of, 612, 877, 882, 915a, 952, 966,
    972, 975, 985, 1024–1054, 1062,
    1113, 1865, 2247, 2772, 2797,
    4410—See also revolution, National
    Socialist
  political parties in, 883, 1788, 1789
  political radicalism in, 252, 880, 881,
    884, 885, 889, 891, 892, 1776–1779,
    2203, 2246, 2411, 2435, 2440, 2446
  racism in, 216, 217, 269
  right-wing opposition in, 179, 887, 2777,
    2789, 2818, 2830
  See also Reichswehr; and under NSDAP
    and elections
Weimarer Blätter, 2604
Wein, Abraham, 5881
Weinberg, Gerhard L., 55, 737, 3929
Weinbrenner, Hans-Joachim, 2863, 3524
Weinert, Erich, 3295, 3646, 3741, 3804
Weinert, Hans, 413
Weingartner, James Joseph, 3227
Weingartner, Thomas, 4414
Weinkauff, Hermann, 1344
Weinreich, Max, 2432
Weinryb, F., 5829
Weinstock, Earl, 5756
Weinstock, Rolf, 6053
Weinzierl, Erika, 5764
Weir, L. H., 1745
Weis, George, 3629
Weise, Gerhart, 4956
Weise, Otto, 3066
Weisenborn, Günther, 2712, 3298, 3320
Weiss, Bernhard, 2919
Weiss, Heinz, 1041
Weiss, Peter, 2702

Weiss, Reska, 6054
Weiss, Wilhelm, 5015
Weissberg, Alex, 6367
Weissbuch über die Erschiessungen des 30.
    Juni, 1108
'Weisse Rose', 2465–2473
Weissmandel, Michael Dov, 5879
Weissmann, Georg, 3673
Weissmann Klein, Gerda, 6252
Weizsäcker, Ernst von, 1224, 3930
Welch, David Albert, 2968
Welickzker, Leon, 5738, 5938
Welisch, Sophie Ann, 4202
Wellems, Hugo, 2205
Weller, Tüdel, 3204
Wellers, Georges, 5813, 5816, 6132, 6513
Wells, Leon—See Welickzker, Leon
Wels, H. Paul, 1537
Welter, Erich, 1614
Weltkriegsbücherei Stuttgart, Bibliothek
    für Zeitgeschichte, 65, 66
Weltliga gegen die Lüge, 245
Weltsch, Robert, 3662, 3674
Wendel, Else, 4668
Wendt, Bernd-Jürgen, 1644, 1655
Wendt, Hans, 1072, 1100, 1123
Wenger, Willo, 6158
Wengst, Udo, 922
Wenn alle Brüder schweigen, 4834
Wenn Judenblut vom Messer
    spritzt . . . ., 939, 1022
Wenzel, Fritz, 761
Wenzel-Burchard, Gertrud, 3613
Wer ist's?, 12
Wer leitet?, 1538
Werber, Rudolf, 2824
Werberat der deutschen Wirtschaft, 2795
Werder, Peter von, 2543
werewolves, 5122
Wermeskerken, H. van, 6281
Werner, Andreas, 3205
Werner, Bruno E., 2691
Werner, Ferdinand, 420
Werner, Gerhart, 3356
Werner, Karl Ferdinand, 2752
Werner, Kurt, 2206, 3326
Werner, Max, 4507, 4639
Wernert, E., 2692
Werth, Alexander, 5078
Wesemann, Hans, 3430
Wessel, Horst, 938, 3201, 3206, 3207
Wessel, Ingeborg, 3207
Wesselsky, Anton, 2071

West, Benjamin, 5896
West Prussia, 1946, 5366, 5380
Westdeutscher Rundfunk, 3411
Westecker, Wilhelm, 2621
Westerbork concentration camp, 5829, 6210–6212
Western Hemisphere, 4519–4523—*See also* individual countries
Westernhagen, A. E., 2805
Westernhagen, Curt von, 2642
Westphal, Siegfried, 4757, 4791, 5111
Westphalia, 972, 973, 1295
Westwall—*See* Siegfried Line
Wetner, Klaus, 5654
Wetzel, Erich, 5213
Wetzel, Heinz, 2882
Wetzel, Kraft, 2738
Wetzlar, 974
Wey, A. van der, 2072
Weygand, Maxime, 3966
Weyl, Stefan, 3394
Wheatley, Ronald, 5022
Wheaton, Eliot Barcule, 1074
Wheeler-Bennett, John W., 1081, 3486, 3848, 3958, 4499
White, Amber Blanco, 2958
White, John Baker, 127, 3037
White, Ralph, 5229
Whiting, Charles, 5122, 5163
Whitton, John B., 3043
Wibald, *pseud.*, 4303
Wichtl, Friedrich, 512
Widmann, Horst, 3797
Wieber, Ida, 1187
Wiechert, Ernst, 2579, 6107
Wieder, Joachim, 5065
Wieneke, Friedrich, 602
Wiener, Peter F., 270, 271, 2243
Wiener Library, 84, 3762, 5621, 5660
Catalogue Series, 78
Wiernik, Yankel, 6204
Wiesel, Elie, 5979, 6055
Wiesemann, Falk, 131, 944, 1173, 3562
Wiesenthal, Simon, 4593, 5612, 5728, 6148, 6409, 6438
Wiesner, Herbert, 2588
Wiest, Hugo, 4715
Wietersheim, Edgar von, 4897
Wighton, Charles, 3239
Wigodor, Geoffrey, 5649
Wilamowitz-Moellendorff, Fanny Gräfin von, 802
Wilde, Harry, 1043

Wilder-Okladek, F., 6439
Wilensky, M., 6291
Wilhelm II, Kaiser, 170
Wilhelm, Hans-Heinrich, 5242
Wilhelm, Theodor, 2244
Wilhelmi, Heinrich, 1862
Wilhelmsburg concentration camp, 3403
Wilhelmy, Herbert, 4082
Will, Irmgard, 2073
Willebrod, Jacques, 5522
Willi, Anton, 2786
Willi, Jost Nikolaus, 3430
Williams, Frederick W., 6471
Williams, R. R., 5223
Willigmann, Karl, 1073
Willikins, Werner, 556
Willim, Ewald, 4897
Willrich, Wolfgang, 553, 586
Willstätter, Richard, 3636
Wilner, Herbert, 5756
Wilser, Ludwig, 196, 197, 200
Wilson, Arnold, 1262
Winghene, Egon von, 446
Winkel, Harald, 1497
Winkel, L. E., 5559
Winkelkemper, Toni, 4899
Winkler, Dörte, 2124
Winkler, Heinrich August, 893
Winkler, Michael, 3777
Winncroft, Eileen, 4668
Winnig, August, 1009, 1719, 1720, 3006
Winschuh, Josef, 1615
Wint, Guy, 4458
Winter, Botho, 2449
Winter, Georg, 249
Winter, M., 1075
Winter, Richard, 2335
'Winterhilfswerk', 1457, 1462–1466
Winterscheidt, Severin, 4541
Wir Fahren gegen Engelland!, 5023
Wir fliegen mit Hitler, 1053
Wirsing, Giselher, 3142, 3161, 4595
Wirth, Andrzej, 6000
Wirth, Fritz, 3017
Wirth, Günter, 1931
Wirth, Herman, 198
Wirtschaftsgruppe Chemische Industrie, 1591
'Wirtschaftsleiter', 1512
'Wirtschaftstreuhänder', 1574
Wise, James Waterman, 3321
Wise, Maurice K., 5196
Wiskemann, Elizabeth, 4089, 4203, 4508

Wiskemann, Erwin, 261, 2749
Wisser, Eva Maria, 2220
Wissmann, Hellmuth, 1564
Witebsk, 5053
Witetschek, Helmut, 1957
Wittels, David C., 4549
Wittelshöfer, Fritz, 1368
Wittken, Jungnik Frhr. von, 1369
Wittland, Hermann, 1322
Wittmann, Klaus, 1657
Wittschier, Bernd, 3328
Witzmann, Conrad, 2228
Wöhrmann, O., 1691
Woerner, Otto, 1689
Wörtz, Ulrich, 522, 865
Wohlfahrt, Erich, 2254
Wohlrab, E. H., 2326
Wojciechowski, Marian, 4324
Wolf, A., 2255
Wolf, Ernst, 1956, 3408
Wolf, Friedrich, 2454, 3812
Wolf, Gerhard, 6354
Wolf, Heinrich, 1485
Wolf, Lore, 3441
Wolf, Werner, 934
Wolfe, Robert, 56
Wolff, Edith, 3621
Wolff, Günter, 4046
Wolff, Helmut, 5140
Wolff, Ilse R., 78
Wolff, Jeanette, 6056
Wolff, Richard, 3700
Wolff, Theodor, 2482, 2797, 3757
Wolff, Willy, 3742
Wolff-Mönckeberg, Mathilde, 4669
Wolffheim, Nelly, 6444
Wolffsohn, Michael, 1721
Wolfskehl, Karl, 3805
Wolhynia, 5219
Wolkovisk, 5880
Wollenberg, Erich, 3863
Wollheim, Norbert, 2727
Wollstein, Günter, 3931
Wolmar, Wolfgang Wolfram von, 4204
Wolters, Rudolf, 2659
Wolzogen, Ernst von, 420
Wolzogen, Hans von, 278
Women, German: general, 2087–2129
  anti-National Socialist, 1833, 2465–
  2467, 2470–2473, 2561, 2678, 3414,
  3418, 6185, 6355
  girls' organizations—See Bund deut-
  scher Mädel

and higher education, 2088, 2097, 2118,
  2444
National Socialist, 1208, 2063, 2090,
  2091, 2099, 2108, 2113, 2116, 3262
in prison, 3296
and war service, 2125–2129, 2360, 3033
as writers, 2537
women in occupied Europe: resistance of,
  5266, 5271, 5401, 5582, 5587, 6043,
  6045
  See also concentration camps: women in
Wonneberger, Günther, 2879
Wood, H. C., 1866
Woodhouse, C. M.,
Woodman, Dorothy, 3973, 4860, 5238
Woodward, David, 4950
Woodward, E. L., 4248
Woolbert, Robert Gale, 3882
Woolf, Leonard, 4155
Wootton, Graham, 4280
workers—See under National Socialism,
  ideology of
workers in Third Reich: general,
  1696a–1759, 2368, 2372, 2381, 3343,
  3344
  laws relating to, 1707–1709, 1750,
  1751
workers' movement—See trade unions
World Alliance for Combating Anti-
  Semitism, 6325
World Committee for the Victims of
  German Fascism, 1082, 1090
World Council for the Welfare of the
  Blind, 6451
World Jewish Congress, 3630, 6459
World Veterans Federation, 6451
World War I, 35, 44, 340, 503, 512, 1636,
  1980, 2298, 2621, 2714, 3103
World War II: general, 36, 45, 2747,
  2751, 4430, 4612–4695
  air war: general, 4861–4919
    allied, against Germany, 4894–4919
    German: general, 4700, 4861–4885,
    4919, 5076
    against Great Britain, 4886–4893
  campaigns, military: general, 4961–
  5136
    in the Balkans (1941), 5032–5039
    in eastern Europe: general, 4804, 4836,
    4842
      Poland (1939), 3893, 4334, 4337,
      4453, 4745, 4820, 4865,
      4961–4977

in Soviet Union, German, 44, 4745, 4836, 5040–5078
Soviet campaigns (1943–1945), 5074, 5084–5090, 5092–5094
in North Africa, 5024–5031
in Scandinavia (1940), 4884, 4981–4990
in Southern Europe, 5080–5082, 5091
in Western Europe (1940), 44, 3850, 4745, 4820, 4991–5015—See also 'Phony War'
allied campaign (1944/45), 5096–5111, 5530
German home front (1939/45), 4654–4669
last days of war, 4624, 5112–5136
and neutral states, 3889, 4214, 4295, 4296, 4366, 4372–4375, 4379, 4380, 4431, 4435–4437, 4535, 4540, 4897
origins of, 4222, 4261, 4409, 4446–4518, 4525, 4628
outbreak of, 4500–4518
and railways, 1316, 4677, 4691, 4692, 5481, 5562
sea war: general, 3120, 4700, 4923–4960
in Mediterranean, 4938–4941
U-boats, 4922, 4952–4960
See also armed forces; New Order; propaganda; and individual countries
Worms, 3551
Wormser (-Migot), Olga, 6057, 6058
Woś, Jan, 5423
Wrede, Franz Otto, 3162
Wright, Gordon, 4640
Wright, S. Fowler, 4047
Wroński, Tadeusz, 5416
Wucher, Albert, 1054, 5707
Wucher, Waldemar, 4343
Wünsch, Georg, 1870
Wünsche, Julius, 3163
Württemberg, 975, 1170, 1914, 1973, 2459, 6044, 6160
Württemberg/Hohenzollern, 3593
Wuescht, Johann, 4179
Wuestenberg, Bruno, 1998
Wuhlheide concentration camp, 3297
Wulf, Josef, 327, 836, 1310, 2544, 2643, 2693, 2716, 2806, 5713, 5905, 5932, 6001, 6383
Wulff, Ernst, 1466
Wulff, Wilhelm Th. H., 149

Wullus-Rudiger, J.-A., 4304, 4305
Wulman, Leon, 5864
Wunderlich, Curt, 3164
Wundt, Max, 603
Wuppertal, 3194, 3356
Wurm, Theophil, 1954, 1955
Wykes, Alan, 128, 3252
Wyl, Hans von, 4444
Wyss, M. de, 5515

Yad Vashem, 3671, 5650, 5657–5659, 5673, 5831, 5881, 5888, 5931
archives, 5647
Yahil, Leni, 5708, 6378, 6381
yellow badge (star), 3674, 5654, 5664, 5669, 5763, 5788, 5812, 5816, 5897
Yellow Spot, The, 3550
Yeo-Thomas, F. F. E., 6035
Yerushalmi, Eliezer, 5943
Yisraeli, David, 4596
Yivo Annual of Jewish Social Science, 5674
Yivo Institute of Jewish Research, 5650, 5657–5659, 5831, 5931
Yogi Mayer, Paul, 3684
Yorck von Wartenburg, Peter Graf, 3383, 3384
Young, A. P., 4286
Young, Gordon, 794
Young, Kimball, 3085
youth: general, 2130–2380, 2735, 4670–4674
'Auslandsdeutsch', 4335
Catholic, 2455–2458, 2809
hostels, 2144, 2649
Jewish, 3593, 3617, 3621, 3688, 5824, 5834, 5909—See also under children, Holocaust
laws relating to, 2137, 2138
militaristic exploitation of, 2142, 2201, 2330, 3866, 3869, 3978, 4672, 4673
oppression and resistance of, 2450–2462
postwar, 6480–6482
Protestant, 2459, 2460
and workers' movement, 2461, 2462
Yugoslav State commission for Investigation of War Crimes, 5901
Yugoslavia: general, 4151, 4155, 4179, 5032, 5033, 5036, 5088, 5299–5315
Federation of Jewish Communities in, 5902
and Jews, 5689, 5833, 5897–5902
resistance in, 5227, 5236, 5274,

5301–5306, 5308–5311, 5314, 5898, 5899, 6280
and 'Volksdeutsche', 4176–4178, 5315, 6412

Zabel, James A., 1904
Zabkar, Joseph, 1998
Zaborowski, Jan, 5363
Zahn, Gordon C., 1974, 3366
Zander, Alfred, 4445
Zanten, Gerth van, 6209
Zapp, Manfred, 4353
Zarnov, Gottfried, 2986
Zassenhaus, Hiltgunt, 6355
Zatloukal, Jaroslav, 5353
Zayas, Alfred M. de, 6414
Zeck, Hans F., 3996
Zeddies, Adolf, 523
Zee, Sytze van der, 4847
Zee-Heräus, Bernhard, 1759
Zeeland, Paul van, 1645
Zehring, Arno, 2928
Zeitler, Ralf, 1285
'Zeitschrift für Geopolitik', 4022
Zeitzler, Kurt, 4757
Zelle, Arnold, 3934, 4349
Zeller, Eberhard, 3520, 3525
Zeller, Edgar, 4921
Zellien, Richard, 1512
Zellmer, E., 2101
Zelzer, Maria, 3591
Zeman, Zbynek A. B., 2959, 2969
Zenner, Maria, 4056
Zentner, Christian, 736, 2207, 4518, 4619, 6505
Zentner, Kurt, 3412
Zentralarchiv der Pioniere, 4812
'Zentralblatt der Bauverwaltung', 2645
Zentrale Stelle der Landesjustizverwaltungen, 5446, 5447, 6253, 6278
Zentralstelle für jüdische Wirtschaftshilfe, 3682
Zentralverband Demokratischer Widerstandskämpfer und Verfolgten Organisationen (ZDWV), 3413
Zentralwohlfahrtsstelle der deutschen Juden, 3682
'Zentrum' party, 1115, 1788, 1789
Zerkaulen, Heinrich, 2712
Zernik, Charlotte E., 3614
Ziebura, Gilbert, 3404

Ziegelmayer, Wilhelm, 1680
Ziegfeld, A. Hillen, 357, 4186, 4343
Ziegler, Hans Severus, 695, 2644, 5646
Ziegler, Janet, 4620
Ziegler, Matthes, 4187, 4730
Ziegler, Walter, 1957
Ziegler, Wilhelm, 2987, 3143, 3944, 4455
Ziegra, K., 573
Zielinski, Henryk, 5394
Ziemer, Gerhard, 6415
Ziemer, Gregor, 2163
Ziemian, Joseph, 5983
Ziff, William B., 4653
Zimmels, H. J., 5709
Zimmermann, Bodo, 4757
Zimmermann, Erich, 3510
Zimmermann, Karl, 391, 2149
Zimmermann, Reinhold, 2623
Zimmermann, Richard, 1565
Zimmermann, Walter, 5197
Zingel, Fritz, 2499
Zinner-Biberach, F., 1075
'Zinsknechtschaft', 539, 540
Zionist movement, 475, 3621, 5824, 5834
Zipfel, Friedrich, 1085, 1129, 1846
Zipperlen, H., 2500
Zischka, Anton, 1580, 1681
Zmarzlik, Hans-Günter, 6494
Zöberlein, Hans, 935
Zöller, Martin, 6280
Zoon, Wilhelm, 5198
Zorn, Gerda, 3340, 3414, 5613
Zorn, Wolfgang, 1171
Zsadanyi, Oszkar, 6254
Zschaetzsch, Karl Georg, 199
Zucht und Sitte . . ., 604
Zuckmayer, Carl, 2589, 3830, 4789
Zugschwert, Hans, 3478
'Zukunft', 3758
Zumpe, L., 3234
Zumpt, F., 498
Zur Geschichte des Kirchenkampfes, 1956
Zuroff, Ephraim, 6331
Zwanzig Briefe an einen jungen Dietwart, 2893
Zwart, Peter, 6207
Zweig, Arnold, 3831, 5737, 5738
Zwerens, Gerhard, 868
Zwickau, 3594
Zwischenspiel Hitler . . ., 1023
Zylberberg, Michael, 5984
Zywulska, Krystyna, 6086